THE OXFORD HAND

CARL SCHMITT

THE OXFORD HANDBOOK OF

CARL SCHMITT

Edited by

JENS MEIERHENRICH

London School of Economics and Political Science

and

OLIVER SIMONS

Columbia University

OXFORD

UNIVERSITY PRESS

OXFORD
UNIVERSITY PRESS

Oxford University Press is a department of the University of Oxford. It furthers
the University's objective of excellence in research, scholarship, and education
by publishing worldwide. Oxford is a registered trade mark of Oxford University
Press in the UK and certain other countries.

Published in the United States of America by Oxford University Press
198 Madison Avenue, New York, NY 10016, United States of America.

Library of Congress Cataloging-in-Publication Data
Names: Meierhenrich, Jens, editor. | Simons, Oliver, editor.
Title: The Oxford handbook of Carl Schmitt / edited by Jens Meierhenrich,
London School of Economics and Oliver Simons, Columbia University.
Other titles: Handbook of Carl Schmitt
Description: New York, NY : Oxford University Press, 2016. |
Includes bibliographical references and index.
Identifiers: LCCN 2016017266 (print) | LCCN 2016029561 (ebook) |
ISBN 9780199916931 (hardcover : alk. paper) | ISBN 9780190943998 (paperback : alk. paper) |
ISBN 9780199916948 (E-book) | ISBN 9780190646509 (E-book) | ISBN 9780199983254 (Online Component)
Subjects: LCSH: Schmitt, Carl, 1888–1985. | Political science—Philosophy—History—20th century.
Classification: LCC JC263.S34 O94 2016 (print) | LCC JC263.S34 (ebook) | DDC 320.01—dc23
LC record available at https://lccn.loc.gov/2016017266

TABLE OF CONTENTS

PART IV THE LEGAL THOUGHT
OF CARL SCHMITT

PART V THE CULTURAL THOUGHT
OF CARL SCHMITT

List of Contributors

Giorgio Agamben is Baruch Spinoza Chair and professor of philosophy at the European Graduate School. His unique readings of literature, literary theory, continental philosophy, political thought, religious studies, and art have made him one of the most innovative thinkers of our time. Educated in law and philosophy at the University of Rome, he has published widely across diverse fields. As a postdoctoral scholar at the University of Freiburg (1966–1968), he participated in Martin Heidegger's seminars on Hegel and Heraclitus and was later a fellow at the Warburg Institute, University of London. His many books include *Homo Sacer: Sovereign Power and Bare Life* (Stanford University Press, 1998); *Remnants of Auschwitz: The Witness and the Archive* (MIT Press, 2000); *State of Exception* (University of Chicago Press, 2005); *The Kingdom and the Glory: For a Theological Genealogy of Economy and Government* (Stanford University Press, 2011); *Stasis: Civil War as a Political Paradigm* (Edinburgh University Press, 2015); and *The Use of Bodies* (Stanford University Press, 2016).

Friedrich Balke is professor of media studies at the University of Bochum, with a special focus on the theory, history, and aesthetics of visual representation. From 2007 until 2012 he was professor of the history and theory of artificial worlds at the Bauhaus University, Weimar. His books include *Der Staat nach seinem Ende: Die Versuchung Carl Schmitts* (Fink, 1996); *Figuren der Souveränität* (Fink, 2009); as coeditor, *Gilles Deleuze: Fluchtlinien der Philosophie* (Fink, 1996) (with Joseph Vogl); *Vom Nutzen und Nachteil historischer Vergleiche: Der Fall Bonn–Weimar* (Campus, 1997) (with Benno Wagner); *Ästhetische Regime um 1800* (Fink, 2008) (with Leander Scholz and Harun Maye); and *Räume und Medien des Regierens* (Fink, 2016) (with Maria Muhle). In 2005 Balke was the Distinguished Max Kade Visiting Professor in the Department of Germanic Languages and Literatures at Columbia University. He is currently codirector of a research group on *"Medien und Mimesis"* and the graduate program *"Das Dokumentarische: Exzess und Entzug,"* both funded by the *Deutsche Forschungsgemeinschaft*, the German Research Foundation.

Joseph W. Bendersky is professor of intellectual and German history at Virginia Commonwealth University and book review editor for *Holocaust & Genocide Studies*. He is the author of *Carl Schmitt: Theorist for the Reich* (Princeton University Press, 1983); *The "Jewish Threat": Anti-Semitic Politics of the U.S. Army* (Basic Books, 2000), a finalist for the National Jewish Book Award; *A Concise History of Nazi Germany* (Rowman & Littlefield, 2014); and a scholarly edition and translation of Schmitt's *On the Three Types of Juristic Thought* (Praeger, 2004). He has authored numerous articles on Carl Schmitt, racial thinking in the U.S. military, American antisemitism, and Friedrich Meinecke. His works have been translated into Chinese, Italian, Japanese, and Polish. Among his most recent publications are "Trajectories in the Study of National Socialism," *German Studies Review* (2016); and "Carl Schmitt and Samuel Huntington's *The Clash of Civilizations* Revisited," in *Carl Schmitt: Hoje, politica, direito e teologia* (Editora Max Limo, 2016).

Aryeh Botwinick is professor of political science at Temple University, specializing in political theory. He studies democratic theory conceived in the broad sense as deriving from both Western monotheistic religious traditions and philosophical skepticism. In particular, he is interested in the relationship between monotheism and skepticism, considered both as a structure of argument and as an ethical content—and in the theoretical and practical intersections between politics and religion. Among other books, he is the author of *Skepticism and Political Participation* (Temple University Press, 1990); *Power and Empowerment: A Radical Theory of Participatory Democracy* (Temple University Press, 1992) (with Peter Bachrach); *Postmodernism and Democratic Theory* (Temple University Press, 1993); *Skepticism, Belief, and the Modern: Maimonides to Nietzsche* (Cornell University Press, 1997); *Michael Oakeshott's Skepticism* (Princeton University Press, 2011); and *Emmanuel Levinas and the Limits to Ethics: A Critique and a Re-Appropriation* (Routledge, 2014).

Horst Bredekamp is professor of art history at Humboldt University, Berlin. He completed his PhD in art history at the University of Marburg. After working at the *Liebieghaus* in Frankfurt am Main as a curator, he became assistant professor of art history at the University of Hamburg, where he was tenured in 1982. Between 2003 and 2012 he was a permanent fellow of the *Wissenschaftskolleg*, the Institute for Advanced Study, Berlin. Since 2012 he has served as director of the cluster *"Bild/Wissen/Gestaltung"* at Humboldt University (with Wolfgang Schäffner), and in 2015 he joined the steering committee of the *Humboldt-Forum*, both in Berlin. The author of twenty-four books, he is a member of several learned societies, including the German National Academy of Sciences and the American Academy of Arts and Sciences. In 2014 he was awarded the *Ordre pour le mérite*.

Rüdiger Campe is professor of German and comparative literature at Yale University. He previously taught at Johns Hopkins University and is the recipient of Aby Warburg and Humboldt research fellowships. His books include *Affekt und Ausdruck: Zur Umwandlung der literarischen Rede im 17. und 18. Jahrhundert* (Niemeyer, 1990); *The Game of Probability: Literature and Calculation from Pascal to Kleist* (Stanford University Press, 2012); and *Baumgarten-Studien: Zur Genealogie der Ästhetik* (August Verlag, 2014) (with Anselm Haverkamp and Christoph Menke). He is also the coeditor of *Re-thinking Emotion: Interiority and Exteriority in Premodern, Modern, and Contemporary Thought* (De Gruyter, 2014) (with Julia Weber) and has edited special journal issues on the work of Hans Blumenberg (*Telos*, 2012), observation in science and literature (*Monatshefte*, 2013), citation (*Germanic Review*, 2014), and other subjects.

David Dyzenhaus is a professor of law and philosophy at the University of Toronto and a fellow of the Royal Society of Canada. He holds the Alfred Abel Chair of Law and was appointed in 2015 to the rank of university professor. In 2014–2015 he was the Arthur Goodhart Visiting Professor in Legal Science at the University of Cambridge. He is the author of *Hard Cases in Wicked Legal Systems: Pathologies of Legality*, 2nd ed. (Oxford University Press, 2010); *Legality and Legitimacy: Carl Schmitt, Hans Kelsen, and Hermann Heller in Weimar* (Oxford University Press, 1997); *Judging the Judges, Judging Ourselves: Truth, Reconciliation and the Apartheid Legal Order* (Hart, 1998); and *The Constitution of Law: Legality in a Time of Emergency* (Cambridge University Press, 2006). He is editor of the *University of Toronto Law Journal* and of the book series "Cambridge Studies in Constitutional Law."

Raphael Gross is director of the Simon-Dubnow-Institute for Jewish History and Culture and holds the Chair for Jewish History and Culture at Leipzig University. He was previously director of both the Jewish Museum (2006–2015) and the Fritz Bauer Institute (2007–2015) in Frankfurt as well as of the Leo Baeck Institute in London (2001–2015). He is the author of *Carl Schmitt and the Jews: The "Jewish Question," the Holocaust, and German Legal Theory* (University of Wisconsin Press, 2007); *Anständig geblieben: Nationalsozialististische Moral* (Fischer, 2010); and *November 1938: Die Katastrophe vor der Katastrophe* (Beck, 2013). His edited collections include *Moralität des Bösen: Ethik und nationalsozialistische Verbrechen* (Campus, 2009) (with Werner Konitzer); *Die Frankfurter Schule und Frankfurt: Eine Rückkehr nach Deutschland* (Wallstein, 2009) (with Monika Boll); *"Ich staune, dass Sie in dieser Luft atmen können": Jüdische Intellektuelle in Deutschland nach 1945* (Fischer, 2013) (with Monika Boll); and *Der Frankfurter Auschwitz-Prozess (1963–1965): Kommentierte Quellenedition* (Campus, 2013) (with Werner Renz).

Duncan Kelly is a reader in political thought in the Department of Politics and International Studies at the University of Cambridge and a fellow of Jesus College, Cambridge. He is the author of *The State of the Political: Conceptions of Politics and the State in the Thought of Max Weber, Carl Schmitt and Franz Neumann* (Oxford University Press, 2003) and *The Propriety of Liberty: Persons, Passions and Judgement in Modern Political Thought* (Princeton University Press, 2010), editor of *Lineages of Empire* (Oxford University of Press, 2009), and coeditor of the journals *Modern Intellectual History* and *Max Weber Studies*. He is currently writing an intellectual history of World War I.

Martti Koskenniemi is Academy Professor of International Law at the University of Helsinki and director of the Erik Castrén Institute of International Law and Human Rights. He was a member of the Finnish diplomatic service in 1978–1994 and of the International Law Commission of the United Nations in 2002–2006. He has held visiting professorships at, among other institutions, New York University, Columbia University, the University of Cambridge, the London School of Economics and Political Science, and the Universities of Brussels, Melbourne, Paris, São Paulo, and Utrecht. He is a corresponding fellow of the British Academy and holds honorary doctorates from the Universities of Uppsala, Frankfurt, and McGill. His main publications include *From Apology to Utopia: The Structure of International Legal Argument* (Cambridge University Press, 1989); *The Gentle Civilizer of Nations: The Rise and Fall of International Law 1870-1960* (Cambridge University Press, 2001); and *The Politics of International Law* (Routledge, 2011). He is currently working on a history of international legal thought from the late medieval period to the nineteenth century.

Matthias Lievens is an assistant professor at the Institute of Philosophy at KU Leuven, Belgium, and a member of Research in Political Philosophy Leuven (RIPPLE). He wrote a doctoral dissertation on Carl Schmitt's concept of the political, and he has published on aspects of Schmitt's work in journals such as *Constellations, Contemporary Political Theory, Philosophy & Social Criticism*, and the *Journal of the Philosophy of History*. His current research concerns the crisis of democracy and the politics of climate change. He is the author of *The Limits of the Green Economy: From Re-inventing Capitalism to Re-politicising the Present* (Routledge, 2015) (with Anneleen Kenis) and has published on Jacques Rancière, governance and democracy, and climate politics in *Thesis Eleven, Political Studies, Environmental Politics*, and *Review of Radical Political Economics*.

Christian Linder is an essayist and literary critic, as well as a radio journalist at *Deutschlandfunk* and *Westdeutscher Rundfunk* in Germany. Educated at the University of Bonn, he has written for the *Süddeutsche Zeitung* and *Frankfurter Allgemeine Zeitung*. He is the author of *Der Bahnhof von Finnentrop: Eine Reise ins Carl Schmitt Land* (Matthes & Seitz, 2008), a deeply researched, unconventional analysis of Schmitt's postwar life in rural Germany presented in the form of a travelogue. His other books include two biographies of Heinrich Böll, *Leben und Schreiben 1917-1985* (Kiepenheuer & Witsch, 1986) and *Das Schwirren des heranfliegenden Pfeils: Heinrich Böll* (Matthes & Seitz, 2009.)

Martin Loughlin is professor of public law at the London School of Economics and Political Science. He was educated at LSE, the University of Warwick, and Harvard Law School and held chairs at the Universities of Glasgow and Manchester before returning to LSE in 2000. Between 2000 and 2002 he held a Leverhulme Major Research Fellowship, in 2007-2008 he was a fellow of the Wissenschaftskolleg zu Berlin, in 2012-2013 he held a Law and Public Affairs Fellowship at Princeton University, and in 2016-2017 he is a EURIAS senior fellow at the Freiburg Institute of Advanced Studies. He is a fellow of the British Academy, and his publications include *The Idea of Public Law* (Oxford University Press, 2003); *Foundations of Public Law* (Oxford University Press, 2010); and *The British Constitution: A Very Short Introduction* (Oxford University Press, 2013).

John P. McCormick is professor of political science at the University of Chicago. He is the author of *Carl Schmitt's Critique of Liberalism: Against Politics as Technology* (Cambridge University Press, 1997); *Weber, Habermas and Transformations of the European State: On Constitutional, Social and Supranational Democracy* (Cambridge University Press, 2007); and *Machiavellian Democracy* (Cambridge University Press,

2011). He is the editor of *Confronting Mass Democracy and Industrial Technology: German Political and Social Thought from Nietzsche to Habermas* (Duke University Press, 2002) and the coeditor of *Weimar Thought: A Contested Legacy* (Princeton University Press, 2015) (with Peter E. Gordon). He has received the following fellowships: a Fulbright scholarship, a fellowship at the Center for European Law and Politics at the University of Bremen, Germany (1994–1995), a Jean Monnet Fellowship at the European University Institute (1995–1996), a Radcliffe Institute for Advanced Study Fellowship at Harvard University (2008–2009), and a Rockefeller Foundation Residential Fellowship in Bellagio, Italy (2013).

Reinhard Mehring is professor of political science at Heidelberg University of Education. He is the author of numerous books, including *Pathetisches Denken: Carl Schmitts Denkweg am Leitfaden Hegels* (Duncker & Humblot, 1989); *Carl Schmitt zur Einführung*, 4th ed. (Junius, 2011); *Carl Schmitt: A Biography* (Polity, 2014); *Kriegstechniker des Begriffs: Biographische Studien zu Carl Schmitt* (Mohr, 2014); and most recently, *Heideggers "große Politik": Die semantische Revolution der Gesamtausgabe* (Mohr, 2016). His edited volumes include *Carl Schmitt: Der Begriff des Politischen* (De Gruyter, 2003); *"Auf der gefahrenvollen Straße des öffentlichen Rechts": Briefwechsel Carl Schmitt/Rudolf Smend 1921–1961* (Duncker & Humblot, 2010); and *Voraussetzungen und Garantien des Staates: Ernst-Wolfgang Böckenfördes Staatsverständnis* (Nomos, 2014) (with Martin Otto).

Jens Meierhenrich is associate professor of international relations at the London School of Economics and Political Science and previously taught for a decade at Harvard University, where he was an assistant professor in the Department of Government and at the Committee on Degrees in Social Studies. He is the author of *The Legacies of Law: Long-Run Consequences of Legal Development in South Africa, 1652–2000* (Cambridge University Press, 2008), which won the American Political Science Association's 2009 Woodrow Wilson Foundation Award for the "best book published in the United States during the previous year in politics, government, or international affairs." His other publications include *Lawfare: A Genealogy* (Cambridge University Press, 2017); and, as editor, *Political Trials in Theory and History* (Cambridge University Press, 2016) (with Devin O. Pendas) and Ernst Fraenkel, *The Dual State: A Contribution to the Theory of Dictatorship* (Oxford University Press, [1941] 2017). In 2012–2013 he was a member in the School of Social Science at the Institute for Advanced Study, Princeton. He is currently writing a book about Carl Schmitt's thought and conduct in Nazi Germany.

Samuel Moyn is Jeremiah Smith Jr. Professor of Law and professor of history at Harvard University. He previously taught in the Columbia University history department for thirteen years, most recently as James Bryce Professor of European Legal History. He is the author of several books in the fields of modern European intellectual history and legal history and for several years has been delving into the history of human rights. He is the author of *Origins of the Other: Emmanuel Levinas between Revelation and Ethics* (Cornell University Press, 2005); *The Last Utopia: Human Rights in History*

(Harvard University Press, 2010); and *Human Rights and the Uses of History* (Verso, 2014). His most recent book is *Christian Human Rights* (University of Pennsylvania Press, 2015).

David Pan is professor of German and chair of the Department of European Languages and Studies at the University of California, Irvine. He is also the book review editor of *Telos*, the executive director of the Telos-Paul Piccone Institute, and a member of the executive council of the Modern Language Association. He has previously held positions at Washington University in St. Louis, Stanford University, Penn State University, and McKinsey & Company. He is the author of *Primitive Renaissance: Rethinking German Expressionism* (University of Nebraska Press, 2001) and *Sacrifice in the Modern World: On the Particularity and Generality of Nazi Myth* (Northwestern University Press, 2012). He has published on Johann Gottfried Herder, Johann Georg Hamann, Johann Wolfgang von Goethe, Heinrich von Kleist, Friedrich Nietzsche, Franz Kafka, Walter Benjamin, Ernst Jünger, Bertolt Brecht, Carl Schmitt, and Theodor W. Adorno.

Stanley L. Paulson was professor of philosophy and William Gardiner Hammond Professor of Law at Washington University, St. Louis, until his retirement in 2011. During the period 1999–2011 he also held, at regular intervals, a Mercator Guest Professorship in the Faculty of Law, University of Kiel, and he is presently a guest at the University's Hermann Kantorowicz Institute. Paulson was awarded an honorary doctorate in Uppsala in 2004 and in Kiel, also in 2004, as well as Germany's Humboldt Research Prize in 2005. He has written nearly two hundred articles and reviews in English and in German, with translations into eight other languages. Presently he is working on a treatise on Hans Kelsen's legal philosophy, under contract with Oxford University Press.

Eric A. Posner is Kirkland and Ellis Distinguished Service Professor of Law, University of Chicago. His current research interests include financial regulation, international law, and constitutional law. His books include *Law and Social Norms* (Harvard University Press, 2000); *The Limits of International Law* (Oxford University Press, 2005) (with Jack Goldsmith); *New Foundations of Cost-Benefit Analysis* (Harvard University Press, 2006) (with Matthew Adler); *Terror in the Balance: Security, Liberty and the Courts* (Oxford University Press, 2007) (with Adrian Vermeule); *The Perils of Global Legalism* (University of Chicago Press, 2009); *Climate Change Justice* (Princeton University Press, 2010) (with David Weisbach); *The Executive Unbound: After the Madisonian Republic* (Oxford University Press, 2011) (with Adrian Vermeule); *Economic Foundations of International Law* (Harvard University Press, 2013) (with Alan Sykes); and *The Twilight of International Human Rights* (Oxford University Press, 2014). He is a fellow of the American Academy of Arts and Sciences and a member of the American Law Institute.

Ulrich K. Preuß is professor emeritus of law and political science at Freie Universität Berlin and at the Hertie School of Governance in Berlin. As a participant in the so-called Round Table negotiations in 1989–1990, he coauthored a constitutional draft for the German Democratic Republic. He has taught at Princeton University, the New School for Social Research, the University of Chicago, and Haifa University. From 1992 until 2011 he served as a judge at the *Staatsgerichtshof* (State Constitutional Court) in the *Land*, or state, of Bremen. His books include *Constitutional Revolution: The Link Between Constitutionalism and Progress* (Humanities Press, 1995); *Institutional Design in Post-Communist Societies: Rebuilding the Ship at Sea* (Cambridge University Press, 1998) (with Jon Elster and Claus Offe); and *Citizens in Europe: Essays on Democracy, Constitutionalism, and European Integration* (European Consortium for Political Research, 2016) (with Claus Offe).

William Rasch is professor of German Studies at Indiana University, Bloomington. His research deals primarily with the theoretical discourse of modernity. He is the author of *Niklas Luhmann's Modernity: The Paradoxes of Differentiation* (Stanford University Press, 2000); *Sovereignty and Its Discontents: On the Primacy of Conflict and the Structure of the Political* (Birkbeck Law Press, 2004); and *Carl Schmitt: Our Untimely Contemporary* (Polity, forthcoming). He has edited a volume of essays by Niklas Luhmann and volumes dedicated to the air war during World War II; postwar German rubble films; and special journal issues on Niklas Luhmann (*New German Critique*, 1994; *Soziale Systeme*, 2008), systems theory (*Cultural Critique*, 1995), and Carl Schmitt (*South Atlantic Quarterly*, 2005). He is currently serving as chair of the Department of Germanic Studies for the third time, having also served as chair of the Department of International Studies.

William E. Scheuerman is professor of political science and international studies at Indiana University, Bloomington, where he teaches political and legal theory. He is the author of *Between the Norm and the Exception: The Frankfurt School and the Rule of Law* (MIT Press, 1994), which won two prestigious awards; *Carl Schmitt: The End of Law* (Rowman & Littlefield, 1999); *Liberal Democracy and the Social Acceleration of Time* (Johns Hopkins University Press, 2004); *Hans Morgenthau: Realism and Beyond* (Polity, 2008); *The Realist Case for Global Reform* (Polity, 2011); and *Frankfurt School Perspectives on Globalization, Democracy, and the Law* (Routledge, 2012). His edited collections include *The Rule of Law Under Siege: Selected Essays of Franz L. Neumann and Otto Kirchheimer* (University of California Press, 1996) and *From Liberal Democracy to Fascism: Legal and Political Thought in the Weimar Republic* (Brill, 2000) (with Peter C. Caldwell). Presently he is writing a book on civil disobedience and the law.

Alexander Schmitz is editor-in-chief of Konstanz University Press. He has published on Hans Blumenberg, Carl Schmitt, and Jurij Lotman. His publications on Blumenberg include, as coeditor, *Hans Blumenberg/Carl Schmitt: Briefwechsel 1971–1978* (Suhrkamp, 2007) (with Marcel Lepper, 2007); Hans Blumenberg, *Der Mann vom Mond: Über Ernst Jünger* (Suhrkamp, 2007) (with Marcel Lepper); Hans Blumenberg, *Geistesgeschichte der Technik* (Suhrkamp, 2009) (with Bernd Stiegler); Hans Blumenberg, *Schriften zur Technik* (Suhrkamp, 2015) (with Bernd Stiegler); 2015); and Hans Blumenberg, *Schriften zur Literatur* (Suhrkamp, 2016) (with Bernd Stiegler). He also edited works of Jurij Lotman, notably Jurij Lotman, *Kultur und Explosion* (Suhrkamp, 2010) (with Susi K. Frank and Cornelia Ruhe); and Jurij Lotman, *Die Innenwelt des*

Denkens: Eine semiotische Theorie der Kultur (Suhrkamp, 2010) (with Susi K. Frank and Cornelia Ruhe).

Oliver Simons is associate professor of Germanic languages at Columbia University and previously taught at Harvard University, where he was an assistant and associate professor in the Department of Germanic Languages and Literatures. His first book, a comparative study of spatial concepts in philosophy, empirical psychology, art history, and literature around 1900, appeared in 2007: *Raumgeschichten: Topographien der Moderne in Philosophie, Wissenschaft und Literatur* (Fink). His second monograph, a book on literary theories, was first published in 2009: *Literaturtheorien zur Einführung*, 2nd ed. (Junius, 2014). He has also coedited *Kolonialismus als Kultur: Literatur, Medien, Wissenschaften in der deutschen Gründerzeit des Fremden* (Francke, 2002) (with Alexander Honold), a collection on German colonialism; *Kafkas Institutionen* (Transcript, 2007) (with Arne Höcker); and *Bachmanns Medien* (Vorwerk, 2008) (with Elisabeth Wagner).

Matthew G. Specter is associate professor of history at Central Connecticut State University and associate editor of the journal *History & Theory*. His research centers on modern European intellectual history, German political thought, human rights, and international relations theory. He earned a BA from Brown University and his MA and PhD from Duke University. His first book, *Habermas: An Intellectual Biography* (Cambridge University Press, 2010), has been widely reviewed and translated. His current project, *Atlantic Realisms, 1890–1960: Political Thought and Foreign Policy*, traces the genealogy of contemporary foreign policy realism through the intellectual careers of Carl Schmitt, Hans Morgenthau, and Wilhelm Grewe. He has also published in *History & Theory* and *Modern Intellectual History*, among other publications. He is a recipient of fellowships from the Wesleyan University Center for the Humanities, the Institute for the Human Sciences, Vienna; the *Internationales Forschungszentrum Kulturwissenschaften*, Vienna; and the Friedrich-Ebert-Stiftung.

Benno Teschke is a reader in the Department of International Relations at the University of Sussex. He is the author of *The Myth of 1648: Class, Geopolitics and the Making of Modern International Relations* (Verso, 2003), which was awarded the 2004 Isaac Deutscher Memorial Prize. In 2011 he led an exchange with Gopal Balakrishnan on Carl Schmitt in the *New Left Review*. His current research projects include a sequel to *The Myth of 1648*, entitled *Grand Strategy and the Political Geographies of Historical Capitalism*. He has held positions as an Andrew Mellon Postdoctoral Fellow at the Center for Social Theory and Comparative History at the University of California, Los Angeles and in the Department of Politics and International Relations at the University of Wales, Swansea. In the summer of 2011 he was a visiting research fellow at the ERC-funded project "Europe, 1815–1914" at the University of Helsinki. In 2013–2014 he served as a visiting professor in the Department of Political Science at the University of Copenhagen.

Johannes Türk is associate professor of Germanic studies and adjunct professor of comparative literature at Indiana University, Bloomington, where he also serves as director of the Institute of German Studies. He is the author of *Die Immunität der Literatur* (Fischer, 2011) and has coedited a special journal issue on figures and figuration of the (un-)dead (*Germanic Review*, 2007) (with Robert Buch). He has published on Marcel Proust, Franz Kafka, Heinrich von Kleist, Carl Schmitt, Thomas Mann, and immunology. He is currently working on projects about immunity as a political concept as well as on political emotions.

Miguel Vatter is professor of politics at University of New South Wales, Australia. He previously taught in the United States and Chile and has held visiting professorships in Germany and China. He works in the areas of political theory and contemporary philosophy, and his books include *Between Form and Event: Machiavelli's Theory of Political Freedom* (Fordham University Press, 2000); *Machiavelli's 'The Prince': A Reader's Guide* (Bloomsbury, 2013); and *The Republic of the Living: Biopolitics and the Critique of Civil Society* (Fordham University Press, 2014). He has also coedited *The Government of Life: Foucault, Biopolitics and Neoliberalism* (Fordham University Press, 2014) (with Vanessa Lam).

Adrian Vermeule is the Ralph S. Tyler Professor of Constitutional Law at Harvard Law School. He has authored or coauthored nine books, including *Mechanisms of Democracy: Institutional Design Writ Small* (Oxford University Press, 2007); *Law and the Limits of Reason* (Oxford University Press, 2008); *The Executive Unbound: After the Madisonian Republic* (Oxford University Press, 2010) (with Eric A. Posner); *The System of the Constitution* (Oxford University Press, 2011); *The Constitution of Risk* (Cambridge University Press, 2014); and *Law's Abnegation: From Law's Empire to the Administrative State* (Harvard University Press, 2016). He is a coeditor of the *New Rambler Review* and a fellow of the American Academy of Arts and Sciences.

CARL SCHMITT'S LIFE: A CHRONOLOGY

1888	Carl Schmitt is born in Plettenberg, Germany (July 11)
1900–1907	Schmitt completes his secondary education at the *Humanistisches Gymnasium*, Attendorn
1907	Schmitt studies law at the University of Berlin
1907–1908	Schmitt studies law at the University of Munich
1908–1909	Schmitt studies law at the University of Strasbourg Schmitt befriends Fritz Eisler
1910	Schmitt passes the first stage of his juridical training (*Erstes juristisches Staatsexamen*) at the University of Strasbourg Schmitt completes his doctoral degree in law at the University of Strasbourg with a dissertation supervised by Fritz van Calker, entitled "Über Schuld und Schuldarten: Eine terminologische Untersuchung" Schmitt begins the second stage of his juridical training at the *Oberlandesgericht* Düsseldorf (August)
1912	Schmitt publishes *Gesetz und Urteil: Eine Untersuchung zum Problem der Rechtspraxis* Schmitt befriends the poet Theodor Däubler
1913	Schmitt publishes, with Fritz Eisler and under a pseudonym, *Schattenrisse*, a collection of parodies Schmitt develops a close friendship with Hugo am Zehnhoff, subsequently minister of justice in Prussia, whom he credits with having taught him what it means to be a lawyer
1914	The death of Fritz Eisler leads to Schmitt's friendship with Georg Eisler, the brother of his close friend World War I begins (July 28)
1915	Schmitt passes the second stage of his juridical training (*Assessorexamen*) (January) Schmitt marries Pawla Carita Dorotić (February 20) Schmitt begins military service at the *Stellvertretendes Generalkommando*, Munich (February 26) Schmitt drafts *Bericht über das Belagerungszustands-Gesetz* for his superiors

1916   On leave from military service, Schmitt commences his *Habilitation* and a temporary lectureship in law as *Privatdozent* at the University of Strasbourg with a *Probevorlesung* titled "Die Einwirkung des Kriegszustandes auf das ordentliche strafprozessuale Verfahren" (February 16)

Schmitt completes the *Habilitation* in law at the University of Strasbourg with a dissertation entitled "Der Wert des Staates und die Bedeutung des Einzelnen"

Schmitt publishes *Theodor Däublers "Nordlicht": Drei Studien über die Elemente, den Geist und die Aktualität des Werkes*

Schmitt publishes "Diktatur und Belagerungszustand: Eine staatsrechtliche Studie"

Schmitt begins a close friendship (which will end in 1933) with the author and editor Franz Blei

1917   Schmitt is promoted to *Assessor* in the *Stellvertretendes Generalkommando*, where he is now in charge of his own department (October 1)

Schmitt attends Max Weber's lecture "Wissenschaft als Beruf" ("Science as Vocation") at the University of Munich (November 7)

Schmitt begins a close friendship with the poet Konrad Weiss

1918   Schmitt befriends Ludwig Feuchtwanger, editor and executive director of the publishing house Dunker & Humblot

Schmitt publishes "Die Buribunken: Ein geschichtsphilosophischer Versuch"

Proclamation of the Weimar Republic (November 9)

World War I ends (November 11)

The University of Strasbourg is dissolved, and Schmitt loses his position (November 11)

1919   The German government relocates to the city of Weimar due to violent unrest in Berlin (January)

The first parliamentary elections in Weimar Germany are held. The democratic political parties gain a large absolute majority, and a center-left majority government (SPD, *Zentrum*, DDP) is formed under Reich chancellor Philipp Scheidemann (SPD) (*Weimarer Koalition*) (January 19)

Schmitt attends Max Weber's lecture "Politik als Beruf" ("Politics as Vocation") at the University of Munich (January 28)

The Weimar parliament convenes as a constituent assembly and unicameral parliament (February 6)

Friedrich Ebert (SPD) is appointed Reich president (February 13)

Schmitt's health suffers due to the revolutionary situation and ongoing state of emergency in Bavaria (May)

The Treaty of Versailles is signed (June 28)

Schmitt declines a civil service position in the *Volkswohlfahrtsministerium* (Ministry of People's Welfare)

Schmitt begins a professional relationship with the macroeconomist Moritz Julius Bonn, the director of the *Handelshochschule*, who becomes a strong supporter

Schmitt is appointed lecturer of law at the *Handelshochschule*, Munich (September 1)

Schmitt publishes *Politische Romantik*

1920   The *Nationalsozialistische Deutsche Arbeiterpartei* (NSDAP) is founded (February 24)

The *"Kapp Putsch,"* a failed attempt by right-wing forces to overthrow the Weimar Republic, takes place (March 13–17)

The *"Ruhraufstand,"* a revolutionary workers' revolt against the *"Kapp Putsch"* and attempt by left-wing forces to establish a dictatorship of the proletariat, fails (March 13–April 12)

In the second parliamentary elections, the *Weimarer Koalition* loses the absolute majority, and a center-right minority government (*Zentrum*, DVP, DDP) is formed under Reich chancellor Constantin Fehrenbach (*Zentrum*) (June 6)

Schmitt loses his position at the *Handelshochschule*, Munich (October 1)

1921   Schmitt begins a professional friendship with Rudolf Smend, the constitutional lawyer, who becomes a mentor

Schmitt is appointed professor of law at the University of Greifswald (fall)

Schmitt publishes *Die Diktatur: Von den Anfängen des modernen Souveränitätsgedankens bis zum proletarischen Klassenkampf*

1922   Schmitt is appointed professor of law at the University of Bonn (spring)

Schmitt completes draft of *Der treue Zigeuner* (*The Loyal Gipsy*), a novella (February)

Schmitt publishes *Politische Theologie: Vier Kapitel zur Lehre von der Souveränität*

Schmitt republishes the first three chapters of *Politische Theologie* in a *Festschrift* for Max Weber

Walter Rathenau is assassinated by right-wing forces, which preoccupies Schmitt (June 22)

Hyperinflation destabilizes Germany (summer)

Schmitt begins a brief friendship (which will end in 1925) with the writer and poet Hugo Ball, cofounder of the Dada movement in European art

Schmitt befriends Erik Peterson, Karl Eschweiler, and other theologians; Blei serves as his most important interlocutor about Catholicism

1923   Schmitt publishes *Die geistesgeschichtliche Lage des heutigen Parlamentarismus*

Schmitt publishes *Römischer Katholizismus und politische Form*

1924   Schmitt publishes "Die Diktatur des Reichspräsidenten nach Art. 48 der Reichsverfassung"

In the third parliamentary elections, the left-wing and right-wing political parties gain significant support, and a center-right minority government (*Zentrum*, DVP, DDP) is formed under Reich chancellor Wilhelm Marx (*Zentrum*) (May 4)

In the fourth parliamentary elections, the democratic political parties gain, the left-wing and-right wing political parties lose some support, and a center-right majority government (DNVP, *Zentrum*, DVP, DDP, BVP) is formed under Reich chancellor Hans Luther (unaffiliated) (December 7)

1925   Schmitt publishes *Verfassungslehre*

The NSDAP is refounded with Adolf Hitler as party leader (February 26)

Reich president Ebert dies (February 28)

In the first presidential elections in Weimar Germany, General Paul von Hindenburg is elected Reich president (April 26)

The Treaty of Locarno is signed (October 16)

The NSDAP creates the *Schutzstaffel* (SS) as a subsidiary organization of the *Sturmabteilung* (SA) (November 9)

1927   Schmitt publishes "Der Begriff des Politischen"

1928   Schmitt is appointed professor of law at the *Handelshochschule*, Berlin

In the fifth parliamentary elections, the democratic political parties gain support, and a left-center-right majority government (SPD, *Zentrum*, DVP, DDP) is formed under Reich chancellor Hermann Müller (SPD) (May 20)

1929   Schmitt publishes *Der Hüter der Verfassung*

Schmitt publishes "Das Reichsgericht als Hüter der Verfassung"

Hitler appoints Heinrich Himmler *Reichsführer* (Reich leader) of the SS (January 6)

Schmitt begins a close professional friendship with the economist Johannes Popitz, a fellow academic-turned-practitioner who initially served and subsequently resisted the Nazi regime

1930   Reich chancellor Müller's left-center-right majority government resigns due to internal disagreements; there is a de facto constitutional transition from parliamentarism to presidentialism (March 27)

Heinrich Brüning (*Zentrum*) is appointed Reich chancellor, and a presidential government (Z, DVP, DDP, BVP, WP, DNVP, KVP) is formed (March 30)

Brüning persuades von Hindenburg to dissolve parliament by invoking Article 48 of the Weimar Constitution, inaugurating a steady rise in the use of presidential *Notverordnungen* (emergency decrees) to govern (July 18)

In the sixth parliamentary elections, the democratic political parties incur heavy losses, the left-wing and right-wing political parties (especially NSDAP) gain significant support, and a presidential government is formed under reappointed Reich chancellor Brüning (September 14)

Schmitt begins a friendship with the writer Ernst Jünger (fall)

Schmitt receives an admiring letter from author and cultural critic Walter Benjamin, who acknowledges an intellectual debt to Schmitt's reflections on the state (December 9)

1931   Schmitt publishes *Der Hüter der Verfassung*

Schmitt publishes "Die Wendung zum totalen Staat"

Schmitt publishes "Die staatsrechtliche Bedeutung der Notverordnung, insbesondere ihre Rechtsgültigkeit"

Schmitt receives, and declines, an offer to succeed Hans Kelsen (who took up a chair at the University of Cologne) as professor of law at the University of Vienna

1932   Schmitt publishes *Der Begriff des Politischen: Mit einer Rede über das Zeitalter der Neutralisierungen und Entpolitisierungen*

Schmitt publishes *Legalität und Legitimität*

Schmitt publishes "Die Verfassungsmäßigkeit der Bestellung eines Reichskommissars für das Land Preußen"

In the second presidential elections, von Hindenburg defeats Hitler (NSDAP) and is elected to a second term as Reich president (April 10)

Brüning resigns as Reich chancellor (May 30), and a presidential government (DNVP, unaffiliated) is formed under Reich chancellor Franz von Papen (unaffiliated) (June 1)

In the so-called *Preußenschlag* (Prussia coup), von Papen persuades Reich president von Hindenburg to dissolve the government of Prussia and seizes power in the state (July 20)

In the seventh parliamentary elections, the democratic political parties incur further losses, the NSDAP emerges as the strongest political party (July 31), and the presidential government continues under von Papen

Schmitt serves as counsel for the German Reich in the case *Preußen contra Reich* at the *Staatsgerichtshof*

Schmitt is appointed professor of law at the University of Cologne (September 19)

The *Reichsgericht* (Constitutional Court) declares the *Preußenschlag* to have been partially unconstitutional (October 25)

In the eighth parliamentary elections, the democratic political parties incur further losses, the NSDAP remains the strongest political party (November 6), and a presidential government is formed under Reich chancellor Kurt von Schleicher (unaffiliated) (December 3)

1933   Schmitt publishes *Staat, Bewegung, Volk: Die Dreigliederung der politischen Einheit*

Schmitt publishes "Das Gesetz zur Behebung der Not von Volk und Reich vom 24. März 1933"

Schmitt publishes "Führertum als Grundbegriff des nationalsozialistischen Rechts"

Schmitt publishes "Die deutschen Intellektuellen"

Schleicher resigns as Reich chancellor (January 28), and a presidential government (NSDAP, DNVP, *Stahlhelm*) is formed under Reich chancellor Hitler (NSDAP) (January 30)

Reich president von Hindenburg dissolves parliament (February 1)

An arson attack on parliament results in the *Reichstagsbrand* (Reichstag fire) (February 27)

Reich president von Hindenburg bestows extraordinary emergency powers on the Hitler government in the "Reichstag Fire Decree" (February 28)

In the first parliamentary elections in Nazi Germany, the NSDAP secures a substantial (but not absolute) majority, and a presidential dictatorship (March 5) is formed

Hitler government abolishes state governments and installs Reich commissars in their stead (March 5–10)

The SS establishes Dachau concentration camp (March 22)

The Nazi parliament adopts *Gesetz zur Behebung der Not von Volk und Reich* (Law for Rectification of the Distress of Nation and Reich), the so-called Enabling Act, formally establishing the Nazi dictatorship (March 23)

Prompted by Popitz, Schmitt begins to contribute to the drafting of the *Reichsstatthaltergesetz* and to the law of criminal procedure (March 31)

The NSDAP and affiliated organizations mobilize for a nationwide anti-Jewish boycott (April 1)

The Nazi parliament adopts *Gesetz zur Wiederherstellung des Berufsbeamtentums* (Law for the Restoration of the Professional Civil Service), excluding most Jews and political opponents from the civil service (April 7)

Schmitt refuses to support a petition seeking to prevent Hans Kelsen's removal from the law faculty at the University of Cologne, the sole faculty member to do so (April 18)

Heinrich Göring establishes the *Geheime Staatspolizei* (Gestapo) (April 26)

Schmitt joins the NSDAP (May 1)

German student associations organize burnings of books by Jews and other presumed enemies of the state (May 10)

Schmitt receives, and declines, an offer to succeed Gerhard Anschütz as professor of law at the University of Heidelberg (May)

Schmitt is appointed *Preußischer Staatsrat* by Hermann Göring (July 11)

The Nazi parliament adopts *Gesetz gegen die Neubildung von Parteien* (Law against the Founding of New Political Parties), establishing a one-party state (July 14)

The Nazi parliament adopts *Gesetz zur Verhütung erbkranken Nachwuchses* (Law for the Prevention of Offspring with Hereditary Diseases), mandating the forced sterilization of disabled persons (July 14)

Schmitt receives, and declines, an offer to become professor of law at the University of Munich (August)

Schmitt is appointed professor of law at the University of Berlin (October)

Nazi Germany leaves the League of Nations (October 14)

Schmitt becomes *Reichsgruppenleiter*, or chair, of the section "University Professors" of the *Bund Nationalsozialistischer Deutscher Juristen* (Association of National Socialist German Legal Professionals) (November)

1934   Schmitt publishes *Über die drei Arten des rechtswissenschaftlichen Denkens*

Schmitt publishes *Nationalsozialismus und Völkerrecht*

Schmitt publishes "Ein Jahr nationalsozialistischer Verfassungsstaat"

Schmitt publishes "Nationalsozialismus und Rechtsstaat"

Schmitt publishes "Nationalsozialistisches Rechtsdenken"

Schmitt publishes "Der Führer schützt das Recht: Zur Reichstagsrede Adolf Hitlers vom 13. Juli 1934"

Himmler is appointed head of Gestapo and of all police forces outside of Prussia (April 20)

Hans Frank appoints Schmitt editor of the *Deutsche Juristen-Zeitung*, Germany's most influential and respected law journal (June 1)

The *"Röhm Putsch,"* a violent purge by the SS of the leadership of the SA, the Nazi paramilitary organization, takes place, and select politicians are assassinated (June 30–July 2)

Von Hindenburg dies, and Hitler becomes Reich president (August 2)

Hitler abolishes the office of Reich president and declares himself *Führer des deutschen Reiches und Volkes* (Leader of the German Reich and People) (August 19)

Himmler establishes the *Inspektion der Konzentrationslager* (Inspectorate of Concentration Camps), the central SS administrative and managerial authority for all Nazi concentration camps (December 10)

1935   Schmitt publishes "Die Verfassung der Freiheit"

Schmitt publishes "Der Rechtsstaat"

The Nazi government adopts the *Reichsstatthaltergesetz* (Reich Governors Law) (January 30)

The Nazi government reintroduces military service, thereby violating the Treaty of Versailles (March 16)

Hitler's government decrees the *Reichsbürgergesetz* (Reich Citizenship Law) and *Gesetz zum Schutze des deutschen Blutes und der deutschen Ehre* (Reich Citizenship Law for the Protection of German Blood and German Honor), the so-called Nuremberg Race Laws (September 15)

1936 Schmitt convenes the conference "Das Judentum in der Rechtswissenschaft" (October 3–4)

Schmitt publishes "Faschistische und nationalsozialistische Rechtswissenschaft"

Schmitt publishes "Die deutsche Rechtswissenschaft im Kampf gegen den jüdischen Geist"

The Winter Olympic Games take place at Garmisch-Partenkirchen (February 6–16)

Nazi Germany occupies the demilitarized Rhineland, thereby violating the Treaty of Versailles (March 7)

Hitler appoints Himmler Chief of German Police (June 17)

The SS establishes Sachsenhausen concentration camp (July 12)

Nazi Germany intervenes in the Spanish Civil War (July 25)

The Summer Olympic Games take place in Berlin (August 1–18)

The *SD-Hauptamt des Sicherheitsdienstes der Reichsführung SS* (Security Service Main Office of the SS High Command) begins investigation of "Prof. Dr. Karl Schmitt" (October 4)

Das Schwarze Korps, the official, weekly newspaper of the SS, publishes the first of two articles calling into question Schmitt's Nazi credentials (December 3)

Das Schwarze Korps publishes the second of two articles calling into question Schmitt's Nazi credentials (December 10)

1937 Schmitt publishes "Totaler Feind, totaler Krieg, totaler Staat"

Schmitt publishes "Der Staat als Mechanismus bei Hobbes und Descartes"

The Nazi parliament extends the Enabling Law by four years (January 30)

The SS establishes Buchenwald concentration camp (July 19)

The Nazi propaganda exhibition *"Entartete Kunst"* ("Degenerate Art") opens in Munich (July 19–November 30)

Hitler decides on a violent solution of the *"Lebensraumfrage"* ("The Question of Living Space") by 1943/1945 (November 5)

The Nazi propaganda exhibition *"Der ewige Jude"* ("The Eternal Jew") opens in Munich (November 8)

1938 Schmitt publishes *Der Leviathan in der Staatslehre des Thomas Hobbes: Sinn und Fehlschlag eines politischen Symbols*

Schmitt publishes *Die Wendung zum diskriminierenden Kriegsbegriff*

Schmitt publishes "Völkerrechtliche Neutralität und völkische Totalität"

Nazi Germany annexes Austria (March 11–13)

The SS establishes Flossenbürg concentration camp (May 3)

The SS establishes Mauthausen concentration camp (August 8)

Nazi Germany, Italy, Great Britain, and France sign the so-called Munich Agreement, forcing Czechoslovakia to surrender its border regions to Nazi Germany (September 29–30)

The NSDAP and affiliated organizations organize a nationwide pogrom against Jews (November 9–10)

The Nazi government issues *Verordnung zur Ausschaltung der Juden aus dem deutschen Wirtschaftsleben* (Decree on the Elimination of the Jews from Economic Life), barring Jews from all economic activities (November 12)

The Nazi government issues *Verordnung über den Einsatz des jüdischen Vermögens* (Decree on the Utilization of Jewish property), forcing Jews to sell any and all of their possessions (December 3)

1939   Schmitt publishes *Völkerrechtliche Großraumordnung mit Interventionsverbot für raumfremde Mächte: Ein Beitrag zum Reichsbegriff im Völkerrecht*

Schmitt publishes "Der Reichsbegriff im Völkerrecht"

Nazi Germany invades the remaining territory of Czechoslovakia and establishes the "Protectorate of Bohemia and Moravia" (March 15)

The SS establishes Ravensbrück concentration camp (May 15)

Nazi Germany invades Poland; World War II begins (September 1)

The SS establishes the civilian prisoner camp (later concentration camp) Stutthof (September 2)

Himmler establishes the *Reichssicherheitshauptamt* (RSHA) (Reich Security Main Office), led by Reinhard Heydrich and subsequently charged with coordinating the destruction of the European Jews (September 27)

Nazi Germany annexes former Polish regions and establishes the *Generalgouvernement* (General Government) to administer these occupied territories (October 26)

1940   Schmitt publishes *Positionen und Begriffe im Kampf mit Weimar—Genf—Versailles, 1923–1939*

Schmitt publishes "Reich und Raum: Elemente eines neuen Völkerrechts"

Schmitt publishes "Die Auflösung der europäischen Ordnung im 'International Law' (1890–1939)"

Schmitt publishes "Raum und Großraum im Völkerrecht"

Nazi Germany invades Norway and Denmark (April 9)

Nazi authorities seal the Jewish ghetto in Lodz (April 30)

Nazi Germany invades the Netherlands, Belgium, Luxembourg, and France (May 10)

The SS establishes Auschwitz concentration camp (Auschwitz I) (May 20)

The SS establishes Neuengamme concentration camp (June 4)

Italy enters World War II as an ally of Nazi Germany (June 10)

Nazi authorities seal the Jewish ghetto in Warsaw (November 15)

Hungary, Romania, and Slovakia become allies of Nazi Germany (November 20–24)

1941   Schmitt publishes "Staatliche Souveränität und freies Meer: Über den Gegensatz von Land und See im Völkerrecht der Neuzeit"

Bulgaria becomes an ally of Nazi Germany (March 1)

Nazi authorities establish and seal the Jewish ghetto in Krakow (March 3–20)

Nazi Germany and its allies invade Yugoslavia and Greece (April 6)

The SS establishes Gross-Rosen concentration camp (May 1)

The SS establishes Natzweiler-Struthof concentration camp (May 21)

Croatia becomes an ally of Nazi Germany (June 15)

Nazi Germany invades the Soviet Union, and mobile killing units (*Einsatzgruppen*) embark on the coordinated mass killing of Jews and other presumed enemies on Soviet territory (June 22)

Heydrich and RSHA are charged with developing plans for the implementation of the "Final Solution" of the "Jewish Question" (July 31)

Nazi authorities establish the Jewish ghetto in Bialystok (August 1)

Nazi authorities seal the Jewish ghetto in Kovno (August 15)

Himmler tasks SS General Odilo Globocnik with implementing *Aktion Reinhardt*, the plan for the destruction of Jews in the General Government (October 15)

Nazi authorities seal the Jewish ghetto in Riga (October 25)

Nazi authorities in the General Government establish extermination camps in Bełżec, Sobibór, and Treblinka (November)

Nazi authorities establish Theresienstadt concentration camp (November 24)

Japan attacks the United States at Pearl Harbor (December 7)

Nazi authorities establish Chelmno extermination camp and begin mass killing of Jews (December)

1942   Schmitt publishes *Land und Meer: Eine weltgeschichtliche Betrachtung*

Heydrich and RSHA convene the so-called Wannsee Conference in Berlin to coordinate the administration of the Holocaust (January 20)

Nazi authorities establish Auschwitz-Birkenau concentration and extermination camp (Auschwitz II) (March 1)

The large-scale deportation and systematic destruction of the European Jews begins (March)

1943   Joseph Goebbels announces "*den totalen Krieg*" in a propaganda speech at the *Sportpalast*, Berlin (February 18)

1944   British and U.S. troops invade Nazi-occupied France (June 6)

1945   SS authorities begin forced evacuations of many concentration camps, so-called death marches, notably in Auschwitz (January 17)

Soviet troops liberate Auschwitz concentration camp complex (January 27)

U.S. troops liberate Ohrdruf concentration camp, a subcamp of Buchen-
    wald (April 4)
British troops liberate Bergen-Belsen concentration camp (April 15)
Hitler commits suicide (April 30)
Schmitt is arrested at his home in Berlin-Schlachtensee by Soviet troops in
    (April)
Nazi Germany surrenders unconditionally (May 7–9)
Schmitt prepares *Das internationalrechtliche Verbrechen des Angriffskrieges
    und der Grundsatz "Nullum crimen, nulla poena sine lege,"* a legal opin-
    ion in support of the defense of Friedrich Flick, a German industrialist,
    at the International Military Tribunal (IMT) (August)
Schmitt is arrested and interrogated by U.S. authorities in Berlin and
    spends almost twelve months in detention there (September 25)
The trial of the major war criminals before the IMT at Nuremberg begins
    (November 20)
Control Council Law No. 10 is adopted (December 20)

1946	Schmitt is released from his first U.S. detention (October 10)
	The IMT delivers its judgment (October 1)
1947	The U.S. military government establishes Military Tribunal III to try *United States v. Josef Altstoetter, et al.*, the so-called Justice Case, under Control Council Law No. 10 (February 13)
	Schmitt is rearrested and interrogated by U.S. authorities; he spends two months in detention in Nuremberg (March 19)
	Schmitt is released from his second U.S. detention (May 6) and retreats to Plettenberg
	Schmitt begins work on the *Glossarium* (August)
	Military Tribunal III delivers its judgment (December 3–4)
1949	Schmitt publishes "Amnestie—Urform des Rechts"
	The resurrected *Vereinigung der deutschen Staatsrechtslehrer* opposes Carl Schmitt's membership
	Otto Kirchheimer visits Schmitt in Plettenberg (December)
1950	Schmitt publishes *Ex Captivitate Salus: Erfahrungen der Zeit 1945/47*
	Schmitt publishes *Donoso Cortés in gesamteuropäischer Interpretation: Vier Aufsätze*
	Schmitt publishes *Der Nomos der Erde im Völkerrecht des Jus Publicum Europaeum*
1952	*Academia Moralis*, a support network for Schmitt, is formally established
1953	Schmitt's isolation lessens and his intellectual contacts and travel increase
	On the occasion of Schmitt's sixty-fifth birthday, friends and supporters publish a bibliography in his honor (July)
	Schmitt assists Johannes Winckelmann with the corrections for the new edition of Max Weber's *Wirtschaft und Gesellschaft*

1954   Schmitt republishes *Verfassungslehre* (May)
        Schmitt publishes "Im Vorraum der Macht"

1955   Schmitt delivers a rare public lecture, on Hamlet, at the *Volkshochschule*,
        an institution of adult education, in Düsseldorf

1956   Schmitt publishes *Hamlet oder Hekuba: Der Einbruch der Zeit in das Spiel*

1958   Schmitt publishes *Verfassungsrechtliche Aufsätze aus den Jahren 1924–
        1954: Materialien zu einer Verfassungslehre*

1959   Schmitt publishes "Nomos—Nahme—Name"
        On the occasion of Schmitt's seventieth birthday, friends and support-
        ers publish the first of two *Festschrifts*, this one edited by Hans Barion,
        Ernst Forsthoff, and Werner Weber

1960   Schmitt publishes *Die Tyrannei der Werte: Überlegungen eines Juristen zur
        Wert-Philosophie*

1962   As founding editors, Ernst-Wolfgang Böckenförde and Roman Schnur
        establish the journal *Der Staat*, a counterpoint to the influential *Archiv
        des öffentlichen Rechts*

1963   Schmitt publishes *Theorie des Partisanen: Zwischenbemerkung zum Begriff
        des Politischen*

1968   On the occasion of Schmitt's eightieth birthday, friends and supporters
        publish the edited collection *Epirrhosis*, the second of two *Festschrifts*,
        this one edited by Hans Barion, Ernst-Wolfgang Böckenförde, Ernst
        Forsthoff, and Werner Weber

1970   Schmitt publishes *Politische Theologie II: Die Legende von der Erledigung
        jeder Politischen Theologie*

1971   Schmitt ends discussions with Propyläen-Verlag, Berlin, about a possible
        edition of his political writings

1978   Schmitt publishes "Die legale Weltrevolution: Politischer Mehrwert als
        Prämie auf juristische Legalität und Superlegalität," his final article

1985   Schmitt dies in Plettenberg (April 7)

LIST OF CARL SCHMITT'S WRITINGS

NOTE: This list of publications is comprehensive but not exhaustive. It is arranged chronologically and across five sections: books and monographs, articles and essays, diaries, correspondence, and interviews. We have excluded minor articles and essays, including most book reviews, the majority of Carl Schmitt's contributions to newspapers, his poems as well as other occasional writings, and his less significant correspondence. Due to space constraints, we have provided only basic bibliographical information.

BOOKS AND MONOGRAPHS

Über Schuld und Schuldarten: Eine terminologische Untersuchung (1910)

Gesetz und Urteil: Eine Untersuchung zum Problem der Rechtspraxis (1912)

Schattenrisse (1913) (with Fritz Eisler)

Der Wert des Staates und die Bedeutung des Einzelnen (1914)

Theodor Däublers "Nordlicht": Drei Studien über die Elemente, den Geist und die Aktualität des Werkes (1916)

Politische Romantik (1919), translated as *Political Romanticism* (1986)

Die Diktatur: Von den Anfängen des modernen Souveränitätsgedankens bis zum proletarischen Klassenkampf (1921), translated as *Dictatorship: From the Origin of the Modern Concept of Sovereignty to Proletarian Class Struggle* (2014)

Politische Theologie: Vier Kapitel zur Lehre von der Souveränität (1922), translated as *Political Theology: Four Chapters on the Concept of Sovereignty* (1985)

Die geistesgeschichtliche Lage des heutigen Parlamentarismus (1923), translated as *The Crisis of Parliamentary Democracy* (1988)

Römischer Katholizismus und politische Form (1923), translated as *Roman Catholicism and Political Form* (1996)

Die Rheinlande als Objekt internationaler Politik (1925)

Die Kernfrage des Völkerbundes (1926)

Volksentscheid und Volksbegehren: Ein Beitrag zur Auslegung der Weimarer Verfassung und zur Lehre von der unmittelbaren Demokratie (1927)

Verfassungslehre (1928), translated as *Constitutional Theory* (2008)

Hugo Preuss: Sein Staatsbegriff und seine Stellung in der deutschen Staatslehre (1930)

Der Völkerbund und das politische Problem der Friedenssicherung (1930)

Der Hüter der Verfassung (1931), translated in part as *The Guardian of the Constitution* (2015)

Freiheitsrechte und institutionelle Garantien der Reichsverfassung (1931)

Der Begriff des Politischen: Mit einer Rede über das Zeitalter der Neutralisierungen und Entpolitisierungen (1932), translated as *The Concept of the Political* (1996)

Legalität und Legitimität (1932), translated as *Legality and Legitimacy* (2004)

Staat, Bewegung, Volk: Die Dreigliederung der politischen Einheit (1933), translated as *State, Movement, People* (2001)

Das Reichsstatthaltergsetz (1933)

Fünf Leitsätze für die Rechtspraxis (1933)

Über die drei Arten des rechtswissenschaftlichen Denkens (1934), translated as *On the Three Types of Juristic Thought* (2004)

Staatsgefüge und Zusammenbruch des Zweiten Reiches: Der Sieg des Bürgers über den Soldaten (1934)

Nationalsozialismus und Völkerrecht (1934)

Der Leviathan in der Staatslehre des Thomas Hobbes: Sinn und Fehlschlag eines politischen Symbols (1938), translated as *The Leviathan in the State Theory of Thomas Hobbes: Meaning and Failure of a Political Symbol* (1996)

Die Wendung zum diskriminierenden Kriegsbegriff (1938), translated as *The Turn to the Discriminating Concept of War* (2011)

Völkerrechtliche Großraumordnung mit Interventionsverbot für raumfremde Mächte: Ein Beitrag zum Reichsbegriff im Völkerrecht (1939), translated as "The *Großraum* Order of International Law with a Ban on Intervention for Spatially Foreign Powers: A Contribution to the Concept of Reich in International Law" (2011)

Positionen und Begriffe im Kampf mit Weimar—Genf—Versailles, 1923–1939 (1940), translated in part as *Four Articles, 1931–1938* (1999)

Land und Meer: Eine weltgeschichtliche Betrachtung (1942), translated as *Land and Sea* (1997 and 2015)

Die Lage der europäischen Rechtswissenschaft (1950)

Ex Captivitate Salus: Erfahrungen der Zeit 1945/47 (1950)

Donoso Cortés in gesamteuropäischer Interpretation: Vier Aufsätze (1950)

Der Nomos der Erde im Völkerrecht des Jus Publicum Europaeum (1950), translated as *The "Nomos" of the Earth in the International Law of the "Jus Publicum Europaeum"* (2003)

Hamlet oder Hekuba: Der Einbruch der Zeit in das Spiel (1956), translated as *Hamlet or Hecuba: The Intrusion of the Time into the Play* (2009)

Verfassungsrechtliche Aufsätze aus den Jahren 1924–1954: Materialien zu einer Verfassungslehre (1958)

Die Tyrannei der Werte: Überlegungen eines Juristen zur Wert-Philosophie (1960), translated as *The Tyranny of Values* (1996)

Theorie des Partisanen: Zwischenbemerkung zum Begriff des Politischen (1963), translated as *Theory of the Partisan: Intermediate Commentary on the Concept of the Political* (2007)

Politische Theologie II: Die Legende von der Erledigung jeder Politischen Theologie (1970), translated as *Political Theology II: The Myth of the Closure of Any Political Theology* (2008)

Das internationalrechtliche Verbrechen des Angriffskrieges und der Grundsatz "Nullum crimen, nulla poena sine lege" (1994), translated as "The International Crime of the War of Aggression and the Principle 'Nullum crimen, nulla poena sine lege'" (2011)

Staat, Großraum, Nomos: Arbeiten aus den Jahren 1916–1969 (1995)

Antworten in Nürnberg (2000)

Frieden oder Pazifismus? Arbeiten zum Völkerrecht und zur internationalen Politik 1924–1978 (2005)

ARTICLES AND ESSAYS

"Über Tatbestandsmäßigkeit und Rechtswidrigkeit des kunstgerechten operativen Eingriffs" (1911)

"Diktatur und Belagerungszustand: Eine staatsrechtliche Studie" (1916), reprinted in *Staat, Großraum, Nomos: Arbeiten aus den Jahren 1916–1969* (1995)

"Die Einwirkungen des Kriegszustandes auf das ordentliche strafprozessuale Verfahren" (1916), reprinted in *Die Militärzeit 1915 bis 1919: Tagebuch Februar bis Dezember 1915* (2005)

"Rechtsbegriff und Rechtsidee" (1916) [book review]

"Recht und Macht" (1917), reprinted in *Die Militärzeit 1915 bis 1919: Tagebuch Februar bis Dezember 1915* (2005)

"Die Sichtbarkeit der Kirche: Eine scholastische Erwägung" (1917), reprinted in *Die Militärzeit 1915 bis 1919: Tagebuch Februar bis Dezember 1915* (2005); translated as "The Visibility of the Church: A Scholastic Consideration" (1996)

"Die Buribunken: Ein geschichtsphilosophischer Versuch" (1918), reprinted in *Die Militärzeit 1915 bis 1919: Tagebuch Februar bis Dezember 1915* (2005); translated as "The Buribunks: A Historico-Philosophical Meditation" (1999)

"Politische Theorie und Romantik" (1921), incorporated into the second edition (1925) of *Politische Romantik* (1919)

"Die Staatsphilosophie der Gegenrevolution" (1922), incorporated into both *Politische Theologie: Vier Kapitel zur Lehre von der Souveränität* (1922) and *Donoso Cortés in gesamteuropäischer Interpretation: Vier Aufsätze* (1950)

"Soziologie des Souveränitätsbegriffes und politische Theologie" (1923), reprinted from *Politische Theologie: Vier Kapitel zur Lehre von der Souveränität* (1922)

"Die geistesgeschichtliche Lage des heutigen Parlamentarismus" (1923), reprinted as *Die geistesgeschichtliche Lage des heutigen Parlamentarismus* (1923) and reprinted in part in *Positionen und Begriffe im Kampf mit Weimar—Genf—Versailles, 1923–1939* (1940)

"Der Begriff der modernen Demokratie in seinem Verhältnis zum Staatsbegriff" (1924), reprinted in *Positionen und Begriffe im Kampf mit Weimar—Genf—Versailles, 1923–1939* (1940)

"Romantik" (1924), reprinted as the preface to the second edition (1925) of *Politische Romantik* (1919)

"Die Diktatur des Reichspräsidenten nach Art. 48 der Reichsverfassung" (1924), incorporated into the second edition (1928) of *Die Diktatur: Von den Anfängen des modernen Souveränitätsgedankens bis zum proletarischen Klassenkampf* (1921)

"Reichspräsident und Weimarer Verfassung" (1925), reprinted in *Staat, Großraum, Nomos: Arbeiten aus den Jahren 1916–1969* (1995)

"'Einmaligkeit' und 'gleicher Anlaß' bei der Reichstagsauflösung nach Artikel 25 der Reichsverfassung" (1925), reprinted in *Verfassungsrechtliche Aufsätze aus den Jahren 1924–1954: Materialien zu einer Verfassungslehre* (1958)

"Die Kernfrage des Völkerbundes" (1925) [book review], incorporated in part into *Die Kernfrage des Völkerbundes* (1926) and reprinted in *Frieden oder Pazifismus? Arbeiten zum Völkerrecht und zur internationalen Politik 1924–1978* (2005)

"Neue Herrschaftsformen im Kampf um den Rhein" (1925), reprinted in part in *Die Rheinlande als Objekt internationaler Politik* (1925)

"Zu Friedrich Meineckes 'Idee der Staatsräson'" (1926) [book review], reprinted in *Positionen und Begriffe im Kampf mit Weimar—Genf—Versailles, 1923–1939* (1940)

"Der Gegensatz von Parlamentarismus und moderner Massendemokratie" (1926), incorporated into the second edition (1926) of *Die geistesgeschichtliche Lage des heutigen Parlamentarismus* (1923) and reprinted in *Positionen und Begriffe im Kampf mit Weimar—Genf—Versailles, 1923–1939* (1940)

"Gerhard Anschütz, 'Die Verfassung des deutschen Reiches vom 11. August 1919'" (1926) [book review]

"Das Ausführungsgesetz zu Art. 48 der Reichsverfassung (sog. Diktaturgesetz)" (1926), reprinted in *Staat, Großraum, Nomos: Arbeiten aus den Jahren 1916–1969* (1995)

"Absolutismus" (1926), reprinted in *Staat, Großraum, Nomos: Arbeiten aus den Jahren 1916–1969* (1995)

"Diktatur" (1926), reprinted in *Staat, Großraum, Nomos: Arbeiten aus den Jahren 1916–1969* (1995)

"Der Begriff des Politischen" (1927), reprinted in part in *Positionen und Begriffe im Kampf mit Weimar—Genf—Versailles, 1923–1939* (1940) and in whole in *Frieden oder Pazifismus? Arbeiten zum Völkerrecht und zur internationalen Politik 1924–1978* (2005)

"Donoso Cortés in Berlin (1848)" (1927), reprinted in *Positionen und Begriffe im Kampf mit Weimar—Genf—Versailles, 1923–1939* (1940) and incorporated into *Donoso Cortés in gesamteuropäischer Interpretation: Vier Aufsätze* (1950)

"Der Völkerbund und Europa" (1927), reprinted in both *Positionen und Begriffe im Kampf mit Weimar—Genf—Versailles, 1923–1939* (1940) and *Frieden oder Pazifismus? Arbeiten zum Völkerrecht und zur internationalen Politik 1924–1978* (2005)

"Der Staat und das Recht auf den Krieg" (1928), reprinted in *Der Begriff des Politischen: Mit einer Rede über das Zeitalter der Neutralisierungen und Entpolitisierungen* (1932)

"Der bürgerliche Rechtsstaat" (1928), reprinted in *Staat, Großraum, Nomos: Arbeiten aus den Jahren 1916–1969* (1995); translated, in part, as "The Liberal Rule of Law" (2000)

"Völkerrechtliche Probleme im Rheingebiet" (1928), reprinted in *Positionen und Begriffe im Kampf mit Weimar—Genf—Versailles, 1923-1939* (1940)

"Wesen und Werden des faschistischen Staates" (1929) [book review], reprinted in *Positionen und Begriffe im Kampf mit Weimar—Genf—Versailles, 1923-1939* (1940)

"Der Hüter der Verfassung" (1929), incorporated into *Der Hüter der Verfassung* (1931)

"Die europäische Kultur im Zwischenstadium der Neutralisierung" (1929), reprinted in *Positionen und Begriffe im Kampf mit Weimar—Genf—Versailles, 1923-1939* (1940)

"Die Auflösung des Enteigungsbegriffs" (1929), reprinted in *Verfassungsrechtliche Aufsätze aus den Jahren 1924-1954: Materialien zu einer Verfassungslehre* (1958)

"Zehn Jahre Reichsverfassung" (1929), reprinted in *Verfassungsrechtliche Aufsätze aus den Jahren 1924-1954: Materialien zu einer Verfassungslehre* (1958)

"Der unbekannte Donos Cortés" (1929), reprinted in both *Positionen und Begriffe im Kampf mit Weimar—Genf—Versailles, 1923-1939* (1940) and *Donoso Cortés in gesamteuropäischer Interpretation: Vier Aufsätze* (1950)

"Das Reichsgericht als Hüter der Verfassung" (1929), reprinted in *Verfassungsrechtliche Aufsätze aus den Jahren 1924-1954: Materialien zu einer Verfassungslehre* (1958)

"Das Problem der innerpolitischen Neutralität des Staates" (1930), reprinted in *Verfassungsrechtliche Aufsätze aus den Jahren 1924-1954: Materialien zu einer Verfassungslehre* (1958)

"Die politische Lage der entmilitarisierten Rheinlande" (1930), reprinted in *Frieden oder Pazifismus? Arbeiten zum Völkerrecht und zur internationalen Politik 1924-1978* (2005)

"Einberufung und Vertagung des Reichstages nach Art. 24 Reichsverfassung" (1930)

"Eine Warnung vor falschen politischen Fragestellungen" (1930)

"Staatsethik und pluralistischer Staat" (1930), reprinted in *Positionen und Begriffe im Kampf mit Weimar—Genf—Versailles, 1923-1939* (1940); translated as both "Ethics of State and Pluralistic State" (1999) and "State Ethics and the Pluralistic State" (2000)

"Reichs- und Verfassungsreform" (1931)

"Die Wendung zum totalen Staat" (1931), incorporated into *Der Hüter der Verfassung* (1931) and reprinted in *Positionen und Begriffe im Kampf mit Weimar—Genf—Versailles, 1923-1939* (1940); translated as "The Way to the Total State" (1999)

"Wohlerworbene Beamtenrechte und Gehaltskürzungen" (1931), reprinted in *Verfassungsrechtliche Aufsätze aus den Jahren 1924-1954: Materialien zu einer Verfassungslehre* (1958)

"Staatsideologie und Staatsrealität in Deutschland und Westeuropa" (1931)

"Die neutralen Größen im heutigen Verfassungsstaat" (1931)

"Die staatsrechtliche Bedeutung der Notverordnung, insbesondere ihre Rechtsgültigkeit" (1931), reprinted in *Verfassungsrechtliche Aufsätze aus den Jahren 1924-1954: Materialien zu einer Verfassungslehre* (1958)

"Die Weimarer Verfassung" (1931)

"Der Völkerbund" (1931), reprinted in *Frieden oder Pazifismus? Arbeiten zum Völkerrecht und zur internationalen Politik 1924-1978* (2005)

"Grundsätzliches zur heutigen Notverordnungspraxis" (1932)

"Legalität und gleiche Chance politischer Machtgewinnung" (1932), reprinted from *Legalität und Legitimität* (1932)

"Der Mißbrauch der Legalität" (1932), reprinted in *Werkstatt—Discorsi: Briefwechsel 1967–1981* (2009) (with Hans-Dietrich Sander)

"Ist der Reichskommissar verfassungsmäßig?" (1932)

"Die Verfassungsmäßigkeit der Bestellung eines Reichskommissars für das Land Preußen" (1932)

"Gesunde Wirtschaft im starken Staat" (1932), reprinted under a different title in *Staat, Großraum, Nomos: Arbeiten aus den Jahren 1916–1969* (1995); translated as "Strong State and Sound Economy: An Address to Business Leaders" (1998)

"Plädoyer Carl Schmitts vor dem Staatsgerichtshof" (1932), reprinted in *Positionen und Begriffe im Kampf mit Weimar—Genf—Versailles, 1923–1939* (1940)

"Inhalt und Bedeutung des zweiten Hauptteils der Reichsverfassung" (1932), reprinted under a different title in *Verfassungsrechtliche Aufsätze aus den Jahren 1924–1954: Materialien zu einer Verfassungslehre* (1958)

"Die Stellvertretung des Reichspräsidenten" (1933), reprinted in *Verfassungsrechtliche Aufsätze aus den Jahren 1924–1954: Materialien zu einer Verfassungslehre* (1958)

"Weiterentwicklung des totalen Staates in Deutschland" (1933), reprinted in both *Positionen und Begriffe im Kampf mit Weimar—Genf—Versailles, 1923–1939* (1940) and *Verfassungsrechtliche Aufsätze aus den Jahren 1924–1954: Materialien zu einer Verfassungslehre* (1958); translated as "Further Development of the Total State in Germany" (1999)

"Machtposition des modernen Staates" (1933), reprinted in *Verfassungsrechtliche Aufsätze aus den Jahren 1924–1954: Materialien zu einer Verfassungslehre* (1958)

"Das Gesetz zur Behebung der Not von Volk und Reich vom 24. März 1933" (1933)

"Der Geist des neuen Staatsrechts" (1933)

"Das gute Recht der deutschen Revolution" (1933)

"Die deutschen Intellektuellen" (1933)

"1 Jahr deutsche Politik: Rückblick vom 20. Juli 1932—Von Papen über Schleicher zum ersten deutschen Volkskanzler Adolf Hitler" (1933)

"Staatsrat Univ.-Prof. Pg. Dr. C. Schmitt über den Staatsrat und die Führerfrage im nationalsozialistischen Gemeinwesen" (1933)

"Frieden oder Pazifismus?" (1933), reprinted in *Frieden oder Pazifismus? Arbeiten zum Völkerrecht und zur internationalen Politik 1924–1978* (2005)

"Führertum als Grundbegriff des nationalsozialistischen Rechts" (1933), reprinted from *Staat, Bewegung, Volk: Die Dreigliederung der politischen Einheit* (1933)

"Richtertum und Politik" (1933)

"Die Ohnmacht des Liberalismus" (1933), reprinted from the second edition (1933) of *Der Begriff des Politischen: Mit einer Rede über das Zeitalter der Neutralisierungen und Entpolitisierungen* (1932)

"Neue Leitsätze für die Rechtspraxis" (1933), reprinted as *Fünf Leitsätze für die Rechtspraxis* (1933)

"USA und die völkerrechtlichen Formen des modernen Imperialismus" (1933), reprinted under a slightly different title in both *Positionen und Begriffe im Kampf mit Weimar—Genf—Versailles, 1923-1939* (1940) and *Frieden oder Pazifismus? Arbeiten zum Völkerrecht und zur internationalen Politik 1924-1978* (2005)

"Der Neubau des Staats- und Verwaltungsrechts" (1933)

"Die Verfassungslage Deutschlands" (1933)

"Ein Jahr nationalsozialistischer Verfassungsstaat" (1934)

"Neuaufbau von Staat und Recht" (1934)

"Das neue Verfassungsgesetz" (1934)

"Nationalsozialismus und Rechtsstaat" (1934)

"Die Logik der geistigen Unterwerfung" (1934)

"Nationalsozialistisches Rechtsdenken" (1934)

"Der Weg des deutschen Juristen: Ein Geleitwort" (1934)

"Unsere geistige Gesamtlage und unsere juristische Aufgabe" (1934)

"Der Führer schützt das Recht: Zur Reichstagsrede Adolf Hitlers vom 13. Juli 1934" (1934), reprinted in *Positionen und Begriffe im Kampf mit Weimar—Genf—Versailles, 1923-1939* (1940)

"Der Vorbehalt beim Abschluß völkerrechtlicher Verträge" (1934) [book review], reprinted in *Frieden oder Pazifismus? Arbeiten zum Völkerrecht und zur internationalen Politik 1924-1978* (2005)

"Auf dem Wege zum neuen Reich" (1934) [book review]

"Gleichberechtigung und Völkerrecht" (1934), reprinted from *Nationalsozialismus und Völkerrecht* (1934)

"Sowjet-Union und Genfer VB [Völkerbund]" (1934), reprinted in *Frieden oder Pazifismus? Arbeiten zum Völkerrecht und zur internationalen Politik 1924-1978* (2005)

"Paktsysteme als Kriegsrüstung: Eine völkerrechtliche Betrachtung" (1935), reprinted in *Frieden oder Pazifismus? Arbeiten zum Völkerrecht und zur internationalen Politik 1924-1978* (2005)

"Über die innere Logik der Allgemeinpakte auf gegenseitigen Beistand" (1935), reprinted in both *Positionen und Begriffe im Kampf mit Weimar—Genf—Versailles, 1923-1939* (1940) and *Frieden oder Pazifismus? Arbeiten zum Völkerrecht und zur internationalen Politik 1924-1978* (2005)

"Die Rechtswissenschaft im Führerstaat" (1935)

"Kodifikation oder Novelle? Über die Aufgabe und Methode der heutigen Gesetzgebung" (1935)

"Die Verfassung der Freiheit" (1935), translated as "The Constitution of Freedom" (2000)

"Was bedeutet der Streit um den 'Rechtsstaat'?" (1935), reprinted in *Staat, Großraum, Nomos: Arbeiten aus den Jahren 1916-1969* (1995)

"Der Rechtsstaat" (1935), reprinted in *Staat, Großraum, Nomos: Arbeiten aus den Jahren 1916-1969* (1995)

"Die geschichtliche Lage der deutschen Rechtswissenschaft" (1936)

"Sprengung der Locarno-Gemeinschaft durch Einschaltung der Sowjets" (1936), reprinted in *Frieden oder Pazifismus? Arbeiten zum Völkerrecht und zur internationalen Politik 1924–1978* (2005)

"Aufgabe und Notwendigkeit des deutschen Rechtsstandes" (1936)

"Faschistische und nationalsozialistische Rechtswissenschaft" (1936)

"Die siebente Wandlung des Genfer Völkerbundes: Eine völkerrechtliche Folge der Vernichtung Abessiniens" (1936)

"Die nationalsozialistische Gesetzgebung und der Vorbehalt des 'ordre public' im internationalen Privatrecht" (1936)

"Vergleichender Überblick über die neueste Entwicklung des Problems der gesetzgeberischen Ermächtigungen (Legislative Delegationen)" (1936), reprinted in *Positionen und Begriffe im Kampf mit Weimar—Genf—Versailles, 1923–1939* (1940)

"Die deutsche Rechtswissenschaft im Kampf gegen den jüdischen Geist" (1936)

"Über die neuen Aufgaben der Verfassungsgeschichte" (1936)

"Politik" (1936), reprinted in *Staat, Großraum, Nomos: Arbeiten aus den Jahren 1916–1969* (1995)

"Totaler Feind, totaler Krieg, totaler Staat" (1937), reprinted in both *Positionen und Begriffe im Kampf mit Weimar—Genf—Versailles, 1923–1939* (1940) and *Frieden oder Pazifismus? Arbeiten zum Völkerrecht und zur internationalen Politik 1924–1978* (2005); translated as "Total Enemy, Total War and Total State" (1999)

"Der Begriff der Piraterie" (1937), reprinted in both *Positionen und Begriffe im Kampf mit Weimar—Genf—Versailles, 1923–1939* (1940) and *Frieden oder Pazifismus? Arbeiten zum Völkerrecht und zur internationalen Politik 1924–1978* (2005)

"Der Staat als Mechanismus bei Hobbes und Descartes" (1937), reprinted in *Staat, Großraum, Nomos: Arbeiten aus den Jahren 1916–1969* (1995); translated as "The State as Mechanism in Hobbes and Descartes" (1996)

"Völkerrechtliche Neutralität und völkische Totalität" (1938), reprinted in both *Positionen und Begriffe im Kampf mit Weimar—Genf—Versailles, 1923–1939* (1940) and *Frieden oder Pazifismus? Arbeiten zum Völkerrecht und zur internationalen Politik 1924–1978* (2005); translated as "Neutrality According to International Law and National Totality" (1999)

"Das neue Vae Neutris!" (1938), reprinted in both *Positionen und Begriffe im Kampf mit Weimar—Genf—Versailles, 1923–1939* (1940) and *Frieden oder Pazifismus? Arbeiten zum Völkerrecht und zur internationalen Politik 1924–1978* (2005)

"Neutralität und Neutralisierungen: Zu Christoph Steding, 'Das Reich und die Krankheit der europäischen Kultur'" (1939) [book review], reprinted in *Positionen und Begriffe im Kampf mit Weimar—Genf—Versailles, 1923–1939* (1940)

"Der Reichsbegriff im Völkerrecht" (1939), reprinted in *Positionen und Begriffe im Kampf mit Weimar—Genf—Versailles, 1923–1939* (1940)

"*Inter pacem et bellum nihil medium*" (1939), adapted and expanded from *Positionen und Begriffe im Kampf mit Weimar—Genf—Versailles, 1923–1939* (1940); reprinted as second corollary to the fifth edition (1963) of *Der Begriff des Politischen: Mit einer Rede über das Zeitalter der Neutralisierungen und Entpolitisierungen* (1932) and in

Frieden oder Pazifismus? Arbeiten zum Völkerrecht und zur internationalen Politik 1924–1978 (2005)

"Über die zwei großen 'Dualismen' des heutigen Rechtssystems: Wie verhält sich die Unterscheidung von Völkerrecht und staatlichem Recht zu der innerstaatlichen Unterscheidung von öffentlichem und privatem Recht?" (1939), reprinted in *Positionen und Begriffe im Kampf mit Weimar—Genf—Versailles, 1923–1939* (1940)

"Reich und Raum: Elemente eines neuen Völkerrechts" (1940), incorporated into the third edition (1942) of *Völkerrechtliche Großraumordnung mit Interventionsverbot für raumfremde Mächte: Ein Beitrag zum Reichsbegriff im Völkerrecht* (1939)

"Die Raumrevolution: Durch den totalen Krieg zu einem totalen Frieden" (1940), reprinted in *Staat, Großraum, Nomos: Arbeiten aus den Jahren 1916–1969* (1995)

"Die Auflösung der europäischen Ordnung im 'International Law' (1890–1939)" (1940), incorporated in part into *Der Nomos der Erde im Völkerrecht des Jus Publicum Europaeum* (1950) and reprinted in *Staat, Großraum, Nomos: Arbeiten aus den Jahren 1916–1969* (1995)

"Das 'allgemeine deutsche Staatsrecht' als Beispiel rechtswissenschaftlicher Systembildung" (1940), reprinted in *Staat, Großraum, Nomos: Arbeiten aus den Jahren 1916–1969* (1995)

"Raum und Großraum im Völkerrecht" (1940), reprinted in *Staat, Großraum, Nomos: Arbeiten aus den Jahren 1916–1969* (1995)

"Die Stellung Lorenz von Steins in der Geschichte des 19. Jahrhunderts" (1940), reprinted in *Staat, Großraum, Nomos: Arbeiten aus den Jahren 1916–1969* (1995)

"Der neue Raumbegriff in der Rechtswissenschaft" (1940), incorporated into the fourth edition (1942) of *Völkerrechtliche Großraumordnung mit Interventionsverbot für raumfremde Mächte: Ein Beitrag zum Reichsbegriff im Völkerrecht* (1939)

"Reich—Staat—Bund" (1940)

"Staatliche Souveränität und freies Meer: Über den Gegensatz von Land und See im Völkerrecht der Neuzeit" (1941), reprinted in part in both (under a different title) *Verfassungsrechtliche Aufsätze aus den Jahren 1924–1954: Materialien zu einer Verfassungslehre* (1958) and *Der Nomos der Erde im Völkerrecht des Jus Publicum Europaeum* (1950) and reprinted in full in *Staat, Großraum, Nomos: Arbeiten aus den Jahren 1916–1969* (1995)

"Das Meer gegen das Land" (1941), incorporated into *Land und Meer: Eine weltgeschichtliche Betrachtung* (1942) and reprinted in *Staat, Großraum, Nomos: Arbeiten aus den Jahren 1916–1969* (1995)

"Die Formung des französischen Geistes durch den Legisten" (1942), reprinted in *Staat, Großraum, Nomos: Arbeiten aus den Jahren 1916–1969* (1995)

"Beschleuniger wider Willen, oder: Problematik der westlichen Hemisphäre" (1942), reprinted in *Staat, Großraum, Nomos: Arbeiten aus den Jahren 1916–1969* (1995)

"Raumrevolution: Vom Geist des Abendlandes" (1942), reprinted from *Land und Meer: Eine weltgeschichtliche Betrachtung* (1942)

"Behemoth, Leviathan und Greif: Vom Wandel der Herrschaftsformen" (1943), reprinted from *Land und Meer: Eine weltgeschichtliche Betrachtung* (1942)

"Die letzte globale Linie" (1943), incorporated into *Der Nomos der Erde im Völkerrecht des Jus Publicum Europaeum* (1950) and reprinted in *Staat, Großraum, Nomos: Arbeiten aus den Jahren 1916–1969* (1995)

"Das international Verbrechen des Krieges in seiner Besonderheit gegenüber dem Kriegsverbrechen (Verletzungen der Regeln des Kriegsrechts und Verbrechen gegen die Menschlichkeit, atrocities)" (1945), incorporated in part into *Der Nomos der Erde im Völkerrecht des Jus Publicum Europaeum* (1950) and reprinted as *Das internationalrechtliche Verbrechen des Angriffskrieges und der Grundsatz "Nullum crimen, nulla poena sine lege"* (1994)

"1907 Berlin" (1946/1947)

"Völkerrecht 1–4" (1948–1950), reprinted in *Frieden oder Pazifismus? Arbeiten zum Völkerrecht und zur internationalen Politik 1924–1978* (2005)

"Gegenwartsfragen der Verfassung" (1949)

"Das Grundgesetz der Bundesrepublik Deutschland" [Part 1] (1949)

"Donos Cortés in gesamteuropäischer Interpretation" (1949), incorporated into *Donoso Cortés in gesamteuropäischer Interpretation: Vier Aufsätze* (1950)

"Francisco de Vitoria und die Geschichte seines Ruhmes" (1949), incorporated into *Der Nomos der Erde im Völkerrecht des Jus Publicum Europaeum* (1950)

"Maritime Weltpolitik" (1949) [book review], reprinted in *Staat, Großraum, Nomos: Arbeiten aus den Jahren 1916–1969* (1995)

"Amnestie—Urform des Rechts" (1949), reprinted under a different title in *Staat, Großraum, Nomos: Arbeiten aus den Jahren 1916–1969* (1995)

"Das Grundgesetz der Bundesrepublik Deutschland" [Part 2] (1950)

"Die Weisheit der Zelle" (1950), reprinted from *Ex Captivitate Salus: Erfahrungen der Zeit 1945/47* (1950)

"Das Problem der Legalität" (1950), reprinted in *Verfassungsrechtliche Aufsätze aus den Jahren 1924–1954: Materialien zu einer Verfassungslehre* (1958); translated as "The Question of Legality" (2001)

"Die geschichtliche Tatsache einer europäischen Rechtswissenschaft" (1950), incorporated into *Die Lage der europäischen Rechtswissenschaft* (1950)

"Die Rechtswissenschaft als letztes Asyl des Rechtsbewußtseins" (1950), incorporated into *Die Lage der europäischen Rechtswissenschaft* (1950)

"Drei Stufen historischer Sinngebung" (1950) [book review], reprinted in *Hans Blumenberg/Carl Schmitt: Briefwechsel 1971–1978* (2007); translated as "Three Possibilities for a Christian Conception of History" (2009)

"Essentielle Geschichtsschreibung: Alexis de Tocqueville" (1950), reprinted from *Ex Captivitate Salus: Erfahrungen der Zeit 1945/47* (1950)

"Der Mut des Geistes" (1950)

"Gesang des Sechzigjährigen" (1951), reprinted from *Ex Captivitate Salus: Erfahrungen der Zeit 1945/47* (1950); translated as "Ex Captivitate Salus" (1987)

"Dreihundert Jahre Leviathan: Zum 5. April 1951" (1951), reprinted in *Staat, Großraum, Nomos: Arbeiten aus den Jahren 1916–1969* (1995)

"Über die Grundrechte im Grundgesetz für die Bundesrepublik Deutschland" (1951)

"Recht und Raum" (1951), reprinted from the first corollary in *Der Nomos der Erde im Völkerrecht des Jus Publicum Europaeum* (1950) and reprinted in *Staat, Großraum, Nomos: Arbeiten aus den Jahren 1916–1969* (1995)

"Die Einheit der Welt" (1952), reprinted in *Staat, Großraum, Nomos: Arbeiten aus den Jahren 1916–1969* (1995)

"Das Schauspiel im Schauspiel" (1952), incorporated into *Hamlet oder Hekuba: Der Einbruch der Zeit in das Spiel* (1956)

"Prologue and Epilogue to Lilian Winstanley, Hamlet, Sohn der Maria Stuart" (1952)

"Nehmen/Teilen/Weiden: Ein Versuch, die Grundfragen jeder Sozial- und Wirtschaftsordnung vom Nomos her richtig zu stellen" (1953), reprinted in *Verfassungsrechtliche Aufsätze aus den Jahren 1924–1954: Materialien zu einer Verfassungslehre* (1958); translated as "Appropriation/Distribution/Production: Toward a Proper Formulation of Basic Questions of Any Social and Economic Order" (1993)

"Im Vorraum der Macht" (1954), reprinted in *Verfassungsrechtliche Aufsätze aus den Jahren 1924–1954: Materialien zu einer Verfassungslehre* (1958)

"Welt großartigster Spannung" (1954), reprinted in *Staat, Großraum, Nomos: Arbeiten aus den Jahren 1916–1969* (1995)

"Der neue Nomos der Erde" (1955), reprinted in *Staat, Großraum, Nomos: Arbeiten aus den Jahren 1916–1969* (1995); translated as "The New 'Nomos' of the Earth" (2003)

"Rechtsfragen der europäischen Einigung" (1955) [book review], reprinted in *Frieden oder Pazifismus? Arbeiten zum Völkerrecht und zur internationalen Politik 1924–1978* (2005)

"Der Barbarei entgegen" (1955) [book review], reprinted in *Frieden oder Pazifismus? Arbeiten zum Völkerrecht und zur internationalen Politik 1924–1978* (2005)

"Machtpolitik" (1955) [book review], reprinted in *Frieden oder Pazifismus? Arbeiten zum Völkerrecht und zur internationalen Politik 1924–1978* (2005)

"Der Krieg der modernen Vernichtungsmittel" (1955), reprinted from *Der Nomos der Erde im Völkerrecht des Jus Publicum Europaeum* (1950)

"Die weltgeschichtliche Struktur des heutigen Weltgegensatzes von Ost und West: Bemerkungen zu Ernst Jüngers Schrift 'Der gordische Knoten'" (1955), reprinted in *Staat, Großraum, Nomos: Arbeiten aus den Jahren 1916–1969* (1995); translated as "The New 'Nomos' of the Earth" (2003)

"Was habe ich getan?" (1957)

"Politische Theorien" (1957), selections reprinted from "Staatsethik und pluralistischer Staat" (1930), *Verfassungslehre* (1928), *Der Hüter der Verfassung* (1931), *Die geistesgeschichtliche Lage des heutigen Parlamentarismus* (1923), and *Staat, Bewegung, Volk: Die Dreigliederung der politischen Einheit* (1933)

"Gespräch über den neuen Raum" (1958), reprinted in *Staat, Großraum, Nomos: Arbeiten aus den Jahren 1916–1969* (1995); translated as "Dialogue on New Space" (2015)

"Gesellschaft und Staat in der verstehenden Soziologie" (1958) [book review]

"Nomos—Nahme—Name" (1959), reprinted in *Staat, Großraum, Nomos: Arbeiten aus den Jahren 1916-1969* (1995); translated as "Nomos—Nahme—Name" (2003)

"Gesammelte politische Schriften" (1959) [book review]

"Kritik und Krise" (1959) [book review]

"Der Gegensatz von Gemeinschaft und Gesellschaft als Beispiel einer zweigliedrigen Unterscheidung: Betrachtungen zur Struktur und zum Schicksal solcher Antithesen" (1960)

"Max Weber und die deutsche Politik" (1960) [book review]

"Dem wahren Johann Jakob Rousseau: Zum 28. Juni 1962" (1962)

"Die vollendete Reformation: Bemerkungen und Hinweise zu neuen Leviathan-Interpretationen" (1965) [book review], incorporated into the second edition (1982) of *Der Leviathan in der Staatslehre des Thomas Hobbes: Sinn und Fehlschlag eines politischen Symbols* (1938)

"Clausewitz als politischer Denker: Bemerkungen und Hinweise" (1967) [book review], reprinted in *Frieden oder Pazifismus? Arbeiten zum Völkerrecht und zur internationalen Politik 1924-1978* (2005)

"Die Prinzipien des Parlamentarismus" (1967), reprinted from the third edition (1961) of *Die geistesgeschichtliche Lage des heutigen Parlamentarismus* (1923)

"Politische Theologie II: Die Legende von der Erledigung jeder Politischen Theologie" (1970), reprinted as *Politische Theologie II: Die Legende von der Erledigung jeder Politischen Theologie* (1970)

"Die legale Weltrevolution: Politischer Mehrwert als Prämie auf juristische Legalität und Superlegalität" (1978), reprinted in *Frieden oder Pazifismus? Arbeiten zum Völkerrecht und zur internationalen Politik 1924-1978* (2005); translated as "The Legal World Revolution" (1987)

DIARIES

Glossarium: Aufzeichnungen der Jahre 1947-1951 (1991)

Tagebücher: Oktober 1912 bis Februar 1915 (2003)

Die Militärzeit 1915 bis 1919: Tagebuch Februar bis Dezember 1915, Aufsätze und Materialien (2005)

Tagebücher 1930 bis 1934 (2011)

Der Schatten Gottes: Introspektionen, Tagebücher und Briefe 1921 bis 1924 (2014)

Glossarium: Aufzeichnungen aus den Jahren 1947 bis 1958 (2015)

CORRESPONDENCE

Jawohl, der Schmitt: Zehn Briefe aus Plettenberg (1988) (with Hansjörg Viesel)
Franz Blei: Briefe an Carl Schmitt 1917–1933 (1995)
Carl Schmitt: Briefwechsel mit einem seiner Schüler (1995) (with Armin Mohler)
Wilhelm Stapel/Carl Schmitt: Ein Briefwechsel (1996)
Werner Becker: Briefe an Carl Schmitt (1998)
Briefe an Carl Schmitt (various correspondents) (1998)
Carl Schmitt/Ernst Jünger: Briefe 1930–1983 (1999)
Jugendbriefe: Briefschaften an seine Schwester Auguste 1905 bis 1913 (2000)
Carl Schmitt/Álvaro d'Ors: Briefwechsel (2004)
Hans Blumenberg/Carl Schmitt: Briefwechsel 1971–1978 (2007)
Carl Schmitt/Ludwig Feuchtwanger: Briefwechsel 1918–1935 (2007)
Ernst Forsthoff/Carl Schmitt: Briefwechsel 1926–1974 (2007)
Gretha Jünger/Carl Schmitt: Briefwechsel 1934–1953 (2007)
Werkstatt—Discorsi: Briefwechsel 1967–1981 (2009) (with Hans-Dietrich Sander)
Auf der gefahrenvollen Straße des öffentlichen Rechts: Briefwechsel Carl Schmitt/Rudolf Smend 1921–1961 (2010)
Jacob Taubes/Carl Schmitt: Briefwechsel (2012)
Carl Schmitt/Ernst Rudolf Huber: Briefwechsel 1926–1981 (2014)

INTERVIEWS

"Gespräch über die Macht und den Zugang zum Machthaber" (1954) (with Günther Neske), translated as "Dialogue on Power and Access to the Holder of Power" (2015) and published in *Dialogues on Power and Space* (2015)
"Gespräch über den Neuen Raum" (1955), translated as "Dialogue on New Space" (2015) and published in *Dialogues on Power and Space* (2015)
"Gespräch über den Partisanen" (1970) (with Joachim Schickel), reprinted in both *Gespräche mit Carl Schmitt* (1993) and *Staat, Großraum, Nomos: Arbeiten aus den Jahren 1916–1969* (1995); translated as "Nomos—Nahme—Name" (2003)
"Gespräche mit Carl Schmitt" (1993) (with Joachim Schickel)
"'Solange das Imperium da ist': *Carl Schmitt im Gespräch mit Klaus Figge und Dieter Groh 1971*" (2010)

PART I

INTRODUCTION

CHAPTER 1

"A FANATIC OF ORDER IN AN EPOCH OF CONFUSING TURMOIL"

The Political, Legal, and Cultural Thought of Carl Schmitt

JENS MEIERHENRICH AND OLIVER SIMONS

INTRODUCTION

CARL SCHMITT was a leading thinker of the twentieth century. He was a theorist, a protagonist, and, above all, an antagonist. A conservative constitutional lawyer with a deep interest in matters of politics and culture, he wrote thought-provoking commentary on the human condition that was revered by some and reviled by others. During his long and eventful life—his work stretched from the beginning to almost the end of the twentieth century—Schmitt left a mark on four different incarnations of his native Germany: the absolutist regime that was Wilhelmine Germany, the failed republic of Weimar Germany, the authoritarian and totalitarian Nazi Germany, and the consolidated democracy of the Federal Republic of Germany.

Only a handful of theorists in history have survived as many radically different regimes as the controversial jurist from Plettenberg. Schmitt has influenced intellectual currents like few other Germans before him or since. Given his ever-broadening international appeal, some have been tempted to add Schmitt's name to the list of "German greats," the list of internationally renowned thinkers of German pedigree that ranges from Immanuel Kant to Jürgen Habermas.

Schmitt was determined to leave a mark not only with his thought but also through his conduct. He was exceedingly driven in this quest—sometimes by considerations of power, at other times by matters of principle. Though repeatedly crippled by self-doubt,

Schmitt desperately wanted to succeed in life, to be someone. And he wanted to be *seen* to be someone.[1] Jacob Taubes called him a "striver from the ostracized minority of Catholics" (*"Aufstreber von der geächteten Minderheit der Katholiken"*; 1987, 75).[2] Hasso Hofmann has argued that nothing was more important to Schmitt "than constantly being 'in touch with the times,' locating the 'intellectual place of the present' in the process of history" (2002, 89). This quest for *Ortung*, or localization and orientation—a key term in Schmitt's book *The "Nomos" of the Earth in the International Law of the "Jus Publicum Europaeum"*—may well have been one of the reasons he was drawn to positions in the echelons of power.

Despite a steadily growing appreciation of his writings in numerous disciplines, dealing with Carl Schmitt remains a challenge, for in addition to having been an incisive thinker, he was a committed Nazi and lifelong antisemite. In light of this increasingly well-documented fact, scholars continue to grapple with the question of what to make of the relationship between Schmitt's thought and his conduct. As with any thinker, both dimensions of his persona were inextricably intertwined. Yet to what extent does one facet of his life invalidate or affect the other? Is it appropriate, or even possible, to make Schmitt's thought usable for our time? As Benno Teschke recently asked, "Can we extricate—beyond either demonization or apologia—Schmittian insights from the odium of their association with Nazism?" (2011, 79). The thirty contributors to this Oxford Handbook have answered this question in very different ways.[3]

This framework chapter sets the stage for what is to come, but it is also an intervention in its own right that seeks to decenter the study of this most hyped thinker of the twentieth century. We advance two interconnected arguments. First, we argue that *the motif of order* is a powerful yet insufficiently utilized heuristic device for making sense of Schmitt's thought. By placing the motif of order at its heart, we contradict the popular belief, articulated most recently by Jan-Werner Müller (2003), that no unifying thread runs through the jurist's oeuvre. Although we do not propose to have found a master key for unlocking the many mysteries that are contained within Schmitt's sprawling body of thought, we do think that much can be gained from searching for an overarching motif—that is, a salient recurring figure—that inspired and holds together the divergent strands of his thought.

Second, we argue that a *trinity of thought* is discernible in Schmitt's writings comprised of his political, legal, and cultural thought. We establish intellectual connections across these three bodies of thought and trace the mutually constitutive relationships that exist among them. Schmitt's thought, we propose, amounted to a veritable network of ideas about the sources of social order, the cement of society. Whenever Schmitt wrote about culture, he also addressed politics; whenever he wrote about politics, he also addressed law; whenever he wrote about law, he also addressed culture; and so forth. He mined these three defining spheres of his life as part of the same trajectory of *orderly thought*. We rely on the neologism to convey a dual meaning, namely the centrality in Schmitt's oeuvre of a systematic (i.e., orderly) line of thinking in which the question of how to create—and maintain—social order also ranked supreme. In an attempt to analytically frame Schmitt's trinity of thought, we have organized this introductory chapter around the motif of order.

Order as a Motif

In music theory, a motif is "the smallest structural unit possessing thematic identity" (White 1976, 26–27). We might say that in the social sciences, a theoretical motif is the shortest subdivision of a theoretical theme that still maintains its identity as an abstract idea. The motif of order in our argument fits this definition and recurs in the vast majority of Schmitt's writings, albeit often indirectly. The concern with order, we argue, was Schmitt's guiding motif, his idée fixe. We are nonetheless reluctant to claim that the idea of order amounts to more in Schmitt's work—to a theme, for example. In music theory, a theme is a more complete artistic expression than a motif. For our purposes, a motif is the substrate of a theme (Dunsby 2002, 910). A brief look at Schmitt's book *Dictatorship* (1921) helps illustrate the distinction. In it, Schmitt returned frequently to the motif of order, although the book addressed primarily the theme of dictatorship. His observations on the history and typology of dictatorship were the foundation for his argument in defense of commissarial dictatorship. The motif of order helped him unify the conceptual and historical sections of his account. In the analysis below, we provide many more examples of order as an overriding motif in Schmitt's thought, highlighting the unifying function it served.

We believe that an integrated analysis of Schmitt's orderly thought has the potential to illuminate new facets of his biography and intellectual output. Although we emphasize coherence at the expense of contradictions in Schmitt's life and work, we are nevertheless mindful of the latter. A long line of scholars has commented on the inconsistencies in Schmitt's oeuvre. It has even been suggested that this "foundational ambivalence" may be the principal draw for many of Schmitt's readers (Lepsius 1994, 360). It would therefore be a distortion of the intellectual record to claim consistency for a body of work that evolved in anything but a straight line.[4] But it is equally problematic to deny the existence of an underlying logic. Even though the themes of Schmitt's many writings changed over the course of his life, the underlying motif—the logic connecting these themes—did not. We therefore conceive of Schmitt as a cartographer of orderly thought. He was taking the measure of the world. He mapped its political, legal, and cultural ideas and rearranged them on a new conceptual grid. The resultant trinity of his orderly thought was not a coincidental outcome; it was the result of a lifelong mapping exercise, the result of theoretical design.

The idea of turning to the motif of order to make sense of Schmitt's convoluted canon is not entirely new. In 1957 Peter Schneider remarked that the idea of order was one of the "immovable reference points" of Schmitt's thought (1957, 294). Three decades later Pasquale Pasquino (1986) returned to the centrality of order in the jurist's writings. With our analysis we pick up where Schneider and Pasquino left off several decades ago. We dig more deeply than they were able to into the origins, nature, and manifestations of Schmitt's orderly thought. We show that Schmitt's oeuvre was centrally concerned with the determinants of orderly existence, but it was also a well-organized line of thinking, the emergence and evolution of which we trace in this chapter.

We locate the origins of Schmitt's preoccupation with order in his socialization on the precipice of the modern age. Schmitt's thinking turned to imagining possible—and impossible—institutional solutions to the problem of social order in a time of "great transformation," as Karl Polanyi (1957) famously dubbed it. Schmitt discarded as unworkable some models of political order (e.g., parliamentary democracy) while embracing others (e.g., commissarial dictatorship). He sought to eradicate the supposedly harmful influence of normativism from Germany's legal order, and he labored hard to reconfigure the country's cultural life by reviving an existentially meaningful social order to combat what George Lukács called the rise of "transcendental homelessness" ("*transzendentale Obdachlosigkeit*"; 1994, 6).[5] In all the meaningful spheres of his life—politics, law, culture—Schmitt assembled theoretical building blocks to construct a conservative bulwark against what he saw as the abomination of liberal modernity.

Although we believe in the importance of identifying guiding motifs in Schmitt's thought, we are wary of arguments that overstate their significance. The tendency to offer interpretative master keys is exemplified by the influential yet problematic work of Heinrich Meier, who asserted that the essence of Schmitt's thought is to be found in his political theology (2011; see also Wacker 1994). Friedrich Balke and other scholars have shown persuasively why Meier's approach is inadequate for locating the overarching "problem" that motivated Schmitt (Balke 1996, 15–18).[6] According to Balke, what Meier has produced is mere "*Abklatsch*," poor copy, the result of too literal a reading of Schmitt's writings (18). If we are serious about seeking a core of Schmittian thought, we must look beyond the themes that Schmitt himself names, because his use of language was directed in almost equal measure to illuminating the phenomena he studied and rendering them obscure.

In short, it is imperative to look at the underneath of things in Schmitt's work. This introductory chapter is an attempt to do just that. By drawing attention to the underlying motif of order, we also hope to inspire more intellectual exchange than currently exists across the many diverse literatures in which Schmitt has come to feature prominently. It is an invitation to think of Schmitt anew, beyond orthodoxies and across boundaries, disciplinary and otherwise.

AN ANTAGONISTIC LIFE

Schmitt was an adversary of many, an enemy to some. This accounts for at least some of the attraction—and unease—the name Carl Schmitt still inspires. Because others have pored over the facts of his life, we draw just a basic sketch here.[7] Schmitt was born in Plettenberg, Germany, on July 11, 1888, to a devoutly Catholic family. He received his university education in law at universities in Berlin, Munich, and Strasbourg. He completed his doctorate at the latter in June 1910 with a dissertation on the question of criminal guilt: "Über Schuld und Schuldarten" ("On Guilt and Types of Guilt"). That summer, Schmitt relocated to Düsseldorf to start the applied portion of his legal training. In the next eight years he published six monographs, three on questions of law, including the *Bericht über das Belagerungszustand-Gesetz*, a report on the law of the state of siege that his military superior commissioned in September 1915; one on politics; and two on literature. In this period of his life, Schmitt was more taken with the changing character of culture than with law or politics. The latter were his bread and butter, the former his passion. Schmitt's most notable literary publication from this time was *Theodor Däublers "Nordlicht"* (*Theodor Däubler's "The Northern Light"*), a close reading of an important epic poem. Three years earlier, in 1913, under the pseudonym Johannes Negelinus, Schmitt had already coauthored *Schattenrisse* (*Silhouettes*), a collection of parodies. In 1917 he added "Die Buribunken" ("The Buribunks"), a satire of detached intellectualism, to his growing list of cultural writings.

Following Germany's defeat in World War I and the founding of the Weimar Republic, Schmitt lost his teaching position at the University of Strasbourg, where he had begun work on his *Habilitation*, but was appointed lecturer of law at Munich's *Handelshochschule*, a business school. In the early 1920s, having published three more books in the meantime—*Politische Romantik* (*Political Romanticism*), *Die Diktatur* (*Dictatorship*), and *Politische Theologie* (*Political Theology*)—Schmitt first took up a position at the University of Greifswald and then accepted a professorship of law at the University of Bonn. In Bonn he witnessed the assassination of Foreign Minister Walter Rathenau by right-wing forces and the hyperinflation that destabilized Weimar Germany in the summer of 1922. Shaken by these signs of the times, Schmitt devoted more of his thinking to questions of governance. His publications in the next three years reveal a man who had begun to fundamentally rethink the meaning of politics. In 1923 he published *Die geistesgeschichtliche Lage des heutigen Parlamentarismus* (*The Crisis of Parliamentary Democracy*) and *Römischer Katholizismus und politische Form* (*Roman Catholicism and Political Form*); two years later his magnum opus in law, *Verfassungslehre* (*Constitutional Theory*), came out.

The best known of Schmitt's works from this period of maturation was his next book, *Der Begriff des Politischen* (*The Concept of the Political*), published in 1927, shortly before his next professional move, to the *Handelshochschule* in Berlin. Finally Schmitt was at the center of things, in the capital, where he had longed to be. Friends opened doors for him, and Schmitt's counsel was sought in the turbulent constitutional crisis of the early 1930s, most formally when he represented the federal government in the case of *Preußen contra Reich*. His brief was to defend the constitutionality of the so-called *Preußenschlag* ("Prussia coup"), the controversial political move in which Reich Chancellor Franz von Papen persuaded President Paul von Hindenburg to dissolve the subnational government of Prussia and seize power there in July 1932. It was this performance on the public stage that earned Schmitt the moniker "*Kronjurist der Papendiktatur*," the crown jurist of Papen's presidential dictatorship (Hiller 1932; see also Meierhenrich n.d.). After the publication of his book *Legalität und Legitimität* (*Legality and Legitimacy*), also in 1932, and after a brief stint on the law faculty of the University of Cologne, where he served alongside Hans Kelsen, Schmitt took up a chair at the University of Berlin on October 1, 1933, following his appointment as *Preußischer Staatsrat* (Prussian state councilor) on July 11, his forty-fifth birthday.

By that time he had already made a name for himself as a rabid defender of Nazi values. In the immediate aftermath of the Nazi "legal revolution" and Hitler's seizure of the title of Reich chancellor, Schmitt left no doubt about where his political allegiance lay. With what Germans call *vorauseilenden Gehorsam*, or anticipatory obedience, he celebrated the "transition to the one-party state" ("*Übergang zum Ein-Parteien-Staat*"), the "spirit" ("*Geist*") and "good law" of the "German revolution" ("*das gute Recht der deutschen Revolution*"), and Hitler as Germany's first "people's chancellor" ("*Volkskanzler*") in Nazi newspapers such as the *Westdeutscher Beobachter* and the *Völkischer Beobachter* (Schmitt 1933a; 1933b; 1933c). One of his most notorious and loathsome publications was a piece entitled "Die deutschen Intellektuellen" ("The German Intellectuals"; 1933d). In it, Schmitt praised the expulsion of intellectuals such as Albert Einstein, denying that they ever belonged to the German people ("*zum deutschen Volk haben sie niemals gehört*") or to the German spirit ("*auch nicht zum deutschen Geist*"; 1933d). Gleefully he welcomed the news that these foreign bodies had now been expelled. Schmitt wrote elatedly that "Germany spat them out for all eternity" ("*Aus Deutschland sind sie ausgespien für alle Zeiten*"; 1933d). The diatribe is surpassed in notoriety only by his article "Der Führer schützt das Recht" ("The Führer Protects the Law") the next year.

In mid-May 1933 Schmitt recorded a notorious event in his diary: the "burning of the disgraceful books" ("*Verbrennung der Schandbücher*"; quoted in Mehring 2009, 323, entry of May 17, 1933). When this description, which was made in private, is read alongside similar pronouncements he made about the promise of the Nazi project and a litany of antisemitic remarks, it is difficult to sustain the still-influential argument that Schmitt was just a fellow traveler, a careerist turncoat who joined the ranks of the new order for instrumental gain, not because he believed in Nazi principles (for a comprehensive analysis, see Meierhenrich n.d.). And this was just the beginning. In the period 1933–1936, Schmitt published forty-seven popular and academic articles defending and legitimating the Nazi regime.

But Schmitt not only wrote, he also *acted* in support of the new order by helping it build some of its institutional foundations. He contributed to the drafting of the *Reichsstatthaltergesetz* (Reichsstatthalter law) and the new law of criminal procedure. In recognition of his order-sustaining thought and conduct, he was chosen, among other things, as *Reichsgruppenleiter* (or chair) of the university professors' section of the *Bund Nationalsozialistischer Deutscher Juristen* (Association of National Socialist German Jurists). However, after several years of climbing the Nazi professional ladder, Schmitt's political career came to an abrupt end. On October 4, 1936, the Security Service Main Office of the SS High Command (*SD-Hauptamt des Sicherheitsdienstes der Reichsführung SS*) began a clandestine investigation of Schmitt. Within a few months he had been dismissed from all of his public posts except his professorship. His sudden downfall was the result of intra-Nazi competition over ownership of the mantle of the crown jurist. The mudslinging was all the more harmful because Schmitt's Nazi credentials were called into question in a very public manner. His rivals supported the publication of several harmful portrayals of him in *Das Schwarze Korps*, the official weekly of the SS (Anonymous 1936a; 1936b). This very public shaming tied the hands of Schmitt's supporters in the Nazi state, including those of Hermann Göring, who had made Schmitt Prussian state councilor just a few years earlier.

However, in the wake of his fall from Nazi grace, Schmitt did not choose a life of "internal emigration" ("*innere Emigration*"). Although he no longer possessed formal political power, he never truly stopped supporting the totalitarian regime. He returned to the theory of the state, a topic he had tackled explicitly at the beginning of his academic career, notably in *Der Wert des Staates und die Bedeutung des Einzelnen* (*The Value of the State and the Significance of the Individual*). In 1937, on the occasion of the 300th anniversary of the publication of René Descartes's *Discours de la méthode*, Schmitt published a noteworthy essay on the state as mechanism in the theories of Thomas Hobbes and Descartes (1936/1937). This proved to be an intermediate step to the publication, in 1938, of *Der Leviathan in der Staatslehre des Thomas Hobbes* (*The Leviathan in the State Theory of Thomas Hobbes*).

During the next seven years Schmitt was busy preparing a series of publications on international law and related themes. He published eighteen titles in this period, excluding his major summation, *Der Nomos der Erde im Völkerrecht des Jus Publicum Europaeum* (*The "Nomos" of the Earth in the International Law of the "Jus Publicum Europaeum;"* hereinafter *The "Nomos" of the Earth*), which did not appear until after the war. His twin concerns—Hobbes and international law—were intimately related. Schmitt used his engagement with the former to make a case for the development of the concept of the Reich in his study of the latter. Building on this new concept of politico-legal order, he developed his *Großraum* theory. Advanced most fully in the 1939 *Völkerrechtliche Großraumordnung mit Interventionsverbot für raumfremde Mächte* ("The *Großraum* Order of International Law with a Ban on Intervention for Spatially Foreign Powers"), Schmitt's tentative solution to the problem of international order hinged on the reterritorialization of the world, the creation of culturally homogenous and spatially expansive territories that would be governed by concrete (and local or regional) facts instead of abstract (and global) norms: "*Reichs* in this sense are the leading and bearing powers whose political ideas radiate into a certain *Großraum* and which fundamentally exclude the interventions of spatially alien powers into the *Großraum*" (2011, 101). Inspired by the U.S. Monroe Doctrine, Schmitt, in a politically less sensitive arena of the Nazi academy, used this ordering principle in his continuing work on the problem of social order.

More specifically, his *Großraum* theory addressed questions Schmitt had raised but left unanswered a year previously in *Die Wendung zum diskriminierenden Kriegsbegriff* (*The Turn to the Discriminating Concept of War*). His spatial theory had the advantage of being compatible with, and legitimating, Nazi international ambition. Schmitt undoubtedly "envisioned a European *Großraum* in which Germany would stand as the pre-eminent power—the *Reich*" (Hooker 2009, 136). As he insisted, "The action of the *Führer* has lent the concept of our *Reich* political reality, historical truth, and a great future in international law" (Schmitt 2011, 111). It is not at all surprising therefore that U.S. prosecutors at the postwar International Military Tribunal (IMT) at Nuremberg were keen to look more closely at the role Schmitt had played in the preparation of "aggressive war" during World War II (Quaritsch 2000; Bendersky 2007; Meierhenrich n.d.).

From a distance, it certainly seemed as if Schmitt might have been the architect of Nazi international law. He had endeavored to garner support for his policy-oriented perspective at numerous talks around the country, especially in 1940, when he delivered lectures in Bremen, Kiel, Rostock, Halle, Naumburg, Cologne, and Berlin (Mehring 2009, 404). His lecture tour was yet another attempt to make his presence—and intellectual prowess—known to the faces of the "Third Reich." However, Nazis better situated than Schmitt, such as Reinhard Höhn and Werner Best, rejected his arguments and advances. Because Schmitt had opted for a certain degree of vagueness in his spatial theory, the recriminations were less severe this time (Bendersky 1983, 255–256).

His last major wartime publication was *Land und Meer* (*Land and Sea*, 1942). Told as a story to his daughter, the stylistically unusual book was a renewed meditation on the spatiality of international order, which Schmitt continued after the war in *The "Nomos" of the Earth* (see Giaccaria and Minca 2016). *Land and Sea* led to his abandonment of the concept of the Reich. *Nomos* was the neologism that replaced it (Mehring 2009, 430–431). Schmitt's choice of literary genre in this preliminary study coincided with—and performed for all to see—his retreat from the intellectual front lines inside the Nazi state.

In the final days of World War II, in April 1945, Schmitt was briefly arrested and interrogated by Soviet troops. Later that year, U.S. military authorities arrested him and detained him in Berlin and Nuremberg. Because in the international perception Schmitt was "Hitler's lawmaker," the question of his individual responsibility for international crimes arose, especially in the context of the newly created IMT (Sherratt 2013, 92–103, esp. 101; Meierhenrich n.d.). After eighteen months of investigations and interrogations by various U.S. authorities, Schmitt was released on May 6, 1947 (see also Quaritsch 2000). He had spent nearly fourteen months in detention since the end of the war, a fact that he neither understood nor ever forgot.

His postwar life in Plettenberg was active. Dirk van Laak, Jan-Werner Müller, and Christian Linder have shown that Schmitt did not retreat into "the security of silence" ("*die Sicherheit des Schweigens*"), as he had so melodramatically announced he would upon exiting the IMT (Laak 2002; Müller 2003; Linder 2008; 2016). Quite the contrary: Schmitt wrote and talked, talked and wrote. He had a need for "publicity" ("*Publizität*"), for the aura that the act of publication had previously bestowed on him.[8] Schmitt had a secondary presence in the fledgling democratic regime; he was out of view, yet he was on people's minds. From the rural depths of Westphalia, he nourished a conservative intellectual community. His peripheral location in postwar Germany made possible the construction of a loose network of intellectually and ideologically like-minded personalities. Regular visitors included constitutional lawyers such as Ernst-Wolfgang Böckenförde (who later became a prominent constitutional court judge), influential historians such as Reinhart Koselleck (who subsequently pioneered the field of *Begriffsgeschichte*, or conceptual history), conservative journalists such as Johannes Gross, and public intellectuals such as Ernst Jünger and Armin Mohler. This network, a veritable epistemic community, encouraged Schmitt to continue his scholarly work—one of its several *Festschrifts* for the fallen jurist was grandly titled *Epirrhosis*, or "encouragement"—and even set up a registered society, the *Academia Moralis*, to collect donations for the fallen jurist (Barion et al. 1968; see also Laak 2002, 52–63; Schmitz 1994). Over time foreign visitors, too, found their way to the boondocks. Schmitt documented many of these encounters, and the ideas to which they gave rise, in hundreds of letters and in a private notebook—the *Glossarium*—which he kept in addition to his diaries from 1947 to 1958 (Mehring 2009, 458). That his home, named San Casciano after the villa in which Niccolò Machiavelli spent his exile from the Florentine Republic, evolved into a travel destination for a certain type of postwar European intellectual eased Schmitt's gripes with the times somewhat. However, this did not stop him from decrying the "tyranny of values" to which he saw himself and his circle subjected (Schmitt 1960).

Despite his complaints, or perhaps because of them, Schmitt wrote with abandon. In 1950 he published two important books, *Ex Captivitate Salus*, his self-satisfied reflections on the years of detention, and the already mentioned *The "Nomos" of the Earth*, his most important postwar work. But soon thereafter Schmitt abandoned the study of international law. The study of literature, especially of Shakespeare, was what preoccupied him during much of the remainder of his life. This rekindled an interest that had lain dormant since his student days. With a typical blend of panache and melodrama, he described himself in this transitional phase of his life as "the King Lear of constitutional law" ("*der King Lear des öffentlichen Rechts*"; quoted in Mehring 2009, 501). His turn to Shakespeare resulted in the publication of the book *Hamlet oder Hekuba* (*Hamlet or Hecuba*) in 1956.

Schmitt's literary studies were a function of his search for historical archetypes for his own fate (Laak 2002, 77).[9] But he also returned to two other themes of his Weimar years: the nature of the political and the role of theology in it. He published *Theorie des Partisanen* (*Theory of the Partisan*) in 1963 and *Politische Theologie II* (*Political Theology II*) in 1970. Many of Germany's postwar intellectuals followed the gradual rehabilitation of Schmitt with concern, most prominent among them Jürgen Habermas (see Habermas 1989, 128–139; Becker 2003; and Specter 2016). Yet Schmitt's Weimar-era writings enjoyed widespread appeal among Germany's countercultural students. The rejection of the supposed trappings of representative democracy struck a chord on the left, where Schmitt's concern with authenticity was also en vogue (most recently, see Felsch 2015, 203–205, 211). His work was anthologized in a leftist reader, and an extended conversation with the Maoist Joachim Schickel appeared as a radio broadcast in 1969 (Schickel 1970; see also Schickel 2008). Slowly an "intellectual normalization" of Schmitt's work set in, driven in part by the conservative *Frankfurter Allgemeine Zeitung*, one of Germany's most influential dailies (Assheuer 2012). However, Habermas scored one victory: he successfully blocked Jacob Taubes's attempt to include Schmitt's writings in a new (and subsequently hugely successful) theory imprint at the Suhrkamp publishing house (Felsch 2015, 213; see also Müller-Dohm 2014, 145–146). Had Taubes's plan succeeded, the so-called Schmitt renaissance of the 1990s might have happened considerably sooner; because of Suhrkamp's affordable paperback editions, no other publisher has had a greater influence on the intellectual life of postwar Germany.

Schmitt published his last article in 1978. In it he returned to the theme of legality and legitimacy. His final years were filled with heartbreak and decrepitude. Schmitt's daughter, Anima, passed away in 1983, and he developed dementia and other illnesses. Schmitt died on April 7, 1985, in the town where he was born. He was ninety-six.

ORDERLY THOUGHT

The eminent historian Hans-Ulrich Wehler once described Carl Schmitt as "a fanatic of order in an epoch of confusing turmoil" ("*ein Ordnungsfanatiker in einer Epoche turbulenter Wirren*"; 2003, 491), a fairly apt summation of a complicated life. The overarching project that cuts across Schmitt's many interventions into political, legal, and cultural affairs was his attempt to come to terms with the problem of social order. "The problem of social order," writes Robert Bates, "is a classic one, and it has been posed in many forms. In political science, it is sometimes cast as a tension between private interests and the public good, between rights and obligations, or between the individual and the collectivity" (1983, 19).[10] In Schmitt's case, the fixation on the problem of social order was both an intellectual concern and private affliction (Meierhenrich 2016). These twin motivations caused him to embark on a long and winding road of (self-)exploration, an intellectual search in different corners of knowledge that netted interrelated (if not always explicitly connected) insights about the determinants of all kinds of social order: political, legal, cultural.

Thinking Orderly

According to the *Oxford English Dictionary*, the noun "order," among other things, refers to "the overall state or condition of something."[11] The word can also connote "the state in which the laws or rules regulating the relationship of individuals to the community, and the public conduct of members within a community, are maintained and observed and authority is obeyed." In its general sense, the noun "order" captures "the condition in which everything has its correct or appropriate place, and performs its proper functions." In this understanding, order is a "force for harmony and regularity in the universe."[12]

During the time Schmitt was attending university and undergoing legal training, the term "*Ordnung*," the German word for "order," became a favorite of right-wing intellectuals in the Weimar Republic (Breuer 2001, 12). The timing was not accidental. Zygmunt Bauman has described the onset of modernity as "a time when order of the world, of the human habitat, of the human self, and of the connection between all three is reflected upon; a matter of thought, of concern, of a practice that is aware of itself, conscious of being a conscious practice and wary of the void it would leave were it to halt or merely relent" (1991, 5). Though the onset of modernity preceded the onset of democracy in

Weimar Germany, it was the conflagration and destructiveness of the first modern and global war—World War I—and the steady rationalization and bureaucratization and democratization of the world in the early twentieth century that impressed upon many observers, including Schmitt, modernity's all-encompassing force and real-world effects. While the publication of Hobbes's *Leviathan* in 1651 is seen by some as the birth of the consciousness of order, the carnage of global conflict heightened this awareness exponentially.[13] The problem of social order came to be perceived with a new and greater urgency as societies tried to avert anarchy and chaos.

But what does it mean to think about order—and did it mean the same at the beginning of the twentieth century? According to the philosopher Paul Weiss, to order is "to subordinate, to encompass from a particular perspective: it is to restrict entities in a definite way. Order allows one to systematize them, and hence to understand and control them" (1968, 18). The historian Frieder Günther has coined the term "radical-order thinking" (*"radikales Ordnungsdenken"*) to describe the tendency in Germany's conservative circles in the period 1920–1960 to imagine institutional solutions to the problem of social order that eschewed any of the supposed trappings of liberalism (2011). Most of the proposed solutions sought to create a purified society that reinstated the norms and values of Wilhelmine Germany at the zenith of its empire.[14] Schmitt's famous case for "concrete-order thinking" (*"konkretes Ordnungsdenken"*) was a specific manifestation of a much broader intellectual phenomenon. With the neologism, Schmitt sought to repudiate the abstract-order thinking of many of his Weimar contemporaries, notably Max Weber. This was in line with broader efforts in the humanities to inscribe to the notion of order a higher truth, to create distance from the formal conceptions of order that the fledgling social sciences were promulgating. By using the old theological notion of the *ordo rerum*, or "the order of things," conservative theorists such as Schmitt hoped to fight the historicism and relativism that modernity had ushered in (Raphael 2004, 119–120). Thus, they engaged in the sacralization of existing orders, for example the attribution of religious or otherwise metaphysical meaning to orderly arrangements they deemed institutionally desirable. In so doing, they invested them with an existential worth, "a worth that transcends rational discussion" (Dyzenhaus 1997a, 45).

A second semantic development is noteworthy. At around the same time, conservative economists such as Franz Böhm, Walter Eucken, and Alfred Müller-Armack appropriated the notion of *ordo*, which was enjoying a renaissance at the heart of neo-scholasticism in Catholic thought. Now known as "Ordoliberals," Böhm and his colleagues called for a strong state that would put in place a stable institutional framework within which market competition could play out in Weimar Germany. Though liberal minded in economic matters, the Ordoliberals were not democrats; what they argued for was "authoritarian liberalism" (Heller 1995).

From 1933 to 1945 all kinds of disciplines contributed to the discourse about order, though they often referred to rather different things. A plethora of new terms emerged, including "ideational order" (*"geistige Ordnung"*), "people's order" (*"Volksordnung"*), "spatial order" (*"Raumordnung"*), and "racial order" (*"Rassenordnung"*). As Lutz Raphael has shown, the term order was used to justify a plethora of interventions into everyday life (2004, 129).

Scholars in the natural sciences, the social sciences, and the humanities contributed equally to this homogenization of different life-worlds. The semantics of order was radicalized in various ways. Thinking in terms of social pathologies became the norm, for example. The substance of the concept of order was grounded in biology, specifically race. The trope of "form" ("*Gestalt*") was popularized to underwrite the supposed importance of the conceptual fusion of the idea of order and concrete existence, the integration of form and substance. Metaphors of "totality" ("*Ganzheit*") abounded. Universal categories were viewed with suspicion and abandoned. The search for "essences" ("*Wesenheiten*"), especially of peoples, was de rigueur. The construction of ever-more orderly visions (e.g., *Volksgemeinschaft*, or people's community) proceeded apace (Raphael 2004, 128–133; Steber and Gotto 2014). These and related language practices were designed to make exclusionary talk—and action—palatable and even desirable. It was the foundation for what became Nazi social engineering.

It is worth pointing out that Schmitt was not doctrinaire in his solutions to the problem of social order. The only requirements he seemed to have were that a given order be stable, durable, and capable of inspiring existential meaning; that is, that it imbued the lives of its members with an authentic, non-instrumental purpose. There is an affinity here with Arnold Gehlen's institutional theory. Gehlen, a contemporary of Schmitt's, argued that humans were "*Mängelwesen*" ("flawed beings") who depended on at least a modicum of form, of institutional structure, for the creation and maintenance of social order: "If one smashes the institutions of a people, all of the fundamental uncertainty, the willingness to transgress, man's chaotic nature will be unleashed" (Gehlen 1986, 23). In Gehlen's argument, culture was this institutional structure. Schmitt was similarly pragmatic, but he also looked to politics and law as order-producing structures for a stable life. Whereas *the good life* was a staple of premodern thought, *the stable life* became the referent of modern (think Hobbes) and anti-modern (think Schmitt) theorists alike, the only difference being that the former were also interested in *the free life* (think John Locke), while the latter generally were not.

Paradoxically, given Schmitt's virulent anti-modernism, the practice of ordering, of categorically and institutionally rearranging entire realms of life, is a product of the march of modernization. As Bauman notes, "Among the multitude of impossible tasks that modernity set itself and that made modernity into what it is, the task of order (more precisely and most importantly, of *order as a task*) stands out—as the least possible among the impossible and the least disposable among the indispensable; indeed, as the archetype for all other tasks, one that renders all other tasks mere metaphors of itself" (1991, 4). It is no wonder that Schmitt felt it necessary to devote a lifetime to thinking about the task of ordering the world.

Although Schmitt was not talented at drawing up integrated blueprints for any type of order, his theoretical proclivities are indicative of a lifelong fascination, obsession even, with getting right the determinants of *all kinds* of orders (Neumann 1988, 567 n56). In an attempt to analytically frame Schmitt's thought about order(s), we distinguish four *ordering practices* in his work. We first tackle Schmitt's practice of categorical ordering, his analytical efforts to render the world comprehensible through concepts and classifications.

Distinguo ergo sum

The principle of *distinguo ergo sum*, once the motto of duelists, played an important role in Schmitt's approach to concept formation. As Helmut Lethen writes, "where Schmitt's *distinguo ergo sum* resounds, fuzzy contours suddenly clear" (2002, 168). For Schmitt, the ability to reach clear distinctions ("*klare Unterscheidungen*") was the essence of classical thought, a tradition to which he was beholden (Schmitt 2009c, 11).[15] In *Glossarium*, he noted that "the first precondition of the ability to arrive at good definitions is a rare ability: to exclude what cannot be circumscribed" (Schmitt 1991, 169, entry of June 22, 1948). Schmitt was a master of exclusion. But whenever he was not in full command of his masterly skill, despair quickly reared its head. Here is an example from July 19, 1948: "I am not in command of what penetrates into my consciousness...I therefore am unable...to distinguish what is in my power and what is not, and, on the basis of this distinction, master the one and accept the other" (1991, 180). Schmitt tried to preempt this lack of control in both his thought and his life by resorting to categorically unequivocal distinctions. "Using the principle of *distinguo*," Lethen remarked, "the decisionist draws a line to mark off the spheres of what he can, and cannot, master" (2002, 183). Bauman put it more drastically: "The typically modern practice, the substance of modern politics, of modern intellect, of modern life, is the effort to exterminate ambivalence" (1991, 7).

As a semantic instrument, categorization can underwrite any imagined order. As Bauman maintains, "Language strives to sustain...order and to deny or suppress randomness and contingency" (1991, 1). Schmitt used conceptual language precisely to this end. Indeed, the principle of *distinguo* was for Schmitt the "proper foundation of both political and personal identity: 'I think, therefore I have enemies; I have enemies, therefore I am myself'" (Müller 2003, 56). In his *Glossarium*, Schmitt asserted that "the indeterminacy of the enemy creates anxiety." For him, "there is no other kind of anxiety, and it is the nature of anxiety to sense an indeterminate enemy." In response to anxiety, says Schmitt, it is incumbent upon "reason" ("*Vernunft*") to "determine the enemy" ("*den Feind zu bestimmen*"). With the help of this response, which Schmitt argued also invariably involved a process of "determining the self" ("*Selbstbestimmung*"), anxiety ceases and all that might remain is fear ("*Furcht*") (1991, 36, entry of October 31, 1947).

But not everything was about enemies for Schmitt. It stands to reason that *any* form of categorization—not just its most extreme variant—provided an element of psychological relief for him, a sense of harmony and regularity that served as a counterpoint to the feeling of "powerlessness" ("*Ohnmacht*") of which he so often wrote in his diary (2005a, 107, entry of August 8, 1915). Lethen remarks that "in the diary Schmitt repeatedly proclaims his favorite motto—*distinguo ergo sum*—but also knows that the certainty it suggests is illusive" (2002, 182). In 1915, a time in his life that was characterized by recurring bouts of depression and existential fears, for example, Schmitt proclaimed that the practice of "categorization" ("*Einteilung*") represented nothing short of "the purpose of life" ("*der Sinn des Lebens*"; 2005a, 31, entry of March 21, 1915). It is also telling, however, that his anxiety appears to have been assuaged whenever he engaged in an exclusionary categorical act such as stigmatizing persons based on their purported lack of desirability or their possession of undesirable attributes.[16] A close affinity between categorizing and "othering" seems to have existed in Schmitt's work.

His capacity to come to terms with the specter of what he perceived as chaos in its concrete form was limited, which is why, we suspect, Schmitt turned as a first resort to the abstract practice of categorical ordering. Categorical ordering was the foundation for his other, substantive ordering practices, his efforts to order the realms of the political, the legal, and the cultural, of which more below. Schmitt's deconstruction and reconstruction of concepts was a necessary first step (and sometimes the only step he took) in the development of his polycentric thought. He was an exemplar of the decisionist as a conceptual type: "The power of definition had been Schmitt's elixir, the axis of his sovereign consciousness" (Lethen 2002, 175).

The "other" of order. "Without the negativity of chaos," according to Bauman, "there is no positivity of order; without chaos no order" (1991, 7; see also Anter 2004, 43–50). This insight helps account for Schmitt's long-standing fascination with the "other" of order, that which any theorist of order fears: disorder. For him, both collectivities and conditions could represent the other. The tropes of the other of order in any life are plentiful; they include ambiguity, ambivalence, confusion, incoherence, and undefinability (Bauman 1991, 7). For Schmitt, and for many other conservatives of his time, the other of order was "the miasma of the indeterminate and unpredictable. The other is the uncertainty, that source and archetype of all fear" (Bauman 1991, 7). Conceptualizing the other of order also requires a conception of the agents of disorder, or worse, of chaos and even anarchy. The more comprehensive a given vision of order, the more important is this act of thinking the exclusion (Kollmeier 2007, 36).

Schmitt gained a clear understanding of who—and what—he was up against. In his public life he identified real and imagined adversaries; they ranged from romantics to liberals to moderns to assimilated Jews. In his private life he lived in an "erotic state of exception" ("*erotischer Ausnahmezustand*"; Mehring 2009, 235). These tumultuous encounters were both unsettling and productive for Schmitt. He had to think about the other of order—about disorder—if he was ever going to be successful in identifying the determinants of social order. In conceptual terms, as we shall see, the inseparable relationship between order and disorder was related to Schmitt's reasoning in antinomies.

The practice of categorical ordering was most obvious in the formation of concepts. Schmitt was both careful and careless with concepts. He was careful in the sense that he made sure to maximize the polemical impact of his conceptual innovations. He was careless in that he was not interested in minimizing conceptual ambiguity when defining his terms. Definition was not a pressing concern for Schmitt. Arriving at an exciting formulation was often more rewarding than producing an exacting one. And conceptual ambiguity, paradoxically, was often a plus. As David Dyzenhaus writes, "Schmitt usually drew back from a decisive clarification of his conclusions, I think both out of a genuine obsession with the arcane and the aphoristic and because he did not want to reveal his hand too clearly" (1997a, 41). The fact that some of Schmitt's concepts cannot be pinned down is one of the reasons for their continued appeal. They can—and do—mean different things to different people. The fact that the aesthetic appeal of Schmitt's concepts often trumps their explanatory power has amplified their reach. Democrats as well as autocrats have been fond of them, rightists as well as leftists. Because of their ostensible timelessness, Schmitt's concepts have traveled across time and space, leaving indelible impressions on dynamics and languages of contention the world over.[17] This is somewhat surprising in light of Schmitt's call for a "sociology of concepts" that reflects usage in a concrete setting, what he called "the general state of consciousness" of a given time and place (2005b, 45).

A few years later, in his critique of Hugo Preuß, the principal architect of the Weimar Constitution, Schmitt elaborated: "All political concepts arise out of a concrete polarity of foreign or domestic politics ["*aus einem konkreten, außen- oder innenpolitischen Gegensatz*"] and without these suppositions are only misunderstood, meaningless abstractions" (1930, 5). He continued more provocatively: "Every political concept is a polemical concept. It has a political enemy in mind and, with respect to its intellectual rank, intellectual force, and historical significance, it is determined by this enemy. Words such as 'sovereignty', 'freedom', 'Rechtsstaat', and 'democracy', obtain their precise meaning only through a concrete antithesis" (5). Timo Pankakoski has shown that for Schmitt concepts not only had to spring from a concrete political, legal, or cultural situation; they also had to be aimed at a particular target, usually a collectivity (2010, 753).

Schmitt's way with words was tied to the motif of order in two ways. First, he engaged in categorical ordering because of an expressive impulse to categorize the world. By simplifying the world, Schmitt made it more comprehensible and, as a result, more manageable. When the nature of politics, for example, is reduced to an inherent and existential conflict between friend and foe, institutional solutions to the problem of political order that emphasize legislative debate over executive decision will seem inadequate and the case for more drastic, even extremist, solutions compelling. In this example, Schmitt's conceptual reductionism can be said to have been indispensable for his political decisionism.

He also engaged in categorical ordering because of an instrumental impulse to change the world. It was ordering for the purpose of more order, of other orders, of simpler and more authentic orders. Schmitt often remarked on the utility of concepts as weapons, especially in political conflicts. In addition to an innate (and socially and historically reinforced) impulse to make sense of the world in order to better comprehend it and find his place in it, Schmitt embraced the strategic use of concepts. He knew that his categorical ordering of the world could help him recast political, legal, and cultural spaces of contention, as well as access to these. Schmitt's method of concept formation, as Müller writes, "was ideological in the sense of aiming at directing political action, and establishing power and dominance over his opponents" (1999, 62).

Schmitt did not invent the language of extreme categorization; it was the wont of both progressive and conservative intellectuals in Weimar Germany. But his talent was the ability to think in semantic antitheses that were evocative and memorable. His invention of concepts that were "perspectively occupiable" (Koselleck 1995, 344) meant that he was noticed during his lifetime—and continues to be noticed today.

When Schmitt first embarked on his conceptual project, the significance of concepts for the purposes of explanation and understanding was a cutting-edge concern in the fledgling social sciences. The publication in 1922 of Weber's magisterial *Wirtschaft und Gesellschaft* (*Economy and Society*) was the culmination of a conceptual turn in the recently founded discipline of sociology begun by Auguste Comte, Ferdinand Tönnies, and Emile Durkheim. In it, Weber singled out and defined a series of basic concepts of sociology in order to introduce analytical rigor into the study of social phenomena. He implored scholars to adopt a "more correct (thus perhaps seemingly pedantic) form of expression" ["*etwas korrekterer (eben deshalb freilich vielleicht pedantisch wirkender) Ausdrucksweise;*" Weber 1972, 1] when formulating concepts. All of this was in the service, according to Weber, of erecting a "thinking order of empirical reality" ("*denkenden Ordnung der empirischen Wirklichkeit*"; 1985, 156). This methodological turn in the social sciences did not bypass Schmitt. It most certainly inspired (or awakened) his fondness for categorization, even if his approach to concepts was very different from that of his admired, if distant, teacher. For one, Schmitt had little use for Weber's insistence on the correct pedantic expression. His conceptual toolkit was built on the precept that formulations had to be truthful in a metaphysical sense, not just in an analytical sense. His was a quest for classical clarity, for a restoration and tightening of conceptual boundaries (Weimayr 1999, 63). In a time of confusing turmoil, Schmitt experienced conceptual order as orientation (Kröger 1988, 163).

A key dimension of Schmitt's conceptual thought was his penchant for binaries. Because every social order consists not just of substance but also of forms (of which concepts are but one example), the proper conceptualization of the world—the creation of semantic order—was of central importance to Schmitt's vision of social order (Freund 1980, 328–329). The imagination of order qua concepts was, for him, the first step toward its attainment in the real world. Following are a few examples culled from Schmitt's categorical universe.

In *Der Wert des Staates und die Bedeutung des Einzelnen* (*The Value of the State and the Significance of the Individual*), he introduced one of the most important antinomies of his categorical thought: the binary "abstraction/concreteness" (Schmitt 2004a, 41). The binaries "activity/passivity" in *Political Romanticism* and "organic/mechanistic" from a 1929 essay appended to the 1932 addition to *The Concept of the Political* pushed in the same theoretical direction (1986, 116–117; 2007b, 95). Better known from Schmitt's political thought are the binaries "democracy/parliamentarism," "norm/decision," and "sovereign dictatorship/commissarial dictatorship." Schmitt's legal thought also employed conceptual opposites; "center/periphery," "decree/statute," "legal determinacy/legal indeterminacy," "legality/legitimacy," "rule/exception," and "state/Reich" come to mind. Schmitt's cultural thought is similarly replete with conceptual antinomies. Among other phenomena, he juxtaposed "myth/history," "*Nahme/Name*," "land/sea," and "tragedy/play," to name but a few.

Schmitt's concept of the political, "the elevation of an adjective into a singular noun," is one of his most enduring contributions to political thought (Jay 2010, 77). This particular example of categorical ordering had emotional significance for Schmitt, but it also illustrates his deep-seated analytical drive. "With the claim that 'the political' had 'a concept,'" writes Martin Jay, "went the implication that it was a categorical mistake and perhaps even a dangerous one at that, to conflate 'the political' with anything else, say, the social, the economic, the aesthetic, the legal, and perhaps most important of all, the moral. So that those political theories that did so were somehow not living up to the pure conceptual meaning of the term" (2010, 77). Schmitt never entirely abandoned his scientific interest in the conceptual method. Some of his writings, particularly *Dictatorship* and *The Concept of the Political*, are grounded, at least superficially, "in etymology and a historicist view of concepts, which foreshadowed some of the central concerns of the German school of conceptual history" (Müller 1999, 62).

But aside from the *analytical* ordering functions concepts fulfilled, Schmitt was convinced that their true significance lay in the *political* ordering functions they served.[18] He described his *Begriffspolitik*, his conceptual politics, as follows:

> All political concepts, images, and words have a polemical meaning; they refer to a concrete opposition ["*konkrete Gegensätzlichkeit*"] and are tied to a concrete situation ["*konkrete Situation*"], the ultimate consequence of which is a grouping into friends and enemies (manifesting in war or revolution), and become empty and ghostlike abstractions when this situation no longer obtains. Words like state, republic, society, class as well as sovereignty, *Rechtsstaat*, absolutism, dictatorship, plan, neutral or total state, etc. are incomprehensible if ones does not know who *in concreto* is to be "hit" ["*getroffen*"], "fought" ["*bekämpft*"], "negated" ["*negiert*"], and "refuted" ["*widerlegt*"] with such a word (Schmitt 2009c, 29).[19]

Shortly thereafter, in the year of his Nazi turn, Schmitt pronounced on the programmatic side of his conceptual project, exclaiming with self-evident satisfaction: "We are rethinking the concepts of law.... We are on the side of things to come" ("*Wir denken die Rechtsbegriffe um.... Wir sind auf der Seite der kommenden Dinge*"; 1934a, 229).

Schmitt was first and foremost a theorist of preservation. Just as "English and American traditions of mind and society," foremost among them Edmund Burke, "stirred against French innovating fury after 1790," Schmitt and his conservative contemporaries steadfastly railed against the modernizing fury after 1918 (Kirk 1952, 187). Jacques Derrida, whose discovery of Schmitt contributed to the jurist's reception by the Left in the late twentieth century, once speculated about why Schmitt's diagnoses of the interwar period possessed captive power: "As though the fear of seeing that which comes to pass take place in effect had honed the gaze of this besieged watchman," Derrida wrote, "lucidity and fear ... drove this terrified and insomniac watcher to anticipate the storms and seismic movements that would wreak havoc with the historical field, the political space, the borders of concepts and countries, the axiomatics of European law" (1997, 107; see also Bates 2005, esp. 17–21). As a "watcher," Derrida surmised, Schmitt was "more attuned than so many others to the fragility and 'deconstructible' precariousness of structures, borders and axioms that he wished to protect, restore and 'conserve' at all costs" (1997, 107).

Because of Schmitt's concern with functioning orders, he was very adept at diagnosing faults with existing orders. He railed trenchantly and with some success against liberalism (a political order), positivism (a legal order), and modernism (a cultural order). He dissected these orders with verve. As Guy Oakes points out, "Schmitt was the consummate 'prosecutorial' thinker and all his major works were developed as attempts to destroy positions he rejected" (1986, xii). But processes of theoretical construction and deconstruction are two sides of the same activity: a quest for order. As humans, we take things apart in order to understand why they do not work, often with an eye to reconstructing them. Most destructive processes (think interventions and revolutions) are not directed against order as such but are aimed at substituting one order for another.

One of the major appeals, then and now, of Schmitt's thought is its parsimony, itself an achievement of categorical ordering. The conceptual reduction of complex phenomena to their supposed essence can contribute to understanding. This, after all, is the conceit of game theory. However, any conceptually excessive simplification of life—whether political, legal, or cultural—also raises the specter of the fallacy of bifurcation. This logical fallacy obtains when a binary distinction or classification is presented as an exhaustive depiction of a given phenomenon despite the fact that alternative representations are possible. Also known as the "black or white fallacy" and the "either/or fallacy," the fallacy of bifurcation is one of omission. It usually takes the following form:

Premise: There are only two options: x and y.

Conclusion: Because x is false, y must be true.

By reducing the universe in question to binaries, this conceptual strategy can lead to fallacious conclusions that are not borne out by empirical reality. It certainly did in Schmitt's case, for as we have seen, he built much of his scholarly reputation on the back of intriguing—but fallacious—binaries. To take but the most famous of his categorical contributions, by declaring that the concept of the political revolves around the distinction between friend and enemy, Schmitt removed from consideration the alternative possibility that the political sphere could be inhabited by social agents whose actions are motivated by neither friendship nor enmity but by neutrality or indifference or yet other motivations. Schmitt's authoritative declarations were intended to manufacture homogeneity and certainty—to create semantic order. Stylistically, evidence for this quest can be gleaned from the language of the first lines in his major works (Anter 1994, 163). These opening salvos often contained the essence of the analyses to come, their quotable argument. They performed ostensible truths about the topics under investigation. They were deigned to impose order on a wide-open intellectual field. Andreas Anter has termed this analytical procedure, after literary theorist Mikhail Bakhtin, Schmitt's strategy of "the authoritative word" (Anter 1994, 160–164). The sovereignty of many of Schmitt's textual beginnings continues to be order-producing to this day. The opening sentences of Schmitt's most famous works are almost always quoted verbatim, and they quickly divide readers into supporters and opponents. And yet despite his performative utterances, the semantic order that Schmitt's practice of categorical ordering conjured is far from stable. As Raphael Gross has argued, "the aura emanating from his work and person…is not at all nourished by a clarity of ideas. To the contrary: his special powers of attraction rested much more strongly on a downright provocative pseudoclarity of concepts open to all kinds of interpretations, and in the impenetrability of his person" (2000, 3).

We now turn to the substance of ordering as practice. As already noted, Schmitt's orderly thought was polycentric. It was oriented toward—and produced separate reflections on—three distinct spheres of social life: politics, law, and culture. Although we do not claim that it is possible to distill the essence of Schmitt's oeuvre, to find a single key to his thought, we do believe that noticeable theoretical threads exist that tie together his many contributions to disparate literatures.

Political Ordering

Schmitt's political thought was centrally focused on the institutional foundations of political order. Across his sprawling oeuvre, he analyzed a series of very different institutions—from the Catholic Church to dictatorship to the sovereign state to the Reich—in order to meet the challenges of what he called "the political." Finding the perfect ordering principle for this (in his view) most fundamental of social realms was a lifelong quest. This particular ordering practice was political in two senses of the word. It was *about* politics, but it was also an intervention *into* politics. Another way of saying this is that Schmitt's habitus was that of a theoretical partisan, not (or not primarily) that of a theoretical analyst. This is not to deny the sophistication and scholarly value of some of his work, but merely to highlight that Schmitt, unlike some contemporaries, such as Weber, was less interested in explanation and understanding than in diagnosis and prescription. Schmitt was a normative institutionalist (Meierhenrich 2016). His overriding objective was not just to interpret the world, but also to change it.

Below we analyze (some of) the institutions that Schmitt, at one point or another, believed could contribute to the task of political ordering. But before we can do so, we must focus on the thing that was to be ordered: the political.

The political of the concept. Of all the concepts that Schmitt made famous, none looms larger than that of "the political." Several commentators have seen in it a key to understanding Schmitt's theoretical canon as a whole. Reinhard Mehring has described the concept of the political as "a fundamental center" of and a summary device for Schmitt's work (2003, 8), and Ernst-Wolfgang Böckenförde, Schmitt's most respected student, has argued that the foregrounding of "the political unity of a people" makes comprehensible the constitutional theory of his former teacher:

> It is a premise of Schmitt's political thought that it is not the constitution which forms the state but, rather, the state which facilitates setting up a constitution. This premise necessarily follows from the concept of the state as a political unity. As a political unity—i.e., a unity of power and peace, vested with a monopoly of coercive power in domestic affairs—the state is something *factually* given; it is given first as a concentration of power. In addition to this—and this seems especially important to me—the relative homogeneity of the people is also factually given rather than a normative postulate or something produced by compliance with the constitution....The legal constitution—as well as the obedience to, and application of, its normative understanding—does not constitute the state; it is much more the case that the state, as a political unity, is the presupposition of constitutional validity....The constitution is not a contract, but a decision. More precisely, it is a decision about the type and form of the political unity. (Böckenförde 1998, 42–43)

As with so many of Schmitt's categories, the notion of the political was an interventionist concept. Schmitt deployed it to conquer—and occupy—semantic terrain. Most immediately, it was an attempt to seize the theoretical high ground in the debate of the 1920s over the nature of the state and its role in the creation and maintenance of political order.

Schmitt's elusive opening sentence in *The Concept of the Political*—"The concept of the state presupposes the concept of the political" (2007a, 19)—was a salvo aimed directly at Georg Jellinek's *Allgemeine Staatslehre* of 1900, the most important Wilhelmine-era publication on the theory of the state. It was a provocative restatement of Jellinek, who had argued the opposite: that the concept of the political presupposed the concept of the state: "'Political' means 'statist'" ("*'Politisch' heißt 'staatlich'*"; Jellinek 1900, 5). Jellinek was adamant that the realm of the political was not thinkable without "the imaginary of the state" (Loughlin 2010, 192–194).

Schmitt believed that the theoretical relationship between the political and the state was in dire need of clarification: "The state...appears as something political, the political as something pertaining to the state—obviously an unsatisfactory circle" (2007a, 20). In an attempt to square the circle, Schmitt subordinated the state to the political. This theoretical move was in recognition of Schmitt's perception that the state was declining in significance. He no longer believed that the "state-form" was "the center of politics" or that the state was "synonymous with political order" (Galli 2015, 2).[20] He did not want to give up on the state, but he believed it was necessary to rethink its role in relation to the creation and maintenance of political order. This involved a transfiguration of the liberal idea of the state. Schmitt believed that "an efficacious order" was one that "would be mobile and not static, open and not closed, tragic and not pacified, transitional and not definitive" (3). What this summation by Carlo Galli highlights is the importance for Schmitt of relating institutional form to lived reality. Without such a fusion, Schmitt was convinced, any public representation of private subjectivities by the state would be inadequate. His causal logic was simple: no authority without representation. This insight inaugurated what Schmitt referred to as the transition "from the concept of the state to the concept of the political" ("*vom Begriff des Staates zum Begriff des Politischen*," quoted in Schönberger 2003, 42).[21]

By substituting the term "the political" for the more conventionally used "politics," Schmitt created ideological distance between himself and liberal theorists of political order whose equation "politics = party politics" he despised (2007a, 32). The belief of liberals in politics as a sphere of cooperation rather than one of confrontation was alien to Schmitt. It had created "the age of neutralizations and depoliticizations," as he put it in a 1929 eponymous essay (2007b). This development was disastrous for the task of solving the problem of social order because, in Schmitt's interpretation, all of the solutions generated by a political system that "rests on compromise . . . are in the end temporary, occasional, never decisive" (Strong 2007, xv). The activity of "politics," for Schmitt, was tied to modernity and rationality, while the activity of "the political" was tied to tradition and mythology. The modern, rational compulsion for form had hollowed out not only the idea of politics, but also its institutions. A misplaced faith in institutional formality (e.g., liberal norms and procedures) was responsible, in Schmitt's view, for the production of meaningless politics, which for him meant a set of activities that were incapable of inspiring existential or metaphysical orientation. Chantal Mouffe has borrowed from the language of Martin Heidegger in her appropriation of Schmitt's distinction between "politics" and "the political," associating the former with "the 'ontic' level" and the latter with "the 'ontological' one" (2005, 9). Writes Mouffe: "By 'the political' I mean the dimension of antagonism which I take to be constitutive of human societies, while by 'politics' I mean the set of practices and institutions through which an order is created, organizing human coexistence in the context of conflictuality provided by the political" (9). Or, put another way, "the ontic has to do with the manifold practices of conventional politics, while the ontological concerns the very way in which society is instituted" (8–9). In this useful definition, Schmitt was not just concerned with the political, as is often claimed, but *also* with politics. The fact that Schmitt distinguished between the operation of the concept of the political at the macro level of governance and the role of "secondary concepts of the political" at the micro level is often overlooked. For he definitely acknowledged the salience of "more banal forms of politics," as he called them. Though characterized by the occasional "antagonistic moment," whether in the form of "tactics," "competitions," or "intrigues," however, the resulting confrontations were merely "parasite- and caricature-like configurations" of the friend/enemy distinction (2007a, 30). For someone who prided himself on bringing concreteness to theory, Schmitt's rendering of the nature of contentious politics was exceedingly abstract. As Jay has pointed out, "like the phenomenological reduction by Edmund Husserl," Schmitt's concept of the political "assumed that the *eidos* or essential idea can be revealed by bracketing all the specific manifestations of political activity" (2010, 79).

Two themes stand out in Schmitt's thought about the nature and demands of the political: political unity and constituent subjectivity (Galli 2015, 2; see also Galli 1996, 733–837). Tied to the motif of order, they are discernible in virtually all of his so-called political writings, thus creating a degree of "permanence within Schmitt's thought"

(Galli 2015, 2). If we zoom out from some of the specific institutions—for example, state, dictatorship, Reich—for treatments of which Schmitt is well known, it quickly becomes clear that the themes of political unity and constituent subjectivity appear over and over in his writings. They lurk just beneath the surface in this quotation from *The Concept of the Political*: "The political is the most intense and extreme antagonism, and every concrete antagonism becomes that much more political the closer it approaches the most extreme point, that of the friend-enemy grouping" (2007a, 29). Interestingly, Schmitt's concept of the political, despite its rejection of liberalism's procedural definition of politics, still hinged on a formal definition, not a substantive one. His logic was thus: "This [concept] provides a definition in the sense of a criterion and not as an exhaustive definition or indicative of substantial content" (26). Continued Schmitt: "The political can derive its energy from the most varied human endeavors, from the religious, economic, moral, and other antitheses. It does not describe its own substance, but only the intensity of an association or disassociation of human beings whose motives can be religious, national (in the ethnic or cultural sense), economic, or of another kind and can effect [*sic*] at different times different coalitions and separations" (38).

At the core of this conceptualization is the assumption that the political is everywhere, to be found in any social interaction that reaches a certain level of intensity. Schmitt's broad understanding of the political is functionally equivalent to Michel Foucault's concept of power. In *The History of Sexuality*, Foucault famously conceptualized power "as the multiplicity of force relations immanent in the sphere in which they operate and which constitute their own organization" (1990, 92). Schmitt, too, was concerned with "force relations," and he also noted the transmutability of the phenomenon with which he was concerned. The political lay beyond politics. Governing the political, Schmitt insisted, required an ordering of unordered, unstable, and unbalanced societal forces. He surmised that few institutions could muster the infrastructural and symbolic power (to borrow a key term from Pierre Bourdieu) necessary to complete the task.

Schmitt's definition of the political did not tie this criterion of intensity to the concept of the state, which is why, in the mid-1930s and beyond, he increasingly examined alternative institutional arrangements that would be able to accommodate his existential understanding of the political, a formal conception he never gave up on. What Christopher Schönberger has called "the moral core" of Schmitt's concept of the political, that is, its contribution to the identity formation of groups, can be achieved by institutions *other than* the state, a theoretical possibility that Schmitt explored at length, including later in life, when he recognized the centrality of nongovernmental institutions in the constitution of political identities (Schönberger 2003, 41–42; Meierhenrich 2016). Immediately related, at a more fundamental level, to this process of constitution was Schmitt's valorization of political activity. As one observer noted, "Schmitt's theoretical reflections are born from the exigencies of practice" (Galli 2015, 3). In contradistinction to Kelsen (1925) and other leading voices in the legal subfield of *Staatslehre* (state theory), Schmitt valued concreteness over abstraction. Jo Eric Khushal Murkens summarizes the intellectual contest in early twentieth-century Germany and Schmitt's intervention well: "Order is not created by legal rules but by the political existence of the state. Whereas Kelsen had demystified legal science through a process of purification, Schmitt remystifies the state as a polity that is instilled with the autonomous will of the people and that is capable of exceptional action in exceptional circumstances" (2013, 41).

The necessity of such exceptional action becomes immediately more plausible, as both a theoretical and practical proposition, if the social realm in which it is to be carried out is viewed through a glass darkly. It is here that the substance of Schmitt's conceptual transformation of "politics" into "the political" comes into play. By portraying this realm as inherently unsafe and by emphasizing "the utmost degree of intensity" that attends the "specific political distinction" between friends and enemies that must be brought to bear on the categorization of "political actions and motives" (2007a, 26), Schmitt wittingly created a demand for decisive—as opposed to deliberative—solutions to the problem of political order. By reframing (and radicalizing) the debate, he engaged in what positive political theorists refer to as agenda setting and control. With a dystopian diagnosis as his starting point, Schmitt was bound to come up with radical prescriptions (see Meier 1988, 552–555). Another way of putting this is that Schmitt, instrumentally or otherwise, invoked what Cass Sunstein has theorized as "the precautionary principle" (2005). Fearful of the specter of disorder, Schmitt made a case for incorporating, in effect, a margin of safety into the institutional structure of a given political order. "It is well established," as Sunstein writes, "that in thinking about risks, people rely on certain heuristics, or rules of thumb, which serve to simplify their inquiry" (2003, 1041). We can think of Schmitt's concept of the political as just such a heuristic.

As Schmitt himself conceded, his reconceptualization of the nature of political inter-action did *not* qualify "as an exhaustive definition" (2007a, 26) of what it meant to act politically; rather, it was a calculated theoretical reduction, a heuristic in Sunstein's sense. It functioned on two levels. First, it enabled Schmitt to persuade himself that decisionism, not parliamentarism, was needed to guide institutional choice and design in the political realm. Second, it made it possible for Schmitt to persuade others (both scholars and practitioners, and not just on the political right) of the need for decisive—rather than deliberate—responses to the specter of disorder in Weimar Germany. Schmitt had already described one dimension thereof a few years earlier, in 1923: "[D]emocracy requires therefore, first, homogeneity and second—if the need arises—elimination or eradication of heterogeneity" (1923, 9). This sentiment was not unusual at the time, but the language that Schmitt used to express it certainly was.

It is not easy to fully appreciate from the perspective of the present the aesthetic and emotional appeal of Schmitt's conceptual interventions. The eminent historian Christian Meier, who was on friendly terms with Schmitt in postwar Germany, described the concept of the political as not only "fascinating" but "seductive"; its arrival in Weimar's intellectual circles, he wrote, provoked astonishment ("*Es gab einen Verblüffungseffekt*"; Meier 1988, 542). Here is Sunstein one more time: "With respect to risks of harm, vivid images and concrete pictures of disaster can 'crowd out' other kinds of thoughts, including the crucial thought that the probability of disaster is relatively small" (2003, 1047). Schmitt knew full well that concepts, especially polemical ones, could have a similar effect.

In view of the exigencies of rule in interwar Germany, a country that was repeatedly teetering on the brink of civil war (see Blasius 2005; Bracher 1960), few citizens needed reminding of the precariousness of life. Having said that, the radicalization in intellectual circles of the critique of "the state of the political"—a process that Schmitt's conceptualization of the political intensified as a catalyst—tapped into a reservoir of existential discontent (see Bolz 1989). By giving voice with hitherto unprecedented eloquence to key tenets of antiliberalism, Schmitt was building a case that institutions should take precautionary measures. On the basis of his well-known intellectual history of the so-called *Konservative Revolution* (Conservative Revolution), Armin Mohler concluded that Schmitt's writings "decisively" shaped the language of this loosely organized, reactionary group whose fellow travelers, for a variety of reasons, opposed both liberalism and socialism and the uncertain democratic experiment that was the Weimar Republic (Mohler 1950, 75). Meier concurs, pointing to the aura-producing effect of Schmitt's conceptualization of the political, which the historian attributes to an "ingenious blend" of empirical insight and distortion (1988, 544).

Schmitt's political thought was systemic to a degree that is not fully appreciated. The friend/enemy binary coexisted in his thought with binaries that defined other realms of the social: the moral was defined by the binary good/evil, the aesthetic by the binary beautiful/ugly, and the economic by the binary profitable/unprofitable (Schmitt 2007a, 26). These binaries, as William Rasch (2004) has pointed out, are similar to modern systems theory, especially to the thought of Niklas Luhmann, whose theory of autopoietic social systems made him one of the most important sociologists of the twentieth century. It is worth noting that systems theory is associated with transdisciplinarity (Klein 2010, 24). Below we show that Schmitt's trinity of thought was constructed on the foundation of an analytical eclecticism that sought to transgress, transcend, and transform disciplinary boundaries.

However, unlike Luhmann, Schmitt was not just after autonomy. His normative theoretical project had two objectives: (1) to theorize the political as an autonomous realm of social life and (2) to theorize the political as a superior realm. As Rasch notes, "Schmitt simultaneously champions the *autonomy* of the political system as well as the *primacy* of the political as something other than merely one system among many" (2004, 5). It was the second emphasis that set Schmitt apart from the liberal thinkers of his time. Because liberal solutions to the problem of social order did not accord primacy to the political, he agitated against them in theory and—eventually—in practice. Schmitt was concerned that the political was reduced to being seen as "a society among some other societies," as "one association among other associations" (2007a, 44). While such a state of being ensured autonomy, that autonomy was bounded. Rasch's analysis of this point is useful: "The power of the political is thus simultaneously absolute—anything can be judged politically and thus processed by the system—and limited—the political stands in a symmetrical, not hierarchical, relationship to the other systems in the network" (2004, 5).

But Schmitt was never one for nonhierarchical organization. Hierarchy was his institutional vade mecum. As we shall see, as an organizing principle, it featured centrally in virtually all of Schmitt's concrete institutional solutions to the problem of political order. This is not surprising; the political thought of Thomas Hobbes, more than that of any other thinker, shaped the development of Schmitt's corpus. We can speculate that Schmitt's exposure at a young age to the hierarchical norms and institutions of the Catholic Church, a sustainable order that fascinated him as a young scholar, further cemented his faith in the institutional logic of hierarchy.

Schmitt's concept of the political must not be imagined as having stood in an antithetical relation to his concept of the state; the relationship was rather an orthogonal one. In *The Concept of the Political*, Schmitt did not give up on the state as a conceptual variable (or a normative institution). Rather, he hoped to renew it. As the heir to Paul Laband's institutional theory of the state, which in the nineteenth century had influenced the so-called *Staatsrecht* (state law) of Wilhelmine Germany but came under attack at the turn of the twentieth century, Schmitt was seized by the idea of radicalizing the theory of the state from the perspective of transcendental philosophy (Schönberger 2003, 27).

If the state decides the normal situation, the inherent uncertainty of the political can be managed. "Absolute uncertainty" can be turned into "organized uncertainty," or anarchy into order (Meierhenrich 2008, 39–41). As Schmitt wrote, "Every norm presupposes a normal situation" ("*Jede Norm setzt nämlich eine normale Situation voraus*"; 1930, 136). Schmitt was convinced that if an entity other than the state decided the normal situation—what he called "this concrete normality of the situation of the individual, the concrete order in which the individual lives" ("*diese konkrete Normalität der Situation des Einzelnen, die konkrete Ordnung, in welcher der Einzelne lebt*")—the state could no longer expect loyalty from its citizens (137). What Schmitt called "the eternal relation of protection and obedience" would be torn asunder (2007a, 52). The Hobbesian contract in which the state provided security in exchange for loyalty would be null and void, with potentially disastrous consequences for the future of social order. If the state is unable or unwilling to cut through—with its sovereign decisions—the veil of ignorance that the state of nature (or an anarchic situation of a comparable kind) has put in place, disorder, or worse, is bound to result.

Schmitt was grasping for two things in particular: insight and impact. He wanted to comprehend how order worked, but he also wanted to *make* order work. His normative quest in the intersecting realms of politics, law, and culture had both a theoretical and an applied dimension. In the political realm, Schmitt performed an orderly two-step: he first redefined the meaning of politics (categorical ordering), then, in successive attempts, drew up blueprints for a redesign of its institutional architecture (substantive ordering). Put differently, his orderly approach to the political took aim at both the *idea* of politics and the *institutions* of politics and the interpenetration of these two things. Given Schmitt's fear-inducing conception of the political, it is not entirely surprising that it produced proto- or quasi-authoritarian solutions to the problem of political order. Let us turn to some of these solutions.

From *eidos* to order. In the first instance, Schmitt attempted to order the political at the level of ideas. By naming the friend/enemy distinction the *eidos* of the political, he advanced a theoretical argument that a transcendental logic of antagonism was characteristic of all the many social practices that have been called political in history. But this is only half of Schmitt's practice of political ordering. In addition to the onto-logical, he also studied the ontic. It was all well and good to reconfigure the idea of the political and the boundaries of the realm in which political contestation is supposed to take place, but a comprehensive restructuring of political order also necessitated his paying attention to the institutions of the political.

One of the most central institutions for Schmitt was the state; with no other insti-tution did he wrestle as intensely—and as often—in his life. For the younger Schmitt, "the impressive thing" ("*das Imponierende*") about the state was the fact that the institution's "factual powers" outranked any individual, including "the most pow-erful despot" (1914, 85). For Schmitt, the state was therefore a "supraindividual" ("*überindividuelle*") structure, not an "interindividual" ("*interindividuelle*") one. The authority of this structure, Schmitt argued in 1914, was innate and did not depend on individual acts of creation: "The state is not a construction made by humans; to the contrary, the state makes a construction out of every human" (93). In his first pass at state theory, Schmitt threw down the gauntlet, challenging the Hobbesian contrac-tual tradition. Schmitt rejected rationalist explanations of the state. He realized early on that the institutional appeal of the state was historically contingent. Although he considered what Robert Jackson and Carl Rosberg (1982) many years later would call "empirical statehood" and Michael Mann (1984) has theorized as "infrastruc-tural power" to be a necessary attribute of the concept of the state, he did not think that a state's ability to broadcast power was *sufficient* as a definitional requirement. In 1971, in the preface to the Italian edition of *The Concept of the Political*, Schmitt recalled the political circumstances in which he had first written about the state of the political in 1927, reiterating that "the classical profile of the state broke apart when its monopoly on politics disappeared" ("*Das klassische Profil des Staates zerbrach, als sein Politik-Monopol entfiel*"; 1971, 271). According to Schmitt, the state's erstwhile centrality as an ordering mechanism had been the result of its unrivaled ability to monopolize the political (politics included).[22] Once this monopoly was broken, once the state was no longer (or nor longer decisively) able to define the exception, to determine which collectivities count as friends and which as enemies in the realm of the political, a new guardian of political order had to be found. This never-ending search is neatly expressed in a favorite line of Schmitt's from Virgil's *Eclogues*, with which he closed, in abbreviated form, his 1929 essay "The Age of Neutralizations and Depoliticizations." His variation on Virgil was "*Ab integro nascitur ordo*" (2007b, 96), or "an order is born from renewal." If ever an inscription were needed to set in stone the guiding maxim of Schmitt as an institutional theorist, the compressed line from Virgil would be a definite contender.

Few political ideas fascinated Schmitt more than the notion of sovereignty. But sov-ereignty, for him, was "not invested in the state as an impersonal and objective legal subject, an aggregate of rules and statutes, but intermittently crystallizes if and when political crises and social disorder—liminal situations—escape constitutional norms. Such constitutional crises require an extra-legal and eminently political executive decision by a single authority for the re-assertion of order, grounded in the state's right to self-preservation" (Teschke 2011, 72).

To return to the metaphor of the system, in his Weimar-era writings Schmitt gave voice to a widely felt fear that "[t]he autonomy of the state as the unity of the difference of society [was being] replaced by the autonomy of the social system which guarantees the differentiation, not the unity of society" (Rasch 2000, 3). He believed that "the pluralist relativization of the legitimacy and sovereignty of the state, coupled with its recommendation that we transfer our loyalties from the state to social groups," including the political parties that he so abhorred, "leaves us all dangerously exposed" (3).

Schmitt cared deeply about integrating form and substance when it came to theorizing about the institutional foundations of political order. Yet it is remarkable that at the same time he was formally and substantively agnostic; that is to say, he did not hold strong views on which particular institutions should be imbibed with what specific substance to safeguard the political. As long as a given political institution (a stable form) was hierarchical and capable of creating and maintaining order undergirded by a political ideology (a meaningful substance) that was organic and capable of creating and maintaining existential meaning, Schmitt was willing to theorize and promote the institutional arrangement as a solution to the problem of political order. The development of Schmitt's institutional theory in the period 1919–1942 (see Meierhenrich 2016) was the product of his search for what we might call "the ideal sovereign." As he put it, "The sovereign is figured as an autonomous entity, an agent, or at least an agency, who has the authority to make decisions. That agent may be a monarch, a dictator, a ruling body, or any of a variety of other decision-making mechanisms" (Rasch 2000, 7–8). To identify the ideal sovereign, Schmitt immersed himself deeply (if selectively) in the theory and history of institutions. In the course of this immersion a series of alternative institutional solutions to the problem of political order left a deep impression on his thought, which space constraints prevent us from discussing here (but see Kelly 2016; Meierhenrich 2016; Vatter 2016).

To sum up our analysis of the logic of political ordering, Schmitt "was engaged in two related but distinct intellectual processes. On the one hand, an analysis of decline and, on the other, a search for new principles to remedy that decline" (Hooker 2009, 9). In the political realm, Schmitt studied the institutions of state, dictatorship, and the Reich and related concepts such as representation for their potential to stave off decline. But as the next section shows, Schmitt was not only concerned with transitions to—and from—decline in the political realm. The specter of decline in the legal realm was of equal theoretical significance in his work—and of immediate relevance to the problem of political order as Schmitt imagined it.

Legal Ordering

In 1912, in *Gesetz und Urteil* (*Statute and Judgment*), Schmitt began the construction of his legal thought with a far-reaching insight about the nature of law: far from constituting a gapless system of rules, the law was full of holes (Schmitt 1912). Such holes, argued Schmitt, make any legal order brittle. Because he believed that legal indeterminacy inevitably resulted in disorder, Schmitt, at least for a while, was emphatic about decisionism as a more appropriate ordering principle for the legal realm: "The best thing in the world is a command, rather than a law" (Schmitt 1991, 274, entry of October 2, 1949). He believed that the involvement of intermediaries—such as judges—in discerning law's meaning created at best ambivalence and at worst chaos. Because the interpretation of legislation can only ever be indirect speech, any legal order that was founded on the sovereignty of law will be inherently unstable, Schmitt argued. Law as theorized by legal positivism can never be more than an ersatz sovereign, an institution "overcompensating" for the absence of a genuine sovereign (see also Lethen 2002, 180). The absence of a true sovereign, or so he claimed, was an inherently unstable situation that sooner or later would require exceptional measures.

Liminal states. The theme of *Ausnahmezustand*, or state of exception, was one of the major topics in Schmitt's legal thought. It had an immediate bearing on his political thought, with which it was intertwined (see Schmitt 1916c; 1916d; 1916a, 263, 310–312). Schmitt once likened the role of the state of exception in legal theory to the role of the miracle in theology (2005b, 36). Schmitt's miserable experience in the military—an ordeal that had brought him to the brink of suicide—was responsible for pushing him toward some of his most memorable thoughts about the problem of legal order (2005a, 125). His first treatment of the topic was solicited; his military superior ordered him to prepare it. Though he was at first apprehensive about the instruction to draft a report that would justify the use of emergency decrees in non-emergency situations, Schmitt took to the topic quickly.

The specific state of exception with which Schmitt was tasked to grapple at the time of his military service in Munich was the *Belagerungszustand*, or state of siege. It was his first exercise in legal ordering. He was instructed to find a way to legitimate use of the machinery of wartime governance during peacetime. Schmitt's gradual theorization of the state of exception was his attempt to rethink the determinants of order at the intersection of law and politics. Schmitt's concept was, quite literally, a call to order. It is important to appreciate, however, that Schmitt did not equate the state of exception with chaos or anarchy. On the contrary, the temporary suspension of a state of normalcy, according to Schmitt, still represented a viable order, at least in the short term: "Because the exception is different from anarchy and chaos, order in the juristic sense still prevails, even if there is no legal order" (2005b, 18).[23]

A state of exception is a liminal state. Temporary by definition and marked by ambiguity and indeterminacy, its direction is open to contestation. The defining feature of an exception, Schmitt claimed, was "principally unlimited authority, which means the suspension of the entire existing order" (2005b, 12). The fact that Schmitt preferred a blank institutional slate could be interpreted as an indication of a certain intolerance of messiness, ambiguity, and, ultimately, reform of an existing order. And according to Paul Noack, Schmitt had no interest in reform; he wanted to get rid of what de deemed objectionable in life (1993, 79). Of course, forming a political order from scratch is a less challenging undertaking than reforming one already in place. If no institutional remnants have to be salvaged, the next institutional design will require fewer compromises.

The state of exception was a vehicle for Schmitt to rethink Weber's concept of the state. For Weber, the state famously referred to "a human community that (successfully) claims the *monopoly of the legitimate use of physical force* within a given territory" (Weber 1921, 78). Schmitt did not think that Weber had captured the essence of the state as a political phenomenon. This essence, Schmitt wrote, was not to be sought in the monopoly of force but in the "monopoly of decision" ("*Entscheidungsmonopol*"), specifically the monopoly of the power "to legally define" ("*juristisch zu definieren*"; 2005b, 19). The ability of the sovereign to make decisions demonstrates an authority to make law without being bound by it, or so Schmitt believed.

The paradox of this monopoly was not lost on Schmitt. The fact that theorists like John Locke and Immanuel Kant in the "rationalistic eighteenth century," as well as the "neo-Kantian" Hans Kelsen, had not thought to theorize the exception left Schmitt flabbergasted (2005b, 19). He wrote in *Political Theology*: "The exception is more interesting than the rule. The rule proves nothing; the exception proves everything. In the exception the power of real life breaks through the crust of a mechanism that has become torpid by repetition" (2005b, 15). The conceptual binary of rule/exception was not just analytically significant, it was also *exciting* for Schmitt, especially the half of the Janus-faced concept that served as a load-bearing column in his conservative architecture of legal order.

The theme of the state of exception is associated not only with some of Schmitt's most important writings, but also with some of his most famous conduct, notably with his appearance in 1932 as a legal representative of the Reich government in the all-important case *Preußen contra Reich* (see Grund 1976; Seiberth 2001), which was heard before the *Staatsgerichtshof* of the German Reich in Leipzig, which in a 1927 ruling had styled itself the "Guardian of the Reich Constitution" ("*Hüter der Reichsverfassung*"). The contending parties litigated the constitutionality of the state of emergency that Reich President Hindenburg had declared in Prussia pursuant to Article 48(1) and (2) of the Weimar Constitution.[24] As part of this declaration, Hindenburg had also appointed Reich Chancellor Franz von Papen as Reich Commissioner for Prussia. The title and text of Hindenburg's executive decree insisted on the necessity of "re-establishing public safety and order" in Prussia's territory. Schmitt believed that in theorizing a legal justification for this usurping of the power of a subnational state, he was on the side of the angels. He was creating order and trying to avert chaos and anarchy. In this well-publicized instance, his theory and his practice were perfectly congruent. Finally he was being noticed on the public stage, even though Schmitt afterward was cut up about the media reporting of his legal performance (see 1932b for the text of his statement in court).

The state of exception, as an analytical construct, was an orderly state suspended between the poles of order and anarchy. It was a conceptual vehicle that prompted Schmitt's turn to the study of dictatorship, in the course of which his thinking about the nature of the state as institutional guarantor of order underwent an important transformation. Although Schmitt was not, in the early years, an adversary of the *Rechtsstaat*, in his legal theory he developed a strong preference for the *Exekutivstaat*, the executive state, as the state form best suited for the creation and maintenance of social order. Two institutional mechanisms that promised to enhance the reach of this executive state, and its contribution to the creation and maintenance of political order, according to Schmitt, were, on the one hand, what political scientists in recent years have referred to as executive decree authority (Carey and Shugart 1998), and on the other, the institution of commissarial dictatorship. Having discussed the political aspects of Schmitt's theory of dictatorship elsewhere (Meierhenrich 2016; see also Kelly 2016), in this subsection we only touch briefly on the book's legal dimensions, in particular the discussion of Article 48 of the Weimar Constitution. Schmitt's detailed analysis of Article 48 did not appear until 1928, as an appendix to the second edition of *Dictatorship*. This venue was entirely fitting because the appendix, which was based on Schmitt's keynote address to the 1924 convention of the *Vereinigung der Deutschen Staatsrechtslehrer* in Jena, was designed to appeal to a legal audience (Hoelzl and Ward 2014, xxi). It was aimed at readers with a primary interest in the doctrinal—as opposed to historical—analysis of law (see also Schmitt 1924). Schmitt's legal analysis was imbued, as was so often the case in his long career, with ideas from his political thought. Interestingly, his interpretation of Article 48 cautioned *against* opening the door to unlimited dictatorship through the constitutional emergency provision and contemplated possible—and impossible—institutional mechanisms that could delimit the article (2014, 180–226).[25] This position is indicative of Schmitt's attempt in the late 1920s to preserve a legal order with limits. Although he was unconvinced that an ordinary act of parliament was legally capable of placing limits on the uses of a constitutional instrument, Schmitt was not intent on doing away with constitutional law (see Bendersky 1983, 76). Even though *Dictatorship* provides evidence that this was precisely Schmitt's objective, in his extensive analysis of Article 48 he showed a greater commitment to the constitution as an institutional pillar of social order:

> The constitution remains, on the whole, not just the end of all the measures in Article 48; it is also decisive as a basis for its requirements. It defines the fundamental organisation of a state; moreover, it decides what order [*Ordnung*] means.... But Article 48 is only one part of a constitution that came into effect. Therefore, according to Article 48, what is normal—together with the decision as to what constitutes public security and order—cannot be arrived at by ignoring the constitution. (2014, 209–210)

Notwithstanding the fact that Schmitt, unlike the majority of Weimar's constitutional lawyers, favored a broad interpretation of Article 48 that bestowed on the president more powers in times of disorder than were enumerated in the provision's second paragraph, Schmitt was aware of the potential abuse of power. "He believed that the president must be unquestionably loyal to the constitution and represent the nation as a whole rather than the interests of a particular party" (Bendersky 1983, 79). The presidents of the Weimar Republic invoked the emergency provision more than 250 times in response to political disorder. Schmitt argued that the Weimar government's reliance on Article 48 was an act of "pure self-defense" ("*reine Notwehr*") against parliamentary abuse and incompetence (1932a, 14).

Schmitt's analysis of Article 48 indicates that he was seriously engaging with thought related to legal ordering in the 1920s and 1930s. Renato Cristi labeled the period of Schmitt's thought when *Dictatorship* and his reflections on Article 48 were conceived as his "early revolutionary conservatism" (Cristi 1998, 12): "Schmitt's conservative thought, nurtured by the substantivist disposition of traditional metaphysics, emphasized the issue of legitimacy and relativized legality. Legitimacy furnished the conditions for the realization of legality" (21). Weber had described the institutional foundations of legal order differently: "Juridical thought holds when certain legal rules and certain methods of interpretations are recognized as binding. Whether there should be law and whether one should establish just these rules—such questions jurisprudence does not answer" (Weber 1922, 144). And yet according to Schmitt, these were *precisely* the questions that jurisprudence should answer, which is why he despised the procedural conception of law to which Germany's legal positivists—Weber included—were wedded (see Meierhenrich 2008, 15–25). Schmitt gradually resolved to reimagine—to revolutionize, in Cristi's parlance—Germany's legal order, starting with its foundational document.

Constitutional identity as order. This brings us to the institution of the constitution, about which Schmitt wrote a great deal during his lifetime but had little positive to say. For him, the constitution was one of the most misunderstood institutions of legal order. He was consumed by a desire to reverse the intrusion of liberal concepts in constitutional theory. "The state does not *have* a constitution," he exasperatedly exclaimed. "The state *is* constitution" (2008c, 60). What Schmitt meant was that the conceptual unity of people, state, and constitution was indivisible. The constitution was the state's "soul" (60). He accused the positivist tradition in constitutional interpretation of destroying this soul. For Schmitt, the liberal understanding of the concept of a constitution turned it into an anti-institution. It could not be an institutional safeguard of order, least of all in Weimar Germany.

Schmitt was determined to bring analytical and normative order to constitutional theory. He believed it "necessary to make an effort to construct a systematic constitutional theory and to treat the field of constitutional [law] as a special branch...of [the study of] public law" (2008c, 53). *Constitutional Theory* is the most systematic of Schmitt's many books, arguably the only truly systematic one. Although his theory of constitutional law was intellectually regressive, it was systematic in its attempt to turn back time.[26] *Constitutional Theory* was far more political than it appeared at first glance. It was occasioned by (and contributed to) what Stefan Korioth has called "the shattering of methods in late Wilhelmine Germany" (2000, 41). This shattering was the remote cause of Schmitt's turn to the theory and practice of constitutional law; the proximate cause was the permanence of constitutional crisis in the Weimar Republic. To bring order to the intellectual mess that he perceived the "*Staatsrechtsdebatte*" to be, a weightier intervention was apparently required (on the contours of this debate, see also Gangl 2011). Schmitt's occasional commentary had proved insufficient to the task at hand. If he wanted his voice to be heard—and to be taken seriously—he needed to publish his own "big book" on constitutional theory.

It is imperative to discuss *Constitutional Theory* in the context of legal ordering because his treatise, as Schmitt wrote at the time, was "neither a commentary nor a series of separate monographs," but "an attempt at a *system*" (2008c, 53). On the foundation of a categorical ordering exercise, Schmitt once again erected a model institutional order. Schmitt's concept of the constitution fundamentally contradicted the liberal understanding prevalent among Weimar's democracy-supporting forces. For any constitution to be deserving of the name, argued Schmitt, it had to achieve a structural unity of people, state, and constitution. "The concept of the constitution is *absolute* because it expresses a (real or reflective) *whole*," he wrote (2008c, 59). The cohesiveness and coherence of a legal order, in Schmitt's argument, derived from a sustainable constitutional existence. As he wrote in 1928, "The state *is* constitution, in other words, an actually present condition, a *status* of unity and order. . . . The constitution is [the state's] 'soul,' its concrete life, and its individual existence" (60). Or, as Ulrich Preuß says, Schmitt mobilized "the 'substance of the constitution' against its functional elements" (1987, 99; see also Preuß 2016).

As "a special type of political and social order" (Schmitt 2008c, 60), the constitution that Schmitt introduced in *Constitutional Theory* upended conventional understandings. As Ellen Kennedy has noted, "The *Verfassungslehre* was unlike any contemporary work on the Weimar constitution. Its analytic power and persuasion came from the fact that it was not an interpretation of that one constitution, nor was it a general theory of the state, but a political science of the dominant constitutional type of the twentieth century, the *bürgerliche Rechtsstaat*" (2004, 119). Like so many of Schmitt's major works, it was a genre-bending publication and an impressive manifestation of what we call the trinity of his thought.

Schmitt's "absolute" constitutionalism is an example of a systematic reordering of constitutional fundamentals. Bendersky suspects that fear coupled with a sense of pragmatism led Schmitt to advance a legal interpretation of the Weimar Constitution that emphasized its essence, not the strictly formal meaning of its provisions. The concrete situation, not the abstract possibility, was Schmitt's guiding principle of constitutional interpretation. As he declared in a radio address on February 24, 1932, "the more formally we approach the constitution, the more it evolves from an instrument of inner liberation ['*Instrument der inneren Befreiung*'] and prevention of civil war into a weapon of intra-political enmity ['*Waffe der innerpolitischen Feindschaften*']" (2003a, 24). Schmitt objected to a "purely tactical-technical conception of legality" (24). From his vantage point, the contribution of law to order had to be of an altogether different nature.

Ernst Rudolf Huber shed some light on Schmitt's (and his own) suspicions about liberal constitutionalism. Many years later, he recalled that "we did not experience 'constitution' as a secure, normative, security-producing order, but as an endangered, contested, overall condition in need of protection as well as reform" (1980, 134). According to Huber, the constant constitutional crises, constitutional conflicts, constitutional takeovers, constitutional beginnings, and yet more constitutional crises meant that conservatives such as Schmitt and himself would never have much confidence in

the liberal constitutional ideal. Not only did the constitution, as an institution, not pro-
duce order, it seemed to spell *disorder*. This required a concerted legal response that
Schmitt was more than willing to craft. As he put it in a lecture to chemical industry
executives in November 1932: "All fundamental institutions [*Einrichtungen*] of the
Weimar Constitution…today are completely denatured. Only the institution of the
Reich President really remains" (1932a, 5). Weimar constitutionalism, according to
Schmitt, was order-producing, but not in a constitutive sense, only in a regulatory sense.
This was the crux of the matter, as far as Schmitt was concerned. He rejected Kelsen's
argument from a basic norm (*Grundnorm*). Schmitt came down on the side of facts, not
norms: "For a legal order to make sense, a normal situation must exist, and he is sovereign who definitely decides whether this normal situation actually exists" (2005b, 13). In
other words, legal order is what the sovereign makes of it.

Schmitt sketched the component parts of this order in great detail, with particular
reference to his anti-liberal conceptualization of the idea of the constitution. His use of
the phrase "the guardian of the constitution" bespeaks a belief in the importance of a
caretaker, that is, an individual or institution that ensures order. In his writings from the
1940s Schmitt, as we shall see, increasingly theorized about another caretaker of order:
the *katechon*.[27] In the Bible, the *katechon* is the restrainer who forestalls the coming of
the Antichrist. According to Schmitt, every age has its own *katechon*, its own caretaker
of order. In Schmitt's legal theory, the most appropriate individual-as-institution for
the job was the Reich president (1996a, 132–159).[28] Although he did not originate the
guardian metaphor, which has a classical pedigree, Schmitt's reliance on it in his 1931
treatise against constitutional review is indicative of his preference for a legal order
that safeguards the sovereign's power to respond to any exception and to do so entirely
unencumbered.

Indeterminacy as disorder. In 1934 Schmitt invented his "concrete-order thinking"
in response to the perceived problem of legal indeterminacy, which he regarded as a
specific manifestation of the disorder of things. This was Schmitt's third major effort to
think creatively about the making of legal order. In this phase, his legal thought underwent an important transformation. He charted a theoretical path beyond normativism
and decisionism. The meaning of law's order, Schmitt was adamant, had to amount to
more than the sum of a given number of rules: "The norm or rule does not create the
order; rather, it only has, on the basis and within the limits of an existing order, a certain regulatory function with a relatively small degree of autonomous validity independent of a given situation" (1934c, 11).[29] Put differently, order constitutes rules. As Schmitt
wrote in *Political Theology*, "Like every other order, the legal order rests on a decision
and not on a norm" (2005b, 10).[30] *Rex* creates *lex*, not the other way around.

For Schmitt, a decision was the *only* way to overcome what he called "concrete *disorder*" ("*konkrete Unordnung*"; 1934c, 25). However, his ruminations about concrete orders
were far less original than they may appear at first glance. The terminology of concreteness was very much of Schmitt's time, and it was indebted to Weimar legal thought
(Lepsius 1994, 205). It tied in with other contemporary intellectual efforts to revive what

Schmitt thought of as Germany's long (but interrupted) tradition of "indestructible order-thinking" (*"unzerstörbares Ordnungsdenken"*; 1934c, 42, 35–43). On the foundation of this centuries-old tradition, he brought concrete-order thinking into position against the "ideas of 1789" (37). It was the opening salvo of yet another battle in his ongoing war of words with liberalism. For Schmitt, a concrete order was a transcendental category, because as an institutional idea (and ideal) it promised to give expression to the true, real identity of a homogenous (or at least homogenized) people (see also Kollmeier 2007, 58). With this vision, Schmitt became the personified link between the abstract-order thinking of Weimar Germany and the racial-order thinking of Nazi Germany. Many analysts feel that he was instrumental in building this bridge, thus actively contributing to the consolidation of authoritarian rule (see, e.g., Kollmeier 2007, 67).

Ordering the global. For Schmitt's final attempt at legal ordering, we must turn to the topic of international law and Schmitt's *nomos* theme (see Koskenniemi 2016; Simons 2016; Teschke 2016). Galli has argued that Schmitt's *nomos* concept describes a "political form born of originary violence, concrete order oriented not by harmony but by a 'cut' that creates political space, instituting normality derived not from law…but from a concrete act of differentiation" (2010, 6). According to Schmitt, there had always been "some kind of *nomos* of the earth" (1995, 518). Schmitt's theory of international law, although deliberately vague and incomplete, hinged on what he called the "unity of order and orientation" (*"Einheit von Ordnung und Ortung"*).[31] The idea of orientation denotes the spatial dimension of international law. The reach of that law, Schmitt argued, was limited: It was valid only within the sphere of influence demarcated by the hegemon (*"Trägermacht"*) that governed it, the Reich.

Schmitt developed his *Großraum* theory in opposition to Kantian and Grotian conceptions of international law that are based on a universalist approach (see Benhabib 2012). He "critiqued the despatializing effects of the universal, moral categories of liberal thought," the liberal internationalism that had ushered in what he called "the discriminating concept of war," by which he meant the rise of just war theory (Minca and Rowan 2016, 164). For Schmitt, facticity as spatiality trumped morality as legality. The *nomos*, he wrote, was not different from a wall "because, like a wall, it, too, is based on sacred orientations" (2003b, 70). Schmitt engaged in categorical reordering: by divorcing the term *nomos* from its existing German meaning, which at the time was tethered to the idea of law, Schmitt outlined a new semantic order for the practice of international law. He strenuously objected to "the functionalization of *nomos* into 'law' in the style of the 19th century," seeking to invest the term instead "with words like tradition, custom, or contract" (72). For Schmitt, the idea captured "a constitutive act of spatial ordering," one with "a connection to a historical process" (71). At other times in Schmitt's theory of international law, the term *nomos* also appears to have stood in for a particular regime type: "nomo*cracy*" (*"Nomokratie"*; 2003b, 71; 1997, 40).

The impetus behind Schmitt's theory of international law was the 1823 Monroe Doctrine. As early as 1932, Schmitt had described the U.S. foreign policy doctrine approvingly as "a unilateral declaration of governance" (*"eine einseitige Regierungserklärung"*;

1932b, 189). Schmitt saw an intellectual opening and set out to normatively turn a historical fact into a theoretical solution to the problem of international order (2011, 87). Schmitt prescribed de facto globalism over de jure universalism. The former "thinks of the planet in spatial terms" ("*raumhaft planetarisch*"), he argued, the latter only in abstract philosophical terms (2011, 87; 2009a, 28).

In the early 1950s Schmitt began to compare three visions for international order: unipolarity, bipolarity, and multipolarity. He gradually came to be in favor of a system of regional *Großräume*, provided that these greater spaces were internally homogenous and externally sovereign (1955, 521–522). By 1962 Schmitt had developed a clear argument about the nature of the new *nomos* of the earth: "It is the division of the earth into industrial and lesser developed zones" (1962, 605). The defining question of this "pluralism of greater spaces" ("*Pluralismus der Großräume*"), argued Schmitt, was not who governs, but who "takes" ("*nimmt*"; 1962, 605, 607). Although the new *nomos* of the earth was an order in the conventional sense of the word, it was not a desirable order in Schmitt's sense of the term. The postwar dispensation was an order devoid of meaning; it was driven by materialistic considerations rather than by metaphysical principles.

In Schmitt's practice of legal ordering, the reference point for his concept of *nomos* changed quite dramatically. The Cold War proved to be a critical juncture. Whereas Schmitt's prewar conception of an orderly *nomos* was tethered to the idea of unity (as exemplified by the *jus publicum Europaeum*), his postwar conception revolved around the idea of plurality. This volte face is quite remarkable and is not always fully appreciated. It underlines one of Schmitt's behavioral trademarks: a ready ability to adapt to changing circumstances, intellectually and otherwise. This ability was facilitated by the general vagueness of most of his theoretical positions. Schmitt never chose to banish conceptual ambiguity from his thought. This intellectual trait is also apparent in his efforts at ordering the realm of culture.

Cultural Ordering

Remarkably for a thinker who is primarily known as a political and legal theorist, throughout his entire career Schmitt was keenly interested in the problem of cultural order. Particularly from 1910 to 1915, "Schmitt's cultural openness," as Kennedy puts it, is "striking, and...his work is more concerned with cultural questions than with strictly legal issues" (2004, 64–65). But even in subsequent years Schmitt pondered questions of literature and culture. Schmitt first became acquainted with artists and authors, including Hugo Ball, Franz Blei, and Theodor Däubler, in the wake of his university education. In this early period of his career, the majority of his publications dealt with cultural matters, notably literary questions. Only *Gesetz und Urteil* of 1912 and *The Value of the State and the Significance of the Individual* of 1914 dealt with politics or law. The ample list of Schmitt's publications on cultural matters is much longer. He worked on a novel with Fritz Eisler, Franz Kluxen, and

Eduard Rosenbaum, though the manuscript is lost. He contributed short prose to *Die Rheinlande*, and he coauthored (with Fritz Eisler) *Silhouettes*, a satire of early twentieth-century culture and a polemical portrait of influential Germans who, in Schmitt and Eisler's eyes, were harbingers of cultural decline. For this broadside, Schmitt hid behind the pseudonym "Johannes Negelinus." Under his real name, he produced an analysis of Richard Wagner's *Meistersinger* in 1914; his book-length study *Theodor Däubler's "The Northern Light"* followed in 1916, and "The Buribunks" was published in Franz Blei's journal *Summa* in 1918. In Blei's preface to *Das große Bestiarum der modernen Literatur* (*The Great Bestiary of Modern Literature*), Schmitt again made an appearance as "Dr. Negelinus" (Blei 1995).

Schmitt produced most of his literary works during this part of his life. But it would be wrong to suggest that his interest in cultural thought was merely a phase. Plenty of evidence of Schmitt's ongoing exploration of literary themes can be found in his diary entries and in some of his later writings. During World War II he worked on *Land and Sea*, the short text that he referred to as a story (*Erzählung*), and in 1956 he published *Hamlet or Hecuba*. The style of the cultural writings from his later period was fundamentally different from that of the experimental efforts of his early years. Gone entirely was the playful and satirical tone of *Silhouettes*. And despite his conception and characterization of *Land and Sea* as a story, Schmitt was insecure about his literary talent: "I am not a good storyteller" ("*Ich bin kein guter Erzähler*"), he noted in 1954 (quoted in Anter 1994, 154). But Schmitt's deep-seated interest in cultural matters was ever present in his thought. His cultural writings were not the products of an early period of intellectual experimentation and search for orientation that he abandoned once he had established himself professionally as a lawyer. Quite the contrary: literature and culture served as important intellectual reservoirs as well as tools for Schmitt that played significant roles in the development of his oeuvre.

Efforts to take Schmitt's cultural thought seriously are very recent and have come mostly, at least in the English-speaking world, from Telos Press in New York City, which published the English translations of *Hamlet or Hecuba* in 2009 and *Land and Sea* in 2015 and dedicated two special issues of its journal to Schmitt's literary output, in 2008 and 2010. In their introduction to the first of these issues, the editors, David Pan and Russell Berman, emphasized the "centrality of culture for his thinking" (2008, 3). They argued that Schmitt's political, legal, and cultural thought were mutually constitutive, a position that we share:

> Cultural issues lie at the heart of Schmitt's concept of the political. This centrality of culture has been difficult to recognize, though, because culture always lies in a space that is essentially inaccessible to political calculations, discussable only in terms of such ideas as the decision or the state of exception. The trajectory of Schmitt's work therefore consists of a series of incomplete attempts to understand the foundations of the decision and of the political in a mythic-theological-cultural dimension.... Although he never achieved a conclusive account of the cultural basis of law and political order, he recognized the inadequacy of considering a political order as a self-sufficient system. (Pan and Berman 2008, 3)

Schmitt engaged in practices of what we term cultural ordering because he believed that cultural disorder was just as inimical to the creation and maintenance of social order as political and legal disorder were. Schmitt's cultural thought formed part of a trinity of thought, even though the connection and transition points among these bodies of thought are not always obvious or even discernible.

In order to make explicit the theoretical interpenetration among all of the different strands of his thought, we unpack Schmitt's cultural thought with particular reference to his theory of modernity, and by singling out two of his key concepts: aesthetics and technology. Both are intimately related to the motif of order, and both enabled Schmitt to conjure the specter of cultural disorder. But Schmitt's theory of culture was the starting point, the intellectual foundation, not only for his political thought, but also for his legal thought. By homing in on what he perceived as perversions of the cultural determinants of social order, Schmitt offered a dystopian portrayal of the early twentieth century. This stark portrayal, in turn, allowed him to construct and legitimate the archconservative theories of politics and law for which he is still primarily known.

Theorizing the modern. Schmitt's cultural criticism amounted to more than mere criticism of culture. For Schmitt, the practice of *Kulturkritik* was inherently political. The focus on order in Schmitt's cultural writings, according to Carsten Strathausen, was always "a response and intervention" (2010, 26)—a response that recorded the perceived state of cultural disorder and an intervention that sought to stem the tide of cultural decline. For Schmitt, the intervention was directly related to the task of reconfiguring the institutional foundations of political order, which could not be renewed without taking into account the cultural function of law.

As an example, although *Hamlet or Hecuba* was a literary intervention, the conceptual binary of tragedy/play that Schmitt theorized therein was important to him because it spoke directly to key themes that lay at the intersection of his political and legal thought. The most important of these was that of representation, a theme that featured centrally in both *The Crisis of Parliamentary Democracy* and *Constitutional Theory*, to name but the most significant works. In *Hamlet or Hecuba*, Schmitt approached the theme again. There, he argued that only the institution of tragedy was capable of *truly* representing the existential meaning of life, political and otherwise. He wrote, "Genuine tragedy has a special and extraordinary quality, a kind of surplus value that no [pure, merely aesthetic] play, however perfect, can attain because a play, unless it misunderstands itself, does not even want to attain it. This surplus value lies in the objective reality of the tragic action itself, in the enigmatic concatenation and entanglement of indisputably real people in the unpredictable course of indisputably real events" (2009b, 45). The political implication Schmitt derived was simple: a polity is ill served by cultural representations of its life and values when they prioritize aesthetics over politics—and play over seriousness. It follows that tragedy is political, and the political is tragic.

Schmitt's cultural writings were inherently political because they guarded and sought to determine the cultural boundaries of social order. They were acts of policing. The cultural domain, in other words, was a battleground for Schmitt. He did not just describe cultural events; he deployed cultural concepts strategically—sometimes to mete out symbolic violence—in his struggle to halt the march of modernity and inspire a renaissance of conservative mores. We illustrate the logic of Schmitt's cultural ordering with reference to three additional concepts from his cultural thought: symbol, tragedy, and *katechon*. But we begin with an analysis of the concept of aesthetics—and Schmitt's strident opposition to mere aestheticism.

Schmitt's practice of cultural ordering sought to uproot the rise of anything that smacked of "the solely aesthetic" ("*des Nur-Ästhetischen*"; 1998, 17). Schmitt coined the term "subjective occasionalism" ("*subjektivierter Occasionalismus*"; 18) to denigrate the Romantic infatuation with the primacy of the solely aesthetic that was popular at the time. For him, "[t]he general aestheticization, sociologically speaking, only served to privatize by way of the aesthetical all of the other areas of thought as well. When the hierarchy of the intellectual sphere dissolves, anything can become the center of intellectual life" (1998, 17). Schmitt was worried about cultural expression for the sake of only itself. As Susanne Heil writes, he feared the subversive force of the solely aesthetic (1996, 33). He was convinced that the disappearance of religious, political, and other socially meaningful concerns from cultural discourse would have destabilizing effects on the existing order (33). His idea of orderly thought was based on the assumption that modernity was hollowing out the soul of the state, a metaphor that, as we have seen, played an important role in *Constitutional Theory*. The modern way of life, with its excessive aestheticism, was a pure play of forms, a superficial order that lacked the substance required for holding together a polity.

Schmitt's book *Political Romanticism* is a good example to illustrate the point. His account of the state of culture around 1800 was not just a description of the disorder of things, as he saw it. *Political Romanticism* was also a kind of roman à clef about Schmitt's own generation (see Kennedy 1988a, 160). Schmitt singled out Adam Müller, a prominent political economist and theorist of the state, as the target for his broadside against Romanticism as a cultural movement. But he was not content with merely depicting the aesthecization of Müller's political writings in the early nineteenth century; Schmitt was intent on drawing attention to the political implications of Romantic deformations in his own century, the early twentieth. His was not an aesthetic analysis of politics, but a political analysis of aesthetics. The analytical interest was overridingly prescriptive, not diagnostic. Schmitt sought to draw lessons from the past, to reimagine the foundations of social order. In *Political Romanticism* he explored the nexus of cultural order and political order and introduced the claim that ideational deformations in a polity's culture can result in institutional deformations of its politics. The early twentieth-century bohemians that Schmitt encountered in Munich, he felt, were just like the "political Romantics" of Müller's generation. The Romantics of his own time included Hugo Ball, Ernst Bloch, and Walter Benjamin (Kennedy 1988a, 161), all of whom were representatives of a political culture, Schmitt claimed, that had lost faith in—and abandoned loyalty to—the state as an institution. As text and genre, *Political Romanticism* is not dissimilar to *Silhouettes* and "The Buribunks." In *Political Romanticism* Schmitt insisted, as he had before, that the vocabulary associated with the cultural movement of aestheticism should be overhauled. To this end, he made a case for a more orderly approach to concept formation. Schmitt's negative depiction of aesthecisism was a theoretical prerequisite for his subsequent formation and deployment of what we call *interventionist concepts* in the battle for the re-equilibration of cultural order.

In his cultural writings, just as in his political and legal writings, Schmitt was concerned with re-establishing an ancien régime, a cultural dispensation that would reimpose—and guard—a "hierarchy of the ideational sphere" ("*Hierarchie der geistigen Sphäre*"; 1998, 17). Without such an orderly orientation of decisive action, *anything* could become the "center of ideational life" ("*Zentrum des geistigen Lebens*"), a prospect that was terrifying to Schmitt. To be sure, Schmitt was hardly alone in painting a gloomy picture of the age. Like many of his contemporaries, he was in agreement with Weber's argument that the rationalization of the world had led to its disenchantment. Together with Benjamin, Bloch, Martin Heidegger, and Georg Lukács, Schmitt was among "the deserters of modernity" (Bolz 1989, 11). But before we turn to illustrate Schmitt's use of interventionist concepts, it is essential to first address another principal target of Schmitt's cultural thought: technology.

If we believe Arnold Gehlen, who influenced Schmitt's cultural thought deeply, technology was akin to an "organ replacement" ("*Organersatz*"). Gehlen believed that it functioned as a bodily appendage with the help of which humans tried to compensate for their natural deficiencies, but he also warned that technology would lead to the gradual eradication of the organic way of life: "The world of technology, so to speak, is the 'great human': witty and cunning, life-promoting and life-destroying like himself, with the same troubled relationship with nature. It is, like the human, '*nature artificielle*'" (Gehlen 1986, 149). As long as humans looked upon technology only as an instrument, it was efficient and could be controlled. But the Industrial Revolution changed all that, removing the limits that culture had placed on technological reasoning. Technology, the conservative Gehlen prophesized, would take on a life of its own, a life that could no longer be contained.

Gehlen's analysis is useful for making sense of Schmitt's perspective on technology. In *Land and Sea*, for instance, Schmitt's wistful description of the changing character of the institution of whaling was a metaphorical device in support of his argument against technology. He mourned the fact that, in the case of whaling, tales about machines were replacing tales about man's engagement with nature: "Here, I must first say a word in praise of the whale and in honor of the whale-hunters. It is not possible to speak of the great history of the sea, and of the human decision for the element of the sea, without commemorating the fabled Leviathan and its equally fabled hunter. This is, admittedly, an enormous theme. My weak praise measures up neither to the whale nor to the whale-fish hunter" (Schmitt 2015, 25). Whaling, Schmitt declared, had become machinized and industrialized, and thus inorganic. Schmitt feared that humans were being robbed, on land as well as at sea, of elementary experiences, that is, of their primal interactions with the elements. The end result, he predicted, was that humans would become alienated from nature, and thus from themselves.

In one sense, Schmitt's account of the dark side of technology, just like his negative account of aestheticism, was entirely conventional. The tropes and language he used will be familiar to anyone who has ever perused the anti-technological literature of the time (for an in-depth treatment, see Herf 1984). Schmitt's critique of technology is thus relevant not on account of its analytical value, but because it served as the intellectual foundation, the theoretical incubator, if you will, for some of the arresting concepts that Schmitt crafted in response to the cultural as well as the more general social malaise that troubled him. His parsing and reinvention of cultural tropes was aimed at alleviating some of the alienation that he had diagnosed as a sign of the times.

The aestheticization of life, in his interpretation, had led to a distortion of language. The increase in abstraction, he believed, had invariably led to a misrepresentation of organic life. The price of modernity in this interpretation was a gradual loss of lived reality, with language no longer adequate to capture the existential depth of this reality. According to Schmitt, the tentacles of technology had also delimited scope for social action. The modern subject had been forced into passivity. Indeed, as John McCormick has argued, "The essence of romanticism, and political romanticism especially, is passivity" (1997, 49). Schmitt deplored this state of affairs, which is what led him to come up with the interventionist concepts that we have singled out and others like them. Schmitt's cultural oeuvre contains theoretical notions that are defined by their opposition to existing circumstances, aesthetic and technological. In general, the rationale of Schmitt's interventionist concepts—which are also plentiful in his other writings—was to break open, up, or through the status quo. In *Political Theology*, Schmitt put it thus with regard to the institution of the state of exception: "In the exception, the power of real life breaks through the crust of a mechanism caught in repetition" (2005b, 35). No less important than the political and legal dimensions of the concept of the state of exception is the metaphor of the "breakthrough" ("*Durchbruch*") that Schmitt used to describe the institutional state of affairs. It was one of the key functions of Schmitt's cultural thought to break through to an elementary level of culture. By means of the interventionist concepts of symbol, tragedy, and *katechon*, among others, Schmitt hoped to do away with (some of) the cultural disorder of his day. All three of the aforementioned concepts harked back to cultural traditions that had already been largely superseded at the time of Schmitt's writing, but which he labored to revive. All three, albeit in different ways, were aimed at transcending existing ways of seeing. They were quintessential examples of a reactionary modernism.

A strategy of symbols. If the culture of modernity was dominated by representations whose signs no longer referenced reality, but only other signs, it is not at all surprising that Schmitt was interested in experimenting with alternative modes of expression—modes that put a premium on the quest for metaphysical meaning. This explains Schmitt's interest in Däubler's "The Northern Light" (Heil 1996, 14). Published in 1910, the lengthy poem (comprised of more than 30,000 lines) was an exploration of the cosmic condition and the question of being. Released in three volumes, the metric epic impressed Schmitt because of its synthetic power (see Türk 2016). "The Northern Light" for Schmitt was more than an artistic act of occasional expressionism. To him, it was a mythical tale about the elements of nature. The poem does not just describe a long-lost time; its appeal, especially to Schmitt, was Däubler's invention of a singularly emotive, poetic language that transcended the purely communicative function of words. It was the kind of meaningful aesthetic representation for which Schmitt had longed.

Poetry was attractive to Schmitt as a medium that was capable of revealing the elementary function of language. Its unique symbolic power, he was convinced, set it apart from the novel, the literary form at the heart of Romanticism, which Schmitt held in low regard. He believed that the novel, as an art form, could never signify more than an act and product of subjective invention. In the hands of the Romantics, the novel was said to have lost all connection to reality; it was seen as a solely aesthetic achievement. Throughout his life, Schmitt's commentary on the novel was always pejorative. For example, when Schmitt, after World War II, dismissed West Germany's new, democratic constitution, its so-called Basic Law (*Grundgesetz*), he wondered whether the constitutional text belonged to the "realm of the pure novel" ("*Reich des reinen Romans*"; quoted in Anter 1994, 153). Moreover, he quipped that the newly democratizing country's state constitutions were "novels of the state" ("*Staatsromane*"). Schmitt's elevation of poetry as a cultural institution in 1916 and his concomitant demotion of the novel was his attempt to reorder—with the help of yet another conceptual binary—existing cultural hierarchies in the dying days of the German empire.

It is possible to draw a straight line from Schmitt's analysis of language in *Theodor Däubler's "The Northern Light"* to his later writings, in which language remained central, but his substantive focus was more explicitly on politics and law. In the case of *The Concept of the Political*, to cite but the most prominent example, already the title was programmatic. "The concept of the state presupposes the concept of the political," Schmitt (2007a, 19) declared early in the text. The famous formulation is usually interpreted from the vantage point of political thought, but it is also significant from the perspective of Schmitt's cultural thought, especially his cultural criticism. If criticism, as the Greek term *krinein* suggests, is a form of distinction, and the essence of the symbol, in its original meaning, is the unification of elements, Schmitt's concept of the political, with its friend/enemy distinction, can be seen as a *critical symbol*, by which we mean an ordering concept that analytically separates two elements while simultaneously relating them to one another. Here is how Schmitt wrote about his friend/enemy distinction: "This provides a definition in the sense of a criterion and not as an exhaustive definition or one indicative of substantial content" (2007a, 26). What this means is that the concept in question—the political—is *not* defined by the phenomenon that it denotes, politics, but by the distinction that it makes possible. Armed with this critical distinction, Schmitt was ready to reorder the discursive foundations of the political. The idea of culture in Schmitt's thought, one might say, served as the foundation for its own critique. Literary texts continuously inspired Schmitt in the construction and reconstruction of the theoretical edifice of his *entire* oeuvre. As Galli writes, "The literary text is always for Schmitt a pretext, an occasion to speak about himself and about his obsession, namely, the ubiquitous and elusive presence of the 'political' in all realms of human activity" (2012, 62).

Another example of Schmitt's practice of cultural ordering is his book on Hobbes's *Leviathan* (most recently, see also McCormick 2016). It was a critical intervention into the history of interpretations of the famous book's metaphorical language. Schmitt reminded his readers of the original meaning of the symbol of the leviathan, calling into question the appropriateness of Hobbes's use of the metaphor. Several aspects of this cultural reordering strategy are noteworthy. With his intervention, Schmitt hoped to excavate cultural foundations that had largely disappeared in the maelstrom of the modernization of the world. More specifically, he wanted to reassign existential meaning to the sign of the leviathan. Schmitt was convinced that Hobbes's use of the metaphor was without value without the kind of cultural meaning that Schmitt insisted concepts should carry. In other words, Schmitt's objective in 1938 was not to add yet another interpretation to the scholarship concerned with the study of Hobbes's political thought. Instead, he wanted to turn back time. More specifically, he endeavored to turn the analytical metaphor of the leviathan into a mythical symbol that hinged on a conceptual binary. Here we see evidence of the interventionist potential of Schmitt's cultural concepts: They are capable of upending existing interpretations of social life and revealing hidden—or reinventing forgotten—layers of meaning.

The mythical as order. Schmitt contrasted the (to him) timeless core concept of myth with the (to him) arbitrary meaning of metaphors. Unlike metaphors, myths were capable of establishing decisive meanings, he claimed. Of course, Schmitt overlooked, or chose to gloss over, the inconvenient fact that myths, too, are open to a multitude of interpretations. Schmitt's pronouncements on the mythical and supposedly unambiguous prehistory of concepts are methodologically dubious, as so many of his claims are. Each of Schmitt's many attempts to locate the "true" (i.e., the original and unambiguous) meaning of a favored concept—from the concept of dictatorship to the concept of *nomos* to the concept of tragedy—ends up referring back to a contested narrative or tradition, usually one that he distorted. Schmitt's solutions to the problem of conceptual ambiguity at most temporarily displaced the problem of definitional uncertainty; they never contributed in any real sense to solving it. He managed only to erect unstable orders of meaning, conceptual edifices that with a little bit of analytical prodding collapse onto themselves. By and large, Schmitt's was a sham conceptualism, and his turn to mythology often a ruse to conceal this methodological flaw.

Schmitt turned to the practice of cultural ordering because he believed that the problem of the modern age was the influx of too many new and untested ideas. He had no interest in understanding the disorienting arguments of the avantgarde and made every effort to avoid them. In this respect, his cultural persona resembled his political and legal ones. Schmitt's habitus was not that of a scholar who devoted his life to deciphering meanings, aware of the inherent limitations of the exercise, the inability of ever knowing for sure. Instead, Schmitt strove to eradicate ambiguity. He handed down definite interpretations of cultural texts in a manner not dissimilar to the way mechanized judges ("automatons") laid down the law. Schmitt was perennially concerned with exercising *interpretive sovereignty*, what Germans call *Deutungshoheit*. By purging the argumentative space of dissident or otherwise divergent interpretations, it became significantly easier for Schmitt to claim that his intellectual position was the superior one—whether in the realm of politics, law, or culture.

His account of Shakespeare's *Hamlet* illustrates this interpretive practice well. Shakespeare's drama tackled a concrete historical situation, whence Schmitt's admiration for the dramatization. However, the philosopher Hans-Georg Gadamer was convinced, with good reason, that our polymath had it all wrong:

> No doubt the historian can take an interest in investigating those relations in the forming of the play of art that weave it into its time. But in my view Schmitt underestimates the difficulty of this task. He thinks that it is possible to recognize that fissure in the work through which contemporary reality shines and which reveals the contemporary function of the work. . . . An eruption of time into the play which would be recognizable as a fissure within it is, it seems to me, precisely what we do not have here. For the play itself there is no antithesis of time and art, as Schmitt assumes. Rather, the play draws time into its *play*. (2013, 519)

As so often with Schmitt, his *Hamlet or Hecuba* was a study in binaries. Most important, he distinguished tragedy from *Trauerspiel*, or mourning play, and also play from *Ernstfall*, or a state of seriousness, the real thing. Shakespeare's *Hamlet* marked a turning point in the transition from the medieval to the modern era. The play's dramatic form powerfully communicated the unprecedented challenges that modernity brought. On a political reading, Shakespeare's tragedy deals with the changing character of sovereignty under the conditions of early modernism. The figure of Hecuba, the queen of Troy, expresses this theatrical intention very clearly. Johannes Türk (2008) argues that Hecuba represents the threat of the political. Associated with the play as play, her character stands for the neutralization of politics by aestheticism. One deplorable effect of this neutralization, according to Schmitt, was the inability to make decisions.

But Shakespeare's tragedy does not simply contrast Hamlet with Hecuba, or one tragic figure with a dramatic character. As Türk writes, "If art can be *political*, then by *staging the difference between political life and aesthetic form*. And the mistake would consist in a politics that follows aesthetic guidelines" (2008, 88). Schmitt's choice of the word "or" in the title of *Hamlet or Hecuba* is theoretically significant in this regard because the two characters do not operate on the same level. Whereas Hecuba, in Shakespeare's tragedy, acts self-interestedly, Hamlet undergoes a transformation and becomes aware of the nature of his preferences (89). Hamlet has a political mission: he must leave behind a merely aesthetic way of life. But this life cannot simply be abandoned; it is the necessary medium for the experience of this transformation. In other words, tragedy transcends the separation of art and politics, while also serving as an institutional link between the two phenomena.

If this reading is correct, Schmitt's concept of tragedy—just like his concept of the political and his concept of sovereignty—served the purpose of representing symbolically what to him was another meaningful manifestation of the *complexio oppositorum*. The tragic figure of Hamlet embodies a contradiction that set it qualitatively apart from the solely aesthetic character of Hecuba. Unlike her, Hamlet is a figure capable of recognizing inner conflict. Tragedy, for Schmitt, was a cultural form capable of meaningfully linking reality and representation. It stands to reason that Schmitt understood the cultural phenomenon of tragedy as an institution rather than merely as a literary genre, which brings us back to the motif of order. If we analyze Hobbes's *Leviathan* and Shakespeare's *Hamlet* side by side and as texts, as Schmitt apparently did, the intersectionality of his political and cultural thought becomes apparent. Schmitt saw contained in *Hamlet* a blueprint for political order, a prescription that he found more compelling than Hobbes's normative institutionalism in *Leviathan*. According to Schmitt, Hobbes's *Leviathan* had failed to deliver an institutional design for the creation and maintenance of sustainable social order. In Shakespeare's *Hamlet*, on the other hand, Schmitt believed he had detected the outline for an institutional order altogether more promising.

According to Schmitt, it was the tragedy's surplus value that distinguished it from pure play, from the merely aesthetic nature of conventional theater. A political reading of Hamlet served his purpose to hold at bay the menace of modern relativism. It was an instrument in this larger quest. The play's tragic action was not "invented" but stood in for the "objective and subject-less event caused by history itself" (Strathausen 2010, 13). In his *Hamlet* interpretation, Schmitt was primarily concerned with re-establishing the connection to reality that had been lost as a consequence of, in his formulation, "the intrusion of the time into the play." However, in order to arrive at his idiosyncratic interpretation of the famous drama, Schmitt frequently engaged in "blunt allegorical reading" (Rust and Lupton 2009, xix), going well beyond the text of the play itself. This reminds us of Gadamer's serious reservations about the Schmittian approach to Shakespeare. Schmitt dove into loopholes of interpretation, but his conclusions were out of step with the study of Shakespeare then, and they remain so today. Schmitt made no meaningful contribution to our understanding of *Hamlet*. But then again, that never was his aim. As so often, he intervened in a scholarly debate because he saw possible implications for the art of orderly governance. Crucially for our argument, Schmitt's interpretation of a lasting cultural contribution to the Western canon highlights structural similarities with his political writings. If the concept of the state of exception defines a liminal institution that simultaneously is—and is not—part of a legal order, then the institution of tragedy can be similarly understood as an institution that is—and is not—part of a cultural order. The latter produces a connection between the real and the imagined in a manner that is similar to the way the state of exception establishes a theoretical nexus between a legal order and the conditions for this order.

The institution of the *katechon*. This brings us to a third and final interventionist concept in Schmitt's cultural quiver. In his second letter to the Thessalonians, the apostle Paul introduced the idea of the *katechon*. The *katechon* is a figure that, by maintaining order, delays the end of the world. Christians need not fear the imminence of the apocalypse; according to Paul's letter, the Antichrist must be revealed before the world can come to an end, but this revelation is contingent upon the overcoming of the restrainer, that is, the *katechontic* figure. In a world of cultural decline and increasing chaos, the *katechon* is a figure that seeks to maintain a concrete order.

The interpretation of the biblical passage in question has raised many questions, primarily because scripture does not specify the identity of this restraining figure and opponent of the Antichrist. Who, or what, is the *katechon*? Paul does not give us an answer. In the history of theological and philosophical interpretations of the *katechon* the restrainer was recognized as the Holy Ghost, the archangel Michael, the Catholic Church, and the name of God, to provide just a few examples. In Schmitt's works, too, the *katechon* is a "most enigmatic concept" (Hell 2009, 283). But it is precisely owing to its vagueness and ambiguity that Schmitt found this concept so appealing. The *katechon* can be associated with political figures, but also with institutions. Schmitt seems to describe it with terms that have both negative and positive connotations. But if one were to ask, with Schmitt, who the *katechon* actually *is*, his works would not offer a definite answer. The restrainer eludes an ultimate definition, and this is why it proves so productive in his oeuvre. Schmitt's *katechon* is a functional term, a figure that is defined by its role and political potential rather than by its identity.

Recognizing the political potential of the *katechon* early on, Schmitt began to develop the concept at the beginning of the 1940s in a series of articles on war, which were part of his sketch for a Nazi theory of international law. The *katechon* figured prominently in "Beschleuniger wider Willen oder: Problematik der westlichen Hemisphäre," an essay from 1942 that appeared in *Das Reich*; in *Land and Sea*; and in a lecture from 1943, "Die Lage der europäischen Rechtswissenschaft," as well as in *The "Nomos" of the Earth*. In *Political Theology II*, published in 1970, Schmitt mentions the *katechon* for the last time.

In each of these texts Schmitt invoked the *katechon* to call for a categorization of historical agents via the conceptual binary of "accelerators" (*"Beschleuniger"*) and "restrainers and delayers" (*"Aufhalter und Verzögerer"*; 1942, 436). Using this terminology, Schmitt classified states as well as individuals. He deemed the Roman Empire and Hegel restrainers and delayers, that is, *katechontic*, along with Emperor Franz Joseph I of Austria-Hungary. The British Empire, according to Schmitt, was "stuck" (*"wie festgebannt"*) in its role as history's twentieth-century *katechon*, and only the entry of the United States into World War II under President Franklin D. Roosevelt dislodged the declining empire from this predicament. If we believe Schmitt, the United States unwittingly transformed from a substitute restrainer and delayer into an accelerator of history, a *katechon*, albeit a reluctant one (*"Beschleuniger wider Willen"*; 1942, 436). Here, Schmitt's use of the *katechon* has a negative meaning because he followed the rise of U.S. hegemony with trepidation. By contrast, whenever Schmitt wrote about the Reich and its role in world history, he accorded the *katechon* a protective role as a restraining force, as a power that withholds (see 2003b, 60; 1997, 29).

Numerous scholars have analyzed Schmitt's *katechon*. Hell, for one, situated the concept "within the context of imperial discourses and their imagery," arguing that the *katechon* is part of a complex of post-Roman imperial imaginaries haunted by the certainty of imperial dissolution (2009, 283–284). Others have argued that Schmitt's reliance on the concept signified a return to his theological foundations (Koenen 1995). According to Raphael Gross, Schmitt's restrainer is an antisemitic figure that was meant to protect the German Reich against the Jews (Gross 2000). Günter Meuter, to mention a final example, has described Schmitt's theory as "katechontic theology" (1994, 214) and emphasizes its regulative role. As an anti-apocalyptic figure, Meuter writes, Schmitt theorized the *katechon* as an institution that averts chaos and has the capacity to re-establish a concrete social order (1994, 212, 214), an interpretation with which we concur.

The figure of the *katechon* re-emerged in Schmitt's work at a time when he was ruminating over the impending decline of the British Empire and the anarchy he feared this systems change would bring to the international order. The appearance of a *katechon*, for Schmitt, was always dependent on developments in a world-historical context, and only in light of these grander developments can its interventionist function be understood. Despite its biblical origin, Schmitt's reading of the *katechon* was not a theological interpretation, but rather an attempt to endow the notion with political meaning.

Already in Paul's letter the appearance of the *katechon* marked a turning point, as an institution capable of interrupting the declining course of history. In Schmitt's appropriation and reconceptualization of the term, the *katechon* always appeared in similar narratives of a deteriorating world order or a modernist aestheticism that must be brought to a halt. All of the strategies of Schmitt's project of cultural ordering were already to a certain degree anachronistic when they found their way into his arsenal. Just as tragedy stood for a dramatic form that predated the institution of the modern play as play, the concept of the symbol conjured ideas of historical depth and rootedness that the notion of the modern metaphor no longer connotes. The concept of the *katechon* was appealing to Schmitt for similar reasons. As a biblical term, it not only represented a theological world order, it also came from an earlier period, from a culture that preceded the modern era. The *katechon*, for Schmitt, was the revenant of a different world order, and this is what defined its narrative function in his writings as a potential restrainer capable of resisting the progress of history. After introducing the binary accelerator/restrainer in 1942, Schmitt saw the *katechon* instantiated in political institutions, such as emperors and empires. Compared to these institutions, the concept of the *nomos* was the most abstract instantiation of the *katechon*. The interventionist role that Schmitt assigned to it, however, was the same: to re-establish order in a time of cultural decline.

Like the concepts of tragedy and of the symbol, Schmitt developed his concept of the *katechon* with a nod to conceptual antecedents. And once again, his analytical reconstruction of the notion was partial, distortive, and instrumental. Schmitt appears to have been driven by the goal to reorient or at least retard the march of progress. With the concepts of symbol, tragedy, and *katechon*, he sought to identify—and occupy—a theoretical position from which to diagnose and intervene in the disorder of things. His was a search for intellectual entry points. Schmitt made all kinds of interventions thinkable in order to make them actionable. In his mind, he was building bridges between theory and practice, between abstraction and concreteness, and between fact and fiction. Schmitt relied on symbolic concepts because for him they had the advantage of being more deeply rooted in the vernacular tradition, and thus more socially meaningful, than simple metaphors. The institution of the *katechon* functioned in precisely this manner. It served Schmitt as a theoretical construct as well as a narrative device—and it conjured the specter of order in an epoch of confusing turmoil.

To conclude, Schmitt's conceptual interventions were not just methodological instruments for the purpose of edification. They were weapons *for* order. As we have seen, Schmitt had many such weapons in his arsenal. According to Lutz Niethammer, they functioned as "polemical devices," facilitating Schmitt's orientation and positioning in political struggles (2004, 43–44). But Schmitt was not just an orderly thinker, as we use the term; he was also a *polycentric* thinker. In the next and penultimate part of this chapter, we state in full our argument about the logic of his polycentrism and the trinity of his thought.

A Trinity of Thought

Schmitt's contributions to political, legal, and cultural theory were mutually constitutive. They formed a trinity of thought (see figure 1.1). The elements of this trinity developed in response to the same fundamental concern—the problem of social order—and therefore must be read not in isolation but in conjunction with each other. We contend that Schmitt did not, as is sometimes assumed, switch back and forth between different ways of seeing—political, legal, cultural—at different moments of his life. He did not pay much heed to disciplinary boundaries, even though it sometimes looked as if he did, as in the case of *Constitutional Theory*, which is sometimes erroneously described as a law textbook. Rather, Schmitt continuously synthesized insights from political, legal, and

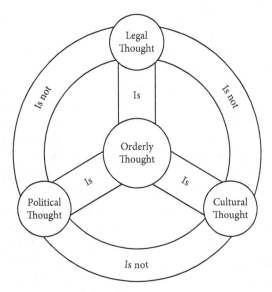

FIGURE 1.1 Carl Schmitt's Trinity of Thought.

cultural thought (although not always convincingly). He viewed the world continuously and consistently through the prism of this trinity. As a result, his thought was refracted in multiple—and not always predictable—ways, depending on how ideas entered his analytical field of vision. Polycentrism and transdisciplinarity comprised Schmitt's habitus. This habitus made his work inchoate but *not* incoherent. Despite inconsistencies in his writings, Schmitt's theoretical project was ultimately coherent, centering on the motif of order. It was a manifestation of orderly thought in all senses of the word: Schmitt's body of work was not only centrally concerned with the determinants of orderly existence, it was also a well-organized line of thinking, the orderly conception of which reveals itself fully only when his oeuvre is viewed contextually—and as a whole.

Schmitt's orderly thought was polycentric. As we have seen, he theorized law as politics and politics as law. At certain moments, "political theory recedes somewhat to bring legal problems to the foreground," and in other instances the obverse is true (Dyzenhaus 1998, 17). And over the course of the evolution of Schmitt's thought, his political theory started to merge with both his legal theory and his cultural theory. Ingeborg Maus and Hasso Hofmann are correct: Schmitt's oeuvre "works as neither an unproblematic unity, nor as a conglomerate of unrelated positions"; instead it is "characterized by steady and uninterrupted development" (Maus 1998, 200; Hofmann 2002). To advance this development, Schmitt pursued a never-ending integration of insights from different spheres of intellectual life. What are we to make of this analytical eclecticism? Are the polycentricism and transdisciplinarity of his body of work the reasons Schmitt continues to be seen as an intellectual provocateur in all sorts of disciplines?

Schmitt accorded equal significance to each of what we consider to be the three constitutive bodies of his thought. The questions of the political, the legal, and the cultural are deeply intertwined in most of his writings. This observation is not new, of course. In an important edited collection about Schmitt, David Dyzenhaus asked contributors to write about "law as politics." In his introduction, he noted that a distinction between Schmitt's political thought and his legal thought was a tenuous one (Dyzenhaus 1997a, 17). Separating one type of thought from another in his oeuvre would be tantamount to misrepresenting both the method and the intention of Schmitt's theoretical project. Schmitt may well have been unique in this regard. Kennedy writes that no other writer in the early twentieth century conceived of law as an expression of a larger intellectual movement (1988b, 234).

But Schmitt did more than oscillate between law and politics, as Volker Neumann (2015) has suggested and Dyzenhaus implied; he also moved between the arts and philosophy of his time (Kennedy 1988b, 234). Pan and Berman echo this position: "Cultural issues lie at the heart of Schmitt's concept of the political.... Although he never achieved a conclusive account of the cultural basis of law and political order, he recognized the inadequacy of considering a political order as a self-sufficient system" (2008, 3). Schmitt had a clear preference for reading—and writing—outside disciplinary boundaries. He searched for and enjoyed constructing transdisciplinary scholarship. We contend that Schmitt's boundary crossings amounted to a habitus of transdisciplinarity because he deliberately staged, time and time again, intellectual encounters between and among disciplines, with the aim of generating novel insights that transgressed, transcended, and transformed disciplinary boundaries (Klein 2010). The results were not always transformative, but often they were. Schmitt's conception of the realm of the political ("*das Gebiet des Politischen*") in terms of enmity is a good example.

One of the consequences of Schmitt's transdisciplinary strategy is the difficulty of classifying his writings. The master of categories is immune to easy categorization. Is there nevertheless evidence of an "order of order" in his thought? Was one discipline superior in the making of his transdisciplinary thought? Martin Loughlin believes so: "Schmitt's primary scholarly contribution was that of a jurist" (2016, 587). It is true that Schmitt never left any doubt that he saw himself as a jurist: "I have been and I am a jurist. I will remain a jurist. I will die a jurist. And all the misfortune of being a jurist is involved therein" (quoted in Agamben 2016). It is reasonable to assume that his vocational background in a profession that tends to be concerned with conserving the status quo was formative and was one of several reasons Schmitt was fixated on the question of social order. After all, as Andreas Anter has pointed out, the law, as an institution, represents "an order of order" (2004, 159). In this order, the constitution has a particular role to play: "It is an order that orders the order of orders" (161). Law, thus understood, does not just create order; it is itself also an expression of order. Is law, then, the key to unlocking the logic of Schmitt's orderly thought?

We are not convinced that a legal lens suffices to be able to truly "see" Schmitt, to bring the entirety of his work into sharp focus. Even if we accept that law, as an institution, is capable of ordering order, it does not follow that a legal way of seeing is appropriate for grasping the logic of ordering in Schmitt's writings, or indeed, of the practice of legal ordering we described above. Even if we assume, with Loughlin, that Schmitt's most important contribution was to the study of law—which many scholars will doubt—this does not mean that a disciplinary approach would be successful in revealing "the real Schmitt," that is, the complicated thinker whose thought knew no boundaries.

Whenever Schmitt attempted to reorder (that is, redirect) a disciplinary approach to a given topic, he deliberately transgressed (and often transcended) the boundaries of whichever discipline he had targeted. For example, a stable legal order, according to Schmitt, was not grounded in law alone. And if Schmitt viewed the sovereign as a political institution that decides the exception, it is impossible to think about this institution without thinking about how it was represented, which in turn is intertwined with cultural understandings embedded in everyday life. In Schmitt's world, any act of representation would be perceived as meaningful only if it was deemed to be appropriate in terms of the social mores of the citizens who were being represented. Schmitt's institution of the sovereign, in other words, is conditioned by politics *and* by law *and* by culture. Unlike the mainstream members of the legal profession, he ventured into uncharted territory. Because his normative institutionalism was ultimately synthetic, Schmitt's trinity of thought should be regarded as an integrated—if not entirely stable—intellectual order.

If we accept that polycentricism and transdiscplinarity were defining features of the man and his method, figure 1.1 is useful for mapping the interconnections among the strands of Schmitt's thought. At first glance, the assignment of Schmitt's writings to any of the three corners of the triangle seems easy and straightforward: *The Concept of the Political* could be assigned squarely to "Political Thought," *Constitutional Theory* to "Legal Thought," and *Hamlet or Hecuba* to "Cultural Thought." On the face of it, each of Schmitt's three bodies of thought centered on unconnected themes.

For example, several major themes in Schmitt's political thought stand out. *The Value of the State and the Significance of the Individual* initiated his focus on the theme of authority. *The Crisis of Parliamentary Democracy* tackled the theme of representation. And from the theme of conflict in *The Concept of the Political*, Schmitt moved to the theme of identity in *Staat, Bewegung, Volk*. In Schmitt's legal writings, he addressed, inter alia, the themes of guilt and responsibility in "On Guilt and Types of Guilt," the concept of law in *Legality and Legitimacy*, and the theme of military intervention in "The *Großraum* Order of International Law with a Ban on Intervention for Spatially Foreign Powers." In his writings associated with cultural thought, Schmitt sounded the theme of space in *Land and Sea*, sovereignty in *Hamlet or Hecuba*, and aesthetics in *Silhouettes* and "The Buribunks."

Yet each of these topoi belongs to *more* than one body of thought. Each of them must be located in more than one of the nodes in the ring of figure 1.1. For example, the concept of *nomos*, unquestionably a product of Schmitt's legal thought, was also informed (and undoubtedly shaped) by his previous thinking about the cultural concept of myth and the political concept of sovereignty. Inasmuch as the three outer nodes in figure 1.1 signify fixed points in Schmitt's thought, the center of which, in each case, coincides with one of the disciplines, the just discussed concepts and themes make plain that Schmitt's writings defy a rigid division into three bodies of thought. Although the terms "political thought," "legal thought," and "cultural thought" are not without value for disentangling, in a first approximation, the different strands of Schmitt's thought, any of his readers must be careful not to overstate the differences between and among these three bodies of thought. As figure 1.2 shows, a high degree of intersectionality characterized the intellectual spaces Schmitt invaded and occupied during his life.

Schmitt's mode of argumentation was transdisciplinary as well as polycentric. This is reflected in the genres of his texts. They are generally ambiguous, because whenever Schmitt wrote about, say, international law, he did not just write from the perspective of a jurist. His most important international legal accounts were also exercises in cultural inquiry and political theory, a fact that set him apart from the disciplinary mainstream of his profession. Likewise, his studies of literature spoke to, implied, or directly referenced his theory of decisionism, which for a long time was the foundation of his legal thought. Most of Schmitt's writings, regardless of whether they nominally belong to his political, legal, or cultural thought, have an air of impalpability about them, as they consistently blur their own generic boundaries. This disciplinary otherness of his writings adds to the appeal of his thought. Schmitt's texts are substantively (if not always stylistically) accessible to readers from a variety of disciplines. Schmitt's thinking at any given time may have been anchored in one of the vertices of figure 1.1, but the vast majority of his many writings managed to break away from their places of origin. Figure 1.2 shows that Schmitt's writings cannot be profitably divided into temporal phases, such as

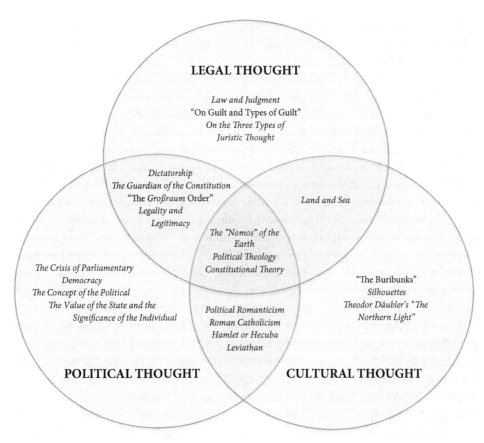

LEGAL THOUGHT

Law and Judgment
"On Guilt and Types of Guilt"
On the Three Types of
Juristic Thought

Dictatorship
The Guardian of the Constitution
"The *Großraum* Order"
Legality and
Legitimacy

Land and Sea

The "Nomos" of the
Earth
Political Theology
Constitutional Theory

The Crisis of Parliamentary
Democracy
The Concept of the Political
The Value of the State and the
Significance of the Individual

"The Buribunks"
Silhouettes
Theodor Däubler's "The
Northern Light"

Political Romanticism
Roman Catholicism
Hamlet or Hecuba
Leviathan

POLITICAL THOUGHT   **CULTURAL THOUGHT**

FIGURE 1.2 Polycentricity and Transdisciplinarity in Carl Schmitt's Major Works, 1910–1956.

a cultural phase, a legal phase, and a political phase. Although Schmitt emphasized different foci over the course of his writing life, his approach did not drastically change. He consistently treated his topics as an interleaving of various strands of thought.

Schmitt's thought was simultaneously disciplined and undisciplined. His writings often were contributions to specific discourses, disciplinary and otherwise, but they were frequently highly unconventional in their execution. As we have shown in earlier sections of this chapter, Schmitt's approach to the world was above all characterized by an attempt to intervene in existing circumstances, to reorder thought or conduct in the world. Not surprisingly, his transdisciplinarity appeals to readers today, a time when law, the social sciences, and the humanities are increasingly embracing multidisciplinarity and interdisciplinarity (see Klein 2010; Frodeman 2010).

It bears emphasizing that Schmitt was *not* an interdisciplinary thinker. This brings us to the undisciplined aspect of his scholarship. Although he excelled at transgressing and transcending the boundaries of a given discipline, he was uninterested in or unable to blend existing bodies of knowledge in a careful, analytical way. He merely dabbled in other disciplines; he did not respect their laboriously acquired stocks of knowledge.

Schmitt's engagement with other disciplines was of a highly selective kind, which is why we use the term "transdisciplinarity" to describe the method and orientation of his boundary-crossing thought.

When one investigates the methodological techniques that were fundamental to Schmitt's theoretical approach, two stand out: the use of conceptual binaries and a preference for concreteness. Schmitt's thinking in antinomies rendered the axes of figure 1.1 as *distance* that produced intellectual separation. His thinking in terms of concreteness had the opposite effect: it produced integration by rendering the axes as *proximity*. The latter insight returns us to his categorical universe, most of which is located, in figure 1.2, at the intersections of the trinity of his thought, as exemplified by "Leviathan/Behemoth" and "existential representation/parliamentary representation." Upon reflection, it becomes clear that Schmitt's binaries (and virtually all others) have transdisciplinary origins, too. Schmitt's model of representation was grounded above all in cultural history. He derived the binary of the sea monster/land monster from the Bible. Even his legal thought contains conceptual binaries, such as "form/substance," "concrete/abstract orders," and "center/periphery," the meaning of which Schmitt in the first instance derived from discourses outside the field of law.

Although Schmitt's concepts were part of a political, legal, or cultural discourse, their paradigm of meaning was frequently associated with a different mode of thought. To give an example, Schmitt interpreted his juristic concepts with non-juristic means. Thus his conceptual antinomies have a peculiar effect: they simultaneously work within their respective contexts as fundamental ideas *and* reference a domain beyond their place of origin. In this sense, the binaries open up a conceptual range that goes beyond the boundaries of the discourse in question. Schmitt constructed argumentative tensions with the help of his antinomies; he contrasted ideas from one discipline with counter-ideas from another.

If one understands antinomies in this sense as a dimension of distance, then these antinomies call for a second method capable of visualizing this distance as cohesion. In our view, Schmitt's "concrete thinking" is such a method. His concrete thinking is, in a sense, the reverse side of his reliance on antinomies, since it attempts to present the connection between the concept and Schmitt's proposed meaning as an unambiguous correlation. In this sense, "concrete" is meant to communicate that Schmitt's newly proposed meaning is neither arbitrary nor metaphorical. In fact, he insisted that his novel conceptualization simply reinstated the "actual" ("*eigentliche*") meaning of a given term. Schmitt's concept of the *nomos* is a good example. If we believe Schmitt, the "concrete" meaning of *nomos* must be derived from its Greek etymology, for the original concept not only has a legal connotation but also connotes the seizure of territory. For Schmitt, the *nomos* was the epitome of justice because it related order to location in a meaningful way. Schmitt claimed that his reading of nomos *concretized* the original meaning of the word *nomos*, and that his concretization of the concept amounted to a *Setzung*, a conceptual settlement, so to speak, of ideational ambiguity.

Often, Schmitt's reading was mere interpretation, not received wisdom, however. Take once again the example of the *nomos* concept. Instead of situating his project within the sizable geospatial Nazi literature and national *nomos* theology, as most scholars would have done, Schmitt, in keeping with his transgressive method, preferred to engage Pindar and Hölderlin instead and to ignore almost entirely the literature on the very theme he set out to theorize. Schmitt's "concretization" of the *nomos* concept is successful *only* because he eradicated inconvenient complexity. Friedrich Balke has shown that Schmitt's discussion of the classical origins of the concept utterly distorted Greek scholarship (1996, 317). Among other questionable strategies, Schmitt ignored the historical fact that the notion of *nomos* also once stood for nomadism, that is, for the exact *opposite* of what he wanted to (and came to) associate with it. Schmitt's frequently deployed strategy of misappropriating ambivalent concepts is evident here. The example also illustrates how Schmitt resorted to myths and stories for his disambiguation of concepts yet failed to properly ground his idiosyncratic interpretations of these problematic sources. Because it is so utterly unperturbed by the demands of verification, we call Schmitt's practice of willfully selective interpretation *authoritarian hermeneutics*. Schmitt's supposedly unambiguous concepts are almost always ambiguous and ambivalent, and as forms of concrete thinking they are for the most part frustratingly non-concrete. Throughout his life, Schmitt attempted to arbitrarily fix the meaning of political, legal, and cultural concepts in his theoretical arsenal without any serious regard for the methodologies of any discipline, his own included. The more "concrete" Schmitt's thought was, the more ambiguous it became.

Conclusion

In this chapter we have advanced an argument that the motif of order is of central importance for making sense of Carl Schmitt's contributions to law, the social sciences, and the humanities. We have further argued that his contributions to diverse disciplines constituted a trinity of thought, that his political thought cannot be understood without reference to his legal thought and his cultural thought; that his legal thought was informed equally by his political and cultural thought; and that his cultural thought contains important traces of his political thought and his legal thought. We have tried to demonstrate that the theoretical and substantive overlap in Schmitt's oeuvre was deliberate. His method resembled what Rudra Sil and Peter Katzenstein have termed "analytic eclecticism" (2010, 411–431). Their definition of the methodological practice goes a long way toward capturing the essence of Schmitt's approach to thinking about the problem of social order. Sil and Katzenstein argue that unlike conventional scholars, who embed their work in research traditions, those who practice analytic eclecticism are not interested in answering narrowly focused research questions and often connect interactions among explanatory factors that are "normally analyzed in isolation from each other within separate research traditions" (212).

Schmitt was an analytic eclecticist par excellence. His adoption of the methodological approach was arguably necessitated by the demands of his overriding intellectual project: solving the problem of social order in all of its complexity, which included devising solutions to the interconnected problems of political order, legal order, and cultural order. But as productive as analytic eclecticism can be, it also carries risks. As Sil and Katzenstein have pointed out, "when drawing upon theories or narratives developed in competing research traditions, there is the danger of theoretical incoherence linked to the problem of incommensurability across traditions" (2012, 214). Evidence of this flaw is detectable in virtually all of Schmitt's writings, where its effect is exacerbated by his analytical carelessness, highly selective reading, and consistent disregard for extant knowledge in the intellectual domains he plundered and strove to reorder.

Understanding the complexity and subtleties of Schmitt's far-reaching oeuvre is a tall order for anyone. Not misunderstanding him is a more manageable goal and should be achievable, and we hope that this chapter, and this volume as a whole, will contribute to that endeavor. In our approach, we are sympathetic to Adam Sitze's recent lament:

> The fewer Schmittian texts we read (the more we constrain our reading of Schmitt, say, to [The] Concept of the Political or Political Theology), and the more carelessly we read these texts (the more our hermeneutic encounter with Schmitt's texts is limited to the extraction of timeless and abstract "logics" of norm and exception, friend and enemy, etc.), the more acutely we will suffer from the illusion that Schmittian thought is adequate for the task of naming our experience today, and the more we will be inclined to prolong "Schmittian logic" past its own immanent expiration date. (2010, 65–66)

We have conceived this collection as a diverse guide to deeper and broader readings of Schmitt. Not all of our contributors are convinced that such an engagement with Schmitt is necessary. Some are content with extracting the timeless and abstract logics from Schmitt's thought that Sitze finds so problematic. Although the chapters in this volume are more than capable of speaking for themselves, we conclude with a brief overview of their organization.

The contributions are organized in four parts. Part I revisits enduring controversies about Schmitt's biography and showcases contending ways of making legible his radically different lives under four successive political regimes. But part I is about more than mere biography; it is also about Schmitt as an institution. Parts II–IV explore a variety of facets of Schmitt's political thought (part II), legal thought (part III), and cultural thought (part IV). Even though a neat tripartite division of Schmitt's oeuvre, for the reasons we elaborated above, is inherently problematic, it affords recognizable entry points into his thought. In one sense, the arrangement of chapters is conventional because it adheres to a customary way of categorizing Schmitt's writings. However, we have been careful not to reify orthodox—and reductive—ways of seeing Schmitt. Our twin goals have been to unify but also to decenter the study of Schmitt. A closer perusal of the contributions will reveal that the structure of this handbook is not as conventional as it may initially appear. It deliberately transgresses and transcends disciplinary boundaries. Schmittian themes such as "modernity," "sovereignty," "democracy," "emergency," "spatiality," and "tragedy" surface in each of this volume's three principal parts, as do such quintessential Schmittian concepts as "commissarial dictatorship," "state of exception," "the political," and "nomos." What this shows is that our handbook can be used in multiple ways by both novices and specialists. We have prepared an extensive index to facilitate the drawing of expected—but also unexpected—connections between and among chapters.

We hope that our handbook will serve as a critical introduction to Carl Schmitt and will inspire a new generation of unorthodox scholarship of Schmitt's trinity of thought. The verb κρίνω ("*krinein*")—the Greek origin of the noun "critique"—deserves a closer look in this context. It can mean, inter alia, "to separate," "to distinguish," and "to pass judgment." It can also mean "to order" and "to arrange." Schmitt's practices of categorical ordering, political ordering, legal ordering, and cultural ordering can be understood as practices of *krinein*. This handbook is also an example of *krinein*. But a few caveats are in order. We are not just interested in reordering the seemingly divergent strands of Schmitt's thought, as we have done in this chapter, nor are we in the business of passing moral judgment on Schmitt. We think of our approach as critical because it is aimed at assembling a varied and sophisticated analytical toolkit with which to cut through the layers of subterfuge in Schmitt's oeuvre (and in the reception thereof during the last hundred years). Arguably the most important tool of all, which several of our contributors have used quite deftly, is that of *contextualization*, both historical and theoretical. Only a contextualization of Schmitt's transdisciplinary thought will allow us to see Schmitt for who he was: a polycentric theorist who responded to a deep-seated fear of disorder with the help of an analytic eclecticism that was inherently undisciplined, in all senses of the word. Schmitt was also unconventional: he consistently defied scholarly conventions by transgressing, transcending, and sometimes transforming the knowledge of his day, and ours.

Our mission was to engage with the critical ordering of Schmitt's writings. The principal purpose was to invest in the proper contextualization of his challenging thought, not to consider the utility of applying it to the postmodern crises of the present. More important than the question of whether Schmitt's positions and concepts are relevant in the twenty-first century is the question of how to read Schmitt so as to grasp the original—rather than the subsequently imputed—meanings of his many publications. Aside from contributing to knowledge about the three strands of Schmitt's thought—and the motif of order that we believe tied them together—we aim to provoke debate about the relevance of his canon for thinking about the present. The contemporary relevance of Schmitt's body of work is widely assumed, but rarely questioned. And yet, like Sitze, we believe that

> the more deeply and widely we read Schmitt's writings, and the more loyal we remain to the kernel of the Schmittian *occasio* in our own thought, the more we will realize how pointless are Schmitt's categories in an epoch in which Schmitt's contradictory oeuvre no longer sustains a relation to the crises from which alone it[s] coherence originates. The use of Schmittian categories to interpret the global age not only betrays what was most alive in Schmitt's thought; it also allows us to comfort ourselves with the reassuring fantasy that contemporary crises will so resemble those of modernity that the critique of the latter will retain purchase on the former as well. (2010, 66)

It is important to read Schmitt, but not in order to understand the present. Schmitt is relevant because his oeuvre helps us better understand the past—*his* past. This handbook is intended as the foundation for a "non-Schmittian Schmittology," the defining challenge of which is "to read Carl Schmitt so completely, so carefully, and so loyally, that we *therefore* close the book on him, turning now to face a set of crises about which Schmitt has, precisely, nothing to say" (Sitze 2010, 66). Locating Schmitt beyond both stigma and enigma is what we are after.

NOTES

1. See, for example, Schmitt 2005a (41, entry of April 5, 1915). See also Mehring 2009 (328). Paul Noack, quite accurately in our opinion, has described Schmitt's belief that he could be more than a mere theorist as a serious misjudgment of his capabilities (and of his temperament). By overestimating his talents—by mistakenly believing that he could succeed in the practical world of politics—Schmitt ensured that his residence in the corridors of power was short-lived (see Noack 1993, 310–311).
2. Unless noted otherwise, all translations of source material by the authors.
3. To our chagrin, this volume ended up being an all-male affair. It was not conceived as such, far from it. Female contributors formed an integral part of the project from the outset, and we extended invitations to numerous junior and senior scholars. Two eminent political theorists accepted. Regrettably, for reasons beyond our control, we were in the end unable to include their important contributions on, respectively, economy and the state in Schmitt's political theory and Schmitt's critique of Immanuel Kant. Other female scholars who we had hoped would join the project, unfortunately, declined our invitations. This explanatory note is not intended to deflect from our editorial and professional responsibility to help reduce gender inequality in the academy, but, rather, to explain why sometimes, despite the best intentions—and concerted efforts over several years—things can nonetheless go awry.
4. It is important to appreciate that the ambivalence in Schmitt's oeuvre was a defining feature of his life. The metaphor of the leviathan—which occupied Schmitt until late in life and inspired some of his most thought-provoking work—has recently been read as a symbol of this ambivalence (see Balke 1996, 10).
5. On the cultural salience of the idea of "transcendental homelessness" in the early twentieth century, see Ulbricht 1998 (47).
6. For a trenchant review, see Laak 1995. Refutations are also provided by Motschenbacher 2000 (esp. 360); Bates 2006 (esp. 416–417); and Roberts 2015 (449–474). For the contrary position, see Schmitt's acolyte, Böckenförde 1997.
7. For an exhaustive, biographical account of his life, see Mehring 2009. A useful intellectual biography is Balakrishnan 2000.
8. Schmitt described this urge in 1941 in a letter to Erwin von Beckerath, commenting on the debilitating effect that the realization of his inability to publish had on him: "*den das Bewußtsein des Mangels jeder echten Publizität völlig lähmt*" (quoted in Laak 2002, 142 n41).

9. Schmitt admitted as much in an informal speech in 1956 that appeared in print in the nationalist Flemish monthly *Dietsland-Europa* a year later: "Was habe ich getan?" Reprinted in Tommissen 1996 (13–19).

10. On the problem of social order more generally, see, among many other contributions, Kuntz 1968; Ellis 1971; Elster 1989; Shapiro and Hardin 1993; Wrong 1994; Soltan et al. 1998; Hechter and Haufler 2003; and Lawler et al. 2015.

11. *Oxford English Dictionary*, s.v. "order, *n.*," http://www.oed.com/view/Entry/132334?rske y=8Y56PU&result=1&isAdvanced=false#eid. The best treatment of the term's etymology and intellectual usage across the centuries remains the four-part entry in Ritter and Gründer 1984 (1251–1303).

12. *Oxford English Dictionary*, s.v. "order."

13. For the argument that the publication of *Leviathan* represented a critical juncture in the evolution of orderly thought in general, see Collins 1989.

14. For the diffusion of radical-order thinking among elites in Nazi Germany, see Raphael 2001.

15. The belief that Romanticism lacked this ability was for Schmitt one of the principal reasons for objecting to its "subjective occasionalism" (see Schmitt 1988, 18). For a good account of Schmitt's juxtaposition of the classical and romantic eras, see Dahlheimer 1998 (56–78).

16. The principal targets of his scorn in the period in question—other than himself, whom he targeted mercilessly—were, in decreasing order of significance, his wife Cari von Dorotić, his military superior, the poet and friend Theodor Däubler, and "the Jews," both individual and collective.

17. Timothy Snyder has recently noted the influence of Schmitt on the development of the ideology of "Eurasianism" in Russia, reportedly "the creed of a number of people in the Putin administration, and the moving force of a rather active far-right Russian youth movement" (2014; see also Sur 2014).

18. Müller correctly noted that "the exigencies of ideological combat and a strategic politics of concepts (*Begriffspolitik*) tended to override Schmitt's *Wissenschaftlichkeit*," i.e., the latter's interest in scientific method (1999, 62).

19. For the sake of accuracy, we have departed from the extant translation in Schmitt 2007a (30–31).

20. While Schmitt distanced himself from the state as a conceptual variable, he "never conceived of a politics completely detached from the State" (Galli 2015, 2). Galli speculates that it was the state-centeredness of Schmitt's chosen profession—law—that "left him incapable of doing away with modern [s]tatuality altogether" (2).

21. Documents among Schmitt's archived papers in the Hauptstaatsarchiv Düsseldorf suggest that he had plans to publish an edition of collected writings under the same title (Schönberger 2003, 42 n60).

22. For an important political science account that bears out this point for the modern state (the only state that Schmitt was ever interested in), see Spruyt 1994.

23. Because George Schwab's English translation is slightly inaccurate here, we have modified it.

24. Verordnung des Reichspräsidenten, betreffend die Wiederherstellung der öffentlichen Sicherheit und Ordnung im Gebiet des Landes Preußen, July 20, 1932, RGBl. I, 377.

25. For a comprehensive analysis of the genesis and usage of Article 48, see Kurz 1992. For a discussion of Schmitt's attitude toward the provision, see Dyzenhaus 1997a and Scheuerman 2016.

26. As Murkens remarks, "Schmitt's observations depicted a bygone era, that of the monarchy prior to the nation state and the constitution. They stem from a time when it was common practice to define the state in socio-historical terms, the constitution in material, non-positive terms, sovereignty as highest might, and *Volk* as a political and homogenous unit" (2013, 55).

27. Schmitt also occasionally relied on the term *demiurge*, the philosophical usage of which goes back to Plato's *Timaeus*, where the figure connotes the *actual* creator of the universe rather than the god who conceived it in the abstract. Schmitt's figure of the sovereign closely resembles Plato's figure of the demiurge. Like the demiurge, the sovereign is faced with imperfect matter.

28. The *katechon* figured prominently in "Beschleuniger wider Willen oder: Problematik der westlichen Hemisphäre," an essay from 1942 that appeared in *Das Reich*; in *Land and Sea*; in a lecture from 1943, "Die Lage der europäischen Rechtswissenschaft"; and in Schmitt 2003b. In *Political Theology II* (1970), Schmitt mentions the *katechon* for the last time.

29. Because it is not entirely accurate, we do not, in this instance, rely on the Bendersky translation of this work (see Schmitt 2004b, 48–49).

30. Note that Schmitt in this context used the terms "norm" ("*Norm*") and "rule" ("*Regel*") interchangeably.

31. The German word *Ortung* combines connotations associated with the English words "orientation" and "localization."

REFERENCES

Agamben, G. 2016. "A Jurist Confronting Himself: Carl Schmitt's Jurisprudential Thought." In *The Oxford Handbook of Carl Schmitt*, ed. J. Meierhenrich and O. Simons.Oxford: Oxford University Press, 457–470.

Anonymous. 1936a. "Eine peinliche Ehrenrettung." *Das Schwarze Korps*, December 3.

Anonymous. 1936b. "Es wird immer noch peinlicher." *Das Schwarze Korps*, December 10.

Anter, A. 1994. "Das Lachen Carl Schmitts: Philologisch-ästhetische Aspekte seiner Schriften." *Literaturmagazin* 33: 153–165.

Anter, A. 2004. *Die Macht der Ordnung: Aspekte einer Grundkategorie des Politischen.* Tübingen: Mohr.

Assheuer, T. 2012. "Zur besonderen Verfügung: Carl Schmitt." *Die Zeit*, September 24.

Balakrishnan, G. 2000. *The Enemy: An Intellectual Portrait of Carl Schmitt.* London: Verso.

Balke, F. 1996. *Der Staat nach seinem Ende: Die Versuchung Carl Schmitts.* Munich: Fink.

Barion, H., et al. eds. 1968. *Epirrhosis: Festgabe für Carl Schmitt.* Berlin: Duncker & Humblot.

Bates, D. 2005. "Crisis between the Wars: Derrida and the Origins of Undecidability." *Representations* 90: 1–27.

Bates, D. 2006. "Political Theology and the Nazi State: Carl Schmitt's Concept of the Institution." *Modern Intellectual History* 3: 415–442.

Bates, R. H. 1983. *Essays on the Political Economy of Africa.* Berkeley: University of California Press.

Bauman, Z. 1991. *Modernity and Ambivalence.* Cambridge: Polity.

Becker, H. 2003. *Die Parlamentarismuskritik bei Carl Schmitt und Jürgen Habermas*, 2nd ed. Berlin: Duncker & Humblot.

Ben-Shai, R. 2009. "Schmitt or Hamlet: The Unsovereign Event." *Telos* 147: 77–98.

Bendersky, J. W. 1983. *Carl Schmitt: Theorist for the Reich*. Princeton: Princeton University Press.

Bendersky, J. W. 2007. "Carl Schmitt's Path to Nuremberg: A Sixty-Year Reassessment." *Telos* 139: 6–34.

Benhabib, S. 2012. "Carl Schmitt's Critique of Kant: Sovereignty and International Law." *Political Theory* 40: 688–713.

Blasius, D. 2005. *Weimars Ende: Bürgerkrieg und Politik 1930–1933*. Göttingen: Vandenhoeck & Ruprecht.

Blei, F. 1995. *Das große Bestiarium der Literatur*, ed. R.-P. Baacke. Hamburg: Europäische Verlagsanstalt.

Böckenförde, E.-W. 1997. "Auf dem Weg zum Klassiker." *Die Zeit*, July 11.

Böckenförde, E.-W. 1998. "The Concept of the Political: A Key to Understanding Carl Schmitt's Constitutional Theory." In *Law as Politics: Carl Schmitt's Critique of Liberalism*, ed. D. Dyzenhaus. Durham: Duke University Press, 37–55.

Bolz, N. 1989. *Auszug aus der entzauberten Welt: Philosophischer Extremismus zwischen den Weltkriegen*. Munich: Fink.

Bracher, K. D. 1960. *Die Auflösung der Weimarer Republik: Eine Studie zum Problem des Machtverfalls in der Demokratie*. Villingen: Ring-Verlag.

Breuer, S. 1993. *Anatomie der Konservativen Revolution*. Darmstadt: Wissenschaftliche Buchgesellschaft.

Breuer, S. 2001. *Ordnungen der Ungleichheit: Die deutsche Rechte im Widerstreit ihrer Ideen 1871–1945*. Darmstadt: Wissenschaftliche Buchgesellschaft.

Carey, J. M., and M. S. Shugart. eds. 1998. *Executive Decree Authority*. Cambridge: Cambridge University Press.

Collins, S. L. 1989. *From Divine Cosmos to Sovereign State: An Intellectual History of Consciousness and the Idea of Order in Renaissance England*. Oxford: Oxford University Press.

Cristi, R. 1998. *Carl Schmitt and Authoritarian Liberalism: Strong State, Free Economy*. Cardiff: University of Wales Press.

Dahlheimer, M. 1998. *Carl Schmitt und der deutsche Katholizismus 1888–1936*. Paderborn: Schöningh.

Derrida, J. 1997. *The Politics of Friendship*, trans. G. Collins. London: Verso.

Dunsby, J. 2002. "Thematic and Motivic Analysis." In *The Cambridge History of Western Music Theory*, ed. T. Christensen. Cambridge: Cambridge University Press, 907–925.

Dupeux, L. 1994. "'Kulturpessimismus', Konservative Revolution und Modernität." In *Intellektuellendiskurse in der Weimarer Republik: Zur politischen Kultur einer Gemengelage*, ed. M. Gangl and G. Raulet. Frankfurt: Campus, 287–299.

Dyzenhaus, D. 1997a. *Legality and Legitimacy: Carl Schmitt, Hans Kelsen and Hermann Heller in Weimar*. Oxford: Oxford University Press.

Dyzenhaus, D. 1997b. "Legal Theory in the Collapse of Weimar: Contemporary Lessons?" *American Political Science Review* 91: 121–134.

Dyzenhaus, D. 1998. "Introduction: Carl Schmitt." In *Law as Politics: Carl Schmitt's Critique of Liberalism*, ed. D. Dyzenhaus. Durham: Duke University Press, 1–20.

Ellis, D. P. 1971. "The Hobbesian Problem of Order: A Critical Appraisal of the Normative Solution." *American Sociological Review* 36: 692–703.

Elster, J. 1989. *The Cement of Society: A Study of Social Order*. Cambridge: Cambridge University Press.

Felsch, P. 2015. *Der lange Sommer der Theorie: Geschichte einer Revolte 1960–1990*. Munich: Beck.

Foucault, M. 1990. *History of Sexuality*, vol. 1: *An Introduction*. New York: Vintage.

Freund, J. 1980. "Der Begriff der Ordnung." *Der Staat* 19: 325–339.

Frodeman, R. ed. 2010. *The Oxford Handbook of Interdisciplinarity*. Oxford: Oxford University Press.

Gadamer, H.-G. 2013. *Truth and Method*, trans. and rev. J. Weinsheimer and D. G. Marshall. London: Bloomsbury.

Galli, C. 1996. *Genealogia della politica: Carl Schmitt e la crisi del pensiero politico modern*. Bologna: Il Mulino.

Galli, C. 2010. "Carl Schmitt and the Global Age." *The New Centennial Review* 10: 1–25.

Galli, C. 2012. "*Hamlet*: Representation and the Concrete." In *Political Theology and Early Modernity*, ed. G. Hammill, J. R. Lupton, and E. Balibar. Chicago: University of Chicago Press, 60–83.

Galli, C. 2015. *Janus's Gaze: Essays on Carl Schmitt*, trans. A. Minervi and ed. with an introduction by A. Sitze. Durham: Duke University Press.

Gangl, M. ed. 2011. *Die Weimarer Staatsrechtsdebatte: Diskurs- und Rezeptionsstrategien*. Baden-Baden: Nomos.

Gehlen, A. 1986. *Anthropologische und sozial-psychologische Untersuchungen*. Reinbek: Rowohlt.

Giaccaria, P., and C. Minca. eds. 2016. *Hitler's Geographies: The Spatialities of the Third Reich*. Chicago: University of Chicago Press.

Gil, T. 1988. "Die gegenaufklärerische Grundperspektive der Rechts- und Staatsphilosophie C. Schmitts." *Archiv für Rechts- und Sozialphilosophie* 74: 521–530.

Gross, O., and F. N. Aolain. 2002. *Law in Times of Crisis: Emergency Powers in Theory and Practice*. Cambridge: Cambridge University Press.

Gross, R. 1993. "Carl Schmitts 'Nomos' und die 'Juden.'" *Merkur* 47: 410–420.

Gross, R. 2000. *Carl Schmitt and the Jews: The "Jewish Question," the Holocaust, and German Legal Theory*, trans. J. Golb. Madison: University of Wisconsin Press.

Grothe, E. 2005. *Zwischen Geschichte und Recht: Deutsche Verfassungsgeschichtsschreibung 1900–1970*. Munich: Oldenbourg.

Grund, H. 1976. *"Preußenschlag" und Staatsgerichtshof im Jahre 1932*. Baden-Baden: Nomos.

Günther, F. 2011. "Ordnen, gestalten, bewahren: Radikales Ordnungsdenken von deutschen Rechtsintellektuellen der Rechtswissenschaft 1920 bis 1960." *Vierteljahrshefte für Zeitgeschichte* 59: 353–384.

Habermas, J. 1989. "The Horrors of Autonomy: Carl Schmitt in English." In *The New Conservatism: Cultural Criticism and the Historians' Debate*, trans. and ed. S. Weber Nicholsen. Cambridge: MIT Press, 128–139.

Hechter, M., and V. Haufler. eds. 2003. *Theories of Social Order: A Reader*. Stanford: Stanford University Press.

Heil, S. 1996. *"Gefährliche Beziehungen": Walter Benjamin und Carl Schmitt*. Stuttgart: Metzler.

Hell, J. 2009. "Katechon: Carl Schmitt's Imperial Theology and the Ruins of the Future." *Germanic Review* 84: 283–326.

Heller, H. 1934. *Staatslehre*, ed. G. Niemeyer. Leiden: Sijthoff.

Heller, H. 1995. "Authoritarian Liberalism?" *European Law Journal* 21: 295–301.

Herf, J. 1984. *Reactionary Modernism: Technology, Culture and Politics in Weimar and the Third Reich*. Cambridge: Cambridge University Press.

Hiller, K. 1932. "Ewiger Friede in Gänsefüßchen." *Die Weltbühne*, September 27.

Hoelzl, M., and G. Ward. 2014. "Introduction." In Schmitt, *Dictatorship: From the Origins of the Modern Concept of Sovereignty to Proletarian Class Struggle*, trans. M. Hoelzl and G. Ward. Cambridge: Polity.

Hofmann, H. 2002. *Legitimität gegen Legalität: Der Weg der politischen Philosophie Carl Schmitts*. Berlin: Duncker & Humblot.

Hooker, W. 2009. *Carl Schmitt's International Thought: Order and Orientation*. Cambridge: Cambridge University Press.

Huber, E. R. 1980. "Verfassungswirklichkeit und Verfassungswert im Staatsdenken der Weimarer Zeit." In *Arbeiten zur Rechtsgeschichte: Festschrift für Gustav Klemens Schmelzeisen*, ed. H.-W. Thümmel. Stuttgart: Klett-Cotta, 126–141.

Jackson, R. H., and C. G. Rosberg. 1982. "Why Africa's Weak States Persist: The Empirical and the Juridical in Statehood." *World Politics* 35: 1–24.

Jacobson, A. J., and B. Schlink. eds. 2000. *Weimar: A Jurisprudence of Crisis*, trans. B. Cooper and P. C. Caldwell. Berkeley: University of California Press.

Jay, M. 2010. *The Virtues of Mendacity: On Lying in Politics*. Charlottesville: University of Virginia Press.

Jellinek, G. 1900. *Allgemeine Staatslehre*. Berlin: Häring.

Kelly, D. 2016. "Carl Schmitt's Political Theory of Dictatorship." In *The Oxford Handbook of Carl Schmitt*, ed. J. Meierhenrich and O. Simons. Oxford: Oxford University Press, 217–244.

Kelsen, H. 1925. *Allgemeine Staatslehre*. Berlin: Springer.

Kennedy, E. 1988a. "Carl Schmitt und Hugo Ball: Ein Beitrag zum Thema 'Politischer Expressionismus'." *Zeitschrift für Politik* 35: 143–162.

Kennedy, E. 1988b. "Politischer Expressionismus: Die kulturkritischen und metaphysischen Ursprünge des Begriffs des Politischen von Carl Schmitt." In *Complexio Oppositorum: Über Carl Schmitt*, ed. H. Quaritsch. Berlin: Duncker & Humblot, 233–251.

Kennedy, E. 2004. *Constitutional Failure: Carl Schmitt in Weimar*. Durham: Duke University Press.

Kirk, R. 1952. "Burke and the Principle of Order." *The Sewanee Review* 60: 187–201.

Klein, J. T. 2010. "A Taxonomy of Interdisciplinarity." In *The Oxford Handbook of Interdisciplinarity*, ed. R. Frodeman. Oxford: Oxford University Press, 15–30.

Kollmeier, K. 2007. *Ordnung und Ausgrenzung: Die Disziplinarpolitik der Hitler-Jugend*. Göttingen: Vandenhoeck & Ruprecht.

Koenen, A. 1995. *Der Fall Carl Schmitt: Sein Aufstieg zum "Kronjuristen des Dritten Reichs"*. Darmstadt: Wissenschaftliche Buchgesellschaft.

Korioth, S. 2000. "Introduction: The Shattering of Methods in Late Wilhelmine Germany." In *Weimar: A Jurisprudence of Crisis*, ed. A. J. Jacobson and B. Schlink. Berkeley: University of California Press, 41–50.

Koselleck, R. 1995. *Vergangene Zukunft: Zur Semantik geschichtlicher Zeiten*. Frankfurt: Suhrkamp.

Koskenniemi, M. 2016. "Carl Schmitt and International Law." In *The Oxford Handbook of Carl Schmitt*, ed. J. Meierhenrich and O. Simons. Oxford: Oxford University Press, 592–611.

Kröger, K. 1988. "Bemerkungen zu Carl Schmitts 'Römischer Katholizismus und politische Form'." In *Complexio Oppositorum: Über Carl Schmitt*, ed. H. Quaritsch. Berlin: Duncker & Humblot, 159–165.

Kuntz, P. G. ed. 1968. *The Concept of Order*. Seattle: University of Washington Press.

Kurz, A. 1992. *Demokratische Diktatur? Auslegung und Handhabung des Artikels 48 der Weimarer Verfassung 1919–1925*. Berlin: Duncker & Humblot.

Laak, D. v. 1995. "Eigentlich beliebig." *Die Zeit*, January 20.

Laak, D. v. 2002. *Gespräche in der Sicherheit des Schweigens: Carl Schmitt in der politischen Geschichte der frühen Bundesrepublik*, 2nd ed. Berlin: Akademie Verlag.

Lawler, E. J., et al. eds. 2015. *Order on the Edge of Chaos: Social Psychology and the Problem of Social Order*. Cambridge: Cambridge University Press.

Lepsius, O. 1994. *Die gegensatzaufhebende Begriffsbildung: Methodenentwicklungen in der Weimarer Republik und ihr Verhältnis zur Ideologisierung der Rechtswissenschaft im Nationalsozialismus*. Munich: Beck.

Lethen, H. 2002. *Cool Conduct: The Culture of Distance in Weimar Germany*. Berkeley: University of California Press.

Linder, C. 2008. *Der Bahnhof von Finnentrup: Eine Reise ins Carl Schmitt Land*. Berlin: Matthes & Seitz.

Linder, C. 2016. "Carl Schmitt in Plettenberg." In *The Oxford Handbook of Carl Schmitt*, ed. J. Meierhenrich and O. Simons. Oxford: Oxford University Press, 147–170.

Loughlin, M. 2010. *Foundations of Public Law*. Oxford: Oxford University Press.

Loughlin, M. 2016. "Politonomy." In *The Oxford Handbook of Carl Schmitt*, ed. J. Meierhenrich and O. Simons. Oxford: Oxford University Press, 570–591.

Lukács, G. 1994. *Die Theorie des Romans: Ein geschichtsphilosophischer Versuch über die Formen der großen Epik*. Munich: Deutscher Taschenbuch Verlag.

Mann, M. 1984. "The Autonomous Power of the State: Its Origins, Mechanisms and Results." *European Journal of Sociology* 25: 185–213.

Maus, I. 1998. "The 1933 'Break' in Carl Schmitt's Theory." In *Law as Politics: Carl Schmitt's Critique of Liberalism*, ed. D. Dyzenhaus. Durham: Duke University Press, 196–216.

McCormick, J. P. 2016. "Teaching in Vain: Thomas Hobbes, Carl Schmitt, and the Theory of the Sovereign State." In *The Oxford Handbook of Carl Schmitt*, ed. J. Meierhenrich and O. Simons. Oxford: Oxford University Press, 269–290.

Mehring, R. 2003. "Vorbemerkung." In *Carl Schmitt, Der Begriff des Politischen: Ein kooperativer Kommentar*, ed. R. Mehring. Berlin: Akademie Verlag, 7–8.

Mehring, R. 2009. *Carl Schmitt: Aufstieg und Fall*. Munich: Beck.

Meier, C. 1988. "Zu Carl Schmitts Begriffsbildung—Das Politische und der Nomos." In *Complexio Oppositorum: Über Carl Schmitt*, ed. H. Quaritsch. Berlin: Duncker & Humblot, 537–556.

Meier, H. 2011. *The Lesson of Carl Schmitt: Four Chapters on the Distinction between Political Theology and Political Philosophy*, expanded ed., trans. M. Brainard. Chicago: University of Chicago Press.

Meierhenrich, J. 2008. *The Legacies of Law: Long-Run Consequences of Legal Development in South Africa, 1652–2000*. Cambridge: Cambridge University Press.

Meierhenrich, J. 2016. "Fearing the Disorder of Things: The Development of Carl Schmitt's Institutional Theory, 1919–1942." In *The Oxford Handbook of Carl Schmitt*, ed. J. Meierhenrich and O. Simons. Oxford: Oxford University Press, 171–216.

Meierhenrich, J. 2017. *Lawfare: A Genealogy*. Cambridge: Cambridge University Press.

Meierhenrich, J. n.d. *In the Belly of the Fish: Carl Schmitt in Nazi Germany, 1933–1945*. Unpublished book manuscript.

Meuter, G. 1994. *Der Katechon: Zu Carl Schmitts fundamentalistischer Kritik der Zeit*. Berlin: Duncker & Humblot.

Minca, C., and R. Rowan. 2016. *On Schmitt and Space*. London: Routledge.

Mohler, A. 1950. *Die Konservative Revolution in Deutschland 1918-1932: Grundlinien ihrer Weltanschauung*. Stuttgart: Vorwerk.

Mouffe, C. 2005. *On the Political*. London: Verso.

Motschenbacher, A. 2000. *Katechon oder Großinquisitor? Eine Studie zu Inhalt und Struktur der politischen Theologie Carl Schmitts*. Marburg: Tectum.

Motschenbacher, A. 2005. *On the Political*. London: Verso.

Müller, J. 1999. "Carl Schmitt's Method: Between Ideology, Demonology and Myth." *Journal of Political Ideologies* 4: 61–85.

Müller, J.-W. 2003. *A Dangerous Mind: Carl Schmitt in Post-War European Thought*. New Haven: Yale University Press.

Müller-Dohm, S. 2014. *Jürgen Habermas: Eine Biographie*. Berlin: Suhrkamp.

Murkens, J. E. K. 2013. *From Empire to Union: Conceptions of German Constitutional Law since 1871*. Oxford: Oxford University Press.

Neumann, V. 1988. "Die Wirklichkeit im Lichte der Idee." In *Complexio Oppositorum: Über Carl Schmitt*, ed. Helmut Quaritsch. Berlin: Duncker & Humblot, 557–575.

Neumann, V. 2015. *Carl Schmitt als Jurist*. Tübingen: Mohr.

Noack, P. 1993. *Carl Schmitt: Eine Biographie*. Berlin: Propyläen.

Oakes, G. 1986. "Translator's Introduction." In Schmitt 1986, ix–xxxv.

Pan, D. 2009. *Carl Schmitt's Hamlet or Hecuba: The Intrusion of the Time into the Play*, trans. D. Pan and J. R. Rust. New York: Telos Press.

Pan, D., and R. Berman. 2008. "Culture and Politics in Carl Schmitt: Introduction." *Telos* 142: 3–6.

Pankakoski, T. 2010. "Conflict, Context, Concreteness: Koselleck and Schmitt on Concepts." *Political Theory* 38: 749–779.

Pasquino, P. 1986. "Bemerkungen zum 'Kriterium des Politischen' bei Carl Schmitt." *Der Staat* 25: 385–398.

Paulson, S. 2016. "Hans Kelsen and Carl Schmitt: Growing Discord, Culminating in the 'Guardian' Controversy of 1932." In *The Oxford Handbook of Carl Schmitt*, ed. J. Meierhenrich and O. Simons. Oxford: Oxford University Press, 510–546.

Polanyi, K. 1957. *The Great Transformation: The Political and Economic Origins of Our Time*. Boston: Beacon Press.

Preuß, U. K. 1987. "The Critique of German Liberalism: A Reply to Ellen Kennedy." *Telos* 71: 97–109.

Preuß, U. K. 2016. "Carl Schmitt and the Weimar Constitution." In *The Oxford Handbook of Carl Schmitt*, ed. J. Meierhenrich and O. Simons. Oxford: Oxford University Press, 471–489.

Quaritsch, H. ed. 2000. *Carl Schmitt: Antworten in Nürnberg*. Berlin: Duncker & Humblot.

Raphael, L. 2001. "Radikales Ordnungsdenken und die Organisation totalitärer Herrschaft: Weltanschauungseliten und Humanwissenschaftler im NS-Regime." *Geschichte und Gesellschaft* 27: 5–40.

Raphael, L. 2004. " 'Ordnung' zwischen Geist und Wahn: Kulturwissenschaftliche Ordnungssemantik im Nationalsozialismus." In *Nationalsozialismus in den Kulturwissenschaften*, vol. 2: *Leitbegriffe—Deutungsmuster—Paradigmenkämpfe*, ed. H. Lehmann and O. G. Oexle. Göttingen: Vandenhoeck & Ruprecht, 119–120.

Rasch, W. 2000. "Conflict as a Vocation: Carl Schmitt and the Possibility of Politics." *Theory, Culture, and Society* 17: 1–32.

Rasch, W. 2004. *Sovereignty and Its Discontents: On the Primacy of Conflict and the Structure of the Political*. London: Birkbeck Law Press.

Ritter, J., and K. Gründer. eds. 1984. *Historisches Wörterbuch der Philosophie*, vol. 6. Basel: Schwabe.

Roberts, A. B. 2015. "Carl Schmitt—Political Theologian?" *Review of Politics* 77: 449–474.

Rossiter, C. 1963. *Constitutional Dictatorship: Crisis Government in the Modern Democracies*. New York: Harcourt.

Rust, J. R., and J. R. Lupton. 2009. "Introduction: Schmitt and Shakespeare." In Schmitt 2009b, xv–li.

Rüthers, B. 1994. "Wer war Carl Schmitt? Bausteine zu einer Biographie." *Neue Juristische Wochenschrift* 47: 1681–1687.

Scheuerman, W. E. 2016. "States of Emergency." In *The Oxford Handbook of Carl Schmitt*, ed. J. Meierhenrich and O. Simons. Oxford: Oxford University Press, 547–569.

Schickel, J. ed. 1970. *Guerilleros, Partisanen: Theorie und Praxis*. Munich: Hanser.

Schickel, J. ed. 2008. *Gespräche mit Carl Schmitt*. Berlin: Merve.

Schmitt, C. 1910. *Über Schuld und Schuldarten: Eine terminologische Untersuchung*. Breslau: Schletter.

Schmitt, C. 1912. *Gesetz und Urteil: Eine Untersuchung zum Problem der Rechtspraxis*. Berlin: Liebmann.

Schmitt, C. 1914. *Der Wert des Staates und die Bedeutung des Einzelnen*. Tübingen: Mohr.

Schmitt, C. 1916a. "Das Gesetz über den Belagerungszustand in der Rechtsprechung." *Preußisches Verwaltungs-Blatt* 37: 263, 310–312.

Schmitt, C. 1916b. *Theodor Däublers "Nordlicht": Drei Studien über die Elemente, den Geist und die Aktualität des Werkes*. Munich: Müller.

Schmitt, C. 1916c. "Diktatur und Belagerungszustand: Eine staatsrechtliche Studie." In Schmitt 1995, 138–162.

Schmitt, C. 1916d. "Die Einwirkungen des Kriegszustandes auf das ordentliche strafprozessuale Verfahren." In Schmitt 2005a, 418–429.

Schmitt, C. 1921. *Die Diktatur: Von den Anfängen des modernen Souveränitätsgedankens bis zum proletarischen Klassenkampf*. Munich: Duncker & Humblot.

Schmitt, C. 1923. "Soziologie des Souveränitätsbegriffes und politische Theologie." In *Hauptprobleme der Soziologie: Erinnerungsgabe für Max Weber*, vol. 2, ed. M. Palyi. Munich: Duncker & Humblot, 3–35.

Schmitt, C. 1924. "Die Diktatur des Reichspräsidenten nach Art. 48 der Reichsverfassung." In *Verhandlungen der Tagung der Deutschen Staatsrechtslehrer zu Jena am 14. und 15. April 1924*, ed. Vereinigung der Deutschen Staatsrechtslehrer. Berlin: De Gruyter.

Schmitt, C. 1930. *Hugo Preuss: Sein Staatsbegriff und seine Stellung in der deutschen Staatslehre*. Tübingen: Mohr.

Schmitt, C. 1931. "Die staatsrechtliche Bedeutung der Notverordnung, insbesondere ihre Rechtsgültigkeit." In Schmitt 1958, 233–262.

Schmitt, C. 1932a. *Konstruktive Verfassungsprobleme: Rede des Professors Dr. Carl Schmitt gehalten auf der Hauptversammlung des Vereins zur Wahrung der Interessen der chemischen Industrie Deutschlands e. V. am 4. November 1932*. Berlin: Maurer & Dimmick.

Schmitt, C. 1932b. "Völkerrechtliche Formen des modernen Imperialismus." In Schmitt 1940, 162–180.

Schmitt, C. 1933a. "Der Staat des 20. Jahrhunderts." *Westdeutscher Beobachter*, June 28.

Schmitt, C. 1933b. "Das gute Recht der deutschen Revolution." *Westdeutscher Beobachter*, May 12.

Schmitt, C. 1933c. "1 Jahr deutsche Politik: Rückblick vom 20. Juli 1932—Von Papen über Schleicher zum ersten deutschen Volkskanzler Adolf Hitler." *Westdeutscher Beobachter*, July 23.

Schmitt, C. 1933d. "Die deutschen Intellektuellen." *Westdeutscher Beobachter*, May 31.

Schmitt, C. 1933e. *Staat, Bewegung, Volk: Die Dreigliederung der politischen Einheit.* Hamburg: Hanseatische Verlagsanstalt.

Schmitt, C. 1934a. "Nationalsozialistisches Rechtsdenken." *Deutsches Recht* 4: 226–229.

Schmitt, C. 1934b. *Staatsgefüge und Zusammenbruch des zweiten Reiches: Der Sieg des Bürgers über den Soldaten.* Hamburg: Hanseatische Verlagsanstalt.

Schmitt, C. 1934c. *Über die drei Arten des rechtswissenschaftlichen Denkens.* Hamburg: Hanseatische Verlagsanstalt.

Schmitt, C. 1936/1937. "Der Staat als Mechanismus bei Hobbes und Descartes." *Archiv für Rechts- und Sozialphilosophie* 30: 622–632.

Schmitt, C. 1940. *Positionen und Begriffe im Kampf mit Weimar—Genf—Versailles, 1923–1939.* Hamburg: Hanseatische Verlagsanstalt.

Schmitt, C. 1942. "Beschleuniger wider Willen oder: Problematik der westlichen Hemisphäre." In Schmitt 1995, 431–440.

Schmitt, C. 1955. "Der neue Nomos der Erde." In Schmitt 1995, 518–522.

Schmitt, C. 1958. *Verfassungsrechtliche Aufsätze aus den Jahren 1924–1954: Materialien zu einer Verfassungslehre.* Berlin: Duncker & Humblot.

Schmitt, C. 1960. *Die Tyrannei der Werte: Überlegungen eines Juristen zur Wert-Philosophie.* Stuttgart: Kohlhammer.

Schmitt, C. 1962. "Die Ordnung der Welt nach dem Zweiten Weltkrieg." In Schmitt 1995, 592–618.

Schmitt, C. 1971. "Der Begriff des Politischen: Vorwort von 1917 zur italienischen Ausgabe." In *Complexio Oppositorum: Über Carl Schmitt*, ed. H. Quaritsch. Berlin: Duncker & Humblot, 269–273.

Schmitt, C. 1978. "Die legale Weltrevolution: Politischer Mehrwert als Prämie auf juristische Legalität und Superlegalität." *Der Staat* 17: 321–339.

Schmitt, C. 1986. *Political Romanticism*, trans. G. Oakes. Cambridge: MIT Press.

Schmitt, C. 1991. *Glossarium: Aufzeichnungen der Jahre 1947–1951*, ed. E. Freiherr von Medem. Berlin: Duncker & Humblot.

Schmitt, C. 1994. *Die Diktatur*, 6th ed. Berlin: Duncker & Humblot.

Schmitt, C. 1995. *Staat, Großraum, Nomos: Arbeiten aus den Jahren 1916–1969*, ed. G. Maschke. Berlin: Duncker & Humblot.

Schmitt, C. 1996a. *Der Hüter der Verfassung*, 4th ed. Berlin: Duncker & Humblot.

Schmitt, C. 1996b. *Roman Catholicism and Political Form.* Westport: Greenwood.

Schmitt, C. 1997. *Der Nomos der Erde im Völkerrecht des Jus Publicum Europaeum*, 4th ed. Berlin: Duncker & Humblot.

Schmitt, C. 1998. *Politische Romantik*, 6th ed. Berlin: Duncker & Humblot.

Schmitt, C. 2003a. "Rundfunkvortrag Deutsche Welle, 24. February 1932 (Fragment)." In *Schmittiana: Beiträge zu Leben und Werk Carl Schmitts*, vol. 8, ed. P. Tommissen. Berlin: Duncker & Humblot.

Schmitt, C. 2003b. *The "Nomos" of the Earth in the International Law of the "Jus Publicum Europaeum,"* trans. G. L. Ulmen. New York: Telos Press.

Schmitt, C. 2004a. *Der Wert des Staates und die Bedeutung des Einzelnen*, 2nd ed. Berlin: Duncker & Humblot.

Schmitt, C. 2004b. *On the Three Types of Juristic Thought*, trans. J. W. Bendersky. Westport: Praeger.

Schmitt, C. 2004c. *Legality and Legitimacy*, trans. and ed. J. Seitzer. Durham: Duke University Press.

Schmitt, C. 2005a. *Die Militärzeit 1915 bis 1919: Tagebuch Februar bis Dezember 1915, Aufsätze und Materialien*, ed. E. Hüsmert and G. Giesler. Berlin: Akademie Verlag.

Schmitt, C. 2005b. *Political Theology: Four Chapters on the Concept of Sovereignty*, trans. with an introduction by G. Schwab. Chicago: University of Chicago Press.

Schmitt, C. 2007a. *The Concept of the Political*, expanded ed., trans. with an introduction and notes by G. Schwab. Chicago: University of Chicago Press.

Schmitt, C. 2007b. "The Age of Neutralizations and Depoliticizations." In Schmitt 2007a trans. M. Konzen and J. P. McCormick, 81–98.

Schmitt, C. 2008a. *Römischer Katholizismus und politische Form*, 5th ed. Stuttgart: Klett-Cotta.

Schmitt, C. 2008b. *The Leviathan in the State Theory of Thomas Hobbes: Meaning and Failure of a Political Symbol*, trans. G. Schwab and E. Hilfstein, with an introduction by G. Schwab. Chicago: University of Chicago Press.

Schmitt, C. 2008c. *Constitutional Theory*, trans. and ed. J. Seitzer. Durham: Duke University Press.

Schmitt, C. 2009a. *Völkerrechtliche Großraumordnung mit Interventionsverbot für raumfremde Mächte: Ein Beitrag zum Reichsbegriff im Völkerrecht*, 3rd ed. Berlin: Duncker & Humblot.

Schmitt, C. 2009b. *Hamlet or Hecuba: The Intrusion of the Time into the Play*, trans. D. Pan and J. R. Rust. New York: Telos Press.

Schmitt, C. 2009c. *Der Begriff des Politischen: Text von 1932 mit einem Vorwort und drei Corollarien*, 8th ed. Berlin: Duncker & Humblot.

Schmitt, C. 2011. "The *Großraum* Order of International Law with a Ban on Intervention for Spatially Foreign Powers: A Contribution to the Concept of Reich in International Law." In Schmitt, *Writings on War*, trans. and ed. T. Nunan. Cambridge: Polity, 75–123.

Schmitt, C. 2014. "Appendix: The Dictatorship of the President of the Reich According to Article 48 of the Weimar Constitution." In Schmitt, *Dictatorship: From the Origin of the Modern Concept of Sovereignty to Proletarian Class Struggle*, trans. M. Hoelzl and G. Ward. Cambridge: Polity, 180–226.

Schmitt, C. 2015. "Dialogue on Power and Access to the Holder of Power." In *Dialogues on Power and Space*, ed. A. Kalyvas and F. Finchelstein. Cambridge: Polity, 23–50.

Schmitz, W. 1994. "Zur Geschichte der Academia Moralis." In *Schmittiana: Beiträge zu Leben und Werk Carl Schmitts*, vol. 4, ed. P. Tommissen. Berlin: Duncker & Humblot, 119–156.

Schneider, P. 1957. *Ausnahmezustand und Norm: Eine Studie zur Rechtslehre von Carl Schmitt*. Stuttgart: Deutsche Verlags-Anstalt.

Schönberger, C. 2003. "'Staatlich und Politisch': Der Begriff des Staates in *Carl Schmitts Begriff des Politischen*." In *Carl Schmitt: Der Begriff des Politischen*, ed. R. Mehring. Berlin: Akademie Verlag, 21–44.

Seiberth, G. 2001. *Anwalt des Reiches: Carl Schmitt und der Prozess "Preußen contra Reich" vor dem Staatsgerichtshof*. Berlin: Duncker & Humblot.

Shapiro, I., and R. Hardin. eds. 1993. *Political Order: NOMOS XXXVIII*. New York: New York University Press.

Sherratt, Y. 2013. *Hitler's Philosophers*. New Haven: Yale University Press.

Sil, R., and P. J. Katzenstein. 2010. "Analytic Eclecticism in the Study of World Politics: Reconfiguring Problems and Mechanisms across Research Traditions." *Perspectives on Politics* 8: 411–431.

Simons, O. 2016. "Carl Schmitt's Spatial Rhetoric." In *The Oxford Handbook of Carl Schmitt*, ed. J. Meierhenrich and O. Simons. Oxford: Oxford University Press, 776–802.

Sitze, A. 2010. "A Farewell to Schmitt: Notes on the Work of Carlo Galli." *New Centennial Review* 10: 27–72.

Snyder, T. 2014. "Fascism, Russia, and Ukraine." *New York Review of Books*, March 20.

Soltan, K., et al. eds. 1998. *Institutions and Social Order*. Ann Arbor: University of Michigan Press.

Specter, M. G. 2016. "What's 'Left' in Schmitt? From Aversion to Appropriation in Contemporary Political Theory." In *The Oxford Handbook of Carl Schmitt*, ed. J. Meierhenrich and O. Simons. Oxford: Oxford University Press, 426–454.

Spruyt, H. 1994. *The Sovereign State and Its Competitors: An Analysis of Systems Change*. Princeton: Princeton University Press.

Steber, M., and B. Gotto. eds. 2014. *Visions of Community in Nazi Germany: Social Engineering and Private Lives*. Oxford: Oxford University Press.

Stolleis, M. 2004. *A History of Public Law in Germany 1914–1945*, trans. T. Dunlap. Oxford: Oxford University Press.

Strathausen, C. 2010. "Myth or Knowledge? Reading Carl Schmitt's Hamlet or Hecuba." *Telos* 153: 7–29.

Strong, T. B. 2007. "Foreword: Dimensions of the New Debate around Carl Schmitt." In Schmitt 2007a, ix–xxxi.

Sunstein, C. R. 2003. "Beyond the Precautionary Principle." *University of Pennsylvania Law Review* 151: 1003–1058.

Sunstein, C. R. 2005. *Laws of Fear: Beyond the Precautionary Principle*. Cambridge: Cambridge University Press.

Sur, S. ed. 2014. *Carl Schmitt: Concepts et usages*. Paris: CNRS.

Taubes, J. 1987. *Ad Carl Schmitt: Gegenstrebige Fügung*. Berlin: Merve.

Teschke, B. 2011. "Decisions and Indecisions: Political and Intellectual Receptions of Carl Schmitt." *New Left Review* 67: 61–95.

Teschke, B. 2016. "Carl Schmitt's Concepts of War: A Categorical Failure." In *The Oxford Handbook of Carl Schmitt*, ed. J. Meierhenrich and O. Simons. Oxford: Oxford University Press, 367–400.

Tommissen, P. ed. 1975. *Over en in zake Carl Schmitt*. Brussels: Economische Hogeschool Sint-Aloysisus.

Tommissen, P. ed. 1996. *Schmittiana: Beiträge zu Leben und Werk Carl Schmitts*, vol. 5. Berlin: Duncker & Humblot.

Türk, J. 2008. "The Intrusion: Carl Schmitt's Non-Mimetic Logic of Art." *Telos* 142: 73–89.

Türk, J. 2016. "At the Limits of Rhetoric: Authority, Commonplace, and the Role of Literature in Carl Schmitt." In *The Oxford Handbook of Carl Schmitt*, ed. J. Meierhenrich and O. Simons. Oxford: Oxford University Press, 751–775.

Twellmann, M. 2004. *Das Drama der Souveränität: Hugo von Hofmannsthal und Carl Schmitt*. Munich: Fink.

Ulbricht, J. H. 1998. "Transzendentale Obdachlosigkeit." In *Ästhetische und religiöse Erfahrungen der Jahrhundertwenden*, vol. 2: Um 1900, ed. W. Braungart, G. Fuchs, and M. Koch. Paderborn: Schöningh, 47–68.

Vatter, M. 2016. "The Political Theology of Carl Schmitt." In *The Oxford Handbook of Carl Schmitt*, ed. J. Meierhenrich and O. Simons. Oxford: Oxford University Press, 245–268.

Vinx, L. 2015. "Prussia contra Reich: Schmitt's Closing Statement in Leipzig." In *The Guardian of the Constitution: Hans Kelsen and Carl Schmitt on the Limits of Constitutional Law*, trans. and ed. L. Vinx. Cambridge: Cambridge University Press, 222–227.

Wacker, B. ed. 1994. *Die eigentlich katholische Verschärfung: Konfession, Theologie und Politik im Werk Carl Schmitts*. Munich: Fink.

Weber, M. 1921. "Politics as a Vocation." In *From Max Weber: Essays in Sociology*, trans., ed., with an introduction by H. H. Gerth and C. Wright Mills. New York: Oxford University Press, 77–128.

Weber, M. 1922. "Science as a Vocation." In *From Max Weber: Essays in Sociology*, trans., ed., with an introduction by H. H. Gerth and C. Wright Mills. New York: Oxford University Press, 129–156.

Weber, M. 1972. *Wirtschaft und Gesellschaft: Grundriß der verstehenden Soziologie*, 5th rev. ed., ed. J. Winckelmann. Tübingen: Mohr.

Weber, M. 1985. "Die 'Objektivität' sozialwissenschaftlicher und sozialpolitischer Erkenntnis." In Weber, *Gesammelte Aufsätze zur Wissenschaftslehre*, ed. J. Winckelmann. Tübingen: Mohr, 146–214.

Wehler, H.-U. 2003. *Deutsche Gesellschaftsgeschichte*, vol. 4: *Vom Beginn des Ersten Weltkrieges bis zur Gründung der beiden deutschen Staaten 1914-1949*. Munich: Beck.

Weimayr, M. 1999. "Carl Schmitt—Sprache der Krise/Krise der Sprache." In *Gegen den Ausnahmezustand: Zur Kritik an Carl Schmitt*, ed. W. Pircher. Vienna: Springer, 53–84.

Weiss, P. 1968. "Some Paradoxes Relating to Order." In ,Kuntz, 16–18.

White, J. D. 1976. *The Analysis of Music*. New York: Prentice-Hall.

Wrong, D. H. 1994. *The Problem of Order: What Unites and Divides Society*. New York: Free Press.

Ziegler, H. O. 1932. *Autoritärer oder totaler Staat?* Tübingen: Mohr.

PART II

THE LIVES OF CARL SCHMITT

CHAPTER 2

A "CATHOLIC LAYMAN OF GERMAN NATIONALITY AND CITIZENSHIP"?

Carl Schmitt and the Religiosity of Life

REINHARD MEHRING

INTRODUCTION

THIS CHAPTER provides a biographical perspective on the multiple meanings of religion, both personal and professional, in Carl Schmitt's long life (cf. Mehring 2009; 2012; 2013a). Schmitt was not a supporter of a "pure" theory of law. He systematically emphasized the metajuridical influence of the contents and forms of legal thought. He likewise did not practice law from an external observer's perspective, but from the internal perspective of a participant in the system and game of justice. He programmatically called his position "political theology."

Occasionally he also called himself a "theologian of jurisprudence" (Schmitt 1991, 23). The dogmatic content of his "theology," however, is highly controversial. Moreover, it is not easy to thoroughly separate "dogmatics" from religious practice and confession. One can see it as a doubly reflexive relationship: a basal religious practice leads to subjective religious confessions, which professional administrators of religion reflect and regulate in complex dogmatics. Belief and denomination are often two very different things, while at the same time, religious convictions reflect religious influences and practices. In a religious biography, the collective religious practice is most often found at the beginnings of religious identity. People grow into confessional practices and influences before they are able to confront them independently and individually. It is therefore hardly possible to draw strict divisions among religious practices, confessions, and dogmatic statements. For this reason, Schmitt regarded religious converts, who had switched from one practice to another dogma, with suspicion and skepticism. It is no easy task to cast off religious socialization and enter into another confession, to convert, for example, from Catholicism or Judaism to Protestantism. As a result, Schmitt always regarded himself as Catholic in terms of his background, even in his later rejections of and distance from the religion. The consistency, scope, and meaning of his "Catholicism" were nevertheless controversial, even among his contemporaries.

This chapter problematizes Schmitt's "Catholicism." It situates the question in Schmitt scholarship, sketches out the complex overall religious situation and the religious mélange in Germany post-1789 and post-Kant, describes Schmitt's tense confessional biography and his distance from the deployment of Catholicism in the interwar period, analyzes his programmatic and systematic self-reflexive statements on his "political theology," and ultimately proposes an alternative "religious" interpretation of his eccentric "life in a state of exception." I differentiate religio-philosophically between a life that is "Catholically" founded and one that is "religiously" experienced and interpreted and regard Schmitt as a religious person who withdrew secularly and heretically from the dogmatically deployed, church-organized majority Catholicism.

It is well-known that Schmitt repeatedly referred to himself as a Catholic. Yet he tended to employ a touch of irony when making this assertion. In his journal of ideas, the *Glossarium*, which Schmitt began in late summer 1947, soon after his return from investigative custody in Nuremberg, and in which he reflected intensively on the "state of intellectual history" after 1945, he called himself a "Catholic layman of German nationality and citizenship" (1991, 283). Each word of this statement calls for a sociologically "concrete" explanation. The emphasis on "German" origins and the differentiation between nationality (*Volksangehörigkeit*) and citizenship (*Staatsangehörigkeit*) is of no small importance. But the true significance here resides in the word "layman." With his self-depiction as a member of the laity, Schmitt alluded to his precarious relationship with the Catholic Church, but at the same time used a formulation particularly in line with his own theological claim. Again and again he referred to himself, often retrospectively, as a "political theologian." Schmitt scholarship has meticulously gathered his various self-descriptions and examined them repeatedly. "Political theology" is a global topic of research. But not every theologian has to be a devout Christian. Following the historical biblical criticism of the nineteenth century, a confession-neutral, non-Christian theology and study of religion is possible (Overbeck 1903). Religions can also be described objectively as social practices.

Even if Schmitt thus somehow voiced "theological" claims, we nevertheless cannot read this simply as a Catholic credo. Even Hugo Ball (1924) did not do so. As Manfred Dahlheimer (1998) in particular has shown, Schmitt was hardly considered a Catholic jurist prior to 1933. During his time in Berlin he received an increased readership as a jurist and political author. After 1945 the controversy regarding his National Socialism had to be dealt with. Hasso Hofmann's (1964) influential portrayal was a problem-based history in legal philosophy. Only more recently has scholarship made the cross-check against the confessional content of *Legality and Legitimacy* (see Meier 1994; 1998; Mehring 1989). Is an alternative "humanistic" reconstruction possible? Was the focal point of the work, following Schmitt's self-depiction, perhaps in *Political Theology*?

Was Schmitt maybe even a devout Catholic? Numerous studies have investigated these questions.[1] In so doing, they have not always kept in mind the diversity of possible perspectives: Should one reconstruct religiosity, confession, metaphysics, theology, and practice? Should these be reconstructed for particular texts and time periods? Should one advocate for a strong unity and consistency or differentiate between stages of development, for instance between a Catholic and a National Socialist phase? Should one limit oneself to published texts? What about correspondence? Should one go through the archives? Or consider biographical elements? Need one take into consideration the context of contemporary discussions and the general relationship of the Catholic Church toward National Socialism? The research dynamic since Schmitt's death in 1985 has been enormously vibrant. Many questions have been put forth and resolved. Many strong claims have also been discounted in the process by newer publications and archival work. Today, a "Catholic" interpretation is risky, to say the least. And if it were to imply a church-oriented perspective and acknowledgment of papal primacy, it would simply be wrong. Let us examine these questions biographically (cf. Mehring 2009; 2010a).

German Idealism

Around 1800 the German Idealists were already overcome by the feeling that "God is dead." Hegel's answer to this sentiment was the "speculative Good Friday" (Hegel 1970a, 432; cf. Mehring 2003) of his philosophy. He hoped to rescue "God" from the Protestant theologians for his own philosophy. In the epoch of restoration after 1815, a confessional reorganization did occur. The churches reacted to the separation of church and state with an increased demarcation and mobilization of their sphere. The ultramontane movement deployed itself against modernity, and German Romanticism migrated to "Rome." However, Christian idealism was supplanted paradigmatically around 1848 by "material" and "biological" ideologies. Cultural pessimism and sociobiology pushed forward, saturating and ultimately drowning the old dogmatic theology and the remnants of Christian cohesion. The foundation of the German Reich in 1871 put the Catholics further on the defensive against the Protestant-Prussian power elite and majority culture. Polemical clusters developed around the dogma of papal infallibility, ultramontanism, and culture-struggle (*Kulturkampf*) Catholicism. Within the *Kulturkampf*, Catholicism certainly asserted itself as a developed worldview, social practice, and worldly sphere. Yet on the whole, the Wilhelmine system around 1900 was not a "Christian state." The ecumenical formula itself is neutralizing. Religiosity, according to a prevalent diagnosis, was in the midst of an upheaval (Nipperdey 1988). Alongside the transformed Christian and Jewish spheres arose a "vagrant" religiosity, in which Christian content survived, but in a secularized form at best. At this time the arts took over ideological functions of religious community development. In response to Wagner's *Parsifal*, Nietzsche declared, "Is this still German?/ Consider! Stay! You are perplexed?/ That which you hear is Rome—*Rome's faith without the text*" (Nietzsche 1982, 673). The old Christianity barely continued to fascinate intellectuals. Instead, there arose a new *Weltfrömmigkeit*, or worldly piety (Eduard Spranger), and a life-reforming search for the "new man" (Küenzlen 1997).

Time after time, Schmitt discerningly and eccentrically emphasized the stages of the "intellectual-historical" development and condition of Germany post-1789 and post-Kant. A pivotal point for his historical conception was the *Vormärz* and the failure of the bourgeois revolution of 1848. The first synopsis of his overall view appears in his 1929 speech "The Age of Neutralizations and Depoliticizations," in which he sketches out a sequence of failed attempts at neutralization and depoliticization: "from the theological to the metaphysical and moral, to the economical" (Schmitt 1963, 88), and refers to "intellectual neutrality" and the "immanence of technology." Later Schmitt would speak again and again of a position "between theology and technology." He illustrates his view in a shockingly radical way in many entries in his *Glossarium*, repeatedly expressing the hope that the products of the "decomposition" of German Idealism—here Schmitt means above all the antithetical constellations and political ideologies of the *Vormärz*—will unleash new "the urgic powers" (1991, 83). "Truly, this philosophy's products of decomposition will be stronger than all of the restorations of the old churches. They will unleash theurgic powers before which our miserable victors and keepers of the law [*Rechtbehaltern*] will shudder" (83). "The line from 1848 to 1948 is the development and intensification of nothingness and nihilism" (203). In many of his notes, Schmitt writes Hitler into his view of the products of decomposition. In doing so, he formulates a peculiar "ruse of reason": the "intellectual-historical key concept of the ingenious enforcer" (151). Schmitt proceeds from a paradoxical dialectic of education and lack thereof, and of civilization and barbarism, insofar as an "educated" people or a civilized society chose Hitler of all people as its "*Führer.*" In this vein, he notes on May 17, 1948:

> The idea takes possession of an individual and thus always appears as a foreign guest. The foreign guest was Adolf. He was strange to the point of caricature. Foreign precisely because of the aseptically empty purity of his ideas of leaders, charisma, genius, and race. He was a presuppositionless enforcer. The masses of the educated were uneducated. They had not yet experienced the crisis of 1848. Bruno Bauer and Max Stirner were considered comical louts. Adolf, however, who was intellectually weaker than Max, was considered by the educated, such as [Johannes] Popitz, to be a genius. And this is how he made his appearance. Existentialism is the appropriate word, that is, it is the death knell for this genialism of the German eighteenth and nineteenth centuries (151).

These kinds of notations demand a thorough and critical commentary. Schmitt's intellectual-historical view of the "decomposition" and paradoxical "enforcement" of German Idealism could be reconstructed in detail, and the result would be an extremely strange book called "From Hegel to Hitler."

German New Humanism would likewise be cast in a harsh light. Schmitt's initial formulation of the idea of a "foreign guest" is a quotation from Goethe. In his *Maxims* and Reflections, Goethe wrote, "every idea appears as a foreign guest, and as it begins to be realized, it can hardly be distinguished from imagination and fantasy" (1909, 177). The same applies to Schmitt's fantastic depictions of Germany's intellectual-historical catastrophe. Most important here is that Schmitt writes of the intellectual history of the "German catastrophe" (Friedrich Meinecke) not primarily from the perspective of the established churches, but rather from that of German Idealism, New Humanism, and the intellectual avantgarde of the Vormärz. He proceeds on the basis of a progressive secularization of Christianity and sees no further chance for the "restoration of the old Church" after 1945. To his mind, Catholicism in the twentieth century was long played out. It was for this reason as well that Schmitt no longer considered himself a dogmatic, politically dutiful Catholic, even though he never denied his Catholic influences and accepted them in the context of secular history as markers of his background and identity.

CATHOLICISM AT HOME

Carl Schmitt was born in 1888. His parents were Catholics. His father's first marriage, however, had been to a Protestant. She died, along with her second child, in childbirth. Schmitt had a half-brother from his father's first marriage, whom he rarely mentions in his writings. He grew up in Plettenberg, Westphalia, in a Catholic diaspora. His social surroundings were primarily Protestant. He then attended a nearby Catholic boarding school, thereby entering an environment with a Catholic majority. He mentions reading authors who were critical of religion during this time. Despite his mother's wishes, he had already decided against studying theology during his school years. Schmitt did not learn Hebrew, nor do we know of any support from or influence by the church. The biographical sources from the years of his university studies and clerkship do not reveal any particularly Catholic inclinations. His artistic interests outweighed the religious. In his relations with women, Catholicism and its sexual morality was not an issue. He first became involved with two Jewish sisters named Bernstein and then fervently began a premarital affair with a cabaret dancer. Only after two years did he legalize this relationship, under extraordinary wartime circumstances. Cari (von) Dorotić, a phony aristocrat, was Protestant, as Schmitt was aware. He therefore chose, just as his father had done in his first marriage, a confessionally "mixed marriage."

Very little about his behavior during this time seemed particularly Catholic. Nevertheless, he saw himself during World War I as a Catholic intellectual. He formulated a state-church dualism (Schmitt 1914) and defended religious individualism against the Church (1917). In contrast to some of his students, Schmitt never developed a clear juridical division of tasks or designation of the relationship between state and church. He comes closest to this kind of institutional dualism in his habilitation treatise, The Value of the State and the Meaning of the Individual, in which he makes a strict distinction between "Times of Means and Times of Immediacy" (1914, 108). Schmitt characterizes the apocalyptic "Times of Immediacy" by a direct relationship of the individual to God, which no longer requires the goods of salvation to be relayed by the institution of a church. Here, too, Schmitt relativizes the religious meaning of the church. Schmitt read a broad spectrum of theologians and church historians; he read works by Kierkegaard, Ernst Troeltsch, and Adolf von Harnack and was in contact with religious authors such as Theodor Haecker and Franz Blei.

In 1921 he met the fervently Catholic, Australian-Irish student Kathleen Murray. At the same time he separated from his wife, whom he had recognized as an impostor with a false identity, and attempted to have his first marriage annulled. Although his marriage was legally annulled in 1924 due to the use of a false identity, he was not yet divorced. His two attempts to have the marriage nullified by the Church failed. Following his civil marriage to the orthodox Serbo-Croatian Dushka Todorović, he was excommunicated in February 1926. It is possible that he even married Dushka in the Orthodox Church. This had at least been his plan and would have been unproblematic according to Orthodox law. Through this marriage he had fallen out with the Catholic milieu.

POLITICAL CATHOLICISM

For a short time he gave lectures for the *Zentrum*, the German Center Party and predecessor to today's Christian Democratic Union (CDU), which was already interdenominational but appealed above all to Catholic voters and was perceived as Germany's Catholic Center Party (cf. older portrayals by Morsey 1966; Huber 1981, 194–196; Lönne 1986).[2] The Center Party was democratically and republican-minded. As a state party and coalition partner, it sought to maintain the Weimar Republic. In the mid-1920s Schmitt sought out political connections in the *Zentrum*, but he rejected the parliamentary course of the Catholic Center Party as well as the offer of a seat in the *Reichstag*. He kept a distance from the political Catholicism of the Weimar Republic and viewed the Church primarily as a form of political power (Schmitt 1923). At this time he positioned himself fairly heretically in Catholic journalism. He tested his own surroundings against their relationship to Romanticism. His work *Political Romanticism* differentiated Romanticism strictly from the Catholic Counter-Reformation (1919). Schmitt dismissed the Catholicizing Romantic movement, along with liberalism and modernity, as an opportunistic arrangement. He rejected every contemporary variation on Catholic Romanticism. He was vehemently opposed—as seen in his correspondence with Waldemar Gurian—to the youth movements in Left Catholicism and the "organic" nationalist ideals of the circles surrounding Othmar Spann, and also to Max Scheler, Romano Guardini, and the Quickborn movement (Binkowski 1981). Furthermore, he condemned Catholic natural law and neo-Thomism and distanced himself from pre-1789 "traditionalism" and old conservatism. The "Catholic" author with whom he found the greatest identification became the solitary Donoso Cortés. According to contemporary attitudes, his standpoint was probably closest to the French "*renou-veau catholique*" and the "*Action Française*" (cf. Kühlmann 2008). Not coincidentally, Schmitt fell out with Gurian over the "*Action Française.*" Gurian coupled his affirma-tion of counterrevolutionary ultramontanism with a sharp reckoning with the "*Action Française*" (1929). He decided in favor of the Catholic Church. Schmitt, however, had been rescinding his state-church dualism since 1925 at the latest and became an advocate of the "total state," even against the church. Although he had been friends with Catholic theologians such as Wilhelm Neuss in his Bonn years, his friendships with Protestant theologians were no less close. Even then he had broken inwardly with the church, the Center Party, and the Catholic milieu, and from Bonn had longed for Berlin. His second wife, Dushka, was critically ill with tuberculosis. As a result, Schmitt dissolved the dif-ficult nexus of love and marriage and decoupled his sexual life from his married life. He took a permanent mistress and frequented the red-light districts of street prostitution in Berlin for several years beginning in 1928. Schmitt dissociated eros and caritas and did not ethicize sexuality through personal ties.

His positions on jurisprudence and the political did not correspond to church doctrine either. Schmitt profoundly rejected Catholic natural law and its juridical representatives (cf. Hollerbach 2004). He did not participate in the Catholic turn to neo-Thomism. Catholic Church dogmatics had long blocked any scholastic or religio-philo-sophical discussion. With the slow acceptance of modernity since the late nineteenth century, a new Catholic movement emerged, which developed primarily into neo-Thomism and revived an interest in St. Thomas Aquinas in its reception of new idealistic philosophy. Through his friendly connection with Karl Eschweiler, Schmitt met Jacques Maritain, a main proponent of neo-Thomism. His translator, Pierre Linn, belonged to the Maritain circle. Here, too, however, Schmitt's interest was delimiting. Nor did he enter the circles of political Catholicism in Berlin. He had no close contact to Center Party chancellor Heinrich Brüning. From 1930 to 1933 Schmitt famously became an important apologist and legal advisor to the presidential system of the Weimar Republic in its final days (Ernst Rudolf Huber). Theoretically, Schmitt supported all three final chancellors of the Weimar Republic: Brüning, Papen, and Schleicher. Yet he actually rejected Brüning. Still up for debate in today's scholarship is only whether Schmitt's primary support went to Papen or Schleicher. Following the publication of his journals written from 1930 to 1934, it has become clearer that Schmitt developed a personal rela-tionship only with Papen and that his juridical support for the presidential system was also meant in terms of legal technique and advocacy (see Mehring 2013b; 2013c).

Politically, Schmitt affirmed the "commissarial dictatorship" of the presidential sys-tem far more than Weimar parliamentarianism. However, this is not enough to con-clude that he gave special support to Weimar in the fight against National Socialism. That which he affirmed as a jurist, he saw more radically and skeptically as a politi-cal thinker. Nonetheless, he was not a clear adherent of National Socialism before the Enabling Act of March 24, 1933. His pre-1933 support of the presidential system was in any case not an expression of adherence to the Center Party. Schmitt was even publicly affronted by party leader Ludwig Kaas in January 1933.

His contact with chancellor Papen was likewise not a sign that he supported the Center. When Franz von Papen became Reich chancellor, Papen had already pulled out of the Center Party. After 1933 Schmitt's break with Catholicism was blatant in his National Socialistic involvement. He had given up his old approach toward a constitutional dualism between state and church. Unlike his students in Bonn—Ernst Rudolf Huber, Ernst Forsthoff, and Werner Weber—Schmitt did not execute or contribute to state-church law. Even his Catholic adepts Karl Eschweiler and Hans Barion argued for political primacy of the state over the institution of the church. Schmitt was also close at the time with Heinrich Oberheid, a bishop appointed by the *Deutsche Christen* (German Christians), a Protestant movement aligned with National Socialism. He desired the political disempowerment of churches through the National Socialist state. But National Socialism and Catholicism are incompatible. National Socialistic antisemitism, racism, and warmongering are deeply unchristian, and Schmitt's salient antisemitism cannot be explained as traditional Christian anti-Judaism. And his National Socialist activities and omissions were scarcely reconcilable with Catholicism. Friends and students, such as Wilhelm Neuss and Erik Peterson, Waldemar Gurian, Werner Becker, and Ernst Friesenhahn, were deeply aware of this and broke with Schmitt (cf. Mehring 2009, 313–315). After 1945, Schmitt's attempt at rapprochement with the Church—which was, if nothing else, tactically important—soon foundered. Of particular importance here were contacts with the Walberberg Dominican monastery. Although Schmitt published some texts in the Dominican journal *Die neue Ordnung* (*The New Order*) about Father Eberhard Welty and was a frequent guest in the monastery, there were soon contentions, and Schmitt broke off contact. After 1950 he withdrew his faint attempts to re-Catholicize his work. His last self-interpretation, *Political Theology II*, also lacks any clear profession of Catholicism.

Schmitt was not a true son of the Church. He did not represent political Catholicism, even as a state teacher did not share the Catholic view of natural law, and had no clear Catholic identity. At most he was a very liberal Catholic. At the time there were certainly quite a few (cf. Bröckling 1993; Schwab 2009). In his *Glossarium* he called himself, with a touch of irony, a "Catholic layman of German nationality and citizenship." Nevertheless, self-definition as Catholic is not at the discretion of the individual believer.

PROGRAMMATIC SELF-DESCRIPTIONS: *POLITICAL THEOLOGY I* AND *II*

Let us transition from a confessional biography to Schmitt's programmatic self-descriptions. To this end, two books on political theology, from 1922 and 1970 respectively, are of foremost importance. The first three chapters of the manifesto from 1922 first appeared in the commemorative publication for Max Weber. Schmitt was in personal contact with Weber in Munich from 1919 to 1920. When one considers that Weber had long since withdrawn from academic teaching and was able only in the final years of his life to exert his influence as a teacher with his interpretative method (*verstehende Soziologie*), Schmitt can be considered one of his few close pupils. Beyond Weber's political writings and sociology of authority (*Herrschaftssoziologie*), Schmitt was doubtless inspired by his sociology of religion. Yet he ignored the "sociological" perspective and did not inquire into the agents and supporting social classes of a religious movement. Schmitt began at the point where Weber rationally and theoretically addressed the objective question of the theodicy problem and the inner-logical rationalization of religious dynamic.[3] Weber emphasized the tension between destiny (*Schicksal*) and merit (*Verdienst*) (Weber 1920b), saw the justification of happiness and suffering as the central topic of the history of religion, and spoke of an "ineradicable need for theodicy" (1920a, 246). In his essays on religious sociology, as concisely formulated in his introduction, Weber sees a rational search for justice as the motive for the development of religion. He thereby relativizes Nietzsche's thesis of "*Ressentiment*" and emphasizes a "theodicy of happiness" alongside the religious representation and valuation of suffering (242). Not only suffering, but also happiness wants to claim "legitimacy" ("[*Auch*] *das Glück will 'legitim' sein*," 242). According to Weber, the "ineradicable need for theodicy" stems not from some opiate feeling of *Ressentiment*, but from the rational awareness of an "incongruence between fate and achievement" (246–247). According to Weber, religious justification closes the void between destiny and merit, insofar as it justifies destiny as merit. Schmitt strongly sensed this very type of religious justification of his own life. In agreement with Weber, he emphasized the religious influence on the horizon of meaning and resources of action. He rejected an autonomous, philosophically justifiable morality, as in Kant, for example. Schmitt carried these questions about the religious sources of action beyond Weber—with and against Hans Kelsen—into legal and political theory.

His central argument in 1922 was a nexus of authoritative decision, personality, and theism (Schmitt 1922). Schmitt developed the hypothesis that an authoritative, juridical decision is only possible within the framework of a theistic and personal worldview. He believed this relationship was threatened by the modern process of secularization, which he saw as destroying theism and personalism, and with them, the necessary prerequisites for jurisprudence. Accordingly, in 1922 Schmitt advocated a Christian personalism with a legal-theoretical purpose. That is to say, he does not religiously presuppose the Christian belief in the individual "soul," but instead, through analytical and transcendental reflection, postulates personality as the condition of possibility for individual and authoritative decisions. Schmitt then short-circuits this necessary precondition of personality with theism. Within the framework of his reflections, he takes on a critical relational definition of theism and personalism and thereby implicitly denies the possibility of a postmetaphysical and secular personalism. Schmitt's short cut from personalism over to theism is of course questionable. Even so, Kant himself advocated a similar logically necessary nexus of God, freedom, and immortality in his critical philosophy and doctrine of postulates. Schmitt's legal postulate of a nexus among theism, personalism, and decisionism seems more loosely applied. He does not make any strong philosophical or transcendental claims, but instead proceeds analytically and hermeneutically, reconstructing prevalent convictions rather than logically necessary ideas. In so doing, he actually only inverted Kelsen's critique of natural law: Kelsen saw "relativism" as an ideological prerequisite for democratization and fought against the alliance among Christianity, monarchism, and the authoritarian state (cf. Schnädelbach 2009). Schmitt considered Kelsen's observations on the relation between form of government and ideology essentially applicable. He, too, saw the ideological validity requisite for political forms, but affirmed state authority against modern democratization for the sake of personalism and theism. He saw his position as defensive and therefore aligned himself with Donoso Cortés and the counterrevolution. He reiterated, notably in his 1938 book on Thomas Hobbes, his claim that theism is a condition for the possibility of personalism. Time after time, Schmitt emphasized Hobbes's personal "piety" and Christianity, but thereby positioned the "image" and "myth" of the leviathan in place of strong dogmatic deliberations.

If the manifesto of 1922 can be read as an essentially political-theoretical civil theology, as an appellative mobilization of religious resources of political authority, then Schmitt's last work, *Political Theology II*, insists upon its own theological competence. This book was often discounted as a clumsy late work. In it, Schmitt very belatedly responds to the criticism of his former Bonn friend, Erik Peterson.[4] Peterson, similar to Schmitt's other Bonn companions (Waldemar Gurian, Wilhelm Neuss), accused Schmitt of having betrayed the differentiation between state and church and having idolized the National Socialist state into a church. In *Political Theology II*, Schmitt rebuffs this "legend" as a typical product of Protestant crisis theology and points out that Peterson for his part argues politico-theologically. Schmitt opposes Peterson's discrimination of "Eusebius as prototype of political theology" and insists that the pious layman cannot be denied his salvation-historical interpretation of political events. Eusebius celebrated the Roman Empire as a "victory of the one true belief in God over polytheism," without confusing God and the emperor. Retrospectively, Schmitt has a similar view of his own role in National Socialism.

Schmitt conceives of the afterword to *Political Theology II*, directed at Hans Blumenberg (2008), as his closing words and a conclusion to the work. He reflects on the relationship of state and society in the mirror of Trinitarian speculations about the relationship of "Creator God and Redeemer God" (*Schöpfergott und Erlösergott*; Schmitt 1970, 120). According to Schmitt's portrayal, in the process of the modern era the political primacy of decision is transferred from the church and the state to society. Hobbes could still find the "clear state alternative." Hegel then faced the problem that the Protestant critique incited revolution. It came to a Left Hegelian reinterpretation of his Christology into a "pseudo-religion of absolute humanity," which—according to Schmitt's dramatizing point of view—opened "the way to an inhuman terror." The completion of the Reformation as emancipation of the individual defines, according to Schmitt, the political-theological dynamic of the modern era. He calls the "metaphysical formula" for this empowerment "political Christology." Unlike Hegel he instead emphasizes the "non-identity of Father and Son" (Schmitt 1970, 71) and the "transcendence" of God. Schmitt's historicizing and anthropological interpretation at that time followed

Young Hegelian religious criticism. His mention of the "transcendence" of God remains theologically very indeterminate and is only clear in its political objective against the modern demand for autonomy and the humanistic self-deification of man.

Even *Political Theology II* is therefore hardly suited for a dogmatic reconstruction of Schmitt's "theology." It is certainly not a clear avowal of Roman Catholicism. Even internally a confessional identification is problematic. Schmitt does not provide his readers with clear terminology, which would allow the identification of a consistent theological position. The ethereal matter of religion, however, is hardly graspable even outside of Schmitt's terminology. Often all sorts of things are chalked up as "theology." Religious practice, churchliness, religiosity, confession, metaphysics, theology, and dogmatics need to be distinguished reasonably precisely. People can carry out religious practices without any inner investment or belief and might go to church only out of traditional custom or to be sociable. Ritualistic religions decouple religious *practice* from belief. This is not the case with Christianity. In distinction to Judaism, it further requires the "spirit" (*Geist*) or sentiment of the religious acts. This is Schmitt's jurisprudential argument against mere legality and the "letter" of the "legitimacy" or "spirit" of the law. Churches ritualize religious belonging in different forms (baptism, communion, confession, etc.). One's denomination can therefore be distinguished as an outward faith separate from belief. No one has to earnestly believe that which he or she purports to believe. The Catholic faith is rhetorically fixed by formulae such as the Apostles' Creed. The Church does not expect from its members any particular sense of meaning or even the capacity for a theological explication of the articles of faith. For Schmitt, however, this kind of outward faith did not suffice as an attestation of Christianity. In his 1938 Hobbes book he rejected the modern dissociation of belief and confession (Schmitt 1938, 84–86).

Theology is the science of God. As such it makes dogmatic demands. It is not only a "doctrine of faith" (*Glaubenslehre*) of sincere and church-compliant religious belief, but also a dogmatic formulation of the religious "truth." Christianity has its truth through Christ. As "core of the apostolic proclamation" (1982, 164, cf. 126), Schmitt pointed repeatedly with Hobbes to the statement "that Jesus is the Christ." Christendom received the revelation of this truth through the Bible. Christian theology is a systematic and dogmatic doctrine of the biblical truth or dictates. This theology formulates its doctrine in the hermeneutic analysis of the text of the "Holy Scripture." Theology is therefore not a kind of historical culture studies. Such an empirical study of religion describes the history of religion undogmatically as a cultural phenomenon.

Metaphysics is a philosophical doctrine or science of the final reasons and purposes of being. It formulates that which must be true, even if theology is not senseless, but instead has an object. Kant elevated "freedom" to a transcendental condition of possibility and made it the subject matter of philosophical metaphysics. He allowed for the religious or mythical justification of this "freedom" through a transcendental "God" "within the limits of reason alone" and within the limits of critical hermeneutics. Even Jürgen Habermas grants the Christian religion today practically important "resources for endowment with meaning" (2001). Philosophical metaphysics and the philosophy of religion (as a subsection of metaphysics) must not be mistaken for theology. Metaphysics does safeguard the transcendental significance of theological hermeneutics, but it can also be pursued entirely independently of the religions and theologies that have been handed down. Philosophy of religion thereby mediates more strongly between philosophical metaphysics and the historically bound religious language and theology.

Schmitt was naturally well-acquainted with such distinctions as have been only roughly outlined here. But he did not address them. Above all, he did not clearly differentiate between theology and philosophy as fields of scholarship, but instead advocated a very broad conception of "theology" that included philosophical discourse. Without differentiating further, he usually saw philosophical methods and claims of validity as a part of the histories of religion and theology. This is an inheritance from the nineteenth century. The Young Hegelians as well as Nietzsche often simply read the philosophical classics as theology. Nietzsche writes in *Ecce Homo*: "In the history of the quest for knowledge the Germans are inscribed with nothing but ambiguous names; they have always brought forth only 'unconscious' counterfeiters (Fichte, Schelling, Schopenhauer, Hegel, and Schleiermacher deserve this epithet as well as Kant and Leibniz: they are all mere veil makers)" (2000, 777).[5] Schmitt did not share Nietzsche's anti-idealistic trajectory, but hardly differentiated between metaphysics and theology, so that a reconstruction of his "theology" is inherently risky.

Theology is often nothing more than a systematized parable. The language of theology requires a philosophical and a juridical-institutional translation. Even though Schmitt changed his stance toward the Church significantly, at the latest from 1925 on, and avoided a theological justification of the "concrete" Church, his avowal of Jesus as Christ and of the salvation-historical view of the present in the "great parallels" to early Christianity was nevertheless unmistakable. He expressed himself particularly clearly in a 1950 commentary on Karl Löwith's book *Weltgeschichte und Heilsgeschehen* (*World History and Salvation History*): "The Christian must uplift the parallels to identity because for him the core events of the Christian Aion—the coming, death on the cross and resurrection of the Son of Man remain alive and unchangedly present" (Schmitt 2007, 163–164).[6] Schmitt argued dogmatically: "Christendom is at its essential core not a moral code or doctrine, nor a penitential sermon, nor a religion in the sense of comparative religious studies, but a historical occurrence of singularity that is infinite and unable to be possessed or occupied. It is the incarnation in the Virgin. The Christian Creed speaks of historical events" (165).[7] Nowhere else does Schmitt express himself in such a decidedly Christian manner. He also names "three possibilities," or criteria, of a "Christian conception of history": "the great parallel, the Katechon and the Christian Epimetheus" (166). His search for a Christian "*Aufhalter*"—one who delays or restrains the "end of history"—is connected with the salvation-historical parallels to the early Christian condition. One finds mention of the *katechon* and "Christian Epimetheus" only in his later works. Whether Schmitt himself was a "delayer" or "catalyst" of the apocalypse is contested. Ever since his early works, however, he consistently adopted the perspective of a religious apocalypticist who saw the "state of things" from the perspective of the state of exception and who distinguished between "times of mediacy" and "times of immediacy" (2004, 107). He saw the law and the state as means with which the state of exception could be overcome and and a normal state of affairs be re-established. But Schmitt did not think normalcy likely. As a religious individual he imagined himself existing in a permanently apocalyptic situation—and he dramatized his life accordingly.

LIFE AS A STATE OF EXCEPTION

Schmitt formulated his religious individuality using several key elements of Christianity. But he was not a pious Catholic. Even the credibility of his minimal or essential Christianity can hardly be discussed conclusively. He certainly did not make strong claims about questions of theological dogma. The debates about his "Catholicism" should therefore be limited to a certain extent. In any case, it would be a mistake to expect to find evidence for an authentic Catholicism in Schmitt's life. Other theological speculations are also abundantly speculative, such as the widespread perception that Schmitt was a "Gnostic."[8] With this, too, an ambiguous label is affixed to an author who eludes such determinations. It would be more reasonable to proceed religio-philosophically from a core definition that seems particularly applicable to Schmitt. "Contingency" would be just such a core. When "religiosity" emancipated itself from Christian dogmatism around 1800 (Krech 2002), the general theories of religion and religious psychology discovered contingency. Friedrich Schleiermacher (cf. 1910) spoke of a feeling of "absolute dependence" (*schlechthinniger Abhängigkeit*) (1821–1822), Rudolf Otto of a "creature-feeling" (*Kreaturgefühl*) and the experience of the "numinous" (*das Numinose*) (1936), and Karl Barth of the "wholly other" (*ganz Anderer*).[9] Wilhelm von Humboldt of course also spoke of religious feelings: "Religious education is less teaching than it is a stimulation of feeling," he wrote in his school plan for Königsberg (Humboldt 1959, 108). The religious is thereby the feeling or experience of the limit, finitude, fragility, or contingency of human existence. Religions thematize this boundary between man and "God." Religiosity can thus essentially be defined, as per Hermann Lübbe, as contingency awareness and "contingency coping practice" (Lübbe 1986). During work on *West-Eastern Divan* in 1816, Goethe, in line with Spinoza, spoke of "absolute submissiveness" to "God's will" (Goethe 1981, 424). By this he meant an active acquiescence or acceptance of one's living conditions.

From the perspective of religio-philosophical systematics and also from the perspective of a general study and sociology of religion that is descriptively comparative and typological, the contingency coping practice is a core criterion for the identification of a religious position. The "contingency" of an individual is admittedly the subject of numerous disciplines. Heidegger elevated the "concern" for one's own "finiteness" and "thrownness" (*Geworfenheit*) to a specification of human existence. Doctors, as well, "cope" with human contingency in a practical way. Here the significance lies in a self-understanding that is religiously reflective and in the practice of cultish "coping" with the problem. The believer trusts in God; he trusts that the ritual forms of devotion will yield a positive coping effect. At the same time, the practical forms of "coping" with the contingency problem are multifaceted and diverse. They need not necessarily be communal. With the modern tendency toward religious privatization and individualization, the traditional and communal rituals are replaced by reflective, intimate forms of religious communication with "God." Hegel called his philosophy religious service: "Dealings with philosophy must be seen as the Sunday of life" (1970b, 412); "Philosophy is in fact religious service, is religion" (1970c, 28). The individualistic traditions of modern mysticism are revived today far from communal dogmatism and practices. Religio-sociologically, this can be described as a trend from churchly organization toward sect movements. Max Weber had already detected such a trend toward mystical "virtuosity." The religious individual interprets human contingency as the divine "destiny" or "truth" of his life. He believes himself to be in a religious relationship through his forms of worship. In the process, his "humility" before God often appears to his contemporaries to be an elite and esoteric conceit or arrogance. Max Weber distinguished two main opposites "in the field of world rejection": "active asceticism: divinely ordained actions as God's instrument on the one hand, and on the other hand, the contemplative healing possession of mysticism, which intends a 'having' rather than an acting, and in which the individual is not an instrument, but rather a 'vessel' of the divine, so that every action consequently appears to be a threat to the completely irrational and other-worldly state of salvation" (Weber 1920b, 538–539). The double register of normalcy and the state of exception allowed Schmitt a double virtuosity, as it were: the jurist acts as an "*Aufhalter*" and tool of God, and the individual sees himself in apocalyptical "times of immediacy" as a mystical vessel. It required the highest religious aptitude and virtuosity to be able to see the borders and differentiate "times of mediacy" and "immediacy." Here Schmitt feared evil "fraud." The modern mystic likes to think of himself as privileged in his religious access. He believes that as a "vessel" of God, he has exclusive knowledge and privileged religious access.

Schmitt was precisely such an individualist and esoteric. In his whole pathos and in his practice of enacting his life as a state of exception, he was permeated by a feeling of contingency and unpredictability. He staged his life as an ongoing state of exception, insofar as he constantly found his way into situations from which he needed "saving" by his contemporaries or by a religiously interpreted coincidence. Schmitt's concept of the state of exception has indisputable great diagnostic importance. The rhetoric of the state of exception is also a problematic crisis scenario from the point of view of legal policy and serves all too often to support the call for a dictator and strong state (Frankenberg 2010). Schmitt officially confronted the theme of the state of siege and exception in Munich in 1915. He was once again distraught over his personal circumstances. He was suffering through military service, doubted and despaired over his wife, was afraid of the front, and felt torn between national "authority" and Schwabing "anarchy." On September 6, 1915, he noted in his diary: "At eight o'clock I was ready to commit suicide, to sink into the world of night and silence, in quiet superiority; then I thought only of carving out a career in the world. A few hours later I was indifferent to everything and wanted to become a soldier—it's enough to drive you mad, this disjointedness; what should I do? In an hour I will shoot myself out of rage over my nothingness" (2005, 125). One day later, he noted: "Afternoon: do a report on the siege law. Justify that the state of siege be maintained for a few years after the war. Me of all people! What providence has destined for me yet" (125).

He is confronted with the topic of the state of siege as an assignment. Schmitt is supposed to say that the state of war requires an exceptional expansion of executive authority, even into the postwar period. This will become a central topic of his work. His entire constitutional theory makes the case that the liberal system of separation of powers can no longer be maintained and that the executive needs the right to take exceptional measures. But in 1915, in the middle of the war, Schmitt first approaches this assignment with astonishment. "Me of all people! What providence has destined for me yet!" The comment is ironic, since Schmitt knows that it was his supervisor who made the assignment. But he already seems to sense that the topic of dictatorship and the transformation of the liberal constitutional state into the executive state belongs to the future. And one can already hear a hint of the existential stabilization that has been ordered of the desperate Bohemian. Schmitt has finally found his life topic. With it, he can find his way and triumph as a "soldier" over the citizens and Bohemians. In this way, his mention of "providence" is not meant merely ironically. It also contains his existential salvation: an inkling of future developments that will give him a goal that he can hold onto.

Political Theology then casts a political-theological light on sovereignty as a "limit-concept" of political science. "The state of exception for jurisprudence has an analogous meaning to the miracle for theology," Schmitt writes at the beginning of his eponymous chapter (1922, 49). The state of exception is an opposite and limit-concept conceived from the expectation of normalcy. There is no strict suspension of all regularities and rules. At a minimum, the laws of nature apply in the godless world. Historically speaking, the political field of activity first emerges as a secular space with the ancient Greeks, through the demystification of the worldview and a separation of God, man, and the world (cf. Meier 1980). In the history of metaphysics, the formula is literally reversed: that which seems incredibly secular, the state of exception, is upon closer inspection actually a metaphysical fiction. Godless nature knows neither the suspension of all rules nor any radical state of exception. Only humans perceive threat situations as catastrophic states of exception. In the dramatization of crises lies a dangerous exaggeration. But life experience also tells us that beyond the horizon life goes on. A secular worldview ultimately views the anthropocentrism of the state of exception soberly and cynically. Nietzsche had formulated the metaphysical scenario of radical finitude succinctly and ironically: "In some remote corner of the universe that is poured out in countless flickering solar systems, there once was a star on which clever animals invented knowledge. That was the most arrogant and the most untruthful moment in 'world history,'—yet indeed only a moment" (1989, 246). Today we constantly expect the end of humanity. But for decades, satellites have been flying in orbit, carrying specific information about human existence to any possible "rational beings" (Kant) even when they have lost radio contact. Humanity today again expects rational beings beyond the human.

Schmitt's sovereignty formula dramatizes the possibility of an amorphous field of action beyond all rules. In this way it is itself a "secularized theological concept." The limit-concept of the state of exception feigns an amorphous randomness that does not actually exist in the social hierarchy. The sovereign wins back the initiative and the "book" of trade like a screenplay or description of stage directions and thereby commands semantic sovereignty and competency for a more detailed configuration of the situation. To speak in terms of antiquity, he performs as a Nomothete or legislator and gains a legislative power and function. That does not necessarily mean full dictatorial power or monarchy. Instead, the gesture of dictatorial sovereignty signals weakness. The true sovereign has no need for rhetorical demonstrations of power or self-aggrandizement. Schmitt's sovereignty formula, with its rhetorical conciseness and openness, lends itself to applicative variations. It also allows for an ethical interpretation and reformulation: a sovereign (a sovereign individual) is someone who withstands diverse challenges in everyday life, primarily and most often with ease. Schmitt escaped from routines into this challenge and in a sense thereby submitted his daily life to a permanent sovereignty test. His stylization of life as a challenge was also a test for his contemporaries. For example, in his sometimes rather careless and chaotic handling of money he occasionally created a test of friendship: a friend is someone who lends money. Schmitt made his happiness a challenge to be tested by the contingencies of his actions. This also has a religious dimension as the test of the good God. In ordinary language, the semantics of sovereignty are usually associated with individual habits and a social performance of personality. A person acts sovereignly; that is, with confidence. As a sovereign individual, one succeeds in maintaining one's composure in various situations. One shows stoic self-control and does not lose one's civil frame of mind even in difficult situations. One restrains oneself and masters everyday and extraordinary situations. No one always succeeds in this in the game for the conditions and contingencies of finite existence. Whoever pretends to do so appears slightly arrogant. The sovereign disposition must be observed socio-historically and in the context of the situation. The mirrors for princes, courtier literature, bourgeois etiquette guides, military standing orders, or *Proletkult* manuals define the maxims of behavior very differently. But sovereignty of one's actions is presupposed in all of these social-psychological characterizations, standardizations, and stylizations.

The game for one's own sovereignty becomes a mere act with behavior inappropriate to the situation. The attempt to protect one's sovereignty at all costs means that it has already been lost. This individual lacks empathy for the moment and inadequately plays a role that reveals itself as a "mask." Sovereign behavior is a game about limits. Bourgeois everyday life attempts to minimize practical challenges through routines. Normalization, embourgeoisement, and routinization sometimes rob life of its charm, kick, vitality, and fleeting charisma, which is complexly interwoven in social structures. Weber had already observed "routinization" (*"Veralltäglichung"*) to mean a loss of "charisma." Schmitt despised bourgeois "security" and wanted to preserve the seriousness of challenge in life. Although he was a "bourgeois" professor, married father, and official who was not conspicuously criminal, his diaries sometimes show quite drastically how

Schmitt put himself in difficult situations and used escapades to flee from the routines of daily life. He sought salvation through his crises. Prior to 1933, the most important rescuers were his Jewish friends Fritz and Georg Eisler. He also perceived the unconditional solidarity of his second wife, Duschka, as constant salvation. He saw the dramatic tension of his life in the form of a dialectic between a state of exception and salvation. Schmitt was aware of this religious theatricality. "*Tout ce qui arrives est adorable*," he often quoted Léon Bloy, and in March 1945 he assured Ernst Jünger, "that man knows no more about his future days than about his life after death" (as quoted in Kiesel 1999, 191).

Schmitt experienced everyday life as a state of exception under the idea of salvation. For this reason he condemned apologetic self-idolization and sacralization of life and despised "bourgeois" security and its view of the future as a stabilized past. He identified his life with the moment of the experience of contingent salvation. His religious feeling of life contradicted stable categories, and here one sees the religious reasons behind his critiques of liberalism and positivism. The double appearance of the normal and the state of emergency is also a religious reassurance. Where the state of normalcy erodes and the capacity of the constitution is called into question, the original religious substance still holds. Even the hubbub makes religious sense and, understood correctly, is still in good order. The end is here, but it comes as salvation. Although Schmitt's "decisionism" was repeatedly read—by Waldemar Gurian (1934–1935), Helmut Kuhn, and Karl Löwith—as a kind of "nihilism" oblivious to nature, Schmitt himself insisted on a religious and Christian interpretation. Andreas Urs Sommer, in *Lexicon of Imaginary Philosophical Works*, wrote about a pamphlet, "The State of Siege" (2012, 33–35). According to Sommer, the imaginary logic of Schmitt's text and its objective possibilities ask the reader to interpret the state of exception ethically and to consider the "biopolitics of the individual" in the form of a commentary on Theresa of Ávila. Sommer reads this "state of siege," this thoughtful self-repression, as a rigid religious asceticism of concern for oneself. Schmitt, the excessive Bohemian, already displays praise for asceticism in "The Concept of the Political." There Schmitt identifies the "coming elite" with a "rebirth" of early Christian "asceticism" and "poverty" (Schmitt 1964, 93). In fact, he perceived his life in a state of exception more as an enormous effort and strain than as the loose luck of libertarian amusement. If one follows Schmitt's autobiographical account of his life, he was seldom if ever happy, before and after 1933, in the everyday sense of relaxed enjoyment of life. But he always considered it religiously fulfilled and meaningful.

Schmitt also conceived of this *religiosity of life as a contingent state of exception* theologically and metaphysical-historically. Regarding the latter, he spoke—especially between 1922 and 1925—of a turn from "rationalism" to "irrationalism." *Die geistesgeschichtliche Lage des heutigen Parlamentarismus* gives an outline of this reversal from rationalism to current, "vitalistically" articulated "irrationalism." He referred to many authors to reflect on his religious irrationalism about the unfathomable transcendence of God, but hardly to any Catholic scholarship (Schmitt 1919, 1926). But even before his acquaintance with Erik Peterson, his understanding of the "*renouveaucatholique*" and post-Kierkegaard crisis-theological discussions led him back to early Christian experiences. Following Bruno Bauer (Mehring 2010b), he later spoke frequently about the "great parallels" between the present and the early Christian situation. The Church as an institution did not yet exist for early Christianity. Therefore, many dogmatic objections are deflected by Schmitt's "ur-Christian" self-conception and attitude toward life. His philosophical intuition is the rough nexus of theism, personalism, and decisionism. Schmitt still believed that man is only really an individual within the framework of Christian theism, through an individual relationship to a personal God. He also viewed guilt and atonement as religious occasions of a personal responsibility toward God. Nevertheless, he publicly rejected moral and political responsibility after 1945.

CONCLUSION

Recent source material and research now present a clearer view of Schmitt's political and theological distance from his social background and his political Catholicism of the interwar period. Schmitt likely only sought out closer contact with Catholic circles during his Bonn years. He always saw himself as a jurist. Schmitt emphasized the dogmatic and political disempowerment of Catholicism in the process of Christian secularization and attributed the history of the German catastrophe to other ideas and powers. Neither before nor after 1933 did he ever aggressively campaign for organized Catholicism. His doctrines of the political and of sovereignty instead reclaimed Christian theism and personalism for legal theory. The semantic re-Catholicization of his work after 1945, with the publication offensive of 1950, was vigorously rejected by postwar German Catholicism. Once again, majority Catholicism would not accept Schmitt as an upstanding partisan and dogmatically convinced Catholic. Schmitt had a similar view and in his later works no longer stylized himself as a true "Catholic" thinker.

If the overall "Catholic" interpretation of his life and work is therefore hardly justifiable today, one can nonetheless apply the common distinction between a "religious" core and a confessional cloak and view Schmitt as a religious author and person. One can then situate his work in relation to the various religious movements of the history of modern faith. Beyond the churches, Schmitt of course did not belong to any organized sect. His religiosity was highly individual. For this reason, a closer consideration of his apocalyptically dramatized, eccentric lifestyle seems to me more important than questionable labels such as "Gnosticism." His constitutional political commitment, too, was determined by this perception of crisis. But Schmitt's methodological definition of the boundary of legal discourse is also systematically important. In his religious discourse, Schmitt did not distinguish extensively between philosophy and theology; he placed philosophy under a (far too) broad conception of "theology" and read all confessional orientations and normative influences religio-historically. He therefore no longer considered his juridical precondition of "personalism" to be capable of justification. He knew no religiously neutral and philosophically justifiable human rights.

His short circuit from "personalism" to "theism" is both systematically and politically problematic.

Translated from the German by Jillian DeMair

NOTES

1. Regarding Schmitt's relationship to the Center Party, his first assessment of Anton Betz's dissertation, dated July 15, 1924, is of interest. Here he states: "A. Betz, Contributions to the History of Ideas and Literary Foundation of the State and Financial Politics of the Center Party 1870–1918. The topic of the dissertation is all the more difficult and interesting, insofar as it concerns a political party that ideologically justifies the crucial points of its platform. The overall problem of the correlation between political idea and political practice could therefore be more clearly demonstrated. In addition, the political-tactical consideration of shifting relations resulting from the changing demands of time and place could be proven in particular with respect to ideational and principal analysis. The author does often vaguely touch on such questions (the anti-unitary tendencies of the Center, its opposition to the expansion of the Reich's jurisdiction, to its monopolies, etc.), but overall he still far oversimplifies the difficulty insofar as he assumes without any hesitation that the politics of the Center are grounded not in the actual political situation, but rather in an 'adamant ideology that is detached from the concrete current circumstances.' The politics of the Center cannot be so easily treated or understood as ideological politics." Unless noted otherwise, all translations of source material by the translator.
2. Following Friedrich Tenbruck, cf. Küenzlen 1980.
3. On Peterson's criticism and emphatic recommendation, cf. Geréby 2008.
4. Kaufmann's footnote: "The name of Schleiermacher (1768–1834), the leading Protestant theologian of the German romantic movement, means literally veil maker."
5. The German original is as follows: "*Der Christ muß die Parallele zur Identität erheben, weil für ihn die Kern-Ereignisse des christlichen Aion, Ankunft, Kreuzestod und Auferstehung des Menschensohnes, in unveränderter Präsenz lebendig bleiben*" (Schmitt 2007, 163–164).
6. The German original is as follows: "*Die Christenheit ist in ihrem Wesenskern keine Moral und keine Doktrin, keine Bußpredigt und keine Religion im Sinne der vergleichenden Religionswissenschaft, sondern ein geschichtliches Ereignis von unendlicher, unbesitzbarer, unokkupierbarer Einmaligkeit. Es ist die Inkarnation in der Jungfrau. Das christliche Credo spricht von geschichtlichen Vorgängen*" (Schmitt 2007, 165).
7. Among others, see Marschler 2004; Manemann 2002; Assmann 2000; Groh 1998; Grossheutschi 1996; Eichhorn 1994; Nicoletti 1990; Taubes 1983.
8. Nevertheless thought-provoking is Groh 1998.
9. For an important religious philosophy of the time, cf. Scholz 1921; 1922.

REFERENCES

Assmann, J. 2000. *Herrschaft und Heil: Politische Theologie in Altägypten, Israel und Europa*. Munich: Fischer.
Ball, H. 1924. "Carl Schmitts Politische Theologie." *Hochland* 21: 263–286.

Betz, A. 1924. *Beiträge zur Ideengeschichte und literarischen Fundamentierung der Staats- und Finanzpolitik des Zentrums 1870–1918*. Regensburg: Manz.

Binkowski, J. 1981. *Jugend als Wegbereiter: Der Quickborn von 1909 bis 1945*. Stuttgart: Theiss.

Blumenberg, H. 1966. *Die Legitimität der Neuzeit*. Frankfurt: Suhrkamp.

Bröckling, U. 1993. *Katholische Intellektuelle in der Weimarer Republik*. Munich: Fink.

Dahlheimer, M. 1998. *Carl Schmitt und der deutsche Katholizismus 1888–1936*. Paderborn: Schöningh.

Eichhorn, M. 1994. *"Es wird regiert!" Der Staat im Denken Karl Barths und Carl Schmitts in den Jahren 1919 bis 1938*. Berlin: Duncker & Humblot.

Frankenberg, G. 2010. *Staatstechnik: Perspektiven auf Rechtsstaat und Ausnahmezustand*. Frankfurt: Suhrkamp.

Geréby, G. 2008. "Political Theology versus Theological Politics: Erik Peterson and Carl Schmitt." *New German Critique* 35: 7–33.

Goethe, J. W. von. 1909. *Maximen und Reflexionen: Nach den Handschriften des Goethe- und Schiller-Archivs*, ed. M. Hecker. Weimar: Goethe-Gesellschaft.

Goethe, J. W. von. 1981. "Sankt-Rochus-Fest zu Bingen." In *Hamburger Ausgabe*, vol. 10, ed. E. Trunz. Munich: Beck, 401–428.

Groh, R. 1998. *Arbeit an der Heillosigkeit der Welt: Zur politisch-theologischen Mythologie und Anthropologie Carl Schmitts*. Frankfurt: Suhrkamp.

Grossheutschi, F. 1996. *Carl Schmitt und die Lehre vom Katechon*. Berlin: Duncker & Humblot.

Gurian, W. 1929. *Die politischen und sozialen Ideen des französischen Katholizismus 1789–1914*. Mönchengladbach: Volksvereins-Verlag.

Gurian, W., and P. Müller. 1934–1935. "Entscheidung und Ordnung: Zu den Schriften von Carl Schmitt." *Schweizerische Rundschau* 34: 566–576.

Habermas, J. 2001. *Glauben und Wissen*. Frankfurt: Suhrkamp.

Habermas, J. 2005. *Zwischen Naturalismus und Religion*. Frankfurt: Suhrkamp.

Hegel, G. W. F. 1970a. "Glauben und Wissen." In Hegel, *Gesamte Werkausgabe*, vol. 2: *Jenaer Schriften 1801–1807*, ed. E. Moldenhauer and K. M. Michel. Frankfurt: Suhrkamp, 287–433.

Hegel, G. W. F. 1970b. "Rede beim Antritt des philosophischen Lehramtes an der Universität Berlin." In Hegel, *Gesamte Werkausgabe*, vol. 10: *Enzyklopädie der philosophischen Wissenschaften III*, ed. E. Moldenhauer and K. M. Michel. Frankfurt: Suhrkamp, 399–417.

Hegel, G. W. F. 1970c. "Vorlesungen über die Philosophie der Religion." In Hegel, *Gesamte Werkausgabe*, vol. 16: *Vorlesungen über die Philosophie der Religion I*, ed. E. Moldenhauer and K. M. Michel. Frankfurt: Suhrkamp.

Hofmann, H. 1964. *Legitimität gegen Legalität: Der Weg der politischen Philosophie Carl Schmitt*. Neuwied: Luchterhand.

Hollerbach, A. 2004. *Katholizismus und Jurisprudenz: Beiträge zur Katholizismusforschung und zur neueren Wissenschaftsgeschichte*. Paderborn: Schöningh.

Huber, E. R. 1981. *Deutsche Verfassungsgeschichte seit 1789*, vol. 6: *Die Weimarer Reichsverfassung*. Stuttgart: Kohlhammer.

Humboldt, W. von. 1959. "Königsberger Schulplan." In *Bildung und Sprache*, ed. C. Menze. Paderborn: Schöningh, 101–110.

Kiesel, H. ed. 1999. *Ernst Jünger und Carl Schmitt: Briefwechsel 1930–1983*. Stuttgart: Klett-Cotta.

Krech, V. 2002. *Wissenschaft und Religion: Studien zur Geschichte der Religionsforschung in Deutschland 1870 bis 1933*. Tübingen: Mohr.

Küenzlen, G. 1980. *Die Religionssoziologie Max Webers: Eine Darstellung ihrer Entwicklung*. Berlin: Duncker & Humblot.

Küenzlen, G. 1997. *Der neue Mensch: Eine Untersuchung zur säkularen Religionsgeschichte der Moderne*. Frankfurt: Suhrkamp.

Kühlmann, W. ed. 2008. *Moderne und Antimoderne: Der Renouveau catholique und die deutsche Literatur*. Freiburg: Rombach.

Lönne, K.-E. 1986. *Politischer Katholizismus im 19. und 20. Jahrhundert*. Frankfurt: Suhrkamp.

Lübbe, H. 1986. *Religion nach der Aufklärung*. Graz: Styria.

Manemann, J. 2002. *Carl Schmitt und die politische Theologie: Politischer Anti-Monotheismus*. Münster: Aschendorff.

Marschler, T. 2004. *Kirchenrecht im Bannkreis Carl Schmitts: Hans Barion vor und nach 1945*. Bonn: Nova & Vetera.

Mehring, R. 1989. *Pathetisches Denken: Carl Schmitts Denkweg am Leitfaden Hegels*. Berlin: Duncker & Humblot.

Mehring, R. 2003. Hegels "'Glauben und Wissen' als Limitation einer Glaubensgeschichte der Moderne." In *Hegel-Jahrbuch 2003: Glauben und Wissen*, ed. A. Arndt et al. Berlin: Akademie Verlag, 104–109.

Mehring, R. 2009. *Carl Schmitt: Aufstieg und Fall. Eine Biographie*. Munich: Beck.

Mehring, R. ed. 2010a. *"Auf der gefahrenvollen Straße des öffentlichen Rechts": Briefwechsel Carl Schmitt und Rudolf Smend 1921–1961*. Berlin: Duncker & Humblot.

Mehring, R. 2010b. "Autor vor allem der 'Judenfrage' von 1843: Carl Schmitts Bruno Bauer." In *Bruno Bauer: Ein "Partisan des Weltgeistes"?*, ed. K.-M. Kodalle and T. Reitz. Würzburg: Königshausen & Neumann, 335–350.

Mehring, R. 2012. "Ein 'katholischer Laie deutscher Staats- und Volkszugehörigkeit'? Carl Schmitts Konfession." In *Carl Schmitt: Análisis Crítico*, ed. H. E. Herrera. Valparaiso: Universidad de Valparaiso, 387–409.

Mehring, R. 2013a. "Das Leben im Ausnahmezustand: Carl Schmitts Repräsentation." In *Ausnahmezustand: Carl Schmitts Lehre von der kommissarischen Diktatur*, ed. R. Voigt. Baden-Baden: Nomos, 144–160.

Mehring, R. 2013b. "Carl Schmitt in Köln: Sinnwandel eines Semesters." In *Kölner Juristen im 20. Jahrhundert*, ed. S. Augsberg and A. Funke. Tübingen: Mohr, 137–161.

Mehring, R. 2013c. "Die Ehre Preußens' in der 'legalen Revolution': Carl Schmitt im Frühjahr 1933." In *Der Tag von Potsdam: Der 21. März 1933 und die Errichtung der nationalsozialistischen Diktatur*, ed. C. Kopke and W. Treß. Berlin: De Gruyter, 113–133.

Mehring, R. 2014. *Kriegstechniker des Begriffs: Biographische Studien zu Carl Schmitt*. Tübingen: Mohr.

Meier, C. 1980. *Die Entstehung des Politischen bei den Griechen*. Frankfurt: Suhrkamp.

Meier, H. 1994. *Die Lehre Carl Schmitts: Vier Kapitel zur Unterscheidung politischer Theologie und politischer Philosophie*. Stuttgart: Metzler.

Meier, H. 1998. *Carl Schmitt, Leo Strauss und der "Begriff des Politischen."* Stuttgart: Metzler.

Morsey, R. 1966. *Die Deutsche Zentrumspartei 1917–1923*. Düsseldorf: Droste.

Nicoletti, M. 1990. *Trascendenza e potere: La teologiapolitica di Carl Schmitt*. Brescia: Morcelliana.

Nietzsche, F. 1982. "Nietzsche contra Wagner." In *The Portable Nietzsche*, trans. W. Kaufmann. New York: Penguin, 661–683.

Nietzsche, F. 1989. "On Truth and Lying in an Extra-Moral Sense." In *Friedrich Nietzsche on Rhetoric and Language*, trans. and ed. S. L. Gilman, C. Blair, and D. J. Parent. New York: Oxford University Press, 246–257.

Nietzsche, F. 2000. "Ecce Homo." In *Basic Writings of Nietzsche*, trans. W. Kaufmann. New York: The Modern Library, 655–800.

Nipperdey, T. 1988. *Religion im Umbruch: Deutschland 1870–1918*. Munich: Beck.

Osterhammel, J. 2009. *Die Verwandlung der Welt: Eine Geschichte des 19. Jahrhunderts*. Munich: Beck.

Ottmann, H. 2004. "Politische Theologie als Herrschaftskritik und Herrschaftsrelativierung." In *Religion und Politik: Zur Theorie und Praxis des theologisch-politischen Komplexes*, ed. M. Walther. Baden-Baden: Nomos, 73–83.

Ottmann, H. 2010. *Das 20. Jahrhundert: Der Totalitarismus und seine Überwindung*. Stuttgart: Metzler.

Otto, R. 1936. *Das Heilige: Über das Irrationale in der Idee des Göttlichen und sein Verhältnis zum Rationalen*, 23rd ed. Munich: Beck.

Overbeck, F. 1903. *Über die Christlichkeit unserer heutigen Theologie*, 2nd ed. Leipzig: Naumann.

Schleiermacher, F. 1821–1822. *Glaubenslehre*. Berlin: Reimer.

Schleiermacher, F. 1910. *Kurze Darstellung des theologischen Studiums*, ed. H. Scholz. Leipzig: A. Deichert.

Schmitt, C. 1914. *Der Wert des Staates und die Bedeutung des Einzelnen*. Tübingen: Mohr.

Schmitt, C. 1917. "Die Sichtbarkeit der Kirche: Eine scholastische Erwägung." *Summa* 2: 71–80.

Schmitt, C. 1919. *Politische Romantik*. Munich: Duncker & Humblot.

Schmitt, C. 1922. *Politische Theologie*. Munich: Duncker & Humblot.

Schmitt, C. 1923. *Römischer Katholizismus und politische Form*. Hellerau: Hegner.

Schmitt, C. 1924. Dissertationsgutachten zu Anton Betz. Archiv der Juristischen Fakultät der Universität Bonn.

Schmitt, C. 1926. *Die geistesgeschichtliche Lage des heutigen Parlamentarismus*, 2nd ed. Munich: Duncker & Humblot.

Schmitt, C. 1938. *Der Leviathan in der Staatslehre des Thomas Hobbes: Sinn und Fehlschlag eines politischen Symbols*. Hamburg: Hanseatische Verlagsanstalt.

Schmitt, C. 1963. *Begriff des Politischen*. Berlin: Duncker & Humblot.

Schmitt, C. 1970. *Politische Theologie II: Die Legende von der Erledigung jeder Politischen Theologie*. Berlin: Duncker & Humblot.

Schmitt, C. 1982. "Die vollendete Reformation." In *Der Leviathan in der Staatslehre des Thomas Hobbes*. Cologne: Hohenheim, 137–178.

Schmitt, C. 1991. *Glossarium*. Berlin: Duncker & Humblot.

Schmitt, C. 2004. *Der Wert des Staates und die Bedeutung des Einzelnen*. Berlin: Duncker & Humblot.

Schmitt, C. 2005. *Carl Schmitt: Die Militärzeit 1915 bis 1919*, ed. E. Hüsmert and G. Giesler. Berlin: Akademie Verlag.

Schmitt, C. 2007. "Drei Möglichkeiten eines christlichen Geschichtsbildes." In *Hans Blumenberg und Carl Schmitt: Briefwechsel 1971–1978*. Frankfurt: Suhrkamp, 161–166.

Schnädelbach, H. 2009. "Zur politischen Theologie des Monotheismus." In *Religion in der modernen Welt*. Frankfurt: Fischer, 100–120.

Scholz, H. 1921. *Die Religionsphilosophie des Als-ob: Eine Nachprüfung Kants und des idealist-ischen Positivismus*. Leipzig: Meiner.

Scholz, H. 1922. *Religionsphilosophie*, 2nd ed. Berlin: Reuther & Reichard.

Schwab, H.-R. ed. 2009. *Eigensinn und Bindung: Katholische deutsche Intellektuelle im 20. Jahrhundert*. Kevelaer: Butzon & Bercker.

Sommer, A. U. 2012. *Lexikon der imaginären philosophischen Werke*. Berlin: andere Bibliothek.

Taubes, J. ed. 1983. *Religionstheorie und politische Theologie*, vol. 1: *Der Fürst dieser Welt, Carl Schmitt und die Folgen*. Munich: Fink.

Weber, M. 1920a. *Gesammelte Aufsätze zur Religionssoziologie*, vol. 1. Tübingen: Mohr.

Weber, M. 1920b. "Zwischenbetrachtung." In Weber 1920a, 536–573.

CHAPTER 3

THE "TRUE ENEMY"

Antisemitism in Carl Schmitt's Life and Work

RAPHAEL GROSS

INTRODUCTION

CARL SCHMITT is one of the best known twentieth-century legal and political thinkers from the German-speaking world. He is certainly the most controversial. This above all reflects his multifaceted participation in the Nazi legal system.[1] As I will argue in this chapter, Schmitt's National Socialist engagement between 1933 and 1945 was closely connected with his attitudes toward Jews, Jewry, and what he deemed, in line with a common perception, "*das Jüdische*," "the Jewish" (Gross 2005; Egner 2013). Schmitt's antisemitism did not first begin in 1933; nor did it end either in 1936, the year he came into conflict with part of the Nazi leadership, or in 1945. For this reason, it should play a role in our understanding of his work as a whole—including his famous texts from the Weimar period and the late work that emerged in the early West German republic. In the following discussion, I shed light on various aspects of Schmitt's grappling with *das Jüdische* and in particular clarify the nature of his antisemitic hatred.

That during the Nazi period Schmitt made frequent, clearly antisemitic statements is a fact acknowledged even by the legal theorist's defenders. Let us consider, for example, the year 1936, when Schmitt was at the height of his academic and political power. That year, hostility toward his Jewish colleagues escalated, as did the intensity of his preoccupation with what he took to be "Jewish law." His intention to ground his antisemitism scientifically now also emerged sharply:

> We need to repeatedly impress on ourselves and our students what the Führer has said about Jewish dialectics, in order to escape the danger of ever-new camouflages and talking a theme to death. A merely emotional antisemitism does not do the job; we need certainty grounded in knowledge [*Erkenntnis*].... We have to liberate the German spirit [*Geist*] from all falsifications, falsifications of the concept of spirit

that made it possible for Jewish emigrants to label Gauleiter Julius Streicher's great struggle [*Kampf*] as something "non-spiritual" [*etwas "Ungeistiges"*]. (Schmitt 1936, 29–30)[2]

This citation is itself reminiscent of the young Adolf Hitler—more specifically of a letter he wrote to Adolf Gemlich on September 16, 1919. Containing Hitler's first known remarks on the "Jewish question," the letter already speaks of an antisemitism based on "knowledge," *Erkenntnis*, rather than "feeling."[3] Whatever its direct source, Schmitt made this distinction between an "antisemitism of reason" and an "antisemitism of feeling" his own. Indeed, he elevated it to a central demand of the conference he organized for the "Reich Group of University Teachers in the National Socialist Association of Legal Guardians" (*Reichsgruppe Hochschullehrer des Nationalsozialistischen Rechtswahrerbundes*) on "Jewry [*Judentum*] in Legal Studies," held on October 3 and 4, 1936 (Gross 2005, 120–135; Mehring 2009a, 372–378; Hofmann 1988, 228–240). Schmitt's embrace of antisemitic policy and practice reveals his enthusiasm for the so-called Nuremberg Race Laws, which he celebrated as a "constitution of freedom" (Schmitt 1935, 1133–1135). Schmitt had in any event never publicly expressed his antisemitism with as much directness and radicalism—also in respect to his Jewish colleagues—as at this convention. He now demanded, for instance, the systematic banning of books by Jewish jurists in German libraries. Already in 1933 he had declined to protect the important legal theorist Hans Kelsen, also teaching at the University of Cologne, from expulsion (Gross 2005, 48).

It is all the more remarkable that for many decades after the war there was no systematic study of Schmitt's antisemitism, either in Germany or elsewhere. One obvious reason for this was a reluctance, extending over that period, on the part of German legal scholars to concern themselves with Nazism and antisemitism within their own ranks. The most important and influential organization in this professional field, the Association of German Public Law Professors (*Vereinigung der deutschen Staatsrechtslehrer*), would only directly address the theme at their annual conference in 2001 (Schlink 2002, esp. 124–144). But another significant reason for this was that after 1945 Schmitt himself managed to sidestep the theme of his own Nazism—and this with great skill and success. On the one hand, on the basis of the above-mentioned setback he endured in 1936—the attack leveled at him by elements within the *Sicherheitsdienst* (SD), the security services of the *Schutzstaffel* (SS), then taken up by the SS journal *Das Schwarze Korps*, which condemned him as a Catholic and, in fact, a philosemite—he laid claim to having himself been, in a basic way, a victim of the Nazi state (and to be sure, of abusive American denazification proceedings). Accordingly, he referred to himself as akin to Benito Cereno, the captain of a Spanish slave-ship in Melville's like-named, haunting tale: as someone who had been ostensibly in control of a ship of state but who had been in fact rigorously controlled, beneath the surface, by—from reader Schmitt's own perspective—wicked barbarians.[4] On the other hand, Schmitt was greatly aided in this sidestepping process by a prevailing long-term lack of interest by German postwar society in any concrete, detailed look at antisemitism as a motivation for Nazism and the

Holocaust. Rather, the preference was for highly vague and generalized formulations (see Meinecke 1946 for a good example of this blending of facts with myth). In addition, many of Schmitt's former friends and students, some of them themselves victims of Nazi antisemitic or political persecution, tended toward a kind of shocked disbelief at both the scale and sheer crudity of Schmitt's antisemitic sentiments. Furthermore, the jurist's adept manipulation of his own legacy was steadily boosted by the solidarity and sometimes ignorance of those who worked on his life and writings in the postwar period. In the Anglo-American world, the biographical work of George Schwab (1970) and Joseph W. Bendersky (1983) was especially important in popularizing the basic interpretive approach being encouraged by Schmitt himself. In this manner, Schmitt the antisemite by conviction emerged in general academic and popular perception as a victim of defamation. This process involved scant attention being paid to at least four central areas of concern:

1. The significance Schmitt's antisemitism had in discriminatory measures taken against German-Jewish legal scholars, including their professional expulsion and their persecution.
2. The biographical significance of Schmitt's antisemitism.
3. The influence of antisemitism on Schmitt's work.
4. The possible continued influence of Schmitt's antisemitism through ongoing reception of his work.

In what follows, I focus above all on the second of these areas, since the necessary sources for exploring it have only recently become available.

SCHMITT AND ANTISEMITISM

Antisemitism has often been described as a modern phenomenon, which is to say as a political phenomenon that rose to prominence in the nineteenth century. In that framework, it is understood as a secular form of traditional Christian anti-Judaism— although historians have also often understood it in that tradition as well, as one pole of a broad phenomenon that extends to social, political, and economic hostility to the Jews and Judaism and onward to Nazism's exterminatory ideology. In its general usage over time, the concept of antisemitism has revealed a similarly broad semantic range: while in the nineteenth-century sources, the concept is mainly used in a context of positive self-description, in the twentieth century, and particularly following the Holocaust, it is almost exclusively ascribed negatively and from the outside. Schmitt never referred to himself as an antisemite. In his personal copy of Hasso Hofmann's study *Legitimität und Legalität*, he put a squiggly line under each instance of the term *antisemitisch*, writing *judenkritisch*—"critical of the Jews"—as a marginal corrective.[5] Nevertheless, any bona fide historian would certainly describe Schmitt's Nazi-era writings and his remarks about Jews and *das Jüdische* in his diary entries for the 1933–1945 period as indisputably antisemitic. A lifelong interest in, indeed a fixation on, the theme of "Jews" is in any event evident in Schmitt's life and work. Sometimes we can observe authentic interest, at other times deepest hatred, sometimes friendship with individual German-Jewish or Austrian-Jewish jurists, sometimes a demand for the expulsion of all Jews from German law and a marking of their ideas as "Jewish." But antisemitism represented a constant presence in Schmitt's thinking: both a sentiment and a key element in his worldview, extending past personal prejudice to inform essential aspects of his writing.

As suggested, a great deal of argumentative effort has been expended by Schmitt's students and friends on avoiding a confrontation with this reality. This has involved, for a start, the invocation of various Jewish acquaintances—not only the unavoidable "good Jewish friend," in this case Fritz Eisler, killed during World War I (on Schmitt and the Eisler family, see Mehring 2009a, 28–30; 2009b). Schmitt in fact dedicated one of his chief works, the *Verfassungslehre* of 1929, to Eisler. The list of the other friends and acquaintances is long; it includes Walter Benjamin, Hans Blumenberg, Moritz Julius Bonn, Georg Eisler, Ludwig Feuchtwanger, Waldemar Gurian, Hermann Heller, Albert Hensel, Erwin Jacobi, Erich Kaufmann, Hans Kelsen, Otto Kirchheimer, Karl Mannheim, Franz Neumann, Eduard Rosenbaum, Leo Strauss, and, last but not least, Jacob Taubes.[6] The nature of the contact here ranged from a single—albeit repeatedly cited—letter of Walter Benjamin to Schmitt to sometimes close friendship with Fritz Eisler's brother George. In the case of Taubes, Schmitt's fascination, unfolding in the post-1945 period, was explicitly with the *Jewish* scholar (see Taubes 1987). In 1933 at the latest, in more or less hasty fashion Schmitt had broken contact with all his Jewish friends and acquaintances. For the most part, he then simply failed to respond to requests for help; following several such requests from his erstwhile close colleague Erwin Jacobi, he agreed to write a reference (see Gross 1994, esp. 139–140).[7] Otherwise I am aware of only one case in which Schmitt seems to have showed an interest in the fate of Jews: the case of the Eisler family in Hamburg, which had been very close to Schmitt for over a decade, during the boycott action of April 1933. We thus read as follows in his diary: "Boycott of Jews [*Judenboykott*], tired and sad.... Telephoned with Georg Eisler, who was very sad and felt dishonored" (2010, 277, entry of April 1, 1933; see Mehring 2009b).

One reading of such possible concern (however rarely expressed) for former Jewish friends is as a sign of Schmitt being "deep down" no antisemite. But this would be an entirely unhistorical understanding of antisemitism: in Nazi Germany, even architects of the "Final Solution," including Hitler himself, could at times be favorably disposed toward one or another Jew. There were naturally, the explanation then usually went, "decent" or "upright" Jews; the problem was posed by Jewry as a whole. Reducing Schmitt's multilayered antipathy toward Jews, Jewry, and Judaism to a *single* conceptual matrix is a problematic endeavor. For in both the uniformly extensive entries in his diaries and his Nazi writings, we find highly varying attitudes articulated toward Jews. We find friendship with individual Jews, anxiety vis-à-vis the same Jewish friends as Jews, anxiety regarding an uncanny Jewish power, aesthetic revulsion at

Jews, feelings of envy and hatred. Alongside traditional Christian-Catholic prejudices about the Jews as "Christ killers" we find themes from the repertoire of Protestant-volkish antisemitism. In short, Schmitt's work contains ideas hostile to Jews and Judaism that can be traced back to left-wing, right-wing, volkish, Catholic, Protestant, and Nazi sources.

SCHMITT'S ANTISEMITISM DURING THE *KAISERREICH*

With the Nazi Party's advent to power in Germany, antisemitism became a political principle of the German state, a principle Schmitt supported in numerous books, brochures, and newspaper articles and through personal appearances. As already suggested, that starting in 1933 Schmitt was an antisemitic legal theorist has never been disputed; but the question of his personal attitude toward both Jews and antisemitism *before* 1933 has been intensely debated. The main reason for this has been the paucity of—above all private—sources, a situation that has changed in recent years. In 2003 his diaries for the 1912–1915 period finally became available, as did those for the 1915–1919 period in 2005. For the question at hand, this meant that the source situation had fundamentally changed. And then in 2010 came publication of the diaries for the years between 1930 and 1934, hence for a decisive period in Schmitt's political and academic engagement. Here again, the newly accessible sources have decisively clarified the factual situation: already before 1933, the personal texts are full of antisemitic outbursts so pronounced and vehement that they emerge as their most central and striking affect. Following, then, both the emergence of these new sources and the massive increase in literature on Schmitt, both in Germany and internationally, after his death in 1985, a new evaluation of the antisemitism question has become urgent. The following remarks constitute an initial effort to analyze the question in light of the new sources.[8]

As we now have them, the diary entries begin in October 1912, when Schmitt was 24. He here comments on his everyday life, with observations on friends and acquaintances and his reading. Two themes form the backdrop to the 1912–1915 entries: Schmitt's great love for the Viennese dancer Carita Dorotić and his pressing financial worries. Although Schmitt was fascinated by the young Austrian genius Otto Weininger and his now notorious bestseller *Sex and Character* (1903), he dismissed the Jewish-born Protestant convert's tract as "truly Jewish" (Schmitt 2003, 38). But Schmitt appears to have found support in Weininger for his own particular sexual fantasies, noting for instance the following: "Women, before whose outstretched receptivity one takes fright and is helpless. These are never Jewish women [*Jüdinnen sind das nie*]" (40; November 11, 1912). Alongside such sentiments, we find expressions of rage directed at Jewish men, for example after a conflict with the jurist Eduard Rosenbaum: "I'm afraid of this sneak, but not differently than I'm afraid of bugs and vermin [*Wanzen und Ungeziefer*]. It's hard to defend yourself against that once they are on your body.... Mankind is riddled with vermin [*Es gibt Ungeziefer unter den Menschen*]" (47; November 21, 1912). Here a conflict between jurists is transformed into a situation without egress, hate grounded in an anxiety and fear that will soon become massive, since as Schmitt sees things he is defenseless. Already at this point, what is at stake is self-defense, self-preservation, and the subject's transformation into a menacing, vermin-like, which is to say dehumanized, collective.[9]

One such hate-filled tirade against Eduard Rosenbaum serves Schmitt as an occasion for calling into question any friendly interaction with Jews: "I can imagine how Rosenbaum would judge my book on the state: as a Jew he knows exactly what pose he needs to take... to be able to... destroy my book. That is dangerous rabble! Maybe Georg is no better" (2003, 250; November 12, 1914). With "Georg" Schmitt is referring to close friend Georg Eisler, the brother of his friend Fritz Eisler, who as mentioned had perished some months earlier in the war. Although Schmitt would dedicate his *Verfassungslehre* to Fritz, this friendship as well was from Schmitt's perspective not always that certain: "Fear of the Jews, of Eisler" (140; January 14, 1914).

Schmitt's social interaction with Jews, even, at that time, in a familial context, was maintained despite such feelings. It is clear that when he spent the Christmas 1914 period with the Eislers he did so above all hoping for financial support (the family was in fact furnishing such support constantly in those years); he nevertheless does indicate "I'm beginning to respect the Jews" (2003, 282; December 26, 1914). And later: "Georg is a splendid chap, a clever, intelligent, decent Jew. They can actually be wonderful fellows, which I hadn't at all suspected" (304; January 24, 1915). With Georg, as later with the Jewish philosopher Jacob Taubes, he ventured on intensive discussions of the "Jewish question," a theme possessing great topicality in the years before the German army's notorious "Jewish census" in World War I. Schmitt also engaged in some reflection on his feelings regarding Jews, at one point noting for instance that "surprisingly, over the course of the day I saw lawyer Weyl twice: might that be tied to my Jewish complex?... There are in fact more educated Jews than Christians." But alongside spontaneous remarks of this sort, appearing to voice a form of philosemitism, the repertoire of relevant feeling in the diary entries is laced with not only extreme aesthetic but also moral disgust, together with a strong sense of confronting a conspiracy. Various layers of negative affect are here combined with the stock antisemitic theme of the Jew as always only a cultural imitator, never a cultural creator, as in the following diary recollection: "While washing I felt fury towards Jews who indulge in art, the counterfeiters, falsifying all genuine growth and twisting [normal] human concepts, the go-betweens and nimble apes, able to imitate everything with such skill you believe in it for months" (245; November 8, 1914).

Covering the February–December 1915 period, the second diary volume contains a great deal of material concerning Jews (2005, 21–175[10]). We here also find use of the term "Aryan," although no real observations tied to racial theory—either in the overwhelmingly negative remarks[11] or the scattered positive ones (for example, the reference to Rudolf Leonhard as a "sensible, highly reasonable Jew"[12]). We see the relationship to the Eislers remaining strong, but also complicated and ambivalent. On one occasion, for instance, we read as follows: "Fräulein Eisler was rather arrogant and treated me badly. For I'm the parasite. Very sad and nasty" (100); and on another, as follows: "Met Georg Eisler in Rosenheim and chatted a few nice hours with him about the Jews, the hard times, the French. I was very happy to hear from him and like him very much" (119). But the extent to which a "Jewish" essence was firmly anchored at this time as a category in Schmitt's thinking, indeed virtually a code for all that he rejects in the world, becomes clear in some remarkable comments on Richard Wagner: "Became enraged about the Jew Wagner, and finally we [Schmitt and his wife Pauline (Cari) Dorotić] went home. I was extremely agitated and almost fell over from agitation. That's so horrible. I'm crazy" (115; August 22, 1915).[13]

In order to tame his emotions, which is to say to get a grip on his "antisemitism of affect," Schmitt drew a clear demarcating line. Nevertheless, peculiar references continue to surface: "Went to Oberaudorf, on seeing the sun another attack. But not so bad if I'm left alone right away (to ease my nerves: a Jew like Weininger committed suicide; that option remains open to me)" (2005, 117; August 25, 1915). Another entry, concerning Ernst Lissauer, the Jewish author of an in its time notorious anti-British song, attests to disbelief at the existence of nationalist German Jews: "Beneath Lissauer's song of hate, which hung on the wall, I wrote *nebbich* next to a ledge" (119; August 29, 1915). The next day he erased *nebbich* (119). In using the Yiddish term, he was indicating that such German-Jewish nationalism could not be taken seriously.

In 1915 Jews were a constant theme in Schmitt's diary. On December 19: "Chatted only about the Jews" (2005, 169–170); the next day, while reading the (in fact himself antisemitic) nationalist historian Treitschke: "Very enthusiastic about this way of writing history, strong and vigorous (but I no longer trust him, it is Jewish-type harlotry [*judenhafte Anhurerei*]. They move with all cultures but themselves are and remain merely little flatterers, sentimental thieves, the most disgusting thing there is" (170; December 20, 1915). And on December 28:

> Perhaps good people are deceived; perhaps there is no justice in history and some great man whose goodness and nobility makes me enthusiastic is in truth a skilled forger who gained his fame like all the little Jews at present who have mastered their tongue and with it history; that is horrible. (175)

But the next year, living in Straßburg, Schmitt seems to have embraced an entirely different attitude: "Just try to imagine a spiritual Germany without Jews: the publisher Lehmann, a pair of major generals and university professors, mining directors as heralds of spiritual Germany" (178; December 21, 1915).[14] To summarize what the diaries up to 1915 tell us about Schmitt and the Jews: although antisemitism is present in the diary entries in a range of facets, it is not present on an everyday basis as it will be in the entries from the Weimar Republic's last phase.

Schmitt's Antisemitism during the Weimar Republic and the Early Nazi State

No Schmitt-diary volumes are extant for the years between 1916 and 1929, hence for the period of his richest work. This forms a contrast to the years between 1930 and 1934. During the later period, Schmitt made a habit of first taking detailed and often lengthy notes, which he would then transfer—it seems promptly—into diary format (see Schmitt 2010; on this edition, VII–IX; diaries, 3–333; pocket calendar, 334–354; parallel diaries, 355–454). The first days set an increasingly aggressive tone: "a horrid East Jew [*ein scheußlicher Ostjude*]" (4; January 19, 1930); "these dreadful Jews" (9; January 25, 1930); "fear and disgust at the Jews" (21; February 17, 1930); "fear of the Jews... Viennese Jews, disgusting" (68–69; December 14, 1930). Things proceed along those lines. Concerning his former mentor Moritz Julius Bonn: "Was startled at the individualism of this Jew" (81; February 21, 1931). Concerning constitutional specialist Erich Kaufmann: "Disgust at Kaufmann" (86; February 3, 1931). The theme is constantly present, in different variations. After a meeting with Ernst Jünger, he notes "no unpleasant taste as almost always with Jews" (90; February 18, 1931), and then, two days later, "[h]ad dinner, good conversation with [Albert] Mirgeler, but was very tired (about the nationalism of the Jews)" (91; February 18, 1931). Again over the following days: "At 5 Tyrel showed up, a poor fellow, probably a Jew; it was fun to listen to him but I don't trust him" (91; February 21, 1931); "strolled through the streets, the bookstores, sadly to the commercial college, fear of the Jews and their hate" (92; February 24, 1931); following a talk by writer and literary critic Friedrich Sieburg: "Revolting Jewish females [*Judenweiber*] as an audience" (92; February 26, 1931). And then the theme of "East Jews," *Ostjuden*: "Landmann is a shrewd *Ostjude*, but already strongly assimilated, told jokes about actors. But all said horrid" (108; May 10, 1931). Sociologist Karl Mannheim falls into the same category:

> Mannheim horrid, ghastly, devious, cowardly, but also impudent enough. But I spoke nicely with him, because I always believe in the intellectual interest of these people. The kind Salomon. Ate lunch with Eisler at home (with Z.) relaxed, in the afternoon raved about Hölderlin with Eisler. At 7 was at Sombart's, a great gentlemen's evening, sat next to old Tönnies. Conversed nicely, afterwards with Mannheim, horrid, miserable *Ostjude*, felt ashamed to have spoken seriously with him. (2010, 109; May 14, 1931)

The brief diary entries rarely allow reflection—but sometimes Schmitt still comments on his aversions: "Read Rosenstock with a great deal of enthusiasm, but probably one more washout with a Jew. Nevertheless spellbound" (2010, 111; May 24, 1931). And again: "Fear of the Jew Martin Wolff" (117; June 13, 1931); "[t]hen Lilienthal also came; embarrassing, this Jew" (117; June 16, 1931). As colleagues or competitors, the Jews are omnipresent, likewise in everyday life as noisy neighbors: "Horrible noise of the Jews above me, they yell and scream" (145; November 18, 1931).

Sometimes antisemitism in the Schmitt house is itself registered and commented upon: "Kirchheimer came over, was impressed because he earns no money. Ate with us in the evening (Duschka speaks foolishly about the Jews). Then went with him to the Dortmunder Klause, we drank beer, chatted nicely, I like him a lot" (2010, 146; November 21, 1931); a year later, Schmitt's attitude toward Kirchheimer, as well, will have drastically changed.[15] In any event, the next day we find an entry concerning a Jew whom Schmitt does not like at all: "Afterwards Valeriu Marcu came as well, a horrid Jew, dumb, superficial chap" (146; November 22, 1931[16]). And then, the day after that, a list of Jews who fill Schmitt with fear and disgust: "Always tired inside, could hardly get up, couldn't reflect, completed desperate, disgust and fear of the Jews (Bonn, Frau von Quednow, Haber and Frau Ehrik). At the university. Exams, then home tired. Desperate. Meeting with Bonn, did not speak with him. Disgust and aversion at a world in which you have to put up with such Jews" (147; November 23, 1931). But a few days later, with philosopher Leo Strauss, a Jew again appears in Schmitt's diary who, although not spared certain imputations, is basically characterized sympathetically: "Dr. Strauss checked in, came at 5, a fine Jew, works on Hobbes, liked his argument, but he will have adjusted it specially for me; he wanted a recommendation for a Rockefeller or another foundation. Anyway a lovely conversation that did me good. He left at 7" (149; November 27, 1931). Often it is clear that in a very classical way Schmitt generalizes from a single experience: "Marcu was very congenial. . . . Did not feel comfortable, he showed me his library. Touching, these Jews" (158; December 18, 1931).

On Christmas Eve 1931, as a summation of his Berlin experiences, Schmitt noted the following in his diary: "We had a lovely dinner, drank Rhine wine with it, lit the tree, sang Christmas songs (I wept with emotion at "Rejoice, oh Christians" from the shame and disgrace at being in this Jew-city [Judenstadt] insulted and defiled by Jews), tired to bed at 11" (2010, 160; December 24, 1931). In this diary volume Schmitt can connect everything with the Jews. On September 11, 1932, for example, he wrote: "Literary Jews' taste [literarischer Judengeschmack], horrid, horrid [scheußlich, scheußlich]" (164). Scheußlich is often tied to Jews like a mantra: "Scheußlich, these Jews" (about Paly; 184; March 11, 1932); "scheußlich, these Jews, their deceitful, plotting, tactless sense of business" (about colleague Hermann Ulrich Kantorowicz; 184; March 8, 1932).

As in the entries for 1915, in this period the relationship with colleagues is often stamped with fear and anxiety. Hans Kelsen, arguably Schmitt's most important theoretical opponent, repeatedly appears in the diary—not as "the Jew Kelsen," Schmitt's way of referring to him later in public, but as a source of anxiety: "All are afraid of Kelsen" (2010, 214; September 6, 1932). Like Kelsen, Moritz Julius Bonn would be of some significance for Schmitt's career, and along with the usual "disgust—Bonn came by at 12:20, disgusting this Jew" (229; October 30, 1932)—we find the same fear attached to him as to Kelsen: "Spoke with Bonn, fear of him, he is very cold towards me" (243; December 10, 1932).

On the basis of the available material, it is difficult to say whether Schmitt's antisemitism was shifting or intensifying in this period. In any event, as the above catalog of examples demonstrates, a broad repertoire of antisemitic stereotypes and expressive forms is manifest here, extending to small asides ("[t]hen Kessler showed up with his wife, unfortunately a Jewess"; 2010, 244; December 11, 1932). The sentiment is in fact present throughout Schmitt's diary, in vehement form. Occasionally we find themes from the repertoire of traditional Christian-grounded antisemitism: "We [Adams and Roßkopf, together with Schmitt] drank lovely Burgundy, remained sitting for a while in the music room, and spoke about the chosenness and crookedness of the Jews" (252; January 14, 1933). But consistently, the Jews and everything "Jewish" are treated as Schmitt's main enemy, privately, emotionally, politically, collegially and professionally, and not least, nationally: "Much love for Munich and the part of Germany not destroyed by Jews. Disgust at Berlin.... Terrible fear of the Jews, including Erwin Jacobi. Grown lonely and weak.... Bought a paper. Disgust at poisoning by the Jews" (255; January 23, 1933). Despite constant oscillation between idealization and abasement, the threat scenario is steadily intensified, until it reaches the acute existential level evident in this passage.

It seems that, in contrast to Paul Noack's description in his biography, Schmitt welcomed the events of January 30, 1933, with relief despite his prior work as an advisor for Schleicher's cabinet: "Then on to Café Kutschera where I heard that Hitler became Reich Chancellor and Papen Vice-Chancellor. Excited, joyously pleased" (2010, 257; January 30, 1933).[17] Often two words in an entry made the next day are cited to suggest a different mood: "terrible state" (257; January 31, 1933). But these words refer to a cold from which Schmitt was suffering at the time, not to Hitler's nomination as German chancellor.

SCHMITT'S ANTISEMITISM, 1945–1985

Schmitt's postwar antisemitism was strongly woven together with his biographical situation. In the early phase of the German federal republic, philosemitism (or at least the fight against antisemitism) was cultivated as part of the official self-understanding, with most people distancing themselves from both philosemitism and antisemitism on a practical level (see the polemic text by Bloch 1965). Schmitt's refusal to distance himself from his Nazi and antisemitic past thus relegated him to an outsider's role. In addition, he had so discredited himself with so many former students of Jewish origin that there was no going back. The personal and academic exchanges that he had been able to cultivate in the Weimar period with Moritz Julius Bonn, Hermann Heller, Erich Kaufmann, Ludwig Feuchtwanger, Ernst Bloch, Karl Mannheim, Waldemar Gurian, Leo Strauss, Franz L. Neumann, and Hans Kelsen were now unthinkable (on the impression Schmitt made within emigrants' circles, see Söllner 1992). Contacts with figures such as Alexandre Kojève, and later Jacob Taubes, were an exception. They mainly rested on inadequate knowledge of his Nazi engagement and actions—this is the case with Raymond Aron, as we know from his autobiography (Aron 1985, 418)—or else on such engagement occupying the center of their interest—this is the case with Taubes, who loved the provocation of meeting, in his status as "arch Jew," with Schmitt the Nazi and antisemite, for most Germans a tabooed gesture.

There was not the slightest hint of any apology by Schmitt for his behavior toward his Jewish colleagues. Such decency would have marked the sharpest contrast to his endlessly repeated reproaches against the "emigrants": "They're throwing us to the emigrants as feed." "The emigrants... are waging a just war, the most horrible sort that human obstinacy has invented. ... I have no desire to steer the hate-affects of that type of human being, supplementing my already endured persecutions, to my poor person" (Schmitt 1993, 115; March 14, 1948; 252; July 4, 1949). Similarly: "Salus ex Judaeis? Perditio ex Judaeis?" Schmitt asks rhetorically. "In the first place enough of this importunate Judaeis!" (290; January 12, 1950). And further:

> When we became disunited, the Jews sub-introduced [*subintroduziert*] themselves. As long as that is not understood, there is no salvation. Spinoza was the first who sub-introduced himself. Today we are experiencing a restoration of this sub-introduction with colossal claims to compensation and repayments. But the sub-introduced individuals are nevertheless even worse than the returned emigrants who are enjoying their revenge. Accepting all those dollars should make them feel shame beneath their collars [*Sie sollten sich was schämen, den Dollar anzunehmen*]. (290)

Such passages themselves emerged from Schmitt's new social situation and are thus not especially surprising. For within his mind, the Jews were really "persecuting" him, as his notes from the period reveal. But they were doing so not as accusers: since his release from arrest in Nuremberg, he had nothing to fear. Rather, they pursued him as his *theme* and metaphysical enemy, against whom he would struggle for the rest of his life. This is made amply clear in the Schmitt archives (see the relevant entries under *Judentum* in van Laak and Villinger 1993, 329).

DEBATING SCHMITT AND THE JEWS

In light of then-available sources, over many decades a prevailing thesis was that in 1933 Schmitt resorted to antisemitism for purely strategic reasons, and that the antisemitism vanished with his disempowerment as a leading "Third Reich" jurist in 1936, or at least with the end of the Nazi state in 1945. Another popular thesis has been that precisely the many above-mentioned Jewish friends and acquaintances, and above all the incriminating references to them emerging from circles tied to the Nazi party's security service, forced radicalization on Schmitt (on this, see Gross 1994). For, so the argument goes, nothing would have better shown him to be a convinced Nazi than a passionately articulated antisemitism that in reality played no extensive role in his ideas.

Still, time and again authors have raised objections to such counterintuitive and apologetic arguments, which we now can consider as refuted by newly published sources.

For instance, both the philosopher of religion Jacob Taubes and the historian and journalist Nikolaus Sombart pointed to a deeply anchored and lifelong hatred of Jews on
Schmitt's part (Taubes 1987; Sombart 1984; see Hofmann 1992, 177–197). In 1991 Schmitt's
notes for the 1947–1951 period appeared under the title *Glossarium*, and the assertion
that Schmitt had ceased being an antisemite in 1945 lost all credibility—the opposite
was clearly the case. When in his postwar publications the jurist kept something secret
or at least veiled, it was inevitably an antisemitism entrusted to the diary volumes and
close friends alone. If anything strategic was at work in Schmitt's writing, it was not his
antisemitism between 1933 and 1945; rather, it was the way he and some supporters tried
to publicly deny it after the war.

In any event, the other part of the Schmitt legend, related to the Weimar Republic,
was not necessarily deflated in this fashion. Generally speaking, researchers did not feel
called on to examine Schmitt's important texts from the Weimar period (*Die Diktatur*;
Politische Romantik; *Römischer Katholizismus und politische Form*; *Die geistesgeschichtliche Lage des heutigen Parlamentarismus*; *Politische Theologie*; *Der Begriff des Politischen*;
Verfassungslehre; *Legalität und Legitimität*; *Der Hüter der Verfassung*) against the backdrop of Schmitt's antisemitism. Consequently one of the potentially important questions in historical work on Schmitt had remained essentially unaddressed. Against that
backdrop of sources that had still not been fully scrutinized, the publication of my doctoral dissertation on Schmitt and the Jews (Gross 2000) generated an intensive public
debate.[18] In the course of this debate it became clear that many Schmitt experts, including those with a critical approach to the jurist, continued to think of a focus on the
jurist's antisemitism as exaggerated. Was it not, after all, legitimate, despite the work's
known antisemitic passages, to engage with it seriously beyond that reality? But that,
in fact, was not the central concern of my book. I did, however, consider it important
to systematically reflect on the antisemitism's significance for the *entire corpus* of the
constitutional theorist. Through the sources that were published after my book's appearance, my underlying premise gained cogency that Schmitt was preoccupied throughout
his life with Jews and *das Jüdische*—something manifest in a readable code in nearly all
his central texts, but that had not always been empirically substantiated in the book as a
result of the sources I had available.

Perhaps the four questions I initially outlined regarding Schmitt's attitude toward
Jews cannot be fully addressed through the material outlined here; but I would argue
that they at least gain distinct contour. The policy of discrimination and expulsion of
Jewish colleagues that Schmitt pursued from 1933 onward is very evident in his pre-1933
antisemitic hatred. Likewise subjective factors already discussed in Reinhard Mehring's
scrupulously detailed biography—personal ambivalence; the theme's violent emotional dimension—come into sharper focus (see Mehring 2009a). Despite efforts by
the diaries' publishers to argue the contrary, the observation that the degree of negative feelings far exceeds the occasionally expressed positive ones seems indisputable.[19]
Schmitt's articulation of antisemitic affect forms a broad spectrum of then widespread
attitudes: comparisons of Jews with vermin; fear of and anxiety sparked by Jews; disgust,
hate, feelings of inferiority and superiority; a resentment-filled sense of being dependent

on Jews; a sense of plotting; ascriptions of intellectual dishonesty and sexual distinctive-ness. Within the years covered by the extant diaries, we can see something deeply obses-sive emerge in certain moments of Schmitt's concern with the theme. But alongside that, we also find phases where the theme recedes entirely before other themes. The antisemi-tism is especially violent in Weimar's closing phase, especially in 1932, thus mirroring the general societal intensification of antisemitic tendencies at the time. But we already find Schmitt expressing many variations of such sentiments before World War I. To that extent a continuously present hatred of and hostility toward Jews can be identified in the diary volumes, a sentiment that constantly alters in intensity and frequency, but gener-ally grows stronger, in the period in question.

What remains is a basic question: that of the meaning of this clear-cut biographical evidence for understanding Schmitt's legal theory. I already offered an answer to this in my 2005 book on the legal theorist. Without being familiar at the time of the book's writing with the violence and emotionality of Schmitt's pre-1933 antisemitism, I did maintain that Schmitt's personal hatreds were tied to the central ideas at work in his writing. Nevertheless, in light of the new information offered by the diaries, a review of the approach I took would now seem useful.

The book is divided into five sections; two focus on Schmitt's writing in a biographi-cal framework, and on both the jurist's political engagement in the Nazi years and his role as an imaginary victim afterward (Gross 2005). Concerning the Nazi years, one of my main concerns in the book was to show that, broadly speaking, Schmitt's engage-ment with National Socialism was aligned with his own inclinations and was not some-thing somehow determined from the outside or indeed forced upon him (ch. 1). When it came to the postwar period, I wished to explore the question of how Schmitt was able to influentially stylize himself into a victim of both the Nazis and Jews, and to examine the fruitful social soil he worked on in this period (ch. 5). Three chapters oriented toward intellectual history develop the book's main argument, its main point of reference being historical contexts in which Schmitt formulated specific positions and concepts. Here I was concerned with analyzing, in each particular case, the role Schmitt assigned Jews as either a historical group or an antagonist in the framework of salvational history. In these chapters three concepts are important for understanding Schmitt's thinking: universalism (ch. 2), particularism (ch. 3), and acceleration (ch. 4). Each concept is examined in an ideational context that was decisive for Schmitt's understanding of con-stitutional theory or the history of ideas: the context of emancipation and counterrevo-lution; that of the Jews and the nineteenth-century Christian state; and that of "katechon and antichrist."

This is the analytic framework I have proposed for grasping the following concep-tualization of the Jews, forming a core explicit and implicit element in Schmitt's legal writing: The Jews are engaged in an effort to postulate putatively universalistic ideas applied to themselves and humanity (human rights, equality, emancipation) in order to pursue their particularistic aims (retention of their specific identity as Jews, uphold-ing Jewish law, and so forth). In this way, Schmitt's argument goes, they increase *accel-eration*: a negative modernization contributing to an escalation of conflicts. Structurally this form of argumentation adheres to Schmitt's famous words from his most famous Weimar text, *The Concept of the Political*: "Whoever says humanity intends to deceive" (Schmitt 1932, 55).

In respect to Schmitt's antisemitism, that dictum forms a backdrop for understanding the connection between his pre-1933 writing and what came afterward. The conceptual structure formed through Schmitt's thematic presentation of "the enemy" in *The Concept of the Political* is highly similar to the conceptual structure of his antisemitism. Two concepts of the enemy are in fact at work in the book: the neutrally understood concept present in his friend/enemy distinction and the anything but neutral concept of the *enemies of this distinction*. The latter are the objects of Schmitt's polemic. Whoever calls the friend/enemy distinction—his construction of the political—into question is the *true enemy*, for with his universalistic vocabulary he is, according to Schmitt, a deceiver. Such a doubling of the "enemy" concept is the basis for the polemic force possessed by this influential essay on politics. Schmitt now defines this "deception" as a secular continuation of the denial of the Christian idea of original sin. In this light, that already in the Weimar writings he viewed the confrontation with his opponents as one between secularized Christian theology and "the others" (Jews, Marxists, anarchists) seems a highly reasonable conclusion. Crucially, the roots of the escalation of this confrontation in the Nazi period, the reasons for Schmitt becoming a highly important Nazi jurist who placed antisemitism at the heart of his reflections starting in 1933, are bound up with specific discussions in German constitutional theory: those centered on the position of the Jews in the secular, modern state. These discussions, however, themselves stemmed from the nineteenth century, when first in France and then in Germany precisely those thinkers came to prominence whom Schmitt would repeatedly evoke as his most important mentors: the radical German Young Hegelians grouped around Bruno Bauer and the conservative French counterrevolutionaries Louis de Bonald and Joseph de Maistre.

We can thus understand Schmitt's work as standing in a highly specific historical context, a context in which antisemitic conceptual currents have a specific meaning. The concepts at work here are increasingly presented in a kind of code. Already in the early works, which contain no open antisemitism, we can identify the code in many passages. At times Schmitt's contemporaries understood the passages in just that way, above all when those readers had similar ideas and feelings. Schmitt even addressed such things directly with Jewish acquaintances to whom he felt close; one good example of this is found in his recently published correspondence with his Jewish publisher Ludwig Feuchtwanger. In 1929 Schmitt wrote Feuchtwanger as follows: "Kelsen's normativism and identification of the state with the law is in fact only possible if one lives not in the state but 'within the law.' The law can or could be the Torah, but certainly hardly the German Civil Code" (Schmitt in Rieß 2007, 313).[20] Such a remark is naturally not overtly antisemitic—why would Schmitt have displayed such open sentiments to his Jewish publisher? But it clearly shows the particular way in which Schmitt perceived his—twice converted—colleague Hans Kelsen as a particularly Jewish jurist: as someone living within the Torah's law and not really being part of the Christian-secular world.

In this manner, confronting the conceptual sweep of Schmitt's antisemitism involved deciphering a specific antipositivist and antiliberal code—one conveying a polemic forming a unifying conceptual framework to the jurist's oeuvre. Legal philosophers or theorists wishing to salvage Schmitt may offer objections along the following lines: whatever the historical setting of Schmitt's work, and whatever the particular valence of his concepts in an antisemitically stamped environment, his texts also have a significance located beyond that framework. In other words, Schmitt's ideas can be freed from their special antisemitic context. We can abstract these ideas from Schmitt's critique, possibly inherent in them, of the "Jews" and "*das Jüdische*"; and inversely, taking up his arguments in a generalized manner, we can use them to show, for instance, the weaknesses and aporias of our own political-legal culture. In theory, such an effort to read Schmitt beyond history is certainly conceivable. After all, why not? (It is also the case that with enough abstraction, any author can be read in that way.) Still, a grave problem appears attached to this particular effort: the possibility—certainly not a remote one—that the codifying process described here did not simply vanish in the decades after the war. In actuality, it would seem incumbent on cultural theorists and others now prone to positively assessing Schmitt—academic authors who prize him as a "thinker," naturally not as a "person"—to be profoundly skeptical when it comes, precisely, to the enthusiasm for the antiliberal, antipositivist, and antisemitic jurist circulating in both Europe and American universities from the postwar period to the present.

Conclusion

Why, in any case, should the antisemitism that Schmitt openly expressed between 1933 und 1945, together with the structurally antisemitic thinking before and after that has now become clear from the diaries, be considered important enough to be addressed at length? For a start, a historiographical response to this question seems to suggest itself: Schmitt, for whom antisemitism evidently counted as one of his deepest convictions, continues to figure as one of the most important authors in German legal history and political thought. For that reason alone, we should not trivialize this central aspect of his life and work. We should not forget that intellectuals like Schmitt were responsible for shaping Nazi antisemitism and played their part in its genocidal development. With a close look at the hatred revealed in Schmitt's texts and diaries, and especially at the racial hatred expressed in the Nazi period, it becomes clear that the jurist did not draw any clear line between "left-wing" and "right-wing" antisemitism, Jew-hatred of the "Protestant," "Catholic," or "religious," "political," or "racial" sort, but fully appropriated all these variants.

Beyond historical considerations, political scientists and constitutional specialists will need to themselves inquire into the relevance of Schmitt's antisemitism for his work as a whole. The historical analysis has in any event already shown that Schmitt tied many of his central ideas extremely closely to the "Jewish question." For example, as David Egner

(2013) recently confirmed in the *Vierteljahrshefte für Zeitgeschichte*, Schmitt's political theology needs to be read very directly in the context of his antisemitic thinking. The concept of the *nomos* is extremely closely connected to the struggle against what Schmitt understood as "Jewish law" or "pure normativism"; in fact it cannot really be understood outside that struggle's framework. His concept of the political can likewise only be removed with great difficulty from the context of his identification of a Jewish enemy.

Without a doubt Schmitt's many-layered and deeply rooted antisemitism also intensified his alignment with Nazism in 1933 in an essential way. In 1932 it was not at all clear whether Schmitt would emerge as a radical National Socialist. But his antisemitism—we see this in, precisely, the diaries—was already very radical long before 1932; it was hatred, a daily obsession with those he considered "the true enemy" (1991, 18).[21] Against this backdrop, I find it difficult, as a historian, to imagine how contemporary political theory could profit from Schmitt's work. Continuing to assimilate and use Schmitt's ideas without an acknowledgment of the strong role antisemitism played in them means passing on elements of that same conceptual substance—albeit for the most part in encoded form.

Translated from the German by Joel Golb

NOTES

1. Cf. Gross 2005 (31–135); Mehring 2009a (304–436); Koenen 1995; Blasius 2001; Bendersky 1983.
2. Unless noted otherwise, all translations of source material by the translator.
3. "As a political movement antisemitism may not and cannot be determined by moments of feeling, but by knowledge of facts. But [the] facts are as follows: first of all Judaism [*Judentum*] is absolutely a race and not a religious association. And the Jew himself never designates himself as a Jewish German, Jewish Pole, or Jewish American, but always as a German, Polish, or American Jew." See the letter from Adolf Hitler to Adolf Gemlich (Munich, September 16, 1919), printed as document 12 in "Hitlers Eintritt in die Politik und die Reichswehr" (1959, 203).
4. Schmitt's analogy here was thus between the Nazis he had worked with and the ship's rebellious African slaves in Melville's fiction. In Melville's work, the slaves, having slaughtered most of their ship's crew in the desperate hope of sailing back to Senegal, secretly control their former master Cereno's every action, on pain of death, in the presence of an unwelcome captain who has boarded from another, well-armed ship; they are portrayed by the novelist with masterful, disturbing ambivalence, as an embodiment of the American white man's bad conscience.
5. This is reported by Hasso Hofmann in the introduction to the 1992 edition of *Legitimität gegen Legalität*, first published in 1964; see Hofmann (1992).
6. Relevant studies of the individual authors include the following: on Benjamin: Palmier (2009); on Blumenberg: Schmitz and Lepper (2007); on Bonn: Hacke (2011); on Eisler: Mehring (2009); on Feuchtwanger: Rieß (2007) and Specht (2006); on Gurian: Hürten (1972); on Heller: Robbers (1983); on Jacobi: Otto (2008); on Kaufmann: Rennert (1987); on Kelsen: Diner and Stolleis (1999); on Kirchheimer: Bavaj (2007) and Neumann (1981); on Neumann: Buckel (2007) and Fishan (1993); on Strauss: Meier (1998); on Taubes: Taubes (1987) and Palzhoff (2009).

7. By contrast, neither Ludwig Feuchtwanger nor Hans Kelsen received any help from Schmitt, and he directly persecuted the jurist Erich Kaufmann—as a "full Jew" and an "existence, aimed solely at concealing origins and at disguise"—through a letter to the Nazi culture ministry (Gross 1994, 26).

8. New collections of letters have also appeared, including Schmitt's correspondence with Ernst Forsthoff (Mußgnug 2007), Hans Blumenberg (Schmitz and Lepper 2007), Auguste Schmitt (Schmitt 2000), Ludwig Feuchtwanger (Rieß 2007), Hans-Dietrich Sander (Lehnert 2008), and Gretha Jünger (Villinger 2007).

9. I thank Dagi Knellessen for clarifying this argument.

10. The volume also contains an appendix covering Schmitt's time in Straßburg in July 1916 (Schmitt 2005, 176–179).

11. See the following entry from March 1915, which takes up the "Aryan" theme in a curious way: "The sharp, clever Aryans laugh, the confidence men and swindlers. They all couldn't form a human society, they are parasites; the good and decent people (i.e. the goodness and decency that many people possess) is the ground on which everything stands and rests. We often are astonished at the scope parasitism can acquire, but it quickly collapses; they then become the evil fertilizer (many of the apes, many Jews, whose fathers are perhaps bankers and who are themselves weak existences, without strength and detached from the world)" (Schmitt 2005, 36).

12. "In the afternoon aphorisms arrived for Herzog. A sensible, highly reasonable Jew. Through Georg Eisler I'll send him my book on the state, because he consistently spoke accurately about social-philosophical problems and sometimes about innocence. Got unusually excited about the whole thing. Crazy desire for power and influence. Nervous, sickly officials' psychosis." Rudolf Leonhard (b. October 27, 1889, in Lissa; d. December 19, 1953 in East Berlin) was a writer and politically active Marxist. He took part in Spartacus League battles and the Spanish Civil War. Following flight from a French internment camp in 1944 he joined the resistance in Marseilles. In 1950 he moved to East Berlin.

13. Cf. December 8, 1915 (164): "We should neither inveigh against Wagner nor praise him, but treat him very generally as a purely internal Jewish affair."

14. Julius Friedrich Lehmann was a German publisher of, for the most part, medical, volkish, and racist literature.

15. See entry of November 6, 1932: "Up at 9, not enough sleep, cheerful while washing, breakfast with Huber, afterwards Kirchheimer came, [talked] with him about his essay in which he reviews my book, the instrumentalization of democratic formulae.... We went to Bahnhof Zoo, it is pointless to speak with him, he simply does not want to see it. Horrid, these Jews" (Schmitt 2010, 231).

16. Valeriu Marcu was a Romanian writer and historian of Jewish origin who wrote mainly in German. In 1941 he emigrated to the U.S., where he died the following year.

17. Contrast with Noack (1993, 160): "Then to Café Kutscherer where everyone was already excited because of Hitler's nomination to be Reich Chancellor. I sent my letter to Kaas with a certain relief."

18. See Balke 2000; Pralle 2000; Busche 2000; Wirz 2000; Kittsteiner 2000; Münkler 2000; Zarusky 2000; Nippel 2000; Maschke 2000; Kalberer 2000; Meyer 2000; Korenke 2000; A. Schmitt 2000; Rumpf 2000; Schwering 2000; Hermann 2001; Deuber-Mankowsky 2001; Sieg 2001; Kuhn 2001; Benöhr 2001; Jabloner 2002; Emden 2009; and Bendersky 2010.

19. The editors of the diaries, Ernst Hüsmert and Gerd Giesler, are inclined to dispute this—for instance especially crassly in the introduction: "Jewish topics and critical material on Jews [*Jüdisches und Judenkritisches*] are interlinked in Carl Schmitt's character.... His many friendships and academic contacts with Jews teach him how much Jewish substance [*Jüdisches*] he himself has within him.... He actually does not hate Judaism, but rather is hostile towards himself" (Schmitt 2005, 4–5). It is striking that the editors appear to simply not recognize Schmitt's antisemitism, even resorting to his own term *judenkritisch* (see note 3).

20. Feuchtwanger was one of the many Jewish friends and acquaintances Schmitt would disappoint and to whom he would deny all assistance starting in 1933. Very soon Feuchtwanger's letters would remain unanswered (see Rieß 2007, 397–398). I thank Martin Jost for drawing my attention to this passage in the letter.

21. The passage in the *Glossarium* where Schmitt uses this phrase is somewhat ambiguous, in that it can conceivably be read as simply pointing to the implications of Peter F. Ducker's account of the usefulness of the Jews as the "demonic enemy" in that author's *The End of Economic Man*. Nevertheless, particularly in light of the newly published diaries, it is perfectly clear that for Schmitt, specialist in the "friend/enemy" distinction, the Jews were the true enemy as the demonic enemy.

REFERENCES

Aron, R. 1985. *Erkenntnis und Verantwortung: Lebenserinnerungen*. Munich: Piper.

Balke, F. 2000. "Kreuzzug und Kartei: Carl Schmitt und die Juden." *Neue Rundschau* 111: 168–179.

Bavaj, R. 2007. "Otto Kirchheimers Parlamentarismuskritik in der Weimarer Republik: Ein Fall von 'Linksschmittianismus'?" *Vierteljahrshefte für Zeitgeschichte* 55: 33–51.

Bendersky, J. W. 1983. *Carl Schmitt, Theorist for the Reich*. Princeton: Princeton University Press.

Bendersky, J. W. 2010. Review of Carl Schmitt and the Jews: The "Jewish Question," the Holocaust, and German Legal Theory by Raphael Gross. *Journal of Central European History* 43: 377–380.

Benöhr, S. 2001. "'Die Vertrauten Eigenen Anderen', Rezension des Buches von Raphael Gross Carl Schmitt und die Juden." *Forum Recht* 3: 91–93.

Blasius, D. 2001. *Carl Schmitt: Preussischer Staatsrat in Hitlers Reich*. Göttingen: Vandenhoeck & Ruprecht.

Bloch, E. 1965. "Die sogenannte Judenfrage (1963)." In *Literarische Aufsätze, Gesamtausgabe*, vol. 9. Frankfurt: Suhrkamp, 549–554.

Buckel, S. 2007. *Subjektivierung und Kohäsion: Zur Rekonstruktion einer materialistischen Theorie des Rechts*. Weilerswist: Velbrück-Wissenschaft.

Busche, J. 2000. "Wie die meisten: Neue Anmerkungen zu Carl Schmitts Antisemitismus." *Badische Zeitung*, June 3.

Deuber-Mankowsky, A. 2001. "Flucht aus der Geschichte und ihre Folgen." *Die Wochenzeitung* 6, February 8.

Diner, D., and M. Stolleis. eds. 1999. *Hans Kelsen and Carl Schmitt: A Juxtaposition*. Schriftenreihe des Instituts für Deutsche Geschichte, Universität Tel Aviv. Gerlingen: Bleicher.

Egner, D. 2013. "Zur Stellung des Antisemitismus im Denken Carl Schmitts." *Vierteljahrshefte für Zeitgeschichte* 61: 345–361.

Emden, C. J. 2009. Review of Carl Schmitt and the Jews: The "Jewish Question, the Holocaust, and German Legal Theory by Raphael Gross. H-German, H-Net Reviews (July) http://www.h-net.org/reviews/showrev.php?id=24782 (accessed December 7, 2011).

Fishan, A. 1993. *Eine kritische Theorie des Rechts: Zur Diskussion der Staats- und Rechtstheorie von Franz L. Neumann.* Aachen: Shaker.

Gross, R. 1994. "Politische Polykratie 1936. Die legendenumwobene SD-Akte Carl Schmitt." *Tel Aviver Jahrbuch für deutsche Geschichte* 23: 115–143.

Gross, R. 2005. *Carl Schmitt und die Juden: Eine deutsche Rechtslehre.* Frankfurt: Suhrkamp.

Hacke, J. 2011. "Ein Vergessenes Erbe des deutschen Liberalismus: Über Moritz Julius Bonn." *Merkur* 65: 1077–1082.

Hermann, U. 2001. "Der Jude als Feind." *Die Tageszeitung*, February 27.

"Hitlers Eintritt in die Politik und die Reichswehr, Dokument 12 (Adolf Hitler an Adolf Gemlich)." 1959. *Vierteljahrshefte für Zeitgeschichte* 7: 177–227.

Hofmann, H. 1988. "Die deutsche Rechtswissenschaft im Kampf gegen den jüdischen Geist." In *Geschichte und Kultur des Judentums,* ed. K. Müller and K. Wittstadt. Würzburg: Schöningh, 228–240.

Hofmann, H. 1992. *Legitimität gegen Legalität: Der Weg der politischen Philosophie Carl Schmitts,* 2nd ed. Berlin: Duncker & Humblot.

Hürten, H. 1972. *Waldemar Gurian: Ein Zeuge der Krise unserer Welt in der ersten Hälfte des 20. Jahrhunderts.* Mainz: Matthias-Grünewald.

Jabloner, C. 2002. "Raphael Gross, Carl Schmitt und die Juden: Eine deutsche Rechtslehre." *Tel Aviver Jahrbuch für Deutsche Geschichte* xxx: 434–441.

Kalberer, G. 2000. "Der frühe Fall des Juristen Carl Schmitt." *Tages Anzeiger*, December 1.

Kittsteiner, H. D. 2000. "Das entdeckte Arcanum: Raphael Gross über Carl Schmitt und die Juden." *Neue Zürcher Zeitung*, August 2.

Koenen, A. 1995. *Der Fall Carl Schmitt: Sein Aufstieg zum "Kronjuristen des Dritten Reiches".* Darmstadt: Wissenschaftliche Buchgesellschaft.

Korenke, T. 2000. "'…nur Israeliten', Raphael Gross: Carl Schmitt und die Juden: Eine deutsche Rechtslehre." *Scociologia Internationalis* 2: 260–263.

Kuhn, M. 2001. "Carl Schmitt und die Juden." *Schweizerische Juristen-Zeitung*, July 1.

Lehnert, E., and G. Maschke. eds. 2008. *Carl Schmitt und Hans-Dietrich Sander: Werkstatt-Discorsi; Briefwechsel 1967–1981.* Schnellroda: Ed. Antaios.

Maschke, G. 2000. "Der subventionierte Amoklauf, Raphael Gross: Carl Schmitt und die Juden." *Junge Freiheit*, October 20, 16.

Mehring, R. 2009a. *Carl Schmitt: Aufstieg und Fall.* Munich: Beck.

Mehring, R. 2009b. *Die Hamburger Verlegerfamilie Eisler und Carl Schmitt.* Plettenberg: Carl-Schmitt-Förderverein.

Meier, H. 1998. *Carl Schmitt, Leo Strauss und "Der Begriff des Politischen": Zu einem Dialog unter Abwesenden.* Erw. Neuausgabe. Stuttgart: Metzler.

Meinecke, F. 1946. *Die deutsche Katastrophe, Betrachtungen und Erinnerungen.* Wiesbaden: Brockhaus.

Meyer, T. 2000. "Eine Studie von Raphael Gross: 'Carl Schmitt und die Juden.'" *haGalil.com*, 10.12., www.hagalil.com/archiv/2000/12/schmitt.htm (accessed December 7, 2011).

Münkler, H. 2000. "Feinde des Politischen: Raphael Gross über Carl Schmitts Antisemitismus." *Die Zeit*, September 14.

Mußgnug, D. R., and A. Reinthal. 2007. *Briefwechsel Ernst Forsthoff und Carl Schmitt (1926–1974)*. Berlin: Akademie Verlag.

Neumann, V. 1981. "Verfassungstheorie politischer Antipoden: Otto Kirchheimer und Carl Schmitt." *Kritische Justiz* 14: 235–254.

Nippel, W. 2000. "Raphael Gross: Carl Schmitt und die Juden." *H-Soz-u-Kult* 27: 10.

Noack, P. 1993. *Carl Schmitt: Eine Biographie*. Berlin: Propyläen.

Otto, M. 2008. *Von der Eigenkirche zum Volkseigenen Betrieb: Erwin Jacobi (1884–1965)*. Tübingen: Mohr.

Palmier, J.-M. 2009. *Walter Benjamin—Lumpenlicht, Engel und bucklicht Männlein: Ästhetik und Politik bei Walter Benjamin*, trans. H. Brühmann, ed. F. Perrier. Frankfurt: Suhrkamp.

Palzhoff, T., and M. Treml. ed. 2009. *Carl Schmitt und Jacob Taubes: Briefwechsel*. Munich: Fink.

Pralle, U. 2000. "Der unsichtbare Feind: Raphael Gross unternimmt eine erste umfassende Erkundung des Antisemitismus bei Carl Schmitt." *Frankfurter Rundschau*, June 17.

Rennert, K. 1987. *Die "geisteswissenschaftliche" Richtung in der Staatsrechtslehre der Weimarer Republik: Untersuchungen zu Erich Kaufmann, Günther Holstein und Rudolf Smend*. Berlin: Duncker & Humblot.

Rieß, R. ed. 2007. *Carl Schmitt und Ludwig Feuchtwanger: Briefwechsel 1918–1935*. Berlin: Duncker & Humblot.

Robbers, G. 1983. *Hermann Heller: Staat und Kultur*. Baden-Baden: Nomos.

Rumpf, M. 2000. "Raphael Gross: Carl Schmitt und die Juden; Ernst Jünger und Carl Schmitt, Briefe 1930–1983." *zeno: Zeitschrift für Literatur und Sophistik* (November): 95–97.

Schlink, B. 2002. *Vergangenheitsschuld und gegenwärtiges Recht*. Frankfurt: Suhrkamp.

Schmitt, A. 2000. "Raphael Gross demaskiert Carl Schmitts theologisch-politischen Antisemitismus." *literaturkritik.de*, October 10.

Schmitt, C. 1932. *Der Begriff des Politischen*. Berlin: Duncker & Humblot.

Schmitt, C. 1935. "Die Verfassung der Freiheit." *Deutsche Juristenzeitung* 40: 1133–1135.

Schmitt, C. 1936. *Das Judentum in der deutschen Rechtswissenschaft: Ansprachen, Vorträge und Ergebnisse der Tagung der Reichsgruppe Hochschullehrer im NSRB am 3. und 4. Oktober*. Berlin: Deutscher Rechts-Verlag.

Schmitt, C. 1991. *Glossarium: Aufzeichnungen aus den Jahren 1947–1951*. Berlin: Duncker & Humblot.

Schmitt, C. 2000. *Jugendbriefe: Briefschaften an seine Schwester Auguste 1905–1913*, ed. E. Hüsmert. Berlin: Akademie Verlag.

Schmitt, C. 2003. *Tagebücher Oktober 1912 bis Februar 1915*, ed. E. Hüsmert. Berlin: Akademie Verlag.

Schmitt, C. 2005. *Carl Schmitt: Die Militärzeit 1915–1919; Tagebuch Februar bis Dezember 1915, Aufsätze und Materialien*, ed. E. Hüsmert and G. Giesler. Berlin: Akademie Verlag.

Schmitt, C. 2010. *Tagebücher 1930–1934*, ed. W. Schuller. Berlin: Akademie Verlag.

Schmitz, A., and M. Lepper. eds. 2007. *Hans Blumenberg und Carl Schmitt: Briefwechsel 1971–1978 und weitere Materialien*. Frankfurt: Suhrkamp.

Schwab, G. 1970. *The Challenge of the Exception: An Introduction to the Political Ideas of Carl Schmitt between 1921 and 1936*. Berlin: Duncker & Humblot.

Schwering, M. 2000. "Studie über Carl Schmitt: Ein unversöhnlicher Antisemit; Raphael Gross untersucht die Haltung des Staatsrechtlers zum Judentum." *Kölner Stadt-Anzeiger*, November 9.

Sieg, U. 2001. "Carl Schmitt und die Juden." *Zeitschrift für Geschichtswissenschaft* 49: 268–270.

Söllner, A. 1992. "'Kronjurist des Dritten Reiches': Das Bild Carl Schmitts in den Schriften der Emigranten." *Jahrbuch für Antisemitismforschung* 1: 191–216.

Sombart, N. 1984. *Jugend in Berlin, 1933–1945: Ein Bericht*. Munich: Hanser.

Specht, H. 2006. *Die Feuchtwangers: Familie, Tradition und jüdisches Selbstverständnis*. Göttingen: Wallstein.

Taubes, J. 1987. *Ad Carl Schmitt: Gegenstrebige Fügung*. Berlin: Merve.

van Laak, D. and I. Villinger. eds. 1993. *Nachlaß Carl Schmitt: Verzeichnis des Bestandes im Nordrhein-Westfälischen Hauptstaatsarchiv*. Siegburg.

Villinger, I., and A. Jaser. eds. 2007. *Briefwechsel Gretha Jünger und Carl Schmitt (1934–1953)*. Berlin: Akademie Verlag.

Wirz, T. 2000. "Ein Fall von reiner Rechtsleere: Einfach unklug; Raphael Gross über Carl Schmitt und die Juden." *Frankfurter Allgemeine Zeitung*, July 31.

Zarusky, J. 2000. "Opportunistischer Held: Der Staatsrechtler Carl Schmitt hinterließ ein zwiespältiges Werk." *Süddeutsche Zeitung*, October 30.

CHAPTER 4

SCHMITT'S DIARIES

JOSEPH W. BENDERSKY

INTRODUCTION

In *Ex Captivitate Salus*, written during his internment after World War II, Carl Schmitt falsely characterizes his personality as "slow, silent, and easy-going" (1950, 10).[1] Those portions of his personal diaries published over the last decade belie such representation. They reveal a historical figure whose inner essence was often a tumultuous cauldron of tormenting anxieties, emotional outbursts, and crudely expressed prejudices. Here was a personality whose doubts, fears, and self-conscious inferiority was inseparable from his intellectual arrogance. Inextricably intertwined with these were the extraordinary erudition and brilliant creative insights for which he had long been known. Indeed, these diaries expose a far more complex, contradictory, and nuanced person and thinker than was ever alluded to in interpretations of him before the availability of this documentation. As such, these long awaited sources have exceeded most expectations in their value to understanding Schmitt as well as various facets of German history throughout the twentieth century. However, until recently these diaries have guarded their secrets from his most intimate friends as well as from those with control of and access to his *Nachlass*. For Schmitt wrote these in Gabelsberger stenography, a nineteenth-century form of shorthand, decipherable to a rare and diminishing few. Even those who have published some of these diaries to date do not know what the thousands of pages yet to be transcribed might reveal.

The chronological breadth of the entire diary collection (published and unpublished) itself is exceptional, extending (with significant gaps) from 1912 to 1979. The earliest extant diaries (late 1912 to early 1915), covering the beginnings of his career as a law clerk to his entry into the army, are available in print (2003). Their revelations about his inner most thoughts and personal relationships, like his intellectual grappling with religion and the cultural crisis of the modern world, speak to the very essence of the man and thinker. Similar insights emerge from his published diaries of 1915 to July 1916, the first years of his military service, where his anti-Prussian, antiwar, and even anti-German sentiments converge with his other anxieties (2005). Both of these volumes are also important in documenting his early attitudes toward and relationships with Jews, a highly contentious aspect of the man and his work. After such crucial revelations, the absence of diaries from mid-1916 to 1921 is truly disappointing. Fortunately, the limited existing diary entries of 1921–1922, related documents from his *Nachlass*, and the almost daily diary entries of 1923–1924, are scheduled for publication as a single volume (2014a; 2014b).[2] What these diary entries might disclose regarding his evolving ideas on parliamentary government and presidential power are anxiously awaited, as are indications of his general attitudes toward Weimar. The partial prepublication documents from this period made available to this author reinforce the image of a cultural pessimist and staunch anticapitalist and elaborate his complicated sentiments about Jews. Schmitt's diaries during the peak of Weimar recovery, stability, and hope (1925–1929) are not accessible to researchers; their publication is unlikely in the near future.

Among all Schmitt's published diaries, those corresponding to the collapse of Weimar and the Nazi seizure and consolidation of power hold a place of distinction. This volume includes not only his detailed diary entries from 1930 to 1934 but also relevant parallel notes of these years gathered from other parts of the *Nachlass* and the brief but invaluable notations in his pocket diary of January to August 1934 (Schmitt 2010). Here, his earlier religious preoccupations had clearly dissipated to a notable degree, while his antisemitism heightened. Otherwise, there is remarkable consistency between these private notations, his published theories, and his own postwar version of his engagement with the presidential system between 1930 and early 1933. Equally significant, his despairing reactions to Adolf Hitler and National Socialism, like his fear of the very Nazi institutions in which he served, make these particular diaries essential reading for anyone assessing Schmitt and the early "Third Reich." Nonetheless, attempts at understanding his Nazi collaboration thereafter, and their subsequent purge of him in 1936, will receive no clarification from Schmitt's private notations, since another serious gap exists in his diaries between 1934 and 1939. That Schmitt's *Nachlass* does contain diary entries from the crucial war years of 1939 to 1945 is of little immediate consolation to scholars because there are no plans currently to transcribe and publish these from their Gabelsberger format. Neither is the transcription and publication of Schmitt's postwar diaries (approximately from the end of the war to 1979) projected for some time. It is not known whether the various gaps in these diaries mean he interrupted his diary transcribing for one reason or another or whether what might have existed perished when his home was destroyed by a Berlin bombing raid. There is no indication that he might have purged entire diaries from these particular years. Given the candidness of the voluminous entries that did survive, it is unlikely he had any inclination to do so.

Schmitt's only postwar private notations available had already been printed in 1991 under the title *Glossarium*. This first publication of his private thoughts was facilitated by the fact that these notations were the only ones not written in Gabelsberger. Though often made daily, Schmitt's *Glossarium* entries are quite distinct from those in his diaries of earlier years because they provide mostly commentaries on present and past events rather than insights into his daily experiences. They are also often scattered retrospectives, lacking the continuity and coherence of the diaries proper. As the first documentation of Schmitt's privately expressed antisemitism, they were shocking; so, too, was his attitude of victimization. Nonetheless, the image of Schmitt that surfaces in these quite embittered postwar utterances must now be considered in light of what the recently published earlier diaries reveal about his complex personality, relationships, attitudes, and ideas as he actually experienced life and events from youth in the *Kaiserreich* through the peak of his career in the 1930s. As the following narrative and analyses will clearly show, there is often a stark and meaningful contrast between the images of the man and thinker reflected in *Glossarium* and that in the other diaries. In other ways, however, these earlier diaries confirm that his *Glossarium* commentaries on the end of Weimar and various aspects of the Nazi experience were not ex post facto rationalizations, in pursuit of exculpation or vindication. In light of his earlier private notations, many of his postwar musings on historical developments now appear to be fairly accurate descriptions of his political thinking in the 1930s, as he analyzed events unfolding around him.

Thus far, the diaries have proven to be a biographer's dream and a documentary windfall that no Schmitt scholar can ignore. Parts of this diary evidence have enriched the narrative in Reinhard Mehring's (2009) recent Schmitt biography and made many of its interpretations more credible. This documentation is also as central to scholars in political and legal thought as it is to historians. While they have more universal influence and applicability, he conceived of many of his core ideas in relationship to the pressing political and legal issues in the various stages of his creativity. Indeed, throughout his lifetime, and in the decades since, his theories have, more often than not, actually been interpreted on the basis of his presumed stand on such contemporary questions or political situations. In themselves, especially when reinforced by an abundance of other revelatory documentation from the Schmitt *Nachlass*, these diaries present a fundamental challenge to many old and more recent interpretations of Schmitt. Among the no longer tenable are, for example, those arguing that Schmitt's theories were aimed at the establishment of a *Führerstaat* that came to fruition in the Nazi *Machtergreifung* (Fijalkowski 1958) or that his ideas committed him to welcoming Hitler (Dyzenhaus 1998; Scheuerman 1999). Certainly, the Marxist interpretation of Schmitt as the theorist of bourgeois capitalist hegemony from Weimar, through the "Third Reich," into the Federal Republic must now forever be cast into the dustbin of history (Maus 1976; 1998). Interpreters of Schmitt as an advocate of the Conservative Revolutionary movement will find no support in these documents, while much of this evidence cast critical doubt on such contentions (Sontheimer 1962; Mohler 1972; Herf 1984). And despite disclosures of the young Schmitt's intense religiosity, the diaries essentially discount any probability that he was a *Reichstheologe* seeking a Christian political order (Koenen 1995) or that he was a Christian eschatological and apocalyptic thinker (Meier 1995; 1998; Lilla 1997; Hooker 2009). Moreover, the diaries now categorically refute interpretations of Schmitt's antisemitism as an opportunistic compromise limited to the Nazi years (Schwab 1970; Bendersky 1983); they demand an entire comprehensive reassessment of this subject. Nevertheless, the available diaries do not substantiate (while reinforcing skepticism about) efforts to place Schmitt's political and legal theory primarily in the context of the Jewish Question (Gross 2007).

Beyond their unprecedented contribution to understanding Schmitt personally, and illuminating certain aspects of his life and thinking, the diaries fall short, however, as a witness to the momentous historical events he experienced. They certainly capture the tenor of the times, disclosing in particular a conservative cultural perspective on, and reaction to, a multiplicity of factors and developments in the dynamically changing modern world. But their style and content make them less informative in the broader sense than one has come to expect given the enriching window to history provided by other recently published diaries. In this respect, Schmitt's diaries are quite distinct in nature, and as historical sources, from Victor Klemperer's *I Will Bear Witness: A Diary of the Nazi Years* (1998) or *Advocate for the Doomed: The Diaries and Papers of James G. McDonald* (2007). In contrast, Schmitt's diaries are typically very personal, with their limited observations on events and historical figures always filtered through his perspectives, emotions, and thoughts. Despite the occasional insightful remark, we receive, for example, no portrayals of the rise of National Socialism, even though this event remained a significant context for Schmitt and his theories.

Nonetheless, as personal diaries, Schmitt's are in their very essence exceedingly rare. Their value cannot be overstated. Other diarists might be more informative on events around them, but few reveal themselves, their lives, their innermost feelings and thoughts with such naked candor as does the private Schmitt in his entries. What is eminently clear throughout these diaries regarding the intellectual, cultural, and political world with which Schmitt interacted is that he saw himself as an isolated loner, a voice crying in the wilderness, whose forewarnings went unheeded with disastrous consequences. Readers will have to judge whether this self-characterization is convincing and his claim to such insights is justifiable.

Youthful Idealism, Cultural Pessimism, and War

The opening pages of the twenty-four-year-old Schmitt's diary in October 1912 set the tone for his entries over the next several years. They are characterized by intense love and friendship, intellectual arrogance and personal doubt, and a pervasive existential *Angst*. Aside from struggling desperately to survive economically and establish a legal career, the young Schmitt is preoccupied with his emotionally demanding inner demons as well as his intensely solipsistic perspectives on his relationships with others and the world in general. That he meticulously detailed so much of this in daily entries that would amount to one-half to one printed page is in itself revealing of his self-absorption. Thus, his diary from October 1912 to February 1915 (2003) offers a window into Schmitt's emotions, thoughts, and perspectives rather than any illuminating political or societal observations of the broader world around him.

During these years, the public Schmitt appeared to be a brilliant young scholar clearly on the path to professional success. The breadth of his reading and erudition—from jurisprudence to literature, philosophy, and theology—was exceptional, even for the fin-de-siècle *Bildungsbürgertum*, about which he had coauthored a parody. He had already published two well-received books in legal theory, and while serving his probationary period as a law clerk in Düsseldorf he published *Der Wert des Staates und die Bedeutung des Einzelnen* (*The Value of the State and the Purpose of the Individual*; 1914), which could be considered his first very abstract excursion into political theory. Yet these publications, like his diary entries, are devoid of any inkling of the specific political issues and events of Imperial Germany or international affairs. The young Schmitt resembled the often-criticized apolitical intellectual of that era. Indeed, while conducting the practical business of a law clerk, his heart and thoughts were of those of abstract intellectual musing and passionate yearning of love and lust reminiscent of early nineteenth-century romantics.

The object of Schmitt's romantic obsession was Pawla (Pauline) Dorotić, his fiancé and soon wife. "I am compelled to love you, Cari....I can't do anything, or feel anything without you," he wrote almost daily in a compulsive style of adulation. It was an emotional love intermingled with strong physical sexual drives: "hunger is the voice of the physiological conscience, sexual love of the biological conscience" (2003, 37). It was a sexual aspect of being that led him to record his ejaculations in the same manner he noted other significant events of his life. It would also be reflected in his future extramarital affairs and visits to prostitutes. The young Schmitt clearly grappled with understanding women, reading Freud and Otto Weininger for solace and guidance but to no avail. His naively adored Cari, as it turned out, who was an over-thirty Viennese-born Serbian dancer of dubious "old noble Croation" lineage. For some time, however, he remained elated by the very thought of her "indescribable charm and elegance" (98).

Schmitt's illusionary visions and relationships with Cari could not compensate for his inherent insecurity and "horrible *Angst* of men and the world" (2003, 124). He vacillates between occasional euphoria over accomplishments or joy in personal relationships and a depressing loneliness. Longing for meaning and psychological consolation, he feels that in his "horrible torment and mental anguish there is no one with whom [he] can speak" (157–158). He described himself as "a poor, helpless, despondent good-for-nothing," who at night cries out to Jesus, the Blessed Virgin, and even unknown gods. Though occasionally panicked by fears of death, he seriously entertained thoughts of suicide. It was, he exclaimed, a "self-destructive *Angst*" (158).

Schmitt's was a crisis of faith and conscience, of ideals and worldly realities, all aggravated by personal insecurity, perhaps inferiority. The search for security that many would later identify as an underlying principle of his political and legal theory was far more than a reaction to the decades of crises and cataclysms following World War I. It was intrinsic to his personality and mental framework long before the outbreak of war. He was not a heroic figure challenging the world but was someone who recoiled from it, seeking escape or protection from the pressures, dangers, and vicissitudes of life. Probably the most reoccurring phrase throughout his diaries is *Angst vor* (fear of, or worried about; 2003, 26, 124, 129). Such a mindset of doubt and fear is not conducive to optimism in political thought

Although the young Schmitt displayed little interest in prewar political issues and conflicts, he was intensely engaged with the cultural and intellectual crises of the modern world. His diary notations epitomize cultural despair. He read Fjodor Dostojevski; he profoundly identified with Sören Kierkegaard's concept of *Angst*. What would culminate in Schmitt's 1916 book *Theodor Däublers "Nordlicht"* had its roots in his earlier reading of the expressionist poet, whose critique of modernity reflected his own disillusionment and despair. Schmitt's subsequent explication of *Nordlicht* described the collision between a relativistic, materialistic, mechanical world of science, technology, and capitalism and a spiritual dimension of eternal values, inherently valuable human beings, and enduring meaning. But his earlier diaries are replete with more visceral scattered expressions of the same sentiments and lamentations. "The age is ripe for dictatorship," as the people merely want to amuse themselves to kill time through frivolity and idleness (2003, 64). "We make out of the equality of all men a foul vitality and demand equality among nations instead of equality of rights. We see in the *Rechtsstaat* a means to undisturbed feeding and prostitutes" (64). The domination of capitalism will collapse upon itself because we lack a purpose: "Acquiring money for the sake of money is senseless" (64). Indeed, "renouncement of anthropomorphism is a renunciation of human nature; the very age of humanity prides itself on destroying everything anthropomorphic in every human form" (91). As such, when mathematics becomes the ideal form of human thought "the result is the machine, which destroys the human countenance.... In the name of humanity one destroys the very image of the human being" (91).

Yet that modern world and the knowledge about nature, men, and society it produced clearly had an impact on Schmitt's religious faith, as did his own intellectual maturation and worldly experiences. Although he would remain for his entire life strongly identified, sentimentally and culturally, with Catholicism, he was already suffering a contentious ambiguity with regard to its dogma and institutions. He still turned to Bible reading for solace in difficult times. After a Christmas mass, he could declare a "renewed belief in the importance of the Catholic Church" (2003, 131). Elsewhere, he would lament that he "could believe in everything, and believe in nothing" (157). He asked, "Where should I flee to the Catholic Church; I cannot do that," any more than he could turn to the "great Dalai Lama of Tibet or to a Mexican god" (157). His experiences with the worldly church exacerbated the existential crisis of faith. "There is no imitation of Christ in the juristic sense," and it was "outrageous" that the papacy legalized its own claim to such." Even more contemptuously, he chastised in the Renaissance tone of Erasmus, "if men had a trace of spirituality and saw the palaces of bishops and comfortable home of priests, they would roar with laughter or rage" (267) when these well-nourished inhabitants preached poverty and designated themselves the councilors of Christ. He was certainly no advocate for the political Catholicism and the Catholic Center Party to which his mentor in Düsseldorf, Hugo am Zehnhoff, was devoted. "This morning we went to church," Schmitt noted, "where a dreadful Catholic cleric preached politics from the pulpit, so that we left the church full of indignation. Cari said: he had a profane attitude" (104). Completely absent in Schmitt's early inner religious turmoil is any evidence for those interpreting him as a *Reichstheologe* whose later works could be explained in terms of a politics motivated by, and directed toward, Christian theology. Likewise lacking are any examples or insinuations of his later political and legal thought being understood in terms of a Christian eschatology in which the search for a *katechon* (or bulwark against the modern world) is the key concept.

Throughout all of this, a deep-seated sincerity pervades his very self-conscious struggles over cultural values and a world that disappoints his faith and his idealism. Similarly, within his own field of jurisprudence, this young scholar grappled for years to sustain his neo-idealist legal philosophy against the predominance of legal positivism. Legal positivists had abandoned eternal universal norms, such as those embodied in natural law theory. To them, law was the creation of the sovereign state, which recognized no higher authority or norm. It was an implicit affirmation of law as an extension of state power or of those who controlled it, even within a democratic system of self-government. In contrast, neo-idealist jurists argued that *Recht* (right law, higher law) existed prior to the state and independent of its power. As a Catholic still immersed in an inner conflict over transcendence, Schmitt found guidance in the neo-Kantianism of scholars such as Heinrich Rickert. Throughout December 1912, Schmitt intellectually wrestled with the question of the origin, nature, and concrete realization of *Recht*. "It is a great mistake," he wrote, "to believe *Recht = Macht*" (2003, 60). Ultimately, he concluded that "*Recht* must exist before the world and exist after it" (60). Two years later, these ideas matured into his book *Der Wert des Staates und die Bedeutung des Einzelnen* (1914), in which he argued that the value of the state emanated not from its sovereign authority or power but rather from its purpose of transforming this transcendent *Recht* into a worldly phenomenon.

Schmitt did not mindlessly adhere to neo-idealist jurisprudence any more than he had to Catholicism, as there were indications of doubt that would lead in the direction of the proclivities of his future political and legal thought. While reflecting on Rickert, Schmitt wondered whether "each definition rested upon a value judgment" (2003, 60). There are even inklings of the future Hobbessian anthropology underlying his later pessimistic political philosophy. He invoked *homo homini lupus* in criticizing Thomas and Heinrich Mann. And before the outbreak of war, he remarked: "I see only evil and vulgarity in the world, perhaps because within myself there is so much evil and vulgarity" (161). "Nothing is more comprehensible and appealing to me than the opinion of Machiavelli. If all men in the world were good, it would be a depravity to lie and deceive. If, however, obviously everything is only the mob and rabble, it would be stupid to be noble and decent. According to this theory, the good, disillusioned man, speaks only of the indignation of a noble soul against the blind, uneducable, irrefutable and impregnable vulgarity, which everyone who stands in the world can observe around him every day and every hour" (163). Moreover, there is already in 1915 a foreshadowing of the devastating critique of political romanticism as "subjective occasionalism," when he recognized the "characteristic intrinsic to romanticism [as] the incapacity to objectivity" (298).

Amid all of his anxiety and alienation, Schmitt found consolation not only in his beloved Cari but equally in his close friendship with Fritz Eisler. It would be difficult to find a more intimate relationship than what is revealed in the diaries of the intellectual and deeply personal interaction of these young men. Schmitt and Eisler, oldest son of a Hungarian-born Jewish publisher in Hamburg, shared the same *Doktorvater* at Strassburg. Thereafter, they corresponded continuously (sometimes daily), as well as visited and traveled, where they occasionally roomed together. They walked and talked for hours, with Schmitt truly cherishing these meetings for which he often anxiously waited and then exclaimed his joy. He depicted Eisler as a marvelous, very decent, and principled person, with whom Schmitt shared his cultural pessimism. Unlike the criticism and sarcasm Schmitt directed at so many others, there was between them a kind of comfortable, often delightful true friendship (2003, 99). They coauthored *Schattenrisse*, a parody of German intellectuals and the *gebildete* bourgeoisie (Schmitt 1913). In 1928, Schmitt dedicated his classic study *Constitutional Theory* to Eisler (Bendersky 1983, 227). Into old age he dreamt of Eisler. After Fritz volunteered at the very outbreak of war, he visited Schmitt in Düsseldorf in September 1914 and, Schmitt worried, lest this "dear, wonderful guy" (2003, 200) would be killed in action. Within a few weeks, he was emotionally shattered by the news that his "dear friend" had fallen. His diary entries capture the anguish of the moment: "It is outrageous. I cry, I scream, I no longer see or hear. It is inconceivable. Oh God, it cannot be.... *Der liebe Eisler, er ist tot.* A Corpse.... It is maddening. I can no longer live. Life is so absurd.... What does it all mean? Am I going mad?... Eisler had sat there... making notes in his diary, cut his nails, combed and cut his hair; and now he is dead.... Why am I still living?" The sadness lingered for a long time, and as Schmitt and Cari withdrew from others and life's "superficialities" he cried himself to sleep (220–223).

Out of this tragedy grew Schmitt's equally intimate, longtime friendship with Eisler's younger brother Georg, who provided him with emotional comfort and intellectual stimulation. Through letters and visits that delighted Schmitt, they sustained their bond. The Eisler family was Schmitt's entry into the world of assimilated European Jews, with which he remained associated professionally and personally until his death. In many ways, Schmitt crossed the German–Jewish cultural divide more often, intimately, and extensively than most professionals and intellectuals. But he was neither culturally blind nor neutral in his attitudes toward Jews. He carried into adulthood the biases of his social background and Catholic cultural milieu, often projected through his own personality quirks as they affected his attitude toward people in general. The few diary references to Jews, dispersed over several years, involve for the most part brief comments on the behavior of individuals or groups specifically identified as "Jews"—respectable and detestable. To him, "Georg is a wonderful guy, a gifted, intelligent Jew" (2003, 304), but "those Jews" who "falsify" artistic currents and "distorted the concept of man" enrage Schmitt (245). In the controversy over whether Schmitt's views on Jews could be interpreted as antisemitism or anti-Judaism, such expressions strongly suggest the former. Nonetheless, his attitudes do not constitute an ideological antisemitism. Nor can one detect any resonance of antisemitism in his theoretical frameworks or publications of this period. He discussed his ideas and books with Fritz and Georg, who found them inspiring, and Jewish editors published his works. Both the men and women in the Eisler family greatly impressed him. After spending Christmas 1914 with the Eisler family in Hamburg, he noted, "I began to respect the Jews" (282). Acknowledging the "Jewish-complex," others attributed to him, he sought discussion with Jews because "there are more educated men among the Jews than among the Christians" (226).

While disclosing the tension between prejudice and intellectual respect, even understanding, these early diaries are nonetheless frustrating for those scholars trying to grasp and explain Schmitt and the Jewish Question. We learn only that he did discuss the subject with Fritz and Georg (rarely with others) as one issue among various topics such as literature and philosophy. He read an unidentified book about Jews that he and Fritz had purchased. In the end, the few brief intriguing references to Jews raise more questions than they answer old ones: "After breakfast we both went to the library, Georg worked diligently on an article about Judaism. He is a thorough, scholarly, talented man.... He read 'psychology.'... Astounded and shocked by the power of Jews. Psychoanalysis is the purest expression of Judaism" (2003, 314–315).

Even before Fritz's battlefield death, the war had turned already emotionally tumultuous Schmitt into a higher state of confusion and anxiety. Particularly noteworthy is the complete absence of any diary observations of public or political events—domestic or international—before the assassination of Archduke Franz Ferdinand. Indeed, the lack of political knowledge or sophistication is astounding for such a brilliant, widely read mind. His entries are totally devoid of references to causation, conflicting interests, or any kind of political explanation for the outbreak or continuation of the war. Never sharing any of the nationalistic euphoria spreading across Europe, his emotions initially swayed between panic over the Russian invasion in the East to exclaiming: "better to lose this war than to win it" (2003, 175). One finds a vague type of political consistency only in his emerging strident anti-Prussian and antiwar sentiments. Otherwise, he remains fearful for his own survival and that of his friends and brother "Jup" in the trenches as well as for the welfare of his Serbian fiancé/wife—an enemy alien. He was relieved when on mobilization he was dispatched to garrison duty in Munich. Aside from his nascent anthropological pessimism nothing suggests a talent for (even slight interest in) political theory, or a future as one of the twentieth century's most incisive and contentious analysts of war, let alone the originator of a friend/enemy theory. His last entry in this diary was a lamentation over the "thousands of men dying" in the trenches and a plea to God or anyone to help him (320).

FROM THE MILITARY TO THE UNIVERSITY IN THE 1920S

The diaries Schmitt wrote during his early wartime service from 1915 to mid-1916 revolved around the intricate triad of Cari, Georg Eisler, and the state as represented by the military. Although most entries retained their solipsistic nature, with significant events ignored, the notable exception was when he lashed out against the war and the "Prussian spirit; this creaking, dashing, completely intellectualless and heartless machine" (2003, 173; 2005, 56), which dominated Germany and transformed men into machines. Meanwhile, the refuge he had found in his new bride turned to misery, leaving Eisler as his sustaining consolation

The young Schmitt was a very humane, sentimental cosmopolitan, who decried, "The barbarism of the Prussians and law clerks, of the moneyed *Mittelstand* with its artistic interests and its windbags, [which were] much more vulgar than the naïve barbarism of the lowliest Slavs" (2003, 175). He could take pity on the French, Slavs, Czechs, and Italians, because they had a kind of tearfulness and innocence but had none for the English or Germans. As the war raged, he contemplated fleeing to Spain or Russia. The various security, geopolitical, or idealistic justifications for war, including the defense of higher *Kultur* touted by prominent intellectuals such as Thomas Mann, never resonated with him. Soaring casualties only heightened his cynicism: "For what reason are the soldiers at the front?... Week after week they lay in the trenches, thousands of decent men are dying in action" so that others can "continue playing the piano...or speculating in cotton" (243). It was a "loathsome war," a "frightful nightmare," which men had to be "crazy" to fight. "For what? For *Vaterland*" (2005, 70, 89, 91, 105–106). Schmitt was an individualist struggling against larger historical, institutional, and societal forces. "I was crazy with rage about the Prussians, militarism.... How horrible it is for an individual to sit within such a prison" (77). He chastised the state for the "cynical," "utilitarian" way it crushed individuals for "miserable and indifferent purposes" (106, 130). The war had consumed thousands of soldiers and left him helpless "against this power apparatus" a callous German state he depicted as a "terrifying, grizzly monster" (2003, 209–210, 320). He now regretted the position he had taken in *Der Wert des Staates und die Bedeutung des Einzelnen*, fearing that the cost of "Germany becoming the land of righteousness would be the destruction of the individual." Moreover, he no longer believed the Catholic Church could serve the role of moral arbiter he had attributed to it in that book, because it lacked "real power" (2005, 24). He wished he had the courage to sacrifice his life as a "demonstration against this awful nonsense" (99).

Yet, agonizingly, he felt trapped into serving a state and war effort he detested. In military intelligence headquarters, his fellow officers laughed at letters to the pope from poor farmers inquiring about peace. Even more ironic, his primary duties involved surveillance and analysis of pacifists and left radicals, especially as these forces worked through neutral Switzerland. He felt privately indignant but still helpless when he had to designate rumors of peace in a German newspaper as "dangerous to the security of the Reich" (2005, 99, 138–139). Or when his office had to back the military authorities in their political intrigues with the chancellor over annexationist policies, which he must have known would prolong the war. Schmitt's wartime predicament foreshadowed similar quandaries disclosed by his diaries from the early 1930s. There, too, one could detect familiar tensions between his own preferences and that of the power apparatuses he served during the Papen government in 1932 and years of collaboration with the early "Third Reich." Although Schmitt continued to publish privately on religion and philosophy, insisting that *Recht* remained essential to the execution of *Macht*, his military duties provided his first excursion into the duplicitous realities of international and party politics. Here sincere pacifist and antiwar movements were cynically manipulated by enemies who sought victory not peace, while radical leftists exploited peace issues as instruments of socialist revolution (393–399).

During these years, his marriage also became a "living hell," with him sarcastically exclaiming: "military and marriage, two splendid institutions" (2005, 23, 90, 120). While still caring for his wife, her hysterics and mistreatment of him became personally unbearable and professionally embarrassing. At points, he contemplated suicide. He found emotional and cerebral refuge only in Georg Eisler with whom he remained in close contact through letters and visits. Next to his own relatives, Schmitt was closest to the Eisler family that had also continuously provided him with financial assistance since 1912. His few entries about Jews remained vague and contradictory, being neither political nor religious nor cultural. He raged against "racial mysticism" and "Wagnerism" (176). "One attempts to imagine an intellectual Germany without Jews," he wrote, "the publisher Lehmann, a few major generals and university professors, mining directors as prophets of the intellectual Germany" (178).

The absence of diaries from mid-1916 to 1921 is unfortunate. Not only did Schmitt write two of his most important works—*Politische Romantik* (1919) and *Die Diktatur* (1921)—during this period, but he experienced the radicalism and violence of the Bavarian Soviet Republic in Munich in 1919, which significantly affected his perspectives on and reactions to communism for the rest of his life. Those documents that do exist from 1921 to 1924 are a mixture of standard diary entries, interspersed letter contents, and introspective commentaries ranging from God to capitalism. They have been transcribed from the Gabelsberger original and are in preparation for publication. Included in this publication will be the diaries from 1923–1924 with their almost daily entries. Unfortunately, the 1923–1924 diaries were not yet available for examination from the archives. They could contain significant material and insights related to his critique of parliamentary government (Schmitt 1985) as well as to the origin and nature of his thoughts on presidential emergency powers in an *Ausnahmezustand* (1924). Likewise inaccessible from the archives are the diaries from 1925 to 1929, a defining stage in his movement away from political Catholicism and toward the Hobbesian realism of his seminal friend/enemy concept. It is also the phase in which his legal thinking coalesced into a coherent theory in his *Constitutional Theory* (2008). Although no date has been scheduled for their publication, these important diaries of the late 1920s will probably amount to 500–600 printed pages. The following is thus based upon the limited diary entries of 1921–1922 and related notes and documents through 1924 (2014a; 2014b).

As his marriage disintegrated toward annulment, he had a passionate affair with the Australian student Kathleen Murray, the subject of the letters in these documents, before falling in love with his second wife, Duška Todorović. Unlike Cari, these women often served as the conduit through which he expressed intellectual musings, particularly concerning religion and Catholicism. But his effusive enunciations of longing and love were just as soppy. Looking over his diaries, he conceded how dependent he had been on women. Though less frequently noted, his anxiety and depression remained as intense as ever. He was a self-proclaimed lost, isolated, and lonely individual fearful of all kinds of people, who still contemplated suicide. He felt helpless against what he believed was this family heritage in his blood (2014a, 25).

His cultural pessimism likewise endured, as he still sought solace in Dostojevski and Kierkegaard. His antipathy toward capitalism and economic modernization became more explicit. Behind the scenes the industrialists and bankers of the economic giants (England, France, and Germany) controlled world politics and economies. He held capitalism responsible for major misfortunes, while his "hatred" of industrialization heightened as he watched its incessant destruction of nature as well as of "human relationships." Momentum, machines, statistics, quantification, and money represented secular gods. While displaying no sympathy for the proletariat, he criticized the modern state as an "empty apparatus" of the bourgeoisie and military. The nationality principle and economics were mere instruments through which this "vampire" state sucked the blood out of both nationality and the economy, causing their deaths. He feared that out of this dissolutionment was emerging a new "age of concentration," as the disintegrating and bohemian gave way to "fascism, discipline, authority" (2014a, 47, 110).

Little is revealed about the origin and nature of his political and legal theory, though he attested he writes against positivism, romanticism, and the enemies of Catholicism. A few passages exist relative to his incipient ideas on sovereignty and the *Ausnahmezustand*. Otherwise, the few manifestations of his political proclivities are suggestive but too brief for analysis: a sarcastic poem on the "majority principle"; the sad impression made by a "ridiculous demonstration" for the defense of the republic; feeling deceived by democracy. More so, he condemned racism and romanticism as "back to nature" frauds (2013a, 128). In 1923, he noted: "Hitler is a hysteric" (93).

In these years, where Schmitt (1996b) conceived of *Roman Catholicism and Political Form*, he both avowed the truth of Catholicism and agonized over his beliefs. In particular, deep devotion to belief, prayer, and ritual pervaded his correspondence with his new beloved, Kathleen Murray, to the extent that Catholicism comprised an important part of their relationship. God and the spiritual realm retained their importance for him; he contrasted this aspect of Catholicism with the worldly orientation of Protestantism. He attended church and read the Bible. Nonetheless, as in his earlier years, Catholicism represented not dogma or an eschatological historical movement but a legacy of law, social order, meaningful identifications and traditions, and a humanity far greater than that of the secular humanists. The overall tone was consistent with the strong moral orientation of his wartime thoughts and the defense of Western civilization and culture he attributed to the Church in *Roman Catholicism and Political Form*. Over time, though, doubts continued to surface: "God is suddenly very far from me" (2014a, 46). "It would be ludicrous to believe," he anguished, "that I am a Christian…I am a skeptic." Then, he seeks God but was impatient; his "atheistic hour" is early morning (57).

During these early years as a professor in Bonn, Schmitt's maintained his intimate personal and emotional contact with Georg Eisler, "my only hope." In a brief entry on pride and humility, Schmitt wrote that "Eisler is also humble, but only so far as he does not have to give up his pride.… How can I hate the Prussians, the Jews, everyone"

(2014a, 9). One day they walked through Frankfurt in search of a synagogue. By this time, Schmitt's close Jewish relationships included his former colleague in Munich, Moritz Julius Bonn, and his publisher Ludwig Feuchtwanger, both of whom furnished him with personal and professional assistance at various points. He held both in very high regard, though more personally for Bonn than intellectually. These circles widened by the inclusion of colleagues in the law faculty at the University of Bonn, particularly the prominent jurist Erich Kaufmann and the young Albert Hensel. These were quite collegial friendships that involved regular socializing, sharing ideas, and discussing their works; they appeared quite receptive to Schmitt's ideas. Although Schmitt eventually began to develop reservations about Kaufmann (very self-centered), he remained fond of Hensel. Yet even when Schmitt severely criticized these colleagues in his private notes, he never referred to their Jewish heritage. Mrs. Kaufmann would attend Schmitt's lectures into the 1930s (2014b, 46, 58–77, 92). The tone and substance of his characterizations of these men, like his relationships with them, differed completely from what he would note in future diaries, where he would vehemently depict Bonn and Kaufmann as Jewish enemies out to get him. And despite the antisemitic undertones of the assassination of Walter Rathenau in 1922, Schmitt suffered a "horrific shock" that this unfortunate, "cultured, splendid" man had been murdered (79).

Consistent with his apparently lifelong conflicting and complex attitudes toward Jews, however, there are scattered throughout these pages the occasional observation suggestive about his existing or evolving thoughts on Jews in society and intellectual life. In an aphoristic note using the automobile, railroad, and propeller as metaphors for the destruction of the organic by the mechanistic world, he compares the elastic function of rubber to the role of the modern Jew. Far more significant for current debates over Schmitt and the Jewish Question were his passing categorizations in 1923 of the theories of Georg Lukács and Freud as revealing the psychology of these "Jewish" thinkers and their "own souls." He rejected both historical materialism and psychoanalysis as similar "ludicrous mythologies" attempting to reduce human relations to questions of consciousness. Lacking in security, Jews, Schmitt alleged, lived only through the contracts they can conclude; they feel they can use the work created only by others. In a further allusion to the often invoked charge of Jewish proclivity toward abstract thinking and logic as opposed to the concrete and culturally embedded, he remarked that "Viennese Jews" such as Kelsen "think essentially in formal juristic" ways—"the inventor is not the one who makes something but the one who registers the invention" (2014a, 70, 73, 110).

AGONY AND TEMPTATION
DURING THE NAZI YEARS

Schmitt's detailed diaries (and parallel notes) from 1930 to 1934 rank among the most important archival evidence regarding crucial facets of his life, thought, and political involvements. It was a period in which he published some of his most influential works, reached the peak of his academic career, attracted public attention as advisor to the presidential system, and began his collaboration with the Nazi regime. If Schmitt personally, or his political and constitutional ideas, exercised any political influence, it occurred during these years. Among its illuminating aspects, this evidence challenges old and more recent interpretations of Schmitt as a Conservative Revolutionary, prophet of the Nazi state, or *Reichstheologe* seeking a Christian political order. Moreover, these diaries yield a substantial amount of revelatory evidence related to debates over his antisemitism. We encounter here the mature Schmitt, an academician in his forties, who, despite success still struggled with his inner demons as well as with critical assaults from intellectual and personal rivals. All of this is aggravated by his political engagements, which, at times, appear to ensnarl him in distressing webs of activities and commitments. With few exceptions, one again learns little of the political events and milieu of the end of Weimar and early years of the "Third Reich," as anything unrelated to Schmitt remains virtually nonexistent throughout these four hundred pages. The disintegrating consequences of the *Parteienstaat*, the Great Depression, and incessant momentum of National Socialism linger as a silent contextual background for his intellectual and emotional responses (Schmitt 2010).

As Schmitt moved from the *Handelshochschule* in Berlin to the University of Cologne and then in 1933 to the University of Berlin, it is clear that his youthful idealism had significantly waned, perhaps completely disappeared. But his almost daily sadness and deep depression remained chronic, with thoughts of suicide occasionally surfacing: "feeling of decline and destruction" (2010, 9, 42–43). He still agonized over his passionate affairs with Hella Ehrik and others (also the temptation of prostitutes), as they complicated his second marriage. Deeply moved by the film *The Blue Angel*, he identified his "own fate" with that film's protagonist Professor Unrat (41–42). But such references were interspersed between overwhelming intellectual, professional, and political concerns. Elated over academic triumphs, he nonetheless feared the "intrigues and slander" of opponents (including former friends Moritz Julius Bonn, Erich Kaufmann, and Rudolf Smend) who attacked his theories of presidential power while they sought to undermine him and his students professionally (204). Still, these entries disclose nothing of his arguments in *Der Hüter der Verfassung* (1931) or *The Concept of the Political* (2007) or those of his detractors. Thus, while his parallel notes occasionally offer insights into his thinking or proclivities, these diaries are not a significant source for understanding the motivations, intentions, or underlying assumptions of his publications from this period. The exception is those few instances during the presidential system and "Third Reich" where others "requested" he produce a specific piece (2010, 276–277). What they do show, however, is a consistency between the tone and general thoughts in his private musings and in his published work, casting serious doubt on those interpretations depicting Schmitt as a deceiver, whose public arguments must be deconstructed to unveil their true meaning.

The limited attention to religion marks a notable departure from Schmitt's earlier diaries. While he retained his Catholic identity, it was unclear how this informed or affected his thinking. Infrequently, certain occurrences "awakened his Catholicism" (2010, 77), but elsewhere a reading of Virgil prompted him to declare "that is my religion" (32). That he alone defined, if only vaguely and erratically, what Catholicism meant to him was illustrated by his following complaint: "The Jew says to me: You must as a Catholic think and mean such and such. He wants to prescribe me, what I have to do" (416). Schmitt associated with German Catholic theologians such as Karl Eschweiler and Romano Guardini and even more closely with Paul Adams, editor of the Center Party paper *Germania* (4, 7, 265). Nothing suggests in the least, however, that he was an advocate, leader, or affiliate of any conservative religious political movement during his Berlin years. The Church's refusal to annul his first marriage still disturbed him. In another context, he chastised the "Roman Church as an empty power apparatus," whose actions he compared to the "Puritan annihilation of the Indians" (81, 94). Always concerned about the politics of the Center Party, particularly its coalition with the Socialists, he felt (by early 1933) that its leaders had unleashed a torrent of hatred against him. He did not go to church on Christmas 1932 (451).

Political circumstances in Germany greatly depressed Schmitt, creating a sense of a "coming catastrophe" (2010, 62). He feared a probable communist triumph, as he did the anticonstitutional political struggles of the National Socialists, against which the legal "neutrality" of the upholders of the parliamentary system, including the Center Party, were unwittingly defenseless. Elsewhere, he discussed the "coming civil war" (59). Often feeling the configuration of conflicting forces made the situation appear hopeless, he nonetheless eschewed any alternative through the party politics he had long disdained. Only when the clique initiating and implementing Hindenburg's presidential system sought his expertise as a constitutional advisor starting in 1930 did he indirectly enter the political arena. Unfortunately, here too, the diaries often disappoint Schmitt scholars and the historical record overall. Aside from brief references to crucial elements such as *Gutachten*, Article 48, or the rejection of a particular plan of his for resolving the political–constitutional deadlock in September 1932, his notations are devoid of informative substance. To identify his political and legal positions, one must still consult his published works, correspondence, or other relevant archival documentation. The frustrated reader is left craving for some details of his many discussions over these years with leaders within various Reich ministries as well as of private conversations of importance with a vast array of thinkers and political figures. No new insights can be gleaned about Brüning, Papen, and Schleicher—the presidential chancellors he served. We discern only snippets of his attitudes toward them; he had mixed feelings about Brüning and did not hold Papen in especially high regard (41, 61, 126–127, 202–248).

These diaries do, however, confirm Schmitt's long-standing assertion of his primary personal and political relationship to the Schleicher circle. When called upon, he might have served Chancellor Papen, but Schmitt's confidence and constant contact lay with Johannes Popitz, and majors Erich Marcks and Eugen Ott. While Marcks and Ott were Schleicher's aides, Popitz served as a minister in Schleicher's cabinet; since 1938, he was part of the conservative German resistance and was executed after July 20, 1944. A stream of entries create a much fuller picture of their interaction far beyond what can be found in Schmitt's correspondence with these men or official government records. Throughout years of private castigation of so many others, Schmitt truly respected and trusted these men. To him, they meant also privileged access to the inner workings and intrigues of government and an avenue of possible influence. Of particular importance are entries from July to December 1932, which capture the dramatic atmosphere within these circles from Papen's seizure of the Prussian state through the trial and supreme court decision on the constitutionality of that action (2010, 202–248). Although Schmitt remained confident in the correctness of his own theories and recent publications on the necessity of such exercise of presidential power, he was perhaps more anxiety ridden over his appointment as a lawyer for the Reich in this case as he had been over any event to date. Surprised by Papen's Prussian action, Schmitt (and often his co-litigators) were greatly depressed by the prospects of failure in court. Exhausted and feeling the process was becoming a "personal disgrace" for him, he almost resigned in the midst of the trial (201, 219, 224–225, 231). He routinely invoked the word *ridiculous* regarding events and predicaments. At times, he distrusted even his close assistant Ernst Rudolf Huber. As Eisler stated, Schmitt no longer had any friends, only "liebste Feinde" (233). He eventually lost faith when Hindenburg ignored his advice on a constitutional ploy to overcome the dilemma of a *Reichstag* no-confidence vote that would paralyze the entire political system. Schmitt "longed for unproblematic peace and quiet" (242).

Consistent with his later contentions that he sought to stabilize and salvage what was left of the Weimar system through presidential authority, a noticeable caution and uncertainty dominated his thinking. But toward the end of Schleicher's chancellorship in January 1933, Schmitt again felt his advice went unheeded. He was "afraid of coming political events" (2010, 256–257), as abandonment of the presidential system opened the prospect of a return to the "swamp of parliamentarianism and social despotism" through the Catholic and Social Democratic parties (254). Instead, he was surprised by appointment of the Hitler cabinet—"the stupid, ludicrous Hitler" (257). Schmitt shared Marcks' despair over "Hindenburg's political passivity" in this decision (258); a few months later, Schmitt alluded to this as the political "suicide of the government" (272). Considering his own future quite doubtful, he thought of an "escape plan" to Italy or Switzerland, to "disappear into nothingness" (260). For three months, he watched developments from the sidelines. These were not the ruminations of someone welcoming the "Third Reich" or seeking realization of his theories through it.

Schmitt did, of course, write several of his more important works from this period with the Nazi danger clearly in focus. But the few brief pre-1933 diary references to Nazis dispersed over three hundred pages disclose only passing suggestions of his attitudes toward this surging movement and its leaders. None were sympathetic. After the Nazi electoral breakthrough in September 1930, he dismissed as ridiculous an invitation to discuss the principles of National Socialism. In 1931, he described the removal of the National Socialist delegation from the *Reichstag* as "*großartig*" (2010, 88). Discussions of the subject usually depressed him, though he made special note that his close colleague Erwin Jacobi, a Protestant of Jewish heritage, found National Socialism appealing.

Elsewhere, he depicted the increasing apprehension of Jews with mounting Nazi successes (50–51, 58, 96, 355).

As he always contended, his association with the Nazi regime began with Papen's March 31 directive that Schmitt participate in the commission to write the "Law for the Coordination of the States with the Reich." By that point, the Enabling Act (granting Hitler extensive dictatorial power) had already signaled the death of the republic and collapse of most realistic opposition. Schmitt's composition of the law depressed him, because he "could not believe the Nazis would understand it" (2010, 276–277). And he published his brochure on that *Reichsstatthaltergesetz* (1933) only at the "shameless" request of the government (2010, 279). Nonetheless, this first act of collaboration advanced the Nazi *Gleichschaltung* of Germany. Shortly thereafter came his first and only up-close view of Hitler at a press conference. Schmitt described that event as the "voracious bull had come into the arena." Quite "shaken by this glimpse into the new regime," he noted: an "absurd affair" (279). May 1, the day he joined the NSDAP, Schmitt was likewise distressed by the "insolence and arrogance" of an SA student speaker: "often afraid of his chthonic brutality and force" (288).

Suddenly, the extensive diary annotations end. One can only speculate about the role that fear might have played in this abrupt interruption. Until the end of 1933, days were reduced to mere brief uninformative words or phrases during this highly significant stage of Schmitt's rise to status of figurehead *Kronjurist* of the "Third Reich." Nothing is revealed of the circumstances or reactions to his appointments to party and government offices or of the establishment of relations with powerful figures (particularly Hans Frank and Hermann Göring). A similar void exists regarding his attempts to analyze, perhaps guide, constitutional developments within the new regime through publications and institutional activities (2010, 289–315). He became, however, "fearful of his persecutors" within the party (315); he was thankful for Göring's protection.

In January and February 1934, he revived his full diary. It was a time of "melancholy and inner despair" (2010, 315) over his activities in Nazi legal institutions and vicious attacks on him from party rivals and officials. This was no mere academic infighting, as some would later contend, but utterly serious, dangerous internal and public assaults on him by powerful men such as *Gauleiter* Erich Koch, "against whose brutality [he felt] defenseless" (328). The reader is struck by the image of a trapped man: "How absurdly I spend my life. Fear of the demons, complete helplessness" (327). Often he sought solace in his old conservative clique of Ott and Popitz. Quite tellingly he had sent Ernst Jünger a copy of André Malraux's *La condition humaine*. Then, except for a few curse entries in May and June, Schmitt ceases his formal diaries until 1939 (315–333).

Also reinforcing the sense of despair conveyed in the diaries, are the terse, though important, references in his pocket diary of January to August 1934 and parallel notes included from elsewhere in his *Nachlass*. The regime's oppressive trends and ideological tendencies came close to home. He worried about proving his Serbian wife's Aryan and non-Jewish heritage. Similarly, "disgusting," "heartrending" stories of acquaintances arrested or interned in concentration camps left him with an "awful feeling" (2010, 344, 353–354). These circumstances, like his continued association with the old Schleicher clique of Ott and especially Popitz, must be considered when interpreting his writing during this period. This is required whether one examines his concessions to National Socialism (particularly his homage to official icons and adoption of Nazi vernacular) or the simultaneous reemphasis of traditional conservative values and perspectives. Both aspects were reflected in *On the Three Types of Juristic Thought* (2004b) and *Staatsgefüge und Zusammenbruch des Zweiten Reiches* (1934b). The former represented a significant theoretical shift from his earlier decisionism to the conservatism inherent in his new concept of concrete orders. The latter reflected his preference for the traditional state and army. His army affiliations quickly caught the eye of the Nazi regime, twice canceling his lectures about or to the *Reichswehr*—one personally preempted by Himmler (2010, 320–321, 357).

The pocket diary also offers some additional insights into one of Schmitt's most infamous works—*"Der Führer schützt das Recht"* (1934a)—written after Hitler's bloody purge of the SA (June 30–July 2, 1934). His initial response was a telephone inquiry to an acquaintance about an unidentified arrest; he spent the evening with Popitz. Later, however, Popitz "angered" him by agreeing with substantial portions of the new law retroactively legalizing the purges. Writing his own legal assessment of these murders, Schmitt noted on July 21: "Article Der Führer schützt das Recht, horrible state of affairs" (2010, 349–350). After showing the piece to his assistant Gustav Schmoller, he felt "both relieved and fearful" (351). Its publication in the *Deutsche Juristen-Zeitung* on August 1 coincided with the death of Hindenburg, the last check on Hitler's legal authority and power. Schmitt had argued that the leader had acted legally in a situation of extreme danger to the country, but he emphasized as well that, to prevent such actions from degenerating in caprice or whims of Hitler or the party, the regular system of justice must be immediately reinstated after such actions. Schmitt also demanded that the injustices of "unauthorized actions" (implicitly the murder of Schleicher and other conservatives) be prosecuted. But Popitz conveyed the general mood: "he found [Schmitt's] article too hopeful" (351).

Although he noted Hans Frank would stand by him, he remained pessimistic and depressed. Travelling to his parental home in Plettenberg and drinking with his brother Jup, he read not Nazi literature but Plutarch and Maurice Hauriou. The institutional theory of the French jurist Hauriou had fundamentally influenced Schmitt's new ideas on concrete orders. Among Schmitt's final entries was: "Frightful doubts, fear of the Juristenbund," the Nazi League of German Jurists he headed (2010, 352–354).

Nevertheless, neither apprehension about the Nazis nor mere opportunistic attempts to ingratiate himself to them alone accounts for the antisemitism that began to surface in his publications and positions in 1933. While both of these factors probably did affect what he said and wrote thereafter, the diaries reveal deep-seated antisemitic prejudices that apparently intensified already by 1930. More so than any previous source, the diaries are replete with revelatory references (*"diese furchtbaren Juden"*; 2010, 9, 184). Colleagues such as Moritz Julius Bonn and Erich Kaufmann, with whom he had close ties previously, he now deprecated as intolerable Jews. Although until his final years Schmitt denied any antisemitism attributed to him, his notations categorically establish that, by any standard definition, he was an antisemite—yet quite an unusual sort. His relationships with and attitudes toward Jews was nuanced, complex (often vague), and certainly inconsistent as well as contradictory. None of this appears to have emerged from any systematic study or analysis of the Jewish Question, though he often discussed the subject, occasionally even with Eisler and his Jewish publisher Ludwig Feuchtwanger. Most of his references were of a very personal nature or situationally reactive rather than founded upon some theoretical framework (20, 47, 200).

While a fuller picture and approximate understanding of Schmitt's antisemitism could be developed only by examining all extant sources, the diaries tentatively suggest a least two possible causes of this intensified antisemitism after 1930. He lived in Berlin, and he felt that he personally, his theories, and his students were under unwarranted hostile assault. "In this *Judenstadt*, I am insulted and defamed by Jews" (2010, 160). He noted a conversation with visitors from Munich about "those parts of Germany that had not yet been destroyed by Jews" (255). The extensive role that Jews played in various aspects of Berlin culture, politics, and society distressed him, occasionally unleashing his preexisting antisemitism into heightened private tirades: "The eternal, ineradicable, cruelty of the Jews against all Christians, all human decency…Jews exploit everything they have" from the "physical and intellectual charm of the Jewess" to the inherently "purely logical, purely juristic, purely scholarly" mode of Jewish thought, which at certain points he alluded to originating in the synagogue (402, 408–409). In a few places, he invoked "ritual murder" to depict Jewish actions in the academic or political spheres (247, 413, 418). In March 1933, he spoke privately of the "danger and cunning" of the Jews and of their hatred of Christians and Germans (252, 271). There are a few references to his fear of the power and "triumph of the Jews" (243, 344, 424). Still, while some Jews were always chastised as such, others were never identified as Jews. The judgmental criteria often appeared haphazard, with no consistent distinction between assimilated and unassimilated or those of only partial Jewish heritage. He disdained even brief interaction with certain individuals (Karl Mannheim, "horrible, wretched *Ostjude*"), yet he enjoyed discussing politics and economics with the Banker Max Warburg (but elsewhere the "impudence of the assimilated"; 109, 172, 271).

Although the persistence of his contempt for Jews was glaring, he also employed similar terminology in lashing out against non-Jews ("disgusted by Smend and Friedrich"; 2010, 205), Freemasons, and Jesuits. For these and others, he likewise jotted down "Angst vor." Jews constituted only one problem of the plethora of concerns over which he agonized, including Social Democrats, naïve Prussian elites, and Catholic political forces (94, 269, 274). Moreover, in the midst of his heightened antisemitism, he sustained sincere, close personal and intellectual relationships with Jews, particularly Georg Eisler. Starting with the Nazi anti-Jewish boycott of early 1933, Schmitt worried about the welfare and future of the Eisler family; Schmitt's wife traveled to Hamburg to console them (274–277). He had high regard for the ideas and work of his publisher and certain fellow jurists of Jewish heritage (e.g., Albert Hensel, Erwin Jacobi, Gerhard Leibholz, Karl Loewenstein). He liked his student Otto Kirchheimer very much, relishing their discussions throughout these years and identifying him as a Jew only in late 1932 when he felt

Kirchheimer had turned against him (97, 116, 146, 210, 231). Schmitt held the young Leo Strauss ("*ein feiner Jude*") and his scholarship in high esteem, gratified by both Strauss's Hobbes study and their discussions. Schmitt recommended Strauss for a Rockefeller Fellowship, as he had done earlier for Kirchheimer (149, 159, 171, 195, 200). Accentuating Schmitt's complex and contradictory sentiments is a 1983 letter in the appendix from Charles Wahl, a Jewish émigré in New York, thanking Schmitt for warning his "non-Aryan" students in 1932 "to take the dangers of National Socialism seriously" (483).

Schmitt's disdain for and concern with certain Jewish jurists and their theories (e.g., Kaufmann and Kelsen) require further examination and explanation. But these diaries do not suggest that one can interpret Schmitt's major works of late Weimar from his perspectives on and sentiments toward Jews, though one cannot discount some relationship. On the other hand, the diaries do require reconsidering the antisemitism that surfaced in his various publications during the Nazi era. Although comprehending the context and motives related to these Nazi-era writings and speeches might involve as much complexity as his general relationship with Jews, the effect of his long-standing antisemitism must now be an integral part of any such analysis.

The frequent references to Jews pervading these diaries also have implications beyond Schmitt. Certain aspects of these entries create the impression that Schmitt's sentiments and concerns were more widely shared beyond obvious antisemitic circles like those around Wilhelm Stapel. The number of apparent discussions about Jews appears symptomatic of a much broader manifestation within the legal profession and intellectual elite. That those privy to these private conversations, particularly those who thereafter shunned him, never alluded to this issue in their references to or criticism of Schmitt, itself raises the suspicion of possible fear of their own potential culpability in perhaps having once shared such sentiments. That Schmitt and others kept this so secret from their Jewish students and colleagues might likewise help explain the shock at the antisemitism exhibited by their former mentors and friends after 1933. This was certainly true of two of Schmitt's most prominent students Kirchheimer and Franz Neumann. Unaware of the true attitudes of the elites they formerly respected, these Frankfurt School intellectuals continued not only to attribute such post-1933 antisemitism to opportunism but also to argue that antisemitism was not popular in Germany, even in the "Third Reich." Their previous experience with German elites had created an enduring illusion (Bendersky 2010, 98–101).

Schmitt's private sentiments, thoughts, and reactions to the escalating anti-Jewish atmosphere and policies of the "Third Reich" in each subsequent year until the outbreak of war will probably never be known. The gap in his diaries between fall 1934 and 1939 is also highly frustrating to historians seeking insights into or clarifications of his commentary on the Nuremberg Laws and his infamous 1936 conference "*Das Judentum in der Rechtswissenschaft*" (Schmitt 1936; Bendersky 1983, 219–242; Gross 2007; Mehring 2009, 358–389). Likewise, what were his innermost responses to Nazi chastisement of his close association with Jews? How is one to interpret the role he attributed to Jews in his *Leviathan* (Schmitt 1996a) and the odious antisemitic images he invoked to convey it? These years cover as well the Nazi campaign against him culminating in his

1936 purge, his inner exile thereafter, the redirection of his thought toward theoretical aspects of war, and the origins of his *Grossraum* concept. Unfortunately, in the absence of private notations, other sources will have to suffice. However, the appendix to the 1930–1934 diaries does provide a noteworthy document relevant to what would follow, an excerpt Schmitt kept from H. Powys Greenwood's *The German Revolution* recounting the British author's 1934 interview with him. Therein, Schmitt amplified his friend/enemy theory, emphasizing that the "horrors of modern war" could be justified only by some truly great issue. Implicitly, though glaringly, challenging the official Nazi glorification of the necessity and heroism of the struggle of 1914, "The Great War," Schmitt said, "was merely a useless waste of human life, due largely to foolish blundering on the part of governments. The recurrence of such a war must be avoided at all costs" (2010, 475–476).

POSTWAR EXILE AND EMBITTERED ALIENATION

Within five years Schmitt experienced a more horrific war that included the deaths of tens of millions, mass suffering and genocide of innocents, and the devastating bombing and defeat of Germany. Access to his contemporaneous private thoughts while witnessing these events must await the transcription and publication of his diaries of 1939–1945, which could rank among his most important. What has been available since 1991 is his *Glossarium*, his private notes of 1947–1951. Although these are often daily entries, they are quite different in style and content from his other diaries, as they do not record the daily events and travails of his personal life as do his other diaries. There is no mention of the return of Kirchheimer in 1947 or the death of Schmitt's wife in 1950, but surely such events stood behind some of his emotional responses in *Glossarium*. While parts are detailed commentaries on events, individuals, and ideas, with clearly discernible meaning and value as historical sources, others are not. Much of *Glossarium* reads like Nietzschean aphorisms. Some of these are insightful in themselves or reveal certain aspects of Schmitt's thoughts, his reactions to specific situations, or the lessons he believed his ideas had offered. But it is difficult to bring much of this together into a coherent or systematic whole. The tone is that of an active intellect that feels unjustly silenced yet cannot resist the urge to comment and write even if it had been denied an audience. And the self-perception of victimization notwithstanding, the breadth and depth of his erudition remain as striking as ever. Throughout, a sense of calm—in his words *Die Stille*—replaces the intrinsic *Angst* of his other diaries (2010, 3).

This *Stille* contrasts dramatically with the two important contexts necessary for understanding *Glossarium*. One is the unprecedented death and destruction caused by a regime with which he had collaborated. The other is his personal fate. Bombing had destroyed his Berlin household in 1943. Interrogated and released by the Russians in

April 1945, he was arrested without charges in September and interned in various camps for the next twelve months. Released in October 1946, after the American authorities certified no grounds existed for holding him, he was subsequently arrested in March 1947 as a potential war criminal by those conducting the Nuremberg Trials. After several interrogations by the émigré prosecutor Robert Kempner, Schmitt was freed from his cell at the end of April. He returned to his hometown of Plettenberg, but his life and future remained as precarious as that of his country. In the years in which he composed this work, it would have been difficult to imagine the subsequent *Wirtschaftswunder* or the great democratic success of German politics and society.

Much of these three hundred pages is fluctuating commentary, widely ranging from James Burnham's *Managerial Revolution* and Aldous Huxley's *Brave New World* to Kafka and Nietzschean nihilism to Heidegger and existentialism as well as theology and technology. Much of the content was his reaction to what he was reading or to the events and intellectual issues with which he grappled at the moment. Interspersed among these, however, are illuminating aspects that go to the core of Schmittian controversies. His first reference of August 28, 1947, for example, quite self-consciously addressed three themes underlying the enduring animosity toward him: Nazis; Jews; and his theories, particularly his friend/enemy perception of politics and insights on war. In each case, he defended his positions as misunderstood or intentionally distorted for political or ideological purposes. The Nazis had condemned him, he wrote, because he had not declared Jews the enemy, whereas Jews had condemned him because he had not proclaimed the Nazis the enemy (1991, 3–5). A year later, his poem "Song of the Sixty-Year Old," summed up his life as one of suffering and terror by reds, browns, and bombings, in which he escaped death three times. The poem also recounts his defamation, blacklisting, and incarceration. A subsequent entry asserted that his enemies were compelled to slander him: "What would they be if I were not what they say about me? They would stand naked in their true existence. Their greatest fear is this exposure" (177, 210).

In his mind, the most egregious misunderstandings, or intentional distortions, regarded his Nazi affiliations, from which other myths about him were extrapolated. Nonetheless, *Glossarium* offers neither details on his activities in the "Third Reich" nor the philosophical musing about his responsibility at the core of *Ex Captivitate Salus* (1950). Instead, his perspectives on his role in the "Third Reich" rarely surface, and then only with enticing assertions that quickly lapse into reflections on other themes. In 1933–1936, he felt so superior to those "poor thieves" seizing power that his "personal problem became identical with the general ontological question of the relationship of spirit and matter, idea and interest" (1991, 18, 244). Or "since 1936 I have experienced the weight and several times have been swallowed by the Leviathan that was the object of my scholarly observations and research" (174). He concurred with Ernst Jünger's "correct diagnosis" that after the Nazis ("the illegitimate powers") seized control, Schmitt's attempt to fill the vacuum left in the position of *Kronjurist* cost him his reputation. Quoting Jünger, "Those are the misfortunes of the profession" (129). The sense of victimhood manifested in other documentation has one quite explicit reference that the "true victims are the defenseless"—that the true victims in Germany were those party members with "membership numbers over two million," who were victims of the Nazis as well as of the persecutors of the Nazis (239). He did not need to cite his own number—2,098,860. Given what his 1930–1934 diaries have recently revealed, such sentiments were not attempts at ex post facto rationalizations or exculpation. All indications are that during the "Third Reich" he had felt trapped by a criminal regime. However, clarifying his predicament through such documentation still falls far short of adequately explaining the choices he made under those circumstances. This is especially vexing considering how frequently he lashes out against the Nuremberg Trials ("the great muddle of justice"; 256), ex post facto law, denazification, and what he perceives as current injustices against him and other Germans in the name of humanity and freedom. He was not beyond comparing the "destruction of the Prussian-German civil service in 1945" with genocide (265, 282).

In Schmitt's own mind, foreign powers and Germans had, contrary to his advice and theories, allowed those Nazis to seize control. The British and French denied the democratic republic the slightest rearmament yet acquiesced in Hitler's major rearmament; an impotent *Reichstag* allowed the president to govern through Article 48 and then voted Hitler dictatorial powers through the Enabling Act of March 24, 1933. Hitler was a "true executor…a collector of outstanding debts…realizer of overdue ideals" (1991, 223–224). He represented a kind of "moral outrage." He was a strange guest, who was a caricature of himself through the "empty ascetic purity of his ideas about a *Führer*, charisma, genius and race" (151). The educated masses were susceptible to such appeals; the less educated were not. Yet Hitler had not invented himself. He was a product of the "genuine democratic brain" that turned this unknown soldier into a mythical figure. National Socialism resounded throughout German history, of which Hitler was the culmination, the "enormous belch of a completely botched millennium." This is where Schmitt placed the responsibility for this "horrible episode" in world history and the "death of 12 million Jews" (267).

Nowhere did Schmitt concede any relationship between his own ideas, affiliations, or compromises and the fate of Europe's Jews. Here, too, he remained the victim of the "terror of Nazis and Jews" (1991, 81). Although the antisemitism in *Glossarium* is far less frequent than his 1930–1934 diaries, it shocked the scholarly world (even his staunchest defenders) not only because of its nature but also because it existed at all. Previous interpretations and extant documentation that had apparently established his Nazi-era antisemitism as sheer opportunism were suddenly challenged. His references to Jews set off a continuing debate over the origin, nature, and significance for his theories of his now undeniable antisemitism. But while inciting this debate, *Glossarium* offers little to settle it. Like so many other themes, Schmitt's references to Jews are dispersed and for long periods nonexistent; they certainly lack systematic attention or cohesiveness. As in Weimar, there are also Jews (Ernst Cassirer, Franz Kafka, Karl Löwith, Walter Rathenau) with whom he apparently had no difficulty. Most brief and detailed commentaries concern returning émigré Jews for whom he has special scorn together with émigrés such as Thomas Mann and hypocritical American and Russian prosecutors. All were participating in the oppression and persecution of Germany, though under the guise of pursuing justice and the cause of universal humanity: "better Adolf Hitler's enmity than the friendship of these returning émigrés and humanitarians" (232). In a short antisemitic ridden poem, he linked "Nürnberg? Hiroshima? Morgenthau?" It continued: "there are only Isra-Eliten" (255). He sarcastically depicted the émigrés as sitting on their "rights like booty and defending them like a prey." Having led a "just war, the most gruesome that human dogmatism had invented," they coveted their rights and "moral outrage." This was their revenge upon Germany (252, 264, 297).

Schmitt was echoing what many Germans of these years believed about their own victimization and returning Jews (Grossmann 2007). One can imagine how such was expressed in private conversations. It was a sentiment shared by many U.S. Army officers in the occupation, who, in keeping with their own longstanding antisemitism, complained about the mistreatment of Germans by occupation policies exploited by Jewish émigrés (Bendersky 2000). In Schmitt's case the subject was more personal because he was being chastised publicly as the Nazi *Kronjurist*. Moreover, most of those army and occupation officials pursuing and handling his arrests, internment, and interrogations were Jewish émigrés, several (e.g., Ossip Flechtheim and Karl Loewenstein) he had personally known during Weimar. Referring to the new American empire that had defeated Germany and was now his new master, Schmitt exclaimed he "had never in the last 5 years spoken with an American but only German Jews" (1991, 264).

The sentiment that surfaces in various parts of *Glossarium* is that the occupation forces, like returning émigrés of all types, depicted Schmitt as something he was not and sought to punish him for something he had not done. In his account, he had never sought or possessed power but had closely observed its exercise throughout his life. His detached scholarship witnessed and analyzed events through conceptual realism (1991, 107–108, 158). Though others denied and condemned his friend/enemy thesis, recent history and contemporary political behavior in occupied Germany and internationally among the emerging superpowers continually vindicated its relevance and truth. His realism contested the nineteenth-century positivism that had still dominated Weimar. Unfortunately, the naiveté inherent in the procedural neutrality of positivist liberal thinking (that ignored his theory of the "equal chance") resulted in radicals destroying democracy through democratic means in 1933 (189, 214). This same liberal thinking was paving the way for the destruction of democracy by the Left around the world after 1945. The 1948 communist coup in Czechoslovakia was a historical repetition of 1929–1933 German events, of which his *Legality and Legitimacy* (2004a) had been the "only adequate scholarly testimony" (1991, 107–108). He proudly noted that the framers of the constitution of the Federal Republic were essentially implementing the core lessons of his *Legality and Legitimacy* but lamented that they had not grasped these in 1932 (214).

As Schmitt told it, whether out of naïve utopian sensibilities or a cynical hypocritical realism deceitfully veiled behind ideals of humanity, justice, and peace, his vital perspective on war continued to be neglected. War had not disappeared, he argued, merely because it had been declared illegal earlier in the century. Now, rather than solving the problem of international conflict, contemporary "just war" theory pursuing the "criminalization of aggressive war" had, like the Nuremberg Trials, significantly intensified conflicts among friend/enemy entities by transforming the enemy into an irredeemable criminal that had to be eradicated (1991, 6–7, 121–122, 137–138). He dreaded the combination of this criminalization of the enemy and the destructive power of the atomic bomb. The great crimes Hitler committed could be surpassed by these new instruments of the Hegelian *Weltgeist* (191). Much of this parallels his *"Nomos" of the Earth* (2006), which he noted "appeared at the right historical moment" (1991, 309). War as a means of rational politics was condemned and outlawed, while presently the accepted "just war" was, in reality, that ideological struggle being waged for world domination between east and west. The mood, as well as much of the substance, of *Glossarium* was summed up in Schmitt's final passages. He had devoted his entire life, he asserted, to expressing carefully considered and disinterested warnings, which were always perceived as inconvenient intrusions, ending with him being hunted down (319). Ironically, he concluded the book with a single word: *Friede!*

CONCLUSION

Schmitt lived another three decades beyond *Glossarium*, publishing and sustaining a prolific correspondence. The content of the diaries he wrote from the end of the war to 1979, amounting to an estimated several thousand pages, will conceal their confidences in the original Gabelsberger for some time, as plans do not yet exist for their transcription and publication. That their potential insights and illuminating information, like their surprises and disappointments to scholars, must await distant disclosure is another indication of how tentative attempts at a comprehensive grasp of this man and thinker will have to remain. What has already been divulged, however, categorically substantiates a consistency between his private thinking and what he argued in his publications. This is perhaps one of the most important contributions the diaries have made to Schmitt scholarship. The available diaries have, however, also raised new, often quite disturbing questions regarding his personality, mode of thinking, and certainly his prejudices, particularly his antisemitism. But here too one must be very cautious not to place undue reliance on these diaries as a source on which to construct grandiose interpretations about him or his theories. The diaries must be read and interpreted in conjunction with his oeuvre, vast correspondence, and other relevant archival documentation. This necessary methodology, like grappling with his ideas, can be a daunting scholarly task. In the process, one must resist succumbing to the temptation of selective usage of the entries in these abundant diaries in an attempt to sustain a particular argument.

The aforementioned cautionary remarks notwithstanding, the voluminous nature, very essence, and historical significance of the available Schmitt diaries already rank them among the most important diary collections of the era. And while their value for historians of German conservatism, Weimar, and Nazi Germany might be self-evident, their wider significance for political and legal theory must assuredly not be underestimated. No scholar grappling with his political and legal thinking can ignore these sources. Though one certainly cannot reduce theoretical questions simply to biography or historical context, neither can one adequately examine the ideas of such a complex and controversial figure as Schmitt without the context of biography and history. In this regard, the diaries are invaluable for acquiring the necessary understanding of the man—of his sentiments, modes of thinking, proclivities, and prejudices, all of which have definitely affected his ideas and work. In addition, so much of his thought is bound to the specific, as well as drastically altering, historical circumstances and developments he encountered over the period of seventy years that constituted his intellectual productivity. Frequently his ideas have been elaborated, analyzed, and criticized (sometimes completely dismissed) on the basis of assumptions about their relationship to such political and historical developments. The same is true concerning his alleged motivations and behavior. And the available diaries do offer clarifications on several significant points related to his life and work. Many of these diary notations, in fact, explicitly contradict, thereby refuting, claims about Schmitt on which widely disseminated interpretations are based.

The recently published diaries have utterly transformed our perceptions of Schmitt's personality, sentiments, and motivations from what had been previously inferred from speculations, readings between the lines of his works, or even from the image of him manifested in *Glossarium*. The newly revealed complexities of his youthful religiosity and agony, so necessary to correctly perceiving the role of Catholicism in his life and thought, differ greatly from interpretations of him as a cosmic eschatological and apocalyptical thinker. They likewise caution us against overestimating the conceptual centrality of the *katechon* often cited from *Glossarium*, then projected back into his earlier work. His now understood lifelong *Angst*, exacerbated by a tumultuous age, also certainly relates to the perennial search for order and security so pervasive in his theory. The sincerity of his youthful idealism and cosmopolitanism are thoroughly illuminating, particularly where he rejects those aspects of the material and theoretical worlds he truly believes are destructive to the very essence of humanity. Does this not have to be considered when interpreting his critique of the very concept of humanity in *The Concept of the Political, Glossarium*, and elsewhere? Similarly, the disclosures of his intense antiwar (occasionally antinationalist) sentiments, apparently carried into the 1930s, undoubtedly undermine those insisting that he was an advocate of perpetual war who hates peace. Nonetheless, it will probably require subsequent confirmation by future publications of the diaries of 1925–1929, 1939–1945, and postwar years to finally put to rest such fervently held and enduring interpretations of Schmitt's stance on conflict and war. And while his pervasive cultural pessimism underscores his elemental conservatism, the surprising depth of his animosity toward capitalism, industrialization, and the detrimental human effects of technology and bourgeois mass culture perhaps further explains the attraction he held for certain members of the Frankfurt School, especially Walter Benjamin, Otto Kirchheimer, and Franz Neumann.

One unavoidable, key conclusion these diaries indicate is that, from the Wilhelmine era through Weimar and the "Third Reich" and into old age, Schmitt perceived himself to be an isolated, often alienated, intellectual loner, whose prescient observations about humanity, politics, and society were ignored. He was definitely a conservative intellectual, with all the characteristics that implies, but for the most part he remained an unaffiliated one of unique quality who, despite a broad network of affiliations from left to right, retained his intellectual autonomy. In this regard, the diaries contain nothing to imply—and much to the contrary—that, though he maintained personal and intellectual relationships with prominent Conservative Revolutionaries, he ever considered himself, or actually was, a part of that intellectual and political cause. Another indispensable revelation is the uncontestable corroboration and disturbing elucidation of Schmitt's antisemitism, dictating a total reassessment of his attitudes toward and affiliations with Jews, including reconsideration of the opportunism thesis. The often crude nature of his expressions, together with the fact that they contain more specific information on the subject than any other extant source, make the diaries essential documentation for any study of Schmitt and the Jewish Question. On the other hand, such notations often raise as many questions or contradictions as they resolve, all of which is further complicated by his truly intimate relationship with the Eislers. Schmitt and the Eislers, like his respect and affinity for particular other Jews, need to be integrated into any attempt at reconciling such paradoxes. Furthermore, though enlightening regarding Schmitt's incessant personal antisemitism (in a few places, also on his perspectives on Jews in history, society, and law), the diaries do not show a preoccupation with the subject or that one can interpret his major works in terms of his viewpoints on Jews.

Although the diaries reveal a definite deception on Schmitt's part in suspiciously hiding his sentiments on Jews, as he did with his personal demons and insecurities, they actually substantiate a consistency between his private thoughts and his published works. Although the diaries do not elaborate as much on his specific publications as we had hoped, sometimes lacking any reference to major works, a good deal of what the diaries embody does relate to his political and legal thought. And this consistency between the candid private diary entries and his public expressions and writings presents a serious problem for those who insist on interpreting Schmitt as a deceiver, whose writings require a peculiar kind of deconstruction to divine their true meaning. This new evidence is thereby, in itself, a major contribution to historiographical and theoretical debates on Schmitt. Similar consistency exists between the contemporaneous diary entries and much of Schmitt's postwar explanations of his political and intellectual engagements at the end of Weimar and in the early Nazi years. In fact, we now know much more than previously about his ambivalent involvement with the Papen government, especially Schmitt's reservations and anxieties regarding the case of Prussia versus Reich, and his close association with the Schleicher circle.

Schmitt's diary references to National Socialism, his fears of that movement and the brutality of its advocates, like his comment on Hitler's appointment as suicide for the republic, do corroborate Schmitt's subsequent references to the Benito Cereno metaphor to explain his quandary and behavior within the "Third Reich." More attention also clearly needs to be paid to his close association with Popitz and conservative military circles during these years as well as to the fundamental shifts in Schmitt's thinking toward traditional conservatism reflected in *On the Three Types of Juristic Thought*. Even two Nazi-era articles significantly damaging to his reputation, often invoked to prove that he truly was the "Third Reich" *Kronjurist*—"Das Reichsstatthaltergesetz" and "Der Führer schützt das Recht"—require a contextual reassessment on the basis of what the diaries indicate about how they were engendered and his motivations for writing them. None of this exculpates Schmitt from the compromises he made: at times his motivations are highly questionable; in other instances, they are not clear at all. Indeed, several entries disclose that a very fearful Schmitt sought the protection of powerful Nazi leaders such as Göring and Frank. But even here there is consistency, as later in life he often publically remarked that he owed his survival in the "Third Reich" to their patronage. Such corroboration of Schmitt's subsequent, apparently fairly accurate, self-narrative of his attitudes toward the Nazis and of his general predicament under their power challenges the perception that he intentionally prepared the way for that regime, welcomed its arrival, and or saw the fulfillment of his ideas in it.

For decades to come, this abundant material will undoubtedly occupy scholars in a variety of fields from philosophy, history, and law to political theory and literature. The research generated due to the intrinsic and indispensable value of these diaries will, in all probability, help ensure that the Schmitt renaissance has not passed its peak as some contend or hope. Serious gaps in the diaries, or their current inaccessibility, of course, preclude the kind of completeness and finality for which scholars strive though rarely achieve. Yet few newly available documentary collections have ever transformed our image of a historical figure to such an extent, clarified significant aspects of his thinking, generated so many new questions and research leads, or forced such momentous alterations in the interpretive historiography of an intellectual as these diaries have already done.

NOTE

1. Unless noted otherwise, all translations of source material by the author.
2. The "Schatten Gottes" notes and his unpublished *Tagebücher* 1921–1922 (RW 265–19585), together with his unavailable *Tagebücher* 1923-1924, reside in the *Nachlass* Carl Schmitt, Nordrhein-Westfälisches Hauptstaatsarchiv, Düsseldorf. An edited collection was recently published as Schmitt (2014c). Citations in this chapter are to the page numbers in the unpublished typed archival manuscripts.

REFERENCES

Bendersky, J. 1983. *Carl Schmitt: Theorist for the Reich*. Princeton: Princeton University Press.
Bendersky, J. 2000. *The "Jewish Threat": Anti-Semitic Politics of the U.S. Army*. New York: Basic Books.
Bendersky, J. 2010. "Dissension in the Face of the Holocaust: The 1941 American Debate over Antisemitism." *Holocaust and Genocide Studies* 24: 85–116.

Dyzenhaus, D. 1998. "Introduction." In *Law as Politics: Carl Schmitt's Critique of Liberalism*, ed. D. Dyzenhaus, Durham: Duke University Press, 1–17.

Fijalkowski, J. 1958. *Die Wendung zum Führerstaat: Ideologische Komponenten in der politischen Philosophie Carl Schmitts*. Cologne: Westdeutscher Verlag.

Gross, R. 2007. *Carl Schmitt and the Jews: The "Jewish Question," the Holocaust, and German Legal Theory*, trans. J. Golb. Madison: University of Wisconsin Press.

Grossmann, A. 2007. *Jews, Germans, and Allies: Close Encounters in Occupied Germany*. Princeton: Princeton University Press.

Herf, J. 1984. *Reactionary Modernism: Technology, Culture, and Politics in Weimar and the Third Reich*. New York: Cambridge University Press.

Hooker, W. 2009. *Carl Schmitt's International Thought: Order and Orientation*. Cambridge: Cambridge University Press.

Klemperer, V. 1998. *I Will Bear Witness: A Diary of the Nazi Years, 1933–1941*. New York: Random House.

Koenen. A. 1995. *Der Fall Carl Schmitt: Sein Aufstieg zum "Kronjuristen des Dritten Reiches."* Darmstadt: Wissenschaftliche Buchgesellschaft.

Lilla, M. 1997. "The Enemy of Liberalism." *New York Review of Books* 44: 38–44.

Maus, I. 1976. *Bürgerliche Rechtstheorie und Faschismus: Zur sozialen Funktion und aktuellen Wirkung der Theorie Carl Schmitts*. Munich: Fink.

Maus, I. 1998. "The 1933 'Break' in Carl Schmitt's Theory." In Dyzenhaus 1988, 196–216.

McDonald, J. 2007. *Advocate of the Doomed: The Diaries of James G. McDonald, 1932–1935*, ed. R. Breitman, B. McDonald Stewart, and S. Hochberg. Bloomington: Indiana University Press.

Meier, H. 1995. *Carl Schmitt and Leo Straus: The Hidden Dialogue*. Chicago: University of Chicago Press.

Meier, H. 1998. *The Lessons of Carl Schmitt: Four Chapters on the Distinction between Political Theology and Political Philosophy*. Chicago: University of Chicago Press.

Mehring, R. 2009. *Carl Schmitt: Aufstieg und Fall*. Munich: Beck.

Mohler, A. 1972. *Die Konservative Revolutionen in Deutschland, 1918–1932: Ein Handbuch*. Darmstadt: Wissenschaftliche Buchgesellschaft.

Scheuerman, W. 1999. *Carl Schmitt: The End of Law*. New York: Rowman & Littlefield.

Schmitt, C. 1914. *Der Wert des Staates und die Bedeutung des Einzelnen*. Tübingen: Mohr.

Schmitt, C. 1916. *Theodor Däublers "Nordlicht": Drei Studien über die Elemente, den Geist und die Aktualität des Werkes*. Munich: Müller.

Schmitt, C. 1919. *Politische Romantik*. Munich: Duncker & Humblot.

Schmitt, C. 1921. *Die Diktatur: Von den Anfängen des modernen Souveränitätsgedankens bis zum proletarischen Klassenkampf*. Munich: Duncker & Humblot.

Schmitt, C. 1931. *Der Hüter der Verfassung*. Tübingen: Mohr.

Schmitt, C. 1933. *Das Reichsstatthaltergesetz*. Berlin: Heymann.

Schmitt, C. 1934a. "Der Führer schützt das Recht." *Deutsche Juristen-Zeitung* 39: 945–950.

Schmitt, C. 1934b. *Staatsgefüge und Zusammenbruch des Zweiten Reiches: Der Sieg des Bürgers über den Soldaten*. Hamburg: Hanseatische Verlagsanstalt.

Schmitt, C. 1936. "Die Deutsche Rechtswissenschaft im Kampf gegen den jüdischen Geist: Schlusswort auf der Tagung der Reichsgruppe Hochschullehrer des NSRB vom 3. und 4. Oktober 1936." *Deutsche Juristen-Zeitung* 41: 1193–1199.

Schmitt, C. 1950. *Ex Captivitate Salus: Erfahrungen der Zeit 1945/47*. Cologne: Greven.

Schmitt, C. 1985. *The Crisis of Parliamentary Democracy*, trans. E. Kennedy. Cambridge: MIT Press.

Schmitt, C. 1991. *Glossarium: Aufzeichnungen der Jahre 1947–1951.* Berlin: Duncker & Humblot.

Schmitt, C. 1996a. *The Leviathan in the State Theory of Thomas Hobbes: Meaning and Failure of a Political Symbol,* trans. G. Schwab. Westport: Praeger.

Schmitt, C. 1996b. *Roman Catholicism and Political Form,* trans. G. L. Ulmen. Westport: Praeger

Schmitt, C. 2003. *Carl Schmitt Tagebücher: Oktober 1912 bis Februar 1915,* ed. E. Hüsmert. Berlin: Akademie Verlag.

Schmitt, C. 2004a. *Legality and Legitimacy,* trans. and ed. J. Seitzer. Durham: Duke University Press.

Schmitt, C. 2004b. *On the Three Types of Juristic Thought,* trans. J. W. Bendersky. Westport: Praeger.

Schmitt, C. 2005. *Carl Schmitt: Die Militärzeit 1915 bis 1919: Tagebuch Februar bis Dezember 1915,* ed. E. Hüsmert and G. Giesler. Berlin: Akademie Verlag.

Schmitt, C. 2006. *The "Nomos" of the Earth in the International Law of the "Jus Publicum Europaeum,"* trans. G. L. Ulmen. New York: Telos Press.

Schmitt, C. 2007. *The Concept of the Political,* trans. G. Schwab. Chicago: University of Chicago Press.

Schmitt, C. 2008. *Constitutional Theory,* trans. and ed. J. Seitzer. Durham: Duke University Press.

Schmitt, C. 2010. *Carl Schmitt Tagebücher, 1930–1934,* ed. W. Schuller and G. Giesler. Berlin: Akademie Verlag.

Schmitt, C. 2014a. Der Schatten Gottes: Aufzeichnungen aus den Jahren 1922 bis 1924. Bestand RW 265-19605, Nachlass Carl Schmitt, Nordrhein-Westfälisches Hauptstaatsarchiv, Düsseldorf.

Schmitt, C. 2014b. Tagebücher 1921–1922. Bestand RW 265–19585, Nachlass Carl Schmitt, Nordrhein-Westfälisches Hauptstaatsarchiv, Düsseldorf.

Schmitt, C. 2014c. *Der Schatten Gottes: Introspektionen, Tagebücher und Briefe 1921 bis 1924,* ed. G. Giesler, E. Hüsmert, and W. H. Spindler. Berlin: Duncker & Humblot.

Schmitt, C., and F. Eisler. 1913. *Schattenrisse.* Leipzig: Otto Meier.

Schwab. G. 1970. *The Challenge of the Exception: An Introduction to the Political Ideas of Carl Schmitt between 1921 and 1936.* Berlin: Duncker & Humblot.

Sontheimer. K. 1962. *Antidemokratisches Denken in der Weimarer Republik: Die politischen Ideen des deutschen Nationalismus zwischen 1918 und 1933.* Munich: Nymphenburger Verlagsbuchhandlung.

CHAPTER 5

CARL SCHMITT
IN PLETTENBERG

CHRISTIAN LINDER

INTRODUCTION

CARL SCHMITT's life in post-World War II Germany began in American captivity in September 1945. Although the Russians had apprehended him five months before in Berlin, they had no idea who was standing before them: the Nazi regime's alleged *Kronjurist*, or leading jurist. This was the man who, fancying himself the only one capable of coming up with a sophisticated national policy, really went to work after Adolf Hitler's assumption of power in 1933. This was the man who, in then and now notorious statements, defended Hitler's orders to assassinate Ernst Röhm and other SA leaders in June 1934 as "true jurisdiction through the Führer" according to the principle of "The Führer protects the law" (Schmitt 1934a, 1).[1] Soon thereafter, in 1936, Schmitt was ousted after being attacked in the SS (*Schutzstaffel*) publication *Das Schwarze Korps*, which accused him of "Catholic thought," opportunism, and having numerous Jewish connections. He was protected from further persecution solely because Hermann Göring, in his capacity as both Prussian minister and second in the Nazi hierarchy after Hitler, had awarded him the (largely nominal) title of Prussian State Councilor (*Staatsrat*) on Schmitt's forty-fifth birthday on July 11, 1933.

The Russians had only interrogated Schmitt in April 1945 because one of his students had visited him after curfew and, after being apprehended, asked Schmitt to corroborate his story to the police. Schmitt, however, assumed he was being questioned about his National Socialist past and immediately launched into a major defense. There are many versions of this interrogation. Josef Pieper, a philosopher and friend of Schmitt's, recounts one:

> In front of the Russian commission, Carl Schmitt claimed that a purported National
> Socialist past must be understood in accordance with von Pettenkofer's experiment.

Naturally, the officer interrogating him had no idea what he was talking about. Max von Pettenkofer was a German natural scientist who at the beginning of the century had argued that infectious diseases were not caused by a bacillus alone; rather, the individual's predisposition toward disease was much more decisive. And in order to prove this thesis, he drank a glass of water contaminated with an entire culture of cholera bacilli in front of his students—and did, indeed, stay healthy. Thus Carl Schmitt's own conclusion was: "You see, I did exactly the same thing. I drank the Nazi bacillus, but was not infected." Which would, if it were true, only make his behavior all the more inexcusable. But one laughed admiringly and ordered his release. (Pieper 1976, 198)

Over the next few months, Schmitt was able to work in peace on his book *The "Nomos" of the Earth in the International Law of the "Jus Publicum Europaeum"*. In a diary entry on September 26, 1945, his wife Dushka noted: "Carl was taken away." By that time, the American troops were already in Berlin. After classifying Schmitt as a "political threat," they first questioned him in the Interrogation Center and then sent him off to internment camps, first Lichterfelde Süd and then later in Wannsee. Although strictly forbidden to write, Schmitt managed to use blocks of prescription paper slipped to him by an American doctor to write notes and letters that he then smuggled out of the camps. In June 1946 he wrote to his wife Duschka:

God has protected me up until now. I must often think of Ernst Jünger's favorite verse, "I give unto you power to tread on serpents and scorpions, and nothing shall hurt you." ... The danger of lifelessness is great. ... But in spite of everything, dearest Duschka, I am not lifeless. Vulnerable, but in nothing annihilated, as Konrad Weiß says. My intellectual work from 1910 to 1945 has prepared me so wonderfully for my present intellectual situation such that God's foreordination continues to amaze me. Everything has had its purpose as spiritual armor.[2]

But on October 7, 1947, in Plettenberg, Schmitt confided to his diary how he really felt:

Towards the end of August 1946, out of desperation with life in the camp, I used to address the sun in the mornings, just as her first rays of light fell upon my plank bed, by saying out loud to her: "You cheater." That was horrible, much like Kierkegaard's father's own remark about God. I am feeling better on the outside since then and the worst abuses have stopped. But is all this a sham? A desperate entanglement in the labyrinth of negativity. A lethal recoil of a throwing stone upon the one hurling it. ... I stand as a ghost and scream without a throat. (Schmitt 1991, 27)

On October 10, 1946, after just over a year, Schmitt was finally released from his internment camp in Berlin. On March 19, 1947, he was once again arrested and transferred to the International Military Tribunal in Nuremburg as a "possible defendant." For five weeks Schmitt sat in solitary confinement in the war criminals' prison. Robert Kempner, the American deputy head prosecutor, questioned him on three occasions; Schmitt was also allowed to defend himself in writing. Solitary confinement and repeated rounds of questioning may well have humiliated him, but they did not break him. If he was to be held responsible for Hitler, he cautioned Kempner, then Rousseau should also be held responsible for the Jacobins. Referring to his own "big name," Schmitt aligned himself with Jean Bodin and Thomas Hobbes, the founding figures of his discipline, international law, constitutional law, and political theory.

Schmitt was eventually released from solitary confinement on May 6, 1947, although he had to stay on in the guesthouse as a witness for the prosecution in the trial against Ernst Weizsäcker, secretary of state in the Foreign Office. "He is now a voluntary witness for office Chief of Counsel for War Crimes," it says in his dismissal letter. On May 7 Schmitt testified in front of Kempner as a witness for the Weizsäcker trial. After some final questioning on May 21, 1947, Schmitt left Nuremberg and returned to the Sauerland, which he had left some forty years earlier in the hope of taming the leviathan. In January 1913, as a twenty-five year old student, he wrote to his sister Auguste that he would surely become a "famous defense lawyer" (2000a, 171). Twenty years down the road, his defendant would be named Adolf Hitler, a man who neither solicited Schmitt's services nor had even heard the name of "his" "famous defense lawyer." So after his release in Nuremberg, Schmitt had little choice but to recapture his homeland in the Sauerland.

STABILITAS LOCI

Back in Plettenberg, Schmitt noted in his diary: "What are you doing here? It was with puerile arrogance that you took on great enemies in this wide world—with Rome and great Jews. And now you are going to throw yourself away to your brothers in the province, you cheapskate. You hold back and then pass, out of indolence and cowardly convenience. You cannot go home" (1991, 91–93). After considering and then quickly dismissing the possibility of emigrating to Argentina, Schmitt ended up staying in his hometown, Plettenberg. He remained there for the next forty years until his death on Easter Sunday in 1985.

In the forty years between his *Abitur* (school leaving examination) on March 2, 1907, and his release from Nuremberg's prison for war criminals on May 21, 1947, it seems unlikely that the famous professor of constitutional law and political author could have foreseen that his life's journey would lead him right back to where he had started. Upon his arrival in Plettenberg, he expressed bewilderment at this experience in the form of monstrous, ejaculatory prayers in which he addressed God in the formal second person and, probably in order to better cope with the feeling of estrangement, in French: "*Seigneur, délivrez-moi, brisez mes chaînes, reconduisez-moi chez mon père, dans ma patrie, dans ma maison, dans mon héritage et faites que ce qui m'appartient me soit rendu, pour que vous soyez glorifié dans votre justice.* [O Lord, deliver me, break my chains, lead me back to my Father, to my fatherland, to my house, to my heritage and see to it that everything that belongs to me shall once again be rendered unto me so that you might be glorified in your justice]" (1991, 29).

In Plettenberg Schmitt moved back into the home built by his parents in 1937, on Brockhauser Weg 10. There he lived at first with his wife Duschka and their daughter Anima and his sisters Auguste, a former elementary schoolteacher, and Anna Margarete, a piano teacher. Conditions were very cramped in the one and one-half story single-family house. The sisters lived on the ground floor; Schmitt and his family took the attic flat. On the few walls that were straight enough there hung paintings, some by Emil Nolde, Werner Gilles, Ernst Wilhelm Nay, and Werner Heldt. Duschka had been able to salvage them from Berlin along with some dark, oaken pieces of designer furniture. But then the walls grew blanker as Schmitt was forced to sell some of the paintings for financial reasons. In the absence of his personal library of 3,300 volumes, which had been confiscated by the Americans in October 1945, Schmitt had to rely on his immense memory in the immediate postwar years. Even in 1977, Schmitt was still speaking of an "enemy seizure" of his library. Although the Americans had returned most of his works to him by the early 1950s, Schmitt ended up reselling many of them because his attic flat in Plettenberg could not accommodate them. What is more, he once again needed the money. To this very day one still stumbles in antiquarian bookshops upon horrendously priced volumes from this library that bear the stamp "Legal division U.S. Group, CC, (Germany) Library—Prof. Carl Schmitt Library."

Schmitt was depressed by the isolation, especially in the first few years after the war. Visits by Anima's classmates were the only change of pace. They used to study and perform plays in Schmitts' garden, such as Gerhard Hauptmann's *Elga*, in which Anima played the main role. Ernst Hüsmert, barely twenty and also from Plettenberg, belonged to Anima's circle of friends. Hüsmert was invited to Schmitt's sixtieth birthday on July 11, 1948. He studied engineering in Hagen and moved to Essen to join the Krupp conglomerate after passing his exams in 1949. He also wrote poetry on the side. His favorite lyricist then was Theodor Däubler, whose newly discovered epic, *Das Nordlicht* (*The Northern Light*), never left his side, even after he fell asleep. At the birthday party Hüsmert raved to Schmitt about Däubler's work and strewed breadcrumbs on the tables and the floor, in the fashion of the poet. Schmitt was amused by this and humored Hüsmert before revealing to him that not only had he been close friends with Däubler before his death in 1934, but he had been the first and only one to dedicate an extensive study to *Das Nordlicht*, which appeared as an eighty-page publication in 1916. "Of course there he had me hooked," laughs Hüsmert. "All wishes come true. Most in a slightly smaller way than expected, but a few in a much grander way," Schmitt told the young Hüsmert. Was this self-commentary? Hüsmert never asked, and in the following forty years he never felt like Schmitt's Eckermann. At Hüsmert's wedding in 1956, Schmitt was his best man.

Hüsmert relates that Schmitt once again took to reading Homer, especially the scene in which the returning Odysseus tells his life's story to the shepherd Eumaeus. Schmitt's life, too, can be read as the exciting story of a strange homecoming that follows a turbulent journey, which many saw as an odyssey. The enmity that Schmitt felt was enormous, and his fear of being banished from German intellectual life was quite justifiable. This is why he embraced any contacts with the outside world, many of which were initially only written correspondence. Schmitt was relieved to be once again able to speak about his situation in the French language. Frenchman Pierre Linn, a friend of his since the 1930s and translator of *Political Romanticism*, had written to him of a general "vaga-bondage." This "vagabondage" also applied to him, Schmitt replied, and was in his own case a problem related to his situation. Schmitt immediately generalized this problem, the phenomenon and even the term "vagabondage," all of which, he argued, were under-going existential changes and "above all on the ground where the opposing impulses and tendencies of this world stormily converge" (1991, 79–81). Particularly in a country like Germany, where the antagonistic forces of the West and East were colliding into and undercutting each other in a region "which is being transformed day by day into both a 'No-man's-land' (i.e., nihilism in Rhenish culture) and an 'Every-man's-land' (i.e., the melee of theogonic forces that was triggered by the decline of Protestantism and idealist philosophy since 1840). I have given a lot of thought to what you said about the idealist state in 1936. The validations that I have found for this are striking. The missing link in the logical and systematic chain is the concept of utopia. Or alternatively: Brave New World!" (79)

Rising again to intellectual heights, Schmitt then informed Linn that their conver-sation could not be that of Boethius (the early Christian philosopher) and the gothic King Theoderic; rather, he likened their conversation to that of one of the senators in Aquitaine with St. Severin, "the eighth century saint who lived around 500 AD in Noricum" (1991, 80). The historical parallel matched Linn's own comparison to the age of Charlemagne. "For if you put aside the 200 years between 1713–1914," Schmitt told Linn, "Christian Europe had always been a pitiful place, invaded from all sides. The interval between 1713–1914 was, anyway, only an ephemeral intermezzo. We are still—as in 500 or 800 AD—in the Christian 'aeon', still in the throes of death, and every major event [and here Schmitt arrived at his favorite subject] is a question of the katechon. . . . It is about a total presence, hidden behind the veil of history" (80).

After this excursion into world history, Schmitt once again came around to speak-ing of his own "vagabondage." He told Linn that he was once again living in his father's house, where he had attended his parents' golden wedding in 1932. He was sleeping in the room where his father had slept and—at the age of ninety-two in the year 1945—died. From his window he could see the Catholic cemetery where his parents rested and where he had had a burial plot reserved for himself and his wife for twenty years. He took the same walks that he had fifty years before. Yet, he told Linn, "our economic situation has changed . . . we have been stripped of everything, and Madame Schmitt is working herself into the ground in the fight for our daily bread. Nevertheless, in a time defined by war and omnipresent nihilism, there is a certain spatial continuity to this, even a 'stabilitas loci' " (1991, 80).

Despite this outward hardship, Schmitt tried to lead his family life entirely through the spirit (*Geist*). "The *Geist* reconciles and drowns out the world," was one of his favor-ite lines from Däubler. "I learnt in the Schmitt household," recalls Christel Hoberg-Heese, a former classmate of Schmitt's daughter Anima, "what my mother had always told me about how spiritual and cultural values are a wonderful counterweight to mate-rial want. In this regard, I still wonder what was going on in the minds of Schmitt and his wife when we 'celebrated' his sixtieth birthday. There were no laudatory speeches, no *Festschrift* and no friends attended. Instead, his sister Ännchen [Anne-Margarete] arranged a small party where we school pupils played music and recited poems."[3] These poems included Annette von Droste-Hülshoff's "An den Mond," Goethe's "Füllest wieder Busch und Tal still mit Nebelglanz," and Clemens Brentano's "Evening serenade" ("*Abendständchen*"): "Hark, the flute whines again,/ And the cool springs sough,/ Golden, the tones drift below—/ Silence, silence, let us listen!" ("*Hör', es klagt die Flöte wieder,/ Und die kühlen Brunnen rauschen,/ Golden wehn die Töne nieder—/ Stille, stille, lass uns lauschen!*")

Shortly after returning from Nuremberg, Schmitt started to keep a diary (as he had since early childhood) to confront the silence that surrounded him and to clarify his thoughts and perhaps also guard them from reality. This was because the dusty printed material that he had saved from his personal archive, especially his correspondence and newspaper articles about him, still had the power to take his breath away. Schmitt asked himself what had brought about this unfathomable enmity toward everything he had ever said and written. While unpacking the moving boxes, he came across a copy of Willy Haas's essay, "Eine neue politische Lehre," which had appeared in the May 1932 issue of the *Literarische Welt*. "Deeply hurt," he noted in his diary on August 28, 1947.

> Haas calls me a nihilist. The friend-enemy theory is a hidden and terrible neutralization, an empty eggshell, because it abstracts from the only concrete source of all enmity—that is, from present materials, namely the class struggle with the bourgeoisie—and thereby neutralizes and thus itself becomes highly political. At the same time, he falsely assumes that the enemy is something "capable of being banished from this world in a war of extermination." How strange. Because of my wariness to identify with his enmity, the enmity of a Marxist civil war, he declares my theory and me to be the enemy. Wonderful confirmation. Everyone agrees with me. If I had said that the Jews were the enemy, then the Nazis would have agreed with me. If I had said that the Nazis were the enemy, then the others would have agreed with me, and so forth. But those are still the somewhat honest ones of the lot. The worst ones are the ones who deny that they have any enmity at all and, on this basis, confirm their enmity. (1991, 4)

He also stumbled upon the French theologian Raymond Bruckberger's thesis that World War III would be a holy war. It occurred to Schmitt that the (at the time) most recent decree from the Holy Office against communism was the official declaration of said war: belief against belief, world religion against world religion. And then Schmitt also thought the following: "The Communist Manifesto contra Syllabus; 'the first act of war is the identification of the enemy.' The modern age had begun with the Jacobins. I am waiting for the Cossacks and the Holy Ghost, Léon Bloy wrote. *Quod custodit Christus [Christus, Jesus] nos tollit Gothus*, wrote the Holy Augustine during a barbarian invasion" (4). Schmitt made the following comment: "In Yalta and Potsdam the Anglo-Saxons pursued a policy of the Third Force, unconscious things thought out to the point of lethargy, an essential characteristic of the Third Force, the mentality of the no-no zone. After working with philosophy and theology for more than twenty years, with the history of the Church and nations, with the documents of the Vatican, after reading Benanos, Péguy and Drumont over and over again, I think I know what I am talking about" (281).

He also thought he knew what he was talking about when he developed the idea of general amnesty at his refuge in Plettenberg. After having unabashedly served the National Socialists, Schmitt was, of course, quick to realize that a wave of anger would sweep through the country should he, of all people, make a public plea for amnesty as "a remembrance of the remnants of sacred law" (1949, 219). So to be on the safe side, he published his thoughts on the subject anonymously in the newspaper *Christ und Welt*. He had to remain hidden in his Plettenberg refuge; he saw himself as an outlaw. From the perspective of somebody stranded in the mountains of the Sauerland, he used his diary to badmouth those around him with a cynical and often malicious wit: "Miracle of the Deutschmark: Thomas Mann has returned to Germany.... Just take a look at this Winston Churchill, that stuffy whisky-drinker" (1991, 242, 256). When he encountered Martin Heidegger's reference to the "locality of essence" (*Ortschaft des Wesens*) he made the following comment: "The locality. He is wary to name names. He does not say Rome and does not say Moscow, and he does not say Geneva and does not say Prague, and he also does not say Lake Success. But I pronounce the names like a child and thereby become the predestined sacrifice of ritual murder, like Kafka's defendant in the trial. I am only still alive because the lemurs that are chasing me no longer have any rites and, hence, are no longer capable of ritual murder. That is my salvation" (1991, 310).

In his isolation Schmitt let his associations run wild, freely blending the distant past with the most recent present. On April 10, 1948, he wrote: "I am currently reading the history of the period of the Diadochi, of the beginning of Hellenistic Greece, for instance the biography of Demtrios Poliorketes from Plutarch: vile immoralities and wild peripeteia, like Adolf's life (*My Life Is a Novel*); more interesting than the history of the Caesars who sat at an already well-organized apparatus of power; the fantastic histrionics; the plurality of such diadochic entities that are no longer capable of unity, for unity for the sake of unity is, as Hegel said, something for the uncultured man who thinks abstractly—that is, globally" (1991, 125–127).

The following day, upon reading a letter written on the occasion of Arnold J. Toynbee's appointment to the American Defense Council, Schmitt encountered Ernst Jünger's view that today philosophers of history were more important than nuclear physicists. Schmitt replied: "You write of Arnold Toynbee and the relationship between philosophers of history and nuclear physicists. Of course, the importance of philosophers of history and their augurs increases with a discriminating ('just') war—that is, through transforming a war between states into a civil war and declaring the enemy a criminal. Undermining the opponent through civil war and shattering his historical-philosophical self esteem is, in the same proportion, a stronger weapon than the atomic bomb" (1991, 127).

After such forays into global politics and world philosophy, Schmitt quickly returned to his own reality and noted in a mood somewhere between depression and haughtiness: "In the loneliness of being the one who leads the way, I make such grave discoveries. I see the polarity of the superhuman [*Übermensch*] and brute [*Unmensch*] and the modern, exterminating notion of the enemy in Karl Marx's 1844 introduction to his criticism of Hegelian legal philosophy. The criticism of Germany 'is not an anatomic knife—it is a weapon. Its object is its enemy, which it does not seek to refute, but destroy'; sic, verbatim, the 26-year-old Karl Marx" (1991, 186). But the effects of such self-adjuration did not last long, and soon Schmitt wrote Linn (again in French) about how he really felt: "I live in a terrible exile, *exul in patria mea*. The Germans are a people of metaphysicians and technicians, but neither jurists nor moralists. When I read some passages in a book by Amédée Ponceau (*Timoleon, Reflexions sur la Tyrannie*) I feel moved to tears. A voice like Ponceau's would be impossible in Germany. To hear this voice from France is, for me, a consolation that borders on a miracle" (1991, 279).

Consoling himself with the words that Machiavelli had written to his friend Francesco Vettori, Schmitt wrote: "At nightfall, I return home and enter my study. Before entering, I take off my workday clothes, covered with mud and dust, and don garments of court and palace. Appropriately attired, I enter the antique courts of ancient men, where, fondly received by them, I nourish myself with the food that alone is mine and for which I live. There I am unashamed to converse with them and to question them about the motives for their actions, and they deign to answer me. And for four hours at a time I feel no boredom at all, I forget all my troubles, I do not fear poverty, and I am not scared of death. I lose myself in them completely....I am wearing myself out and I cannot keep it up much longer without becoming despised because of poverty. Whoever has been loyal and honest for forty-three years, as I am, is hardly able to change his nature...San Casciano, December 10, 1513, Niccolò Machiavelli" (Hüsmert 1988, 40–42).

CULPABILITY

Schmitt was fifty-nine when he returned to Plettenberg. Like Machiavelli, he underscored the inalterability of destiny and character. He signed many a letter with, "Your old, unchangeable, identical Carl Schmitt." Nevertheless, he had the need to continuously prove to himself in his diary entries that his identity, the innermost core of his worldview (*Weltanschauung*), and his life's interpretations had survived the Nazi period (and his involvement in it) unscathed, that the old conception of the enemy had remained intact. "The Jews will always be Jews," he noted on September 25, 1947. "Whilst the Communist can always better and change himself. This has nothing to do with the Nordic race, etc. It is precisely the assimilated Jew that is the true enemy. He has no intent on disproving the Elders of Zion's rallying cry" (1991, 18). As a further affirmation, he added that the compulsion to find a total enemy was correct, "but just one, not two: the East and the West at the same time, the Russians and Anglo-Saxons, both communists and Jews at once—that was too much" (18). No, he was not mistaken, of which he arrogantly assured himself in his diary the next day: "In the years 1933–36, I forgave myself and the dignity of my thoughts less than Plato had forgiven his during his Sicilian travels" (18). Already in his solitary confinement at the war criminals' tribunal, Schmitt had justified himself by claiming that the spirit was free and brought with it its own freedom. He invoked Thomas More as a kind of patron saint of this spiritual freedom. Schmitt noted that he had "overcome numerous obstacles and made extraordinary concessions to the tyrant before he was ready to become a martyr and saint" (1950a, 21).

This was how Schmitt dodged questions about his culpability after 1945, attempting to shirk responsibility for his role in National Socialism by saying that a researcher and scholar could not choose political regimes as he pleased. Even then, he made one of his many appeals to Plato, who while working with the people of Syracuse had taught tyrants to never deprive an enemy of good advice. But did Schmitt give Hitler and the Nazis advice as "enemies?" As a result of Schmitt's clear stance, very few people (with the exception of the SS) came to this conclusion back then, and certainly nobody did after 1945.

Schmitt insisted, however, that this was not a matter of free will, because free will led to the stenciled templates and dead ends of conventional philosophy. He explained this, for instance, in a conversation with Alfred Andersch in Frankfurt in 1951, during a conference celebrating the 300th anniversary of *Leviathan*, at which Andersch upheld man's free will. "You mean something completely different than determinism and indeterminism," Schmitt said to Andersch. "You mean something that every decent man does. What you and I have always done, when we fell in love, when we were inspired politically, when we buckled down. In truth, that was not free will—it was a blind pre-commandment ["*blindes Vorgebot*"]. That is the word and with that the matter and situation: blind pre-commandment" (1991, 314). Schmitt's attempts to use this concept of "blind pre-commandment" to explain away his dedication to the Nazis (who had supposedly "betrayed" him) were, however, dismissed as monstrous. Schmitt was and would remain "the monster."

And his suspicion that people wanted to banish him from German intellectual life was not without grounds. When the Association of German Constitutional Law Teachers was re-established in 1949, the union did not solicit Schmitt for membership. "The membership application had been drafted," reports Wolfgang Abendroth, "but was withdrawn after it was pointed out to fellow members in private conversations that if they approved the application, their own writings from the time of the Third Reich would be possibly re-read and cited. This argument was sufficient to convince the fellow members" (1976, 213). In 1951 the West German President Theodor Heuss even interceded in the debate, demanding that a man like Schmitt should never again be permitted to stand behind a lectern. It would not have done Schmitt any good to point out that whereas he himself had never facilitated Hitler's rise to power, Heuss had voted for the Enabling Act in 1933 while a representative in the Reichstag. "A few decades ago," explained Heuss in 1951:

> Carl Schmitt squeezed the "essence of the political" into the tenuous formalism of the "friend-enemy" relationship. This throttled the infinite variety of interrelations

and interactions in political life because the dynamic tension, which can also belong to this infinite variety, was isolated and over-emphasized. This infinite variety, which does not just look to the friend-enemy relationship, but goes beyond the limits of formal logic to the place where the substance of public life can be seen—a substance that carries values and is carried by values that are, by nature, transcendent. (1963, 302)

Following Heuss's verdict, which came from the most preeminent political position in postwar Germany, it was clear that it would be necessary to cut Schmitt in order to avoid coming under suspicion oneself. In 1952, after the magazine *Merkur* published Schmitt's essay "The Unity of the World," eighty of its employees protested and threatened to resign should more of Schmitt's work be printed. In 1953 Hans Schomerus, the director of the Protestant Academy in Bad Herrenalb, invited Schmitt to attend a conference and give the closing lecture, "The Antichrist and What Is Holding Him Back." Walter Strauß, the state secretary for the Federal Ministry of Justice at the time, personally intervened with Baden's regional bishop and warned of "far-reaching consequences" for the academy should Schmitt actually give a presentation. A copy of this letter was even sent to Hermann Ehlers, the president of the Bundestag. Schomerus was subsequently forced to retract the invitation. In 1954 the weekly Hamburg newspaper *Die Zeit* became the stage of a heated discussion between Richard Tüngel, the editor-in-chief, and the Countess Marion Dönhoff, who ran the political section. Schmitt was to blame. While the countess was on vacation, Tüngel had published and sensationalized a text by Schmitt entitled "In the Antechamber of Power" ("Im Vorraum der Macht"). Dönhoff protested, and Tüngel was forced to leave the paper soon thereafter. "Alarm bells went off for me," said Dönhoff, "when a man who writes for *Die Zeit* continuously opposes the civic, rational constitutional state with mythical theories of an intrinsic unity of the *Volk*."[4] At the 1954 Frankfurt Book Fair, Paul Hühnerfeld, editor of the arts section at *Die Zeit*, even threatened to smash Neske-Publishing House's stand to pieces for displaying a new title by Schmitt.

Alarm bells continued to "ring" for many people well into the 1960s and 1970s whenever Schmitt's name was mentioned. In a summary of the various reproaches of Schmitt, Jürgen Habermas states that the superficial debate about Schmitt's reductive enemy/friend concept of the political was not provocative for the Federal Republic's understanding of itself as a constitutional democracy; rather, it was that political theology "that rejects a secularized notion of politics and, in so doing, the democratic process as a basis for legitimacy of law; it distorts a democracy that has been bereaved of one of its deliberative cores into just an acclamation of deployed masses; it opposes the myth of born national unity with social pluralism; it denounces the universalism of human rights and the moral code of humanity as criminal hypocrisy" (Schmitt 1939, 116). Schmitt was never to shake off his National Socialist past and get rid of the reputation of being somebody who had committed a breach of civilization. The development of German postwar society into "the most liberal democracy" stood in opposition to the ideas of a man who called the "struggle for a catholic intensification...against the neutralizers, the aesthetic *Schlaraffen*, the abortionists, the cremators, and pacifists" the "secret keyword" of his spiritual and journalistic existence (1991, 165).

Schmitt countered these animosities with the construction of his own myth. In his 1950 work *Ex Captivitate Salus*, which was his most personal book, Schmitt put together his writings from his time in the internment camps in Berlin and Nuremberg prison. Here is where he started to construct this postwar myth. Schmitt felt he was (Quincy Wright notwithstanding) the world's only teacher of law who had apprehended and experienced the problem of the just war, including the civil war, in all its depths and causes. He was the last, conscious representative of European international law, of the *jus publicum Europaeum*; its last teacher and researcher in an existential sense, whose end was similar to that of Benito Cereno (the eponymous protagonist from Hermann Melville's 1855 novella) aboard the last voyage of the slave ship *San Dominick*. After mutinying and deposing Cereno, the *San Dominick*'s black crew torments the Spanish captain and then keeps him alive because of his vital seafaring knowledge. Cereno is eventually saved, and the mutineers are put on trial and then hanged. Yet at the trial Cereno only gives sparse evidence and subsequently withdraws into silence. This parable, in which the captain (Schmitt) is kept by the mutineers (the Nazis) for his technical knowledge and constantly held under duress, was immediately recognized as a mythical distortion and duly dismissed.

Despite his postwar announcement in Nuremberg about retreating into the safety of silence, Schmitt really only kept silent about his involvement with the National Socialist authorities. He never expressed any kind of regret. "I understand the prophet Jonah, who refused to do the Lord's bidding and go to Nineveh and preach to the people there. I also do not want to do to this, preach penitence; I also do not want go to Nineveh" (1991, 8–10), he noted in his diary on September 3, 1947. And so Schmitt simply continued to work, seeing himself as an independent scholar. He further developed his political theories in works such as *The "Nomos" of the Earth*, which, although first published in 1950, had been almost entirely complete since 1945. In 1963 he published the *Theory of the Partisan*, an addendum to *The Concept of the Political*, and in 1970 came *Political Theology II*.

VISITORS

Since the beginning of the 1950s, people had begun to pluck up the courage to visit Plettenberg. Many were students from Marburg, notably Rüdidger Altmann and Johannes Gross, both of whom went on to be well-known publishers. The conversations that arose from these visits were Schmitt's lifeblood. The discussions would begin with dinner, a celebrated occasion for Schmitt, and the table could not be cleared until they were over, which did not happen until late in the night, if at all. The discussions would often resume the following morning, and the visitors stayed in hotels in and around Plettenberg.

The few public appearances Schmitt made were organized by the "Academia moralis," a registered association founded in 1947 whose sole purpose was to offer material support to Schmitt after his return from Nuremberg. It was in the unlikeliest of venues that the renowned professor for national and international law and former Prussian councilor of state made appearances, such as the backroom of a restaurant on Venloerstraße in Cologne, close to the train station Westbahnhof: "The lecture hall has been offered to the Academy by the proprietor on the promise that a minimum amount of revenue is generated. Accordingly, 2.00 DM vouchers shall be issued before the beginning of the presentation. These will be accepted as payment by the proprietor," says one invitation from the "Academia moralis" on July 28, 1951, with the announcement of a presentation "by Professor Dr. Carl Schmitt, Plettenberg, Westphalia, on the topic of 'Impressions of travels in Spain'" (Schmitz 1994, 147).

In 1957 Ernst Forsthoff, a former student of Schmitt's, held a vacation course in Ebrach, Upper Franconia. Because Schmitt (unlike Heidegger) was prohibited from teaching after 1945, Forsthoff, who taught constitutional and administrative law at the University of Tübingen at the time, sought to put the notorious professor in contact with colleagues such as Arnold Gehlen, Pascual Jordan, and Werner Conze, as well as with interested students. The Münster philosopher Joachim Ritter also invited Schmitt to the seminars held by Ritter's "Collegium Philosophicum." It was there that Schmitt met people like Hermann Lübbe, Robert Spaemann, and Odo Marquard. The young philosopher Günter Rohrmoser, born in 1927, encountered Schmitt in both Ebrach and Münster. It was in Ebrach that Rohrmoser (having written his dissertation on Shakespeare in 1955) wanted to investigate the connection between tragedy and utopia in Shakespeare's work. Schmitt sat next to him during a presentation, Rohrmoser recalls, "and did what he was always wont to do. He had a piece of paper in front of him on which he drew strange symbols that were nearly impossible to decipher for an outsider. His restlessness grew ever more apparent in the course of the presentation, and towards the end he left the room in a hurry with a bright red face, making a dash for fresh air. I was quite startled, for I was aware of no misdeed" (1998, 147–149). Rohrmoser quickly ran after him and discovered Schmitt "breathing heavily" outside. "A lengthy discussion about Shakespeare ensued. At the time, I did not know that Carl Schmitt had repeatedly worked on Shakespeare, especially in his *Hamlet or Hecuba* monograph. On a large piece of paper he drew an arrangement of symbols and connecting lines, of which the only thing that has remained in my memory is the end: Pope Paul V = Hamlet. And the last line was: Europe = Hamlet? Here is where one of Carl Schmitt's fascinating capabilities was made visible—that is, not only the ability to think in a larger context, but also being able to make connections that an averagely gifted mind would neither be capable of making, nor dare to think of making" (147). He summarized:

> What I found so fascinating about Carl Schmitt was not so much what he thought, but rather what he saw. Perhaps the strength of his intellectual perception has something to do with the way his work always leaves us puzzled: on the one hand, we find sentences and concepts of unusual conciseness and lucidity, and yet we are confronted with the enigmatic quality of his entire oeuvre which, in the face of the innumerable interpretations, begins to crumble and dissolve.... In my encounters with

Carl Schmitt, I came to know him as a warm-hearted and extraordinarily witty indi-vidual who, like all of us, doubtlessly had his faults, to which a certain vanity unmis-takably belonged; but all it took was just a few minutes of conversation to forget this all too earthly trait. Then one could only be fascinated by the never before seen or imagined inter-connections which spanned millennia, and with which he kept sur-prising us. (1998, 147–149)

These significant conversations did not take place in Münster or Ebrach, but in and around Schmitt's Plettenberg. Starting in the mid-1950s, an ever-increasing stream of visitors made the journey to see the "monster" in the flesh. Here they could have a private experience with Schmitt, taking part in a sort of conspiratorial collective. According to Habermas, it was as if a subversive undercurrent to the political intellec-tual history of the Federal Republic had developed here. Habermas traced Schmitt's influence as "a brilliant mind in the self-styled role of the outlaw" back to the notion that, in the "defiance of the self-consciously conquered" (1995, 118–119), Schmitt (like Heidegger) knew how to render the causes of defeat understandable and how to con-vincingly represent the continuity of German traditions that had been called into question. The early Federal Republic had witnessed no reckoning with the Nazi era, no change of elite, Habermas argued.

Carl Schmitt, therefore, formed in a social-psychological sense a functionally neces-sary supplement to the implicit integration of the former base in so far as he repre-sented an antitype onto which rehabilitated Nazis and fellow travellers [Mitläufer] could productively foist their own biographies. Conversely, Schmitt held an under-valued advantage over his favored colleagues. And it is from this angle that his enor-mous reception history and renewed relevance after 1989 can be understood: as he did not have to be denazified, Carl Schmitt also did not have to remain silent like the others; he could broach the German continuities that others were content to leave unspoken. (1995, 120)

Schmitt stayed in the attic flat on Brockhauser Weg until 1970. Unless he was enter-taining company, he would mainly communicate with the outside world in writing. Telephone, radio, and television were not permitted in the apartment; nothing "unsolic-ited like waves or radiation" was allowed to penetrate his space (Hüsmert 1988, 40–42). The last move came in 1970; the family relocated to Pasel, a village on the outskirts of Plettenberg. He moved into house number 11c, a modest flat-roof bungalow designed by friend and architect Hans de Vries. Pasel was a former farming village with a one-room schoolhouse. Strangers rarely got lost when they visited, because the only road that led into the village also happened to be the only one that led out. This is probably why Pasel's locals may have been initially puzzled by the many visitors following Schmitt's arrival: Americans, Englishmen, Frenchmen, Spaniards, Chinese, Thais, Koreans, and Japanese. Like Jünger's Wilfingen or Heidegger's Todtnauberg, it was as if Pasel became a kind of pilgrimage site.

The villagers of Pasel eventually got used to the fact that their neighbor, the cordial and gentle "Herr Professor," simply knew lots of people, some of whom the locals were no doubt also proud to recognize: Georg Kiesinger, the former chancellor, or Rudolf Augstein, *Spiegel's* publisher. The mailman, whom Schmitt eagerly awaited every morning, was likewise soon no longer surprised by the mountain of mail he had to deliver to the house. If all of Plettenberg had been Schmitt's refuge, his "San Casciano," up until 1970, it was now only his house that he called "San Casciano," which is the name of the town where Machiavelli had fled after the Florentine Republic no longer had any use for his services. The famous name could be read on a wooden panel hanging out back, facing the garden. Close friends knew that this name did not just allude to Machiavelli's country estate in San Andrea di Percussina, near San Casciano, but also commemorated the holy St. Cassian of Imola. Persecuted by the emperor Diocletian and condemned to death for his Christianity, St. Cassian eventually died at the hands of his own pupils, who murdered him with iron styli. Occasionally Schmitt also spoke of a Spanish monk by the name of San Casiano and his 1499 manuscript, "*Vocabulario de Santaelle*," in which San Casiano had cataloged the burdens of age.

ARCANUM

The last fifteen years of Schmitt's life in Pasel were marked by external serenity and inner turmoil. His growing international reception allayed his fear of being an intellectual outcast. In the late 1960s and early 1970s the ever-elusive and mysterious Schmitt offered a glimpse into his *Arcanum*, into his most private of private beliefs, when he revealed the secret of his worldview in *Political Theology II*. Two reasons account for this more daring attitude. On the one hand, it was a response to an old wound that his erstwhile friend, Erik Peterson, had inflicted upon him. In his essay *Monotheism as a Political Problem* (1935), Peterson had declared all political theology to be over and done with. His claim rested on the argument that no dualistic political theology, such as Schmitt's, was compatible with the doctrine of the trinity—a rather bold claim, according to Schmitt. On the other hand, Schmitt was forced to come out into the open after being challenged by Hans Blumenberg in *The Legitimacy of the Modern Age*. Blumenberg did this by criticizing Schmitt's *Political Theology* from a scientific (and not theological) perspective and by assigning the work a place beyond modernity.

In his dispute with Peterson and Blumenberg, Schmitt let the cat out of the bag when he revealed his last myth in the afterword to *Political Theology II*, which above all contains his response to Blumenberg. Schmitt refers to Marcion, a leading gnostic from AD 85–160 who postulated the existence of two different gods: a god of the Old Testament and a god of the New Testament, both of which, according to Marcion, could have nothing in common with each other. By taking up and further developing Marcion's theories, Schmitt betrays his belief in a god that embodies not "unity" but "duality" (1984, 109–111).

Based on Goethe's epigraph in the fourth volume of his autobiography, *Truth and Poetry: From My Own Life* ("*nemo contra deum nisi deus ipse*"), Schmitt interprets this "egregious dictum" as an upheaval ("stasis") of the redeemer-god against the creator-god. Schmitt reminds his readers that the history of the word and concept "stasis" ranges from Plato to the neo-Platonists, especially Plotinus, right up to the Greek Church Fathers. Firstly, "stasis" means calm, a position of rest, standpoint, and status; the antonym "kinesis" means movement. Yet at the same time, "stasis" also means unrest, motion, turmoil, and civil war. Although most lexicons merely juxtapose these two contradictory meanings without further commentary, "the mere juxtaposition of numerous examples of such a contradiction offers a rich source for recognizing political and political-theological phenomena. Here we encounter a true political-theological stasiology at the core of the trinity doctrine," wrote Schmitt. "Which is why," he concludes, "the enmity problem and the problem of the enemy cannot be concealed" (1996, 92).

Earlier he had quoted Gregory of Nazianzus as an additional source: "The One (*to Hen*) is always in upheaval (*stasiatson*) against himself (*pros heauton*)" (1996, 116). And so here Schmitt returns once again to the gnostic dualism that he defended against Peterson and Blumenberg. "Gnostic dualism puts a god of love, an unworldly god, as the redeemer-god up against the just god, the lord and redeemer of this evil world. Both behave, if not with mutually active and combatant enmity, then certainly with an unbridgeable foreignness, in a sort of dangerous cold war whose enmity can be even more intense than that enmity which manifests and asserts itself in the naivety of a pure pitched battle" (93). The "toughness" of and "difficulty to refute" gnostic dualism was, according to him, based less on the evidence of old mythic and metaphoric images of lightness and darkness, and "more…on the fact that an omnipotent, omniscient and infinitely good creator-god could not be identical with a redeemer-god. Augustine shifts the difficulty from the deity to the freedom of man, to a creature created by God and endowed with freedom. By virtue of the freedom endowed to him, this creature makes the world of god, otherwise not in need of redemption, in need of redemption in the first place. Man, the creature that is capable of this, retains his freedom not through deeds, but rather misdeeds. The doctrine of the trinity enshrouds the identity of the creator-god and the redeemer-god in the unity of father and son who, although not absolutely identical, are nevertheless 'one,' whereby a dualism of two natures, 'god-man,' becomes a unity in the second person" (93).

In every world in need of change and renewal, this "structural, central problem" of the gnostic dualism of a creator-god and redeemer-god was, Schmitt summarized, "intrinsically given, unescapably and ineradicably so." He draws the following conclusion: "The enmity between people cannot be eliminated by prohibiting state wars of every sort, by propagating a world revolution and by attempting to transform global policy into a global police. Revolution, in contrast to reformation, reform, revision and evolution, is a hostile conflict. The master of a world in need of change (that is, of a misguided world), the one to whom this need to change is ascribed because he does not give in to the change but resists it, cannot be good friends with the liberator, the one who is to bring about a changed, new world. They are, so to speak, enemies *of their own accord*" (1996, 93–95). Schmitt thus affixed his friend/enemy theory to his concep-tualization of God and at the same time made clear that he was not on the side of the unworldly god of love. Rather, he put his chips on the creator-god of an "evil" world in which friend and enemy had to be distinguished. "Until Jesus returns, the world shall be amiss."[5] This is why Schmitt went up against an enemy whom he had exactly identi-fied and whose "real possibility I continue to recognize in a[n] utterly de-theologized antithesis" (96). In this sense, Schmitt could not use Jesus Christ, who had made his promise to the meek and peaceful, for his theory. More fitting to his concept was an insight he formulated on April 27, 1948, in his diary: "Even Satan's power is…as such from God and not evil. How could Burkhardt arrive at the opposite conclusion? The 'will to power' would be the good will! Indeed, if it's a divine will and the will sub-ordinates itself; there is only one evil will: the will to impotence, that is forgoing an execution" (1991, 139). How curious indeed: Schmitt as the mouthpiece and executor of the creator-god's will? A god whose quintessence is justice, yet one that he exercises according to the law of love?

After reading Schmitt's commentary on his work *The Legitimacy of the Modern Age*, Blumenberg was so provoked and inspired that he wrote his first private letter to him. "After opening a dialogue between us in *Political Theology II*," Blumenberg confessed, "there is much that I can no longer write as I would have written it earlier."[6] In return, Schmitt sent him his small study *Three Stages of the Attribution of Historical Meaning* along with the question discussed therein: "whether eschatological faith and histori-cal consciousness can coexist?" (1950b, 930). While most people denied this question, Schmitt saw the "possibility of a bridge" that lies in imagining a force that holds back the end and the evil power that precedes it. This was Schmitt's old notion of the *katechon*.

Blumenberg eagerly read Schmitt's reference to the second epistle to the Thessalonians in which the *katechon*, which seemed important to Blumenberg, can be found both per-sonally and neutrally. "Is this mysterious notion of somebody holding back the final events and restraining the forces not itself an eschatological notion," Blumenberg asked. "Or is it rather an interpretation of and justification for the non-appearance of the end and its promises?" Blumenberg also gave the same answer:

> The most important transition is this: the signs of the end of the world become more negative the more one feels disappointed by the expectation of this end. And no sooner, some mysterious force gets credited with deferring and holding back the end. I have repeatedly pointed out that both Paul and John's theology take up the non-appearance of the end in various ways by announcing the goods of salvation of this end as already realized: the justification [acquittal at the final judgment] and life. It will not be long before the Christians start praying for a deferral of the end and not the coming of Christ in order to eventually posit themselves as the force that the Roman Empire maintains by constantly staying God. After they become identical with the power of the Empire, the "katechon" will, as a sheer consequence, also repre-sent itself in this power. But all of this is just forms, not of the simultaneity of history and eschatology, but of the inversion of the eschatological promise into the promise of deferring the eschata. (1950b, 930)

Blumenberg was intent on getting to the bottom of their differences through this correspondence by showing that he was opposed to the idea, "that a simultaneity of historical consciousness and genuine eschatology were possible" (930). The old man in Pasel must have been utterly content (and his notations in the Blumenberg letter support this assumption) upon reading that one of the reasons for Blumenberg's interpretation lay in the admission that "every eschatology is, by its very nature, gnostic, for it presupposes a dualism between the creator and the judge. There cannot be, as Marcion saw, an identity between the God of the Old Testament and the God of the New Testament because the horrors of the end implicate the discriminations of the beginning" (930). After speaking of Schmitt's "pessimism of old age," Blumenberg entreats him with the following words: "How urgent it seems to me that you insist upon your interpretation of and emphasis on the 'katechon'. It would indeed be important to put to the test 'what I can withstand' because—forgive me—an opponent of this dignity is what a thinker must wish for above and beyond all acclaim. I am presumptuous enough to have and express this wish" (930).

Another important correspondent and friend of Schmitt's was the Russian-French Hegel scholar Alexandre Kojève. In 1967 Kojève attended a conference in Berlin. Jacob Taubes, a Jewish philosopher, was charged with taking care of him.

> I asked him in Berlin: where are you heading from here? (He had come to us directly from Beijing). His answer: "To Plettenberg." I stared at him in bewilderment, even though I was used to surprises with Kojève. Kojève proceeded: "where else should one go in Germany? Carl Schmitt is the only one worth talking to." That stung me, because I forbade myself from visiting Carl Schmitt and envied . . . Kojève the impartiality with which he consorted with him. But in the end, Kojève was Russian, originally Kojevnikoff, and wrote his dissertation under Jaspers in Heidelberg about Wladimir Soloview, the "Russian Hegel" and friend of Dostoyevsky. Ergo a member of an apocalyptic nation—just as Carl Schmitt was a member of the German Reich with healing claims—and me, the son of the true chosen people that just arouses the envy of the apocalyptic nations; an envy that puts phantasmagoria into the world and denies the true chosen people's right to exist. It is no question for me that the Jewish problem occupied Carl Schmitt his whole life, that 1936 was merely an occasion to take a "timely" stand on the problem, which, for him, possessed quite other dimensions. It was Christ of the Gentiles who stared upon those with hate and envy 'to whom pertaineth the adoption, and the glory, and the covenants, and the giving of the law, and the service of God, and the promises; whose are the fathers, and of whom as concerning the flesh Christ came.'[7]

For Schmitt, Christianity was "Judaism for Gentiles whose power he always desired to stand up to. But Schmitt's appreciation of how impotent such a 'protest' against God and history is grew ever deeper" (Taubes 1987, 24–26).

It was only later—"much later, much too late" (25) according to Taubes—that he decided to follow Kojève's example and visit Schmitt in Plettenberg. In Schmitt's house, Taubes says he had the fiercest conversations in the German language: it was historiography in a nutshell, shoved into the mythical image. "It is the prejudice of the gild that mythical images or terminology are called vague oracles, pliant and obedient to the will of all, whereas the scientific language of positivism has a lease on the truth.... Nothing can be further from the actual situation than this historical prejudice" (25).

In Taubes's eyes, Schmitt was both a "legitimate catholic anti-Semite" and an anti-bolshevist:

> If I understand his work at all, he is the only one who said what was going on—that is, a global civil war was in the works. Right after World War I. He could have become a Leninist, but he had what it took to become the only relevant anti-Leninist. That all of this got lost in the Hitler-mush is the most fatal consequence, but not the only one. That means the history of the Weimar republic was steering toward an end. That has a fatalistic character. That was one possibility—and it was the worst one. So, I am truly not qualified to teach or even defend German history, but to say that German history (be it since Luther, Bismarck, Charlemagne or Schmitt) was leading up to Hitler, well, that is something I just cannot believe. These genealogies are cheap and cost nothing, just time in the library. That is not the case; there were open possibilities that were buried alive. (1987, 71–73)

It was in this spirit that Taubes, after another long conversation with Schmitt in Plettenberg, wrote on September 18, 1979:

> Dear Mr. Schmitt, please allow me to thank you once again for your friendly, indeed amicable reception, for your patience and for the openness with which you discussed the failures in the long life of a legal expert. Even in his failures, "an incomparable, political teacher" (and I permitted myself the variation of a word that still resounds in my ears from my college years). As an arch-Jew, I hesitate to roundly condemn someone because, in all the unspeakable horror, we were saved from one thing. We had no choice: Hitler had declared us a total enemy. But where there is no choice, there can also be no judgment, much less on others. That does not, however, mean that I am not concerned with understanding what "actually" happened (and not in an historic sense, but rather in an eschatological one). Where were the foundations laid for (our and your) catastrophe? (39)

Another visitor in Plettenberg was the French novelist Jean-Pierre Faye, whose theory of narration, *L'introduction aux langues totalitaires* (1977), an introduction to totalitarian language, was based on a very critical reading of Schmitt's works. Faye experienced Schmitt as an affable man who enjoyed a good laugh. Faye recalled that Schmitt could not help but laugh at the notion of a "Conservative Revolution" as well as at the idea that there could be a dialogue between Jünger and Heidegger. Heidegger was, according to Schmitt, the "milker of language," the "milker of meaning," and between the two only a few drops of this milk could fall.

Schmitt was in a similarly exuberant mood on July 11, 1978, on the occasion of his ninetieth birthday, which was held in the Tanneneck, a Plettenberg mountain hotel. All of his friends were gathered and several addressed him as *"Herr Staatsrat,"* which pleased Schmitt, for he remained proud of the title, telling anyone who would listen how grateful he was to be a *Preußischer Staatsrat* and not a Noble Prize Laureate.

NIGHTFALL

Schmitt's daughter predeceased him by two years; she had been fighting cancer for a long time. Schmitt's housekeeper, Anni Stand, and Hüsmert, broke the news to him softly. "He took the news with composure," relates Hüsmert, "even though it must have taken him by surprise because we had hidden from him the hopelessness of her condition. Schmitt said: 'I sensed it,' and walked into the bedroom silently. There hung a picture of a twelve-year-old girl. The picture dated back to the days when he used to read to her from his most beautiful book, *Land and Sea* (*Land und Meer*), which he had also dedicated to her. After returning, he did not want to speak of his child" (Hüsmert 1988, 40–42). According to Hüsmert, her death broke Schmitt for good.

Yet Schmitt's state of consciousness was still calm. The chapter "Carl Schmitt and the Jews" was closed for him, even though memories were occasionally stirred up. Similarly, his masochistic hate for the Jews had finally oozed out of him, save for the occasional outbreak well into the 1970s. The Jewish question came up again one evening in Pasel. Altmann and Gross were there with Hüsmert. Altmann exclaimed: "Herr Professor, I will not take part in this discussion. You dedicated your 'constitutional theory' to your Jewish friend, Fritz Eisler, who fell in World War I for Germany. This ought to prohibit you from speaking in such a way here." "Schmitt fell silent," recalls Hüsmert (1988, 40–42). Since that time, Hüsmert continues, Schmitt had finally made his peace with the Jews because ever since they "got a piece of land under their feet and possessed their own state, they started behaving like every other nation." What was behind Schmitt's love/hate relationship with the Jews, which gushes forth from many of his texts, especially the diary entries? Had the man with so many close Jewish friends (not just Eisler) dreamt of being a Jew himself? In the mid-1930s, after letting himself get carried away and making a fiercely antisemitic statement in the company of his family, his brother, Jup, cut him off and said: "But you are a Jew yourself!" Even then Schmitt fell silent.

In the summer of 1984 Schmitt fell seriously ill: cerebral sclerosis with accompanying hallucinations. According to Hüsmert,

> it was never people and events of the past that made the sick man's life a living hell, day and night. The origin of the enemy who was afflicting him remained obscure, however real he might have seemed to him or however concrete the pain was that he inflicted upon him.…Sound waves were entering into the house from every which way; rays from every imaginable electronic device were conveying exceptionally clear voices from a distance of over a hundred kilometers. There were bugging devices hidden all over the house. His enemies were closing in on him for the kill. Nothing was hidden from them; they intruded on the most intimate of affairs. They were primitive, yet technically savvy and incredibly dangerous. They were neither Nazis, nor emigrants nor members of an established party. They condemned him to death. He awaited his execution. But the fusiliers did not show up. He was condemned and simultaneously pardoned. (1988, 40–42)

The leader of these unidentifiable enemies was a "tall, strong guy with a roaring voice" whom Schmitt called "Kra." Although this "Kra" organized the terror, he was himself merely the "agent" of powerful men behind the scenes. One day Schmitt even apprehended this "Kra," although he did not manage to find out his true name. At the time Hüsmert thought he recognized in this clamor about Kra and his people the Ra-drama from Theodor Däubler's *Nordlicht*. "The way it steadily goes *ra-ra-ra-rat*, and how Ra's herold, Chuenaten, hears the piercing and horrid clamor of the riotous crowd in twenty seven rhymes. Power and noise, all in one. That was the Kra who was now taking shape and whom Schmitt had been challenging all his life with the power of his mind."

Schmitt extracted his knowledge of Ra from Däubler's depiction in *Nordlicht*. As an Egyptian sun god and the "first, still entirely wild and unbridled manifestation" of the power of the sun, Ra was the "manly, violent ruler who founded his state upon this brutal power and, in the end, consumed himself in his own fire. Chuenaten, his servant, king and priest, the despiser of everything feminine, the raging fanatic of the cult of Ra," sets his capital, Thebes, on fire after "the senseless power of the life of the sun, which is dictated by no spiritual goal, had exhausted itself in the horrible orgies of emasculation at the 'festival of the castrated.' As a logical progression to this madness, he turns his wrath upon himself and allows the priests of Ammon to slice open his belly" (Däubler 1991, 19–21). As Schmitt had known since 1916, "his cry while the priests were slaughtering him and rummaging around his guts was horrible" (1991, 45).

Conversations with Schmitt were only possible with some difficulty, not least because he was hard of hearing. He was nearly deaf and blind, writes Jünger in one of his last letters. He consoled himself with verses from Konrad Weiss (1948): "on the dark track, time gathers its light with inaudible steps." From time to time he was also given to monologues, as when Hüsmert visited him on Christmas Eve in 1984. According to Hüsmert, Schmitt did not even register his visit. This is why Hüsmert was so perplexed when Schmitt, with remarkable awareness, announced loud and clear: "After World War I said: 'sovereign is the one who determines the state of exception.' After World War II, in the face of my death, I now say: 'sovereign is the one who commands the room's waves'." Hüsmert tried to get him to expound upon this view, but his efforts were in vain. Schmitt's last sentence on this Christmas Eve was: "My last days have been very sad. It pains me that people mistreat my daughter because of me. The poor child." (At the time, Anima had already been dead for one and a half years.) Hüsmert relates further: "Then Schmitt took his leave from me very formally by excusing himself for being tired, and after getting up from the sofa with some difficulty, he shuffled into his bedroom" (1988, 40–42).

On New Year's Eve, just a few days later, Schmitt fell in his room and broke his thigh and pelvis. Hüsmert had just visited him that afternoon. Werner Böckenförde, the canon from Limburg, had also come. Along with his brother Ernst-Wolfgang Böckenförde, the influential and well-regarded constitutional court judge, Werner belonged to Schmitt's closest circle of friends. Schmitt always reserved the second day of Christmas for the two brothers. On the afternoon of New Year's Eve, Böckenförde (who would later give Schmitt a Catholic burial) presented Schmitt with a volume of the literary remains of Hans Barion, the canon lawyer with whom Schmitt had been friends since his time in

Bonn. Böckenförde himself was the book's editor, and he had dedicated the preface to Schmitt. "Too late," recalls Hüsmert, "he no longer acknowledged it. Here is somebody that is almost hundred years old and is still going to die too young."

According to Hüsmert, after Schmitt's fall on New Year's Eve, he was bedridden and resolved to die without really understanding the state of his condition. He refused to eat and lay in the throws of death, only to come around again without the ability to recognize visitors, not even his friend of many years, Hüsmert. One day before his death on Easter Sunday Schmitt received one last visit from Hüsmert in the Evangelical Hospital in Plettenberg. Upon entering the ward in which Schmitt was stationed, Hüsmert could already hear his moans and cries from the distance. The cries of a nearly ninety-seven year old man were enough to bring down the whole hospital. When Hüsmert entered the room, he bore witness to a hideous sight. He ran straight to the doctor in charge and demanded that Schmitt be given a sedative. He never went back into the hospital room. Schmitt's death throws haunted Hüsmert: "[T]he dialectic opposition, which dominated all of his thought, was also in his body and at work until the end." Or, as Hüsmert later put it, "Surely one cannot say that Carl Schmitt died believing in redemption" (1988, 40–41).

Translated from the German by Benjamin Dorvel

NOTES

1. Unless noted otherwise, all translations of source material by the translator.
2. Letter from the Hauptstaatsarchiv Düsseldorf, Nachlass Carl Schmitt, RW 265–13773.
3. Christel Hoberg-Heese, from a lecture given on November 6, 2004, at a meeting of the "Siedlinghauser Kreises", which was founded in the 1930s by the country doctor Franz Schranz, in the Sauerland; quotes taken from the manuscript.
4. Bucerius 1966; the comment can be found in a letter by the Countess Dönhoff to Richard Tüngel in July 1954.
5. Letter to Linn, as quoted in Koenen 1995 (823).
6. The correspondences with Blumenberg can be found among Schmitt's literary remains in the Hauptstaatsarchiv Düsseldorf, RW 265–1498/1–6.
7. Romans 9:4–5, King James Bible.

REFERENCES

Abendroth, W. 1976. *Ein Leben in der Arbeiterbewegung*. Frankfurt: Suhrkamp.
Bucerius, G. 1966. "ZEIT-Geschichte—wie sie uns in Atem hielt." *Die Zeit*, February 18.
Däubler, T. 1991. *Nordlicht*. Munich: Müller.
Faye, J. P. 1977. *Theorie der Erzählung: Einführung in die totalitären Sprachen*. Frankfurt: Suhrkamp.
Habermas, J. 1995. "Carl Schmitt in der politischen Geistesgeschichte der Bundesrepublik." In Habermas, *Die Normalität einer Berliner Republik*. Frankfurt: Suhrkamp, 112–122.
Heuss, T. 1963. *Erinnerungen*. Tübingen: Wuderlich.

Hüsmert, E. 1988. "Die letzten Jahre von Carl Schmitt." In *Schmittiana: Beiträge zu Leben und Werk Carl Schmitts*, vol. 1, ed. P. Tommissen. Berlin: Duncker & Humblot, 40–54.

Koenen, A. 1995. *Der Fall Carl Schmitt: Sein Aufstieg zum "Kronjuristen" des Dritten Reiches*. Darmstadt: Wissenschaftliche Buchgesellschaft.

Peterson, E. 1935. *Der Monotheismus als politisches Problem: Ein Beitrag zur Politischen Theologie im Imperium Romanum*. Leipzig: Hegner.

Pieper, J. 1976. *'Noch wußte es niemand:' Autobiographische Aufzeichnungen 1904–1945*. Munich: Kösel.

Rohrmoser, G. 1998. "Der Hegelsche Staat ist tot." In *Schmittiana: Beiträge zu Leben und Werk Carl Schmitts*, vol. 6, ed. P. Tommissen. Berlin: Duncker & Humblot, 147–155.

Schmitt, C. 1934a. "Der Führer schützt das Recht." *Deutsche Juristen-Zeitung*, August 1.

Schmitt, C. 1934b. *Über die drei Arten des rechtswissenschaftlichen Denkens*. Hamburg: Hanseatische Verlagsanstalt.

Schmitt, C. 1939. *Völkerrechtliche Großraumordnung mit Interventionsverbot für raumfremde Mächte: Ein Beitrag zum Reichsbegriff im Völkerrecht*. Reprinted in Schmitt 1995, 269–371.

Schmitt, C. 1949. "Amnestie oder die Kraft des Vergessens." In Schmitt 1995, 218–221.

Schmitt, C. 1950a. *Ex Captivitate Salus*. Cologne: Greven.

Schmitt, C. 1950b. "Drei Stufen historischer Sinngebung." *Universitas* 5.8: 927–931.

Schmitt, C. 1979a. *Der Begriff des Politischen*. Berlin: Duncker & Humblot.

Schmitt, C. 1979b. *Politische Theologie*, 3rd ed. Berlin: Duncker & Humblot.

Schmitt, C. 1991. *Glossarium*, ed. E. von Medem. Berlin: Duncker & Humblot.

Schmitt, C. 1995. *Staat, Großraum, Nomos: Arbeiten aus den Jahren 1916–1969*, ed. G. Maschke. Berlin: Duncker & Humblot.

Schmitt, C. 1996. *Politische Theologie II*. Berlin: Duncker & Humblot.

Schmitt, C. 2000. *Jugendbriefe: Briefschaften an seine Schwester Auguste 1905–1913*, ed. E. Hüsmert. Berlin: Akademie Verlag.

Schmitz, W. 1994. "Zur Geschichte der Academia Moralis." In *Schmittiana: Beiträge zu Leben und Werk Carl Schmitts*, vol. 6, ed. P. Tommissen. Berlin: Duncker & Humblot, 119–156.

Taubes, J. 1987. *Ad Carl Schmitt: Gegenstrebige Fügung*. Berlin: Merve.

Weiß, K. 1948. *Gedichte*. Munich: Hegner.

Wieland, C.-D. 1987. "Carl Schmitt in Nürnberg." *Zeitschrift für Sozialgeschichte* 1: 96–122.

PART III

THE POLITICAL THOUGHT OF CARL SCHMITT

CHAPTER 6

FEARING THE DISORDER OF THINGS

The Development of Carl Schmitt's Institutional Theory, 1919–1942

JENS MEIERHENRICH

INTRODUCTION

JEREMY WALDRON recently bemoaned the state of contemporary political theory, deploring its disregard of institutions. Unhappy with the achievements of his field, he presented a case for the pursuit of "*political* political theory" (Waldron 2013). Waldron argued that a firmer grasp of the means through which democratic order is realized was needed. This is what he was after: "theory addressing itself to politics and to the way our political institutions house and frame our disagreements about social ideals and orchestrate what is done about whatever aims we can settle on" (Waldron 2016, 6). Carl Schmitt was more innovative than most when it came to theorizing about the logic of institutions.[1] He devoted a considerable portion of his scholarship to understanding what Waldron has termed "the ordering presence" of institutions, that is, their contribution to the creation and maintenance of political order. Despite Schmitt's fervent antiliberalism (not to mention antisemitism), he, too, was concerned with democratic order, though few contemporary political theorists would countenance Schmitt's understanding of what democracy meant, and with good reason (see, e.g., Rasch 2016). In the course of his intellectual life, Schmitt's conception of democracy became ever more exclusionary, culminating in his advocacy of racial dictatorship in Nazi Germany. This does not per se invalidate Schmitt's institutional theory, but it forces us to read him with great care, not least because "Schmitt's arguments always require some excavation" (Dyzenhaus 1999, 77).

A close reading of Schmitt's institutional theory is timely because of the continued interest in the twenty-first century in some of the institutional solutions to the problem of political order that he favored, notably the state of exception, commissarial dictatorship, and the decisive sovereign.[2] For several decades now, Schmitt's oeuvre has been mined by critics of liberalism on both the left and the right. Seeing that Schmitt's institutional ideas in this process of appropriation have frequently been taken out of context, I restore them to their context in this chapter. I relate Schmitt's institutional thought not only to the historical conflagration to which it responded, but also to the intellectual socialization that caused him to develop a predilection for orderly thought (see also Meierhenrich and Simons 2016). If Schmitt's writings are placed in a developmental perspective, what emerges is the picture of a theorist who was—despite his preconceived notions about what makes the world hang together—surprisingly undogmatic in his unstinting search for institutional responses to the specter of disorder in his native Germany and elsewhere. Over the span of the twenty-three years under investigation, his institutional solutions evolved quite dramatically, often in an ad hoc fashion, but nonetheless organically, in keeping with his orderly quest. This chapter is dedicated to a reconstruction and critical analysis of this evolution of Schmitt's normative institutionalism.

I advance three interrelated arguments. First, I depart from conventional analyses according to which Schmitt only embarked on an "institutional turn" in the early 1930s, in the context of his legal theory (see, most recently, Croce and Salvatore 2013, 102). I submit that this interpretation, especially widespread in legal scholarship, is founded on a reductionist understanding of institutionalism. I show that Schmitt's institutional theory cannot be reduced to the publication in 1934 of *Über die drei Arten des rechtswissenschaftlichen Denkens* (*On the Three Types of Juristic Thought*), as the existing literature is wont to do. I refute the juxtaposition of Schmitt's decisionism and his institutionalism. Instead, I maintain that the latter encompasses the former, and that its genesis dates back to the beginning of Schmitt's career. Instead of conceiving of Schmitt's institutionalism as an intellectual stage of his thought, I posit that it constituted—as his predominant theoretical approach—its essence. This institutional focus was germane, in one form or another, to almost all of Schmitt's Weimar-era as well as Nazi-era publications. It is reflective of an ontological consistency in Schmitt's thought that has not been fully appreciated to date.

Second, I argue and demonstrate that Schmitt's institutional theory underwent a gradual transformation from what I call *pragmatist institutionalism* to *extremist institutionalism* in the period 1919–1942. Taking a leaf from the late Hans Mommsen, I argue that Schmitt's institutional theory was subject to a cumulative radicalization.[3] I account for this dynamic intellectual development by incorporating insights from what social scientists refer to as the logic of consequences as well as the logic of appropriateness. I propose that Schmitt based his turn to what I call his *racial institutionalism* (as a subtype of extremist institutionalism) on a personal consideration of means and ends as well as norms and values. The radicalization of his institutional theory in the run-up to, and its racialization in the aftermath of, the Nazi seizure of power (the so-called *Machtergreifung*) was, in my argument, a strategic but also an expressive choice. Ultimately, it was an outcome of structured contingency. By this I mean that Schmitt made instrumental and meaningful choices in the 1930s and 1940s, but within the constraints of his intellectual field of vision. Schmitt's conservative socialization and his concomitant fear of disorder had a pre-structuring effect on the range of Schmitt's thinking about viable options in the transition from democracy to authoritarianism and eventually to totalitarianism in his native Germany. The emergence of his racial institutionalism as a subset of a broader extremist institutionalism was not inevitable; it was not a predetermined outcome. But it was not a purely contingent outcome either, because it was neither entirely unexpected, nor accidental, nor unforeseen.[4] This becomes obvious when his writings are placed in longitudinal perspective.

Third, and related to my evolutionary account of Schmitt's normative institutionalism, I submit that decontextualized treatments of Schmitt are highly problematic. I find that neither the metaphor of the "break" nor that of "continuity" fully captures the relationship between Schmitt's Weimar-era writings and his Nazi-era writings.[5] While I argue that the motif of order provided a great deal of intellectual consistency across the 1933 juncture, we must be careful to avoid retrospective determinism when analyzing the form and substance of Schmitt's institutionalism. As David Bates has opined, "it would be a mistake to draw a straight line between Schmitt's 'decisionism' and the German state organized around the decisive power of the Führer" (2006, 416). I demonstrate in this chapter that Schmitt traveled on a long and winding theoretical road to cover the distance between his advocacy of decisionism in the early 1920s and of the racial state in the early 1930s. I provide a detailed road map, highlighting critical junctures and theoretical turns along the way. As morally reprehensible as Schmitt's Nazi-era writings are, their place in the development of his institutional theory begs contextualization, not just condemnation.

The remainder is organized as follows. In the first section I introduce the motif of order—and its "other," the idea of disorder—as a heuristic device for framing my analysis of the development of Schmitt's institutional theory. In the second section I then explicate Schmitt's concept of the institution and reflect on the nature and role of institutional theory in his oeuvre as a whole. The third section turns from the general to the particular, especially to Schmitt's political thought. In the context of the latter, I trace in depth the logic and evolution of Schmitt's institutional theory, starting in the revolutionary year 1919. I conclude the textual analysis in 1942, the year in which Schmitt began using the concept of *nomos* (Mehring 2009, 430–431), which saw him largely withdraw from scholarship. A few years before that, with the publication of *Der Leviathan in der Staatslehre des Thomas Hobbes* (*The Leviathan in the State Theory of Thomas Hobbes*), Schmitt had embarked on a halting transition from racial institutionalism to a less overtly antisemitic (though still deeply illiberal and also extremist) form of normative institutionalism.[6] I summarize the findings of my longitudinal analysis of Schmitt's institutional ideas in the fourth section, where I also consider implications.

THE DISORDER OF THINGS

In its most general sense, the noun "order," according to the *Oxford English Dictionary*, captures "the condition in which everything has its correct or appropriate place, and performs its proper functions."[7] In this understanding, order is a "force for harmony and regularity in the universe."[8] Schmitt longed for such harmony and regularity in his life, even though he self-destructively undermined the stability he achieved time and again.[9] Schmitt's "orderly thought" (see Meierhenrich and Simons 2016 for an all-encompassing treatment) was also inexorably linked to what I have elsewhere called his "orderly conduct" (Meierhenrich n.d.), including transgressions thereof.

The problem of social order seized Schmitt very early in the development of his thought. In intellectual terms, the failure of the "Second Reich," Wilhelmine Germany, was "the central existential topic" of Schmitt's life (Sombart 1991, 10). It was this historical experience that informed his quest for order, political and otherwise. Described once as the "last Bismarckian," Schmitt attributed great meaning to the decline of absolutism. The decay of the Wilhelmine state to him was the "enormous background to our entire political situation" ("*gewaltigen Hintergrund unserer politischen Gesamtlage*"; Schmitt 1934a, 203).[10] He bemoaned the "hopelessness of this political structure" ("*Hoffnungslosigkeit dieses politischen Gebildes*"), of the state lacking a "solid constitutional order" ("*feste verfassungsmäßige Ordnung*"; 1934b, 26).

Schmitt was thirty years old when Wilhelmine Germany gave way to what became Weimar Germany. Having spent his formative years in an era in which premodern mentalities were the norm, the dissolution of political, legal, and cultural certainties was confounding, even frightening, to him. As Jacob Taubes recalled, "Carl Schmitt thinks apocalyptically, but from above, from the powers" ("*Carl Schmitt denkt apokalyptisch, aber von oben her, von den Gewalten*"; 1985, 22). Schmitt's vision of history, like Taubes's, was heavily influenced by the absolute uncertainty that attended the early twentieth century. The experience of World War I, the revolutionary upheavals that followed, the Great Depression, and other disconcerting developments created existential fears of a severity hitherto unknown to the German population. The late Detlev Peukert, a respected historian of Weimar Germany, declared uncertainty "the sign of the epoch" (1987, 266). The era's unprecedented uncertainty, Taubes recalled, gave rise to their—his and Schmitt's—thinking in terms of extremely short time-horizons: "We have in common this experience of time and history as time limit, as last respite" ("*Uns beiden gemeinsam ... ist jene Erfahrung von Zeit und Geschichte als Frist, als Galgenfrist*"; Taubes 1987, 22). This is not surprising, for as Peter Gordon and John McCormick recently reminded us, "[a]bject material deprivation during the era of hyper-inflation, occupation by foreign forces, and psychological burdens associated with war guilt, all conspired to intensify the perception of a broad-scale crisis of culture and civilization" (2013, 7; see also Eley et al. 2016). This crisis threatened to destroy everything that people had, everything they knew, and everything they were.

Schmitt's "trinity of thought" (Meierhenrich and Simons 2016, esp. 49–55), in the construction of which his institutional theory played an important part, was a response to this chaotic state of the world, though his response to the perceived malaise was far from coherent. It was polycentric and not without contradictions. Schmitt's engagement with the specter of what Oswald Spengler in dystopian terms had described as the "decline of the West" played out in different intellectual spheres, across dozens of publications; explored multiple themes; and made use of a variety of stylistic means. The eclectic (what some have been tempted to call interdisciplinary) nature of his thought was a function of the fact that Schmitt was actively searching—and in all directions—for "models of order" ("*Ordnungsmodellen*") that could halt the march of modernity and the disorder that Schmitt feared was lurking in its wake (Heil 1996, 15).

But the fear of disorder was not just a professional concern of Schmitt's. It was also a private affliction. Schmitt's diary entries between 1912 and 1934 are replete with descriptions of despair and disillusionment, of a life lacking an orderly form. They bespeak an ongoing existential quest on Schmitt's part to find his place in the world. For much of this time, he lived in a "productive state of emergency" and engaged in risky transgressions in his private life. As Mehring puts it, "Marital trust and bourgeois calm and order he did not find" (2014, 4). Nicolaus Sombart has argued that for Schmitt and the conservative men of his generation, the most serious threat to any order was disorder. They feared nothing more than chaos hollowing out the fundamental institutions of social order of their time: family, church, and state (Sombart 1991, 232). In his diary the young Schmitt wrote disparagingly, and fearfully, about both the "*Generalkommando*," where he served his military service, and his wife, "*Cari*," referring to them ironically as "two lovely institutions" ("*Militär und Ehe; zwei schöne Institutionen*"; 2005, 90). In Sombart's psychoanalytical account, Schmitt's fear of disorder in reality was the fear of being overwhelmed by his innermost desires (Sombart 1991, 232). These desires included a penchant for transgression and a fascination with the "other."

Given his ambivalence, both public and private, toward the order of things in interwar Germany, Schmitt throughout his life searched for "existential stabilizations" ("*existentielle Stabilisierungen*"; Mehring 2014, 9). He turned to a slew of successive institutions to find them. Institutions are sometimes thought of as "sets of implicit or explicit principles, norms, rules, and decision-making procedures around which actor expectations converge" (Krasner 1982, 186). Defined as such, rationalist scholars generally assume that they reduce uncertainty: "Social institutions affect strategic decision making by establishing social expectations, and they do so through two mechanisms: the provision of information and sanctions. Through these mechanisms social actors learn the information necessary to formulate expectations about the actions of those with whom they interact. With these expectations they choose the strategies that they think will maximize their individual benefits" (Knight 1992, 49). But institutions do not only confer competitive advantage by reducing transaction costs; they also create social meaning, a contribution in which interpretivist scholars are particularly interested. As Alan Sica observes, "[b]ecause man is the meaning-making animal, he gravitates to loci (or institutions) where meaning is likely to be found or created" (1992, 264). Schmitt,

I contend, looked to institutions for *both* of these reasons. To him, they promised to provide informational stability and existential stability. Living orderly was about stability *and* orientation for Schmitt. It is probably not coincidental that the idea of orientation emerged as a supporting concept in the *The "Nomos" of the Earth in the International Law of the "Jus Publicum Europaeum"* at precisely the time that Schmitt was casting about for a new orientation in his own life. As a heuristic device for framing my analysis of the development of his institutional theory, the motif of order has the advantage of interpreting Schmitt in terms that were very much of his life—and of his time.

THE ONTOLOGY OF INSTITUTIONS

A great deal of Schmitt's theoretical project revolved around the ontology of institutions, that is, in Waldron's words, "the ordering presence that they have among us in what might otherwise be a crushing scramble for individual advantage, the roar of millions of blind mouths, shouting slogans and threats to one another, bellowing out to get out of each other's way" (2013, 15). The stability of a political order, Schmitt was convinced, rested on the quality of the institutional framework that underpinned it. Starting from this premise, he theorized in his long career a variety of institutions, from dictatorship to international law.

I do not analyze all of these institutions in this chapter. But is worth pointing out that Schmitt's reflections on all of them shared a concern with improving *really existing* social order, especially political order. "Belying his reputation as a 'decisionist,'" Bates has found, "Schmitt observed that those who tried to trace 'order' to the act of decision usually assumed the existence of at least some institutional form" (2006, 420). Or, as Schmitt himself put it, "Concepts like king, ruler, overseer, or governor, as well as judge and court, shift us immediately into concrete institutional orders that are no longer mere rules" (Schmitt 2001, 50; translation modified). This formulation is an apt summary of the essence of Schmitt's institutionalism.

Hauriou's Institutionalism

Maurice Hauriou, a French scholar of administrative law, is said to have greatly influenced the development of Schmitt's institutional theory.[11] In fact, Schmitt himself acknowledged this debt, in *The Crisis of Parliamentary Democracy* in 1923, again in *Legality and Legitimacy* in 1932, and also in *On the Three Types of Juristic Thought* in 1934. But the debt is apparent in other works as well, certainly in *Roman Catholicism and Political Form*. In 1947 Schmitt recalled privately his "ideational relation" ("*gedankliche Verwandtschaft*") with Hauriou, who, like him, had placed great stock in the institution of the Catholic Church (Schmitt 1991, 12).[12] He admired most of all the fact that Hauriou had not arrived at his theoretical maxims "through a normativistic-positivistic way of squeezing something out of isolated legal texts," but rather had developed his institutional theory on the foundation of practical experience, from a "concrete view of a concrete order" (Schmitt 2001, 87).

Describing the depth of his intellectual bond, Schmitt went as far as naming the French institutionalist his "elder brother," a clear indication of the size of the theoretical debt (1991, 13).[13] A few months later Schmitt went further yet, declaring, "Maurice Hauriou is for his age more important than all others" (108).[14] Although Roscoe Pound, from 1916 until 1936 the dean of Harvard Law School, dismissed Mauriou's anti-individualist theory of institutions, continental institutionalists like Schmitt immediately grasped the theoretical potential of the Frenchman's writings (Pound 1959, 342).[15] But what about Hauriou's institutionalism *in particular* left a mark on Schmitt's thought?

Perhaps the most important element that influenced Schmitt was the notion of the animating idea ("*idée directrice*"), usually translated into German as "*Leitidee*."[16] Hauriou's animating idea (sometimes referred to in English as "directing idea") is not to be confused with the function or instrumental purpose of an institution. Rather, the concept speaks to the non-rationalist origins of institutions. Institutions will only be stable and endure, according to Hauriou, to the extent that they embody a strong institutional culture. Such a culture, in turn, depends on "manifestations of communion" ("*la manifestation de communion*"). These manifestations will only be forthcoming if an institution's life bears out, in the eyes of the members of the social group that it is intended to serve, the animating idea to which it owes its founding. In many respects, Hauriou outlined what we would today call a constructivist theory of institutions. Influenced by Henri Bergson's work on *le vitalisme*, or the idea of social vitalism, Hauriou, not unlike Schmitt, anthropomorphized institutions, regularly emphasizing that a given institution "was born, lives and dies as well as any other organism" (Croce and Salvatore 2013, 97).

Despite a superficial resemblance to Emile Durkheim's work in the late nineteenth and early twentieth centuries, notably the idea of the "collective conscience," Hauriou's argument about the collective internalization of the animating idea was distinct, for as he remarked, "movements of communion cannot in any sense be analyzed as manifestations of a collective conscience. It is individuals who are moved by their contact with a common idea and who, by a phenomenon of interpsychology, become aware of their common emotion" (1925, 107). Upon closer inspection of Schmitt's institutional theory, his intellectual debt to Hauriou becomes gradually apparent. Though he did not adopt the language of the animating idea, Schmitt borrowed its logic. In *Constitutional Theory*, for example, he made a strong claim for the importance in constitutional governance of "a type of being that is higher, further enhanced, and more intense in comparison to the natural existence of some human group living together" (Schmitt 2008a, 243). The political unity of such "a special type of being" can be derived "by virtue of a strong and conscious similarity, as a result of firm natural boundaries, or due to some other reason.... [T]he political form of the state defines itself by the idea of an identity. The nation *is* there" (239, 243). According to Schmitt's argument, only a unified people held together by an animating idea is worthy of representation: "Something dead, something inferior or valueless, something lowly cannot be represented. It lacks the enhanced type of being that is capable of an existence, of rising into the public being" (243). With this and similar formulations, Schmitt added an archconservative twist to Hauriou's ultimately liberal understanding of the *idée directrice*.[17]

Volker Neumann has recently observed that Hauriou's institutionalism amounts to a "curious combination of idealism and realism" (2015, 368), which is precisely why it was so appealing to Schmitt in his pursuit of a pragmatist institutionalism. It did not hurt that Hauriou, in contradistinction to Hans Kelsen, assigned only a secondary role to legal norms, and in fact is said to have contributed to the "dethronization of the legal norm," a move (and result) that was completely in line with Schmitt's effort to combat the rise of legal positivism (368). And like Schmitt, Hauriou was a proponent of properly ordering the social *as a whole*: "Established social order is what separates us from catastrophe" ("*L'ordre social établi est ce qui nous sépare de la catastrophe*"; Hauriou 1986, 49). On several scores, then, Hauriou, to Schmitt, was a brother in arms in the intellectual battle with modernity.

For Hauriou, as for Schmitt, institutions were "liminal entities, forms of order with a concrete presence in the world of materiality, but incarnating an organizational structure that is spiritual and therefore immaterial" (Bates 2006, 426). Political order for him depended on the existential character of the state, not just on the monopoly of the legitimate use of physical force (Hauriou 1904, 564–581; see also Speth 2001, 126). Hauriou allowed Schmitt to theoretically relate identities to institutions, especially in the case of the state as an institution *primus inter pares* (see Hauriou 1896, 367). Schmitt used Hauriou's scholarship *selectively* to bolster his argument—the significance of which, as we shall see, waxed and waned during the development of his institutional theory—about the centrality of the state for the creation and maintenance of political order: "For the institutional mode of thinking, the state itself is no longer a norm or a system of norms, nor a pure sovereign decision, but the institution of institutions, in whose order numerous other, in themselves autonomous, institutions find their protection and their order" (Schmitt 2004, 88).[18] This formulation and the analysis that it concludes are generally taken as evidence for the claim that Schmitt's so-called institutionalist turn occurred in "the early 1930s" (Croce and Salvatore 2013, 102). After all, it was Schmitt himself who insisted that the "restoration of a concept of [the] institution overcomes both the previous normativism as well as decisionism and with it ... positivism, which is composed of both" (2004, 88). But one should not always take Schmitt at his word.

Pace Schmitt and also Bates (2006), as well as Croce and Salvatore (2013) and most recently Martin Loughlin (2016), the genesis of Schmitt's institutionalism long predated the Nazi revolution of 1933. It would be a categorical mistake (in all senses of the word) to claim, as Bates does, that "Schmitt developed his concept of the institution just as the National Socialists were consolidating and developing their power" (2006, 420). It is true that Schmitt articulated his concept of "concrete orders" ("*konkrete Ordnungen*") in 1934, but this was but one of *many* institutions that played a role in Schmitt's institutional theory. The fact that Schmitt eschewed the *language* of institutions until the mid-1930s does not mean that he was not engaged in what the social sciences (and also the humanities) have come to call institutional theory.[19] Having said that, Bates is undoubt-edly correct when he claims that "Schmitt's thinking about institutions was his way of conceptualizing a stable governmental system that would nonetheless preserve a space for decisive interventions to protect this prevailing order in exceptional circum-stances" (2006, 422). However, this interpretation is valid for the *entirety* of Schmitt's institutional theory, not just for his invention of the institution of concrete orders.

Schmitt's Institutionalism

Schmitt was an institutionalist from inception. Institutionalists, whether new or old, are scholars "who place special emphasis on the role institutions play in structuring behav-iour" (Steinmo 2008, 123). Some institutionalists are primarily interested in formal insti-tutions, such as organizations; others study informal institutions, such as international regimes. What all institutionalists agree on is, first, the centrality of institutions for the creation and maintenance of political order (as well as social order more generally), and, second, their centrality as conceptual variables for making explanatory or interpretive sense of this order. Institutions, or so institutionalists believe, are the rules of the game: they determine who gets to participate in politics and how decisions are made. But in addition to shaping the strategic behavior of anyone who is affected by the political game, institutions also encase—and constitute—identities.

It becomes clear very quickly from reading any of Schmitt's major works that he shared both of the above assumptions about the role of institutions. His quest was to find the institution *primus inter pares*, the institution best suited to the task of creating and sustaining political order. To this end, he searched far and wide in the annals of theory and history. As a result of this far-reaching quest, his institutionalism was inherently dynamic, not static. It evolved in response to changing contexts and stimuli and thus was marked by theoretical twists and turns. Yet despite Schmitt's many contributions to thinking about the *concept* of the institution, he spurned the *term* of the institution, the word itself. Although he was deeply admiring of, and influenced by, Hauriou's 1925 essay "La théorie de l'institution et de la fondation," Schmitt felt that a translation of the French term *"l'institution"* was not appropriate for his purposes: "For us Germans, the word 'institution' has all the disadvantages and few of the advantages of a foreign word" (2001, 89). Instead of speaking of institutions—terminology that to him smacked of superannuated conservatism—Schmitt proposed a forward-looking neologism: concrete orders. He also quickly retired the term "institutionalist thinking" ("*institu-tionelles Denken*"), which he had previously used, and introduced in its stead the rather awkward phrase "concrete-order and formation thinking" ("*konkretes Ordnungs- und Gestaltungsdenken*"; 90; translation modified). However, these semantic quibbles, as important as they are, should not distract us from the fact that Schmitt's thought at its core was institutionalist and remained so for most of his career.

In the modern social sciences, institutions are understood, at the most general level, as stable patterns of behavior that define, govern, or constrain social action.

Sometimes, but not always, institutions are organizations, which is the case when institutions are embodied, that is, are possessed of an institutional structure and a degree of differentiation. The subtleties and varieties of institutional theory need not concern us here, except to help us locate Schmitt in the theory of institutions. Schmitt's institutional sketches and more elaborate designs, as different as they are, all at one point seemed socially appropriate to him as solutions to the problem of political order, not only because the institutions in question were, to him, the most politically or legally efficient for the task at hand, but also because they reflected, and seemed capable of sustaining, culturally specific practices that he considered desirable for the German polity.

In some respects Schmitt, like Max Weber, was practicing, at least in his more deeply analytical works, a rudimentary version of what a century later would come to be known in political science as "historical institutionalism." Sven Steinmo has summarized the essence of this analytical perspective: "Historical institutionalism is neither a particular theory nor a specific method. It is best understood as an *approach* to studying politics and social change. This approach is distinguished from other social science approaches by its attention to real-world empirical questions, its historical orientation and its attention to the ways in which institutions structure and shape behaviour and outcomes" (2008, 118). Without going into the nuances of this variant of the so-called new institutionalism, it is worth emphasizing that historical institutionalists have a view of social action according to which agents are not merely interest-driven (as rational choice institutionalism would have it) nor primarily norm-driven (as sociological institutionalism holds), but motivated by reason *and* emotion.

From his 1912 *Habilitation* onward, Schmitt consistently homed in on all of these aspects, notably in the context of a diverse set of formal institutions: from the state in *Der Wert des Staates und die Bedeutung des Einzelnen* (*The Value of the State and the Significance of the Individual*; 1914), to parliament in *The Crisis of Parliamentary Democracy* (1988), and from the League of Nations in *Die Kernfrage des Völkerbundes* (*The Key Question of the League of Nations*; 1926), to plebiscite in *Volksentscheid and Volksbegehren* (1927) and the constitution in *Constitutional Theory* (2008b), to name but a few. But even informal institutions made the cut in Schmitt's trinity of thought. He studied the institution of tragedy for its political implications (2009b), and the opening volley of his political thought was a critical inquiry into the institution(s) of Romanticism (1919; see also Ziolkowski 1990). The affinity between his approach and historical institutionalism notwithstanding, Schmitt's brand of institutionalism is more fittingly categorized as *normative institutionalism*, that is, the kind of institutionalism that Waldron hopes to resurrect in political theory.[20] The moniker is a more fitting label for the classification of Schmitt's institutional theory because his analytical interest was neither explanation nor understanding, but prescription.[21] As such, it resembles less historical institutionalism than what is now known as old institutionalism, that is, the largely descriptive form of institutional theory that preceded the rise of the new institutionalism in the aftermath of the behavioral revolution.[22]

Virtually all of Schmitt's writings explored possible—and impossible— institutional designs for the construction of political order. The development of his institutional theory was owed partially to what Norbert Bolz has referred to as the "philosophical extremism" of the interwar period (1989). But Schmitt's intellectual project was also borne of personal experience in the transition from absolutist rule. As a consequence of this transition, he lived with "an almost chronic fear of political disorder" (Bendersky 1983, 96). This being so, he was normatively inclined in his institutional theory, which, as John McCormick has pointed out, is somewhat ironic "given his aversion to normativism" (1997, 215).

This does not mean that Schmitt did not deal in facts, but his explanatory and interpretive accomplishments were rudimentary at best. More important to him, and a more significant accomplishment of his, was the production of knowledge for the purpose of prescription, hence my use of the label normative institutionalism to capture the essence of his institutional approach. Put differently, Schmitt's institutional theory, like the rest of his thought, was action-guiding and idealizing. It was oriented toward *directly* affecting the construction of his imagined orders in the real world. Schmitt's was "a quest for some ideal state of the world" (Goodin 1996, 34). His institutional designs were "theories about what a good (indeed, perfect: optimal) arrangement would be" (34).

The history of political thought commonly distinguishes three solutions to the problem of political order. As Dennis Wrong reminds us, "Hobbes's solution was coercive, Locke's stressed mutual self-interest, and the Rousseau of *The Social Contract* gave primacy to normative consensus" (1994, 9). What all of Schmitt's institutional solutions to the problem of political order shared was an anthropological view of man as a "dangerous" being, a "risky" creature (Schmitt 2007, 58).[23] This assumption about the state of man in nature undoubtedly was attributable to Hobbes's "warre of every one against every one," though Schmitt devised non-rationalist solutions that differed in important respects from the rationalist solutions that Hobbes had theorized in *Leviathan* almost three hundred years earlier.[24] But Schmitt agreed with Hobbes that man needed to be put on a leash. As he put it in *Roman Catholicism and Political Form*, man is "a cowardly rebel in need of a master" (1996b, 33). Inasmuch as Schmitt favored institutional over individual solutions to the problem of political order, the figure of the master was a recurring theme in his institutional theory. It resurfaced in the form of the king, the president, the dictator, and the sovereign. The most abstract manifestation was the leviathan, the most concrete the Führer. In his institutional theory, in other words, Schmitt recognized the need to blend both agency and structure in any plausible prescription for the creation and maintenance of political order—and social order writ large.

Over the course of his life, Schmitt favored very different institutional solutions to the problem of political order, most of them national in character, some supranational. For the period under investigation, I illustrate this observation in four steps: first, by taking a closer look at Schmitt's theory of sovereignty, as expressed most cogently in *Dictatorship* and *Political Theology*; second, by exploring how Schmitt, especially in *Roman Catholicism and Political Form*, drew on the ordering principles of the Catholic Church for his institutional design of a stable anti-modern order; third, by tracing

Schmitt's return to a secular—though eventually racial—institutionalism centered on a non-rationalist concept of the state; and fourth, by analyzing the postnational constellation of the Reich that was the hallmark of Schmitt's later writings, notably of *The "Nomos" of the Earth in the International Law of the "Jus Publicum Europaeum"* (hereinafter *The "Nomos" of the Earth*). The conceptual development from the institution of commissarial dictatorship to the institution of the Reich as Schmitt's preferred solution to the problem of political order proceeded via several important theoretical junctures. But the road connecting these junctures was long and winding.

A CUMULATIVE RADICALIZATION, 1919–1942

Schmitt's institutional theory underwent a gradual transformation from pragmatist institutionalism to extremist institutionalism in the period 1919–1942. In this part of the analysis I trace this cumulative radicalization in detail. I demonstrate why, and when, in Schmitt's theoretical trajectory institutional pragmatism gave way to institutional extremism. To be sure, no straight line led from one end of the theoretical continuum to the other. Schmitt's racial institutionalism, as a more radical instantiation of his extremist institutionalism, in Nazi Germany was not a preordained outcome; it was the result of structured contingency. By this I mean that Schmitt's intellectual development predisposed him to orderly thought. This confining condition—and the conservative intellectual mores of his time into which he was socialized—meant that he was highly likely to embrace a form of extremist institutionalism to respond to the political disorder of things. But it was not obvious in the 1920s—neither from Schmitt's thought nor from his conduct—that he would become an ardent intellectual performer on behalf of the Nazi regime. This outcome, I argue, was contingent on more proximate developments.

Pragmatist Institutionalism, c. 1920

In March 1920 the archconservative Gustav Ritter von Kahr, state president (*Ministerpräsident*) of Germany's second-largest *Land*, created the *"Ordnungszelle Bayern,"* or "Orderly Cell Bavaria" (see most recently Nerdinger 2015, 30–31, 402–403). This spatial construct, established as a southern bastion against "red Berlin," became a rallying point for diverse conservative and right-wing forces intent on restoring monarchical or an otherwise non-liberal order. After the failed so-called *Kapp Putsch* in Berlin, for example, General Erich Ludendorff and his supporters relocated from Prussia to the periphery in response to the problem of political order at the center. But the *Ordnungszelle Bayern* did not just carry the promise of a re-equilibration of erstwhile political order. It also channeled resistance to the cultural disorder that the modernization of the arts was said to have wreaked in Germany courtesy of the unconventional, avantgardist, and otherwise "degenerate" (*"entartete"*) art that was emanating from the "cesspool" (*"Sündenbabel"*)

Berlin (Nerdinger 2015, 30). For in the capital, "[t]he arts formulate[d] their opposition to the rigidity of the old symbolic order by mimetically appropriating the forces of social disorganization," which exacerbated fears of disorder on the right (Lethen 2002, 23; generally, see Dupeux 1994). Schmitt, too, was frightened and began to write about institutional designs that might have the potential of solving what he perceived to be an especially pernicious variant of the problem of political order—one that haunted not just his native Germany but endangered polities everywhere. His first imagined solution revolved around the institution of dictatorship; his second around the idea of decisionism. What both solutions had in common was a preoccupation with the sovereignty of the state. They were the products of what I call Schmitt's pragmatist institutionalism.

I argue that Schmitt's thinking in this early phase of his institutional theory was pragmatist in the sense that it combined anti-skepticism and fallibilism into a problem-driven approach to institutions, as defined by Jack Knight and James Johnson: "On a pragmatist view, our ideas, principles, practices and institutions simply are tools for navigating a social and political world that is shot through with indeterminacy. Roughly, one can say that pragmatists treat those tools that prove most reliable over time as 'true.' But all tools—even our most reliable ones—can fail or prove inadequate or inappropriate" (Knight and Johnson 2007, 49). Schmitt's normative institutionalism was, on one level, grounded firmly in a logic of consequences. In keeping with this instrumental approach, he moved to theorizing about new institutions (or about modified institutional designs of preferred institutions) when he thought that a previously favored institution had become ill suited to the task of ordering the political. All in all, this was a decidedly pragmatist approach to a real-world problem.

Schmitt's turn to the institution of dictatorship as a potentially viable solution to the problem of political order was directly related to the historical events leading up to the establishment of the *Ordnungszelle Bayern* in 1920. Prior to the proclamation of the Weimar Republic, the constitutional monarchy of Wilhelmine Germany had evolved "into a military dictatorship that was virtually unassailable" (Heiber 1993, 3). In the uncertain interregnum between the end of Wilhelmine order and the advent of Weimar order, Munich was a premier site of violent contention in Germany. In November 1919, "[t]hree modes of government were at loggerheads," namely military incumbents, social democratic challengers, and communist insurgents (Hoelzl and Ward 2014, xii). The establishment of the so-called *Bayerische Räterepublik*, a socialist republic, in Bavaria was violently crushed by right-wing paramilitaries in May 1919. Schmitt was in Munich at this time, in military service. At a time when he was "pursuing the concept of sovereignty in terms of the evolving nature of dictatorship, nowhere was sovereignty a matter of the moment more than in Munich" (xvi). Schmitt's theoretical prescription of commissarial dictatorship was thus indirectly also a practical (and pragmatist) solution to a problem of political disorder that he was witnessing firsthand. Put more abstractly, the problem of political *dis*order represented for Schmitt the flip side—the corresponding "other"—of the problem of political order. By the time he put pen to paper, two of Weimar Germany's major emergencies—the Kapp Putsch and the collective violence in Munich—had been "contained."

Neither the idea nor the practice of dictatorship was new to Germany when Schmitt was drafting his eponymous study. To respond to the constant threats to the new political order, Friedrich Ebert, the country's first and social democratic Reich president, relied extensively on what Clinton Rossiter a quarter of a century later would refer to as the institution of "constitutional dictatorship," that is, the temporary and limited use of emergency powers pursuant to Article 48 of the Weimar Constitution (Rossiter 1948; Watkins 1939). This practice of constitutional dictatorship, combined with the communist theory of dictatorship that was gaining ground at the time, provided *some* of the impetus to Schmitt's thinking about the logic of imposing institutional order from above, from sovereignty. But his ambition was, as so often, also categorical. He believed it important to order the conceptual landscape in which talk about institutions was taking place at the time: "[T]he material has not been gathered as an end in itself, but rather in order to document the development of a concept that has systematically proved to be essential" (Schmitt 2014a, xliv, emphasis added).[25]

Dictatorship's most referenced contribution is Schmitt's conceptual distinction between "commissarial dictatorship" and "sovereign dictatorship." Unhappy with the conflation of dictatorial subtypes and the negative connotations that he believed were a result of this conflation, Schmitt endeavored to return to the contemporary debate the classical understanding of dictatorship, by which he meant the idea that dictatorship was *not* synonymous with arbitrary despotism and entirely compatible with democracy. To make usable the classical understanding of dictatorship in the Weimar debate about emergency rule, Schmitt introduced the concept of commissarial dictatorship. It shared with the sovereign type of dictatorship the attribute of purposive action ("*Aktionscharakter*"), that is, the decisive intervention by way of *whatever* means necessary into the domestic affairs of a given polity: "Both in sovereign dictatorship and in commissarial dictatorship, the idea of a situation that ought to be created by the practice of the dictator is implicit in the concept. Its legal nature consists in the fact that, in view of the end to be achieved, legal restrictions and restraints that, in a given situation, are an ill-considered hindrance to achieving the goal are *in concreto* [in practice] eliminated" (Schmitt 2014b, 117; translation modified).

The defining feature of Schmitt's commissarial type was the proviso that dictatorship would only be imposed for a limited period of time, in a specific situation, and for the sole purpose of restoring in times of extraordinary crisis a status quo ante. The historical inspiration for his neologism was the Roman Republic, a political order that Schmitt idealized and where, in his interpretation, "the dictator was not a tyrant and dictatorship was not a form of absolute government but rather an instrument to guarantee freedom, which was in the spirit of the Republican constitution" (2014b, 4).

The most important puzzle in the theory of dictatorship, Schmitt believed, was the "problem of the concrete exception" ("*Problem der konkreten Ausnahme*"; 2014a, xliii). Although Schmitt only tackled this problem head-on in *Political Theology*, his treatment of dictatorship saw him explore the question of "which highest authorities have the power to grant such exceptions" (xliii). In answer, he built a theoretical argument emphasizing the "*rettende Tat der Staatsgewalt*," the rescuing act of sovereign intervention qua dictatorship (xliii; translation modified). It is here that we witness the aforementioned theme of the master resurface. The imposition in a moment of extraordinary crisis of commissarial dictatorship, and the abrogation of the *Rechtsstaat* that it invariably brings, was justified, according to Schmitt, because its purpose was the preservation and re-equilibration of an existing political order, *not* the creation of a new order. In this view, the sovereign state's arbitrary tampering with a polity's legal safeguards is legitimated by the fact that the imposition of emergency rule is an act of institutional maintenance. "In practice the commissarial dictatorship suspends the constitution in order to protect it—the very same one—in its concrete form" (Schmitt 2014b, 118; translation modified). Such an intervention is conservative (in all senses of the word) in character, not revolutionary. Here is Schmitt: "In order to achieve a concrete result, one has to interfere in the causal order of things using means whose justification is given by their degree of appropriateness and depends exclusively on the actual contexts of this causal patterns" (2014a, xlii). The practice of commissarial dictatorship—although it necessarily constitutes an exception to the authority of law— is institutionally bounded because "it is genuinely designed to resolve a very particular problem" and temporally delimited (xlii). Once the problem has been solved, and the state of exception (*Ausnahmezustand*) weathered, the practice of dictatorship by the sovereign state comes to an end, and ordinary governance resumes. Any dictatorship that "does not seek to make itself redundant," argued Schmitt, amounts to "arbitrary despotism" (xlii). We see here that Schmitt's institutionalism in the 1920s did not yet show signs of extremism, at least not of the kind that came to characterize his later institutional theory.

For Schmitt, arbitrary despotism was the hallmark of sovereign dictatorship, the other major type of dictatorship that Schmitt unpacked conceptually and theoretically. In this type, the sovereign intervention is not about institutional maintenance or rescue but about revolution, that is, about the fundamental overhaul of social norms and institutions. Its purpose is "to break off the existing social order," he claimed (2014b, 113). The occasion to act is not a concrete exception but the wish to respond permanently to an absolute exception, whether real or imagined. Whereas in the case of the commissarial type the institution of dictatorship "protects a specific constitution against an attack that threatens to abolish this constitution," in the case of the institution's sovereign variant, "dictatorship does not appeal to an existing constitution, but to one that is still to come" (118, 119). In Schmitt's institutional theory, commissarial dictatorship was about the *re-equilibration* of a political order, sovereign dictatorship about the *replacement* of such an order.[26] Schmitt was convinced that the historical cases of the dictatorships of Sulla and Caesar, as well as those of Cromwell and Napoleon, among others, were exemplars of the sovereign type of dictatorship—a solution to the problem of political order for which, at this stage of his career, he felt nothing but disapprobation (80–147). He was wary in particular of the spirit of 1793 and French revolutionary theorists like Abbé Gabriel Bonnot de Mably and Abbé Emmanuel-Joseph Sieyès, who, not unlike the communist theorists of his own time, had agitated for a dictatorship of the people. "In Schmitt's view, they advocate[d] a sovereign dictatorship that destroys an old order and creates a new one not on the authority of a specific constitutional arrangement or legal charge, but rather as the agent of a vague entity such as 'the people' " (McCormick 2004, 200).

Interestingly, and somewhat surprisingly given the depth of his sentiment, in the ensuing years Schmitt transitioned from a normative position that advocated limited and temporary dictatorship (what he called, as we have seen, commissarial dictatorship) as a solution to the problem of political order to one that centered, in effect, on absolute and permanent dictatorship (what he termed sovereign dictatorship). He developed the second solution in *Political Theology*. However, the earlier historical study already contained the seeds of his subsequent, more extreme position. As John McCormick writes, "Schmitt intimates toward the close of *Dictatorship* that perhaps what should confront the sovereign notion of dictatorship, touted by domestic and foreign revolutionaries, is not a notion of commissarial dictatorship at all, but perhaps a counter-theory of sovereign dictatorship" (2004, 201). These ideas, I show, formed the intellectual nucleus of Schmitt's extremist institutionalism in the final Weimar and early Nazi years, but they must not be equated with them. Although theoretical affinities are evident, so are theoretical differences.

Be that as it may, *Political Theology*'s infamous opening sentence—"Sovereign is he who decides on the [state of] exception"—marked an important and often overlooked transition in Schmitt's theory of dictatorship (Schmitt 2005, 5). It "signals Schmitt's endorsement of something much closer to sovereign than commissarial dictatorship" (McCormick 2004, 203). It also explicitly linked two of Schmitt's separate, yet intimately related, institutional theories: his theory of dictatorship and his theory of sovereignty.

Schmitt further cemented the link between the two institutional theories in the second edition of *Dictatorship*, published in 1928, to which he appended a careful legal interpretation of Article 48 of the Weimar Constitution, one of the document's emergency provisions (Schmitt 2014c). Article 48 authorized the Reich president to govern by way of so-called emergency decrees (*Notverordnungen*) if and when he deemed it necessary "for the restoration of public security and order." This is noteworthy because in *Political Theology* Schmitt advanced "a notion of sovereignty embodied in the *Reichspräsident*, who is not encumbered by constitutional constraints but only the demands of a political exception" (McCormick 2004, 202). It is possible to identify in *Dictatorship* "some of the key elements of Schmitt's later theory of law, and in particular of his decisionism" (Hoelzl and Ward 2014, xiv). The 1928 appendix accentuated this theoretical prefiguration, reducing somewhat the theoretical dissonance that existed between the first edition of *Dictatorship* and *Political Theology*. For it is undeniable that in the latter book, Schmitt made a theoretical case for "the very fusing of popular sovereignty and emergency powers that he [had previously shown] to be potentially abusive in *Dictatorship*" (McCormick 2004, 202).

Having said that, Schmitt's interpretation of Article 48, even though it was published in the wake of *Political Theology*, did *not* contain an argument for sovereign dictatorship, which is why Schmitt, in my interpretation, had not yet entirely abandoned his pragmatist institutionalism. (He mentioned at one point that "the dictatorship of the President of the Reich ... was by necessity one of the commissarial kind.")[27] The contrasting styles (and arguments) of *Dictatorship* and *Political Theology* arguably expressed a normative ambivalence on Schmitt's part about his preferred institutional response to the specter of disorder in general and in his beleaguered country in particular. By contrast, this ambivalence is absent in *The Guardian of the Constitution*, published in 1931, in which Schmitt responded decisively to Weimar Germany's most recent bouts of instability and unrest. "By the conclusion," McCormick notes, "Schmitt has formulated a popularly legitimated sovereign dictatorship of the nation in the person of a purportedly charismatic German president" (2004, 208). This guardian, this defender of the constitution, Schmitt argued, was indispensable to addressing the far-reaching social and economic, not to mention political, dislocations that the preceding years had brought. In the book he repeatedly made reference to how "ten years" of case law and legal scholarship favored a new interpretation of Article 48, one that put to rest the "pre-war clichés of the Weimar Constitution" (Schmitt 1996a, 116, 118, 120). Schmitt adamantly rejected the role of the *Reichsgericht* as the alternative guardian of the constitution (158). By this point in time, Schmitt appears to have lost faith in all the legal institutions of Weimar's political order save the institution of the sovereign as constitutional dictator, whence began his search for a more suitable institutional *katechon*.

The publication of *Legality and Legitimacy* in 1932 was an important turning point in the development of Schmitt's institutional theory (Schmitt 2004). It marked the beginning of the transition from pragmatist institutionalism to extremist institutionalism in his institutional theory. McCormick summarizes the book's significance well: "The possibility of a commissarial dictatorship is no longer mentioned either as it was for substantive purposes in 1921 or as it was for cosmetic purposes in the mid-twenties. The unlimited extent of power that was previously reversed for extraordinary moments is now invoked as the ordinary competence of an executive answerable only to the acclamation of plebiscitary moments" (McCormick 2004, 209). From here it was but a short theoretical step to justifying Nazi dictatorship and to the virulence of his racial institutionalism. But before I analyze the extremist end of Schmitt's institutionalism, a final contextualization of his pragmatist institutionalism is in order.

Although Schmitt's totalitarian turn was not preordained, it cannot be understood without an appreciation of the nature and changing character of his Weimar-era thought. The increasingly dystopian descriptions of the political condition that characterized it account, among other things, for his embrace of charismatic authority (at the expense of legal authority) in his institutional theory. Not unlike Weber, Schmitt gradually moved to a strong-man theory of the state—one with an institutional master at the helm. But it is important to appreciate that by the mores of their time, *both* theorists had advanced what most contemporary observers would have regarded as pragmatist institutional designs. Rudolf Speth (2001, 137) has pointed out that in Schmitt's institutional theory, the state was initially assigned the role of the *katechon*, only to be replaced in the role of the restrainer of history by the institution of the Reich, and subsequently by the *nomos*.

The first three chapters of Schmitt's *Political Theology* initially appeared in a commemorative volume for Weber (Schmitt 1923, 3–35; see also Motschenbacher 2000, 61). In his contribution to the collection, Schmitt recast his erstwhile teacher's concept of the state. Schmitt replaced Weber's emphasis on the monopoly of the legitimate use of physical force with a new emphasis on the monopoly of the decision. However, if we are to fully grasp the array of solutions to the problem of political order that Schmitt proposed in his early Weimar writings, it is essential that we read *Political Theology* alongside *Roman Catholicism and Political Form*, one of his most neglected writings, especially in the English-speaking world. The next section delves deeper into the nature and development in the 1920s of Schmitt's pragmatist institutionalism, of which his "positivistic 'Catholicism of order'" (*"positivistischer 'Ordnungskatholizismus'"*; Maier 1969, 3) formed an integral part.

A Positivistic Catholicism of Order, c. 1923

After the publication of *Dictatorship* and *Political Theology* in the early 1920s, Schmitt's search for political ordering principles continued in his 1923 book on the institutional foundations of the Catholic Church. In this little book, which the constitutional lawyer Josef Isensee has declared a "key work" for making sense of Schmitt's thought, Schmitt recognized that the problem of social order—whether political, legal, or cultural—is inexorably intertwined with the question of institutional form: "Every order is an order of forms," as Julien Freund (1980, 328) put it.[28] The formlessness of politics in Weimar Germany, where the state was under threat from multiple directions, led to Schmitt's casting about for institutional transplants, for design features conducive to stability that could be replicated in the conflictual realm of politics, in interwar Germany and elsewhere (Noack 1993, 73). Interestingly, given his arguments in *Dictatorship* and *Political Theology*, Schmitt, in *Roman Catholicism and Political Form*, voiced serious doubts about the appropriateness of a purely Hobbesian solution to the problem of order: "Once the state becomes a leviathan, it disappears from the world of representation," he warned (1996b, 21; translation modified). Schmitt, as we shall see, never entirely recovered from his reservations about the role of the state in the process of ordering the political.

The next and third institutional form to which Schmitt was drawn in his exploration of political order is the *complexio oppositorum* of the Catholic Church. The idea of the "complex of opposites" that Adolf von Harnack had identified as the governing principle of the controversial yet enduring religious organization intrigued Schmitt. Because the decay of the Wilhelmine state was the most vexing analytical question around which his orderly thought revolved at that time, Schmitt was drawn to the logic of what he considered to be a highly functioning supranational order. He idealized the institutional history of the Catholic Church—notably for its strong ideational foundation—and searched for a functional equivalent to govern the politics of the early twentieth century (Niethammer 2004, 63; see also Cooney 2015).

Schmitt was not alone in his admiration for the religious determinants of order. As Eric Weitz reminds us, "Protestants and Catholics alike evinced a nostalgia for a bygone age when, supposedly, order existed and Christian spirituality permeated every sphere of life. In the churches' view, Germans had forsaken a deep connection with God and nature; instead, the modern society they inhabited was mechanistic, rationalist, ego-tistical, individualist" (2007, 339). This was also Schmitt's view, though on account of his upbringing, he leaned toward the institutional teachings of Catholicism, not Protestantism. In Plettenberg, where he grew up, the devout Catholic Schmitt family had been on the receiving end of a "sectarian Protestantism" (Dahlheimer 1998, 411). The family home became a "bastion of Catholicism" in the midst of what Schmitt and his parents perceived to be enemy territory (411). Not surprisingly, Schmitt received his entire secondary education in Catholic school. Due to both nurture and learning, he became and remained a loyal, though never a devout, Catholic.[29] It is entirely plausible that the introjection of parental injunctions, combined with this experience of ostra-cism, caused Schmitt to regard as socially appropriate—and worthy of replication—the institutional structure of the Catholic Church. Biographically primed in this manner, it was a short step toward theorizing about the transplantation of institutional insights from the religious to the secular realm.

Schmitt was heartened by the formal affinity between the institution of the Catholic Church and the institution of law. He noted approvingly that "the permeation [of the former] with juridical elements goes very deep" (1996b, 29). It is in this context that Schmitt also spoke of jurists as "theologians of the existing order" (29). But as impor-tant as form was for Schmitt's political ordering, a modicum of substance was no less significant. Hence Schmitt's veneration of the Catholic Church as an institutionalized order with a social purpose: "[T]he essence of the Roman Catholic *complexio opposito-rum* lies in a specific, formal superiority over the matter of human life such as no other imperium has ever known. It has succeeded in constituting a sustaining configura-tion of historical and social reality that, despite its formal character, retains its concrete existence at once vital and yet rational to the *n*th degree" (8). Schmitt was not unduly concerned with the *exact* nature of the substance to which the purpose-built institu-tion gave form. *Roman Catholicism and Political Form* was first and foremost about the practice of political ordering and only tangentially about Catholicism as dogma or faith. As Gopal Balakrishnan notes, Schmitt's ideas "owed very little to the theological tradi-tions of the Church" (2000, 55). His was "a secular apotheosis of 'Roman' Catholicism" that bracketed the religious in Catholicism (Mehring 2009, 149; Isensee 1988, 174–176). More relevant for Schmitt was the fact that the Catholic Church managed to create—and maintain—a stable and hierarchical order:

> There appears to be no antithesis it does not embrace. It has long and proudly claimed to have united within itself all forms of state and government; to be an autocratic monarchy whose head is elected by the aristocracy of cardinals but in which there is nevertheless so much democracy that... even the least shepherd of Abruzzi, regardless of his birth and station, has the possibility to become this autocratic sovereign. Its history knows examples of astounding accommodation as well as stubborn intransigence, the manly ability to resist and womanly compli-ance—a curious mixture of arrogance and humility.... [T]his *complexio opposito-rum* also holds sway over everything theological: the Old and New Testament alike are scriptural canon; the Marcionitic either-or is answered with an as-well-as....

> The union of antitheses extends to the ultimate socio-psychological roots of human motives and perceptions. The pope is called the Father; the Church is the Mother of Believers and the Bride of Christ. This is a marvelous union of the patriarchal and the matriarchal, able to direct both streams of the most elemental complexes and instincts—respect for the father and love for the mother—toward Rome. (Schmitt 1996b, 7–8)

The social mechanism responsible for this institutional durability, according to Schmitt, was the accommodation of seemingly irreconcilable ideas via the principle of representation. Disenchanted with the theory and practice of the liberal idea of representation ("every type of representation disappears with the spread of economic thinking"), Schmitt was in awe of the Catholic Church's power of representation: "It represents the *civitas humana*. It represents in every moment the historical connection to the incarnation and crucifixion of Christ. It represents the Person of Christ Himself: the God who in historical reality became man. Therein lies its superiority over an age of economic thinking" (1996b, 19; translation modified). Although Schmitt asserted that his own vocation, law, "can easily assume a posture similar to Catholicism with respect to alternating political forms," he regretted that it had "lost both its meaning and the specific concept of representation during the popular struggle with the king for representation in the nineteenth century" (26, 29; see also Speth 2001, 131). As a result of this loss of representative capacity, wrote Schmitt, "The Catholic Church is the sole surviving contemporary example of the medieval capacity to create representative figures—the pope, the emperor, the monk, the knight, the merchant" (1996b, 19).

Schmitt admired and praised the marriage of form and substance and concreteness in the institution of the Catholic Church (1996b, 8).[30] Its *potestas* derived from its *auctoritas* (Motschenbacher 2000, 56). He believed its response to the problem of political order was superior to that of the Hobbesian solution because of the ideational grounding that it provided. Schmitt detected a metaphysical void in the theory of the modern state, and, following Georges Sorel, declared the absence of "myth" a structural weakness of leviathan, a liability that diminished, in Schmitt's view, the institution's capacity to create or maintain political order. In his eyes, the Hobbesian state was an abstract form without substance. The mythology of Catholicism, by contrast, supplied a veritable cornucopia of substance that promised to ensure that political order was not just stable and durable but also culturally meaningful.

According to Schmitt, the most appealing formal feature, from the perspective of institutional transplantation, of the structure of the Catholic Church was "the great trinity of form" that it achieved, notably by enshrining, in one and the same institution, "the aesthetic form of art; the juridical form of law; and...the glorious shine of a world-historical form of power" (1996b, 21; translation modified). Some of the ideas in *Roman Catholicism and Political Form* are of a piece with those developed in *The Crisis of Parliamentary Democracy* (Schmitt 1988), also published in 1923, in which Schmitt critiqued vehemently the principle of *parliamentary* representation. He returned to the theme in *Constitutional Theory* in 1928, when he theorized the concepts of representation and identity as institutionally linked and the most important "principles of political form" (2008b, 239–248). He explained their interrelationship as follows: "The idea of representation rests on a people existing as a political unity, as having a type of being that is higher, further enhanced, and more intense in comparison to the natural existence of some human group living together" (243). It was a trenchant elaboration on his critique of parliamentarism, the logic of representation of which Schmitt had wholeheartedly rejected a few years earlier: "That X steps in for the absent Y or for a few thousand such Ys is still not an instance of representation.... If the representative is handled only as a delegate, who acts as a trustee of the interests of voters for practical reasons (because it is impossible that all voters could always and at the same time come together), then representation is [not]...present" (243, 246). This is so, added Schmitt, because representation "is not a normative event, a process, and a procedure. It is, rather, something *existential*" (243). The emphasis is in the original, which underscores the importance that Schmitt attributed to the substance, the cultural meaning, of institutional form, and by implication, of political order—a thought first articulated fully in *Roman Catholicism and Political Form.*

His entire life, Schmitt reasoned consistently from what the modern social sciences call the logic of appropriateness, repudiating the rise of the logic of consequences in the twentieth century in both scholarship and practice. In *Roman Catholicism and Political Form*, he pitted "Catholic rationality" against "economic rationality," building a case for a theory of institutional design that celebrated the role of ideas, not just of technology: "To the political belongs the idea, because there is no politics without authority and no authority without an ethos of conviction" (1996b, 17; translation modified). The idea of Catholicism to him seemed an ingenious (and desirable) example of anti-modern order. Schmitt's admiration for the institutionalism of the Catholic Church (as he conceived of it) knew few bounds at the time. In *Political Romanticism*, of 1919, he had described it gushingly as a "miraculous structure of Christian order and discipline, dogmatic clarity and precise morality" ("*Wunderbau christlicher Ordnung und Disziplin, dogmatischer Klarheit und präziser Moral*"; 1919, 9). The structural feature of the *complexio oppositorum* to him represented an ideal organizing principle for *any* political polity. The ability to contain disorder to Schmitt meant that Catholicism was in possession of a transhistorical ordering principle that, if reproduced elsewhere, might be capable of avoiding the instability of the modern polity that he had diagnosed and found so problematic in *Dictatorship, Political Theology*, and *The Crisis of Parliamentary Democracy* (see also Heil 1996, 51).

However, neither dogma nor faith was at the heart of *Roman Catholicism and Political Form*. The book was only tangentially about the Catholic Church, properly understood. Schmitt's understanding of the religious institution as an organization was shallow, his depiction of it theoretically and empirically skewed. He had, as so often in his writings, a distorted view of the Catholic Church, "always preferring his own intellectual picture to actually existing Catholicism" (Balakrishnan 2000, 57).

Toward the Racial State, c. 1931

Misgivings about Roman institutionalism quickly tempered Schmitt's enthusiasm for the Catholic solution to the problem of political order. In response to the exigencies of life in Weimar Germany, he began to think about political order increasingly in the particular (as opposed to universal) and secular (as opposed to religious) sense. This contingent evolution of his political thought eventually led to Schmitt's "abandonment of the Church" (Roberts 2015, 464).[31] From theology he returned to philosophy for inspiration, especially to the secular institutionalism of *Leviathan*, which he radically reimagined in the ensuing years. Schmitt brought the state back in, as it were, but in the process bolted a decidedly constructivist element to Hobbes's rationalist theory of the state. By "socializing" the state, so to speak, he carved out a definitional space to be filled by a culturally appropriate belief system. Schmitt's new interventionist state (formed in pursuit of an overarching but non-economic idea) was all-encompassing: "[T]he state that has turned into the self-organization of society, and...is consequently no longer materially separable from it, comes to encompass everything social, i.e. everything that concerns the collective life of human beings" (Schmitt 2015, 132).

In 1927 Schmitt referred to his theory of the state as a "Hobbes crystal" (as quoted in Lethen 2002, 170). Hobbes will forever be tied to the political thought of Carl Schmitt because, in the eyes of some, "[t]he former founded the theory of the modern state, [while] the latter issued its death certificate" (Maschke 1982, 180–181). Though admiring of it, Schmitt rejected the purely Hobbesian solution to the problem of political order because it ignored the question of social meaning. Absent a social purpose, order, for Schmitt, was nothing more than stability—instrumentally desirable but culturally meaningless. Hobbes, by contrast, thought about political order in terms of quantities, not qualities, as Aristotle and the ancients had. He was after a science of social order, a *scientia civilis* (see, most importantly, Skinner 1996, 1; 2002). It was this mechanical approach that Schmitt opposed. We might say that, according to Schmitt, Hobbes's solution to the problem of political order was *undersocialized*. It was institutional form without substance.

Schmitt was not opposed to the idea of the state per se, however. At this juncture, it is perhaps useful to distinguish among contending concepts of state, as elaborated by Schmitt in, most notably, *The Guardian of the Constitution* (1931a) and *Legality and Legitimacy* (2004). When read in conjunction, the two slim volumes, published in 1931 and 1932 respectively, find Schmitt defending his idea(l) of the authoritarian state against the "absolute state" of the seventeenth and eighteenth centuries, the "neutral state" of the nineteenth century, and the "total state" of the early twentieth century. Schmitt considered the latter a manifestation of the third and latest phase of the "dialectical development" of the modern state (1931a, 79).[32] For Schmitt, and this is not always fully appreciated, the increasingly popular notion of the total state in pre-Nazi Germany was misguided from the perspective of theory as well as practice. He vehemently criticized the far-reaching "turn" in state theory that had brought it about (1931b). What Ernst Jünger termed the phenomenon of "total mobilization" and the resultant collapse of the distinction between state and society, their complete interpenetration, which is a hallmark of the total state, according to Schmitt was a sure recipe for state weakness, not state strength. This "structural transformation," as Schmitt called it, for him carried the risk of unmitigated disaster, especially in economic terms. Unbeknown to most, Schmitt in this context even wrote worriedly about the inevitable termination of the "self-regulating mechanism of a free economy and a free market" ("*sich selbst regulierende Mechanismus der freien Wirtschaft und des freien Marktes*") that the realization of the total state would bring (1931a, 80; see also Bentin 1972). In support of his argument, he cited as a witness his close friend Johannes Popitz, an "expert of the greatest authority," who in 1930s Berlin maneuvered him closer to the "intellectual circuitry of the German far Right and the halls of government power."[33]

To be sure, Schmitt *did* advocate an interpenetration of state and society, but he was unconvinced that a complete—total—interpenetration was required to put in place a stable and durable political order. In November 1932 he observed that the Weimar state was a "curious amalgam" ("*sonderbare Verbindung*") of total state and weak state (1932, 8). The totalization had not yet reached "Bolshevik" or "fascist" levels, remarked Schmitt, but he was perturbed by the dominance of political parties in every sphere of life (9–10). In an essay published in February 1933, Schmitt elaborated on his critique of what he called Weimar Germany's "quantitative total state" (1933b, 361). This variant of the total state was characterized, in Schmitt's argument, by "a totality only in the sense of mere volume"; it represented "the opposite of power or strength," a totality born out of weakness and the inability to resist capture by social forces, especially political parties (362). According to Schmitt's assessment, the defining attribute of the quantitative total state was the inability "to distinguish," which relates to his methodological practice of categorical ordering: *distinguo ergo sum* (364; for an analysis, see Meierhenrich and Simons 2016, 15–21).

Because, Schmitt argued in 1933, the modern state was "at its core executive" ("*in seinem Kern Exekutive*"), what was needed to replace the failed party political state was a strong state, independent of political parties, but one that granted a modicum of autonomy to subsidiary institutions (1933c, 367; 1923, 11). Inspired by the institutional logic of Italian fascism, he dubbed this institution the "qualitative total state." Since Schmitt, after the Nazi seizure of power, scrambled to make forgotten this particular institutional prescription (and put in its place, as we shall see, an alternative vision), it is worthwhile to quote him verbatim: "What is required is that the state becomes the state again, and that that, which is not the state, no longer be forced to be political in order not to be trampled to death" ("*Es handelt sich nämlich darum, daß der Staat wieder Staat wird und das, was nicht Staat ist, nicht mehr gezwungen wird, politisch zu sein, um nicht totgetreten zu werden*"; 1932, 11). Schmitt's prescription was unambiguous: "clear and strict separation" of spheres of life, of state and society (11). What the *Volk* needed, wrote Schmitt, was "self government" ("*Selbstverwaltung*"). The role of the state was to create and protect the space necessary for a vibrant associational life (15). Schmitt believed that the authoritarian state (though he avoided the term) was a superior solution to the problem of political order (as it presented itself in interwar Germany) than the totalitarian state, a position that evinced a variant of pragmatist institutionalism, albeit with strong overtones of extremism.[34]

Schmitt advanced his idea of the qualitative total state in direct opposition to Otto Koellreuter, another leading constitutional lawyer in Nazi Germany, and the theorist of the idea of a "national *Rechtsstaat.*" However, shortly thereafter, he began to parody and avoid the loaded term entirely, using the word "strong state" instead.[35] Adds Michael Stolleis: "Even if Carl Schmitt was still using the phrase 'total state' at the time as an invective directed against a state that was seemingly liberal but intervened everywhere, he had supplied the slogan for Ernst Forsthoff's *Der totale Staat*" (2004a, 374). Forsthoff, a student of Schmitt's, was by no means any more enamored with the total interpenetration of state and society than his teacher: "What Forsthoff envisaged was not totalitarian despotism, but the authoritarian state of the 'conservative revolution' that would reconcile conservatism and modernity, a commitment to values *and* efficiency" (Stolleis 2004a, 374, emphasis added). This came close to Schmitt's own vision of what the ideal Nazi state should look like. Although some Nazi intellectuals were wary of the concept of the state (preferring instead that of *Gemeinschaft*, or community; see also Steber and Gotto 2014), Schmitt stuck with it, although he altered his position once more, making the theoretical leap toward a particularly unsavory subtype of extremist institutionalism, to what I call racial institutionalism.

Racial Institutionalism, c. 1933

In the 1933 pamphlet *Staat, Bewegung, Volk* (*State, Movement, People*), Schmitt imbued the idea of the emergent racial state with *völkisch*, that is, racial values. What previously had been "just" an example of extremist institutionalism he retrofitted with the trappings of National Socialism, including some of the ideological tenets that combined with the regime's "eliminationist racism" (Smith 2008, 167–210).[36]

This was easily done because Schmitt's institutional theory was largely agnostic about the content of the form. Despite his frequent insistence on the importance of relating form to content in the theoretical—and practical—design of institutions, he was astonishingly indifferent to the ideological nature of the substance that was to sustain political order. This relative nonchalance is indicative of a substantive vacuity in his institutional theory, a hollowness that raises the question of whether Schmitt's institutionalism has more in common with procedural approaches to social order than is commonly assumed.

Regardless, Hitler appears to have shared Schmitt's attitude toward the state as guarantor of political order: "What I am contending against," Hitler had declared in his 1923 Beer Hall Putsch trial, "is not the form of a state as such, but its ignominious content" (as quoted in Caldwell 1994, 404). To appease the Nazi rulers, Schmitt delivered, in forty-six pages, a theoretical justification for the racial order that was being constructed while he stood by. He invented the institutional triad state-movement-people to legitimate it (1933a). His was a manifesto for the racial state. Schmitt introduced "racial equality" ("*Artgleichheit*") as the first defining attribute of the Nazi state, and as the second defining principle the leadership of the Führer ("*Führertum*"; 1933a, 32–46). In constructing what I call his racial institutionalism, Schmitt borrowed from Hermann Göring, his Nazi benefactor, who had once described the institutions of state, movement, and people as the three great "motion wheels" ("*Schwungräder*") of National Socialism. Schmitt asserted that the "political unity" of the German polity could only be normatively realized (and analytically grasped) with the help of said institutional triad. The interrelationship among its components was thought to be simple: "differentiated, but not divided, linked, but not fused" ("*[u]nterschieden, aber nicht getrennt, verbunden, aber nicht verschmolzen*"; 32). According to Schmitt, the three institutional wheels were turning side-by-side, each according to its own logic, all powered by Nazi ideology (32). The intended theoretical consequence of this imaginary construct was the conceptual removal of any and all boundaries between the public sphere and the private sphere. It was "confusing and dangerous," Schmitt now warned, in a remarkable volte face, to continue to think in terms of the "the old divisions" between state and society, between public and private (21).

In keeping with this latest solution to the problem of political order, Schmitt hailed the *Führerprinzip*, the Nazi perversion of the institution of charismatic authority. It represented the apex of the institutional structure of the racial order. Schmitt praised this sovereignty of will by revisiting the so-called *Preußenschlag*, in the final months of the Weimar Republic, in which he had been involved as a legal representative of the pre-Nazi Reich:

> Even though the decision of the Staatsgerichtshof of October 25, 1932, did not restore the Weimar System, it was unable to give the Reich government what it was lacking and what it did not dare to take; this decision also refused to recognize, and help to eliminate ["*unschädlich zu machen*"], the enemy of the state. Only when the Reich President on January 30, 1933 appointed the Leader of the National Socialist Movement, Adolf Hitler, as Reich Chancellor, did the German Reich gain a political leadership and the German state find the energy to destroy state-hostile ["*staatsfeindlich*"] Marxism. (1933a, 31)

Hitler's appointment, maintained Schmitt, marked the critical juncture when the "nineteenth century Hegelian bureaucratic state" gave way to a new "state construction," the Nazi state (31–32). Schmitt proclaimed that January 30, 1933, was the day that "Hegel died" (32). He was quick to add that the decline of the Hegelian state did *not* mean that the state *as such*, as an institution, was irrelevant. Its bureaucratic form would persist, but the nineteenth-century norms that governed it had been "disposed of" ("*beseitigt*") and replaced by new (and more concrete) institutional ideas—the Nazi principles of "leadership" ("*Führertum*") and "racial equality" ("*Artgleichheit*") (32, 32–46). The day that (figuratively speaking) Hegel is said to have died marked the transition from the era of the bureaucratic state to that of the racial state, a transition that Schmitt unreservedly endorsed. Elsewhere in his pamphlet *Staat, Bewegung, Volk*, he returned explicitly to the question of order, emphasizing the legality of the

"German revolution," an ostensible fact that he attributed to the "German sense of order" (*"deutschem Sinn für Ordnung"*; 8).

Schmitt's institutional design for the new political order had no place for "the laws and procedures of formal institutions" (Caldwell 1994, 411). The relationship between form and substance became skewed in favor of the racial idea, the ideological foundation of political order. Caldwell offers a concise summary of the institutional logic at play:

> The "state in a narrower sense" was a bureaucratic apparatus, which carried out the political demands of the *Führer*. The state "apparatus," Schmitt argued, was static, but set in motion by the "movement" of National Socialism. The latter, in turn, was the "politicized" and organized element of the "unpolitical" *Volk*. By using the terms "State" and *"Volk"* separated by the mediating "Movement," Schmitt seemed to maintain the distinction between state and society that had permitted the notion of formal constitutional organization in the first place. But the moment of the Movement actually destroyed the system. (1994, 417, emphasis added)

In 1935 Schmitt attempted to accelerate this destruction by making a case for abandoning the concept of the *Rechtsstaat*. To take its place, Schmitt proposed, unsuccessfully as it turns out, the term "ideological state" (*"Weltanschauungsstaat"*) (1935, 201). A year later he very noticeably avoided the term state altogether and praised instead the "political order of racial leadership by the *Führer*" (*"politische Ordnung eines völkischen Führertums"*; 1936, 21). By attempting to provide the theoretical foundations for the racial order, Schmitt abandoned (or at least concealed) not only his deeply held beliefs about the relationship between form and substance, but also those about the appropriate relationship between state and society. Whereas Schmitt's *original position* in the debate about the nature of the Nazi state saw him promoting the idea of a partially independent authoritarian state, his *eventual position* was altogether different. Gone were the intimations of institutional limits on constitutional reform in the Nazi state and the case for a modicum of associational life. Schmitt gave up on authoritarianism and backed wholeheartedly the Nazi project of a new totalitarianism. His extremist institutionalism, which was characterized by a normative belief in the necessity of radical or exclusionary solutions to the problem of political order, evolved into racial institutionalism. I propose that a form of institutionalism deserves the adjective "racial" when it is normatively oriented in its promotion of institutional ideas and designs toward advancing, directly or indirectly, the purification of a given polity on racial grounds. It is extremist, but in a very particular way.

I believe the moniker racial institutionalism is apt when describing the substantive ideas of most (though not all) of the strands of Schmitt's institutional theory during the Nazi dictatorship.[37] The slogan "state, movement, people," for one, was an attempt at ingenuous trickery: "With the phrase 'state, movement, people,' Schmitt had articulated the trinity that also pervaded the entire propaganda apparatus of the regime. To that extent he was not an innovator, but he succeeded in monopolizing this phrase and filling it, in a sleight of hand, with his own positions critical of 'Weimar,' thus creating the impression that the Nazi state was offering the substantive decision he too had long hoped for" (Stolleis 2004a, 342). Schmitt suppressed any intellectual reservations he previously had about the totalization of society and became a vociferous and public advocate of the *Führerstaat*. Accommodating himself with the regime, he embraced, one month after the adoption in Nazi Germany of the so-called Enabling Act (*Ermächtigungsgesetz*) on March 24, 1933, the complete and utter eradication of the state-society boundary for which it stood (Schmitt 1933d, 455–458).[38] Though at least in part opportunistic in nature, Schmitt's theoretical move was *also* fully in accordance with one of his long-standing intellectual desires: "to affirm the myth of the state as an autonomous will capable of extraordinary action in an emergency" (Caldwell 1997, 52).

In 1934 Schmitt's next major publication, *On the Three Types of Juristic Thought*, saw him side with Hegel against Hobbes, a precursor of intellectual things to come. (Schmitt's book-length treatment three years later deepened his criticism of the Hobbesian solution to the problem of political order.) As already noted, Schmitt thought Hobbes a decisionist whose power-based solution to the problem of political order, in the form of an omnipotent leviathan, he found plausible but ultimately inadequate. In its stead, Schmitt brought into position the Hegelian state, which he likened to a political order that is "neither mere sovereign decision nor a 'norm of norms,' nor a changing combination of [these] notions of the state, alternating between the state-of-exception (*Ausnahmezustand*) and legality. It is the concrete order of orders, the institution of institutions" (2001, 78–79).

In 1937, after his star on the Nazi firmament had been dismantled, Schmitt published, largely overlooked in the literature, an article on the state "as a mechanism," in which he further distanced himself from Hobbes (1937, 622–632). The mechanization of the image of man initiated by René Descartes, argued Schmitt, ought to be rejected. Its incorporation into theories of political order, such as Hobbes's, can only have dire consequences. According to Schmitt, it could only ever result in a cheap imitation ("*böse Nachäffung*") of Christian order (1917, 80). The problem, as he saw it, was the following: "No mechanism is capable of totality" ("*Ein Mechanismus ist keiner Totalität fähig*"; 1937, 631). After his fall from Nazi grace, Schmitt returned, in this respect at least, to the position of his pre-1933 writings (631). This also brings us back to Hobbes, with whose political thought Schmitt had grown increasingly disenchanted.[39] He doubted that the provision of security qua statehood was enough to establish political order, as he understood it. Years later, in 1948, in an entry in the *Glossarium*, Schmitt was dismissive of the declared purpose of the state in Hobbes's *Leviathan*, which he took to be "organization for the elimination of fear; *securité*" (1991, 95).[40] Schmitt approvingly quoted St. Augustine's maxim "*plena securitas in hac vita non expectanda*," according to which one should not expect security in life, a formulation that is often read to have been a commentary on Schmitt's Nazi experience (94).[41] It would be equally suitable to read it as Schmitt's summation of one of his life's fundamental driving forces: a fear of the disorder of things.

Schmitt's admiration for Hobbes never appears to have entirely ceased, but in his institutional theory he did not remain in agreement with the Englishman for long. Whereas Schmitt learned to think in terms of *concrete* orders, Hobbes forever remained a theorist of *abstract* orders. Schmitt, or so it appears, felt that Hobbes's rationalist solution to the problem of order, while intellectually exciting and hugely stimulating, ultimately said nothing to him about the exigencies of the twentieth-century world, notably his native Germany. As Schmitt remarked in midlife, again in the *Glossarium*, "The machine is not the key to happiness, but to utopia" (1991, 95).[42] To him, the Hobbesian state was functional, but not meaningful. And for Schmitt, life was *all* about the pursuit of meaning. For this reason, an expressive, not an instrumental, solution to the problem of political order had to be devised. Although Schmitt did, up until 1938, display in his writings a strong predilection for the state as guarantor of political order, his sovereignty formula was *not* tied exclusively to this institutional choice. That formula identified "the moment of order creation as an act of recognition of the power to decide," as Mehring (2014, 13) writes, and the power to decide can be vested in all kinds of institutions, including supranational ones, which brings me to Schmitt's "planetary" turn.[43]

Extremist Institutionalism, c. 1938

In 1938, in his book on Hobbes, Schmitt dispatched one of his preferred institutional guarantors of political order—the state—to the dustbin of theory. Because "the Jews" ("*die Juden*"), according to Schmitt, had "hunted down" ("*erlegt*") and "disemboweled" ("*ausgeweidet*") the mythical creature of the leviathan, Hobbes's once arresting idea of the state was now dead to him (1938, 124).[44] But Schmitt's preoccupation with the institutional foundations of political order was far from over. Although the state as a conceptual variable no longer held the appeal for him that it once did, the really existing challenge of creating and maintaining political order remained. In the years following his exit from "the belly of the fish," as he referred to his years in the proximity of Nazi power (Meierhenrich n.d.), Schmitt turned his theoretical attention increasingly to the problem of international order. Although the virulence of his extremist institutionalism abated somewhat in this period, and he returned to a form of pragmatist institutionalism, his move beyond the racial state was halfhearted, as I explain below.

Schmitt's solution to the problem of international order was the idea of the "Reich." In 1939 Schmitt declared the notion to be "the new ordering concept for a new international law" ("*[d]er neue Ordnungsbegriff eines neuen Völkerrechts*"; 2009a, 63).[45] It is important not to misunderstand the nature and purpose of the concept, however, especially in relation to the contending concept of the state. Inasmuch as Schmitt had lost faith in the ordering function of the latter and regularly bemoaned its political salience, he did not give up on the state completely. He did not abandon the state as an ordering mechanism *as such*; he merely subordinated it to other elements in this latest conceptual turn of his evolving institutionalism (see figure 6.1). Schmitt embraced the *marginality* of the state as a conceptual variable, so to speak. It was a significant transition from what J. P. Nettl (1968), several decades later and in a different context, would term the centrality of the state as a conceptual variable, a centrality that Schmitt had confidently asserted at the beginning of the twentieth century, in *The Value of the State and the Significance of the Individual* (1914). All the while Schmitt was fully cognizant of the fact that even a supranational institution needed an administrative core.

Figure 6.1 underscores that for Schmitt the concept of "space" ("*Raum*") did not itself represent a concrete order, a fact that is sometimes missed in the literature. Instead the

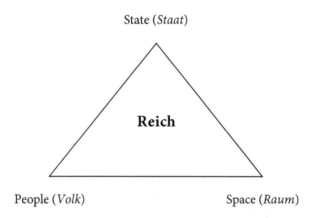

FIGURE 6.1 Carl Schmitt's Concept of the Reich.

concept of space—in the concrete form of the "large space" ("*Großraum*")—served as the foundation for a new way of thinking about international law that proceeded from the concept of "the people" ("*Volk*") and retained the elements of order inherent in the concept of "the state" ("*Staat*"). By incorporating the concept of space as a constitutive element into his concept of the Reich, Schmitt sought to do justice "to the spatial conceptions of today," to create a language for thinking orderly in "planetary" terms (2011, 111).

Interestingly, Schmitt's theoretical turn to the concept of the Reich, even though it formed a part of his extremist institutionalism, was not so much a new beginning as a return to a previously favored solution to the problem of political order, and thus shared traits with his pragmatist institutionalism. Schmitt had first announced his commitment to the idea of the Reich as an ordering principle for the German polity in a public address on January 18, 1933, and reiterated it shortly thereafter in a radio interview conducted on February 1, 1933.[46] His participation on behalf of the central government in the legal proceeding against Prussia to defend the so-called *Preußenschlag* of 1932 is further indicative of Schmitt's deeply felt desire to rescue the idea of the Reich, as first instantiated in the Holy Roman Empire, the *Sacrum Romanum Imperium Nationis Germanicae* or *Heiliges Römisches Reich Deutscher Nation*, between 911 and 1806, and subsequently—in geographically vastly more circumscribed form—in the *Deutsches Kaiserreich*, the German Empire, between 1871 and 1918.[47] The "*Sacrum Imperium*," as it was known in Weimar Germany, served as a political countervision to the modern concept of the state (for an expression of this vision, see Dempf 1929). To Schmitt's dismay, Samuel von Pufendorf, who in the seventeenth century had disparagingly described the institution of the Reich as "an irregular body reminiscent of a monster" (Pufendorf 1976, 106), and other foundational thinkers of the Enlightenment had dismissed the notion of the Reich as an institutional structure—in his view to the detriment of political order. As Schmitt exhorted in characteristically dramatic fashion, "The modern concept of the state destroyed the old Reich" (1933e, 191). With this remark, Schmitt closed ranks with the young Hegel, who in 1802 had begun his essay "Critique of the Constitution of Germany" ("Kritik der Verfassung Deutschlands") with the words "Germany is no longer a state" ("*Deutschland ist kein Staat mehr*"; Hegel 1999, 6).[48] Yet Schmitt at the same time chastised Hegel for giving up on the concept of the Reich, complaining that "even the greatest philosopher, Hegel, flees from the now incomprehensible empirical reality of the Reich toward a more sensible concept of the state" (Schmitt 1933e, 192).

It is therefore not at all surprising that Schmitt exclaimed that "[t]he concept of the state is the true enemy of the concept of the Reich" (1933e, 192). The conceptual enmity was troubling to Schmitt because he believed that the latter concept was not just an abstract notion—a type of conceptual innovation that he utterly despised—but a "real" ("*echt*") concept, one that was "full of life" ("*lebensvoll*") and "substantial" ("*wesenhaft*"; 191). The difference was far from trivial. For as Schmitt had famously declared at the decisive moment of his turn to racial institutionalism: in political struggle, concepts matter, especially those that are "full of energy" ("*energiegeladene*"; 191). They are expressions of "sharply and precisely rendered opposites and friend-enemy constellations" (191). Words-turned-concepts, for Schmitt, were "sharp weapons" ("*scharfe Waffen*"; 191). For this reason he warned that changes in conceptual meaning and usage, however slight, had to be monitored with great care, because they could have unexpected and far-reaching political consequences. The, from his perspective, unfortunate shift from the concept of the Reich to that of the state (and the concomitant rise of the concept of the "*Bund*," or "union," with which that of the state was often paired) to depict Germany's institutional realm was one such political consequence, one to which Schmitt attributed grave significance. It is not an overstatement to suggest that for him, at this moment in time, the conceptual death of the Reich spelled the beginning of the end of the most ideal form of political order that he was capable of imagining at that juncture in history. He mourned the loss of this institutional ideal, performing "a long literary farewell" from the Reich concept (Mehring 2009, 429).

But Schmitt's intellectual imagination was vivid, and undogmatic theorist that he was, he reconfigured his institutional theory once more—moving on to another supranational solution, the institution of the *nomos* (for recent analyses from three different disciplinary perspectives, see Koskenniemi 2016, Simons 2016, and Teschke 2016). In so doing, he continued to "contemplate the earth" ("*Ich betrachte die Erde*") and renewed his search for its "global division and order" ("*ihre globale Einteilung und Ordnung*"; 1955, 518, 519). But seeing that Schmitt only completed his theory of international institutions (including international law) one decade after the end of World War II (2006), I restrict myself here to analyzing the theoretical interregnum—the institutional bridge—between the *pre*war concept of the Reich and the *post*war concept of the *nomos*.

In this period, Schmitt published, aside from *Land and Sea* (2015; see also Simons 2016), *Völkerrechtliche Großraumordnung mit Interventionsverbot für raumfremde Mächte* ("The *Großraum* Order of International Law with a Ban on Intervention for Spatially Foreign Powers"; 2011). I end my analysis of the long and winding road of Schmitt's institutional theory in the period 1919–1942 with a brief examination—and contextualization—of a few writings that inaugurated a halting, and ultimately incomplete, transition from racial institutionalism to extremist institutionalism. To this end, I must return to the concept of the *Großraum* and some of the unexamined tropes of the institutional theory at the center of which it stood—the arguments for which Schmitt first presented at the University of Kiel on April 1, 1939. Mehring found a fitting formulation to capture the performative dimension of Schmitt's attempted retreat (by way of his international thought) from what I have analyzed as his racial institutionalism, calling it the "literary staging of an exit" (*"literarische Inszenierung des Abgangs"*; Mehring 2009, 424).

To begin with, Schmitt's institutional theory of the *Großraum* (which noticeably evolved across multiple editions between 1939 and 1941; on which see Stirk 1999, 361–362) contained a normative argument for a territorially defined way of life that was "capable of restraining terminal formlessness" (Hooker 2009, 126–127). This imaginary order, argued Schmitt, held the promise of recasting the institutional fundamentals of the international system and of Nazi Germany's position within it. By proscribing in his normative treatise the violation of the sovereign borders of these expansive institutional structures, Schmitt legitimated imperial conquest. On this there is agreement in the literature. The question that continues to divide scholars of Schmitt's international thought is whether this final contribution to his institutional theory in the period 1919–1942 also legitimated, or was otherwise implicated in, in the Nazi conquest of *Lebensraum*. It is on this question that I primarily focus here.

As a publication, "The *Großraum* Order" is open to divergent interpretations. As a political intervention, it was an unsuccessful attempt to effect a return to prominence and influence in the Nazi regime. For a brief period Schmitt was seen and heard and debated, both at home and abroad, but neither he nor his institutional theory ever became decisive again. This fact—the irrelevance of Schmitt's institutional theory of the *Großraum*—has been taken by some, including the literary theorist Julia Hell, as evidence that the international turn of Schmitt's late-Nazi era institutionalism was, to use my categories of analysis, pragmatist, possibly extremist, but certainly not racial in either substance or intent. Instead, Hell believes that "Schmitt was not a National Socialist theorist of *Lebensraum* and genocide, but a theorist of empire, imperial mimesis, and imperial imaginaries" (2009, 298).

Lending further support to this view is the historical fact that the Nazi approach to international law "was far from coherent, developing in tandem with German expansion and subject to vying factions within the regime, and making it difficult for those trying to theorize the development of Nazi rule to keep apace" (Minca and Rowan 2015, 278–279). Schmitt was among the dozen or so theorists who were vying with one another to keep up. He "appeared to be chasing events and trying to provide legitimation after the fact, as opposed to influencing, let alone driving, policy developments" in the making of Nazi international law (279). Adds Hell: "Schmitt's reactionary vision of a German continental *Reich* in the wake of the German-Soviet Pact, which included the resettlement, ghettoization or deportation of Jews, was quickly transformed into a genocidal nightmare administration administered by [Heinrich] Himmler's SS [*Schutzstaffel*]" (2009, 298; on the gestation of the "Final Solution," see, most important, Browning 2004; Longerich 2010; and Gerlach 2016).

In these readings of "The *Großraum* Order" and related publications, Schmitt appears as a proponent of extremist institutionalism, especially in overseas territories, whose ideas had been misappropriated by the Nazi dictatorship. While this interpretation has some merit, a less sanguine interpretation of Schmitt's final wartime performance of institutional theory is also possible, and in the final analysis, more plausible (most unequivocally, see Schmoeckel 1994; Blindow 1999). For example, even Anthony Carty, who has a favorable view of Schmitt's theory of international law, has pointed out that the theoretical invocation of terms such as "völkisch particularity" ("*volkshafte Eigenart*") in "The *Großraum* Order" "refer to race" (2001, 40). The most recent account that comes to a similar conclusion stems from two geographers, Claudio Minca and Rory Rowan. It is worth quoting their analysis at length because they avoid analytically simplifying an ambiguous text, finding that this final example of Schmitt's wartime institutionalism was neither mere scholarship nor mere propaganda, but a combination of both:

> [D]espite the apparent conceptual distance separating *Großraum* and *Lebensraum* the relationship between them is nonetheless tricky to disentangle. Schmitt developed his ideas in support of the Nazis' genocidal imperial expansion and, even if he did not adopt the crude biological reductionism of the Party line, he was happy to single out Jews as a separate "racially alien" group who stood outside a new European order of "national groups."…Indeed, while Schmitt showed no interest in the concept of *Lebensraum* he nonetheless expressed support for a political order based upon "the natural growth of living peoples."… Further, he was ready to employ the biopolitical language of "achievement space" ["*Leistungsraum*"], "living space" ["*Lebensraum*"] and *Lebensrecht* ["the right to live"], particularly in his *Großraum* writings. The distinction between the "political idea" of *Großraum* and the racial and biological categories of *Lebensraum* in fact appears to dissolve when viewed in relation to the context in which Schmitt was writing and the bitter anti-Semitism that came to light when his private post-war diaries were published recently.…Although there were clear differences between Schmitt's conceptualization of *Großraum* and the popular theories of *Lebensraum*—and there were indeed internal differences within Nazi spatial thought—these theoretical differences counted little when faced with the brute realities of Nazi policy, which Schmitt was willingly throwing his intellectual support behind. (Minca and Rowan 2016, 173–174)

In addition, the contemporary literature on overseas empires, to which Hell saw Schmitt making a contribution with his institutionalist writings from the late 1930s and early 1940s, also "was permeated by racist ideas: the formation of empires was supposedly based on race struggles in which the 'superior' race shaped the territory it ruled and imposed its own international law on the peoples it subjugated" (Stolleis 2004b, 206). Inasmuch as Schmitt, during the next, postwar turn in the development of his institutional theory—that is, his elaboration of an integrated theory of international law as *nomos*, published in 1955—managed a successful return to the pragmatist institutionalism of his Weimar years, with what amounted to the final stand of his wartime institutional theory, he failed to fully transcend the extremist and racial institutionalisms that had preceded it.

CONCLUSION

Carl Schmitt's institutional theory underwent a radical transformation in the interwar years. His pragmatist institutionalism of the early 1920s gave way to an extremist institutionalism in the early 1930s. The latter took on explicitly racial overtones in 1933 during the transition from authoritarianism to totalitarianism in Germany. This theoretical shift came about not suddenly, but gradually, as the result of a cumulative radicalization of Schmitt's institutional project and his outlook on the prospects for political order, which is why the long-standing, rather simplistic debate over a "break" or "continuity" in his thought in the period 1919–1942 and beyond has largely missed the mark.

Insisting on a break glosses over the fundamental consistency in Schmitt's institutional theory in the period 1919–1942, as set out above. Despite numerous changes in his theoretical foci, not to mention his positions and concepts, Schmitt never ceased to work toward "a unified idea of form" (Ulmen 2001, 24). His fear of the disorder of things was prevalent before 1933, and it remained so afterward. His quest to find an institutional solution to the problem of political order was the intellectual hinge that connects his Weimar-era writings with his Nazi-era writings. And yet it would be an overstatement to claim continuity in Schmitt's thought beyond the persistent salience of the motif of order. His approach was consistent, but his arguments were subject to change. Speaking of continuity in Schmitt's thought implies that it was characterized by a degree of intellectual cohesion that the textual and historical evidence does not bear out. The term consistency, by contrast, is epistemologically less demanding, which is why I use it here. It is sufficient for challenging revisionist arguments that seek to exonerate Schmitt by insisting on an evolutionary rupture in the development of his oeuvre. But it also avoids the deterministic connotations that the term "continuity" carries.

In the 1919–1942 period, Schmitt's institutional theory was concerned with two related but distinct intellectual processes: "[o]n the one hand, an analysis of decline and, on the other, a search for new principles to remedy that decline" (Hooker 2009, 9). Most of the principles that he invented or recycled were more procedural in nature than they were substantive. Although both form *and* content mattered in Schmitt's institutionalism, the two conceptual halves did not always exist in a theoretical balance. Form, I find, ranked supreme in his theoretization of (and normative designs for) political-order-creating institutions.

As we have seen, the ordering principles that he found worthy of in-depth investigation (and propagation) ranged from the institution of representation to that of dictatorship, and from the institution of the state to that of the Reich.[49] Schmitt stayed remarkably true to a *minimalist approach* to the problem of political order in this period, that is, a normative position that is more concerned with form than it is with substance, one that was more invested in stability-cum-identity than in ideology. To be sure, none of this is to suggest that substantive ideas did not matter to Schmitt, because clearly they did. Rather, my point is that the phenomenon of sustainable order, not ideological order, was the thing with which he sought to come to terms in his evolving institutional theory. It was his explanandum, his motif, and his obsession. It is entirely fitting that one of Schmitt's favorite maxims was "*ab integro nascitur ordo*" ("an order is born from renewal"), from Vergil's Fourth Eclogue (Strong 2007, xxx; Mehring 2009, 397). Schmitt's institutional theory, too, was born from renewal. His pragmatist institutionalism morphed into a variant of extremist institutionalism in the final years of Weimar Germany. This exclusionary approach to institutional design then became a despicable example of racial institutionalism upon the establishment of Nazi dictatorship. Even Schmitt's updated vision of the state as a non-rationalist solution to the problem of political order was fully compatible, if not identical, with the ideology of National Socialism, which is why some scholars do believe in a continuity of Schmitt's thought across the temporal chasm of 1933 (for this argument, see Maus 1969 and the expanded English translation in Maus 1998).

Schmitt tempered somewhat the excesses of his institutional theory in the late 1930s. This is not to say that he abandoned his racial institutionalism after 1936. Though Schmitt was excluded from Nazi Germany's polycratic rule, his loyalty to the racial state does not seem to have wavered much. It is worth recalling in this context that Schmitt, though an antisemite for most of his life, was never a fanatic of racial order *as such*. This distinguished him from the likes of Koellreutter and Reinhard Höhn, his intellectual rivals in the Nazi legal universe.[50] But engineers of racial institutions, to qualify as such, do not need to possess bona fide credentials as eugenicists. Schmitt gave more than his tacit consent to the Nazi dictatorship, even after his removal from the front lines of the academy. He scaled back his public appearances, but give them up, he did not. As Jan-Werner Müller writes, despite the fact that Schmitt's "power dreams" were shattered, he "still did his part for Nazi propaganda. In 1943 and 1944 he criss-crossed Europe from Lisbon to Bucharest to lecture to foreign lawyers and dignitaries as part of the Nazis' cultural policies. . . . Everywhere, he defended a vision of Europe asserting itself against Anglo-Saxon fake universalism in the West and Bolshevist nihilism in the East" (2003, 45). For reasons that may never be entirely known to us, "the 'foremost proponent of *Geojurisprudenz*,'" apparently under no duress, "provided concepts and categories to legitimise Hitler's decisions" (34).

The fact that Schmitt's contributions to the theory of Nazi international law did not curry favor with either higher-ups (Nazi decision makers) or lower-ups (his academic rivals) in the racial state is only of secondary relevance for the argument at hand. Even an unsuccessful variant of racial institutionalism remains an example of racial institutionalism. To offer an analogy, the fact that Ernst Röhm, the commander of the *Sturmabteilung*, or SA, was assassinated in 1934 (incidentally a concrete decision that Schmitt subsequently legitimated in writing), and that his personal vision for Nazi order thus ground to a halt, does not make Röhm any less of a Nazi functionary. By the same logic, just because Schmitt's intervention in the debate over the shape of Nazi international law was rebuffed by intra-regime rivals, we must be careful not to underestimate Schmitt's expressive commitment to Nazi international order. He may well have acted to a large extent out of an instrumental motivation to make ends meet and to keep his head above murky Nazi water, and he may even have been wary of the regime's increasingly violent solutions to the "Jewish problem," but it is a distortion of the historical record to claim, as some commentators do, that Schmitt embarked on some form of internal emigration in the period 1936–1945 (see, e.g., Ulmen 2001, 30).

It is possible that Schmitt "never became an ideological convert to Nazism" (Bendersky 1983, 208), in the narrowest sense of that phrase, but his "[t]aking a leave of the state did not mean that there were no other authoritarian political forms left for Schmitt to advocate, as he tried to regain a position of intellectual leadership in the "Third Reich." Toward the end of the 1930s, he turned his attention primarily to international affairs" (Müller 2003, 41). And let us not forget that Raphael Gross has made a compelling (if not always *entirely* convincing) case that Schmitt not only succumbed to a strain of "biological racism," but had been also infected with the bacillus already prior to the advent of Nazism (Gross 2000; 2016).[51] While more careful and contextual research is needed, and text and content analyses will continue to be contested, there is no doubt that Schmitt, with a slew of publications, for several years advocated strongly for a state and related institutional forms in which, in the words of Michael Burleigh and Wolfgang Wippermann (1991, esp. 44–74), "barbarism" became "institutionalised."

Whether Schmitt's racial institutionalism was the result of a long incubation, a self-serving move to gain and sustain entry to the antechamber of power, or a combination of the two, the evidence of racial undertones and *völkisch* overtones in his writings from the mid-1930s to the early 1940s is substantial enough to warrant the application of the label to a considerable portion of this output. Bates is right: "Schmitt's institutional theorization in 1933 and 1934 was not ... merely opportunistic, nor was it intrinsically fascist" (2006, 416). But the theoretical positions and concepts that Schmitt advanced in those years and in the subsequent decade either directly encapsulated, or indirectly enabled, visions of racial order. They were the structurally contingent outcomes of a *political* political theory (Waldron 2013; 2016) that was addressed *not* to questions of justice, liberty, and equality, but—above anything else—to coming to terms with the disorder of things. Schmitt's primary objective in this period was to identify a sustainable *ordo ordinans*—an order of ordering—nothing more and nothing less.[52] All along, delineating the institutional foundations of this self-enforcing order was of greater importance to him than defining the values that it would protect. As long as *some* form of cultural content was married to a sustainable institutional form, all was in order. It is this substantive vacuity of Carl Schmitt's institutional theory that accounts for its widespread appeal, then and now.

NOTES

1. On the topic's revival in the late twentieth century, see, most important, Evans et al. 1985; Elster and Slagstadt 1988; March and Olsen 1989; North 1990; Powell and DiMaggio 1991; Steinmo, Thelen, and Longstreth 1992; Goodin 1996; and Rhodes et al. 2006.
2. For examples of recent scholarly treatments, see, among others, Ferejohn and Pasquino 2004; Lazar 2009; Levinson and Balkin 2010; and Posner and Vermeule 2011; see also Posner and Vermeule 2016.

3. For a recent restatement, see Mommsen 1997. Mommsen's original formulation of the concept of cumulative radicalization dates from 1976.

4. For relevant methodological treatments, see Shapiro and Bedi 2009.

5. For opposing perspectives in the debate over "break" and "continuity" in Schmitt's thought, see, most important, Maus 1969 and Schwab 1970. For an apologia disguised as an alternative third position in this debate, see Ulmen 2001. Despite Ulmen's problematic denial of the evidence demonstrating the existence of Schmitt's virulent antisemitism even prior to 1933 and the highly questionable logic of his argument, I believe he was right in concluding that Schmitt espoused "a consistent approach to changing legal and political questions" (Ulmen 2001, 31). Indeed, this chapter is dedicated to demonstrating this consistency in the case of Schmitt's institutional theory and its development across the juncture that was 1933.

6. In this chapter I focus primarily on Schmitt's institutional *political* theory. Due to space constraints, I largely gloss over the development of Schmitt's institutional *legal* theory, including his constitutional theory. For a comprehensive analysis, see Meierhenrich n.d. In addition, see the chapters in part IV of this volume. Farther afield, see Schneider 1957; Maus 1980; Dyzenhaus 1997; and Croce and Salvatore 2013.

7. *Oxford English Dictionary*, s.v. "order, *n*.," http://www.oed.com/view/Entry/132334?rskey= 8Y56PU&result=1&isAdvanced=false#eid.

8. *Oxford English Dictionary*, s.v. "order, *n*."

9. As Freund (1980, 337) points out, disorder can be alluring because it promises freedom without responsibility.

10. Unless noted otherwise, all translations of source material by the author.

11. See, most important, Hauriou 1925 (93–124). For a brief discussion of Schmitt's theoretical borrowing, see Neumann 2015 (366–370).

12. Entry of September 9, 1947.

13. Entry of September 9, 1947.

14. Entry of March 2, 1948.

15. Schmitt identified the following three of Hauriou's works as having been important to him: *La science sociale traditionnelle* (1896), *Principes du droit public* (1910), and *La théorie de l'institution et de la fondation* (1925). See Schmitt 2001 (112).

16. For a similar observation, see Böckenförde 1984 (1313). For a contrary argument, see Neumann 2015 (370).

17. On Hauriou's liberal credentials, see Croce and Salvatore 2013 (103–104).

18. Most important, Schmitt let fall by the wayside Hauriou's central emphasis on the importance of two secondary institutions for achieving political order: the separation of powers and the institution of representation. See Hauriou 1925 (105–106). For a more detailed discussion than can be provided here of Schmitt's very selective borrowing from Hauriou, see Croce and Salvatore 2013 (94–108).

19. For influential contributions to institutional theory that originated in the humanities, see, for example, Levin 1946 (159–168); Dickie 1974; Hohendahl 1982; Weber 1987; Graff 1987; and Rainey 1999. For an important study of distant relevance to this chapter's topic, see Ziolkowski 1990.

20. As Waldron emphasizes, "The study [of institutions] that I am envisaging is emphatically normative" (2013, 10). My usage of the term "normative institutionalism" differs from that of Guy Peters, for whom, rather oddly, the foundational contribution to institutional theory by March and Olsen qualifies as an example of normative institutionalism because of

their analytical emphasis on the role of norms and values. However, the latter is usually, and more appropriately, categorized as a forerunner of sociological or historical institutionalism or both. See Peters 2013 (25–46).

21. See also Thelen 1999 (369–404). Applied examples of the approach include Thelen 2008; Meierhenrich 2008; and Mahoney 2010.

22. For the eponymous article that gave the novel theoretical approach to institutions its name, and which is still illuminating, see March and Olsen 1984.

23. As Lethen 2002 (48) writes, "The view of man as harmless, according to Carl Schmitt, is either the quaint touch of a naïve anthropology or the symptom of an infantile disorder, such as expressionism or some other comparable radicalism."

24. On Schmitt's debt to Hobbes, see also McCormick 2016. Aside from Hobbes, Schmitt also cites Machiavelli, the French theologian Jacques-Bénigne Bossuet, Johann Gottlieb Fichte, Joseph de Maistre, the Spanish diplomat and political theorist Juan Donoso Cortés, the French literary theorist Hippolyte Taine, and Hegel as progenitors of "the idea of a problematic human nature." See Schmitt 1996c (61).

25. On the book's argument and place in Schmitt's thought, see also Kelly 2016.

26. On the idea of institutional re-equilibration, see Linz 1978 (esp. 87–98).

27. Schmitt 2014c (207). He also criticized the fact that "a delimitation" (206) of the commissarial dictatorship had not yet transpired.

28. The Isensee remark can be found in Isensee 1988 (174). Other participants at the 1986 conference in Speyer, Germany, concurred, including Hennis 1988 (168) and Kröger 1988 (159).

29. In 1948, Schmitt put it plainly: "For me the Catholic faith is the religion of my fathers. I am a Catholic not just out of belief, but also on account of my historical heritage, of, if I may say so, my race" (1991, 131, entry of April 20, 1948). Bendersky 1983 (506) has suggested (and Bernd Rüthers disputed) that Schmitt's concept of the political, with its defining friend/enemy distinction, can be traced back to this family experience. See also Rüthers 1994 (1683).

30. Note, however, that the translation is imperfect. For the original, see Schmitt 2008a (14).

31. A key development in his private life, his excommunication from the Catholic Church, contributed to this abandonment.

32. It is important not to conflate in this context the meanings of "total state" and "totalitarian state."

33. The first quote is from Schmitt 1931a (80); the second a formulation from Minca and Rowan 2015 (16). Popitz became minister of finance in Prussia in 1933, and later, to Schmitt's great consternation when he found out after the fact, a participant in the failed plot of July 22, 1944, to assassinate Hitler. See Bendersky 1983 (263).

34. Schmitt mentioned the idea of "the authoritarian state" in *Legality and Legitimacy* (2004, 90), but he did not elaborate on it. Schmitt was clearly influenced by, if critical of, Ziegler 1932 (see Schmitt 2004, 87). Stefan Breuer summarizes well Schmitt's dismissive attitude toward Ziegler's pragmatic argument in defense of a total state, noting also Schmitt's casual antisemitism. In his diary, Schmitt referred to the young sociologist pejoratively as "*Salonjüdchen*," or "little salon Jew" (Breuer 2013, 161). Schmitt had the unfortunate habit of treating intellectual rivals as true adversaries, occasionally even as enemies.

35. Koellreutter 1932; Schmitt 1933a. On this important intra-Nazi debate, see Caldwell 1994. For a broader analysis of contending concepts of state in Nazi Germany, see Hilger 2003.

36. Exemplary of a sizable literature on racial ideology and practices in Nazi Germany are Hutton 2005 and Kühl 1994.

37. One very important such strand—Schmitt's institutional approach to questions of international law and of international relations—is beyond the confines of this analysis. A comprehensive treatment is available in Meierhenrich n.d. See also Koskenniemi 2001 and 2016.

38. Despite their acceptance of the tenets of Nazi rule, "the early formulation of both Koellreutter and Schmitt contained phrases that might have suggested limits to the Führer's power" (Caldwell 1994, 411).

39. On Schmitt's reception of Hobbes, see, for example, Rumpf 1972; Dyzenhaus 1994; Strong 2008; Voigt 2009; Trelau 2010. Most recently, see McCormick 2016.

40. Entry of February 10, 1948.

41. Entry of February 10, 1948.

42. Entry of February 10, 1948.

43. For a brief intellectual history of Schmitt's so-called spatial turn, see Breuer 2013 (257–272).

44. I have, in this instance, not relied on the English translation because of its inaccurate rendering of the original.

45. Once more, I have not relied on the recent English translation of this monograph due to a number of imprecise or otherwise problematic formulations that it contains in the section referenced here. See Schmitt 2011 (110–111).

46. A transcript of the radio interview is available in Tommissen 1975 (113–119).

47. See also Koenen 1995b. For a recent and reliable history of the German Reich and its emergence from the remnants of the Holy Roman Empire, see Whaley 2012. Note that Schmitt referred to the German Empire pejoratively as "*Bundesstaat*," a, in his view, problematic attempt at fusing two incompatible visions of order. See Schmitt 1933e (193).

48. The first edition of Hegel's pamphlet, which originally had no title, was published in 1893 as "Critique of the Constitution of Germany" ("Kritik der Verfassung Deutschlands"). The title was subsequently shortened to "The Constitution of Germany" ("Die Verfassung Deutschlands"). In Nazi Germany, the republication of the essay was entitled "The Constitution of the German Empire" ("Die Verfassung des Deutschen Reiches"). See Avineri 1972 (34–35).

49. As already noted, space constraints disallowed an extension of this institutional analysis across the entirety of Schmitt's trinity of thought, which is why I have given pride of place to the institutional dimensions of his political thought, broadly defined. I mostly sidestepped the role and place of Schmitt's institutional theory in his legal thought and cultural thought.

50. On Schmitt's rivalry with Koellreutter, see Caldwell 1994; on his rivalry with Höhn, see von Lösch 1999 (429–470). For an integrated analysis, see Meierhenrich n.d. Also relevant is Koenen 1995a.

51. Some context may be helpful here: In the early 1980s, Bendersky had controversially claimed that Schmitt "never succumbed to a belief in the biological racism of National Socialist ideology" (1983, 208).

52. For pertinent discussions of the idea of *ordo ordinans*, in general or in relation to Schmitt, see Anter 2004 (200–259); Meierhenrich and Simons 2016; and Loughlin 2016.

References

Anter, A. 2004. *Die Macht der Ordnung: Aspekte einer Grundkategorie des Politischen.* Tübingen: Mohr.

Avineri, S. 1972. *Hegel's Theory of the Modern State.* Cambridge: Cambridge University Press.

Balakrishnan, G. 2000. *The Enemy: An Intellectual Portrait of Carl Schmitt*. London: Verso.

Bates, D. 2006. "Political Theology and the Nazi State: Carl Schmitt's Concept of the Institution." *Modern Intellectual History* 3: 415–442.

Bendersky, J. W. 1983. *Carl Schmitt: Theorist for the Reich*. Princeton: Princeton University Press.

Bentin, L.-A. 1972. *Johannes Popitz und Carl Schmitt: Zur wirtschaftlichen Theorie des totalen Staates in Deutschland*. Munich: Beck.

Blindow, F. 1999. *Carl Schmitts Reichsordnung: Strategie für einen europäischen Großraum*. Berlin: Akademie Verlag.

Böckenförde, E.-W. 1984. "Konkretes Ordnungsdenken." In *Historisches Wörterbuch der Philosophie*, vol. 6, ed. J. Ritter and K. Gründer. Basel: Schwabe & Co., 1312–1315.

Bolz, N. 1989. *Auszug aus der entzauberten Welt: Philosophischer Extremismus zwischen den Weltkriegen*. Munich: Fink.

Breuer, S. 2013. *Carl Schmitt im Kontext: Intellektuellenpolitik in der Weimarer Republik*. Berlin: Akademie Verlag.

Broderick, A. ed. 1970. *The French Institutionalists: Maurice Hauriou, Georges Renard, Joseph T. Delos*, trans. M. Welling. Cambridge: Harvard University Press.

Browning, C. R. 2004. *The Origins of the Final Solution: The Evolution of Nazi Jewish Policy, September 1939–March 1942*, with contributions by J. Matthäus. London: Heinemann.

Burleigh, M., and W. Wippermann. 1991. *The Racial State: Germany 1933–1945*. Cambridge: Cambridge University Press.

Caldwell, P. 1994. "National Socialism and Constitutional Law: Carl Schmitt, Otto Koellreutter, and the Debate over the Nature of the Nazi State." *Cardozo Law Review* 16: 399–427.

Caldwell, P. 1997. *Popular Sovereignty and the Crisis of German Constitutional Law: The Theory and Practice of Weimar Constitutionalism*. Durham: Duke University Press.

Carty, A. 2001. "Carl Schmitt's Critique of Liberal International Legal Order between 1993 and 1945." *Leiden Journal of International Law* 14: 25–76.

Cooney, T. A. 2015. "The Priority of Form in Carl Schmitt's Early Theological Perspective." PhD diss., Boston University.

Croce, M., and A. Salvatore. 2013. *The Legal Theory of Carl Schmitt*. London: Routledge.

Dahlheimer, M. 1998. *Carl Schmitt und der deutsche Katholizismus 1888–1936*. Paderborn: Schöningh.

Dempf, A. 1929. *Sacrum Imperium: Geschichts- und Staatsphilosophie des Mittelalters und der politischen Renaissance*. Munich: Oldenbourg.

Dickie, G. 1974. *Art and the Aesthetic*. Ithaca: Cornell University Press.

Dupeux, L. 1994. "'Kulturpessimismus', Konservative Revolution und Modernität." In *Intellektuellendiskurse in der Weimarer Republik: Zur politischen Kultur einer Gemengelage*, ed. M. Gangl and G. Raulet. Frankfurt: Campus, 287–299.

Dyzenhaus, D. 1994. "'Now the Machine Runs Itself': Carl Schmitt on Hobbes and Kelsen." *Cardozo Law Review* 16: 1–19.

Dyzenhaus, D. 1997. *Legality and Legitimacy: Carl Schmitt, Hans Kelsen and Hermann Heller in Weimar*. Oxford: Oxford University Press.

Dyzenhaus, D. 1998. "Introduction: Carl Schmitt." In *Law as Politics: Carl Schmitt's Critique of Liberalism*, ed. D. Dyzenhaus. Durham: Duke University Press, 1–20.

Dyzenhaus, D. 1999. "Putting the State Back in Credit." In *The Challenge of Carl Schmitt*, ed. C. Mouffe. London: Verso, 75–91.

Eley, G. et al. eds. 2016. *German Modernities from Wilhelm to Weimar: A Contest of Futures.* London: Bloomsbury.

Elster, J., and R. Slagstadt. eds. 1988. *Constitutionalism and Democracy.* Cambridge: Cambridge University Press.

Evans, P. B., et al. eds. 1985. *Bringing the State Back In.* Cambridge: Cambridge University Press.

Ferejohn, J., and P. Pasquino. 2004. "The Law of the Exception: A Typology of Emergency Powers." *International Journal of Constitutional Law* 2: 210–239.

Freund, J. 1980. "Der Begriff der Ordnung." *Der Staat* 19: 325–339.

Gerlach, Christian. 2016. *The Extermination of the European Jews.* Cambridge: Cambridge University Press.

Goodin, R. E. ed. 1996. *The Theory of Institutional Design.* Cambridge: Cambridge University Press.

Gordon, P. E., and J. P. McCormick. 2013. "Weimar Thought: Continuity and Crisis." In *Weimar Thought: A Contested Legacy,* ed. P. E. Gordon and J. P. McCormick. Princeton: Princeton University Press, 1–11.

Graff, G. 1987. *Professing Literature: An Institutional History.* Chicago: University of Chicago Press.

Gross, R. 2000. *Carl Schmitt und die Juden: Eine deutsche Rechtslehre.* Frankfurt: Suhrkamp.

Gross, R. 2016. " 'The True Enemy': Antisemitism in Carl Schmitt's Life and Thought." In *The Oxford Handbook of Carl Schmitt,* ed. J. Meierhenrich and O. Simons. Oxford: Oxford University Press, 96–116.

Hauriou, M. 1896. *La science sociale traditionnelle.* Paris: Larose.

Hauriou, M. 1904. "Le régime d'état." *Revue Socialiste* 39: 564–581.

Hauriou, M. 1910. *Principes de droit public.* Paris: Larose & Tenin.

Hauriou, M. 1925. "The Theory of the Institution and the Foundation: A Study in Social Vitalism." In Broderick 1970, 93–124.

Hauriou, M. 1929. "The Social Order: The Formal Organization of the Social Order Conceived as a System Endowed with a Slow and Uniform Movement." In Broderick 1970, 132–138.

Hauriou, M. 1986. "L'ordre social, la justice et le droit." *Revue trimestrielle de droit civil. Reprint in Hauriou, Aux sources du droit: Le pouvoir, l'ordre et la liberté.* Caen: Bibliothèque de philosophie politique et juridique, 43-71.

Hegel, G. W. F. 1999. "The German Constitution." In *Political Writings,* ed. L. Dickey and H. B. Nisbet. Cambridge: Cambridge University Press, 6–101.

Heiber, H. 1993. *The Weimar Republic,* trans. W. E. Yuill. Oxford: Blackwell.

Heil, S. 1996. *"Gefährliche Beziehungen": Walter Benjamin und Carl Schmitt.* Stuttgart: Metzler.

Hell, J. 2009. "Katechon: Carl Schmitt's Imperial Theology and the Ruins of the Future." *Germanic Review* 84: 283–326.

Hennis, W. 1988. "Aussprache." In *Complexio Oppositorum: Über Carl Schmitt,* ed. H. Quaritsch. Berlin: Duncker & Humblot, 168–169.

Hilger, C. 2003. *Rechtsstaatsbegriffe im Dritten Reich: Eine Strukturanalyse.* Tübingen: Mohr.

Hoelzl, M., and G. Ward. 2014. "Introduction." In Schmitt 2014b, x–xxix.

Hohendahl, P. U. 1982. *The Institution of Criticism.* Ithaca: Cornell University Press.

Hooker, W. 2009. *Carl Schmitt's International Thought: Order and Orientation.* Cambridge: Cambridge University Press.

Hutton, C. M. 2005. *Race and the Third Reich: Linguistics, Racial Anthropology and Genetics in the Dialectic of Volk.* Cambridge: Polity.

Isensee, J. 1988. "Aussprache." In *Complexio Oppositorum: Über Carl Schmitt,* ed. H. Quaritsch. Berlin: Duncker & Humblot, 172–174.

Kelly, D. 2016. "Carl Schmitt's Political Theory of Dictatorship." In *The Oxford Handbook of Carl Schmitt*, ed. J. Meierhenrich and O. Simons. Oxford: Oxford University Press, 217–244.

Knight, J. 1992. *Institutions and Social Conflict*. Cambridge: Cambridge University Press.

Knight, J., and J. Johnson. 2007. "The Priority of Democracy: A Pragmatist Approach to Political-Economic Institutions and the Burden of Justification." *American Political Science Review* 101: 47–61.

Koellreutter, O. 1932. *Der nationale Rechtsstaat: Zum Wandel der deutschen Staatsidee*. Tübingen: Mohr.

Koenen, A. 1995a. *Der Fall Carl Schmitt: Sein Aufstieg zum "Kronjuristen des Dritten Reiches."* Darmstadt: Wissenschaftliche Buchgesellschaft.

Koenen, A. 1995b. "Visionen vom 'Reich': Das politisch-theologische Erbe der Konservativen Revolution." In *Metamorphosen des Politischen: Grundfragen politischer Einheitsbildung seit den 20er Jahren*, ed. A. Göbel, D. van Laak, and I. Villinger. Berlin: Akademie Verlag, 53–74.

Koskenniemi, M. 2001. *The Gentle Civilizer of Nations: The Rise and Fall of International Law 1870–1960*. Cambridge: Cambridge University Press.

Koskenniemi, M. 2016. "Carl Schmitt and International Law." In *The Oxford Handbook of Carl Schmitt*, ed. J. Meierhenrich and O. Simons. Oxford: Oxford University Press, 592–611.

Krasner, S. D. 1982. "Structural Causes and Regime Consequences: Regimes as Intervening Variables." *International Organization* 36: 185–205.

Kröger, K. 1988. "Bemerkungen zu Carl Schmitts 'Römischer Katholizismus und politische Form.'" In *Complexio Oppositorum: Über Carl Schmitt*, ed. H. Quaritsch. Berlin: Duncker & Humblot, 159–165.

Kühl, S. 1994. *The Nazi Connection: Eugenics, American Racism, and German National Socialism*. New York: Oxford University Press.

Lazar, N. C. 2009. *States of Emergency in Liberal Democracies*. Cambridge: Cambridge University Press.

Lethen, H. 2002. *Cool Conduct: The Culture of Distance in Weimar Germany*. Berkeley: University of California Press.

Lethen, H. 2014. "Zeitspeicher der Entleerung: Carl Schmitts Tagebücher als Quelle der Werkdeutung." *Sinn und Form* 66: 293–303.

Levin, H. 1946. "Literature as an Institution." *Accent* 6: 159–168.

Levinson, S., and J. M. Balkin. 2010. "Constitutional Dictatorship: Its Dangers and Its Design." *Minnesota Law Review* 94: 1790–1866.

Linz, J. J. 1978. *The Breakdown of Democratic Regimes*, vol. 1: *Crisis, Breakdown, and Reequilibration*. Baltimore: Johns Hopkins University Press.

Longerich, P. 2010. *The Holocaust: The Nazi Persecution and Murder of the Jews*. Oxford: Oxford University Press.

Lösch, A.-M. Gräfin von. 1999. *Der nackte Geist: Die Juristische Fakultät der Berliner Universität im Umbruch von 1933*. Tübingen: Mohr.

Loughlin, M. 2016. "Politonomy." In *The Oxford Handbook of Carl Schmitt*, ed. J. Meierhenrich and O. Simons. Oxford: Oxford University Press, 570–591.

Mahoney, J. 2010. *Colonialism and Postcolonial Development: Spanish America in Comparative Perspective*. Cambridge: Cambridge University Press.

Maier, H. 1969. " 'Politische Theologie?' Einwände eines Laien." In *Diskussion zur "politischen Theologie,"* ed. H. Peukert. Mainz: Grünewald, 1–25.

March, J. G., and J. P. Olsen. 1984. "The New Institutionalism: Organizational Factors in Political Life." *American Political Science Review* 78: 734–749.

March, J. G., and J. P. Olsen. 1989. *Rediscovering Institutions: The Organizational Basis of Politics*. New York: Free Press.

Maschke, G. 1982. "Zum 'Leviathan' von Carl Schmitt." In Schmitt 1982, 179–244.

Maus, I. 1969. "Zur 'Zäsur' von 1933 in der Theorie Carl Schmitts." *Kritische Justiz* 2: 113–124.

Maus, I. 1980. *Bürgerliche Rechtstheorie und Faschismus: Zur sozialen Funktion und aktuellen Wirkung der Theorie Carl Schmitts*, 2nd, expanded ed. Munich: Fink.

Maus, I. 1998. "The 1933 'Break' in Carl Schmitt's Theory." In Dyzenhaus 1998, 196–216.

McCormick, J. P. 1997. *Carl Schmitt's Critique of Liberalism: Against Politics as Technology*. Cambridge: Cambridge University Press.

McCormick, J. P. 2004. "From Constitutional Technique to Caesarist Ploy: Carl Schmitt on Dictatorship, Liberalism, and Emergency Powers." In *Dictatorship in History and Theory: Bonapartism, Caesarism, and Totalitarianism*, ed. P. Baehr and M. Richter. Cambridge: Cambridge University Press, 197–220.

McCormick, J. P. 2016. "Teaching in Vain: Carl Schmitt, Thomas Hobbes, and the Theory of the Sovereign State." In *The Oxford Handbook of Carl Schmitt*, ed. J. Meierhenrich and O. Simons. Oxford: Oxford University Press, 269–290.

Mehring, R. 2009. *Carl Schmitt: Aufstieg und Fall*. Munich: Beck.

Mehring, R. 2014. "Ein Leben im Ausnahmezustand." In *Kriegstechniker des Begriffs: Biographische Studien zu Carl Schmitt*. Tübingen: Mohr, 1–29.

Meierhenrich, J. 2008. *The Legacies of Law: Long-Run Consequences of Legal Development in South Africa, 1652-2000*. Cambridge: Cambridge University Press.

Meierhenrich, J. n.d. *In the Belly of the Fish: Carl Schmitt in Nazi Germany, 1933–1945*. Unpublished book manuscript.

Meierhenrich, J., and O. Simons. 2016. "'A Fanatic of Order in an Epoch of Confusing Turmoil': The Political, Legal, and Cultural Thought of Carl Schmitt." In *The Oxford Handbook of Carl Schmitt*, ed. J. Meierhenrich and O. Simons. Oxford: Oxford University Press, 3–70.

Minca, C., and R. Rowan. 2015. "The Question of Space in Carl Schmitt." *Progress in Human Geography* 39: 268–289.

Minca, C., and R. Rowan. 2016. *On Schmitt and Space*. London: Routledge.

Mommsen, H. 1997. "Cumulative Radicalisation and Progressive Self-Destruction as Structural Determinants of the Nazi Dictatorship." In *Stalisnism and Nazism: Dictatorships in Comparison*, ed. I. Kershaw and M. Lewin. Cambridge: Cambridge University Press, 75–87.

Motschenbacher, A. 2000. *Katechon oder Großinquisitor? Eine Studie zu Inhalt und Struktur der Politischen Theologie Carl Schmitts*. Marburg: Tectum.

Müller, J.-W. 2003. *A Dangerous Mind: Carl Schmitt in Post-War European Thought*. New Haven: Yale University Press.

Nerdinger, W. 2015. ed. *München und der Nationalsozialismus: Katalog des NS-Dokumentationszentrums München*. Munich: Beck.

Nettl, J. P. 1968. "The State as a Conceptual Variable." *World Politics* 20: 559–592.

Neumann, V. 2015. *Carl Schmitt als Jurist*. Tübingen: Mohr.

Niethammer, L. 2004. "Die polemische Anstrengung des Begriffs: Über die exemplarische Faszination Carl Schmitts." In *Nationalsozialismus in den Kulturwissenschaften*, vol. 2: *Leitbegriffe—Deutungsmuster—Paradigmenkämpfe*, ed. O. G. Oexle and H. Lehmann. Göttingen: Vandenhoeck & Ruprecht, 41–82.

Noack, P. 1993. *Carl Schmitt: Eine Biographie*. Berlin: Propyläen.

North, D. C. 1990. *Institutions, Institutional Change and Economic Performance*. Cambridge: Cambridge University Press.

Peters, B. G. 2013. *Institutional Theory in Political Science: The New Institutionalism*, 3rd ed. London: Bloomsbury.

Peukert, D. J. K. 1987. *Die Weimarer Republik: Krisenjahre der Klassischen Moderne*. Frankfurt: Suhrkamp.

Posner, E. A., and A. Vermeule. 2011. *The Executive Unbound: After the Madisonian Republic*. Oxford: Oxford University Press.

Posner, E. A., and A. Vermeule. 2016. "Demystifying Schmitt." In *The Oxford Handbook of Carl Schmitt*, ed. J. Meierhenrich and O. Simons. Oxford: Oxford University Press, 612–626.

Pound, R. 1959. *Jurisprudence*, vol. 3. St. Paul: West.

Powell, W. W., and P. J. DiMaggio. eds. 1991. *The New Institutionalism in Organizational Analysis*. Chicago: University of Chicago Press.

Pufendorf, S. von. 1976. *Die Verfassung des Deutschen Reiches*, trans. and ed. H. Denzer. Stuttgart: Reclam.

Rainey, L. 1999. *Institutions of Modernism: Literary Elites and Public Culture*. New Haven: Yale University Press.

Rasch, W. 2016. "Carl Schmitt's Defense of Democracy." In *The Oxford Handbook of Carl Schmitt*, ed. J. Meierhenrich and O. Simons. Oxford: Oxford University Press, 312–337.

Rhodes, R. A. W., et al. eds. 2006. *The Oxford Handbook of Political Institutions*. Oxford: Oxford University Press.

Roberts, A. B. 2015. "Carl Schmitt—Political Theologian?" *Review of Politics* 77: 449–474.

Rossiter, C. 1948. *Constitutional Dictatorship: Crisis Government in Modern Democracies*. Princeton: Princeton University Press.

Rumpf, H. 1972. *Carl Schmitt und Thomas Hobbes: Ideelle Beziehungen und aktuelle Bedeutung mit einer Abhandlung über: Die Frühschriften Carl Schmitts*. Berlin: Duncker & Humblot.

Rüthers, B. 1994. "Wer war Carl Schmitt? Bausteine zu einer Biographie." *Neue Juristische Wochenschrift* 47: 1681–1687.

Schmitt, C. 1914. *Der Wert des Staates und die Bedeutung des Einzelnen*. Tübingen: Mohr.

Schmitt, C. 1917. "Die Sichtbarkeit der Kirche: Eine scholastische Erwägung." *Summa* 2: 71–80.

Schmitt, C. 1919. *Politische Romantik*. Munich: Duncker & Humblot.

Schmitt, C. 1921. "Preliminary Remarks to the First Edition." In Schmitt 2014b, xxxvii–xlv.

Schmitt, C. 1923. "Soziologie des Souveränitätsbegriffes und politische Theologie." In *Hauptprobleme der Soziologie: Erinnerungsgabe für Max Weber*, vol. 2, ed. M. Palyi. Munich: Duncker & Humblot, 3–35.

Schmitt, C. 1926. *Die Kernfrage des Völkerbundes*. Berlin: Dümmler.

Schmitt, C. 1927. *Volksentscheid and Volksbegehren*. Berlin: De Gruyter.

Schmitt, C. 1931a. *Der Hüter der Verfassung*. Tübingen: Mohr.

Schmitt, C. 1931b. "Die Wendung zum totalen Staat." In Schmitt 1940, 146–157.

Schmitt, C. 1932. *Konstruktive Verfassungsprobleme: Rede des Professors Dr. Carl Schmitt gehalten auf der Hauptversammlung des Vereins zur Wahrung der Interessen der chemischen Industrie Deutschlands e. V. am 4. November 1932*. Berlin: Maurer & Dimmick.

Schmitt, C. 1933a. *Staat, Bewegung, Volk: Die Dreigliederung der politischen Einheit*. Hamburg: Hanseatische Verlagsanstalt.

Schmitt, C. 1933b. "Die Weiterentwicklung des totalen Staats in Deutschland." In Schmitt 2003, 359–366.

Schmitt, C. 1933c. "Machtpositionen des modernen Staates." In Schmitt 2003, 367–371.

Schmitt, C. 1933d. "Das Gesetz zur Behebung der Not von Volk und Reich." *Deutsche Juristen-Zeitung* 38: 455–458.

Schmitt, C. 1933e. "Reich—Staat—Bund." In Schmitt 1940, 190–198.

Schmitt, C. 1934a. "Der Führer schützt das Recht." In Schmitt 1940, 199–203.

Schmitt, C. 1934b. *Staatsgefüge und Zusammenbruch des zweiten Reiches: Der Sieg des Bürgers über den Soldaten.* Hamburg: Hanseatische Verlagsanstalt.

Schmitt, C. 1935. "Was bedeutet der Streit um den 'Rechtsstaat'?" *Zeitschrift für die gesamte Staatswissenschaft* 95: 189–201.

Schmitt, C. 1936. "Die geschichtliche Lage der deutschen Rechtswissenschaft." *Deutsche Juristen-Zeitung* 41: 15–21.

Schmitt, C. 1937. "Der Staat als Mechanismus bei Hobbes und Descartes." *Archiv für Rechts- und Sozialphilosophie* 30: 622–632.

Schmitt, C. 1938. *Der Leviathan in der Staatslehre des Thomas Hobbes: Sinn und Fehlschlag eines politischen Symbols.* Hamburg: Hanseatische Verlagsanstalt.

Schmitt, C. 1940. *Positionen und Begriffe im Kampf mit Weimar—Genf—Versailles, 1923–1939.* Hamburg: Hanseatische Verlagsanstalt.

Schmitt, C. 1955. "Der neue Nomos der Erde." In Schmitt 1995, 518–522.

Schmitt, C. 1982. *Der Leviathan in der Staatslehre des Thomas Hobbes: Sinn und Fehlschlag eines politischen Symbols*, ed. G. Maschke. Cologne: Hohenheim.

Schmitt, C. 1985. *Der Hüter der Verfassung*, 3rd ed. Berlin: Duncker & Humblot.

Schmitt, C. 1988. *The Crisis of Parliamentary Democracy*, trans. E. Kennedy. Cambridge: MIT Press.

Schmitt, C. 1991. *Glossarium: Aufzeichnungen der Jahre 1947–1951*, ed. E. Freiherr von Medem. Berlin: Duncker & Humblot.

Schmitt, C. 1995. *Staat, Großraum, Nomos: Arbeiten aus den Jahren 1916–1969*, ed. G. Maschke. Berlin: Duncker & Humblot.

Schmitt, C. 1996a. *Der Hüter der Verfassung*, 4th ed. Berlin: Duncker & Humblot.

Schmitt, C. 1996b. *Roman Catholicism and Political Form.* Westport: Greenwood.

Schmitt, C. 1996c. *The Concept of the Political*, trans. G. Schwab. Chicago: University of Chicago Press.

Schmitt, C. 1998. *Politische Romantik*, 6th ed. Berlin: Duncker & Humblot.

Schmitt, C. 2001. *On the Three Types of Juristic Thought*, trans. J. W. Bendersky. Westport: Praeger.

Schmitt, C. 2003. *Verfassungsrechtliche Aufsätze aus den Jahren 1924–1954: Materialien zu einer Verfassungslehre*, 4th ed. Berlin: Duncker & Humblot.

Schmitt, C. 2004. *Legality and Legitimacy*, trans. and ed. J. Seitzer, with an introduction by J. P. McCormick. Durham: Duke University Press.

Schmitt, C. 2005. *Political Theology: Four Chapters on the Concept of Sovereignty*, trans. with an introduction by G. Schwab. Chicago: University of Chicago Press.

Schmitt, C. 2006. *The "Nomos" of the Earth in the International Law of the "Jus Publicum Europaeum,"* trans. G. L. Ulmen. New York: Telos Press.

Schmitt, C. 2007. *The Concept of the Political*, expanded ed., trans. with an introduction and notes by G. Schwab. Chicago: University of Chicago Press.

Schmitt, C. 2008a. *Römischer Katholizismus und politische Form*, 5th ed. Stuttgart: Klett-Cotta.

Schmitt, C. 2008b. *Constitutional Theory*, trans. and ed. J. Seitzer. Durham: Duke University Press.

Schmitt, C. 2008c. *The Leviathan in the State Theory of Thomas Hobbes: Meaning and Failure of a Political Symbol*, trans. G. Schwab and E. Hilfstein, with an introduction by G. Schwab. Chicago: University of Chicago Press.

Schmitt, C. 2009a. *Völkerrechtliche Großraumordnung mit Interventionsverbot für raumfremde Mächte: Ein Beitrag zum Reichsbegriff im Völkerrecht*, 3rd ed. Berlin: Duncker & Humblot.

Schmitt, C. 2009b. *Hamlet or Hecuba: The Intrusion of the Time into the Play*, trans. D. Pan and J. R. Rust. New York: Telos Press.

Schmitt, C. 2011. "The *Großraum* Order of International Law with a Ban on Intervention for Spatially Foreign Powers: A Contribution to the Concept of *Reich* in International Law." In *Writings on War*, trans. and ed. T. Nunan. Cambridge: Polity, 75–124.

Schmitt, C. 2014a. "Preliminary Remarks to the First Edition (1921)." In Schmitt 2014b, xxxvii–xlv.

Schmitt, C. 2014b. *Dictatorship: From the Origins of the Modern Concept of Sovereignty to Proletarian Class Struggle*, trans. M. Hoelzl and G. Ward. Cambridge: Polity.

Schmitt, C. 2014c. "Appendix: The Dictatorship of the President of the Reich According to Article 48 of the Weimar Constitution." In Schmitt 2014b, 180–226.

Schmitt, C. 2015. "The Guardian of the Constitution: Schmitt on Pluralism and the President as the Guardian of the Constitution." In *The Guardian of the Constitution: Hans Kelsen and Carl Schmitt on the Limits of Constitutional Law*, trans. and ed. L. Vinx. Cambridge: Cambridge University Press, 125–173.

Schmoeckel, M. 1994. *Ein Beitrag zur Geschichte der Völkerrechtswissenschaft im Dritten Reich, insbesondere der Kriegszeit*. Berlin: Duncker & Humblot.

Schneider, P. 1957. *Ausnahmezustand und Norm: Eine Studie zur Rechtslehre von Carl Schmitt*. Stuttgart: Deutsche Verlags-Anstalt.

Schwab, G. 1970. *The Challenge of the Exception: An Introduction to the Political Ideas of Carl Schmitt between 1921 and 1936*, 2nd ed. Westport: Greenwood Press.

Sica, A. 1992. *Weber, Irrationality and Social Order*. Berkeley: University of California Press.

Simons, O. 2016. "Carl Schmitt's Spatial Rhetoric." In *The Oxford Handbook of Carl Schmitt*, ed. J. M. and O. Simons. Oxford: Oxford University Press, 776–802.

Shapiro, I, and S. Bedi. eds. 2009. *Political Contingency: Studying the Unexpected, the Accidental, and the Unforeseen*. New York: New York University Press.

Skinner, Q. 1996. *Reason and Rhetoric in the Philosophy of Hobbes*. Cambridge: Cambridge University Press.

Skinner, Q. 2002. *Visions of Politics*, vol. 3: *Hobbes and Civil Science*. Cambridge: Cambridge University Press.

Smith, H. W. 2008. *The Continuities of German History: Nation, Religion, and Race across the Long Nineteenth Century*. Cambridge: Cambridge University Press.

Sombart, N. 1991. *Die deutschen Männer und ihre Feinde: Carl Schmitt—Ein deutsches Schicksal zwischen Männerbund und Matriarchatsmythos*. Munich: Hanser.

Speth, R. 2001. "Der Mythos des Staates bei Carl Schmitt." In *Mythos Staat: Carl Schmitts Staatsverständnis*, ed. R. Voigt. Baden-Baden: Nomos, 119–140.

Steber, M., and B. Gotto. eds. 2014. *Visions of Community in Nazi Germany: Social Engineering and Private Lives*. Oxford: Oxford University Press.

Steinmo, S. 2008. "Historical Institutionalism." In *Approaches and Methodologies in the Social Sciences: A Pluralist Perspective*, ed. D. Della Porta and M. Keating. Cambridge: Cambridge University Press, 118–138.

Steinmo, S., K. Thelen, and F. Longstreth. 1992. *Structuring Politics: Historical Institutionalism in Comparative Analysis*. Cambridge: Cambridge University Press.

Stirk, P. 1999. "Carl Schmitt's *Völkerrechtliche Großraumordnung*." *History of Political Thought* 20: 357–374.

Stolleis, M. 2004a. *A History of Public Law in Germany 1914–1945*, trans. T. Dunlap. Oxford: Oxford University Press.

Stolleis, M. 2004b. "International Law under German National Socialism: Some Contributions to the History of Jurisprudence 1933–1945." In *East Asian and European Perspectives on International Law*, ed. Stolleis and M. Yanagihara. Baden-Baden: Nomos, 203–213.

Strong, T. B. 2007. "Foreword: Dimensions of the New Debate around Carl Schmitt." In Schmitt 2007, ix–xxxi.

Strong, T. B. 2008. "Foreword: Carl Schmitt and Thomas Hobbes: Myth and Politics." In Schmitt 2008c, vii–xxviii.

Taubes, J. 1985. "Carl Schmitt: Ein Apokalyptiker der Gegenrevolution." *Die Tageszeitung*, July 20, 1985. Reprinted in Taubes 1987, 7–30.

Taubes. J. 1987. *Ad Carl Schmitt*. Berlin: Merve.

Teschke, B. 2016. "Carl Schmitt's Concepts of War: A Categorical Failure." In *The Oxford Handbook of Carl Schmitt*, ed. J. Meierhenrich and O. Simons. Oxford: Oxford University Press, 367–400.

Thelen, K. 1999. "Historical Institutionalism in Comparative Politics." *Annual Review of Political Science* 2: 369–404.

Thelen, K. 2008. *How Institutions Evolve: The Political Economy of Skills in Germany, Britain, the United States, and Japan*. Cambridge: Cambridge University Press.

Tommissen, P. ed. 1975. *Over en in zake Carl Schmitt*. Brussels: Economische Hogeschool Sint-Aloysisus.

Trelau, J. ed. 2010. *Thomas Hobbes and Carl Schmitt: The Politics of Order and Myth*. London: Routledge.

Ulmen, G. 2001. "Between the Weimar Republic and the Third Reich: Continuity in Carl Schmitt's Thought." *Telos* 119: 18–31.

Voigt, R. ed. 2009. *Der Hobbes-Kristall: Carl Schmitts Hobbes-Interpretation in der Diskussion*. Stuttgart: Steiner.

Waldron, J. 2013. "*Political* Political Theory: An Inaugural Lecture." *Journal of Political Philosophy* 21: 1–23.

Waldron, J. 2016. *Political Political Theory: Essays on Institutions*. Cambridge: Harvard University Press.

Watkins, F. M. 1939. *The Failure of Constitutional Emergency Powers under the German Republic*. Cambridge: Harvard University Press.

Weber, S. 1987. *Institution and Interpretation*. Minneapolis: University of Minnesota Press.

Weitz, E. 2007. *Weimar Germany: Promise and Tragedy*. Princeton: Princeton University Press.

Whaley, J. 2012. *Germany and the Holy Roman Empire*, vol. 2: *The Peace of Westphalia to the Dissolution of the Reich 1648–1806*. Oxford: Oxford University Press.

Wrong, D. H. 1994. *The Problem of Order: What Unites and Divides Society*. New York: Free Press.

Ziegler, H. O. 1932. *Autoritärer oder totaler Staat?* Tübingen: Mohr.

Ziolkowski, T. 1990. *German Romanticism and Its Institutions*. Princeton: Princeton University Press.

CHAPTER 7

....

CARL SCHMITT'S POLITICAL THEORY OF DICTATORSHIP

....

DUNCAN KELLY

INTRODUCTION

....

CARL SCHMITT developed a concept of dictatorship both to attack the general weaknesses of modern liberalism and to engage critically with particular debates about
Article 48 of the Weimar Constitution. This much is well known, but what remains
underappreciated in Anglophone scholarship is how important the concept of dictatorship was to Schmitt's attempt to rewrite the history of modern political thought. This
matters because such a rewriting the history of modern political thought provided the
foundations upon which his pointed criticisms of liberalism and Weimar constitutionalism were built. To show this, my chapter first explains the intellectual and historical background of his analysis of dictatorship and tries to measure the ambition of his
enterprise. It was an ambition readily apparent to those, like Moritz Julius Bonn, who
helped foster Schmitt's early career in quite powerful ways.

In 1919, as a highly polished and entrepreneurial director of the relatively recently
established *Handelshochschule* in Munich, Bonn called the precocious young legal
scholar Carl Schmitt away from Strasbourg to a new academic position as *Dozent
der Rechtslehre*. It would not be the last time he would be instrumental in furthering
Schmitt's career, and within a few years Bonn would also bring him to the *Hochschule
für Politik* in Berlin. In Berlin, Schmitt's powerfully compressed account of the concept
of the political received an early hearing in a seminar series on the foundational problems of modern democracy. Here, Schmitt pitted his arguments against those of ideological opponents like Hermann Heller and others interested in the integrative power

of the modern state like Rudolf Smend, who in turn became something of a mentor (Mehring 2010, 60–62).[1] Moreover, the themes that were encompassed within the 1927 Berlin seminar series, *Probleme der Demokratie*, were close to Moritz Bonn's own interests. He had also written engagingly of the problems of interwar politics in terms of the interrelated crises of state, democracy, and liberalism (Bonn 1925).[2]

Nevertheless, thanks to his new appointment it was in Munich that Schmitt's powerful and compressed histories of modern political thought were first presented. His study of the history and theory of dictatorship, *Die Diktatur*, appeared in 1921, and this early call to Bavaria thrust Schmitt into a highly charged and clearly highly productive atmosphere. Returning to the city where he had been stationed during the war and that was now in the throes of revolution, into a teaching post with no internal prospects of promotion or advancement, he found both a platform and a challenge. And like many ambitious young academics, he set out to develop his earlier work by practicing his arguments on students in lectures and cultivating a particular style.[3] Perhaps most importantly, he used these lectures as the basis for academic publications.

In October 1919 Schmitt gave a lecture on the history of political ideas since the Reformation, which built on the account of modern political theory outlined in his highly polemical *Politische Romantik* published earlier that year. This moved him toward a consideration of the rise of political absolutism in the form of the modern unified state (*Einheitsstaat*), considered by Bodin, Hobbes, and Montesquieu. Over the course of the same year, he taught classes on political ideas since the French Revolution, constitutional law, the foundations of the social welfare state, labor law, and the legal forms of economic administration. Schmitt was soon offered (but declined) a contract with *Drei Masken Verlag* to write the book on liberalism in its series *Der deutsche Staatsgedanke*. He tried to pass the commission on to Kurt Wolzendorff, the historian whose views on minority rights and parliamentary democracy he would shortly criticize in his own work on German parliamentarism (Mehring 2009, 119, 612 n21, 612 n26). In combination, however, these obligations and opportunities provided him with the intellectual bedrock of *Die Diktatur*.

Clearly, Schmitt had established a reputation as a sharp critic of liberalism, and in the same year as the publication of his book on dictatorship a précis of his attack on *Political Romanticism* appeared in the *Historische Zeitschrift* (Schmitt-Dorotic 1921; Schmitt 1919, 109–162; also Mehring 2009, 119–120). Putting the two arguments together, it is clear that Schmitt's critique of liberalism relied upon a distinctive assessment of the rise of German romanticism and liberalism in the aftermath of the French Revolution. It is to these connections that my attention now turns, because they allow us to see Schmitt thinking about liberalism as either a passive or an active form of politics, and that active or passive construction will open up a space into which Schmitt can reconceive dictatorship as either an ordinary technique of political management or the active creation of a new political order. He will claim that liberalism has forgotten the former and cannot cope with the latter.

ROMANTICISM AND THE FRENCH
REVOLUTION IN GERMANY

If Schmitt is understood as a sharp critic of the conceptual ambiguities of liberalism as a political theory, the original contours of his criticism are typically ignored by much of the political theory that has developed it. For the point Schmitt was engaging in this early critique of *Political Romanticism*, a typically rapid-fire production, was directly concerned with the origins of liberalism in Germany as a form of post-revolutionary and restoration era politics (Mehring 2009, 243).[4]

Restoration politics, he suggests, began as an explicit rejection of romanticism, because romanticism was less a liberal and more of an anti-political theory that developed in the aftermath of the French Revolution (cf. Jainchill 2008). If romanticism was a source for liberal individualism, it was grounded in claims about cultural uniqueness and the centrality of historicism. But Schmitt wants to show how the true sources of a robust liberalism might to be found in the realist, rather than utopian and romantic, writers associated with the Restoration. Here, figures like Friedrich Gentz, the translator of Edmund Burke, and certain claims by arch-reactionaries Karl Ludwig von Haller and Joseph de Maistre, became the embodiment of significant truths about the realities of politics and the need for sovereignty, according to Schmitt, but they had in fact been taken to embody a form of romanticized and aestheticized politics according to self-designated liberals. By contrast, Schmitt saw the historicist moves of liberal political romanticism to be the real expression of a claim to aestheticize politics, so the liberal critique of restoration politics needed to be clarified. If one can extract an ideal-typical view of modern German liberalism from the celebrated *Staatslexicon* of Karl von Rotteck and Karl Welcker (1840, vol. 9, 713–730 and passim), then post-restoration and nationally based liberalism was explicitly defined as a form of politics grounded in public reason, toleration, and equality through law. What Schmitt effectively claimed, however, is that such self-styled liberals misunderstood the origins of their own form of politics, which had everything to do with the character of the modern European state outlined in the writings of Bodin and Hobbes and less to do with ideas of a naturally developing desire for popular sovereignty. Neglecting this, he suggested, misjudged what had made liberalism realistic rather than utopian.

Schmitt argued that the political theories of the restoration showed that politics could be legitimately founded only on historical prudence. Claiming that they were instead straightforwardly reactionary, as the liberals did, was therefore misplaced. In fact, he continued, only a position that was a "conscious rejection of every adequate causal relationship" ("*bewußter Ablehnung jedes adäquaten Kausalzusammenhanges*") in both theory and practice could assume the mantle of a romantic, "subjectified," and "occasional" response to any political event and make it into a form of romantic "production" (Schmitt-Dorotic 1921, 392; cf. Schmitt 1919, 160).[5]

Thus, Schmitt engaged in a twin process of historical and political redescription. First, he reviewed and revised what were, in fact, thoroughly conventional views of nineteenth-century public law and politics, exemplified by the synthesizing Swiss jurist Johann Kaspar Bluntschli, one of his sources. Bluntschli had claimed both that the origins of the distinctively modern state were to be found elsewhere than in the politics of Machiavelli, Hobbes, and Rousseau and that the theory and practice of the state required both a legal analysis of its structure and form analytically and a political focus on the requirements entailed in its movement (cf. Schmitt 1927a, 102–105). But if he rejected Bluntschli's temporal reorientation of the origins of the modern state and its fulcrum as psychologically "liberal," Schmitt maintained Bluntschli's claim that any general theory of the state (*Allgemeine Staatslehre*) required both a descriptive account of its status in public law (*Staatsrecht*) and a political (*Politik*) component that could understand its dynamism. Only together could one jointly analyze the interconnections between justice (*Iustitia*) and public safety (*Salus Populi*; see Bluntschli 1901, 58–61, 69). This required from both a rejection of extreme forms of restoration thinking, exemplified in the work of Karl Ludwig von Haller, as well as the defense of a certain form of reconceived and realistic liberalism.[6]

By reinterpreting historically prudential political thinking as foundational for any realistic appraisal of politics, Schmitt rejected both romanticism as well as abstract liberalism. Claiming that romanticism applied to politics was little more than particularism, any liberalism that saw its foundations there would be fatally flawed. This could easily be read as a sideways blow aimed at Friedrich Meinecke (1911), whose account of the centrality of German romanticism for developing a cultural theory of the German nation played such a prominent role in his genealogy of the German nation-state, published as *Weltbürgertum und Nationalstaat*. Meinecke was someone whose work Carl Schmitt would regularly set his face against because Meinecke's combination of historicism and nationality viewed liberalism as both necessary and sufficient for the tasks of a German form of politics, which could cultivate a sphere of individual and national autonomy without falling into the disastrous terror of the French Revolution. In short, it was a highly moralized form of politics, and one that Meinecke further developed in his treatise on the intellectual origins of raison d'état (1925, 24–27, 31–60, 461–468). In a similar vein, Schmitt also rejected the developmental history of liberalism offered by Immanuel Kant's successor, Wilhelm Traugott Krug, which was an attempt to open a space for politics grounded on the interconnection between the principles of nationality and political autonomy at the level of the state and whose justificatory principles as well as actual practices could be historically understood (Krug 1823, 149).

By avoiding the neo-Roman freedom of the French that led to Napoleonic tyranny and despotism, Meinecke sought to provide an account of how a moral understanding of reason of state and of cosmopolitanism, filtered through Hegel and Fichte, offered a pathway between coldly utilitarian reasoning about the interests of state on one hand and rampant nationalism on the other. Modern, post-restoration liberalism offered for Meinecke the possibility of cultivating a particularly German idea of freedom out of this moralized historicism. This moralizing of key political doctrines, however, was precisely what Schmitt rejected. In Schmitt's second act of redescription, then, it is not surprising to find in his review of Meinecke's book on reason of state a defense of a more starkly Weberian, ideal-typical method of historical writing in the service of contemporary political and legal theory (Schmitt 1926a, 51–59, esp. 54).

Strict conceptual boundaries were the absolute sine qua non of historically informed research that could engage with contemporary problems at all, but at the same time politics was one of those concepts that defied the sort of limits that Meinecke wanted to place on it. Meinecke would have some semblance of revenge by noting that Schmitt's work on romanticism depended upon a "laughable caricature" of his own analysis of romanticism and the wars of liberation.[7] The two men were destined to disagree, but Schmitt's criticisms of Meinecke would be foundational for the development of new arguments about reason of state and modern politics in the twentieth century (see Koselleck 1973, 124, 156; 2004, 58–71, 119–125, esp. 56–57, 62–63).

Rather than being constrained to serve a morally defensible end like the national interest or the common good, the autonomy of the political would always resist a priori limitations. As Schmitt pointed out, the sphere of reason of state was necessarily similar to the sphere of prerogative, and in as much as nationalists or liberals forgot this they moved toward a form of liberalism that was at quite some remove from the ideas of such intellectual precursors as John Locke. As they did so, their attempts to constrain the political and render it technically neutral and morally beneficial opened up a space for Schmitt to later, and very famously, attack both the development of parliamentary democracy and forms of German liberalism associated with the nineteenth-century *Rechtsstaat*. This became clearer in his discussions of the historical connections and parallels between the constitutional dictatorship of France in 1793 and the "dilatory formal compromise" (*"dilatorische Formelkompromiß"*) of the second part of the Weimar Constitution of 1919. For him, the principle of nationality understood as a principle of political autonomy was simply an updated form of reason of state, and one whose structure provided the foundation for thinking about dictatorship (1993, 32–34; 2008a, 85–86). Dictatorship was a tool that could be used either for managing politics or for transforming politics, and it could therefore possess either a commissarial or a sovereign form. This was a point he had first begun to think about during World War I, when distinguishing between dictatorship and the state of siege (1993, 58–60; 2008a, 108–111).

STATES OF SIEGE AND DICTATORSHIP

While stationed in Munich during the early stages of World War I, Schmitt was concerned with the political and legal status of the military commander during a state of siege. His arguments at this time bear the marks of still earlier discussions from his doctoral work, undertaken in the legal and political borderland of Strasbourg, which downplayed the role of the individual in law and looked instead at broader structures of authority. In Munich, however, academic thinking about the nature of political and legal authority came into contact with the harsh psychic practicalities of having to obey the orders of a real military commander, when Schmitt was assigned to administrative duties in the *Generalkommando* of the First Bavarian army. As his tortured private notebooks all too clearly attest, Schmitt found the work intellectually stupefying and personally difficult. Whether writing hack propaganda for the foreign press or censoring the mail—all the while pining for his new lover, Cari—he tried to keep up his cultural and intellectual interests by working and writing on Theodor Däubler and Hugo Ball, but he was clearly working out ideas about the state of siege.

The military diaries with their personal longings and marked self-loathing continue for the first year and a half of the war, and around September 6, 1915, he even records that he is thinking of suicide. His personal antipathy toward militarism generally, and military personnel particularly, comes across very sharply in these texts (2005a, 125). The very next day, however, he prepares a report on the law of the state of siege, which he finds ironic given that the country has already been at war for over a year. Yet there is some further irony to the fact that Schmitt clearly recognized that this report was something he could develop to try making his way in the world.

A new job was on the horizon in Strasbourg. So he set about writing up very quickly his "report" on the state of siege and reconnected with his doctoral supervisor, Professor Fritz von Calker. Also Robert Redslob's supervisor, Calker had taken Schmitt under his wing as a student, offering him the role of *Dozent* when he was first at Strasbourg between 1908 and 1910. One might plausibly trace Schmitt's analysis of parliamentarism some years later back to this moment and see it as an attack on Redslob's famous thesis of a "true" form of English parliamentarism (1918).[8] Yet although the place held some painful personal memories, when the order came to write on the situation of the Bavarian military commander and then the state of siege, he was nevertheless keen to use the work to carve out a path back to the border city.

His very early work on causal reasoning in the law, on the relationship between the state and individual, on guilt, and on the connections between legal interpretation and legal judgment mirrored closely the sorts of themes and questions that had been taken up by Max Weber when discussing juridical questions of "adequate causation" in the work of Gustav Radbruch in particular (Weber 1922, 276–290, 269, 290). Radbruch had laid out a deeply skeptical foundation, of relevance to contemporary legal theory, about the possibility of ever truly "knowing" what was at issue in the reality of causation. To assume we could answer the question with recourse to a notion of a power that determined or caused an action, counterfactually or otherwise, was thoroughly "metaphysical." And the rejection of metaphysics in favor of probable, and probably adequate, causation is the terrain upon which both Weber and Schmitt operate.[9] However, where Weber thought that legal formalism was perfectly adequate when applied to the sphere of law but not to other disciplines, it was Schmitt who expressed the much more polemical rejection of a technically formal, politically neutral, understanding of law and its history, beginning with siege and dictatorship (Ghosh 2008, 299–347, esp. 329–333; cf. Egon Zweig 1907, 130; 1909, 2; Schmitt 1923, 3–36).[10]

Schmitt's early essays on the various states of siege, war, and dictatorship were of clear contemporary resonance in the aftermath July 1914 and were published in the *Zeitschrift für die gesamte Strafrechtswissenschaft*, where Werner Rosenberg's recently published essay on the subject in the same journal was a clear target (Caldwell 1997, 56). The first essay, developed from a sample lecture given to colleagues at Strasbourg, assessed the state of war and its effects on military command and procedure, effectively concluding that there was no legal "right" to command that could be derived from the state, and which would grant the military commander his authority. Rather, such authority was simply practical and dependent upon his control and assessment of the military situation (Schmitt 2005a, 429; Mehring 2009, 90). Schmitt's report for the Bavarian army command was developed into an essay for the same journal, becoming a slightly better known paper comparing dictatorship with a state of siege. It would be foundational for his later book on the subject.

In the state of siege, principally a military situation, traditional justifications for the separation between legislation and implementation were sidelined, and transferred as well as centralized in the singular body of the executive. Under dictatorship, although the conceptual distinction between legislation and implementation remains, any separation is in practice eliminated because either the legislative or the executive completely takes over (Schmitt 1916, 16). Because this conceptual separation remains, however, the figure of the dictator occupies an almost liminal space, and in Schmitt's rather portentous Hegelian formulation this means that although "the division of powers is the negation [of a previously unified state apparatus]; the state of siege signifies (for a delimited space) a return to this position, while the dictator is the negation of the negation, which is to say, the division of powers is indeed transcended but also presupposed and assumed" (19). Therefore, although the political consequences may be similar, from a legal point of view one needs to differentiate between a military state of siege and its possible use as a political tool on the one hand, and on the other to notice whether the legislative power has superseded the executive, or if the executive has superseded the legislative, so as to fully grasp the matter (20).

This early separation of dictatorship from a state of siege looks slightly disconcerting given the later, and better known, moves away from such a position in his work toward a distinction between types of dictatorship (commissarial and sovereign), alongside his apparent conflation of dictatorship with the liberal *Rechtsstaat*. But discussing executive power in wartime was, of course, the central concern of many constitutional lawyers, and Gaston Jèze in France, for example, published a major comparative review of contemporary English, Italian, Swiss declarations of war and legal formulations of the fullness of power (*pleins des pouvoirs*), which also took up similar questions (cf. Jèze 1917, 5–43, 209–268, 404–442). In practice, Schmitt's writings differed in that they pinpointed not only the emergence of a real military dictatorship in the period of 1793, when the French state was encircled by its enemies, but also the idea of dictatorship as the complete combination of legislative with executive power (Caldwell 1997, 58–59).

The technicalities of his distinctions were well received by one of the preeminent figures in Wilhelmine *Staatsrechtslehre*, Paul Laband, which is something of a surprise to those who know Schmitt's work only through his later, ferocious polemics with Laband-inspired legal positivism.[11] Thanks to these essays, Schmitt was invited back to Strasbourg to begin lecturing (admittedly to rather empty lecture halls) in *Strafprozessrecht* during the academic year 1916–1917.[12] He was listed as lecturing on *Strafrecht* again in the 1918 summer semester. However, thanks to his application in March 1917 to rejoin the war effort in Munich, he was once again attached to the military assessor's unit of the *Generalkommando* in Bavaria, writing propaganda and monitoring mail as well as posting various other pieces in the Catholic journal *Summa* (on the "visibility" of the Church, Theodor Däubler, and rather muted satire; see 2005a, 403–472).

It is unsurprising that Schmitt should have be engaged in a topic of general European concern during his brief time at Strasbourg, but he quickly noted how German laws on the subject were governed by arguments that had first been made in France between the revolutionary epochs of 1789 and 1848. In France, writers concerned with real and fictive uses of the state of siege—that is, the distinction between a military and a political-constitutional state of siege or dictatorship—were writing during the war about this very topic as part of the connection between national history and constitutional law. For Schmitt, as well as for his sources, a pivotal moment for understanding this development was the period between the first revolutionary constitution of 1791, where legislative authority determined something akin to a state of exception to deal with domestic disturbances in Titre IV, Articles 10–11, and the promulgation of the infamous declaration of October 10, 1793, that the provisional government would be revolutionary until the peace.[13] This state of siege idea would be reasserted legislatively in the aftermath of the 1848 revolutions.

In his early essay on the subject, Schmitt engaged in minor technical criticisms of French scholarship, but his smaller points were developed more expansively in *Die Diktatur*.[14] Differentiating between states of war, political states of siege, and the question of dictatorship provided his boundary positions. He noted that the idea of the state of siege was mentioned on July 10, 1791, while other French authors argued that the principles of the state of siege were only formally outlined in the first article of an April 3, 1878, law. The conceptual point was the crucial one, however, and claiming that the state of siege "can only be declared in the case of imminent peril or danger resulting from a foreign war or the insurrection of the army" was exactly how Schmitt discussed the justification for the state of siege declared in 1914 (Carret 1916, 35, 37).

For many of the French lawyers discussing this problem, there was an apparent "paradox": parliamentary oversight of the state of siege in the republic seemed most necessary at exactly the moment where legislative authority was to be given over to executive power. The best they could propose was that there should be a proscribed time limit upon the suspension of power (Carret 1916, 49, 133, 135). This was, of course, a classical concern. Another early French study, this time a doctoral thesis by Fernand Velut, examined the state of siege propounded in the August 9, 1849, law. Velut focused on the Roman dictator as a precursor or model, taking his cue from Theodor Mommsen's analysis of Roman law, for an account of Bonaparte's neo-Roman legislation (Velut 1910, 10–14, 117–118). Velut's conclusion, however, about the distinction between a political state of siege on one hand and a military state of siege on the other was quite suggestive. The former were governed by "conventions of the new law" (*"dispositions de la nouvelle loi"*) and the latter by the "laws of the republic and the empire" (*"lois de la République et de l'Empire"*; 1910, 132–133).

Schmitt followed suit, echoing the work of both Theodor Reinach and Paul Romain, who had distinguished between a "real" military state of siege and an artificial or "fictitious" (and hence political) state of siege (Reinach 1885, 110, 147; Romain 1918, 23–24). He would hardly discuss Bonapartism as a political problem, though, and this distinguished him from French scholars.[15] But in 1918, both Schmitt and Romain were concerned with differentiating between an illegal state of siege (which did not follow due process) and one that arose simply from a faulty diagnosis of the situation. Put in these terms, the difference between the two spheres of siege and dictatorship presupposed a distinction between "morality and politics" (Romain 1918, 182, 185). As Schmitt began to develop his own position out of a critical engagement with the "details" (*Ausführungen*) of these various French arguments, Reinach's in particular, two issues came to the fore. First, they provided for him an early intimation of the importance of 1793–1794 and the French Revolution for the rise of a sovereign, legislative dictatorship (Reinach 1885, 27, 86–87, 91–92). Second, the obviously classical sources for the idea and the practice of dictatorship, public enmity, and the distinctions between the fictive political state of siege, the military state of siege, and the concept of dictatorship seem to have prompted Schmitt to examine more closely the work of Theodor Mommsen on authority and Roman law.

The discovery of a fragment concerning the *auctoritas* of Augustus between 1914 and 1924 in Anatolia, known as the *Res Gestae Divi Augusti*, reinvigorated the study of the term in German classical scholarship and focused attention on the legitimating role of *auctoritas* as traditional or conventionally established supreme power, in contrast to the power of the magistrates or senate (Nippel 2007, 28–29). By looking at the question of dictatorship and supreme political authority in tandem, Schmitt was compelled to think about the nature of modern, democratic political authority and its sources. He therefore tried to develop Mommsen's arguments about constituent power and *auctoritas* and to apply them to the period of the French Revolution. This provided the real transmission mechanism for his theory.

CONSTITUENT POWER AND DICTATORSHIP

As some scholars have suggested, we would also do well to read Schmitt's use of Mommsen's work on Roman public law (*Staatsrecht*) in light of Mommsen's own reading of revolutionary authors like Mably, Rousseau, and Sieyès.[16] Schmitt was not alone in connecting these topics, for he also developed his thinking about dictatorship through close readings of works on Sieyès and constituent power by Egon Zweig and Bernhard Braubach.[17]

By combining ancient and revolutionary source material drawn from Mommsen and Sieyès, Schmitt began to construct an opposition between the demands of a modern democracy based on liberal constitutionalism and the historical account of constituent power and constitutional control in Roman legal and political institutions.[18] He continued to use and often transpose this combination of ancient and modern in other works, noting how an opposition between classical democracy, mass democracy, and parliamentarism produced a crisis of the modern state (cf. 1926b, 52–66, esp. 65; 1927b, 48, 32). His analysis required, though, the erection of an often rather strained and even tendentious account of Sieyès's theory of constituent power (Thiele 2003, 165–167, 220–221, 223). Sieyès's complex system of election, representation, and authorization, particularly in Year Three of the Revolution, sanctified both the nation and its people as the ground of political legitimacy and the expression of "public reason" but de facto constrained the political power of its major sovereign figurehead, which he termed the Grand Elector, after Thermidor (Sieyès 2007, 501, 504 n9, 552, 557, 565; see also Thiele 2003, 273–274).

Schmitt then applied these thoughts about the constituent power of the people as a nation into his own frame of reference, offering a much more obviously Hobbesian account of representation of the people by the sovereign. Ironically, this meant that Schmitt offered a more politically romanticized version of Sieyès than his writings permit. Making the Abbé into something of a "procedural anarchist," with an idea of a formless mass of constituent power as the legitimate grounds of a constitutional order, rather transforms the reality of Sieyès's project of constitutional guardianship into a rhetorical fantasy. But it offered Schmitt a potentially revolutionary theory of counter-revolution, through which he could explain and simultaneously constrain the idea of popular constituent power through political theology (Schmitt 2005b, esp. 51–66; cf. Thiele 2003, 225, 232; Nippel 2008, 184; Roques 2009, §§50, 57). That is, it allowed him to present the anti-Jacobin theory of constituent power outlined by Sieyès as the true source of political legitimacy, only to immediately claim that such power must be represented by a unitary national sovereign (Schmitt 2006, 142; Pasquino 1986, 371–385). Because of this, Schmitt absolutely separated constituent and legislative power, or what Sieyès considered *pouvoir constituant* and *pouvoir constitué*, but made their conflict the site for what some scholars have thought of as a permanent revolution (Thiele 2003, 226). For the background to this, the very detailed *Habilitationsschrift* published by Zweig on constituent power was fundamental to formulating Schmitt's analysis.

Yet it is precisely Zweig's attempt to see Sieyès as a "rationalist" with an Enlightenment-inspired theory, one that attempts to manage and constrain constituent power by explosively combining Montesquieu and Rousseau, that Schmitt rejects. He does so for the same reasons he rejects Enlightenment political thinking in general, namely, its inattention to contingency.[19] If Schmitt's attacks on romanticism had attempted to undermine the individualistic foundations of one version of modern post-restoration liberalism, with its concomitant rejection of theism and a newly minted theory of democratic legitimacy, then his attack on its political and constitutional foundations would continue and develop in his book on dictatorship.[20] Having now considered many of its sources and contexts for its development, it is to that book, finally, that my discussion turns.

RECONCEPTUALIZING DICTATORSHIP
AND CONSTITUENT POWER

After defending the primacy of practice in terms of his interpretation of the state of siege and the condition of dictatorship and having considered the pivotal moment of the French Revolution, Schmitt could now develop his account of dictatorship in a more rigorous conceptual manner. Differentiating between what he proposed as "commissarial" and "sovereign" models of dictatorship, *Die Diktatur* proposed a history of political thought that could account for the origin and development of these ideas. It remains one of the outstanding, yet ultimately puzzling, works by Schmitt, and it has certainly divided opinion. Franz Neumann used it in his analysis of National Socialism, but while he found it extraordinarily stimulating, it was, for reasons he failed to give, deemed "not acceptable" (1957, 254 n1).[21]

Later scholars such as Maurice Duverger (1961, 120–127, 156–158, 206), who tried to conceptualize dictatorships of left (revolutionary) and right (reactionary) from past to present in terms of nascent belief structures and socioeconomic foundations, mostly to account for the relationship between France and Algeria in the early 1960s, found it little more than a pamphlet (*surtout un pamphlet*). By contrast, Alfred Cobban (1939, 337, 339–341), for whom it was inchoate, incomplete, and far too obviously Germanic, thought it a work of theory and not of history, although one whose temporal location of sovereign dictatorship in the French Revolution he nevertheless agreed with. More recently still, Pasquale Pasquino (1998, 198) has noted its central role in understanding Schmitt's history of liberalism, though adding that it was "historically mistaken and conceptually misleading." Finally, John McCormick (1997b, 169, 176–177, 181) has focused on its place in Schmitt's oeuvre as a hinge between his jurisprudential defense of constitutional management and a later, more rigid form of political existentialism.

In its own terms, however, Schmitt's theory and history of dictatorship simply continued his interest in explaining the rise of the modern state as unified, centralized power. He proposed Bodin as the originator of a view of the commissarial dictatorship of the public person and Rousseau as the progenitor of sovereign dictatorship. Bodin offered Schmitt a distinction, from his *Six Livres de la République* (1576), between the commissar and the official and thus between the techniques available to the magistrate and the commissar (Schmitt 2006, 33–35). On his terms, a dictator under such an account would be like the "absolutist action commissar," or a "conceptually necessary commissar, whose activity is legally observed," strictly delimited and presupposed by the distinction between law and ordinance (38–39). In the move toward the unified modern nation-state, Bodin's limiting framework of commissarial action for dealing with the emergency situation laid conceptual foundations that were developed, according to Schmitt, in the writings of both Locke and Sidney.

Schmitt then moved to discuss what he saw as princely commissarial dictatorships down to the eighteenth century. Beginning with a discussion of analogous cases to the *plenitudo potestatis* of the papacy, this is where Schmitt writes about Catholic political phi-losophy as well as judicial (*richterliche*) activity. Both focus on the activity that takes place under a heading of commissarial action, which is so "general" that it could cover the activity of both princes (*Fürsten*) and estates (*Stände*; 48). The aim is very clearly to show the long-standing acceptance of a defense of *salus populi* with the techniques of prerogative or commissarial, and hence powerful but strictly limited, political authority in the history of legal and political thought. Making use of his comparative local advantage, Schmitt illus-trated his claim by using materials in the *Staatsarchiv* in Munich, particularly those show-casing Ludwig, Duke of Bavaria, dealing with the Bohemian rebels in a "commissarial" fashion (2006, esp. 62–65). He also undertook a similar reappraisal of the celebrated gen-eral Wallenstein, rejecting historical arguments about his "dictatorship," from Pufendorf onward and focusing instead on his legally specific status as military commander-in-chief. Wallenstein's actions had temporarily practical sovereign status, but he was nevertheless expressly under the orders of the Kaiser (78, 83, 87–88). He would have been a dictator, in the unusual situation in which he found himself, "if he had, in his actions, made an objec-tive legal judgment about what sort of significance the state of exception would have signi-fied."[22] His was, however, a "purely objective and technical" assumption of command, in the absence of any other prior claims having been made by the prince (92).

In the next two chapters of his book, Schmitt outlines the transition to what he calls "sovereign" dictatorship. This is a move away from the idea of a dictatorship as the legal means to restore an extant constitutional structure, and toward its development as a means of creating a new legal order. In this transition from commissarial to sovereign dictatorship, there are broadly three stages. He begins first with the claim that the abso-lutist monarch in France in fact ruled through commissars (2006, 95). But only occa-sionally, and "in opposition to its usual" activities, would the executive authority of a so-called *Aktionskommissar* be known as the office of a dictator (97). The sources for his account vary from contemporary legal histories of European public law to the canoni-cal sources of political philosophy, from Gierke on Althusius to Montesquieu and his legacy in France. All are brought forward to show the predominance of the view that, although the king has majesty, where the real source of authority begins the legal actions of a monarch are buttressed de facto by the balancing functions of Montesquieu's *pou-voirs intermédiaires* (more broadly, see Kelly 2010, ch. 2).

The second claim he makes concerns the updating of this conceptual vocabulary in the eighteenth century, showing how dictatorship quickly became a synonymous term of opprobrium to be used with reference to despotism. It was then transfigured into the "dictatorship of reason" under the aegis of an enlightened absolutism. Such a framework could explain both Voltaire's anti-parliamentarism on the one hand and Mably's attempt to use a powerful monarchy to bring about social equality on the other (2006, 100–101 n14, 107, 110–111, more generally 101–111). The shared justification behind these other-wise differing responses to the question of despotism and dictatorship, nevertheless, lay in a view of man as "naturally evil" ("*der natürlichen Bosheit der Menschen*").

Such a view would be opposed and refracted by Rousseau most famously, and Rousseau's political theory is the third and crucial hinge in the transition toward a political theory of sovereign dictatorship for Schmitt. Yet he is also at pains to point out that Mably's hatred for the executive had, in his book of 1756 on the *Droits et devoirs des citoyens*, also outlined a claim about the necessity of popular representation that presaged by decades what became known as the Jacobin terror of the National Convention. Mably's claim that a sovereign dictator not bound by representation would be "more like a king" (*mehr als ein König, denn mit seinem Amt hätten die Funktionen aller übrigen Magistrate aufgehört*) shows to Schmitt that the transition toward a "new concept of dictatorship" was present in his work (2006, 114). Rousseau, however, was the progenitor of the ideal of the sovereign dictator who was above and beyond the law, that is, for whom "the dictator is total power without law, unlimited power" ("*die Diktatur ist Allmacht ohne Gesetz, rechtlose Macht*"; 126). Even if Rousseau was "unconscious" of the opposition, his account was no less influential for it.

There is, however, a triple irony in Schmitt's threefold presentation of the political thought of the French Revolution in this way. First, to the extent that the absolutism of both sovereignty and representation under the Terror corresponds to confusion between both private and public spheres in law, both considerations actually oppose Rousseau's project, thereby making the claim that it was the intellectual support for the Terror confused at best (Beaud 1993, 3–18, at 14). Second, as Cobban suggested some time ago, Schmitt "does not really produce a single pre-revolutionary writer who supports his conception" of sovereign dictatorship even when he writes about Mably and Rousseau (Cobban 1939, 339; Nippel 2011, 130). Third, it was Sieyès who saw this problem most clearly, but his arguments were ultimately rejected by the Jacobins for avowedly dethroning the nation in place of the state through his complex model of representation, constituent power, and the division of labor and citizenship. This fact makes the Jacobin model of sovereignty a resolutely anti-Rousseauvian politics in theory as well as in practice. It therefore also makes Sieyès's anti-Jacobin politics of representation much closer to certain ways of reading the analysis of representation offered by Hobbes, particularly in the *De Cive*, with which Sieyès would have been familiar. Even more obvious were the linguistic and metaphysical resources he found in Locke, in modern political economy and also in German idealism, that helped to make up his specific language of politics as the explication of practice (Guilhaumou 2002, esp. 127–128, 133–136, 213; Hont 2007, esp. 493–494, 498, 508).

These complex connections back to classical political philosophy are precisely the sorts of connections that Schmitt sought to exploit. And just as political philosophy today often attempts to read Rousseau as cleverly updating Hobbes's arguments about sovereignty and the general will, the nineteenth-century lawyers with whom Schmitt was thoroughly familiar had already thought the same. They therefore rejected both. Hobbes's politics was absolutist, had no economics, and was part of the old world, not the new. Rousseau was the modern Hobbes and the ideological penumbra of the revolutionary terror in France. Bluntschli had said as much, though for Bluntschli modern politics was to be made safe through being reorientated to a liberal yet simultaneously cosmopolitan principle of nationality. For Schmitt, this was altogether far too hopeful a conclusion when faced with the realities of political struggle, and the puzzle of reconciling Hobbes and Rousseau for modern politics remained central.

His account of Hobbes in *Die Diktatur* considers *Leviathan* as the "substantial bearer of all rights," in order to see how it might be allied to the "less systematic" but avowedly metaphysical and puritan system of Locke. Schmitt thought that the rationalization of society and individuality is made possible under a particular and representative form of sovereignty, and therefore seeking out Hobbesian representation and Lockean prerogative were ways of thinking about how to rationalize the politics of a potentially incoherent liberalism. For Rousseau, by contrast, there could be no representative sovereignty. Rather, the general will of the people simply is sovereignty and is famously incapable of being represented in theory, even if it might just result in a majoritarian democracy in practice (cf. Schmitt 2006, 117, 116; Jouanjan 1993, 137). Schmitt then notes the similarity between aspects of Hobbes's presentation in *De Cive* and Rousseau's analysis of sovereignty, but he comes to a hyperbolic conclusion (Schmitt 2006, 117, 119–120; cf. Tuck 1999, 197–207). He claims that Rousseau's focus on the "direct self-rule of a free people" ("*unmittelbare Selbstherrschaft des freien Volkes*") supports sovereign dictatorship but is therefore ultimately the "despotism of freedom" ("*diente so zur Rechtfertigung einer Diktatur und lieferte die Formel für den Despotismus der Freiheit*"; Schmitt 2006, 121). Schmitt focuses on this rather than on Rousseau's admittedly rather weak attempt to derive an appropriately classical lineage for the dictator, as a figure who restores order but who is temporarily above the law (122 n45).[23]

In sum, for Schmitt the dictator in Western political thought and practice typically operates under a form of commission, or is commissarial. Sovereign dictatorship, however, appears through Rousseau's vision of the legislator who somehow exists both outside of and prior to the constitution itself. The dictator as legislator certainly does not act under a commission in the traditional sense, and this means that sovereign dictatorship might be a tool with which the general will could transform the structures of politics altogether (2006, 123, 125). When thinking about what could justify such a form of sovereign dictatorship, Schmitt came to focus upon the idea of constituent power, both to examine how the very idea of the constituent power of the people had transformed modern politics, but also to see how it could be controlled (143).

He considers the French Revolution to be the central moment during which a modern conception of constituent power emerges and first examines the activities of those whom he terms people's commissars, or *Volkskommissare*, though in France they were known as *représentants en mission*. This was clearly done with one eye on contemporary people's commissars in revolutionary Germany and more importantly in Russia. He suggests that the various decrees of the National Convention, particularly those relating to the declaration of enemies of the fatherland, and the reorganization of administrative and representative functions were the transitional elements in a move toward the "dictatorship of the representatives" ("*Diktatur der Repräsentanten*"). Alongside their imperative mandate, this was akin to a commissarial dictatorship within the sovereign dictatorship of the National Convention (2006, 162–163; Cobban 1939, 338). Having begun this historical reconceptualization, he concludes the book with a long chapter on the interconnections between the politics of the French revolution and the state of siege. It begins by repeating his standard claim about the technical and straightforwardly legal mechanism of martial law in the name of necessity. However, it quickly moves into the "remarkable history" of a concept that has "not yet been written," namely, the "concept of a combined law of official activity" ("*Der Begriff der zusammengesetzten Amtshandlung hat eine merkwürdige Geschichte, die noch nicht geschrieben ist*"; Schmitt 2006, 170–171, 173).

Such a compound concept can connect, he writes, both the practical actions of Wallenstein with the abstract state theory of Georg Jellinek, where each citizen is at the same time a particular "organ" of the state (184, cf. 142). By doing so, the concept of dictatorship becomes a framing device for historical work and a critical tool in contemporary legal scholarship, both of which seem to have been in his mind as he wrote about the state theory of the French Revolution. Indeed, the progressive militarization of the state from Thermidor to the coup of 1797 was, for Schmitt, indicative of the transformation of the external laws of war and state of siege into a new language of domestic politics, one which points to the incorporation of military technique into political matters. This is about the primacy of national security for domestic politics.

Finally, as a result of the Napoleonic coup of 18 *brumaire*, Schmitt claimed that with the suspension of the constitution the practical irrelevance of the state of siege as a political tool under Napoleon had become obvious. In fact, Napoleon had no need for it as a "means for political struggle" ("*Napoleon hat den Belagerungszustand nicht als Mittel für politische Kämpfe benutzt*") because his government simply used exceptional courts or tribunals (*Ausnahmegerichte*) to justify policy (2006, 184, 185). This in turn paved the way for Napoleon's fateful war with Russia and also highlighted the legal difficulties of ascribing public enemy status (*die hostis-Erklärung*) to the enemies of France under such a system. If no individual was named as the enemy, nobody could thereby be legally accountable as *hostis*, which means that the laws of war become uncoupled and abstracted from the disciplining realms of ordinary political conflict, and move into a utopian world where judgments might be based on the idea of whether one is a friend or enemy of humanity (187).

These developments, Schmitt argues, explain why the state of siege (*Belagerungszustand*) didn't appear in the French Constitution until 1815, and then specifically as something dealing either with military emergency or domestic unrest (2006, 187). Schmitt cites the declaration of a state of siege by the military commander in Grenoble in May 1816 as an illustration of the combination of discretionary powers given to both the military and the civil authorities under these circumstances. He remains keen to show that, although this was called a dictatorship by many, such an expression of sovereignty is "in truth neither a commissarial nor a sovereign" form of dictatorship but rather a mere pretense of sovereignty.[24] Here, unlike the original situation of the time-limited and juridically constrained dictator, the military commander under such a siege *is* limited, but those who authorize his activity are not. The commander takes on the mantle of one who bears original constituent power because he is authorized by the constituent assembly, but the assembly remains without limit and without constitutional sanction or control (197).

A pretention to sovereign status on the part of the people was, however, the major worry animating Schmitt's political thinking about the nineteenth century. What had taken place by 1829–1830 concerning the state of siege and limits to press freedom in particular, and what would be made explicit in the various reactions to 1848, was presented as a conflation of the "fictional" political state of siege with the "real" military emergency. In addition, the artificial unity of the people through their original constituent power was precisely what could be constrained by the real unity provided by the political sovereign. The concept of dictatorship remained central in the nineteenth century only because everybody knew, writes Schmitt, that when "dictatorship was mentioned, what was really meant was the so-called fictive state of siege."[25] It becomes clear at this point that he is attempting to dethrone a liberal historiography of the *Rechtsstaat* and perhaps even to claim the *Rechtsstaat* as a fictive state of siege itself, a confusion that could best be solved with the application of an alternative understanding and exercise of dictatorship.

The question of how theoretically unlimited constituent power could or should be constrained remained the central point at issue, and when Schmitt (2006, 198–201) came to close his study with contemporary reference to Article 48 of the Weimar Constitution, the resonance of the history and theory of dictatorship he had traced seemed obvious to him. The difference between the French Constitution of 1814 and the Weimar Constitution of 1919, for example, was to be found in this fact: whereas the French Crown claimed absolute sovereignty and "unlimited fullness of power" ("*unbegrenzten Machtvollkommenheit*") in determining the emergency situation, now it is unclear whether the *Reichspräsident* or the parliament has such fullness of power, and because of the confusion, a potentially boundless state of exception (*Ausnahmezustand*) exists. It is therefore also not clear who bears the representative weight of original constituent power according to Article 48, either the *Reichspräsident* or the *Reichstag*, but without such clarity the constitutional order will "remain precariously provisional" ("*prekäres Provisorium bleiben*").

Article 48 of the Weimar Constitution and the Politics of Anti-Communism

Article 48 of the Weimar Constitution was the unspoken beginning as well as the most obvious end point of Schmitt's theory and history of dictatorship. The opening preface to *Die Diktatur*, for example, offered a polemical encapsulation of his attack on both radical communists and liberals. To the extent that liberals simply equate dictatorship with Bonapartism, Caesarism, and military rule, they neglect the useful technical history of commissarial dictatorship as a form of political management. Similarly, to the extent that the communists recognize the force of dictatorship against the liberals, they understand dictatorship as a technical and temporally limited procedural mechanism, albeit one that is linked to the realization of a future goal, namely the transition to communism. He is talking here, of course, about the idea of the dictatorship of the proletariat (2006, xiv, xv, xvi).

The major difference from the classical or commissarial model, however, is that the communists (and Schmitt is happy again to conflate German communists with Russian revolutionaries) envisage using this political tool to create a new situation. Liberal amnesia about the theory and history of dictatorship creates practical problems of constitutional form, which Article 48 in its lack of clarity about the managerial as well as the exceptional sovereign power of the *Reichspräsident* expresses. By contrast, the communist theory of sovereign dictatorship radically transforms the structure and function of political thought and its history by considering the liberal order to be itself a type of dictatorship, a form of regime that liberals would otherwise decry (xii). His fear, unsurprising given his appreciation of the role of political myth, seems to have been that the inherent voids within liberal political theory would be filled by the "irrationalist" and mythical ideologies of Bolshevism and anarcho-syndicalism, allowing communism to capture the language of dictatorship for itself entirely. One of his principal motivations when writing about parliamentary democracy, therefore, was his clear recognition of the power of these ideas and of an assumed need to challenge them (1996b, esp. chs. 3–4).

If liberalism is for the communists what Bonapartism was for the liberals, the status of any future communist dictatorship is nevertheless transposed onto the plane of future history and politics. According to Schmitt, communist sovereign dictatorship is justified by reference to a historical telos that has yet to be realized, and pitted against a particular historical-political formation (liberalism), whose norm of the rule of law is said to lack foundational legitimacy. This is why, for example, Schmitt can so easily conflate the liberal *Rechtsstaat* of the nineteenth century with a sovereign form of dictatorship, seeing it as an inverted representation of what he takes to be the communist critique of liberal democracy. He is concerned with the political tactics of both.

His target in the text is Karl Kautsky's essay on *Terrorismus und Kommunismus*, though Kautsky's essay of a year earlier, *Demokratie oder Diktatur*, would appear more germane (Kautsky 1918, 32, 36–37). Through this and in line with his wider political commitments, Schmitt tries to transpose the situation of 1917 in Russia and 1919 in Germany onto the history of the French Revolution and to trace (in a different register) an alternative genealogy of what many have seen as the long shadow of Thermidor. In so doing, he operates on a plane that is curiously analogous to the way that François Furet later discussed the problems of the French Revolution. This refers in particular to Marxist interpretations of 1789 as the foundation for a sort of secular theodicy, which was still being played out in terms of the more recent Russian Revolution.[26] The connection is not as surprising as it might seem, given that the radical historiography of the French Revolution with which Schmitt was familiar did at least mistakenly suggest (even if it did not fully develop) the idea that Sieyès paved the way for Jacobin dictatorship (e.g., Mathiez 1929; and recently Gauthier 2008). Schmitt in turn thought that the Bolshevik transition toward a sovereign form of dictatorship had to be traced to the revolutionary movements in thought and action inspired in part by Cromwell but predominantly by Mably, Rousseau, Sieyès, and Robespierre, as my discussion has aimed to show.

Furet developed his critique of predominant Marxist interpretations of the French Revolution in a similar fashion, vigorously rejecting what he saw as teleological history in the service of an illusory passion, a passion concerned with the inevitable realization of a radical project of democratic equality. He suggested, in a unique self-refashioning of nineteenth-century interpretations of the revolution that ran together Tocqueville and Thiers as well as Cochin and Quinet, and which was powerfully mediated through the postwar French political philosophy of Clade Lefort and Marcel Gauchet, that this was little more than a revolutionary catechism (cf. Prochasson 2012, 100, 106–110, 112–114, 117; Moyn 2008, 7, 9–12). As such, it was also hopelessly anachronistic in anchoring a passionate attachment to an outdated nineteenth-century model of politics as the messianic victory of the autonomous will, with an outdated model of political explanation based on the rigid determinism of Marx's theory of history. It was a view, he famously exclaimed, whose absence was the specter at the feast of the revolutionary bicentennial (Furet 1999, 159–162, 184–188; discussion in Prochasson 2012, 114).

The politics of the past, and in particular the politics of the memory of the past, had been radically recast and with ironic implications for both Schmitt and Furet, though for different reasons. Whereas the Bolsheviks fancied themselves to have interred the Jacobin theory of revolution in 1917, the French revolutionary bicentennial simply served to inter the Bolsheviks to better defend the not yet realized legacy of the Jacobins. To keep to one of the dominant tropes of Furet's analysis, one that relied heavily on Marx's account of the tragi-comic elements of the French revolution, history had been farcically rewritten to avoid confronting its bloody realities in both revolutionary situations.

Schmitt saw in the radical politics of contemporary Germany and Russia the same sort of attempt to posit a utopian vision of politics as unrestrained, based on the will and focused on purity of intention. It was an argument equally similar to that presented by Max Weber in his attack on the politics of what he decried as a revolutionary carnival in Munich and Berlin. What Schmitt highlights, though, when refocusing comparative attention on the connections between revolutionary France and contemporary Germany, are the legal and political implications of Sieyès's attempts to find and constitutionalize a revolutionary order based on a constituent power that is, in principle, neither manageable or controllable at all (*das unorganisierbar Organisierende zu finden*). He focuses on this opposition to highlight the disjunction between popular sovereignty, or constituent power, and the power of the representative sovereign, or *Reichspräsident*, in relation to the constitution. He effectively recasts Sieyès's analysis of *pouvoir constituant*, following interwar debates about heresy, Spinozism, and Catholicism, and renders sovereignty based on constituent power into something with quasi-mystical power, whose demotic source could be formless but whose representation could not (Schmitt 2006, 139, 117, 142).[27] His thoughts on this soon hardened over the course of the 1920s, as debates about Spinoza and Spinozism in Europe radicalized in antisemitic form, but that is another story.[28]

Meanwhile, in focusing on paragraph 2 of Article 48 in his 1924 lecture to the *Vereinigung der deutschen Staatsrechtslehrer*, Schmitt recalled the original claim about the dictatorship of the *Reichspräsident* made by Hugo Preuß (1924, 63–104).[29] Preuß had claimed that the military could be placed at the disposal of the president for the restoration of order, offering purely and simply an updated form of *salus populi* as justification for a constitutional dictatorship (Schmitt 1924, 222; 2011, 304). Schmitt's focus instead is on the legal specificity of constitutional suspension, which can occur only through the prerogative of the executive or in unexceptional and discretionary moments where constitutional norms are not suspended but merely deviated from. Schmitt gives the example of the pardon. To pardon, he writes, is not to suspend a norm but to deviate in a particular case and thereby to prove the solidity and preeminence of the constitutional norm itself.

He had already made similar claims about how sovereignty and the state of exception typically serve to prove the rule of the normal situation, which he would later transpose into a more general claim about the political as a gauge for measuring degrees of antagonism between public friends and enemies (Schmitt 1923, 5, 7, 10–11, 13–16; 2005b, 5–6, 9, 11–12, 18–20; 1928, 5–6; 1996a, 28–30; Kennedy 1997, 44–47). At this point, when discussing the constitution in front of colleagues, he simply wished to claim that the constitution outlined what the normal legal situation of the state is and that his focus was on the way Article 48 appeared to allow the *Reichspräsident* a mixture of both commissarial and sovereign dictatorial powers—commissarial to the extent that the capacity and authority to suspend the constitution was explicitly limited to the emergency situation, but seemingly sovereign in its suspension of basic fundamental rights to create new norms. Nevertheless, the normal situation of the state is already described by the constitution itself, just as the standard nineteenth-century legal theorists had suggested.[30]

What this means in terms of contemporary practice is that suspension by the executive of constitutional powers would allow for administrative and military action to occur in the various *Länder* without the direct involvement of the president (Schmitt 1924, 227–228; 2011, 306–307). But just as the initial constitutional convention debates concerning the Weimar Constitution clearly noticed that the original Article 49, which then became Article 48 Part II, allowed for executive suspension in cases of emergency, it also seemed clear that the executive creation of new norms through the active suspension of fundamental rights was possible. This meant that the concept of the emergency or exceptional situation had clearly spread far beyond the immediate circumstance of domestic political or military emergency and into a de facto act of prerogative political will. Part II effectively adds extra powers to Part I of Article 48 and offers de facto unlimited power until new decrees are enacted or expressed (1924, 230–232; 2011, 308–309).

What this also means is that the *Reichspräsident* is not a sovereign dictator in the manner of the revolutionary assembly leaders whom Schmitt had earlier discussed. Such a model would be incompatible with the existence of a constitution such as the Weimar Constitution (Schmitt 236; 2011, 311). Yet because the limitations placed upon the president by Article 48 end only when new decrees are enacted and signatory assent is granted, constitutional activity might be de facto dictatorial in the sovereign sense that Schmitt has outlined, even if de jure it cannot be so described. This is why, in Schmitt's eyes, Article 48 renders the entire Weimar Constitution precarious. It oscillates between the role of legal judgment, which is grounded on norms, and legal measures, which are grounded in circumstance (1924, 246, 250–251; 2011, 317, 319).

Standard legal thinking about this problem had tended to support one of two arguments. One focused on questions of contemporary interpretation of the text itself, while another defended constitutional originalism. For many at the time, the fact that reference was made to specific articles concerning fundamental rights that could be suspended under emergency conditions (Articles 114, 115, 117, 118, 123, 124, 153) was enough to make the rest of the constitution safe from the problems of dictatorship (*diktaturfest*) that Schmitt had raised. This at least is how Schmitt presents the position of Hugo Preuß, and in particular his formulation of the authoritarian state (*Obrigkeitsstaat*) as the principle danger to be avoided in the modern state, when claiming that the question of dictatorship could be constrained within the confines of the constitution. As Preuß put it, the choice was between democracy and Bolshevism, or Wilson and Lenin, and the major issue was how to understand the concept of a (constitutional) dictatorship (see Preuß 1918, 73–75; 1923, 526–527). But Schmitt also clearly thought that contemporary practice made a mockery of these kinds of legal and conceptual arguments. Article 48 was naturally deemed to be valid law in terms of the constitution despite the apparently ambiguous preconditions it was based on. In fact, though, constitutional practice since the constitution was enacted had seen far more extensive use of presidential powers, particularly over the various *Länder*, than either the more or the less limited readings of Article 48 had indicated.

The major boundary positions of the dispute were of course ideological and concerned arguments about the constitution as grounded either in popular sovereignty or in the representative capacities of the president and the Reich. Thus, democracy, constitutional monarchy, or the authoritarian state became the pivots around which legal scholars debated questions of political unity and statehood in the transition from a monarchical to a democratic-republican constitution (see Grau 1922; Anschütz 1923).[31]

Conclusion

The various threads of political discourse that underlie Schmitt's analysis of dictatorship were pulled taut by the framing idea of crisis. The idea that liberalism and the state were in crisis across Europe, and particularly in Weimar, occupied writers from Alfred Weber and Hans Kelsen to Moritz Julius Bonn and motivated Schmitt very clearly in his critique of parliamentary democracy. The basic structure of that book is determined by its focus on a threefold crisis in thinking about the state, democracy, and parliamentarism and is in fact closely related in theme and in content to Moritz Bonn's now relatively unknown argument about the destruction of (as well as the destructive tendencies within) the modern state. Bonn, as my earlier discussion noted, was one of Schmitt's most important supporters and interlocutors.

Yet where Bonn favored representative democratic institutions, argued against Sorelian myth, and was more sympathetic to Weber's attempted solution to the need for charisma and competence to be balanced in a plebiscitary democratic system, Schmitt chastised an apparently revolutionary and identity-based concept of homogeneous democracy, counter posing this to the parliamentary institutions of contemporary representative liberalism. He nevertheless found both wanting, and this structured his analysis of the opposition between legality and legitimacy in the Weimar Constitution.[32] He could generate such an argument only after having rewritten the history of modern political thought as a history of the idea of dictatorship in theory and practice, however, because that allowed him to focus attention on the exceptional situation.[33]

It has been my aim here to show how Schmitt contrived to write such a history of political thought, with the concept of dictatorship at its heart, by moving from a practical engagement with the state of siege during World War I toward a polemical distinction between commissarial and sovereign forms of dictatorship under the fledgling Weimar Republic. It is an account of a mind moving toward those positions for which he would become famous, then infamous, but which can best be grasped by taking the measure of these early and substantive foundations. His defense of the representative sovereignty of the *Reichspräsident* and his dictatorial powers came directly from a re-visioning of both early modern political thought and the French Revolution. This allowed him to develop a claim that would defend the idea of the constituent power of the people as the foundation of the modern state, but which simultaneously denied to them the capacity to act upon that power. Constituent power alone was, in his mind, a rather formless mass, which could only be unified and given active form, as Thomas Hobbes had suggested, through the substantial unity of a representative sovereign figure. Thus, although the people were sovereign in theory, they were not sovereign in practice. They had form at all only when they were either represented by a sovereign body or took part in moments of extraordinary constitutional founding. The latter had happened during the major moments of constitutional transformation in Germany since 1848, and that is why democracy and liberalism became the foundational issues of modern politics for Schmitt.

By developing his concept of dictatorship in this way, Schmitt could both strengthen and attack liberalism at the same time. To liberals who thought that dictatorship was anathema to legitimate politics, his work could show that, far from being marginal to it, commissarial dictatorship had a major place in the liberal canon. Conversely, sovereign dictatorship could be related to the foundations of modern democratic politics by reorienting it toward the space occupied by constituent power. Such a conceptual innovation allowed Schmitt both to take liberalism seriously on its own terms at the same time as he sought to undermine it. In particular, his relentless focus on the paradoxes of presidential dictatorship under Article 48 of the Weimar Constitution illustrated the importance of clarifying what sort of dictatorship one was talking about, how it might be understood, and how liberalism itself had few plausible answers to how one might constitutionally limit the necessity of prerogative or dictatorship. Using his conception of dictatorship as a framework for rewriting the history of modern political thought, Schmitt was able to render dictatorship both historical and contemporary at precisely the same time, and that capacity to connect the history of political thought to contemporary political and legal practice is precisely what gives his thought its particular power.

Notes

1. See, for example, Schmitt 1928 and Heller 1928, for evidence of this dynamic.
2. Cf. Hacke 2010 (26–59, esp. 28, 35 n24, 40 and n39). See also Bonn 1949 (330). On Bonn's centrality to Schmitt's work prior to 1933, see Mehring 2009 (esp. 115–120, 134, 148, 201–203, 230, 233–235, 325). See also the correspondence between Schmitt and Smend, in Mehring 2010 (19, letter 1, May 11, 1921; 23, letter 6, May 6, 1923; 62, letter 34, June 26, 1927).
3. On Schmitt's lecturing style and his cultural connections, see Lethen 2002 (171–176, 181) and 2006 (241, 252).
4. For an illustration of Schmitt's contractual dealings with Ludwig Feuchtwanger and therefore Duncker & Humblot, see Ludwig Feuchtwanger's letter to Schmitt, June 25, 1927 (Rieß 2007, followed by Schmitt's reply, 211–213).
5. Unless noted otherwise, all translations of source material by the author.
6. See Schmitt 1993 (208–209, author's notes); 2008a (242). See also von Haller 1821 (537–539). Cf. Hegel 2010 (§258, §§278–281); Bluntschli 1869 (464–471, esp. 466–467, 469); 1876 (601, 605); 1901 (69); Triepel 1926 (11, 16).
7. Meinecke 1919 (292–296, 295): "*Das ist eine lächerliche Karikatur meiner Auffassung.*" See also Clark 1996 (550–576).
8. On Redslob at Strasbourg, and his development of a theory of "true parliamentarism," see Le Divellec 2008 (128–158); Stirk 2002 (497–516, esp. 503–510); cf. Spann 1921, whom Schmitt also countered. On Schmitt in Strasbourg, see Mehring 2009 (25, 600 n20).
9. Radbruch 1902 (408, though see also 355, 382), for his critique of von Kries (another major source for Max Weber) on probability. Cf. von Kries 1886 (87) for the distinction between "nomologic" and "ontologic" ideas and their relation to "objective" or "physical" causes.
10. For a discussion, see Ulmen 1985 (3–57). On Schmitt as a Catholic-inspired critic of Weber, see McCormick 1997a.
11. Paul Laband, letter to Schmitt, January 6, 1917, in Schmitt 2005a (501).
12. Mehring 2009 (92–93); see also Caldwell 1997 (13–40), and more briefly Kelly 2003 (86–88).
13. For a brief summary of the transition, see Saint-Bonnet 2001 (285–316).
14. Schmitt, "Die Einwirkungen" (2005a, 418 n1; 2006, 191 n1; citing Reinach 1885). Reinach, a celebrated classicist, appears fleetingly in de Waal 2010 (103).
15. Schmitt 1916 (11 n25); cf. Baehr and Richter 2004.
16. For the connections to Mommsen's work, see Nippel 2011 (105–139, esp. 133); 2005 (253–255). On Mably's construction of the idea of revolution as conscious and directive enterprise, see Michael-Baker 1990 (esp. 97–99).
17. Schmitt 2006 (134–139, 176–189); Zweig 1909 (147, 396, 407); cf. Redslob 1912 (31–33, 49). On Egon Zweig, see Kelly (2014); cf. Jellinek 1909 (392). On Braubach, see Schmitt, "Gutachten für Bernhard Braubach," University of Bonn, July 25, 1923, which details Braubach's subsequent work on Sieyès and the French Revolution (2010, 162–164, n5). Related work by Braubach was also taken up by Smend 2002 (213–248, 376, n108, n115). On the contemporary use made by Schmitt of Sieyès's theory of representation, see Kelly 2004 (113–134).
18. Cf. Nippel 2011 (133 n136).
19. Zweig (1909, 137) wrote of Sieyès that he used "*die Terminologie Montesquieus auf einen Rousseauschen Gedanken angewendet und so die politische Begriffswelt gründlich desorientiert hat.*"

20. This development also came shortly after having attended Max Weber's celebrated vocational lectures and his private seminar on the state (Schmitt 2005a, 51, 495). See also Mehring 2009 (118).
21. On Neumann's connections to Schmitt, see Kelly 2003 (ch. 4).
22. *"Diktatur wäre sie nur dann gewesen, wenn sie in ihrer Wirkung auf die objektive Rechtslage einen Ausnahmezustand bedeutet hätte"* (Schmitt 2006, 92).
23. Rousseau 2003 (Book IV, ch. 6, 138–140); cf. Reinach 1885 (20 n2), who writes that we must "relegate to the world of fantasy" (*"On relèguera dans la domaine de la fantaisie l'explication de J.-J. Rousseau"*) Rousseau's attempt to relate this to anything that resembled the reality of classical dictatorship.
24. *"In Wahrheit ist es weder kommissarische noch souveräne Diktatur, sondern einfach die Prätention der Souveränität als der prinzipiell unbegrenzten Staatsgewalt"* (Schmitt 2006, 189–190).
25. *"Wenn aber im 19. Jahrhundert von Diktatur gesprochen wird, versteht man darunter den sogenannten fiktiven Belagerungszustand"* (Schmitt 2006, 197).
26. On the "long shadow of Thermidor" in the history of democracy, see Dunn 2005 (esp. 130–147).
27. For the context of interwar debates about Spinoza, Schmitt, and crisis theology, see Lazier 2008 (esp. 80–82, 103–106); Rosenthal 2008 (94–112); Vatter 2004 (161–214). See also Heerich and Lauermann 1991 (97–160); Walther 1993 (361–372). On one idea of mysticism central to Schmitt, see Janetzky 1922.
28. The work of Johan Carp is central to this story. See his early essay 1921 (81–90); for discussion, Mommen 2011 (87–102); see also Koekkoek 2014. Cf. Schmitt 2008b (56–61).
29. This is predominantly reprinted in the second edition (1928) of *Die Diktatur* (2006, 213–257) and cited here. There is also an English translation (2011).
30. *"Die Verfassung besagt, was normale Ordnung im Staat ist"* (1924, 241; 2011, 314).
31. English edition in Jacobson and Schlink 2002 (134, 139). See Jacobi 1924 (105–136, esp. 134), on the threat of dictatorship to both *"Rechtseinheit und Reichseinheit."*
32. Bonn 1921; Schmitt 1996b (16–17, 18–21, 68, 79); 1993 (204–220, on identity and representation as the two modern political forms); 2008a (239–252); discussion in Hacke 2010 (35–37, 42–43, 45–8, on the connection between Bonn and Weber, 52–53); cf. Mehring 2009 (198–200).
33. The analysis is summarized in Schmitt 1916 (33–37), and expanded in 1925/1995 (24–27); 1926c (41).

References

Anschütz, G. 1923. *Drei Leitgedanken der Weimarer Verfassung.* Tübingen: Mohr.
Baehr, P., and M. Richter. eds. 2004. *Dictatorship in History and Theory: Bonapartism, Caesarism and Totalitarianism.* Cambridge: Cambridge University Press.
Baker, K. 1990. *Inventing the French Revolution.* Cambridge: Cambridge University Press.
Beaud, O. 1993. "Ouverture: L'histoire juridique de la Révolution française est-elle possible?" *Droits* 17: 3–18.
Bluntschli, J. K. 1869. "Demokratie und repräsentative Demokratie." In *Staatswörterbuch in drei Bänden auf Grundlage des deutschen Staatswörterbuchs von Bluntschli und Brater in elf Bänden,* ed. E. Löning. Zurich: Schulteß.

Bluntschli, J. K. 1876. *Lehre vom Modernen Staat*, Teil III: *Politik*. Stuttgart: Klett-Cotta.

Bluntschli, J. K. 1901. *The Theory of the State*. Oxford: Oxford University Press.

Bonn, M. J. 1921. *Die Auflösung des modernen Staats*. Berlin: Duncker & Humblot.

Bonn, M. J. 1925. *Die Krise der europäischen Demokratie*. Munich: Meyer & Jessen.

Bonn, M. J. 1949. *Wandering Scholar*. London: Cohen & West.

Caldwell, P. 1997. *Popular Sovereignty and the Crisis of German Constitutional Law*. Durham: Duke University Press.

Carp, J. 1921. "Naturrecht und Pflichtbegriff nach Spinoza." *Chronicon Spinozanum* 1: 81–90.

Carret, J. 1916. *L'Organisation de L'État de Siège Politique d'après la Loi du 3 Avril 1878*. Paris: Librairie de la société du Recueil Sirey.

Clark, C. 1996. "The Wars of Liberation in Prussian Memory: Reflections on the Memorialization of War in Early Nineteenth-Century Germany." *Journal of Modern History* 68: 550–576.

Cobban, A. 1939. *Dictatorship: Its Theory and History*. London: Jonathan Cape.

Dunn, J. 2005. *Setting the People Free*. London: Grove.

Duverger, M. 1961. *De la dictature*. Paris: Julliard.

Furet, F. 1999. "1789–1917: aller et retour." In *La Révolution en débat*. Paris: Gallimard, 155–188.

Gauthier, F. 2008. "Albert Mathiez, historien de la révolution française." *Annales historiques de la révolution française* 353: 95–112.

Ghosh, P. 2008. "Max Weber and Georg Jellinek: Two Divergent Conceptions of Law." *Saeculum* 59: 299–347.

Grau, R. 1922. *Die Diktaturgewalt des Reichspräsidenten und der Landesregierungen auf Grund des Artikels 48 der Reichsverfassung*. Berlin: Liebmann.

Guilhaumou, J. 2002. *Sieyès et l'ordre de la langue: L'invention de la politique modern*. Paris: Éditions Kimé.

Hacke, J. 2010. "Ein vergessener Erbe des deutschen Liberalismus: Über Moritz Julius Bonn." *Mittelweg 36* 19: 26–59.

Haller, K. L. von. 1821. *Restauration der Staatswissenschaft*, vol. 3: *Makrobiotik der Patrimonial-Staaten*, 2nd ed. Winterthur: Steinersche Buchhandlung.

Heerich, Th., and M. Lauermann. 1991. "Der Gegensatz Hobbes-Spinoza bei Carl Schmitt." *Studia Spinozana* 7: 97–160.

Hegel, G. W. F. 2010. *Elements of the Philosophy of Right*, ed. A. W. Wood. Cambridge: Cambridge University Press.

Heller, H. 1928. "Politische Demokratie und soziale Homogenität." In *Probleme der Demokratie. Schriftenreihe der Deutschen Hochschule für Politik und des Institutes für Auswärtige Politik in Hamburg*, vol. 5. Berlin-Grunewald: Rothschild, 35–47.

Hont, I. 2007. *Jealousy of Trade*. Cambridge: Harvard University Press.

Jacobi, E. 1924. "Die Diktatur des Reichspräsidenten nach Art. 48 der Reichsverfassung." In *Der deutsche Föderalismus: Die Diktatur des Reichspräsidenten*. Berlin: Duncker & Humblot, 105–136.

Jainchill, A. 2008. *Reimagining Politics after the Terror*. Ithaca: Cornell University Press.

Janetzky, C. 1922. *Mystik und Rationalismus*. Munich: Duncker & Humblot.

Jellinek, G. 1909. "Review of Egon Zweig, *Die Lehre vom Pouvoir Constituant*." *Archiv für öffentliches Recht* 25: 389–392.

Jèze, G. 1917. "L'exécutif en temps de guerre: les pleins pouvoirs." *Revue du droit public et de la science politique d'étranger* 34: 5–43, 209–268, 404–442.

Jouanjan, O. 1993. "La suspension de la constitution de 1793." *Droits* 17: 125–138.

Kautsky, K. 1918. *Demokratie und Diktatur*, 2nd ed. Berlin: Cassirer.

Kelly, D. 2003. *The State of the Political: Conceptions of Politics and the State in the Thought of Max Weber, Carl Schmitt and Franz Neumann*. Oxford: British Academy.

Kelly, D. 2004. "Carl Schmitt's Political Theory of Representation." *Journal of the History of Ideas* 65: 113–134.

Kelly, D. 2010. *The Propriety of Liberty: Persons, Passions and Judgment in Modern Political Thought*. Princeton: Princeton University Press.

Kelly, D. 2014. "Egon Zweig and the Intellectual History of Pouvoir Constituant." In *Constitutionalism, Legitimacy and Power: Nineteenth-Century Experiences*, ed. K. Grotke and M. Prutsch. Oxford: Oxford University Press, 332–350.

Kennedy, E. 1997. "*Hostis*, not *Inimicus*: Towards a Theory of the Public in the Work of Carl Schmitt." *Canadian Journal of Law and Jurisprudence* 10: 35–47.

Koekkoek, R. 2014. "Carl Schmitt and the Challenge of Spinoza's Pantheism Between the World Wars." *Modern Intellectual History* 11: 333-357.

Koselleck, R. 1973. *Kritik und Krise*. Frankfurt: Suhrkamp.

Koselleck, R. 2004. *Futures Past: On the Semantics of Historical Time*, trans. K. Tribe. New York: Columbia University Press.

Kries, J. von. 1886. *Die Principien der Wahrscheinlichkeits-Rechnung: Eine Logische Untersuchung*. Freiburg: Mohr.

Krug, W. T. 1823. *Geschichtliche Darstellung des Liberalismus alten und neuen Zeit*. Leipzig: Brockhaus.

Lazier, B. 2008. *God Interrupted*. Princeton: Princeton University Press.

Lethen, H. 2002. *Cool Conduct: The Culture of Distance in Weimar Germany*, trans. D. Reneau. Berkeley: University of California Press.

Lethen, H. 2006. *Der Sound der Väter: Gottfried Benn und seine Zeit*. Berlin: Rowohlt.

Le Divellec, A. 2008. "Robert Redslob, juriste alsacien entre la France et l'Allemagne." *Annales de la Faculté de droit de Strasbourg* 9: 128–158.

Mathiez, A. 1929. "La révolution française et la théorie de la dictature: La Constituante." *Revue historique* 161: 304–315.

McCormick, J. 1997a. *Carl Schmitt's Critique of Liberalism*. Cambridge: Cambridge University Press.

McCormick, J. 1997b. "The Dilemmas of Dictatorship: Carl Schmitt and Constitutional Emergency Powers." *Canadian Journal of Law and Jurisprudence* 10: 163–187.

Mehring, R. 2009. *Carl Schmitt: Aufstieg und Fall*. Munich: Beck.

Mehring, R. ed. 2010. "*Auf der gefahrenvollen Straße des öffentlichen Rechts*": *Briefwechsel Carl Schmitt und Rudolf Smend (1921–1961)*. Berlin: Duncker & Humblot.

Meinecke, F. 1911. *Weltbürgertum und Nationalstaat*. Munich: Oldenbourg.

Meinecke, F. 1919. "Review of Carl Schmitt-Dorotic, *Politische Romantik*." *Historische Zeitschrift* 121: 292–296.

Meinecke, F. 1925. *Die Idee der Staatsräson*. Munich: Duncker & Humblot.

Mommen, A. 2011. "Van spinozist tot nationaal-socialist: de Nederlandse rechtsfilosoof Johan Herman Carp (1893–1979)." *Vlaams Marxistisch Tijdschrift* 45: 87–102.

Moyn, S. 2008. "The Intellectual Origins of François Furet's Masterpiece." *Tocqueville Review* 29: 1–20.

Neumann, F. 1957. "Notes on the Theory of Dictatorship." In *The Democratic and Authoritarian State*, ed. H. Marcuse. New York: Free Press, 233–256.

Nippel, W. 2005. "'Rationeller Fortschritt' auf dem 'antiquarischen Bauplatz': Mommsen als Architekt des 'Römischen Staatsrechts.'" In *Theodor Mommsen: Wissenschaft und Politik im 19. Jahrhundert*, ed. A. Demandt, A. Goltz, and H. Schlange-Schöningen. Berlin: De Gruyter, 246–258.

Nippel, W. 2007. "The Roman Notion of *Auctoritas*." In *The Concept of Authority: A Multidisciplinary Approach: From Epistemology to the Social Sciences*, ed. P. Pasquino and P. Harris. Rome: Fondazione Olivetti, 1–34.

Nippel, W. 2008. *Antike oder moderne Freiheit?* Frankfurt: Fischer.

Nippel, W. 2011. "Carl Schmitt's 'kommissarische' und 'souveräne Diktatur': Französische Revolution und römische Vorbilder." In *Ideenpolitik: Geschichtliche Konstellationen und gegenwärtige Konflikte*, ed. H. Bluhm, K. Fischer, and M. Llanque. Berlin: Oldenbourg, 105–139.

Pasquino, P. 1986. "Die Lehre vom 'Pouvoir Constituant' bei Emmanuel Sieyès und Carl Schmitt." In *Complexio Oppositorum*, ed. H. Quaritsch. Berlin: Duncker & Humblot, 371–385.

Pasquino, P. 1998. "Locke on King's Prerogative." *Political Theory* 26: 198–208.

Preuß, H. 1918. "Volksstaat oder verkehrter Obrigkeitsstaat." In *Gesammelte Schriften*, vol. 4, ed. D. Lehnert. Tübingen: Mohr, 73–75.

Preuß, H. 1923. "Reichsverfassungsmäßige Diktatur." In *Gesammelte Schriften*, vol. 4, 523–535.

Prochasson, C. 2012. "François Furet, the Revolution, and the Past Future of the French Left." *French History* 26: 96–117.

Radbruch, G. 1902. *Die Lehre von der adäquaten Verursachung*. Berlin: Guttentag.

Redslob, R. 1912. *Staatstheorie der französischen Nationalversammlung von 1789*. Leipzig: Veit.

Redslob, R. 1918. *Die parlamentarische Regierung in ihrer wahren und in ihrer unechten Form: Eine vergleichende Studie über die Verfassungen von England, Belgien, Ungarn, Schweden und Frankreich*. Tübingen: Mohr.

Reinach, Th. 1885. *De l'État de Siège: Étude historique et juridique*. Paris: Pichon.

Rieß, R. ed. 2007. *Carl Schmitt und Ludwig Feuchtwanger: Briefwechsel 1918–1935*. Berlin: Ducker & Humblot.

Romain, P. 1918. *L'État de siège politique: Histoire, Déclaration, Effets, Levée*. Albi: Imprimerie des Orphelins Apprentis.

Roques, C. 2009. *"Radiographie de l'ennemi: Carl Schmitt et le romantisme politique."* *Astérion* 6. Online publication: DOI: 10.4000/asterion.1487

Rosenthal, M. A. 2008. "Spinoza and the Crisis of Liberalism in Weimar Germany." *Hebraic Political Studies* 3: 94–112.

Rotteck, K. von, and K. Welcker. 1840. *Staatslexicon, oder Encyclopädie der Staatswissenschaft*. Altona: Johan-Friedrich Hammerlich.

Rousseau, J-J. 2003. *The Social Contract and other later political writings*, ed. V. Gourevitch. Cambridge: Cambridge University Press.

Saint-Bonnet, F. 2001. *L'État de l'exception*. Paris: PUF.

Schmitt-Dorotic, C. 1921. "Politische Theorie und Romantik." *Historische Zeitschrift* 123: 377–397.

Schmitt, C. 1916. "Diktatur und Belagerungszustand." In Schmitt 1995, 3–23.

Schmitt, C. 1919. *Politische Romantik*. Berlin: Duncker & Humblot.

Schmitt, C. 1923. "Soziologie des Souveränitätsbegriffes und der politische Theologie." In *Hauptprobleme der Soziologie: Erinnerungsgabe für Max Weber*, ed. M. Palyi. Berlin: Duncker & Humblot, 3–36.

Schmitt, C. 1924. "Die Diktatur des Reichspräsident nach Art. 48 der Reichsverfassung." In *Der deutsche Föderalismus: Die Diktatur des Reichspräsidenten*. Berlin: Duncker & Humblot, 63–104.

Schmitt, C. 1925. "Reichspräsident und Weimarer Verfassung." In Schmitt 1995, 24–27.

Schmitt, C. 1926a. "Zu Friedrich Meineckes Idee der Staatsräson." In Schmitt 1988, 51–59.

Schmitt, C. 1926b. "Der Gegensatz von Parlamentarismus und moderner Massendemokratie." In Schmitt 1988, 60–74.

Schmitt, C. 1926c. "Das Ausführungsgesetz zu Art. 48 der Reichsverfassung." In Schmitt 1995, 38–41.

Schmitt, C. 1927a. "Macchiavelli: Zum 22. Juni 1927." In Schmitt 1995, 102–107.

Schmitt, C. 1927b. "Volksentscheid und Volksbegehren: Ein Beitrag zur Auslegung der Weimarer Verfassung und zur Lehre von der unmittelbaren Demokratie." In *Beiträge zum ausländischen öffentlichen Recht und Völkerrecht*, Heft 2. Berlin: De Gruyter.

Schmitt, C. 1928. "Der Begriff des Politischen." In *Probleme der Demokratie. Schriftenreihe der Deutschen Hochschule für Politik und des Institutes für Auswärtige Politik in Hamburg*, vol. 5. Berlin-Grunewald: Rothschild, 1–34.

Schmitt, C. 1988. *Positionen und Begriffe im Kampf mit Weimar—Genf—Versailles, 1923–1939*, 2nd ed. Berlin: Ducker & Humblot.

Schmitt, C. 1993. *Verfassungslehre*, 8th ed. Berlin: Duncker & Humblot.

Schmitt, C. 1995. *Staat, Großraum, Nomos: Arbeiten aus den Jahren 1916–1969*, ed. G. Maschke. Berlin: Duncker & Humblot.

Schmitt, C. 1996a. *The Concept of the Political*, trans. G. Schwab. Chicago: University of Chicago Press.

Schmitt, C. 1996b. *The Crisis of Parliamentary Democracy*, trans. E. Kennedy. Cambridge: MIT Press.

Schmitt, C. 2005a. *Die Militärzeit 1915 bis 1919: Tagebuch Februar bis Dezember 1915*, ed. E. Hüsmert and G. Giesler. Berlin: Akademie Verlag.

Schmitt, C. 2005b. *Political Theology*, trans. G. Schwab. Chicago: University of Chicago Press.

Schmitt, C. 2006. *Die Diktatur*. Berlin: Duncker & Humblot.

Schmitt, C. 2008a. *Constitutional Theory*, trans. and ed. J. Seitzer. Durham: Duke University Press.

Schmitt, C. 2008b. *The Leviathan in the State Theory of Thomas Hobbes: Meaning and Failure of a Political Symbol*, trans. G. Schwab and E. Hilfstein. Chicago: University of Chicago Press.

Schmitt, C. 2011. "The Dictatorship of the Reich President According to Art. 48 of the Reich Constitution." *Constellations* 18: 299–323.

Sieyès, E.-J. 2007. "Discussion sur la constitution, l'an III." In *Des Manuscrits de Sieyès, Tome II, 1770–1815*, ed. C. Fauré. Paris: Honoré Champion.

Smend, R. 2002. "Constitution and Constitutional Law," trans. B. Cooper et al. In *Weimar: A Jurisprudence of Crisis*, ed. A. Jacobson and B. Schlink. Berkeley: University of California Press, 213–248.

Spann, O. 1921. *Der wahre Staat: Vorlesungen über Abbruch und Neubau der Gesellschaft*. Leipzig: Duncker & Humblot.

Stirk, P. 2002. "Hugo Preuß, German Political Thought and the Weimar Constitution." *History of Political Thought* 23: 497–516.

Thiele, U. 2003. *Advokative Volkssouveränität: Carl Schmitts Konstruktion einer 'demokratischen' Diktaturtheorie im Kontext der Interpretation politischer Theorien der Aufklärung*. Berlin: Duncker & Humblot.

Triepel, H. 1926. *Staatsrecht und Politik: Beiträge zum ausländischen öffentlichen Rechte und Völkerrecht*, ed. Institut für ausländlisches öffentliches Recht und Völkerrecht im Berlin. Berlin: De Gruyter.

Tuck, R. 1999. *The Rights of War and Peace*. Oxford: Oxford University Press.

Ulmen, G. 1985. "The Sociology of the State: Carl Schmitt and Max Weber." *State, Culture and Society* 1: 3–57.

Vatter, M. E. 2004. "Strauss and Schmitt as Readers of Hobbes and Spinoza: On the Relation Between Political Theology and Liberalism." *New Centennial Review* 4: 161–214.

Velut, F. 1910. *Le régime de l'état de siège avant la loi du 9 août 1849*. Paris: Jouve & Cie.

Waal, E. de. 2010. *The Hare with the Amber Eyes*. London: Vintage.

Walther, M. 1993. "Carl Schmitt et Baruch Spinoza ou les aventures du concept du politique." In *Spinoza au XXième siècle*, ed. O. Bloch. Paris: PUF, 361–372.

Weber, M. 1922. *Gesammelte Aufsätze zur Wissenschaftslehre*. Tübingen: Mohr.

Zweig, E. 1907. *Studien und Kritiken*. Vienna: Braumüller.

Zweig, E. 1909. *Die Lehre vom Pouvoir Constituant: Ein Beitrag zum Staatsrecht der französischen Revolution*. Tübingen: Mohr.

CHAPTER 8

THE POLITICAL THEOLOGY OF CARL SCHMITT

MIGUEL VATTER

INTRODUCTION

OF ALL the new concepts introduced by Carl Schmitt into the vocabulary of political and juridical thought, perhaps the most controversial one is that of political theology. As Schmitt acknowledged, the concept did not exist before he coined it in 1922 with his book *Political Theology*.[1] The term itself seems to have appeared previously only in the polemical use given to it by Mikhail Bakunin in his attack on Giuseppe Mazzini. As a concept, Schmitt intended the term to refer to the structural identity of the concepts employed by the sciences of theology and jurisprudence in medieval thought. "This is exactly what is at stake in my *Political Theology*. The scientific conceptual structure of both of these faculties has systematically produced areas in which concepts can be transposed, among which harmonious exchanges are permitted and meaningful" (Schmitt 2008a, 108). On the basis of this analogy between theology and public law, Schmitt claims that "all significant concepts of the modern theory of the state are secularized theological concepts not only because of their historical development—in which they were transferred from theology to the theory of the state ... but also because of their systematic structure" (1988, 36). The study of these analogies is the subject matter of political theology understood as a way to do the sociology of concepts, and this is how the concept has been generally understood by readers of Schmitt as early as Hans Kelsen through Ernst Kantorowicz and up to Hans Blumenberg and Giorgio Agamben.[2]

But Schmitt also believed that "all political concepts, images, and terms have a polemical meaning. They are focused on a specific conflict and are bound to a concrete situation" (2007, 30). The concept of political theology is no exception: its polemical meaning is acquired in the late nineteenth-century context in which the nation state comes under stress from the combined fronts of working-class transnational organizations and various forms of Catholic revival, a context best captured by Bakunin's devise of God and state. The polemical meaning of political theology was clear to theologians like Erik Peterson and political theorists like Leo Strauss from early on; it was later picked up by Jacob Taubes (1983; 1993) and Jan Assmann (2002) and has been brought to prominence recently in the interpretation of Heinrich Meier.[3] Considered in the light of this polemical usage, the term political theology refers to the age-old question of religious legitimation of political power, or what Peterson (2011) called monotheism as a political problem (see also Metz et al. 1970). In most of his works Schmitt moves between the scientific and the polemical registers without always taking care to elucidate the transitions in the argument. Thus, in *Political Theology II* he explicitly acknowledges the manifold equivocations that the term political theology can give rise to, since "there are many political theologies because there are, on the one hand, many different religions, and, on the other hand, many different kinds and methods of doing politics" (2008a, 66).

In this chapter I discuss the scientific and the polemical meanings of political theology by taking as my guiding thread what Schmitt calls the problem of "political unity and its presence or representation" (2008a, 72). For him, the parallelism between theology and jurisprudence reflects the necessary unity of religion and politics in the representation of what he calls concrete (normative) orders, such as the *respublica Christiana* in the medieval period and the modern Westphalian system of nation-states in the early modern period (1995; 2003; 2008a, 108; Kervégan 2009, 96–97). Perhaps Schmitt's central thesis in jurisprudence is that the representation of political unity makes possible a concrete legal order. In turn, he understands this concept of representation to have a distinct theological origin, reflecting the peculiar situation of a legal organization (the Catholic Church) that conceives of itself as standing in for the kingdom of God.

Such a juridical understanding of political theology also has direct polemical referents. My second thesis is that the most important such referents for Schmitt's conception of legal order are not drawn from the nineteenth-century representatives of "anti-Roman temper" (from Bismarck to Bakunin) but are strictly juridical: Kelsen's legal positivism; Gierke and the English school of pluralism; and Peterson's juridical understanding of Christology. All three (not just Peterson) argue on juridical grounds that a "scientific" concept of political theology is impossible, that there is no reality to the parallelism between God and state, and for that reason they needed to be addressed, scientifically and polemically, by Schmitt in his role as a self-appointed "theologian of jurisprudence" (1991, 23). This chapter is accordingly structured in three sections, each of which focuses on one essential component of the juridical conception of political theology advocated by Schmitt. The first section discusses the polemic with Kelsen over the juridical concept of legal person and its parallelism in theology with the idea of God's incarnation; the second section treats the juridical concept of representation as developed in Schmitt's defense of Hobbes against the critiques of sovereignty found in Gierke and in English pluralism; the third section uncovers the significance of Trinitarianism in Schmitt's later polemic against Peterson. At stake here is the possibility of giving the concepts of legal personality and of representation a democratic turn antithetical to their monarchic construals found in Schmitt's earlier work. The chapter concludes with a brief discussion of the recent post-Schmittian transformation of political theology into economic theology, which is centered no longer on the problem of the state and its personality but on that of governmentality and the impersonal social orders, like markets, through which it acts.

POLITICAL THEOLOGY AND LAW: SCHMITT AND KELSEN ON LEGAL PERSONALITY

Although Schmitt claims that already in his first book *Der Wert des Staates* of 1914 he had drawn attention to the existence of "systematic and methodical analogies" (1988, 37) between jurisprudence and theology, he dedicates the second and third chapter of *Political Theology* to a refutation of Kelsen, who "has the merit of having stressed since 1920 the methodical relationship of theology and jurisprudence" (39).[4] Kelsen had not only mentioned the existence of such analogies but also had actually tried to explain them in his 1922 book *Der soziologische und der juristische Staatsbegriff.* Thus, at least as concerns the scientific treatment of political theology, Schmitt is reacting to Kelsen rather than the other way around.[5]

In an early article dedicated to juridical fictions (*fictio juris*) Kelsen argues that there are two ways law can use fictions. In a first sense, the fiction takes the form of a reference in law to an objective, legally independent reality. The classic example of such a juridical fiction is the idea of a juridical person, understood as a substance existing independently of the system of norms and endowed with duties and rights (Kelsen 1919, 631). For Kelsen, this juridical person is merely a useful "personification of a complex of norms" (631); it is a fiction that has no corresponding reality. Yet Kelsen points out that it is the most natural of mistakes to "hypostasize" this fiction and consider it "as if" it were a real person: the same happens when one hypostasizes mental functions into the idea of a "soul" or, in the case of physical motion, into the idea of a "force" (634–635). In all these cases two entities are made out of one tautology.

A second sense of juridical fictions is at stake when the law considers one category of persons "as if" they were another for the purposes of law (e.g., someone stands in for the "father" of another person although this person is not its biological progeny) (1919, 639–641). Whereas the latter fiction is legitimate because the reference is internal to the system of norms, Kelsen considers that the former sense of juridical personality is entirely problematic because it transcends the legal system. A scientific or objective approach to the law is possible only on the basis of "the sovereignty of the law ["*Souveränität des Rechts*"] (or, what is the same, of the state), that is, when one recognizes the legal order [*Rechtsordnung*] as *a self-standing system of norms not derived from a higher order*" (652).[6] For Kelsen, the condition of possibility of a scientific approach to jurisprudence depends on unmasking the role played by the fiction of juridical personality within a legal system. Without the critique of the hypostasis of such legal persons, there is no true science of law.

Only three years later, in 1922 in *Der soziologische und der juristische Staatsbegriff*, Kelsen advances his radical claim that the idea of a "unique-single [*"einig-einzigen"*] state" is a hypostatization of the legal order parallel to the hypostatization of the unity of nature in the person of the monotheistic God (1981, 220). In both cases, there is a juridical person (God or state) that transcends a complex of norms and presents itself as endowed with an "absolute will" (sovereignty) claiming to have "created" this norm complex (222–223). In that discussion, which carries no reference to any of Schmitt's texts but does contain references to Bakunin, Kelsen argues that the hypostatization of the juridical person is foundational to both theology and to the theory of the state (*Staatslehre*). Both discourses seek to relate the hypostasis back to the complex of norms from which it had previously been separated: the person of God with the legal order of nature, the person of the sovereign with the system of positive law.

Once God is separated from the order of nature and the state from the legal order, the hypostasis of personification requires a concept of representation so as to make present and render visible the substance (the hypostasis) that is not visible as such in the empirical world. As he explains in his celebrated essay "God and the State," originally published in *Logos* in 1922 (which takes up large parts of the arguments outlined previously in *Der soziologische und der juristische Staatsbegriff*), "God transforms Himself into the world, or into its representative, man, in that the divine essentially splits into two persons, God-the-Father and God-the-Son...This theory of God's incarnation in the world is put forward in theology under the aspect of the self-limitation or self-obligation of God" (Kelsen 1973, 73). The same structure is replicated to account for the relation between sovereign and law: "the state is the creator or sustainer of law, and is therefore above the law; but on the other hand is again of the same nature as the law, is subject to the law" (72). Kantorowicz (1997) later gives this structural feature of sovereignty the poetic name of the "king's two bodies." Political theology is possible only as an answer to the question of whom or what represents and bears the person of the state or of God. Political theology depends on representation and is impossible without it. This result is also central to Schmitt, except that for Kelsen representation becomes essential only because of the prior fallacy that mistook the person of the state for a real thing, for someone standing apart and above the legal order. Schmitt's "problem of representation" merely denotes "the pseudo-existence of a metalegal, supralegal state." Sovereignty is a pseudo-solution to a pseudo-problem (Kelsen 1973, 70).[7]

For Kelsen, the dualism of state and law is not a scientific result: it serves a political purpose; it is merely ideological. The fiction of the state as person is useful only for purposes of ascribing to human acts the character of acts of state. But "the criterion of ascription to the state can only be a legal one. A human action can be accounted an act of state only when and insofar as it is qualified in a specific manner by a legal norm, is decreed in the system of the legal order" (Kelsen 1973, 76). Therefore, the doctrine of "reason of state," which ascribes a "legal" or state-like character to human acts that stand in a relation of exception to the legal order, essentially makes "a legal act out of a naked act of power" and is merely the theoretical expression of "an autocratic order directed against a law essentially customary" (77). Here Kelsen indicates the historical context in which the doctrine of sovereignty (the *jus publicum Europaeum*) is born: in the late medieval confluence of Christian doctrine, scientific interpretations of the *corpus iuris civilis*, and practice of feudal common law. But it was Gierke's genealogy of the *jus publicum* and its reception by the English school of pluralism, to which I turn in the next section, that deals a fatal blow to the doctrine of sovereignty. Furthermore, since political theology lacks a scientific basis, Kelsen ironically suggests that its only support must lie in faith: "God and the state *exist only if and insofar as they are believed in*, and all of their enormous power…collapses if the human soul is able to rid itself of this belief" (80). With this remark, Kelsen's critique of sovereignty touches on the doxological and liturgical basis of Christology later uncovered by Peterson, which I discuss in the third section of this chapter.

Schmitt's *Political Theology* erects its defense of sovereignty entirely on the idea of representation, which made only a fleeting but crucial apparition in Kelsen's argument. In *Roman Catholicism and Political Form*, composed slightly before, Schmitt presented his conception of representation and made it the condition for the possibility of legal order, but *Political Theology* has the harder task of reconceiving the idea of legal order in such a way that the appeal to representation and thus to the person of the state, the sovereign, is inevitable: at least, this is the scientific task of the treatise. Schmitt agrees with Kelsen that "power proves nothing in law" (1988, 17, 18); however, precisely for this reason "the connection of actual power with the legally highest power is the fundamental problem of the concept of sovereignty." In other words, political theology, with its central concept of sovereignty, is a theory that claims to explain how an abstract complex of norms (jurisprudence) connects to a concrete complex of power (sociology): this is what it means for political theology to be "a sociology of juristic concepts" (37, 42). If the system of norms is not to remain a ghostly abstraction, if this normative system is to become a concrete legal order, then it needs to link up with a real person who must also be a real representative of the entire juridical order. This order depends on the king's "two bodies" *not* being a mere *fictio juris* but actually having a real juridical substance.

Schmitt's entire argument rests on the jurisprudential thesis that norms connect to social reality (to existence) at the point of their application, for he posits that every ascription to a law is based "on a command" (1988, 20). Thus, to deny the difference between state (the representative person who commands) and law (the point of ascription), as Kelsen suggests, is to "disregard the independent problem of the realization of law" (21), that is, the problem of legal application.[8] For Schmitt, the state is different from law because the state exists to apply law, to decide on its interpretation, to give law its force. If a system of norms is going to make up one legal order, this is possible only if all laws are applied by the state. Since application requires decision, a juridical person who represents the unity of the state is unavoidable.

Legal form or legal application of principles of justice (legal ideas) calls for a conception of personality:

> All these objections [to juridical personality made by Kelsen] fail to recognize that the conception of personality and its connection with formal authority arose *from*

a specific juristic interest, namely, an especially clear awareness of what *the essence of the legal decision* entails.... The legal interest in the decision as such should not be mixed up with the kind of calculability. It is rooted in the character of the normative and is derived from the necessity of judging a concrete fact concretely even though what is given as a standard for the judgment is only a legal principle in its general universality. Thus a transformation takes place every time. That the legal idea cannot translate itself independently is evident from the fact that it says nothing about who should apply it. In every transformation there is present an *auctoritas interpositio* (Schmitt 1988, 30; emphasis added).

Schmitt's critique of Kelsen is contained in the move from the problem of the legal application of a principle of justice (the legal idea) to the solution afforded by a juridical person who is authorized to make this application or to take this decision. It is in this transition that Schmitt reveals the strictly juridical background of his understanding of authority: the idea of *auctoritas interpositio* refers to the Roman law conception of a tutor who is authorized to act for a minor who lacks, by definition, a *sui juris* status. The reference to this figure of Roman law is a clear indication that Schmitt understands the state as the sole legal representative of society, the sole legal person who is authorized to act for the society as a whole because this society exists as a unity only in the person of its representative and consequently only its sole representative can legislate for it.[9]

POLITICAL THEOLOGY AND REPRESENTATION: SCHMITT AND THE PLURALIST QUARREL WITH HOBBES

This idea of a vicariate or presidential representative as *personam alicuius repraesentare* (Hofmann 2007, 255) has its origin in the medieval fiction theory of corporations initiated by Innocent IV. In *Political Theology* Schmitt admits that only one other theory could potentially provide a solution to the problem of how a system of norms links up to social life, and this was the theory proposed by Gierke, for whom associations were endowed with a real personality. Therefore, they did not need to be represented by their rector, nor did they owe their existence to a concession of the sovereign: "the will of the state or sovereign is not the final source of law but is the organ of the people convoked to express legal consciousness as it emerges from the life of the people" (Schmitt 1988, 24). According to Schmitt, only Gierke "answered the basic question on their [law and state] mutual relation by asserting that both are independent factors of human communal life" (24). Only Gierke did not evade the problem of sovereignty as Kelsen evaded it. Does society make law spontaneously, as Gierke thinks, or does the state have to make law for it due to its condition of tutelage, as Schmitt argues? This is the fundamental question treated by *Political Theology*. Schmitt answers it by recovering an idea of representation as *personam alicuius repraesentare* and opposes it to the idea of representation advanced by Gierke according to which a society can legislate for itself because its people can be convoked "in person" through legislative assemblies that "are identical" to the people itself.[10] Gierke's point is that if every association develops a real group personality spontaneously then it is clear that no sovereign can represent it. Indeed, no representation in the sense of an external political unity is ever needed for it: no sovereign can bring it into presence.

Perhaps it was Harold Laski who drew most clearly the radical implications from Gierke's theory of group personality. These implications are already stated in his first book, *Studies in the Problem of Sovereignty*, which was originally published by Yale University Press in 1917, that is, five years before Schmitt's *Political Theology: Four Chapters on the Concept of Sovereignty*. Even the mere comparison of both titles indicates that Schmitt's book is polemically addressing Laski's critique of sovereignty.[11] Laski's starting point is Gierke's idea that "any group of people leading a common life" develops a "personality that is beyond the personalities of its constituent parts. For us that personality is real. Slowly its personality has compelled the law to abandon the theory of fiction" (1968, 4). The importance of Laski's *Studies*, published the very same year as Kelsen's article on juridical personality, rests precisely in its ambition to demonstrate the illusion of sovereign authority. His radical thesis is that there is no such thing as sovereignty if by this one understands an attribute of a political entity that elicits obedience in its subjects: such an idea of sovereignty is a fiction that has never existed historically and that gives the lie to the Hobbesian (later Schmittian) conceit that the essence of law is command. "There is no sanction for law other than the consent of the human mind" (14). As a consequence, there is no "a priori justification which compels their allegiance [to the state] more than the allegiance to Church or to other groups—it [the state] wins the allegiance pragmatically" (19). In hindsight, Laski's *Studies* appears as the first exercise in proving the impossibility of political theology.

The discussion of Laski's thesis takes up an entire chapter of *The Concept of the Political*: Schmitt must have hardly considered it a matter of indifference. By that time, Schmitt was even willing to concede that Laski's critique of the illusions of sovereignty "is largely justified. The juridical formulas of the omnipotence of the state are, in fact, only superficial secularizations of theological formulas of the omnipotence of God" (Schmitt 2007, 42). But he is unwilling to admit that there is no "fact of the matter" to sovereignty because in Laski's analysis "the question remains unanswered: which social entity...decides the extreme case and determines the decisive friend-and-enemy grouping? Neither a church nor a labor union nor an alliance of both could have forbidden or prevented a war....Such an opposition would have risked being treated as an enemy" (43). As he reiterates at the end of his life, "Hobbes' all-deciding questions: *Quis judicabit? Quis interpretabit?*" are unavoidable (Schmitt 2008a, 51). Again, implicit in Schmitt's answer to Laski is the idea that there must exist a representative who gives to the plurality of groups conforming a society its unity, and such a representative makes the state into a separate entity with regard to all associations of civil society. The answer to pluralism is always Hobbes's theory of representation: "the absolute prince is also *the sole representative* of the political unity of the people. He alone represents the state. As

Hobbes puts it, the state has 'its unity in the person of the sovereign'; it is 'united in the person of the sovereign.' Representation first establishes this unity" (Schmitt 2008b, 247). To Gierke's and Laski's thesis that any truly representative system necessarily will reject a sovereign entity, Schmitt responds that unless a legal system is focused on the apex of sovereignty it will not be representative at all. The representative has authority because it represents to all members their unity or state; no representative as such can represent the members against the state for then they cease being a representative of the whole and become an advocate of the part.[12]

Perhaps the most important claim made by Schmitt's early political theology is that representation cannot be democratic, in neither an indirect nor direct sense of the term. In *Constitutional Theory* Schmitt postulated that "the state as a political unity rests on the connection of two opposing formative principles. The first is the principle of identity (specifically the self-identity of the existing people as a political unity, if, by virtue of its own political consciousness and actual will, it has the capacity to distinguish friend and enemy), and the other is the principle of representation, through which the government represents the political unity" (2008b, 247). In the ideal and extreme case of pure identity or homogeneity (between rulers and ruled as in direct democracy) there can be no representation. Representation is possible only when unity (*complexio*) must be forged out of oppositions, out of contradictions (*oppositorum*), and thus where a decision is always required. The decision can come only from a juridical person who decides for the whole people or community (*civitas*), not subjectively or arbitrarily but in virtue of being the representative of this whole.[13] The representative must stand for a people because "there is no state without people, and that a people, therefore, must always actually be existing as an entity present at hand" (239).

In *Roman Catholicism and Political Form*, Schmitt argues that the Catholic Church resolves the dilemma caused by the fact that the representative must be both superior to the people it represents and at the same time must be the representative of these people because it was an organization that understood itself as a *complexio oppositorum* and whose politics was always "a strict realization of the principle of representation" (1996b, 8).[14] The reason that the church so understood itself lies in the fact that what the church represents is "Christ reigning, ruling, and conquering" (31). The church "represents the Person of Christ Himself: God become man in historical reality" (18). The church is the representative of Jesus as king of a kingdom that is of this *aion* or age (as opposed to the previous age under the rule of Mosaic law) but that is not yet realized on earth as it is in heaven. The juridical problem of the age after the resurrection of Christ is that the truth of "Jesus is the Christ" requires that his kingdom be proclaimed also on earth by his people. The goal of the true church, that is, of whoever is his actual representative, is to make visible the realm of an invisible king: "to represent means to make an invisible being visible and present through a publicly present one" (2008b, 243). A representative, in other words, not only personifies, in a "fictional" way, a body politic or corporation but also does so insofar as he stands in for (is the vicar of) the real person of God. "The Church is a concrete personal representation [by the priesthood, and above all the Pope] of a concrete personality" (1996a, 18). Here Schmitt confirms Kelsen's original intuition, namely, that the theory of legal personality is inseparable from Christology because only if the transcendent God limits itself by incarnating itself is it at all possible to have a human representative or vicar of Christ.[15]

This theological subtext clearly informs Hobbes's discussion of representation in chapter 16 of the *Leviathan*. Hobbes defines a person as an actor who performs actions or utters words either his own, in which case the person is natural, or those of someone else, in which case the person is artificial and "is said to beare" the other person and "act in his name." Hobbes identifies this artificial person with the terms "Representative, a Lieutenant, a Vicar, an Attorney... and the like" (2010, 81, 98). Artificial persons perform actions or speak words that belong to others, as their author; in other words, they act or speak by authority of the person represented. But it is not necessary to be a person to be represented by another person: Hobbes calls the person or representative fictional when what is to be represented is an inanimate thing (a church, a hospital, a bridge) or an individual who cannot give his consent to being impersonated (children, fools, and madmen).

At this point Hobbes introduces the two central possibilities for representation, one after the other. The first is that "the true God may be personated" (2010, 82, 100). Hobbes claims that this happened on three occasions: first by Moses; then by Jesus Christ; last by the Holy Spirit found in the apostles and their legal successors (the Holy Spirit is a person sent by both God and his Son). Immediately after theological representation, he introduces the famous consideration about political representation: "A Multitude of men are made *One* Person, when they are by one man, or one Person, Represented; so that it be done with the consent of every one of that Multitude in particular. For it is the *Unity* of the Representer, not the *Unity* of the Represented, that maketh the Person *One*. And it is the Representer that beareth the Person, and but one Person: And Unity, cannot otherwise be understood in Multitude" (82, 100). Thus, Hobbes places in parallel God's representatives and the state's or people's representatives. For this very reason it is not implausible for Schmitt to claim that Hobbes is engaging in the exercise of political theology, understood as reaffirming the "unity" of politics and religion, "the power of the sovereign as the lieutenant of God... that brings about the unity of religion and politics" (2008c, 55).[16]

The construction of the leviathan in the following chapter 17 does not ultimately help in deciding which way to understand the contraposition of God and state in the previous chapter. Hobbes famously argues that to achieve peace it is necessary that all the individuals:

> Reduce all their Wills... unto one Will: which is as much to say, to appoint one Man, or Assembly of Men, to beare their Person... and therein to submit their Wills, every one to his Will, and their Judgment to his Judgment. This is more than Consent, or Concord; it is a reall Unitie of them all, in one and the same Person.... This done, the Multitude so united in one Person, is called a Common-wealth, in latine Civitas. This is the generation of that great Leviathan, or rather (to speak more reverently) of that Mortall God, to which we owe, under the Immortall God, our peace and defence.... And he that carryeth this Person, is called Soveraigne. (2010, 87–88, 104–105)

The passage lends itself to confusion insofar as Hobbes here is speaking of two artificial persons and therefore also of two relations of representation: the person of the *civitas* or people understood as one group personality; and the artificial person of the sovereign, who bears or impersonates the group personality of the *civitas* or people. As has been noted by several commentators (Pitkin 1967; Runciman 2005; Skinner 2005; Hofmann 2007), the consent between individuals in appointing one person (the sovereign) to represent each of them singly is not enough to warrant the claim that this same sovereign represents the person of all of the individuals as a whole, as a united people. Schmitt already makes the same point: "The state is more than and something different from a covenant concluded by individuals.... The sovereign-representative person is much more than the sum total of all participating particular wills.... To this extent *the new god is transcendent vis-à-vis all contractual partners...obviously only in a juristic and not in a metaphysical sense*" (2008c, 98).

The English followers of Gierke argued that such a transcendence on the part of the Hobbesian state with respect to society or to the people was an illusion: the sovereign bears a purely fictional, unreal person of the people; he impersonates "a mere ghost of a fiction" in the words of F. W. Maitland (Runciman 2005, 101). That is why, as Schmitt argues in *The Leviathan in the State Theory of Hobbes*, Hobbes is forced to give a "body" to this ghostly apparition of the people and conjures the "mythical symbol" of the leviathan for such a body politic: "The image of the Leviathan is being asked to provide the state with an identity apart from the identity of its representative" (Schmitt 2008c, 21). But the leviathan cannot really be thought of on the model of an organic body of the people because then Hobbes could not argue that the people or *civitas* exists by virtue of its representative, of its sovereign. Hobbes would have had to return to the medieval Conciliarist view that the rector of a corporation may be, considered as a single individual, greater than each member of the corporation but is smaller (has less authority) than the entire body when it is collected in an assembly or council. For that reason, Hobbes must designate the sovereign as the soul of a mechanical, not an organic body politic: the machine state of the leviathan.[17] To make sense of the Hobbesian sovereign as the soul of a people, Maitland uncovered the old legal figure of the corporation sole, that is, the strange idea of a corporation (the Crown) composed of only one person (the king). As an officer of the Crown the physical king is below the law and serves it; as the incarnation of the Crown, the king is above the law, a mortal God.

If this reading of the dilemmas of Hobbes's theory of representation is correct, then it is easy to see the force of the pluralist critique of Hobbes. Maitland had identified in Gierke's account of medieval law as a function of representative assemblies of associations based on solidarity the outlines of a legal theory that could make sense of the English developments in common law that had tried to undermine the absolute sovereignty of the English king granted him thanks to juridical fantasies like the corporation sole and the king's two bodies. For Maitland, the reason Hobbes's construction failed to spread in England was that the English political system gave rise to its own immunitary reaction against fictional theories of incorporation—namely, the idea of an unincorporated body, such as a trust, which has a real personality separate from the individuals composing the trust yet is not dependent on the concession of the sovereign, which is the case when the personality is only fictional (Runciman 2005, 67–69). The idea of real personality of the group is there-fore crucial for two reasons. First, since the body politic, or association of individuals, is a group personality, it is also a living body that is self-steering and not a machine (indeed Maitland and the other English pluralists toyed with the idea that such associations evolved along Darwinian lines—a conception that has now been revived by systems the-ory). Consequently, it requires no external, sovereign-appointed rector or tutor as its legal guide. This theory of group personality was the historical, real refutation of Hobbes's the-ory of representation: for here was a multitude that, in representing itself to itself, acquired unity. Pluralist theorists of group personality were on the verge of discovering a third con-cept of representation, a democratic form of representation that Schmitt had banned from conceptual existence—hence, the enormous threat that they represented to his political theology.[18] This threat was posed at the juridical level and precisely on the two points that motivated Schmitt's political theology: the relation of law to social life (jurisprudence to sociology); and the problem of political unity through representation.

To show that the Hobbesian sovereign is not simply an impersonator of a ghost or fic-tion (i.e., of an absent people), as the pluralist critique charged, Schmitt had to return to the liturgical conception of a vicariate representative of Christ as head of the mysti-cal body of his people (Kantorowicz 1997, 59, 102, 159–160; Hofmann 2007, 139, 192–193). When a bishop takes on the mask or person of the Lord and repeats the words of the Lord, he "personifies a role" in that he stands in for the person of Christ and in this sense makes visible again the invisible head of Christ. But in so doing the bishop also does something more: he brings back to ("eternal") life an assembly of believers in and through the glo-rification of the Christ who had defeated death. As Kantorowicz shows, the liturgical conception of sovereignty is essentially preoccupied with accounting for the immortal-ity of the mystical body of Christ's people—an idea later transposed from theology to jurisprudence to account for the secular immortality of the *civitas*. This is the democratic dimension of Christology that becomes decisive for the later Schmitt.

Schmitt's treatment of political theology begins with the study of the transfer of theo-logical concepts to the field of political and juridical concepts, but, with the Hobbes book, a shift occurs whereby he becomes more interested in the transfer of political and juridical concepts to theological ones. It is as if, between *Political Theology* and *Political Theology II*, Schmitt reads Hobbes's decisive sixteenth chapter of the *Leviathan* back-ward, from the problem of representation of the people in the sovereign to the problem of representation of God in the Trinity.

Recent interpretations of Hobbes's *Leviathan* have confirmed that the Trinity plays a cru-cial role in Hobbes's model of representation.[19] Hobbes links God to the people because he considers both to be invisible and silent entities if considered independently of their rep-resentatives: "(in the current era) God, too, did not speak or act. God was personated pre-cisely because he did not intervene directly in politics" (Garsten 2010, 529). But precisely this absence of God in history only heightens the importance of the persons of the Trinity (Moses, Jesus, and the Holy Spirit) who impersonate him on earth: "Hobbes's account sug-gested that there was no relation of identity between the one God and three members of the Trinity, but instead relations of representation" (538). The question is whether Hobbes intended the association of political representation with the representation of the Trinity in a serious way or whether he did so with an ironical intention, intending thereby to undermine the political representative. Garsten takes the latter position: "To worship a representation as if it were real was, according to Hobbes, to commit the sin of idolatry. How could citizens obey a sovereign representative without idolizing it? By keeping in mind that it was only a representation" (540). But this understanding of representation, which folds the impersonator into the figure of the impostor, seriously downplays the liturgical, sacramental origin related to the impersonation of the mystical body of Christ.

Schmitt would have understood Hobbes's link between Trinity and political representation otherwise. In so doing he would have followed Peterson's claim that, in the Christian understanding of the "(Unum Necessarium) Onely Article of Faith...that Jesus is the Christ" (Hobbes 2010, 325, 356), it is not the case that Jesus came to earth to announce a future kingdom of God but to the contrary that it is the Apostles who announce the "fact" that Jesus is already the king by virtue of his death on the cross, passage through Hell, and resurrection to Heaven and that this event puts an end to one age (of sin) and opens another age (of grace). Hence, from this perspective the problem of political representation consists in understanding its function in relation to the real kingdom of Jesus Christ. That Hobbes may have taken seriously the liturgical dimension of representation is also indicated in the sixteenth chapter by the claim that God's political action in history is *never* apart from his personations (Martel 2007, 129). Hobbes understood all too well that the Trinity, in Christian political theology, means nothing other than God's knowable praxis (as opposed to his unknowable essence). Indeed, it is only if God is really present in history through his representative persons that it makes sense to say that the people are really present in history through their representative person (i.e., the civil sovereign).[20] Such a liturgical reading of the Hobbesian sovereign understands sovereignty as a function of representing (Max Weber would say: routinizing or secularizing) the charismatic gift of power granted to all Christians in virtue of their baptism. In short, sovereign is he who can arouse the acclamation of an assembled people (an *ekklesia*). Additionally, this liturgical reading of the Trinity makes it unavoidable to consider the function of the Hobbesian sovereign in light of the problem of the *katechon*, that is, of that historical agent who keeps the end of history at bay by slowing down the definitive second coming of the king. These are the problems that occupy the later Schmitt, and his reorientation of political theology toward the Trinity reflects his continued preoccupation with Peterson's critique of political theology from the standpoint of Christian theology.

POLITICAL THEOLOGY AND DEMOCRACY: SCHMITT AND PETERSON ON THE TRINITY

Political Theology II was written as a belated response to Peterson's 1935 *Monotheism as a Political Problem,* which, according to Schmitt, put in circulation the legend that political theology had reached its end. Peterson argues that Christian theology could not possibly be secularized in the form of a political theology, as Schmitt had attempted to do, because the essence of this theology is its Trinitarianism and not the doctrine of monotheism understood as a divine monarchy. The three persons of God (Father, Son, and Holy Spirit) do not fit the one-to-one match between divine king (God as king of the universe) and human king that is the paradigm for monotheism understood as a political problem. This was the concise conclusion at which Peterson's treatise arrived after providing a genealogy of the idea of divine monarchy that found its origin in the adoption of Aristotle's theology in Hellenistic conceptions of divine monarchy and climaxed with Philo's Hellenistic Judaism (Peterson 2011, 71–77). The early Church fathers like Origen and Eusebius who tried to reconcile theologically the peace promised by the Gospel with the Pax Romana were wrong: "Only on the basis of Judaism and paganism can such a thing as a 'political theology' exist.... The peace that the Christian seeks is won by no emperor, but is solely a gift of him who 'is higher than all understanding'" (104–105).

The polemical object of this assertion is clearly Schmitt's *The Concept of the Political* and its claim that the legitimacy of sovereignty rests in its power to bring peace and security to its subjects by wielding the monopoly of decision as to who is friend and who is enemy (*protego ergo obligo*). But the last sentence of Peterson's treatise invites another political reading of Christian theology.[21] The reason that political theology qua divine kingship came to an end is that the Christian Gospel had announced the advent of a new kingdom that closed the age of human kingdoms (the age of leviathan and behemoth, to speak mythically). This new kingdom, at whose head was the resurrected Jesus, brings about a Christian idea of peace that is guaranteed not by a human emperor but exclusively by the charismatic power of Jesus the Christ Emperor and by the gift of grace. As Peterson (1997) argues at length in his lectures on the *Letter to the Romans*, the charisma of Christ is experienced by all Christians exclusively through the sacrament of baptism, which consequently makes all those who accept Jesus as their king into a people (an *ekklesia* as opposed to a *synagogue*) endowed with full powers. On this account, the *plenitudo potestatis* (fullness of powers), before being taken up by pope or king, is an endowment of the mystical body of the Church, whose head is Jesus Christ, the Son of God. The bishop of Rome as much as the Holy Roman Emperor are granted plentitude of powers only vicariously over the children of God and only until the Second Coming of the King when all the children shall be, like the Son of God, also themselves kings (i.e., will attain the same glory of the resurrected body). Peterson's point is that, if a Christian political theology is at all possible, then it can take such a democratic and antimonarchical form only when centered on the political and juridical interpretation of the Trinity.

Schmitt and Peterson entertained friendly relations throughout the 1920s and early 1930s, and judging from Peterson's 1925 and 1928 lectures on the *Letter to the Romans* the picture of the Catholic Church that emerges there is not far removed from the ideals voiced in *Roman Catholicism as Political Form*. So, apart from Schmitt's sympathy with the attempt to find common ground between Germany's Christians and the Nazi regime and Peterson's profound antipathy to that particular *complexio oppositorum*, what led to their public breakup in 1935 must have its roots in their differing ideas with respect both to peace (i.e., to the distinction between friend and enemy in relation to the Gospel) and to the idea of God's kingdom and its nonarrival in history, namely, the problem of the *katechon* and of secularization (of Christ's charisma).[22]

When Schmitt defended his concept of political theology forty years after Peterson's attack, in the book *Political Theology II*, his central claim was precisely that Peterson had made a gross mistake in reducing political theology to the question of divine monarchy, for in so doing he minimized the democratic essence of political theology as Schmitt understood it. The fundamental parallelism in political theology, so said Schmitt, is not that between one God and one king, but between one God and one people. Political theology, Schmitt now says, as a theory of sovereignty is not a doctrine of monarchism "but has to be oriented towards political unity and its presence or representation" (2008a, 72). In other words, the question of Christian political theology is the question of who represents the *political unity of a people*: it is a representative *of the people* who is charged with ultimate authority. As Schmitt argues in *Constitutional Theory*, the principle of monarchism entails the idea that the dynasty itself—the physical body of the king and its passage from one man to another—is the representative of the realm (2008b, 138). The principle of monarchism, in fact, calls for the divinization of the physical kings. Schmitt is entirely aware that the important development in medieval jurisprudence goes in the opposite direction, namely, toward the humanization of the body of the physical king and the divinization (the glorification) of the body politic and its representative (King-in-Parliament). But the divinization of the political body (as opposed to the divinization of the political leader) is an idea that makes sense only under the assumption that this body is somehow "eternal" by virtue of the sacraments that tie it with the salvational acts of its head, Jesus the Christ. The eternal life granted to the body of the believers in virtue of the incarnation of God in the person of Jesus becomes the decisive point in this democratically inflected reading of political theology: it is the very development that would become the topic of Kantorowicz's narrative.[23]

In *Political Theology II* Schmitt takes up the question of whether such a Christian peace is brought about by the doctrine of the two cities of church and state established by Augustine, as Peterson implies. This doctrine is clearly intended to separate the power of the sovereign or emperor from the authority of the Church and in that way relegates the state and politics to the sole purveyance of physical indemnity to sinful individuals because it cannot provide them with the "gifts" or "sacraments" that assure their eternal salvation in Christ's kingdom. Schmitt contests whether this Augustinian doctrine is the correct political understanding of Trinitarian theology. For Schmitt, Peterson's supposedly Augustinian critique of political theology inevitably gets caught in a conflict of competences that already Pope Gelasius I had tried to pacify unsuccessfully through his formula according to which authority belongs to priests and power to kings and emperor. In *The "Nomos" of the Earth* Schmitt explains what it is that disallows the separation of church from empire: nothing less than the function of the *katechon* or restrainer of the Antichrist that befalls charismatically to a Christian king when he is ascended to the office of emperor in order to fight the "holy" enemy. Augustine's division of church and state reiterates the very problem for which Hobbes is the only solution: as Schmitt says, the problem of the conflict of competences between theology and politics can only come to a real end "in the same way as the confessional civil wars of the sixteenth and seventeenth century: either in a precise answer to the big question *quis judicabit?* Or in an equally precise *itio in partes* [return to the region]—that is, a spatially clear territorial or regional demarcation, in accordance with the principle *cuius regio eius religio*" (Schmitt 2008a, 114). For Schmitt, Augustine's doctrine of the two cities is unable to give an answer to the question of who decides what is spiritual and what is temporal: "this is the big question posed by Thomas Hobbes, which is at the centre of my treatise *Political Theology* from 1922 and which led to a theory of decisionism and of the inner logic of the act" (114). Only the Hobbesian solution has a chance of bringing about real peace, until the Second Coming of Christ.

This entire argument entails, of course, that the political commandment to recognize one's true enemy and fight it in a life-and-death struggle is compatible with the Christian Gospel and its commandment to "love thy enemies." Schmitt's solution, in *The Concept of the Political*, is to argue that enemy means something different in the Gospel than it does in the theory of sovereignty: one ought to love one's enemies—in the private sense of enmity (*inimicus*), where the enemy is internal to the concrete juridical order and belongs within private right—but one must fight one's public enemies (*hostis*), where the enemy is external to that order (and is therefore a matter of public law).[24] But this solution is hardly satisfying for anyone who reads, like Peterson, all the concepts of the Gospel as having a public law meaning since they must all refer, necessarily, to the public law event embodied by the elevation to the throne of Jesus the Christ. And it is no surprise that the problem of how to unite together the Gospel and the political, love and militancy, reappears also in anti-Schmittian Christian political theologies like those of Eric Voegelin, Jacques Maritain, and most recently Alain Badiou and Slavoj Žižek.[25]

Perhaps because he knew that his distinction between *inimicus* and *hostis* begged the question once it was assumed that the age of earthly kingdoms had come to an end with the new age of Christ's kingdom (which sets up a universal public law that no longer permits heathens to stand outside of God's kingdom), in *Political Theology II* Schmitt makes one last attempt to show how a Christian idea of peace is inseparable from the sovereign function of declaring war on the enemy. First, he points out that the Trinity may contain an inner stasiology or doctrine of civil war (*stasis*) between the three persons of God. Second, he closes his discussion of Hans Blumenberg's critique of the secularization thesis with an obscure reference to Goethe's motto, which opens the fourth book of *Dichtung und Wahrheit, Nemo contra deum nisi deus ipse* (no one can fight God except God himself). According to Meier (2011, 190–191), this motto suggests that the civil war contained in the Trinity obtains when the Son (or God of salvation) appeals to man to undermine the kingdom of the Father (or God of creation) and to ascend Him to the throne from which He was sent by his Father and overthrow him. According to this reading, Goethe is advocating that the human being side with Jesus as rebel, as revolutionary, against the monarchy of the Father (who created a cosmic order that is good). The implication is that the Church or *katechon* should step in and act as a restrainer of the anarchic Gospel of Jesus and in that way act as Dostoyevsky's Grand Inquisitor to Dostoyevsky's Christ (Hohendahl 2008, 19).

Such a reading interprets the problem of the stasiology in the late Schmitt purely polemically, whereas it is possible to give an interpretation that is more juridical in nature and brings one closer to the scientific sense of political theology.[26] On this alternative reading, Schmitt is using the stasiology of the Trinity to point out the following dynamic. The Father's love for human beings first takes the form of Jewish theocracy with the personation of Moses; this form is in reality a "tyranny" of the law, which is resisted (indeed, the ancient divine law is both fulfilled and abolished) by the personation of Jesus as Christ. But this antinomian moment in the Trinity, this resistance of the Son to the Father, need not mean that the Son is taking up the mantle of anarchy as Meier suggests. Rather, two elements can help to make sense of the resistance. The first element is the gnostic traces within the Trinity that Schmitt points out: Goethe's motto would then refer to the way the redeemer God (the second person) has to struggle against the nature created by God the Father. Divine providence as personified by the Holy Ghost is the name given to this struggle against nature that redeems nature.

The second element concerns the juridical status of the second person. If Moses imposes the law of God the Father tyrannically, then, by opposition, Jesus the Christ cannot impose his kingdom on human beings in the same way: it is a kingdom that requires the consent of his people. This second element refers to a discovery of Peterson, to which Schmitt himself appeals, in accordance with which the Christian liturgy is a transposition of imperial acclamation to the case of Jesus as Christ Emperor: hence prayer would be the only way one can "impose" on earth the kingdom of Jesus Christ (Peterson 2012). At this point, one rejoins Kelsen's suggestion that God exists only insofar as He is believed in. This claim now means, when interpreted juridically and liturgically, that Christ ascends into His glory through the glorification of Him as king by his people. In this last permutation of political theology, all sovereign power and authority turn on the category of glory or *doxa* (*Herrlichkeit*), indeed, of popular opinion. Goethe's dictum could therefore also mean that only by the elevation of the dignity of human beings, and thus of the rights of man against divine monarchs, would Jesus be elevated to His throne and His kingship established on earth.

This is clearly not the sense that Schmitt wants to give to Goethe's motto. It can safely be said that Schmitt never could transform his political theology in the direction required by this Christology, which would have meant separating the medieval problem of government (*gubernaculum*) entirely away from the scheme of the *lex regia* and retranslating it to the problem of self-government by the people of Christ.[27] This problem is foreshadowed by Kantorowicz in his narrative of how the dignity of the kingdom of Christ is secularized into the dignity of man, thus eventually giving rise to constitutional regimes based on the rights of man. It seems to me more likely that Schmitt's defense of the democratic permutation of political theology remains Hobbesian until the very end and thus in this respect is monarchical. But this is not because Schmitt would be calling for the return of the Father and of theocracy. It is Hobbesian simply because at any given historical turning point everyone must decide who or what is their representative that upholds the belief that "Jesus is the Christ" and on the basis of that belief this vicar of God is granted by the people the monopoly of the political decision.

CONCLUSION

The democratic turn taken by the discussion of political theology thanks to Peterson's intervention leads into what has been called economic theology, which has recently found a new basis in Agamben's (2007; 2010) interpretation of Trinitarianism.[28] Agamben brings out the two crucial elements of stasiology previously highlighted: the reconciliation with nature in the form of divine providence; and the juridical interpretation of prayer. His thesis is that Trinitarian theology advances a theory not of divine kingship but of divine government: the Trinity represents God's action in history, but this action is not political (as in Schmitt). Rather, God acts in history on the basis of the "mystery of the economy" of the divine dispensations or gifts leading to salvation (Agamben 2007, 62–82). The political theology of Jesus as Christ is not political at all but economical: Jesus Christ governs in the absence of the Father, and indeed this government shows the ultimate emptiness of the throne. One can see that Agamben is here putting forward yet another interpretation of the Goethean maxim, where the rebellion of the Son against the Father, the conquest of the empty throne, is not a harbinger of disorder. Rather, it takes place in and through seeing in created nature a conception of immanent, providential order, the order of economy (Hayek calls it *catallaxy*; cf. Nishiyama and Leube 1984, 367) that depends on the unpredictable emergence of networks and regularities caused by the externalities of the rational choices of individuals with asymmetrical sources of information, as the decisive ground for politics in the new age (Agamben 2007, 126–148).

In *Monotheism as a Political Problem*, Peterson characterizes the Aristotelian divine monarch by employing the nineteenth-century liberal motto of constitutional monarchy: "le roi règne mais il ne gouverne pas" ("The king reigns but he does not govern"; 2011, 71). For Peterson, this aptly indicates the gnostic vein of divine monarchy: the good God as king does not meddle with the affairs of the world, leaving the government of worldly affairs to the evil archons. In *Political Theology II* Schmitt rejects the formula as anachronistic and as indicative of a hatred of order, but above all as a typical liberal misunderstanding of the unity of state and government in the sovereign representative. Agamben, instead, argues that the dualism between kingdom and government contains the essence of the political significance of the Trinity, namely, that divine government through the "economy" of natural order takes over from divine kingship and God's transcendence is no longer separable from His immanence. In this sense, Agamben's thesis sheds new light on Kantorowicz's central claim, namely, that sovereignty in medieval political thought is never simply a function of being above the law but also of being below the law: if the sovereign appeals to God the Father for its prerogative to make law from above (this is Schmitt), then it is equally true that such sovereignty is internally limited by the necessary reference to the sonship of Christ, which orients sovereignty below the law and in the direction of the economic or providential government of the affairs of the realm. This is no doubt the reason that Kantorowicz's fundamental problem of how to secure the eternity of the mystical body of the people first takes the economic form of the eternalization of the "fisc" and why, to this day, "fiscal" policy (political economy) remains the key to all politics. This shift from political to economic theology and the priority of the transfer from political to theological concepts (rather than from theological to political concepts)—made possible by Peterson's juridical analysis of Trinitarian theology—opens a new horizon for the problem of political theology. In that sense, perhaps it does bring to a closure the discourse on political theology as understood by Schmitt.

NOTES

1. See Schmitt's statement according to which *Political Theology* "introduced the phrase 'political theology' to literature" (2008a, 35); see also his claim in a letter to a student that "the coining of the term 'political theology' in fact comes from me" (Mohler 1995, 119), as quoted by Meier 2011 (202 n48), who discusses at length the history of the term.
2. See the article "God and State" in Kelsen 1973; see also Kantorowicz 1997. For an early use of the concept, seemingly without reference to Schmitt, see Oakley 1968. Most recently, see the discussion of Schmitt's scientific use of the concept in Agamben 2008. This meaning of political theology is also discussed in Böckenförde 1983; Blumenberg 1996; Schmitz and Lepper 2007; Galli 1996; Kervégan 2005; Kahn 2011.
3. The polemical concept of political theology takes as it object the "hatred" of power, which develops in the late nineteenth-century Russian nihilist and anarchist tradition culminating in many ways with Bakunin and that finds in Dostoyevsky's novels its most influential depiction. On this Russian context of Schmitt's polemical use of political theology, see Palélogue 2004; McCormick 2010 and now Forti 2012. A related literary context that is important for Schmitt's polemical use of political theology is now discussed in Hoibraaten 2011. The importance of the Russian development of political theology was already pointed out by Voegelin 1952.
4. For instance, the claim that "the modern constitutional state triumphed together with deism, a theology and a metaphysics that banished the miracle from the world" (Schmitt 1988, 36). This thesis has now been taken up by Milbank 2006 and Taylor 2007, in particular the claim—originally directed against the "monistic" metaphysics Schmitt thought he detected in Kelsen's jurisprudence—that "all the identities that recur in the political ideas and in the state doctrines of the nineteenth century rest on such conceptions of immanence" (Schmitt 1988, 49).
5. For recent interpretations of Schmitt's scientific approach to political theology, see Chen 2006; Espejo 2010. The importance of Kelsen for Schmitt's conception of political theology is highlighted in Baume 2009.
6. Unless noted otherwise, all translations of source material by the author.
7. For a discussion of the question of the state's extralegality in Kelsen, see now Tanguay-Renaud 2010.

8. On the problem of application and its significance for Schmitt's jurisprudence, I refer to Vatter 2008 and the literature cited therein.

9. For a discussion of Schmitt's concept of representation in terms of the problem of application of law to life see Weber 2005; Kahn 2011, although neither contextualizes this problem within the medieval juridical understanding of representation, where in no case is the representative to be thought in existentialist terms. If the person who decides were merely the "decisional intervention of a singular subject" (Weber 2005, 35), then Schmitt could not confront Kelsen's objection concerning the hypostatization of legal form in the form of a singular being who makes the singular decision.

10. Skinner (2005) traces this alternative concept of representation in English Parlamentarian theorists roughly contemporary with Hobbes. Hofmann (2007, 253) traces this idea of representation as *repraesentatio identitatis*, whereby the representative assembly is "identical" to the represented people and does not merely incarnate the fiction of their juridical personality, as with vicariate representation, back to Bartolus and Marsilius of Padua. On all of these questions, see also Duso 2003.

11. For someone who is otherwise so attentive to Schmitt's polemical interventions, it is curious that neither Laski nor any of the English pluralist thinkers appear in the index of names in Meier's book on Schmitt's political theology.

12. Schmitt (2008, 247) accuses Gierke of having confused representation with advocacy. On early English understanding of representation as advocacy before the king's court, see Clarke 1936. The representative as advocate has been recently defended in Urbinati 2006.

13. "The political unity of the people as such can never be present in actual identity and, consequently, must always be represented by men personally" (Schmitt 2008b, 239); "the presentation of the political unity is an intrinsic part of the form. In every state there must be persons who can say 'L´État c'est nous'" (241).

14. Whether one follows Ullmann's 1980 view that medieval political thinking is characterized by the conflict between an ascendant (from people to king) or a descendant (from king to people) form of jurisdiction or whether one takes the view that law is essentially *constitutio populi*, the self-ordering of a people as it reflects itself in common law and in divine or natural law (which law is then merely applied or interpreted, but not made, by kings), the tension between the people or the king as fountain of law is present throughout. For the former view, see Ullmann 1980; for the latter view, see the seminal formulation, directed against Kantorowicz's politico-theological reading of medieval jurisdiction, in Lewis 1964. According to Kantorowicz, political theology in its scientific meaning emerges in the thirteenth century with the attempt of kings (starting with Frederick II) to become considered "the sole legitimate legislator and ultimate interpreter of the law" and in that sense to take away from the people its jurisdictional prerogatives (1997, 104).

15. On the current discussion with regard to representation in Christology, see Deuser 1999.

16. Kantorowicz speaks of the king as "the perfect impersonator of Christ on earth" given its "dual" nature (human by nature, divine by grace; 1997, 58). Whether the Hobbesian unity of religion and politics is a Christian political theology and how this relates to the claim that "the Jews brought about unity from the side of religion" (Schmitt 2008b, 10), these are some of issues at stake in Schmitt's debate with Strauss over the nature of Hobbesian political science. On this issue, see the different interpretations found in Meier 1995; 2011, 101–121; Vatter 2004; Galli 2008; Dotti 2009.

17. On this point, again, Schmitt's insistence on the mechanical nature of the leviathan seems to be correct. I refer to his essay "The State as Mechanism in Hobbes and Descartes" (2008c, 91–103). See now Stanton 2011 on Schmitt's overall reading of Hobbes.

18. This threat posed by the English pluralist interpretation of Hobbes is visible throughout Schmitt's *The Leviathan in the State Theory of Hobbes*. Laski argues that all law depends on the "opinion of the members of the State, and they belong to other groups" (1968, 12). In his Hobbes book, Schmitt will say that this Spinozist belief overturns the priority that Hobbes had established between public confession over private faith, thereby making the state's highest duty that of protecting the freedom of thought of each individual: the religion of the state is only an external cult that must leave the individual free to believe and speak publicly what she wants. This was the first "death" of the "mortal God" (Schmitt 2008c, 56). And it is still the English pluralists who are accused of bringing about the "second" death of the leviathan by reviving Gierke's notion that associations make law spontaneously:

> The old adversaries, the "indirect" powers of the church and of interest groups, reappeared in that century as modern political parties, trade unions, social organizations, in a word as "forces of society." ... The "private" sphere was thus withdrawn from the state and handed over to the "free," that is, uncontrolled and invisible forces of "society." ... From the duality of state and state-free society arose a social pluralism in which the "indirect powers" could celebrate effortless triumphs. ... The leviathan, in the sense of a myth of the state as the "huge machine," collapsed when a distinction was drawn between the state and individual freedom. That happened when the organizations of individual freedom were used like knives by anti-individualistic forces to cut up the leviathan and divide his flesh among themselves. Thus died the mortal god for the second time. (2008c, 73–74)

Clearly, Schmitt thought that the detour taken by political theology through the concept of the political did not succeed in protecting Hobbes's conception of political form and of representation from the attacks of democratic representation. The continuity of pluralism as the polemical object in Schmitt's work is a decisive textual argument against those interpretations of Schmitt that wish to establish a major break between that work and the earlier *Political Theology*. On this question see McCormick 1998; 2010.

19. Apart from Martel 2007 and Garsten 2010 discussed later herein, see also Edwards 2009; Colodrero 2011.

20. Martel also argues that for Hobbes the sovereign person may be an idol when compared to the personations of Moses and Jesus. But unlike Garsten this is not because the device of personation is an imposture as such. On the contrary, for Martel the reason that Hobbes ironically undermines the sovereign personation is because he understands the personations of God as "a completely alternative notion of representation set amid the discussion of terrestrial sovereignty" (2007, 133).

21. The discussion of Peterson's alternative Christian political theology was first put forward in several essays in Taubes 1983 and then was discussed at length in Nichtweiss 2001 and recently again in Schmidt 2009. Schmidt downplays the juridical and political understanding of Christ's kingship in Peterson, essentially reducing the legitimate political action by the church to an "apocalyptic intervention of martyrdom" (Schmidt 2009, 123). Missing from this perspective, as from Geréby 2008; Hohendahl 2008, is the idea that the dualism of church and empire conforms the concrete order of Jesus's kingdom and that

their law is the law of the people of Jesus Christ. Meier dedicates one footnote to the entire question of Peterson's theopolitics (2011, 172 n145).

22. On the *katechon*, see now the latest discussion in Cacciari 2013; Esposito 2013.
23. I therefore disagree with Kahn (2009, 84–86), who sees a major distinction here between Schmitt and Kantorowicz. The centrality of the idea of the mystical body for Schmitt's reinterpretation of political theology in a democratic sense explains Schmitt's claim, in a 1969 letter, that "the problem of political theology concerns an inherently Christian problem, which, only through the Reformation (namely, through the battle for the jus reformandi) reached the historically concrete stage of reflection on which I operate. Expressed theologically it is a Christological problem and immanent to Christian theology of the Trinity as such: the two natures of the actual God-Man as a single person. Those you named (beginning with Varro and Augustine…) did not know it" (as quoted in Meier 2011, 202 n48). The reason that Christology attains a climax in the Reformation is because of the Puritan attempt to realize the kingdom of God on earth in and through a democratic revolution that accelerates the end of history, putting an end to both church and empire. This is the specter against which Voegelin and Löwith write their critiques of secularization, and to which Schmitt is belatedly reacting to as well; see for instance Schmitt's last published interpretation of Hobbes in "Die vollendete Reformation: Bemerkungen und Hinweise zu neuen Leviathan-Interpretationen" published in 1965 and now found in Schmitt 1982.
24. On the different senses of enemy and the tension with the Christian commandment to love one's enemy, see Taubes 1993; Schmitt 1996a; Derrida 1997; Meier 1998.
25. For the case of Maritain, see Vatter 2013.
26. Paradoxically, Bakunin seems to reject this polemical reading. With regard to the question of stasiology in the Trinity, he writes: "[A]gainst that God the Son in whose name they [church and state] assume to impose upon us their insolent and pedantic authority, we appeal to God the Father, who is the real world, real life, of which he (the Son) is only a too imperfect expression" (1970, 35). In other words, Bakunin sides with God the father and not God the son, whereas on Meier's 2011 reading of Christ as rebel and anarchist he should side with the latter. Since Schmitt had read Bakunin and was surely aware of this passage, it would hardly make sense if he had understood the Goethean motto as a call to resist the Son, for that would have placed him in the same camp as Bakunin. So much for Meier's interpretation of Goethe's motto.
27. On the problem of government in medieval and early modern jurisprudence, see McIlwain's 1947 classic work and more recently Duso 2006.
28. But see the Prologue by Dotti to Schmitt 2009 where an attempt is made to link Schmitt's theory of representation with the question of the economy.

References

Agamben, G. 2007. *Il Regno e la Gloria: Per una genealogia teologica dell'economia e del governo.* Rome: Neri Pozza Editore.

Agamben, G. 2008. *Signatura Rerum: Sul metodo.* Torino: Bollati Boringhieri.

Agamben, G. 2010. *La Chiesa e il Regno.* Roma: Nottetempo.

Assmann, J. 2002. *Herrschaft und Heil: Politische Theologie in Altaegypten, Israel und Europa.* Frankfurt: Fischer.

Bakunin, M. 1970. *God and the State.* New York: Dover.

Baume, S. 2009. "On Political Theology: A Controversy between Hans Kelsen and Carl Schmitt." *History of European Ideas* 35: 369–381.

Blumenberg, H. 1996. *Die Legitimität der Neuzeit*. Frankfurt: Suhrkamp.

Böckenförde, E.-W. 1983. "Politische Theorie und politische Theologie." In *Der Fürst dieser Welt: Carl Schmitt und die Folgen*, ed. J. Taubes. Munich: Fink, 16–25.

Cacciari, M. 2013. *Il potere che frena*. Milan: Adelphi.

Chen, J. 2006. "What Is Carl Schmitt's Political Theology?" *Interpretation: A Journal of Political Philosophy* 33: 153–176.

Clarke, M. V. 1936. *Medieval Representation and Consent*. London: Longman.

Colodrero, A. 2011. "Theology and Politics in Thomas Hobbes's Trinitarian Theory." *Hobbes Studies* 24: 62–77.

Deuser, H. 1999. "Inkarnation und Repräsentation: Wie Gott und Mensch zusammengehören." *Theologische Literaturzeitung* 124: 355–370.

Derrida, J. 1997. *Politics of Friendship*. London: Verso.

Dotti, J. 2009. "Jahvé, Sion, Schmitt: Las tribulaciones del joven Strauss." *Deus Mortalis* 8: 147–240.

Duso, G. 2003. *La rappresentanza politica: Genesi e crisi del concetto*. Milan: Angeli.

Duso, G. 2006. "La democrazia e il problema del governo." *Filosofia Politica* 20: 367–390.

Edwards, J. J. 2009. "Calvin and Hobbes. Trinity, Authority, and Community." *Philosophy and Rhetoric* 42: 115–133.

Espejo, P. 2010. "On Political Theology and the Possibility of Superseding It." *Critical Review of International Social and Political Philosophy* 13: 1–37.

Esposito, R. 2013. *Due: La macchina della teologia politica e il posto del pensiero*. Turin: Einaudi.

Forti, S. 2012. *I nuovi demoni: Ripensare oggi male e potere*. Milan: Feltrinelli.

Galli, C. 1996. *Genealogia della politica: Carl Schmitt e la crisi del pensiero politico moderno*. Bologna: Il Mulino.

Galli, C. 2008. *Lo sguardo di Giano: Saggi su Carl Schmitt*. Bologna: Il Mulino.

Garsten, B. 2010. "Religion and Representation in Hobbes." In *Thomas Hobbes: Leviathan*, ed. I. Shapiro. New Haven: Yale University Press.

Geréby, G. 2008. "Political Theology versus Theological Politics: Erik Peterson and Carl Schmitt." *New German Critique* 35: 7–33.

Hobbes, T. 2010. *Leviathan*, ed. I. Shapiro. New Haven: Yale University Press.

Hofmann, H. 2007. *Rappresentanza-Rappresentazione: Parola e concetto dall'antichità all'ottocento*. Milan: Giuffrè Editore.

Hohendahl, P. 2008. "Political Theology Revisited: Carl Schmitt's Postwar Reassessment." *Konturen* 1: 1–28.

Hoibraaten, H. 2011. "Carl Schmitt, Henrik Ibsen und die Politische Theologie." In *Henrik Ibsens "Kaiser und Galileaer": Quellen—Interpretationen—Rezeptionen*, ed. H. H. Faber. Würzburg: Königshausen & Neumann.

Kahn, V. 2009. "Political Theology and Fiction in *The King's Two Bodies*." *Representations* 106: 77–101.

Kahn, P. 2011. *Political Theology: Four New Chapters on the Concept of Sovereignty*. New York: Columbia University Press.

Kantorowicz, E. H. 1997. *The King's Two Bodies: A Study in Medieval Political Theology*. Princeton: Princeton University Press.

Kelsen, H. 1919. "Zur Theorie der juristischen Fiktionen: Mit besonderer Berücksichtigung von Vaihinger's Philosophie des Als Ob." *Annalen der Philosophie* 1: 630–658.

Kelsen, H. 1973. *Essays in Legal and Moral Philosophy*. Dordrecht: Reidel.

Kelsen, H. 1981. *Der soziologische und der juristische Staatsbegriff: Kritische Untersuchung des Verhältnisses von Staat und Recht*. Amsterdam: Scientia.

Kervégan, J.-F. 2005. *Hegel, Carl Schmitt: la politique entre spéculation et positivité*. Paris: PUF.

Kervégan, J.-F. 2009. "¿Qué significa ser un teólogo de la jurisprudencia?" *Deus Mortalis. Cuaderno de Filosofía Política* 8: 91–102.

Laski, H. 1968. *Studies in the Problem of Sovereignty*. London: Allen & Unwin.

Lewis, E. 1964. "King above Law? 'Quod Principi Placuit' in Bracton." *Speculum* 39: 240–269.

Martel, J. 2007. *Subverting the Leviathan: Reading Thomas Hobbes as a Radical Democrat*. New York: Columbia University Press.

McCormick, J. P. 1998. "Political Theory and Political Theology: The Second Wave of Carl Schmitt in English." *Political Theory* 26: 830–854.

McCormick, J. P. 2010. "From Roman Catholicism to Mechanized Oppression: On Politico-theological Disjunctures in Schmitt's Weimar Thought." *Critical Review of International Social and Political Philosophy* 13: 391–398.

McIlwain, C. H. 1947. *Constitutionalism: Ancient and Modern*. Ithaca: Cornell University Press.

Meier, H. 1995. *Carl Schmitt and Leo Strauss: The Hidden Dialogue*. Chicago: University of Chicago Press.

Meier, H. 1998. *The Lesson of Carl Schmitt: Four Chapters on the Distinction between Political Theology and Political Philosophy*. Chicago: University of Chicago Press.

Meier, H. 2011. *The Lesson of Carl Schmitt: Four Chapters on the Distinction between Political Theology and Political Philosophy*, expanded ed. Chicago: University of Chicago Press.

Metz, J. B., J. Moltmann and W. Oelmueller. 1970. *Kirche im Prozess der Aufklärung: Aspekte einer neuen "Politische Theologie."* Munich: Kaiser.

Milbank, J. 2006. *Theology and Social Theory*, 2nd ed. London: Blackwell.

Mohler, A. ed. 1995. *Carl Schmitt: Briefwechsel mit einem seiner Schüler*. Berlin: Akademie Verlag.

Nichtweiss, B. ed. 2001. *Vom Ende der Zeit: Geschichtstheologie und Eschatologie bei Erik Peterson*. Berlin: Lit.

Nishiyama, C., and K. Leube. eds. 1984. *The Essence of Hayek*. Stanford: Hoover Institution Press.

Oakley, F. 1968. "Jacobean Political Theology: The Absolute and Ordinary Powers of the King." *Journal of the History of Ideas* 29: 323–346.

Palélogue, T. 2004. *Sous l'oeil du Grand Inquisiteur: Carl Schmitt et l'héritage de la théologie politique*. Paris: Les Éditions du Cerf.

Peterson, E. 1997. *Der Brief an die Römer*. In *Ausgewählte Schriften*, vol. 6, ed. B. Nichtweiss. Würzburg: Echter.

Peterson, E. 2011. *Theological Tractates*. Stanford: Stanford University Press.

Peterson, E. 2012. *Heis Theos: Epigraphische, formgeschichtliche und religionsgeschichtliche Untersuchungen zur antiken "Ein-Gott" Akklamation*. In *Ausgewählte Schriften*, vol. 8, ed. C. Markschies. Würzburg: Echter.

Pitkin, H. 1967. *The Concept of Representation*. Berkeley: University of California Press.

Runciman, D. 2005. *Pluralism and the Personality of the State*. Cambridge: Cambridge University Press.

Schmidt, C. 2009. *Die theopolitische Stunde*. Munich: Fink.

Schmitt, C. 1982. *Der Leviathan in der Staatslehre des Thomas Hobbes*. Stuttgart: Klett-Cotta.

Schmitt, C. 1988. *Political Theology: Four Chapters on the Concept of Sovereignty*, trans. G. Schwab. Cambridge: MIT Press.

Schmitt, C. 1991. *Glossarium: Aufzeichnungen der Jahre 1947–1951*. Berlin: Duncker & Humblot.

Schmitt, C. 1995. *Les trois types de pensée juridique*. Paris: PUF.

Schmitt, C. 1996a. *The Concept of the Political*, trans. G. Schwab. Chicago: University of Chicago Press.

Schmitt, C. 1996b. *Roman Catholicism and Political Form*, trans. G. L. Ulmen. Westport: Greenwood Press.

Schmitt, C. 2003. *The "Nomos" of the Earth in the International Law of "Jus Publicum Europaeum,"* trans. G. L. Ulmen. New York: Telos Press.

Schmitt, C. 2007. *The Concept of the Political*, trans. G. Schwab, expanded ed. Chicago: University of Chicago Press.

Schmitt, C. 2008a. *Political Theology II: The Myth of the Closure of Any Political Theology*. Cambridge: Polity Press.

Schmitt, C. 2008b. *Constitutional Theory*, trans. and ed. J. Seitzer. Durham: Duke University Press.

Schmitt, C. 2008c. *The Leviathan in the State Theory of Thomas Hobbes: Meaning and Failure of a Political Symbol*, trans. G. Schwab. Chicago: University of Chicago Press.

Schmitt, C. 2009. *Tiranía de los valores*, ed. J. Dotti. Buenos Aires: Hydra.

Schmitz, A., and M. Lepper. eds. 2007. *Hans Blumenberg und Carl Schmitt: Briefwechsel 1971–1978*. Frankfurt: Suhrkamp.

Skinner, Q. 2005. "Hobbes on Representation." *European Journal of Philosophy* 13: 157–184.

Stanton, T. 2011. "Hobbes and Schmitt." *History of European Ideas* 37: 160–167.

Tanguay-Renaud, F. 2010. "The Intelligibility of Extralegal State Action." *Legal Theory* 16: 161–189.

Taubes, J. 1993. *Die Politische Thelogie des Paulus*. Munich: Fink.

Taubes, J. ed. 1983. *Der Fürst dieser Welt: Carl Schmitt und die Folgen*. Munich: Fink.

Taylor, C. 2007. *A Secular Age*. Cambridge: Harvard University Press.

Ullmann, W. 1980. *Jurisprudence in the Middle Ages: Collected Studies*. London: Variorum.

Urbinati, N. 2006. *Representative Democracy: Principles and Genealogy*. Chicago: University of Chicago Press.

Vatter, M. 2004. "Strauss and Schmitt as Readers of Hobbes and Spinoza: On the Relation between Liberalism and Political Theology." *New Centennial Review* 4: 161–214.

Vatter, M. 2008. "The Idea of Public Reason and the Reason of State: Schmitt and Rawls on the Political." *Political Theory* 36: 239–271.

Vatter, M. 2013. "Politico-Theological Foundations of Universal Rights: The Case of Maritain." *Social Research* 80: 233–260.

Voegelin, E. 1952. *The New Science of Politics*. Chicago: University of Chicago Press.

Weber, S. 2005. *Targets of Opportunity: On the Militarization of Thinking*. New York: Fordham University Press.

CHAPTER 9

....

TEACHING IN VAIN

Carl Schmitt, Thomas Hobbes,
and the Theory of the Sovereign State

....

JOHN P. McCORMICK

INTRODUCTION

....

CARL SCHMITT's *The Concept of the Political* (2007) attempts to reformulate the intellectual basis of the state in the midst of its twentieth-century crisis—a basis whose founding Schmitt attributes to the great English philosopher, Thomas Hobbes of Malmesbury. According to Schmitt, over the course of several centuries liberal theory and practice has undermined the unity, the integrity, of the state and has put European nations, particularly Germany, back in circumstances similar to those that confronted Hobbes during the English Civil War and the continental Wars of Religion. In particular, Schmitt seeks to return to the sovereign state the monopoly over *the political* that liberalism wrested from it during intervening centuries. He draws upon Hobbes in his effort to restore the state's monopoly over violence and, more problematically, over the subjective disposition of individuals who might be inclined to use violence unilaterally.

Schmitt famously insists that the political corresponds to the fact of human enmity—the factuality, the facticity, of the eternal human propensity to make distinctions between friends and enemies. The political pertains to the existential reality that humans resort to mortal violence, lethal force, to make or sustain friend/enemy dissociations, us-versus-them groupings. Since the age of absolutism that Hobbes helped initiate and solidify, social groups, invoking universal rights, have progressively weakened the sovereign state's monopoly over friend/enemy decisions. In the middle of what he asserts to be the state's final, most decisive crisis in Germany's Weimar Republic, Schmitt endeavors to recast the bargain that Hobbes offered the would-be subjects of his leviathan state. By recasting this political bond on collective rather than individualist grounds, Schmitt aspires to render the sovereign state securely authoritarian again and to definitively inoc-ulate it against all future liberal subversions.

Liberals, Schmitt charges, have selectively emphasized the fundamentally unstable aspects of Hobbes's political theory in order to weaken his leviathan state with deleteri-ous results for domestic peace and international order: they insist that the state is gov-erned by an economic rationality that posits a social contract from which individual parties may defect, more or less at their whim. On the contrary, Schmitt asserts that subjects are tethered more securely to the sovereign state by two other elements that are prevalent in Hobbesian political philosophy: a quasi-Catholic juridical rationality that renders the sovereign a representative person who amounts to something much more qualitatively than the sum total of the wills that created or empowered him; and the irra-tional element of *myth* that allows individuals to perceive themselves to be part of a col-lectivity with a historical or providential mission.

By the time he devotes an entire book exclusively to Hobbes, *Der Leviathan in der Staatslehre des Thomas Hobbes (The Leviathan in the State Theory of Thomas Hobbes)* (2008a), Schmitt, who had joined the ascendant Nazi Party he once publicly criticized, expresses serious reservations about Hobbes's state theory and, by extension, salient aspects of his own earlier appropriation of it. Schmitt, now thoroughly discredited with and, he fancied, physically threatened by the party, implies that the Nazi regime was no state at all. His book on *Leviathan*, which may be interpreted, somewhat perversely, as both his most Nazi and least Nazi intellectual effort under the "Third Reich," very subtly criticizes the Reich for resembling nothing remotely so noble as a leviathan state but rather for becoming a mechanized, bureaucratic apparatus that was seized by partisan social forces and put to the thuggish ends of pure intolerance and oppression. Schmitt intimates that the "Third Reich" more closely approximates the fundamentally dys-functional, disordered political entity that Hobbes described in *Behemoth; or the Long Parliament* (1889) rather than the one he endorsed in *Leviathan; or, The Matter, Forme and Power of a Commonwealth, Ecclesiasticall and Civill* (1991).[1]

However, Schmitt attributes ultimate blame for the demise of the classical European, leviathan state and the rise of the extraordinarily oppressive, behemoth-like "Third Reich" neither to the Malmesbury philosopher nor to himself, Hobbes's Plettenberg devotee. Instead, in this overtly, virulently, almost cartoonish antisemitic book, liberals—especially liberal Jews—fiendishly perverted Hobbes's state theory, permit-ting more radical political movements like anarchism, Bolshevism and, even, Schmitt intimates, Nazism to appropriate the leviathan for their own ends. In so doing, they ren-dered hopelessly ineffective any supposedly good faith attempts, like Schmitt's, to revive the Hobbesian state.

In what follows, I trace Schmitt's attempt in *The Concept of the Political* to quell the near civil war circumstances of the late Weimar Republic and to reinvigorate the sover-eignty of the German state by reinstilling within German citizens the Hobbesian bargain of *protection for obedience*. Schmitt's efforts, I suggest, were challenged by two powerful forces: the intellectual critique of the young Leo Strauss; and the historical fact of Nazi ascendance in Germany. For Strauss, Schmitt's effort to refortify the Hobbesian state was insufficiently fundamental: Schmitt's attempt to revive Hobbesian state theory as a solution to the crisis of liberalism, according to Strauss, "remained within the horizon of liberalism" (1952a, 105). To get beyond the sociopolitical crisis engendered by the failings of contemporary liberalism, Strauss averred, Schmitt needed to get beyond Hobbes, who stood as the founder of modern liberalism, not as a potential resource in its overcoming.

Strauss insisted that a nightwatchman's state of the kind Hobbes proposed and Schmitt sought to revive—however authoritarian Hobbes and Schmitt thought that state to be—was destined to permit society to rebel against the state in one form of civil war or another. Modern state theory, on the contrary, Strauss insists, required resources drawn from classical Platonic philosophy and biblical religion to justify the imposition of substantive notions of truth, beauty, and justice upon society—resources that Hobbes, the enemy of religious authority, radically undermined in his state theory and that Schmitt, the embarrassed former Roman Catholic, conspicuously eschewed in his revival of the Hobbesian state. For its part, National Socialism, quite simply, as I demonstrate, first appeared to Schmitt as the solution to the failings of liberalism and then represented the very culmination of those failings. I conclude the essay by examining Schmitt's responses to both Strauss's critique and to Nazi ascendance in his *Leviathan* book.

THE ACCOMPLISHMENTS
OF THE HOBBESIAN STATE

As the first line of Schmitt's 1932 book makes plain, the Plettenberg jurist apparently considers the political to be more fundamental than the state: "the concept of the state presupposes the concept of the political" (2007, 19). Before the modern state, and before Hobbes's elegant and eloquent theorization of it, the political was fluid and completely unruly; the political was barely controllable by multifarious secular and ecclesiastical authorities, whose borders and jurisdictions were overlapping, incoherent, and inefficient. Different groups within the same polity had the right and authority to inflict bodily harm and even kill for social, political, or religious reasons. The Hobbesian state, Schmitt suggests, was founded in a particular moment when the sphere of religion took on political intensity—a moment when members of the same society would kill fellow subjects or citizens because they were Catholic or Protestant or, for that matter, the wrong kind of Protestant. Hobbes and the modern state make it possible, in a historically unprecedented fashion, to govern the political more effectively: not eliminate it—because, as Schmitt insists, the political can never be eliminated from human affairs—but rather institutionalize it.

The Hobbesian state monopolizes decisions over the political; it removes the prerogative to use lethal force from the subjective domain of social groups. Catholics and Protestants, monarchists and parliamentarians, aristocrats and bourgeoisie will not take up arms against each other within the strictly defined geographical borders of the state. The sovereign state now has a monopoly on the use of violence within a territorially defined realm. The state secures this monopoly by promising its subjects protection in exchange for their obedience. Just as modern philosophy is founded on the Cartesian presupposition "I think, therefore I am," modern politics, Schmitt avers, is founded on the Hobbesian principle "protection, therefore obedience" (2007, 52). The state assures its subjects that private parties will never threaten their bodily integrity; in fact, neither will the state itself threaten the bodily integrity of subjects unless such subjects threaten the well-being of others or the stability of the state.

Hobbes proposes this bargain to individuals who constitute antagonistic groups, thus neutralizing the affective allure of such attachments as well as the virulence of such groups' animosity toward others. No longer primarily members of a religious community or a social class, individuals contract directly with each other to create a sovereign. Once they pledge obedience to the sovereign state, the latter protects individuals from inquisitions and witch trials, from reckless and overbearing aristocrats, and eventually, in theory, from exploitative captains of industry. Henceforth, no private person, group, or institution will decide the political; only the state decides who is friend and who is enemy. Schmitt consciously echoes Max Weber here: Through territorial contiguity and a monopoly on domestic violence, the state vacuums up political remnants from all corners and crevices of society, consolidates them in the single person of the sovereign, and directs the now unified political externally into conflict with enemies in the international realm.

So effective is the modern state as an institution, according to Schmitt, that the international order also becomes effectively regulated as a result of its development. The balance of power that results from independent sovereign states aligning with and against each other, the so-called Westphalian state system, manages the political on an international level. Sovereign states that control the political within their own borders recognize each other's right of existence in the international arena. This system deters wars of conquest and annihilation on European soil, even as such wars continue to be prosecuted mercilessly on distant continents and oceans during the age of exploration and colonization.[2]

Eighteenth- and nineteenth-century wars within Europe, Schmitt posits somewhat romantically, were waged not to subjugate or eliminate enemy states but only to alter the relative weight of each within the international balance of power. Hence, Schmitt claims that these conflicts were not "total" wars (2007, 34–35); besides guaranteeing the continued existence of combatants, potential and real, these wars rarely involved whole populations, and civilians remained largely unmolested. Professional armies engaged on a field of battle, after which swords were transferred from the vanquished to the victor. Treaties were signed, borders rearranged, and eventually alliances reconfigured. This economy of violence began to break down, Schmitt suggests, only with the French Revolution, which made civil wars international wars, initiating a process of desovereignization and depoliticization that culminated disastrously in World War I.

THE DECLINE OF THE
HOBBESIAN STATE SYSTEM

On Schmitt's understanding, for centuries the sovereign state effectively defused civil wars domestically, and the state system efficiently managed interstate conflict internationally. Nevertheless, Schmitt suggests that both the sovereign state model and Hobbes's philosophical formulation of it were flawed. Both allowed the state to be undermined from within and from without. As subjects surrender their subjective opinions over the political to the state, Hobbes granted them an ostensibly less volatile subjective freedom: individuals are free to think whatever they want so long as they do not act and especially resort to violence on the basis of what they think. This freedom of conscience is followed soon by economic rights: in pursuit of commodious living, subjects may rightfully engage in commercial exchange with rather than armed conflict against their fellow subjects. According to Schmitt, freedom of conscience and economic activity eventually threaten the state and upset the state-secured equilibrium of the political.

On one hand, freedom of conscience spawns Kantian normativism, deeply subjective in its origin and expansively universal in its claims. On the other hand, commercial activity allows particularistic interests to grow in power and stymie the state's supervision of society. Moreover, economic activity contributes to the emergence of the capitalist and working classes, a development that portends a new era of civil war. Thus, domestically, the state was beset by a crisis of parliamentary government: justified by liberal rights, particularist interests gained a foothold against the state in parliament, gumming up its works and threatening to topple it.

Internationally, the more commercially successful nations, especially the Franco–Anglo–American alliance, instrumentalize universal morality with the purpose of disrupting the Westphalian order and crippling so-called bestial, criminal, and rogue states like Germany. Instead of mutual recognition of sovereign states, universal ideals of perpetual peace and human rights allow liberal nations to stigmatize vanquished nations as aggressive war criminals, indeed, as enemies of humanity (2007, 35). After World War I, the victorious allies vilified Germany from the standpoint of morality rather than treating it in objective political terms simply as a defeated enemy. At Versailles, Germany was most certainly *not* considered an equal member of the Westphalian brotherhood of states who simply happened to lose a war. On the contrary, Schmitt seethes, Germany was treated as a monster that must be not only defeated but also humiliated—and perhaps destroyed.

In World War I, known by some as the Great War, the liberal capitalist nations fought a so-called war to end all wars and therefore changed the rules of engagement (2007, 36). Drastic means, Schmitt complains, which are unprecedented in the history of warfare, must be enlisted in a struggle to end war as such; draconian punishments, unprecedented in the history of diplomacy, must be enforced against the enemies of humanity.

Thus, potentially devastating total wars against criminals necessarily supplant the more civilized eighteenth-century type of war between mere enemies. Subsequently, the liberal nations replace the no-fault surrender characteristic of the eighteenth century with the kind of vengeful peace inflicted on Germany at Versailles. It is tempting to reduce Schmitt's complaints here to base resentment. But he certainly has a point: compare Germany's treatment of defeated France in 1870 with France's treatment of vanquished Germany in 1919.

Schmitt's point is that Hobbes's state of nature has returned in both the domestic and international realms. He notes that workers now look to Moscow, a foreign capital, for guidance against their own state, just as traitorous Catholics once looked to Rome. Clever states now cynically use universal morality, whether free trade or international revolution, to cover their imperialist designs, just as princes once used the similar transnational cover of religion. According to Schmitt, honesty regarding the political has evaporated, with devastating results. To restore such honesty, and consequently restore order, a new cogito of the state is required—one that will permit the state to neutralize the political, domestically, so that it might prosecute the friend/enemy distinction more effectively abroad. In *The Concept of the Political*, Schmitt attempts to restore the Hobbesian status quo ante—or, rather, to institute an amended version of the Hobbesian project, one less susceptible to internal subversion and external exploitation.

The Place of Hobbes in Schmitt's *The Concept of the Political*

In *The Concept of the Political*, Schmitt sets forth his most famous thesis: "the specific political distinction to which political actions and motives can be reduced is that between friend and enemy" (2007, 26). Yet despite the apparent novelty of this proposition, one finds the shadow of Hobbes cast quite prominently over this famous treatise. As Hobbes maintained, in humanity's natural condition, "every man to every man, for want of a common power to keep them all in awe, is an Enemy" (1991, I. 15, 102).[3] Indeed, Schmitt's friend/enemy distinction is intended to serve a theoretical-political role analogous to Hobbes's state of nature. If Hobbes predicated the modern state on the natural condition, Schmitt again declares that "the concept of the state presupposes the concept of the political." Any inquiries into the "essence" of the state that do not first consider this foundation are necessarily premature (2007, 19). Whether the state is "a machine or an organism, a person or an institution, a society or a community, an enterprise or a beehive"—questions in which Schmitt is quite interested must be, he insists, provisionally set aside (19).

Schmitt thus understands his formulation of the political as an Archimedean point not unlike what Hobbes located in the state of nature. The political, according to Schmitt, is irreducible to any other element. It is distinct from the aesthetic, the economic, the moral, and the theological spheres of human life as well as the antithesis that constitutes its essence differs from those corresponding with those other spheres: good and evil in the moral sphere, beautiful and ugly in the aesthetic sphere, and so on. Human enmity is simply beyond good and evil in the moral realm; it exists independent of categories such as beautiful and ugly in the aesthetic realm. Schmitt assures readers that the enemy need not be evil or ugly (2007, 27). The enemy is simply the embodiment of an alternative, "different and alien," way of being, one that by virtue of its inherent otherness potentially threatens one's own (27).

However, even though the political stands independent of these other concepts that constitute the various spheres of human life, these spheres may at some point become, in an existential sense, political if groups of people were to raise the possibility, the threat, of deadly force in pursuit of any of these other distinctions. If religious distinctions, economic distinctions, even, theoretically, aesthetic distinctions, develop into potentially mortal distinctions among groups, then they are no longer strictly religious, economic, or aesthetic but now primarily political (2007, 36). Thus, the political derives its content, its substance, from the potential for life-threatening violence posed by various human groupings, *not* from the specific issue over which that violence might be deployed. In the end, Schmitt envisions the friend/enemy distinction as so fundamental and elementary that in the course of his argument he feels compelled at particular points to remark on the self-evidence of his thesis: "nothing can escape this logical conclusion of the political" (36).

"Terrible Times of Civil War": Stuart England and Weimar Germany

The Hobbesian quality of Schmitt's project derives in no small part from the similar sociopolitical situations shared by the Malmesbury philosopher and the Plettenberg jurist. Schmitt observes that Hobbes formulated his political theory "in the terrible times of civil war" where

> all legitimate and normative illusions with which men like to deceive themselves regarding political realities in periods of untroubled security vanish. If within the state there are organized parties capable of affording their members more protection than the state, then the latter becomes at best an annex of such parties, and the individual subject knows whom he has to obey (2007, 52).

This also happens to be an excellent description of Weimar Germany during its most acute crisis years. Schmitt recognizes in the context of Hobbes's thought a parallel with his own and hence a parallel in their projects.

Hobbes, in *Leviathan*, sought "to instill in man again 'the mutual relation between Protection and Obedience'" (52) and thus to forestall the strife and chaos that arises when armed autonomous groups confront each other as enemies. This is not far removed from Schmitt's own intentions. The exceptional situation of civil war reveals normally concealed political realities such as human behavior in the absence of authority: "in it, states exist among themselves in a condition of continual danger, and their acting subjects are evil for precisely the same reasons as animals who are stirred by their drives (hunger, greediness, fear, jealousy)" (59). Because civil war reveals man's fundamental evil, Schmitt argues, all "genuine" political theories—those that have confronted head-on the normally concealed "political realities"—presuppose "man to be evil," meaning "dangerous and dynamic" (61).

Schmitt thus shares with Hobbes not only a similar theoretical context (i.e., civil war) but also a similar, pessimistic outlook on humanity (i.e., human evil). What are the ramifications of this? This outlook points the way out of the natural condition, civil war, or impending civil war. Of the genuine political philosophers who take the view that human beings are essentially dangerous, Schmitt writes, "their realism can frighten men in need of security" (2007, 65). This is precisely the point. Schmitt recognizes, as did Hobbes, that by frightening men one can best "instill" in them that principle, "the *cogito ergo sum* of the state," *protego ergo obligo* (52). In other words, fear is the most fundamental source of political order. "Fear," Hobbes wrote, is "the Passion to be reckoned on" (1991, I. 14, 99). Human beings, once confronted with the reality of their own dangerousness, will be terrified into the arms of authority, however imperfect they may previously have thought such authority to be.

Thus, as Schmitt explains, "For Hobbes, truly a powerful and systematic political thinker, the pessimistic conception of man is the elementary presupposition of a specific system of political thought" (2007, 65). But systematic most decidedly does not mean scientific or technical, Hobbes's Euclidean, Galilean, or geometrician pretensions notwithstanding. As Schmitt observed concerning Hobbes a decade earlier, in *Political Theology*:

> It is striking that one of the most consequential representatives of abstract scientific orientation of the seventeenth century became so personalistic. This is because as a juristic thinker he wanted to grasp the reality of societal life just as much as he, as a philosopher and a natural scientist, wanted to grasp the reality of nature.... Juristic thought in those days had not yet become so overpowered by the natural sciences that he, in the intensity of his scientific approach, should unsuspectingly have overlooked the specific reality of legal life. (2006, 34)

As far as Schmitt is concerned, Hobbes the philosophical and juristic thinker who grapples with human reality takes precedence over Hobbes the mechanistic and mathematical thinker concerned with logic and natural science.

The stakes of this distinction are high for Schmitt. After all, he argues, natural science and technology have helped foster the liberal conception of man that undermined Hobbes's greatest accomplishment, the sovereign state. Natural-scientific and technical thinking have enhanced the faulty view that, with wealth and abundance, humanity's dangerousness can be ameliorated and hence blinds humanity to the eternal reality of

the political (2007, 61). Technology, according to Schmitt, has aided in the neutralization of the state and the European order of states, again concealing the nature of the
political (90–93). In this spirit, he chides Eduard Spranger for taking "too technical"
a perspective on human nature, for viewing it in light of "the tactical manipulation of
instinctive drives" (59). Hobbes's insight, on the contrary, is neither "the product of a
frightful and disquieting fantasy nor of a philosophy based on free competition by a
bourgeois society in its first stage but is the fundamental presupposition of a specific
political philosophy" (65).[4]

Schmitt's task then is to elaborate and reformulate Hobbes's specific political philosophy, one that exhibits a juridical interest in the specific reality of legal life. He seeks to
revive the fear that is characteristic of man's natural condition: by demonstrating the
substantive affinity between his concept of the political and Hobbes's state of nature;
by making clear the ever-present possibility of a return to that situation in the form of
civil war; and by convincing individuals—partisans and nonpartisans alike—that only
a state possessing a monopoly on decisions regarding the political can guarantee peace
and security. Schmitt seeks to accomplish all this while avoiding the elements of natural
science and technology often associated with Hobbes, elements that eventually undermined the Hobbesian state.

Radical Subjectivity
and Remissly Governed Subjects

The radical subjectivity characteristic of the political heightens the danger regarding
Schmitt's concept of the political and consequently intensifies the fear that it inspires.
"Only the actual participants can correctly recognize, understand, and judge the concrete situation and settle the extreme case of conflict. Each participant is in a position to
judge whether the adversary intends to negate his opponent's way of life and therefore
must be repulsed or fought to preserve one's own form of existence" (Schmitt 2007, 27).
In the absence of a centralized power, there is no standard by which one can judge
another as an enemy or be so judged by them. Hence, one must always be ready to be
attacked, or, more reasonably, one is compelled to be the first to strike. This scenario
obviously revives the Hobbesian "condition of meer Nature" where all "are judges of the
justnesse of their own fears" (Hobbes 1991, I. 14, 96).

The persistence of this kind of subjectivity within society implies the continued threat
of war and the fear that it engenders. As Hobbes makes explicit, it is a "diseased" commonwealth that tolerates the doctrine, "That every private man is Judge of Good and Evil
actions" (I.29, 223), and worse, that allows persons to resort to violence to defend such
judgments, "for those men that are so remissely governed, that they dare take up Armes,
to defend, or introduce an Opinion, are still in Warre" (I.18, 125). Schmitt saw in the pluralist theories of the early twentieth century a justification for precisely such thinking

and acting (2007, 52), and like Hobbes, evaluated the outcome of such thinking as state vulnerability both domestically and with regard to foreign powers:

> The intensification of internal antagonisms has the effect of weakening the common identity vis-à-vis another state. If domestic conflicts among political parties have become the sole political difference, the most extreme degree of internal political tension is thereby reached; i.e., the domestic, not the foreign friend-and-enemy groupings are decisive for armed conflict. The ever present possibility of conflict must always be kept in mind. If one wants to speak of politics in the context of the primacy of internal politics, then this conflict no longer refers to war between organized nations but to civil war. (2007, 32)

Hobbes (1991, II.22, 164) adamantly maintains that the existence of violent factions, whether constituted by familial ties, religious affiliation, or economic status, is "contrary to the peace and safety of the people, a taking of the Sword out of the hand of the Sovereign." And it is precisely these kinds of armed antagonisms that characterized Weimar during its most intense periods of crisis: trade union members versus company goons; communist versus fascist paramilitaries; political party partisans versus their rivals, and so on. Each had declared the right to evaluate self-protection in its own way and to act accordingly. Each had claimed the right to judge the political (Schmitt 2007, 37).

Schmitt wants desperately to demonstrate that this situation portends a likely eruption into all-out civil war and return to Hobbes's natural condition. He must revive the fear that led to the termination of the natural condition to prevent a full-scale reversion to it. If groups other than the state have power, particularly power over declaring war— or worse, if they do not possess it themselves but can prevent the state from exercising that power itself—then the state disappears:

> It would be an indication that these counterforces had not reached the decisive point in the political if they turned out to be not sufficiently powerful to prevent a war contrary to their interests or principles. Should the counterforces be strong enough to hinder a war desired by the state that was contrary to their interests or principles but not sufficiently capable themselves of deciding about war, then a unified political entity would no longer exist. (2007, 39)

Schmitt's implicit reading of Hobbes, therefore suggests that a return to the state of nature is an ever-present possibility for any society. Both thinkers view the state of nature not as a factually historical past but rather as a politically possible present. Buttressing Schmitt's reading of Hobbes on this point more clearly demonstrates his own intentions. Schmitt seeks to make real the terror of what is and what might be so as to strengthen the existing order. For both Hobbes and Schmitt, the threat of danger is always present, even when the actual danger is not. As Hobbes remarks, the essence of war within the natural condition "consisteth not in actuall fighting; but in the known disposition thereto" (1991, I.13, 88–89); Schmitt, for his part, maintains that "to the enemy concept belongs the ever present *possibility* of combat" (2007, 32; emphasis added). The fear that one experiences while actually fighting, while engaging in combat for one's life, is not nearly so excruciating as the fear, or rather the anxiety, arising from the uncertainty over when the next such struggle will be necessary. In this light Schmitt endeavors to emphasize the conditions under which the following takes place: subjects give up their epistemological uncertainty regarding the totality of human nature in the natural condition, their fear of everything and everyone at every moment, for the much more tolerable knowledge within a state that it is only the sovereign that is to be feared and then only under certain conditions.

The radical subjectivity of individuals Hobbes identifies who exist without a central authority is the source of the danger Schmitt's political poses. The potential for war among human beings and the uncertainty arising from radical subjectivity intensify fear because they make felt the constancy of danger. Hence, according to Schmitt the citizens of Weimar must reaffirm the pact that delivers human beings out of the natural condition and into civil society by transferring their illegitimately exercised subjectivity regarding friend and enemy back to the sovereign state. "To the state as an essentially political entity belongs the *jus belli*, i.e., the real possibility of deciding in a concrete situation upon the enemy and the ability to fight him with the power emanating from the entity" (2007, 45). The state, and the state alone, decides on internal enemies (46) and external ones as well (28–29).

Regarding internal enemies, Schmitt seeks to refute the pluralist doctrine that posits the state as merely one interest group among many others within society or even as a mere servant of the latter (2007, 44). On the contrary, he insists, the state must stand above society as a quasi-objective entity rather than help precipitate civil war by conducting itself as one subjectivity among others. Regarding external enemies, just as Hobbes had Catholics in mind when he warned against allegiance to extra-national powers, Schmitt surely thinks of the communists when he writes that one should not "love and support the enemies of one's own people" (29). Moscow should come before Berlin no more than Rome before London or Paris. Only one's own state can ask one to surrender one's life for it (46), and Schmitt mocks liberal individualism for not being able to command this from citizens (71). But here he parts company with Hobbes, who is the most famous exponent of this kind of right—the right *not* to lay down one's life in response to a political command.

SOVEREIGN SUBJECTS: FROM DISCRETE INDIVIDUALS TO FIGHTING COLLECTIVITIES

How might, according to Schmitt, the state reappropriate social subjectivity over the political without granting society at least a trace of the dangerous subjective freedom that inevitably threatens the state? His answer is that obedience to the state must be pledged not by the free choice of individual subjects but rather by the acclamation of the people as a whole (2007, 38–39, 48–49). Schmitt often declared that the age of liberal individualism and of general ideas is over. The new democratic age demands that the people, the demos, rule themselves through the most direct means, namely, through a plebiscitarianly elected executive. The terms by which the people define themselves shall be concretely specific, not abstractly normative. The people should be first and foremost members of a homogeneous identity organization, not individual rights-bearing citizens (70–71). This means that identity trumps protection in the consolidation of the political community; Hobbes's strongest power, the most powerful individual capable of consolidating authority in the natural condition, becomes the strongest group.

In other words, Schmitt thinks he solves the crisis of the state by replacing Hobbes's individualism with a revived and radicalized version of Aristotelian social solidarity. He revives a notion of the natural human tendency toward sociality that Hobbes in many ways sought to dissolve. The predisposition of some groups of humans to live together according to specific ways of life allows Schmitt to postulate an unassailable collective existence of humans congregated around specific forms of life; those groups transpose to state authority something more existentially vital and willfully binding than could the contracting individuals in Hobbes's natural condition. Even though Hobbes does not formally permit any defection on the part of the individuals who have compacted to create a supreme authority, the individualism of the Hobbesian model of human social life persists within the commonwealth and renders it fundamentally unstable.

However, unlike Aristotle, Schmitt willfully resists any moral assessment of the particular substance that brings a specific collectivity together or, conversely, of the particular grounds on which they fight other collectivities bound by some other organizing substance. Schmitt will not even supply an account of the mechanisms, moral or not, that bring such people together to begin with and that keep them together; that is, he ignores what we conventionally understand as *politics*. At a more abstract level, Schmitt promotes social solidarity through the invocation at some points of a quasi-Catholic, juridical notion of "representation,"[5] and at others of a quasi-irrational "myth of the nation" (1923, 11–19)—and sometimes the two simultaneously.[6]

In Schmitt's early Weimar writings, such as *Political Theology* (2006) and *The Crisis of Parliamentary Democracy* (1985, 65–76), he suggested that there exist two competing forms of political integration available in the contemporary historical moment: Russian, class-based nationalism; or European nationalism mediated by culture, religion, ethnicity, or morality. This constitutes a choice, in practice, between Vladimir Lenin and Benito Mussolini, between Mikhail Bakunin and Juan Donoso Cortés, but a choice for nationalist identity in either case. The decision for nationalist homogeneity is not a rational choice, as was the original Hobbesian bargain, a strategic assessment calculated by bourgeois individuals. Democratic acclamation called for by the present moment is a spontaneous, existential choice by the people en masse for identity with the nation—a political choice empowering, in the Weimar Republic, the directly elected *Reichspräsident* to deal with heterogeneous entities domestically as well as with political forces abroad that pose threats to national existence (Schmitt 2007, 46–47). The president should be afforded full discretion to decide who are internal enemies and who are foreign enemies.

Within the text of *Concept of the Political*, Schmitt never specifies how domestic heterogeneity should be handled, how domestic enemies should be treated. Schmitt, as he did in *The Crisis of Parliamentary Democracy*, in 1923, appears to be agnostic regarding the specific substance of democratic homogeneity. He suggests that an appropriately political way of life could be constituted by identities formed around the phenomena of class, language, religion, or ethnicity. The people themselves decide the substance of their existence through the authority of the single individual they collectively acclaim to embody and transcend their wills and to act as a unified agent on their behalf. Nevertheless, actions speak more clearly than words.

As he prepared the book-length *The Concept of the Political* in 1932, Schmitt was advising the conservative aristocrats in President Paul von Hindenburg's circle how domestic enemies should be treated. Chancellor Franz von Papen, in particular, was encouraging Nazi Stormtroopers to beat down and intimidate communists, social democrats, and union members to suppress their electoral turnout; he then overthrew the legitimately elected social democratic government of Prussia to reduce that party's influence within national politics. Schmitt served as the administration's legal advocate and justified such measures before the German Supreme Court (see Dyzenhaus 1997, 121–134). When the Hindenburg clique failed to ensure the Republic's stability by violating its constitution in the ways that Schmitt advised, he offered his services to those who would altogether destroy both.

THE BARELY VISIBLE CRACK: SCHMITT'S *DER LEVIATHAN*

For several years, Schmitt held prominent judicial posts within Adolf Hitler's Reich and wrote notable treatises in its support. By 1936, however, Schmitt's unorthodox National Socialism, his past connection with political Catholicism, and his previous public denunciations of the party eventually ran him afoul of the SS. Schmitt, who had so eagerly justified Nazi policies of intimidation, brutality, and murder (especially after the notorious Röhm Purge, or "Night of the Long Knives"; see Schmitt 1934, 227–232), returned to Hobbes as the Reich's ever more vengeful and suspicious eye turned to the Plettenberg jurist himself.

Schmitt declares Hobbes's leviathan to be the "earthly" and "mortal" god that must time and time again bring man out of the "chaos" of the "natural condition" (2008a, 22). Hobbes asserted that leviathan was the "Mortall God," which "hath the use of so much Power and Strength conferred on him, that by terror thereof, he is enabled to conforme the wills of them all, to Peace at home, and mutuall ayd against their enemies abroad" (1991, II.17, 120–121). In *Der Leviathan*, we still find Schmitt defending Hobbes against those who would interpret him "superficially" as strictly a "rationalist, mechanist, sensualist, individualist" (2008a, 22). But Schmitt is more forthright in admitting that these elements, particularly the mechanistic, are present—in fact, ultimately decisive (30)—even though they do not constitute Hobbes's theory as a whole.

Schmitt emphasizes that there are three leviathans in Hobbes's book: the mythical monster; the representative person; and the machine (2008a, 30). Schmitt suggests that leviathan as myth or even as juridical person is an entity sufficiently capable of keeping men bound together in a stable commonwealth; however, these entities are superseded historically by the image of leviathan the machine, which comes to be viewed as a mere tool to be used by various social groups (54). In other words, Schmitt admits that his Weimar attempt to divorce the mechanistic elements from the vital or personalist elements in Hobbes and to elevate the latter over the former has proven historically untenable—he even implies that this outcome was inevitable. Compare, for instance Schmitt's (2006, 34) statement on the personalism of Hobbes's state theory in *Political Theology*, cited previously, with this quote from *Der Leviathan*:

> In Hobbes, the state is not in its entirety a person. The sovereign-representative person is only the soul of the "huge man" state. The process of mechanization is not however, arrested but completed by this personification. This personalistic element too is drawn into the mechanization process and becomes absorbed by it.... The "huge man" as the sovereign-representative person could not prevail in history. (2008a, 34)

However, Schmitt is determined to give the juridically representative and substantively mythical elements of Hobbes's state theory their due. For instance, against both pluralist defenders and authoritarian detractors of Hobbes, Schmitt insists that the sovereign power that emerges out of the natural condition possesses a suprarational, quasi-theological quality:

> The terror of the state of nature drives anguished individuals to come together; their fear rises to an extreme; a spark of reason flashes, and suddenly there stands in front of them *a new god....* What comes about as a result of this social covenant, the sole guarantor of peace, the sovereign-representative person is *much more than the sum total of all the participating particular wills.* (2008a, 31, 33; emphasis added)

Yet because the soul of the representative person was man-made, because the god created by social consensus was a man-become-god rather than a god-become-man, the theological and juridical qualities of Hobbes's state were overwhelmed by the rationalist-mechanistic elements (32–33). The juridical logic of representation that Hobbes borrowed from his Roman Catholic enemies and the myths he invoked to captivate the human mind proved paltry imitations of their premodern predecessors that possessed genuine transcendental substance. They proved no match for the techno-scientific aspects of Hobbes's project. Consequently, Schmitt concludes that the Leviathan state was "the first product of the age of technology.... The typical, even prototypical, work of the new technological era" (34). Hobbes hoped that the juridical and mythic aspects of the leviathan would unify particularist elements of society and keep them from becoming fully autonomous of the state and from making demands against it. Now, however, the leviathan is reduced to the failure that Schmitt's title suggests.

The neutralization of Hobbes's state—its transformation into mere machine—begins, Schmitt posits, as a response to the wars of religion, but this process led inevitably to "the neutralization of every truth" (2008a, 64). Religious, metaphysical, juristic, and political considerations eventually come to mean nothing to the "clean" and "exact" workings of the state mechanism. Now, Schmitt declares, liberals and communists both agree that the state is a mere machine, an apparatus that the most "varied political constellations can utilize as a technically neutral instrument" (62–63). Going further, and resorting to an antisemitism not present in his Weimar writings, he blames in particular "the Jew" Spinoza for accelerating the neutralizing process of converting the leviathan from a myth into a machine.

In 1921, Schmitt concludes his book on dictatorship with a footnote favorably citing Spinoza as a crucial intellectual link in the development of modern notions of sovereignty. In a 1929 lecture, he places Spinoza side by side with Hobbes as a chief representative of "the heroic age of occidental rationalism" (included in Schmitt 2007, 83). Yet in *Der Leviathan* Schmitt (2008a, 55) labels Spinoza a *Jewish philosopher* and the *first liberal Jew*, and, furthermore, he assigns Spinoza the central role in an esoteric Passion play. Schmitt posits Hobbes's absolutist state as a "mortal god" that was betrayed by Spinoza on behalf of "his own Jewish people" with dramatically detrimental consequences for Christian Europe (2008a, 60). According to Schmitt, the man-become-god leviathan state emerged upon the earth to bring peace and security to humanity, to redeem human kind from its own dangerousness. This mortal god asked its subjects not simply to exchange obedience for protection but also, Schmitt now claims, to believe, genuinely, that "Jesus is the Christ" (14). Schmitt here reveals the true reason that Hobbes cannot be fully blamed for turning the leviathan into a morally neutral, and hence potentially oppressive, totalitarian state: Hobbes affirmed the historical truth of the incarnation of Christ and asked the subjects of his leviathan to do the same (83).

On the contrary, that liberal Jew Spinoza, according to Schmitt (2008a, 57), perpetuated the fateful demise of God on Earth, the sovereign state. Spinoza, who could not accept the doctrine of the incarnation, used the qualified subjective freedom of conscience permitted by Hobbes to turn particularist societal forces against the unity of what were fundamentally Christian states, all in the subversive interests of assimilating Jews (57; see Vatter 2004, 190–192). According to Schmitt's blood libel narrative, Spinoza and the Jews effectively recrucify divinity incarnate, the leviathan state, on the cross of private conscience. As a result, they unleash chaos and disorder on the Christian world in the form of the Enlightenment, the age of revolutions, world wars, and even at the deepest levels of the text the mechanically oppressive and abusive Nazi state itself (Schmitt 2008a, 62). The Jews—not Hobbes and certainly not Schmitt himself—the Plettenberg jurist reprehensibly insinuates, are ultimately responsible for the eventual emergence of the "Third Reich."

How exactly did Spinoza accomplish this betrayal of the leviathan? What precisely constituted the treacherous kiss that he placed upon its cheek? As Schmitt explains it, Hobbes, the socio-religious insider (a nominally Christian Englishman), formulated the state–civil society relationship in the following stable manner:

> public peace and sovereign power
> ensures
> individual freedom

Spinoza, the socio-religious outsider (a secular Jew), inverts the priorities to make the relationship fundamentally unstable:

> individual freedom
> ensured by
> public peace and sovereign power

Thus, Spinoza made it possible historically for the dangerous subjectivity—which so concerned Schmitt in his reformulation of Hobbes in *The Concept of the Political*—to acquire preeminence over the state, which was founded precisely to keep the former in check. Spinoza and the emancipated Jews associated with the German Enlightenment (e.g., Moses Mendelssohn, Friedrich Julius Stahl) exploit the freedom of conscience granted by Hobbes's leviathan to weaken the unitary state and empower the multifarious subjective forces of society. They effectively take a crowbar, Schmitt implies, to "the barely visible crack" at the foundation of the leviathan state, ultimately toppling it and in so doing destroying the peace and security of modern Christian nations (2007).

As radical social subjectivities proliferated and gained in power over the course of modernity, Schmitt argues, they demanded of the state objectivity—objectivity toward its own existence—the logical result of which is the complete neutrality of the state. According to Schmitt, Kant finally saps the state of any substantive content of its own, disentangling the political organism from the political mechanism, just as, simultaneously, Schilling and the Romantics were disentangling art from mechanics (2008a, 61). After Kant, the reigning image for jurisprudence would no longer be a dignified judge pronouncing moral decisions but rather would be a mechanism dispensing rules: "The *legislator humanus* becomes a *machina legislatoria*" (100).

In his Weimar works, Schmitt treats the breakdown of the Hobbesian state and the Westphalian state system as a possibly contingent historical development; early in *Der Leviathan*, Schmitt implies that it was inevitable that the mechanistic elements within Hobbes's state would undermine the mythic-theological and juridical-representative ones. However, at this juncture of the text, he suggests that all of these elements might have resided together within the Hobbesian state to foster a stable order, one not susceptible to decline and moreover, that was substantively moral and not technically neutral. But the Jews intervened to make the state vulnerable to its worst attributes, which, Schmitt implies, have become especially salient in the inconvenient conditions under which Schmitt presently lives.

Because, Schmitt states, the modern state no longer possesses moral content, neither do the laws it thereby produces: "for the technically represented neutrality it is decisive that the laws of the state become independent from every substantive content, from religious or legal truth and prophesy, and should be valid only as a result of the positive determinations of the state's decision in the form of commands" (67). If a state is purely mechanical, if no value inheres within it other than efficiency, then that state knows no boundaries or limits—not even what theoretically restrained the Hobbesian state: the protection of individual life. Schmitt remarks rather coldly: "Such a state can be tolerant or intolerant but neutral nonetheless. It has its truth, and justice in its technical perfection. The state machine either functions or does not function" (68–69).

Ironically, to Schmitt's mind, precisely because the Hobbesian state grants both a subjective realm and a right of resistance to individuals so that they may better preserve their lives, the security of those lives and of the state itself become threatened all the more grievously. Had Hobbes recognized, as Schmitt wished, the danger posed to both state and subjects by granting individuals subjective determination of self-preservation, his state might have held for itself the moral content of protecting the lives of individuals. But as the state permitted the subjective entities of civil society to demand more objectivity from the state, they drained it of even this limited content.

Schmitt paints the following picture of what likely ensues in such circumstances: one of these subjective entities, justified by their guaranteed subjective freedom of conscience, seizes the neutralized but still efficient state and then disregards the boundary separating the state from its subjects, with horrific results. Such circumstances approximate a state of nature where each individual is *not* equal to every one else in his ability to kill and be killed. Those who possessed the state apparatus in such circumstances would exhibit both the radical subjectivity of the natural condition and the objective efficiency of the sovereign state. As Schmitt's *The Concept of the Political* so masterfully describes the predicament of late Weimar in Hobbesian terms, here too he sets forth a Hobbesian depiction of National Socialism.

In Hobbesian terms, the "Third Reich" is no sovereign state but rather a perverted powerful form of the state of nature, where no one is sure if he is friend or enemy to his fellow citizen or to the regime and where no one is bound by morality of any kind to act as he sees fit. It is, as Schmitt intimates in *Der Leviathan*, and as his former student Franz Neumann charged in his magnificent critique of National Socialism, a behemoth, "a non-state, a situation of lawlessness, disorder and anarchy" (Neumann 1944, xii).

DER LEVIATHAN: GENUINE MEA CULPA OR SELF-SERVING APOLOGIA?

As already indicated, Schmitt is not simply the historically legitimated prophet of doom he implicitly presents himself to be in *Der Leviathan*. Rather, he was also an active contributor to the state of affairs he criticizes under National Socialism. He criticized in earlier writings the appropriation of the state by non-neutral forces that would "seize" the apparatus of "state will-formation" for themselves, "without themselves ceasing to be social and non-state entities" (1931a, 73). He even described such a coup in terms of a deposition of the leviathan: "When the 'mortal god' falls from his throne and the realm of objective reason and civil society becomes 'a great gang of thieves,' then the parties slaughter the powerful Leviathan and slice pieces from the flesh of his body" (see 1930, 28–29). Furthermore, Schmitt insisted that a state that integrates itself into every facet of society is hardly a state at all. For a state to be a genuine state, Schmitt argued, it must stand over and above society, governing it—no doubt firmly and vigilantly—as a separate entity. The state formation that Schmitt endorsed in 1933 became precisely the worst form of state that he criticized in the 1920s—not a healthy "qualitative total state" but a varyingly weak yet oppressive "quantitative" one (see 1931b; 1933).

But Schmitt's intellectual efforts contained no safeguards to prevent his political prescription from bringing forth the outcomes he most sought to avoid. In Weimar, Schmitt promoted the *Reichspräsident* as the "neutral" force to keep the greedy, ravenous, anarchic social elements at bay—a force that was neutral only with regard to the competing parties, but that was not neutral toward its own authority power. Yet as Schmitt's Weimar theoretical adversary, Hans Kelsen, so presciently asked at the time: what is to prevent such a supposedly neutral entity from behaving as a rather biased participant in the social conflict Schmitt describes? (1930–1931, 1917–1918) Schmitt offered no real answer in Weimar, and he still poses none under National Socialism in his *Der Leviathan*.

Thus, the stance of Hobbesian neutrality that Schmitt maintained throughout the 1920s and 1930s turns out to be somewhat misleading. An important difference between the natural condition and the friend/enemy confrontation is this: in the former, despite some occasional references by Hobbes to families or professions, there exist no friends and hence no antagonistic groupings. The abstract individualism of Hobbes's "war of all against all" points up his ultimate agnosticism regarding the respective combatants in the English Civil War: *Leviathan* was written, for the most part, in support of the king but was easily converted by Hobbes into a justification for Oliver Cromwell.[7] Schmitt had much stronger preferences regarding the participants in Weimar's near civil war. It *did* matter to him, for instance, that the Social Democrats, let alone the Communist Party, not gain long-lasting victory. Groups who would be the enemies of these groups would necessarily be, according to Schmitt's concept of the political, better friends of the state. Should, moreover, these state "friends" gain control of the state, it would be appropriate for them to suppress the enemies of that state. This is in fact what the National Socialists did once gaining power, albeit in a manner more ruthless than Schmitt could have foreseen. To this effect, then, Schmitt's theory encouraged as much as it forewarned against the seizure of the leviathan state by radically subjective social forces.

Moreover, the potentially lethal results of such a seizure are compounded by Schmitt's theoretical tampering with the Hobbesian formula of *protego ergo obligo*. Had Hobbes originally formulated the state in the way Schmitt wished in 1932—by not granting to the individual the subjective right of self-protection, even for the sake of better ensuring that individual's life—the logic of the leviathan would have broken down. Only the retention of some of that subjectivity regarding self-preservation that rules completely in the natural condition is what encourages Hobbesian man to make a compact and submit to sovereign authority.

Schmitt was correct to recognize in *Der Leviathan* that the state was, in a way, ultimately the product of the age of technology; it was an *instrument*, a tool. It served as a means to something else, namely, security and stability, preservation and peace. The state itself could not, without most unfortunate results, be what he wanted it to be, namely, the mythic or representative embodiment of these things and not the means thereto. Such formulations are potentially as politically dangerous to modern subjects as they are rationally incoherent to modern ears. The state could not be expected to absorb all of the right to self-preservation from the natural condition and at the same time guarantee it. The radical subjectivity, the dangerous right to judge, accruing to the state as it does in Schmitt's interpretation of Hobbes, only increases that subjectivity's volatility exponentially. Schmitt may blame the Jews for facilitating this development in *Der Leviathan*, but the blueprint for such an outcome was laid out in his own Weimar writings (see, e.g., Schmitt 2004).

Schmitt abhorred the liberal critique of the authoritarian state. Nevertheless, he might have heeded, to some extent, the warnings posed centuries before by John Locke:

> I desire to know what land of Government that is, and how much better it is than the State of Nature, where one Man commanding a multitude, has Liberty to be Judge in his own case, and may do to all his Subjects whatever he pleases, without the least liberty to anyone to question or controle those who Execute his Pleasure? And in whatsoever he doth, whether led by Reason, Mistake or Passion, must be submitted to? Much better it is in the State of Nature wherein Men are not bound to submit to the unjust will of another. (1988, §13)

In Locke's reformulation of Hobbes, unaccountable rule, not the state of nature, is the actual state of "Warre." The state of nature where each individual has an equal chance of remaining alive must surely be better than a situation where one has completely given over one's right to and capacity for self-protection to an inordinately stronger force that offers no guarantee, no assurance of protecting one's life. Schmitt surely must have come to understand that Weimar, for all of its crises, and all of his criticisms of it, was certainly better than the "Third Reich"; there, whatever the social disturbances and economic fluctuations, Schmitt's academic controversies did not cause him to fear for his life.

CONCLUSION

In his writings on Hobbes from the 1920s and 1930s, Schmitt attempts to preserve, strengthen, and even redefine the sovereign state by reviving the source of its development, the fear of violent death, and by recasting its foundations on collective rather than individual grounds. To avoid recreating the conditions that brought about the crisis of the sovereign state to begin with, Schmitt attempts to refound the state solely on juridically rational representative grounds or upon this vital and inevitably mythic element of fear, divorcing the latter from the neutralizing elements of modern science and technology. By presenting man as an incorrigibly dangerous being who inevitably forms violently aggressive groups, Schmitt hoped to eradicate the justification for a subjective autonomous realm cultivated by science and technology and governed by the right of self-protection, which might grow to rival the power of the state and threaten to bring about the chaos of the natural condition.

But this project suffered from fateful flaws. Drawing upon his Weimar writings, Schmitt sought to make the "Third Reich" that he endorsed in 1933 conform to his definition of representation—he wanted the *Reichsführer* to behave in the juridically authoritarian manner he had previously prescribed for *Reichspräsident*. However, it soon became clear that Hitler was no Hindenburg. The "Third Reich" would draw much more extensively on irrational myth than juridical rationality in conducting its business. Hence, certain elements of Schmitt's Weimar theories—like those of Hobbes before him—came to overwhelm others and transformed in ways that their author could not himself control. But, if in Hobbes's case, the mechanistic aspects of the leviathan came to overwhelm the mythic, in Schmitt's, it was the mythic elements that took precedence over the rational.

More specifically, Schmitt's revival of the myth necessary to instill fear, terror, awe in subjects for the sake of creating or strengthening sovereign authority provides no real guarantee of eventually allaying that fear in the manner that Hobbes intended: it does not abolish the state of nature but rather perpetuates it. Indeed, such efforts may not diminish the role of technology in modem politics but instead may serve to expand that role many times fold (see Benjamin 2008). Schmitt's project unwittingly facilitated not the elimination of but rather potentially the very *institutionalization* and *manufacture* of chaos. Rather than, in Hobbes's words, ensuring "Peace at home," and simply fostering "mutuall ayd" against external enemies, Schmitt's aestheticization and elevation of conflict to the status of myth helped inspire war, ghastly in manner and scale, on Germany's own citizens, and in unprecedented global terms on other nations.

Thus, Schmitt's Weimar attempt to supplant liberalism through a reinterpretation of Hobbes proves a catastrophic failure in two ways. First, he tampers with one Hobbesian formula: the protection/obedience relationship that had already been improved by the liberalism that succeeded Hobbes. Second, he experiments with another Hobbesian formula—the myth/technology relationship—to which post-Hobbesian liberalism continues to be oblivious. In both cases he renders the reformulation more dangerous than the original, supposedly unstable proposition, and the historical reality with which it corresponds was undeniably disastrous.

After the war, Schmitt attempted to justify his collaboration with National Socialism by appealing to the Hobbesian standard of obedience for protection. He merely offered allegiance to a new regime, which he assumed would in turn protect him. It is almost fitting then that—as reward for making that unforgivable political choice—this Hobbesian, who sought to theorize into oblivion the protection component of the protection/obedience formula, came to fear for his security and, in his more dramatic moments, for his life under the "Third Reich." Instead, Schmitt lived well into his nineties, claiming until the end that he had always been simply misconstrued.

Carl Schmitt closed his *Der Leviathan* of 1938 by offering comfort and assurance, "across the centuries," to Thomas Hobbes, who died deeply concerned that he had been misunderstood (2008a, 86). He exclaims, on the contrary, that if no one else understood the Malmesbury philosopher then Schmitt certainly does: "Thomas Hobbes, now you do not teach in vain!" (86) The contents of that work and the political career of its author suggest that, in highly critical historical circumstances, Hobbes's lessons did indeed fall upon a rather deaf pairset of ears.

NOTES

1. At various junctures in the text Schmitt attempts to dissociate his own philosophy from Nazi practice. For instance, here he invokes the year but not the book, *Political Theology*, where he first appropriated Hobbes's state theory: "*Auctoritas...non veritas*...often cited since 1922, as expressed by Hobbes, is anything but a slogan of irrational despotism" (Schmitt 2008a, 44).
2. These arguments were later more fully elaborated by Schmitt in *The "Nomos" of the Earth in the International Law of the "Jus Publicum Europaeum"* (2003).
3. The language of friend and enemy is quite prevalent in *Leviathan*, for instance: "when either [a group of people] have no common *enemy*, or he that by one part is held for an *enemy*, is by another part held for a *friend*, they must needs by the difference of their interests dissolve, and fall again into a war among themselves" (Hobbes 1991, II.17, 119, emphases added).
4. In his celebrated 1932 commentary on *The Concept of the Political*, the young Leo Strauss agrees with Schmitt that Hobbes's thought results not from fantasy, incipient capitalism, and especially *not* natural science, but rather a fundamental philosophical orientation. In his commentary on Schmitt, he identifies this orientation as a rather thin moral basis, because, he asserts, Hobbes has no notion of "sin." However, in his full-length book on Hobbes from 1936, Strauss identifies a kind of sin, a quasi-Christian moral antipathy to pride, as the source of Hobbes' philosophical orientation. See Strauss 1952a (97–122); 1952b.
5. Quasi-Catholic because in Schmitt's early writings the Catholic basis is explicit, whereas after his break with the church in 1926 his theory of representation seems to merely imitate Catholic juridical thinking. Compare Schmitt 1996 with Schmitt 2008b.
6. Unless noted otherwise, all translations of source material by the author.
7. See Hobbes 1991 (483–490); on the dating of this book see Skinner 1972.

REFERENCES

Benjamin, W. 2008. *The Work of Art in the Age of Its Technological Reproducibility, And Other Writings on Media*, trans. E. F. N. Jephcott. Cambridge: Harvard University Press.

Dyzenhaus, D. 1997. "Legal Theory in the Collapse of Weimar: Contemporary Lessons?" *American Political Science Review* 91: 121–134.

Hobbes, T. 1889. *Behemoth; or the Long Parliament*. London: Simpkin.

Hobbes, T. 1991. *Leviathan; or, The Matter, Forme and Power of a Commonwealth, Ecclesiasticall and Civill*, ed. R. Tuck. Cambridge: Cambridge University Press.

Kelsen, H. 1930–31. "Wer soll der Hüter der Verfassung sein?" *Die Justiz* 6: 1917–1918.

Locke, J. 1988. *Second Treatise on Government*, ed. P. Laslett. Cambridge: Cambridge University Press.

Neumann, F. 1944. *Behemoth: The Structure and Practice of National Socialism, 1933–1944*. New York: Oxford University Press.

Schmitt, C. 1921. *Die Diktatur: von den Anfängen des modernen Souveränitätsgedankens bis zum proletarischen Klassenkampf*. Berlin: Duncker & Humblot.

Schmitt, C. 1923. "Die politische Theorie des Mythus." In Schmitt 1994, 11–19.

Schmitt, C. 1930. "Staatsethik und pluralistischer Staat." In Schmitt 1994, 28–29.

Schmitt, C. 1931a. *Der Hüter der Verfassung*. Tübingen: Mohr.

Schmitt, C. 1931b. "Die Wendung zum totalen Staat." In Schmitt 1994, 146–157.

Schmitt, C. 1933. "Weiterentwicklung des totalen Staates in Deutschland (January 1933)." In Schmitt 1994, 211–213.

Schmitt, C. 1934. "Der Führer schützt das Recht." *Deutsche Juristen-Zeitung* 39: 945–950.

Schmitt, C. 1985. *The Crisis of Parliamentary Democracy*, trans. E. Kennedy. Cambridge: MIT Press.

Schmitt, C. 1994. *Positionen und Begriffe im Kampf mit Weimar—Genf—Versailles, 1923–1939*, 3rd ed. Berlin: Duncker & Humblot.

Schmitt, C. 1996. *Roman Catholicism and Political Form*, trans. G. L. Ulmen. Westport: Praeger.

Schmitt, C. 2003. *The "Nomos" of the Earth in the International Law of the "Jus Publicum Europaeum"*, trans. G. L. Ulmen. New York: Telos Press.

Schmitt, C. 2004. *Legality and Legitimacy*, trans. and ed. J. Seitzer. Durham: Duke University Press.

Schmitt, C. 2006. *Political Theology: Four Chapters on the Concept of Sovereignty*, trans. G. Schwab. Chicago: University of Chicago Press.

Schmitt, C. 2007. *The Concept of the Political*, expanded ed., trans. G. Schwab. Chicago: University of Chicago Press.

Schmitt, C. 2008a. *The Leviathan in the State Theory of Thomas Hobbes: Meaning and Failure of a Symbol*, trans. G. Schwab. Chicago: University of Chicago Press.

Schmitt, C. 2008b. *Constitutional Theory*, trans. and ed. J. Seitzer. Durham: Duke University Press.

Skinner, Q. 1972. "Conquest and Consent: Thomas Hobbes and the Engagement Controversy." In *The Interregnum*, ed. G. E. Aylmer. London: Archon Books, 79–98.

Strauss, L. 1952a. "Notes on Carl Schmitt's *The Concept of the Political*," trans. J. H. Lomax. In Schmitt 2007, 97–122.

Strauss, L. 1952b. *The Political Philosophy of Hobbes: Its Basis and Genesis*, trans. E. Sinclair. Chicago: University of Chicago Press.

Vatter, M. E. 2004. "Strauss and Schmitt as Readers of Hobbes and Spinoza: On the Relation between Political Theology and Liberalism." *New Centennial Review* 4: 161–214.

CHAPTER 10

....

CONCEPTS OF
THE POLITICAL IN
TWENTIETH-CENTURY
EUROPEAN THOUGHT

....

SAMUEL MOYN

INTRODUCTION

....

OF CARL Schmitt's many provocations to political thought in the twentieth century, one stands out for being as epoch-making as it is ambiguous: his desire to disengage what he called "the political" (*das Politische*) from mere politics or policy and to redeem it from potential loss. In titling what remains perhaps his most influential book precisely *The Concept of the Political*, Schmitt signals his clarificatory venture as clearly as he possibly can even as he interprets his new concept in an intensive manner that indicates a longing for a return before or a way beyond its dissipation in the modern age. Because Schmitt's insistence on the primacy of the political has returned in recent thought in so many different guises, it deserves continuing study and interrogation.

For Schmitt's fervent desire to place the political first, both analytically and experientially, begs a host of questions and concerns. What exactly is the political, for a start? Is it distinct from politics? What is at stake in a contrastive or invidious concept of the political such as Schmitt insisted he needed to achieve? What might it mean to retrieve the concept from its threatened obsolescence (presupposing that it could wane or depart in the first place)? Does it make sense to champion the political as a matter of intensity, as if our experience of the political could, let alone should, be a matter of more rather than less (or vice versa)? Finally, could anything remain of the desire to foreground the political if Schmitt's own commitment to define it intensively, as well as through a famous logic of necessary enmity, proves unpersuasive?

This chapter argues that much of the twentieth-century fate of the political in European thought can be followed as a process in which Schmitt's will to identify the political was retained even as other features of his approach were dropped. Schmitt's concept of the political remains one of his major and lasting bequests, affecting modern and contemporary thought fundamentally, as Hannah Arendt's case most immediately shows. But it fell to another major thinker, Claude Lefort, working from different traditions, to elaborate a theory of the political that set out on a very different path from the one Schmitt marked out in 1922—one that may remain more compelling now.

The discussion begins by recalling the main outlines of *The Concept of the Political*, with emphasis on conceptual ambiguities in Schmitt's argumentation that others would identify and exploit. The chapter then turns to a recent debate about which young German Jew—Hans Morgenthau or Leo Strauss—most influenced the revisions Schmitt made to his text as it went from edition to edition, concluding that the role of both has been overstated. The balance of the chapter reconstructs an alternative—and in some ways opposed—French tradition of conceptualizing the political with roots in the thought of Raymond Aron. Culminating in Lefort, this tradition among other things decentered the role of enmity that Schmitt wanted to define the political, a point the chapter dramatizes in conclusion with discussion of international relations theory and how the French tradition conceived of warfare and strife.

CARL SCHMITT'S CONCEPT
OF THE POLITICAL

"The Concept of the Political" originally appeared in 1927 as an essay in the *Archiv für Sozialwissenschaft und Sozialpolitik*, a central organ in the genesis of the discipline of sociology. Schmitt then revised it for publication by Mohr Siebeck, the reputable German publisher, as a freestanding volume in 1932 (as well as again in 1933, in an openly Nazified version that Schmitt chose not to reprint after the war). Opening his essay, Schmitt signals that he will attempt a transcendental argument from the first sentence of the venture: "The concept of the state presupposes the concept of the political" (2007, 18). Conceptualizing the state—in so-called *Staatsrechtslehre*—had long been a central concern of German legal theorists and early political scientists. Schmitt now claims that such inquiry presupposed a deeper one into what he calls "the political" (*das Politische*).[1]

To be sure, one could claim that this notion had been implicit since Aristotle first defined man as a political animal. The Greek term Πολιτικά meant "concerning the city," and Aristotle uses the term to refer as much to a distinguishing feature of human life he is concerned to theorize as to a specific regime form he contrasted to other ones (democracy most notably). It was a sign that Schmitt was operating within the terms of modern state theory that he presumed that, whatever it was, the political was essential to identifying the entity associated with a people in executing specific functions. In other words, it matters utterly that Schmitt frames the inquiry as one getting to the transcendental presuppositions of the modern state or even nation-state.

Schmitt's trouble is that in conducting this inquiry most prior attempts fell prey to the objection that they were circular. In the most characteristic definitions, the state was understood as a political entity, while politics typically connoted state functions. For example, Schmitt notes that Max Weber, in his classic "Politics as a Vocation," defined politics in terms of power within or among states (1958, 20–21n). But then, as Schmitt comments, "The state thus appears as something political, the political as something pertaining to the state—obviously an unsatisfactory circle" (2007, 20). The goal, given this vice, was to search for the transcendental presupposition of the state without simply defining the political in its terms.

It is worth noting that, while Schmitt uses the political as a contrastive item from the start of his essay (opposed to economy, morality, and law), he does not place special emphasis on the novelty of speaking of *das Politische* as opposed to some other level of politics. Indeed, he seems to have reflected explicitly on his use of the adjectival noun *Politische* for his title rather than the more traditional term *Politik* only forty years later, in the preface to an Italian translation of the book (Schwab 2007, 12–13). Unlike for a number of French and later global authors beginning circa 1980, there is for Schmitt no fetishized terminological difference between the political and mere politics. In fact, Schmitt goes on to suggest that the main problem is not so much a distinction he wants to draw within the concept of politics as a historical transformation that had destabilized the notion that politics were a separate and isolable domain. In the eighteenth century, Schmitt suggests, a conceptual distinction between what was the realm of politics (the state) and what was not (civil society) was indeed defensible because it corresponded to real facts (2007, 22). The nineteenth-century interpenetration of the state and its others now gave way to an obliteration of any borders to politics. As Schmitt observes in a celebrated essay published in between the article and book versions of *The Concept of the Political*, his generation was witnessing "the turn to the total state" (1931).

It is here that Schmitt turns from a merely descriptive to an explicitly evaluative agenda. The muddying of once stable distinctions between the politics of the state and other phenomena required what *made* the state a political entity to be a critical analytical imperative, and apparently for the first time.[2] But how to disengage what made the state political once it extended beyond its prior limitations to embrace the totality of social life was not simply an analytical puzzle. For insofar as boundary between the state and society fragments, Schmitt fears, it likewise opens the risk that other domains could engulf the political in what Schmitt calls neutralization. The interpenetration of hitherto separate domains could be a recipe for depoliticization, one to which the contemporary assertion of the rise of the total state offered an implicit response—insisting that neither managerial economy nor religious vocation nor moral conscience could fully define what had made the state political in the first place (2007, 22). Where everything is political, it could follow that nothing is. Schmitt's analytical goal of specifying the essence of the political is thus prompted by an evaluative anxiety that it might disappear.

The argumentative setting had thus been prepared for Schmitt's most memorable and debated claim in the essay: the distinction between friend and enemy provides the key to the concept of the political. Yet already in these preparatory steps many potential confusions lurked. For one thing, it remained strange to frame the search for the political as the search for the presuppositions of the modern state at all, given that many forms of political organization antedated modernity. Ancient sources of the term itself and straightforward historical reflection suggest that there was a huge range of political associations before the modern state ever came about.

More important, the exact nature of the transcendental argument Schmitt implied remained unclear. As Leo Strauss puts it in a letter to Schmitt in September 1932, it was unclear whether "presupposition" meant "constitutive principle" or "causal precondition" (as quoted in Meier 1995, 125). If it meant the former, then enmity was what made the state a distinctive entity. But this possibility was one that the much broader historical inquiry into the alternative forms of political organization other than the state—an inquiry Schmitt fails to carry out in framing his discussion—seemed to rule out. History suggested that there was no way to claim that the political actually constituted and distinguished the state as a specific formation. It was more plausible, Strauss notes, to think of the political as the condition that established the possibility of the state—but not the exclusive principle of its meaning.

Further, and perhaps more important, Schmitt allows a negative, or contrastive or invidious, conception of the political to constrain the definition of the concept, even as he insists that it was the very emphasis on what the political was not that haunted the definitions of his predecessors. Thus, for example, much turned for Schmitt on the fact that an economic, moral, or religious criterion could not amount to a political one. Yet it is rare that, precisely when it comes to a transcendental condition, its analytical identification will exclude (as opposed to allow) amalgam phenomena.

For example, suppose it is a precondition of aesthetic experience that some distinction between beautiful and ugly obtain. But identifying that condition for aesthetic experience couldn't possibly rule out the category of religious art or suggest that it threatens the project of analytically disengaging what makes something aesthetic as opposed to political—a phenomenon like religious art could be both. Correspondingly, to insist on the necessity of a criterion of political by no means implies that a new sort of welfare state fails to meet it simply because it intrudes into hitherto private economic affairs.

The upshot is that Schmitt insists that identifying the political went beyond negative or contrastive definitions, but his actual project was framed to achieve an invidious distinction between political entities and ones defined by economics, ethics, or religion. Among other things, Schmitt assumes, a criterion of the political would show why the liberal state was depoliticized even though this conclusion could not possibly follow from the bare discovery of such a criterion. It would help only to explain how the new form of state that intruded into hitherto private relations now required multiple categories to make sense of it (as amalgam phenomena always do).

Finally, the very way Schmitt structures the problem of identifying what the political implied was a definition that was not simply invidious but also intensive in content. If what made something political or not depended on historical circumstances in which (in Schmitt's own example) state and civil society were self-evidently separate phenomena, then the passing of those circumstances would endanger the concept itself. Thus, the collapse of the boundary between the state and its opposite numbers would risk the loss of the experiential intensity that the autonomy of the state had allowed.

At stake in this dimension of the essay was Schmitt's motivated confusion of analytical clarity and experiential intensity, as if the latter required the former. Yet this requirement remained entirely without explanation. By Schmitt's own argument, the era of the autonomy of the state from civil society had allowed the concept of the political to remain unspoken. If there was some motivation for disengaging the political, it was hard to agree with Schmitt that it was the integration of state and society that provided it. Schmitt relies on his anxiety that the intensity of the experience of the political might wane to encourage the reader to care about an analytically distinct politics, a stance that in turn encouraged an intensive account of the topic.

Enmity as an Existential Fact of Life

Heedless of these complications, yet having introduced a novel agenda all the same, Schmitt presses ahead to his claim about friends and enemies. Much of the rest of Schmitt's essay details his argument about the primordiality of the distinction between friends and enemies—a real rather than metaphorical distinction—as the decisive criterion of politics. And the implication of this criterion meant that a truly political relationship did not obtain absent the threat of violent battle (Schmitz 1965).

Stating that his theory of enmity as the condition of the political implied neutrality about how enmity is lived out (it could accommodate peace treaties and cold wars as easily as military engagement), Schmitt is clear that it made war an ever-present possibility—or perhaps, more accurately, one never fully dispensable from human affairs so long as humans could not befriend one another except in contrast to already subjugated animals or not yet encountered aliens (2007, 34). Schmitt then writes:

> A world in which the possibility of war is utterly eliminated, a completely pacified globe would be a world without the distinction of friend and enemy and hence a world without politics. It is conceivable that such a world might contain many very interesting antitheses and contrasts, competitions and intrigues of every kind, but there would not be a meaningful antithesis whereby men could be required to sacrifice life, authorized to shed blood, and kill other human beings. For the definition of the political, it is here even irrelevant whether such a world without politics is desirable as an ideal situation. The phenomenon of the political can be understood only in the context of the ever present possibility of the friend-and enemy grouping, regardless of the aspects which this possibility implies for morality, aesthetics, and economics. (35)

In spite of his official neutrality about the proximity of the threat of open warfare in political relationships, Schmitt also implies that certain forms of maintaining this threat inevitably tends to make it experientially peripheral. In this way, when he establishes this criterion, Schmitt anticipates others who are trying to hew out a lexical distinction in the French language between politics and the political. For he insists that superficial sorts of public enmity, such as a contrast of two alternative policy groups or even organized parties, does not qualify as the radical or root enmity that alone made relationships political. Indeed, Schmitt goes so far as to claim that insofar as such superficial divisions intensified, the more fundamental enmity that made politics possible at all risked submersion. "The equation politics = party politics," he notes dismissively, "is possible whenever antagonisms among domestic political parties succeed in weakening the all-embracing political unit, the state" (2007, 32). Thus, Schmitt's establishment of the friend/enemy criterion as the essence of the political makes a liberal politics of compromise and negotiation seem like not just an evasion of the political but downright threatening to its experience.

There were a number of new difficulties in Schmitt's specification of the primordiality of the friend/enemy distinction, especially insofar as he avers it is an "existential" fact necessarily portending real violence (Kennedy 2004, ch. 4). Where, to begin with, does the line between groups come from? Schmitt refers easily to *peoples* as if they were built-in categories of world society and as if humanity itself were a later and superficial ideal. In case this inference is not clear, Schmitt (2007, 54, §6) famously repeats the jarring aphorism of Pierre-Joseph Proudhon: "whoever invokes humanity wants to cheat." And he devotes a large part of the balance of the essay to harsh criticism of those who willfully misunderstood the League of Nations to promise or achieve the unification of humanity.

Schmitt does note that his insistence on conflict cannot mean that "one particular nation must forever be the friend or enemy of another specific nation" (2007, 34). But even that formulation, like the rest of his discussion, implies that the nations themselves were durable and perhaps eternal equipment of the world order. Nations constructed the world through enmity but were not themselves constructed. Just as his transcendental approach to the political threatened to reduce the inquiry to the presuppositions of the modern state, so Schmitt's later definition of the political in terms of friends and enemies risked assuming the modern nation-state as something more than the historically contingent feature of the landscape than it is. Schmitt offers no theory of nationalism and appears willing to grant the truth of its myths.

Then there was the matter of why the different sorts of internal distinctions in a polity—quarrels among friends, so to speak—were not dignified enough to count as political. One possible interpretation is that Schmitt assumes that the international space of war was the exclusive site of the political, whereas domestic antitheses and contrasts, presupposing the working unity of those squabbling over their arrangements, were simply something else. But aside from being oddly stipulative, this clarification would ruin the prospect of a single definition of politics that would cut across the divide between the international and domestic spheres. Indeed, to the extent Schmitt sees politics as possible within the domestic space, it can take only the form of the threat of open violence. "If one wants to speak of politics in the context of the primacy of internal politics, then this conflict no longer refers to war between organized nations but to civil war" (2007, 32). Making the specter of outright violence the criterion of the political at home—as if the substance of conflict were not germane to its political status—begs the question of how it is that suddenly a hitherto unified group could fragment into enmity and over what causes: unless, of course, Schmitt believes that civil war primarily occurred in the case that there were an already extant and clearly defined internal enemy requiring purgation.

At this point, Schmitt finally acknowledges that other factors colored and at times evolved into political differences in which violence beckoned. In doing so, he goes beyond his initial framing by acknowledging that the political could merge with or at least arise out of other sorts of bases for group membership like economic or moral or religious opinion or identity. If pacifists were serious about their cause, he notes, they would have to fight to advance it, showing that their cause had become political for the first time (though the war they would declare would contradict their program). Similarly, economic, moral, and religious differences could "transform" into political ones, creating enmity where there had been none before (2007, 37). If Marxists had their way, the class distinction of bourgeois and proletariat could become political, even within a single state. Overall, then, Schmitt now not only acknowledges but also insists that politics can "derive its energy from the most varied human endeavors, from the religious, economic, moral, and other antitheses" (38).

These clarifications offer another way than the natural and prepolitical existence of peoples that inimical groups could come about. However, if they do not explain what justified the assumption of apparently autochthonous peoples in the first place, neither do his clarifications about elective sorts of community interfere with Schmitt's stark assumption that politics exist at home solely when the threat of violence occurs. Instead, they merely explain that civil war could come to pass, and political distinction would come about domestically, when new enmity following from hitherto constrained economic, moral, and religious difference intensified into political form.

It must have been Schmitt's continuing debt to a contrastive and exclusionary conception of the political that his text implies that, the moment other sorts of conflicts became political, they cease being what they were before. It was as if, when it came to the political, the substantive matters that divided groups suddenly became pretextual to their existential enmity. And that enmity, in turn, was defined in terms of the novel availability of the prospect of mortal combat. What the friend/enemy distinction, and the threat of war, provided, was a criterion of *intensity* that alone demarcated what was not political from what was.

PHILOLOGY AND POLITICS: THE ROLE OF HANS MORGENTHAU AND LEO STRAUSS

The impact of Carl Schmitt's essay on German thought was, as Hans Morgenthau puts it, "sensational" (1978, 67; see also Rohe 1978). Yet only recently have the alterations

Schmitt made to his text as he published it as a book in 1932 and 1933 become the object of sustained scholarly inquiry. The differences between the texts have been overstated, as if Schmitt moves from one model or paradigm to another. In a well-known recent book, for example, Heinrich Meier (1995) claims that Schmitt moved by 1933, thanks to Leo Strauss's criticisms, from a model of the political as a separate domain to a model of the political as experiential intensity. Meier's argument, however, overstates the extent of transformation that occurred, and uncritical reliance on its effort to emphasize the profundity of Leo Strauss has ended up distorting both the discussion of Schmitt's text and the history of its reception.

Already in the original version of the essay, as I have shown, Schmitt remains quite undecided about how far to ban substantive concerns from the domain of the political. Though always interested in a contrastive understanding of the concept, and ruling out amalgam phenomena, Schmitt ultimately allows for some sort of theory of the economic, moral, and religious basis of the rise of political enmity—even in the first version of the essay. His revisions make this agenda more pronounced, to be sure. Further, Schmitt's ultimate goal was always an intensive definition. The revisions for the book editions of *The Concept of the Political* were thus far more a matter of clarification under pressure of implicit possibilities in the text, after critics suggested implausibilities and incompatibilities in the original version. And in any event, Schmitt's commitment to the *autonomy of the political* either resounded successfully in his original articulation or survived his revisions sufficiently to shape much later thought—and most notably the entire outlook of his most complex and interesting later disciple in this regard: Hannah Arendt.[3]

If it is a matter of emphasizing that a critic drove revisions of the text, credit apparently falls not to Strauss but to Morgenthau, who—as William Scheuerman (1999, ch. 9) usefully shows—offers a serious criticism of Schmitt in his doctoral dissertation between the essay and book versions of *The Concept of the Political*.[4] In his dissertation, which was later found in Schmitt's library, Morgenthau insists that it was Schmitt's emphasis on the specific intensity of dispute between enemies that distinguished political from other sorts of relationships. And it does seem clear that the latter altered his text in view of the former's argument that the political was not a special domain but instead "a *quality*, a tone, which can be peculiar to any object and which attaches itself with some preference to certain objects, but which does not by necessity attach itself to any of them" (Morgenthau 1929, 67; 1933, in English as 2012, 101).

Notwithstanding the emphasis on the move from autonomy to intensity in Schmitt's revision, a much more fundamental change has been lost in the shuffle: Schmitt attempts to drop what Strauss later calls the constitutive interpretation of the book's transcendental argument. I do not have an explanation as to why this change occurred in the history of the text. But when Schmitt adds the following clarification to his argument, he evidently is repulsing the interpretation of the political as constitutive and endorsing the interpretation as conditional: The distinction between friend and enemy, Schmitt now writes, "provides a definition in the sense of a criterion and not as an exhaustive definition or one indicative of substantial content" (2007, 26). (Curiously, Strauss does not mention this passage in criticizing the first sentence of Schmitt's book for its ambiguous transcendental argument.)

If Schmitt attempts to untangle the meaning of his transcendental arguments before Strauss puts the dilemma so well in his letter, then what further significance does Strauss play in the reception? It is absolutely true that—as Meier points out and as is unsurprising in the revision of any text—the 1932 version of *The Concept of the Political* that Strauss anatomizes still offers remnants of Schmitt's primary original goal of singling out the political as an autonomous domain alongside others. But (to repeat) it was true neither that an intensive emphasis was altogether lacking from the first version nor that it fully displaced a prior paradigm in the second version nor even that Strauss's essay caused a fuller shift in the direction of intensity in the third version. The truth is that both arguments were there to differing extents in all three versions of the text. Far more important was that Schmitt drops any sense that the clarification of the political would provide an exhaustive account of the modern state (as opposed to one of its conditions). But it is not clear that Strauss drives this change, since he does not mention the need for making it even more pronounced in his review, doing so only on reflection in the previously cited letter.

Strauss's main contribution, instead, lies in his claim that only a premodern search before the modern state—and Thomas Hobbes's modern liberalism—could vindicate Schmitt's critique of contemporary depoliticization. Famously, in his notes on Schmitt's text, which are published in the same journal where it had originally appeared, Strauss (1932) claims that Schmitt was too liberal. A full-fledged critique of liberalism, Strauss contends, one that did justice to Schmitt's insight that modern politics proceeded from too optimistic an anthropology, would have to begin with ancient thought. Strauss's self-transformation into a champion of an ancient alternative to a bankrupt modernity lay before him from this point in his career, but it is neither the case that Strauss continued to speak in terms of the political nor that his critique influenced the reception of Schmitt until Meier's book itself.

TOWARD A FRENCH TRADITION

Prior to recent decades, there was no conceptual distinction in French between politics and the political, though (just as in German and in Schmitt's original usage) it was always linguistically possible to refer to the latter without any technical meaning. The dominant meaning of *le politique* all along referred to the politician rather than any special domain, whether in a general or technical sense. And while the percolation of Schmitt's ideas should not be discounted, it is probably true that the vogue of structuralism played a more important role in the rise of a notion of politics as deeper fund for superficial withdrawals on its basis—much as in the relationship of *language* and *speech* in linguist Ferdinand de Saussure's theory. But the most surprising and curious fact about the trajectory of the political is that it was set off initially by non-Schmittian sources, into which a later Schmitt revival fed.

Schmitt's own French contacts and disciples—Raymond Aron and Julien Freund are the best examples of those respective categories—were certainly familiar with the tremendous debate caused by *The Concept of the Political*.[5] Aron later testified that he had read the book in Germany in 1931, and he sponsored its translation into French four decades later (Jenkins 2014). At first, however, it was not Aron but his doctoral student Freund—a more or less faithful disciple of Schmitt's—who made it his distinctive project to transmit the notion of the political as an analytically distinctive domain in French circles, especially in his dissertation published as *L'essence du politique* in 1965. Yet Freund was generally without much influence in his own right, in an era in which Schmitt was usually still regarded as toxic and his European network remained discreet.[6]

The same year as Freund published his Schmittian dissertation, Aron's lecture course on democracy and totalitarianism reached print, with its crucial introductory chapter on the different meanings of the concept of *politique*—which arguably led in the end to a strongly different tradition from what Schmitt inaugurated of conceptualizing the theme. It is worth spending some time with it before turning to Lefort. In his opening lecture, Aron starts out by noting some ambiguities in the French term *politique*, nestled as it is uncertainly between the idea of policy or specific programmatic endeavor and politics as the horizon against which or space within policies jostled and competed. Of these, the relationship Aron singles out between "on the one hand, a particular sector of the social scene and, on the other, the social scene itself, seen from a particular point of view," seems now of most interest (Aron 1968, ch. 1, 5; cf. Palonen 1990; Donégani and Sadoun 2007). For even when all different political entities subject to analysis by political scientists were grouped together, they occupied part of the overall realm of the social, beside family, religion, or work. But of course, Aron acknowledges, those things were political too in a more general sense: "politics is the major feature of the entire community because it conditions any cooperation between men" (1968, 5–6). And given the more general definition in everyday speech, it would then follow that politics would have a certain primacy.

If this is a transcendental argument, it is neither of the constitutive nor conditional version, of the sort Schmitt seeks to make sense of the relationship between the state and the political. It is not constitutive in the sense outlined already because it does not account for the distinctive character of the state or other ordinary features of political life; it begins with the premise that, whatever the legitimacy of distinguishing those features, it is nonetheless true that politics pervades society and each and every aspect of it rather than inhabiting some distinguishable zone. In this vein, Aron harkens more authentically to classical understanding since, as he notes, by the term Aristotle means "the manner in which the whole community is run" rather than merely a specific domain or intensity level. So Aron's goal is especially not, therefore, a contrastive understanding; instead politics is *foundational* of any possible domain of social life. The difference is arguably decisive, for it does not give rise to inquiry into a contrastive definitional criterion. And while it might make sense to speak of the definitional autonomy of the political in Aron's sense too, his foundational understanding of the political makes the analytical goal to understand how it related to what was built on its ground. Just as a foundation is not autonomous from whatever structures arise upon it, so Aron's notion of the political emphasizes the political determination of apparently different social domains.

Aron recognizes that his definition could lead to a detailed account of the relationship between politics and society analogous to the base and superstructure relationship some Marxists saw between ownership of the means of production (or the economy generally) and the rest of social life. But he certainly does not proceed in this direction himself. Long most concerned intellectually to struggle with Marxist theory, Aron does realize that his attempt to reverse any account of the primacy of economy failed as an account of the Soviet Union itself (1968, 7–9; 2002). True, Aron insists that "it is not a question of exchanging the doctrine of unilateral economic determination of society for the doctrine of political determination of society, which would be just as arbitrary" (1968, 10). But at this point in his analysis Aron reverts to an understanding of politics as public powers. If he had stuck with his broader conception of politics as *regime form*, then he would have had to acknowledge his reversal of Marxism into a doctrine of the political determination of society. For Aron is indeed suggesting that politics in the broadest conception is the fundamental basis of social life. As Aron concludes: "Politics in a restricted sense, that is the particular sector in which governors move and act, does not determine all the interactions of men in society. ... However, even if we do not agree with the Greek philosophers who held that human life is essentially politics, it remains true that the way authority is exercised ... contributes more than any other institution to mold personal relations" (12). In short, as Roberto Unger, a founder of the so-called Critical Legal Studies movement, argues, "It's all politics" (1997, 72–91).

A fundamentally unphilosophical theoretician, Aron is content to leave the matter there. Several other French thinkers once schooled in Marxism, however, soon attempted to spell out just such a foundational theory of the political. One towered over them: Claude Lefort. His sources in doing so were primarily phenomenological: Lefort, though formally a doctoral student of Aron's, was a follower of Maurice Merleau-Ponty, the celebrated phenomenologist. But Lefort, a teenage Trotskyist who throughout the era after World War II sought a radical alternative first to Stalinism then to Marxism of any sort, also combined the interest in social form characteristic of the new human sciences with a theory of the symbolic that gave him many more conceptual resources than Aron had for theorizing the primacy of politics and the different regime forms. The symbolic, unlike Marxist reduction of the social to economic relations but also unlike Aron's simpler approach to politics as the allocation of authority, referred to how intellectual principles and not just material factors framed the social order (Tarot 2003; Breckman 2013).

CLAUDE LEFORT'S CONCEPT
OF THE POLITICAL

Lefort is best understood as a sophisticated elaborator of Aron's attempt to shift to a foundational understanding of the political, going so far as to credit him for recovering it, even as the former imposed a lexical distinction between politics and the political that the latter had not used (Lefort 2007b, 995; cf. Anderson 1997). The rise internationally of the notion of the political, in spite of the Schmittian precedent, is traceable to events around 1980, at which time French disciples of German existentialist Martin Heidegger Philippe Lacoue-Labarthe and Jean-Luc Nancy founded a Center for Philosophical Research on the Political, whose proceedings Lefort attended.[7] These figures were probably the first to mobilize a categorical distinction between politics and the political, in ways that Lefort and others connected to their ongoing theorizing and which eventually intersected the slow then massive Schmitt revival (cf. Lefort and Gauchet 1971; Lefort 2007c). Later mobilizations of the political by philosophers like Alain Badiou and Jacques Rancière, for example, certainly flow from this conjuncture (Badiou 1985; Rancière 2003, in English as Rancière 2007).

It is convenient to skirt the detailed elaboration of Lefort's approach to examine it fully formed by the early 1980s. "The word 'political,'" Lefort (1988c) writes, "brings us face to face with an ambiguity that must be resolved if we are to know what we are talking about. The fact that we can choose to say *the political* [*le politique*] or *politics* [*la politique*] is, as we all know, an index of this ambiguity" (216).[8] Lefort is in effect referring to the same ambiguity Aron pointed out between restricted and comprehensive meanings of the political, now augmenting it with a lexical distinction—but he resolves this ambiguity in a somewhat different way.

Lefort's own perspective on the problem begins, quite strikingly given the Schmittian search for a contrastive or exclusionary criterion of the political, with a critique of the entire enterprise of seeking a definition that would distinguish what is political from what is not:

> What is certain is that the delimitation of the domain known as "the political" does not result from methodological criteria alone. The very notion of "limits" in fact derives from a desire for an "objective" definition—a desire that lies at the origin of the political theory, political science, and political sociology that have developed in the course of our century. No matter whether we attempt, for example, to circumscribe an order of social relations which are intelligible in themselves, such as power relationships; to conceive of a body of social functions whose necessary articulation signals the coherence of a system; to distinguish a superstructural level, based upon relations of production at which class domination is at once expressed and disguised by institutions, practices, and representations which supposedly serve the general interest; or, finally, to identify from empirical observation which of the mass of social facts relate directly or indirectly to the exercise of power, the underlying assumption is always the same: we assume that the object can have substance only if it is particular.... The criterion of what is *political* is supplied by the criterion of what is *nonpolitical*, by the criterion of what is economic, social, juridical, aesthetic, or religious. (1988c, 216–217)

Lefort's primary targets are empirical political scientists who wanted to classify phenomena positivistically as belonging to different domains as well as Marxists who wanted to make specifically political facts and processes causally posterior to a more basic economic set of determinants. But it is striking that, in arguing against the whole enterprise of defining the political against things that were not political, Lefort takes umbrage at what Schmitt tried to achieve several decades before. The criticism held even if, as Lefort goes on to observe, the point of the distinction was to allow for amalgam phenomena in which specifically political entities crossed into other domains—much as Schmitt did in the later parts of his book. "It need scarcely be pointed out," Lefort comments, "that this disposition has never prevented anyone from looking for articulations between that which pertains to politics and that which pertains to different realities and different systems; on the contrary, it usually acts as an encouragement to do so" (1988c, 217).

To be sure, such a criticism says nothing about any alternative proposal for defining the political. But it points in a foundational direction, in which the political grounded all other social domains. Indeed, the criticism points even further in this direction than in Aron (who vacillates about whether to reverse the primacy of politics and economics and also preserves a Weberian note in his description of the broader political field since he associated regime forms primarily with the criterion of authority). Nonetheless, like Aron, Lefort claims the authority of the first Western thinkers of politics in saying that his alternative to the implausible search for a contrastive principle of distinction would be faithful to "philosophy's oldest and most constant inspiration," by using the term political to refer to "the principles that generate society or, more accurately, different forms of society" (1988c, 217). Much as in Aron before him, Lefort's ancient reference for a concept of the political forces him to make it a theory of regime form—and thus everything in a given regime—rather than a theory of the presuppositions of the modern state.

What follows in Lefort's thought, of course, departs far from ancient understandings of politics, especially insofar (as he acknowledges) as classical theorists were preoccupied with the basis for the artifice of politics in a natural or anthropological foundation. If the political provides a theory of the foundations of social life, it is not one with natural grounds. For the same reason, it also departs far from the modern device of positing natural man at least far enough to generate a thought experiment about the origins of the social on its basis. With its alimentation drawing on twentieth-century phenomenology and psychoanalysis, whose details are too involved to cover here, Lefort's rival conception of the political differs primarily in supposing the impossibility of stabilizing politics with reference to extrapolitical criteria. For this reason, the basic issue of political theory is not what role different societies accorded political institutions but how different societies were structured in the first place. In Lefort's terms, "it is impossible, in the eyes of the philosopher, to localize the political *in* society" (1988c, 217). If a given society distinguishes between religion and politics, this is itself due to a prior political distinction. Where Schmitt fears that everything is becoming politics due to the novel rise of the interventionist state in the twentieth century, Lefort contends that everything has been politics since the beginning of humanity. In this light, it appears as if Schmitt's entire inquiry were premised on a local contingency that distinguishes the sphere of politics (or state) from those of economics, morality, and religion. But if that distinction is itself a political development, then the local inquiry (however fruitful) has neither analytical nor prescriptive implications for the status or meaning of politics generally.

Perhaps even more interestingly, Lefort argues that the very availability of the premise that politics need to be restricted to some delimited portion or contrastive feature of social experience presupposes a political revolution—quite literally. In the essay, devoted to the fate of religion in modern circumstances, Lefort claims that prior to an emancipatory revolution there had been no distinction between religion and politics for most of humanity's history. Today there is one. Far from showing that the very distinction between religion and politics is not political, the appearance of the debate about how far to separate realms presupposes a political event in which the truth that humans make the social order (and thus can remake it) became apparent. As Lefort puts it, "The fact that something like *politics* should have been circumscribed within social life at a given time has in itself a political meaning, and a meaning which is not particular, but general" (1988d, 11). In this sense, Schmitt's transcendental project is not transcendental enough, for it inquires into the conditions for the possibility neither of the distinction between politics and other realms nor of proposing to isolate the essence of the distinction—conditions that inevitably lay in the political making of society and its political remaking in history.

Lefort's most faithful heir, Pierre Rosanvallon, titled his chair at the Collège de France "the modern and contemporary history of the political."[9] When he gave his inaugural lecture at the institution in 2001, he made clear that his understanding of *le politique* did share Aron's sense of politics as "everything that constitutes political life beyond the immediate field of partisan competition for political power, everyday governmental action, and the ordinary function of institutions" (Rosanvallon 2006, 36). And while he never developed as richly philosophical an understanding of the political, Rosanvallon also incorporated Lefort's notion of the political as the basic terms of coexistence, which alone explained, in turn, both what social domains there were at a given place and time, and how the domain designated politics related to others. The political, Rosanvallon concludes,

> means the process whereby a human collectivity, which is never to be understood as a simple "population," progressively takes on the face of an actual community. It is constituted by an always contentious process whereby the explicit or implicit rules of what they can share and accomplish in common, rules which give a form to the life of the polity, are elaborated. One cannot make sense of the world without making room for the synthetic order of the political, except at the price of an exasperatingly reductive vision. The understanding of society, in fact, can never be limited to adding up and connecting together the various subsystems of action (economic, social, cultural, and so forth). These latter are, for their part, far from being easily intelligible by themselves, and only become so as part of a more general interpretive framework. Whatever the catalogue of cultural and social facts, economic variables, and institutional logics, it is impossible to decipher society at its most essential level without bringing to light the nerve center from which the very fact of its institution originates. (2006, 35)

It is a far cry from Schmitt's contrastive agenda. If anything, its comprehensive aspirations suggests that this new concept of the political, though still transcendental, courts precisely Schmitt's charge that because the political touches everything it risked counting as nothing at all.

THE INTERNATIONAL POLITICS
OF ENMITY AND WARFARE

In spite of their various criticisms, it is a striking fact that many of Schmitt's interlocutors in Weimar and after became central figures in the invention of international relations theory in the second half of the twentieth century. In this much-researched story of recent years, it was Morgenthau, especially, who imported Schmitt's account of necessary enmity as the specifically political distinction into theoretical understandings of the international realm. Of course, it may have been quite plausible to do so in the Cold War's heat. In any case, it is rather interesting that, if contemporary scholarship is right, Schmitt exerted massive though unavowed influence on Cold War international relations theory, retrieved for the sake of domestic politics and the potential activation of agonism only after 1989 when the new problem seemed not too much conflict in the international realm but too little at home (Pichler 1998; Schmidt 1998; Guilhot 2010).

As noted already, Schmitt does not theorize in *The Concept of the Political* how to connect his putatively transcendental account of the notion with the hoary distinction of domestic from international politics. He allows that a pacified domestic space could verge on a distinctively political one when its conflicts began to portend war, bringing it into analogy with the international realm. Morgenthau, though he indicted Schmitt's contrastive account of the political, does so for the sake of further emphasizing the role of enmity in international affairs. And, as Martti Koskenniemi (2001, ch. 6) emphasizes, as Morgenthau left Europe and his training in international law and devoted himself to the construction of international relations, his reliance on Schmitt remained essential.[10] Aron, Morgenthau's French opposite number in the field, owed Schmitt much too (Tommissen 2001).[11] Even Arendt, devoted more deeply than either Aron or Morgenthau to supplementing Schmitt's account of the political with a domestic civic republicanism emphasizing non-violent action, could find no way in the Cold War to escape his premise of necessary enmity and warfare in international affairs, especially as Schmitt turned himself to international affairs theory himself (Bates 2010).

For his part, Lefort never seriously considered international politics.[12] Neither did he ever mention (let alone comment on) Schmitt at any point, because he forged his theory out of different sources than were available or popular prior to the recent surge of interest in the German thinker.[13] In doing so, I have been suggesting, he allied with a different sort of transcendental approach than Schmitt offered, which ultimately sought to make the political foundational rather than conditional. But before concluding, it is nonetheless worth considering what Lefort might have made of Schmitt's more specific approach to enmity as the essence of the political. For arguably, Lefort's thought also usefully reveals some of the limits of making enmity a core feature of the political even for someone equally committed to placing the political first.

As in Arendt's parallel work, the Lefortian concept of the political displaces Schmitt's claim that the essence of the political is the distinction between friend and enemy—even as, like Arendt, Lefort attempts to make much room for agon and dissensus within political communities. According to Lefort's symbolic approach to the constitution of political community, however, it is a prior problem how a group could take on its identity at all—requiring a kind of external reference but not one that demands any rival communities for subjectivity to form. Put boldly, where Schmitt insists that community depended on *real externality*, Lefort insists on *symbolic externality*, which also allows him to dispense with the premise of necessary enmity. In this way, Lefort's symbolic theory of the political identifies the conditions for communities to take shape *in the first instance*—for friends to be together independently of the existence of enemies.

One way to get clear about the difference is to examine briefly the treatment by an anthropologist friend and colleague of Lefort's, Pierre Clastres, of intergroup war. The setting of Clastres's work was the primitive world, which he theorizes in the Lefortian manner as involving political community attained through symbolic constitution (Moyn 2004). Interestingly, however, as a premodern community, so-called savage tribes could not have politics as a delimited space because their politics involved as radical a suppression as possible of the fact that humans make their social world. In fact, it was as following from just this premise that Clastres interprets the endemic warfare of the tribes he studied.

In Clastres's ethnography, intergroup conflict, for all its spilled blood, nevertheless plays a *homeopathic* function. Rejecting the theses that war is natural (Thomas Hobbes's thesis, supposedly confirmed by accounts of savages) and economic arguments that war arises over scarce resources or because of a breakdown of exchange, Clastres proposes the need for a political interpretation that does justice to how integral war is to primitive life while understanding its true function. "In its being, primitive society wants dispersion," Clastres (1994, 153) argues, accounting for the recourse to war as a guarantee for small communities that needed to remain separate. For it was only on condition of membership in bounded entities that primitive men can preserve their antipolitical politics, through which Clastres sees them rejecting hierarchy and keeping the modern state at bay—the very state Schmitt takes as the occasion for his own transcendental argument.

Far from society following from natural warfare, as Hobbes had it, violence followed politically from society: it was necessary not for the community to exist at all but to avoid its dissolution. For its existence and coherence in the first instance, Lefort comments on Clastres's work, primitive communities do need to look outside themselves, but at least in the first instance only to a representation of their own making (Moyn 2012). The same is true, in spite of a series of other differences, in modern politics. To make the enemy the foundation of collective politics is to leave unexplained whether and why the enemy is needed.

CONCLUSION

There can be no doubt that Carl Schmitt opened a consequential twentieth-century debate in proposing to put something called the political first. But the story of his concept of the political is as much that Schmitt could not control the legacy of that concept. In any case, as I have tried to show, the intellectual trajectory of the political proceeded in part because Schmitt says so little about the concept in his book on the subject, reducing it to a transcendental inquiry into the conditions of the state before moving rapidly to his indictment of welfarism for putting enmity at risk. And what Schmitt does say in his brief introduction of the concept raised as many questions as it answered.

One clear trend in the reception of Schmitt's *Concept of the Political* is the attempt to extricate both the search for an autonomous political realm and even Schmitt's distinction between friend and enemy from the assumption of ethnically homogeneous peoples to which he was tempted to tether it. And perhaps the reasons for this trend, after the collapse of the particular brand of German nationalism Schmitt supported, are straightforward (cf. Gross 2007). Arendt provides an early case in point here, but two contemporary examples in the massive and uncharted contemporary Schmitt revival also do so.

In her famous leftist appropriation of Schmitt, Chantal Mouffe (1993; 2005) seeks to retrieve Schmitt's agonism for the sake of a theory of the political that overcame the new age of depoliticizations and neutralizations that, she feared, the end of the Cold War brought about. Paul W. Kahn, to take a second interesting case, cites Schmitt for the analytical recovery of "the autonomy of the political in the modern nation-state," in which politics affords a "complete system of meaning that is its own source and end," alongside concurrent but distinct systems (2004, ch. 6, 280). Unlike Mouffe, Kahn disclaims any prescriptive interest in the political and its agonistic essence but insists that it is crucial to understand the workings of modern life for the sake of a more honest liberalism. A modern nation-state like the United States certainly defines its system of political meaning through identifying friends and promoting self-sacrifice against mortal foes, even as Kahn emphasizes that "American political experience has been directly to the contrary" of an ethnic nationalist—one Schmitt illicitly imports into his otherwise exportable approach. For this reason, Kahn concludes, "While the structure of Schmitt's theory of the political offers a useful set of concepts, the content of his theory is not similarly useful" (2004, 20).[14]

It should have been clear from the beginning, however, that an emphasis neither on autonomy nor enmity was the sole path available to a theory of the political. In the alternative tradition initiated by Aron and continued by Lefort—though returning, as Leo Strauss first emphasized the need to do, to classical sources—the political is neither a contrastive nor an intensive concept. It is also therefore not one that is susceptible of disappearing before the threat of liberalism, as Schmitt himself feared, and post-Cold War Schmittians (even tame ones) were also tempted to worry. In forging a foundational concept of politics, of course, Lefort inherited the difficulties that Marxism had faced in placing economics first. But his concept of the political at the very least began with a central problem that both Schmitt and many of his followers skirted, which is how to account for communal identity—including versions in which the political appeared as a topic of inquiry and site of experience potentially separate from others—in the first instance.

NOTES

1. For background on German *Staatsrecht* and Schmitt's thought in relation to it in English, see, for example, Caldwell 1997 (ch. 1); Kelly 2003. See also Galli 1996 (ch. 14, esp. 754–755). On the nature of transcendental arguments, see, for example, Taylor 1995.

2. In a brilliant recent book, David Bates 2011 shows that it was precisely in the Enlightenment that the autonomy of the political was first theorized, challenging Schmitt's view that only late nineteenth-century developments prompted the need to discover its essence.

3. Since Arendt's relationship to Schmitt has been canvassed in much earlier scholarship, I leave it aside here for other matters. Though the commentary that follows locates many discontinuities between the two thinkers, everyone agrees that Arendt adopted Schmitt's exclusionary or contrastive notion of the political, even as she hoped for ways to revive the ancient intensity of politics (which she did not read in terms of enmity) within the framework of modern constitutionalism. See Scheuerman 1998; Kalyvas 2008; Moyn 2008a; Sluga 2008; zum Kolk 2009.

4. Note, however, that Scheuerman also overemphasizes how much Schmitt changes his mind and about what—adopting Meier's framework and simply assigning Morgenthau credit for the paradigm shift.

5. For a bibliographically rich but rather different survey of the twentieth-century trajectory of the political, which omits Raymond Aron and describes Claude Lefort as offering an aesthetic doctrine, see Jay 2010 (ch. 2).

6. See Freund 1965 (esp. 751) for his Schmittian definition of the political. For this I rely on Jenkins forthcoming. See also Müller 2003.

7. See Balibar et al. 1981 (esp. 15) on terminology; Lacoue-Labarthe and Nancy eds. 1983—the latter with Lefort's paper "The Question of Democracy," which also deploys the terminological distinction. Some useful materials about and from this center appear in English as Lacoue-Labarthe and Nancy 1997; see also Marchart 2007 (esp. ch. 2). I am very grateful to Danilo Scholz for information about the center and to Wim Weymans for help identifying the evolution in Lefort's terminology.

8. Note that the collection this citation is taken from *Democracy and Political Theory*, which in French was simply titled *Essais sur le politique (XIXe–XXe siècles)* (Lefort 1986). I am working on a historical study about the origins of Lefort's approach to the political; for now, see Moyn 2008b.

9. On Rosanvallon's career, see my essay, coauthored with Andrew Jainchill; Moyn and Jainchill 2004; also Palonen 2009.

10. See also Koskenniemi's chapter in this volume (2016). Compare the corrective but not fully convincing alternative reading of Morgenthau in Scheuerman 2009; Brown 2007.

11. See also the special issue of *Études internationales* of September 2012 on Raymond Aron and international relations, esp. De Ligio 2012.

12. See the few post-Cold War pieces from late in his life on the subject collected in Lefort 2007a.
13. Lefort did devote escalating attention to Arendt over the second half of his career, beginning with Lefort 1988b.
14. See later Kahn's 2011 much more full-blown engagement with Schmitt, in a similar spirit.

References

Anderson, Brian. 1997. *Raymond Aron: The Recovery of the Political.* Lanham: Rowman & Littlefield.

Aron, R. 1968. *Democracy and Totalitarianism*, trans. V. Ionescu. London: Littlehampton.

Aron, R. 2002. *Le marxisme de Marx.* Paris: Editions de Fallois.

Badiou, A. 1985. *Peut-on penser le politique.* Paris: Seuil.

Balibar, E., L. Ferry, P. Lacoue-Labarthe, J. F. Lyotard, and J.-L. Nancy. 1981. *Rejouer le politique: Travaux du Centre de recherches philosophiques sur le politique.* Paris: Galilée.

Bates, D. 2010. "Enemies and Friends: Arendt on the Imperial Republic at War." *History of European Ideas* 36: 112–124.

Bates, D. 2011. *States of War: The Enlightenment Origins of the Political.* New York: Columbia University Press.

Breckman, W. 2013. *Adventures of the Symbolic: Postmarxism and Democratic Theory.* New York: Columbia University Press.

Brown, C. 2007. "'The Twilight of International Morality': Hans J. Morgenthau and Carl Schmitt on the End of the Jus Publicum Europaeum." In *Realism Reconsidered: The Legacy of Hans Morgenthau in International Relations*, ed. M. C. Williams, New York: Oxford University Press, 42–61.

Caldwell, P. 1997. *Popular Sovereignty and the Crisis of German Constitutional Law: The Theory and Practice of Weimar Constitutionalism.* Durham: Duke University Press.

Clastres, P. 1994. *The Archeology of Violence.* New York: Semiotext(e).

De Ligio, G. 2012. "La vertu politique: Aron, penseur de l'ami et de l'ennemi." *Études Internationales* 43: 405–420.

Donégani, J.-M., and M. Sadoun. 2007. *Qu'est-ce que la politique?* Paris: Gallimard.

Freund, J. 1965. *L'essence du politique.* Paris: Sirey.

Galli, C. 1996. *La genealogia della politica: Carl Schmitt e la crisi del pensiero politico moderno* Bologna: Il Mulino.

Gross, R. 2007. *Carl Schmitt and the Jews: The "Jewish Question," the Holocaust and German Legal Theory*, trans. J. Golb. Madison: University of Wisconsin Press.

Guilhot, N. 2010. "American Katechon: When Political Theology Became International Relations Theory." *Constellations* 17: 224–253.

Jainchill, A., and Moyn, S. 2004. "French Democracy between Totalitarianism and Solidarity: Pierre Rosanvallon and Revisionist Historiography." *Journal of Modern History* 76: 107–154.

Jay, M. 2010. *The Virtues of Mendacity: On Lying in Politics.* Charlottesville: University of Virginia Press.

Jenkins, D. 2014. "Why Did Raymond Aron Write that Carl Schmitt Was Not a Nazi? An Alternative Genealogy of French Liberalism." *Modern Intellectual History* 11: 549–574.

Kahn, P. 2004. *Putting Liberalism in Its Place.* Princeton: Princeton University Press.

Kahn, P. 2011. *Political Theology: Four New Chapters on the Concept of Sovereignty*. New York: Columbia University Press.

Kalyvas, A. 2008. *Democracy and the Politics of the Extraordinary: Max Weber, Carl Schmitt, Hannah Arendt*. Cambridge: Cambridge University Press.

Kelly, D. 2003. *The State of the Political: Conceptions of Politics and the State in the Thought of Max Weber, Carl Schmitt and Franz Neumann*. New York: Oxford University Press.

Kennedy, E. 2004. *Constitutional Failure: Carl Schmitt in Weimar*. Durham: Duke University Press.

Koskenniemi, M. 2001. *The Gentle Civilizer of Nations: The Rise and Fall of International Law 1870–1960*. Cambridge: Cambridge University Press.

Koskenniemi, M. 2016. "Carl Schmitt and International Law." In *The Oxford Handbook of Carl Schmitt*, ed. J. Meierhenrich and O. Simons. Oxford: Oxford University Press, 592–611.

Lacoue-Labarthe, P., and J.-L. Nancy. 1997. *Retreating the Political*, ed. S. Sparks. New York: Routledge.

Lacoue-Labarthe, P., and J.-L. Nancy. eds. 1983. *Le retrait du politique: Travaux du Centre de recherches philosophiques sur le politique*. Paris: Galilée.

Lefort, C. 1986. *Essais sur le politique (XIXe–XXe siècles)*. Paris: Seuil.

Lefort, C. 1988a. *Democracy and Political Theory*, trans. D. Macey. Minneapolis: University of Minnesota Press.

Lefort, C. 1988b. "Hannah Arendt and the Question of Political." In Lefort 1988a, 45–56.

Lefort, C. 1988c. "The Permanence of the *Theologico-Political?*" In Lefort 1988a, 213–255.

Lefort, C. 1988d. "The Question of Democracy." In Lefort 1988a, 9–20.

Lefort, C. 2007a. *Le temps présent: Écrits 1945–2005*. Paris: Belin.

Lefort, C. 2007b. "Raymond Aron et le phénomène totalitaire." In Lefort 2007a, 993–999.

Lefort, C. 2007c. "Repenser le politique—Entretien avec E. A. El Maleh." In Lefort 2007a, 359–368.

Lefort, C., and M. Gauchet. 1971. "Sur la démocratie: le politique et l'institution du social." *Textures* 2–3: 7–78.

Marchart, O. 2007. *Post-Foundational Political Thought: Political Difference in Nancy, Lefort, Badiou, and Laclau*. Edinburgh: Edinburgh University Press.

Meier, H. 1995. *Carl Schmitt and Leo Strauss: The Hidden Dialogue*, trans. J. H. Lomax. Chicago: University of Chicago Press.

Morgenthau, H. 1929. *Die internationale Rechtspflege: Ihr Wesen und ihre Grenzen*. Leipzig: Universitätsverlag Noske.

Morgenthau, H. 1933. *La notion du "politique" et la théorie des différends internationaux*. Paris: Sirey.

Morgenthau, H. 1978. "An Intellectual Autobiography." *Society* 15: 63–69.

Morgenthau, H. 2012. *The Concept of the Political*, trans. M. Vidal, ed. H. Behr and F. Rösch. New York: Palgrave Macmillan.

Mouffe, C. 1993. *The Return of the Political*. New York: Verso.

Mouffe, C. 2005. *On the Political*. New York: Routledge.

Moyn, S. 2004. "Of Savagery and Civil Society: Pierre Clastres and the Transformation of French Political Thought." *Modern Intellectual History* 1: 55–80.

Moyn, S. 2008a. "Hannah Arendt on the Secular." *New German Critique* 105: 71–96.

Moyn, S. 2008b. "Marxism and Alterity: Claude Lefort and the Critique of Totality." In *The Modernist Imagination: Essays in Intellectual History and Critical Theory*, ed. W. Breckman et al. New York: Berghahn, 99–116.

Moyn, S. 2012. "Claude Lefort, Political Anthropology, and Symbolic Division." *Constellations* 19: 37–50.

Müller, J.-W. 2003. *A Dangerous Mind: Carl Schmitt in Post-War European Thought*. New Haven: Yale University Press.

Palonen, K. 1990. *Die Thematisierung der Politik als Phänomen: Eine Interpretation der Geschichte des Begriffs Politik im Frankreich des 20. Jahrhunderts*. Helsinki: Societas Scientiarum Fennica.

Palonen, K. 2009. "The Two Faces of Contingency: La Politique and Le Politique in the Work of Pierre Rosanvallon." *Contributions to the History of Concepts* 5: 123–139.

Pichler, H.-K. 1998. "The Godfathers of 'Truth': Max Weber and Carl Schmitt in Morgenthau's Theory of Power Politics." *Review of International Studies* 24: 185–200.

Rancière, J. 2003. *Aux bords du politique*. Paris: Folio.

Rancière, J. 2007. *On the Shores of Politics*, trans. L. Heron. New York: Verso.

Rohe, K. 1978. *Politik: Begriffe und Wirklichkeiten*. Stuttgart: Kohlhammer.

Rosanvallon, P. 2006. *Democracy Past and Future*, ed, S. Moyn. New York: Columbia University Press.

Scheuerman, W. 1998. "Revolutions and Constitutions: Hannah Arendt's Challenge to Carl Schmitt." In *Law as Politics: Carl Schmitt's Critique of Liberalism*, ed. D. Dyzenhaus. Durham: Duke University Press, 252–280.

Scheuerman, W. 1999. *Carl Schmitt: The End of Law*. Lanham: Rowman & Littlefield.

Scheuerman, W. 2009. *Hans Morgenthau: Realism and Beyond*. Cambridge: Polity Press.

Schmidt, B. 1998. *The Political Discourse of Anarchy: A Disciplinary History of International Relations*. Albany: State University of New York Press.

Schmitt, C. 1931. "Die Wendung zum Totalen Staat." *Europäische Revue* 7: 241–250.

Schmitt, C. 2007. *The Concept of the Political*, trans. G. Schwab. Chicago: University of Chicago Press.

Schmitz, M. 1965. *Die Freund–Feind Theorie Carl Schmitts*. Cologne: Westdeutscher Verlag.

Schwab, G. 2007. "Introduction." In Schmitt 2007, 3–16.

Sluga, H. 2008. "The Pluralism of the Political: From Carl Schmitt to Hannah Arendt." *Telos* 142: 91–109.

Strauss, L. 1932. "Anmerkungen zu Carl Schmitt, *Der Begriff des Politischen*." *Archiv für Sozialwissenschaft und Sozialpolitik* 67: 732–749.

Tarot, C. 2003. *De Durkheim à Mauss: l'invention du symbolique*. Paris: Decouverte.

Taylor, C. 1995. "The Validity of Transcendental Arguments." In *Philosophical Arguments*. Cambridge: Harvard University Press, 20–33.

Tommissen, P. 2001. "Raymond Aron face à Carl Schmitt." In *Schmittiana: Beiträge zu Leben und Werk Carl Schmitts*, vol. 7, ed. P. Tommissen. Berlin: Duncker & Humblot, 111–129.

Unger, R. M. 1997. *Politics: The Central Texts*, ed. Z. Cui. New York: Verso.

Weber, M. 1958. "Politics as a Vocation." In *From Max Weber: Essays in Sociology*, ed. H. H. Gerth and C. W. Mills. New York: Oxford University Press, 77–128.

zum Kolk, P. 2009. *Carl Schmitt und Hannah Arendt: Ausnahme und Normalität*. Frankfurt: Lang.

CHAPTER 11

CARL SCHMITT'S DEFENSE OF DEMOCRACY

WILLIAM RASCH

INTRODUCTION

THE HISTORY of the modern European state, Michael Oakeshott asserts, is the history of a continuous search for the sources of power and authority. Of the two, power has received the greatest attention, but authority is the most important, for it demands recognition and obligation even when assent or approval is lacking. "Most constitution makers and constitutional reformers in modern times," he writes, "have not been disposed to think of a constitution as that in terms of which a government may be acknowledged to have authority" (Oakeshott 1990, 192). Rather, they have viewed it "merely as a piece of machinery," an "apparatus of governing" (192). Historically it has been the strong leader who created the conditions for authority, either by eliminating or going into partnership with rivals and creating or consolidating statewide legal uniformity, for it is in law that Oakeshott finds authority. After providing a list of what authority is not,[1] Oakeshott asserts that "*Respublica* [political association] as a system of law...contains rules in terms of which the authority of other rules may be recognized, and the recognition of its authority begins in what may be called the recognition of the validity of its prescriptions" (150). To borrow a phrase from Niklas Luhmann (1983), whom Oakeshott stunningly resembles on this point, a state's authority arises as a form of "legitimation through process." Indeed, Oakeshott concludes in true Luhmannian fashion: "And should it be asked how a manifold of rules...may be acknowledged to be authoritative, the answer is that authority is the only conceivable attribute it could be indisputably acknowledged to have. In short the only understanding of *respublica* capable of evoking the acceptance of all *cives* [members] without exception, and thus eligible to be recognized as the terms of civil association, is *respublica* understood in respect of its authority" (1990, 154). Authority is not the infinite regress of hierarchy, but takes the shape of a virtuous circle.

Oakeshott concedes that authority is seldom durable, no matter the form of political organization achieved. Anarchy always lurks "just below the surface," and once authority is questioned or denied, civil war becomes a real possibility (1990, 190). Because of a feared "disintegration of the association and the self-alienation of its components," there "have always been people...who have wanted the state to be an integrated community set on a common course and pursuing a common purpose" (188). Carl Schmitt is one of those people in whom the threat of resurgent disorder occasions the desire for a more substantial source of authority. For him, authority is the source, not the result, of law, because in the end, law cannot protect itself or the association it governs. The consequences of World War I certainly heightened Schmitt's fears. Germany—with restricted sovereignty, relieved of chunks of its territory, deprived of an effective military, occupied (the Rhineland, and then the Ruhr), denied membership in the promised land of the League of Nations (until 1926), stripped of its merchant fleet, under foreign economic supervision (reparations), and fighting border wars in the east as well as insurrectionary battles not "just below the surface" but on the streets of its major cities—was faced with basic questions of political order and survival. To assume that the "self-authenticating property of *respublica*"—especially in liberal form, with its postulated autonomy of the individual equipped with prepolitical rights and consumer desires—would be sufficient to hold a political association together was a luxury, Schmitt felt, that Germany could ill afford. A more substantial source of authority (of *legitimacy*, to use Schmitt's language) was needed, and during the 1920s and early 1930s Schmitt increasingly found that source to be "the people," a collected political body (not simply a collection of bodies) with felt obligations to "the nation." The authority of *respublica* was to be located not in law but in the popular constituent power that animated the law.

On the other side of the Atlantic, the situation was quite different. The United States had become the globe's preeminent power. Domestically, however, the country had been traumatized. If the war's aftermath had inspired Schmitt's most brilliant dissections of liberal individualism and (moral and economic) deceit, in the United States the opposite occurred. The governmentally organized surveillance, violence, and vigilantism during Woodrow Wilson's disastrous second term (1917–1921) sparked an American liberal rights revolution.[2] At the conclusion of his fine study on World War I and the making of modern American citizenship, Christopher Capozzola muses about the relative merits of obligation and rights. "These days," he writes, "some Americans wish for obligations, hoping to renew among Americans a sense of commitment toward our fellow citizens. Ninety years, they tell us, have put rights, and not obligations, at the center of our political life. Individualism has corroded our common culture and our civic associations; we even bowl alone" (Capozzola 2008, 213). The complaint resonates with us, he admits. "From such a perspective, the sense of voluntarism and obligation in the political culture of early twentieth-century America must astound" (213). But, he insists, the humiliation, persecution, imprisonment, and murder of German Americans and other immigrants; the stepped-up terror waged against African Americans; the flare-up of antisemitism; the violation of religious conscience; and the violent destruction of the radical labor movement and the Socialist Party tell a different story. "Those who seek something beyond the rights revolution must understand the political culture that existed before rights talk, when obligation still held sway. In a divided and unequal society, civil society could be an arena for negotiating political obligation; it could also be a weapon wielded against the weak" (214). Capozzola's is a necessary reminder and warning, not least because his example is not taken from one of the usual totalitarian suspects. The coupling of civil society and the state can be brutal, even in liberal democracies. But, alas, rights themselves are no magic shield. Beyond their negative, fragmentary consequences, ones that turn citizens into consumers and politics into slogans about the *oikos* ("Are you better off today than you were four years ago?"—"It's the economy, stupid!"), rights frequently not only *fail* to protect individuals and groups (African Americans, Japanese Americans, Muslim Americans), but can *also* become weapons (the right to private property, for instance) wielded against the weak.[3] Most alarming, however, at least to Schmitt, is the sense that a reliance on rights (civil, human, or other) threatens to enfeeble popular political will, thereby replacing political decision with legal, bureaucratic procedure. And indeed, in the world in which we now live, "human rights" trump self-determination (Moyn 2010).

Reading Carl Schmitt becomes an exercise in contemplating contradictions: the public versus the private, duties versus rights, collective equality versus individual liberty. These are the contradictions that Hegel and Marx unsuccessfully attempted to sublate. At the beginning of the twenty-first century, we are left with the wreckage of the dialectic. Nevertheless, unlike the noble defenders of the liberal consensus, Schmitt was not content to let the right-hand column of alternatives dominate over the left, and that is why some political philosophers who are discontented with the current lack of theoretical alternatives are still—or rather, once again—interested in him. Accordingly, the tension between the private and the public, between the expansiveness of liberty and the self-disciplinary demands of equality, which lies at the heart of Schmitt's views on liberalism and democracy, structures what follows. First, I use Norbert Bobbio to outline the logical incompatibility of substantial equality and liberty. The second section outlines Schmitt's radical discontent with nineteenth-century liberal thought (using Benjamin Constant as an example). This is followed by an exploration of Schmitt's arguments, outlined primarily in *Constitutional Theory* (2008), on "the people" as the constituent power of a modern constitution. Since in Schmitt's view, good governance requires plebiscitary leadership, in the last main section I investigate Schmitt's notions of representation and acclamation. The conclusion describes two attempts at plebiscitary leadership, one successful but pernicious, and a second, failed attempt, the consequences of which lead back to my opening deliberations on the unresolved relationship between private liberty and common, public responsibility. The two examples give no clear signal, which is why theoretical contemplation beyond the norms of liberal orthodoxy may once again be worth entertaining.

DEMOCRATIC EQUALITY
VERSUS LIBERAL FREEDOM

With more than just a hint of impatience, the Italian political theorist Norberto Bobbio firmly insisted that modern democracy is necessarily formal and procedural. "I have stated on other occasions," he wrote in the mid-1980s, "and I will never tire of repeating it, that it is impossible to ever understand anything about democracy until it is realized that a democratic system nowadays signifies first and foremost a set of procedural rules, among which majority rule is the main, but not the only one" (Bobbio 1987, 63). Perhaps "nowadays" is the key word in that proclamation, because Bobbio is keenly aware of the history of an antagonism between the ideal of democracy based on a "social" or "sub-stantial" notion of equality and liberalism as a political movement that emerged at the beginning of the nineteenth century in opposition to *both* the monarchical principle and popular sovereignty. Individual liberty, formal equality before the law, and consti-tutional government (understood primarily as the separation of powers and guarantee of select subjective rights) were advanced to combat the absolutist "tyrant" as well as the "tyranny of the mob." Of course, democracy too saw itself as the implacable enemy of monarchy; hence during the course of their common nineteenth-century battles, a com-promise or synthesis occurred—not without its radical critics, chiefly Marx—between the two uneasy allies. As Bobbio describes it, the compromise was worked out on a ter-minological terrain, though of course it had its political and social correlates.

The battle between liberalism and democracy is the battle between the hegemony of liberty over equality, on the one hand, and equality over liberty, on the other. According to Bobbio, "liberty and equality are antithetical values, in the sense that neither can be fully realized except at the expense of the other: a liberal laissez-faire society is inevi-tably inegalitarian, and an egalitarian society is inevitably illiberal" (1990, 32). To fuse the two political ideologies, one needs to tweak definitions, primarily by weakening the meaning of equality. "There is only one form of equality—equality in the right to lib-erty—which is not only compatible with liberalism but equally demanded by its view of freedom" (33). Thus, "nowadays" democracy must restrict its desire for equality to the aforementioned liberal ideals of equality before the law and equal rights. A problem that this hybrid creature called liberal democracy cannot examine is the fact that just because one has a *right* to equality does not mean that one necessarily has the material means to enjoy its concrete exercise. Liberalism habitually brushes this inconvenient detail aside and thereby wins its battle with democracy, for whereas liberal ideals seem-ingly need no alteration, older, "substantial" definitions of democracy are discredited or simply disappear. Modern liberal-democracy in its "juridical-institutional" sense is "procedural," in that it emphasizes a "body of rules," Bobbio maintains; it is a formal "government *by* the people." What liberal democracy supplants is an "ethical" vision that promotes "substantial" equality not only of opportunity but also of achievement and therefore exerts itself to be a "government *for* the people" (31–32; emphasis added). This latter, older version, Bobbio says, is to be rejected, for "today non-democratic lib-eral states would be inconceivable, as would non-liberal democratic states" (38). Like "nowadays" above, "today" here accepts the liberal definition of equality and thus the liberal modification—or mollification—of democracy as an irreversible (and of course desirable) fait accompli. Based on this victory, then, Bobbio can decry Carl Schmitt's "withering critiques of democracy" (1987, 122), even though by the late 1920s, especially in his *Constitutional Theory* (a text Bobbio often cites), Schmitt saw himself as a classic democrat at war with liberalism's enervating assault on all things political.

What follows examines Schmitt's renewal of the war between democracy and liberalism; for during the Weimar Republic, after some hesitation, Schmitt wrapped himself, like some modern Robespierre, in the mantle of democracy. This cloak, like all the capes of political theory, is a patchwork quilt, stitching this with that while leaving the other behind, but the pattern that emerges is coherent, even, some might think, aesthetically pleasing. At any rate, it challenges the tireless certitude of Bobbio's insistence. Therefore, whatever its immediate practical value or potential threat, its contemplation may serve to stimulate the modern political imagination, if, that is, such a thing as political imagination still exists at all "nowadays."

The Threat of Liberalism

As political theorists and classical scholars well know, the idea of liberty was articulated quite differently in Greek antiquity than it is today. In Athenian democracy, citizens (nonforeign, nonslave, adult males, i.e., a small percentage of the total population) were the true source of all political decisions, as they participated directly and often in open-air assemblies to discuss and make laws, set policies, hold leaders accountable, and even declare war or make peace. As M. I. Finley states, the members of the *polis* felt themselves to be members of a community (*koinonia*), "in which the bonds were not merely propinquity and a common way of life but also a consciousness of common destiny, common faith" (Finley 1985, 29). Educated by all Athenian institutions small (the family) and large (the political assembly itself), a young man gained a *paideia* (formation or *Bildung*), a sense of civic responsibility that fostered the virtues of public service (29–31). The distinction between the public and the private certainly existed, but refusing one's public duties in favor of private pleasures was considered pathological. In the words of Thucydides: "We consider anyone who does not share in the life of the citizen not as minding his own business but as useless" (cf. Finley 1985, 30). Liberty, then, meant citizenship, the right and duty to participate directly in political decision. Liberty meant integrating oneself in one's community.

Quite the opposite is the modern view, which raises the importance of the individual up over the whole, the private above the public. There is perhaps no better champion of the modern view than Benjamin Constant, though his advocacy is couched in language so honest that it betrays a twinge of regret, a nod, perhaps, to a "nobler" time that cannot be recaptured and thus should now never be attempted.[4] That it was attempted—by the leaders of the French Revolution—and so disastrously so, is the motor that drives Constant's fear of political power, which he wishes to brake with the force of commerce. He therefore highlights the distinction between the public and private spheres, between the political community and the private individual as *homo oeconomicus*. For the ancients, Constant asserts, liberty "consisted in exercising collectively, but directly, several parts of the complete sovereignty" (1988, 311, 102); thereby communal well-being was elevated over faction or self-interest. The individual was free in his "active participation in collective power"; thus his liberty consisted in his ability to take part in communal deliberation and exercise political decision. For the privilege of this active and public liberty, however, he paid by renouncing "private independence... since to enable a people to enjoy the widest possible political rights, that is that each citizen may have his share in sovereignty, it is necessary to have institutions which maintain equality, prevent the increase of fortunes, proscribe distinctions, and are set in opposition to the influence of wealth, talents even virtue" (103). For the ancients, then, liberty was a public and political quality, not a private pleasure.

For the moderns, the poles are reversed. Private pleasures wholly replace political participation, for modernity no longer permits direct, public citizenship. Based on property rights and grown to a size that is unmanageable by communally deliberative methods, the modern state, Constant says, has happily hit upon the idea of representative government, which removes from the citizen the burdensome necessity of political knowledge and intimate participation. Popular sovereignty, no matter how stridently proclaimed, is at best illusory. "Lost in the multitude," Constant writes, "the individual can almost never perceive the influence he exercises. Never does his will impress itself upon the whole; nothing confirms in his eyes his own cooperation" (1988, 311). Accordingly, the pleasure afforded the ancients by their exercise of political rights is no longer attainable. Rather, *our* pleasure is taken privately. Whereas "the aim of the ancients was the sharing of social power among the citizens of the same fatherland," the "aim of the moderns is the enjoyment of security in private pleasures; and they call liberty the guarantee accorded by institutions to these pleasures" (312). It is almost as if he were singing us lullabies: "The sole aim of the modern nations is repose, and with repose comfort, and, as a source of comfort, industry" (54). The citizen becomes the bourgeois; the political actor the passive consumer. Hush little baby, don't you cry. Or rather, and much more to the point, the interests of the political subserve those of the economy. With disarming honesty, Constant exults: "The effects of commerce extend even further: not only does it emancipate individuals, but, by creating credit, it places authority itself in a position of dependence.... Power threatens; wealth rewards: one eludes power by deceiving it; to obtain the favours of wealth one must serve it: the latter is therefore bound to win" (325). Constant leaves us in no doubt whose interests the representatives of representative government represent.

For Carl Schmitt, Benjamin Constant's lineaments of modernity produce a consumptive portrait of a pale humanity engaged only in passive pleasures, eschewing public responsibility. Throughout his work and often with a fine and elegant pathos, Schmitt knew how to eviscerate this liberal ethos of wealth and property buffed with the patina of self-assured morality. To say, as does the consistent liberal, that all vice lies on the side of the state and all virtue with civil society is to elide the necessary efficacy of the public—that is to say—of the political altogether. As did Kant before him and John Rawls since, Constant believed that commerce was inherently pacific and brought people and peoples together. Unlike Kant and Rawls, he seems to have been more honest about what commercial pacification entailed. "War and commerce," he writes,

> are only two different means of achieving the same end, that of getting what one wants. Commerce is simply a tribute paid to the strength of the possessor by the aspirant to possession... an attempt to conquer, by mutual agreement, what one can no

longer hope to obtain through violence...a milder and surer means of engaging the interest of others to agree to what suits his own. (Constant 1988, 313)

But why should the replacement of war by trade, force by industry, even when used as a means of covert subjugation, be such a problem? Surely the devastation of World War I might have had the same or similar impact on Schmitt as the revolutionary and Napoleonic wars had on Constant. What was Schmitt trying to rescue from the cunning of commerce?

In the last section of *The Concept of the Political*, Schmitt deals directly with Constant, citing one of the texts I have used above, *The Spirit of Conquest* of 1814. For Schmitt, Constant's views are not unique but rather stand as exemplary of a common eighteenth- and nineteenth-century view. Freedom, progress, and reason in alliance with the economy, industry, and technology are prized and pitted against the evils of feudalism, reaction, force, state, war, and politics. What emerges from this confrontation is the triumph of parliamentarianism (liberalism) over dictatorship (of the monarch or the people; Schmitt 2007a, 75). The result, in other words, is the desired victory of civil society as the repository of all that is good over the state and the sinister machinations of politics. Schmitt denies the absoluteness of the distinction and questions the judgment. "[O]ne could," he notes, "just as well the other way around define politics as the sphere of honest rivalry and economics as a world of deception" (77). After hesitating briefly, he in fact does just that. Almost as if mimicking Heidegger, he continues as follows: "Exchange [*tauschen*] and deception [*täuschen*] are often not far apart. A domination of men based upon pure economics must appear a terrible deception if, by remaining nonpolitical, it thereby evades political responsibility and visibility" (2007a, 77; 1963, 76). The issues of responsibility and visibility are crucial. A state can be held accountable only if its actions are seen and recognized as state actions, that is, as political actions, and these deeds can be visible as political actions only if they do not mask themselves as private commercial transactions or as embodied moral precepts. One may wish to put it this way: The political is a stage upon which actors display the making of decisions and their explicit and implicit consequences. The audience is comprised of spectators or perhaps participant-spectators, depending on the form of political organization prevalent in a given state. Economic activity occurs in the lobby where buying and selling goes on. If actual political decisions are made by the various transactions occurring in the lobby rather than the actions portrayed on the stage, then the audience is deceived as the actors hide the fact that they are mere marionettes manipulated from afar.

But even if the theater analogy strikes home, we might still ask ourselves why this transfer of power from political actors to economic agents should *eo ipso* be a *pernicious* deception. Why would we not welcome a pacified if inegalitarian globe, whether honestly or dishonestly achieved? The continuation of the above passage from *The Concept of the Political* gives us a strong clue regarding the specific interest behind Schmitt's fundamental complaint:

Exchange by no means precludes the possibility that one of the contractors experiences a disadvantage and that a system of mutual contracts finally deteriorates into a system of the worst exploitation and repression. When the exploited and the repressed attempt to defend themselves in such a situation, they of course cannot do so by economic means. And it is equally evident that the possessor of economic power would consider every attempt to change its power position by "extra-eco-nomic" means as violence and crime, and would seek methods to hinder this. (2007a, 77–78; translation modified)

The deceit of the economic conqueror is the insistence that economic measures further the civilizing process and are therefore *not* political weapons of cultural or physical destruction. To claim otherwise, to resist the blandishments of trade with violence and in the name of political necessity, would simply be immoral and criminal. It is not difficult to see in persistent hymns to commerce of whatever provenance the invisible hand of imperialism, and Schmitt does not hesitate to raise contemporary examples, such as the neocolonial mandate and protectorate systems of the League of Nations or the semicolonized areas of the Western Hemisphere subject to American dollar and, when necessary, gunboat diplomacy. But it is also crystal clear that the exploited and subjugated area that lay nearest his heart was located in post–World War I central Europe; the contracts and treaties to which he indirectly refers bear the names Versailles, Kellogg-Briand, and Dawes, among others, as we can easily detect in the conclusion of this bitter disquisition: "[N]ot all things possess an exchange value. No matter how large the financial bribe may be, there is no money equivalent for political freedom and political independence" (78).

We have, therefore, two reasons to resist the apotheosis of civil society. First there is the existential ground. Not everything has an exchange value, because not every "value" in life has a market value. The interests of *homo oeconomicus* or of a rationalized and thoroughly calculable technological society do not exhaust the definition of humanity. For someone like Schmitt, there is always also a religions dimension to terms like "debt" and "guilt" (*Schuld*) and of course "redemption." But one need not be a supposed "political theologian" to uphold the belief that there is more to man than money; one could, for instance, be quite simply a teacher attempting to conduct courses in the humanities for contemporary students. As it becomes increasingly difficult to justify liberal arts education to parents and administrators *except* on instrumentalist grounds, one becomes correspondingly sympathetic to Schmitt's overheated pathos. That aside, the second reason for opposing the economization of society and politics has already been touched upon, namely Schmitt's patriotism, his defense of a semicolonized Germany against what he perceived to be the moral sophistry used to justify economic exploitation and political hegemony. Liberalism, then, has the characteristics of a double-edged sword. In the hands of the economically strong, it becomes an apolitical form of conducting political conquest; for the economically weak, it serves as the solvent that dissolves a people into a random collection of self-serving private individuals, rendering them politically defenseless.

A politically united people becomes, on the one hand, a culturally interested public, and, on the other, partially an industrial concern and its employers, partially a mass of consumers. At the intellectual pole, government and power turns into propaganda and mass manipulation, and at the economic pole, control. (72)

To condemn liberalism, then, is simultaneously to condemn a politics that refuses to show its colors and to bemoan the loss of any kind of political maneuverability at all in the attempt to secure collective independence. To preserve political unity, Schmitt concludes, requires locating the sovereign constituent power.

THE PEOPLE AS CONSTITUENT POWER

The distinction between liberty and equality that Norberto Bobbio identified as the irreconcilable contradiction separating liberalism and democracy is the focus of Schmitt's preface to the 1926 second edition of *The Crisis of Parliamentary Democracy* and one of the driving forces of his *Constitutional Theory*. It is not that liberty ceases to exist in a democracy or that equality has no place within liberalism; rather, each must alter its basic definition in order to be welcome on the other's terrain. If within a *liberal* democracy, as advocated by Bobbio, equality must be reduced to a formal "equality in the right to liberty," within Schmitt's democracy liberty must become a public, not private, virtue, a collective freedom of the political body and a freedom on the part of the citizen to participate as a member of that collective.[5] Liberty, as a quality, is to be removed from the interiority and authority of conscience and placed at the disposal of the body politic. Within democracy, therefore, liberty becomes a political virtue that subserves equality, which provokes the necessary question: What is democratic equality?

"Democracy requires ... first homogeneity and second—if the need arises—elimination or eradication of heterogeneity. ... A democracy demonstrates its political power by knowing how to refuse or keep at bay something foreign and unequal that threatens its homogeneity" (Schmitt 1985, 9). The contemporary reader, who claims definitive knowledge of the moral lessons of twentieth-century history and is convinced of the unshakable quality of learned norms that are said to be innate human rights, will be chilled by the notion of homogeneity and the seeming brutality of the language of exclusion contained in these two sentences. In fact, if you are reading these lines for the first time, one can well imagine the colors and the shape that now flit through your mind. Though Schmitt can give example after example of democracies that exclude in order to include, above all ancient Athens, but also 1920s Turkey, Australia, and the British Empire, to which list the United States could easily be added, *we* take our bearings not from the present or the past but from the future, from the "democracy to come," whose features we mercifully do not yet know and therefore do not have to define. Consequently, we condemn totalitarian homogeneity and sing hymns to pluralist heterogeneity. No doubt we are right to do so. Indeed, perhaps doing so is a mark of our contemporary homogeneity, though we would call it "consensus." But if we rest here, we miss the point.

For Schmitt, homogeneity is a necessary feature of equality. "Equality is only interesting and valuable politically so long as it has substance, and for that reason at least the possibility and the risk of inequality" (1985, 9). Again, for the contemporary reader, the word "substance" as a limiting term will raise a red flag. We will again wish to intervene and say that the human being qua human being is the common subject and only legitimate "substance" of equality, that all men and women are created equal by virtue of their humanity. As a charitable ethic or even tenet of Christian love, such a claim might meet with Schmitt's approval. As a political postulate, however, it has no purchase. "The equality of all persons as persons is not democracy but a certain kind of liberalism, not a state form but an individualistic-humanitarian ethic and *Weltanschauung*" (13). In this view, the formal equality offered by the ideological "monism" of humanity (see Schmitt 2007a, 44) does not and cannot provide the proper subject for democratic identity, for that subject, namely "the people," needs the nonidentical in order to form itself. The people must be *a* people, not all persons, and for a people to understand itself *as* a people, as an identity of ruler and ruled, it needs, as Chantal Mouffe repeatedly states, a "constitutive outside… an exterior to the community that makes its existence possible" (1993, 114).[6] Thus, while Schmitt consistently uses the term "substance" to evoke the identity of the people as if it had always already been present, in his attempt to offer us a picture of what such a "substance" might look like, he generally gives us a menu of options that operate as sides of a distinction. For "the people" to be the subject of political action, it needs some common medium or, as he says elsewhere, a "central sphere" (Schmitt 2007b) such as a common history or language or religion or ethnicity or even a moral quality like civic virtue (1985, 9; 2008, 258–263).

Furthermore, in the modern (post-Westphalian, European) world, lines of demarcation are not merely ideal but territorial. "Germany" has (an ever-changing) physical shape with an (ever-changing but) continuous history and identity. Without such a ground around which a people can form (in opposition to others with other common grounds), equality would be a formal term that promises much but delivers precious little. This may someday end—Germany (say) may cease to exist as a political unity—but if it does, a new entity (Europe?) will emerge as the subject of political identity, and it will do so only by finding a common ground by means of which it can establish its identity in contradistinction to other, now non-European identities. All along the way, differences remain. Homogeneity does not mean that heterogeneity disappears. Protestants will be Protestants, Catholics Catholics, Jews Jews, and Muslims Muslims. Bavarians will fiercely define themselves in opposition to Prussians, Prussians to Rhinelanders. Workers will rail against capitalists; the bourgeois entrepreneur will disdain union workers as spoiled, lazy, and unkempt. But which distinction serves as the prime distinction, worker/capitalist, Bavarian/Prussian, Christian/non-Christian, or German/non-German? In Schmitt's world, for "a people" to exist, it must pick the national distinction around which to rally, if for no other reason than that the national distinction is (or has become) the territorial distinction and thus the physically defensible distinction. In a world of nation-states, the nation-state is supreme. To raise another distinction above all others—one's Christianity, one's class, one's "local" territory—would be to incite civil war, which would make the collective vulnerable to forces and pressures coming from the outside. The democratic community, in Schmitt's view, is forever defined by this threat.

In the ideal world of normative political theory, we still may not be satisfied with this answer. And perhaps we are right not to be. But it is neither a bizarre nor inherently dangerous notion, despite repeated attempts to see nothing but fascist ideology in anything and everything Schmitt writes. In fact, in Schmitt's ideal of homogeneity as a necessary means of political agency and survival, one may easily recognize a family resemblance to Laclau's and Mouffe's theory of hegemony, the construction of an overarching (if temporary and strategic) political association uniting disparate social movements and agendas under a single name or sign (Laclau and Mouffe 2001). Nevertheless, even if homogeneity (perhaps under a less suspicious name) could be salvaged as a plausible category, it will not have escaped the reader's attention that the notion of *economic* homogeneity is conspicuous by its absence. The issue of class conflict is never far from the surface in early twentieth-century Europe, not least Weimar Germany. The economic inequalities of 1920s Germany were at least as stark as those of twenty-first-century America, but then, unlike now, there were alternatives on the Left that directly addressed the perceived causes of these disparities. Schmitt is hardly unaware of economic issues and debates; they are shot through the Weimar Constitution, party battles, and the political theory of the time, and some of his best students and sometime admirers, like Otto Kirchheimer and Franz Neumann, were socialists or at least social democrats. Yet "class" never appears on Schmitt's menu of homogeneous options. On the surface, the reason is obvious. If the idea is to preserve the nation by identifying the constituent power with the collective called "the people," then dividing the people into warring classes could lead to nothing but civil war. Schmitt, then, could use class as an operative principle *only* if he could accept the Marxian philosophy of history, which prophesizes the apocalyptic elimination of economic strife. But for Schmitt,[7] the conflict between liberalism (liberty) and democracy (equality) is not historically contingent, caused by the contradictions of capitalism, but logically constitutive. Sadly, perhaps, but without a doubt, there will be no cancellation of that tragic opposition in a projected future when a completely transparent society will host a fully emancipated human being. We must therefore look to other means of dealing with economic inequality when such inequality disturbs political homogeneity, as this intriguing passage in *Constitutional Theory* mandates:

> According to democratic principles, equality in private law is dominant only in the sense that the same private law statutes are valid for everyone, not, on the contrary, in the sense of *economic* equality of private wealth, property, or income. In its consequences and applications, democracy as an essentially political concept involves, to begin with, only the public law. However, the superiority of the public over the private results unconditionally from democracy's essentially political character. As soon as political equality is destroyed or endangered by economic inequalities or by the social power of private property, it can become politically necessary to eliminate, by statute or measure, that type of disturbance or threat. In regard to this necessity, appealing to the sanctity of private property would be undemocratic. Still, such an

appeal would be in accord with the principles of the bourgeois Rechtsstaat, whose sense lies precisely in hindering the logical consequences of a political principle, as with democracy, and to transform democracy into a constitutional democracy, which is limited by constitutional law. (2008, 283)

Here Schmitt unravels the contradiction between liberty and equality by contrasting public and private law. Liberal rule of law (the constitutional *Rechtsstaat*) establishes the primacy of the private sphere and thus the sanctity of private property, come what may. Democracy, however, relies on the primacy of the public, and in the name of public necessity, (private) property rights may be violated. Put another way, if the aim of liberalism's struggle with the monarchy was to integrate the bourgeoisie into the power structure of the state, the aim of modern, mass democracy is to integrate the proletariat (see Schmitt 1995, 47). Though no social democrat, Schmitt understood the need for economic harmony even if, under capitalism, economic "homogeneity" was not possible.

In *Constitutional Theory*, the distinction between liberalism and democracy is starkly portrayed as the difference between the private and the public, between civil society and the state, between the economically driven denial of politics and the existential necessity of the political. This distinction is organizationally portrayed by the juxtaposition of Section II, "The Rechtsstaat Component of the Modern Constitution," and Section III, "The Political Component of the Modern Constitution." Under the "Political Component," Schmitt gives a thorough definition of his conception of democracy, to which we will shortly turn. In the former, however, he informs us that the *Rechtsstaat*, the state governed by the liberal rule of law, is not really a state form at all, but rather the enumeration of means by which civil society and the private, pleasure-seeking individual can keep any hint of the state at bay. As a *Rechtsstaat*, the "state appears as the strictly regulated servant of society" (Schmitt 2008, 169). "[B]ourgeois freedom" is the guiding value, which leads to the following formulation of the essence of liberalism: "The individual's sphere of freedom is presupposed as something prior to the state, in particular the freedom of the individual is *in principle unlimited*, while the authority of the state for intrusions into this sphere is *in principle limited*" (170; 1995, 45). Organizationally this priority of the individual over the state is guaranteed, on the one hand, by a series of basic rights, and on the other, by the so-called separation or balance of powers.

Though Schmitt means his definition to be a critique, a consistent liberal would find here little with which to argue. Basic rights—now commonly called human rights—are generally thought of as prepolitical, and fear of state power and the desire structurally to limit its extent motivates all liberal constitutions. Again, Constant can be our guide. "No authority on earth is unlimited," he admonishes us, "neither that of the people, nor that of the men who declare themselves their representatives, nor that of the kings, by whatever title they reign, nor, finally, that of the law.... The individuals possess individual rights independently of all social and political authority, and any authority which violates these rights becomes illegitimate" (1988, 180). Not only is "the sovereignty of the people...circumscribed within the limits traced by justice and by the rights of individuals," but even "God, if he intervenes in human affairs, can only sanction justice"

(182). In the liberal world so depicted, the single most important political imperative is to place limits on the political. Therefore, if one's reaction to Schmitt's description is a simple shrug of the shoulders and the question, "So?," then one affirms the seemingly obvious, namely that the liberal world is, in fact, the world we comfortably inhabit and most likely wish to continue inhabiting. In *The Crisis of Parliamentary Democracy*, even Schmitt admits that "[t]here are certainly not many people today who want to renounce the old liberal freedoms, particularly freedom of speech and the press" (1985, 50), and as any reader of his diaries will see, Schmitt enjoyed his share of the private pleasures granted to the comfortable bourgeois. Yet even if the affirmative shrug is conceded, one can still ask whether the equal right to the individual pursuit of happiness is the be-all and end-all of the political. And even if the answer to *that* is "yes," one may still legitimately ponder whether such a pursuit can best be executed in a strictly liberal society in which private pleasures are inextricably linked to (though not exclusively determined by) the accumulation of private property. Do communities exist so that some, and *only some*, may become wealthy?

These concerns—some explicitly, others implicitly addressed by Carl Schmitt—point to questions raised by that other Karl, Karl Marx, and his answers produce a similarly impatient negative evaluation of the triumph of the bourgeois individual over the citizen. In "On the Jewish Question," the young Marx also negatively contrasts the rights of man with the rights of the citizen. The former "are simply the rights of a member of civil society, that is, of egoistic man, of man separated from other men and from the community" (Marx 1972, 40). The right to liberty, he continues, is the "right of the *circumscribed* individual, withdrawn into himself" (40). Likewise, the right to property is founded upon "self-interest" (40). Most tellingly, equality is nothing but "the right to liberty," as long as liberty is confined to its liberal definition (40). To what purpose, then, does the political community exist in this self-interested view of the world? With no little indignation Marx concludes:

> The matter becomes still more incomprehensible when we observe that the political liberators reduce citizenship, the *political community*, to a mere *means* for preserving these so-called rights of man; and consequently, that the citizen is declared to be the servant of egoistic "man," that the sphere in which man functions as a species-being is degraded to a level below the sphere where he functions as a partial being, and finally that it is man as a bourgeois and not man as a citizen who is considered the *true* and *authentic* man. (41)

The liberal state, then, has no other function than preserving the rights of the "egoistic" individual pursuing his or her private pleasures, and both K/Carls, for different reasons, have a problem with that. Schmitt's antidote is not Marx's, not the achievement of perfection by way of the emancipation to come; rather, it is the "muscular" democracy to be shored up in the here and now. It is therefore not surprising that Section III of *Constitutional Theory*, "The Political Component of the Modern Constitution," is the section in which democracy receives its fullest definition. For the Schmitt of 1928, democracy is all but coterminous with the political. In the heart of every modern constitution, then, the putatively prepolitical rights of the individual are pitted against the political decision of the people, or, more succinctly: private property and private pleasure confront the public, common good in a fight over who controls the political apparatus and to what purpose.

Stripped of all its qualifying phrases modifying the subject, the preamble to the Weimar Constitution of 1919 reads: "The German people…has given itself this constitution" ("*Das deutsche Volk…hat sich diese Verfassung gegeben*"), a statement to which Schmitt often refers.[8] The constitution thereby unequivocally announces who the constituent power is, "*das Volk*," that is, "the people" as a collective singular ("The German people…*has*"), not a collection of individuals (i.e., *not* "have").[9] Without using the term (which did not yet exist), Schmitt specifically *denies* that naming the people the author of the constitution is a performative act. "It is not the case that the political unity first arises during the 'establishment of a constitution'" (2008, 75). Rather, the constitution results from an "*act of the constitution-making power*," an act that "*constitutes* the form and type of the political unity, the existence of which is presupposed….Such a constitution is a conscious decision, which the political unity reaches *for itself* and provides *itself*" (75–76).

Schmitt's pronouncement is both direct (indicative sentences), purportedly descriptive (not normative), yet slippery. "The German people" is both the subject of the utterance—the German people has given itself this constitution—and what the utterance presupposes—there is a German people that has the power to give itself this constitution. A political unity is said to exist prior to the shape its peculiar political identity takes. This preexistent political body gives itself distinct political form by way of a politically conscious act of giving itself a constitution. The inarticulately political becomes articulated, delineated. We may think of "the people" as the state. A state does not cease to exist when a constitution is superseded and a new one written, as happened in Germany in 1918/1919. If Bismarck's constitution of 1871 gave the German people a political form (constitutional monarchy), with the Weimar Constitution nearly fifty years later the German people gave itself a different form (republic), but at no time did "the German people" cease to exist as a political unity. It is true that the socialist and social-democratic leaders who declared the founding of a German Republic in November 1918 wished, for a variety of reasons having to do with keeping order and negotiating with the Allies, to see the abdication of the *Kaiser* as a kind of transfer of legitimacy, but in reality, no fiction of legal continuity was necessary. A new constitution is not authorized by the old one or by an interim government; it is authorized by the political unity that underlies and underwrites all constitutions, namely, "the German people." The "people" as constituent power necessarily precedes the act of this formal creation, which has to be seen, therefore, as a deliberate political decision and not simply as the resolution of some self-evident logical syllogism. The German people has given itself *this* and no other constitution at *this* and no other particular time by *this* and no other deliberate act. "The people," then, as the subject of political decision, must be thought of as more than just the historically contingent state.

At one point in *Constitutional Theory*, Schmitt finds "nation" to be a "clearer" term, for it "denotes, specifically, the people as a unity capable of political action, with the consciousness of its political distinctiveness and with the will to political existence, while the people not existing as a nation is somehow only something that belongs together ethnically or culturally, but it is not necessarily a bonding of men existing *politically*" (2008, 127). Whether "nation" is clearer or not, at least here we have a distinction between "people" referring to a social or familial group and "people" as a collective that is politically self-conscious and thus the subject of political decision. It is surely not coincidental that "nation" is the operative term used by Emmanuel Sieyès, a term that in fact answers the question of his most famous pamphlet: *What Is the Third Estate?* It could in fact plausibly be argued that large sections of *Constitutional Theory* are extended elaborations of the following passage from that text by Sieyès:[10]

> But how…is it possible to claim that the nation itself ought to have been given a constitution? The nation exists prior to everything; it is the origin of everything. Its will is always legal. It is the law itself. Prior to the nation and above the nation there is only natural law. To have a proper idea of the sequence of *positive* laws, all emanating solely from the nation's will, the first in order of precedence will be the *constitutional* laws, which will be divided into two parts. Some will regulate the organization and functions of the *legislative* body; others will fix the organization and functions of the various *active* bodies. These laws are said to be *fundamental*, not in the sense that they can be independent of the national will, but because bodies that can exist and can act only by way of these laws cannot touch them. In each of its parts a constitution is not the work of a constituted power but a constituent power. No type of delegated power can modify the conditions of its delegation. It is in this sense and no other that constitutional laws are *fundamental*.… Thus all the parts of a government are answerable to and, in the last analysis, dependent upon the nation. (2003, 136)

With the concept "nation," Schmitt would say, we have something a good deal more "concrete" than a hypothesized basic norm, something that can really, "existentially," legitimate the political and legal order. The nation exists (*ist*), it is not merely "valid" (*gilt*). As the constituent power, the nation creates a political form for itself by founding a constitution. The constitution is fundamental in the sense that it organizes procedures, rights, and duties for its citizens. Citizens within the order that the nation constitutes can alter laws but cannot alter the form of the political that finds its ground in the constitution. According to Sieyès, the people-as-nation, however, never disappears:

> A nation never leaves the state of nature and, amidst so many perils, it can never have too many possible ways of expressing its will.… [A] nation is independent of all forms and, however it may will, it is enough for its will to be made known for all positive law to fall silent in its presence, because it is the source and supreme master of all positive law.… A nation should not and cannot subject itself to constitutional forms. (138)

As constituent power, the nation rests in the state of nature, unlimited, incapable of being limited, yet forever capable of setting limits on and within the order it creates. Thus all constituted order and the agents acting within it are in a commissarial relationship to this original, natural force called the people. In *Constitutional Theory*, under the heading "The Constitution-Making Power," Schmitt makes a first pass at rendering Sieyès's basic assertion.

> [T]he issuance of a constitution can no more exhaust, absorb, or consume the constitution-making power than an organizational decree can exhaust the organization's power, which its supreme command and authority holds. The constitution-making power is not thereby expended and eliminated, because it was exercised once. The political decision, which essentially means the constitution, cannot have a reciprocal effect on its subject and eliminate its political existence. This political will remains alongside [*neben*] and above the constitution. (2008, 125–126; translation modified; compare with the original German, Schmitt 1993, 76–77)

Then, in Section 18, under the heading "The People and the Democratic Constitution," Schmitt delineates, using clear spatial metaphors, the three ways a people appear within and yet also outside of the constitution. First, as original subject of the constitution-making power, the people stand *vor* and *über* the constitution, that is, "anterior" to and "above" it. Second, once the constitution exists, the people are of course included "within" (*innerhalb*) the constitution as they exercise "constitutionally regulated powers," chiefly as the electorate (Schmitt 2008, 268). Yet these two moments no more exhaust the capacities of the people for Schmitt than they do for Sieyès. The nation, the people as constituent power, remains *neben* or "next to" the constitution. That is, the people can never be wholly reduced to a mere state "organ" or "functioning bureau," but rather "persists as an entity that is unorganized and unformed" (271).[11]

For those who, with Giorgio Agamben, see Schmitt engaged in an ongoing if clandestine conversation with Walter Benjamin, we can use the following imagery to visualize the relationship of (the) people to the political order. Recall that in his "Critique of Violence," Benjamin contrasts mythic with divine violence. Under mythic violence he subsumes lawmaking and law-preserving violence, equating this with the pernicious political order that is utterly reprehensible (1996, 248–252). Using Schmitt's terms, we could identify the people within the constitution with both lawmaking violence and law's preservation, that is, with the legislative branch of government and the judicial apparatus (including the police). If divine violence could signify the people's initial creation of the constitution, then "the people" or "nation" remains in the state of nature "next" to the constitution, ever able to intervene, destroy, and create anew. As Schmitt wrote, appealing to Jefferson and Mazzini, " 'the people's voice is the voice of God' " (2008, 267) and God's power is absolute.

Be that as it may, for Schmitt the essential feature of democracy is the demos. How the people become activated as a force within the state is the last feature examined here.

THE IDEAL OF PLEBISCITARY LEADERSHIP

Schmitt works words like "substance," "concrete," and "will" quite hard (see 2008, e.g., §1, §8, §17). They are meant to support an essential distinction between legitimacy and legality, thereby overcoming the perceived shortcomings of legal positivism and the reduction of the state to the legal system. Neither law's simple existence (law is law) nor its posited, logically reconstructed normative ground serves as an adequate legitimation, because neither sheer facticity nor the abstraction of normative expectations has binding force or political power. Constant, to return to him one last time, would disagree. "[W]e may affirm," he writes, optimistically, "that when certain principles are clearly and completely demonstrated, they tend to become their own guarantee" (1988, 182). Perhaps, sometimes, here and there, but what we call history as well as current events seem to serve up enough contrary examples to cause hesitation and doubt, if not brute skepticism. Does the "nation" or "the people" fare any better? After reading Rousseau, Sieyès, and above all Schmitt, what do we say when we come to the realization that the people, whether gathered under the proverbial oak in some primeval forest or represented by delegates to a constitutional assembly in a nondescript convention center, complete with bottled water and stale cookies, what do we say to ourselves when we admit that "the people" is also, like the norm, a fiction?

What do we say? We ask: What function does the concept "people" serve, and does it fulfill its purpose? If so, how? For all his hammering on the notion of substance, "the people" (like "homogeneity," its cohort) is "merely" a functional placeholder. It is, in Schmitt's eyes, the only possible nonliberal, democratic placeholder. The people—again, as a collective singular, not as private, interest-pursuing individuals—must be thought of as the source and subject of political decision. Nevertheless, that the people can err, fall victim to usurpation, fail to protect its own status as constituent power, also seems clear. Nor is it always possible for it to remain "next to" the constitution as guardian of its own sovereignty—again, citing "history" as evidence. What favors opting for the people over norms, law, or any other candidate for the surety that legitimacy promises?

Schmitt proffers the notion of representation, which he defines in a way that Hanna Fenichel Pitkin would consider to be "symbolic," a form of "standing for" rather than the more conventional "acting for" (1967, 92–111). "Symbols," she writes, "are often said to represent something, to make it present by their presence, although it is not really present in fact" (92), which is precisely Schmitt's definition of representation. "To represent," Schmitt claims, "means to make an invisible being visible and present through a publicly present being. The dialectic of the concept is that the invisible is presupposed as absent and nevertheless is simultaneously made present" (2008, 243; translation slightly modified). The pope, for instance, "represents" Christ by bringing him forth in a public manner, by making his presence visible to the gathered community of believing Christians.[12] Similarly, the leader of a political community—the monarch in premodern Europe, the *Reichspräsident* in the Weimar Republic—represents or bodies forth the "*political unity as a whole*. . . . Only he who *rules* [*regiert*] takes part in representa-tion. The government [*Regierung*] distinguishes itself from administration and business management by presenting and rendering concrete the spiritual principle of political existence. . . . [E]very genuine government *represents* the political unity of a people, not the people in its natural presence" (245).[13] Indeed, it is precisely *to* people in their every-day aspect that the political unity of *a* people is represented. The invisible constituent power that remains inchoately *next to* the constitution is coaxed out of the shadows and makes its presence known.

Perhaps we can better visualize this rather amorphous—some would say mystical—concept by using the theater analogy I briefly introduced above. It is evening. As indi-viduals we enter the lobby, which is still part of the private, economic sphere. We buy tickets and, if in Europe, a program. During intermission we return to the lobby for more economic exchange—a drink, sweet pastries. Within the theater itself something else happens, however. The space becomes a public space, a space in which we see and are seen. At first we are still private citizens, spectators of the action on a public stage. The actors present to us the actions of embodied characters. The actors are of us—we mingle with them before and after the play—but now stand before us engaged in public speech and action. In full theatrical majesty and dignity they make present and visible the collective—the "we-the-people"—as a political unity. Each individual now sees the whole of which it is a part. The citizen-spectator, however, need not, indeed, should not remain passive. For the representative of the people to have adequately made the invisi-ble visible, the publicly gathered citizen-spectator must recognize and acclaim the deed. If not, if the attempt has gone awry, then the gathering must reject the attempt. Required is either the recognition that those who are charged with representing the people to the people have in fact done so or the recrimination that they have failed. Those in the the-ater either cheer and applaud or boo and whistle.

Almost incredibly, Schmitt makes much of the notion of acclamation. "The natu-ral form of the direct expression of a people's will is the assembled multitude's decla-ration of their consent or their disapproval, the *acclamation*" (2008, 131). The ancient, Germanic practice is described by Tacitus: "On matters of minor importance only the chiefs debate; on major affairs the whole community. . . . If a proposal displeases them, the people shout their dissent; if they approve, they clash their spears. To express appro-bation with their weapons is their most complimentary way of showing agreement" (1970, 110–111).[14] In our fictional theater, acclamation, whether positive or negative, could be direct; in modern mass democracy, such gatherings of the whole are impos-sible. Hence, the modern mode of acclamation, according to Schmitt, is public opinion. We must keep in mind the distinction Schmitt wishes to uphold, namely that between the people as organized electorate *within* the constitution and the people as constituent power *next to* the constitution. The modes of administering government (through par-liament, executive branches, courts, etc.) and the basic rights of individuals, including the right to assemble, are all manifestations of the constituted order and mark the place of the people within that order. Even voting by secret ballot is essentially an expression of the private interests of the individual (in the "privacy" of the voting booth) and not the voice of "the people." Public opinion as the modern form of acclamation embodies the voice of the people outside of these organized, essentially private, administrative functions. To be able to secure the clear distinction between liberal forms of limiting the will of the people in the interest of the individual, on the one hand, and democracy as the political form of the collected people, on the other, public opinion must remain "uncontrolled," "diffuse," "unorganized." "Precisely like acclamation, [public opinion] would be deprived of its nature if it became a type of official function.... [I]t can never be recognized legally and made official" (Schmitt 2008, 275), which is why Schmitt—surprisingly for a "conservative" thinker observing the relative dysfunction of party politics in the Weimar era—links public opinion to the function of political parties (which, as he notes, are mentioned nowhere in the Weimar Constitution). "There is no democracy without parties," he declares,

> but only because there is no democracy without public opinion and without the people that are always present as the people. Just as a party cannot transform itself into an official organ without losing its party character, so public opinion cannot permit its transformation into an official jurisdiction, in particular because even the people cannot allow itself to be transformed into an official body without ceasing to be the people. (275)

In our fictional theater, the outburst of bravos or catcalls must not be orchestrated by the management.

Modern democracy therefore requires representation to be symbolic, bodying forth the invisible essence of the demos, and carried out by a popularly elected leader whose bearing exhibits the necessary dignity and gravitas. The people function within organized politics as interested individuals, but also, through their leader's (or leaders') acts of representation, recognize their public, collective stature as constituent power and make that power visible and effective through "unofficial" channels of public opinion, which dictates either approval or disapproval of the government's actions, plans, or behavior. This arrangement corresponds exclusively neither to representative democracy (though it cannot do without the more mundane notions of representation) nor to direct democracy. It preserves, or so Schmitt proposes, the idea of democracy, the idea of the public citizen over the private individual and the public body over the masses with divided interests. Liberal participation—deliberation in parliament, for instance, which because of its "empty formality" functions, Schmitt says, "like a superfluous decoration, useless and even embarrassing, as though someone had painted the radiator of a modern central heating system with red flames in order to give the appearance of a blazing fire" (1985, 6)—is trumped by democratic participation, which does not directly make political decisions, but simply affirms or rejects decisions that are made elsewhere. Some will find his critiques of liberalism, even if here and there accurate, infuriating, because some will always be guided by the assumption that political ideologies should be judged by their original design, not by how they actually work. Most will find Schmitt's notion of democracy frightening. It is not surprising, for instance, that Pitkin finds in symbolic representation, when taken to the extreme, the fascist theory of representation (as exemplified by the leadership principle). "Representation is a power relation, that of the leader's power over his followers," she writes, with reference to symbolic representation; "Hitler claimed that he had greater right to say that he represented his people than did any other statesman" (Pitkin 1967, 108).[15] The judgment implied in that statement appears definitive, for whoever attempted to defend Hitler's claim would be thereby revealed as either a fascist ideologue or an inveterate Germanophobe. The parsing of differences, like Schmitt's insistence that public opinion be unofficial, unorchestrated, and linked to parties (note the plural), is easily ignored, given his own political decision of May 1933. Should it therefore be simply disregarded?

Conclusion

As an abstract model, Schmitt's affirmation of plebiscitary democracy has little appeal, even as we continue to suffer the massive dysfunction of liberal governance. The gamble involved in trading our right to private pleasures for public duties has all the allure, in our cynical age, of betting our life savings at the craps table. Yet dismissing his thought through the evocation of the great Satan of the twentieth century serves us ill. Schmitt's *Constitutional Theory* and other writings on political form during the 1920s and early 1930s were neither prophesies of the nightmare to come nor conservative fantasies projecting an impossible past on an intractable present. Rather, they are perceptive, conceptual readings of what modern, democratic governance both might look like and, in some respects, *does* look like. As such, they can be used as critical and diagnostic tools.[16] In particular, the plebiscitary leader, who professes to represent the general will of the people in a more articulate way than the people themselves are able to do, has become a feature of what the American political historian Jeffrey Tulis has called "the rhetorical presidency" (1987, esp. 117–137; see also Hogan 2006).

Tulis claims that Woodrow Wilson, as scholar and president, initiated a new mode of presidential leadership by changing the president's relationship to both Congress and the American public. Readers of Schmitt will be struck by some common themes to be found in Wilson's writings. Wilson too found discussion as conducted in the U.S. House of Representatives a false façade, behind which all political decisions are executed in private committees, though he never officially doubted the epistemological value of the ideal of discussion for democracy (Wilson 2006, 68–73; cf. Schmitt 1985, 3–8, 48–50). And he believed the separation or "balance" of powers to be both antiquated and debilitating. "The makers of the Constitution," Wilson wrote just a few years before his presidency,

> constructed the federal government upon a theory of checks and balances which was meant to limit the operation of each part and allow to no single part or organ of it a dominating force; but no government can be successfully conducted upon so mechanical a theory.... The government of the United States was constructed upon

the Whig theory of political dynamics, which was a sort of unconscious copy of the Newtonian theory of the universe. (1908, 54–55; cf. Schmitt 1985, 39–41; 2008, 220–224)

It is within this context that Wilson also condemns divided sovereignty. "Leadership and control must be lodged somewhere," he emphasizes (Wilson 1908, 54). The "division of authority" and the resultant "concealment of responsibility" lead to "a very distressing paralysis in moments of emergency." Therefore: "*Power and strict accountability for its use* are essential constituents of good government," for "the only fruit of dividing power [is] to make it irresponsible" (2006, 186, 187). The interesting question to ask, then, is this: If power and authority is to remain undivided, not "checked" or "balanced" by countervailing, equally powerful governmental controls, who or what holds the leader accountable? The answer would seem to be "the people," expressed through some form of "acclamation." For Wilson too, popular opinion served this function.

In short, in the 1880s Wilson despaired of the presidency as an institution and advocated a revision of American government along the lines of British parliamentarianism, in which a strong leader at the head of a majority party could rule with full transparency and responsibility. By 1900, however, things had changed, and he saw a renewed chance for executive leadership. The catalyst was the war with Spain. In the preface to the fifteenth printing of *Congressional Government* (dated August 15, 1900), Wilson notes that "the greatly increased power and opportunity for constructive statesmanship given the President, by the plunge into international politics and into the administration of distant dependencies [e.g., the Philippines], which has been that war's most striking and momentous consequence" raises hopes for an integration of power that will "substitute statesmanship for government by mass meeting." After all, no one but the president "represents the people as a whole" (cf. Schmitt 2008, 369–372). Therefore: "Let him once win the admiration and confidence of the country, and no other single force can withstand him.... If he rightly interpret the national thought and boldly insist upon it, he is irresistible.... [The country's] instinct is for unified action, and it craves a single leader.... A President whom it trusts can not only lead it, but form it to his own views" (Wilson 1908, 68). What Wilson craves is "common understandings, common interests, common impulses, common habits," "common consciousness," "common standards of conduct," and "the habit of concerted action, which will eventually impart to it in many more respects the character of a single community." What calls forth all these commonalities is representation. Elizabeth created England as a nation for "a great ruler made great subjects" and she was England's "embodiment." Frederick the Great did the same for Prussia; he "called it into consciousness" (1908, 32, 33). This is what a leader is, a man (or woman, presumably) who is the "embodiment" of the nation, "who understands his own day and the needs of the country, and who has the personality and the initiative to enforce his views both upon the people and upon Congress" (65). Ultimately, leadership is interpretation, for a leader must impute to the people the opinion that they genuinely hold and then represent that opinion before them. The leader must "arouse" the community from its slumber. "The forces of the public thought may be blind: he must lend them sight; they may blunder: he must set them right" (Wilson 1952, 45).

I have stressed the commonality of themes and language between Wilson and Schmitt not to equate them in the form of a one-to-one relationship. The cultural, historical, and political differences of their environments lend varying shades of meaning to their words, and their political commitments are certainly not identical.[17] Furthermore, Wilson's ruminations (and later actions) are meant to be in the service of the form of government outlined by the American Constitution; Schmitt's, though occasioned by the Weimar Constitution, seem to question more thoroughly the basis of political form in general. Nevertheless, there is enough here to show that Schmitt's views were neither aberrant nor singularly and teleologically linked to fascism. The idea of representation as "standing for" rather than merely "acting for" may be more common than modern political philosophers are willing to acknowledge. So, considering the historical judgment concerning Wilson's presidency during World War I and immediately thereafter,[18] if one wants a poster child for what is wrong with Schmitt's notion of representation and plebiscitary democracy, then that child need not sport the obligatory mustache.

But in fact, the idea of plebiscitary leadership, as articulated by Schmitt or Wilson, is neither inherently negative nor positive. It is a feature of the political life we currently lead, altered no doubt by technology and history to make it perhaps utterly unrecognizable to the two above-named protagonists. Since negative examples of successful plebiscitary leadership spring easily to mind, I leave you with an example of a *failed* attempt, one that, *because of its failure*, is an indirect cause of the radically unchecked pursuit of private, economic interests that we call freedom today, a form that Schmitt (and, I would venture to say, Wilson too) so thoroughly loathed.

On July 15, 1979, U.S. President Jimmy Carter addressed the nation in a televised speech.[19] In it he responded to a series of crises, environmental and economic, each firmly linked to energy, which is to say, to the use of nonrenewable fossil fuel. He emphasized the country's increased dependence on oil beyond its capacity to produce it and the connection among consumption, energy use, and environmental hazards, all issues that continue to occupy our political and private concerns today. He claimed that the United States faced "a fundamental threat to American democracy." That threat was not aimed at "our political and civil liberties," nor was our "outward strength," that is, our military might or economic power challenged. Rather: "The threat is nearly invisible in ordinary ways. It is a crisis of confidence. It is a crisis that strikes at the very heart and soul and spirit of our national will. We can see this crisis in the growing doubt about the meaning of our own lives and in the loss of a unity of purpose for our Nation." He went on to say that "[o]ur people are losing...faith...in the ability as citizens to serve as the ultimate rulers and shapers of our democracy," and that "too many of us now tend to worship self-indulgence and consumption." He concluded: "[W]e must face the truth," because "[w]e are at a turning point in our history. There are two paths to choose. One is a path...that leads to fragmentation and self-interest. Down that road lies a mistaken idea of freedom, the right to grasp for ourselves some advantage over others. That path would be one of constant conflict between narrow interests ending in chaos and immobility." In contrast,

he said: "[A]ll the promises of our future point to another path, the path of common purpose.... That path leads to true freedom for our Nation and ourselves."

Carter's speech is a remarkable document, one that Tulis (1987, 3, 136, 141) alludes
to, as does Andrew J. Bacevich (2009, 31–36), ruefully pointing to the consequences of
Carter's failure. It lays out concrete legislative proposals, including import quotas on oil,
tax incentives for fuel efficiency and conservation, and investments in alternate sources
of energy and public transportation, all with specific targets and dates that now, given
our present paralysis, boggle the mind. But its specific policy suggestions are not important here, for I am more interested in Carter's general intention. In remarkably clear
terms, ones that no American president would dare use today, Carter clearly drew a distinction between the freedom of private interest and the duty of public, collective action,
reminiscent of, if not roughly equivalent to, the distinction Schmitt makes between liberalism and democracy. To today's ear, his language rings prophetic. What he feared has
come to pass: "fragmentation," "self-interest," "chaos," and "immobility." What he advocated seems completely out of reach and sounds profoundly dissonant, perhaps dangerous to most, vaguely "fascist" or "socialist."

But his words also sound archaic, harking back to the language spoken much earlier
in the century, the language of Schmitt's notion of democracy as the action of a people
who see themselves—no, sees *itself*—guided by a "common purpose," as opposed to the
freedom of unbridled, individual self-interest. Furthermore, in this speech Carter presented himself as the representative of the American people, attempting, with a sense of
urgency, to make the collective political unity visible and present. In Wilson's terms, he
wished to "interpret" or channel the general will so as to make it active for the crisis at
hand. As "symbolic" representative of the American people, Carter acted, as it were, as
this constituent power's commissar, not as commissarial dictator, for he hoped to operate strictly within normal constitutional structures, but as one who sought to carry out
the will of the whole for the good of the whole in a time of crisis. In the act of representing the people he called it to self-consciousness as a unity and not as a conglomeration
of individual parts. In representing that unity, he was set to act "decisively." But first, he
needed the people to recognize that in fact he was its representative and thus authorized
to exercise his commissarial duties. He therefore delivered the speech orally, by television, in front of the entire nation. Carter then awaited acclamation.

He did not receive it. The spectator-citizens, carriers of public opinion, booed and
whistled. The speech was dubbed the "malaise" speech, though Carter never used that
word. From both the Left and the Right, from within his party and from the Republicans,
from the full spectrum of the press, he was mocked, ridiculed, scorned. In the
Democratic primaries of 1980 he was challenged by Ted Kennedy. In the general election he was defeated by Ronald Reagan, who had repeatedly assured the conglomeration
of American individuals, whom he pitted one against the other—white against black,
Christian against nonbeliever, rich against poor—that the first path Carter had outlined,
the path that was lit by the false idea of freedom and that leads to fragmentation and self-
interest, would be the path we could all painlessly take. We do not know what the consequences of positive acclamation at the time would have been, perhaps as disastrous as

accepting Wilson's call to action in 1917. But we *do* know the consequences of Carter's failure, because we still live in its shadows.

NOTES

1. His list of false candidates includes the state's putatively contractual origins, the beneficial conditions it produces (security, welfare), the sovereign's will, and an ultimate or basic norm. See Oakeshott 1990 (149–150, 152–153).
2. Classic studies include Murphy 1979 and Peterson and Fite 1968. More recent work includes Capozzola 2008, McCoy 2009, and Thomas 2008.
3. In the United States, so-called religious conservatives claim the right, based on their "moral" beliefs, to harass and bully homosexuals.
4. My reading of Constant is guided by my goal of elucidating Schmitt. That there are more complicated readings of Constant I am fully aware. See, e.g., Kalyvas and Katznelson 2008 (146–175).
5. Helpful here is not only the Athenian tradition rehearsed above but also Quentin Skinner's *Liberty Before Liberalism* (Skinner 1998), though "participate" means something different for Schmitt, as we shall see, than it did in Athens or does for Skinner. However, for a critique of Skinner, see Kalyvas and Katznelson 2008.
6. See also Mouffe 1993 (141); 2000 (21); 2005 (15, 18–19). Mouffe uses the Derridean notion to alter and rework (not just explain) Schmitt's notion of homogeneity and identity. See, e.g., Mouffe 1993, 128–130.
7. And, for that matter, Bobbio. Recall: "[A] liberal laissez-faire society is inevitably inegalitarian, and an egalitarian society is inevitably illiberal" (32).
8. Oddly, given its importance in Schmitt's analysis, the preamble is omitted in the copy of the constitution reproduced in *Constitutional Theory* (Schmitt 2008, 409–439).
9. The much-maligned German term *Volk* has the virtue of serving as a singular term (the plural, *Völker*, means "peoples"), and not, like "people," also as the plural of a singular (i.e., "person/people"). My use of verbs following "people" in the third-person singular ("The German people…has") is thus deliberate.
10. For Schmitt on Sieyès, see Schmitt 1994 (137–141); 2008 (126–129). I am fully aware that Sieyès cannot be limited to the uses Schmitt makes of him, that there are aspects of his thought that Schmitt neglects.
11. Andreas Kalyvas has alerted us to the importance of distinguishing these three moments of the people as constituent power before and next to the constitution, and as constituted power within it (2009, 79–186). The English translation obscures this spatial imagery by translating "neben" as "in comparison with" in the most important passage (Schmitt 2008, 271), though elsewhere it comes closer by using the word "alongside" (125, 140).
12. The example given by both Schmitt 1984 (23–24) and Pitkin 1967 (105).
13. Compare with Hobbes: "A Multitude of men, are made *One* person, when they are by one man, or one Person, Represented; so that it be done with the consent of every one of that Multitude in particular. For it is the *Unity* of the Representer, not the *Unity* of the Represented, that maketh the Person *One*" (1996, 114).
14. It is not chiefly from the Germanic tradition that Schmitt's idea of acclamation comes, but from the Christian tradition, namely Erik Peterson's study of the "One-God" acclamation. See Peterson 2012.

15. See also Nadia Urbinati's fleeting references to Schmitt, often associating him with fascism; e.g., Urbinati 2006 (22 and 235 n25).
16. See, e.g., the way Posner and Vermeule use him in this volume (2016) and in Posner and Vermeule 2010.
17. Though perhaps not as antithetical as common opinion might believe.
18. See again the works cited in note 1.
19. http://www.eoearth.org/article/Jimmy_Carter's_%22malaise_speech%22?topic=49485 (accessed March 19, 2011).

References

Bacevich, A. J. 2008. *The Limits of Power: The End of American Exceptionalism*. New York: Henry Holt.

Capozzola, C. 2008. *Uncle Sam Wants You: World War I and the Making of the Modern American Citizen*. Oxford: Oxford University Press.

Benjamin, W. 1996. "Critique of Violence." In *Selected Writings*, vol. 1, ed. M. Bullock and M. W. Jennings. Cambridge: Harvard University Press, 235–252.

Bobbio, N. 1987. *The Future of Democracy: A Defence of the Rules of the Game*, trans. R. Griffin. Minneapolis: Minnesota University Press.

Bobbio, N. 1990. *Liberalism and Democracy*, trans. M. Ryle and K. Soper. London: Verso.

Constant, B. 1988. *Political Writings*, trans. and ed. B. Fontana. Cambridge: Cambridge University Press.

Finley, M. I. 1985. *Democracy Ancient and Modern*, revised ed. New Brunswick: Rutgers University Press.

Hobbes, T. 1996. *Leviathan*, revised student ed., ed. R. Tuck. Cambridge: Cambridge University Press.

Hogan, J. M. 2006. *Woodrow Wilson's Western Tour: Rhetoric, Public Opinion, and the League of Nations*. College Station: Texas A&M University Press.

Kalyvas, A. 2009. *Democracy and the Politics of the Extraordinary: Max Weber, Carl Schmitt, and Hannah Arendt*. Cambridge: Cambridge University Press.

Kalyvas, A., and I. Katznelson. 2008. *Liberal Beginnings: Making a Republic for the Moderns*. Cambridge: Cambridge University Press.

Laclau, E., and C. Mouffe. 2001. *Hegemony and Socialist Strategy: Towards a Radical Democratic Politics*, 2nd ed. London: Verso.

Luhmann, N. 1983. *Legitimation durch Verfahren*. Frankfurt: Suhrkamp.

Marx, K., and F. Engels. 1972. *The Marx–Engels Reader*, ed. R. C. Tucker. New York: Norton.

McCoy, A. W. 2009. "President Wilson's Surveillance State." In *Policing America's Empire: The United States, the Philippines, and the Rise of the Surveillance State*. Madison: Wisconsin University Press, 293–346.

Mouffe, C. 1993. *The Return of the Political*. London: Verso.

Mouffe, C. 2000. *The Democratic Paradox*. London: Verso.

Mouffe, C. 2005. *On the Political*. London: Routledge.

Moyn, S. 2010. *The Last Utopia: Human Rights in History*. Cambridge: Harvard University Press.

Murphy, P. L. 1979. *World War I and the Origin of Civil Liberties in the United States*. New York: Norton.

Oakeshott, M. 1990. *On Human Conduct*. Oxford: Clarendon Press.

Peterson, E. 2012. *Heis Theos: Epigraphische, formgeschichtliche und religionsgeschichtliche Untersuchungen zur antiken "Ein-Gott"-Akklamation*. Würzburg: Echter.

Peterson, H. C., and G. C. Fite. 1968. *Opponents of War, 1917–1918*. Seattle: Washington University Press.

Pitkin, H. F. 1967. *The Concept of Representation*. Berkeley: California University Press.

Posner, E. A., and A. Vermeule. 2010. *The Executive Unbound: After the Madisonian Republic*. London: Oxford.

Posner, E. A., and A. Vermeule. 2016. "Demystifying Schmitt." In *The Oxford Handbook of Carl Schmitt*, ed. J. Meierhenrich and O. Simons. Oxford: Oxford University Press, 612–626.

Schmitt, C. 1963. *Der Begriff des Politischen*. Berlin: Duncker & Humblot.

Schmitt, C. 1984. *Römischer Katholizismus und Politische Form*. Stuttgart: Klett-Cotta.

Schmitt, C. 1985. *The Crisis of Parliamentary Democracy*, trans. E. Kennedy. Cambridge: MIT Press.

Schmitt, C. 1993. *Verfassungslehre*. Berlin: Duncker & Humblot.

Schmitt, C. 1994. *Die Diktatur*. Berlin: Duncker & Humblot.

Schmitt, C. 1995. "Der bürgerliche Rechtsstaat." In *Staat, Großraum, Nomos: Arbeiten aus den Jahren 1916–1969*, ed. G. Maschke. Berlin: Duncker & Humblot, 44–54.

Schmitt, C. 2007a. *The Concept of the Political*, trans. G. Schwab. Chicago: Chicago University Press.

Schmitt, C. 2007b. "The Age of Neutralizations and Depoliticizations." In Schmitt 2007a, 80–96.

Schmitt, C. 2008. *Constitutional Theory*, trans. and ed. J. Seitzer. Durham: Duke University Press.

Sieyès, E. J. 2003. *Political Writings*. Indianapolis: Hackett.

Skinner, Q. 1998. *Liberty before Liberalism*. Cambridge: Cambridge University Press.

Tacitus. 1970. *The Agricola and the Germania*, trans. H. Mattingley. Harmondsworth: Penguin.

Thomas, W. H. Jr. 2008. *Unsafe for Democracy: World War I and the U.S. Justice Department's Covert Campaign to Suppress Dissent*. Madison: University of Wisconsin Press.

Tulis, J. K. 1987. *The Rhetorical Presidency*. Princeton: Princeton University Press.

Urbinati, N. 2006. *Representative Democracy: Principles and Genealogy*. Chicago: Chicago University Press.

Wilson, W. 1908. *Constitutional Government in the United States*. New York: Columbia University Press.

Wilson, W. 1952. *Leaders of Men*, ed. T. H. Vail Motter. Princeton: Princeton University Press.

Wilson, W. 2006. *Congressional Government: A Study in American Politics*. Mineola: Dover.

CHAPTER 12

SAME/OTHER VERSUS FRIEND/ENEMY

Levinas contra Schmitt

ARYEH BOTWINICK

INTRODUCTION

To MORE fully appreciate what is at stake in Carl Schmitt's vocabulary of friend/enemy for diagnosing the Western philosophical, ethical, and political tradition (or series of traditions),[1] it is illuminating to compare it with Emmanuel Levinas's categorial dichotomy of same/other which has also been invoked as the key to Western philosophy, ethics, and politics.[2] On a sheerly abstract theoretical level, the terminology seems to be fairly interchangeable—or, at least, friend/enemy appears as a dominant subdivision within same/other. Either friend/enemy seems to be synonymous with the other (i.e., it has to be acknowledged as either a friend or an enemy), or else the larger category of the other has to be subdivided into the dichotomous categorial pair of friend/enemy. I shall argue that the depth content of same/other and friend/enemy yield antagonistic metatheoretical perspectives upon Western political theory that situate this theory in radically opposed ways.

The personalizing of human thought and institutions to the level of same/other or friend/enemy results from a common impulse. Many of the cognitive dilemmas and paradoxes that confront us when we are engaged in thought can be alleviated, if not resolved, by noticing how assigning different views to different personal perspectives reduces the problematic elements in our conjectures and constructions. For example, to take an issue that preoccupies Plato in the *Theaetetus*, skepticism from the perspective of the individual philosophical inquirer (what Plato denominates as the same) poses what look like insuperable philosophical obstacles toward rational elucidation and justification. The skeptic is skeptical of everything but his own doctrine of skepticism. His very effort to formulate his position undermines his ability to state it.

Skepticism self-destructs. Once you take a third-person perspective into account and not just a first-person approach (you acknowledge that there are others and not just the self), then the inability of rational individuals considered singly to state skepticism coherently can be discounted in the face of their mutual awareness that the limitations of logic and language attendant to skepticism do not need to be (and perhaps cannot be) overcome. The mutual awareness that skepticism is the furthest we can go in grounding a common world (it is the doctrine we converge upon in an inchoate, not fully artic- ulable form) enables us to circumvent skepticism as a metaphysical challenge and to transform its fractured, scaled-down version as a humanly sustained precondition for interpersonal communication. The implicit Platonic response in *Theaetetus*, *Sophist*, and *Timaeus* to the centrality of skepticism is that to salvage a universe suffused by skep- ticism all one needs is otherness (the acquiescence or mutual implication of others in our limited epistemological horizons)—not certainty.[3]

Schmitt in *The Concept of the Political* can be understood as following a formally simi- lar set of moves to what I have just outlined with regard to the same and the other. Schmitt begins *The Concept of the Political* by stating that "the concept of the state presupposes the concept of the political" (1976, 19). The political in its technical, historically evolved sense is coextensive with the unit of relationship and governance called the state. The state enjoys a monopoly of force and authority within the larger community that makes it not only quantitatively superior to all other relationships but also, most importantly, qualita- tively unique. How do we account for the singular configuration of relationships typified by the state? How do we theorize even the temporary suspension of moral accountability typified by the monopolistic structure of state power and authority? The friend/enemy distinction in Schmitt can be viewed on analogy with the genesis of the same/other dis- tinction in Plato and its usage by Levinas as a displacement unto a plural perspective what from a solitary perspective appears as intensely problematic. The apparent aberrations of the concentration of power and the sanctioning of violence represented by the state can be accounted for if we see the state (in contrast to all other types of human relationship) as predicated upon dealing with enemies rather than on accommodating the needs and aspirations of friends. Invoking the particular constellation of attitudes and approaches represented by the notion of enemy helps to rationalize and perhaps to a limited extent even justify state behavior. As in the case of Platonic skepticism, deflecting upon a new set of human relationships what initially appears as philosophically or morally problematic helps to defuse the alien or exotic character of the human stance in question (the skep- tic's questioning; the political official's assertion of state authority) by assimilating it to a broadened repertoire of human relations.

Plato goes on, especially in the *Sophist*, to render problematic the whole same/other relation in a manner that influences Levinas's shaping of the concept of infinity in his book *Totality and Infinity* (1969). In the *Sophist*, the Stranger asks:

> But then, what is the meaning of these two words,
> "same" and "other"? Are they two new kinds other
> than the three ["being," "rest," and "motion"], and

yet always of necessity intermingling with them,

so that we must inquire into five kinds instead of

three; or when we speak of the same and other,

are we unconsciously speaking of one of the three

first kinds? (Plato 1964, 254e–255a, 409)

The Stranger responds to his own query a little later on by saying (using the example of motion) that it is both the same and the other, that it cannot be coherently theorized as belonging exclusively under the one rubric rather than the other:

Then we must admit, without grumbling, the statement

that motion is the same and yet not the same; for when

we apply these expressions to it, our point of view is

different. We call it the same in relation to itself,

because it partakes of sameness; whereas we call it not

the same because, having communion with otherness,

it is thereby severed from the same, and has become

not that but other; so that it is with equal justice

spoken of as "not the same." (256a–256b; 411)

In this passage, Plato emphasizes that from two different angles of vision motion can be spoken of as both the same and the other. We call it the same because it conforms to some law of identity: It is what it is. At the same time, in relation to what is not itself, it can be characterized as the other. But for Plato otherness is never complete and unqualified. The taint of the same cannot be fully transcended even in the acknowledgment of the other. Sameness and otherness are humanly established categories designed to make our experience of the world more recognizable and assimilable, but reflecting no intrinsic order or scheme of creation. Ontologically speaking, sameness is still the overarching category, because it is in response to our needs that otherness is created.

The upshot of Plato's analysis is that the same overtakes the other. Virtually every phenomenon that we encounter in the world can be subsumed from each perspective, depending on the angle and the purpose with which we approach it. Sameness and otherness are instrumental—not intrinsic—concepts. They are probes that help us pinpoint what we have previously conceptualized for ourselves. The other does not disclose to us a reality that is absolutely, unqualifiedly, unconditionally different from ourselves. It reflects to us who we are—what we have invested conceptually and otherwise in the persons and things of this world.

The prevalence of the same yields a universe dominated by totality. What creates the space for Levinas for the emergence of infinity is the instability of the skeptical dynamic lurking in the concept of totality. If even the other is tainted by its conceptual association with the notion of the same—if the intrusion of selfhood mars the sustainability of an objective concept of otherness—then we are willy-nilly thrust into a skeptical position where only the same or self has indubitable reality. Skepticism, however, is an inconsistent philosophical doctrine. The skeptic is skeptical of everything but his own skepticism.

One version of skepticism that might be taken to circumvent this difficulty is a generalized agnosticism. A generalized agnosticism is a version of skepticism that includes self-interrogation within its ambit of skepticism. All of our beliefs and affirmations—including our questioning of our beliefs and affirmations—remain indefinitely in suspended animation from generation to generation, awaiting further specification, elaboration, and possible confirmation from a continually evolving future. What I have just described constitutes Levinas's notion of infinity that emerges as a kind of horizontal transcendence, with each human present becoming hostage to future human presents, without a final resolution of any of those presents guaranteed anywhere along the line. The live human others of our lives as well as the metaphoric conceptual others of our lives get deferred in their autonomy and self-subsistent character from moment to moment and (potentially) from generation to generation. We could say that a generalized agnosticism releases us into an infinitely protracted present.

In *Totality and Infinity*, Levinas displaces the concept of the other unto the concept of infinity. It is precisely this displacement that is missing in Schmitt. Even though in a formal sense he begins his theorizing by following the same Platonic moves that Levinas does—the theoretical conundrum posed by the existence of the state is resolved by introducing two divergent perspectives (that of friend and enemy) from which the defiant material composing political theory could be approached, Schmitt does not proceed to take the further steps of showing how friend and enemy are mutually parasitic concepts, that one notion always forms the underside of the other. Because of the enduringly complex interplay between the contrasting concepts in pinning down what we want to refer to by invoking the categories of friend and enemy, we can appreciate how neither category names or flags a reality all by itself. The recourse to acts of naming, to words, to conjure up reality for us means that reality remains endlessly distanced, poised between an explicit verbal *what is* and a suppressed verbal *what isn't*, but in any case not directly appropriated or accessed by us. Because words do not directly deliver reality to us, they need to be continually reassessed and reexamined to maximize our opportunities to deflect and rechannel reality along lines that we deem most favorable in the light of our values and aspirations. This second half of the Platonic picture developed by Levinas is what remains dormant in Schmitt.

The tradition of Western political theorizing that goes from Plato to Nietzsche shapes up very differently when viewed from the perspective of same/other than when approached from the vantage point of friend/enemy. In contrast to John McCormick, who reads liberalism from Schmitt's perspective as "technology's infiltration of politics" (1997, 121–289), I propose to show that Schmitt can be used as an interpretive probe to disclose the skeptical, pacific elements within liberalism and to argue that it is not liberalism but Schmitt who is misguided. Sustaining our awareness of the taint of the same in all depictions of otherness makes us sensitive to the idea that there are few brutely given configurations on the political landscape. The epistemological, strategic, and tactical contexts in which we situate political events and phenomena are crucial for determining the identity of those events and phenomena and the menu of responses that they appropriately occasion. In terms of interpreting some of the classic texts of Western political theory, if we highlight the skeptical currents present in them we can then reinterpret them as veering in a much more peaceful liberal direction than an excessive focusing on their political rhetoric might lead one to believe. This is especially true in the cases of Machiavelli, Hobbes, and Nietzsche. I shall offer some illustrations of this reading a little later on in this chapter.

I shall focus here on an exposition and critique of the friend/enemy dichotomy in Schmitt's thought and shall compare it with a reading of some central passages in Western political theory (primarily from Hobbes and Machiavelli) in the light of the same/other dichotomy. I shall argue against Schmitt that, instead of "the ability to distinguish between friends and enemies" becoming "the criterion for the existence of political consciousness" (Cristi 1998, 133), it is rather how liberalism copes with its awareness that virtually all decisions, both personal and political, have to be made in a climate of uncertainty that is its strongest drawing card in shaping and evoking the loyalty of a mass following.

At the outset, it is important to clarify that friend/enemy cannot simply be restricted to a way of reading the behavior of states but, willy-nilly, extends to individual perception, judgment, and behavior. As someone fixated on the idea of power that he takes to be an extension of Hobbesian political theory, Schmitt appears to be suspicious of the role of ideas in politics and to be simultaneously committed to the nominalistic view that all reifications and abstractions need to be broken down to their most elementary, accessible components for us to adequately grasp what they are about. From this perspective, for us to comprehend how the dynamics of friend/enemy operates on the state level, we need to notice how it propels individual behavior that, when suitably magnified, gets attributed to the state as a collective actor. On the level of both motivation (i.e., the friendly or hostile behavior exhibited by a state) and outcome (i.e., the results that the state's friendly or hostile behavior nets) state action needs to be deconstructed to the level of individual action for us to gain a clearer, less ideologically distorted view of what calculations are driving state action and what types of response would appropriately engage them.

In what follows, I shall make the case that Hobbes, who looms as such a central figure for Schmitt in his development of the friend/enemy distinction, needs to be viewed as the philosophical founder of modern liberalism. I contextualize Hobbes differently from Schmitt in relation to both his successors and his predecessors. In my reading, Machiavelli serves as a significant precursor for Hobbes in his denigration of overt means of power as a means of dealing with suspicious or hostile forces both inside and outside the state. I endeavor to show that the relevant contrasting term to *friend* in liberal political theory is not *enemy* but *self*. Given the skepticism that both suffuses and surrounds liberal theory, the self remains an endlessly problematic construct that gives us ongoing opportunities for reimagining and reconstructing what the behavior of both friends and enemies is truly like. I examine key terms in the liberal epistemological vocabulary such as *skepticism, empiricism, nominalism,* and *conventionalism* to clarify their import for the liberal conceptions of personal identity, friend, and enemy. Throughout, I try to show how the Levinasian deployment of the same/other distinction with its devolution upon the concept of infinity offers us a revealing guide to liberal political thought and practice and thereby also constitutes an important implicit critique of Schmitt.

In my reading of Levinas, I differ sharply from Slavoj Žižek, who sees Levinas as deliberately crafting a large wedge between ethics and politics:

> Far from preaching an easy grounding of politics in the ethics of the respect and responsibility for the other, Levinas instead insists on their absolute incompatibility, on the gap separating the two dimensions: ethics involves an asymmetric relationship in which I am always-already responsible for the other, while politics is the domain of symmetrical equality and distribution of justice. (Žižek, Santner, and Reinhard 2005, 149)

In my reading, the incoherence and contradiction attached to Levinas's conception of the ethical (divorced from any consideration of his political theory) requires a reconstruction of his ethical theory in a manner that facilitates a smoother transition to his politics.

I also address issues where Schmitt takes a determined stand against liberalism such as liberalism's preference for partial as against total redemption, its proceduralism, and its delegitimation of antisemitism within the larger setting of Levinas's same/other distinction versus Schmitt's friend/enemy distinction. For Schmitt, "in order for the political to emerge, the ground must be cleared. Or, rather, as Schmitt would have it, the political is itself this clearing, the erasure of substantial difference at a threshold of intensity" (Shapiro 2003, 107). In contradistinction to Schmitt, I try to show through the application of Levinas's same/other distinction and its devolution upon the concept of infinity that the goal of *erasure of substantial difference* ignores the vulnerability residing in the concept of the same. The same itself consists in a tissue of irreconcilable differences and tensions that establishes common ground with all of the other standard-bearers of the same existing in any given society and serves as a spur to work toward achieving compromise and reconciliation of differences animating each of us and defining the terrain between us.

LEVINAS AND THE
SAME/OTHER DISTINCTION

In his essay "Philosophy and the Idea of the Infinite," Levinas uses the Platonic terminology of the same and the other to level a broad indictment against Western philosophy. He condemns it for being "indissolubly bound up with the adventure that includes every other in the Same" (Peperzak 1993, 99). What Levinas means by this is that through conceptualization—recourse to language (as "the house of being" in the Heideggerian sense)—the otherness of what lies outside or beyond human beings is subdued and domesticated to conform to the ordering mechanisms of language. In Levinas's formulation (which is evocative simultaneously of Hobbes and Nietzsche), "reason, which reduces the other, is appropriation and power" (98).

The same thus overwhelms the other. In addition, the same is not even able to preserve its viability as the same. The problem with the same consists of several interrelated components. First, it situates the relationship between theory and fact-language and world-words and objects in a way that virtually guarantees the underdetermination of the former by the latter. The reason that the original delineation of the problem cannot be reformulated—so that we describe what is at stake in our recourse to concepts and language as a matter of straightforward reportage or reflection of what confronts us in the world—is that the choice of organizing frameworks itself remains underdetermined by factors outside itself. Again, whether the vocabulary of choice or constraint is appropriate at this juncture is also underdetermined by factors outside of the elements going to constitute the choice situation itself. The vocabulary of underdetermination itself remains underdetermined, which in a negative sense provides Levinas with an opening wedge for considering alternatives that are *otherwise than being* (the master category of the same)—namely, genuine unassimilable human otherness and God.

The paradox and irreconcilable tension upon which Levinas's theorizing rests is that it is only by manifesting the full panoply of powers of the same that he is able to make room for the other. A central presupposition of Levinas's thought is that the same always triumphs over the other. As a result, the questionings of the same always triumph over the certainties of the same. In our idiom, the thesis of the underdetermination of theory by fact (language by reality) is exposed as being itself underdetermined. This skeptical questioning of skepticism is what enables Levinas in a negative sense to point to what might lie beyond being. To make his argument for what is otherwise than being, Levinas needs to invoke precisely what the conclusion of the argument seeks to rule out: the primacy of the same over the other.

In being a captive of this dilemma, Levinas's argument resembles Maimonides's case for negative theology (that we can say only what God is not, not what he is) in *The Guide of the Perplexed* (Maimonides 1963).[4] To show that none of the attributes that monotheistic theology traditionally ascribes to God can be applied literally, Maimonides needs to presuppose the subsistence of that very God himself so that the endless disownings of the literal significations of attributes can take place. Analogously, to make his case for the other, Levinas has to persistently exploit the argumentative resources residing in the same. He needs the same to be able to call forth the other.

The idea of the *infinite* in Levinas follows a Maimonidean trajectory—and is invoked for reasons parallel to Maimonides's emphasizing this constitutive element in God's makeup as integral to the biblical and rabbinic conceptualization of him. As long as God is theorized as finite, he does not bring the explanatory quest to a halt. One can always attempt to penetrate to what lies above and beyond him that is responsible for the phenomenon that one is examining. The idea of infinity is introduced to render God on a literal level conceptually inaccessible to us and therefore the factor beyond which by definition one can no longer inquire. God achieves ultimacy—and his total Otherness from things human is guaranteed—once the metaphor of infinity is conjoined with the whole panoply of attributes (e.g., omnipotence, omniscience) that biblical religion ascribes to him.

One can discern a parallel movement of argument taking place in Levinas. "The Other," he says, "who provokes this ethical movement in consciousness and who disturbs the good conscience of the same's coincidence with itself compromises a surplus which is inadequate to intentionality. Because of this inassimilable surplus, we have called the relation that binds the I to the Other (*Autrui*) *the idea of the infinite*" (1996, 19). To properly affirm and respect the otherness of the other, we cannot resort to purely egoistically determined psychological processes that yield to us our sense of the other, which then becomes the basis for the moral judgments we make concerning him. At some point, there is a need to break out of the circuit of the self to both grasp our notion of the other and to affirm the moral priority that Levinas claims he has over us. The metaphor of infinity (encapsulating as it does unfathomable and irreducible distance) becomes the appropriate symbolic vehicle for both fixing the genuine otherness of the other and for dramatizing the priority that his claims exert upon us.

Once we acknowledge that Levinas introduces the idea of infinity as a metaphor for rhetorically working his way around the limits of logic and language to be able to embrace both the authentic otherness and the moral superiority of the other, we notice that (just as with Maimonides) the idea of infinity obfuscates and mystifies more than it clarifies. In Maimonides, God's infinity enables us to achieve ultimacy in our explanatory quest, but only by sacrificing intelligibility. If God's ultimacy were indeed to bring our search for explanations to a satisfactory arrest, we would have to be able to show what by definitional postulation we are debarred from doing, namely, how the infinite intersects with the finite. If, *per impossibile*, we would be able to do this, however, it would only restart (give a new impetus) to the explanatory quest because then God would cease to be the final factor in explanation.

Similar vicissitudes of argument bedevil Levinas's strategy. If it is the metaphor of the infinite that gives us our idea of the human other and accentuates the notion of his moral priority over us, how do we rescue an intelligibly relatable other from the metaphoric thicket of infinity? The moment we begin to pursue our usual moral deliberations in trying to determine how to act, the metaphor of infinity with its inscrutability and unchartable and irrecoverable distances becomes unactionable and untranslatable. With regard to our moral quandaries and dilemmas centering on the issue of how to escape the taint of self in our moral theorizing and deliberating, we find ourselves in precisely the same location that we were in before the metaphor of infinity was introduced. Levinas at this point in his exposition confronts a choice between two equally unpalatable alternatives. While fully acknowledging the metaphoric character of the infinite, he can declare that it is an indispensable category for accounting for ethical judgment and deliberation. Levinas appears to be pursuing this approach in the following passage: "the Other resists my attempt at investiture, not because of the extent and obscurity of the theme that it offers to my consideration but because of the refusal to enter into a theme, to submit to a regard, through the eminence of its epiphany" (1996, 12). In other words, the metaphor of infinity helps to fix my relationship to the other for me. But, in this case, if one needs to invoke the humanly delineated metaphor of the infinite to gain conceptual and moral access to the other, this constitutes the weightiest declaration of the triumph of the same imaginable.

Or, alternatively, Levinas could be opting for a remapping of the philosophical landscape, with the idea of infinity (its unintelligibility unrelieved, so that only its rhetorical adaptation for human ethical uses lies in the foreground) being invested with obdurate—if cognitively inaccessible—reality and primacy so that it overshadows key standard categories in the lexicon of philosophy. Levinas also seems to opt for this way of dealing with infinity: "In this way, we rediscover the Cartesian itinerary, which moves from the Cogito to the World by passing through the idea of the infinite. In a more general way, the priority of the idea of the infinite is asserted over the idea of being and ontology" (12).

Levinas seeks to accommodate the "surplus which is inadequate to intentionality" (19)—a conceptualization of the other as genuinely other, either by rigorously extending the domain of metaphor or by rezoning reality to make room for new categories and new priorities. The first approach is counterproductive (and recognized by Levinas to be such) because the proliferation of metaphors is one of the major ways through which the empire of the same is extended. The second approach is ineffective because it can be understood only as a variation upon the first approach. By making sense of our relationship to the other under the aegis of the category of infinity, Levinas is not deciphering the notion of infinity for us—which would be logically impossible because infinity can be described only in negative terms by inventorying what it is not—but is trading upon some of its metaphoric connotations to buttress his understanding of the primacy of the ethical. Maimonides's theorizing of biblical monotheism invokes a notion of the infinite that is neither analytically nor emotionally sublimatable to a set of higher, more overarching terms and is not reducible to a set of familiar categories that would enable us to immediately domesticate it. So, too, Levinas's reference to the infinite in making sense of our relationship to the other cannot be extrapolated to a more general, inclusive level that would give us a more secure grip on the infinite, and it cannot be collapsed to a set of familiar ways of making sense of and conceiving the other. Infinity, in both Maimonides's and Levinas's hands, reflects to us limits to reason from which we must now seek to find our bearings.

In early modern political thought, Machiavelli and Hobbes emerge as crucial figures who help us find our bearings with regard to the concept of infinity by their implicit translation of it as horizontal transcendence. In his exposition of the friend/enemy distinction as constitutive of the political relation, Schmitt brackets Hobbes with Machiavelli (1976, 61, 65). It is important to note in the light of the argument of this chapter that Machiavelli's implied embrace of the totality versus infinity distinction in his theorizing of power facilitates the birth of modernity. Machiavelli theorizes power in such a way that the more fully it is displaced, the more effective it becomes. Where appearance, reputation, and deterrence do the job of more overt mobilizations of power, then one is truly powerful. His model political animal is the fox rather than the lion— where stratagem substitutes for brute force (Machiavelli 1961, ch. 18, 99). The lion is a devotee of totality, and the fox represents infinity—infinite substitutions for an unrealizable brute force.

According to Machiavelli, the tests to apply whether power has been maximized or undermined in a particular situation are a series of counterfactual probings. If one had acted different from the way one did on a particular occasion, would one have reached the same outcome with more or less violence? Would more or fewer lives have been spared? It is the invocation of counterfactual tests that determines the degree of power at the disposal of a state. The Machiavellian paradox consists in showing how power is present the more fully it is absent.[5]

One of the things that Hobbes and subsequent social contract theorists learned from Machiavelli is that state-making consists in minimizing overt uses of power. This insight is institutionalized in classical liberal theory in the imagery and argument of the social contract, where the assertion of power is depicted as a prepolitical, precivil act. What marks the fashioning of civil society is the containment of power in its unbridled, menacing forms.

In the liberal state, the public sphere plays a formally subordinate, instrumentalized role in relation to the private sphere. Liberalism is associated with the design of governmental institutions that facilitates the pursuit of the priority of the right over the good, and assigns primacy to "process" and "procedure" above "substance." These features seem to be responsive to the Machiavellian understanding that the more power is dispersed and deferred, the more enduring it becomes.

The conception of power that animates Machiavelli's thought can be viewed as his response to the dilemmas of self-referentialism haunting formulations of skepticism in Western thought. If formulations of contained, limited skepticism open up onto scenes of unmitigated, open-ended skepticism via the medium of a shift from validationist to vindicationist paradigms of doing philosophy[6]—so that what makes sense in terms of a set of premises internally applied becomes skeptically vulnerable once one invokes an external questioning of the categories employed in the premises—then even limited knowledge statements and claims can be skeptically challenged. The skeptical critique of these statements alerts us to the traces of unrationalized, unredeemed power in our theoretical formulations. A key metatheoretical vulnerability of a skeptical critical perspective is that for skeptical canons to be applied consistently they end up engulfing and consuming themselves. One needs to be skeptical of skepticism as well as of its competitors. If a not fully successfully executed skeptical critique of our concepts and theories issues forth in a recognition of the tremendous role played by power considerations of various sorts in our structuring of the world, then the trick becomes to theorize power in such a way that echoes of this not fully achieved devolution of skepticism onto power are erased. Machiavelli theorizes power in such a way that all vestiges—all remainders and reminders—of the issue of self-referentialism have been folded onto our envisioning of power. He conceives of power as involving endless deferral. The foundationless character of reason displaces onto power, and power in turn displaces onto an endless displacement of itself. We might describe what I just summarized as the Machiavellian encapsulation of the Levinasian notion of infinity.

We might say that power in Machiavelli registers the same sort of ambiguity that the other does in Levinas's thought. Power stands poised somewhere between tautology and objective description. On one hand, to refer to power as shaping the outcome of a situation is just a way of redescribing that whatever happened happened. Power becomes a kind of neutral conceptual currency into which the self-images and official proclamations of participants in events can be translated. On the other hand, though, the vocabulary of power seems to partake of the character of objective description precisely in terms of what it rules out—the inflated pretensions of those directly involved in events. Analogously, the notion of the other in Levinas seems to be situated somewhere between a further conceptual artifact claimed by autonomy (the same) and a potential manifestation (an experience or expression or reminder or conjuring up) of heteronomy (being grasped by the other).

The conceptualization of power that Machiavelli bequeaths to Hobbes engenders a theorizing of the liberal state as the custodian of a movement toward horizontal transcendence—of time stretching endlessly forward to infinity. Liberal democracy has been described in the writings of Kant and of John Rawls as the form of state that institutionalizes "the priority of the right over the good" (1971, 449).[7] The state is officially debarred from embracing a conception of the good of its own but must instead assign priority to individuals and groups in the private sphere to elaborate and pursue conceptions of the good of their own constrained by what their noumenal, or ideal, selves would choose. From Rawls's perspective, these noumenal selves choose organizational principles for the basic structure of society that reflect their own self-respect and their own preoccupation with cultivating their highest selves—that is, they select as their optimal societal framework Rawls's individualist, contractarian society. The state's role is to be instrumental to the individuals and groups going to compose the private sphere to exercise the primary right to their separateness (including the right to formulate separate and divergent visions of the good) and to the whole panoply of rights that this more basic right spawns—and to renounce any independent visions of the good of its own except those that support the basic neutral social structure. Thomas Nagel and others have argued that this stance of subordination of the public sphere in relation to the private sphere is itself grounded in some conception of the good that identifies the good with neutrality (1973, 220–234). Nagel does not offer us a very ample discussion of what the background conception of the good animating the liberal state's policies and priorities is. I would submit that at least in metaphysical terms we could describe it as the pursuit of horizontal transcendence opening up to infinity. The liberal state is structured in such a way as to ensure endless deferral of such issues as sovereignty, truth, and justice. The public sphere defers to the private sphere, which in turn has its wants and demands processed by multiple tiers and branches of government that contribute to both dispersing and deferring a concerted stand on any of the overarching issues affecting the life of the community. The diffusion of decision-making across generations also contributes toward dispersal and deferral.

Translating this image of the liberal state into a more narrowly epistemological idiom, we might say that the liberal state resists embracing a more positive conception of the good because of its implicit grounding in skepticism. The problem with skepticism is that it is an unsustainable philosophical thesis. To be consistently skeptical requires one to be skeptical of one's own skepticism—and thus to disengage from the very position one is seeking to define and defend. The version of skepticism that is able to accommodate these scruples is a generalized agnosticism, which interweaves skepticism of itself into its formulation of skepticism. A generalized agnosticism in turn requires what I am calling a *horizontal transcendence*. If every present crystallization of meaning and reference needs to be displaced onto future crystallizations, since we need to take into account the possibility that the returns are not fully in with regard to our theoretical formulations, and if *vertical transcendence* is ruled out by skepticism or negative theology (the idea that the whole divine vocabulary is metaphoric in character), then horizontal transcendence would constitute a most plausible candidate for carrying the conceptual weight of a consistent skepticism. Horizontal transcendence is integral to a liberal politics. The future is needed as a continual balancing and corrective mechanism to the past—a kind of institutionalization of a pattern of reverse causation. Every present moment in human existence remains radically incomplete—with later events, occurrences, and discoveries being required to render more precise (more filled in with content) our present understandings and formulations themselves. A generalized agnosticism establishes the future as an indispensable resource for rendering our statements (in the present) more perspicuous and more objective.

Hobbes's projection of the leviathan state as a progressively developing society that persists into the indefinite future harbors the motif of a generalized agnosticism.[8] His widespread skepticism, which can be sustained only as a generalized agnosticism, guides him to postulate a nondisruptive future as a continuing resource for filling in with content a not fully realized or specified present. In Levinas's arresting formulation, "The awaiting of the Messiah is the duration of time itself" (1989, 203). Hobbes cements the link between a negatively constituted political society and a generalized agnosticism.

Infinity, which is the value implicit in Machiavelli's conception of power as endless deferral, turns out to be the most promising candidate for the category of supreme good underlying liberalism's embrace of the priority of the right over the good. The normative basis for liberal-democratic politics might be conceived as a nurturance of time to enable the play of contingency to be redeployed again and again without succumbing to either premature abstraction or closure or underresponding by failing to notice and capitalize upon the range of possibilities residing within current constellations of forces. The political in a technical, nonmetaphysical sense has to do with keeping the prospect of successive presents endlessly alive.

SCHMITT AND THE
FRIEND/ENEMY DISTINCTION

For Schmitt, the category of *enemy* clearly predominates over that of *friend*. Schmitt actually speaks only of what *foe* or *enemy* means and restricts its usage to a public enemy or enemy of the state. *Friend* is inferable and reconstructible from what sorts of people enable a nation to ward off its enemies. Where does the ontological primacy of enemy over friend derive from in Schmitt? One way of making sense of this is to notice how in its origins it might be an illegitimate response to skepticism, the thesis that our knowledge claims can never be fully grounded. Schmitt takes over from Hobbes the nominalism (the theory that only individuals and no abstract entities, such as essences, classes, or propositions exist) and the conventionalism (the notion that some of the most enduring institutions of social life such as language and government are formed by agreement or compact) that, in their skeptical import, converge in highlighting how theory is underdetermined by fact and words are underdetermined by things. Schmitt then uses these skeptical epistemological premises to buttress his decisionism—to ground political authority in the sovereign decision, which from Schmitt's perspective includes the sovereign delineation of an enemy (or enemies) that confers an authentic political identity upon the state. In other words, skepticism points to arbitrariness as being our epistemological fate, and Schmitt reifies this arbitrariness in terms of the sovereign decision that includes the specification of an enemy.

Schmitt's decisionism predicated upon his skepticism is evident in a passage such as the following: "only the actual participants can correctly recognize, understand, and judge the concrete situation and settle the extreme case of conflict. Each participant is in a position to judge whether the adversary intends to negate his opponent's way of life and therefore must be repulsed or fought in order to preserve one's own form of existence" (1976, 27). Restricting knowledge of a situation to only the actual participants is suggestive of the absence of any neutral, objective means to test the validity of one's perceptions and judgments. Why are such means unavailable? A cogent and persuasive answer to this question would be that Schmitt takes over from Hobbes without directly alluding by name the factors that are encapsulated in terms such as nominalism and conventionalism, which indicate why an objective picture of the universe (including the political world that we inhabit) is unavailable to us. If, as the doctrines of nominalism and conventionalism suggest, the words that we use to refer to things can never be corroborated as the uniquely and authentically right words to refer to those things because those things could always be described in alternative ways and if we were persevering and consistent enough in applying these alternate vocabularies our worlds would still hold up, then there is never a secure, nonquestion-begging way to justify one's perception or judgment of anything. The stage is thus set for the political sovereign to step forward to announce and enforce who the political community's friends and enemies are and thereby enable the state to come into being.

The skeptical background affecting the Schmittian notion of the decision can be expanded even further and used to call into question Schmitt's concept of the decision itself. If it is the skeptical factors that I have just alluded to that nudge Schmitt to assign centrality to the idea of the decision, then the notion of the decision cannot be enlisted to perform the tasks that Schmitt has outlined for it. The way Schmitt wants to use the concept of decision presupposes a previously known and identifiable sovereign and his plan of action through an identification of an enemy and his propagation of an appropriate enemy narrative to justify such a categorization so the sovereign is able to galvanize his people into an authentic political stance. But if it is skepticism that propels Schmitt to decisionism, then skeptical postulates should prod us to question how there could be a sovereign decider pursuing a fully worked-out decision concerning how to instigate the formation of the political before the enactment of the decision itself. From a systematic Hobbesian skeptical perspective, words follow deeds and do not perspicuously precede them. Words open up in so many different directions that they do not fix the meaning of anything. It is only by assigning priority to doing that our words (our acts of interpretation) take off since they at least have an immediate frame of reference that to a limited extent helps to focus our interpretations. The counter-Schmittian point to notice is that the skeptical background to the concept of decision suggests that words begin and end in flux and that in the end decision decides far less than the sovereign decider had in mind. In Derrida's words, "If there is a decision, it presupposes that the subject of the decision does not exist and neither does the object. Thus with regard to the subject and the object, there will never be a decision" (1996, 84). Thus, decision emerges as a kind of circular trap. If you have to come on to "decision" to overcome the destabilizing effects of skepticism, this ensures that "decision" will never be able to do the work that the theorist assigns to it.

My reading of Schmitt on the objectivity of the political receives support from the remainder of the paragraph in which the previously cited text is embedded. Schmitt goes on to say in this paragraph that the objectivity of the concept of the political is confirmed by its resting upon an indigenous distinction, as it were—that of friend and enemy—instead of embodying or reflecting or relating to distinctions that are crucial in any adjacent realm that might impinge upon the political: "the morally evil, aesthetically ugly, or economically damaging need not necessarily be the enemy; the morally good, aesthetically beautiful, and economically profitable need not necessarily become the friend in the specifically political sense of the word. Thereby the inherently objective nature and autonomy of the political becomes evident by virtue of its being able to treat, distinguish, and comprehend the friend-enemy antithesis independently of other antitheses" (1976, 27). The objectivity of the political for Schmitt is not a function of its resting upon a neutral set of criteria that confirm it in its identity as the political. In a strange and paradoxical way, it is rather the absence of such criteria that renders the objectivity of the political possible. From Schmitt's perspective, the political in his sense as the embodiment of the friend/enemy distinction is triumphantly objective because it *excludes* reference to all other criteria (especially moral, aesthetic, and economic) in its delineation and differentiation of itself. One might almost say that for Schmitt it is the absence of objective criteria in the conventional sense—those stemming from adjacent disciplines and sectors of experience such as morality, aesthetics, and economics—that makes the political objective in his sense. Schmitt has to first subvert objectivity before he can claim it for his conception of the political. The missing intervening premises between that subversion and his revised conception of the political as institutionalizing the friend/enemy distinction appear to be the Hobbesian postulates concerning skepticism.

It is important to note that Schmitt takes over from Hobbes only the limiting effects of skepticism but not its self-limiting effects. From a more critical philosophical perspective than the one pursued by Schmitt, one would have to say that if Hobbes is persuasive in his argument for skepticism then one has to immediately confront the implication that skepticism is unsustainable as a philosophical thesis (to be coherently and consistently skeptical one has to be skeptical of the tenets of skepticism themselves as well as of all other philosophical theses) and can survive only in the form of a generalized agnosticism which questions its own questioning. In other words, properly conceived, Hobbesian skepticism calls into question equally (on a level of ontological parity) notions of the self, friend, and enemy. As names applied to phenomena within the psyche and the interpersonal, social, and political worlds, they are all equally insecure, equally unmoored—underdetermined by the phenomena that they seek to capture and represent. It is only Schmitt's illicit transmutation of skepticism into the throwaway, arbitrary gesture of decisionistically designating an enemy that allows him to feel that he has remained faithful to the mandate of skepticism, whereas in fact he has already violated it through this very designation.

From the perspective that I am developing here, liberalism's position on the friend/enemy distinction can be seen to be diametrically opposed to Schmitt's—but not at all for his suggested reasons relating to his being faithful to what he considers to be Hobbes's friend/enemy distinction and liberalism modifying or abandoning it. Hobbesian liberalism is epistemologically predisposed neither to conceive of friend as a foil for enemy nor of enemy as a foil for friend—but to question the epistemological self-sufficiency of both categories. In classical liberal theorizing, the notion of a self (as well as the allied notions of friend and enemy)—like the kindred container notions of *thing, substance,* and *physical object*—are all highly questionable. In this stream of theorizing, there is always presumed to be an unwarranted leap between experiencing both an individual sense-datum and a phenomenologically grasped putative physical object or person, and naming. One can never be sure that the name exhausts or even covers the experience—and one even has to question one's questioning of the adequacy of the name.

In his discussion of Hobbes, Schmitt realizes that Hobbes is not only the theorist of the great leviathan in his sense of a state totally structured to accomplish and committed to achieve the evisceration of its enemies but is also the theorist of the evisceration of leviathan who reconciles its existence with the preservation of individual freedom. Schmitt says that, for Hobbes, "the state's power...determines only the external cult. Hobbes laid the groundwork for separating the internal from the external in the sections of the *Leviathan* that deal with a belief in miracles and confession" (1996a, 57). Schmitt goes on to say more direly, "The leviathan, in the sense of a myth of the state as the 'huge machine,' collapsed when a distinction was drawn between the state and individual freedom. . . . Thus did the mortal god die for the second time" (74). For Schmitt, the belligerent character of the leviathan state confers upon it an activist, totalistic, substantive stance that is belied by Hobbes's countervailing gestures of reticence and deference motivated at least partially by his skepticism.

The inner–outer distinction that Schmitt chafes against as undermining the structure and purpose of the leviathan state (see 1996a, chapters 5–7) is a manifestation of the same urge toward minimalism that is manifested elsewhere in the metaphysics, epistemology, and political theory of *Leviathan*. Outward assent to dogma on the part of all citizens (and not inner acquiescence and affirmation) is all that is required for the public fabric of the leviathan state to remain intact and to enable it to function as the final repository of authority and power within the political community. Requiring and enforcing inner assent to religious and political dogma would be counterproductive. To achieve the end of inner conformity on the part of its citizens, the leviathan state would have to reduce itself to the level of co-combatant alongside the religious and sociological forces it would be attempting to tame and discipline. By waxing maximal with regard to religious and political content and practice, the leviathan state would be forfeiting the strategic high ground of minimalism that enables it to solidify its power in the form of assuring ongoing stability. By striving for formal rather than substantive control of its citizens, the leviathan state works to foster its own longevity—to achieve the eternity connoted by its name. Since it is pitched to assure rather than to prescribe the commodious living of its citizenry—citizens in the private sphere fill this phrase in with divergent contents of their own—the leviathan state in its fastidious and elegant withdrawal contributes toward perpetuating its own undisturbed continuity. By having very little of overt substance to perpetuate, the Hobbesian state ensures its own perpetuation.

LEVINAS CONTRA SCHMITT

Schmitt's antiliberalism constitutes an interrelated family of notions, just as liberalism constitutes an interrelated family of notions. One important (but often unnoticed) member of both families is Schmitt's paradox of sovereignty on one side and liberalism's unparadoxical conceptualization of sovereignty on the other. For Schmitt, the sovereign constitutes the sovereign exception: since it defies both reason and logic, how he can be both outside its rubric in terms of setting it up and included within its purview once it is established? The concept of sovereignty, which leaves no person falling under the territorial unit of the state out of account, has to be theorized in such a way (to ward off an infinite regress) that the sovereign institutor falls outside it to make sense of how it gets established, whereas once it is in operation in many respects he comes under it. The paradox is most dramatically heightened at the moment of institution. How does one rationalize that moment when the sovereign inescapably, paradoxically has to be conceived as being both inside and outside of sovereignty?

This paradox sets the stage for Schmitt's irrationalist political vocabulary to come into play. In the context of this paradox, the state and the political (with its designation of an enemy) can be temptingly conceptualized as decisionistic leaps that are moving along tracks distinct from and alternative to the pathways sanctioned by the restraining protocols of reason. In tandem with the decisionistic vocabulary is an irrationalist stripping of the human person as the embodiment and harbinger of reason down to the prerationalist level of the emotionally charged stereotypes of friend and enemy. The target membership for a political community that is born in the throes of the collapse of reason and the community of nations to which it will belong has to be rationally denuded. Instead of being composed of persons, it can consist only of friends and enemies.

Liberalism, by contrast, can be theoretically reconstructed on the basis of the skeptical understandings that are integral to its articulation as circumventing the paradox of sovereignty at the cost of deepening its own skepticism. Schmitt's paradox emerges when one cuts off the philosophical analysis of sovereignty at the moment of institution. Then, it becomes intensely problematic to conceive how the sovereign can be simultaneously both inside and outside his own creation. But there is nothing intrinsic to the concept of sovereignty to mandate that our conceptual slicing has to be narrowly circumscribed to the moment of institution. When one broadens the frame of analysis, the paradox gets dissipated. If one expands the framework of analysis beyond the moment of institution to encompass sovereignty (the sovereign state) as a going concern (how its rules operate in the course of the ongoing life of the state and not how they can be rendered coherent in the instant of creation), then the position of the sovereign as founder or chief executive or chief legislator or chief magistrate of the state becomes fully intelligible. While he might enjoy certain privileges and immunities stemming from his exalted status within the political community, for other purposes (e.g., when he steals money from a private person for purposes of enjoying a more affluent vacation) he comes within the purview of the state's system of laws and is as vulnerable to its penalties and punishments as any private citizen. That the sovereign bears a differentiated relationship to the state rather than a univocal one is not in the least paradoxical.

An important feature to notice about this liberal reconstruction of the concept of sovereignty is that it flows from a deeper and more consistent version of skepticism than Schmitt's theorizing of sovereignty. The relationship between words and the phenomena that they purport to describe is so underdetermined that there is nothing intrinsic to the words that we use and to their possible relationships to the phenomena that they are ostensibly about that requires us in moments of philosophical reflection to cut our frame of analysis at one point rather than another. Our skepticism is so deep-seated that it is not just the answers that are up for grabs but also how to formulate the questions. If one denominates (as both Plato and Levinas do) human rational assertiveness as an expression of the same, then we notice in the course of our pursuit of philosophical reasoning how the arguments that we advance persistently coil in upon themselves, managing to keep themselves afloat only at the cost of sustaining the questions that surround them. In this way, the liberal idea of sovereignty can be kept intact only at the cost of acknowledging the irresolvability of the prior question of the conceptual slicing upon which the theory is predicated.

This provisional sustaining of answers only within the penumbra of questions that surround them haunts our metaphysical, ethical, and political vocabularies from start to finish. The notion of a self can be floated, but only at the cost of recognizing that the movement from individual impressions of engagement in thought and action to the extrapolation of a self involves a leap whose distance can never be rationally neutralized. The notion of a self might be a total fiction, or we might be constituted by multiple and successive selves. The other in the guise of friend or enemy involves comparable leaps and elisions. The skepticism that undermines the macro leap from impressions of multiple individual engagements in thought and action to the concept of a self also undermines the myriad micro leaps from interactions with self and others to the imposition of a specific, self-contained identity upon each of these engagements from which the larger concepts of self and other get inferred and generalized.

Skepticism itself is vulnerable to a series of irresolvable questions that is comparable to what affects applications of skepticism to individual cases. To comply with requirements of consistency means that one needs to be skeptical of skepticism itself and not just of the array of targets to which skepticism is applied. Addressing issues of reflexivity—the need to be skeptical of skepticism and not just of its targets—means that the vocabulary of sameness and otherness remains inextricable. In all of our skeptical bracketing off of the other—in settings ranging from our modes of identification of individual engagements in thought and action to the positing of self and other (in all of these cases where we notice the taint of the same)—we are not able to exit the intellectual assertions and theoretical designs and visions of the same into a secure domain of at least skeptical otherness because skepticism debars us from even making that connection. We have to remain as skeptical of skepticism as we are of everything else. From the perspective of the skepticism animating liberalism, one remains mired forever in the aborted circuit between sameness and otherness. One never gets to a friend/enemy vocabulary. It is only by abrogating issues of reflexivity that one is able to move beyond same/other to friend/enemy.

Social Contract Theory and Empiricism

The difficulties of opting out of the same and genuinely engaging the other, in this case the otherness of the elements composing the world in which we live, is evident in the theory of knowledge historically associated with social contract theory, namely, empiricism. It is no accident that in different ways (and in different combinations with other epistemological views) social contract theory in Hobbes and in Locke goes hand in hand with a doctrine of empiricism. One way to conceive of empiricism as a theory of knowledge is to notice how the emphasis on sense impressions as the source of knowledge suggests a continuing orientation toward the future for corroboration and rectification of our knowledge claims. Empiricism as a theory of knowledge emphasizing the centrality of sense data in the formation and validation of knowledge symbolically encodes a relationship of excess between knowledge and its sources. Sense data suffuse the world of lived experience. They are virtually everywhere and can be instantly generated through engagement in daily human activities. This relationship of excess can be formulated from either direction: starting with words or starting with sense data. We can say either that there are always more materials (sense data) out of which words and concepts can be formed than there are words and concepts or, alternatively, that there are always (at least potentially) more words and concepts to apply to events and experiences than there are events or experiences to apply them to. Empiricism highlights for us the infinite prospect of generating sense data through normal interaction with the world and thus encapsulates the notion of excess. As a result, in relation to these hypothetical sense data as they get registered on human sensory apparatuses at any given moment in time, we can always generate more descriptions than there are things to describe; alternatively, we can always redescribe the same set of things so that their persistent identity as the same set of things can be called into question.

If empiricism is read as flagging an orientation toward the future, then its strategic point as a doctrine is to call itself into question at the same time that it calls opposing doctrines into question. Sense impressions that need to be juxtaposed and correlated with other sense impressions are as evocative of infinity as verbal formulations that need to be juxtaposed to and correlated with other verbal formulations. From within an infinite horizon of inquiry, one can imagine the supersession of the category of empiricism itself in relation to accumulated bodies of experience that together with the imaginative possibilities that they engender and render plausible call empiricism itself into question. In addition, it is worth noting that empiricism as a philosophical theory and doctrine about the nature and sources of knowledge has already left brutely experienced sense impressions far behind and, in its transformation into a theory about knowledge, has already penetrated deeply into the precincts of its idealist philosophical opponents.

In contradistinction to Schmitt, in liberalism, which in key respects is the political theory of empiricism, the category of enemy is not primary, but neither is the category of friend in a direct, literal sense. The silent other posited by the category of friend in liberal thought is not enemy but self. What limits the category of friend in liberal theorizing is not the adversarial category of enemy but the ontologically prior category of self. If one cannot securely get to the self in liberalism, then how can one get to a friend? And enemy seems at least equally remote.

The epistemological slack attendant to the categories of *self, friend*, and *enemy* in liberalism is suggestive of a philosophical opportunity that has Levinasian resonances. If epistemology cannot secure its own ground, perhaps this can be regarded as a tacit invitation to invoke and explore ethical categories as a means for mapping the terrain of the self and the other and their sustainable patterns of interrelationship. Perhaps ethics can become relevant (if not primary) by default—as a result of theorizing the simultaneous nonnegotiability and unexitability of epistemology. The imperative for action in the face of unconsummated and unconsummable thought leads us to ethics. Everything from the self on upward to friend and enemy is a charitable posit. Liberalism harbors the promise that we can begin to deploy and manipulate these charitable posits in ways that nurture the consensual moral judgments of humankind over the centuries and that are epitomized in the values of life and peace.

LIBERALISM AND DEPOLITICIZATION

Schmitt's analytical framework is skewed and distorted on other grounds as well. His moral–metaphysical–political indictment of liberal society is that it is depoliticized—and therefore weak, apathetic, materialistic, directionless, and disoriented. By contrast, a political society that has clearly identified its enemies and has psychologically if not yet fully materially girded itself up to do battle against them has attained properly speaking to the level of the political. For Schmitt, the fault line for differentiating between properly political societies and improperly political societies is the delineation of enemies and the preparation and readiness for war in the first case and the neglect (or un- or undercultivation) of enemies and the consequent lack of preparation for war in the second case.

Schmitt is correlating politicization with readiness to wage war only because he is working with a tacit background premise—namely, inequality. Schmitt affirms descriptively and cherishes normatively the inegalitarian nature of human societies. Therefore, preparation for war legitimizes for indigenous elites the unequal share of political power they exercise and reinforces for the masses the imperative of their subordination and galvanizes and energizes them within that subservient status to contribute their utmost to the state's war effort. The premise of inequality is carried over into the international political arena as war-making elites seek to assert and preserve their hegemony not only vis-à-vis their immediate constituents but also in relation to foreign powers.

Once one sheds the premise of inequality and substitutes instead the premise of equality, one is poised to notice the ways liberal society is also politicized. Modern philosophical liberalism is predicated in the thought of Thomas Hobbes upon an inversion. Instead of the passions being subordinate to reason and thereby validating hierarchical, inegalitarian orderings of human beings, Hobbes conceives of reason as being subordinate to the passions. He thus discloses and implicitly embraces a vista of radical human equality. Reason that is an active set of capacities differentially distributed among human beings divides us from one another. The passions that refer to a common set of susceptibilities or vulnerabilities such as to pleasure and pain broadly distributed among human beings unite us—and establish our most enduring claim to equality. If what makes us authentically, properly speaking human has more to do with our capacity to feel (to experience joy—and suffering) than our capacity to think, then a focus has been established for justifying greater and greater equalization of human societies. Hobbes, who in his personal predilections and social ties was an aristocrat, makes an aristocratic case (through the application of his own privileged rational faculties) for the enlargement of the scope of the irrational in our analysis of individual and collective life.

From the perspective of Hobbes's philosophical liberalism, the politicized nature of liberal society finds expression in the progressive waves of equalization that have characterized modern liberal societies. The theme of politicization in liberal society is bound up with more and more excluded and disenfranchised groups juxtaposing their socioeconomic experience and status as members of liberal society to the premise of equality and then finding their experience and status wanting. Politicization in liberal society has to do with a diminution or erosion of the false consciousness that accepts such subordination as natural or justifiable and the attempt to achieve greater socioeconomic parity with the more advantaged members of society. Because liberal society provides a basis with its organizing premise of equality for its own self-improvement and self-transformation, the atmosphere for effectuating political change and economic redistribution (to the extent that these have succeeded at all) while charged with tensions, resentments, and hostilities do not exhibit that full-blown bellicose character that is Schmitt's hallmark of the political. As a result, Schmitt condemns liberal society for being unpoliticized. What Schmitt's judgment reflects is that he has drawn his analysis to the scale of inequality, and liberalism expresses its politicizing impulses within the framework of equality as norm and as good.

STATE OF NATURE AND CIVIL SOCIETY IN HOBBES AND IN SCHMITT

Schmitt misconstrues the role of the state of nature in Hobbes's thought and its relationship to civil society (the society of the social contract). Schmitt regards the Hobbesian state of nature as a state of war, meaning the readiness to engage in conflict and not the actual eruption of hostilities. He contrasts the warlike environment of the state of nature with the mechanisms conducive to accommodation and peace constitutive of civil society, and he identifies the authentically political state with the Hobbesian state of nature rather than with Hobbes's vision of civil society. Schmitt misses the role and function of the state of nature in Hobbes's thought. Hobbes's political theory and the character of philosophical liberalism as a whole are predicated upon the changes that take place in the course of the transition between the state of nature and civil society occurring on a secondary rather than on a primary level. The image of human nature that pervades both the state of nature and the fully developed civil society is constant. In both cases, you have human beings in whom the passions predominate over reason and the ends of human life are grounded in the passions. The people who pursue commodious living in the Hobbesian social contract society have a similar psychological profile grounded in a common metaphysical reading of the limits of human reason as the people who inhabit the state of nature society. Where they differ is in terms of the development of a unique faculty, which in actuality is an evolutionary outgrowth of one of their original capacities—namely, the passions. This new faculty can be called instrumentalized reason or rationalized passion, and what it exemplifies is a calculating mechanism that enables the passions to proceed more smoothly and efficiently to the ends to which they are antecedently, atavistically driven than would be the case if only unmitigated passion were in control. Instrumental reason is passion's other as it seeks to replicate itself within the human psyche in ways that assure both its continuing hegemony and effective management of its environment.

In the transition between the state of nature and civil society in Hobbes's political theory there is no radically altered psychological profile and no rearticulation of human ends from what prevailed in the state of nature. Human beings are still seeking to maximize pleasure and to minimize pain—except that they are going about their business with a greater awareness of the need for constant adjustment between means and ends. In the course of moving out of the state of nature society with its destructive impact on their lives, the calculating capacities of the erstwhile members of such a society become more finely honed. The most momentous manifestation of this environmentally nurtured capacity for adjustment is in the general acknowledgment of the need for a coordinated environment represented by the establishment of government that enjoys a monopoly of force and authority within the community to wield sanctions against recalcitrants who seek to reap the benefits of social cooperation without having to shoulder any of the costs. But who people are and the ends that they pursue remain remarkably consistent between the state of nature and civil society.

SCHMITT AND THE QUEST
FOR TOTAL REDEMPTION

Schmitt refuses to see or to endorse the homogeneity of metaphysical, psychological, and political content governing the relationship between the state of nature and civil society because unlike Hobbes who is a theorist of partial redemption Schmitt is after total, gnostic regeneration and redemption of humankind. This is the way Strauss phrases the point:

> Affirmation of the state of nature does not mean affirmation of war, but "relinquishment of the security of the status quo." Security is relinquished, not because war is something "ideal," but because one must return from "dazzling representation," from the "comforts and convenience of the existing status quo," to the "cultural or social void," to the "mysterious, unimpressive origin," to "undefiled, uncorrupted nature," so that "by virtue of pure, unpolluted knowledge...the order of human things" may arise afresh. (Strauss in Schmitt 1976, 101)

Schmitt's dualistic reading of Hobbes's political theory and his patterning of his own political theory upon what he takes to be Hobbes's reading of the state of nature and his (Schmitt's) rejection of Hobbesian civil society is forcefully exemplified in the centrality that Schmitt assigns to a readiness to die for the state. Hobbes, by contrast, discredits and delegitimates this readiness in his political theory. In wartime situations when self-preservation and the defense of the state come into conflict, Hobbes assigns priority to the life of the individual member over the life of the society. The state does not have a right to make its citizens die for it. Given the continuity between the state of nature and civil society in Hobbes that I have emphasized, it is merely dishonorable, rather than unjust, for an individual citizen to refuse to risk his life to safeguard the state (Hobbes 1946, 142–144). The primacy of the passions that remains a constant in both phases of Hobbes's political theory (the state of nature and civil society) ensures that the establishment of systemic restraints institutionalized in state political authority can be undertaken and justified only instrumentally, not substantively or unconditionally. For Hobbes, in both the state of nature and civil society death remains "the greatest evil" (Strauss in Schmitt 1976, 88–89).

Does Liberalism Rest upon a Performative Contradiction?

The affirmation of life in Hobbes is reinforced from the direction of his metaphysics and epistemology. As we have seen, the consistent version of skepticism that Hobbes adheres to is a generalized agnosticism that emphasizes that all of our claims to knowledge are transitory and provisional. The openness to the future, which is endemic to a generalized agnosticism, places a premium on continuing investigations in all fields of knowledge and inquiry since no sets of results are foreclosed in advance. The critical apparatus of skepticism neutralizes itself under a generalized agnosticism so that the field (all the manifold fields of human inquiry) remains open for new conceptualizations and empirical work done under their auspices. This suggests that the future is needed as an indispensable ongoing resource to replenish and recast the past. Every human present is epistemologically hostage to the future to crystallize more fully as a present. While the overall metaphysical picture conjured up by a generalized agnosticism is one of incompleteness (unless this too gets altered in the course of time), in more restrictive time frames futures revise and reconfigure pasts even though as those futures become pasts they are likely to be revised and reconfigured in their turn. All of this presupposes an undisrupted fabric of human life that proceeds endlessly. Hobbes's moral psychology, metaphysics, and epistemology point in the direction of the primacy of human life.

Hobbes's monistic metaphysics and political theory take the sting out of the performative contradiction that Schmitt suggests bedevils opponents of his view of the political. To eliminate the political in Schmitt's sense of designating an enemy and preparing one's country to go to war against him—to pursue antipolitical pacifism rather than a belligerent, militant politics—also requires one to go to war against those who favor the politicized, warlike stance of the state, which proves from Schmitt's perspective the primacy and unavoidability of the political in his sense. This performative contradiction has force and point for adherents of Schmittian dualism but not for followers of Hobbesian monism. For those who project a rabid contrast between a politicized state of nature and a depoliticized civil society, it makes sense to assume that members of the latter community to contain participants of the former community might be condemned in extremis to resort to violent means to sustain their nonviolent mode of existence. For adherents of Hobbesian monism, however, there is no sharp break between the state of nature and civil society in terms of what guides and drives human beings. Civil society is just the state of nature itself purged over time of its self-defeating excesses by the human beings that populate it who unpremeditatingly learn something that contributes to the containment of its most debilitating features. The descriptive–normative continuum that Hobbes's monism projects displaces the Schmittian character type who is a pure product and embodiment of the state of nature onto a self-correcting personality type who puts the sublimation maneuvers he learns in the course of transition to civil society at the service of his id-inspired, pre-contractarian self.

Schmitt identifies the public sphere with hatred and consigns love to the private sphere: "Never in the thousand-year struggle between Christians and Moslems did it occur to a Christian to surrender rather than defend Europe out of love toward the Saracens or Turks. The enemy in the political sense need not be hated personally, and in the private sphere only does it make sense to love one's enemy, that is, one's adversary" (1985b, 28–29). Here, as elsewhere, liberalism reverses the Schmittian priorities. Hatred (competition, aggressiveness) in the prepolitical, anarchistic state of nature is private. Love (in the attenuated form of minimalistic social cooperation) is public and is a function of (is registered by) the institutionalization of the public sphere by entry into the social contract. Liberalism is predicated upon the unreality of both love and hatred (how they both constitute premature reifications). The sublimated, structured mirror that the social contract holds up to the state of nature (after all, according to both Hobbes and Locke, the motivational profile and psychological propensities of human beings remain fairly constant in both cases) is how with a few channelings and nudgings hate can be transmuted into love. And, presumably, with some contrary tinkerings, a degenerative dynamic is equally possible and likely with love being transmuted back into hate. What is quintessentially human—and the central datum about human nature that politics needs to take into account and to address—is the ease and fluency with which the transmutations between love and hatred occur in both directions.

THE PRIMACY OF PROCEDURE
WITHIN LIBERALISM

The centrality assigned to procedure within liberalism is initially a reflection of its ontology—of what it considers to be more real than other things. The insecure negotiation of the other in liberalism rather than his premature reification as the enemy leads liberalism to take the movement (the deconstructing and rechanneling of energies in both directions) between love and hatred to be more real and enduring than love and hatred themselves. For Schmitt, proceduralism that keeps the political society focused on the promotion of individual interests and the safeguarding of individual rights represents the apotheosis of everything he detests about liberal politics: "the negation of the political" is inherent in every consistent individualism (Strauss in Schmitt 1976, 82). From a liberal perspective, its proceduralist emphasis represents the consummation of the political considered as individual participation in and assumption of responsibility for the affairs of the larger society. Proceduralism is geared toward sustaining an instrumentalized, subordinate relationship between the private sphere and the public sphere and maps out free zones wherein the individual can engage in self-enactment and self-disclosure[9] in ways that augment his individuality and deepen his sense of personal responsibility. The gap between the unknown and unknowable individual (who is always in the process of becoming) and the substantive agendas and priorities of collective action can be filled in only by the proceduralist sanctionings, which enable individuality to flourish and the public agenda to be formed from the initiatives, interventions, and acquiescences of people who have had the formal opportunity to cultivate individuality in the sense described.

In the end, Schmitt via the medium of his summary of Hegel has provided us with the best account as to why liberalism differs from him: "Hegel has…advanced a definition of the enemy which has in general been evaded by modern philosophers. The enemy is negated otherness."[10] This summary of Hegel captures the point just right as to why liberalism has charted a theoretical course that is radically different from Schmitt. Since (as we have seen) in liberal epistemology and metaphysics the other in all of his forms remains only incompletely validated (including all of the internal others posited by the self on an ongoing basis in order to achieve greater self-awareness and self-mastery so that the concept of the self also remains incompletely transparent), the concept of negated otherness and consequently of the enemy does not have the opportunity to get formed.

In what from a liberal perspective must appear as the very perversity and wrongheadedness of his stance, Schmitt unwittingly confirms liberalism: movement (what is enshrined in the notion of procedure) has priority over substance. As I suggested earlier, one way of making sense of Schmitt's understanding of the political as a decisionistic leap pursuant to the collective delineation of and psychological mobilization for doing combat with an enemy is as following from the skeptical nominalistic and conventionalistic premises that he shares with liberalism. If the relationship between words and things (theory and fact) is as underdetermined as nominalism and conventionalism stipulate, then the triumph of skepticism gets figured as an irrational leap (a baptism through fire, or at least the readiness to enter the fire) that becomes the hallmark of the political. I have argued how the most coherent reconstruction of liberal thought highlights how at this point it makes a detour. To remain consistent, skepticism must be reformulated as a generalized agnosticism that disenchants the inverted certainty attendant to full-fledged skepticism and legitimates deferral and procedure (the endless deferral encoded in the priority assigned to procedure) as the constitutive categories in the formation and maintenance of the state. The way that Schmitt inadvertently attests to the validity of liberal understandings is that in his rejection of a generalized agnosticism he becomes a gnostic. "He affirms the political [in his sense] because he realizes that when the political is threatened, the seriousness of life is threatened" (Strauss in Schmitt 1976, 99). There is no middle ground for Schmitt. When he rejects a generalized agnosticism, he does not move to some middle ground between not knowing with certainty (but still claiming to know) and passionately knowing. His very arguments that establish his jettisoning of a generalized agnosticism are the ones that communicate to us his intoxication with the certainty born of passionate commitment. Schmitt thereby unconsciously dramatizes for us a teaching that is central to the priority that liberalism assigns to procedure: that the movement is all—whether for good or for evil.

Conclusion

Derrida points to a new problematic that Schmitt's theory of the political confronts in a multicultural world: "all the concepts of this [Schmitt's] theory of right and of politics are European.... Defending Europe against Islam, here considered as a non-European invader of Europe, is then more than a war among other wars, more than a political war. Indeed, strictly speaking, this would be not a war but a combat with the political at stake, a struggle for politics" (Derrida 1997, 89). Schmitt's conceptual linkage of the political with overcoming an enemy works only in a European and a European-inspired cultural setting (such as North America) where the concept of enemy has an intersubjectively affirmed set of meanings. Then Schmitt's grand gesture of irrationally conceiving the political as a readiness to go to war against a collective enemy has at least the surface resonance that he wants it to have. How does Schmitt's theory square in relation to a real-world Islamic adversary? Does the Muslim see himself and you in these same terms from the vantage point of his own Islamic categories? What if he does not see you as an enemy in the conventional sense but as a child-like infidel who has not yet seen the light of conversion? What if Islam sees the whole world as its territory—a globe of spiritual seekers whose consciousness only has to be raised for Islam to triumph?

Placing Schmitt's theory of the political in a multicultural setting of this sort points in unsuspected ways to the perils and limits of irrationalism in politics. The irrationalist also requires a rationally communicable context in which his irrationalism can be understood as irrationalism and not as groping or stumbling in the dark. The self-image of the targeted nation has to match in crucial respects the self-image of the aggressor nation for Schmitt's theory of the political to carry the connotations and valences that it does. In a multicultural world, the mediated, conceptually dependent character of even an irrationalist political program becomes apparent and compels its perpetrators to reconfront the dilemmas of skepticism that they felt they had surmounted once and for all through their lurch into irrationalism. Instead, in the multicultural global setting that we currently inhabit, the old epistemological problem returns: how can you confirm that the self-images of the other correlate with the projections of the same? Schmitt's discussion presupposes exactly what it was designed as a solution to address and to effectuate: that by virtue of pure, unpolluted engagement of the enemy, the order of human things would arise afresh and humanity would be regenerated. The emergence of a multicultural world discloses how Schmitt's irrationalist solution works only if it is already in place—if the grasp of the notion of enemy by aggressor and victim already match—before it is officially decided upon and put into effect.

Notes

1. The works by Schmitt considered in this chapter are the following: Schmitt 1976; Schmitt 1985a; Schmitt 1985b; Schmitt 1986; Schmitt 1996a; and Schmitt 1996b.
2. See my discussion of Levinas's use of the same/other distinction in Botwinick 1998 (79–104).
3. The concepts of same and other are taken from Plato *Sophist* (254b–256b); *Timaeus* (35ab); and *Theaetetus* (185cd).
4. See the discussion of this work in Botwinick 1997.
5. For a further discussion of Machiavellian minimalism and its influence on Hobbes and the subsequent social contract tradition, see Botwinick 1990 (94–103).
6. For an elaboration of the distinction between *validation* and *vindication*, see Feigl 1952.
7. "The indeterminacy in the notion of rationality does not translate itself into legitimate claims that men can impose on one another. The priority of the right prevents this" (Rawls 1971, 449).
8. See the discussion of the meaning of the symbol of leviathan in Schmitt 1996a (5–15, especially at 9). I present a critique of Schmitt's reading of Hobbes in Botwinick 2010.
9. These terms are those of Michael Oakeshott 1975 (70–78).
10. See Derrida's summary of Schmitt's notion of the enemy in Derrida 1997 (83–92).

References

Botwinick, A. 1990. *Skepticism and Political Participation*. Philadelphia: Temple University Press.

Botwinick, A. 1997. *Skepticism, Belief, and the Modern: Maimonides to Nietzsche*. Ithaca: Cornell University Press.

Botwinick, A. 1998. "Religion and Secularism in Liberalism." *Telos* 113 (Fall): 79–104.

Botwinick, A. 2010. "Shakespeare in Advance of Hobbes: Pathways to the Modernization of the European Psyche as Charted in *The Merchant of Venice*." *Telos* 153 (Winter): 138–143.

Cristi, R. 1998. *Carl Schmitt and Authoritarian Liberalism: Strong State, Free Economy*. Cardiff: University of Wales Press.

Derrida, J. 1996. "Remarks on Deconstruction and Pragmatism." In *Deconstruction and Pragmatism: Simon Critchley, Jacques Derrida, Ernesto Laclau, and Richard Rorty*, ed. C. Mouffe. London: Routledge.

Derrida, J. 1997. *Politics of Friendship*, trans. George Collins. London: Verso.

Feigl, H. 1952. "Validation and Vindication: An Analysis of the Nature and the Limits of Ethical Arguments." In *Readings in Ethical Theory*, ed. W. Sellars and J. Hospers. New York: Appleton-Century-Crofts, 667–680.

Hobbes, T. 1946. *Leviathan*, ed. M. Oakeshott. Oxford: Basil Blackwell.

Levinas, E. 1969. *Totality and Infinity: An Essay on Exteriority*, trans. A. Lingis. Pittsburgh: Duquesne University Press.

Levinas, E. 1987. "Philosophy and the Idea of Infinity." In *Collected Philosophical Papers*, trans. Alphonso Lingis. Dordrecht: Martinus Nijhoff, 47–59.

Levinas, E. 1989. *The Levinas Reader*, ed. S. Hand. Oxford: Basil Blackwell.

Levinas, E. 1996. *Basic Philosophical Writings*, ed. A. T. Peperzak, S. Critchley, and R. Bernasconi. Bloomington: Indiana University Press.

Machiavelli, N. 1961. *The Prince*, trans. G. Bull. Baltimore: Penguin Books.

Maimonides, M. 1963. *The Guide of the Perplexed*, trans. S. Pines. Chicago: University of Chicago Press.

McCormick, J. P. 1997. *Carl Schmitt's Critique of Liberalism: Against Politics as Technology*. Cambridge: Cambridge University Press.

Nagel, T. 1973. "Review of John Rawls, *A Theory of Justice*." *Philosophical Review* 82: 220–234.

Oakeshott, M. 1975. *On Human Conduct*. Oxford: Clarendon Press.

Peperzak, A. 1993. *To the Other: An Introduction to the Philosophy of Emmanuel Levinas*. West Lafayette: Purdue University Press.

Plato. 1964. *Sophist in The Dialogues of Plato*, 4th ed., trans. B. Jowett. Oxford: Clarendon Press.

Rawls, J. 1971. *A Theory of Justice*. Cambridge: Harvard University Press.

Schmitt, C. 1976. *The Concept of the Political*, trans. G. Schwab, with comments by L. Strauss. New Brunswick: Rutgers University Press.

Schmitt, C. 1985a. *The Crisis of Parliamentary Democracy*, trans. E. Kennedy. Cambridge: MIT Press.

Schmitt, C. 1985b. *Political Theology: Four Chapters on the Concept of Sovereignty*, trans. G. Schwab. Cambridge: MIT Press.

Schmitt, C. 1986. *Political Romanticism*, trans. G. Oakes. Cambridge: MIT Press.

Schmitt, C. 1996a. *The Leviathan in the State Theory of Thomas Hobbes: Meaning and Failure of a Political Symbol*, trans. G. Schwab and E. Hilfstein. London: Greenwood Press.

Schmitt, C. 1996b. *Roman Catholicism and Political Form*, trans. G. L. Ulmen. London: Greenwood Press.

Shapiro, C. 2003. *Sovereign Nations, Carnal States*. Ithaca: Cornell University Press.

Žižek, S, E. L. Santner, and K. Reinhard. 2005. *The Neighbor: Three Inquiries in Political Theology*. Chicago: University of Chicago Press.

CHAPTER 13

....

CARL SCHMITT'S
CONCEPTS OF WAR

A Categorical Failure

....

BENNO TESCHKE

INTRODUCTION

THE LITERATURE on Carl Schmitt has not yet generated an in-depth study of his conceptual history of war in the context of his geopolitics of international law. This is perhaps surprising given that war is, according to him, the ultimate expression of the friend/enemy binary and therefore the "leading presupposition" of his notion of the political (1996, 34). The elision of this central Schmittian category in the wider Schmitt literature indicates a distinct political chronology in the reception of his work, which cleaves into an early phase, which revolves largely around the domestic aspects of Schmitt's opus, and a more contemporary phase, which seeks to recover his international thought. While a voluminous and growing first wave of *Schmittiana* dominates the field, including studies on his conception of political theology (Meier 1998); constitutionalism and law (Dyzenhaus 1997, 1998, 2006; Scheuerman 1999; Koskenniemi 2001; Kennedy 2004); and liberalism, democracy, and the state (Holmes 1996; McCormick 1997; Kalyvas 2008) and extending to his collusion with National Socialism (Rüthers 1990; Blasius 2001), antisemitism (Gross 2007), intellectual reception in postwar Germany and Europe (van Laak 2002; Müller 2003), and possibilities of his left appropriation (Mouffe 1999; 2005; Balakrishnan 2000; Hardt and Negri 2000; Buck-Morss 2008), Schmitt's texts on war have received very little explicit attention.[1]

This absence of what must count as the neuralgic center of Schmitt's thought, especially in midcareer, has been partly remedied after the more recent publication of English translations of his key writings on the subject, *The "Nomos" of the Earth in the "Jus Publicum Europaeum"* (2003) and *Theory of the Partisan* (2007), as well as some of his lesser known tracts, *The Turn to the Discriminatory Concept of War* (1937), "The *Großraum* Order of

International Law with a Ban on Intervention for Spatially Foreign Powers" (1939–1941), *The International Crime of Aggression and the Principle "Nullum Crimen, Nulla Poena sine Lege"* (1945), "Forms of Modern Imperialism in International Law" (1933), and *"Großraum versus Universalism: The International Legal Struggle over the Monroe Doctrine"* (1939).

These translations, partly prompted by the George W. Bush Doctrine and his "War on Terror," have thrown Schmitt's contemporary relevance into sharp relief. They occasioned a second wave of *Schmittiana*—centering either on Schmitt's influence, mediated via Leo Strauss, on neoconservative ideology (Norton 2005; Drolet 2011); or on Schmitt as a critic of liberal imperialism and the U.S.-led perversion of an alleged classical legal category of public war among sovereign states (Rasch 2004; Stirk 2005; Scheuerman 2006; Odysseos and Petito 2007; Hooker 2009; Slomp 2009; Legg 2011; de Benoist 2007). Here, Schmitt is validated as the prescient diagnostic of a trend line that began with the dissolution of a territorially defined *jus publicum Europaeum* around the turn of the century, the rise of a legal liberal universalism during the interwar period, and the invention of the discriminatory concept of war; was codified in the Treaty of Versailles and the League of Nations; and ended in the grotesqueries of U.S.-American pan-interventionism after 9/11. Schmitt's Weimar writings on the turn to discriminatory warfare have been mobilized to understand the conceptual genealogies of the contemporary neologisms of rogues states, liberal interventionism, irregular warfare, geographies of extralegality, unlawful combatants, asymmetric warfare, and the political justice of the War Crimes Tribunals in The Hague and elsewhere. However, the contemporary Schmitt literature, particularly in the discipline of International Relations (IR), has rather uncritically accepted and passively relied on the historical plausibility and conceptual coherence of Schmitt's wider historical narrative.

This was best set out in *The "Nomos" of the Earth*, which traced changes in the category of war from the Middle Ages to the Cold War. This history of international law is often adduced to lend historical depth and intellectual legitimacy to Schmitt's more conjunctural interventions into interwar international politics. In fact, one prominent and discerning Schmitt scholar, while qualifying some aspects of Schmitt's history, suggests that "what Schmitt claims for this period has been corroborated by historians of international relations" (Scheuerman 2004, 538). Others claim that "the *Nomos* is widely regarded as the masterpiece of Schmitt's intellectual production and offers perhaps the most compelling history of the development of international law from the ashes of the Middle Ages to the beginning of the Cold War" (Odysseos and Petito 2007, 1). And most recently, a serious study concurs that "the great breadth and erudition of what is, in a self-evident sense, Schmitt's *magnum opus* appears destined to guarantee a place for *Nomos of the Earth* in the canon of essential IR reading" (Hooker 2009, 3). Much of the neo-Schmittian revival takes Schmitt's antiliberal historical counternarrative at face value, applying Schmittian categories of analysis to contemporary affairs without having sufficiently interrogated their intellectual provenances and plausibility. In the process, the reproduction of the tired jargon of the Westphalian state system is performed by the invocation and assimilation of Schmitt's depiction of the *jus publicum Europaeum* to IR's most cherished master category: *Westphalia Redivivus*. One myth is chasing another.

This chapter, by contrast, explores the historical veracity of Schmitt's conceptual history of the category of war in the context of the permutations of international public law from the late Middle Ages to the early Cold War. It examines furthermore whether this history is secured by the theoretical shifts that accompanied his thought on the subject during the Weimar and Nazi periods. For if Schmitt's theoretically informed historical counternarrative is to a large degree flawed, representing more of an ideological construction than a reliable and verifiable grand narrative, then much of the neo-Schmittian literature's celebration of Schmitt's prophetic genius across the social sciences—from the left to the right—requires reconsideration.

READING SCHMITT

Carl Schmitt's thought on war and political violence developed across three distinct stages, each positioning his evolving conceptions of war in response to concrete world-historical conjunctures and each grounding these conceptual readjustments and realignments in more fundamental theoretical shifts. His defense of the classical legal concept of war in his revisionist interwar writings against the Versailles turn toward a discriminatory concept of war, reliant on the retrieval of just war considerations, was tied to his conception of executive sovereignty. This was theoretically secured by decisionism and his concept of the political. By the mid-1930s, this gave way to a fascist concept of territorial *Landnahme* (land capture)—brute acts of seizure and occupation that repartition the world—in which war was reconceived transhistorically as a legality-constituting uract of legitimacy, establishing through a series of *Raumrevolutionen* (spatial revolutions) new interstate *nomoi*. These unities of space, law, and political order were forged by wars of conquest, establishing radical titles to land. This move was theoretically anchored in Schmitt's turn away from decisionism toward concrete-order thinking as a new type of juristic thought. In the post-World War II period, this was to be followed by examinations of the figure of the partisan as the last authentic and legitimate political bearer of physical violence in a largely depoliticized and spaceless world, grounded, if more casually, in a return to the concept of the political.

Schmitt's writings on war form interventions into and adaptations to specific geopolitical constellations but remain unified in the continuity of a deep underlying leitmotif: the quest for the autonomy of the political, which informed his views on the polemical nature of concept formation:

> All political concepts, images, and terms have a polemical meaning. They are focused on a specific conflict and are bound to a concrete situation; the result (which manifests itself in war or revolution) is a friend–enemy grouping, and they turn into empty and ghostlike abstractions when this situation disappears. Words such as state, republic, society, class, as well as sovereignty, constitutional state, absolutism,

dictatorship, economic planning, neutral or total state, and so on, are incomprehensible if one does not know exactly who is to be affected, combated, refuted, or negated by such a term. (Schmitt 1996, 30–31)

Schmitt's polemical (i.e., combative) approach to concept formation, most clearly exemplified in his rejection of the self-professed and seemingly value-neutral and depoliticized rendition of the political and legal terminology of American imperialism, is decisive for understanding his hyperpoliticized mode of knowledge production. It was conceived as an explicit program to forge a countervocabulary and counternarrative against the faux semantic neutralizations of liberal universalism. For Schmitt, political science and jurisprudence are subject to and in the service of his definition of the political—the public friend/enemy distinction—that demands an existential act of decision, politically and intellectually. "It is one of the most important phenomena in the entire legal and intellectual life of humanity that whoever has real power is also able to appropriate and determine concepts and words. *Caesar dominus est supra grammaticam*: the emperor is ruler over grammar as well" (1933, 44). Schmitt's method of concept-formation is consequently not simply devised as an analytic to capture the history of thought, but deliberately designed to fabricate counter-concepts in the political and conceptual battles for intellectual hegemony (Pankakoski 2010). Schmitt's method has to be turned against himself to reveal the political construction of an anti-liberal history of the evolution of the concept of war in international law.

For Schmitt, political combat blends into conceptual combat. Partisan intellectual commitment is intrinsic to the intensification of collective differences and identities—the essence of the political—whose ultimate resolution escalates to the level of war and physical killing. War defines the very possibility of a political community and constitutes the highest expression of the political (Schmitt 1996, 32–35). Schmitt's "intransigence" (Anderson 2005) reflects a personal temperamental disposition and a deep existentialist concern for the question of German independence and, after defeat, the figure of the partisan—the vanishing point of the political. This generated Schmitt's acute fixation on the defense of the autonomy of the political, domestically and internationally, encapsulated in Germany's self-determined decision and capacity to conduct war.

This chapter suggests that the mutations in Schmitt's concept of war can be productively read against the temporal exigencies of this polemical epistemological background. His reflections on the subject cannot be dissociated from his deeper theoretical presuppositions and his ideologically motivated attempt to retrace and redefine the evolution of the concept of war within a revised history of international law and order for specific political purposes. But here a specific problem arises. Any objections to Schmitt, which are themselves primarily politically driven, run the danger of confirming Schmitt's basic insight that no intellectual agreement can be reached by following the liberal protocols of removing "extraneous" political commitments from sober "scientific" debate—into the light of the suasive force of the better argument and its suprapolitical chimera of dispassionate objectivity and value neutrality. Max Weber's irrational demons (i.e., those ultimate value convictions) loom too large. Avoiding this Schmittian trap—reading any critique as an a priori validation of his basic epistemological pre-suppositions, or the idea of ultimately irreconcilable intellectual combat grounded in existential differences—requires therefore the deployment of the method of imma-nent critique: (1) assembling and reconstructing Schmitt's premises and concepts from within, or internal according to their own self-definitions and declared purpose; (2) developing and exposing the internal limits and contradictions of these premises and concepts according to their own logic, forcing the concepts to a crisis; (3) and interro-gating and registering the distance between explananda and explanantia (the match or mismatch between the object of inquiry and the method of explanation) until both cap-size. This method of immanent critique will be supplemented by an external standard of critique (i.e., using the accumulated state of historical scholarship)—some of which was available to Schmitt at the time—to ascertain the plausibility of his conceptual history of war within the framework of his history of international law and order.

The Schmittian project will therefore be assessed in the light of three questions. First, what is the explanatory power of his triple core theoretical axiomatics to capture the his-tory of sovereignty, war, geopolitics and international law? We take these axiomatics to include decisionism, the concept of the political, and concrete-order thinking, reflected in their substantive analogues: sovereignty defined in terms of the declaration of the state of emergency; the agonal friend/enemy binary; and the notion of the *nomos* as a unity of law, space, and order established by acts of land grabs. Second, how credible is Schmitt's history of international law and order when checked against the current record of historical, juridical, economic, diplomatic, and sociological scholarship? And third, what are the contextual conditions that shaped Schmitt's ideologically supercharged view of concept formation as political combat, and what are its intellectual liabilities?

In answer, I argue that the conjunction of immanent critique, external critique (i.e., exposure to historical counterevidence), and ideology critique reveals that Schmitt's triple axiomatics are too restrictive to grasp the phenomena under investigation and too opportunistically deployed to provide for consistency and coherence. This opens up a gap between explanatory premises and historical narrative. Schmitt's theoretical architecture cannot sustain the explanatory burden of the task at hand. It therefore leads to a specious, selective, and defective history of war, geopolitics, and international law. This failure is ultimately grounded in Schmitt's consistent suppression of social relations as a relevant category of analysis, which the ultrapoliticist cast of his premises system-atically elided. This disabled any attempt to relate transformations in modes of warfare, geopolitics, and law to transformations and crises in lived social relations. As a result, the abstraction of power from domestic and international social contexts and its eleva-tion to the neuralgic center of Schmitt's thought leads ultimately to the reification and fetishization of the political and the geopolitical. More specifically, decisionism and the definition of sovereignty in terms of the declaration of the exception exclude the agency of social forces meant to be excepted from the normal rule of law, rendering decision-ism a desocialized, depoliticized, and one-sided concept outside any sociopolitical con-text. The notion of the political externalizes any specification as to what activates the intensification of differences to a condition of potential killing, rendering the notion formalistic, abstract, and empty. Concrete-order thinking identifies the concrete with the factual rather than with the analysis of the confluence of multiple determinations, and it removes any explanation of the question of what drives land captures (i.e., what causes war?) from its explanatory remit. It thereby regressed into a descriptive affirmation of occupation *tel quel* as a pristine and metajuridical act of legitimacy.[2]

The remainder is organized as follows. I start by providing an outline of Schmitt's wider narrative of the history of war and its relationship to geopolitics and international law. I then explore and critique the theoretical presuppositions Schmitt put in place to secure this distorted narrative. The chapter then delves more deeply into this problematic narrative by unpacking in detail the flaws in Schmitt's invented history of geopolitics both empirically and theoretically. I conclude by identifying the misreadings, contradictions, and omissions in his theoretically informed treatment of war from 1492 to the early Cold War.

Schmitt's History of War

Schmitt's thought on war is embedded in his history of international law and order, revolving around the centrality of the *jus publicum Europaeum*—the body of maxims and praxes of early modern international law that prevailed, roughly, throughout the period from 1492/1648 to World War I—as a functioning system of legal norms (Schmitt 2003). Its achievement, according to Schmitt, resided in its ability to regulate the excesses of interstate anarchy in a geopolitical pluriverse without erasing the essence of sovereign statehood: the public and sovereign decision to conduct war. The *jus publicum*—a unity of space and law termed by Schmitt a *nomos*, in contradistinction to the medieval and liberal-capitalist *cosmos*—revolved around five core categories: the state, as the only legitimate subject of war and peace; secularized and absolute state sovereignty; the executive, as the final locus of reason of state and the arbiter over the state of exception; the idea of *justus hostis* (just enemy), the just enemy; and the associated concept of nondiscriminatory war.

What distinguished the early modern international legal and political order was that the monopolization of warfare by states—*jus belli ac pacis*: the rights to war and peace—removed violent conflict from the ideological struggles of civil society and reconcentrated organized violence at the level of the state. Absolutism for him referred to a state strong enough to depoliticize and neutralize civil wars domestically. Its historical achievement was to have carried through and institutionalized the separation between the private—the world of clashing ultimate validity claims—and the public, the sphere of a morally neutered raison d'état, whose overriding interest resided in the security of the state itself, codified in the exclusive right to make war and peace. This arrogation of the monopoly of violence by absolutist states formalized therefore a double distinction: first, that between public and private, delegitimizing and demilitarizing private actors (lords, cities, estates, pirates, military orders) while elevating the public state as the only subject of international law and politics; and second, between inside and out-side, separating a domestically neutralized and pacified civil society from an international sphere of interstate rivalries.

This dualism fortified the distinction between public international law and private criminal law. Since the absolutist state was prerepresentational or preparliamentarian, conceiving of itself as *legibus solutus*, it provided the ideal type for Schmitt's theory of the modern state, encapsulated in its decisionist nature, absolved from law. Correlatively, as the domestic sphere was rationalized, its international flipside led to the rationalization of interstate conflict by means of a nondiscriminatory concept of war. The rise of the *jus publicum* was premised on the concrete order of this state-centric spatio-political revolution (Schmitt 2003, 126).

While war remained an indispensable and irreducible manifestation of concrete political communities—indeed, the essence of the political—it was the crowning achievement of early modern public law to have channeled generalized collective violence (i.e., an ongoing European civil war) into a "war in form" (2003, 141), conducted exclusively among legally recognized states according to certain rules and conventions. This move entailed, according to Schmitt, a clear distinction between belligerents and neutrals, combatants and noncombatants, states of war and states of peace. Schmitt referred to these achievements as the bracketing of war or a war in form, which he lauded as the civilization, rationalization, and humanization of war. Modern interstate warfare came to be conducted among equals, according to certain intersubjectively agreed and commonly binding legal conventions—a combination of the right to war (*jus ad bellum*) and rights in war (*jus in bello*)—which also implied the positive making of peace. The *jus ad bellum* came to be divorced from just cause (*justa causa*) considerations, which were declared immaterial for determining the legitimacy of war.

This gave rise to the notion of a nondiscriminatory concept of war (2003, 152), which superseded medieval just war doctrines. Thus, juridically externalized, the reasons for war declaration were placed outside any legal, moral, or political judgment, implying the retention of the status of the enemy, even during the fighting, as a just enemy rather than its demotion as a foe, criminal, or barbarian. Morality, in that sense, came to be divorced from politics proper. A destructive moral universalism, as expressed in the fifteenth- and sixteenth-century wars of religion, was replaced by a salutary moral relativism in interstate relations. Accordingly, the *jus publicum* implied a decisive rupture with medieval just war theories, grounded in the moral universalism of the *res publica christiana*.

This new concept of war—at once public (i.e., restricted to interstate war), bracketed (i.e., circumscribed by rational rules of conduct), and nondiscriminatory (i.e., morally neutral)—contrasted sharply with the anterior medieval practice of violence. Within feudal Christian Europe, the arms-bearing status of the nobility and, in particular, the instrument of the feud, rendered all distinctions futile between the private and the public as well as between the domestic and the international. A feud was not a war, since it was regarded as an instrument for the execution of justice. Outside feudal Christian Europe, the enemy was categorically rendered as a barbarian, which included, by definition, the threat of his annihilation, exemplified in the Crusades. This shift from the medieval *jus gentium* (law of the peoples) to the *jus inter gentes* (law between peoples) established a historically unprecedented and exemplary *nomos*, capable of combining untrammelled state sovereignty with the anarchy-mitigating effects of international law.

This line of reasoning was powerfully invoked by Schmitt (1988; 1996) against the post-World War I criminalization of the German Reich as an outlaw nation, whose political status as a sovereign state was revoked by the perceived *Versailles Diktat*. Since Germany was not admitted to the peace negotiations and war guilt and war crime were not juridical concepts in interstate relations (*nullum crimen, nulla poena sine lege*), their formulation and intrusion into international law after 1919 transformed public inter-state law into an incipient world domestic law, which started to domesticate, remoralize, and juridify the interpolitical by introducing a new discriminatory concept of war (Schmitt 2003, 259–299; 1937). This reinserted just war considerations into the definition of the legality of warfare. This move, according to Schmitt, castrated the essence of the political—the sovereign decision to go to war against an enemy. Versailles thereby abrogated the cornerstone of the classical *jus publicum*, undermining war's status as the autonomous, purest, and highest form of interstate relations. It transformed war into a policing exercise and thus redomesticated it. Worse, the Wilsonian invocation of the concept of humanity reconnected post-Versailles conceptions of international law to medieval just war doctrines, which contained a tendency toward the total negation of the just enemy and its degradation to an enemy of mankind—a nonhuman (Schmitt 1996). Correlatively, it generated a new and distinct liberal way of war, more total in its aims than the bracketed and limited wars of pre-1914 Europe, since it aimed—next to the killing of nonhumans—at the direct transformation of politics, society, and subjectivities: the making of liberal subjects. For Schmitt, the Versailles Peace Treaties declared a *status mixtus* between war and peace—a continuation of war by other means.

The development of the discriminatory concept of war was for Schmitt closely tied to the historical trajectory of U.S. foreign policy, shaped by the 1823 Monroe Doctrine toward the Western Hemisphere, rendering the sovereignty of Latin American countries conditional on the domestic maintenance of private property and free trade; otherwise, U.S. intervention beckoned. This precedent was inflated to universal proportions in the League of Nations' redefinition of the category of war with its morally recharged discourse of law states versus outlaw states, good versus evil, humanity against terrorists, and the impossibility of neutrality. This was further entrenched in liberal humanitarian law, notably in the 1928 Kellogg-Briand Pact, which sought to outlaw wars of aggression. The invocation of a common humanity leads, paradoxically but logically, to the depoliticization of former just enemies (Schmitt 2003, 266), their criminalization as outlaws, even their dehumanization as foes, and to the radicalization of warfare through its transformation into an annihilatory exercise of unqualified killing and the structural impossibility of concluding peace in the absence of a legal enemy—a war without end. Wilson's "war to end all wars," laconically derided by Schmitt as "the last war of humanity" (1996, 70), is paradoxically total in purpose and unending in space and time.

According to Schmitt, the totalizing character of liberal war invariably includes the liberal transformation of targeted states, societies, and subjectivities. It is structurally incapable of leaving a defeated enemy state and its society intact or of readmitting it into the international community—a historical practice ideal typically exercised with post-Napoleonic France's readmission into the Concert of Europe, agreed at the Vienna Congress—without its constitutional and social alignment with liberal norms. In this perspective, liberal war no longer deserves the appellation war but is repackaged in pacifist terminology and transformed into a series of policing actions, otherwise known as humanitarian intervention. This opened up the prospect of the return to the global civil wars of the pre-Westphalian period, even though American world unity had immeasurably expanded the efficacy of universal law in a cosmopolitan age, defined as a spaceless universalism driven by the ideology of pan-interventionism (Schmitt 1996; 1933; 1939; 1939–1941). These developments are inscribed in the long-term logic of the world-historical departure from Schmitt's golden age of limited interstate wars, which then appears in retrospect as—and is accordingly elevated to the status of—the highest achievement of European civilization: the genius of European jurisprudence.

Schmitt's critique of liberalism's discriminatory and total category of war forced him to reconcile his definition of conventional war in the context of the rise of National Socialism and his personal complicity with Hitlerism, as he joined the National Socialist German Workers' Party on May 1, 1933. While his Weimar writings against Versailles relied on the classical notion, as he saw it, of early modern sovereignty and nondiscriminatory warfare, portraying Germany as a revisionist and defensive power concerned to reestablish the status quo ante, this position became intellectually increasingly indefensible in the light of Adolf Hitler's main foreign policy moves and the final descent into open warfare during the late 1930s. For while Schmitt's early embrace of Nazism emphasized its anti-universalism as a defensive project, designed to protect ethnic differences and "German blood" on the customary grounds of national self-determination (1934, 391–423), he now had to justify and rationalize the offensive wars for German *Lebensraum* beyond the original geography of ethnic German settlement, which broke with all conceptions of just enmity and many conventions of *jus in bello*—brute wars of conquest, murder, and plunder.[3] Schmitt closed this discrepancy through a double adjustment, invoking the Monroe Doctrine as a model for German regionalism, articulated as a German *Großraum*—a greater territorial space or a pan-region—to argue for a new planetary pluriverse composed of multiple greater regions (1995; 1939; 1939–1941), and by replacing the liberal discriminatory concept of war with a more primitive and transhistoricized notion of war as land capture and effective occupation, sanctioned as an original legal order founding act of legitimacy, creating a *nomos* (2003; 1997). Wars of aggression and wars of conquest, quite simply, were the historical norm—"a constitutive process of international law" (2003, 80). "World history," Schmitt declared in 1942, "is a history of territorial conquests" (1997, 39). Both conceptual mutations realigned Schmitt's legal and political thought with ongoing developments.

The anti-universalist category of the *Großraum* came to form the fulcrum of the theoretical structure of Nazi international law, designed to revolutionize the international system. Schmitt was prescient enough and faithful to his own radical historicism not to harbor any nostalgic notions of a return to the classical interstate civilization, as he saw it. The age of (nation-)states and the post-Versailles *Kleinstaaterei* (proliferation of mini-states) was irretrievably over. The future, he argued, belonged to a different type of political unit, for which the Monroe Doctrine provided the historical and legal precedent. Schmitt's normative agenda for a pluriverse of pan-regions was most clearly set out in his 1939 work "The *Großraum* Order of International Law with a Ban on Intervention for Spatially Foreign Powers" (1939–1941), published before the signing of the Molotov–Ribbentrop Pact in August 1939. Schmitt lambasted the legal double standards entertained by the United States at Versailles: simultaneously advocating the notions of national self-determination and nonintervention, conditional upon the acceptance of democracy and capitalism, while declaring the Western Hemisphere—South and Central America and the Pacific—an exclusive American zone. The Western Hemisphere was *hors de la loi*, that is, outside the league framework and outside any intervention by European powers. Inversely, this American greater space would serve as the foil for Schmitt's notion of a German *Großraum*—a self-contained and autarchic German security zone, immune and off-limits to any intervention by *raum-fremde* (alien) powers. For the Monroe Doctrine not only had prohibited interference by European powers in American affairs but also had articulated a legal concept of American intervention and limited sovereignty for other states within the Western Hemisphere. Against the threat of an American spaceless universalism, Schmitt developed during his fascist period the notion of a *Großraum* as the elementary building block for an anti-cosmopolitan, anti-universal organization of the international order based on a plurality of coexisting *Großräume*, each one under the leadership of one imperial nation. Pan-regions are meant to provide guarantees against the homogenization of the world into a liberal flatland—essential for the maintenance of difference and pluralism, indeed, essential for the very possibility of the political, the friend/enemy distinction, encased in mutually exclusive regional blocs.

Since Germany, in contrast to the United States, had first to carve out its greater space, Schmitt returned to the question of how the preliberal European legal order—the *jus publicum Europaeum*—was itself established, identifying 1492—the discovery of the New World—as the last great spatial revolution of world-historical proportions, premised on a simple but effective act of seizure and occupation (Schmitt 2003). Schmitt conjoined Nazi expansionism with the history of war as a law antecedent act of legitimacy, which refounds territorial and legal international orders. Wars of conquest, wars of aggression, and acts of land capture precede any legal order, forming their material-terrestrial basis and establishing radical title to land. World history itself is now reconceived as a series of wars between land and sea powers, allowing Schmitt (1997) to insert the German quest for Lebensraum in a transhistorical continuum from which there is no liberal escape. War is therefore reinstated as a quintessentially political and not a juridical concept. War precedes law.

Schmitt's Theoretical Premises: Decisionism, the Concept of the Political, Concrete-Order Thinking

This account was theoretically framed by Schmitt through three distinct, chronologically successive, but substantially partly overlapping theoretical perspectives: his conception of sovereignty derived from political theology and decisionism; his concept of the political defined as the agonal friend/enemy binary; and his concrete-order thinking, understood as a more sociological perspective on the constitution of a *nomos* as a unity of space, power, and law (i.e., an international order). The exposition of these theoretical perspectives will be followed by their immanent critique to specify their explanatory limits and to ascertain whether this triple theoretical architecture can carry the burden of the narrative above.

In his 1922 *Political Theology*, which reconceived the state of law and sovereignty from the angle of the exception, Schmitt programmatically announces that "sovereign is he who decides on the emergency situation" (1985b, 5). Not Max Weber's classical definition of sovereignty as the legitimate monopoly over the means of violence but the monopoly of the decision moves center stage. Schmitt develops this key thesis in his attempt to defend and strengthen Article 48 of the Weimar Constitution— executive government by emergency decrees—against legal positivism. This theme cuts across Schmitt's major writings from his Weimar period: *Dictatorship* (2010); *The Crisis of Parliamentary Democracy* (1985b); *The Concept of the Political* (1996); *Constitutional Theory*; *The Guardian of the Constitution*; and *Legality and Legitimacy*. Since legal norms could function only in normal situations, legal positivism was liable to a depersonalized, apolitical, and ahistorical blindness. Sovereignty, according to Schmitt, is not invested in the state as an impersonal and objective legal subject, an aggregate of rules and statutes, but intermittently crystallizes if and when political crises and social disorder—liminal situations—escape constitutional norms. Such constitutional crises require an extralegal and eminently political executive decision by a single authority for the reassertion of order, grounded in the state's inalienable right to self-preservation. Moments of indeterminacy and indecision in the objective legal order require rapid and firm, discretionary if not arbitrary, fact-setting acts of subjective decision: *Auctoritas, non veritas facit legem*. Decisionism captures the idea that sovereignty resides ultimately in that power that can declare and enforce the state of exception, suspending the constitution in an emergency. Its declaration cannot be derived from extant legal norms and standard procedures of decision-making. The gap between legal norm and decision inserts an indeterminacy that can be closed only by an interpretation of the sovereign. The sovereign decision is a self-referential, self-empowering, and unmediated act of authority—singular, absolute, and final. Jurisprudentially, it appears ex nihilo. This discretionary element of political surplus value reestablishes the primacy of politics over the rule of law. Legality does not exhaust legitimacy.

Decisionism was complemented in 1927 by Schmitt's (1996) concept of the political. It was formally defined in terms of an intensification of latent antagonisms escalating to the friend/enemy distinction, which demands at some unspecifiable point a political decision on the identification of the internal and external enemy to forge a decisive political unit and maintain existential collective autonomy. The decision activates the differentiation between inside and outside and, within the inside, what must be externalized and excluded. This precipitated a redefinition of the meaning of democracy. For Schmitt, "democracy requires therefore, first homogeneity and second—if the need arises—elimination or eradication of heterogeneity" rather than the "perennial discussions" of parliamentary democracy, grounded in liberal pluralism (1985b, 9). This instantiated the consolidation of an otherwise intensely fragmented industrial and mass-democratic society into a socially homogeneous political community—and, ultimately, an ethnically defined (*artgerecht*) *demos*—through the joint first principles of autonomous executive sovereignty: external war and internal repression.

The politics of the exception transmuted into the politics of fear as a socially integrative device. By appealing to the *prima ratio* of self-preservation, the overriding threats to security and independence demote and flatten all domestic differences and generate the required unity and unanimity. Democracy, according to Schmitt, is thus redefined in identity terms as the direct representation of a unified people (*Volk*) by the political leadership. This may be mediated by irregular acts of spontaneous acclamation or plebiscitary elements, intermittently renewing the bond between leader and led—the national myth of direct democracy. Schmitt systematically deconstructs the bourgeois state of law in favor of the total state to resolve the crisis of the Weimar Republic.

After his ousting from power in 1936, Schmitt resumed his academic work and produced three major texts: "The *Großraum* Order of International Law with a Ban on Intervention for Spatially Foreign Powers"; *Land and Sea*; and *The "Nomos" of the Earth*, written 1943–1945 but published in 1950; as well as the edited 1940 volume, *Positionen und Begriffe* (*Positions and Concepts*), collecting the essays written in his struggle against Weimar, Geneva, and Versailles. This turn toward international law and international history was premised on a paradigmatic move away from political decisionism, which criticized legal normativism from above, to concrete-order thinking, which attacked legal normativism and decisionism from below. This was first announced in 1934 in a somewhat obscure but theoretically important book, *On the Three Types of Juristic Thought* (2004). Schmitt first deployed this new type of juristic thought to replace the liberal and universalist idea of the rule of law—and its increasingly threatened principles of generality and predictability—by a situation-bound deformalization of law, upheld and encased in different nationally homogeneous legal cultures.

As Schmitt's preoccupations moved from constitutional to international law during the mid-1930s, he realized that political decisionism was insufficient to capture the politics and geopolitics of land appropriations and spatial revolutions, which he now privileged as foundational and constitutive acts of world ordering to rewrite the history of international law as an antiliberal and antinormative tract. This revealed another weakness in normativism, for which the original formation of statehood—indeed, the very presence of sociopolitical normalcy—appeared as an extralegal and non-jurispru-dential problem. Neither normativism nor decisionism had an answer to the question: what foundational act of legitimacy precedes acts of legality? What constitutes territo-rial order? Any answer had to revise constitutional law in the direction of a sociologi-cally and politically expanded notion of jurisprudence as a new type of juristic thought, which Schmitt referred to as concrete-order thinking. Here, the term *nomos*, in contra-distinction to an undifferentiated universal cosmos, was designed to fill this deficiency in conventional jurisprudence: "[N]omos is precisely the full immediacy of a legal power not mediated by laws; it is a constitutive historical event—an act of legitimacy, whereby the legality of a mere law is first made meaningful" (2003, 73). This conception of a law-antecedent act of legitimacy came to inform Schmitt's interpretation of the history of international law—from the New World discoveries to the *Großraum*—for it put the question of the *origins* of spatial and legal order as the focus.

What is concrete-order thinking as a sociologically enhanced jurisprudence in international law? Schmitt exemplified his paradigmatic turn most clearly in *The "Nomos" of the Earth*. It is premised on a single overarching thesis, stating that all legal orders are concrete, territorial orders, founded by an original, constitutive act of land capture. This establishes a primary and radical title to land: a *nomos*, a unity of space, power, and law. Acts of land appropriation and distribution, their parti-tion and classification, form the material matrix that constitutes a *nomos*. Schmitt derives the term—in contradistinction to law as statute (*Gesetz*)—from the Greek verb *nemein*, meaning the tripartite act of appropriating, dividing, and pasturing. "*Nomos* is the immediate form in which the political and social order of a people becomes spatially visible—the initial measure and division of pasture-land, i.e. the land appropriation as well as the concrete order contained in it and following from it" (2003, 70). *Nomos* connotes the situative unity of a spatial order (*Ordnung*), and the position or orientation (*Ortung*) of any community, creating a unity of space and law. Against the prevailing aspatial, ahistorical, and depoliticized legal positivism—which conceived of domestic and international law as an abstract web of norms, tied together in a seamless hierarchy, ultimately derived from the *Grundnorm* of the con-stitution to which even the state is subjected. Schmitt explicitly opts for this brute act of seizure and occupation to argue for the metalegal origins of any international order that grounds its law in a material-terrestrial reality. Legal orders have spatial and martial origins. Might generates right.

Schmitt conjoined concrete-order thinking to his critique of the post-Versailles order and the Monroe Doctrine, in setting out the intellectual terrain for his geopo-litical vision of a new greater territorial order. This was encapsulated in his notion of *Großraum*, which argued for the coexistence of several pan-regions, one of which included Central and Eastern Europe, under Germany's imperial hegemony. The turn to the category of the *nomos* had a dual function. First it offered a revisionist history of international law and order, as revolving around a series of land grabs and spatial

revolutions, which also served to heap up intellectual resources and arguments to legitimize Hitler's *Raumrevolution* and *Großraumpolitik*. Second, it detonated all the pieties
of the League of Nations, as Nazi German expansion was now inscribed within the
trans-historical recurrence of primeval *nomos*-constituting acts of conquest and land
appropriations. History is rewritten in the light of Schmitt's (geo-)politics, and this historical revisionism justifies German imperialism.

SCHMITT'S THEORETICAL
PRESUPPOSITIONS: A CRITIQUE

To which degree can Schmitt's theoretical perspectives (i.e., decisionism, the concept of
the political, concrete-order thinking) and his key concepts (i.e., sovereignty as exception, friend/enemy, *nomos,* and pan-region) function as generic analytics, able to theoretically secure the rewriting of the history of statehood, war, and international law?
Clearly, the central axis of Schmitt's intellectual project revolves around the insufficien-
cies of legal positivism in answering the question of the state and war in historical perspective. He formulated this critique, prior to 1934, from the vantage point of political
decisionism and thereafter from the angle of concrete-order thinking, as a new type of
juristic thought—the two methods that frame the aforementioned categories.

Analytically, Schmitt's notion of the extralegal decision that instantiates the politics
of the exception—while jurisprudentially an important corrective to the depoliticized
world of legal positivism—is little more than a passe-partout that can be applied to an
indiscriminate range of polities, which under duress turn to emergency powers. The
application of Schmittian concepts to the exception can only descriptively confirm, a
posteriori, an already instituted state of affairs as a fait accompli. The explanation of
the emergency is outside their remit; its critique cannot be formulated from within the
Schmittian vocabulary. Why is that the case? Since Schmitt's method—be it decisionism, the friend/enemy distinction, or concrete-order thinking—is bereft of any sociology of power, decisionism lacks the analytics to identify what constellation or balance of
sociopolitical forces can activate, in what kind of situation, the politics of the exception
and fear. For the declaration of the state of exception is never a non-relational creation
ex nihilo—a unique and self-referential event, equivalent to the miracle in theology. It
remains bound to the social by an indispensable act of calculation, preceding its declaration, as to its chances of implementation and daily public compliance or resistance by
those upon whom it bears: the social relations of sovereignty.

The exception remains quintessentially inserted in a relation of power whose reference point remains the social. The decision alone is never decisive. Of the two sides of
the exception—the power that invokes it and the power that is being excepted from
the normal rule of law—Schmitt theorizes only the first. Social relations remain theoretically exterior to, and systematically excluded from, his conception of sovereignty,

as formalized in political decisionism. Sovereign is he who decides over the state of exception—"an absolute decision created out of nothingness" (1985a, 66). This definitional narrowing—in fact, erasure—of the net of determinations of the decision to an unmediated subjective act is the essence of Schmitt's idea of sovereignty. *Quis iudicabit?* Who will decide? Social forces do not enter Schmitt's definition of the extra-normative declaration of the state of emergency, which remained analytically a supra-sociological, extra-constitutional (as well as ideologically antisocial) device—a liminal concept—for the restoration of order by executive force.

Desocialized, Schmitt's conception of sovereignty also remains curiously depoliticized: he seeks to identify an Archimedean point not only outside society but also equally outside politics—superinsulated from any sociopolitical contestation—to neuter domestic politics altogether: ultrasovereignty. This extra-political vantage point is deliberately chosen—and here political theology and hyper-authoritarianism converge—to pinpoint that chimerical location that restabilizes social processes from nowhere, ex nihilo, yet with overwhelming force: the apotheosis of the state. But this "place beyond" belongs to the sphere of theology proper. Here, at the latest, political theology—the conception of sovereignty modeled on absolutism and the papal *plenitudo potestatis*—collapses into arbitrary state terror. Schmitt's restrainer, conceptualized as the force that "holds back," transmogrifies into the Antichrist (2003, 59–62).

Schmitt's conception of sovereignty constitutes a normative prescription, designed specifically for a hyperauthoritarian solution to the intractable crisis of the Weimar state, and cannot function as a generic analytic for ubiquitous invocations of emergency powers. In this context, it should be recalled that Schmitt's decision to define sovereignty in terms of the exception was not the result of a dispassionate and scholarly inquiry into the ultimate locus of power but instead was a politicized intervention into the jurisprudential debates on the interpretation of the Weimar Constitution's Article 48, on the scope of presidential emergency powers and executive government by decree. For Schmitt, sovereignty *should* reside in the authoritative decision, rendering it a nonrelational concept, outside society and even outside politics—analogous to the miracle in theology. Schmitt explicitly related his notion of the exception to political theology rather than a historical sociology of public law. His ultra narrow definition of the exception failed to develop a theoretical perspective on sovereignty that would enlarge its scope to incorporate the historicity of differential and contested social relations of power. Schmitt developed a legal-political register, unsupported by sociological or political-economic analogues. This does not per se invalidate this register, but it leaves it suspended in midair. Schmitt constructed legal-political concepts *against* the crisis of the Weimar state rather than concepts *of* the crisis. Sovereignty as exception is singularly unable to incorporate the social forces that contest sovereignty and to gauge the different constellations and transformations between political authority and social relations as well as geopolitics and international law.

But this was the task set by The *"Nomos" of the Earth* and the turn toward concrete-order thinking in the mid-1930s, generating a reinterpretation of history as a succession of spatial-legal *nomoi* that tied Schmitt's present to a seemingly remote and recondite past. Schmitt's glorification of the classical age of the European interstate civilization—the *jus publicum Europaeum*—served the purpose of depicting the Anglo-American conception of international law as degenerate and total, with Nazi Germany and *Großraumpolitik* as their rightful historical nemesis—in fact, the torch bearer of geopolitical pluralism. Between the two central axes that sustain Schmitt's ideas of sovereignty—the brute act of land appropriation and the extra-political state of exception—his invocation of the *jus publicum* finds no systematic position. His approach to constitutional and international law receives its illumination from these two vantage points—above and below—but not from positivistic law itself. Schmitt's reinterpretation, from his discussion of the discoveries of the New World through to the *Großraum* regional blocs, oscillates permanently between two mega-abstractions: the literal acceptance of the *jus publicum*, endorsing a legal positivism and formalism that he otherwise violently contested; and the abstraction of spatial concretion, which was originally meant to provide an antidote to the former. Between these two reifications, any determinate social content and process disappears from view.

Concrete-order thinking fails to provide guidance on what processes *drive* the politics of land appropriation and world ordering. What causes war? This leads to an asociological and curiously non-geopolitical—in the sense of geopolitics as an intersubjective conflict—stance: the nature of sixteenth-century Spanish absolutism, the relations between the *conquistadores* and the Spanish Crown, and the interimperial relations between the expanding European overseas empires remain unexamined. The concrete processes of land appropriation, distribution, and property relations in the Americas—the geopolitical clash with the natives as historical subjects—remain not only off-screen but by definition also outside any purely political or geopolitical notion of conquest as concretion. In this sense, concrete-order thinking remains blunt, since the concepts for specifying the dynamics of the social property and authority relations that drive overseas expansion are nowhere developed or deployed. Schmitt's non-sociological account of the New World discoveries is compounded by the absence of an inquiry into the interpolitical nature of the encounter. The native Amerindians remain missing from his account of the regionally differentiated resolutions of land and property conflicts. They are not even acknowledged as passive bearers and victims of the incoming Spaniards and Portuguese but instead are nullified and written out of history. Schmitt conceives of the Americas as a desubjectified vacuum.

In the end, Schmitt provides no answer to his own question: what processes established the order of the *jus publicum*? The "concrete" is largely the factual. The descending journey from the concrete to its manifold inner determinations and the ascending return journey to the concrete as a concrete in thought, captured in its rich inner determinations, are never undertaken. The concrete—facticity—turns into an abstraction in Schmitt's work. But this cannot really be surprising: concrete-order thinking remains, throughout Schmitt's work, strictly extrasociological since the lateral dynamics of geopolitics and land appropriations remain abstracted from, and non-articulated with, the vertical dynamics of social relations and surplus appropriation. In fact, it is self-consciously antisociological, in line with Schmitt's generic *Weltanschauung* as a counterrevolutionary *étatist* thinker. This suppression and elimination of social relations was, of course, already prefigured in his concept of the political, which now informed his concept of the geopolitical. Both detach the political, or geopolitical, from the social—in fact, prioritize and valorize the political and geopolitical over and against the social. This renders both the jargon of the exception (the reformulated essence of sovereignty) and the jargon of the concrete (the reformulated essence of territorial orders) abstract, formalistic, and explanatorily empty.

THE INVENTION OF SCHMITT'S GEOPOLITICAL HISTORY

Given the self-limitations of Schmitt's theoretical architecture, to which degree is his history of sovereignty, war, and law still plausible? Is his history consistent with and carried by his triple theoretical axiomatics? And what is the ultimate ideological motive behind and fallout of Schmitt's revision of the history of international law and order? This section argues that his historical narrative is flawed because the New World Discoveries did not precipitate, as Schmitt admits, the spatial revolution that drove the construction of the new *nomos* of the *jus publicum*. Furthermore, it argues that Schmitt's account of the absolutist state as an archetypical decisionist polity has long been historiographically discredited and suggests that his acceptance and glorification of the *jus publicum* as a binding system of international law is empirically untenable and inconsistent with his general critique of legal positivism and normativism. It further shows that the practice of early modern warfare was diametrically opposed to Schmitt's definition of nondiscriminatory war as a rationalized, civilized, and humanized affair, subject to the laws of war, and that the attempt to hedge and regulate war was de facto the achievement of international humanitarian law forced by liberal-constitutional states from the late nineteenth century onward. It argues that Schmitt's ascription of the category of total war to liberal states is historically problematic and conceptually misconstrued, as Schmitt deflected attention from Nazism's self-declared total war as a new class of war on which he remained silent. It finally suggests that Schmitt had to abandon concrete-order thinking—without any admission—to theorize the deterritorializing nature of American imperialism, adopting a political-economic theoretical register on loan from Marxist theories of informal imperialism. Inversely, he refused to theoretically ground Germany's turn toward new wars of aggression and conquest in a political economy of German *Lebensraum/Großraum*, opting instead for a pure invocation of the friend/enemy distinction to rationalize Nazi expansionism. It concludes by proposing that these inconsistencies and theoretical failures are grounded in the systematic suppression of social relations as a category of analysis to fully comprehend the history of war, geopolitics, and international law, rendering his narrative empirically defective, theoretically flawed, and ultimately ideological.

Did the Conquest of the New World Establish the *Jus Publicum Europaeum*?

While the *Wehrmacht* marched toward Moscow and Stalingrad, Schmitt (1940; 2003) invoked in the early 1940s the Spanish discoveries of the Americas to exemplify his thesis that revolutions in the structure of international law follow spatial revolutions, which are themselves grounded in the fact-setting acts of land captures: wars of conquest. But as soon as this thesis was announced, it was descriptively immediately qualified and retracted by Schmitt himself in his much subtler historical analytics of the impact of the colonial discoveries on the demise of the medieval cosmos and the rise of the new interstate *nomos*. In fact, the latter history negates the former thesis.

Any closer reading of *The "Nomos" of the Earth* shows not only that Schmitt was deeply ambivalent in his explanation of the European interstate system—vacillating between the *Conquista* (1492), the rise of the absolutist state (1648), and English balancing (1713) as the formative moment—but also that he explicitly excluded the conquests of the Americas from the constitution of early-modern Europe. His discussion of the rationalization—jurisprudential and material—of the colonization process by Spain and Portugal reveals, paradoxically, that the conquests did not precipitate the spatial revolution and the subsequent rise of the new European interstate *nomos* that he generically associated with the enclosure processes overseas. This is most clearly expressed in his differentiation between the *rayas* (divisional lines) and the amity lines. The first repartition of the oceans after the discoveries in the form of the *rayas* was laid down in the 1494 Treaty of Tordesillas between Spain and Portugal, establishing a dividing line a hundred miles west of the Azores and Cape Verde: all the land west of the line should go to Spain and all the land east of it to Portugal (2003, 88–89; 1997, 41). This meant the conditional territorialization of both the seas and the newly discovered lands, as required by feudal land-holding patterns and social property relations (Teschke 1998). The Americas, the Atlantic, and the Pacific remained firmly within the reach of the late-medieval law-governed cosmos of the *res publica Christiana*, including the papal missionary mandate and the just war doctrine against non-Christians. "The later antithesis of firm land and free sea, decisive for spatial ordering in international law from 1713–1939, was completely foreign to these divisional lines" (Schmitt 2003, 89). All land and sea remained jurisprudentially firm. At least formally, the Vatican was still the central supraterritorial source of adjudication in Catholic Europe. Against Schmitt's express purpose—the centrality of land appropriations for the constitution of the law-governed European interstate civilization—he shows that this causal nexus does not hold.

The quantum leap to the *jus inter gentes* is precipitated not by the Salamanca School but by Dutch and English secular jurisprudence, notably Grotius and Selden, in the Spanish–Dutch/English debate on *mare clausum versus mare liberum*. The initial post-conquest partition of the world between the Catholic powers along the *rayas* was challenged only by the Spanish–French Treaty of Cateau-Cambrésis (1559) and the subsequent seventeenth-century Anglo-French and Anglo-Spanish treaties that fixed the amity lines, dividing the world into a civilized (i.e., law-governed) zone within these lines and an anarchic zone, a state of nature, "beyond the line" (2003, 94). This designated not only the land but also the sea beyond the line as free and lawless. *Res nullius* is also *res omnium*—up for grabs by the strongest taker. It should be understood that the arguments for mare liberum had nothing to do with free capitalist competition, as Schmitt obscured the distinction between free and open seas. The notion of free sea simply referred to its non-law-governed status and implied permanent military rivalry over the control of trading and shipping routes, as states tried unilaterally to territorialize the seas rather than declaring them multilaterally open. Free trade across open seas had to wait until the nineteenth century. Irrespective of this misreading, he therefore locates the decisive break from medieval Christian to early-modern practices of spatial ordering not in the fact of the Discoveries per se but in the transition from the Spanish–Portuguese *rayas* system to the Anglo-centric amity lines. This initiated America's redefinition from an integrated appendix of the Eurocentric Old World to a distinct New World to be reappropriated and divided in a morally neutral agonal contest according to the law of the stronger. Schmitt provides ample evidence—*rayas*, scholasticism, *res publica Christiana*—that rather than dissolving the old medieval and catholic *cosmos*, his purported spatial revolution of 1492 was jurisprudentially assimilated to prevailing discourses of Christian expansion and aligned to late-medieval customs of conditional territorialization.

The *Jus Publicum* and the Absolutist State: Decisionism or Social Collaboration?

Schmitt's history of the rise and decline of the *jus Europaeum* evinces another paradox. It consists in the contradiction between Schmitt's interpretation and idealization of the absolutist state as a decisionist polity (literally absolved from law; *legibus absolutus*), which gave free rein to rulers in imposing domestic law and order, and his simultaneous embrace of the *jus publicum* as a system of international laws and norms, which prescribed absolutism's external (i.e., nondiscriminatory, civilized, and limited) wars and wider foreign affairs as law-abiding, rationalizing military conduct subject to the *jus belli ac pacis*. A logical problem is here compounded by a historical one. How, given Schmitt's lifelong antipathy against legal positivism, could he suddenly embrace legality over political legitimacy? How could a system of mere norms tame the absolutist war machines of continental Europe? How could Schmitt assign executive sovereignty to omnipotent absolutist rulers while simultaneously celebrating a European-wide legal formalism that he otherwise castigated intellectually in his debates with Hans Kelsen? This pretense to legality by the Great Powers is characteristically un-Schmittian. Logically speaking, the legal groundlessness of the subjective decision should have operated in external relations as much as in internal affairs—a conclusion that Schmitt failed to draw but that is much closer to the historical record.

How does Schmitt's account of absolutism and early modern warfare square with historical research? Schmitt defined absolutism as a fully rationalized, secularized, and morally neutralized public order. Assisted by its pre-parliamentarian constitutional nature, which exalted monarchical executive government, Old Regimes had successfully carried through the distinction between the domestic and the international, the public and the private, overcoming the religious and civil wars of the sixteenth century (1926; 2003, 140–151). But since Schmitt was unconcerned with the social relations of sovereignty and power, his interpretation of the classical period of European interstate civilization, abstracted from the clashing value claims and competing interests of civil society, turns out to be a historical fiction. Absolutist states, rather than institutionalizing a secularized notion of depersonalized sovereignty that neutralized domestic politics and rationalized interstate relations, remained personalized, sociopolitically highly contested, legitimized by divine authority, and embodied in the persons of their respective princes. And the multiplicity of these dynastic houses across Europe—and their interdynastic relations—patterned the intense geopolitical conflicts over land and people across the period of the *jus publicum*.

Why does a social interpretation of absolutism lead to this conclusion? And why is it more in sync with the contemporary literature, Marxist and non-Marxist alike, on absolutism that has dominated the historiographical debate since the 1980s (Beik 1985; Bonney 1995; 1999; Parker 1996; Ertman 1997; Gerstenberger 2007)?[4] Class relations had developed in France along a specific trajectory since the late Middle Ages (Brenner 1985).[5] Here, social conflict over the distribution of peasant surplus had replaced by the seventeenth century the feudal rent regime between lords and peasants in favor of an absolutist tax regime. Peasant communities benefited from competition between the monarchy and local nobles for their surplus, gaining freedom in the process and establishing inheritable tenures that owed fixed dues that subsequently lost value with inflation. With the waning of the old feudal powers of lordly domination and extraction, the monarchy became the central institution that could force income from the peasantry through taxation. However, the relations of exploitation remained governed throughout the *ancien régime* (and even beyond) by political conflicts between the monarchy and the aristocracy over the terms and the distribution of the rights of appropriation, though now in the form of state-sanctioned privileges. Taxation became the key arena of domestic political conflict. The logic of political accumulation—the extortion of surplus from direct producers through extra-economic coercion—continued to rest on personalized praxes of domination, revolving around the personalized sovereignty of the Crown: *L'État, c'est moi!*[6] In the context of this social property regime, a formal separation between the political and the economic, the public and the private, state and civil society, could not be carried through.

Since the pressures for political accumulation persisted internally, the logic of geopolitical accumulation, that is, the predatory accumulation of territories and control over trade routes, characterized foreign policy as well. The normal way to expand the tax base was to acquire territory and control over its taxable population, driving a territorial-demographic (extensive) mode of taxation. But since absolutist sovereignty came to be personalized in the figure of the king, he also remained enmeshed in the Westphalian logic of dynastic unions through royal marriage policies and its wars of succession. Warfare was endemic. Territorial redistributions were a constant of early modern international relations.

The old sword-carrying aristocracy (*noblesse d'épée*), especially during and after the crisis of the seventeenth century, came to be increasingly domesticated, absorbed, and integrated into the tax/office state through office venality and other channels of privilege, while a new office nobility (*noblesse de robe*) was promoted by the Crown. These complex and ungovernable forms of interruling-class cooperation created over time a very unstable and regionally differentiated modus vivendi between the privileged classes and the Crown, which William Beik (2005) refers to as social collaboration. Its center became the court society at Versailles—a jamboree of patronage, clientilism, and nepotism. Feudalism, based on the regionally and locally autonomous powers of the militarized lordly class, was replaced by the institutionalization of aristocratic power in estates and other representative and corporative bodies, whose powers had to be continuously renegotiated in relation to the Crown. Autonomous lordly powers of domination were replaced by state-sanctioned privileges. Feudalism was dead, yet absolutism never materialized (at least not in its orthodox meaning). To remain financially afloat and to pacify the office nobility, French monarchs sold and auctioned off public offices in ever-greater numbers. Over time, venal offices were held in perpetuity and heredity and became thus a privatized source of income. The Crown thus lost control over its fiscal, financial, and juridical administration. It failed to establish a central bank or secure lines of credit and was also forced to borrow on short-term loans at high interest rates from a class of wealthy financiers, who were themselves often taxfarmers.

As a result, during every war, French kings were obliged to resort to the artificial creation and then the sale of more and more offices to raise money. They effectively mortgaged the extractive powers of the state to private financiers and tax farmers. This led to the Byzantine and hopelessly bloated nature of the French semiprivate–semipublic state apparatus. This ruled out any progress toward a modern, rationalized, and efficient bureaucracy that would administer a uniform and countrywide tax code (i.e., a public rule of law) or would establish a state-controlled standing army, staffed by salaried professional soldiers. At the same time, the peasantry had to carry ever-higher rates of taxation so that the agrarian economy—the tax base—remained mired in stagnation. While war thus increased the absolutist claims of French monarchs over their subjects, it simultaneously paralyzed their long-term financial and administrative capacity to rule.

Since early-modern states were not rationalized public apparatuses but were confessional dynastic-composite constructs claiming a sacralized form of sovereignty, public power was not detheologized and neutralized (Gorski 2000). While the age of absolutism did break with the transterritorial theological absolutism of the Vatican, it simultaneously fragmented the unitary confessional papal claims and reassembled them across the spectrum of a pluriverse of creedal mini-absolutisms, after 1555 and again after 1648. The Augsburgian formula *cuius regio, eius religio* did not endorse religious toleration for private subjects but sanctioned the right of regional rulers to determine and enforce the faith of the land. In the French case, the nascent absolutist state did not simply guard over the de-politicized and neutral character of domestic politics and religion but actively established during the Reformation and the Wars of Religion (1562–1598) its Catholic absolutism in violent, directly politicized, century-long campaigns, culminating in the repression and expulsion of the Huguenots with the Revocation of the Edict of Nantes (1685). Absolutism did not rise above the warring civil parties but repressed one of them, giving rise to mono-confessionalized, even sacralized states. Against this background, Schmitt's rendition of absolutism as the embodiment of a decisionistic polity cannot be sustained.

Was Early Modern War a Rational and Civilized Affair?

Correlatively, the praxis of *ancien régime* warfare contrasts sharply with Schmitt's nondiscriminatory concept of war as a bracketed war in form: civilized; rationalized; limited; and humanized. While there is some evidence to suggest that the notion of *Kabinettskriege* attempted to rationalize the conduct of battle, the pairing of limited and total—more precisely, absolute—war, which Schmitt adopted from Clausewitz, is too coarse to capture the nature of early modern warfare.[7] Clearly, Napoleonic and post-Napoleonic warfare marks a qualitative shift in the nature of military affairs, though this does not mean that prerevolutionary warfare can be generically referred to as bracketed or limited in Schmitt's sense. His idealization of *ancien régime* warfare is compromised by the frequency, magnitude, duration, and intensity as well as the costs and casual-ties of early-modern conflicts. For example, at the end of the Seven Years' War, casu-alty figures in the Prussian Army stood at 180,000 soldiers, which was the equivalent of two-thirds of its total size and one-ninth of the Prussian population (Anderson 1988). This was partly due to innovations in military technology, including the development of firearms, artillery, and new techniques like infantry volley fire, and partly to the exis-tential threat of territorial dismemberment and repartition posed by defeat to dynastic Houses. While casualty figures in early-modern wars do not by themselves discredit the category of bracketed warfare, Schmitt's purely legal category is unable to decipher the social sources of and real nature of Old Regime warfare, powered by the requirements of precapitalist geopolitical accumulation.

Military praxes render Schmitt's claim of its civilized, rationalized, and humanized character implausible, given the noncompliance with the nominal conventions of war, the non-distinction between combatants and noncombatants, the customs of recruit-ment, and the problems of provisioning (Kroener 2000). The effects of war on civilian populations were devastating. Since war logistics were not properly developed and sol-diers lacked permanent provisioning, early-modern armies lived off the land, either by looting and pillaging on foreign soil or by way of sequestration and ransom. Armies tended to ransack civilian areas in an effort to feed themselves, causing plunder, rape, famines, and population displacement. *Bellum se ipse alet* ("War feeds off itself") cap-tures this predicament. The absence of a clear set of rules and powers of enforcement con-cerning the treatment of prisoners and noncombatants implied their ransom for money or other prisoners, if they were not killed outright.[8] Forced conscription of civilians was a common practice. Any sociology of contemporary armies shows that, in spite of all the Weberian and Foucauldian emphasis on the increasingly rationalized, professionalized, and disciplined character of the new standing armies, soldiers were generally not salaried bureaucrats but were in pay of noble officers who had usually themselves bought their military commissions. Armies were not public armies but precisely the king's armies yet were essentially beyond their disciplinary control (Kroener 2000, 205).

While most of these wars of succession and trade wars were largely redistributional, in terms of land and control of trade routes, and thus were limited in their war aims, they were simultaneously total insofar as whole regions and kingdoms vanished (cf. the partitions of Poland). The notion of *justus hostis* (a just enemy) whose territory and order would remain intact after defeat was a legal fiction. This manifested itself by an imperial, if not totalizing, drive toward the infinite accumulation of land and booty, as evidenced in aggressive outward orientation—colonialism. Most of these wars of succession, from the Wars of the Spanish and Austrian Succession to the Seven Years' War, were multilateral if not world wars. This would also qualify Schmitt's thesis that the assignment of the lands and seas beyond the line—the externalization of the international state of nature from Europe—caused the civilization of intra-European warfare, as codified in the *droit public de l'Europe*.[9]

It is furthermore unclear how Schmitt's argument on early modern limited war can be squared with the standard historical argument that Old Regime permanent war states or fiscal-military states succumbed to their military expenses, leading—with the important exception of capitalist Britain—to fiscal crises, bankruptcies, and state collapse (Skocpol 1979; Brewer 1988; Contamine 2000a; Glete 2002; Storrs 2009). Early modern intra-European wars were not occasional rule-governed contests—prettified by Schmitt as gentlemanly duels—narrowly circumscribing the external relations of states within an essentially stable interstate order but were a continuous, structural presence, deeply rooted in the nature of social relations that reached into and finally transformed their very sociological cores. *Ancien régime* polities were not only sociologically transformed under the pressure of military rivalries but also eventually were exhausted and destroyed by the combination of spiraling war expenditures, mounting public debts, fiscal crises, repressive rates of taxation, and social discontent, leading in the case of France to 1789. Wars eventually devoured their own masters—dynastic Houses. The idea of nondiscriminatory warfare regulated by the *jus publicum* is a fiction, designed to promote the early-modern epoch as the paragon of civilized warfare against which the subsequent descent to the liberal era of total war can appear only as a decivilizing perversion. Schmitt's whole account of the Westphalian system is both empirically and theoretically deeply flawed.

Who Civilized War?

Throughout his narrative, Schmitt stresses that the delimiting of war, its escape from the confines of the *jus publicum*, was a result of the total wars perpetrated by liberal states, driven by a reversal to just war thinking, which turned former just enemies into mere foes, criminals, and outlaws. This unleashed the absolute moral judgments that characterized the new discriminatory concept of war after 1919. The limited and civilized wars of yore were replaced by the total wars of liberal states. Schmitt imputes throughout that absolutist states, rather than liberal states, articulated, codified and practiced the *jus in bello*. But any closer inspection suggests—and standard histories of international humanitarian law confirm (Roberts and Guelff 2000; Neff 2005, 159–214; Kalshoven and Zegveld 2011)—that the attempt to civilize and regulate the conduct of armed hostilities (to codify war as a legal institution) did not originate within the *jus publicum Europaeum* but was the distinct achievement of primarily liberal-constitutional states in the context of the rise of legal positivism. This was enshrined in the growing body of multilateral treaty law throughout the second half of the nineteenth century: the 1856 Paris Declaration Respecting Maritime Law abolished privateering, a standard practice fully supported by early-modern states as they regularly enlisted pirates as corsairs and privateers in the service of monarchies, blurring the distinction between public armed forces and private subjects, combatants, and noncombatants; the 1864 First Geneva Convention proscribed rules for the amelioration of the wounded and sick in armed forces in the field; the two Hague Conventions of 1899 and 1907, the two most substantial pre-World War I agreements on the laws of war, specified rules, among others, for the pacific settlement of disputes, the opening and closing of hostilities, the laws and customs of war on land, the rights and duties of neutral powers and persons in case of war, the status of enemy merchants ships, the laying of automatic submarine contact mines, the bombardment by naval forces, and the adaptation to maritime war of the principles of the Geneva Convention; the 1925 Geneva Protocol prohibited the use in war of asphyxiating, poisonous and other gases, and of bacteriological methods of warfare; and the 1929 Geneva Convention pertained to the treatment of prisoners of war.

None of these multilateral and open-ended treaties outlawed wars per se and left therefore the sovereignty of liberal and illiberal states (the *jus ad bellum*) intact. Furthermore, the series of conventions and protocols that litter the second half of the nineteenth century constitute in their majority innovations rather than codifications of existing practices. Schmitt either consciously suppressed or simply failed to note the fact that all major multilateral treaties on the laws of war and international humanitarian law were suggested and enacted primarily by liberal-constitutional states. Inversely, his discussion of the laws of war during the early modern period relied primarily on the textual exegesis of moral philosophy, political theory, and scholastic thought, conducted without any attempt to pursue the question whether these deliberations—from the Salamanca School to Grotius and Vattel—were ever codified in international treaty law or abided to on the battleground. Pre-World War I "liberal" international law developed a nondiscriminatory concept of war brought into form by a positivistic *jus in bello*, governing armed hostilities. Schmitt's attempt to identify a liberal concept of discriminatory war with just war, and both with total war, suppressed the admission that liberal states themselves sought to de-totalize liberal war by hedging and bracketing the conduct of war.

TOTAL WAR, AMERICAN
IMPERIALISM, FASCISM

This critique objects to only one aspect of Schmitt's analysis of liberalism's total wars—the assignment of the *jus in bello* to absolutism rather than to liberalism's attempt to bring wars into form—and leaves his argument of liberal wars as polity and society-reshaping exercises untouched. But even here, Schmitt's argument is misleading. While his Weimar writings targeted U.S. imperialism, he reserved special venom in his fascist period for the British practice of total war, grounded in its maritime tradition of conducting naval warfare. Since Britain—amphibious and autothalassical in nature—was never fully integrated into the continental tradition of limited land warfare, it was the arch-representative of total war: "naval wars were based on the idea of the necessity of treating the enemy, trade and economy as one. Hence the enemy was no longer the opponent in arms alone, but every inhabitant of the enemy nation, and ultimately, every neutral country that had economic links with the enemy" (Schmitt 1997, 47). Maritime powers not only reformulated international law but also pioneered the praxis of total war and the category of the total enemy, including the non-distinction between combatants and civilians and the non-distinction between acts of war and acts short of war (blockades, capture of merchant men, economic sanctions). According to Schmitt (1994; 1943), liberal wars were total, presupposing a total enemy as the total population became the target of war.

But while Schmitt's legal dissection of Anglo-American imperialism, the Treaty of Versailles, the League of Nations, and the new notion of discriminatory war was effective, it could not be reconciled with his method of concrete-order thinking. For the analysis of American imperialism was now shifted onto a much deeper sociological terrain that gave Schmitt a privileged insight into the structural transformations of international law and order at the start of the twentieth century. These revolved around the developing dualisms between international public law and transnational private law, a territorial interstate order and a subterritorial world economy, a public pluriverse and a private universalism, grounded in the separation between the political and the economic across the member states of the international system. Schmitt (2003, 235, 255) lays bare the structural correspondence between a transnationalizing capitalism and American postwar grand strategy. These structural complementarities inform Schmitt's analysis of the American vacillation between isolationism and internationalism, encapsulated in the dialectic between political absence and economic presence, ethical pathos and economic calculation: informal empire.

The United States, after Versailles, was politically absent in Europe, both as a League member and as an occupying power, yet it was economically present by its inscription of free trade and its political precondition: the generalization of liberal constitutionalism, private property relations, the rights-bearing and free individual, and the rule of law into the League's Covenant. This strategy, according to Neil Smith (2004), presented a political project of global domination—the rationalization of global space driven by a nonterritorial capitalist imperialism for American economic *Lebensraum*. This rested on the central insight that economic expansion could be decoupled from territorial aggrandizement, divorcing political geography from international accumulation. In this way, the flattening of differentially organized political territories and their submission to common legal principles sanctioned a constitutive dualism between the proliferation of liberal-constitutional states and the expansion of a borderless private world market.

But if Schmitt's argument demonstrated the structural preconditions for global American domination, it simultaneously imperiled and transformed three core assumptions of his theoretical-historical axiomatic: an unwitting erasure of his account of the classical *jus publicum*; a retraction from concrete-order thinking; and a turn toward a transnational economism, selectively applied to the United States and bracketed for Germany. For if the separation between the public interstate and the private substate became recognized in international law in the course of the nineteenth century and politically operationalized by the United States post-1919, then this overturned his generic thesis of the status of the *jus publicum* as genuinely public interstate law.

Second, Schmitt's theoretical excursion into the field of international political economy forced him to change theoretical register—a volte face not licensed by his method of concrete-order thinking. Where Schmitt excavates the roots of the new universal order, he is pressed into an analysis of the international political economy of American world order—falsifying his axiomatic statement that every international legal order is grounded in an original act of land appropriation. The predominantly non-territorial nature of the U.S. restructuration of the interwar European order provided a direct refutation of Schmitt's axiomatic thesis of international orders based on land grabs: Germany, though trimmed in size and regime changed, like Austria-Hungary and the Ottoman Empire, was neither occupied nor annexed. Schmitt's account of the dissolution of the *jus publicum*— suggesting a constitutive nexus between the space-canceling tendencies of transnational capital and the transition from the *jus publicum* to the age of international law—directly unhinges the premise of his concrete-order thinking. This abrupt turn toward international political economy constitutes a theoretically uncontrolled move, not licensed by his own method. This forces him to deploy a Hegelian-Marxist figure of thought: the separation between the political and the economic, with its international analogue; the separation between a territorialized interstate system and a private, transnational world market (Schmitt 2003, 293–294). Simultaneously, this turn toward the separation argument cancels his central thesis that the *jus publicum* rested already on the differentiation between public statehood—with the institutionalization of the early-modern interstate system—and private civil society. Capitalism's border-canceling tendency also cancels Schmitt's core method and core thesis. As the novelty and distinctiveness of U.S. world order is not rooted in a logic of territorialization—but in an attempt to promote informal empire—this negates and transcends Schmitt's now curiously anachronistic notion of concrete-order thinking and his spatialized counterproject: a German *Großraum*.

Third, Schmitt had pressed too far the argument about the geopolitics-dissolving effects of capitalist expansion. For the period between 1880 and Versailles and beyond did not simply constitute a passage, however chaotic and disorderly, from the *jus publicum* to a universal international law or, alternatively, from interstate geopolitics to a space-canceling economic universalism. It rather experienced first the intense interimperial rivalries among the capitalist European empires and their associated reterritorializations of the world, before the settlement of World War I launched a supremely power-political project of the American state. This involved the territorial, military, political, and constitutional reconfiguration of Europe as an ongoing grand strategy of American power projection. The result was not a depoliticized liberal spaceless universalism but an attempt to reconstitute and align European political geography with American economic and security concerns, including the creation of the *cordon sanitaire* as a buffer zone against the Soviet Union. Schmitt overinterprets the space and geopolitics—dissolving impact of Anglo-American capitalism after Versailles and effectively embraces a trans-national economism that out-Marxed Marx. Schmitt failed to see the difference between a spaceless universalism—a universal liberal empire—and a U.S.-supervised European interstate system. The combination of the League of Nations system and American grand strategy did not lead to an apolitical and deterritorialized spaceless universalism during the interwar period. Rather, it only reconstituted and aligned European political geography with American economic and security concerns without erasing the interstateness of the continent—as German *Großraumpolitik* itself was to demonstrate.

How was that possible? As Weimar Germany was already fully integrated into the world economy when *Großraum* thinking started to preoccupy Schmitt in the 1930s, he was forced into yet another theoretical volte face. He turned away from international political economy and re-embraced a spatial-legalistic register that capitalist imperialism, by his own reasoning, either had long dissolved or—but this could not feature in Schmitt's theory—had regenerated through the general capitalist crisis of the 1929 Great Depression, sweeping fascism to power. But as the precepts of international political economy were reserved by Schmitt to Anglo-American imperialism and never applied to German imperialism, his legal-political argument about the desirability of a universalism-blocking concept of German *Großraum* remained strictly beyond the confines of the analysis of capitalism. Although Schmitt (1939–1941) gestured inconclusively toward the transcendence of the classical concept of the territorial state driven by the economic imperatives of a *Großraumwirtschaft* (economic greater space) as a sphere of economic performance (*Leistungsraum*), he was theoretically unable to ground the turn toward German continental autarchy in a series of successive German strategic policy choices within the wider context of the post-1929 crisis of the world economy (Opitz 1977). Consequently, the legal concept of the *Großraum* had to be de-economized and anchored in a reassertion of the political in the abstract, the friend/enemy distinction, arising like a deus ex machina from an identity-based notion of *völkisch* democracy.[10]

But this raises the final question of why Schmitt (1940; 1999), as a trained constitutional and international jurist, never sought, two short diatribes apart, to categorize and place the specific form of Nazi warfare within his legal and political history of warfare. Total war as a distinct class of warfare—normally defined as the complete mobilization of society and economy for the war effort, the non-separation between civilians and combatants, the non-distinction between military and civilian targets and the partial suspension of the laws of war, possibly involving the complete annihilation of the enemy—was the express purpose of the Nazi regime, officially since 1943 at the latest. While Joseph Goebbels gave his infamous 1943 *Sportpalast* Speech, declaring total war, Schmitt ruminated on the Spanish *Conquista*.[11] Given that Schmitt himself drew a line from French revolutionary warfare via General Ludendorff's 1935 World War I memoir *Der Totale Krieg* to World War II, why did he not define total war—perhaps in the calmer waters of the 1950s German Federal Republic when *The "Nomos" of the Earth* was eventually published—as the ultimate perversion of any achievements, absolutist or liberal, in the evolution of international humanitarian law? It is surely a moral monstrosity and intellectual obscenity to wrongly ascribe limited warfare to absolutism and castigating liberal warfare as total, while Nazi Germany conducted a total war and wars of extermination, systematically ignoring the most minimal conventions of war, pursuing scorched earth tactics, and perpetrating state terror and mass killing on an industrial scale. What is Schmitt's legal and political concept of war in German total warfare? Since it is now compared to the *Conquista*—however cryptically—it appears as a prejuridical act without any *justa causa* and without any laws of war, not even a papal mandate.

And what is Schmitt's concept of the German enemy? If it is no longer *justus hostis*, then it must have been a new type of foe—not even the alleged liberal criminal and nonhuman but a total enemy and more likely the subhuman. While the Nazi conception of the enemy was racialized, demoted, and perverted to the status of a subhuman (at least on the Eastern Front), Schmitt felt obliged to denounce Anglo-American war as total: "[T]here is an Anglo-Saxon concept of enemy, which in essence rejects the differentiation between combatants and non-combatants, and an Anglo-Saxon conception of war that incorporates the so-called economic war. In short, the fundamental concepts and norms of this English international law are total as such and certainly indicative of an ideology in itself total" (1999, 34). While Schmitt's transition from the classical interstate war to the liberal wars of pan-interventionism conferred the title of total war to the Anglo-Americans, Schmitt preferred to remain silent throughout his life on Nazi warfare—the alleged land captures designed to bring about a new *nomos* of interregional legality.

CONCLUSION

Schmitt's evolving conceptualizations of war are the intellectual product of an ultra-intense moment in his friend/enemy distinction in the passage from his struggle against Weimar, Geneva, and Versailles to his embrace of National Socialism—the forging and reforging of concepts and positions conceived as intellectual combat. These concepts were flanked by deeper theoretical shifts—from decisionism and his concept of the political to concrete-order thinking—meant to secure and ground concept formation. This led to a tendentious and often falsifying account of war within a revised history of international

law and order. Schmitt inscribed Hitler's spatial revolution into a full-scale reinterpretation of Europe's geopolitical history, grounded in land appropriations, which legitimized
Nazi Germany's wars of conquest. Consequently, Schmitt's elevation of the early modern
nomos as the model for civilized warfare—the golden age of international law—against
which American legal universalism can be portrayed as degenerated, is conceptually
and empirically flawed. Schmitt devised a politically motivated set of theoretical premises to provide a historical counternarrative against liberal normativism, which generated
defective history. The reconstruction of this history reveals the explanatory limits of his
theoretical vocabulary—friend/enemy binary, sovereignty as exception, *nomos*–universalism—for past and present analytical purposes. Its ultra-politicist and spatial-*étatist* cast
remained too restrictive to capture the phenomena at hand, as the reading of history in
horizontal terms failed to incorporate social relations into the dynamics of war and peace.

Wherever Schmitt attempts to penetrate the social, he either mobilizes a geomy-
thological register—British maritime existence, land versus sea—or betrays his own
method, borrowing liberally from political economy. At crucial moments in this large-
scale reinterpretation—1492, absolutist sovereignty, early-modern warfare, British seventeenth-century sovereignty, the classical period of the new imperialism, the origins of
World War I, U.S. informal imperialism, the crisis of the Weimar Republic, Hitler's spatial
revolution—the methods of decisionism, the friend/enemy binary, and concrete-order
thinking disintegrate. They simply fail to reveal the social dynamics that drive transformations in the nature of authority and sovereignty relations, the social sources of land
appropriations and spatial reconfigurations, or developments in the historical genealogy of war and peace. Furthermore, world-historical events that upset Schmitt's spatial-
étatist perspective—the origins of capitalism and the Industrial Revolution; the French
Revolution and Napoleon; the late nineteenth-century New Imperialism and interimperial rivalry; the interwar Great Depression; the Bolshevik Revolution; fascist Economic
Grand Strategy—are either expunged from his account or receive short shrift. Schmitt's
international political thought and historical narrative are empirically untenable and
theoretically flawed—replete with performative contradictions, subterranean reversals
of theoretical positions, omissions and suppressions, mythologizations and flights into
épreuves étymologiques. Schmitt's concrete-order thinking constitutes a rudimentary and
failed attempt to develop a history of international law and geopolitics, which ultimately
regresses into a Eurocentric historico-legal theory of geopolitical occupation *tel quel*.

NOTES

1. Münkler 1992 remains an exception, though his account is restricted to a summary of
   Schmitt's argument. His later work, which introduces the distinction between Old Wars and
   New Wars, relies on Schmitt's conception of early modern wars as classical state-to-state
   affairs (Münkler 2002, 68, 114).
2. For a more detailed exposition of the following argument, see Teschke 2011a; 2011b; 2011c
   and Balakrishnan's 2011 reply.
3. Unless noted otherwise, all translations of source material by the author.

4. It should be noted that the argument for the de-absolutization of absolutism is not restricted to contemporary revisionist historians but was already widely proposed in the German literature in the interwar period and thus was available to Schmitt. See, for example, Joseph Schumpeter's 1955 essay on the "Sociology of Imperialism," which, in spite of its key thesis that imperialism constitutes the objectless disposition toward unlimited forceful expansion, provides a convincing analysis of the structurally bellicose nature of absolutism, grounded in class relations. See also Hans Delbrück's 1990 classic work. Schumpeter was a colleague of Schmitt at the University of Bonn in the 1920s, and Schmitt cited his "Imperialism" essay in his *The Concept of the Political*. See also Scheuerman 1999 (198). In earlier writings, Schmitt himself qualified the decisionistic character of absolutism by noting that the king had to pay heed to the aristocracy, the bureaucracy, customary law, and natural law (1926, 98).

5. For an alternative history and theory of the rise and decline of the Westphalian system, see Teschke 1998; 2002; 2003; 2006.

6. The concept of political accumulation was originally developed by Robert Brenner (1985, 238–239), to capture the fact that under feudal social property relations the transfer of surplus from producers in possession of their means of reproduction (peasants) to non-producers in possession of the means of violence (lords) had to rely on *extra-economic* coercion, a term originally suggested by Karl Marx (1981, 926–927) to grasp the nature of reproduction in all non-capitalist communities. Political accumulation is therefore not so much an anti-economistic concept but rather indicates that the political (the state) and the economic (the market) were not separate institutional spheres in precapitalist Europe with their own distinct logics (power and market competition via prices). The rate of surplus appropriation therefore always involved social conflict over the normative and political terms and obligations of the producer–appropriator relationship. This included also tendencies to the "build-up of larger, more effective military organization and/or the construction of stronger surplus-extracting machinery" (Brenner 1977, 238) in the late Middle Ages, leading in some cases from the parcelized sovereignty of the feudal *Personenverbandsstaat* (state of associated persons) to the more centralized Old Regime states. The classical debate over whether to define feudalism as a political phenomenon revolving around a particular type of domination or as an economic phenomenon revolving around a particular mode of production is therefore misplaced.

7. For critiques of the hedged nature of so-called cabinet warfare, see Göse 2007; Externbrink 2011.

8. See Contamine 2000b for the slow and uneven growth of state control in relation to these practices.

9. Schmitt's idea of no peace beyond the line appears as yet another myth. See Fisch 1984; Stirk 2011.

10. Cf. Schmitt's cryptic statement: "The United States believed it could turn the political into an external façade of territorial borders, that it could transcend territorial borders with the essential content of the economic. But, in a decisive moment, it was unable to prevent the political grouping of friend and enemy from becoming critical" (2003, 258). This politicism sits rather uneasily with Schmitt's position on the academic advisory board of the *Gesellschaft für Europäische Wirtschaftsplanung und Großraumwirtschaft* (Society for European Economic Planning and the Greater Space Economy), founded in 1941; Opitz 1977 (930–933).

11. The analogy is explicitly drawn by Schmitt in 1940 (388) as the expected spatial revolution of World War II is directly likened to the spatial revolution of 1492.

References

Anderson, M. 1988. *War and Society in Europe of the Old Regime, 1618–1789*. Leicester: Leicester University Press.

Anderson, P. 2005. "The Intransigent Right: Michael Oakeshott, Leo Strauss, Carl Schmitt, and Friedrich Hayek." In *Spectrum: From Right to Left in the World of Ideas*, ed. P. Anderson. London: Verso, 3–28.

Balakrishnan, G. 2000. *The Enemy: An Intellectual Portrait of Carl Schmitt*. London: Verso.

Balakrishnan, G. 2011. "The Geopolitics of Separation: Response to Teschke's 'Decisions and Indecisions.'" *New Left Review* 68: 57–72.

Beik, W. 1985. *Absolutism and Society in Seventeenth-Century France: State Power and Provincial Aristocracy in Languedoc*. Cambridge: Cambridge University Press.

Beik, W. 2005. "The Absolutism of Louis XIV as Social Collaboration." *Past and Present* 188: 195–224.

Blasius, D. 2001. *Carl Schmitt: Preussischer Staatsrat in Hitler's Reich*. Göttingen: Vandenhoeck & Ruprecht.

Bonney, R. ed. 1995. *Economic Systems and State Finance*. Oxford: Clarendon Press.

Bonney, R. ed. 1999. *The Rise of the Fiscal State in Europe, c. 1200–1815*. Oxford: Oxford University Press.

Brenner, R. 1977. "The Origins of Capitalist Development: A Critique of Neo-Smithian Marxism." *New Left Review* 104: 25–92.

Brenner, R. 1985. "The Agrarian Roots of European Capitalism." In *The Brenner Debate: Agrarian Class Structure and Economic Development in Pre-Industrial Europe*, ed. T. H. Aston and C. H. E. Philpin. Cambridge: Cambridge University Press, 213–327.

Brewer, J. 1988. *The Sinews of Power: War, Money and the English State, 1688–1783*. New York: Knopf.

Buck-Morss, S. 2008. "Sovereign Right and the Global Left." *Cultural Critique* 69: 145–171.

Contamine, P. ed. 2000a. *War and Competition between States*. Oxford: Clarendon Press.

Contamine, P. 2000b. "The Growth of State Control: Practices of War, 1300–1800: Ransom and Booty." In *War and Competition between States*, ed. P. Contamine. Oxford: Clarendon Press, 163–193.

De Benoist. A. 2007. *Carl Schmitt Actuel: Terrorisme, Guerre "Juste," État d'Urgence, "Nomos de la Terre."* Paris: Éditions Krisis.

Delbrück, H. 1990. *History of the Art of War in the Context of Political History*, vol. 4: *The Dawn of Modern Warfare*. Lincoln: University of Nebraska Press.

Drolet J.-F. 2011. *American Neoconservatism: The Politics and Culture of a Reactionary Idealism*. London: Hurst.

Dyzenhaus, D. 1997. *Legality and Legitimacy: Carl Schmitt, Hans Kelsen and Herman Heller in Weimar*. Oxford: Oxford University Press.

Dyzenhaus, D. ed. 1998. *Law as Politics: Carl Schmitt's Critique of Liberalism*. Durham: Duke University Press.

Dyzenhaus, D. 2006. *The Constitution of Law: Legality in a Time of Emergency*. Cambridge: Cambridge University Press.

Ertman, T. 1997. *Birth of the Leviathan: Building States and Regimes in Medieval and Early Modern Europe*. Cambridge: Cambridge University Press.

Externbrink, S. 2011. "Die Grenzen des 'Kabinettkrieges': Der Siebenjährige Krieg 1756–1763." In *Handbuch Kriegstheorien*, ed. T. Jäger and R. Beckmann. 350–358. Wiesbaden: Verlag für Sozialwissenschaften.

Fisch, J. 1984. *Die Europäische Expansion und das Völkerrecht*. Stuttgart: Steiner.

Gerstenberger, H. 2007. *Impersonal Power: History and Theory of the Bourgeois State*. Leiden: Brill.

Glete, J. 2002. *War and the State in Early Modern Europe: Spain, the Dutch Republic and the Sweden as Fiscal-Military States, 1500–1660*. London: Routledge.

Gorski, P. 2000. "Historicizing the Secularization Debate: Church, State, and Society in Late Medieval and Early Modern Europe, c. 1300 to 1700." *American Sociological Review* 65: 138–167.

Göse, F. 2007. "Der Kabinettskrieg." In *Formen des Krieges: Von der Antike bis zur Gegenwart*, ed. D. Beyrau, D. Hochgeschwender, and D. Langewiesche. Paderborn: Schöningh, 121–147.

Gross, R. 2007. *Carl Schmitt and the Jews: The "Jewish Question," the Holocaust, and German Legal Theory*. Madison: University of Wisconsin Press.

Hardt, M., and A. Negri. 2000. *Empire*. Cambridge: Harvard University Press.

Holmes, S. 1996. *The Anatomy of Antiliberalism*. Cambridge: Harvard University Press.

Hooker, W. 2009. *Carl Schmitt's International Thought*. Cambridge: Cambridge University Press.

Kalshoven, F., and L. Zegveld. 2011. *Constraints on the Waging of War: An Introduction to International Humanitarian Law*, 4th ed. Cambridge: Cambridge University Press.

Kalyvas, A. 2008. *Democracy and the Politics of the Extraordinary: Max Weber, Carl Schmitt, and Hannah Arendt*. Cambridge: Cambridge University Press.

Kennedy, E. 2004. *Constitutional Failure: Carl Schmitt in Weimar*. Durham: Duke University Press.

Koskenniemi, M. 2001. *The Gentle Civilizer of Nations: The Rise and Fall of International Law, 1870–1960*. Cambridge: Cambridge University Press.

Kroener, B. 2000. "The Modern State and Military Society in the Eighteenth Century." In *War and Competition between States*, ed. P. Contamine. Oxford: Oxford University Press, 195–220.

Legg, S. ed. 2011. *Spatiality, Sovereignty and Carl Schmitt: Geographies of the Nomos*. London: Routledge.

Marx, K. 1981. *Capital: A Critique of Political Economy*, vol. 3. London: Penguin.

McCormick, J. 1997. *Carl Schmitt's Critique of Liberalism: Against Politics as Technology*. Cambridge: Cambridge University Press.

Meier, H. 1998. *The Lesson of Carl Schmitt: Four Chapters on the Distinction between Political Theology and Political Philosophy*. Chicago: Chicago University Press.

Mouffe, C. ed. 1999. *The Challenge of Carl Schmitt*. London: Verso.

Mouffe, C. 2005. *On the Political*. London: Routledge.

Müller, J.-W. 2003. *A Dangerous Mind: Carl Schmitt in Post-War European Thought*. New Haven: Yale University Press.

Münkler, H. 1992. *Gewalt und Ordnung: Das Bild des Krieges im Politischen Denken*. Frankfurt: Fischer.

Münkler, H. 2002. *Die Neuen Kriege*, 3rd ed. Reinbek: Rowohlt.

Neff, S. 2005. *War and the Law of Nations: A General History*. Cambridge: Cambridge University Press.

Norton, A. 2005. *Leo Strauss and the Politics of American Empire*. New Haven: Yale University Press.

Nunan, T. ed. 2011. *Schmitt: Writings on War*. Cambridge: Polity.

Odysseos, L., and F. Petito. eds. 2007. *The International Political Thought of Carl Schmitt: Terror, Liberal War and the Crisis of Global Order*. London: Routledge.

Opitz, R. ed. 1977. *Europastrategien des Deutschen Kapitals, 1900–1945*. Cologne: Pahl-Rugenstein.

Parker, D. 1996. *Class and State in Ancien Régime France: The Road to Modernity?* London: Routledge.

Pankakoski, T. 2010. "Conflict, Context, Concreteness: Koselleck and Schmitt on Concepts." *Political Theory* 38: 749–779.

Rasch, W. 2004. *Sovereignty and Its Discontents: On the Primacy of Conflict and the Structure of the Political*. London: Birkbeck Law Press.

Roberts, A., and R. Guelff. eds. 2000. *Documents on the Laws of War*, 3rd ed. Oxford: Oxford University Press.

Rüthers, B. 1990. *Carl Schmitt im Dritten Reich: Wissenschaft als Zeitgeistverstärkung?* Munich: Beck.

Scheuerman, W. 1999. *Carl Schmitt: The End of Law*. Boston: Rowman & Littlefield.

Scheuerman, W. 2004. "International Law as Historical Myth." *Constellations* 11: 537–550.

Scheuerman, W. 2006. "Carl Schmitt and the Road to Abu Ghraib." *Constellations* 13: 108–124.

Schmitt, C. 1926. "Absolutismus." In Schmitt 1995, 95–101.

Schmitt, C. 1933. "Forms of Modern Imperialism in International Law." In Legg 2011, 29–45.

Schmitt, C. 1934. "Nationalsozialismus und Völkerrecht." In Schmitt 2005, 391–423.

Schmitt, C. 1937. "The Turn to the Discriminating Concept of War." In Nunan 2011, 30–74.

Schmitt, C. 1939. "Großraum versus Universalism: The International Legal Struggle over the Monroe Doctrine." In Legg 2011, 46–54.

Schmitt, C. 1939–1941. "The *Großraum* Order of International Law with a Ban on Intervention for Spatially Foreign Powers: A Contribution to the Concept of Reich in International Law." In Nunan 2011, 75–124.

Schmitt, C. 1940. "Die Raumrevolution: Durch den totalen Krieg zu einem totalen Frieden." In Schmitt 1995, 388–394.

Schmitt, C. 1943. "Strukturwandel des internationalen Rechts." In Schmitt 2005, 652–700.

Schmitt, C. 1945. "The International Crime of Aggression and the Principle 'Nullum Crimen, Nulla Poena sine Lege.'" In Nunan 2011, 125–197.

Schmitt, C. 1985a. *Political Theology: Four Chapters on the Concept of Sovereignty*. Cambridge: MIT Press.

Schmitt, C. 1985b. *The Crisis of Parliamentary Democracy*. Cambridge: MIT Press.

Schmitt, C. 1988. *Positionen und Begriffe im Kampf mit Weimar—Genf—Versailles, 1923–1939*. 2nd ed. Berlin: Duncker & Humblot.

Schmitt, C. 1994. "Über das Verhältnis der Begriffe Krieg und Feind." In Schmitt 1988, 245–258.

Schmitt, C. 1995. *Staat, Großraum, Nomos: Arbeiten aus den Jahren 1916–1969*, ed. G. Maschke. Berlin: Duncker & Humblot.

Schmitt, C. 1996. *The Concept of the Political*, trans. G. Schwab. Chicago: University of Chicago Press.

Schmitt, C. 1997. *Land and Sea*, trans. S. Draghici. Washington: Plutarch Press.

Schmitt, C. 1999. "Total Enemy, Total War, and Total State." In *Carl Schmitt: Four Articles, 1931–1938*, ed. S. Draghici. Corvallis: Plutarch, 28–36.

Schmitt, C. 2003. *The "Nomos" of the Earth in the International Law of the "Jus Publicum Europaeum."* New York: Telos Press.

Schmitt, C. 2004. *On the Three Types of Juristic Thought*, trans. J. W. Bendersky. New York: Praeger.

Schmitt, C. 2005. *Frieden oder Pazifismus: Arbeiten zum Völkerrecht und zur Internationalen Politik, 1924–1978*, ed G. Maschke. Berlin: Duncker & Humblot.

Schmitt, C. 2007. *Theory of the Partisan: Intermediate Commentary on the Concept of the Political*, trans. G. L. Ulmen. New York: Telos Press.

Schmitt, C. 2010. *Dictatorship*. Cambridge: Polity.

Schumpeter, J. 1955. "The Sociology of Imperialism." In *Social Classes, Imperialism: Two Essays*. Cleveland: Meridian, 3–99.

Skocpol, T. 1979. *States and Social Revolutions: A Comparative Analysis of France, Russia and China*. Cambridge: Cambridge University Press.

Slomp, G. 2009. *Carl Schmitt and the Politics of Hostility, Violence and Terror*. Basingstoke: Palgrave.

Smith, N. 2004. *American Empire: Roosevelt's Geographer and the Prelude to Globalization*. Berkeley: University of California Press.

Stirk, P. 2005. *Carl Schmitt, Crown Jurist of the Third Reich: On Pre-Emptive War, Military Occupation, and World Empire*. Lampeter: Edwin Mellen.

Stirk, P. 2011. "No Peace Beyond the Line." In Legg 2011, 276–283.

Storrs, C. 2009. *The Fiscal-Military State in Eighteenth-Century Europe: Essays in Honour of P. G. M. Dickson*. London: Ashgate.

Teschke, B. 1998. "Geopolitical Relations in the European Middle Ages: History and Theory." *International Organization* 52: 325–358.

Teschke, B. 2002. "Theorising the Westphalian System of States: International Relations from Absolutism to Capitalism." *European Journal of International Relations* 8: 5–48.

Teschke, B. 2003. *The Myth of 1648: Class, Geopolitics and the Making of Modern International Relations*. London: Verso.

Teschke, B. 2006. "Debating the 'Myth of 1648': State-Formation, the Interstate System, and the Rise of Capitalism—A Rejoinder." *International Politics* 43: 531–573.

Teschke, B. 2011a. "Fatal Attraction: A Critique of Carl Schmitt's International Political and Legal Theory." *International Theory* 3: 179–227.

Teschke, B. 2011b. "Decisions and Indecisions: Political and Intellectual Receptions of Carl Schmitt." *New Left Review* 67: 61–95.

Teschke, B. 2011c. "The Fetish of Geopolitics: Reply to Gopal Balakrishnan." *New Left Review* 69: 81–100.

van Laak, D. 2002. *Gespräche in der Sicherheit des Schweigens: Carl Schmitt in der politischen Geistesgeschichte der frühen Bundesrepublik*, 2nd ed. Berlin: Akademie Verlag.

CHAPTER 14

CARL SCHMITT'S CONCEPT OF HISTORY

MATTHIAS LIEVENS

INTRODUCTION

How TO make sense of Carl Schmitt?[1] Can we isolate those parts of his work that are of remaining relevance for contemporary political-theoretical endeavors from the controversial political positions he adopted during his life, such as his advocacy of plebiscitary presidency under the Weimar Republic or his alliance with the Nazis? And if so, how to identify the key that can enable us to make such a distinction?

My contention is that to understand what is fundamentally at stake in Schmitt's work, one should try to come to grips with his philosophical strategy and his understanding of what political philosophy fundamentally is. The crux of the matter is that this strategy is situated on a metalevel: in his most philosophically relevant texts, Schmitt is not so much concerned with taking sides in ongoing conflicts or with opening and intensifying certain lines of battle against a concrete political opponent. He rather engages in a strange kind of struggle around the very conditions of possibility for conflict and struggle to become visible and recognizable. His is a struggle, in other words, to make struggle visible and give it a place. For Schmitt, this can be only a philosophical struggle, as the conditions of possibility of conflict are inevitably spiritual in nature. Schmitt famously defines the political as the "degree of intensity of a union or separation, of an association or dissociation" (1996a, 26). This intensity is produced symbolically, through the way the enemy is morally or spiritually "put into question" (1995e, 533).[2] *The political* therefore entails a certain spirit, structuring the relations and institutions between inimical (groups of) human beings and governing their self-understanding. The fight that is central in Schmitt's philosophy is the fight for that spirit.

From that perspective, it does not make so much sense to approach Schmitt's philosophy as a "polemic in favor of *pólemos*, of war to the death against a real, blood-spilling enemy" (Pourciau 2006). Schmitt rather engages in what could be called a metapolitical struggle against depoliticizing types of spirit or ways of thinking and for the particular spiritual form that makes conflicts political in the first place. Important in this regard is that Schmitt does not take an Archimedean standpoint, from where he judges particular conflicts or conflicting parties and establishes the conditions of possibility of political conflict. Instead, he starts in the middle: he intervenes on the level of the existing spirit to come to grips with the way the latter obfuscates or enables conflict. What makes Schmitt's theoretical production interesting is not the concrete struggles he wages against particular enemies. It is rather his defense of the political and his critique of depoliticization as such, which provide the conditions of possibility for enmity to appear in the first place.

Crucially, this defense of the political takes place through polemic interventions within the existing "spiritual" conjuncture. Although to a certain extent they were always also interventions in concrete political battles, Schmitt's main books of the twenties, but also some of his later works, are philosophically located on a metalevel: they are philosophical struggles against certain ways of thinking or "types of spirit," as Schmitt (1996b, 11) calls them, which threaten to undermine the political. In *Political Theology* or in *Roman Catholicism and Political Form*, for example, Schmitt criticizes economic and technical ways of thinking, because they are incapable of thinking political decision or conflict. Similarly, in *The Concept of the Political*, he attacks liberalism for not being able to give a place to genuinely political conflict. In this latter book, but also in other works, he mainly polemicizes against ways of thinking that tend to intensify the friend/enemy relation so strongly that the latter moves beyond the political (*"über das Politische hinausgehend"*).[3] Schmitt situates his concept of the political on a scale of increasing intensity between a prepolitical level, on which the social relation is not yet interpreted as a friend/enemy opposition, and what could be called a hyperpolitical level, where the antagonism is intensified to such a degree that the conflict is no longer political but enmity is being moralized or theologized (Schmitt 1991a, 190; 1996a, 36; 2002, 89; 2004, 67, 66; Taubes 2003, 25). Schmitt's philosophical strategy thus consists of the attempt to find a way of thought or "spirit" that is genuinely political, through a polemic with depoliticizing and hyperpoliticizing ways of thinking, seeking a middle ground between these extremes. This strategy remains a conflictual and polemic one, but it is situated on a metalevel.

Through this metapolitical struggle, a formal way of thinking the political comes to the fore. Many readers of Schmitt have stressed the formal and even nihilistic character of Schmitt's concept of the political (Koselleck 1990, 226–227; Löwith 1995, 150; McCormick 1999, 112; Llanque and Münkler 2003, 14). Yet it is important to underline that for Schmitt the political is worthy of a fight: its loss as a result of de- or hyperpoliticization can be dangerous. The argument driving this chapter is that it is exactly because of its formal character that Schmitt's philosophical approach to the political can be supported without having to endorse the problematic political positions Schmitt adopted during his life. Evidently, Schmitt engages in "spiritual" conflict to make real conflict visible and recognizable, but there is no necessary relation between Schmitt's metapolitical strategy and the concrete political stances he adopted (such as German nationalism or plebiscitarian democracy). On the contrary, his argument in favor of the political is situated on the metapolitical or metaphilosophical level of the struggle concerning the spiritual or symbolic figuration of political relations, and this metapolitical dimension can be studied and endorsed even though one does not agree with Schmitt's concrete political stances.

In previous publications I have developed the argument that Schmitt actually makes two clearly distinguishable theoretical moves: first, he wages a metapolitical fight for the political; and second, he tries to place or territorialize the political plurality in a specific way (Lievens 2013). This placing yields a particular distribution of politicizations and depoliticizations that inevitably leads to the misrecognition of specific political subjects (particular enemies). Concretely, Schmitt's aim was to territorialize the political in such a way as to give the monopoly of the political decision to the state again. The counterpart of this is that society could then remain depoliticized. I contend that Schmitt's most problematic ideas concerning the strong state, sovereignty, or the central role of executive power should be understood on the basis of this tension between the political and its territorialization and therefore do not directly follow from his advocacy of the political as a kind of spirit as such.

This chapter focuses on Schmitt's political-philosophical struggle for the political on the particular terrain of the meaning of history. For him, the signification or symbolization of history is a crucial device through which the relation between enemies is given meaning, and thus it is of central importance in his metapolitical approach. This is a terrain that he cannot leave untouched: even though he strongly rejects the predominant philosophies of histories (especially to the extent that they rely on the notion of progress), he understood that historical meaning is a key object in his struggle for the political and that he thus also had to provide an answer to the question of how to signify and symbolize history. As is the case with other politically relevant concepts, the notion of history and the meaning that it receives in a certain context have an inevitably polemical character (Schmitt 1996a, 30–31). Moreover, for Schmitt, the political has an intrinsic relation to time and history, because of its connection with processes of social change.[4] It is thus inevitable to engage in the process of struggle around the meaning of history, a battlefield dominated by Marxists during Schmitt's lifetime (1950a; 1931, 261).

The analysis is organized into four parts. First, Schmitt's struggle for a political conception of history will be reconstructed, showing in particular how he attempted to develop an image of history that gives a place to the defeated. Against ideologies of progress or the idea that history repeats itself or that there are lessons to be learned from history, Schmitt especially wanted to think historical singularity, which he considered as crucial for a political conception of history, as will be shown in the second section. His ideas on history are scattered throughout his oeuvre, from his Weimar texts until his later, post–World War II writings. Yet his engagement to develop a sober and profane image of history that accentuates singularity, relative contingency and openness, and the plurality of social temporalities is certainly a red thread throughout his oeuvre that will be reconstructed in the third section. He systematically counterposes this image to attempts to think history as a process that can be studied in a strictly scientific way in terms of causal relations. The final section discusses the enigmatic concept of the *katechon*, which is the linchpin of his political conception of history. As will be shown, this concept is a crucial discursive device through which Schmitt tries to develop an extremely minimalistic yet symbolically very powerful approach to historical meaning.

SCHMITT AND BENJAMIN AGAINST IDEOLOGIES OF PROGRESS

Although both authors have widely divergent views on a large number of matters, a fascinating convergence exists between how Walter Benjamin and Carl Schmitt conceive of history. Both radically dismiss ideologies of progress and aim at rescuing the defeated of history. They both try to develop a political image of history to overcome prevailing historical narratives that often conceal history's political dimension. For them, historical meaning and even historiography are battlefields, and in their struggle for a political conception of history they in particular attempt to rescue the position of the defeated.

In his *Passagenwerk* (*Arcades Project*), Benjamin famously stated that "from now on, the political crowns history" (1989, 405). Yet he observed how the political character of history tended to become invisible under the influence of the dominant ideologies of progress, which were especially advocated by Stalinism and social democracy (1968, 258). Ideologies of progress rely on an empty and homogenous concept of time, Benjamin argued, and this leads to passivity or fatalism. They threaten to disempower political actors when confronted with fascism and war, which advocates of these ideologies tended to understand merely as a detour on the progressive course of history. In contrast to this, he advocated a full and broken conception of time and a vision of history as made up of discontinuities, moments of crisis, and bifurcations: a vision that makes it possible to understand the need and the scope for conscious political decision (Bensaïd 1990).

Benjamin understood that genuine political action presupposes a conception of time that fundamentally breaks with the notion of progress. As an alternative, he advocated a dialectical image of history, which makes us acutely aware of the need to politically decide here and now and of the fact that such decision can have a redemptive effect with regard to the downtrodden of the past. It is by engaging in the full and broken time of the present that we rescue the latter from oblivion and reactualize their past struggles. The idea of progress is a centerpiece of the victors' ideology, according to Benjamin. It suggests the course of history could not have been different from what it actually is. The result is a historical narrative that focuses on the powerful and makes the defeated invisible as, with hindsight, their defeat appears as inevitable. History thus appears as a judge and rationalizes victory and defeat. A redemptive approach to history and historiography, in contrast, ought to rescue the defeated from forgetfulness by conceiving of history as essentially political and contingent: in this way, a space is created for thinking the plurality of political forces involved in the historical process, which could have taken a radically different course depending on the contingent outcome of their struggles.

Historiography thus becomes a profoundly political (and we might add metapolitical) undertaking. This is also true for Schmitt, who in *The Concept of the Political* states that "all spirit is present spirit" (1996a, 62). Even history is always written from a present perspective, from which it also derives its intensity (1991b, 79). In that sense, historical knowledge is inevitably knowledge of the present. In this present, it is always the winners who write history, he argues, and they also determine its vocabulary and terminology (1991c, 52; 2002, 25).

In contrast to Benjamin, who is especially concerned about rescuing the defeated of the past by rewriting history in terms of what had been forgotten, Schmitt is more interested in the political effects of historical discourses in the present. He criticizes ideologies of progress especially because they threaten to subvert the specifically political nature of the symbolic relation between friends and enemies. More in particular, ideologies of progress tend to strip the enemy or the defeated of their political subjectivity by depicting them in nonpolitical terms and by making the plurality of political forces behind the historical process invisible.

In his book *Ex Captivitate Salus* written shortly after World War II, Schmitt (2002, 60) tells about his own experience as a defeated in front of the victors' judge and argues that he is in a good position to understand the rightlessness that this position entails: "The suffering, which humans inflict on each other, is terrifying. We cannot simply turn away from it. But how will we endure its appearance? Especially, how will a man, for whom the knowledge of the law has become a part of his existence, bear the mere fact, yes the mere possibility of being totally outlawed, whoever undergoes it in a singular case?" These statements are evidently very ambiguous if one remembers Schmitt's membership of the Nazi Party in the thirties. Yet they do shed an interesting light on how Schmitt viewed the enemy and the defeated. In this text, he develops a rather austere vision of history: many people lose, some of them turn into martyrs, and suffering and need become the driving force for subsequent generations to realize new things. "World history is not the basis of happiness," Schmitt soberly concludes (60). In contrast to Benjamin, Schmitt does not see possibilities to redeem those who were defeated in the past, even though some of them can be remembered as martyrs. What is interesting, however, is that Schmitt in this text presents the defeated enemy as an object of ethical consideration. Schmitt even empathizes with the defeated and naked human being who is confronted with the victor: "nudest is the human being, who is put undressed before a dressed human being, unarmed before an armed, powerless before a powerful one" (79).

This concern for the defeated was already present in his work written during the interwar period. He considered himself one of the defeated of World War I and of the Treaty of Versailles, and that undoubtedly turned the political dignity of the defeated enemy into one of his central concerns. According to Schmitt, the war was not concluded with a genuine peace treaty but rather with "a damning judgment of the victors on the defeated, who were marked even more as enemies afterwards, the more they were defeated" (1938, 279). In his later work, too, this concern remained present. After

World War II, he wrote several texts on the tendency toward universalism, cosmopolitanism, and world unity, which he saw as central characteristics of twentieth-century global politics. According to him, this tendency resulted in an increasingly unbearable *vae victis* (woe the defeated; 1988a, 33).

Schmitt's goal was not to develop a redemptive type of historiography as Benjamin did but to open a space to think the present in a political way. He was mainly interested in how visions of history impact upon the symbolic constitution of the relation between friend and enemy. Like all political discourses, philosophies of history such as that based on the notion of progress produce subjects: "the planning and leading elites produce themselves and the masses they lead with the help of historical-philosophical meanings" (1950b, 927–931). This discursive production of subjects has an important political effect, according to Schmitt. When history is thought of in terms of progress and of the inexorable trend toward world unity, this will have an impact on how struggling subjects and their mutual relations will be symbolically represented. Indeed, the struggle for world unity as it is waged by certain cosmopolitans is based on a specific historical and philosophical self-understanding (1995d, 500). "More than any other magnitude, self-interpretation is an element of the current world situation," Schmitt argues (501). A self-understanding in terms of progress threatens to undermine the specifically political nature of the relation between struggling subjects, as it tends to locate the enemy in a past that is irrevocably lost: "All mass propaganda seeks its evidence in the proof that it lies at the side of things to come. All mass belief is merely the belief to be situated rightly, while the opponent is situated falsely, as time and history and development work against him" (1950a, 12). The fight between the old and the new on the line of progress can impossibly be a struggle between two equal political subjects who mutually recognize each other as such. Especially when progress is depicted in terms of a growing technical mastery of the world, the enemy threatens to become a mere technical source of disturbance that should simply be identified and done away with. In an era where technical thinking predominates, Schmitt explains, those who hold power tend to depict the defeated as mere disturbers (2002, 84). They project a world according to their own ideals, the ideals of the victor, in which the defeated no longer have a place. One of Schmitt's main polemical targets in this regard was communism, and especially its intention to realize "the unity of the planet and . . . its submission to one sole master" (1990, 242).

As suggested already, there is no politics without social change over time. Yet when change is symbolized in terms of progress this leads to de- or hyperpoliticization. In his article "The Legal World Revolution," Schmitt posits that the concept of progress functions as a legitimizing device that tends to make invisible what is politically at stake: "*progress* in the sense of accelerated scientific, technical and industrial development . . . can become an all-out global legitimation of opposing political means and ends" (1987, 76). Although he refers to the detrimental environmental and health effects of current society, Schmitt's main goal is not to develop a critique of modern industrialism or capitalism. He especially aims to underline how the notion of progress threatens to make a genuinely political symbolic order impossible. Within the range of different possible notions of progress, he especially targets the concept of political progress, which, according to him, is part of the program of parties that pursue world unity after the 1917 October revolution. He forecasts that this process will be tantamount to a "planetary appropriation of industry," whose methods of conquest will be "more intensely aggressive and of greater destructive potential in terms of the means of power utilized" (80). Realizing world unity will not imply any ethical or moral progress, Schmitt argues: "The day *world politics* comes to the earth, it will be transformed into a *world police power*. That is a dubious progress!" (80). Inevitably, this project ends up with forms of hyperpoliticization: the enemy is turned into a criminal rather than a political opponent, or he even becomes an enemy of humanity, the most radical kind of enemy imaginable (De Wit 2001, 117; Lievens 2010).

Schmitt's concern with the effect of philosophies of history on the political is a constant throughout his oeuvre. From his early criticisms of Georg Lukács' (1992) philosophy of history in his book on the crisis of parliamentarism through his articles on the Treaty of Versailles until his later work on the notion of world unity, he develops a strong awareness of the potentially disastrous effects of images of history that do not recognize the position of the enemy or the defeated.

HISTORICAL SINGULARITY VERSUS REPETITION

Schmitt does not merely criticize nonpolitical philosophies of history but also seeks an alternative vision of history that can symbolize the present in a political way. One option he investigates is the new paganism of the Nietzschean theory of eternal return. He readily dismisses this approach, however, because it tends to misrecognize history and historical change as such (Schmitt 1990, 246). He argues that it draws human beings back into the orbit of nature, whereas political existence is exactly about transcending the latter. There is no politics in nature: a political relation arises only when one puts the other spiritually into question (1995e, 533).

According to Schmitt, the notion that history repeats itself is fundamentally problematic, even when one does not follow a Nietzschean conception of eternal return. He addresses this topic when discussing which pathways for future development can be chosen within the current epoch of space revolution. There is a tendency, he argues, to repeat the answers that were given to earlier transformations of the global spatial order. The Treaty of Versailles, for example, produced an outcome between war and peace, as it relied on a reductive conception of peace, merely consisting of the end of physical fighting. The real historical task, according to Schmitt, was to establish a new spatial order to replace the previous one, which had fallen apart, as World War I had clearly shown. The early modern Eurocentric order of sovereign states (the *jus publicum Europaeum*) had become obsolete by the end of the nineteenth century, and a new spatial ordering principle was needed. Realizing peace in such a situation entailed more than the end of fighting (1995b, 389). Real peace was not possible, Schmitt argues, without the establishment of a new spatial configuration of the world.

World War I was a watershed event for Schmitt. It could be ended only with a type of peace that would similarly entail a historical event, distinguishing a before and after. "In the great history of humankind, each true peace is only true once," he argues. "Peace which really brings an end to a war around spatial order can only be a peace based on a new spatial order" (1995b, 389). The war could not be ended by repeating the previous answers to the wars that had occurred within the demised global spatial order. In other words, peace has a historically specific meaning within different historical-spatial configurations. It was clear for Schmitt that the protagonists of the Treaty of Versailles were completely unaware of the singularity of the historical moment they were faced with.

The concept of historical singularity is an important one for Schmitt, and it pops up in a number of his post–World War II writings. It represents a crucial dimension of his political understanding of history. If there would be repetition in history, political action would merely consist of the mechanic application of preexisting answers. For Schmitt, in contrast, politics requires the capacity to think the singularity of historical situations and events and to act in circumstances that have never been seen before. In that sense, it is impossible to develop a general theory of history that provides transhistorically valid lessons on how to act in certain situations. Time and again, Schmitt stresses that thinking history is about thinking unique situations and unique truths (1995e, 531): "[T]he big events are unique, irrevocable and unrepeatable. A historical truth is true only once" (1994b, 55).

As a result, counterfactual reasoning is meaningless, according to Schmitt. The attempt to imagine what would have happened if Germany had won World War I or if the Industrial Revolution had come about in France instead of England is a mere act of fantasy. It especially threatens to disregard what genuinely historical thinking is about, namely, to grasp the singular event. Historians who advocate counterfactual reasoning commit "absurdities, because they forget the uniqueness and unrepeatability of historical events" (1995e, 531).

Similarly, the temptation always exists to think historical events with the help of historical parallels, but for Schmitt one should use the latter only to lay bare the unicity of a singular historical event. There is always a risk, he argues, that such parallels are turned into the basis of "a more general lawfulness, a functional sequence, which does not exist in history" (1995e, 531). Schmitt recognizes that man also has "an almost irresistible need to eternalize his last great historical experience." But he adds, "Precisely my sense of history guards me from such repetitions. My sense of history especially maintains itself by recalling to memory the unrepeatable uniqueness of all great historical events. A historical truth is true only *once*. But also the historical call, the challenge which opens a new epoch, is true only once and is correct only once" (1994b, 61). Schmitt's focus on historical singularity does not dissolve history, as is often the case with postmodern discourses on the now, which lacks historical roots (Bensaïd 2001). For him, it remains possible to theorize history, for example, by theoretically grasping the rise and fall of global spatial orders or *nomoi*. Fredric Jameson (2005, 202) shows there is a significant parallel between Schmitt's concept of the *nomos* and the Marxist notion of mode of production in this regard.[5] This last notion is a transhistorical concept that acquires its specific meaning only within an analysis of a concrete social formation. It therefore is at the basis of a very open theorization of history (Sayer 1987, 31). This problematic strikingly resembles Schmitt's postwar work on the theory of how spatial orders or *nomoi* arise and demise, each spatial order involving its own, historically specific mode of operation. Like social and political revolutions in Marxism, the space revolutions in between the *nomoi* are singular historical moments or events.

It is important to underline, however, that Schmitt's focus on singularity and difference in history is not primarily grounded in epistemological considerations. What he is really interested in is how historical meaning operates politically and to what extent it opens a space for real political thought and action. His insistence on the singularity of historical events results in a very particular understanding of what political action is about, namely, to give a "unique concrete answer to the call of a similarly unique concrete situation" (1995e, 532). According to Schmitt, this call/answer structure of historical events is dialectic and should be opposed to the kind of polarity present in theories of history that start from the eternal return of the same. "Every historical action and act of a human being is the answer to a question which is raised by history.... Every human word [*Wort*] is an answer [*Antwort*]" (532). The meaning of the answer is drawn from the question that precedes it, and the meaning of this question resides in the specific situation from which it arises.

Schmitt's representation of history thus radically discards the idea that history would contain lessons for future generations. Drawing on Schmitt's work, Reinhart Koselleck (1990, 41) calls this latter conception of history *historia magistra vitae* and shows how it is fundamentally based on repetition. This vision of history has become especially outdated with the rise of modernity, Koselleck states. He refers to de Tocqueville (1986, 657) in this regard, who argues that it is impossible to compare the advent of democracy with previous historical occurrences: "I go back from century to century until the earliest antiquity; I do not see anything which resembles what I face today. When the past no longer enlightens the future, the spirit marches in darkness."

In his understanding of the call of history, Schmitt (1995e) is clearly inspired by but at the same time departs from the work of R. G. Collingwood (1993), which he criticizes for being too individualistic and psychological, and from that of Arnold Toynbee (1987), whose challenge/response structure in history threatens to downplay historical singularity. Schmitt suggests that Hegel's dialectical vision had the potential to let this singularity reappear but that, as a result of the speculative and systematic nature of Hegel's philosophy of history, this chance was lost: historical singularity was again absorbed within a greater historical sequence. In that sense, Schmitt is certainly not a Hegelian dialectician, for whom the crisis is only a moment in the unfolding of contradictions toward higher syntheses. For Schmitt, not all contradictions can be rationally mediated, as Carlo Galli (1996) shows. It is no coincidence that the notions of sovereignty and constituent power, which denote ruptures and discontinuities in time, were so central to his thinking, while Hegel, for example, refused the concept of constituent power (Bensaïd 2008, 73).

Of course, stressing historical singularity against the notion that history repeats itself does not suffice to establish a genuinely political vision of history. Thinking the uniqueness of historical events could perfectly go together with a vision of history that is based on progress (Koselleck 1990, 47). According to Schmitt, the idea of progress has pervaded contemporary society and has even become a mass ideology. He calls it a *religion of technicity* based on the belief in progress and infinite technical perfectibility (Schmitt 1995d, 503). It undergirds the depoliticizing slogan for world unity. Although he appears to be quite pessimistic about the predominance of this ideology, he still tries to develop an alternative vision that gives a more truthful account of historical singularity, thinking it as an event: "History is not the unfolding of natural-scientific, biological or other rules and norms. Its essential and specific content is the event, which arrives once and does not repeat itself. Here, experiences do not count, neither do functionalisms, nor hypothetical proportions combined in order to see what would have happened when this or that fact would not have happened" (1990, 258). Schmitt's aim is to think of history without taking any recourse to historical automatisms or general laws. He thus strongly opposes positivistic depictions of history in terms of lawful generalizations, as in the work of Auguste Comte. Very often, the formulation of general laws of history entails the illegitimate generalization of a very concrete historical experience. According to Schmitt, Marx, for example, had tended to generalize his historically determined experience and understanding of industrialization into an overall theory of historical necessity (1995e, 536).

What both such visions and ideologies of progress do is to subordinate historical singularity to generalities. Although ideologies of progress sometimes do recognize the uniqueness of a historical moment, they nevertheless threaten to destroy its singularity by locating it on a rationalistically understood ascending line of progress (Schmitt 1990, 258). Yet real history always prevails over such speculative philosophies, Schmitt (1995d, 505) argues (see also Kervégan 1999, 71). Even though he particularly targets Enlightenment philosophies of history in this regard, he argues that this criticism is equally applicable to the Christian vision of history (1995d, 504–505; see also 1990, 249).

As already stated, Schmitt's stress on historical singularity and on its eventful character is not merely meant to provide a more "adequate" picture of history, but it is especially intended as a polemical weapon against ways of thinking that undermine the political character of the spirit. His aim was to resymbolize the present in such a way as to enable it to become political, creating the symbolic conditions for struggles between more or less equal political subjects who recognize each other as such and do not dehumanize or discredit each other. That is the problem of visions of history based on repetition: they tend to depict one of the antagonists as rightful from the outset. With his insistence on historical singularity, Schmitt tries to develop a symbolic device in order to undermine the victors' vision of history. Indeed, the idea that history repeats itself is often the spontaneous philosophy of history of the victors, who "will not easily understand that also their victory is only true once" (1994b, 61; see also 1995e, 544). In contrast, thinking historical singularity undermines the victor's claim to eternal domination and opens a space for the enemy or the defeated. Confronted with the alternative between "eternal recurrence on the one side, uniqueness and unrepeatability of historical events and epochs on the other side," Schmitt clearly advocates the second (1995e, 544–545; see also Vad 1996, 104). He also strongly criticizes utopian thinking, because it tends to subordinate the present to a pregiven image of the future and thereby obfuscates current conflicts and enmities (1996a, 31).

What is fundamentally at stake for Schmitt is that the stress on historical singularity makes it possible to radically historicize political defeat: today's victors can become tomorrow's defeated. In the end, history does not judge but remains open. Furthermore, thinking historical singularity is also crucial for recognizing historical contingency, as human beings each time have to provide new answers to the call of history. This contingency is not absolute: according to Schmitt, in the current era of space revolution, only a limited number of alternatives exist between which one has to choose. At the same time, however, no image of history can dissolve this very need to make a decision or a choice. Schmitt thus attempts to find a middle ground between the dominant philosophies of history and the loss of the sense of history. For him, history is composed of events, but the event is not "pure": it always appears within particular historical circumstances, even though it cannot be reduced to these.

A Plural and Contingent View of History

In different parts of Schmitt's wide-ranging oeuvre, one can find attempts to develop a political conception of history. Some of them are mere fragments, and others, especially in his later work, are more elaborated. Throughout his work, however, a constant attempt can be found to develop a vision of history that is not a transparent and predestined totality based on its own immanent laws of development. Instead, history appears as a contingent process, characterized by a full concept of time that is broken up by multiple temporalities, related to different social spheres that have their own rhythms, discontinuities, and accelerations. Even the sphere of (political) ideas has its own rhythm, in which "there are epochs of great energy and times becalmed, times of motionless status quo" (Schmitt 1992, 8). Political action is about dealing with these multiple temporalities and the moments of crisis that their discordance produces, about judging and deciding within always specific circumstances.

For Schmitt, historical time is not transparent but is characterized by desynchronization and non-contemporaneity, features that appear very clearly in the unavoidable anachronism of the spirit. All spirit is present spirit, Schmitt states, while he equally stresses that spirit is also struggle, differentiation, and nonidentity. In his seminal text on "The Age of Neutralizations and Depoliticizations," Schmitt argues that during the past centuries the central domain of spiritual life shifted several times. The central role of the theological in the sixteenth century gave way to the metaphysical in the seventeenth century, the humanitarian-moral spirit in the eighteenth, and via a short phase of the romantic-aesthetic to the economic and technical spirit from the nineteenth century onward. The motor force of this succession of phases was the search for a neutral sphere, "in which the struggle was brought to a close, and people settle their disputes, reach agreement and convince each other" (1991b, 88). Schmitt explicitly warns that this depiction of modern history should not be understood as a philosophy of history but that it is merely an a posteriori attempt to grasp the history of concrete conflicts and their outcomes. In this sense, the sequence of "stages" should not be understood in terms of linear progress or regress, but rather as a relatively contingent struggle between elites (81).

Interestingly, Schmitt's own position within this historical sequence is peculiar: he clearly brushes history against the grain with his defense of the concept of sovereignty in an epoch characterized by the predominance of depoliticized, technical thinking. His defense of the political thus appears as very anachronistic with regard to the contemporary spirit. This triggers interesting questions. How can Schmitt, in an epoch whose metaphysics, "the most intensive and the clearest expression of an epoch," is impregnated by a mechanical and technical way of thinking and in which the machine is thought to "run by itself" (1988b, 48), take a distance from it and defend the political?[6] In the same vein, how was it possible for Donoso Cortés, the nineteenth-century Spanish thinker admired by Schmitt, to uphold "the theological mode of thought of the Middle Ages, whose construction was juristic" (52)? Schmitt's polemic against the spirit of technicity pluralizes and impurifies historical time. In general, he was very conscious of the temporal plurality of modernity: "Actually, it would also be a misunderstanding to explain the succession of stages in such a way as if in each century there would have been nothing else than the central sphere. There exists rather a pluralist co-ordination of different stages which are already traversed; people of the same time and the same country, yes even of the same family live next to each other in different stages, and contemporary Berlin for instance is closer in cultural respect to New York and Moscow as to Munich or Trier" (1991b, 81–82). Different social spheres, but also different social subjects, are thus characterized by different historical temporalities. Not all people have to go through the same succession of stages that the European elite has passed through. In actual facts, the masses made a leap from one type of magic spirit to another: from traditional religion to the new mass religion of technological progress.

This plural nature of history and of time is a theme that recurs in several of Schmitt's texts: from his interwar work that emphasizes the different temporalities of law, the military and the economic to his later distinction between different types of progress in his article on the "Legal World Revolution" (1978).

Schmitt thus breaks history open as a process characterized by various possibilities. As already argued, this contingency is not absolute, and not everything is equally possible. Despite its openness, history is characterized by a certain structure, which has as its effect that not all ideologies can be equally effective within a specific epoch. It is certainly possible for a certain spirit to be really obsolete, according to Schmitt. In his book *The Crisis of Parliamentary Democracy*, he (in)famously argued for example that the metaphysical underpinnings of parliamentarianism have lost their validity and effectiveness with the rise of the proletariat and mass society. Of course, parliamentary institutions can continue in existence despite the fact that their "spiritual" foundations are no longer effective. This is similar to how monarchy had become a merely external apparatus when the "sense of the principle of kingship, of honor, has been lost, if bourgeois kings appear who seek to prove their usefulness and utility instead of their devotion and honor" (Schmitt 1992, 8). It is certainly possible to search for new, pragmatic justifications for monarchy, but the latter is thereby inevitably enfeebled: other institutions might be much better adapted to realize the same pragmatic goals: "The same holds true of the 'social-technical' justifications for parliament. If parliament should change from an institution of evident truth into a simply practical-technical means, then it only has to be shown via *facta*, through some kind of experience, not even necessarily through an open, self-declared dictatorship, that things could be otherwise and parliament is then finished" (8). History thus has a certain structure or materiality; therefore, historical judgment remains possible. Yet it cannot be expressed in the language of the existing philosophies of history, as these tend to undermine the political understanding of history. In the previous example, it is important to stress that Schmitt's judgment is grounded in a factual analysis of the forces that are politically relevant in the concerned epoch (e.g., the proletariat) and of how they can become integrated within a political unity that is yet to be formed. It is not history that judges but rather concrete political subjects who need to decide when confronted with the call of history and the limited range of possibilities that are inscribed in the historical present.

Time and again, Schmitt stresses how in the twentieth century the need for effective decision increasingly posited itself as a result of events that constitute discontinuities and ruptures and that fundamentally challenge the existing political order: "war and post war, mobilization and demobilization, revolution and dictatorship, inflation and deflation" (1943/1944, 404). These events put a lot of pressure on the legal system and its capacity to stabilize social relations (Maus 1976, 24; Schmitt 1936, 244). War and economic developments tend to accelerate history, while law has difficulties to follow pace: the results are dangerous and are ultimately vain attempts to "motorize" law, Schmitt (1943/1944, 407) argues.

In such a context of rapidly succeeding new events, the defense of the status quo has become impossible (Schmitt 1991b, 80). Whether one likes it or not, the time of events, ruptures, and discontinuities imposes political action. This is the "full time" Benjamin (1968) speaks about in his theses on the concept of history and that looks like a politicization of the romantic concept of time the young Schmitt aptly describes as follows: "In every moment, time determines the human being and confines the most powerful human will. As a result, every moment becomes an overwhelming, irrational, ghost-like event. It is the ever-present and incessant negation of the countless possibilities that it destroys" (1986, 69). Schmitt is sharply aware of the nature of modern time, and especially its ephemeral, fluid, contingent, rapidly changing character (1932, 293). The decisionism he advocates constitutes a political-juridical answer to this full and pluralized temporality of modernity, which he thinks in terms of a discontinuous process of ruptures and accelerations of events. Fundamentally, a genuinely political decision is an intervention in this multiplicity of temporalities, which ruptures the continuum of empty time.[7]

Because of his decisionism and the concepts of time and history it is based on, Schmitt is an exceptional figure compared to other right-wing thinkers such as Joseph de Maistre or Louis de Bonald. His profoundly modern understanding of time makes it impossible for him to believe in traditions and the slow flow of history, as Louis de Bonald did, for example. Therefore, Schmitt's thought is very different from conservatism. In his book *Konservativismus*, Panajotis Kondylis, who is strongly influenced by Schmitt, draws the opposition between conservatism and the notion of sovereignty very sharply: the sovereign, Kondylis (1986, 76) states, has to be understood as the demiurge of history (*Geschichtsdemiurg*). In this sense, sovereignty and historicity are closely related.[8] Sovereign decisions show that "history is not a circle which is accomplished and brought to a close from the very beginning in the womb of the eternal order of being, but that it is an open and dynamic movement" (76). According to Kondylis, conservatism is to be understood as a vision that defends *societas civilis*, whereby law is strongly anchored within a natural and divine order of being. The advent of the notion of sovereignty inevitably disrupts this order and opens the door for an entirely different conception of time.

Unsurprisingly, Schmitt (1970, 8) admits that conservatism is no longer a credible option in modern society. Already in his early work of the 1920s, he rather located concepts that were central to his thought, such as dictatorship, in the sphere of "revolutionary democratism" (1927, 96). Similarly, he develops his understanding of decisionism as a genuinely historical way of thinking law, which makes it possible to relate law and legal decision to a singular point in time, in contrast to the incapacity to do so for normativism and concrete-order thinking (1993b, 31).

A *KATECHONTIC* VIEW OF HISTORY

As explained already, Schmitt's struggle around the meaning of history has a metapolitical stake: its objective is to ward off visions of history that make a political self-understanding of the present impossible. But he evidently needs an alternative to the natural-scientific and philosophical accounts of history he rejects. Schmitt is conscious of the need to occupy a proper position within the field of struggle around historical meaning. He needs his own perspective on historical meaning, in order to strengthen and intensify his metapolitical struggle against the dominant, depoliticizing approaches to history. His sober vision of history in terms of plural times, contingency and historical singularity does not by itself suffice to reach the polemic intensity required to successfully combat the images of history he opposes.

It is at this point that the enigmatic notion of the *katechon* enters our reconstruction of Schmitt's political conception of history. Many authors have been puzzled about the seeming impossibility of finding any coherence in Schmitt's use of this notion (e.g., Grossheutschi 1996; Paléologue 2004). As with all polemic concepts, it must primarily be understood in terms of what it is opposed to. Throughout Schmitt's (later) work, the *katechon* appears time and again as a force that has to ward off the possibility of a world without politics, be it in the form of cosmopolitan world unity, nihilistic centralization, total functionalization of law, or eschatological paralysis (Schmitt 1950a, 930; 1943/1944, 429; 1991b, 165). World unity, total mechanization, and the end of history are elements that stand in strong opposition to Schmitt's advocacy of a political understanding of the present. It is against these that Schmitt mobilizes the image of the *katechon*. The latter provides a strong image of what Schmitt's metapolitical endeavor fundamentally is about: to save history from being de- or hyperpoliticized.

In the following reconstruction of Schmitt's use of the notion of the *katechon*, I will part ways with approaches that interpret the *katechon* as being the centerpiece of a conservative or authoritarian outlook. According to these approaches, the *katechon* constitutes a force that merely maintains the current order, the empire or the state. In contrast, my contention is that it is not so much a particular manifestation of the political (the empire, or the state) that is at stake in Schmitt's theorization of the *katechon*, but the political as such.[9] Indeed, a crucial passage in *Glossarium* underlines that the *katechon* manifests itself not only in authoritarian power but also in its radical opposite—the hungry and powerless people who resist. To represent the people as a *katechontic* force against technical planning underscores that what is at stake in regard to the *katechon* is the political as such, in its opposition to depoliticization: "The *katechon* is shortage, hunger, misery and powerlessness. It is those who do not govern, it is the people; all the rest is a mass and an object of planning" (1991a, 272). Strikingly, Schmitt states that even anarchist chaos is "better than nihilist centralization and regulation" (272).[10]

The notion of the *katechon* was in a dormant state when Schmitt took it up in the 1930s.[11] It was originally coined by St. Paul in his second letter to the Thessalonians, whom he wanted to warn against the false idea that the second coming of Christ was nigh. This second coming would be preceded by the appearance of the Antichrist: "There come a falling away first, and that man of sin be revealed, the son of perdition; Who opposeth and exalteth himself above all that is called God, or that is worshipped; so that he as God sitteth in the temple of God, shewing himself that he is God" (2 Thessalonians 2:2). Before Christ's second coming, the Antichrist will appear in a concealed way, taking the place of God in the world. There is a force, however, that restrains it: the *katechon*. Although Paul suggests to the Thessalonians that they know who or what the *katechon* is, we do not, and many divergent hypotheses have been put forward for what or whom Paul was hinting at: belief, God himself, the proclamation of the gospel, and even the Roman Empire (Grossheutschi 1996, 24–25). Throughout the history of Christianity, from the Church fathers to Luther and Calvin, very diverse forces or persons have been considered to be the *katechon*. After the Reformation, though, the notion of the *katechon* tended to be forgotten. Schmitt played a central role in resurrecting it as a central category in the Catholic understanding of history.

However, Schmitt's use of the notion of the *katechon* is no less complex than his predecessors'. Indeed, at first sight it seems to lack any systematic character or coherence, to the extent that, according to Théodore Paléologue, "properly speaking, there is no *doctrine of the katechon* in Schmitt" (2004, 64). In his very valuable work on the *katechon*, Felix Grossheutschi (1986) shows how the notion appears in nine texts of Schmitt's, and functions very differently in each one of them. It seems almost impossible to extract a single meaning from these many passages. Sometimes Schmitt speaks of the *katechon* in a positive way, as a force that restrains the functionalization of the law for example (see, e.g., Schmitt 1943/1944, 429). On the other hand, he also uses the notion in a negative, critical way, as when he deems England to be the *katechontic* force restraining the rise of Germany (Schmitt 1995c, 435). In this latter case, England (and later the United States) tried to restrain the tendency toward great spaces, represented by Germany, and to maintain the empire with its universalist ambitions.

Sometimes the *katechon* appears as a real historical figure (the *katechon*) (e.g., Hegel, emperor Franz Joseph I, Masaryk, or Pilsudski); sometimes Schmitt understands it in a more impersonal way (the *katechontic*). Sometimes it is a person, sometimes a collectivity (e.g. a state or the Roman Empire). There are full *katechons* and forces that are *katechon* only in a weak or "splintered and fragmentary" way (Grossheutschi 1996, 79). Some worldly powers are *katechon*, while others definitely are not, according to Schmitt; he refers to Churchill or John Foster Dulles as examples of the latter (Schmitt 1991c, 63). The *katechon* can be a global power or a local one (Grossheutschi 1996, 80). Ultimately, as already suggested, the *katechon* can even be anarchist chaos, restraining the trend toward centralization (272; see also 85).

Sometimes, the *katechon* appears within the framework of an eschatological image of history; sometimes it does not. In *Land und Meer*, Byzantium appears as the *katechon* because it stopped the rise of Islam, but Schmitt (1993a, 19) does not refer to any image of history in this text. Sometimes the *katechon* is understood religiously: the German emperors had a clear understanding of themselves as the literal restrainers of the Antichrist. Sometimes it appears outside of any religious framework: Hegel and Savigny are thought to be *katechons* simply because they restrained a certain development in thinking about law, notably its trend toward "total functionalization" (1943/1944, 429). Schmitt praises Hegel and Savigny, despite their deep differences, because both maintain a sense of history against the ahistorical vision of the purely functional. Elsewhere, Hegel is considered to have a direct role in fighting atheism: in "Die andere Hegel-Linie" Schmitt (1957, 2) picks up Nietzsche's idea that Hegel is "the greatest delayer of Germany's course towards atheism."

At first sight, the concept of the *katechon* thus seems to be profoundly ambiguous.[12] This lack of clarity has made it possible to interpret it in rather creative ways. The Italian philosopher Paolo Virno mobilizes the *katechon*, for instance, to deconstruct the Hobbesian notion of the sovereign. According to Virno (2005, 14), the pessimistic anthropology at the basis of Hobbes's theory of sovereignty makes his notion of sovereignty deeply problematic. When it is governed by an evil human being, the civilian state can be even more dangerous than the state of nature.

In an attempt to deal with this ambivalence, Virno understands the *katechon* as a force that is situated between the two states. He underlines that the *katechon* is very ambiguous: it holds back the Antichrist, that is, radical evil, but it thereby also holds back the *parousia*, the second coming of the Messiah. In a certain way, the *katechon* thus keeps human beings bad: it restrains evil by tolerating it. The *katechon* oscillates between the civil and the natural state and thus stands in a tense relation to the sovereign, who is supposed to guarantee the overcoming of the state of nature and thus reduce the space for human wickedness. The *katechon* is the force that maintains the tension between law and the exception, good and evil, Messiah and Antichrist. It maintains the openness to the world of the human animal: "the *katechon*, a radically anti-eschatological theological-political concept, opposes the 'end of the world,' or better, the atrophy of the openness towards the world, the diverse ways in which the crisis of the present can manifest itself" (Virno 2005, 33).

In Virno's interpretation of Schmitt, the *katechon* becomes a generic force that is present in all institutions and not only in the state. Wherever it manifests itself, it keeps off the final abolition of human evil. This restraining role can be present in many different institutions, "from an anarchic commune to a military dictatorship" (32). "If the concept of the *katechon* is equated with the apotropaic function present in every political (and non-political) institution, it becomes necessary to conclude that it also runs through and exceeds the institution of state sovereignty. There subsists an insurmountable breach between the two concepts, the same as that separating the genus from the species, the syntagm 'linguistic animal' from the syntagm 'university professor'" (32). In this way, one might say that the concept of the *katechon* precedes the concept of sovereignty, just as Schmitt (1996a, 19) states that the concept of the political is presupposed by the concept of the state. The *katechon* appears as a force that has as its specific function the retention of an openness, an ambiguity situated between the state of nature and the civil state. It safeguards the possibility of the arrival of ever-new conflicts or exceptions. Virno shows the *katechon* to be an essential presupposition for the exception still to be possible within a Hobbesian state. He thus decisively detaches the notion of the *katechon* from its original theological framework to introduce it within a discussion on the foundations of political theory. It seems indeed more interesting to investigate how the notion of the *katechon* functions within the contemporary polemical field of political concepts in which Schmitt intervenes, than to focus on its historical genesis, by relating Schmitt's position to the historical tradition from the Church fathers to Luther.

One of the texts in which Schmitt discusses the *katechon* most systematically is his article "Drei Stufen historischer Sinngebung" (1950b). Here he develops a Christian image of history as an alternative to the dominant philosophies of history at the basis of planning programs, centralizing tendencies and trends toward world unity. On the basis of his reading of Karl Löwith's (1949) book *Meaning in History*, Schmitt briefly develops some ideas for such an alternative image of history. One of the questions he asks is whether eschatological belief on the one hand and historical consciousness and political action on the other can ever go together. They seem to be at odds with each other: "the lively expectation of the immediately approaching end seems to strip history of its meaning and leads to an eschatological paralysis, of which there are many historical examples" (Schmitt 1950b, 929).

For Schmitt (1950b), the *katechon* is precisely the force that has to keep off this eschatological paralysis. He states that the *katechon* functions as a bridge between an eschatological vision and a political understanding of history. It is a necessary pre-supposition if one wants to maintain the possibility of political commitment in this world while at the same time acknowledging that modernity thrives on the idea of a final salvation (Tronti 2000). The notion of the *katechon* is then a symbolic weapon for a polemical intervention within a spiritual configuration characterized by a strong eschatological penchant: a weapon that paradoxically has to repress this penchant by somehow making use of it.

If one wants to safeguard a political form of historical consciousness while at the same time maintaining the reference to an eschatological perspective (even if it is only to intensify the consciousness of the dangerousness of such a perspective), one needs a gatekeeper in between. That is exactly the role the *katechon* fulfills, as a force restrain-ing the end and making relative evil possible by suppressing its radical counterpart. Therefore, the *katechon* is a presupposition for worldly commitment and is not a con-servative or reactionary force as such: "we have to be careful not to turn the word into a general designation for merely conservative or reactionary tendencies," Schmitt (1950b, 930) states.

The *katechon* is thus the gatekeeper between a profane and political understanding of history on the one hand and the dangerous illusion of salvation through the final struggle of humanity on the other. It is the bridge between eschatology and historical conscience. It is the minimal rest of an eschatological vision needed to keep history and theology apart and to maintain an open and profane understanding of history. The image of the *katechon* is very ambiguous, however. Although it only makes sense within an eschatological view on history, it functions in such a way as to keep off the detri-mental effects of eschatological ideas on human political affairs. Indeed, the *katechon* is what makes the political as such possible. Its polemical aim is to ward off the idea that humans can definitively judge over the world, history, and morality and announce the end of history. The political is conditional on such a refusal of the theologization of history.

The *katechon* thus becomes a crucial element of Schmitt's metapolitical polemic strategy. It must not be understood in a theological sense in the narrow meaning of the word.[13] William Rasch asks the right question in this regard: "[W]hat if the *katechon* were not primarily a theological figure, but a political one, or rather a figure of the politi-cal itself?" (2004, 100) For "denying God—or at least denying His intervention in the world of the political—is precisely what the *katechon* does." And, it could be added, it is only through this denial that the political can arise in the first place.[14] The *katechon* has this effect not only because it keeps history open and profane but also because it throws us back onto the here and now, away from eschatological or utopian visions, which obliterate the present and inhibit the self-understanding required for genuine political action. The time of political action is now.[15]

The utmost the narrative on the *katechon* does is to represent the future in the pres-ent in a specific way, namely, as open and profane, while at the same time recalling the dangers of its closure. A genuinely political understanding of time presupposes not only its emancipation from mythical origins but also the rejection of myths about the future. In this sense, Schmitt's image of history is a very sober and profane one. It is difficult to conceive of a more minimal image of history: its sole function is a negative one, namely, to keep final ends away and to throw us back onto ourselves here and now. Below this minimal level, there seems to be only nihilism.

CONCLUSION

Schmitt is not the only author who strategically uses a word of theological provenance to think the temporal conditions of the political. Jacques Derrida does something similar in his reconceptualization of Benjamin's notion of messianism. In his seminal book *Specters of Marx*, Derrida speaks of "messianism without religion, even a messianic without messianism, an idea of justice" (1994a, 59). In *Marx & Sons*, Derrida (1999) coins the term *messianicity* to refer to the same idea. Derrida borrows the notion of the messianic from Benjamin to conceptualize a specific experience of time ("political temporality properly conceived"; Jameson 1999, 36). Derrida adjusts it to refer to the indeconstructibility of the idea of justice and to the experience of promise: "the messianic appeal belongs properly to a universal structure, to that irreducible movement of the historical opening to the future" (1994, 167).

For Derrida, the messianic is not a religious category but a profane structure of historical experience. It is strictly anti-utopian,[16] as its basic thrust is to keep history open and undecided. To that extent, one could say there is even something *katechontic* to it, as it strictly refuses the idea of an end time and keeps the present open for political intervention. Both the messianic and the *katechon* are to be clearly distinguished from utopia. For Derrida, messianicity is "anything but utopian," as it "mandates that we interrupt the ordinary course of things, time and history, the here-now" (1999, 248).

Schmitt (1996a, 31) was also very critical of utopian thinking, especially when it was mixed up with a belief in technical progress. In their rejection of progress and utopia, Schmitt's conception of the *katechon*, Benjamin's "weak messianic force" and Derrida's "messianism without religion"[17] strikingly converge.[18] Of course, there are clear differences between their approaches, in the first place because Benjamin's and Derrida's goal is to rethink emancipation, while Schmitt's vision is more soberly about the political as such.[19]

However, like Derrida's notion of messianicity, Schmitt's notion of the *katechon* can perfectly be understood outside of an explicitly religious framework. One could oppose something like a Schmittian *katechonticity* to Derrida's messianicity. Indeed, just as Virno underlined the generic character of the notion of the *katechon*, messianicity distills a similar generic dimension from messianism: messianicity "refers to an undoing of all possible messianisms: messianicity is merely what remains as the affirmation and the passion of justice beyond every possible subjectification of it" (Moreiras 2004, 73).

The question remains, however, why Schmitt felt the need to use a word originating from eschatology. Why could he not just advocate a political conception of history against tendencies toward neutralization and functionalization without taking recourse to an image that is part of an eschatological outlook? In other words, why did it not suffice to criticize ideologies of progress and repetition and to underline the contingency and plurality of history, as explained already? Why introduce such an enigmatic theological image into the struggle around historical meaning?

It might be of interest to look at why Walter Benjamin turned to a theological image to think history. His motivation to do so sprang from a dissatisfaction with Horkheimer's materialist conception of history (Löwy 2001). According to such a conception, what is past is definitively past. It can never be redeemed. Benjamin's theological image of history was an attempt to remedy this. He needed such an image to intensify the present and to disclose the weak messianic force we as contemporary political actors and writers of history are imbued with: we are able to take up the fight of the oppressed and downtrodden of the past and rescue them from becoming forgotten. In the end, this has nothing to do with theology in the strict sense of the word. It is just an image that generates a totally different perspective on history and should spur people to become engaged and act politically.

Schmitt, too, feels the need to use a theological image of history. Its objective is different from Benjamin's, of course: it is to intensify the consciousness of the danger that is implied in hyperpoliticizing philosophies of history that forecast a last struggle of humanity. It remains paradoxical, however, that a figure drawn from eschatology is needed to ward off eschatology. One can understand this paradox only by stressing that even a metapolitical struggle has to produce its own symbols that give this struggle a certain intensity. The image of the *katechon* can generate an awareness of how much is actually at stake: it produces a sharp perception of the metapolitical enemy and its dangers, namely, the chaos that a world without politics would inevitably bring as it would open a struggle that is interminable (Lievens 2013). The *katechon*, in other words, is a polemical weapon in the struggle on this metalevel and thus contributes to Schmitt's fundamental endeavor: to fight for the political.

NOTES

1. Some of the ideas in this chapter were first developed in Lievens 2011.
2. Unless noted otherwise, all translations of source material by the author.
3. I translate the phrase "*über das Politische hinausgehend*" (Schmitt 1991b, 37) as "beyond the political" because the currently available English translation "transcending the limits of the political framework" (Schmitt 1996a, 36) does not have the strong and concise meaning as the original German.
4. If there would not be social change, jurisprudence would overrule politics, Schmitt argues. In such a situation, there would no longer be a state in the specific sense of the word, but only an "unpolitical legal community" (Schmitt 1932, 267).

5. Schmitt (1995e, 539) also uses the concept of the *suprastructure* to refer to what arises out of the "historically essential," for example, the choice for a maritime or a terrestrial principle of spatial ordering.

6. Every epoch has its "general state of consciousness," Schmitt 1988b (46) argues. Colliot-Thélène 1999 believes that for Schmitt "the identity of a period is of a metaphysical nature" (144).

7. As Schmitt 2003a (143) states in one of his early quasi-Kantian texts, there is a time of immediacy and one of mediation.

8. See also Benjamin's 1980 statement: "The Sovereign represents history. He holds the course of history in his hand like a scepter" (245).

9. According to Schmitt, one cannot in advance fix the *katechontic* function to any particular instance. One must presuppose there has always been a *katechon*: "It must be possible to identify the *katechon* of each epoch of the last 1948 years. The place of the *katechon* has never been unoccupied, or we would no longer be here" (1993a, 63). But who or what instance has *katechontic* force can change: "there are no rightfully acquired rights to the position of the *katechon*" (65).

10. Schmitt states in the introduction to a bundle of texts on Donoso Cortés published in 1950 that in the 1920s the opposition between anarchism and authority was still central while in the meantime a new contradiction had become actual, namely, the one between anarchism and nihilism. Faced with the nihilism of a centralized order mastering the modern means of destruction, anarchy seems the lesser evil and can even be salutary (Schmitt 1950, 9–10).

11. As Schmitt states—in French—in his notebooks, "Vous connaissez ma théorie du *katechon*, elle date de 1932" ("You know my theory of the *katechon*; it dates from 1932"; 1991c, 80).

12. In his attempt to categorize Schmitt's uses of this concept, Paléologue distinguishes between a personal and an impersonal *katechon*, a direct and an indirect *katechon*, a political and a spiritual *katechon*, and a *katechon* within and outside the church. In addition, he also distinguishes between weak and strong *katechons*. Crucial for him is the relation the *katechon* upholds with the law: "the *katechon* is … the guarantee of a legal order" (2004, 65).

13. The contention that the *katechon* should be understood in political rather than theological terms follows from an analysis of the field of concepts within which Schmitt intervenes with his concept of the *katechon*. It is striking how he consistently opposes the *katechon* to world unity or planning and never mentions the Antichrist. *The "Nomos" of the Earth* is one of the few books published by Schmitt in which he discusses the concept of the *katechon* with an explicit mention of the Antichrist. He does this, however, in a chapter devoted to the medieval Christian Empire as the restrainer of the Antichrist (Schmitt 2003b, 59).

14. According to Paléologue, who wrote a whole book on the problem of the topic, the *katechon* has a political dimension, but the political does not necessarily have a *katechontic* dimension. The reason is, according to him, that there is a politics of the Antichrist. However, even if it can be said that the Antichrist decides on an enemy to annihilate her, it is precisely in this annihilation that his nonpolitical character lies. What Paléologue does not see (similarly to most "theological" readings of Schmitt) is that Schmitt distinguishes the political from a "beyond," an intensity leading the enemy to be annihilated. It is not true that, as Paléologue 2004 states, "The political is neutral with regard to eschatology, just as it is neutral with regard to morality" (115). Eschatology, humanitarian moralism, and ideologies of progress do lead beyond the political. The Antichrist is a figure of this hyperpolitical level par excellence.

15. "The present is the central temporal category of an open history. Emancipated from the myths of the origin and the end, it is the time of politics, which 'attains primacy over history' as a strategic approach to struggle and decision" (Bensaïd 1996, 70).

16. This is contrary to how Jameson 1999 (33) understood it.

17. Messianisms without religion have to be distinguished from Benjamin's concept of weak messianic force, according to Derrida (cf. Bensaïd 2001, 175–176).

18. Theo De Wit 1992 (336) observes a parallel between Schmitt's *katechon* and Benjamin's Messiah: the *katechontic* aspect of dictatorship in Schmitt and Donoso Cortés resembles the task Benjamin attributes to the proletariat, namely to pull the emergency brake of the train of capitalist progress.

19. On the other hand, Balibar 2001 (172) in a very Schmittian fashion suggests that these messianic conceptions actually reproduce their ethical and religious origins and are thus also tributary to the contemporary end of politics: "But aren't eschatology and myth actually simply driven back one step, moving from a religious belief or hope to an ethical hypothesis and command?"

References

Balibar, E. 2001. *Nous, citoyens d'Europe? Les frontières, l'Etat, le peuple.* Paris: La Découverte.

Benjamin, W. 1968. "Theses on the Philosophy of History." In *Illuminations.* New York: Shocken, 253–264.

Benjamin, W. 1980. *Ursprung des deutschen Trauerspiels.* In *Gesammelte Schriften*, vol. 1: *Abhandlungen*, ed. R. Tiedemann and H. Schweppenhäuser. Frankfurt: Suhrkamp.

Benjamin, W. 1989. *Paris Capitale du XIXe Siècle: le livres des passages.* Paris: Editions du Cerf.

Bensaïd, D. 1990. *Walter Benjamin: Sentinelle messianique.* Paris: Plon.

Bensaïd, D. 1996. *Marx l'Intempestif: Grandeurs et misères d'une aventure critique (XIXe–XXe siècles).* Paris: Fayard.

Bensaïd, D. 2001. *Résistances: Essai de taupologie générale.* Paris: Fayard.

Bensaïd, D. 2008. *Eloge de la politique profane.* Paris: Albin Michel.

Collingwood, R. G. 1993. *The Idea of History.* Oxford: Clarendon Press.

Colliot-Thélène, C. 1999. "Carl Schmitt versus Max Weber: Juridical Rationality and Economic Rationality." In *The Challenge of Carl Schmitt*, ed. C. Mouffe. London: Verso, 138–154.

Derrida, J. 1994. *Specters of Marx: The State of the Debt, the Working of Mourning, and the New International.* New York: Routledge.

Derrida, J. 1999. "Marx & Sons." In *Ghostly Demarcations: A Symposium on Jacques Derrida's Spectres of Marx*, ed. M. Sprinker. London: Verso, 213–269.

De Wit, T. 1992. *De Onontkoombaarheid van de Politiek: De Soevereine Vijand in de Politieke Filosofie van Carl Schmitt.* Ubergen: Pomppers.

De Wit, T. 2001. "Op zoek naar de vijand: De agressiviteit van de vooruitgang volgens C. Schmitt." In *Onbehagen met de moderniteit*, ed. A. Braeckman. Kapellen: Pelckmans, 116–144.

Galli, C. 1996. *Genealogia della politica: Carl Schmitt e la crisi del pensiero politico modern.* Bologna: Mulino.

Grossheutschi, F. 1996. *Carl Schmitt und die Lehre vom Katechon.* Berlin: Duncker & Humblot.

Jameson, F. 1999. "Marx's Purloined Letter." In *Ghostly Demarcations: A Symposium on Jacques Derrida's Spectres of Marx*, ed. M. Sprinker. London: Verso, 26–67.

Jameson, F. 2005. "Notes on the Nomos." *South Atlantic Quarterly* 2, 199–204.

Kervégan, J.-F. 1999. "Carl Schmitt and 'World Unity.'" In Mouffe 1999, 54–74.

Kondylis, P. 1986. *Konservativismus: Geschichtlicher Gehalt und Untergang*. Stuttgart: Klett-Cotta.

Koselleck, R. 1990. *Le futur passé: Contribution à la sémantique des temps historiques*. Paris: Editions de l'Ecole des Hautes Etudes en Sciences Sociales.

Lievens, M. 2010. "Carl Schmitt's Two Concepts of Humanity." *Philosophy and Social Criticism* 36: 917–934.

Lievens, M. 2011. "Singularity and Repetition in Carl Schmitt's Vision of History." *Journal of the Philosophy of History* 5: 105–129.

Lievens, M. 2013. "Carl Schmitt's Metapolitics." *Constellations* 20: 121–137.

Llanque, M., and H. Münkler. 2003. "'Vorwort' von 1963." In *Carl Schmitt: Der Begriff des Politischen*, ed. R. Mehring. Berlin: Akademie Verlag, 9–20.

Löwith, K. 1949. *Meaning in History: The Theological Implications of the Philosophy of History*. Chicago: University of Chicago Press.

Löwith, K. 1995. "The Occasional Decisionism of Carl Schmitt." In *Martin Heidegger and European Nihilism*, ed. R. Wolin. New York: Columbia University Press, 137–159.

Löwy, M. 2001. *Walter Benjamin: Avertissement d'Incendie*. Paris: PUF.

Maus, I. 1976. *Bürgerliche Rechtstheorie und Faschismus: Zur sozialen Funktion und aktuellen Wirkung der Theorie Carl Schmitts*. Munich: Fink.

McCormick, J. P. 1999. *Carl Schmitt's Critique of Liberalism: Against Politics as Technology*. Cambridge: Cambridge University Press.

Mouffe, C. ed. 1999. *The Challenge of Carl Schmitt*. London: Verso.

Moreiras, A. 2004. "A God without Sovereignty: Political Jouissance—The Passive Decision." *New Centennial Review* 4, 71–108.

Paléologue, T. 2004. *Sous l'oeuil du grand inquisiteur: Carl Schmitt et l'héritage de la théologie politique*. Paris: Editions du Cerf.

Pourciau, S. 2006. "Bodily Negation: Carl Schmitt on the Meaning of Meaning." *MLN* 120: 1066–1090.

Rasch, W. 2004. *Sovereignty and Its Discontents: On the Primacy of Conflict and the Structure of the Political*. London: Birkbeck Law Press.

Sayer, D. 1987. *The Violence of Abstraction: The Analytic Foundations of Historical Materialism*. Oxford: Blackwell.

Schmitt, C. 1927. "Donoso Cortes in Berlin, 1849." In Schmitt 1994a, 84–96.

Schmitt, C. 1931. "Die staatsrechtliche Bedeutung der Notverordnung, insbesondere ihre Rechtsgültigkeit." In Schmitt 1985, 235–262.

Schmitt, C. 1932. "Legalität und Legitimität." In Schmitt 1985, 263–350.

Schmitt, C. 1936. "Vergleichender Überblick über die neueste Entwicklung des Problems der gesetzgeberischen Ermächtigungen; 'Legislative Delegationen.'" In Schmitt 1994a, 244–260.

Schmitt, C. 1938. "Über das Verhältnis der Begriffe Krieg und Feind." In Schmitt 1994a, 278–285.

Schmitt, C. 1943/1944. "Die Lage der europäischen Rechtswissenschaft." In Schmitt 1985, 386–429.

Schmitt, C. 1950a. *Donoso Cortés in gesamteuropäischer Interpretation: Vier Aufsätze*. Cologne: Greven.

Schmitt, C. 1950b. "Drei Stufen historischer Sinngebung." *Universitas* 5: 927–931.

Schmitt, C. 1954. *Materialien zu einer Verfassungslehre*. Berlin: Duncker & Humblot.

Schmitt, C. 1957. "Die andere Hegel-Linie: Hans Freyer zum 70. Geburtstag". *Christ und Welt* 10: 2.

Schmitt, C. 1970. "Von der TV-Demokratie: Die Aggressivität des Fortschritts." *Deutsches Allgemeines Sonntagsblatt*, June 28.

Schmitt, C. 1985. *Verfassungsrechtliche Aufsätze aus den Jahren 1924–1954: Materialien zu einer Verfassungslehre*, 3rd ed. Berlin: Duncker & Humblot.

Schmitt, C. 1986. *Political Romanticism*, trans. G. Oakes. Cambridge: MIT Press.

Schmitt, C. 1987. "The Legal World Revolution." *Telos* 72: 73–89.

Schmitt, C. 1988a. *Die Wendung zum diskriminierenden Kriegsbegriff*. Berlin: Duncker & Humblot.

Schmitt, C. 1988b. *Political Theology: Four Chapters on the Concept of Sovereignty*, trans. G. Schwab. Cambridge: MIT Press.

Schmitt, C. 1990. "L'unité du monde (II)." In *Du Politique: "Légalité et légitimité" et Autres Essays*, ed. A. de Benoist. Puiseaux: Editions Pardès, 237–249.

Schmitt, C. 1991a. *Glossarium: Aufzeichnungen der Jahre 1947–1951*. Berlin: Duncker & Humblot.

Schmitt, C. 1991b. *Der Begriff des Politischen*. Berlin: Duncker & Humblot.

Schmitt, C. 1991c. *Völkerrechtliche Grossraumordnung mit Interventionsverbot für raumfremde Mächte: Ein Beitrag zum Reichsbegriff im Völkerrecht*. Berlin: Duncker & Humblot.

Schmitt, C. 1992. *The Crisis of Parliamentary Democracy*, trans. E. Kennedy. Cambridge: MIT Press.

Schmitt, C. 1993a. *Land und Meer*. Stuttgart: Klett-Cotta.

Schmitt, C. 1993b. *Über die Drei Arten des rechtswissenschaftlichen Denkens*. Berlin: Duncker & Humblot.

Schmitt, C. 1994a. *Positionen und Begriffe im Kampf mit Weimar—Genf—Versailles, 1923–1939*, 3rd ed. Berlin: Ducker & Humblot.

Schmitt, C. 1994b. *Gespräch über die Macht und den Zugang zum Machthaber/Gespräch über den neuen Raum*. Berlin: Akademie Verlag.

Schmitt, C. 1995a. *Staat, Grossraum, Nomos: Arbeiten aus den Jahren 1916–1969*, ed. G. Maschke. Berlin: Duncker & Humblot.

Schmitt, C. 1995b. "Die Raumrevolution. Durch den totalen Krieg zu einem totalen Frieden." In Schmitt 1995, 388–394.

Schmitt, C. 1995c. "Beschleuniger wider Willen oder: Problematik der westlichen Hemisphäre." In Schmitt 1995a, 431–440.

Schmitt, C. 1995d. "Die Einheit der Welt." In Schmitt 1995a, 496–512.

Schmitt, C. 1995e. "Die geschichtliche Struktur des heutigen Welt-Gegensatzes von Ost und West: Bemerkungen zu Ernst Jüngers Schrift 'Der Gordische Knoten.'" In Schmitt 1995a, 523–551.

Schmitt, C. 1996a. *The Concept of the Political*, trans. G. Schwab. Chicago: University of Chicago Press.

Schmitt, C. 1996b. *Politische Theologie II: Die Legende von der Erledigung jeder Politischen Theologie*. Berlin: Duncker & Humblot.

Schmitt, C. 1996c. *Roman Catholicism and Political Form*. Westport: Greenwood Press.

Schmitt, C. 2002. *Ex Captivitate Salus: Erfahrungen der Zeit 1945/47*. Berlin: Duncker & Humblot.

Schmitt, C. 2003a. *La valeur de l'état et la signification de l'individu*. Genève: Librairie Droz.

Schmitt, C. 2003b. *The "Nomos" of the Earth in the International Law of the "Jus Publicum Europaeum."* New York: Telos Press.

Schmitt, C. 2004. "Theory of the Partisan." *New Centennial Review* 4: 1–78.

Schmitt, C. 2005. "Die Ära der integralen Politik." In Schmitt, *Frieden oder Pazifismus? Arbeiten zum Völkerrecht und zur internationalen Politik 1924–1978*, ed. G. Maschke. Berlin: Duncker & Humblot, 464–468.

Taubes, J. 2003. *En divergent accord: A propos de Carl Schmitt.* Paris: Payot et Rivages.

Tocqueville, A. de. 1986. *De la démocratie en Amérique; Souvenirs; l'Ancien Régime et la Revolution.* Paris: Laffont.

Toynbee, A. 1987. *A Study of History.* New York: Oxford University Press.

Tronti, M. 2000. *La politique au crépuscule.* Paris: Editions de l'Eclat.

Vad, E. 1996. *Strategie und Sicherheitspolitik: Perspektiven im Werk von Carl Schmitt.* Opladen: Westdeutscher Verlag.

Virno, P. 2005. "Il Cosidetto Male e la Critica dello Stato." *Forme de Vita* 4: 9–35.

CHAPTER 15

WHAT'S "LEFT" IN SCHMITT?

From Aversion to Appropriation in Contemporary Political Theory

MATTHEW G. SPECTER

INTRODUCTION

WHEN *TELOS*, a philosophical journal of the New Left, in 1987 devoted an entire issue to "introducing" Carl Schmitt to its readers, few left-wing American social or political theorists considered Schmitt a major resource for contemporary theory. But twenty-five years later, the modest Schmitt "renaissance" initiated by the small-circulation *Telos*, has "turned into a virtual tsunami" of interest globally (Bernstein 2011, 403). In Richard Bernstein's words: "Schmitt's work is actively and passionately discussed throughout the world. He has been hailed as the most incisive, relevant, and controversial political and legal theorist of the twentieth century—and the enthusiasm for Schmitt is shared by thinkers across the political spectrum from the extreme Left to the extreme Right" (403).

While a sketch of the global reception of Schmitt is beyond the scope of this chapter, and the reasons for Schmitt's appeal to thinkers on the extreme right are not hard to discern, this chapter will explore the more vexing, yet intriguing problem of the resurgence of left interest in Schmitt's writings. Broadly speaking, what makes left interest in Schmitt potentially problematic is the question of whether Schmitt's texts can be divorced from their contexts, "insights" from the intentions behind them? Can his analyses of the weaknesses of liberal democracy in the Weimar Republic be disentangled from either his theoretical defense of the Nazi state between 1933 and 1936 or his deep-seated antisemitism? How to approach a "master-thinker" of political theory, who is at the same time, in Peter Caldwell's phrase, a representative of Germany's unmastered past

(Gross 2007)? Can a political thinker be both intellectual friend and political enemy? To what extent does a contextual reading of Schmitt's political theory circumscribe its meanings and thereby limit its utility for progressive theorizing?

A quarter-century ago, the Western Left was deeply averse to the appropriation of ideas from Schmitt; today, the Left's spectrum of responses ranges from aversion to appropriation. The first half of this chapter analyzes the writings of Jürgen Habermas, the preeminent social and political thinker of the Federal Republic of Germany from the 1960s to the present, whose profound aversion to Schmitt has been paradigmatic for a generation of leftists and left liberals. Habermas sought to make leftists deeply skeptical of any effort to defend, appropriate, or critically reconstruct Schmitt for a progressive politics (Müller 2003, 195), and he was successful in this endeavor.[1] It is quite ironic therefore, that more than one close study of Habermas's career as political and legal theorist has revealed that his intellectual animus toward Carl Schmitt was one of the defining enmities of his career.[2] This is not to say that Habermas is covertly, or at some deep level, a Schmittian, as some have claimed, but it is to recognize that there is a historical interrelationship between the two thinkers that is not captured by either the gesture of unveiling influence on one hand or of refusal to acknowledge any Schmittian influence on the other. For Habermas, Schmitt was always an enemy, never a friend, but as with many enmities it was constitutive of his identity, and a relationship of intimate familiarity. In this section I argue that Habermas has at times used Schmitt as a mere foil for his own arguments but that, more often, working through Schmitt seems to have been actually constitutive of his thought. Since at least some of Habermas's engagements of Schmitt have been productive, there is a tension between his principled aversion to Schmitt and his practice of appropriation. Insights are successfully separated from intentions in Habermas, implying that others could do the same. Thus, it would be hypocritical for leftists to consider the only ethically or politically responsible position to be to declare Schmitt's thought a priori taboo or unworthy of engagement. On the other hand, the last twenty years of left appropriation of Schmitt, as I argue next, have not yielded impressive results.

In the second half of the chapter, I analyze the recent appropriations of Schmitt by three Western political theorists who self-identify as part of a Left political project: Chantal Mouffe, Gopal Balakrishnan, and Andreas Kalyvas. Here I try both to reconstruct the historical contexts behind their surprising turn from aversion to appropriation and to offer a critique of what may be described as the recent Left-Schmittianism in political theory. The new Left-Schmittians generally describe their approach as separating Schmitt's insights from his intentions, rescuing the classic status of the former from the contingent failures of Schmitt's own political judgment. In this section, I argue that the salvage operations performed by Balakrishnan, Kalyvas, and Mouffe fail to deliver on this promise: either because they underestimate the extent to which the contexts of German history circumscribe these texts' possible meanings or by refashioning Schmitt into a theorist of class struggle, extraordinary democratic politics, or pluralism, respectively, they so dilute Schmitt's meanings that the resulting syntheses cannot any longer be considered "Schmittian."

The transformation of Schmitt into a political "classic" was initiated shortly after his death in 1985 (Müller 2003, 196). The new, left interest in Schmitt can be traced to the identical moment, for very different political reasons, but also benefited from Schmitt's public rehabilitation as a classic. But the project of normalizing Carl Schmitt as a political classic still runs aground on the politics of postwar memory. While Habermas emphasizes the continuities in Schmitt's pre-1933 and post-1933 thought, Balakrishnan, Kalyvas, and Mouffe assert that there is a clear break. While an older generation of intellectual historians placed Schmitt within the conservative revolution in Weimar, intellectual-historical argument is today used as much to justify one's appropriations of Schmitt as it is to anchor one's aversions (see Herf 1986; Mosse 1998). While Mouffe and Kalyvas go so far as to claim that Schmitt's Weimar writings were intended to save the Republic, most accept the consensus view of contextual intellectual historians that Schmitt aimed with his texts to sharpen the contradictions between liberalism and democracy and thereby shorten the republic's life. The new Left-Schmittians therefore use intellectual history when it suits their purposes and dispute its relevance when it does not. Most establish their bona fides by acknowledging Schmitt's "personal" failures of political judgment—his deep-seated antisemitism, his theoretical defense of the Nazi state between 1933 and 1936—but imply that these choices are contingencies of the life, not the motivating lifeworlds of the thought.

The erosion of the taboo on reading Schmitt affirmatively is also a function of our temporal distance from the "Third Reich" and the Holocaust: today it seems less risky to read Schmitt ahistorically because professional scholars have already done their due diligence, as it were, in excavating the depths of Schmitt's antisemitism and identifying his complicity with the Nazi state. But there is still something deeply unsettling about accounts of Schmitt that seek to "normalize" him by emphasizing the prominence or liberal credentials of his interlocutors in the Weimar Republic, or as Raphael Gross writes, "to refine Schmitt into a classic" (2007, 231).[3] It was not for nothing that Schmitt was banned from teaching in Germany from 1945 to his death. As the political scientist Kurt Sontheimer eulogized Schmitt, "He who cares about liberal democracy has no need of Carl Schmitt" (Müller 2003, 195).

Recent appropriations of Schmitt by left political theorists thus raise challenging questions at once methodological and political: to what extent can Schmitt's corpus be disassembled and reassembled for purposes alien to Schmitt's intentions? Are the new political projects that draw on these infusions still Schmittian—or have their original ideological meanings been expunged? What have leftists of the last twenty years found in Schmitt that they consider useful? How do we historicize and evaluate these appropriations? In short, what's "left" in Schmitt?

LEFTIST AVERSIONS: HABERMAS'S
RECEPTION OF SCHMITT, 1957–1996

In his recent essay on Habermas, William Scheuerman notes that most Anglophone commentators (he names my 2010 *Habermas: An Intellectual Biography* "an important exception") have missed the importance of West German legal and political contexts for understanding Habermas's political theory: "It would be a mistake to overlook the crucial fact—Habermas came of age intellectually in 1950s and early 1960s Germany and that his political theory can be fruitfully reconstructed not only as an effort at creatively 'superseding' (in the Hegelian sense) the earlier theoretical accomplishments of the German Marxist Left but also as an attempt to respond critically to the German Right and its foremost midcentury representative Carl Schmitt" (Scheuerman 2011, 241).

Habermas's first encounters with Schmitt were shaped by the writings and teaching of Wolfgang Abendroth (1906–1985) an isolated Marxist professor of political science at the University of Marburg in the late 1950s and the only figure in the Association of German Public Law Professors (*Vereinigung der deutschen Staatsrechtslehrer*) constituted after the war who had actively resisted the Nazis. After it became clear that Max Horkheimer was alarmed by Habermas's political radicalism and would not support his *Habilitationsschrift*, Habermas sought out Abendroth in Marburg as a replacement supervisor. Thus, it was in part through a fortuitous accident of academic politics that Habermas found his way to Abendroth, and through him to the debates in Weimar political and legal theory in which Carl Schmitt figured so centrally. In another respect, however, Habermas's path to Abendroth was indicative of the broader deficit of normative political theory in the West German intellectual field of the 1950s, of which his conflict with Horkheimer was but one symptom (Specter 2010, 29–34). This field was aporetically structured by an empirical and positivist political science on one hand and a conservative statist constitutional theory on the other. One of the major questions Habermas asked in *The Structural Transformation of the Public Sphere* (1961) was whether democracy had become little more than the periodic plebiscitary acclamation of decisions already made by elites, and if so, what normative perspective was required to critique it? Which institutional reforms were necessary to arrest this disintegration? These questions led him in search of a *normative* theory of the political, something he did not find in American political science. On this point, German constitutional theory seized Habermas's interest, despite its being dominated by the statist approach. Thus, it was the limited positivistic character of contemporary political science that prompted Habermas to investigate the traditionally conservative discipline of *Staatsrechtslehre*. As he explained, "In contemporary political science, in contrast to classical social philosophy and the older *Staatsrechtslehre*, democracy is not derived from principles" (1961, 14).[4] Habermas considered the influence of the positivist trend in American political science on the newly refounded German discipline a strongly negative one, leaving it without resources to arrest the decline of the public sphere. In context, therefore, Habermas's appropriation of conservative constitutional theory was a result of a historical lacuna. As Habermas wrote in response to a question about the influence of some of the leading contemporary German political scientists on his work: "It is true that I was very much influenced in the late '50s by the Weimar *Staatsrechtslehrerdiskussion* and its aftermath (C. Schmitt, Forsthoff, Weber vs. Abendroth), but less so by Kirchheimer, Fraenkel and Neumann...I hadn't read much of [the] contemporary stuff in the field of political science and theory (except the American literature on mass communication and political sociology—Kornhauser,

Lipset, C. W. Mills etc.). Until I discovered Rawls in the late '70s, I was nourished in political theory almost only by the German *Staatsrechtslehre*."[5]

What to make of the influence of Schmitt and the Schmittians on Habermas's early political writings has been a controversial question since the 1980s, but setting these writings back in the context of the intellectual field of the 1950s, especially with regard to the *Staatsrechtslehre*, illuminates these appropriations better than the notion that Habermas was a secret Left-Schmittian, as political scientist Ellen Kennedy famously charged (Kennedy 1987). The first references to either Schmitt or his students in Habermas's writings are in his 1958 essay "On the Concept of Political Participation," which formed the introduction to an Institute for Social Research study on the political consciousness of Frankfurt University students, *Students and Politics*; the next appear in his *Habilitationsschrift, The Structural Transformation of the Public Sphere*, completed in 1961.[6] The essay originally published by Kennedy in 1986 sparked heated controversy over the interpretive significance of these passages.

Kennedy claimed the deep resemblances between Habermas's critique of parliamentary democracy and Schmitt's illustrated a fundamental illiberalism in Habermas's thought that compromised his image as "the man who brought [Germans] Locke and Mill" (Kennedy 1987, 66). Ulrich Preuß, Alfons Söllner, and Martin Jay leapt into the fray to defend Habermas from the charges, noting that Marxism had its own critique of parliamentarism that coincided at points with Schmitt's and that the proposed Schmitt—Habermas genealogy was therefore not a convincing one. Nearly twenty years later, Jan-Werner Müller argued that the presence of Schmitt in Habermas's work could not be denied, but neither was it proof of scandal: "There could be no doubt that in the late 1950s and early 1960s, Habermas had drawn on Schmitt's thought, alongside others like Arnold Gehlen, Ernst Forsthoff and Hans Schelsky. There was also no doubt that Habermas, at that time, regarded Schmitt as a formidable opponent who had seen through the logic of parliamentarism and correctly diagnosed its decline" (Müller 2003, 195).[7] Moreover, it is true that Habermas admitted in 1992 that he had not escaped the influence of some aspects of Schmitt's *Verfassungslehre*: "In Germany the discussion over the generality of legal statutes is still colored by the rather extreme views found in Carl Schmitt's 1928 *Verfassungslehre*. This view became influential in the Federal Republic through the direct efforts of Ernst Forsthoff and indirectly through Franz Neumann. I did not escape this influence myself at the end of the fifties; see my introduction to . . . *Student und Politik*" (Habermas 1998b, 563 n75).

Müller is correct that Habermas's use of Schmitt's diagnoses of decline did not amount to an endorsement of that decline, nor did pointing to an unresolved tension between parliamentary rule and democratic sovereignty mean that one wished for the destruction of parliamentarism and liberalism altogether. In fact, we know from Habermas's biography that *Structural Transformation* was written under the guidance of Wolfgang Abendroth—whose democratic socialist program called for a democratic deepening and reinvention of the liberal welfare state, not its replacement by dictatorship or plebiscitarian democracy—and that the concluding section clearly aligns Habermas with Abendroth's program (see Habermas 1989, ch. 23; Scheuerman 2011, 244).

The influence of both the Schmitt and Abendroth schools on Habermas's thought in the period from 1957 to 1963 is clear, abundant, and direct. But Habermas appropriated these thinkers in a specific context that in retrospect had a specific logic, to wit: Habermas's appropriations from Schmitt and the Schmitt school were clearly guided by an Abendrothian hermeneutic strategy, that is, to interpret the social state clauses of the Basic Law to maximum effect. For nearly a decade in the 1950s, Abendroth had defended the notion that the *Rechtsstaat* and *Sozialstaat* concepts outlined in Articles 20 and 28 were not contradictions as the Schmittians argued but moments of a higher unity: in the "binding of these three moments, *Rechtsstaat, Sozialstaat,* and democracy—we catch a glimpse of the legal heart of our system" (Specter 2010, 43). Since Habermas sided with Abendroth in the Forsthoff/Abendroth debate, which he cited in his 1958 and 1961 works, Habermas's appropriations of Forsthoff must also have aimed not to bury the *Rechtsstaat* but to reinvent it.

In Forsthoff's writings on the welfare state and administrative law, Habermas found an expert witness to the breakdown of the separation of powers in general and the state–society distinction in particular. With enabling laws and supplementary legislations, the legislator handed over powers to administration. Thus, legislation and administration, deemed separate in Montesquieu, began to appear indistinct. If the line between state and society was becoming ever blurrier, then the idea that a private, prepolitical sphere could be clearly demarcated from a public one was equally fictitious. On the basis of Forsthoff's reading of the deformalization of law, Habermas concluded that a unified state–society had arrived. What remained was to recognize the *already* politicized character of the social sphere.

Because of their conservative intentions and pedigree, Habermas held the Schmitt students at arm's length. Nevertheless, he appropriated their radical critique of the welfare state against the grain of their intention. Like Forsthoff, Werner Weber, and Rüdiger Altmann, Habermas was repelled by the influence of powerful interest groups—but there the similarities end. Where Schmitt and his students criticized the vacuum of state authority, Habermas did not seek to reconstruct a strong executive branch and instead saw the legislative branch as his preferred guardian of the constitution. Habermas learned from the Schmittians that the spheres of state and society had interpenetrated one another.[8] If public and private spheres were collapsing in on one another, Habermas reasoned, the idea of prepolitical, negative liberties had ceased to be meaningful. Negative liberties could be reinvented only as positive guarantees of participation with a unified state–society. The collapse of the classical liberal society/state divide required government intervention in the economy to democratize it, to support social rights, and revive the public sphere (Specter 2010, 59–86; Scheuerman 2011, 244).

Therefore, while Habermas says he did not escape the influence of Schmitt's critique of legal deformalization in his constitutional theory of the 1920s—and as the textual evidence makes clear, the influence of Schmitt's students who updated that critique for the West Germany of the 1950s—Habermas adopted the critique of the generality of the legal norm (i.e., that executive power commonly deformalized or sought exceptions to the norms created by the legislature). This critique had already been adopted by one of the Frankfurt School's legal theorists, Franz Neumann, who had learned from Schmitt's critique too.[9] But whereas Neumann employed the concept as a tool for describing an empirical process that could be arrested or reversed, Schmitt reified the process, discerning it an expression of the underlying weakness of all legal forms everywhere when confronted with the power of the political. In short, while Habermas did not need Schmitt to teach him to be critical of the classical nineteenth-century ideal of the *Rechtsstaat*, the paucity of Marxist theoretical discourse in West Germany in the late '50s and early '60s meant that the most up-to-date critique of the concept was more easily found on the right than on the left. Coming from an Abendrothian perspective, however, Habermas's objective was not to exacerbate the contradiction between *Rechtsstaat* and democracy to augment executive power but to lessen it. In this Habermas followed Abendroth's strategy (which was itself indebted to the Weimar theorist Hermann Heller), namely, to insist that there could not be real democracy without a socialist transformation of the economy (Specter 2010, 66). Liberal constitutionalism could not be completely discounted since it contained an intention that pointed beyond capitalism.

REINHART KOSELLECK AS SOURCE FOR HABERMAS'S RECEPTION OF SCHMITT

Habermas's introduction to Schmitt in his early political development, therefore, occurred mostly in a mediated fashion, through the figures of Forsthoff, Weber, and Altmann on the right and Neumann on the left. But Habermas also encountered Schmitt by another avenue, via the writings of Schmitt pupil (and later major intellectual historian and historical theorist) Reinhart Koselleck. In 1959, as he worked on *Structural Transformation*, Habermas read and critiqued Koselleck's dissertation, *Critique and Crisis*, a tour de force history of the Enlightenment that aimed to uncover the genealogy of modern totalitarianisms of both the Left and Right. Koselleck believed that a study of eighteenth-century Enlightenment would shed light on both National Socialism's "loss of reality and Utopian self-exaltation" and the "Utopian roots" of the Cold War that "prevented the two superpowers from simply recognizing each other as opponents" (1988, 2).

In eighteenth-century France, Koselleck detected social groups coalescing into a new bourgeois stratum that would form a constituency for Enlightenment ideologies. Excluded from full participation in the old Absolutist order, the members of society would meet at nonpolitical localities such as the exchanges, coffeehouses, academies, clubs, salons, and Masonic lodges—all exemplary bearers of Enlightenment sociability. The secrecy and seclusion characteristic of the lodges in particular "led to a form of existence which included the moral qualification to sit in judgment on that outside world....In their rejection of politics the Masons simultaneously established themselves as the world's better conscience.... They did nothing but think, enlighten, embody the spirit and act as carriers of light....But...political absence in the name of morality turned out to be an indirect political presence....Filled with the pathos of innocence, [their secrecy] concealed a revolution" (1988, 83). Koselleck argues that the Enlightenment failed to recognize its own political will-to-power. His diagnosis of the ongoing crisis was that from the time of the Enlightenment state power has been sub-jected to critique in a way that tends to promote instability and unleash civil war. Before the tribunal of reason, the bourgeois spirit "functioned simultaneously as prosecutor, as court of last resort, and—as a party" (10). Koselleck's critique was that in denying its own political interests the bourgeoisie had presumed to embody a spurious universality.

Thus, the Enlightenment spirit of criticism positioned itself on the side of the sphere of morality against the sphere of politics. Criticism, claiming to be nonpolitical (i.e., purely moral) concealed its own political will and claims access to the truth. "The King as ruler by divine right appears almost modest alongside the judge of mankind who replaced him, the critic.... The critic saw himself as the King of Kings, the true sovereign" (1988, 118–119). Koselleck claimed that the bourgeoisie failed to understand that their ongoing critiques would actually cause a revolution. The dialectic of morality and politics con-cealed as it intensified the prospect of revolution. In calling for the rule of law, "moral legitimacy is the politically invisible framework along which society, as it were, climbed up.... Being directly non-political, society nevertheless wants to rule indirectly through the moralization of politics" (154).

Although Koselleck's thesis about the relationship of Enlightenment and revo-lution was mostly original, his conceptual vocabulary was largely borrowed from Schmitt. The structure of his argument—how the Protestant development of an individual realm of conscience undermined political order by creating a space free from the sovereign in which the moralization of political discourse, with all its attendant destabilizing consequences, could begin—clearly replicates Schmitt's thesis in *The Leviathan in the State Theory of Thomas Hobbes* (2008). One of Schmitt's central theses—the irreducibility of the "political element"—is the clear inspiration behind Koselleck's critique of the false historico-philosophic con-sciousness of the Enlighteners. He claims that there was a widening breach between state and society, leading to the critique of the political by the social and the crisis of the political as such. It is striking how much of *Structural Transformation* one can discern, as if in outline, in Habermas's critical review of Koselleck's *Critique and Crisis*:

> In short the thesis of this book, that the indirect political power of established criti-cism necessarily instigates crisis, is not, in fact, convincing. This all-encompassing critique did in fact embrace politics, but at the same time did not renounce its own apolitical world, i.e., that which was reasonable, natural or moralistic. [By] identi-fying private convictions with public opinion and [by] discrediting the principle of public discussion as the outcome of the civil war, he misjudges the objective inten-tions of the public, which develop a new sphere based on a state emancipated from bourgeois society.... The intention was not the moralization of politics as such, but the arrangement of rationalization by the principle of publicity. (1960)

Where Koselleck labeled the interaction of state and society a hypocritical moralization of politics—of critique promoting while concealing crisis—Habermas argued that the classic bourgeois public sphere had successfully mediated between society and state. At the very time Habermas was searching for a new answer to a question Schmitt had posed in Weimar—What are the implications of the contemporary crisis of parliamentary democracy?—his reading of Koselleck directed him to the eighteenth-century social spaces of political critique. Where Koselleck updated Schmitt and Hobbes for the postwar German Right, Habermas stood Koselleck on his head, formulating the crisis of modern capitalist democracies for the Left in opposite terms: society did not have *enough* criticism to guide it, more legitimation through the rationalization of political domination.

THE SALIENCE OF SCHMITT IN HABERMAS'S POLITICAL THEORY, 1961–1992

In the 1960s and '70s, the terms of Habermas's reception of Schmitt changed from one set of problems—parliamentarism/plebiscitarianism, generality of the legal norm/arbitrary discretion of the executive branch, morality/politics, critique/crisis—to another problematic more focused on the concepts of decisionism and technocracy (Specter 2010, ch. 3). In a series of essays from the early 1960s Habermas continued to update a Schmittian trope—"the growing scope for pure decision"—by suggesting that the greatest obstacle to democracy was the short-circuiting of political praxis by technocratic elites (Habermas 1971, 43–81). Further, a contextual reading shows that the question of decisionism was the central motivation for Habermas's interest in the pragmatists. Throughout the 1960s and '70s, Habermas engaged in debates over university reform that often pitted him against Hermann Lübbe and Helmut Schelsky, two figures he regarded as modernizers of Schmittian decisionism (Moses 2008).

The 1970s were also the decade of Habermas's intellectual debate with Niklas Luhmann, the other most important social theorist of his West German generation. In 1971, Habermas and Luhmann together published their debate over the emancipatory potential of Luhmann's systems theory, which ended only with the publication of Habermas's *Theory of Communicative Action* (1984) and Luhmann's *Social Systems* (1995) and which left deep marks on Habermas's philosophy to this day. In *Legitimation Crisis* Habermas professed concerns about aspects of Luhmann's systems theory that he considered reminiscent of Schmitt: "[In Luhmann] the belief in legitimacy thus shrinks to a belief in legality: the appeal to the legal manner in which a decision comes about suffices" (1975, 98). In *Theory of Communicative Action*, Habermas notes Weber's "positivistic equation of legality and legitimacy," which he claims "lands him in an embarrassing situation," namely, "how can a legal domination whose legality is based on a law that is viewed purely in decisionistic terms (that is, a law that devalues all grounding in principle) be legitimated at all? Weber's answer, which has found adherents from Carl Schmitt to Niklas Luhmann, runs as follows: 'through procedure'" (1984, 265).

From the early 1970s through the early 1980s, Habermas often deployed the categories "neoconservative" and "Schmittian" interchangeably to describe a range of phenomena that concerned him. The problematics of decisionism, the relationship of legality to legitimacy, and the juridification of the welfare state are not central to Habermas's philosophical development in the 1970s, but they remain important touchstones in his political writings and to some extent in his social theory (Scheuerman 2011, 249). Throughout the 1970s, Habermas was politically preoccupied with the *Tendenzwende* (ideological shift), a description of a cluster of social trends: the polarizing effect of protests and counter-protests about university reform in 1968–1969; the economic contraction of 1973 and the accompanying backlash against the Social Democrat-Liberal coalition's expansion of the welfare state; the controversy over the Ban on Radicals (*Berufsverbot*) in the civil service; and the state's response to Red Army Faction terrorism in 1977 (*Deutscher Herbst* (Habermas 1985a; 1981, 311–465)).[10] In October 1982, Habermas delivered a lecture "Neoconservatism in the U.S. and the Federal Republic," in which he surveyed both the domestic and foreign policy dimensions of neoconservatism, attributing paternity for much of it to Schmitt (1985a). On the domestic side, technocratic leadership still threatened democracy, whereas on the foreign policy side, decisions made by the Kohl government to station nuclear missiles on German soil foregrounded the high stakes of the friend/enemy distinction in German politics. While neoconservatives exploited fears about internal and external security to legitimate their opposition to university reforms and curtailment of civil liberties (e.g., restrictions on the right of demonstration), the neoconservatives, following Hobbes and Schmitt, "proceed from the claim that the state must legitimize itself by defending itself against foreign and domestic enemies. This perspective explains the priority of the problem of inner security, above all the stylization of a competition between *Rechtsstaat* and democracy" (1985a, 50). It was in this context—of protestors who practiced civil disobedience to contest their government's decision about nuclear strategy—that Habermas began his decade-long re-investigation of the relationships of *Rechtsstaat* to democracy and *Rechtsstaat* to *Sozialstaat*.

In 1983, the *Rechtsstaat* appeared to Habermas threatened by authoritarian legalism in a manner reminiscent of the previous decade. He accorded the jurists a leading role in the drama that surrounded the citizen mobilization against the Euromissiles and described German jurisprudence as originating in "that curiously effective Hobbesianism elaborated in German constitutional theory by Carl Schmitt" the defining characteristic of which was that "questions of legitimation are subsumed under the problem of the guarantee of their legality, permitting politicians to avoid them" (Habermas 1985b, 107, 108). One problem in Habermas's formulations is that he characterizes the same line of statist German constitutional theory as at once Schmittian and legal positivist, when it is clear that Schmitt was not a legal positivist at all (Specter 2010). If it is the "legal positivist misunderstanding of militant democracy, which seeks to do away with the ambiguity of civil disobedience"—the "law is the law mentality"—that is to blame, it is not clear that Schmitt is the culprit, though it is true that the representatives of the mainstream postwar statist tradition in German jurisprudence were directly or indirectly influenced by Schmitt (Habermas 1985c, 35). Schmitt did not collapse legitimacy into legality but rather counterposed the primordiality of the former to the superficiality of the latter.

In any case, it is clear that Habermas in the early 1980s was, inspired in part by Rawls to rethink the liberal *Rechtsstaat*, in order to oppose the Schmittians whom he believed responsible for three major obstacles into a civic culture in Germany: stylizing the competition of *Rechtsstaat* and democracy in the name of social order; attempting to isolate a pristine *Rechtsstaat* uncontaminated by an expensive social welfare state (*Sozialstaat*); and misunderstanding the paradox of the *Rechtsstaat* by collapsing the discrete dimensions of legitimacy and legality. Habermas's breakthrough in 1983 was to emphasize the *Rechtsstaat's* dynamic, unfinished character—only thus understood would such a constitution be deserving of the citizen's patriotic devotion: no constitutional patriotism could be justified without a public culture of tolerance and respect for the progressive force of civil disobedience (Specter 2010, 133–170).

Between Facts and Norms: Contributions to a Discourse Theory of Democracy is Habermas's mature work in political theory and first sustained treatment of legal theory. In it, he returns to the theme of structural transformation but now from the vantage point of his theory of communicative action rather than the Hegelian–Marxist framework of the former. One of the purposes of the work was to rebut complaints that "his model of moral reasoning had no implications, or merely 'anarchistic' ones, for legal and political institutions" (Outhwaite 2009, 146). Taking up jurist Ulrich Preuß's definition of a constitution as a "fallible learning process," Habermas (1998b, 444) makes systematic insights he had obtained during the Euromissile crisis about the importance of civil disobedience in eliciting constitutional states' capacity to evolve. This model, which emphasizes the dynamic interrelationship between legality and legitimacy and between constitutional state and civil society, implicitly responds to the Schmittian critique. Where Schmitt had sought to exploit the alleged contradiction between legality and legitimacy, Habermas acknowledges the tension, but dissolves the paradox into a progressive dialectic between institutions and citizens.

Implicitly responding to the Schmittian juxtaposition of rule of law (*Rechtsstaat*) and welfare state (*Sozialstaat*), Habermas devotes a major section of *Between Facts and Norms* to transcending the two major postwar German legal paradigms: one focused on the negative rights of property; and the other concentrated on positive duties of material provision (Specter 2010, 171–202; Scheuerman 2011). Arguing that these paradigms have been in crisis since the 1970s, Habermas says that "the opaque and inconsistent structure of [today's] legal order has thus stimulated the search for a new paradigm beyond the familiar alternatives" (1998b, 390). Absent from both was a crucial supplement: individual autonomy requires civic participation in lawmaking; it cannot be secured merely through material redistribution.

Finally, to the Schmittian juxtaposition of *Rechtsstaat* and democracy, or rule of law and popular sovereignty, Habermas proposed a proceduralization of sovereignty that would break up sovereignty into a plurality of locations. He used words like *desubstantialized, disembodied,* and *fully dispersed* to characterize a popular sovereignty that should "withdraw" into democratic procedures (1998b, 486). Breaking up legislative power into institutionalized and non-institutionalized spaces—the parliament and a plurality of public spheres—was the only way to preserve the democratic ideal of popular self-determination, he believed, while eschewing the holism he found in certain forms of republicanism. Habermas's procedural reinterpretation of the republican tradition was designed in part as a rebuttal of Schmitt's theory of a homogeneous nation, anchored in a consciousness of its past, a "prepolitical" datum. Thus, on Habermas's reading it is Schmitt who fails to think politically enough about the becoming conscious of the demos, which creates itself by engaging insisted in "constitution-founding praxis" (486). In general, Habermas's mature statement of political theory was nourished by an engagement with Schmittian arguments that he considered uniformly dangerous.

THE SALIENCE OF SCHMITT IN HABERMAS'S INTERNATIONAL POLITICAL WRITINGS, 1996–2004

Rolf Wiggershaus dates the beginning of his cosmopolitan phase to Habermas's retirement from the university (2004, 131–141). In a footnote, his translator Ciaran Cronin notes that Habermas "has punctuated his writings on cosmopolitanism and international law with sharp polemics against Carl Schmitt" (Wiggershaus 2004, 194 n4). Cronin understates the relationship between the two thinkers because it reduces Schmitt's appearances to contingent and unnecessary ones, whereas Habermas indicates that Schmitt poses one of the most incisive challenges to Kant's moral universalism and belongs to a right-Hegelian tradition: "Carl Schmitt gave this argument (the critique of Kant's moral universalism) its most incisive formulation and offered a justification that is in part insightful, in part confused" (1998a, 188). Habermas's critical interrogations of Schmitt are thus better viewed as sites of creative work than mere occasions for polemic.

In 1999, Habermas argued in favor of the North Atlantic Treaty Organization (NATO) intervention in Yugoslavia, insisting that such an action would be legitimate even absent the Security Council resolution on which its legality would depend. The NATO action was criticized by many on the European left, some from a left-Schmittian perspective, who argued that it cloaked contingent political objectives in the dress of universal morality (Zolo 2002). Three years earlier, Habermas had an opportunity to rehearse these arguments in an essay written in honor of the bicentennial of Kant's famous essay of 1796 on the theme of perpetual peace (1998a, 165–202). He argued that Schmitt's critique of just war theory as the moralization of politics was mooted by the ratification of the United Nations (UN) charter. Since the charter provides the guidelines for defining whether wars are legal or illegal—not just or unjust—Schmitt's argument loses its force, insisted Habermas (see also 2006, 102).

In 2004, Habermas published several essays under the title *The Divided West* (2006); these take the events of September 11, 2001, and the beginning of the wars in Afghanistan and Iraq as their subject and once again point to major differences between his views about the utility of Schmittian ideas and those of other commentators on the left.[11] In these essays he restates the Kantian cosmopolitan vision of a world society he had already articulated in 1996 and 1999, but now with a greater sense of urgency about the stakes of failure. Once again, Habermas not only represents but also seems genuinely to perceive current events through the lens of a schematic choice between antipodes: Kant or Schmitt. To avoid the fragmentation of the globe into the endless and deadly competition of regional hegemons (and presumably also the depressing scenario in which progressives accept this as the only "realistic" option), Habermas implores the United States to return to the genuine internationalist path pioneered by Presidents Woodrow Wilson and Franklin Roosevelt (2006, 85). He argues that critics who emphasize the long-term continuities in U.S. imperialism risk trivializing the uniqueness of the George W. Bush Administration's break with international law, but Habermas's move also risks trivializing the history of U.S. imperialism in Latin America, Southeast Asia, the Pacific Rim, and Africa (95, 102, 181).

While some critics on the left thus suggested that the Bush Administration was simply admitting to an imperial mindset and behavior that the mainstream of U.S. policymakers had always shared, Habermas insists on the pace-setting role of the United States. He seems to envision the United States, once chastened and returned to its correct path, as the midwife of a cosmopolitan future. It is as if he is forced by his own logic—Kant or Schmitt?—to exaggerate the likelihood of the U.S. ability or willingness to bind itself to international law in a meaningful sense. Indeed, he argues that a self-abnegating superpower can be the midwife of cosmopolitanism. Since Habermas understands that a Schmittian hermeneutics of suspicion thrives where cosmopolitanism is too easily linked to the particular interests of an empire, it is a weak move to place his cosmopolitan bet on a far-sighted American empire. Thus he insists on a bright line of demarcation between self-asserting and self-transcending (or better, self-sublating) hegemons. Although "specific hegemonic acts that promote the juridification of international relations" may serve the interests of the hegemon, he observes, "hegemonic law is still law" (2006, 182; emphasis added). To this analysis, the probable left-Schmittian rejoinder would be to emphasize the obverse: "hegemonic law is still hegemonic." One's decision to follow Habermas or the left-Schmittian path in assessing our moment in American empire, humanitarian intervention, and international law is, one might say, a function of where one puts the stress in that sentence.

In sum, Habermas argued with Schmitt throughout his career because his many-faceted legacy in jurisprudence and political theory in the Federal Republic alarmed him, both as ideology and as political mood. Arguing with Schmitt provided a means of managing these anxieties by identifying a Schmittian etiology for numerous political pathologies. However, Habermas seems to recognize that the interest in Schmitt is symptomatic of a cluster of underlying problems (the right-Hegelian critique of Kantianism, the temptation of *Großraum* theory) that cannot be finally inoculated against.

LEFTIST APPROPRIATIONS OF SCHMITT SINCE THE MID-1980S: BALAKRISHNAN, MOUFFE, AND KALYVAS

Gopal Balakrishnan, Chantal Mouffe, and Andreas Kalyvas would all agree that the robustness of contemporary liberal democracies has been compromised and that Schmitt offers unique resources for their revival. Schmitt, the enemy of liberal democracy, is thereby reinvented as its friend. But this project fails to convince, because all three thinkers press on the tension Schmitt first identified in liberal democratic theory between liberalism and democracy. As is well-known, Schmitt in *The Crisis of Parliamentary Democracy* (1923) describes the two as inherently unrelated and in fact contradictory. Each of the thinkers discussed in this section wishes to emphasize the tension between liberalism, constitutionalism, or civic rights on the one hand and democracy and popular sovereignty on the other, rather than to deepen the bonds between them. While most liberal and democratic theorists recognize the tensions between the two traditions, they tend to look for ways to reconcile them. All three, by contrast, find inspiration and pathos in the dialectic of norm and exception and the furtive appearance of the demos.

The collapse of the USSR is the key historical factor behind the contemporary revival of Schmitt. From it emerge both the unipolar moment and the acceleration of processes of globalization dating back to the 1970s. Without the friend/foe polarity that had defined world politics for four decades, some worried about a dissolution of the world into a formless space. For others, the emergence of a U.S.-led neoliberal trade order under U.S. presidents George H. W. Bush and Bill Clinton was the real stimulus to the discovery of Schmitt.

If Bush's New World Order and Clinton's neoliberal trade agenda abroad and dismantling of welfare programs at home were rallying points for many on the left, the "War on Terror" launched by the United States and the George W. Bush Administration in the wake of the September 11, 2001 attacks represented a second historical turning point in the Western Left reception of Schmitt. If the end of the actual Cold War was one source of the Schmitt renaissance, the reappearance of mentalities reminiscent of the Cold War lent plausibility (and radical cachet) to the interpretation of Schmitt as a nonpartisan realist—a social scientist alert to the human penchant to divide societies into "us" and "them," or of the powerful to except themselves from the rules of the game.

Much as the Kosovo intervention had divided the Left, the Iraq War reiterated and deepened the split. For Balakrishnan and Danilo Zolo, Schmitt's epigram, "he who invokes humanity wants to cheat," seemed the most apposite description for NATO intervention; the ability of defenders and critics of the Iraq War alike to claim international law or human rights in their support seemed to underscore the conjunction of legal indeterminacy and imperial might (Zolo 2002). As Seyla Benhabib notes, "In the period before and after George Bush's Iraq War, Schmitt's work has found receptive audiences" (2011, 252 n12), among them the left political theorists Chantal Mouffe (1993; 1999a; 1999b; 2005a; 2005b) and Susan Buck-Morss (2008). An entire issue of *South Atlantic Quarterly* (2005) is devoted to discussion of Schmitt's *The "Nomos" of the Earth*. On the question of what's "left in Schmitt," the editor of the special issue, William Rasch, oscillates between two positions, which together reveal the difficulties that attend answering it. On the one hand, "Reading Schmitt, one quickly realizes that his prejudices and allegiances do not necessarily match one's own. Yet one also soon learns that one need not always sympathize with his sympathies to profit from his insights" (Rasch 2005, 180). On the other hand, though, "Carl Schmitt is an acquired taste.... It remains an intriguing and much-debated issue whether Schmitt can be harnessed by what's left of the Left in its attempt to think alternatives and strategies of resistance to the contemporary monolith.... The scholars in this collection are decidedly divided on this issue" (182).

One major theme that appears in the sections to follow is the unresolved tension between the Left-Schmittian critique of intrastate democratic politics and their critique of interstate politics. While Left-Schmittians recoil from the formlessness of the *pax Americana* or biopolitical empire because it appears to entrap us in universalizing discourses like those of human rights or humanitarian intervention, when it comes to politics within the nation-state formlessness becomes an important moment in democratic politics—the exceptional and unbounded moments which precede and renew the formal rules and regularities of quotidian or normal politics. Their refusal of explicit normative argument has allowed this contradiction to pass unnoticed.

BALAKRISHNAN'S RECEPTION OF SCHMITT

In the year 2000, a member of the *New Left Review* editorial board, the intellectual historian Gopal Balakrishnan, published the first English-language intellectual biography of Carl Schmitt in over a decade. In it, he made it clear that Schmitt warranted serious critical engagement because his writings offer fundamental insights to leftists concerned about the quality and depth of liberal democracy and the problem of empire in international relations. Schmitt's accounts, he contends, "are, at the very least, timely antidotes to the inebriating consensus which surrounds these big issues today" (Balakrishnan 2000, 261). Balakrishnan elaborates by arguing that Schmitt's emphasis on the foundational power of the sovereign people (*pouvoir constituant*) is therapeutic for today's Left:

> The Left can invoke this idea in its original radical democratic form as a concentrated public power capable of reining in the powers of private property. Those who thought of democracy as a dangerous, overreaching and unstable political system, even from an enemy perspective, have more to say about the meaning of radical democracy than an effete, incorporated, and culturalist Left. (2000, 265)

In short, since "the shrewdest analysts of democracy are sometimes its enemies," Schmitt's work offers resources to a Left creative enough to put him to uses other than those to which he was himself committed (265). Thus, while Schmitt explicitly rejected liberalism and Marxist socialism, never defended in theory or in practice any of the ideals historically defining of the Western Left since 1789—neither liberty, equality, nor fraternity, neither solidarity nor the dignity of labor, enfranchisement or participation, gender equality, a consistent anti-imperialism or the class struggle—Balakrishnan insists that Schmitt can be made a kind of intellectual ally despite himself.

Balakrishnan's reading of Schmitt through a Gramscian lens seems to recall the strategy employed by Mario Tronti, an Italian left reader of Schmitt, already in the early 1970s. As Müller writes: "Tronti pointed out that Schmitt's friend–enemy distinction could be mapped onto a new understanding of class antagonism…[and] to that end, any existing political and economic crisis also had to be radicalized in the direction of a real state of exception" (2003, 179). Balakrishnan argues that Habermas has misunderstood Schmitt's conception of homogeneity, which has no intrinsic anthropological (i.e., ethnonational) meaning. Instead, what homogeneity really meant to Schmitt was "the minimal threshold of political unity beneath which 'the people' dissolves into warring parties, each claiming to represent the whole" (2000, 263). Though Schmitt feared dissolution into civil war, "in his own way he recognized that it is only in the struggle for hegemony over 'the people'…that it [the people] becomes something more than an empty signifier of an imagined community" (263).

Redescribing Schmittian antagonism as Marxist class struggle raises questions about the feasibility of this synthesis. On what normative basis can one claim a privileged status for the standpoint of the proletariat (or if you prefer, the oppressed or exploited), if all universal norms have been reduced by the Schmittian logic to an expression of particular interests, profane, and having no abstract purchase on those who are not oppressed or exploited? On what basis is it possible to form hegemonic, cross-class coalitions when the category of justice has been stripped of any immanent or transcendent, or quasi-transcendental (*pace* Habermas) support? Perhaps this is another way of making the point Habermas (2006) makes in *The Divided West*: there is a key difference between a Schmittian and a Marxian critique of universality. And this difference is what gets lost in the Left's current enthusiasm for Schmitt: "Just as every objection raised against the selective or one-sided application of universalistic standards must already presuppose these same standards, so too does any deconstructive unmasking…actually presuppose the critical viewpoints advanced by these same discourses."[12] Philosopher Richard Bernstein (2011, 413–415, 422–424) makes the same point a different way, pointing out that Schmitt's political theory smuggles normative-moral commitments into his purportedly neutral diagnoses. For example, the force of Schmitt's critique of absolute enmity depends on a crypto-normative judgment, namely, that the more limited enmity secured by the *jus publicum Europaeum* was superior because it did not lead to the degradation of the enemy but entailed recognition of his status as legitimate combatant, a status connected to the humanistic tradition of respect for the dignity of persons.

Balakrishnan goes equally astray in his appropriation of Schmitt for a critique of the U.S. role in contemporary international relations. For example, he makes the astonishing claim (and untenable given the existence of transnational networks which traverse and embed states, denaturing them quite thoroughly) that the international arena is best described as a "state of nature." As he writes, "Here we leave behind the rule of law and enter the state of nature—a zone where the fictions of legality can be particularly pernicious" (Balakrishnan 2000, 265). This emphasis on the international realm as a state of nature recalls Hobbesian arguments that had long since been incorporated into the dominant strand of the realist tradition in international relations theory exemplified by Hans Morgenthau.[13] The problem with the wave of realism that arose on the antiwar Left was that it ended up replicating the pessimism about international institutions and cynicism about international law already characteristic of many neoconservatives and realists. At the moment of convergence between neoconservative critiques and left-Schmittian critiques of international law, Habermas's countervailing defense of universal principles in international affairs was a valuable corrective to both. Habermas eschewed some realists' obsession with the alleged naturalness of the nation-state and its unquestioned and clearly reified "national interests" and the Leftist analogues that mirrored it.

Written one year before Habermas's work, *A Dangerous Mind*, by Jan-Werner Müller, reflected cogently on the weaknesses of the new left-Schmittian critique of international relations:

> It remained unclear whether the Left was celebrating the return of open international conflict because anything was preferable to the triumph of the global market, or whether the inevitably conflictual nature of politics had to be reasserted.... Unable to live with the organized hypocrisy and "legal fictions" of the international order, some seemed to wish for the great immediate cataclysm, rather than live with the ambiguities of piecemeal progress in a highly complex and highly mediated world. (Müller 2003, 231)

On the one hand, Müller locates an impatience with melioristic politics at the root of the left-Schmittian appeal, psychologizing it as a despairing "apocalyptic temperament" (231). On the other hand, he posits a sociological basis for the return of Schmitt—the deterritorialization of power in an age of globalization: "As the spatial structures of politics became reconfigured in unpredictable and unsettling ways, the craving for a return to an 'episteme of separation' increased," a craving which "united forces on the Left and the Right" (231). What Müller calls this episteme links Agamben's anxiety about the formation of zones of indistinct sovereignty—Guantanamo, for example, to Hardt and Negri's concern about the erasure of barriers to empire, and also to Huntington's mid-1990s prediction of a coming clash of civilizations that would give the lie to the false confidence in unipolarity, unilateralism, and universal human rights. One irony of Balakrishnan's (2000) appropriation of Schmitt of international law, therefore, is that while it is made anxious by formlessness, and thus driven by a longing for form, it is the formalism of international law—its implicit promise that all like cases will be treated alike—that most excites its contempt.[14]

KALYVAS'S RECEPTION OF SCHMITT

In 2009, political theorist Andreas Kalyvas published *Democracy and the Politics of the Extraordinary: Max Weber, Carl Schmitt, Hannah Arendt*. While Balakrishnan (2000) finds value in Schmitt's writings on international law during the "Third Reich," Kalyvas cordons off the post-1933 theorist for the Reich altogether. Both agree on the value of his Weimar-era reflections on the relationship of liberalism, democracy, and constitutionalism, and Kalyvas further insists on the "huge differences between Schmitt's political and legal theory and the politics of the NSDAP" (2009, 148–149 n80). He continues, "Although aspects of Schmitt's theory remain unattractive, especially those referring to a plebiscitarian executive, his professed concern before 1933 to 'safeguard and assure the constitution of the Reich in force' against the centrifugal political forces of the communist and Nazi parties should not be disregarded" (162). But if this is so, how to account for the pathos of the attack on liberalism in both *Crisis of Parliamentary Democracy* and *The Concept of the Political*, which provided no respite for the Republic, written as they in the brief parenthesis of stability in Weimar's history, when the Republic was stabilized by international loans and had a chance of survival? Further, of what value is a theory of democratic constitutionalism that has no place for what Habermas calls public discussion guided by arguments (as Kalyvas, to his credit, admits in a concession to Habermas's critique of Schmitt; see 2009, 125)? Kalyvas himself blurs the pre- and post-1933 Schmitt when he asserts that Schmitt's theory of the president as guardian of the constitution "clouds his notion of normal politics and could partly explain his infamous turn to Nazism" (159).

Like Balakrishnan, Kalyvas writes that Schmitt "was captivated by the genuine capacity of the groundless creative power of the multitude, the unformed [*formlos*] form of all forms to create order out of chaos" (Kalyvas 2009, 134). To be sure, Kalyvas wants us to note that there is a less familiar Schmitt, who "was equally attentive to [the multitude's] need for self-limitation, that is, to the second, ordinary face of democratic politics" (134). But the major objective of his book is to emphasize the creative power in extraordinary democratic politics. Like Balakrishnan, Kalyvas argues that one can "reconstruct" a thinker like Schmitt against the grain, "disassociating [him] from [his] explicit political motivations and objectives, intellectual contexts and philosophical assumptions" (13). What value does Schmitt have for democratic theory? Kalyvas explains that he relies "upon and further [develops] Schmitt's attempt to extricate constitutionalism from the liberal tradition in order to take it in a more democratic direction" (14). Elsewhere, he elaborates that "Schmitt never described his project in terms of a rejection of constitutionalism. Before his 'turn' in 1933, he never provided a theoretical or political justification of permanent dictatorship" (129). Quite the contrary, Schmitt's major constitutional treatise, the *Verfassungslehre* of 1928, is one piece of a broader "effort to redefine the nature of constitutionalism," in terms broader and more positive than "government limited by the rule of law" (130). Thus, in Kalyvas's revisionist interpretation, Schmitt emerges not only as a resource for the Left in thinking moments and levels of extraordinary politics but also as a theorist who recognizes the value of the regular dimensions of politics too: "Schmitt was fully aware that democracy requires a stable, predictable, and secure political order, where laws will guarantee regularity and diminish indeterminacy" (135). As Kalyvas continues, "The people do not need to be constantly mobilized and activated. With a constitution they can rest. Against the model of an excessive politicization of society, he proposed the temporal limitation and juridical containment of the popular constituent sovereign during ordinary times" (133). At the level of abstraction at which he here reads him, Kalyvas quietly discards Schmitt's distinctive and dangerous baggage. Schmitt's theory of democratic politics is said to "share some remarkable similarities with Bruce Ackerman's theory of 'dualist democracy,'" the notion that politics divides into two different ideal-typical phases: that of higher and normal lawmaking. Obscured therefore is the centrality to Schmitt's system of what Kalyvas anodynely names his "authoritarian preferences."

All of this reasonableness and moderation reaches its apex in Kalyvas's depiction of Schmitt as an advocate of constitutional patriotism *avant la lettre*: "Schmitt argued, in a tone that anticipates today's discussions about constitutional patriotism that 'unity rests, therefore, before anything first in the Constitution, recognized by all parties; in fact, the constitution, which is the common foundation demands an unconditional respect'" (2009, 161).[15] But how to distinguish between the essential and the conditional, the amendable and the nonamendable, in any constitution? Kalyvas argues that Schmitt's key distinction between the constitution (*Verfassung*) and the constitutional law (*Verfassungsgesetz*) performs this work (139). Citing similar distinctions in the work of John Rawls, Carl Friedrich, and Andrew Arato, Kalyvas concludes that the belief that there is a substantive core to any constitution sets limits to the amending powers, which stems from the lower "procedural" part of any constitution (142–143). Schmitt's distinctions therefore strengthen, not handicap, constitutionalism: "The constitution, in its 'absolute' form, is not a formal list of abstract principles and individual rights juxtaposed to the state and the political sphere, nor a set of neutral procedures aimed at encircling and policing political power. Rather it is a positive document that embodies the fundamental, substantive values and founding popular decisions of a political community" (132).

Kalyvas is not the first thinker to suggest that Schmitt may in fact be considered the father of the Basic Law: that constitution established a clear hierarchy between the substantive and procedural sections of the constitution (2009, 132; see also Lietzmann 1988). In a 1953 essay, Schmitt took credit for having developed one of the signature features of the Basic Law (the constitution that governed West Germany after 1949): the so-called eternity clause, or Article 79, Section 3, which declares the Basic Law's commitment to a "free, democratic basic order," unchallengeable in perpetuity (Schmitt 1958, 345). While Schmitt himself sought to claim paternity for this aspect of the postwar German constitution, a number of historical facts discount this genealogy. First, while the drafters of the Basic Law may have drawn on Schmitt, they probably found more inspiration in Karl Loewenstein (1937), who articulated the more historically proximate notion of a militant democracy. Schmitt was not the only theorist asserting that Bonn should not be Weimar. And although he may have retrospectively tried to portray himself as a theorist of stability (much as Kalyvas does), there is evidence that this was either an expression of vanity, duplicity, or both. Second, Forsthoff and Weber, Schmitt's students, rejected the Bonn constitution as the product of an exogenous decision imposed by the Allies too weak to contain the force of the political (Müller 2003, 66). In short, the claim that the Basic Law was fundamentally a Schmittian text is belied by the resistance to it of the most visible Schmittians in the Federal Republic.[16] The wording of the eternity clause leaves no doubt that Schmitt's claim to its paternity is fallacious since among the provisions it guarantees in perpetuity is Article 20, which defines the Federal Republic as a democratic, legal, and social state (*Sozialstaat*); the *Sozialstaat* was an unremitting target of critique in the 1950s by both Schmitt and his pupils. Militant democracy was and is problematic in many ways, but not because it illustrated an excess of Schmittian commitment.

Moreover, the attempt to make Schmitt a precursor of both the Basic Law's fundamental commitments and the notion of constitutional patriotism, or a moderately conservative avatar for Ackerman, misses the more complex story of Schmitt's reception on both the left and right in the Federal Republic. As Preuß argues, Schmitt's "main distinction" was between the "political essence of the constitution which confers superior legality of certain values, and which he calls legitimacy—and those parts which embody the rights, institutions and procedures of an inferior notion of legality, which essentially apply to the practice of pluralist democracy" (1999, 167). In the late 1960s and early 1970s, Preuß was one of a number of left-wing critics of West German society and the Constitutional Court, who found in Schmitt's legality/legitimacy distinction a useful vocabulary for naming the emergence of a new enemy: superlegality, or a superconstitution, which had gained supremacy in the Federal Republic.

By the late 1990s, however, Preuß had arrived at a much more critical estimate of Schmitt's value. Drawing any such boundary line within the constitution is inherently dangerous, not because it precludes a socialist transformation of the economy or reveals the "latent dictatorship of the bourgeois state" (as quoted in Müller 2003, 185 n14) but rather because it abets the most powerful conservative forces in society. "This approach implies the inescapable consequence that in the case of a serious conflict or a crisis, the substantive values claim priority," entailing that "those social and political forces which are in a position to assert successfully that they are the exponents of the 'true,' 'genuine,' or 'authentic' spirit of the constitution have the power to define the 'enemies' of the constitution, and hence to demarcate the realm of...'legitimate' and loyal democratic dissent" (Preuß 1999, 167–168). The major Schmittian legacy in the Federal Republic, Preuß argues, is the statist tendency in German constitutional reasoning, which he characterizes in terms that directly refute Balakrishnan and Kalyvas. This tendency, "more or less consciously, relies on the doctrine of the pre-constitutional political existence of the people and its incarnation in the state, being concerned in the first instance with the preservation of the unity, homogeneity and integrity of its power" (169). As we saw already, Habermas argues that Schmitt describes the demos as a homogeneous prepolitical datum usually ethnic or national in character and therefore insufficiently inclusive to be suitable for modern pluralist societies. Kalyvas, by contrast, argues that "too much ink has been wasted over [Schmitt's] alleged glorification of substance, homogeneity, and identity. What he advocated was much more prosaic and commonsensical: democracy can only exist in the movement toward the elimination of political inequalities and political conflict, and the removal of the distance between rulers and ruled" (2009, 155).

The price of reading Schmitt at such a high level of abstraction is that Kalyvas brackets something as fundamental as Schmitt's rejection of pluralism. But to claim that this is what Schmitt really meant (i.e., what he advocated) is contradicted by the findings of intellectual history. Given what the historian Raphael Gross (2007) and others have discovered about the depth of Schmitt's investments in a specifically ethno-national form of homogeneity, namely, the Aryan–German one cleansed of Jewish membership, it is difficult to stomach the claim that Schmitt's requirement that democracies be homogeneous is only common sense.

MOUFFE'S RECEPTION OF SCHMITT

In a plethora of books and articles written between 1991 and 2008, political theorist Chantal Mouffe argued that Carl Schmitt is the most relevant and profound theorist of democracy and pluralism for our time. Like Balakrishnan, Mouffe considers Schmitt's writings especially timely tools for resisting the two primary arenas of depoliticization since the end of the Cold War: the post-1990 narrowing of the spectrum of Western political debate toward the center (e.g., Clinton's presidency or UK prime minister Tony Blair's tenure); and the arrogant American conflation of its status as sole remaining superpower with the triumph of liberal democratic values, in short, of unipolarity misrepresented as universalism. "*The Concept of the Political* was originally published in 1932 [sic], but Schmitt's critique is more relevant now than ever. If we examine the evolution of liberal thought since then, we ascertain that it has indeed moved between economics and ethics" (Mouffe 2005a, 12). Mouffe appears fascinated with Schmitt because of his perceived relevance to diverse theaters of contemporary life. Schmitt's concept of the political seems as relevant to the contest between different models of democracy in the academy (i.e., the aggregative interest model and the deliberative reasoning one) as it is to the projection of U.S. power in the post-Cold War world (neoliberal economic policies accompanied by moralistic deployments of state violence against other states and terrorists). Her texts imply the question: Can a theory that dovetails so well with contemporary discourses be prudently neglected, let alone shunned? Mouffe's rendering of the contemporary situation in democratic theory and global politics yields a close fit between the two spheres but one that is more an artifact of her own reading of Schmitt than inherent in these spheres.

Further, it is unclear why, given her assessment of the theory's specific historicity and timeliness, Mouffe distills Schmittian insights into sweeping transhistorical generalizations: "By 'the political' I refer to the dimension of antagonism that is inherent in all human society.... 'Politics' consists in trying...to defuse the potential antagonism that exists" (1999a, 754). She continues: "All politics creates an 'us' by determination of a 'them'; agonistic politics does not try to overcome it through discussion or deliberation, but to recognize the legitimate adversary" (755).

Like Kalyvas, Mouffe does her due diligence, making all the necessary caveats about Schmitt's professional choices, personal prejudices, and political intentions, insisting that a theorist's use of Schmitt, thus koshered, as it were, should be uncontroversial: "I would have thought everybody should be able to understand that it is possible to use Schmitt against Schmitt—to use his insights of his critique of liberalism in order to consolidate liberalism—while recognizing that this was not, of course, his aim" (1999a, 52 n2). Mouffe's claim that one can use Schmitt's insights to strengthen or consolidate liberal democracy is a curious one given his fundamental antipathy to liberalism. While Mouffe equivocates between rejecting liberalism and claiming to consolidate it, it would be more accurate to say that she aims at a redescription of modern democratic practice—"a new understanding of democratic politics" (2005a, 14). In place of deliberative democracy, she offers her "agonistic" politics, a theory that she claims reconciles essential Schmittian insights with the pluralism of modern multicultural societies. But on closer scrutiny, her new understanding merely utilizes Schmitt's transgressive vocabulary to redescribe the agonistic political practice long conventional to all Western democracies.

Mouffe argues that the deliberative democratic model common to Rawls and Habermas denies, devalues, or underestimates the centrality of antagonism in human society and politics, and offers an illusory fantasy of rational consensus in its place. Transforming potentially violent antagonisms into manageable agonisms is hardly a radical or novel idea (consider the *Federalist Papers*), but Mouffe believes that the dominance of the deliberative model in some sections of the academy warrant a reminder of it:

> When we accept that every consensus exists as a temporary result of a provisional hegemony, as a stabilization of power, and that always entails some form of exclusion, we can begin to envision the nature of a democratic public sphere in a new way. An approach that reveals the impossibility of establishing a consensus without exclusion is of fundamental importance for democratic politics [because it] forces us to keep the democratic contestation alive. (1995b, 756–757)

Mouffe again runs into a contradiction: if the key advantage of her understanding of democratic pluralism is that it foregrounds rather than camouflages the exclusions that result from every consensus implemented (her provisional hegemony), then why does she restrict the field of democratic contestation to those who agree on the ground rules of democracy in the first place?

> The novelty of democratic politics is not the overcoming of this us/them distinction—which is what a consensus without exclusion pretends to achieve—but the different way in which it is established. What is at stake is how to establish the us/them distinction in a way that is compatible with pluralist democracy. In the realm of politics, this presupposes that the "other" is no longer seen as an enemy to be destroyed, but as an "adversary."... This category of the "adversary" should be distinguished from the liberal notion of the "competitor" with which it is sometimes identified. An adversary is a legitimate enemy, an enemy with whom we have in common a shared adhesion to the ethico-political principles of democracy. (1995b, 755)

The banality of Mouffe's formulations of agonistic politics suggests an idealist distortion of the issues at stake. As a close reading of the journal *Telos*'s early reception of Schmitt also reveals, frustration with Habermasian and Rawlsian ideas within the academy—and not a failure of liberal democratic institutions *per se*—appears to be the real problem preoccupying many Left Schmittians.

Mouffe's description of international relations mimics her description of politics within nation-states; the common denominator is her commitment to agonistic pluralism. In "Schmitt's Vision of a Multipolar World Order," Mouffe applies insights she finds in Schmitt's wartime *The "Nomos" of the Earth* to challenge the hegemony of the United States in its unipolar moment: "The central problem that our current unipolar world is facing is that it is impossible for antagonisms to find legitimate forms of expression. It is no wonder, then, that those antagonisms when they emerge take extreme forms" (2005b, 250–251). Mouffe acknowledges that al-Qaeda's terrorism—one such expression of dissent—has multiple sources, but she gives pride of place to neoliberal globalization under an American aegis: "To create the channels for legitimate expression of dissent, we need to envisage a pluralistic world order constructed around a certain number of great spaces and cultural poles" (250–251). Here we see a perfect example of the fatal *Zeitgeist* appeal of Carl Schmitt's theory of great spaces, as Habermas calls it in *The Divided West* (2006). Mouffe's error recapitulates Balakrishnan's (2000): In the name of anti-imperialism, a preemptive strike is made against the cosmopolitanism with which it is conflated, and all that remains is classical realism's balance of power, now rewarmed and served *à la* Schmitt.

CONCLUSION

That the most influential architect of aversion to Schmitt, Jürgen Habermas, also exemplifies creative appropriation from him is one important irony that springs from the effort to answer the question, what's "left" in Schmitt? But there is also a second such irony. The journal that almost single-handedly sparked the Schmitt renaissance with its

1987 issue—*Telos*—arrived at its iconoclastic decision to revive Schmitt in part out of the editors' frustration with the ascendance of Habermas's own theory of communicative action (see Habermas, 1981) within critical theory. This is evident in both the journal's 1987 issue and in the forum *Telos* generated for its hundredth issue in 1994.[17] However, today Rawls seems to be as important an antagonist for the new Left-Schmittians as is Habermas. As Richard Bernstein notes, "Part of the attraction of Schmitt by Left thinkers is that he provides sharp weapons for criticizing the normativism and rationalism of thinkers such as John Rawls and Jürgen Habermas" (2011, 404). Today's Schmitt revival on the Left is motivated not only by professionals who feel suffocated by Habermasian or Rawlsian ideas in the academy but also by many thoughtful leftists who believe that politics within the North Atlantic democracies and in international relations alike can benefit from the sobering tonic that Schmitt's so-called realism provides (404). At its narrowest, the new Left-Schmittianism represents a protest against the intellectual hegemony of Habermas and Rawls in some political theory circles. I presented evidence for the latter in the writings of Mouffe, Bernstein, Rasch, and Balakrishnan.

The Schmitt revival of the last quarter-century precedes the collapse of the Soviet Bloc but was intensified by it. Generalizing broadly, one might say that the pulling up of one of the symbolic anchors of the twentieth-century's political imagination disoriented or demoralized many leftists. The revolutions in 1989 unmoored the communist Left but also weakened the morale of the democratic noncommunist Left that found itself on the defensive. From the early 1970s, the steering capacity of national welfare states in an increasingly globalized economy declined. The traditional electoral strength and ideological salience of the postwar Social Democratic Left also declined through the 1980s, and some leftists may have felt cowed by the prevailing mood of Cold War triumphalism. Since Rawls and Habermas were connected in some minds with this postwar Social Democratic consensus (even if their thought was never reducible to these social projects), their thought also became a target of critique. The end of the Cold War resulted in a unipolar moment of U.S. hegemony that seemed to invite a critique in the name of multipolarity.

All of these factors converged in the rise of a post-Marxist Left of poststructuralist or postmodernist type. Mouffe's exploration of Schmitt's utility for the Left began with her *Hegemony and Socialist Strategy* (1985). For Mouffe (1999b, 752–754), Schmitt is a poststructuralist *avant la lettre*, a thinker who eschews the weaknesses of orthodox Marxism by remaining alert to the relational (and therefore antiessentialist qualities of political identities) and thus the desire for an illusory final reconciliation or social harmony (the world beyond class struggle). While the post-Marxist Left threw out Marx with the Stalinist bathwater, representatives of the noncommunist democratic Left like Habermas did not experience the collapse of the Soviet Bloc in 1989 as an intellectual crisis. This differential experience of 1989 is one of the historical roots of the divergence between appropriations and aversions to Schmitt.

Some may wonder if Habermas's aversion to Schmitt reflects an overinvestment in a left/right distinction salient before 1989 but obsolescent since. Left-Schmittians then might appear to be displaying an admirable audacity in the face of outdated labels.

But a reading of the 1990s suggests Habermas was not the only thinker stuck on the left/right distinction. At the national-political level, Schmitt also spoke to theorists concerned in the 1990s with a perceived ideological constriction of the political spectrum, the much discussed notion of convergence on a "Third Way" in the Clinton/Blair era. Thus contextualized, the Left's turn to Schmitt does not provide evidence of a desire to rethink the meaning of left and right so much as a nostalgia for a truly Left position that can resist the blandishments of the center. For Balakrishnan and Mouffe, Schmitt was the thinker who could re-anchor the Left that was drifting unmoored toward the center of the political spectrum.

Beyond the intradisciplinary context and the national-political one is the international context for the Schmitt revival. I have emphasized the advance of globalization since 1989, the war on Iraq begun in 2003, and the ongoing war on terror as sources of Schmitt's appeal. Leftists have discovered a passing affinity between Carl Schmitt's resentment of Wilsonian moralism and their own frustrations with the moralistic hubris of the sole remaining superpower and have mistaken the affinity of the moment for transhistorical truths about a mythological abstraction—"the political." Schmitt is only the most recent practitioner of the hermeneutics of suspicion to capture the imagination of Western academics seeking contact with the hard surfaces of reality. But Schmitt's so-called realism about international affairs is in fact a set of ontological assumptions about the perpetuity of struggle that evacuates history of agency and contingency and any recognition of the facticity of normative claims. In short, he who aspires to be realistic about politics has no need of Carl Schmitt.

In the struggle for the Left's broader ideals critical reason, private autonomy, democratic self-determination, and solidarity with the oppressed, is it really Habermas and Rawls who stand in the way of their realization? Left-Schmittians succumb to a kind of exaggerated idealism in making Rawls and Habermas the touchstone of their critique of the weaknesses of contemporary liberal democracy and international law. Not only do they misdiagnose liberalism's core challenges, but they also choose the wrong remedies: tempted by Schmitt's pathos-laden rhetoric, Left-Schmittians have struggled in vain to formulate appropriations of Schmitt that can transcend the conspicuous weaknesses, aporias—and inconsistencies with traditional left values—of the master.

Notes

1. Jan-Werner Müller asserts that Habermas's "The Horror of Autonomy: Carl Schmitt in English," published in *The New Conservatism* in 1994, represented a "preemptive strike" against a broader Schmitt reception in the Anglo-American world—"trying to preempt those on the left tempted by the Schmittian antithesis" (2003, 195).
2. Thus does my work on Habermas concur with Scheuerman's 2011 observations: "Habermas's similarly reveal an impressive familiarity with Schmitt's far-flung writings along with deep political and moral revulsion.... In any event, opposition to Schmitt runs like a red thread throughout his political and legal theorizing" (Specter 2010, 248).

3. See, for example, Strong, who argues that before 1934–1935 Schmitt "had been of importance to thinkers across the entire political spectrum.... Important liberals such as Carl Friedrich and Hans Morgenthau found significant insights in Schmitt" (2011, 33).

4. Unless noted otherwise, all translations of source material by the author.

5. Author's private correspondence with Habermas, October 24, 2008. He is referring to Kornhauser 1959; Lipset 1960.

6. The 1958 text has never been translated; it was first published in 1961. A *Habilitation* is the second doctoral-length dissertation that was traditionally required of German academics to qualify for a professorship.

7. Peter Caldwell seconds this: "Habermas's discussion of the rise and all of democratic republicanism and the 'public' made use of both Schmitt's concept of representation and his assessment of what happens when interest groups occupy and structure public discussion. While Habermas was certainly aware of Schmitt's personal involvement with Nazism, Schmitt's antisemitic worldview played no role in Habermas's analysis" (as quoted in Gross 2007, ix).

8. Thus, Ellen Kennedy's observation is correct about genealogy but not about the significance of the appropriation because it misses the purpose to which it is put: "In *Student und Politik*, Habermas draws on Forsthoff's analysis of the development of the liberal state into an agent of collective welfare; he incorporates Schmitt's arguments that the attendant structural changes imply a decay of (1) the generality of norms (2) individual rights and (3) the division of powers to protect both" (1987, 58).

9. In *Student und Politik*, "Habermas updated a core thesis that Neumann and Ernst Fraenkel (both also Sinzheimer students) had formulated in the 1930s: With the transition from competitive to monopoly or organized capitalism, the classical rule of law and especially the central place of the general legal norm necessarily found itself under attack" (Scheuerman 2011, 245).

10. Moses 2008 is the best source on the contests over university reform in the 1970s.

11. Habermas 2006 (except for chs. 1, 2, and 7, which were first published elsewhere).

12. "What fascists seem to overlook and what Marx clearly saw, is the other aspect of a [universalistic] discourse: the peculiar self-reference that first makes it into a vehicle for self-correcting learning processes" (Habermas 2006, 24).

13. For the Schmitt–Morgenthau link, see Koskenniemi 2000; for a dissenting, rehabilitative view, see William Scheuerman's book on Morgenthau (2009) which defends a non-Schmittian realism for the Left.

14. For a sampling of Schmitt-inspired critiques of U.S. imperialism and the War on Terror, see Rasch 2005. Rasch's essays on the subject date back to 2002.

15. Finally, as Preuß—one of the German Left's most attentive students of Schmitt—clarifies, there were "ambiguities" in Schmitt's concept of the "spirit of the constitution," which the framers of the Basic Law took pains to eliminate (1999, 166).

16. See the discussions in *Telos*: de Benoist 1995 (73–89).

17. See Piccone and Ulmen 1987; Luke 1994 (101–108); Gross 1994 (110–116); Ost 1994 (137–154). As Ost remarks, "Coming a scant five years after the disillusionment with the victorious communist regimes in Southeast Asia, the failure of the Solidarity movement in Poland was the last straw turning most of the Western New Left toward liberalism and modernity. The *Telos* editorial board split on this issue. The dispute focused around Habermas and the concept of civil society" (1994, 140).

452   MATTHEW G. SPECTER

References

Balakrishnan, G. 2000. *The Enemy: An Intellectual Portrait of Carl Schmitt*. London: Verso.

Benhabib, S. 2011. *Dignity in Adversity: Human Rights in Troubled Times*. Cambridge: Polity Press.

Benoist, A. de. 1995. "End of the Left–Right Dichotomy: The French Case." *Telos* 102: 73–89.

Bernstein, R. 2011. "The Aporias of Carl Schmitt." *Constellations* 18: 403–430.

Buck-Morss, S. 2008. "Sovereign Right and Global Left." *Cultural Critique* 69: 145–171.

D'Amico, R. 1994. "Is there a 'Telos' left in *Telos*? Reflections after 100 Issues." *Telos* 101: 97–109.

Gross, D. 1994. "Where Is *Telos* Going?" *Telos* 101: 110–116.

Gross, Raphael. 2007. *Carl Schmitt and the Jews: The "Jewish Question," the Holocaust, and German Legal Theory*, trans. J. Golb. Madison: University of Wisconsin Press.

Habermas, J. 1960. "Zur Kritik an der Geschichtsphilosophie (R. Koselleck, H. Kesting)." *Merkur* 14: 468–477.

Habermas, J. 1961. *Strukturwandel der Öffentlichkeit*. Neuwied: Luchterhand.

Habermas, J. 1961. "Reflexionen über den Begriff der politischen Beteiligung." In *Student und Politik*, ed. L. v. Friedeburg et al. Neuwied: Luchterhand, 11–55.

Habermas, J. 1971. "The Classical Doctrine of Politics and its Relation to Social Philosophy." In *Theory and Practice*, trans. J. Viertel. Boston: Beacon Press, 41–81.

Habermas, J., and N. Luhmann. 1971. *Theorie der Gesellschaft oder Sozialtechnologie: Was leistet die Systemforschung?* Frankfurt: Suhrkamp.

Habermas, J. 1975. *Legitimation Crisis*, trans. T. McCarthy. Boston: Beacon Press.

Habermas, J. 1981. "Vol. III: Tendenzwende." In *Kleine Politische Schriften I-IV*, ed. J. Habermas. Frankfurt: Suhrkamp, 311–466.

Habermas, J. 1984. *The Theory of Communicative Action*, vol. 1: *Reason and the Rationalization of Society*, trans. T. McCarthy. Boston: Beacon Press.

Habermas, J. 1985a. "Die Kulturkritik der Neokonservativen in den USA und in der Bundesrepublik." In *Die Neue Unübersichtlichkeit: Kleine Politische Schriften V*, ed. J. Habermas. Frankfurt: Suhrkamp, 30–58.

Habermas, J. 1985b. "Recht und Gewalt—ein Deutsches Trauma." In *Die Neue Unübersichtlichkeit: Kleine Politische Schriften V*, ed. J. Habermas. Frankfurt: Suhrkamp, 100–120.

Habermas, J. 1985c. "Ziviler Ungehorsam—Testfall für den demokratischen Rechtsstaat: Wider den autoritären Legalismus in der Bundesrepublik." In *Die Neue Unübersichtlichkeit: Kleine Politische Schriften V*, ed. J. Habermas. Frankfurt: Suhrkamp, 79–99.

Habermas, J. 1985d. "Über den doppelten Boden des demokratischen Rechtsstaates." In *Eine Art Schadensabwicklung: Kleine Politische Schriften VI*, ed. J. Habermas. Frankfurt: Suhrkamp, 18–24.

Habermas, J. 1989. *The Structural Transformation of the Public Sphere: An Inquiry Into a Category of Bourgeois Society*, trans. T. Burger with F. Lawrence. Cambridge: MIT Press.

Habermas, J. 1998a. *The Inclusion of the Other: Studies in Political Theory*, ed. C. Cronin and P. De Greiff. Cambridge: MIT Press.

Habermas, J. 1998b. *Between Facts and Norms: Contributions to a Discourse Theory of Law and Democracy*, trans. W. Rehg. Cambridge: MIT Press.

Habermas, J. 2006. *The Divided West*. Cambridge: Polity Press.

Herf, J. 1986. *Reactionary Modernism: Technology, Culture, and Politics in Weimar and the Third Reich*. Cambridge: Cambridge University Press.

Kalyvas, A. 2009. *Democracy and the Politics of the Extraordinary: Max Weber, Carl Schmitt, and Hannah Arendt*. Cambridge: Cambridge University Press.

Kennedy, E. 1987. "Carl Schmitt and the Frankfurt School." *Telos* 71: 37–66.

Koselleck, R. 1988. *Critique and Crises: Enlightenment and the Pathogenesis of Modern Society*. Cambridge: MIT Press.

Koskenniemi, M. 2000. "Carl Schmitt, Hans Morgenthau and the Image of Law in International Relations." In *The Role of Law in International Politics: Essays in International Relations and International Law*, ed. M. Byers. New York: Oxford University Press, 17–34.

Lietzmann, H. 1988. "Vater der Verfassungsväter?" In *Carl Schmitt und die Liberalismuskritik*, ed. K. Hansen and H. Lietzmann. Opladen: Leske und Budrich.

Loewenstein, K. 1937. "Militant Democracy and Fundamental Rights, II." *American Political Science Review* 31: 638–658.

Luhmann, N. 1995. *Social Systems*. Stanford: Stanford University Press.

Luke, T. 1994. "Toward a North American Critical Theory." *Telos* 101: 101–108.

Mosse, G. 1998. *The Crisis of German Ideology: Intellectual Origins of the Third Reich*. New York: Howard Fertig.

Moses, D. 2008. *German Intellectuals and the Nazi Past*. Cambridge: Cambridge University Press.

Mouffe, C. 1993. *The Return of the Political: Radical Thinkers*. London: Verso.

Mouffe, C. 1999a. "Carl Schmitt and the Paradox of Liberal Democracy." In *The Challenge of Carl Schmitt*, ed. C. Mouffe. London: Verso, 38–53.

Mouffe, C. 1999b. "Deliberative Democracy or Agonistic Pluralism?" *Social Research* 66: 745–758.

Mouffe, C. ed. 2005a. *On the Political*. New York: Routledge.

Mouffe, C. 2005b. "Schmitt's Vision of a Multipolar World Order." *South Atlantic Quarterly* 104: 245–251.

Mouffe, C. 2007. "Carl Schmitt's Warning on the Dangers of a Unipolar World." In *The International Political Thought of Carl Schmitt: Terror, Liberal War and the Crisis of Global Order*, ed. L. Odysseos and F. Petito. London: Routledge, 147–153.

Müller, J.-W. 2003. *A Dangerous Mind: Carl Schmitt in Post-War European Thought*. New Haven: Yale University Press.

Ost, D. 1994. "Search for Balance." *Telos* 101: 137–154.

Outhwaite, W. 2009. *Habermas: A Critical Introduction*. Palo Alto: Stanford University Press.

Piccone, P., and G. Ulmen. 1987. "Introduction to Carl Schmitt." *Telos* 72: 3–14.

Preuss, U. 1999. "Political Order and Democracy: Carl Schmitt and His Influence." In *The Challenge of Carl Schmitt*, ed. C. Mouffe. London: Verso, 155–189.

Rasch, W. 2005. "Carl Schmitt and the New World Order." *South Atlantic Quarterly* 104: 177–183.

Scheuerman, W. 2009. *Morgenthau*. Cambridge: Polity, 2009.

Scheuerman, W. 2011. "Jürgen Habermas: Postwar German Political Debates and the Making of a Critical Theorist." In *Political Philosophy in the 20th Century: Authors and Arguments*, ed. C. Zuckert. Cambridge: Cambridge University Press, 238–251.

Schmitt, C. 2004. *Legality and Legitimacy*, trans. and ed. J. Seitzer. Durham: Duke University Press.

Schmitt, C. 2008. *The Leviathan in the State Theory of Thomas Hobbes: Meaning and Failure of a Political Symbol*, trans. and ed. G. Schwab and E. Hilfstein. Chicago: University of Chicago Press.

Specter, M. 2010. *Habermas: An Intellectual Biography*. New York: Cambridge University Press.

Strong, T. 2011. "Carl Schmitt: Political Theology and the Concept of the Political." In *Political Philosophy in the 20th Century: Authors and Arguments*, ed. C. Zuckert. Cambridge: Cambridge University Press, 32–43.

Ulmen, G. 2001. "The Military Significance of September 11." *Telos* 121: 174–184.

Wiggershaus, R. 2004. *Jürgen Habermas*. Reinbek: Rowohlt.

Zolo, D. 2002. *Invoking Humanity: War, Law and Global Order*, trans. F. and G. Poole. London: Continuum.

PART IV

THE LEGAL
THOUGHT OF
CARL SCHMITT

CHAPTER 16

A JURIST CONFRONTING HIMSELF

Carl Schmitt's Jurisprudential Thought

GIORGIO AGAMBEN

INTRODUCTION

THE TEXTS and interviews that were gathered in the collection *A Jurist Confronting Himself* offer the reader keys with which to unlock the mysteries surrounding one of the most controversial figures of the twentieth century.[1] The image they offer—particularly in the interviews in which Schmitt speaks of himself with an unprecedented, and an at least apparently unfeigned, directness—is not like that of a mug shot, which would once and for all present the identifying traits of the author's personality. Instead, each text can best be seen in light of what Walter Benjamin called the "now of knowability"—that is to say, in a constellation formed by the decisive political problems of our time. The challenge these texts thus propose is akin to that of finding figures hidden in a landscape painting, or like that of looking at drawings in which a second image replaces an initial one if we keep our gaze fixed on it for long enough. Or that challenge might be compared to something else: those illustrations found in old treatises on physiognomy in which a human face shows its true nature by progressively revealing the features of another animal therein. The hidden figures, or *facies inumana*, in Carl Schmitt's works designate those points at which their contemporary relevance is greatest. And it is only in this constellation that the crux of Schmittian exegesis—that of a fascist thinker who continues to concern contemporary society profoundly—can be fully experienced. This uneasy proximity ceases to be embarrassing only at the point—which lies beyond facile dismissal and facile lionization—when we show ourselves capable of remaining on the crest of a present moment that at once unites and divides the watershed of history.

JURIST

"I have been and I am a jurist. I will remain a jurist. I will die a jurist. And all the misfortune of being a jurist is involved therein" (Schmitt 2005, 183). This imperious declaration, which closes the interview Carl Schmitt gave Fulco Lanchester in November 1982, leaves little room for doubt about how Schmitt saw himself. This was neither as a political scientist nor as a political philosopher (as he has often been considered), but as a *jurist*. But what does it mean to be a jurist? Just as in the history of philosophy *being* "is said in many ways," in the history of jurisprudence *jurist* also "is said in many ways."[2] To be a jurist, however, can only mean something within the context offered by a specific conception of law. In this connection two clarifications are in order. As Schmitt made clear as early as his second book, *Gesetz und Urteil*, published in 1912 when he was a mere twenty-four-years old, *law* means not only *norm*, but also—and more important—*decision* and *judgment*. Schmitt's so-called decisionism—which, beginning with Karl Löwith's essay "Political Decisionism" from 1935, was to give rise to so many misunderstandings—has its roots in a conception of law that privileges, as concerns the idea of *norm*, practical action clearly directed toward the making of a *decision*. For this reason, Schmitt's thought is bound to remain misunderstood as long as its interpreter fails to identify therein a conception of law (*diritto*) based on an element that is antagonistic to laws (*legge*, *Gesetz*, as opposed to *nomos*).[3] In the essay from 1950 entitled "The Problem of Legality," Schmitt evokes the equation of law and war in Laberthonnière's posthumously published *Critique of the Notion of Sovereignty*, and in so doing shows how far such an antagonism might be pushed (1958, 440–451).[4] If the state of exception comes to occupy such an important place in Schmitt's thought, this is because by suspending the norm, the state of exception "reveals with absolute purity a specifically juridical formal element: the decision" (Schmitt 1922, 13). This means that for Schmitt, as for Franz Kafka (just as for the great Italian jurist Salvatore Satta), law is essentially praxis and "trial." This is to say that law can never be entirely determined by a norm. (In this regard, it is instructive that in the interview from 1982 Schmitt evokes Kafka's *Trial*, calling it "one of the most brilliant novels ever," and that in Kafka's novel no norm ever appears as such, so this norm comes to be identified, more or less unjustly, with the work's protagonist.)

Every bit as important as the above is Schmitt's declaration in a radio interview given on February 1, 1933, that "my work derives its true meaning from the fact that I am nothing other than the vehicle of the substantive law of the people of whom I am a part" (2005, 35). If law is decision, then the jurist is not only an impartial interpreter of the existing norms, he is also a vehicle contributing to the formal elaboration of new substantive law created through social praxis. (The jurist is then, in other words, a vehicle and an interpreter of the constituting power of a people of which he is a part.) Schmitt argues without reservation for this involvement of the jurist in the material constitution of his times. The work of a jurist who, like Schmitt, works in public law,

> concerns questions whose consequences affect domestic and international politics. As a result they are directly exposed to the problem of the political. And this is a

danger which the jurist in these disciplines cannot avoid, not even by disappearing into the nirvana of pure positivism.... The material from which his concepts are made and upon which his scholarly work necessarily ties him to political situations, whose favor or disfavor, victories and defeats, concern the scholar and the professor, and determine his personal destiny. (1950a, 55–56)

The jurisprudential tradition in which Schmitt locates himself is the *jus publicum Europaeum*, born of the civil wars of religion that devastated Europe from the sixteenth through the eighteenth centuries. The father of this juridical science is "Roman law reborn," and "the mother is the Roman Church" (69). This tradition, whose end was marked by the positivism and the technical focus of the twentieth century, is one to which Schmitt swore his allegiance, more or less sincerely, to the very end. "I am the final representative of this *jus publicum Europaeum*, the last to have taught and studied it in a fundamental sense, and I'm living through its end as *Benito Cereno* experienced the voyage of the pirated ship" (75). It is at the very least noteworthy—and reflects a contradiction that is one of the most puzzling aspects of Schmitt's juridical activity— that it is precisely the final representative of this *jus publicum Europaeum* who, writing *State, Movement, People* in 1933, took on the task of delineating, in his role as vehicle of the substantive rights of the German people, the fundamental principles of a National Socialist state that spelled the irrevocable end of that law. Schmitt the jurist never chose, never *decided*, between these two contradictory identities—or rather, he attempted up until the very end to reconcile them, even at the cost of having recourse to a myth.

BENITO CERENO

At the end of the 1982 interview Schmitt invoked Benito Cereno, who in the intervening period (and thanks in part to the essays of Enrique Tierno Galvan and Sava Klickovic in the *Festschrift* for the jurist's eightieth birthday) had attained something of the status of a "myth" (Galvan 1968, 345–347; Klickovic 1968, 265–267). Referring to his place in twentieth century German and European history, Schmitt remarked, "it seems to me apt to invoke the myth of Benito Cereno.... Do you know Melville's story, the myth of unresolved situations?" (2005, 182–183). According to this mythographic interpretation, the *St. Dominick* (the ship Benito Cereno commanded until the slaves led by the ferocious Babo revolted and forced him to collaborate in their enterprise) is a symbol of an aging European culture that has fallen prey to barbarism and terror. The "myth" is an ad hominem justification that explains the "unresolved situation": why "the final representative of the *jus publicum Europaeum*" so readily and actively collaborated with the Nazi regime. In a diary entry of October 18, 1941, which Ernst Jünger made after a conversation with Schmitt, he notes how Schmitt "compared himself to the white man dominated by the black slaves in Melville's *Benito Cereno* and then cited the motto: '*Non possum scribere contra eum, qui potest proscribere*'" (1960, 275).

It is possible that this interpretation of the myth, clearly opposing good and evil, order and disorder, is not the correct one—or at least that it presents an exoteric meaning that does not exhaust its significance. As the reader of Melville's tale well knows, an obscure affinity and an almost occult solidarity seem to bind Benito Cereno to his slave and jailer, Babo. In the ambiguity of the unhappy captain's situation, Tierno Galvan sought the key to Schmitt's position as representative of the European elite during the Nazi regime, unable either to abandon the ship or to accept the barbarism taking place on it:

> In this myth Benito Cereno symbolizes the conscience of the *élite* that sees and suffers. The unfortunate captain has not chosen to enter into the farce.... He knows that the ship is not heading in any direction and that it is pointless to try and control it. Thence his prolonged downfall and self-sacrifice. Thence also his continued oscillation between resistance, surrender and fear. But resistance in the name of what? In the name of reason, certainly. Reason counsels fleeing the ship at the first occasion, to emigrate to the friendly ship of Mr. Delano. But can the *élite*, Europe's conscience, even were it materially possible, simply bid adieu to Europe? (Galvan 1968, 354; cf. Klickovic 1968, 270–271)

It seems likely that this justification too is insufficient for Schmitt's purposes. Unlike Don Benito, Schmitt was at no point forcibly made to take part in the farce. He willingly collaborated with the government of the pirated ship and repeatedly sought to give juridical form to the new constitution of National Socialist Germany. "The Weimar Constitution is no longer in force" (Schmitt 1935, 5) he wrote in 1933 in his work on the tripartite division of the new national political reality, and at no point did he express doubt or regret concerning the latter's legitimacy. In a series of works published between 1916 and 1922 Schmitt had in fact already elaborated his theory of the state of exception that the activities of the Weimar government and the National Socialists seemed secretly to share. What is more, in Melville's tale, Don Benito is in some sense conscious of the fact that the legality he has left behind was not morally superior to the disorder (which appears orderly) that followed it, but is ultimately indistinguishable from it. During the entire voyage, Babo remains so inseparably close to him as to become something like his shadow. Ultimately, the return to normality is so intolerable to him that he does not survive the hanging of his erstwhile companion and enemy. The ship of *jus publicum Europaeum* seems at this point to have reached a point where it can neither continue its voyage nor turn back.

CHRISTIAN EPIMETHEUS

The essay "Three Possibilities for a Christian Conception of History," first published in 1950 in the journal *Universitas*,[5] offers unique insight into Schmitt's conception of history. Schmitt begins therein with a review of Löwith's recently published *Meaning in History*. Under the pretext of expanding upon his enthusiastic appraisal of the book, he defines three potential paradigms for a Christian conception of history. The first concerns an analogy between the manner in which the twentieth century seemed to conceive of itself and of Christian eschatology: that is, to an end of time, an "expired time" ("*erschöpfte Zeit*"; Schmitt 1950b, 929). This idea is in clear opposition to a modern one of planning. To the eschatological paralysis of the present Schmitt opposed something taken from the Christian vision of history: the image of the *katechon* from Paul's Second Letter to the Thessalonians and its idea of a dynamic power that delays and defers the end of time. In *The "Nomos" of the Earth*, published that same year (although, as the *Glossarium* shows, Schmitt first elaborated his "theory of the *katechon*" in 1932; cf. Paléologue 2004, 66), this idea is placed at the center of Schmitt's conception of a Christian empire:

> I do not believe that any historical concept other than *katechon* would have been possible for the original Christian faith. The belief that a restrainer holds back the end of the world provides the only bridge between the notion of an eschatological paralysis of all human events and a tremendous historical monolith like that of the Christian empire of the Germanic kings. (Schmitt 1997, 29; 2006, 60)

However, in the essay from *Universitas* dating from that same year, this *katechon* is superseded by a third paradigm. This paradigm is expressed through a new image: that of the Christian Epimetheus, which, after that of Benito Cereno, is both Schmitt's most extreme attempt at a self-justification via myth and the key to his esoteric conception of history. The image of the Christian Epimetheus comes from a poem of that name by Konrad Weiss published in 1933. Strangely, Schmitt seems to know it only through Friedhelm Kemp's essay on Weiss and the poems published along with it in the April 1949 issue of the Viennese journal *Wort und Wahrheit*, from which are drawn all the citations Schmitt uses in the 1950 essay and in *Ex Captivitate Salus* (Kemp 1949). For Schmitt, the Christian experience of history has its foundation in the Incarnation, understood as a "historical event of infinite...uniqueness" ("*ein geschichtliches Ereignis von unendlicher, unbesitzbarer, unokkupierbarer Einmaligkeit*"; 1950b, 930). Employing an image that seems to recast that of the angel of history from Benjamin's "Theses on the Philosophy of History" (republished that same year, after an initial and no longer readily available publication in *Neue Rundschau* from 1942), Schmitt writes: "Christ looks backward towards completed events and sees there an internal reason and a symbolic nucleus the active contemplation of which allows the obscure meaning of our history to develop itself" (930).[6] This a posteriori look at history is, for Schmitt, that of a Christian Epimetheus who finds himself in the paradoxical position of needing to respond to something that had always already been predestined and completed. To understand the meaning of this image, it is necessary to turn to the essay by Kemp (which Schmitt characterized as "an excellent introductory essay";

930). According to the Christian conception of history dominated by the idea of divine providence, "our acts are at once an *a posteriori* completion and an anticipation. In the eyes of God they execute what is already predetermined... an execution of that which was already prescribed and, in the blind knowledge of our freedom, a trusting and courageous anticipation" (Kemp 1949, 284–285). It is in this context that Kemp cites the passage from Weiss's poem, which Schmitt will place at the end of "Two Tombs" in *Ex Captivitate Salus* as the ultimate form for his self-justification:

> *Complete that which you must, and which was already*
> *From the beginning completed and to which you could but reply.* (Schmitt 1950a, 53)

Like Epimetheus, Schmitt's Christian must react to an action that has, in fact, no possibility of affecting history and always occurs, so to speak, *post festum*. Benjamin's image of an activity turned toward the past is taken literally here. But whereas in Benjamin this position confers on the gesture its peculiar and real, albeit weak, messianic force, in Schmitt the historical activity of humankind can have no redemptive value whatsoever. Instead, Schmitt's vision obliges humankind to respond to that which is not so much done as carried out. Like the anticipatory decision of the Heideggerian being-toward-death, the Schmittian decision decides something ineluctable; it anticipates something already decided. That is, strictly speaking it decides nothing (thus the appearance of occasionalism and opportunism that so annoyed Löwith).

It is at this point that Schmitt's conception of history reveals its peculiar theological structure. The *katechon*, which suspends and contains the end of time, initiates a time in which nothing can truly happen because the meaning of any historical progression—whose only meaning is to be had in the *eschaton*—is indefinitely deferred. That which happens during the suspended time of the *katechon* is something undecidable that happens, so to speak, without really happening, because its happening can derive meaning only from a ceaselessly deferred *eschaton*. Schmitt's katechological time is that of a frozen messianism. This frozen messianism, however, reveals itself as the theological paradigm of the time in which we live, and its structure is none other than that of Derridean *différance*. Christian eschatology gave a meaning and a direction to our conception of time. By suspending and deferring this meaning, *katechon* and *différance* render it undecidable.

Schmitt's adoption of the figure, or myth, of the Christian Epimetheus neglects an important theological legacy and resembles the status of irresponsible guilt (or innocent responsibility) that seems to define the ethical tenor of our times, and which Nazi officials, beginning with Adolf Eichmann (who declared himself guilty before God, but not before the law), consistently invoked to justify their acts. A decision that decides something always already decided, a historical act that has lost its meaning in history, can only either take responsibility for an error whose price it is not obliged to pay or discount the importance of the suffering for which it is responsible.

CONSTITUTIVE POWER

In his interview with Fulco Lanchester, Schmitt stops for a moment to pose a question of his own: "Do you know my essay *Die legale Weltrevolution* [The Legal World Revolution]?" (Schmitt 2005, 154). This essay, published in the journal *Der Staat* in 1978, is one of the points at which the topicality of Schmitt's interests appears with maximal clarity. At its center is the ascendancy of legality in modern times to the paradoxical point that revolutions—that is, transformations of the formal and material constitutions of countries—occur that are carried out in full accordance with the law. Not only are fascism and National Socialism two examples of such revolutions (Schmitt shows in an abbreviated historical sketch how Hitler succeeded in legally taking power, only to then close the door of legality behind him, thereby using legal means to force his political enemies into illegality), but all strategies for the seizing of state power (e.g., that of the Communist Party) show this. All the important sociopolitical transformations of our time thus tend, in Schmitt's view, to legitimate the state "in exchange for the benefit to have a legal revolution of the state" (2005, 188; 1978, 322). "In our age of rapid scientific, technical and industrial progress," wrote Schmitt in the ample preface to the Italian anthology, "it is no longer possible to distinguish between constitution, law and measure, which have simply been transformed into so many methods for the permanent transformation of values" (1972, 22). The dialectic between constitutive power and constituted power, which beginning with the French Revolution had governed the grand political transformations of our times, thereby enters into a state of crisis. Thanks to the progressive legalization of the coup d'état and the processes for transforming material constitutions, the need for a revolution to traverse a constitutive phase has been radically eliminated: "The legal revolution becomes permanent and the permanent state revolution becomes legal" (2005, 188; 1978, 322).

Let us try to better understand this eclipse of constitutive power in favor of the increasingly dominant category of legality. Thirty years later Schmitt's analyses are, if anything, still more relevant than when they first appeared. We need only think of the problems raised by the proposed European constitution currently at the center of a host of political debates. What the *no*-votes of the French and Dutch citizens recall is that a new constitution cannot be introduced through "legal" agreements between governments, but must pass through a constitutive phase. A new constituted power without a constitutive power may be legal, but it will not be legitimate. And nothing is so disconcerting as the recklessness with which Western democracies, after having descended between the two World Wars into fascism, pretend today to move just as legally into practices and forms of government for which there are as yet no names and about which there is no certainty that they represent an improvement on what preceded them.

It is notable that while vehemently criticizing legalism, Schmitt nonetheless had an easy time demonstrating how a European constitutive power would imply something like a "European patriotism" (2005, 210; 1978, 336) capable of overwhelming the identities of individual nation-states and of which, neither then nor now, is there the slightest trace.

Here too Schmitt was fighting on two opposing fronts. Whereas on the one hand he criticized legal revolution, on the other hand, he rejected with equal tenacity the possibility of a constitutive power capable of countervailing the primacy of such legal revolution.

State, Movement, People

The text in which all the contradictions of Schmitt the jurist come together to the point of inextricability and thereby reveal with maximal clarity their rationale is *State, Movement, People: The Triadic Structure of Political Unity*, published in 1933 and, despite its indisputable theoretical relevance and its durable topicality, never republished after the war. By publishing it in Italian in 1935, alongside selected other texts, under the title *Political Principles of National Socialism*, Delio Cantimori made clear that he had perfectly understood Schmitt's intention, which was nothing less than to formulate the fundamental principles of a new National Socialist constitutional order. And yet the attentive reader of today is confronted by the uneasy but unavoidable realization that this text also describes the constitutional principles of the postdemocratic societies of the twentieth century in whose wake we still move today. If the interpretation of this text I am proposing is correct, it contains the esoteric center and what we might call the *arcanum* of Schmitt's theory of public law. And if Schmitt chose not to reprint it, it was not to conceal what was already perfectly clear—his complicity with Nazism—but rather because the truths to which it gives voice are too disagreeable today to find an audience either on the right or the left.

The text begins by registering the end of the Weimar Constitution and with it the entire liberal-democratic tradition. (According to Schmitt, democracy and liberalism—essentially distinct in identity and representation—had mutually corrupted one another.) The political unity that replaced this earlier order was founded on the articulation of three elements or members: *state*, *movement*, and *people*. The relationships among these three elements (the second of which contends for a special rank and is clearly defined for the first time in constitutional doctrine) is not to be understood, Schmitt stresses, after the fashion of the separation of powers in the liberal tradition, "in which the political sense is the revocation or at least the relativization of the political totality" (2005, 265; 1935, 12). The three elements do not, in fact, run parallel to one another, but "one of them—movement—supports, imbues and guides the state and the people" (2005, 265; 1935, 12) and is thereby the constitutive element. At this point Schmitt proposes a definition of the three elements that appears anodyne, but which on the contrary contains nothing less than the paradigm for the evolution of democratic-liberal constitutions in the new form of government, of which fascism and National Socialism are but first instances: "The State can be considered in a strict sense as the *state-focused political* element, the movement as the *dynamic political* element and the people as the *non-political side* [*unpolitische Seite*] growing under the protection and in the shadow of political decisions" (2005, 265; 1935, 12).

The implications of this tripartite articulation of a political unit are worthy of reflection. The *people*, which in the democratic tradition is the bearer of sovereignty and political legitimacy, becomes a nonpolitical element. It is no longer the "body politic," but instead the biological body or population, which "grows in the shadow and under the protection" of the *movement*. It would be difficult to imagine a better definition of that which Michel Foucault was later to call "biopolitics" (or the passage from a state based on the concept of sovereignty to one based on the concept of population). The primacy of the movement, to become the bearer of political decisions and which finds in the party its specific form, is a function of the fact that the people have become unpolitical—which in turn is a function of the definitive eclipse of constitutional democracy. The movement—and this is the paradox that defines it—is not simply the movement of the people (subjective genitive), but it is that which "bears," "imbues," and "guides" the people and thus constantly is deciding, protecting, and governing its unpolitical character. In a significant reversal of the democratic tradition that marks its entry into a biopolitical dimension, politics is at this point that which decides the unpolitical ("deciding if something is unpolitical is a specifically political decision"; 2005, 272; 1935, 17).

This paradoxical declaration implies a new and decisive reformulation of the definition of the political that Schmitt had proposed in 1927: the opposition between friend and enemy. In the context of the material constitution of National Socialism, this opposition coincides with the inscription of the division political/unpolitical in the place once occupied by the people. This division is not the arbitrary act of a subject, but rather something like the crest that the movement's wave ceaselessly delineates in the life of a specific people. Deciding what constitutes the political is the same as deciding what constitutes the unpolitical. People and movement, body politic and unpolitic body, are in this respect the two edges of the blade on which is figured the Janus head of the Führer: not a subject, but something like the pure expression of the movement, the unending decision of what is political and what is unpolitical. The Western biopolitical machine has perhaps never appeared in such a clear light. Politics is ultimately nothing other than the decision concerning bare life (*la nuda vita*), and the production of an unpolitic body is not the shadow (as in Schmitt's metaphor), but the very substance of the political decision.

We can now understand why Schmitt, with what might easily appear to have been irresponsible opportunism, chose at precisely this point to adopt the National Socialist race doctrine in his analysis of the Reich's new constitution, introducing the concept of *Artgleichheit* ("species identity") "as the most indispensable of presuppositions." As early as his 1976–1977 seminar *Il faut défendre la société*, Foucault observed how *racism* was the means through which the new biopower presenting itself as care for life was reconciled with the earlier sovereign model of the power of life and death. In Schmitt's presentation, however, the link between the two elements is even more fundamental. Species identity, or racial purity—which according to Schmitt both intensifies and absolutizes a democratic principle of identity—is that which ensures the unified articulation of state, movement, people, and Führer. The movement can "bear" the people, and its leader can guide the movement, only because they share an "unconditional species unity":

> For this reason [the concept of *Führung*], in its political urgency, also implies an *absolute species identity between Leader and followers*.... Only this species unity

prevents the Leader's power from becoming arbitrary or tyrannical; and only it distinguishes that power from the domination of some heterogeneous will, be that will ever so advantageous or intelligent. (2005, 307; 1935, 42)

In the same manner as in medieval theology *gubernatio divina* governs the world through the very nature of its creatures, the Führer guides the movement—not from outside of it, but by virtue of species identity. Species identity is thus the means through which the friend/enemy division is inscribed in the depoliticized body politic in the form of a threshold over which the impolitical constantly passes into the political, while at the same time remaining distinct from it. For this very reason there remains an unsubsumable remnant that is foreign to the species (*Fremdart*):

> An element foreign to the species is capable of attaching itself and of cleverly engaging itself as much as one likes; it may read books and write them; but it thinks and understands in a different manner because *it has a different nature [geartet]*, and in any ordering of essential ideas remains in the existential conditions of its own species [*Art*]. (2005, 311; 1935, 45)

The identity principle of modern mass democracy, pushed to its limit, necessarily implies, for Schmitt, an exclusion.

The embarrassing contemporary relevance of Schmitt's thought finds here its ultimate confirmation. When—as is the case today under the dominion of the biopolitical—the political is nothing other than the decision concerning what is unpolitical, then the excluded part becomes ever larger and more difficult to control. Schmitt's thesis concerning the primacy of the movement and the party can be seen in its full significance—and thereby becomes all the more disquieting—only when we recall that National Socialism shares with it traditions that are, at least apparently, antagonistic to it, such as workers' movements, Marxism, and social democracy, which all were based on a bracketing of the people as body politic and on their transformation into a biopolitical entity. Even today extra-parliamentary currents find their sole source of legitimization through a concept of the movement, which, however, remains completely undefined and whose blatant complicity with its enemy is never investigated. Here, too, the overcoming and the decision of this promiscuity can occur only through a lucid analysis of that which epochally unites and separates modern democracy from fascism.

ON THE *St. Dominick*

At the end of his essay *State, Movement, People*, Schmitt introduces perhaps for the first time the image of a dangerous sea voyage, referring to the historical situation of that European public law of which he considered himself the last, misfortunate representative. He writes that all legal concepts have entered into an indeterminate phase that renders their application difficult. If, on the one hand, the legalistic illusion of a codification and normification free from gaps, applicable in any situation and for any case, has forever disappeared, on the other hand the increasingly frequent recourse to provisions referring to a specific situation (such as "security and public order," "dangerous state," "necessary state," and so on—all formulae in which it is easy to recognize the paradigm so dear to Schmitt of the state of exception) push the uncertainty of law to its extreme. Schmitt suggests therein that the contemporary condition of public law is that of a ship forced to seek a passage between Scylla and Charybdis:

> All application of laws is done between Scylla and Charybdis. The way forward seems to lead to a limitless sea and to distance itself ever more from the terra firma of juridical security and legal compliance... the way back, towards a formalistic superstition in regard to the laws which has been recognized is recognizable as senseless and, historically speaking, long ago supervened, is not for as much worthy of consideration. (2005, 309; 1935, 44)

It is interesting to observe that of the two mythical monsters in question, one is the formalism and juridical positivism that Schmitt has not ceased to oppose, and the other is the state of exception, whose theorization was precisely the jurist's tenacious response to the crisis of European public law and which, in the years when he is writing, has become common practice in Germany. In this respect as well, the book from 1933 occupies a special position because it represents an attempt to find the difficult and perhaps impossible passage between the Scylla of legalism and Charybdis of the state of exception, between the sovereignty of law and the sovereignty over law.

It would perhaps then be worthwhile to attempt to reflect in this context on the "myth of the unresolved situation" through which Schmitt sought his personal justification, as well as the justification for law in general: a final, desperate "nomodicy" (*nomodicea*). The *St. Dominick*, that Spanish "strange ship" that Amasa Delano, representative of the New World, observed with supreme unease for his entire eleven hours aboard, is the ship of European public law. But what happened on board? The situation on board the *St. Dominick* could be defined less as disorder and lawlessness than as a state of indistinction in which law and the state of exception, law and violence, were indistinguishable. The captain, Don Benito Cereno, who conserves all the outward signs of power, is—like law in Europe between the two World Wars—a powerless sovereign, one who reigns but does not govern. For this reason the sword with the silver hilt hanging at his hip ("apparent symbol of despotic command"), just as on the frontispiece of *Leviathan*, is in truth without a blade, and the key suspended from his neck, symbol of the *jus ligandi et solvendi* ("so, Don Benito—padlock and key—significant symbols, truly"), is useless because, in reality, the lock is already open. All effective power is in the hands of the ferocious Babo, who shadows Don Benito—who shadows legality—to the point of intimacy, inseparability, and finally, indistinguishability. (When Amasa Delano asks Don Benito, "What has cast such a shadow upon you?," he responds simply, "The negro.") Just as in the grip of National Socialism, the state of exception has become the rule and the revolution pretends to be in every respect legal. Don Benito and his obscure *partner* stand on the deck of *St. Dominick* ("not only his constant attendant and companion, but in all things his confidant"), where law and terror have become completely intertwined. Nothing expresses this secret and abject solidarity better than the contract that, at a certain point, Don Benito and Babo draft and sign, in which the captain commits himself to an impossible task (lead the slaves to Senegal) and Babo to an equally impossible relinquishing of violence. And Amasa Delano does not succeed in getting to the heart of matters, uncertain until the end whether Don Benito is a gentleman or a pirate, a representative of a weakened law and completely incapable of exercising his function or, on the contrary, an excessively ferocious leader, "a bitter hard master."

In this perspective the true symbol of the *jus publicum Europaeum* is not Don Benito, but the gigantic Negro Atufal, who pretends to be bound by chains to which the captain holds the key, but which in reality can be set aside at any moment. And there is perhaps no more powerful allegory of the situation of law in Nazi Germany—and perhaps in the world in which we today live, where "the whole world is the San Dominick" ("*der ganze Globus ist 'San Dominick'*"; Klickovic 1968, 272)—than the farcical ceremony in which Don Benito and Atufal, under the vigilant gaze of Babo, present themselves every two hours to display the false chains and, at the same time, bear witness to irreducible insubordination.

Between 1933 and 1935 Schmitt wrote *State, Movement, People*, as well as a series of articles in which, in addition to winning favor with those in power, he aspired to give form to the constitutional principles of socialism. In so doing he sought to guide the *St. Dominick* between the Scylla of legality and the Charybdis of the state of exception. The theory of *Führung* is not a "baroque allegory" (a clear allusion to Benjamin's image of the baroque sovereign incapable of deciding anything), nor "the domination of a foreign will," because it is founded on the "absolute species identity between leader and followers." Schmitt's attempt to respond to the division—which in Melville's story takes precisely the form of a racial division—is to give the ship of European public law a leader and a pilot who can be neither the uncertain Don Benito nor the purely violent Babo. To understand the full meaning of the allegory that the *St. Dominick* presented to Schmitt's eyes, we would do well not to forget that for the jurist, from the moment that identity was viewed as the identifying mark of democracy (National Socialism was, in this sense, for Schmitt nothing but democracy in a more extreme form) and representation of liberalism, the misfortunate ship was truly the symbol of Weimar Germany, torn between two principles that had become irreconcilable.

Ultimately, Schmitt's attempt could only reveal itself as bankrupt. As a more attentive reading of Melville's tale would have revealed, the pirated ship can go nowhere. It is with prophetic prescience that Babo substituted for the ship's figurehead, an image of Christopher Columbus, symbol of the New World, the skeleton of the assassinated master, Alexandro Aranda, under which he had inscribed "Seguid vuestro jefe" ("Follow your leader"). The true Führer of the ship of the *jus publicum Europaeum* in its extreme phase is death. Schmitt doubtless knew this well and knew that he, playing the one mythographic mask against the other, must, like the Christian Epimetheus, respond to a decision whose outcome went without saying.

Translated from the Italian by Leland de la Durantaye

Notes

1. This essay was originally published in Italian as a preface to *Un giurista davanti a se stesso: Saggi e interviste*, a collection edited by Agamben (2005) of interviews with, and essays and texts, by Carl Schmitt that were hitherto unavailable in Italian. Reprinted in translation with permission of the publisher.
2. *Translator's note*: Agamben trusts his reader to recognize this allusion to Aristotle's claim in the *Metaphysics* that "being says itself in many ways" (VII.1, 1028a 10).
3. *Translator's note*: Italian, like German, possesses two terms that are both generally translated into English as *law. Diritto*, like the German *Recht*, is an abstract conception of the law. *Legge*, like the German *Gesetz*, refers to specific laws or sets of laws. In some cases the Italian *diritto*, like the German *Recht*, can be translated as *right*, but systematically doing so here would have obscured the meaning of both Agamben's and Schmitt's thinking.
4. Laberthonnière's remark that Schmitt cites is "*La maxime: c'est la loi, ne diffère en rien au fond de la maxime: c'est la guerre.*" Cf. Laberthonnière 1947.
5. *Translator's note*: Schmitt's essay was originally published under the title "Drei Stufen historischer Sinngebung" ("Three Stages of Historical Justification"; 1950b, 927–931). Upon republication the title was changed to "Drei Möglichkeiten eines christlichen Geschichtsbildes" ("Three Possibilities for a Christian Conception of History"). It is this revised title that Agamben uses here.
6. Unless noted otherwise, all translations of source material by the translator.

References

Agamben, G. ed. 2005. *Un giurista davanti a se stesso: Saggi e interviste*. Venice: Neri Pozza Pozza.

Galvan, E. T. 1968. "Benito Cereno oder der Mythos Europas." In *Epirrhosis: Festgabe für Carl Schmitt*, ed. H. Baron et al. Berlin: Duncker & Humblot, 345–356.

Jünger, E. 1960. *Tagebücher II: Strahlungen. Sämtliche Werke*, vol. 2. Stuttgart: Klett-Cotta.

Kemp, F. 1949. "Der Dichter Konrad Weiss." *Wort und Wahrheit* 4: 280–292.

Klickovic, S. 1968. "Benito Cereno: Ein moderner Mythos." In *Epirrhosis: Festgabe für Carl Schmitt*, ed. H. Baron et al. Berlin: Duncker & Humblot, 265–273.

Laberthonnière, L. 1947. *Sicut ministrator: Critique de la notion de souveraineté de la loi*. Paris: Vrin.

Löwith, K. 1935. "Politischer Dezisionismus." *Revue internationale de la théorie du droit/ Internationale Zeitschrift für Theorie des Rechts* 9: 101–123 (published under the pseudonym Hugo Fiala).

Paléologue, Th. 2004. *Sous l'oeil du grand Inquisiteur: Carl Schmitt et l'héritage de la théologie politique*. Paris: Cerf.

Schmitt, C. 1912. *Gesetz und Urteil: Eine Untersuchung zum Problem der Rechtspraxis.* Berlin: Liebmann.

Schmitt, C. 1922. *Politische Theologie: Vier Kapitel zur Lehre von der Souveränität.* Munich and Leipzig: Duncker & Humblot.

Schmitt, C. 1935. *Staat, Bewegung, Volk: Die Dreigliedrigkeit der politischen Einheit.* Hamburg: Hanseatische Verlagsanstalt.

Schmitt, C. 1950a. *Ex Captivitate Salus: Erfahrungen der Zeit 1945/1947.* Berlin: Duncker & Humblot.

Schmitt, C. 1950b. "Drei Stufen historischer Sinngebung." *Universitas* 5: 927–931.

Schmitt, C. 1958. "Das Problem der Legalität." *Die neue Ordnung*: 270–275; repr. *Verfassungsrechtliche Aufsätze aus den Jahren 1924–1954: Materialen zu einer Verfassungslehre.* Berlin: Duncker & Humblot, 440–451.

Schmitt, C. 1972. *Le categorie del 'politico': Saggi di teoria politica.* Bologna: Il Mulino.

Schmitt, C. 1978. "Die legale Weltrevolution: Politischer Mehrwert als Prämie auf juristische Legalität und Superlegalität." *Der Staat* 3: 321–339.

Schmitt, C. 1997. *Der Nomos der Erde im Völkerrecht des Jus Publicum Europaeum*, 4th ed. Berlin: Duncker & Humblot.

Schmitt, C. 2005. "Un giurista davanti a se stesso." In Agamben 2005, 151–183.

Schmitt, C. 2006. *The "Nomos" of the Earth in the International Law of the "Jus Publicum Europaeum,"* trans. G. L. Ulmen. New York: Telos Press.

....

CHAPTER 17

CARL SCHMITT AND THE WEIMAR CONSTITUTION

....

ULRICH K. PREUß

INTRODUCTION

....

THE WEIMAR Constitution of August 11, 1919, was the outcome of a social and political revolution that pushed Germany into the twentieth century. Although this constitution did not ratify the most radical demands and practices of the revolution, most notably the system of council democracy, it sanctioned and gave rise to deep social, political, and juridical changes, the most evident being expressed in its first article: "The German Reich is a republic. State authority derives from the people." The democratic republic replaced the autocratic, semi-parliamentary monarchy and thus created a completely new political universe. It set the seal on the "entry of the lower classes into the arena of national politics" (Bendix 1977, 89–90) and opened the gates for deep political, socio-economic, cultural, and institutional transformations (Dyzenhaus 1997a, 17–37). The democratic principle was specified as a combination of parliamentary, presidential, and plebiscitary elements through which the "necessarily heterogeneous will of the citizens should transform into a necessarily unified decision" (Gusy 1997, 90–91).[1] Arguably the most salient political thrust of the constitution was its ambition to establish a new order not just for the organization of the state but for all spheres of society. In the eyes of its founders, the democratic republic required corresponding societal institutions that would extend the scope of the responsibility of the polity into society. Thus the constitution not only contained—for the first time in Germany—a bill of rights, but also a normative frame for community life, including marriage and family, religion and religious communities, schooling and education, and, most important, the economic relations within a capitalist economy (Gusy 1997, 298–369). Aspirations to order the economic sphere played a pivotal role. Being the product of a rupture, which was as much a social as a political revolution, the Weimar Constitution aimed at taming the class struggle by reconciling, or at least mitigating, the tension between capitalism and political democracy through the creation of universal suffrage, a competitive party system on the basis of proportional representation, institutions of collective bargaining, and workers' codetermination in large business enterprises.

One and a half years before the end of World War I, Max Weber had foreshadowed several elements of this turn in a series of journal articles published between April and June 1917: a new political order would be based on "active democratization of the masses," including political parties, professional politicians, "mass demagogy," and parliamentary government, as well as plebiscitary forms of political articulation and their corollary tendency toward Caesarism. He named it mass democracy (Weber 1994, 209–233). Mass democracy, in fact, was the political order of the Weimar Constitution.

As a consequence, the Weimar Constitution posed a serious challenge to traditional constitutional law scholarship. For almost two generations—roughly since the enactment of the constitution of the German Reich of 1871—this discipline had been dominated by legal positivism, which excluded historical, philosophical, sociological, and political considerations from legal reasoning (Stolleis 1992, 337–348; Caldwell 1997, 1339). Such a depoliticized state law could have existed only in the serenity of an age of stable bourgeois saturation and domination, a world that was still a far cry from the predicament of the German postwar society of 1919 and the years that followed. A few public law scholars of the younger generation had challenged basic assumptions of legal positivism already before the outbreak of the war—among them Schmitt (1912; see Korioth 1992; Stolleis 1992, 445–447; Caldwell 1997, 52–62)—but now the rejection of "constitutional formalism in favor of an approach that set questions of public law within politics and history" had become a plain methodological necessity for a scientific discipline whose subject had become a politicized mass society (Kennedy 2004, 5; Stolleis 1999, 153–186; Caldwell 1997, 78–84).

Even more challenging than the innovations of the Weimar Constitution as a juridico-political institution was the fact that it had to take on deep crises throughout its short-lived existence between 1919 and 1933. It had to cope with the consequences of military defeat in war, most notably the very harsh conditions of the Treaty of Versailles and attendant international isolation; a strong domestic anti-republican and anti-constitutional opposition from both right and left extremist forces, in the last years of the republic ever more frequently carried out in violent street fights among their tightly organized supporters; the erosion of the economic foundations of the middle class through inflation and economic crisis; recurrent strikes and social unrest of the impoverished popular masses; and a fractured party system that complicated the formation of parliamentary majorities and created the notorious Weimar governability problems (see the documents in Kaes et al. 1994; Jacobson and Schlink 2000, 8–21; Winkler 2005; for a politico-economic analysis of the crisis, see Abraham 1986). During the fourteen years of the Weimar period, no less than twenty cabinets held office, including sixteen parliamentary and four presidential governments (Huber 1981, 328–329). Thus, Arthur Jacobson and Bernhard Schlink have rightly identified the attempts of the German constitutional lawyers of the 1920s to conceptualize the new constitution as "a jurisprudence of crisis."

The subject of this chapter is Schmitt's view of the crisis and his response to it as a political, legal, and constitutional theorist. It does not deal with Schmitt's much-debated role as a political advisor in the final months of the Weimar Republic between July 1932 and January 30, 1933. This is a matter of historical research that lies outside my professional expertise (cf. Berthold 1999; Pyta and Seiberth 1999; Grimm 1992). The chapter's aim is rather the reconstruction of Schmitt's conceptual edifice of the Weimar Constitution, which led him to the conclusion that the founding document did not provide an appropriate political system for the German people. I start with an account of Schmitt's perception of the constitutional innovations of the Weimar Constitution and his earliest theoretical response to them, which focuses on the two varieties of the concept of dictatorship: commissarial and sovereign. Thereafter I discuss Schmitt's construction of an inherent connection between dictatorship and the constituent power of the people, both of which he viewed as authentic expressions of democracy.

In the following section I discuss the implications of Schmitt's claim of the superiority of the constituent power of the German people over the constitution as a means to protect the unity of the nation against the constitution's divisive effects. The subject of the section following that is Schmitt's conceptual construction of the relationship between the principle of democracy and parliamentarianism and his contention that the latter was an obstacle to "genuine" democracy, because it embodied the pluralist divisions of a society divided by class. I maintain that Schmitt's argument for presidential dictatorship in the critical months of 1932—a regime that was to become the slippery slope toward Hitler's takeover in January 1933—was not an inescapable choice for an interim arrangement in an extraordinary time of emergency, but rather a blueprint for the kind of constitutional framework he had, right from the outset, regarded as appropriate constitutional setup to govern the political life of the German people even in ordinary times.

SCHMITT'S VIEW OF THE POLITICAL ORDER OF WEIMAR

Schmitt shared the skeptical view of most of his colleagues about the Weimar Republic. But while they regarded the revolutionary transition of 1919 from the Wilhelmine monarchy to the democratic republic as a deep (and mostly unwelcome) rupture of the political order, which undermined the stability of society (Stolleis 1999, 79–80), Schmitt took a radically different position. In his view the Weimar Constitution was neither a revolutionary breakthrough to a modern type of liberal democracy nor merely a modified continuation of the Bismarckian-Wilhelmine regime, the "Second Reich." In his opinion, it belatedly transplanted the ideas of the liberal movement of 1848 into the twentieth century and, but, inevitably, fell short of the requirements of the time. In a 1928 article, he states quite bluntly that what would have been timely in 1848, and in part perhaps still in 1871, was totally inept in 1919. He declares the Weimar Constitution "in a sense something posthumous" and compares this constellation with the situation of a young man who courted a girl of the same age but was rejected in favor of a rival and who decades later wins the widow (1928, 44–45; see also 2008, 54–55, 357–358). But what would the historical situation of 1919 have required, in Schmitt's mind? Writing six years later, after the Nazis had seized power and he had delivered himself to the regime, he was, of course, quite outspoken and identified the "revolution" of the National Socialists, which he believed had "liberated the German people from the centennial bewilderment of the bourgeois constitutionalism," as the solution to the historical problem created by the "belated" revolution of 1918 (2011b, 47). Arguably that was not the answer he had had in mind in the period between the founding of the Weimar Republic in 1919 and its definitive downfall on January 30, 1933, the day Hitler was sworn in as chancellor of the republic.

A preliminary approach to an answer leads us to the first book by Schmitt that makes explicit reference to constitutional problems, which he wrote after the downfall of the Wilhelmine regime: *Die Diktatur* (*Dictatorship*), with its subtitle "From the Beginnings of the Modern Idea of Sovereignty to the Proletarian Class Struggle." In fact, the relationship between sovereignty and class struggle became the leitmotif of Schmitt's stance on the Weimar Constitution. As he remarks in the preliminary note to the first edition, he wrote this text in the summer of 1920 (1978, xiii). It was the year of the first major crisis of the republic, an attempted putsch of *Freikorps* soldiers (irregular voluntary military units), following mass strikes and uprisings in the Ruhr region, the industrial heartland of Germany, and in other parts of Germany (Winkler 2005, 109–142). These instances of disorder could only be mastered by the use of the extraordinary powers bestowed on the *Reichspräsident* by Article 48(2) of the Constitution[2] (Huber 1984, 95–96, 112–114). Interestingly enough, they were commonly referred to as his dictatorial powers, and their usage as the "dictatorship of the *Reichspräsident*" (Huber 1981, 687–705). Thus, beyond the methodological originality of *Die Diktatur*, which approached the problem of dictatorship from a constitutional angle, in this period it amounted to a statement about the viability of the first democratic constitution in Germany's history.

For Schmitt dictatorship is not in itself an abnormal political status; it is rather a mode of "overcoming an abnormal state of affairs" by exercising "state authority unburdened of legal barriers for [that] purpose" (1926, 33). He defines dictatorship as the personal rule of a single person, based on an induced or presupposed consent of the people, "thus on a democratic fundament," who "uses a centralized governmental machinery which is indispensable for the control and administration of a modern state" (1978, xii). His key concept is the exception; a state of exception requires exceptional means for its overcoming. The dictator disregards norms that are valid in a normal situation but an obstacle to the efforts to end the state of exception. It is the purpose of the dictator to restore a normal situation that is more or less tacitly presupposed in the normativity of legal norms. Thus the essence of dictatorship consists of the separation of norms of law from the method of their realization through extralegal, purposeful, factual, and mostly coercive means (Schmitt 1978, xvi–xvii; McCormick 1998, 218–230; Hofmann 2010, 49–64). In *Political Theology*, published one year later, Schmitt pointedly paraphrases and sharpens his concept of the exception, asserting that "[t]he exception appears in its absolute form when a situation in which legal prescriptions can be valid must first be brought about....For a legal order to make sense, a normal situation must exist" (Schmitt 2005, 13; see McCormick 1997, 121–156; Caldwell 1997, 96–100).

In that statement the relationship between the state of exception and a normal situation has significantly changed. While the juristic element in *Die Diktatur* consisted in the linkage of dictatorship to its *telos* to restore normalcy—that is, to render itself superfluous—Schmitt's interest now turns to the question of how generally a normal situation comes into being in which legal norms are valid. Building on the above distinction between legal norms and the means of their realization, he points out that since "the legal idea cannot realize itself, it needs a particular organization and form before it can be translated into reality" (Schmitt 2005, 28, 31). First and foremost, there must be somebody who "definitively decides whether the normal situation actually exists" (13). That can only be someone who has the requisite resources at his command to restore normality, because only he would be in the position to enforce any kind of decision. This is the sovereign. "The sovereign," Schmitt argues, "produces and guarantees the situation in its totality. He has the monopoly over this last decision" (13). No predetermined normative standard for this decision exists. "Looked at normatively, the decision emanates from nothingness" (31–32). This amounts to a reversal of the original relationship between normalcy and exception: it is not the normal situation and its normativity that define the standard according to which the dictator has to restore order in an exceptional situation; rather, it is the decision of the dictator that defines the standards of normality— a normality he has to create in the first place (McCormick 1998, 224–225). This is the meaning of the famous first sentence of *Political Theology*: "Sovereign is he who decides on the exception" (Schmitt 2005, 5).

Within the conceptual framework of *Die Diktatur*, the distinction between dictatorship that restores a preexisting standard of order and dictatorship that defines order "from nothingness" is equivalent to the distinction between commissarial and sovereign dictatorship. A commissarial dictator is authorized by an existing constitution that defines the conditions under which that dictator may claim a state of exception, and which specifies the constitutional norms that he may suspend in order to restore constitutional normalcy. Sovereign dictatorship, by contrast, rejects the validity and authorizing force of an existing constitution and aims at the creation of a new, "genuine" or "true" constitution (1978, 130–152; cf. Nippel 2011). The paradigmatic pattern of sovereign dictatorship is the Marxist concept of the dictatorship of the proletariat, which serves as a vehicle for the achievement of the desired final communist society (1978, xiii, 137). Schmitt views it as an example for his recurring claim that dictatorship is not antithetical to democracy (1988a, 51–64, also 17, 28, 32). Thus he regards the notion of democratic dictatorship as an appropriate analytical tool for the study of the Weimar Constitution (2011a, 310–311; 1926, 35; see Kennedy 2011, 288–292).

In this view dictatorship and democracy meet historically in the constituent assemblies, which roused his interest because they embodied the original, "untainted," preconstitutional, "unified and indivisible" power of the people (Schmitt 2008, 126). He regarded the Weimar constituent assembly as a "sovereign dictator" who is the "sole constituted power of the political unity of the German people" (109, 110). Note that the constituent assembly, despite its designation, is actually a constituted power, if a quite extraordinary one. The constituent power proper remains with the people; they are the ultimate source of all political power. But as an unorganized multitude they cannot have a clear will.

Thus the sovereignty of the people is delegated to a constituent assembly, which is empowered to exercise the plenipotentiary capability of the people's constituent power. By implication the constituent assembly has not just to interpret, but also to form, the constituent will of the people in the first place. This entails the paradoxical status of a body that exercises delegated power without being restricted by instructions of the principal or being responsible to him; indeed, "who even dictates his constituent without ceasing to appeal to its legitimacy" (1978, xviii, 143–144). This is the essence of Schmitt's concept of the constituent assembly as a sovereign dictator: sovereign because plenipotent, dictator because dependent on the commission of the bearer of the constituent power, unified and inherently democratic because it embodies the unity of the preconstitutional people (Schmitt 1978, 139–150; 2011a, 311; 1926, 35; 2008, 109–110; Caldwell 1997, 99–102; Cristi 1998, 183–185; Kalyvas 2008, 79–100). Moreover, this is also Schmitt's ideal of a democratic institution.

The problem is, of course, that such an institution is transitory; it is its purpose to be replaced by the powers established by the constitution, hence to make itself superfluous. At least in the case of Weimar this instance aroused Schmitt's political frustration, because he observed that the outcome of the Weimar constituent assembly, the Weimar Constitution, was quintessentially an instruction manual for the political life of a plural, disjointed, class-divided, and culturally split mass society. Most unfortunately, as Schmitt had to realize, the presupposed preconstitutional unity of the German people had disappeared with the accomplishment of the mandate of the agents of this very political unity; that is, with the entry into force of the constitution. From a liberal viewpoint this is exactly what constituent assemblies are all about: they are commissioned to create the institutional conditions for the free development of societal life, which includes the recognition and permission of value and interest diversity and conflicts and the provision of institutional means to cope with them in a civilized manner. This is what the Weimar Constitution did to a more or less satisfying degree.

By contrast, in Schmitt's view the constitution deprived the German people of its democratic identity. He missed the spirit of unity of the constituent power of the people within the framework of the constitution. Since Schmitt regarded the Weimar Constitution as a paradigm of the liberal-democratic type of constitution (2008, 54; 1965, vii), we can safely assume that he generally doubted the capacity of a liberal constitution to preserve the substantial unity of the people, presumed by him as an inherent and comprehensive quality of its constituent power. Consequently his constitutional reasoning focused on how to preserve political unity against the—in his view—dissociating forces of the constitution itself. Schmitt used several conceptual strategies to pursue this aim, including, inter alia, the theoretical assumption of the permanence and permanent supremacy of the political will of the constituent power over the constituted powers and the dissociation of democracy and parliamentarianism, especially through the assertion of the normative superiority of what he called "extraordinary lawgivers" over the system of parliamentary legislative legality. They will be outlined successively in the following sections.

The Permanence of the Constituent Power and the Need for Dictatorship

In textbooks on constitutional law the notion of constituent power usually has a rather marginal status. Some authors claim that after the enactment of a constitution the constituent power's mission has been completed and its productive force and authority have been metamorphosed into the constitution; hence the constituent power has expired. Others assume that indeed the constituent power of the people continues to exist after the enactment of a constitution, but that its unmediated and untamed character must be contained and channeled to protect the integrity of the constitution (Böckenförde 1991, 98–107). Schmitt, on the contrary, is predominantly concerned about the preservation of the immediateness and amorphousness of the constituent power. In *Constitutional Theory* he claims the "continuous presence (permanence) of the constitution-making power," which cannot be absorbed or consumed by the constituted powers; he contends that it "expresses itself in continually new forms, producing from itself these ever renewing forms and organizations ... without ever subordinating itself, its political existence, to a conclusive formation" (2008, 140, 128).

At first glance this assertion seems to have a merely academic significance. It is a truism that a people has the "right" to shake off a political regime and to establish a new one by way of constitution-making at any time—after all, one cannot forbid a revolution. But Schmitt's claim is different (cf. Kennedy 2004, 92–109[3]). He contends that the constituent power not only has temporal and logical precedence over the constitution, but also outranks it in normative terms. This is not meant in the sense of Kelsen's hierarchy of norms, which Schmitt of course rejected, but in the sense of the "superiority of the existential element over the merely normative one.... Whoever is authorized to take such actions and is capable of doing so, acts in a sovereign manner" (2008, 154; cf. Cristi 1998, 191–192). The distinction between the existential and the normative is mirrored in Schmitt's contrasting of the relative and the positive concept of the constitution: according to the former the constitution is "a multitude of individual, formally equivalent constitutional laws" that renders constitutional rank to whatever is written in the text of the constitution. "It is no longer generally asked why a constitutional provision must be 'fundamental'" (2008, 67)—this is a feature of the relative constitutional concept, which Schmitt labels the "constitutional law," as distinct and opposed to the positive concept of the constitution according to which it "originates from an *act of the constitution-making power*."[4] It does not contain individual normative provisions, but rather an existential decision about the political form of the political unity of the people. The essence of the constitution "is not contained in a statute or in a norm" (75, 77). From this it follows that the continuing constituent power "stands alongside and above every constitution derived from it and any valid constitutional provision of this constitution" (140).

Although, Schmitt argues, the Weimar Constitution contains a series of mere constitutional laws in the sense of the relative concept of the constitution (2008, 70), it also includes several fundamental decisions concerning the political existence of the German people, most importantly the decisions for democracy, for the republic, for federalism (77–78), and against the "dictatorship of councils" and the "proletarian class-based state" (83–84), which had been the program of the radical Left. It is only due to these decisions that the Weimar Constitution is "actually a constitution and not a sum of disconnected individual provisions, which the parties of the Weimar governmental coalition agreed to insert into the text on the basis of some 'compromise'" (78). These decisions contain the substance of the constitution, which must be protected against the bent toward disunity and division made possible by its relative components. In Schmitt's opinion the main cause of these divisions is the party-dominated parliament, which "increasingly ceases to be representative of the political unity" and "becomes an exponent of the interests and moods of the masses of voters" (337). Consequently, the permanence of the constituent power is a reminder of the ever-present potentiality for its interference in the affairs of the constituted polity (cf. Kalyvas 2005, 230).

In this way the constituent power operates as a permanent observer that checks the conformity of the actions of the constituted powers with the existential decisions the constituent assembly made in the founding period of the polity. Hence the constitution is exposed to a permanent latent challenge to its normative validity. Such a theoretical construction is only plausible on the premise of a deep distrust in the legitimacy of the constituted powers. Schmitt actually disliked the Weimar Constitution because in his view it opened the door for the erosion of the people's unity. He contrasted the unity of the constituent power of the German people as allegedly manifested in the Weimar National Assembly of 1919 with the disunity of political life as it was expressed in the fragmentation of the *Reichstag* parties (Schmitt 2008, 364–366; more explicit, 2004, 85–88). After the expiration of the Weimar National Assembly (the constituent assembly) he looked for a custodian of the German people's political unity within the framework of the constitution. Only someone who, similar to the constituent assembly, is "authorized and capable" to act in an existential manner, which means as the authentic delegate of the unified people's will, came into question. In Schmitt's conceptual framework this is a democratic dictator—a curator of the unity and identity of the people in times of constitutional crisis.

In Schmitt's constitutional theory the barriers for the self-proclamation of any populist leader as the authentic mouthpiece of the people were not very high. After all, the "natural form of the direct expression of a people's will is the assembled multitude's acclamation." In modern expanded societies it finds its expression in public opinion (2008, 131, 275); obviously that is almost as much susceptible to manipulation as an

assembled multitude's mood. The immediacy of these more or less articulate manifestations elevates them above all mediated forms of expression, because "as long as a
people have the will to political existence, the people are superior to every formation
and normative framework" (131, 271). Even if, due to their unorganized state and their
amorphous disposition, the people may not be capable of expressing a determinative
and recognizable will, "the tacit consent of the people is also always possible and easy to
perceive" (131, 139).

This, then, is an open invitation to those who struggle for political power to claim that
they have understood the silence or the diffuse acclamation of the people correctly or,
respectively, the overwhelming feelings of public opinion, and hence are legitimized to
act on their behalf outside the constitution. An induced or presupposed consent of the
people satisfies Schmitt's condition for a democratic fundament of dictatorship (1978,
xiii). It opens the path toward the translation of the potency of resourceful elites into
extra-constitutional political power in the name of the supremacy of the constituent
power of the people. This is a scarcely concealed option for populist dictatorship—in
Schmitt's conceptual frame, democratic dictatorship—in the worst case even for latent
or manifest civil war.

It is a matter of debate whether Schmitt's conception of the constituent power and
its relationship to the constitution followed from his love for democracy or for dictatorship. In his constitutional theory there is no contradiction between these seemingly
antithetical versions of political rule: the purest form of democracy—the acclamation of
the "present, genuinely assembled people" (1978, 272)—requires dictatorship, which, in
turn is the indispensable agent for the formation and realization of the will of the formless people. Paradoxically, this antiliberal constitutional theory (Kennedy 1988, xxxiv;
Holmes 1996, 37–50; Scheuerman 1996; 1999, 61–84; Seitzer 1998, 297) conforms to the
liberal belief that a constitution is a device for constraining and eroding the people's
power. This belief, however, neglects the fact that the binding devices of a constitution
are predominantly enabling means of a people's self-determination rather than of their
disempowerment (Holmes 1993, 227–235).

PARLIAMENTARIANISM: A LIBERAL
CAMOUFLAGE OF DEMOCRACY

A further key element of Schmitt's slightly depreciative view of the Weimar Constitution
is his conception of the relationship between democracy and parliamentarianism.
According to his reasoning, the "parliamentary system" rests on the application and
mixture of different and even opposing elements (monarchical, aristocratic, democratic), among which the democratic element is largely located in the residual power
of the plebiscitary decision of the people in cases of conflict between parliament and
government. Parliamentarianism is "*the* political system of the bourgeois Rechtsstaat,"

which suffers "from the deficiency that is unique to this *Rechtsstaat* idea generally, for it intends to evade the ultimate, inevitable political decision and logical consequence of the principles of political form" (2008, 330).

Schmitt distinguishes two principles of political form through which political unity can be achieved: identity and representation (2008, 239; Dyzenhaus 1997b, 51–58). The former predominates where the people are the subject of the constituent power—in other words, identity is the genuine principle of democratic rule. It is defined by a series of identities: "of ruler and ruled, governing and governed, commander and follower. In pure democracy, there is only the self-identity of the genuinely present people, which is not a type of representation" (2008, 264). Referring to Rousseau, Schmitt claims that the people cannot be represented "because they must be *present*, and only something absent, not something present, may be represented" (272; see also 289). Not only does no particular relationship exist between democracy and representation; the latter "contains the genuine opposition to the democratic principle of identity" (251). What is represented is "the political unity as a whole," not the people. Thus, in the constitutional monarchy of the nineteenth century, the parliament was " 'the people's advocate', but not the representative of the political unity of the people," because in the monarchy the "totality of the subjects are in fact not supposed to be the political unity" (245).

Accordingly, the representative system of the liberal *Rechtsstaat* of the nineteenth century, which presupposed "a genuine representation of the . . . nation," was not a variety of democracy; rather, it had the "meaning of a representative elite, of an aristocratic assembly with representative character," and only its opposition to the absolute monarchy made it appear to be a democratic institution (2008, 250). When the monarchy fell with the rise of mass democracy, the liberal conception of the parliament as an association of economically and socially independent, intellectually autonomous, and judicious notables also collapsed. This appearance could no longer be sustained. For Schmitt "rising democratization"—that is, the metamorphosis of the deputy into "a dependent agent of voters and interest organizations" (250)—could not undermine the democratic quality of the parliament, because this had never existed. Yet it undercut its representative-aristocratic character, which had functioned as the representation of political unity. In Schmitt's view, in the twentieth century political unity can only be regained on the basis of the democratic principle of identity.

Note that Schmitt did not acknowledge as proof of the democratic character of the parliament the fact that in Weimar it rested upon general, equal, immediate, and secret elections for men and women older than twenty years pursuant to the principle of proportional representation. This had a major impact on the integration of the hitherto largely excluded popular masses into the political system. Not so for Schmitt. "The election or vote . . . is a *secret individual vote*. The method of the secret individual vote, however, is not democratic. It is, rather, an expression of liberal individualism" because it transforms the citizen, a political man, into a private person (2008, 273). He contends that even those constitutional procedures through which the electorate intends to express its political will—elections, referenda, popular initiatives—do not fully exhaust the democratic quality of the constitution. These procedures imply certain competences for the people, but through them the popular will "comes into being only as a result of a system of validations or, indeed fictions" ("*Geltungen oder gar Fiktionen*") (279). Schmitt insists that in a democracy "the people cannot become…a mere state 'organ'" and that "*outside* all such normative frameworks, the people continue to exist as an entity that is directly and genuinely *present*, not mediated by previously defined normative systems, validations, and fictions" (271).

However, Schmitt acknowledges that no state can exist without elements of representation (2008, 241). Thus, in modern large states the people's will is no longer directly conveyed through acclamation but "expresses itself as 'public opinion'" (131, 275). He even acknowledges political parties as elements of democracy, despite his contempt for them in connection with parliaments: "There is no democracy without parties, but only because there is no democracy without public opinion and without the people that are always present as the people.…The current superiority of the party organizations in contrast to parliament rests on the fact that these party organizations correspond to the democratic principle of identity insofar as they, like the people, are always present and at hand without representing" (276–277; see also 251). Thus, when genuine democracy, as Schmitt argued, is defined by the continuous existence and activity of the unformed people in its twofold role as "subject of the constitution-making power" and "bearer of public opinion and subject of acclamations" (279), then the role of the people as the constitutionally formed and organized political actor and stakeholder, most importantly of course in the form of a parliament, becomes secondary and, arguably, even dispensable.

This, in fact, is the conclusion Schmitt drew when the political crisis of the Weimar Republic escalated, after the breakdown of the last parliamentary coalition in March 1930. In *Der Hüter der Verfassung* (*The Guardian of the Constitution*) he states more precisely what had already been the underlying assumption in his *Constitutional Theory* (2008, 251), namely that with the disappearance of the distinction between state and society the nineteenth-century presupposition of the parliament's claim to represent the people has eroded. As the state has become a medium of the self-organization of the society, the disunity of society has migrated, as it were, into the political sphere, most visibly into the parliament. It has become an "arena of a pluralist system," dominated by political parties, which he portrays as strictly organized power machines with a bureaucratic apparatus and a disciplined mass of followers without concern for political unity and the formation of a common political will (Schmitt 1969, 82–91). They frustrate the expectation that they can and will transform conflicting social, economic, cultural, and confessional interests, values, and opinions into a single political unity. Heterogeneous momentary and special interests have replaced a unitary and homogeneous state will; the Weimar parliamentary party state is, he writes, an "unstable coalition-party-state" (88).

In the political situation of 1930–1931, in which the *Reichstag*, hampered by serious economic crisis and deep social divisions, proved unable to find a stable governing majority, Schmitt looks for a neutral actor, one superior to the plurality of social, economic, and political forces. He finds him in the *Reichspräsident*. He has, Schmitt argues, the authority to preserve the constitutional order, because he is "the center point of a system of plebiscitary and nonpartisan institutions through which the constitution aims at establishing a counterpoise to the pluralism of social and economic powers on the basis of democratic principles" (1969, 159). While this observation as such was certainly true, Schmitt here betrays his well-known antiparliamentary thrust, dismissing the Weimar Constitution's institutional architecture, which aimed at producing a minimum of political unity for a deeply divided society through the combination of parliamentary, presidential, and plebiscitary elements. The political meaning of the construction of the Weimar Constitution would wear away, indeed be turned upside down, if Schmitt's assertion were true: that the constitution "*presupposes* the whole German people as a unity which is directly capable of acting, not just through the mediation of social organizations, and which can express its will and in the decisive moment shall come together and assert itself despite all pluralistic divisions" (159; emphasis added).

This tendency to downgrade the parliamentary pillar of the Weimar Constitution's democratic architecture was carried forward with considerable conceptual sophistication in *Legality and Legitimacy* (2004). Schmitt attached importance to the fact that he had completed this treatise on July 10, 1932, ten days before the *Preußenschlag* (the so-called Prussia Coup) occurred—a coup d'état in which the *Reichspräsident*, using his emergency powers under Article 48(2) of the Constitution, ordered the replacement of the democratic government of Prussia with the *Reichskanzler* (chancellor of the Reich) von Papen as the "*Reichskommissar für das Land Preußen*" (Reich commissioner for the State of Prussia). Papen actively fostered the takeover of the Nazi Party and a few months later became a member of the first Hitler government. In fact, *Legality and Legitimacy* can be read as the juristic blueprint for the transformation of the Weimar Constitution into an authoritarian state, which, as history has shown, proved to be the starting point for the totalitarian regime of the Nazi Party.

Schmitt's argument relies on a narrative of Weimar's political system that verges on caricature. It tells a suggestive story about the antagonism between the empty normativism of parliamentary legality and the plebiscitary legitimacy of a saving executive authority "in which one can have confidence that it will pose the correct question [to the people] in the proper way and not misuse the great power which lies in the posing of the question" (2004, 90). More specifically, Schmitt's argument goes as follows: the Weimar Constitution is a "parliamentary legislative state," which is just another term for the notion of *Rechtsstaat* (3, 12, 17–26). Within this *Rechtsstaat* context the parliament embodies the dignity of a legislator and stands for a political system in which ideally laws, not men or authorities, governs—this is the meaning he assigned to the principle of legality (4). The *Reichstag* can only live up to its responsibility as a legislator and preserve the "dignity of legality" when it enacts general pre-established norms (10–11). These norms elicit the obedience of the citizens, who trust that these laws are just and reasonable. "All the dignity and majesty of the statute depends exclusively and directly...on this trust in the justice and reason of the legislature itself and in all the organs of the legislative process" (21).

If this trust exists, Schmitt argues, then even a formal and value-neutral concept of law is acceptable according to which any will of the current majority of the citizenry is law, although not unconditionally. The condition is that there is an intact connection of "confidence between the parliamentary majority and the will of the homogeneous people" (2004, 24; cf. also 27). This is so because, "by virtue of being part of the same people, all those similarly situated would in essence will the same thing" (28). If, however, this condition is not fulfilled, "the 'law', then, is only the present decision of the momentary parliamentary majority" and would amount to the tyrannical absolutism of a majority over a suppressed minority (20, 28). In other words: in a heterogeneous, deeply divided society such as Germany after World War I, the majority decision in the parliament is not able to obligate the whole citizenry because it acts only for the majority, while the "suppressed" minority regards the majority party in legal control of state power as illegal. "So at the critical juncture, each denounces the other, with both playing the guardian of legality and the guardian of the constitution" (34).

Such was the situation in Schmitt's perception of the crisis in the summer of 1932. Of course he had been critical of parliamentarianism in general and of Weimar parliamentarianism in particular since the very origin of the Weimar political system. Now the political situation offered him plausible reasons to invoke three "extraordinary lawgivers of the Weimar Constitution," all of which have the function to displace or relativize, respectively, the "legislative state legality"; that is, the authority of the *Reichstag*. As the first lawgiver he identifies the second part of the constitution itself, headed "The Fundamental Rights and Duties of the Germans," which he calls a "Second Constitution" (2004, 37), because due to its fundamental principles of "supralegal dignity" it "contains an assortment of different types of *higher legality*.... It also contains part of a *counterconstitution*" (57–58; emphasis added). The second "extraordinary lawgiver" is, as Schmitt admits, somewhat fuzzily embodied in the power of one-tenth of the enfranchised voters to initiate legislation (Article 73.3), which, Schmitt argues, constitutes a distinct sphere of plebiscitary-democratic legitimacy that competes with the system of "legislative state legality" (59–66). Finally, and most important, the third lawgiver is the dictatorial authority of the popularly elected *Reichspräsident*, pursuant to article 48, para. 2, to take the necessary measures to reestablish law and order (67–83).

Schmitt is convinced that "plebiscitary legitimacy is at present the single last remaining accepted system of justification," which presupposes "a government that...has the authority to properly undertake the plebiscitary questioning at the right moment" (90). Hence he regards the dictatorship of the *Reichspräsident* as the best solution of the crisis. Viewed from a purely formal standpoint, this was still a commissarial dictatorship. Within the logic of Schmitt's constitutional theory, however, it amounted to a sovereign dictatorship. In Schmitt's vision the Weimar Constitution, with its parliamentary system and its liberal "distortion" of the principle of democracy, could obviously not embody the standard of normality, which a commissarial dictator would have to accomplish through his extralegal instruments. Why should a genuinely "democratic dictator" who represents the unity of the people lead the polity back to a constitutional system that cannot uphold the presupposed unity of the people? Indeed, in a speech given to an audience of German industrialists in November 1932 Schmitt spoke of the "outrageous constructional defects of the Weimar constitution," which would have to be avoided in future constitutional reforms expected from the dictatorial powers of the *Reichspräsident* (Schmitt 1932, 55). Unsurprisingly, shortly afterward he hailed the transition from the ostensibly commissarial dictatorship of *Reichspräsident* Hindenburg to the explicitly sovereign dictatorship of Hitler on January 30, 1933, most clearly in his infamous article in 1934, "Der Führer schützt das Recht" (1988b).

Thus, dictatorship on a democratic foundation, which he had devised as an appropriate form of government at the dawn of the Weimar Republic, remained his answer in the final crisis of its dusk. As we know, and as could hardly have escaped Schmitt's sharp intellect, it was tantamount to a "wholesale disempowerment" of the people (McCormick 2004, xxxv; cf. also Scheuerman 1999, 85–112).

The epilogue of the constitutional drama of Weimar, in which Schmitt played a pivotal role as a constitutional theorist, was his performance as a counsel for the Reich in the trial on the constitutionality of the Prussian Coup at the *Staatsgerichtshof* (Seiberth 2001, 97; Dyzenhaus 1997a). Here he acted as a constitutional practitioner in defense of the use of the dictatorial powers by the *Reichspräsident* against the *Land* Prussia, whose acting center-left, so-called Weimar coalition government had come under fierce siege by the National Socialists, which had become the largest party group of the Prussian parliament in the elections of April 1932. The Prussian Coup of the Reich government significantly weakened the defenders of Weimar democracy, frail and self-destructive as it had become in March 1930, when the last parliamentary government collapsed due to the failure of the democratic parties to reach a compromise over the issue of public unemployment insurance (Huber 1984, 722–726). In his defense before the court Schmitt argued, inter alia, that the Prussian government, qua party government, was unable to make objective, just, and fair decisions about the legality of the National Socialists. Referring to the current Prussian government and its coalition partners, he claimed that the Reich president has to save the independence of a *Land*, which is jeopardized if "tightly organized and centralized political parties seize the *Land* and delegate their agents, their attendants into the *Land* government" (*Preußen contra Reich* 1976, 39, 468). It is a matter of debate whether he acted bona fide or ruthlessly. In any case, he was consistent in that he defended in the juridico-political realm what he had established theoretically with great sophistication throughout the whole lifespan of the Weimar Constitution—namely, the superiority of "democratic" dictatorship over parliamentary democracy (Dyzenhaus 1997b, 125–127).

CONCLUSION

In his afterword to a reprint of *Legality and Legitimacy*, written in 1957, Schmitt marked this treatise as "a despairing attempt to safeguard the last hope of the Weimar Constitution, the presidential system, from a form of jurisprudence that refused to post the question of the friend and enemy of the constitution" (2004, 95). For a naïve reader this statement might create the impression that Schmitt had been a passionate defender of the Weimar Constitution who had mobilized the last reserves of his intellectual resources to rush to the republic's rescue. In fact, however, it is self-apologetic, at least self-delusive. In his reasoning the transformation of the parliamentary mode of governance into the order of presidential dictatorship was not a response to an exceptional case of emergency, but a deeply hailed overcoming of what he had criticized time and again as the structural defect of the Weimar Constitution—namely, the establishment of the parliament as the core institution of modern democracy. Already its renaming as the "system of legality of the parliamentary legislative state" distorted its essentially democratic function to represent the people in their plurality and to bring into balance the multiplicity of their political intentions and antagonisms. What he called "the value neutrality of a functionalist majority system" could only be overcome by the establishment of a "substantive order" (94), ranking above any kind of parliamentary legality and its sources, viz. the compromises among the pluralism of competing social forces.

By excluding social and political pluralism from the concept of democracy and mistaking the *Reichstag* as a liberal institution in decline, Schmitt's alleged rescue plan for the democratic republic could only end up in a kind of authoritarian, Caesarist, or dictatorial regime. Max Weber, too, had been sympathetic to a "democratic caesar," but he had conceived of Caesar as a political leader arising from the parliament of a mass democracy. In contrast, for Schmitt the democratic dictator was the alternative to parliamentarianism. True, Schmitt did not openly challenge the legitimacy of the Weimar Constitution. Jeffrey Seitzer, the translator of the American edition of Schmitt's *Verfassungslehre*, argues that Schmitt—at least in this opus—recast "liberal constitutionalism so that the Weimar constitutional system, defined as liberal in *his* terms, can respond to the German State crisis as *he* understands it" (Seitzer 2001, 3; see also 1998, 298). This claim is not convincing because it disregards the fact that Schmitt's reading of the Weimar Constitution ignores and rejects its basic political intentions and spirit (for a more relativizing assessment, see Seitzer and Thornhill 2008, 2, 34–35). This constitution was established as an attempt to reconcile, at least to make compatible, mass democracy and capitalism, which meant the incorporation of the hitherto excluded lower classes into the political system of a deeply divided post-authoritarian and post-war society according to the basic principles of Western constitutionalism. For that purpose parliamentarianism was devised as the pivotal pillar of the political system.

Fundamental propositions of Schmitt—for instance that democracy and parliamentarianism are antipodes (2008, 289, 292); that the working class is inapt for being integrated into the political system through the institution of parliament (337); or that genuine leadership should be "directly borne by the confidence of the masses," which, as he rightly observes, would arise "in opposition to parliament" (337)—are compelling indicators that he understood the Weimar Constitution as a futile approach to solving the problems of a modernizing mass society, inferior to any authoritarian version of polity. In other words, for him the Weimar Constitution was not a tool for the solution of the crisis of the republic, but rather a central part and cause of that very crisis itself (Stolleis 2004, 332–355).

In a pointed manner one could say that for Schmitt the constitutional system of Weimar *was* in fact the true crisis. This belief was not the upshot of the experience of the collapse of

Weimar's parliamentarianism. Already in 1928, at a time when the Weimar Republic experienced a short period of relative stability, Schmitt spelled out what Hasso Hofmann, one of the most erudite analysts of his work, rightly called the "core of his seemingly purely academic constitutional theory" (2010, xxxii). In an article about the "bourgeois *Rechtsstaat*" Schmitt affirmed that the democratic element of the Weimar Constitution was still strong enough to enable the people to find its political form, despite the constraints that had been imposed on them by the ideas of the bourgeois *Rechtsstaat*. However,

> [f]or the constitutional development of the near future the point is to save democracy from its disguise through liberal moments. Only in this way...the new situation which has been produced by the new significance of the proletariat can be mastered and the political unity of the German people reestablished....Each democracy presupposes the homogeneity of the people. Only such a unity can be the bearer of political responsibility. If, as in the existing state, the people is a heterogeneous entity, then the integration of these masses into a unity becomes the challenge of the day. The genuine democratic method is not a method of integrating heterogeneous masses. However, the present-day people are multiply split with respect to culture, social status, class, and religion. Hence, a solution outside of those democratic-political methods must be found, or the parliament will become the stage which has precisely the function of exacerbating these antagonisms....It is exactly the pivotal task of integrating the proletariat into this state that reveals the deficiency of the methods of the bourgeois Rechtsstaat. (Schmitt 1928, 49–50)

In other words, a nondemocratic way to integrate the heterogeneous masses into the polity had to be discovered and applied in order to create a homogeneous people. Five years later he believed (or pretended to believe) that the right response to that challenge had been found on January 30, 1933.

Notes

1. Unless noted otherwise, all translations of source material by the author.
2. Article 48.2 reads: "In case public safety is seriously threatened or disturbed, the Reich President may take the measures necessary to reestablish law and order, if necessary using armed force. In the pursuit of this aim he may suspend the civil rights described in articles 114, 115, 117, 118, 123, 124 and 154, partially or entirely."
3. Kennedy uses the unusual term "constitutional power" for the concept of *pouvoir constituant*, constituent or constitutive power, *verfassungsgebende Gewalt*.
4. That is, constituent or constitutive power in the sense of the previous note.

References

Bendix, R. 1977. *Nation-Building and Citizenship: Studies of our Changing Social Order.* Berkeley: University of California Press.
Berthold, L. 1999. *Carl Schmitt und der Staatsnotstandsplan am Ende der Weimarer Republik.* Berlin: Duncker & Humblot.

Böckenförde, E.-W. 1991. "Die verfassunggebende Gewalt des Volkes: Ein Grenzbegriff des Verfassungsrechts." In *Staat, Verfassung, Demokratie: Studien zur Verfassungstheorie und zum Verfassungsrecht*, ed. E.-W. Böckenförde. Frankfurt: Suhrkamp, 90–112.

Böckenförde, E.-W. 1998. "The Concept of the Political: A Key to Understanding Carl Schmitt's Constitutional Theory." In Dyzenhaus 1998, 37–55.

Caldwell, P. C. 1997. *Popular Sovereignty and the Crisis of Constitutional Law: The Theory and Practice of Weimar Constitutionalism*. Durham: Duke University Press.

Cristi, R. 1998. "Carl Schmitt on Sovereignty and Constituent Power." In Dyzenhaus 1998, 179–195.

Dyzenhaus, D. 1997a. *Legality and Legitimacy: Carl Schmitt, Hans Kelsen and Hermann Heller in Weimar*. Oxford: Clarendon Press.

Dyzenhaus, D. 1997b. "Legal Theory in the Collapse of Weimar: Contemporary Lessons?" *American Political Science Review* 91: 121–134.

Dyzenhaus, D. ed. 1998. *Law as Politics: Carl Schmitt's Critique of Liberalism*. Durham, NC: Duke University Press.

Grimm, D. 1992. "Verfassungserfüllung—Verfassungsbewahrung—Verfassungsauflösung: Positionen der Staatsrechtslehre in der Staatskrise der Weimarer Republik." In *Die deutsche Staatskrise 1930–1933: Handlungsspielräume und Alternativen*, ed. by H. A. Winkler and E. Müller-Luckner. Munich: Oldenbourg, 183–199.

Gusy, C. 1997. *Die Weimarer Reichsverfassung*. Tübingen: Mohr.

Hofmann, H. 2010. *Legitimität gegen Legalität: Der Weg der politischen Philosophie Carl Schmitts*, 5th ed. Berlin: Duncker & Humblot.

Holmes, S. 1993. "Precommitment and the Paradox of Democracy." In *Constitutionalism and Democracy*, ed. J. Elster and R. Slagstad. Cambridge: Cambridge University Press, 195–240.

Holmes, S. 1996. *The Anatomy of Antiliberalism*. Cambridge: Harvard University Press.

Huber, E. R. 1981. *Deutsche Verfassungsgeschichte seit 1789. Vol. VI: Die Weimarer Reichsverfassung*. Stuttgart: Kohlhammer.

Huber, E. R. 1984. *Deutsche Verfassungsgeschichte seit 1789: Ausbau, Schutz und Untergang der Weimarer Republik*. Stuttgart: Kohlhammer.

Huber, E. R. 1988. "Carl Schmitt in der Reichskrise der Weimarer Endzeit." In *Complexio Oppositorum: Über Carl Schmitt*, ed. H. Quaritsch. Berlin: Duncker & Humblot, 33–50.

Jacobson, A. J., and B. Schlink. eds. 2000. *Weimar: A Jurisprudence of Crisis; Philosophy, Social Theory, and the Rule of Law*. Berkeley: University of California Press.

Kaes, A., et al. eds. 1994. *The Weimar Republic Sourcebook*. Berkeley: University of California Press.

Kalyvas, A. 2005. "Popular Sovereignty, Democracy, and the Constituent Power." *Constellations* 12: 223–244.

Kalyvas, A. 2008. *Democracy and the Politics of the Extraordinary: Max Weber, Carl Schmitt, and Hannah Arendt*. Cambridge: Cambridge University Press.

Kennedy, E. 1988. "Introduction: Carl Schmitt's *Parlamentarismus* in Its Historical Context." In Schmitt 1988a, xiii–l.

Kennedy, E. 2004. *Constitutional Failure: Carl Schmitt in Weimar*. Durham: Duke University Press.

Kennedy, E. 2011. "Emergency Government within the Bounds of the Constitution: An Introduction to Carl Schmitt, 'The Dictatorship of the Reich President According to Article 48 RV.'" *Constellations* 18: 284–297.

Korioth, S. 1992. "Erschütterungen des staatsrechtlichen Positivismus im ausgehenden Kaiserreich: Anmerkungen zu den Arbeiten von Carl Schmitt, Rudolf Smend und Erich Kaufmann." *Archiv des öfffentlichen Rechts* 117: 212–238.

McCormick, J. P. 1997. *Carl Schmitt's Critique of Liberalism: Against Politics as Technology.* Cambridge: Cambridge University Press.

McCormick, J. P. 1998. "The Dilemmas of Dictatorship: Carl Schmitt and Constitutional Emergency Powers." In Dyzenhaus 1998, 217–251.

McCormick, J. P. 2004a. "From Constitutional Technique to Caesarist Ploy: Carl Schmitt on Dictatorship, Liberalism, and Emergency Powers." In *Dictatorship in History and Theory: Bonapartism, Caesarism, and Totalitarianism,* ed. P. R. Baehr and M. Richter. Cambridge: Cambridge University Press, 197–220.

McCormick, J. P. 2004b. "Identifying or Exploiting the Paradoxes of Constitutional Democracy? An Introduction to Carl Schmitt's Legality and Legitimacy." In *Carl Schmitt: Legality and Legitimacy,* trans. and ed. J. Seitzer. Durham: Duke University Press, xiii–xliii.

Nippel, W. 2011. "Carl Schmitts 'kommissarische' und 'souveräne' Diktatur: Französische Revolution und römische Vorbilder." In *Ideenpolitik: Geschichtliche Konstellationen und gegenwärtige Konflikte,* ed. H. Bluhm et al. Berlin: Akademie Verlag, 105–139.

Preußen contra Reich. 1976. *Preußen contra Reich vor dem Staatsgerichtshof: Stenogrammbericht der Verhandlungen vor dem Staatsgerichtshof in Leipzig vom 10. bis. 14 und vom 17. Oktober 1932.* Glashütten: Auvermann.

Pyta, W., and G. Seiberth. 1999. "Die Staatskrise der Weimarer Republik im Spiegel des Tagebuchs von Carl Schmitt." *Der Staat* 38: 423–448, 594–610.

Scheuerman, W. E. 1996. "Carl Schmitt's Critique of Liberal Constitutionalism." *Review of Politics* 58: 299–322.

Scheuerman, W. E. 1999. *Carl Schmitt: The End of Law.* Lanham: Rowman & Littlefield.

Schmitt, C. 1912. *Gesetz und Urteil: Eine Untersuchung zum Problem der Rechtspraxis.* Berlin: Liebmann.

Schmitt, C. 1926. "Diktatur." In Schmitt 1995, 33–37.

Schmitt, C. 1928. "Der bürgerliche Rechtsstaat." In Schmitt 1995, 44–50.

Schmitt, C. 1932. "Konstruktive Verfassungsprobleme." In Schmitt 1995, 55–64.

Schmitt, C. 1936. "Der Führer schützt das Recht." In Schmitt 1988b, 199–203.

Schmitt, C. 1965. *Verfassungslehre,* 4th ed. Berlin: Duncker & Humblot.

Schmitt, C. 1969. *Der Hüter der Verfassung,* 2nd ed. Berlin: Duncker & Humblot.

Schmitt, C. 1978. *Die Diktatur: Von den Anfängen des modernen Souveränitätsgedankens bis zum proletarischen Klassenkampf,* 4th ed. Berlin: Duncker & Humblot.

Schmitt, C. 1988a. *The Crisis of Parliamentary Democracy,* trans. E. Kennedy. Cambridge, MA: MIT Press.

Schmitt, C. 1988b. *Positionen und Begriffe im Kampf mit Weimar—Genf—Versailles, 1923-1939,* 2nd ed. Berlin: Duncker & Humblot.

Schmitt, C. 1995. *Staat, Grossraum, Nomos: Arbeiten aus den Jahren 1916-1969,* ed. G. Maschke. Berlin: Duncker & Humblot.

Schmitt, C. 2004. *Legality and Legitimacy,* trans. and ed. J. Seitzer. Durham: Duke University Press.

Schmitt, C. 2005. *Political Theology: Four Chapters on the Concept of Sovereignty,* trans. G. Schwab. Chicago: University of Chicago Press.

Schmitt, C. 2008. *Constitutional Theory,* trans. and ed. J. Seitzer. Durham: Duke University Press.

Schmitt, C. 2011a. "The Dictatorship of the Reich President According to Art 48 of the Reich Constitution," trans. E. Kennedy. *Constellations* 18: 299–323.

Schmitt, C. 2011b. *Staatsgefüge und Zusammenbruch des zweiten Reiches: Der Sieg des Bürgers über den Soldaten*, ed. G. Maschke. Berlin: Duncker & Humblot.

Seiberth, G. 2001. *Anwalt des Reiches: Carl Schmitt und der Prozess "Preußen contra Reich" vor dem Staatsgerichtshof*. Berlin: Duncker & Humblot.

Seitzer, J. 1998. "Carl Schmitt's Internal Critique of Liberal Constitutionalism: *Verfassungslehre* as a Response to the Weimar State Crisis." In Dyzenhaus 1998, 281–311.

Seitzer, J. 2001. *Comparative History and Legal Theory: Carl Schmitt in the First German Democracy*. Westport: Greenwood Press.

Seitzer, J., and C. Thornhill. 2008. "An Introduction to Carl Schmitt's *Constitutional Theory*: Issues and Context." In Schmitt 2008, 1–50.

Stolleis, M. 1992. *Geschichte des öffentlichen Rechts in Deutschland: Staatslehre und Verwaltungswissenschaft, 1800–1914*. Munich: Beck.

Stolleis, M. 1999. *Geschichte des öffentlichen Rechts in Deutschland: Staats- und Verwaltungsrechtswissenschaft in Republik und Diktatur, 1914–1945*. Munich: Beck.

Stolleis, M. 2004. *A History of Public Law in Germany 1914–1945*, trans. T. Dunlap. New York: Oxford University Press.

Weber, M. 1994. "Parliament and Government in Germany under a New Political Order." In *Max Weber Political Writings*, ed. P. Lassmann and R. Speirs. Cambridge: Cambridge University Press, 130–271.

Winkler, H. A. 2005. *Weimar 1918–1933: Die Geschichte der ersten deutschen Demokratie*, 4th ed. Munich: Beck.

CHAPTER 18

....

THE CONCEPT OF THE RULE-OF-LAW STATE IN CARL SCHMITT'S *VERFASSUNGSLEHRE*

....

DAVID DYZENHAUS

INTRODUCTION

....

CARL SCHMITT'S *Verfassungslehre* is considered by many to be his greatest work and one of the major contributions to legal and political theory of the twentieth century. For example, in *The Constitution of Liberty*, Friedrich August Hayek sought to state systematically "the essential conditions of liberty under the law." "Mankind," he said, learned from long and painful experience that the law of liberty must possess certain attributes" (1990a, 205). In support of this claim, Hayek cited more than a page of scholarship in English, French, and German, including Schmitt's *Verfassungslehre*, of which he said: "the conduct of Carl Schmitt under the Hitler regime does not alter the fact that, of the modern German writings on the subject, his are still among the most learned and perceptive" (485).[1] However, in *Law, Legislation and Liberty*, Hayek also issued a strong *caveat lector* through expressing his agreement with the 1935 observation of a Nazi lawyer, Georg Dahm, that all of Schmitt's works are "from the ground up trained on one target: the unmasking and destruction of the liberal, rule-of-law state and the conquest of the statutory state" (1990b, 161).[2] In my view, Hayek was right in both respects, and I will explore this claim by focussing on Schmitt's treatment of the rule of law in the *Verfassungslehre*.

It is important to note at the outset that Hayek's second set of remarks were directed at an essay in which Schmitt was making a conscious effort to ingratiate himself with the Hitler regime after the 1933 seizure of power (Schmitt 1934). But Hayek is clear that the tension is not between Schmitt's scientific or scholarly legal writings, on the one hand, and his polemical and opportunistic interventions in German political debate after 1933, on the other. Rather, the latter, Hayek suggests, bring to the surface in a final formulation Schmitt's "central belief" that "law is not to consist of abstract rules which make possible the formation of a spontaneous order by the free action of individuals through limiting their range of actions, but is to be the instrument of arrangement or organization by which the individual is made to serve concrete purposes" (1990b, 71).

After the war, Hayek became the preeminent theorist of the liberal, rule-of-law state, what Schmitt, as we will see, termed the bourgeois *Rechtsstaat*. His remarks suggest that Schmitt helps us to appreciate that the rule of law should not be confused with the requirement of "mere legality in all government action" since that confusion leads to the claim that a government acts under the rule of law simply because a law has given it "unlimited power to do as it pleased" (1990a, 205). The rule of law is more than mere legality and "more than constitutionalism": "it requires that all law conform to certain principles" (205).

Another way of putting Hayek's point is that one should not confuse the formal conception of the *Rechtsstaat* (or rule-of-law state) that prevailed at the end of the nineteenth century in Germany, a conception that Hayek regarded as "emasculated," with "the ideals which inspired the liberal movement of the first half of that century or with "the theoretical conceptions that guided the reform of administrative jurisdiction in Prussia" (1990a, 202, 484). This distinction is the reason I translated Dahm's "*des liberalen Rechtsstaates*" as "liberal, rule-of-law state": namely, that for Schmitt, as for Hayek, if the *rechtsstaatlich* or rule-of-law conception of state is to escape being a vacuous, merely formal conception, it had to protect the liberal ideals associated in the English tradition with the rule of law.

One might even say that *because* of Schmitt's determination to destroy the liberal state he captures more clearly than do friends of liberalism a tension internal to liberalism between a substantive and a merely formal conception of the rule of law. For Schmitt, this is a distinction that has to be drawn if liberalism is to preserve itself but that forces immanent within its historical development and its self-understanding prevent it from maintaining.

I will rely in my analysis on Jeffrey Seitzer's most welcome, recent translation of the *Verfassungslehre* as *Constitutional Theory* (2008). But I will from time to time amend his translation, mainly because of the notorious difficulties in translating German terms for rule of law and associated ideas—difficulties that largely spring from the complexity of the distinction to which Hayek, following Schmitt, wishes to draw our attention.[3]

I will start by setting out Schmitt's critique of liberal legal theory, in which he seeks to show how a conception of the rule of law that once tied that rule to the protection of individual liberty has deteriorated into one in which any valid law is considered legitimate just because it is valid. I will then show how this critique is driven by Schmitt's conception of politics, a conception he claims exposes a chink in liberalism's rule-of-law armor through the recognition within legal order of the need for the president in a time of exception or emergency to act as the guardian of the Constitution. In the following section, I highlight the main features of Schmitt's position through examining the role it played in his oral argument in a crucial constitutional case of 1932, which helped prepare the legal ground for the Nazi seizure of power in 1933. Since the position is one that affirms that law cannot be more than a mere instrument of political power and one that can stabilize politics only if the political power is exercised to bring about a substantive homogeneity in the population subject to the law, I then confront the question why legal theorists and others should find that position a fruitful one with which to engage. I conclude by suggesting that Schmitt's own substantive position has nothing to offer. However, his critiques of liberalism and its conception of the rule of law point to genuine weaknesses in the liberal tradition that require an elaboration of a secular conception of authority in which principles of legality play a central role.

SCHMITT'S CRITIQUE OF THE RULE-OF-LAW CONCEPTION OF STATUTE

In §13 of *Constitutional Theory*, Schmitt discusses what he calls the "rule-of-law conception of statute," and he begins with the claim that the "bourgeois *Rechtsstaat* is based on the 'supremacy of statute law'" (2008, 181).[4] This claim is deeply polemical, as are all Schmitt's claims and definitions. It is not that it is inaccurate: the liberal state is based in part on the supremacy of statute law. It is a "statutory state"—one committed to the ideal that all acts of public officials must be able to show a warrant in a statute that delegates them the authority so to act. Schmitt is right also that the bourgeois *Rechtsstaat* is just one form of such a statutory state, since an illiberal state can be committed to the same ideal. But, as we will see, the point of his claim is to show that the liberal ideals of that state, the ideals suggested in the idea that it is a rule-of-law state, reduce to the form of the statutory state. Moreover, that reduction in turn shows that the liberal attempt to construct a state based on the supremacy of statute law must fail, since political sovereignty is always prior to law, a fact that makes it possible for liberalism's enemies to weaken, even seize control of, the state in accordance with the law.

In this section, and indeed in the book as a whole, Schmitt's main opponent is the great legal philosopher of the last century, Hans Kelsen, though he does not make an appearance by name in the section. But it is Kelsen's conception of constitution that Schmitt opposes to his own in the opening paragraph of *Constitutional Theory*. The argument of §13 is Schmitt's attempt to hammer in the final nail in Kelsen's coffin, an act that does double duty since he takes Kelsen's legal positivism to be the best possible statement of the legal and political theory of the rule-of-law state.

On the one hand, there is Schmitt's conception of a constitution as the state, "an individual, concrete state," the expression of "the political unity of the people," the "*complete condition* of political *unity* and *order*" (2008, 59). On the other hand, there is Kelsen's conception of a constitution as a "closed *system of norms*," one that does not describe a unity or anything that has a concrete existence since it is a unity that exists only as an ideal construct (59). These are both, says Schmitt, "*absolute*" conceptions of constitution since they seek to express a *"whole"* (59). But he remarks on a tendency, "a form of expression dominant today," that he clearly associates with Kelsen, to call any "series of specially constituted *statutes* a constitution," thus treating "constitution and constitutional law as identical" and at the same time making the absolute conception of constitution *"relative"* (59).

The argument of §13 is crucial since it, above all, shows why the appropriately absolute Kelsenian conception of a constitution must, because it envisages a closed system of norms, be reduced to an inappropriately relative conception of a series of statutes. In §13, Schmitt seeks to dismantle Kelsen's identity thesis, namely, that the state is not a natural individual or set of natural individuals but an artificial person which can act in that role if and only if its actions comply with the constitutive or regulative, that is, legal, conditions of that role. In sum, the state is identical with the law in the sense that acts of state that are not legally authorized do not count as such. This identity thesis is tied to a unity thesis, that the legal order is a hierarchically organized system of norms, with a basic norm at the apex of the hierarchy to which all other legal norms can trace their validity. The unity of legal order gives rise to the unity of the state.

In §1, Schmitt claims that the unity thesis in Kelsen's hands is an attempt to transform a substantial and authentically political being, one brought into existence in the bourgeois victory over the monarchy in the seventeenth and eighteenth centuries, into a formal legal functionalism. I will quote at some length from his remarks, as I think this passage is one of two in *Constitutional Theory* that are key to understanding the work as a whole. Schmitt says that in the seventeenth and eighteenth centuries

> the bourgeoisie mustered the strength to establish an effective system, in particular the individualistic law of reason and of nature, and formed norms valid in themselves out of concepts such as private property and personal freedom, which should be valid prior to and above every political being, because they are *correct* and *reasonable*, and can contain a genuine *command* without regard to the actually existing, that is, positive-legal reality. That was a logically consistent normative order. One was able to speak of system, order, and unity. With Kelsen, by contrast, only *positive* norms are valid, in other words, those which are *actually* valid. Norms are not valid because they *should* properly be valid. They are valid, rather, without regard to qualities like reasonableness, justice etc., only, therefore, because they are positive norms.... Something is valid when it is valid and because it is valid. That is "positivism."... A normative unity or order is only derivable from systematic, *correct* principles, which are normatively consistent and, therefore, valid in themselves by virtue of reason and justice without regard for their "positive" validity. (2008, 63–64)

In this passage, Schmitt seems to make some surprising concessions to liberalism and its ideal of the rule of law, given his general anti-liberalism and his claims about the political as a status that liberalism cannot achieve. He seems to concede, that is, that there is, or at least was, a liberal ideal of the rule of law that is not merely formal but also substantive. It follows by definition from the concession of substance that this ideal corresponded at one time to a political position. Moreover, while in §3 he asserts that the

Weimar Constitution is full of "dilatory compromises" (2008, 84–88), compromises in regard to the kinds of issues that have to be decided if a constitution is to have an authentically political basis, he also says that if it contained nothing besides such compromises "its value would certainly be illusory, and one would have to understand that the fundamental political decisions are to be reached *outside* of the constitutionally provided procedures and methods" (2008, 87; 1989, 35).

> However, the substance of the Weimar Constitution lies in the fact that it reaches the fundamental political decisions concerning the political form and principles of the bourgeois Rechtsstaat clearly and unambiguously. Without this political decision, its organizational provisions would only be the norms of something that merely functions without substance, and its individual provisions would only mean a tactical victory, which was achieved by some party coalition in a favorable moment in order to protect its partisan special interests against shifting parliamentary majorities. (2008, 87)

It thus seems to follow that the bourgeois *Rechtsstaat* authentically represented a political unity, which brings me to the second passage that I believe to be key to understanding the argument of *Constitutional Theory*, in Schmitt's discussion in §16 of "Bourgeois Rechtsstaat and Political Form." If liberalism were genuinely political, then, following §16, liberalism would also amount to something *existential,* not merely "a normative event, a process, and procedure" since it makes an "invisible being visible and present through a publicly present one" (243). But Schmitt's contrast with existential reality is clearly the liberalism of his day, incapable of achieving a "higher type of being" since "something dead, something inferior or valueless, something lowly cannot be represented... What serves only private affairs and only private interests can certainly be advocated. It can find its agents, attorneys, and exponents. However, it is not represented in a specific sense" (243). So the question which Schmitt seems to seek to answer in §13 is how did liberalism journey from existential "majesty, fame, dignity, and honor" (243) to dead, substanceless formalism? The clue to his answer is, first, that liberalism as an authentically political phenomenon is confined to the moment when it achieved ascendancy over monarchy and, second, that even that political ascendancy is qualified in ways that set it inevitably on the journey toward Kelsenian vacuity. Liberalism never achieved and could never achieve the quality of being truly political. For to escape vacuity, that is, to achieve political substance, the rule of law has to oppose something real, which in liberalism's case is the rule of persons. And Schmitt traces the degeneration of liberalism from rule-of-law substance to vacuity in the following passage:

> The supremacy of statute law means above all and in the first place that the legislature itself is bound by its law and its authority to legislate does not become the instrument of a system of arbitrary rule. The bond of the legislature to statute law, however, is only possible so long as the statute is a norm with certain properties, such as rectitude, reasonableness, justice, etc. All these properties presuppose that the statute is a *general* norm. A legislature, whose individual measures, special directives,

dispensations, and breaches are just as valid as its statutes containing general norms, is in no conceivable manner bound by its statutes; the "bond to statute law" is a meaningless way of speaking when in issue is one who can make "statutes" as he pleases. (2008, 181; 1989, 139)[5]

In this passage we see displayed two rhetorical moves to which Schmitt was prone. The first involves asserting that in dealing with any serious problem in political or legal theory we have to make a choice between two radically opposed alternatives, one of which is asserted to be vacuous or wholly unattractive or both; hence, there is no real choice. The second, which usually works in combination with the first, consists of using conditional claims to state a possibility that liberals must find totally unacceptable but whose antecedent Schmitt thinks is not merely possible but either already exists or will inevitably come to exist. His point here is that one has to choose between the rule of general norms and rule by directives and other particularized norms. If the latter choice is made, we would have in place not the rule of statute law but the rule of persons, which the rule of statute law was designed to escape. But, he goes on to suggest, the latter choice has been made and moreover could not be avoided.

Schmitt advances two rather different reasons for liberalism's predicament. The first is that the principles of generality and of reasonableness and justice "cannot substitute for natural law convictions" in "politically and economically difficult times" (2008, 183–184). The second is that these principles cannot be maintained, since even the principle of generality has to give way to government by directives, thus giving up on "the last residue of the bourgeois Rechtsstaat's ideal foundation generally" (183–184).

Schmitt then adds a claim that makes clear the polemical nature of the first sentence of §13. The problem with the liberal idea of the supremacy of statute law is not only that it degenerates from a commitment to generality into "helpless formalism" but also that it has to coexist in the bourgeois constitution with a "*political*" concept of law, because it is not sufficient by itself (184). The liberal or formal concept of statute law is only a "so called one" (184).

Schmitt has in mind a commonly observed phenomenon. In a legal order in which the only criterion for the validity of statutes is that they be enacted in proper form, any statute is valid no matter its content as long as it is properly enacted. It thus seems to and is often taken to follow that a statute that grants vast discretion to officials to act as they please is valid. Schmitt seems to suggest that we should reject this implication: it is "improper and false" that "legislative officials can empower themselves for anything if it is given the form of a statute" (187). However, his basis for doing so is mysterious, as he moves immediately to a different topic, the "political concept of statute law" (187).

In dealing with this topic, he hastens to reassure the reader that the political concept is not meant as a "contradiction to a juristic concept of statute law" (187). Both concepts are proper objects of scholarly treatment, but it is clear that he thinks that the upshot of his treatment of the formal or juristic concept is that it is not a genuine concept. Law in the political sense is not general; rather it is "concrete *will* and *command* and an act of sovereignty" (187): "A logically consistent and complete Rechtsstaat endeavours to suppress the political concept of statute law, in order to set up a 'sovereignty of statute law' in the place of a concrete existing sovereignty. Hence, it endeavours in fact not to answer the question of sovereignty and to leave open the question of which political will makes the appropriate norm into a positively valid command. As noted…, this must lead to concealments and fictions, with every instance of serious conflict posing anew the problem of sovereignty" (2008, 187; 1989, 146–147).[6]

Schmitt then adds that the political concept always stands alongside of the *Rechtsstaat* element and that the latter is incapable of eliminating the political concept.[7] This is important because his point is precisely that the political element can and will eliminate the *Rechtsstaat* element. The political element comes about because the bourgeoisie could not simply set up legal principles against absolutism to vanquish it but also had to put in place a different political order—the order of democracy. So one gets blended the *Rechtsstaat* concept of statute law as a "*norm* characterized by certain qualities" with the "democratic concept of statute law as the *will* of the people," that is, the "will…of the parliament" (2008, 188).

The rule of law was meant to be a guarantee against absolutism of all kinds. It should protect not only against the tyranny of monarchs but also against the tyranny of the majority. But to achieve the first aim, it delivers itself into the hands of the majority. Thus, to cut a long story short, the qualities of legality that are meant to act as a check on the kind of law that may be enacted, get reduced to the proposition that a law has been properly enacted, because it is inevitable that a "political concept of statute law proves itself stronger in opposition to the Rechtsstaat concept of statute law" (190). A merely formal concept of law "would transform the rule of law into an absolutism of legislative offices, and any distinction of legislation, administration, and adjudication would be eliminated. If that were valid constitutional law today, the entire Rechtsstaat struggle against the absolutism of the monarch would be ended in the sense that the multiheaded absolutism of the transitory partisan majority would replace monarchical absolutism" (191). Here we see again the rhetorical moves I identified earlier as part of Schmitt's argumentative strategy. The choice has already been made and had to be made since the distinction crucial to the *Rechtsstaat* between general statutory norms and application of these norms by judges or administrative officials cannot be preserved. For the equality of citizens before the law which "*is immanent to the Rechtsstaat concept of statute law*" is tied to generality, in that there is "no equality before the individual command" (194). Moreover, the independence of the judiciary "has its essential correlate in the *dependence* of judges on the *statute*" (195), so that guarantee of the *Rechtsstaat* goes when judges become subject to particular directives. Thus, Schmitt concludes that all that "protects the bourgeois Rechtsstaat against complete dissolution in the absolutism of shifting parliamentary majorities is the…factually still present residue of respect for this general character of the statute" (196).

Of course, this is no protection at all. In Schmitt's view, the liberal constitution, and in particular the Weimar Constitution, is helpless before the first enemy of liberalism who is determined and powerful enough to use the tool of legislative authorization to give itself legislative authority. And so it came to pass—the Enabling Act of 23 March 1933, celebrated by Schmitt as an act in which Hitler established himself as the guardian of right in his 1934 essay, "The Führer as Guardian of Right" (1988a, 199).

THE PRIMACY OF THE POLITICAL IN SCHMITT'S CONSTITUTIONAL THEORY

As we can see, for Schmitt the political element in a constitution has primacy. In §16, he makes it clear that liberalism never achieved an authentic political existence. It had to compromise not only with parliamentary democracy, which is not an authentic mode of representation, but also with an authentic form—the monarchical form of government embodied to some extent in the executive, and represented in Weimar by a state president. The Weimar Constitution is on this view doomed to fail, since it is an attempt to establish through law a political order that is not and cannot be authentically political, incapable as it is of making the fundamental distinction of politics between friend and enemy (1996).

Schmitt seemed to make exactly this point in 1932, four years after the publication of *Constitutional Theory*, in the last lines of his book *Legality and Legitimacy* (see also 2004, 94):

> Once one is made aware that the Weimar Constitution is two constitutions, thus offering a choice between the two, so must the decision fall for the second constitution and its attempt at a substantive order. The core of the second part of the Weimar Constitution deserves to be freed of inner contradictions and failed compromises and to be developed in accordance with its internal logic. If this is successful, so then is saved the idea of a constitution as a German work. If not, the end is at hand both for the constitution and the fictions of a functionalism of the majority with its posture of neutrality against value and truth. Then truth will take its revenge. (1988b, 98)

What does Schmitt mean here? If one puts this passage together with §3 of *Constitutional Theory* (2008, 82–88), he seems to be suggesting that the authentic German constitution will be one that sheds the organizational structure of the *Rechtsstaat* contained in the first part and then also sheds those elements in the second part that render the core of rights contradictory. That is, what he wanted saved was the rights of social units that could form the basis of what he would soon call a concrete order—rights of family, religious education, church, army—which were recognized in the second part but only in the tension-ridden fashion of liberalism because it cannot manifest itself in the public sphere without contradiction (Schmitt 1934).[8]

In my view, the means for this salvage operation are clear. They reside in the emergency powers provision, Article 48. Curiously, Article 48, which is at the center of much of Schmitt's work (e.g., Schmitt, 1988d), gets comparatively little attention in *Constitutional Theory*. His main claim is in §3 and §11 where he rejects the theory that the president's authority under Article 48 is limited to suspending the seven basic rights enumerated in Article 48(2); Articles 114 (freedom of the person); 115 (sanctity of the home); 117 (privacy of communication); 118 (freedom of expression); 124 (freedom of association); and 153 (protection of private property).

In line with his critique of Kelsen's conception of constitutionalism, Schmitt says that this theory is "tenable as long as the constitution is confused with every individual constitutional law and a distinction is not made between a principle like 'the German Reich is a Republic' (Article 1) and individual provisions like 'the civil servant is protected from intrusion into their personal papers' (Article 129)" (2008, 80–81). This confusion misconstrues altogether the "essence" of a commissarial dictator because it elevates the "individual statute above the entirety of the political form of existence" and that "twists the meaning and purpose of the state of exception into its opposite" (80–81). Schmitt clarifies this point by saying that the president may act as he sees fit under Article 48(1), whereas Article 48(2) just gives him a specific power also to place certain statutory provisions in abeyance (157–158).

Now Schmitt could be understood as saying that the president is able to suspend less important provisions (e.g., Article 129) but obviously not fundamental provisions (e.g., Article 1). But he also could be saying that, since it is absurd to suppose that the president's authority does not extend to Article 129, it is absurd to suppose that it is limited to the seven basic rights; hence it must extend further, with the question of the limits of its extension left open, to be decided by an exercise of sovereign will.

If there are doubts on this score, we can note that in §8, "Constituent Power," Schmitt makes it clear that the "constitution-making power" cannot be exhausted in the making of a constitution: it hovers above the constitution, ready to make the fundamental decision (2008, 125–126). He also says that when a constitution is democratic, that is, when the people is the bearer of such power, its will, recognized in the act of acclamation, transcends any normatively regulated procedure (131–132).

The idea here is clearly that the president, as guardian of the constitution, will decide when and how Article 48 is to be applied and the people will either choose to acclaim him or not depending on his success in articulating a vision of the identity of the people, one that makes the distinction between friend and enemy that Schmitt takes to be the essence of the political. Thus, as Kelsen pointed out in a devastating criticism of Schmitt's 1931 monograph in which Schmitt argued that the president was the true "guardian of the constitution" (1987), Schmitt's conception had to "peak in an apotheosis of Article 48" (1930–31, 623). It leads to the paradoxical conclusion that the condition for the application of Article 48, a threat to the parliamentary system, is fulfilled by the existence of that system, thus allowing Schmitt to assert that a decision to overthrow the Weimar Constitution in fact saves it as an authentic German work (627).[9]

The accuracy and exceptional prescience of Kelsen's critique was vindicated in the stance adopted by Schmitt in his argument in 1933 to the *Staatsgerichtshof*, the court with its jurisdiction to adjudicate disputes between the federal government and the states or *Länder*, in the matter triggered by the *Preußenschlag*, the strike against Prussia. More accurately, this was a coup d'état in which the conservative forces at the helm of the federal government took over the machinery of the Prussian government, made up of a coalition dominated by the Social Democratic Party (SPD). Schmitt appeared in the matter as the legal advisor to the chief architect of the coup, General Kurt von Schleicher, the Minister of Defence in the cabinet headed by Franz von Papen.

SCHMITT BEFORE THE *STAATSGERICHTSHOF*

The presidential decree of July 20, 1932, that initiated the *Preußenschlag* purported to rest on the authority granted the president by the emergency powers section of the Weimar Constitution—Article 48.[10] It declared Papen to be the commissioner for Prussia—the largest and most powerful of the German *Länder*—and gave him authority to take over its political machinery.[11] The decree responded to the alleged inability and unwillingness of Prussia's government to deal with the state of political unrest and violence within Prussia. Because this government was made up of a SPD-dominated coalition, it was the most important base of institutional resistance to the National Socialist march to power and it was removed at the stroke of a pen.

Schleicher and others in Papen's cabinet of right-wing aristocrats intended the coup as the first move in a plan to rid politics of the SPD. They would then be able to crush the communists and simultaneously tame Adolf Hitler by drawing him within the control of an increasingly authoritarian cabinet. The strategy would be complete once Hitler was neutralized and the cabinet, having eliminated all internal opposition and obstacles (including the *Reichstag*), ruled Germany by decree.

The *Preußenschlag* was a crucial moment in the breakdown of Germany's first experiment with democracy. Michael Stolleis calls it a "milestone in the constitutional history of the downfall of the Republic" (2004, 101). Both democrats who wrote accounts of the episode on the basis of their firsthand experience and leading historians of the period agree that Weimar was destroyed by the exploitation of its structural problems by those opposed to parliamentary democracy rather than doomed to failure because of the structural problems. And they agree that right up until Hitler's seizure of power displays of democratic commitment by important institutional actors, including the courts, could have made a difference to the course of events.

That the court gave the stamp of legality, however blurred that stamp was, to an executive seizure of power in 1932 by the aristocratic right in Germany can thus be said to have laid the foundation for the more dramatic seizure of power the following year and for the idea that the 1933 Enabling Law was a perfectly legal means of handing supreme and unlimited legislative power to Hitler. It also, as Stolleis says, "was a preview of the equally violent *Gleichschaltung* [political alignment]...of the *Länder* by the National Socialists once they had come to power" (2004, 102).

Papen's case for action rested on the allegation that the Prussian government was, in collaboration with the communists, bringing about a state of disorder by acting unfairly against the National Socialists. Indeed, the SPD together with the Center Party had, while in government, secured a change in the Prussian electoral law just prior to an election in correct anticipation that the National Socialists would become the largest minority party. The law ensured that the old government would continue as a caretaker government until the point when there was a majority vote of no confidence, a state of affairs that depended on the toleration of the Communist Party's representatives.[12]

It is important to understand that the decree was just part of an intricate plan in which political disorder would provide the excuse for dealing first with the Left and then with the extreme Right. Prior to issuing the decree, Papen's government had lifted a ban on the SA or *Sturmabteilung*, Hitler's paramilitary organization, while a similar ban on the communist Red Front organization remained in force. The decree unbanning the SA was followed by one on June 28 that prohibited *Land* governments from imposing their own bans on National Socialist organizations. In that month, street battles became the order of the day, as the triumphant return of the National Socialist paramilitary to the streets brought a furious and bitter response from the communists.[13] On July 14, Papen secured the emergency decree from Hindenburg. He kept it in his pocket until the outbreak of violence gave him the excuse he wanted. On July 20, the Prussian government was forcibly removed from office and Papen became commissioner for Prussia.

The court did not in its judgment accede totally to all of the legal arguments made on behalf of the federal government. Had it done so it would have had to give up on any claim to be a court of law, let alone the guardian of the Weimar Constitution, since Papen's case rested on the assertion that there were no legal limits on its use of the emergency powers provision of the Weimar Constitution, Article 48. But the court gave the federal government control of the internal machinery of Prussian government, and its reasoning wobbled precariously between saying that it could and could not enforce legal limits on action under Article 48.

Despite the fact that in substance his argument had won the day, Schmitt greeted the judgment with sorrow in his diary, bemoaning in particular the fact that the court left to Prussia the right to represent itself in the *Reichsrat*, the upper house of the German parliament in which the *Länder* were represented (2010, 227; entry for 25 October 1932.) His reaction can be explained only by the fact that his argument to the court presupposed that the court should recognize that it had no jurisdiction to second-guess the president when it came to claims about both the existence of a state of emergency and the means required to respond to it. And that argument depended directly on themes that we have seen were developed in his work since the early 1920s but that had become more distinct and explicit in late Weimar: that the primary distinction of the political is the distinction between friend and enemy; that the political sovereign is the person who is able to make that distinction; that liberal democratic institutions are incapable of making the distinction, hence incapable of being sovereign, hence cannot be the guardian of the constitution; that all of this find expression in section 48 of the Weimar Constitution, since that section recognizes the need for the exercise of sovereign authority on existential questions but seeks in a liberal legalist or *rechtsstaatlich* fashion to set limits to an exercise of executive discretion that cannot be legally circumscribed.[14]

Perhaps the most significant moment in Schmitt's argument came when he responded to Arnold Brecht, the distinguished public servant and democrat, who appeared for Prussia. In his opening statement to the court, Brecht claimed that Schmitt's (1988b) position as outlined in *Legality and Legitimacy* published earlier that year, supported the Prussian attempt to deal with its political enemies since Schmitt had suggested that it was absurd for a parliamentary democracy to permit an equal chance of gaining power to a political party that was committed to the destruction of that political system (*Preußen contra Reich* 1976, 11–28).

Schmitt responded, first, that Brecht failed to see that his question was who should decide which party to a conflict should be dealt with as illegal because it is an enemy of the state, the people, or the nation. That decision cannot, he said, be taken by one of the parties to the conflict, since it will then be taken in a purely self-interested way. The decision had to be taken by an independent government (*Preußen contra Reich* 1976, 39). He responded, second, that the issue was not merely one in which a party-political conflict threatened to explode into civil war. Rather, two states confronted each other, one of which was "occupied" by one of the conflicting parties. It was a situation in which both demanded the right to make politics and then politics in the most far-reaching and intensive sense involved in answering the question of who was an enemy of the state and the Constitution (40–44). Schmitt accused the SPD of a subterfuge in its bid to preserve parliamentary democracy in Prussia. On his view, Prussia itself, more accurately, the SPD's role in Prussia, was the threat to which the Reich government was reacting rather than the breakdown or threatened breakdown in public safety and order within Prussia (469).[15]

Thus, Schmitt held that it was irrelevant that it was in a bid to preserve democracy in Prussia and in Germany as a whole that the Prussian SPD had engineered a role for a caretaker government in the event of the republican parties not being able to command a parliamentary majority. The issue for Schmitt had nothing to do with the Prussian government's inability to command majority support because, in his view, the legitimacy of a state institution stemmed from its independence from parliamentary politics, which rendered only the federal government capable of dealing with its enemies, who included those who wished to save parliamentary democracy as well as the Communist Party. Indeed, for Schmitt it is political parties in general that pose a threat to the sovereignty of the state. A decision to intervene to preserve parliamentary democracy would perpetuate the struggle between political parties that, according to Schmitt, could poison Germany. A government that enjoyed a parliamentary mandate was part of the problem since such a government is under the control of one or more political parties (*Preußen contra Reich* 1976, 39).

Hence, Schmitt's response to Brecht is that he did not mean in that prior work that a parliamentary democracy must make the friend/enemy distinction if it is to save itself. Rather, his claim is that a parliamentary democracy is by nature potentially suicidal since it cannot make the distinction necessary for self-protection. The point of Schmitt's distinction between friend and enemy is to bring about the substantive homogeneity of the German people. More accurately, the decision as to who is friend and who is enemy is an existential one in the sense that it makes substantive homogeneity in the first place possible. It brings "the people" into existence at the same time as ensuring their preservation. And once substantive homogeneity is in place, the individuals who make up the group will find that their lives have a worth that far transcends anything that a liberal democratic society can offer. Thus, the only constraint on a decision being a genuine political decision is that it must make the friend–enemy distinction. Ruled out is an attempt to perpetuate the situation of parliamentary democracy, for parliamentary democracy adopts what Schmitt considers to be the pretense of liberal legalism. It pretends that the distinction between friend and enemy has no place in its politics. It then subverts itself by permitting interest groups to flourish that are dedicated to the kind of ideology that seeks to eradicate the idea of substantive homogeneity altogether.

Thus, while Kelsen's critique of Schmitt's 1931 claim that the president is the guardian of the constitution responded to a work published three years after Schmitt's *Constitutional Theory*, and while three years in Weimar politics was a very long time indeed, Kelsen, like Hermann Heller, another leading public law theorist and philosopher of law of Weimar, was right to regard Schmitt's position during Weimar's death throes as hardly different from his position in the late or early 1920s. In my view, and as we saw Dahm suggest, it is plausible that Schmitt's position did not change other than becoming progressively more radical and more explicit from his very first publication in 1911 (1969). But if my analysis in this and the last section is right, the question naturally arises about why we should bother with Schmitt at all—the topic of my final section.

Why Read Schmitt?

One answer to this question might be that Schmitt offers a fruitful methodology, one that does not shy away from the complex relationships between law, power, and politics or from the fact that this relationship will change from context to context, from historical period to period. But Kelsen was just as aware of these facts as Schmitt. He differed only in that he thought it important as a philosopher of law to work out the juristic standpoint appropriate for understanding a highly developed legal order from the inside—from the perspective of the individual who regards the directives of the legal order as binding.

Kelsen not only knew that there were many other questions to be answered, for example, about the relationship between law, power, and politics but also wrote at length on these issues. Moreover, as Lars Vinx shows, it is plausible that Kelsen's answer to what he took to be the questions of law's normativity informs his work on democracy, thus creating a rich resource that could contribute to our contemporary debates in legal and political philosophy (2007).

One can make much the same point about other Weimar contemporaries of Schmitt, for example, Heller, who shares with Schmitt the claim that legal theory is a branch of political theory, but, like Kelsen, regards Schmitt's understanding of the political as both dangerous and theoretically unfruitful, and again, like Kelsen, is concerned to elaborate the special kind of legitimacy of a political order that is legally constituted (see Dyzenhaus 1997a). Put differently, both Kelsen and Heller, whatever their differences, are concerned to understand the way liberal democratic legal orders have developed a scheme of legality that make it reasonable for individuals subject to the power of the state to obey its law even when they disapprove of the content of particular laws. Their legal theories thus answer the question: What attributes does law—that is, rule according to law—have that sustains the legitimacy of law under conditions of individual and group pluralism?

Schmitt, of course, does not seek to answer that question because his political theory is first and foremost about the eradication of pluralism in the cause of bringing about the achievement of the substantive homogeneity of the people that he thought was essential to maintaining a stable political and legal order. Law, on his view, is simply the instrument of legitimacy, the content of which is established or not in the moment of constituent power. Thus, there is no reason for him to engage at any deep level with the juristic thought of those who take this internal perspective on legal order, in particular with what they took to be the dynamics of legal order, and their view of the special kind of authority that inheres in legality. And because he did not so engage, he was unable or unwilling or both to engage with the way the juristic component of their thought is also an important element of their understanding of the political.

In Schmitt, this unwillingness is in part based on the understandable fact that refuge in legality looked very precarious in the circumstances of late Weimar, but with him the unwillingness goes deeper—it is, as it were, constitutional; and, as I suggested earlier, his skepticism about legality goes back to 1911. For him, only an authentic political entity can have authority, and its authenticity comes through recognition or acclamation, the "*Ja*" of the "*Volk.*" We could call this charismatic authority or, better, revelatory authority. Authority is revealed as such in a quasi-religious or mystical way, whatever is appropriate in a secular, disenchanted age. This is a political theological conception of authority, which is contentless in that it does not specify what content the legitimating ideology of the ruler should have, other than to rule out liberalism, as Leo Strauss pointed out in his critique of Schmitt (1996, 107). It is only this constitutional principle of Schmitt's thought that can explain his obsession with the exception, since the exception is for him the secular and ineliminable relict of the power to work miracles, the prerogative power that monarchs had enjoyed in virtue of the fact that the basis of their authority is divine grace. Since he accepts that appeals to divine sources of authority are no longer plausible in a secular age, he finds that the source perforce is a claim made in an existential moment. And when we call the content of what is asserted in that moment democratic, what we really mean is that its success depends on its recognition as an authentic expression of identity by a substantial proportion of the population of a given, that is, geographically bounded, territory.

Given this, Schmitt's current popularity among legal scholars and political theorists is somewhat puzzling since it is rare to find anyone in the academy who endorses this profoundly anti-liberal and indeed anti-democratic position. However, there are two explanations for this popularity.

The first and rather problematic one is that Schmitt's position can be reconfigured so that it is no longer liberalism with a minus sign: substantive homogeneity, the core of which is anything but liberalism. Rather, it is liberalism with a vengeance in which the test of whether one is part of "the people" and thus entitled to the protections and benefits of the liberal democratic state, including the rule of law, is whether one is a patriot of the principles of liberal democracy.

This kind of liberal patriotism might seem at first sight unproblematic since it merely takes seriously Schmitt's claim that a state has to make the friend–enemy distinction but rejects his thought that a liberal state is incapable of making the distinction. But when one takes into account that liberal patriotism manifests itself in stances such as "the rule of law is for us but not for those 'enemy combatants,' " or that "constitutionally protected rights and freedoms are for us but not for those Muslim immigrants," one has to become aware that the position preserves a precarious distance from Schmitt's. Still, to notice this phenomenon is important because one can then see that Schmitt's position raises starkly a question for liberal democracies. How can they respond to anti-liberals and remain true to liberal ideals, including (if this is one such ideal) not forcing people to be liberal in ways that would not be considered legitimate if they were visited on the individuals who make up the people?

The more attractive explanation is that Schmitt is an acute analyst of the problem of legality and constitutionalism, so we can detach his analysis fruitfully from his politics. For example, one might concede that Schmitt's distinction between sovereign and commissarial dictatorship makes no or little sense either from the perspective of his quasi-theological understanding of the political, or in terms of his idea that the constituent power of the people is the true source of a legal order's authority, so that it can assert itself at any time. However, one might also suppose that his attempt to work out the implications of the distinction, particularly his account of the legal constraints on a commissarial dictator, are highly interesting, especially in the post-9/11 era.

There is a lot to this explanation. Schmitt despite himself could not help but see that there was more to the *Rechtsstaat* concept of statute law than he thought politically possible, perhaps even more than some liberal theorists of the time thought legally possible. Recall, for example, his claim that it is "improper and false" that "legislative officials can empower themselves for anything if it is given the form of a statute" (2008, 187). Here, as in consideration of the first explanation, Schmitt's either–or strategy in argument, either the liberal *Rechtsstaat* or the substantive homogeneity of the people, poses a fruitful question for political scientists and lawyers alike.[16]

Schmitt thus raises challenges for liberals and democrats that are still pertinent and important. But while a lot of constructive work can be done in answering these challenges, its inspiration will not be found in Schmitt's own work except in that, somewhat ironically, he indicates a more fruitful path when he says in *Constitutional Theory* that the rule-of-law idea has to be understood as standing in a "certain tradition" (2008, 181–183), the tradition of natural law. Schmitt contrasts this path with "state *absolutism*," whose "classical formula" he claims is coined by Thomas Hobbes in the maxim, "auctoritas, non veritas facit legem," which Schmitt paraphrases as: "The law is will and command, not a wise council," that is, "valid merely as command, not by virtue of moral or logical qualities" (182).

But what Schmitt fails to notice here is that Hobbes's account of the authority of law is built on the basis of laws of nature that do not come from outside of law but that are necessarily part of the structure of legality—of governing through law—and that constitute the political power concentrated in the absolutist state in a particular way (see, e.g., Dyzenhaus 2009, 488; 2010, 453). Kelsen may be best interpreted as falling within this rule-of-law tradition in Western political thought, with its most articulate presentations in English in the twentieth century in the works of Michael Oakeshott and Lon L. Fuller.

This is the tradition that regards government by law as a normative or authoritative project, one that sees particular laws not primarily as commands backed by power but as artifacts that get their authority from the fact of their compliance with legality—from the qualities that are constitutive of the practices of both lawmaking and law interpretation.[17] Thinkers in this tradition are after a relentlessly secular conception of authority, one in which legality has a special role. Government under law has an authority that makes it possible for legal subjects to take seriously their obligation to obey the law, even though they regard its content as misguided.

In both Hobbes and Kelsen, these are qualities that inhere in legality, for Hobbes located in the laws of nature in Kelsen in what he calls the principle of legality. These qualities are by no means the sole source of legitimacy, but they are important. Law's authority is in part what makes it possible for such important issues as whether to opt for socialist or capitalist economic order to be left to political decision.[18] What Schmitt regarded as one of the weaknesses of the Weimar Constitution, that it did not decide this issue, is from Kelsen's and Hermann Heller's perspective precisely one of its strengths.

I do not want to assimilate Hobbes and Kelsen totally, of course. Kelsen saw in a way that Hobbes could not, given his personal history and his experience of the Civil War, that democracy is a political order in which this secular account of the authority of law is most at home. But what they shared is the idea that the fundamental choice in politics is between theology and secularism. That might seem in a disenchanted era to make the choice for us, and Schmitt's theoretical and personal career in late Weimar helps us understand why we should look not to Schmitt but to the thinkers in the rule-of-law tradition for our positive clues about how to go forward. Nevertheless, Schmitt's thought, as Hayek suggested, remains one of the richest resources for understanding why "the law of liberty must possess certain attributes" (1990a, 205).

CONCLUSION

As Hayek saw, Schmitt's *Constitutional Theory* has to be taken seriously because it sets out so clearly problems that a liberal account of the rule of law has to surmount if it is to prove adequate in an era where statutes dominate the legal landscape and often delegate vast powers to administrative officials to interpret and implement the statutes. If all that liberalism can manage in the age of statutes and the administrative state is to bestow legitimacy on any validly enacted statute and on anything that is done in its name by an administrative official, the rule of law would, as Schmitt claimed, have become something completely vacuous.

These insights have not lost their freshness or their pertinence since Hayek paid Schmitt the compliments I set out at the beginning of this chapter. Consider that in one of the most important books on public law of the last thirty or so years, Martin Loughlin's *Foundations of Public Law* (2010), Schmitt's critique of liberal legalism, especially the insights sketched here from his *Constitutional Theory*, play a central role perhaps even the central role in an account of public law in which *Recht* or public right is reduced to maxims of political prudence, the calculation of which seems to be in the prerogative of those who happen to have power. But, as I have argued here and in a review of Loughlin (Dyzenhaus 2013), the turn from Schmitt's negative critique to an embrace of aspects of his account of politics that lies behind it is not only politically hazardous but also requires a neglect of the rich resources within the liberal tradition that offer much help when it comes understanding how, in an age of statutes, the administrative state can be subject to the rule of law. And here subjection to the rule of law is not to something vacuous but to a set of secular principles of legality that are constitutive of individual liberty—liberty under a public order of law.

Acknowledgments

This paper was initially prepared for a class in Andrew Arato's seminar on Carl Schmitt's *Constitutional Theory* at the New School for Social Research. It has been revised in light of the discussion at the class, especially in response to remarks by Arato, Nehal Bhuta, and Jean Cohen. I am particularly grateful to Lars Vinx for a set of customarily careful and extensive written comments as well as to further discussions about Schmitt.

Notes

1. Hayek referred also to Schmitt, *Der Hüter der Verfassung* (1933).
2. Quoting from a review by Dahm. Unless noted otherwise, all translations of source material by the author. Dahm was a member of the Kiel school of law, which had the reputation of being a "shock troop university" for the construction of National Socialist law. See Michael Stolleis 2004 (291–295). Dahm, of course, meant his observation to be laudatory.
3. For Seitzer's own view of this difficulty, see 2008 (xvii–xviii).
4. I have substituted *conception of statute* throughout for Seitzer's "concept of law" and *supremacy of statute law* for Seitzer's "rule of law," as *Gesetzesbegriff* is a conception of a particular kind of law, not of law in general, and rule of law does not convey the kind of law that is supreme when we have *Herrschaft des Gesetzes* (1989, 138). I will signal other changes in the

notes and will on each occasion that I make a change other than those set out in this note cite the relevant pages from *Verfassungslehre*.

5. I have amended the translation at several points including adding the words after the semicolon in the last sentence, as these are omitted in *Constitutional Theory*.

6. Translation slightly modified.

7. At this point (2008, 187), the translation gets Schmitt's claim the wrong way round as it says that the political concept of law must not only stand "alongside the Rechtsstaat concept" but also is "not capable of eliminating" it (see 1928, 147).

8. There was thus much to Richard Thoma's critique of Schmitt's *The Crisis of Parliamentary Democracy* (1988c), included as an appendix at 77–83. Schmitt responded that Thoma's claims were "utterly fantastic" (1). Seitzer and Christopher Thornhill suggest in their Introduction to *Constitutional Theory* that it is in large part a response to Thoma's critical review (2008, 29–30).

9. Does this mean that Schmitt did not think that a distinction between commissarial and sovereign dictatorship could really be drawn? I think that the logic of his decisionism at best makes the distinction unstable, perhaps even untenable, whatever he himself suggested at times.

10. This section summarizes for the most part arguments I have made elsewhere, see Dyzenhaus 1997b.

11. One grave structural weakness in the federal system was that it perpetuated a prewar problem by leaving Prussia intact as a political entity. For Prussia contained almost two-thirds of the German population and occupied almost two-thirds of German territory. In addition, the seat of federal government continued to be the Prussian capital—Berlin. This created a severe imbalance in intergovernmental relations that the framers of the Weimar Constitution left to politics to work out.

12. Until an April 1932 election, an SPD-dominated coalition could count on majority support in the Prussian parliament. In anticipation of a situation in which the National Socialists would be the strongest minority party, the coalition changed the electoral regime, replacing the requirement that a prime minister could be elected by a relative majority if, on the first ballot, the incumbent had been voted out, with the requirement that the new prime minister be chosen by an absolute majority. In that election, the National Socialists increased their representation in the Prussian parliament to the point where they and the German Nationalists controlled about two hundred votes in contrast to the SPD and the Centre Party's one hundred and sixty. Since the Communist Party had fifty votes and would oppose a government dominated by either the National Socialists or the SPD, majority support could not be found for a new government. The old coalition government then resigned, but under the Prussian electoral law it continued to run the affairs of state as a caretaker government until a new prime minister had been chosen and had named his cabinet.

13. Ninety-nine were killed and more than one thousand wounded in skirmishes, most dramatically on Sunday, July 17, in Altona, a communist-dominated suburb of Hamburg, where the battle in the streets left seventeen dead.

14. It has been claimed in recent scholarship that Schmitt was hamstrung in his argument to the court by being forced to operate within confines set by Papen that did not permit him to represent his own position and that in the wake of the court's decision Schmitt was with Schleicher in trying to save the constitution rather than with Papen who wished to change it; see Seiberth 2000; Berthold 1998. It is obviously true that Schmitt's legal argument had

to accept the parameters of the case, and it is clear from his diary that he was frustrated by the case. See Schmitt 2010's entry for October 15, 1932 (224). It is also likely that Schmitt conceived of himself as acting to save the constitution. But his frustration was in large measure because his theoretical position was so radical that it could not be accepted in toto by a court, and it is not that easy to discern what he had in mind when it came to the "constitution" he wanted to save other than the fact that it was *not* the liberal democratic elements of the Weimar Constitution. For relevant discussion, see Caldwell 2005 (368–373).

15. For strikingly ambiguous claims in this regard, see *Preußen contra Reich* 1976 (290–291). Compare Hermann Heller's response (292–294). Schmitt also indignantly rejected the "insulting equation" of the National Socialists with the Communist Party (and thus the Prussian attempt to discredit Papen). He maintained that when the Reich government had decided to change its practice in regard to its dealings with the National Socialists, this was simply in "rightful and objective" recognition of the simple fact that millions of Germans supported their movement (39).

16. William Scheuerman (1997) underestimates this complexity of this question, and thus the reason to take both Schmitt and Hayek seriously, in an otherwise very perceptive essay.

17. Eric Posner and Adrian Vermeule (2016) see Schmitt's insights as a kind of forerunner to contemporary game-theoretic understandings of constitutionalism, coupled with a form of legal positivism that regards legality as the control of behavior by determinate legal rules so that when a rule does not have a determinate content that applies to a particular situation, the decision as to what to do in that situation is political not legal. They are right that Schmitt shares much with such accounts of law since in both all the action, as it were, takes place outside of law, in the realm of the political. Where they differ from Schmitt is that they are sanguine about liberal democracy's ability to flourish in the absence of the legal constraints on politics that are associated with the rule-of-law tradition in political thought. They acknowledge that on this view the executive is largely unbound by law; indeed, they seem to celebrate this aspect of Schmitt's thought. And that should be enough to make one wonder whether Schmitt can be demystified or defanged in the way they claim.

18. Schmitt is right that this liberal concept of the rule of law requires that law to be such must exhibit special qualities but is wrong insofar as he supposes that these qualities are tied to the preservation of a particular political ideology, the ideology of negative liberty centered on the protection of private property of an emerging bourgeoisie. To this extent, Hayek's formulation, which we encountered earlier, of the rule of law as making "possible the formation of a spontaneous order by the free action of individuals" (1990b, 71) is too narrow if it is confined to securing to individuals the ability to order their private affairs. It has to be broadened to include what we can think of as the principle of democracy, which requires securing the background conditions for making possible collective decisions about the public good.

REFERENCES

Berthold, L. 1998. *Carl Schmitt und der Staatsnotstandsplan am Ende der Weimarer Republik.* Berlin: Duncker & Humblot.

Caldwell, P. 2005. "Controversies over Carl Schmitt: A Review of Recent Literature." *Journal of Modern History* 77: 357–387.

Dyzenhaus, D. 1997a. *Legality and Legitimacy: Carl Schmitt, Hans Kelsen and Hermann Heller in Weimar.* Oxford: Clarendon Press.

Dyzenhaus, D. 1997b. "Legal Theory in the Collapse of Weimar." *American Political Science Review* 91: 121–134.

Dyzenhaus, D. 2009. "How Hobbes Met the 'Hobbes Challenge." *Modern Law Review* 72: 488–506.

Dyzenhaus, D. 2010. "Hobbes's Constitutional Theory." In *Leviathan*, ed. Ian Shapiro. New Haven: Yale University Press.

Dyzenhaus, D. 2013. "The End of the Road to Serfdom?" *University of Toronto Law Journal* 63: 310–326.

Hayek, F. A. 1990a. *The Constitution of Liberty*. London: Routledge.

Hayek, F. A. 1990b. *Law, Legislation and Liberty*, vol. 1. London: Routledge.

Kelsen, H. 1930–31. "Wer soll der Hüter der Verfassung sein?" *Die Justiz* 6: 576–628.

Preußen contra Reich. 1976. *Preußen contra Reich vor dem Staatsgerichtshof: Stenogrammbericht der Verhandlungen vor dem Staatsgerichtshof in Leipzig vom 10. bis. 14 und vom 17. Oktober 1932*. Glashütten: Auvermann.

Loughlin, M. 2010. *Foundations of Public Law*. Oxford: Oxford University Press.

Posner, E. A., and A. Vermeule. 2016. "Demystifying Schmitt." In *The Oxford Handbook of Carl Schmitt*, ed. J. Meierhenrich and O. Simons. Oxford: Oxford University Press, 612–626.

Scheuerman, W. 1997. "The Unholy Alliance of Carl Schmitt and Friedrich A. Hayek." *Constellations* 4: 172–188.

Schmitt, C. 1934. *Über die drei Arten des rechtswissenschaftlichen Denkens*. Hamburg: Hanseatische Verlagsanstalt.

Schmitt, C. 1969. *Gesetz und Urteil: Eine Untersuchung zum Problem der Rechtspraxis*. Munich: Beck.

Schmitt, C. 1987. *Der Hüter der Verfassung*. Berlin: Duncker & Humblot.

Schmitt, C. 1988a. "Der Führer schützt das Recht." In *Positionen und Begriffe in Kampf mit Weimar—Genf—Versailles 1923–1939*. Berlin: Duncker & Humblot.

Schmitt, C. 1988b. *Legalität und Legitimität*. Berlin: Duncker & Humblot.

Schmitt, C. 1988c. *The Crisis of Parliamentary Democracy*, trans. E. Kennedy. Cambridge, MA: MIT Press.

Schmitt, C. 1988d. *Political Theology: Four Chapters on the Concept of Sovereignty*, trans. G. Schwab. Cambridge: MIT Press.

Schmitt, C. 1989. *Verfassungslehre*. Berlin: Duncker & Humblot.

Schmitt, C. 1996. *The Concept of the Political*, trans. G. Schwab. Chicago: University of Chicago Press.

Schmitt, C. 2004. *Legality and Legitimacy*, trans. and ed. J. Seitzer. Durham: Duke University Press.

Schmitt, C. 2008. *Constitutional Theory*, trans. and ed. J. Seitzer. Durham: Duke University Press.

Schmitt, C. 2010. *Tagebücher 1930–1934*, ed. W. Schuller. Berlin: Akademie Verlag.

Seiberth, G. 2000. *Anwalt des Reiches: Carl Schmitt und der Prozess "Preußen contra Reich" vor dem Staatsgerichthof*. Berlin: Duncker & Humblot.

Stolleis, M. 2004. *A History of Public Law in Germany: 1914–1945*. Oxford: Oxford University Press.

Strauss, L. 1996. "Notes on Carl Schmitt, *The Concept of the Political*," trans. J. H. Lomax. In Schmitt 1996, 81–107.

Vinx, L. 2007. *Hans Kelsen's Pure Theory of Law: Legality and Legitimacy*. Oxford: Oxford University Press.

CHAPTER 19

HANS KELSEN AND CARL SCHMITT

Growing Discord, Culminating in the "Guardian" Controversy of 1931

STANLEY L. PAULSON

INTRODUCTION

IT CANNOT come as a surprise that Hans Kelsen (1881–1973) and Carl Schmitt should offer altogether different solutions to the problem of the "guardian of the constitution," the most celebrated of the many points of contention between them. Their respective views in legal and political theory differ in every imaginable way, beginning with their points of departure.[1] Kelsen commences his inquiry with the legal norm, taking up its proper construction and its presuppositions.[2] The result, regarded by many in European jurisprudential circles as the most elegant statement extant on the structure of the legal norm, reflects a far-reaching development of methodological dualism, that is, the radical separation of "is" and "ought," of *Sein* and *Sollen*, where "*Sein*" is understood as a reference to matters of fact and "*Sollen*" as a reference to the normative import of valid law.[3]

One point of departure in Schmitt's work is his means of ascertaining the "sphere of the political" (Schmitt 1927, 1–33; 1932a; 1976).[4] He contends that the political is identified by the juxtaposition of "friend or foe,"[5] whose *relata* take their meaning from "the real possibility of physical killing" (1927, 6; 1932a, 20; 1976, 33). The very existence of the state presupposes "the political," understood in this peculiarly Schmittian way (see 1927, 1, 19; 1932a, 7, 17, 41; 1976, 19–20, 29–30, 53).[6] The familiar antithesis of *Sein* and *Sollen*, defended by Kelsen and the neo-Kantian philosophers,[7] is supplanted, as Hasso Hofmann neatly puts it, by the antithesis of *Sein* and *Nicht-Sein* (1992, 21, see also 39, 48, 87).

A second contrast between Kelsen and Schmitt, following naturally upon the first, emerges from their respective views on sovereignty. In Kelsen's work, the traditional doctrine of legally illimitable sovereignty yields to a peculiarly Kelsenian concept of constitution, comprising the constitutional norms of the positive law (see Alexy 2005, 333–352)[8] and the juridico-logical constitution underlying them.[9] Kelsen is quick to dismiss the views of his Hungarian colleague, Felix Somló, who was well known in his day for a treatise that counts, inter alia, as a defense of an Austinian doctrine of sovereignty, replete with numerous references to John Austin's *Lectures on Jurisprudence* (Somló 1917).[10] Schmitt, by contrast, develops his concept of sovereignty with special attention to two of Austin's intellectual ancestors, Jean Bodin and Thomas Hobbes.[11] Sovereignty, which is personalized, decisionistic, and above the law, manifests itself whenever a decision is taken on the exception (*Ausnahmezustand*). "Sovereign is he who decides on the exception" (Schmitt 1922, 9; 1934, 11; 1985b, 5), and, Schmitt continues, "the legal system rests on a decision, and not on a norm" (1922, 11; 1934, 16; 1985b, 10). The question of the state's existence calls in the end for an absolute decision "free of all normative ties" (1922, 13; 1934, 19; 1985b, 12).

A third general contrast turns on the profound differences between Kelsen and Schmitt on the theory of democracy. Whereas Kelsen is a convinced proponent of parliamentary democracy,[12] Schmitt sees parliamentarianism as a reflection of liberalism, which he subjects to a savage critique.[13] In place of liberalism, Schmitt offers a theory of democracy the central premise of which is identity, namely, "the identity of the governing with the governed" (1922, 44; 1934, 63; 1985b, 49). Not only is democracy to be understood as an alternative to liberalism, but since "the core of democracy" is "the identity of law and the people's will," and since a dictator's decrees can be identified with the "properly recognized, properly formed, and correctly expressed" will of the people, then "democracy and dictatorship are not antithetical."[14]

A fourth contrast between Kelsen and Schmitt may be drawn from their respective views on unity. Questions about how to determine the unity of the state, the nation, a people—questions as to which indicia count and why—were a motif in politics and the law over a very long period of time,[15] of especial import for the multicultural Austro-Hungarian Empire. Kelsen's deep and abiding interest in unity[16] was informed by these questions. His answers are grounded in the theory of knowledge. "[T]he postulate of the *unity* of cognition is unconditionally valid for the normative sphere, too, and finds expression here in the unity and exclusivity of the system of norms presupposed as valid" (Kelsen 1920a, §25, 105). Thus understood, Kelsen's unity of law thesis is pervasive in his legal philosophy, dictating, inter alia, his doctrine of legal monism in public international law (see 1920a, §§25–51, 102–241; 1926, 289–320).[17]

A prominent theme for Schmitt is his steadfast interest in political unity. In *Constitutional Theory*, he speaks of the act of establishing a constitution as a decision that gives expression to political unity. "This act *constitutes* the form and the nature of political unity, whose existence is presupposed" (Schmitt 1928a, §3.I, 21; 2008, 75). The reading of political unity that Schmitt sets out here is overshadowed by his contention that, as a factual matter, political unity has been completely undermined by political pluralism. "In three horrific centuries, the *political unity* of the Germans has gone to *rack and ruin*,"[18] and this has led, in the Weimar period, to the undiscriminating identity of state and society, to what Schmitt calls the "quantitative" or "weak" total state.[19] The only solution, Schmitt contends, is wholly to supplant the parliament, dysfunctional in any case,[20] by means of the Reich president, yielding the "qualitative" or "strong" total state.[21]

The contrasts between Schmitt and Kelsen are clearly sharpened in 1922, with Schmitt's publication of *Political Theology*.[22] In very early work, however, Schmitt stands in a certain proximity to Kelsen. This is particularly evident in Schmitt's treatise of 1914, *The Value of the State*,[23] in which he unequivocally endorses certain motifs familiar from Kelsen and the neo-Kantians.

Against this background, the present chapter delineates and explains the evolution of the contrasts between Schmitt and Kelsen. It charts growing discord, with particular reference to its culmination in the "guardian" controversy of 1931, that is, the sharp disagreements between the two thinkers in the wake of the publication of Schmitt's monograph *The Guardian of the Constitution*. In the first part of this chapter I focus on two of Kelsen's juridico-philosophical motifs, dualism and "points of imputation," along with positions of Schmitt's that are in part analogous. In the second part I take up Schmitt's criticism, above all in *Political Theology*, of Kelsen's Pure Theory of Law. Schmitt's stance in this work, published in 1922, is very different from his view in the 1914 monograph *The Value of the State*, and the shift in his attitude toward Kelsen can scarcely be missed. Schmitt's earlier dualism, not far removed from Kelsen's, disappears without a trace. And while Schmitt drew on Kelsen's doctrine of "points of imputation" in an altogether friendly way in his earlier work, the doctrine now ignites what proves to be formidable criticism of Kelsen's legal philosophy. In the third part, an excursus on Kelsen's major role in the formation of the Austrian Federal Constitution of 1920, including his most noteworthy contribution, centralized constitutional review, I anticipate the "guardian" controversy. The controversy itself is front and center in the fourth part. I examine Schmitt's central arguments on behalf of the Weimar Reich president as the guardian of the constitution, and I also take up Kelsen's rejoinders to these arguments. From our current perspective, Schmitt's position in the "guardian" controversy, in particular his categorical rejection of constitutional review, is hard to get a handle on. The explanation here—as distinct from a justification—turns at least in part on Schmitt's role in promoting the Weimar *Präsidialsystem*, or presidential constitutional framework, an issue to which I turn in my conclusion. The great differences between Kelsen and Schmitt on the merits of the presidential constitution mark the culmination, in the Weimar period, of the ever greater discord between them.

SCHMITT'S PROXIMITY TO TWO MOTIFS IN KELSEN'S EARLY WORK

In the monograph *The Value of the State* (1914), Schmitt defends a *dualistic* position in legal theory.[24] Dualism is reflected in the familiar juxtapositions, for example, of *Sein* and *Sollen*, fact and value, reality and idea (*Wirklichkeit und Idee*), as they are under-stood in the work of fin-de-siècle neo-Kantians, whose position is manifest in the arguments they adduced against the myriad psychologistic and naturalistic theories of the day.[25]

But why emphasize dualism in a comparison of Kelsen's legal philosophy with that of the early Schmitt[26] when Kelsen's philosophy is a prominent example of a monistic position? The answer here turns on an ambiguity. Within the confines of his legal phi-losophy, his Pure Theory of Law, Kelsen attacks dualisms at every turn: the dualism of objective law and subjective right,[27] of public and private law (see 1925a, §17, 80–91), of legal person and human being (see 1992, §25, 46–52; 1960, §33, 172–195), of public international law and municipal law,[28] and indeed, of law and state (see 1992, §§18–24, 37–46; 1960, §41, 289–320). By contrast, whenever Kelsen is addressing both the natural world, the world of *Sein*, as well as the law, the world of *Sollen*, his position is dualistic, reflecting a "two worlds" doctrine, at any rate in his earlier work.[29] And it goes with-out saying that the natural world reaches to and includes much of the law. That is, the daily activities of the law—the mechanics of discovery (oral depositions, depositions on written interrogatories, and the like), the joinder of claims, the cross-examination of witnesses, and so on and so forth—are found not in the ideal world of *Sollen* but in the natural world of *Sein*. Thus understood, Kelsen's position is a clear case of methodologi-cal dualism, familiar from the neo-Kantians. The point of interest here is that Schmitt, in *The Value of the State*, defends dualism along lines similar to Kelsen's, even if his defense proves to be short-lived.

Schmitt, at an early point in the monograph, takes up the problem of law and power. Which comes first? The question is no more helpful than the overworked chicken-and-egg query (Schmitt 1914, 39). The real question, Schmitt argues, is

> whether the law can be derived [*abgeleitet*] from facts. Even if recognition of the law by human beings is simply a fact, the question arises of whether facts can establish law. If the question is answered in the negative, the opposition of two worlds is given. If the law is self-sufficient and independent vis-à-vis power, then dualism follows, corresponding to the antitheses of *Sollen* and *Sein*, of perspectives normative and genetic, of the critical perspective and the perspective of natural science. (1914, 20)

Taking the conditional statements in the quotation at face value, one is inclined to inter-pret them hypothetically: *If* the law is self-sufficient, then dualism follows. Schmitt, however, expressly affirms a categorical, as distinct from a merely hypothetical, position on dualism: "The difference between law and non-law is established only by the intro-duction of a norm, not by nature. The sun shines on the just and the unjust alike" (1914, 31). Schmitt continues:

> If the law can be derived from facts, then there is no law. The two worlds stand in opposition to one another. ... Legal norms, in seamless unity, must be independent of everything empirical, so that an empirical fact as such can never be subject to the law's judgment. (31)

In a word, there is common ground between Kelsen and the Schmitt of 1914. Both endorse dualism, the world of *Sein* and the world of *Sollen*. Dualism gives rise, however, to a serious philosophical problem. As Schmitt rightly observes: "[T]he problem lies in bringing the two spheres together" (1914, 38). If there is no basis for taking up content from the one world into the other world, then a legal pronouncement (*Sollen*)—in Kelsenian parlance, an individual legal norm[30]—addressed to an actual state of affairs (*Sein*) is impossible. In attempting to resolve this problem within a dualistic framework, Kelsen fares better than Schmitt in at least one respect, to wit: He, unlike Schmitt, addresses the issue with arguments. I begin with Kelsen's proposed resolution.

Kelsen is keenly aware of the problem posed by the complete separation of *Sein* and *Sollen*. In 1911 he wrote:

> The opposition of *Sein* and *Sollen* is a formally logical opposition, and as long as one remains within the boundaries of the logico-formal perspective, no path leads from the one world to the other, the two are separated from each other by an unbridgeable chasm.[31]

Kelsen seeks to resolve the problem by means of the "modally indifferent substrate,"[32] arguing that this doctrine provides the required link between the two spheres. In *The Problem of Sovereignty*, a very early statement of the doctrine,[33] he amalgamates *Sein* and *Sollen* as distinct worlds with *Sein* and *Sollen* as distinct forms of thought,[34] arguing:

> Although *Sein* and *Sollen* are two altogether distinct *forms* of thought, neither reducible to the other, they can still have the same *content*. Human action can be imagined as the content of *Sein*, as a part of nature or history, that is, as the subject matter of natural science or the study of history, or it can be imagined as obligatory, as the content of norms and therefore as the subject matter of legal science. It is only because of this common "substrate"—in and of itself indifferent, and *in abstract terms completely unimaginable*—that an actual state of affairs can be evaluated and, in particular, can be legally judged. (Kelsen 1920a, §24, 99 n1)

Thus, so Kelsen is arguing, "an actual state of affairs" (*Sein*) can be "legally judged" (*Sollen*). The substrate underlies content both in the world of *Sein* and in that of *Sollen*, making possible the move from one world to the other.

However, there is a problem with the argument, and perhaps Kelsen is alluding to it in the italicized phrase of the quotation.[35] The problem is that "substrate" remains something of a mystery. Kelsen finds himself in good company here. No less a figure than John Locke, in his *Essay on Human Understanding*, speaks of substance or *substratum* and, in the same breath, of our ignorance of "the secret and abstract Nature of Substance."[36]

There may be a way out of the thicket. Many years later, in the early 1940s, Kelsen introduces legal propositions (*Rechtssätze*) as a means of describing legal norms.[37] With this shift, Kelsen arguably anticipates developments that would become familiar from speech act theory or pragmatics. The point can be illustrated by appeal to machinery set out by Richard Hare in *The Language of Morals* (1952). There Hare introduces the *phrastic*, understood as a gerundial phrase—for example, "your shutting the door" (see Hare 1952, ch. 2, 17–31)—and the *neustic*, which means, roughly, "to nod assent." Hare then employs the neustic in the course of distinguishing between the assertion (nodding as if to say "you are shutting the door") and the command (nodding as if to say "shut the door"). In a word, the neustic is shorthand for whatever species of illocutionary act is at hand—the act of making an assertion or of issuing a command.[38] The phrastic, the descriptive component, is Hare's counterpart to Kelsen's substrate. Just as the phrastic is common to the indicative and the imperative in Hare's scheme, the substrate is common to the modi that correspond to Kelsen's world of *Sein* and world of *Sollen*.

To be sure, all of this presupposes that Kelsen in introducing legal propositions has moved from the hyletic conception of norms, which embraces an ontology of norms in the world of *Sollen*, to the expressive conception, that is, to speech act theory or pragmatics as adumbrated above. Leaving aside a host of complex issues, the important point for my purposes is that there are arguments on behalf of the thesis that this shift did indeed take place in Kelsen's work, marked initially by his introduction of legal propositions.[39]

Schmitt, too, attempts to find a way out of the quandary posed by dualism. In sharp contrast to Kelsen, who has the makings of an argument, Schmitt rests content with bald assertions. His key notion is the state. Hinting in this direction at the outset of *The Value of the State*, he writes that "the state gives effect to the link between this world of thought (*Gedankenwelt*) and the world of real empirical phenomena" (Schmitt 1914, 2). He goes on to say that the essence of the state is "to mediate the link between the two spheres" (38) and that furthermore, what follows "from the juxtaposition of the norm and the real empirical world is the status of the state as the point connecting the one world with the other" (52). The state is, therefore "the framework of the law whose sense consists exclusively in the task of realizing the law" (52, emphasis in original omitted). Schmitt emphasizes here that his "definition, which renders the state dependent on the law," provides a role for purpose in the concept of the state, holding the state to be "an instrument for the influence of the law on reality." Indeed, he continues, "the state is the sole construction of the law that incorporates purpose into its concept" (53). Schmitt concludes, from this, that every state is a *Rechtsstaat* (53).[40]

Kelsen, too, claims that every state is a *Rechtsstaat*,[41] but his reasoning is different. Stephen Holmes would have us believe that Kelsen is claiming thereby that every state manifests constitutionalism. Holmes asserts: "Kelsen made a notorious statement that even the Nazi regime qualified as a *Rechtsstaat*—a constitutional state in which the rule of law prevails" (Holmes 1995, 698). But Kelsen made no such statement. The statement Holmes attributes to Kelsen represents a misunderstanding. Kelsen clearly distinguishes between *Rechtsstaat* qua identity of law and state and, as the concept is ordinarily understood, *Rechtsstaat* qua constitutional state embracing the rule of law. When Kelsen says that every state is a *Rechtsstaat*, he has the first reading in mind.

The important Danish legal philosopher Alf Ross (1899–1979), in a major treatise of 1933 (ch. III, §2, 52–53; see also Hommes 1984, 171–172), develops a powerful rejoinder to Kelsen's effort to bridge the gap between *Sein* and *Sollen*. Arguably, Ross's criticism does not apply after the shift in Kelsen's thinking in 1941, but it clearly applies to the earlier

Kelsen and to Schmitt as well, underscoring Schmitt's difficulties in invoking the state as his means of bridging the gap between the worlds of *Sein* and *Sollen*. Ross's argument runs as follows. In dualism, the worlds of *Sein* and *Sollen* are together exhaustive of the field, and they are altogether distinct. Thus, there can be no third kind of thing—*tertium non datur*—and, what is more, the two worlds cannot share any element; that is, there can be no common element linking them.

The putative link, the state, in Schmitt's response to the problem can be evaluated from the standpoint of Ross's criticism. Either the state is a part of the world of fact or it is a part of the normative world. The state always finds itself in the one world or the other and cannot, therefore, serve as a link between them. Or the alternative, which is this: The state is introduced as something that goes beyond the two worlds. But this is tantamount to introducing a third world, contrary to the hypothesis that the worlds of *Sein* and *Sollen* are together exhaustive. In short, all of Schmitt's remarks on the state's linking *Sein* and *Sollen* give rise to the question: *How* does the state count as the required link between the natural world and the law? Schmitt has no answer. To be sure, there is a significant shift in his work, coming, for some purposes, as early as 1916 and clearly entrenched in focus and in attitude by 1922. Thereafter, dualism plays no role in Schmitt's theorizing.

There is, in addition to *Sein* and *Sollen*, a second context that underscores Schmitt's proximity to Kelsen in 1914, namely the significant and peculiarly Kelsenian doctrine of "points of imputation" (*Zurechnungspunkte*), to which Schmitt refers in *The Value of the State* (1914, 4, 99). The fact that Schmitt takes up Kelsen's doctrine in an altogether friendly way in the monograph of 1914 invites attention to Schmitt's receptivity, at this early point, to other aspects of Kelsen's legal philosophy. Eight years later, in *Political Theology*, Schmitt takes up Kelsen's doctrine of points of imputation again, but this time around the doctrine in Schmitt's hands gives rise to powerful criticism of Kelsen's position.

The general notion of imputation, as distinct from points of imputation, is familiar in both moral and legal contexts, above all from Kant (1900–, vol. 6, 211–228; 1999, 7–24). In Kant's *Rechtslehre*, an individual is responsible in a moral sense for those acts that are attributable to him. Similarly, mutatis mutandis, in Kant's legal context. If a material fact that counts as an instance of a type of act proscribed by law is attributed or *imputed* to an individual in the legally required way, the individual is deemed to be legally liable (see Kant 1900–, vol. 6, 227; 1999, 21). Kelsen takes things further, shifting from persons— human beings—to normative counterparts, where "normative" flags entities in the world of *Sollen*.

> When certain acts of particular physical persons count, from a legal standpoint, not as acts of these persons but as acts of another person distinct from them, this is a special case of *imputation*. The material fact in the activity of these persons is imputed not to these persons themselves but to another person. The point of imputation, however, is not within another human being. Imputation proceeds, so to speak, through the physical actors and their psychical acts of will without stopping in another physical person, as is the case, for example, with liability for harm wrought by children or employees and imputed to the father or the employer, respectively. Rather, all strands

of imputation unite in a common conceptualized point outside every physical subject. (Kelsen 1911a, 183; 2008, 293–294)[42]

What is this "common conceptualized point"? In the first sentences of the quotation, where Kelsen speaks of "another person," he is not referring to a human being at all. Rather, he has in mind a legal subsystem (*Teilrechtsordnung*), say, a municipality. The acts of particular persons are imputed to the legal subsystem, the municipality. This subsystem, this cluster of legal positions or points of imputation, is imputed in turn to a legal subsystem at a more fundamental level. Ultimately, points of imputation representing a legal subsystem make reference to the greater legal system, to the will of the state qua legal system, which counts as the endpoint of imputative reference, the "common conceptualized point" that lies beyond every physical subject.

This is an elaborate explanation of a doctrine that Kelsen, in later work, replaces for the most part with "peripheral imputation," which he links to certain other doctrines.[43] It is Kelsen's early work, however, that is of interest in the present context—with Schmitt following Kelsen here, introducing points of imputation several times in *The Value of the State*. For example:

A time that presents itself as skeptical and precise cannot in the same breath call itself individualistic.... If one can speak of individuality at all, it is found in a definition of subject matter that is predicated on individuality as a point of imputation (*Zurechnungspunkt*) for valuations made according to norms. (Schmitt 1914, 4)

Individuality is a point of imputation. It is thereby relegated to the ideal world, the world of *Sollen*, with an eye to "valuations made according to norms" (1914, 99; see also Jaitner 1996, 482). To be sure, Schmitt is not engaged in Kelsen's enterprise of imputing acts to legal subsystems and ultimately to the state. Still, points of imputation in Schmitt's monograph represent a concept that is on all fours with Kelsen's own understanding of the concept; both thinkers resort to it in the world of *Sollen*.

Franz Weyr, in a review of *The Value of the State*, remarks that the respective inquiries of Kelsen and Schmitt agree in their results to an extent that is "well nigh baffling" (1914, 579).[44] Weyr (1879–1951), the leading figure in the Brno School of Legal Theory,[45] a sister school to Kelsen's Vienna School of Legal Theory, was in 1914 *the* expert on Kelsen's work. He had been profoundly influenced by Kelsen, and he wrote, in three languages, in a Kelsenian vein.[46] It is understandable, then, that Weyr would dwell on what he saw as similarities between Kelsen and Schmitt in the latter's treatise. What is more, Weyr welcomes the fact, as he saw it then, that "the direction inaugurated by Kelsen is gaining ground among the writers in the field" (579).

I have looked thus far at Schmitt's proximity in very early work to Kelsen, in particular the proximity found in Schmitt's monograph of 1914, *The Value of the State*. There is, in addition, Schmitt's review, appearing in 1916, of Julius Binder's *Legal Concept and Legal Idea* (1916a, 431–440). Binder wrote as a neo-Kantian in his early work (see Dreier 1987, 435–455; 1991, 142–167), and his treatise is a sustained critique of Rudolf

Stammler's *Theory of Legal Science* (1911). Stammler, the whipping boy of an entire generation of legal theorists, philosophers, and social theorists, including Kelsen, Hermann Kantorowicz, Hermann Cohen, Max Weber, and Georg Simmel, did not escape Binder's attention. Of special interest is the fact that Schmitt's arguments in the review, directed first to Stammler's position and then to Binder's, count as immanent criticism, that is to say, criticism developed within the framework of those whom he is criticizing. Stammler and Binder's standpoint was the transcendental philosophy of Kant and the neo-Kantians. And Schmitt proceeds from a transcendental standpoint, arguing that Stammler "conflates formal and empirico-psychological elements" (Schmitt 1916a, 434), thereby undermining the ostensibly transcendental dimension of his legal philosophy. Schmitt turns then to Binder, arguing that Binder's distinction between the factual dimension of the law and its transcendental dimension amounts to nothing more than a definition, with the result that the ostensibly "'constitutive import' of the legal norm vanishes without a trace" (437). Here, Schmitt adds, Kelsen's position is to be preferred:

> Binder's professed allegiance to the Kantian philosophy and his adoption of the distinction between natural and cultural sciences—in contrast to the resoluteness with which, for example, Kelsen juxtaposes jurisprudence as a normative science with the sociologico-explicative sciences—has no practical significance whatever. (437)

In these lines, too, Schmitt's receptive attitude toward Kelsen's work is abundantly clear. Still, this common ground is ephemeral. By 1922, in *Political Theology*, Schmitt is engaged in hard-headed criticism of Kelsen, now treating some of the Kelsenian doctrines he had taken up in *The Value of the State* in altogether unfavorable terms.

SCHMITT'S SHIFT, IN 1922, TO CRITICISM OF KELSEN

In *Political Theology* (1922), far and away Schmitt's most rewarding critical discussion of Kelsen, he takes up two closely related issues: first, the problem of sovereignty writ large, and second, Kelsen's points of imputation as one aspect of the problem of sovereignty. The first issue, sovereignty writ large, is of no special interest here, for Schmitt's argument is weak. However, when Schmitt turns to points of imputation, he engages in unusually effective criticism, and this stands in sharp contrast to his tacit endorsement of points of imputation in *The Value of the State*. I begin, very briefly, with the first issue, Schmitt's criticism of Kelsen on sovereignty writ large.

Schmitt addresses the problem of how "factual power" stands to "the highest legal power," a motif familiar in English-speaking circles as a fundamental problem of sovereignty.[47] But, Schmitt contends, Kelsen proceeds with what purports to be "a simpler solution,"[48] a solution that turns on the "opposition" between sociology and

jurisprudence: "The old juxtaposition of *Sein* and *Sollen*, of causal and normative perspectives, is…recast in terms of the opposition between sociology and jurisprudence"
(1922, 20; 1934, 27; 1985b, 18).

This position of Kelsen's, Schmitt concludes, represents the "negation" of the problem
of sovereignty (1922, 22; 1934, 31; 1985b, 21). Schmitt's conclusion is, I think, less than
helpful. Kelsen dismisses all naturalistic notions of sovereignty and introduces in their
place a normative counterpart, represented by constitutional norms and the underlying juridico-logical constitution or basic norm. Sovereignty is dispersed, so to speak,
over a range of legal norms, and the complexities of Kelsen's view are underscored by
the role he assigns to the "greater constitution" (*Gesamtverfassung*; see 1927b, 128–143)
on the one hand and to constitutional review on the other. Thus, Kelsen explicates sovereignty in a manner strikingly different from Schmitt's view. To be sure, the problem of
sovereignty that Schmitt rightly poses in the name of the competing claims of "factual
power" and "the highest legal power" remains. But this problem lies in the nature of
things. Institutional arrangements may diminish its effects, but they offer no solution.

A different criticism of Schmitt's, both at this point in chapter two of *Political Theology*
and in chapter three, takes us back to imputation and to the notion, drawn from Edmund
Bernatzik, that the state "posits itself." What, Schmitt asks, has become of the state in
Kelsen's theory? Answering on Kelsen's behalf, Schmitt refers to the peculiarly Kelsenian
notion of points of imputation: "The state, that is, the legal system, is a system of imputations [*Zurechnungen*] [leading] to a final point of imputation [*Zurechnungspunkt*] and
to a final basic norm" (1922, 21; 1934, 28; 1985b, 19). This statement reflects Kelsen's well-
known doctrine of the identity of the law and the state.

Schmitt, drawing on Bernatzik, works up a brilliant criticism of Kelsen's legal philosophy that turns on the idea of a system of norms that "posits itself." The first hint of the idea
that "a norm or a system [of norms] 'posits itself'" comes near the end of the first chapter
in *Political Theology* (1922, 14; 1934, 21; 1985b, 14). Although Schmitt at this point in the
text is in fact addressing a different issue, the question arises as to how the state, the final
point of imputation, "posits itself." In the second chapter Schmitt reverts to the "imputation problem" again, adumbrating Kelsen's position: "From the legal perspective, there
are neither real or fictitious persons but only points of imputation [*Zurechnungspunkte*].
The state is the endpoint of imputation [*Endpunkt der Zurechnung*]."

Finally, in the third chapter of *Political Theology*, Schmitt takes up what might be
termed a bootstrap operation, turning directly to Kelsen's erstwhile advisor in Vienna,
Bernatzik,[49] who, quoted by Schmitt, writes: "It lies in the concept of legal competence
that its source, the state legal system, must posit itself as the subject of all law, thus, as a
legal person."[50]

This claim, which Schmitt attributes to Kelsen, gives rise to what Schmitt rightly
regards as a rhetorical question, to wit: How is the state to "posit itself"? Of course it
cannot posit itself; the bootstrap operation makes no sense. What is more, Schmitt sees
clearly the transition, in Kelsen's work, from imputation—represented by points of
imputation—to the basic norm. Schmitt's criticism, that the bootstrap operation is nonsense, carries over to the basic norm: How does the basic norm enable the state to "posit

itself"? No consensus—not today, let alone in 1922—has emerged on what, exactly, the doctrine of the basic norm comes to,[51] and Schmitt's criticism stands as a formidable case against the viability of the doctrine.

As already noted, Schmitt's most powerful and detailed criticism of Kelsen's legal philosophy is found in *Political Theology*. Six years later, in *Constitutional Theory*, Schmitt is equally outspoken in his criticism of Kelsen, but now the tone has changed. In *Constitutional Theory*, it is less a matter of detailed analysis than of impatient dismissal. Schmitt contrasts the tradition in legal philosophy with Kelsen's philosophy. In the tradition, a thoroughgoing normativity is reflected in the "individualistic law of reason and natural law," forming valid norms "from such concepts as private property and individual freedom" (Schmitt 1928b, 8; 2008, 64). What one finds in Kelsen's philosophy is diametrically opposed.

> Here *Sollen* suddenly ceases to be and normativity is cut off; instead of normativity there appears the tautology of a crude facticity: Something is valid if it is valid and because it is valid. *This* is "positivism." One who is serious in insisting that "the" constitution is supposed to be valid as the "basic norm" and that everything else that is valid is supposed to be derived [*ableiten*] from it is not allowed to take just any given concrete provisions as the basis of a pure system of pure norms simply on the ground that they have been set down by a certain organ, that they are recognized, and that they are therefore characterized as "positive," that is, as factually efficacious. (1928b, 8; 2008, 64; emphasis added)[52]

The idea that "everything else that is valid" is somehow *derived* from the basic norm is a common misunderstanding of Kelsen's position, stemming from the familiar charge that Kelsen's legal philosophy is formalistic (see Paulson 2002, 109–113; 2008, 9–16). Despite all the puzzles and problems that arise in connection with Kelsen's basic norm, some things can be said with confidence, for example, that he set out no fewer than six different basic norm forms, to wit:[53] the basic norm qua ultimate ground of legal validity, where the "validity" of a legal norm refers to its membership in a legal system; the basic norm qua ultimate ground of legal validity, where the "validity" of a legal norm refers to bindingness, the idea that one ought to obey the commands of the law; the basic norm qua ultimate ground for the move from the merely subjective sense of an act to its objective or legal sense; the basic norm qua ultimate ground for the empowerment to issue legal norms; the basic norm qua ultimate ground for the empowerment to impose sanctions; and finally, the basic norm qua ultimate ground of the unity of law. Given this complexity, it is not helpful to proceed, as Schmitt in fact proceeds, as though the basic norm were nothing more than a fig leaf, shrouding from view "a crude facticity." For an argument here—as distinct from a straw man—Schmitt would have to address the very neo-Kantian underpinnings of Kelsen's legal philosophy that he, Schmitt, had adumbrated in some of his own early work.

I now turn to a self-contained excursus on Kelsen's leading role in Austrian constitutional law in the immediate aftermath of World War I. The exposition sets the stage for the controversy with Schmitt over the question of who ought to be the "guardian" of the constitution. Kelsen's position in the controversy turns, in particular, on his defense of centralized constitutional review,[54] an institutional practice that he expressly incorporated into the Austrian Federal Constitution of October 1920. The practice, in Kelsen's day, was entirely new.[55] The excursus begins with a handful of historical details.

ANTICIPATING THE "GUARDIAN" CONTROVERSY

The Austro-Hungarian Empire collapsed in October 1918. Following the death of Franz Joseph, Kaiser Karl had become emperor in 1916. His last effort to save the old order took place on October 16, 1918. He proclaimed that the Austrian part of the empire be established in the form of a federal state "in which each ethnic group, in its own region, would form its own community [*Gemeinwesen*] in the federal state."[56] Thus, each ethnic group would have its own member state in a federal union.

The emperor's effort came too late. The non-German peoples of the empire had already begun forming states that were altogether independent of it, prompting those in the German-speaking regions to form, on October 21, 1918, the Provisional National Assembly of the independent German-Austrian state (see Kelsen 1920b, 245–246; 1923a, 74–76). Nine days later, on October 30, 1918, the Provisional National Assembly declared that it would assume power in the German-speaking regions of the empire. This major step marked the founding of the postwar Austrian state, "German-Austria" (*Deutsch-Österreich*), as it was known in the immediate post–World War I period.

The constitution of German-Austria, the "provisional constitution" as it is sometimes called, consisted not of a single document but of a number of decisions taken by the Provisional National Assembly and embodied in statutes. These included the foundational decision of October 30, 1918, and a decision of November 12, 1918, in which the Provisional National Assembly declared that the state would adopt a republican form of government.

The Assembly did not take up its central task of developing a full-fledged constitution for Austria until the spring of 1919. Kelsen, who had been serving since November 1918 as legal consultant to Chancellor Karl Renner, was now called upon by Renner to draft a new federal constitution. In Kelsen's own words:

> In May of 1919, I received instructions from the Chancellor to draft a federal constitution, following up on my earlier preparation of certain preliminary studies. During the summer of 1919, with the help of the constitutional department in the Chancellor's offices, I completed the draft, supplementing it throughout the fall with several other drafts that were intended to present variations of the basic draft and to take into account the various political options. My guideline was to retain everything usable from the previous constitution, to preserve to the greatest possible extent the continuity of the constitutional institutions, to incorporate the principle of

federalism into the existing tried and true, and thereby to lean on the Swiss but even
more on the new German [Weimar] Constitution as far as I could, considering the
differences in historico-political presuppositions. (1922, 236; 1923a, 160–161)

These lines of Kelsen's capture his own role succinctly, and he was, indeed, active during
all three phases of the work on the constitution.[57] The first phase is marked by prepara-
tions carried out in Renner's government between the spring and the fall of 1919. During
this first phase, Kelsen works up no fewer than five drafts of the federal constitution
(see Schmitz 1981), whose differences reflect the different perceptions of the parties
in Renner's coalition government. For example, in the first draft Kelsen accords particularly favorable treatment to the *Länder*, whereas in the second draft he strengthens
the ties of the *Länder* to the federal unit and inserts a supremacy clause. In the fifth of the
drafts Kelsen draws on the new Weimar Constitution to a greater extent than in the
other drafts.[58] A second phase, reaching into the spring of 1920, is marked by discussions
with representatives of the *Länder*, who tried unsuccessfully to take control of the proceedings. Kelsen, although not present at the Länder conference in Salzburg, is called as
constitutional expert to the *Länder* conference in Linz. Discussion there prompts him,
along with Renner and others, to work up still another draft. Finally, a third phase, during the summer and fall of 1920, is marked by negotiations between the parties in parliament. During this period Kelsen works out a compromise between the views of the
Social Democratic Party and those of the Christian Social Party, melding their respective drafts into a single instrument that ultimately wins the approval of the Provisional
National Assembly and emerges as the Austrian Federal Constitution of October 1, 1920.

In his work on the Constitution of 1920, as Kelsen remarks many years later, the provisions on constitutional review, Articles 137–148, had meant the most to him (1974,
50). The review powers of the Constitutional Court are in part familiar from the earlier
Reichsgericht or High Court of the Empire and are in part entirely new.[59] I leave aside the
review powers carried over from the earlier *Reichsgericht* and confine myself to a handful of details of the newly introduced review powers.[60]

Of special significance among the new provisions are Articles 139 and 140. Article 139
confers power on the Constitutional Court to hear, on the application of a lower court,
a challenge to the legality of ordinances issued by a federal or a Land authority. Article
140 confers power on the Constitutional Court to hear, on the application of the federal government, a challenge to the constitutionality of a Land law and to hear, on the
application of a Land government, a challenge to the constitutionality of a federal law. If
either a Land law or a federal law is rescinded as unconstitutional by a judgment of the
Constitutional Court, the Land minister in question or the federal chancellor, respectively, is to publish the rescission without delay. If the Constitutional Court does not
itself set an effective date for rescission, the effective date may not exceed six months
beyond the publication date of rescission. The Court is also empowered to decide ex
officio, that is, on its own initiative, on the constitutionality of a Land or a federal statute
insofar as this is required in order to pass on the constitutionality of a statute in a case
before the Court. It is, in particular, the powers conferred on the Constitutional Court in

article 140 that Kelsen counts as "the high point of [the Court's] function as the guarantor of the constitution [*Garant der Verfassung*]" (1922, 264).

I shall return to constitutional review for a look at Kelsen's effort to justify the
practice qua protector of the constitution. First, however, it is well briefly to examine
Kelsen's concept of the positive law constitution. Presupposed in Kelsen's inquiry into
the concept of the constitution is his *Stufenbaulehre* or doctrine of hierarchical structure, according to which "the law regulates its own creation."[61] That is, a legal norm
governs the process whereby another legal norm is created, and the idea applies all
the way up and down the normative hierarchy. This is the dynamic conception of the
law, a characterization of the law in terms of how it is created (see 1992, §43, 91). The
dynamic conception of the law serves to relativize the differences between creation
of law and application of law, thereby relativizing the standing of the different species
of law themselves. In particular, legislation, the standard-bearer of later nineteenth-
century statutory legal positivism (*Gesetzespositivismus*) in Europe, loses its privileged position.

It is only from the vantage point of this "theory of hierarchy," Kelsen argues, that the
immanent meaning of the concept of the constitution is accessible.[62] For it is the constitution that serves as the fundamental positive-law rule—more precisely, the set of fundamental positive-law rules—that determines the organs and procedures of legislation,
which in turn provide for the remaining levels or *Stufen* of the hierarchy. Kelsen understands the constitution in its "original" concept in terms, above all, of the allocation of
powers:

> [The constitution] is the rule that determines the creation of the statutes, the general
> norms, whose enforcement is the activity of state organs, in particular of courts and
> administrative officials. This rule for the creation of the legal norms that shape, above
> all, the system of the state, this determination of the organs and procedures of the legis-
> lature—this is the actual, original, and narrower concept of the constitution. (1929c, 36)

Along with this "actual, original, and narrower concept of the constitution," namely, the
constitution qua means of allocating legal powers, there is a broader concept of the constitution. It includes, alongside the norms addressing the powers and procedures of legislation, a catalog of basic rights. As Kelsen writes:

> If in the positive law there is a specific constitutional form that differs from statutory
> form, then nothing stands in the way of using this form even for norms that do not
> fall within the concept of the constitution in the narrower sense, above all for norms
> that determine not the creation of statutes but their content. Thus, a concept of the
> constitution in the broader sense emerges. This is the case where modern constitu-
> tions include not only norms that address the organs and the procedures of legisla-
> tion but also a catalogue of basic rights. (1929c, 37)

Here Kelsen mentions the equality of citizens before the law, freedom of expression, freedom of belief and conscience, and the inviolability of property.[63] As Kelsen understands

them, basic rights and freedoms represent certain constraints on the scope and manner of the exercise of legal powers.[64]

How does Kelsen justify these far-reaching review powers, which together represent centralized constitutional review? Thanks to several key papers written by Kelsen during his time in Vienna and then in Cologne (1929c; 1930/1931), we have a rough picture of his explication and defense. Constitutional review, he writes, serves as "a judicial guarantee of the constitution." It is, in other words, one of a number of juridico-technical measures the purpose of which is to assure the "legality" or "constitutionality" of those governmental functions carried out in the name of the law (see 1929c).

The problem of legality writ large is the problem of assuring that application of law comports with the law being applied. Thus, the question in constitutional law is whether an application of the constitution in the form, say, of a statute comports with the constitution itself. This issue, legality, can be recast in the language of the doctrine of hierarchy, where creation and application of law are understood not as distinct kinds in opposition to one another but as "merely two levels in the process of law creation, standing to one another in a relation of subordination and superordination" (31). Recast in these terms, legality is simply the "relation of correspondence" between lower and higher levels in the normative hierarchy.

The idea, then, is to provide for legality to the greatest possible degree, thereby holding arbitrariness to an absolute minimum. Two presuppositions are understood: first, constitutional law is binding law and not simply a program of goals, and second, the normative hierarchy distinguishes between constitutional law and statutory law, treating them as distinct kinds of law, so that the application of the maxim *lex superior derogat legi priori* will serve to recognize the "superiority" and thus the priority of constitutional law over statutory law. Another way of putting this is to note that the appeal to constitutional law marks an appeal to something independent of the statutory provision in question, exactly what justification requires. With this machinery in place, Kelsen is arguing, the prospects of enhancing legality are greater with a constitutional court than without one. Suppose, as Kelsen argues in the Vienna lecture, that the parliament enacts a statute that is constitutionally doubtful. Since the parliament is ill-equipped to monitor itself, it is appropriate that the constitutional court assume the role of monitor. In summary, nothing short of an independent organ with power to invalidate an unconstitutional statute will be in a position to meet the demands imposed by legality, and this independent organ, Kelsen is arguing, is a constitutional court (53). With this background in mind, I next turn to the controversy between Kelsen and Schmitt over the "guardian of the constitution."

THE "GUARDIAN" CONTROVERSY OF 1931

Schmitt's strategy generates the controversy.[65] He purports to show that Kelsen's candidate for the guardian of the constitution, namely, a constitutional court with review powers reaching to federal legislation, is impossible or unworkable. And then, having disposed of Kelsen's candidate, Schmitt turns to his own candidate and underscores the significance of the Reich president as *pouvoir neutre*.

The central text reflecting Schmitt's strategy is his monograph of 1931, *The Guardian of the Constitution*. As has been noted in the literature, Schmitt anticipates the monograph of 1931 with a lengthy paper, two years earlier, that bears the same title (Schmitt 1929b, 161–237). Still earlier, rarely noted in the literature, is a paper that Schmitt completed in August 1928, "The High Court as Guardian of the Constitution" (Schmitt 1929a). The stimulus for this paper may well have been Kelsen's lecture on the nature and viability of constitutional review,[66] delivered at the 1928 meeting of the Association of German Public Law Professors (*Vereinigung der deutschen Staatsrechtslehrer*), held that year in Vienna.[67] In his paper Schmitt attempts, for the first time, to make the case on behalf of the Reich president as guardian of the constitution by showing that the alternative, Kelsen's doctrine of constitutional review, is unworkable. The argument is a tad more reserved than in the monograph of 1931, although to be sure, the central motif in *Guardian*, the model of subsumption, is already evident in this early article.

To assume, however, that Schmitt's defense of the Reich president as guardian of the constitution is prompted solely by Kelsen's endorsement of constitutional review would be a mistake. On the contrary, Schmitt's program in support of what became the Weimar "reserve constitution" or *Präsidialsystem*, was in place long before Kelsen's 1928 lecture in Vienna. I return to Schmitt's program below.

The arguments in Schmitt's *Guardian* and in Kelsen's reply[68] manifest fairly clearly four themes, the first being Schmitt's model of subsumption, the second his unduly narrow reading of "material fact," the third Kelsen's rejoinder to Schmitt on the political dimension of the judicial decision, and the fourth the putative neutrality of the head of state, specifically, the Reich president.

1. **Schmitt on the model of subsumption.** How does Schmitt support his claim, scarcely comprehensible from our current perspective, that constitutional review is impossible or unworkable? He argues that adjudication is possible only if it meets the requirements of the model of subsumption, and since so-called constitutional adjudication cannot meet these requirements, it does not count as adjudication at all.

This first requirement of the model is *derivation*. It stems from an aspect of the nineteenth-century understanding of the *Rechtsstaat*, namely, the role of derivation within a statutory framework. As Schmitt asserts:

> The special position of the judge in the *Rechtsstaat*, namely, his objectivity, his disinterested stance vis-à-vis the parties, his independence, and his immunity to dismissal—all of this rests on the following alone: that he decide on the basis of a statute and that the content of his decision be *derived* from another decision...already contained in the statute. (1931a, 37–38)

Kelsen replies that Schmitt's notion of "derivation" counts as deduction. The idea, Kelsen writes, that "the judicial decision is already contained, in finished or complete form, in the statute," and that its derivation from the statute is simply "an operation of logic," amounts to "judicial decision-making qua slot machine [*Rechtsautomat*]!" (1930/1931, 591–592). Rudolf von Jhering also used colorful language in deprecating so-called mechanical jurisprudence. In a parody directed at legal constructivism, von Jhering suggests as a model for the judicial decision the digestive process of the duck. "From the front, the case is inserted into the judgment-making machine, and then the case qua judgment comes out at the rear" (Jhering 1893, 394).

Summarizing thus far, Kelsen interprets "derivation," the first requirement of Schmitt's model of subsumption, as deductive inference and then proceeds to dismiss the model of subsumption, thus understood, as mechanical jurisprudence. Criticism along these lines cannot come as a surprise. Kelsen is not only familiar with the criticism leveled at mechanical jurisprudence—*Begriffsjurisprudenz*—by the Free Law Movement, he expressly endorses this criticism, following the lead of Kantorowicz.[69]

The second requirement of Schmitt's model of subsumption is that the subsuming norm not be "questionable" or "controversial" in the context in question: "The work of the judiciary is bound to legal norms, and it ends where the norms themselves come to be questionable or controversial in their content" (Schmitt 1931a, 19).

It is worth noting that Schmitt, in his very early work, did not believe a word of this. In *Statute and Judgment* (1912), he wrote that "the countless revisions of statutory language" and their "saturation with a thousand juridico-scientific concepts" preclude the notion that the "subsuming norm" is free of controversy. And by the same token, the idea that the judge might be a "subsumption machine," a "statutory *Automat*," is fanciful.[70]

Kelsen, turning to Schmitt's requirement that the subsuming norms cannot be questionable or controversial, expresses great surprise:

> [I]t is little short of astonishing that Schmitt appears to be of the opinion that civil courts, criminal courts, and administrative courts, whose character vis-à-vis adjudication he does not wish to call into question, only apply norms whose content is neither doubtful nor controversial; and that in the case of a legal dispute to be decided by one of these "courts," what arises is always simply a question of fact and never a so-called question of law. (1930/1931, 588)

In Schmitt's view, as expressed in *Guardian*, the question put before the court is *always* a question of fact, since a question of law would arise only if the content of the norm to be applied were questionable or controversial. Kelsen finds this astonishing, and I dare say he is not alone.

In the course of his criticism, Kelsen employs one of his favorite argumentative strategies, the *inversion*. In his *Habilitationsschrift* of 1911, in the name of an inversion, he turns the traditional legal positivist's or voluntarist's view of the law on its head (see 1911a, 133–144, 172–188, et passim), arguing that whereas the traditional theorist had contended that *if willed, then legally valid*, it is in fact the other way around: *if legally valid, then willed*. "Will," the explicatum of the law in traditional legal positivism or voluntarism, survives in Kelsen's work merely as a sop to the tradition, shorn of any substantive import.[71] So likewise, mutatis mutandis, in Kelsen's reply to Schmitt's claim that the subsuming norm cannot be either doubtful or controversial. "It is only with the inversion of this claim that one is led back to a truth simple and clear to everyone: Adjudication first begins when the norms become doubtful and controversial in their content. Otherwise there would only be disputes over material facts and no genuinely 'legal' disputes at all" (589). As the language of inversion suggests, this is precisely the opposite of Schmitt's view.

In summary, Kelsen is of the opinion that Schmitt has stacked the deck, proceeding in such a way as to assure that constitutional review is impossible or unworkable. As Kelsen puts it:

> To conclude from a concept of "judicial decision," however it be conceived, that the institution characterized as a "constitutional court" is impossible or unworkable, would be a typical case of conceptual jurisprudence (*Begriffsjurisprudenz*), seen today as outmoded. (584)

2. **Schmitt's narrow reading of "material fact."** Kelsen suggests that Schmitt's notion of material fact stems from the criminal law,[72] where the typical determination is whether or not the behavior of the accused counts as an instance of the type of material fact characterized by the criminal law as an offence.

Kelsen argues that constitutional adjudication can be understood, mutatis mutandis, in the same way. That is, the material fact in question is an issue of either procedure or content: "The unconstitutionality of a statutory provision can consist ... either in the fact that it was not issued according to the constitutionally prescribed *procedure*, or in the fact that its *content* is not constitutionally allowed" (1930/31, 590).

Whether the unconstitutionality of a statutory norm is owing to a defect in its procedure or in its content, it will be true to say that the norm was not issued in accordance with the constitution. The review of constitutionality, as Kelsen puts it, is always a decision on the question of "[w]hether the manner of issuance of the statute is constitutional" (590).

Thus, Kelsen is arguing, Schmitt reads "material fact" far too narrowly, failing to see that the issuance of a norm is itself a material fact (590–591). Schmitt's own model can be extended straightaway to include the issuance of the legal norm as the "material fact" of adjudication. Baldly to deny this, as Schmitt does, simply begs the question.

3. **Kelsen's rejoinder to Schmitt on the political dimension of the judicial decision.** The political dimension of the judicial decision represents another facet of the model of subsumption, and here Kelsen draws on an aspect of Schmitt's "decisionism." It is well to begin with Kelsen's notion of the *Stufenbau* or hierarchical structure of the legal system, adumbrated above. As I suggest there, the dynamic conception of the law reflected in the *Stufenbau* invites attention to a property unique to the law: that it regulates its own creation. The result of this dynamic conception, Kelsen argues, is a relativization of the differences between law creation and law application. This is not to say, however, that the issuance of the lower-level norm is governed entirely by the higher-level norm. On the contrary, there is an irreducibly "decisionistic" component

in the judicial decision; here Kelsen and Schmitt are on common ground.[73] For example, Schmitt writes: "In every decision, even in the decision of a court that proceeds by means of subsuming the material fact, there lies an element of *pure decision* that cannot be derived from the content of the norm. I have characterized this as 'decisionism.'"[74]

Kelsen argues that this "element of *pure decision*" means that the judicial decision, like the statute, is properly represented as *law creation*. Like the legislative enactment, the judicial decision is, then, political in character, and the greater the role of "pure decision," the larger the political dimension.[75] Schmitt's objection to constitutional review on the ground that it is political in character (Schmitt 1931a, 22) collapses now of its own weight. All forms of law are political in character—and, Kelsen is arguing, Schmitt's talk of an "element of *pure decision*" underscores the point.

Kelsen completes his argument with a rhetorical question: If Schmitt grants that all forms of law are political in character, how can he contend in the same breath that constitutional adjudication, owing to its political character, cannot count as genuine adjudication? Kelsen's reply is that

> [Schmitt's] claim that constitutional review is not adjudication is of central importance to him, and he maintains it even in the face of his own theoretical views [showing the contrary], for it serves as the presupposition of [his] *legal policy*: Because the decision on the constitutionality of a statute and the overturning of an unconstitutional statute in a judicial proceeding are not matters of "adjudication", they *may not* be turned over to a group of independent judges. They must, instead, be turned over to another organ. (1930/1931, 593)

For Schmitt, the organ in question is of course the Reich president. And this leads in turn to the last of the motifs in Schmitt's *Guardian* and Kelsen's rejoinder.

4. **The putative neutrality of the head of state, namely, the Reich president.** Here, in chapter three of *Guardian*, Schmitt sets out his case on behalf of the neutrality of the Reich president.

> The differences of opinion between those empowered to take political decisions or exercise political influence…do not, in general, lend themselves to adjudication. Either these differences of opinion are eliminated by a greater political power, one that stands over [them], thus, a *higher*, third body. This, however, would not be the protector of the constitution; rather, it would be the sovereign head of state. Or these differing opinions are eliminated or coped with by means of a *neutral* third body—this is the sense given to a neutral power, a *pouvoir neutre et intermédiaire*, which does not stand over the other powers established by the constitution. Rather, it stands alongside them, but with its own powers and means of exercising influence. (Schmitt 1931a, 132)

In this last round, on Schmitt's contention of neutrality, Kelsen tends to lose patience. Indeed, at one point he is unwilling to lend any measure of credibility to Schmitt's case at all. With an eye to posing a question, Kelsen refers to nineteenth-century constitutions that confer powers and prerogatives on the monarch and then, at the same time, attribute to one and the same monarch the status of *pouvoir neutre*. The monarch is "the possessor of a greater part of state power or, indeed, the whole of state power." He exercises this power, he issues a law. And now he is to be regarded as "a neutral authority" and is, in virtue of his neutrality, "alone called upon to review the constitutionality of the law?" (Kelsen 1930/1931, 578–579). This flies in the face of Kelsen's point that the law-making body is ill-equipped to monitor itself, and objections inevitably arise. What is the claim of neutrality based on? Is it not an "intolerable contradiction," in Kelsen's words, to attribute this greater part of state power to the monarch and then to add, in the same breath, that the monarch's exercise of this power will be guided by the strictures of neutrality?

Kelsen does not, sensu stricto, raise this objection. Rather, he addresses its character: "The objection that this is an intolerable contradiction would, however, be entirely inappropriate. [To raise] such an objection would lend a measure of (juridico-)*scientific knowledge* to something that can only be understood as *political ideology*" (578–579). The tenor of much of Kelsen's discussion of the "neutrality" of the Reich president is of a piece with what I am quoting here.

Kelsen's assessment of Schmitt's effort to show that constitutional review is impossible or unworkable is harsh but not, I think, unjustified. In order fully to appreciate the cogency of Kelsen's assessment, it is helpful to have a picture of Schmitt's more general position, particularly in the later Weimar years, even if my statement in what follows is so brief as barely to qualify as a sketch.

Conclusion

A fundamental aspect of the beginnings of the constitutional crisis in the Weimar Republic in the summer of 1930 is Article 48 of the Weimar Constitution. On its face, Article 48 appears clearly to address emergency situations. The key provision is Section 2, which reads:

> If public safety and order in the German Reich are seriously disrupted or endangered, the Reich President can take the measures necessary to restore public safety and order and, if required, can intervene by force of arms. For this purpose, he may temporarily suspend, in whole or in part, the fundamental rights established in articles 114, 115, 117, 118, 123, 124, and 153.[76]

By June 1930, as Gotthard Jasper writes, the financial situation of the Weimar Republic had become so severe and unemployment so massive that "new measures to address the situation were imperative."[77] The legislative bill proposed by the Brüning cabinet— curbs on spending along with tax increases—proved to be unacceptable to the *Reichstag* and was rejected. Chancellor Heinrich Brüning then turned to Reich President Paul von Hindenburg with the request that he pass the bill by invoking the provisions of article 48, section 2. Hindenburg agreed, and on July 16 the bill was passed in the form of an emergency decree. On July 18 the Social Democrats in the *Reichstag*, exercising power under Article 48, Section 3,[78] rescinded the emergency decree. Brüning had anticipated the Social Democrats' reaction. He held in his hand an express order for the dissolution, by the Reich president, of the parliament. It read: "Now that the Reichstag has resolved to demand that my 16 July emergency decrees be overturned, I hereby order the dissolution of the Reichstag on the authority of Article 25."[79] The dissolution of the parliament proceeded henceforth, and just a few days later, the decree that had been rescinded by the Social Democrats in the *Reichstag* was reissued by the Reich president.

These moves reflect a pattern that became all too familiar during the last two and one-half years of the Weimar Republic: (a) emergency decrees in place of parliamentary legislation, (b) their rescission by the parliament, and (c) the dismissal of the parliament by the Reich president, followed by (d) the reissuance of the emergency decrees, this time without any danger of rescission. The effect was to supplant parliamentary government.

The new framework—amounting to a "reserve constitution," a *Präsidialsystem*—is a scheme that Schmitt had been moving toward over a considerable period of time. His paper of 1916 on "Dictatorship and the State of Siege" represents a shift in focus away from the orthodox motifs of the very early work. Now he is focusing on executive action—and indeed, on the most palpable case of executive action, the emergency situation. What is more, Schmitt's shift in focus is not a passing fancy. He devotes an entire monograph, *Die Diktatur* of 1919, to the explication of the notion of dictatorship. In *The Crisis of Parliamentary Government*, first published in 1923, Schmitt argues that parliamentary government is dysfunctional. A year later, in "The Dictatorship of the Reich President according to Article 48 of the Weimar Constitution" (1924, 63–104),[80] Schmitt sets out, on the one hand, his very broad reading of emergency powers, which he argues are not limited to the scheme set out in Article 48, while adding, on the other hand, a constraint to the effect that emergency decrees are mere "measures" (*Maßnahmen*) without statutory import.[81] In the treatise of 1928, *Constitutional Theory*, Schmitt contrasts the "two political leaders" in the Weimar Constitution. He disparages the chancellor, who is in a position to define policy only insofar as "he maintains the confidence of the Reichstag," which, however, amounts to "a shifting and unreliable coalition." By contrast, he praises the Reich president, who "has the confidence of the entire people," not mediated by "a parliament splintered into parties" (Schmitt 1928a, §27.III.4, 351; 2008, 370). And in late July 1930 Schmitt drafts an advisory opinion in which he abandons the constraint to which he had given voice in the 1924 lecture, namely, that emergency decrees had no statutory import but were merely to be understood as "measures." On July 28, 1930—on the heels of the extraordinary events that transpired earlier in the month in the name of the *Preußenschlag*—he announces that decrees issued in accordance with Article 48, Section 2, are to be recognized as "regulations with statutory import" (*gesetzvertretende Verordnungen*; Schmitt 1930b). This, too, was no passing fancy. Schmitt incorporates the entire advisory opinion into *Guardian* (see 1931a, 117–130). In October 1932 Schmitt represented the Federal Government in the case concerning the takeover of the Prussian state.[82]

The *Präsidialsystem*, does not lead inevitably and unavoidably to the Hitler regime. Indeed, the Papen and Schleicher governments (during the period June 1932 to January 1933) concocted schemes, however ineptly, that would have Hindenburg dismissing the *Reichstag without* provisions for new elections within sixty days, as the Weimar Constitution required. Each of these schemes was understood as a device for circumventing the threat posed by the Nazis. Each, needless to add, failed.[83] Schmitt's role in these schemes, a subject of discussion in some of the literature, is not clear.[84] What is clear is that he sought an alternative to parliamentary government—and from a fairly early point in his career.

The risk undertaken by those who sought to establish a *Präsidialsystem* was not lost on Kelsen. At the outset of his reply to Schmitt in the 1931 exchange, Kelsen refers to the liberties being taken with the Weimar Constitution and adds that it is hard to see how the constitution "can avoid the danger of being blown apart" (1930/1931, 579). Tragically for the world, Kelsen's prediction proved to be accurate.

ACKNOWLEDGMENTS

I wish to express my gratitude to Jörg Kammerhofer, Iain Stewart, and especially Bonnie Litschewski Paulson, all of whom read a draft of my text and gave me helpful comments and criticism. Theo Öhlinger advised me on aspects of the formation of the Austrian Federal Constitution of October 1920.

NOTES

1. I draw these contrasts from Kelsen's writings, beginning in 1911, and from Schmitt's, beginning in 1922, but I make no effort in this opening section to speak to the niceties of these contrasts, which are set out here simply for purposes of illustration.
2. Kelsen broaches the question of the proper construction of legal norms in his first major work, *Hauptprobleme der Staatsrechtslehre* (1911a, 237; repr. 2008, 353). For details on how Kelsen proceeds with the construction, see Paulson 2012a (78–85). The presuppositions of the legal norm can be summarized under the rubric "normativism," which reaches to Kelsen's well-known basic norm with, ideally, support stemming from a neo-Kantian argument (102–111).
3. On the distinction between *Sein* and *Sollen*, "is" and "ought," see Paulson 2012a (66–71).
4. My quotations from Schmitt's texts are drawn from the German with a single exception (see next endnote); I have added citations to the English-language editions of these texts for the reader's convenience.
5. The concept of the political is to be understood "in the sense of a criterion, not as an exhaustive definition or a specification of content" (Schmitt 1932a, 14; 1976, 26). In Schmitt's writings, this is the standard reading of the doctrine (even if the express reference to a "criterion"

does not turn up in the initial version of *Der Begriff des Politischen*, 1927). At one point, however, Schmitt stands the doctrine on its head: Here the "friend or foe" juxtaposition does not purport to serve as a criterion but is instead determined by appeal to a criterion. As Schmitt writes: "For 'the political', correctly understood, is only the degree of intensity of a unity. Political unity can contain and comprehend different contents. But it always designates the most intensive degree of a unity, from which, consequently, the most intensive distinction—the grouping of friend and enemy—is determined" (1930a, 36; 1940, 133–145, at 141; 1999, 203). I have followed the Dyzenhaus translation, which is excellent.

6. On Schmitt's characterization of the political, see generally Karl Löwith 1960 (104–111); first publ. 1935 under the pseudonym H. Fiala); Matthias Kaufmann 1988 (§3, 46–55); Hasso Hofmann 1965 (17–39); also the essays in *Carl Schmitt: Der Begriff des Politischen* (Mehring 2003).

7. On the characterization of neo-Kantianism, see Paulson 2012b (141–145). See also Beisler 2011; Makkreel and Luft 2010; and Paulson 2012c.

8. For some details on Kelsen's role vis-à-vis the Austrian Federal Constitution of October 1920, including its provisions on constitutional review, see the third part of this chapter.

9. On the "juridico-logical constitution" or basic norm, see, e.g., Kelsen 1925a (§42e, 307). With respect to the positive law constitution, Kelsen distinguishes a narrower, primary reading, from a broader, secondary reading.

10. Felix Somló, very much at home in European jurisprudence, nevertheless refers to John Austin more frequently than to any other theorist. Kelsen 1920a (§7, 31–36), engages in hard-headed criticism of Austinian legal positivism as portrayed by Somló, and Kelsen's treatment lends itself to comparison with H. L. A. Hart's celebrated critique.

11. Schmitt 1928b (25–42, 118–119, et passim). See also Schmitt 1922 (10–12, 19); 1934 (13–16, 25); 1985b (8–10, 16–17).

12. Kelsen 1920b (50–85); 1929b; 1925a; 1925b; 1927a (37–68, 113–118); 1955 (1–101). With the exception of 1925b; all of these works are reprinted in Kelsen 2006.

13. Schmitt 1926; 1985a. See also Schmitt 1928a (§17.III, 234–238); 2008 (264–267).

14. Schmitt 1926 (37); 1985a (28). See generally Kaufmann 1988 (ch. II, 132–217).

15. See, e.g., Johann Gottfried Herder, *Briefe zur Beförderung der Humanität*, Brief No. 57 (1795), in Herder 1991 (301–307).

16. As Kelsen writes: "It may be that I arrived at [my] view [of legal theory] not least of all because the state I was closest to and from personal experience knew better than any other—the Austrian state—was clearly nothing other than a legal unity (*Rechtseinheit*). Considered in light of the Austrian state, composed of so many groups differing in race, language, religion, and history, those theories that attempted to establish the unity of the state on the basis of some socio-psychological or socio-biological connection among the persons belonging in a legal sense to the state proved very clearly to be fictions. In so far as [my] theory of the state [i.e. the state qua legal unity] is an essential component of the Pure Theory of Law, the Pure Theory of Law can be regarded as a specifically Austrian theory" (2007, 59–60).

17. According to Kelsen, legal monism comes in two different forms: with the priority of international law and with the priority of state law. The choice between these two forms is a question of politics and does not, therefore, belong to legal science. This is Kelsen's standard view. At one point in *Das Problem der Souveränität*, however, he makes it abundantly clear that he has taken a juridico-scientific position on the question. Pursuing a line of argument familiar from Schopenhauer, Kelsen contends that monism with the priority of

state law leads to "solipsism" (1920a, §63, 314–317). On Kelsen's monism, see also the papers by Kelsen, Joseph G. Stark, and H. L. A. Hart in Paulson and Litschewski Paulson 1998 (525–581).

18. Schmitt 1932b (15); 1995 (72–73). Schmitt's overblown rhetoric ("*in drei erbärmlichen Jahrhunderten*") in this lecture of November 23, 1932, given to a group of Ruhr industrialists, is perhaps a reflection of zeal in his effort to win his audience over to his position. Elsewhere Schmitt offers a more straightforward statement of essentially the same position: "The colossal shift [to the "quantitative" or "weak" total state] can be construed as part of a dialectical development that unfolds in three stages: from the *absolute* state of the seventeenth and eighteenth centuries, by way of the *neutral* state of the liberal nineteenth century, to the *total* state [in the Weimar period, which is marked by] the identity of state and society" (1931a, 79). Schmitt, at this point in 1931a (78–91), has incorporated the text of "Die Wendung zum totalen Staat" (1931b).

19. See Schmitt 1932c (96); 2004a (92); 1932b (18, 20); 1995 (74–75, 76).

20. This is Schmitt's theme in 1926.

21. Late in 1933, in *Staat, Bewegung, Volk* (1933, §II, 11–22), Schmitt boasts that political unity qua "qualitative" or "strong" total state is now a fait accompli. See generally Volker Neumann 1980 (147–154) and Kaufmann 1988 (§18 (a), 347–354). The systematic ambiguity of "total state"—the "quantitative" or "weak" total state and the "qualitative" or "strong" total state—has of course not gone unnoticed; see, e.g., Quaritsch 1991 (24, 41).

22. More precisely, there is over time a twofold shift in Schmitt's work. First is a shift in focus in his area of concentration, coming as early as "Diktatur und Belagerungszustand" ("Dictatorship and State of Siege"), which appeared late in 1916 (see 1916b). At this point in time, Schmitt is still receptive to such legal concepts as *Rechtsstaat*, separation of powers, and the like, as they were understood in the nineteenth century. Later, but no later than *Political Theology* in 1922, Schmitt's work reflects not only this shift in focus but also a notable shift away from his earlier tacit endorsement of legal concepts understood traditionally. If, as Schmitt will now claim again and again, the important issues are clustered around the "exception" rather than the "normal situation," then the colossus on which Kelsen is busy at work is all but irrelevant—or so Schmitt would have us believe. Schmitt's attitude toward Kelsen is no doubt also colored by personal factors, as exemplified in Schmitt's irritation with Franz Weyr, a close associate of Kelsen's. In a review, Weyr writes that the extent of the similarities between *Der Wert des Staates* (1914) and Kelsen's philosophy is "wellnigh baffling," and, Weyr adds, Schmitt refers to Kelsen only once in the entire monograph (see 1914, 77), intimating that Schmitt may have copied from Kelsen without acknowledgment. Schmitt, nothing if not prickly, expresses his indignation in the preface to the 1921 edition of *Die Diktatur*, writing that "a scholar as important as Weyr" has identified straightaway "my concept of law with Kelsen's positivistic form, which, in my opinion, involves a *contradictio in adjecto*." Schmitt continues, alluding now to the motif of his 1921 monograph, that for Kelsen, "in accordance with his relativistic formalism, the problem of dictatorship can be no more a legal problem than a brain operation can be a logical problem" (1921, xi; in the 2nd printing [1928, xix]). And Schmitt's contempt for Kelsen and his circle grows. In 1926, in correspondence with his publisher Ludwig Feuchtwanger, Schmitt addresses the dismal state of legal science: "It is indeed very bad, but even worse in Vienna and Austria than elsewhere. These people—Kelsen, Sander, Verdross—are fertile and multiplying like fleas. Every month a new book, arguing for 500 pages that the state is a legal system; for all their historical breadth and garrulity, they are superficial and downright lazy" (Schmitt in Rieß 2007, 194).

23. The book served, in 1916, as Schmitt's *Habilitationsschrift* in Strassbourg. It was reprinted in 1917, and a new printing (with, absurdly, a different pagination) has appeared (see 2004b). As Mehring (1990, 38, 54) rightly points out, *Der Wert des Staates* is a philosophical treatise. It is perhaps Schmitt's only genuinely philosophical work.

24. This very early development in Schmitt's work has not received much attention. The leading statements are Hofmann 1992 (44–56) and Jaitner 1996 (479–487).

25. On the Baden neo-Kantians, see Beisler 2011 (365–467), a magisterial statement. On the Marburg neo-Kantians, see Makkreel and Luft 2010 and Paulson 2012b.

26. On Schmitt's very early work, see Nicoletti 1988 (109–128); Kiefer 1990 (479–489); Ulmen 1991 (102–117); Dahlheimer 1998 (44–48); Mehring 2004 (2–7); 2009 (32–36, 38–40, 60–65); and Neumann 2010 (741–744).

27. "Subjective right" (*subjektives Recht*), that is, an individual's legal right. I preserve the literal counterpart of the German expression for the sake of Kelsen's contrast with "objective law." On the juxtaposition, see Hans Kelsen, *Introduction to the Problems of Legal Theory*, a translation of the first edition of the *Reine Rechtslehre* (1934) by Paulson and Litschewski Paulson 1992 (§24, 43–46); Kelsen 1960 (§33, 174–175).

28. Kelsen defends "legal monism" in the context of public international law; see, e.g., Kelsen 1992 (§50, 111–125). This is, however, an altogether different reading of "monism," that is, legal monism versus legal dualism *within* the normative sphere. Thus understood, monism is not to be confused with monism in the juxtaposition of monism and dualism in the early paragraphs of the present section.

29. On Kelsen's "two worlds" doctrine, see below. On the periodization of Kelsen's phases of development, see Paulson 1998 (153–166); 1999 (351–365).

30. The distinction between legal norms and legal rules is made by appealing to the individual or singular legal norm (*individuelle Rechtsnorm*), say, a judicial holding, contrasting it with a general legal norm, such as a statutory provision. Legal norms come, so to speak, in both sizes, whereas legal rules are by definition general. See Joseph Raz 1972 (79, repr. in Paulson and Litschewski Paulson 1998, 451).

31. Kelsen 1911a (6; repr. 2008 3, 22–55, at 27–28). See also Kelsen 1925a (§13 [b], 62).

32. Kelsen 1920a (§24, 99 n1). See also Kelsen 1916 (123–124 [1209–1210], repr. in Jestaedt, *Kelsen Werke*, vol. 3, 2010, 578–579). From this paper it is fairly clear that Kelsen has drawn the notion of a substrate from the Baden neo-Kantian Emil Lask. Kelsen's modally indifferent substrate also turns up in his posthumously published work; see Kelsen, *General Theory of Norms* (1991, ch. 16, ii, 60, and ch. 51, 194–198, along with Kelsen's note no. 138, 376–380). To be sure, the posthumously published work represents, for many purposes, an altogether different legal theory. See Paulson 1992; 2013a.

33. This is in fact a very early statement, even earlier than the publication date of 1920 would suggest. A good part of the text was already complete in 1916, just five years after the publication of *Hauptprobleme der Staatsrechtslehre* (1911a).

34. The amalgamation is a reflection of Kelsen's idealist proclivities, which are particularly pronounced in the earlier work. Kant is there in the background, of course, and so is the philosopher Johann Friedrich Herbart (see Kelsen 1916, 95 [1181]; repr. 2010, 553). One of Kelsen's immediate sources in this connection is Georg Simmel, *Einleitung in die Moralwissenschaft*, ch. 1: "Das Sollen"; Simmel 1989– (vol. 3, ch. 1). For Kelsen's reception of Simmel, see Kelsen 1911a (4, 7–8, 13, 20–21 et passim; repr. 2008, 81, 86–87, 92, 100–101 et passim).

35. Kelsen quotes these lines two years later in "Rechtswissenschaft und Recht" (1922–1923, 211–212), and there he adds the emphasis in the last sentence.

36. Locke writes: "We have as clear a Notion of the Substance of Spirit, as we have of Body; the one being supposed to be (without knowing what it is) the *Substratum* to those simple *Ideas* we have from without; and the other supposed (with a like ignorance of what it is) to be the *Substratum* to those Operations, which we experiment in our selves within" (*An Essay Concerning Human Understanding*, bk. II, 23, at §5; see McMann 2007, 157–191).

37. The concept, legal proposition, is new, but the expression, "*Rechtssatz*," was there from the beginning. Kelsen often uses it in the earlier writings simply as a synonym for "*Rechtsnorm*," but sometimes as his device for flagging the reconstructed legal norm; see, e.g., Kelsen 1992 (§11[b], 23–25). The introduction of the legal proposition is found in Kelsen 1941–1942 (51); 1957 (266–287, 390 [notes], 268). To be sure, the first clear statement of the doctrine of legal propositions awaits the second edition of his *Pure Theory of Law*; see Kelsen 1960 (§16, 73–77).

38. It is well known that there are many types of illocutionary act (command, assertion, request, question, etc.). I confine my discussion to the assertion and the command, for they serve my purposes in mapping directly onto the worlds of *Sein* and *Sollen*, respectively. On illocutionary acts, see Austin 1961 and Searle 1969; 1979.

39. See Alchourrón and Bulygin 1981; reprinted in Paulson and Litschewski Paulson 1998 (383–410). Ota Weinberger is perhaps the most distinguished proponent, among recent norm-logicians, of the hyletic conception. For his views, see, e.g., Weinberger 1979; 1988; 2000, part I. For a reply to Alchourrón and Bulygin, see Weinberger 1985 (165–191), reprinted in Paulson and Litschewski Paulson 1998 (411–432).

40. Literally: "Thus, there is no state other than the *Rechtsstaat*" (*Darum gibt es keinen anderen Staat als den Rechtsstaat*).

41. As Kelsen writes: "The attempt to legitimize the state as a *Rechtsstaat* is exposed as completely inappropriate, since every state must be a *Rechtsstaat*—if one understands by '*Rechtsstaat*' a state that 'has' a legal system. There can be no state that does not have, or does not yet have, a legal system, since every state is only a legal system (this is not a political value-judgment of any kind). Of course, one must not confuse this concept of the *Rechtsstaat* with the concept of a legal system having a particular content, namely, a legal system comprising certain institutions, such as individual liberties, guarantees of legality in the functioning of organs, and democratic methods of creating law" (1992, §48[e], 105).

42. In the first line of the quotation, Kelsen speaks of "physical persons." Elsewhere in *Hauptprobleme*, the reference is to "a zoologico-psychological person" (Kelsen 1911a, 145, repr. 2008, 251). Later, however, the physical person turns up as one species of legal person, see Kelsen 1992 (§25[a], 48).

43. In particular, peripheral imputation, along with a developed doctrine of empowerment and the basic norm, displaces in most contexts the original doctrine, now dubbed "central imputation," along with the related notion of "points of imputation." See Paulson 2012a (106–109).

44. For more on the import of this remark of Weyr's and also Schmitt's later reaction thereto, see n. 22 above.

45. On the Brno School, see Kubeš and Weinberger 1980.

46. For a selection of Weyr's papers in German and French on issues in legal theory, see Métall 1974. Weyr's major works and also a three-volume autobiography appeared in Czech.

47. See Bryce 1901 (vol. 2, ch. 10, 51–111), which distinguishes legal or de jure sovereignty from practical or de facto sovereignty. The same distinction is evident in Dicey 1915 (ch. 1, 68–82, ch. 14, 424–434).

48. Here the expression is the comparative "simpler," in "a simpler solution" (*eine einfachere Lösung*), not, as the English translation has it, "a simple solution."

49. Kelsen refers to Bernatzik in his autobiography; see Kelsen 2007 (37, 40, 43–44, 54, 57).

50. Bernatzik 1890 (244, quoted by Schmitt 1922, 39; 1934, 53; 1985b, 40).

51. See Dreier 1986 (42–90 et passim); Dias 2005 (169–183 et passim); Paulson 1993; 2012b (85–87); 2013a, 2013b, 2013c; 2014.

52. Schmitt's reference to the basic norm in connection with a constitution marks an ambiguity that Kelsen himself recognized: the basic norm qua positive-law constitution and the juridico-logical basic norm. The latter turns out to be the peculiarly Kelsenian basic norm. In his first introduction of the basic norm, however, Kelsen had the positive-law constitution in mind. On the ambiguity, see Kelsen 1923b (xv); 1998 (13); and on the initial introduction see Kelsen 1914 (216–217). See also Dias 2005 (171–172); Walter 1993 (87–88).

53. These forms are evident as early as Kelsen 1928.

54. The locus classicus on the distinction between centralized and decentralized constitutional review is Mauro Cappelletti, *Judicial Review in the Contemporary World* (1971, esp. ch. III, 45–68). In countries with centralized constitutional review, a single "constitutional court" is empowered to hear constitutional questions, and courts of ordinary jurisdiction refer constitutional questions to the constitutional court. In countries with decentralized constitutional review, a constitutional review power is recognized in the courts of ordinary jurisdiction.

55. If the claim "entirely new" is directed not to the practice of centralized constitutional review but to the Austrian Constitutional Court, it is not, without qualification, entirely accurate. That the Austrian Constitutional Court was the first of its kind in the world had long been assumed in some circles, but scholarship has invited attention to the Czech Constitutional Court, established by the Czech Constitution of February 29, 1920, which thereby antedates the Austrian court by seven months. See Haller 1979 (30–33, 61–67); Öhlinger 2002 (583–585). The Austrians' rejoinder, however, is that the Czech court remained largely inactive during the entire period 1920–1939. See Osterkamp 2009. The European intellectual origins of constitutional review include the remarkable work of Robert von Mohl. Mohl, in his major treatise *Das Bundes-Staatsrecht der Vereinigten Staaten von Nord-Amerika* (1824), recognized the slowly emerging system of decentralized constitutional review in America, whereby the Supreme Court—and ultimately all courts of ordinary jurisdiction, both federal and state courts—acquired power to "set aside," for the case at hand, a statutory provision that the court deems to be contrary to the Constitution (see Mohl 1824, 298). In Germany at the midpoint of the nineteenth century, the developments of the Revolution of 1848 included a draft of a new constitution for the German federation, the Frankfurt or Paul's Church Constitution (*Paulskirchenverfassung*) of 1848–1849. On March 30, 1848, a National Assembly met in Frankfurt with an eye to the formation of a new federal constitution for Germany, and late in May of that year the National Assembly elected thirty persons to serve on a drafting committee. The constitution stemming from the committee's work comprised 197 articles, including, in articles 125–129, the introduction of a *Reichsgericht* or High Court with far-reaching constitutional review powers; the court, however, never came to fruition. See generally Faller 1974 (827–866); Kühne 1985. Thirty-five years before the Austrian Constitutional Court was established, the leading figure in public law theory (*Staatsrechtslehre*) at the turn of the century, Georg Jellinek wrote a short monograph entitled *Ein Verfassungsgericht für Österreich* (1885). On Jellinek's significance in public law theory, see Stolleis 2001a (440–444 et passim).

56. Kaiserliches Manifest, October 16, 1918, in *Wiener Zeitung* no. 240 (Extra-Ausgabe), October 17, 1918, quoted in Walter and Mayer 1992 (23).

57. See generally Schefbeck 1995 (88–107); Öhlinger 2002; 2003.

58. In particular, the initial sections on "the administration of the federal government" and "basic rights and obligations" reflect the Weimar Constitution's sections on "the Reich administration" (Arts. 78–101) and "basic rights and obligations" (Arts. 109–165) respectively; see Schmitz 1981 (58). On constitutional review in the Weimar Republic, see Dreier 2014, a well-nigh definitive statement.

59. See Kelsen 1922 (263–267); Kelsen, Froehlich, and Merkl 1922 (249–284).

60. See Kelsen, Froehlich, and Merkl 1922 (46–49). This partial sketch of the powers of the Constitutional Court stems from the original Austrian Federal Constitution of October 1, 1920. For a full account of the Court's powers today, see Öhlinger 2009 (ch. XI, §2, 456–493).

61. See generally Kelsen 1925a (§§32–36, 229–255); 1992 (§31, 63–75); 1960 (§35, 228–282). The *Stufenbaulehre* or doctrine of hierarchical structure stems from Adolf Julius Merkl. For his last full statement of the doctrine, see Merkl 1931 (252–294).

62. See, in particular, Kelsen 1929c (69). This paper is Kelsen's contribution to the 1928 meeting in Vienna of the *Association of German Public Law Professors*.

63. In the same paper, Kelsen expresses scepticism about whether "the ideals of 'justice', 'liberty', 'equality', 'equity', 'morality', and the like" are legally explicable at all. He argues, in particular, that these "formulae" or "open-ended clauses," as they have often been termed, represent nothing "more than a typical political ideology" (1929c, 69).

64. H. L. A. Hart's view is similar, quite possibly reflecting Kelsen's influence on Hart; see Hart 2012 (69–70 et passim).

65. Given the lively interest in constitutional review on the one hand and in the work of both Kelsen and Schmitt on the other, the lack of attention to their exchange in 1931 comes as a surprise. The important literature on the exchange begins, I believe, with Mantl 1982 (196–199), then Wendenburg 1984 (129–136, 179–183), followed by Dyzenhaus 1997 (108–123), an insightful discussion. Then, a decade after Dyzenhaus, there are important statements by Jestaedt 2007 (155–175), and Schönberger 2007 (177–195). Most recently, there is hard-hitting criticism directed to Schmitt in Neumann 2010 (747–750). Dyzenhaus 2006 (1–65), in an unusually rich and rewarding contribution, addresses the stakes—and competing claims of emergency powers versus constitutionalism—in emergency situations generally.

66. Although both papers, "Hüter" (1929b) and "Reichsgericht" (1929a), appeared in 1929, the latter is clearly the older paper. Completed in August 1928, only three months after the association's meeting in Vienna, the text of Kelsen's lecture had not yet been published, and Schmitt in his paper relied on reports stemming from the meeting. By contrast, in the "Hüter" paper (1929b) Schmitt had access to, and quoted from, the published version of Kelsen's lecture.

67. An illuminating account of the beginnings and development of the association, the forum for much of what took place in the name of the Weimar politico-constitutional debates, is found in Stolleis 2004 (178–197). This is the third volume in Stolleis's monumental four-volume treatise on the history of German public law theory. On the Weimar politico-constitutional debates generally, Stolleis's treatise is a reliable and rewarding guide. On aspects of Stolleis's exposition, see Paulson 2005. See also Stolleis 2001a; 2001b; 2011 (545–566) and Schefold 1998.

68. Kelsen 1930/1931 (576–628). The paper was also published as a booklet: Kelsen, *Wer soll Hüter der Verfassung sein?* (1931), and it contains an additional, opening paragraph, which

has been included in the Klecatsky reprinting (1873–1922). Kelsen wrote this paper during his brief tenure in Cologne, which was brought to an end by the notorious Nazi statute of April 7, 1933, on the "restoration of the professional civil service." The statute called for the dismissal of civil servants—a category including university professors—who were either "politically unreliable" or of Jewish ancestry. Kelsen was deemed to qualify on both counts.

69. See Kelsen 1929a (1723–1726); Paulson 2008 (9–23). See also Kelsen 1992: "Particular norms of the legal system cannot be logically deduced.... Rather, they must be created by way of a special act issuing or setting them" (§28, 56). In short, Kelsen emphatically rejects derivation qua deduction as a characterization of the judicial process. This position is to be distinguished, however, from subsumption as a post factum reconstruction of a judicial decision already taken. Kelsen has no objections here, and he says as much at one point in the reply to Schmitt; see Kelsen 1930/1931 (589). The idea of subsumption qua reconstruction is familiar from some of the more recent European literature, dubbed "internal justification." See, e.g., Wróblewski 1974 (39); Alexy 1989 (221–230); Bäcker 2012 (302–304). See also the papers in Gabriel and Gröschner 2012. For a full rehearsal of nineteenth-century views in Germany on the ostensibly "logico-mechanical" nature of the judicial decision, see Ogorek 1986. Long-standing stereotypes respecting *Begriffsjurisprudenz* or "mechanical jurisprudence," as ostensibly defended by such nineteenth-century figures as Puchta and Jhering during the latter's first phase, are addressed and corrected in Haferkamp 2004.

70. Schmitt 1912 (9 et passim). See also Schmitt 1913 (804–806); 1917 (157–158). This early view of Schmitt's has been noted in the literature; see, e.g., Wendenburg 1984 (182). Unless noted otherwise, all translations by the author.

71. For a more detailed development of this theme, see Paulson 1996 (797–812); Paulson and Litschewski Paulson 1998 (23–43).

72. This is in any case a reasonable assumption, and it is of interest in this connection that Schmitt wrote his doctoral dissertation in the field of criminal law; see Schmitt 1910.

73. For Kelsen's decisionism, see Kelsen 1930/1931 (592). Although Kelsen does not employ the language of "decisionism" elsewhere, his position, that a "range of discretion" is inevitably and unavoidably left to the lawmaker is clear. See Kelsen 1929a; 1992 (§§33, 78); 1960 (§45(a), 347).

74. Schmitt 1931a (45–46; emphasis added; quoted by Kelsen 1930/1931, 592).

75. Kelsen 1930/1931 (586, see 592). The law, in Kelsen's view, is political in nature. It is the *theory* of law that is "pure" and therefore free of politics. If, however, the law is political in nature, is there any room for a claim respecting the autonomy (*Eigengesetzlichkeit*) of the law? See, e.g., Kelsen 1992 (§11[b], 23). Kelsen ascribes the latter, the autonomy of law, to his *reconstructed* version of the law. Once the reconstruction of the law is complete, its autonomy is a mirror image of the purity of legal theory. To be sure, a great many details of the proposed reconstruction remain utterly obscure.

76. On the background and significance of Article 48, see, e.g., Boldt 1971; Kaiser 2011. The provisions that may be temporarily suspended, according to Section 2, are personal liberty (Article 114), inviolability of the home (Article 115), privacy of communications (Article 117), freedom of expression (Article 118), freedom of assembly (Article 123), freedom of association (Article 124), and the right of private property (Article 153).

77. Jasper 1986 (36). I have drawn generally on Jasper's rewarding statement of these developments. The locus classicus on these developments is Bracher 1971.

78. Article 48, Section 3, provides that the Reich president must immediately inform the *Reichstag* of measures adopted under the earlier sections (section 1 addresses the Reich

president's control over the *Länder*), and such measures shall be rescinded at the demand of the *Reichstag*.

79. Quoted in Jasper 1986 (37). Article 25 of the Weimar Constitution confers power on the Reich president to dissolve the *Reichstag*, with new elections to take place no later than sixty days after the dissolution.

80. The companion lecture at the 1924 meeting was held by Erwin Jacobi. On Jacobi's role, see Otto 2008 (ch. 9, 83–98).

81. See Huber 1974 (31–52). Huber compares the more progressive Weimar theorists, who rejected a broad reading of emergency powers going beyond the letter of Article 48 while recognizing the statutory import of the Article 48 provisions, with Schmitt and Ernst Jacobi, who held precisely the reverse position (see Schmitt 1924).

82. See *Preußen contra Reich* 1976 (39–41, 130–134, 175–181, 288–291, 311–322, 350–355, 466–469); Kelsen 1932 (65–91). It is not clear, however, that Schmitt and Kelsen on the *Preußenschlag* can be treated as a second round in their greater exchange, for Kelsen's discussion is largely analytical and descriptive; see generally Dyzenhaus 1997 (123–132). What is clear is that Schmitt, particularly during the years of the Nazi regime, made appalling references to Kelsen couched in antisemitism. See Gross 2005 (ch. I, §4, 120–134). Here Gross writes at length about the 1936 conference, "Judaism in Legal Science" (*Das Judentum in der Rechtswissenschaft*). Less well known, but clear from Schmitt's recently published diaries from the years 1930–1934, is the fact that his frank and unreserved antisemitism precedes the Nazi period. For example, in December 1930 Schmitt in a reference to Kelsen combines antisemitism and obscenity. See Schmitt 2010, 73, entry of December 28, 1930.

83. See, e.g., Pyta 2007 (701–805), a rewarding statement.

84. See, e.g., Huber 1974 (33–70); Pyta and Seiberth 1999 (423–448, 594–610); Berthold 1999.

References

Alchourrón, C. A., E. and Bulygin. 1981. "The Expressive Conception of Norms." In *New Studies in Deontic Logic*, ed. R. Hilpinen. Dordrecht: Reidel, 95–124.

Alexy, R. 1989. *A Theory of Legal Argumentation*, trans. R. Adler and N. MacCormick. Oxford: Clarendon Press.

Alexy, R. 2005. "Hans Kelsens Begriff der Verfassung." In *Hans Kelsen: Staatsrechtslehrer und Rechtstheoretiker des 20. Jahrhunderts*, ed. S. L. Paulson and M. Stolleis. Tübingen: Mohr, 333–352.

Austin, J. L. 1961. *How to Do Things with Words*. Oxford: Clarendon Press.

Bäcker, C. 2012. *Begründen und Entscheiden*, 2nd ed. Baden-Baden: Nomos.

Beisler, F. C. 2011. *The German Historicist Tradition*. Oxford: Oxford University Press.

Bernatzik, E. 1890. "Kritische Studien über den Begriff der juristischen Person und über die juristische Persönlichkeit der Behörden." *Archiv des öffentlichen Rechts* 5: 169–318.

Berthold, L. 1999. *Carl Schmitt und der Staatsnotstandsplan am Ende der Weimarer Republik*. Berlin: Duncker & Humblot.

Boldt, H. 1971. "Article 48 of the Weimar Constitution, Its Historical and Political Implications." In *German Democracy and the Triumph of Hitler*, ed. A. Nicholls and E. Matthias. London: George Allen and Unwin, 79–97.

Bracher, K. D. 1971. *Die Auflösung der Weimarer Republik*. Villingen: Ring Verlag.

Bryce, J. 1901. *Studies in History and Jurisprudence*. 2 vols. Oxford: Clarendon Press.

Cappelletti, M. 1971. *Judicial Review in the Contemporary World*. Indianapolis: Bobbs-Merrill.

Dahlheimer, M. 1998. *Carl Schmitt und der deutsche Katholizismus 1888–1936*. Paderborn: Schöningh.

Dias, G. N. 2005. *Rechtspositivismus und Rechtstheorie*. Tübingen: Mohr.

Dicey, A. V. 1915. *Introduction to the Study of the Law of the Constitution*, 8th ed. London: Macmillan.

Dreier, H. 1986. *Rechtslehre, Staatssoziologie und Demokratietheorie bei Hans Kelsen*. Baden-Baden: Nomos.

Dreier, H. 2014. "Verfassungsgerichtsbarkeit in der Weimarer Republik." In *Schutz der Verfassung: Normen, Institutionen, Höchst- und Verfassungsgerichte*, ed. T. Simon and J. Kalwoda. *Der Staat*, Beiheft 22. Berlin: Duncker & Humblot, 317–372.

Dreier, R. 1987. "Julius Binder (1870–1939): Ein Rechtsphilosoph zwischen Kaiserreich und Nationalsozialismus." In *Rechtswissenschaft in Göttingen*, ed. F. Loos. Göttingen: Vandenhoeck & Ruprecht, 435–455.

Dreier, R. 1991. *Recht—Staat—Vernunft*. Frankfurt: Suhrkamp.

Dyzenhaus, D. 1997. *Legality and Legitimacy*. Oxford: Oxford University Press.

Dyzenhaus, D. 2006. *Constitution of Law*. Cambridge: Cambridge University Press.

Eikema Hommes, H. J. van. 1984. "The Development of Hans Kelsen's Concept of Legal Norm." In *Rechtssystem and gesellschaftliche Basis bei Hans Kelsen*, ed. W. Krawietz and H. Schelsky. *Rechtstheorie*, Beiheft 5. Berlin: Duncker & Humblot, 159–178.

Faller, H. J. 1974. "Die Verfassungsgerichtsbarkeit in der Frankfurter Reichsverfassung vom 28. März 1849." In *Menschenwürde und freiheitliche Rechtsordnung: Festschrift für Willi Geiger zum 65. Geburtstag*, ed. G. Leibholz et al. Tübingen: Mohr, 827–866.

Gabriel, G., and R. Gröschner. eds. 2012. *Subsumtion*. Tübingen: Mohr.

Gross, R. 2005. *Carl Schmitt und die Juden*. Frankfurt: Suhrkamp.

Haferkamp, H.-P. 2004. *Georg Friedrich Puchta und die "Begriffsjurisprudenz"*. Frankfurt: Klostermann.

Haller, H. 1979. *Die Prüfung von Gesetzen*. Vienna: Springer.

Hare, R. 1952. *The Language of Morals*. Oxford: Clarendon Press.

Hart, H. L. A. 2012. *The Concept of Law*, 3rd ed. Oxford: Clarendon Press.

Herder, J. G. 1991. "Briefe zur Beförderung der Humanität (1793–1795)." In *Werke in zehn Bänden*, vol. 7, ed. H. D. Irmscher. Frankfurt: Klassiker Verlag, 9–753.

Hofmann, H. 1965. "Feindschaft—Grundbegriff des Politischen?" *Zeitschrift für Politik* 12: 17–39.

Hofmann, H. 1992. *Legitimität gegen Legalität*, 2nd printing with a new preface. Berlin: Duncker & Humblot.

Holmes, S. 1995. "Kelsen, Hans." In *The Encyclopedia of Democracy*. vol. 2, ed. S. M. Lipset. London: Routledge, 697–699.

Huber, E. R. 1974. "Zur Lehre vom Verfassungsnotstand in der Staatstheorie der Weimarer Zeit." In *Im Dienst an Recht und Staat: Festschrift für Werner Weber zum 70. Geburtstag*, ed. H. Schneider and V. Götz. Berlin: Duncker & Humblot, 31–52.

Jaitner, A. 1996. "Rechtsnorm und Staatsmacht." *Staatswissenschaften und Staatspraxis* 7: 479–487.

Jasper, G. 1986. *Die gescheiterte Zähmung: Wege zur Machtergreifung Hitlers 1930–1934*. Frankfurt: Suhrkamp.

Jellinek, G. 1885. *Ein Verfassungsgericht für Österreich*. Vienna: A. Holder.

Jestaedt, M. 2007. "Der 'Hüter der Verfassung' als Frage des Rechtsgewinnungsverständnisses." In *La controverse sur "le gardien de la Constitution" et la justice constitutionnelle: Kelsen contre Schmitt*, ed. O. Beaud and P. Pasquino. Paris: Editions Panthéon Assas, 155–175.

Jestaedt, M, ed. 2007–. *Hans Kelsen Werke*. 33 vols. (projected). Tübingen: Mohr.

Jhering, R. von. 1893. *Der Zweck im Recht*, 3rd ed., 2 vols. Leipzig: Breifkopf & Härtel.

Kaiser, A.-B. 2011. "Die Verantwortung der Staatsrechtslehre in Krisenzeiten—Art. 48 WRV im Spiegel der Staatsrechtslehrertagung und des Deutschen Juristentages 1924." In *Zur Aktualität der Weimarer Staatsrechtslehre*, ed. U. J. Schröder and A. von Ungern-Sternberg. Tübingen: Mohr, 119–142.

Kant, I. 1900–. *Gesammelte Schriften*, ed. Preussische Akademie der Wissenschaften. Berlin: Reimer.

Kant, I. 1999. *Metaphysical Elements of Justice*, trans. J. Ladd, 2nd ed. Indianapolis: Hackett.

Kaufmann, M. 1988. *Recht ohne Regel?* Freiburg and Munich: Karl Alber.

Kelsen, H. 1911a. *Hauptprobleme der Staatsrechtslehre*. Tübingen: Mohr. Reprinted in Kelsen 2008.

Kelsen, H. 1911b. *Über Grenzen zwischen juristischer und soziologischer Methode*. Tübingen: Mohr. Reprinted in Kelsen 2010, 22–55.

Kelsen, H. 1914. "Reichsgesetz und Landesgesetz nach österreichischer Verfassung." *Archiv des öffentlichen Rechts* 32: 202–245, 390–438. Reprinted in Kelsen 2010, 359–425.

Kelsen, H. 1916. "Die Rechtswissenschaft als Norm- oder als Kulturwissenschaft." *Schmollers Jahrbuch für Gesetzgebung, Verwaltung und Volkswirtschaft im Deutschen Rechte* 40: 95–153. Reprinted in Kelsen 2010, 551–605.

Kelsen, H. 1920a. *Der Problem der Souveränität und die Theorie des Völkerrechts*. Tübingen: Mohr. Reprinted in Kelsen 2013, 263–572.

Kelsen, H. 1920b. "Die Verfassung Deutschösterreichs." *Jahrbuch des öffentlichen Rechts der Gegenwart* 9: 245–290.

Kelsen, H. 1920c. "Vom Wesen und Wert der Demokratie." *Archiv für Sozialwissenschaft und Sozialpolitik* 47: 50–85.

Kelsen, H. 1922. "Die Verfassung Österreichs." *Jahrbuch des öffentlichen Rechts der Gegenwart* 11: 232–274.

Kelsen, H. 1922–1923. "Rechtswissenschaft und Recht." *Zeitschrift für öffentliches Recht* 3: 103–235.

Kelsen, H. 1923a. *Österreichisches Staatsrecht*. Tübingen: Mohr.

Kelsen, H. 1923b. *Vorrede zur 2. Auflage der Hauptprobleme der Staatsrechtslehre*, v–xxiii. Tübingen: Mohr. Reprinted in translation in Paulson and Paulson, 1998, 3–22.

Kelsen, H. 1925a. *Allgemeine Staatslehre*. Berlin: Julius Springer.

Kelsen, H. 1925b. *Das Problem des Parlamentarismus*. Vienna and Leipzig: W. Braumüller.

Kelsen, H. 1926. "Les rapports de système entre le droit interne et le droit international public." *Recucil des cours* 14: 227–331.

Kelsen, H. 1927a. "Demokratie." In *Verhandlungen des 5. Deutschen Soziologentages vom 26. bis 29. September 1926 in Wien*. Tübingen: Mohr, 37–68, 113–118.

Kelsen, H. 1927b. "Die Bundesexekution." In *Festgabe für Fritz Fleiner zum 60. Geburtstag*, ed. Z. Giacometti and D. Schindler. Tübingen: Mohr.

Kelsen, H. 1928. *Die philosophischen Grundlagen der Naturrechtslehre und des Rechtspositivismus*. Charlottenburg: Pan-Verlag Rolf Heise.

Kelsen, H. 1929a. "Juristischer Formalismus und reine Rechtslehre." *Juristische Wochenschrift* 58: 1723–1726.

Kelsen, H. 1929b. *Vom Wesen und Wert der Demokratie*, 2nd ed. Tübingen: Mohr.

Kelsen, H. 1929c. "Wesen und Entwicklung der Staatsgerichtsbarkeit." *Veröffentlichung der Vereinigung der Deutschen Staatsrechtslehrer* 5: 30–88.

Kelsen, H. 1930/1931. "Wer soll Hüter der Verfassung sein?" *Die Justiz* 6: 576–628.

Kelsen, H. 1931. *Wer soll Hüter der Verfassung sein?* Berlin-Grunewald: Walther Rothschild.

Kelsen, H. 1932. "Das Urteil des Staatsgerichtshofs vom 25. Oktober 1932." *Die Justiz* 8: 65–91.

Kelsen, H. 1941/1942. "The Pure Theory of Law and Analytical Jurisprudence." *Harvard Law Review* 55: 44–70.

Kelsen, H. 1955. "Foundations of Democracy." *Ethics* 66: 1–101.

Kelsen, H. 1957. *What Is Justice?* Berkeley and Los Angeles: University of California Press.

Kelsen, H. 1960. *Reine Rechtslehre*, 2nd ed. Vienna: Deuticke.

Kelsen, H. 1974. "Wiedergabe einer Sendung des österreichischen Rundfunks." In *Hans Kelsen zum Gedenken*, ed. W. Antoniolli et al. Vienna: Europaverlag, 49–74.

Kelsen, H. 1991. *General Theory of Norms*, trans. M. Hartney. Oxford: Clarendon Press.

Kelsen, H. 1992. *Introduction to the Problems of Legal Theory*, trans. B. Litschewski Paulson and S. L. Paulson. Oxford: Clarendon Press.

Kelsen, H. 1998. *Foreword to the Second Printing of Main Problems in the Theory of Public Law*, trans. and ed. B. Litschewski Paulson and S. L. Paulson, 3–22.

Kelsen, H. 2006. *Verteidigung der Demokratie*, ed. M. Jestaedt and O. Lepsius. Tübingen: Mohr.

Kelsen, H. 2007. *Hans Kelsen Werke*. vol. 1, ed. M. Jestaedt. Tübingen: Mohr.

Kelsen, H. 2008. *Hans Kelsen Werke*, vol. 2, ed. M. Jestaedt. Tübingen: Mohr.

Kelsen, H. 2010. *Hans Kelsen Werke*, vol. 3, ed. M. Jestaedt. Tübingen: Mohr.

Kelsen, H. 2013. *Hans Kelsen Werke*, vol. 4, ed. M. Jestaedt. Tüebingen: Mohr.

Kelsen, H., G. Froehlich, and A. J. Merkl. 1922. *Die Bundesverfassung vom 1. Oktober 1920*. Vienna: Deuticke.

Kiefer, L. 1990. "Begründung, Dezision und Politische Theologie: Zu drei frühen Schriften von Carl Schmitt." *Archiv für Rechts- und Sozialphilosophie* 76: 479–499.

Klecatsky, H., et al. eds. 1968. *Die Wiener rechtstheoretische Schule*. 2 vols. Vienna: Europaverlag.

Kubeš, V., and O. Weinberger. eds. 1980. *Die Brünner rechtstheoretische Schule*. Vienna: Manz.

Kühne, J.-D. 1985. *Die Reichsverfassung der Paulskirche*. Frankfurt: Metzner.

Löwith, K. 1960. "Der okkasionelle Dezisionismus von C. Schmitt." In *Gesammelte Abhandlungen*. Stuttgart: Kohlhammer, 93–126.

Makkreel, R. A., and S. Luft. eds. 2010. *Neo-Kantianism in Contemporary Philosophy*. Bloomington: Indiana University Press.

Mantl, W. 1982. "Hans Kelsen and Carl Schmitt." In *Ideologiekritik and Demokratietheorie bei Hans Kelsen*, ed. W. Krawietz et al. Berlin: Duncker & Humblot, 185–199.

McMann, E. 2007. "Locke on Substance." In *The Cambridge Companion to Locke's "Essay Concerning Human Understanding,"* ed. L. Newman. Cambridge: Cambridge University Press, 157–191.

Mehring, R. 1990. *Carl Schmitt*. Hamburg: Junius.

Mehring, R. ed. 2003. *Carl Schmitt: Der Begriff des Politischen*. Berlin: Akademie Verlag.

Mehring, R. 2004. "Macht und Recht: Carl Schmitts Rechtsbegriff in seiner Entwicklung." *Der Staat* 43: 1–22.

Mehring, R. 2009. *Carl Schmitt: Aufstieg und Fall*. Munich: Beck.

Merkl, A. J. 1931. "Prolegomena einer Theorie des rechtlichen Stufenbaues." In *Gesellschaft, Staat und Recht: Untersuchungen zur Reinen Rechtslehre*, ed. A. Verdross. Vienna: Springer, 252–294.

Métall, R. A. ed. 1974. *33 Beiträge zur Reinen Rechtslehre*. Vienna: Europaverlag.

Mohl, R. 1824. *Das Bundes-Staatsrecht der Vereinigten Staaten von Nord-Amerika*. Stuttgart and Tübingen: Cotta.

Neumann, V. 1980. *Der Staat im Bürgerkrieg*. Frankfurt: Campus.

Neumann, V. 2010. "Theoretiker staatlicher Dezision: Carl Schmitt." In *Festschrift 200 Jahre Juristische Fakultät der Humboldt-Universität zu Berlin*, ed. S. Grundmann et al. Berlin: De Gruyter, 733–754.

Nicoletti, M. 1988. "Die Ursprünge von Carl Schmitts 'Politischer Theologie.'" In *Complexio Oppositorum*, ed. H. Quaritsch. Berlin: Duncker & Humblot, 109–128.

Ogorek, R. 1986. *Richterkönig oder Subsumtionsautomat? Zur Justiztheorie im 19. Jahrhundert*. Frankfurt: Klostermann.

Öhlinger, T. 2002. "Die Entstehung und Entfaltung des österreichischen Modells der Verfassungsgerichtsbarkeit." In *Der Rechtsstaat vor neuen Herausforderungen. Festschrift für Ludwig Adamovich zum 70. Geburtstag*, ed. B.-C. Funk et al. Vienna: Verlag Österreich, 581–600.

Öhlinger, T. 2003. "The Genesis of the Austrian Model of Constitutional Review of Legislation." *Ratio Juris* 16: 206–222.

Öhlinger, T. 2009. *Verfassungsrecht*, 8th ed. Vienna: Facultas WUV.

Osterkamp, J. 2009. *Verfassungsgerichtsbarkeit in der Tschechoslowakei (1920–1939)*. Frankfurt: Klostermann.

Otto, M. 2008. *Von der Eigenkirche zum Volkseigenen Betrieb: Erwin Jacobi (1884–1965)*. Tübingen: Mohr.

Paulson, S. L. 1992. "Kelsen's Legal Theory: The Final Round." *Oxford Journal of Legal Studies* 12: 265–274.

Paulson, S. L. 1993. "Die unterschiedlichen Formulierungen der 'Grundnorm.'" In *Rechtsnorm und Rechtswirklichkeit: Festschrift für Werner Krawietz zum 60. Geburtstag*, ed. A. Aarnio et al. Berlin: Duncker & Humblot, 53–74.

Paulson, S. L. 1996. "Hans Kelsen's Earliest Legal Theory: Critical Constructivism." *Modern Law Review* 59: 797–812.

Paulson, S. L. 1998. "Four Phases in Hans Kelsen's Legal Theory? Reflections on a Periodization." *Oxford Journal of Legal Studies* 18: 153–166.

Paulson, S. L. 1999. "Arriving at a Defensible Periodization of Hans Kelsen's Legal Theory." *Oxford Journal of Legal Studies* 19: 351–365.

Paulson, S. L. 2002. "Neumanns Kelsen." In *Kritische Theorie der Politik*, ed. M. Iser and D. Strecker. Baden-Baden: Nomos, 107–128.

Paulson, S. L. 2005. "The Theory of Public Law in Germany 1914–1945." *Oxford Journal of Legal Studies* 25: 525–545.

Paulson, S. L. 2008. "Formalism, 'Free Law', and the 'Cognition' Quandary: Hans Kelsen's Approaches to Legal Interpretation." *University of Queensland Law Journal* 27: 7–39.

Paulson, S. L. 2012a. "A 'Justified Normativity' Thesis in Hans Kelsen's Pure Theory of Law?" In *Institutionalized Reason*, ed. M. Klatt. Oxford: Oxford University Press, 61–111.

Paulson, S. L. 2012b. "Hans Kelsen und Gustav Radbruch: Neukantianische Strömungen in der Rechtsphilosophie." In *Marburg versus Südwestdeutschland: Philosophische Differenzen zwischen den beiden Hauptschulen des Neukantianismus*, ed. C. Krijnen and A. J. Noras. Würzburg: Königshausen & Neumann, 141–161.

Paulson, S. L. 2012c. Review of *Neo-Kantianism in Contemporary Philosophy*, ed. R. A. Makkreel and S. Luft. *European Journal of Philosophy* 20: 508–513.

Paulson, S. L. 2013a. "Das Ende der Reinen Rechtslehre? Zum Umbruch im Werk Hans Kelsens." In *Kölner Juristen im 20. Jahrhundert*, ed. S. Augsberg and A. Funke. Tübingen: Mohr, 53–74.

Paulson, S. L. 2013b. "Die Funktion der Grundnorm: Begründend oder explizierend?" In *Gedenkschrift Robert Walter*, ed. C. Jabloner et al. Wien: Manz, 553–573.

Paulson, S. L. 2013c. "The Great Puzzle: Kelsen's Basic Norm." In *Kelsen Revisited: New Essays on the Pure Theory of Law*, ed. L. Duarte d'Almeida et al. Oxford: Hart, 43–61.

Paulson, S. L. 2014. "Das regulative Prinzip als Rettung der Reinen Rechtslehre Hans Kelsens?" In *Wissenschaftstheorie und Neukantianismus*, ed. C. Krijnen and K. W. Zeidler. Würzburg: Königshausen & Neumann, 222–244.

Paulson, S. L., and B. Litschewski Paulson. eds. 1998. *Normativity and Norms: Critical Perspectives on Kelsenian Themes*. Oxford: Clarendon Press.

Preußen contra Reich. 1976. *Preußen contra Reich vor dem Staatsgerichtshof: Stenogrammbericht der Verhandlungen vor dem Staatsgerichtshof in Leipzig vom 10. bis. 14 und vom 17. Oktober 1932*. Glashütten: Auvermann.

Pyta, W. 2007. *Hindenburg: Herrschaft zwischen Hohenzollern und Hitler*. Munich: Siedler.

Pyta, W., and G. Seiberth. 1999. "Die Staatenkrise der Weimarer Republik im Spiegel des Tagebuchs von Carl Schmitt." *Der Staat* 38: 423–448, 594–610.

Quaritsch, H. 1991. *Positionen und Begriffe Carl Schmitts*, 2nd ed. Berlin: Duncker & Humblot.

Raz, J. 1972. "Voluntary Obligations and Normative Powers." *The Aristotelian Society* 46, suppl: 79–102.

Rieß, R. ed. 2007. *Lion Feuchtwanger und Carl Schmitt: Briefwechsel 1918–1935*. Berlin: Duncker & Humblot.

Ross, A. 1933. *Kritik der sogennanten praktischen Erkenntnis*. Copenhagen: Leven & Munksgaard; Leipzig: Meiner.

Schefbeck, G. 1995. "Verfassungsentwicklung 1918–1920." In *75 Jahre Bundesverfassung: Festschrift aus Anlaß des 75. Jahrestages der Beschlußfassung über das Bundes-Verfassungsgesetz*, ed. Österreichische Parlamentarische Gesellschaft. Vienna: Österreichische Staatsdruckerei, 53–107.

Schefold, Dian. 1998. "Geisteswissenschaften und Staatsrechtslehre zwischen Weimar und Bonn." In *Erkenntnisgewinne, Erkenntnisverluste: Kontinuitäten und Diskontinuitäten in den Wirtschafts-, Rechts- und Sozialwissenschaften zwischen den 20er und 50er Jahren*, ed. K. Acham et al. Stuttgart: Steiner, 576–599.

Schmitt, C. 1910. *Über Schuld und Schuldarten: Eine terminologische Untersuchung*. Breslau: Schletter.

Schmitt, C. 1912. *Gesetz und Urteil: Eine Untersuchung zum Problem der Rechtspraxis*. Berlin: Liebmann.

Schmitt, C. 1913. "Juristische Fiktionen." *Deutsche Juristen-Zeitung* 18: 804–806.

Schmitt, C. 1914. *Der Wert des Staates und die Bedeutung des Einzelnen*. Tübingen: Mohr.

Schmitt, C. 1916a. Review of Julius Binder, *Rechtsbegriff und Rechtsidee. Kritische Vierteljahresschrift für Gesetzgebung und Rechtswissenschaft* 53.17: 431–440.

Schmitt, C. 1916b. "Diktatur und Belagerungszustand." *Zeitschrift für das gesamte Strafrechtswissenschaft* 38: 138–162.

Schmitt, C. 1921. *Die Diktatur*. Leipzig: Duncker & Humblot.

Schmitt, C. 1922. *Politische Theologie*. Munich: Duncker & Humblot.

Schmitt, C. 1924. "Die Diktatur des Reichspräsidenten nach Artikel 48 der Weimarer Verfassung." *Veröffentlichungen der Vereinigung der Deutschen Staatsrechtslehrer* 1: 63–104. Reprinted in Schmitt, 1928b, 213–254.

Schmitt, C. 1926. *Die geistesgeschichtliche Lage des heutigen Parlamentarismus*, 2nd printing with new foreword. Leipzig: Duncker & Humblot.

Schmitt, C. 1927. "Der Begriff des Politischen." *Archiv für Sozialwissenschaft und Sozialpolitik* 58: 1–33.

Schmitt, C. 1928a. *Verfassungslehre*. Leipzig: Duncker & Humblot.

Schmitt, C. 1928b. *Die Diktatur*, 2nd printing with new foreword. Munich: Duncker & Humblot.

Schmitt, C. 1929a. "Das Reichsgericht als Hüter der Verfassung." In *Die Reichsgerichtspraxis im deutschen Rechtsleben: Festgabe der juristischen Fakultäten zum 50jährigen Bestehen des Reichsgerichts*, ed. O. Schreiber, vol. 1, *Öffentliches Recht*. Berlin and Leipzig: De Gruyter, 154–178.

Schmitt, C. 1929b. "Der Hüter der Verfassung." *Archiv des öffentlichen Rechts* 55 (N.F. 16): 161–237.

Schmitt, C. 1930a. "Staatsethik und pluralistischer Staat." *Kant-Studien* 35: 28–42. Reprinted in Schmitt, 1993a, 133–145.

Schmitt, C. 1930b. "Verfassungsrechtliches Gutachten über die Frage, ob der Reichspräsident befugt ist, auf Grund des Art. 48 Abs. 2 WRV finanzgesetzvertretende Verordnungen zu erlassen." Unpublished manuscript, Berlin

Schmitt, C. 1931a. *Der Hüter der Verfassung*. Tübingen: Mohr.

Schmitt, C. 1931b. "Die Wendung zum totalen Staat." *Europäische Revue* 7: 241–250.

Schmitt, C. 1932a. *Der Begriff des Politischen*, 2nd, enlarged ed. Munich: Duncker & Humblot.

Schmitt, C. 1932b. "Gesunde Wirtschaft im starken Staat." *Mitteilungen des Vereins zur Wahrung der gemeinsamen wirtschaftlichen Interessen in Rheinland u. Westfalen* 21: 13–32.

Schmitt, C. 1932c. *Legalität and Legitimität*. Munich and Leipzig: Duncker & Humblot.

Schmitt, C. 1933. *Staat, Bewegung, Volk*. Hamburg: Hanseatische Verlagsanstalt.

Schmitt, C. 1934. *Politische Theologie*. Munich: Duncker & Humblot.

Schmitt, C. 1940. *Positionen und Begriffe Im Kampf mit Weimar—Genf—Versailles, 1923-1939*. Hamburg: Hanseatische Verlagsanstalt.

Schmitt, C. 1969. *Gesetz und Urteil: Eine Untersuchung zum Problem der Rechtspraxis*. Munich: Beck.

Schmitt, C. 1976. *The Concept of the Political*, trans. G. Schwab. New Brunswick: Rutgers University Press.

Schmitt, C. 1985a. *The Crisis of Parliamentary Democracy*, trans. E. Kennedy. Cambridge: MIT Press.

Schmitt, C. 1985b. *Political Theology*, trans. G. Schwab. Cambridge: MIT Press.

Schmitt, C. 1988. *Positionen und Begriffe Im Kampf mit Weimar—Genf—Versailles, 1923-1939*. Berlin: Duncker & Humblot.

Schmitt, C. 1993a. *Positionen und Begriffe*. Hamburg: Hanseatische Verlagsanstalt.

Schmitt, C. 1995. *Staat, Großraum, Nomos*, ed. G. Maschke. Berlin: Duncker & Humblot.

Schmitt, C. 1999. "Ethics of State and Pluralistic State," trans. D. Dyzenhaus. In *The Challenge of Carl Schmitt*, ed. C. Mouffe. London: Verso, 195–208.

Schmitt, C. 2004a. *Legality and Legitimacy*, trans. and ed. J. Seitzer. Durham: Duke University Press.

Schmitt, C. 2004b. *Der Wert des Staates und die Bedeutung des Einzelnen*. Berlin: Duncker & Humblot.

Schmitt, C. 2008. *Constitutional Theory*, trans. and ed. J. Seitzer. Durham: Duke University Press.

Schmitt, C. 2010. *Tagebücher 1930 bis 1934*, ed. W. Schnuller and G. Giesler. Berlin: Akademie Verlag.

Schmitz, G. 1981. *Die Vorentwürfe Hans Kelsens für die österreichische Bundesverfassung.* Vienna: Manz.

Schönberger, C. 2007. "Die Verfassungsgerichtsbarkeit bei Carl Schmitt und Hans Kelsen: Gemeinsamkeiten und Schwachstellen." In *La controverse sur "le gardien de la Constitution" et la justice constitutionnelle: Kelsen contre Schmitt*, ed. O. Beaud and P. Pasquino. Paris: Editions Panthéon Assas, 177–195.

Searle, J. 1969. *Speech Acts.* Cambridge: Cambridge University Press.

Searle, J. 1979. *Expression and Meaning.* Cambridge: Cambridge University Press.

Simmel, G. 1892–1893. *Einleitung in die Moralwissenschaft.* 2 vols. Berlin: Hertz.

Simmel, G. 1989–. *Gesamtausgabe*, ed. O. Rammstedt. Frankfurt: Suhrkamp.

Somló, F. 1917. *Juristische Grundlehre.* Leipzig: Meiner.

Stammler, R. 1911. *Theorie der Rechtswissenschaft.* Halle: Waisenhaus.

Stolleis, M. 2001a. *Public Law in Germany 1800–1914*, trans. P. Biel. Oxford and New York: Berghahn.

Stolleis, M. 2001b. *Der Methodenstreit der Weimarer Staatsrechtslehre—Ein abgeschlossenes Kapitel der Wissenschaftsgeschichte?* Stuttgart: Steiner.

Stolleis, M. 2004. *A History of Public Law in Germany 1914–1945*, trans. T. Dunlap. Oxford: Oxford University Press.

Stolleis, M. 2011. *Ausgewählte Aufsätze und Beiträge*, ed. S. Ruppert and M. Vec. Frankfurt: Klostermann.

Ulmen, G. L. 1991. *Politischer Mehrwert.* Weinheim: VCH, Acta Humaniora.

Walter, R. 1993. "Die Grundnorm im System der Reinen Rechtslehre." In *Rechtsnorm und Rechtswirklichkeit: Festschrift für Werner Krawietz zum 60. Geburtstag*, ed. A. Aarnio et al. Berlin: Duncker & Humblot, 85–99.

Walter, R., and H. Mayer. 1992. *Grundriß des österreichischen Bundesverfassungsrechts.* 7th ed. Vienna: Manz.

Weinberger, O. 1979. *Logische Analyse in der Jurisprudenz.* Berlin: Duncker & Humblot.

Weinberger, O. 1985. "The Expressive Conception of Norms: An Impasse for the Logic of Norms." *Law and Philosophy* 4: 165–198.

Weinberger, O. 1988. *Norm und Institution.* Vienna: Manz.

Weinberger, O. 2000. *Aus intellektuellem Gewissen: Aufsätze von Ota Weinberger*, ed. M. Fischer et al. Berlin: Duncker & Humblot.

Wendenburg, H. 1984. *Die Debatte um die Verfassungsgerichtsbarkeit und der Methodenstreit der Staatsrechtslehre in der Weimarer Republik.* Göttingen: Otto Schwartz.

Weyr, F. 1914. "Review of Carl Schmitt, *Der Wert des Staates und die Bedeutung des Einzelnen.*" *Österreichische Zeitschrift für öffentliches Recht* 1: 578–581.

Wróblewski, J. 1974. "Legal Syllogism and Rationality of Judicial Decision." *Rechtstheorie* 5: 33–46.

CHAPTER 20

....

STATES OF EMERGENCY

....

WILLIAM E. SCHEUERMAN

INTRODUCTION

....

FEW THINKERS have been as preoccupied with the political and legal challenges posed by emergencies, and perhaps none has garnered both as much favorable and unfavorable press for his reflections as Carl Schmitt. Particularly since the 9/11 terrorist attacks on the World Trade Center and Pentagon and similar attacks in Spain and the United Kingdom, Schmitt's ideas about states of emergency have come to play a major role in political and legal debate. His has become a household name even among Anglophone political and legal scholars who otherwise evince little interest in recent continental European political and legal thought.

Contemporary fascination with Schmitt's ideas about states of emergency derives in part from two distinct theses, each of which he rigorously advanced. Schmitt argued for the unavoidability and ubiquity of dire crises or emergences while linking this fundamentally empirical claim to a far-reaching legal skepticism. Schmitt believed that liberalism's so-called normativistic quest to subject wide swaths of human affairs to general law—that is, the rule of law—is both conceptually misguided and historically obsolescent. Liberalism's legalistic inclinations rob it of the conceptual and institutional materials necessary for mastering ever-more widespread crisis scenarios, whose imperatives inevitably explode the ordinary paraphernalia of law-based government. Manifold emergency situations demand state action inconsonant with the rule of law: liberalism's various attempts to circumscribe emergency action (e.g., constitutional emergency power clauses like Weimar's Article 48) regularly fail. Emergencies—potentially of a life-or-death nature—demand unexpected and sometimes unforeseeable exercises of far-reaching discretionary executive power. Since emergencies are both irrepressible and commonplace and liberalism's arsenal of legalistic restraints necessarily founders, Schmitt's remark that the "exception is more interesting than the rule" was intended as much more than a clever aphorism (1985a, 15).[1] Not only do emergencies, which "cannot be circumscribed factually and made to conform to a preformed law," increasingly constitute the normal rather than exceptional state of political and legal affairs, but also their proliferation highlights the structural advantages of an executive-dominated authoritarian institutional alternative, liberated from obsolete legalistic (and especially liberal) ideals (6).

Here I chiefly focus on the roots of Schmitt's views about emergency power in three crucial historical and biographical conjunctures: World War I, when Schmitt served in Munich with the military authorities responsible for overseeing Germany's wartime emergency regime; the Weimar debates about Article 48, and particularly a prominent 1924 lecture, "Die Diktatur des Reichspräsidenten nach Artikel 48 der Weimarer Verfassung" ("The Dictatorship of the Reich President According to Article 48 of the Weimar Constitution"), in which he offered a latitudinarian account of presidential prerogative; and Weimar's dying days (1930–1933), when he defended—and sometimes advised—the German president in support of his reliance on far-reaching emergency measures. My aim is not the crudely historicist one according to which we can attempt to explain Schmitt's ideas by reducing them to their context. Yet without close attention to these three decisive political (and personal) moments, we cannot make proper sense of them, which—as I hope to show—exhibit far more continuity than widely asserted.[2] In particular, their core elements were already sketched out in his initial foray into the topic during World War I. Despite some shifts in Schmitt's thinking about emergency government, continuities outweigh discontinuities: precisely when Schmitt appears to make concessions to the view that emergencies can be regulated or reined in by legal or constitutional means, he in fact typically suggests the impossibility of effectively doing so. Schmitt regularly masks his radical hostility to modern and especially liberal ideals of law-based government behind a superficial legalistic veneer.

Since 9/11, Schmitt's views of emergency power have been employed to serve an astonishing variety of political and theoretical ends. Yet one general result has been a tendency to downplay their normative limits by means of a decontextualized and dehistoricized reading, apparently oblivious to their deleterious political implications. Given this trend, careful attention to the specific political and historical contexts in which Schmitt's views initially emerged seems particularly timely today. In a concluding section, I consider Schmitt's prominent status in recent U.S. debates on emergency powers, underlining the ways even those authors who try to distance themselves from their disturbing normative and political implications struggle with mixed results to do so.

Jurist for Military Dictatorship, 1916–1917

World War I resulted in a vast expansion of emergency authority within all participating states. Even in liberal democracies like the United States and United Kingdom, it generated relatively novel legal forms (e.g., legislative emergency delegations to the executive) and also dramatically accelerated the general developmental tendency for de facto emergency power to transcend conventional de jure restraints (Rossiter 2002, 242). Most striking perhaps, the exigencies of modern total warfare demanded its extension well beyond strictly military- and security-related matters: essential features of modern warfare (e.g., propaganda and extensive state economic regulation) rapidly became objects of emergency regulation. In Germany, where the war's outbreak led to the declaration of a state of siege (*Belagerungszustand*), state officials were promptly given vast authority to suspend basic rights and to exercise an effectively unlimited right to issue directives in myriad political and social arenas.[3] The distinction between temporary military decrees and general legislation was soon blurred, with the courts condoning military promulgations of administrative orders having the force of law (*gesetzesvertretenden Charakter*). In contrast to liberal democracies like the United States, where wartime dictatorial measures remained at least in principle subject to a popularly elected president, in Germany they for the most part entailed—despite some legitimate disagreements among scholars about its scope and severity—military dictatorship.

Schmitt spent much of the war in Munich working for the regional *Generalkommando*, the military authority responsible for exercising emergency rule in Bavaria's great metropolis and, by war's end, the site of massive political and social turmoil. Although his diaries suggest that he was bored by the day-to-day bureaucratic routines, in September 1915 he was assigned the task of providing a justification for an expansive interpretation of emergency powers with the aim of extending them for "a few years after the war."[4] In a pair of 1916 publications, "Die Einwirkungen des Kriegzustandes auf das ordentliche strafprozessuale Verfahren" ("The Impact of the State of War on Ordinary Criminal Law Procedure") and "Diktatur und Belagerungszustand: Eine staatsrechtliche Studie" ("Dictatorship and State of Siege: A Study in Public Law"), both of which probably helped land him his first teaching position at the University of Strasbourg, Schmitt did just that. More generally, the two essays vividly mirror the dramatic shifts in emergency power that occurred during World War I. They outlined ways relatively traditional legal instruments—most important, the state of siege—could be theoretically retailored to fit novel conditions. In Schmitt's account, they could do so only if interpreted as permitting vast administrative (and especially military) discretion. Many of Schmitt's subsequent ideas about emergency rule, including the key intuition not only that the legitimate scope of emergency action is irrepressibly broad but also that conventional legal devices are unlikely to contain it effectively, were already part and parcel of his 1916 and 1917 writings.

The first and more conventional of the two pieces deals with the impact of the military state of siege on the ordinary criminal law, a subject Schmitt taught at Strasbourg. Initially given as an introductory lecture (*Probevorlesung*) to his would-be colleagues on the legal faculty, Schmitt pleads—not surprisingly, given the lawyers and jurists making up his audience—for the preservation of a modicum of judicial independence. However, its compass turns out to be somewhat narrow. Schmitt dutifully recounts that under the state of siege German military authorities are put in charge of the state administrative apparatus. They can legally abrogate civil liberties and basic protections and set up special courts (1917a, 785–787). Without critical comment, he notes that the military government has been exercising far-reaching power not simply in the political and military but also in economic realms (787–788). In fact, their measures have taken on a quasi-legislative status, efforts by critics to maintain a clear separation between general law and emergency decrees notwithstanding (784–785). For most areas of governance, the only real restraint on them is their sense of duty and professional responsibility: military officials are expected to act in the public interest. In short, Schmitt reminds his readers what they surely already knew: wartime Germany was being governed in many spheres of life by a military dictatorship.

However, he quickly notes, the state of siege still prohibits military authorities from disbanding the ordinary criminal courts. Despite the fact it enjoins them to search homes without a warrant, censor newspapers, issue decrees having the force of law, detain suspects absent regular legal checks, and set up some extraordinary courts, the ordinary criminal courts still maintain a modicum of institutional autonomy. Consequently, Germany's military should not try to hire and fire ordinary criminal judges at will. Even if criminal prosecutors should be made subordinate to the military government, Schmitt claims, the emergency regime should not jettison the ordinary courts altogether and simply appropriate to themselves the job of punishing those found guilty of crimes, notwithstanding massive transformations necessarily taking place elsewhere on the country's political and legal terrain (1917a, 788–796).

During 1916 and 1917, Schmitt shuttled back and forth between his military and academic duties in Munich and Strasbourg. On one reading of the *Probevorlesung*, his position provides a justification for an alliance between the military government and criminal lawyers along the lines he temporarily embodied. Military authorities should properly recognize the advantageous political and legal functions exercised by the ordinary courts as "junior partners" in the wartime emergency government—hardly an implausible expectation, given the profoundly conservative and nationalistic predilections of his legal colleagues. Ordinary courts can and should continue to hear criminal cases and punish the guilty. Addressing his fellow jurists, Schmitt defends a measure of judicial integrity. Yet, crucially, he does so not to challenge the military regime head-on by subjecting it to judicial review or blocking its activities but instead to maintain a role for his colleagues in Germany's wartime legal system: they should be allowed to continue to punish and sentence criminals.

The second and more provocative essay from the same period, "Dictatorship and State of Siege," sheds the legalistic contours still haunting Schmitt's remarks on wartime criminal law. Unfairly neglected in much of the massive secondary literature, it anticipates central features of his mature thinking about emergency rule.[5]

Initially, the essay neatly separates the state of siege from dictatorship (Schmitt 1917b, 138–156).[6] "Under the state of siege a concentration takes place within the executive while the separation of legislation and execution is maintained; under dictatorship the difference between legislation and execution continues to exist, but the separation is removed insofar as the same authority [*Stelle*] has control of both decree and execution of laws."[7] During the state of siege, executive power is concentrated, while the separation of powers between the legislative and executive branches remains in principle intact. In a dictatorship, legislative and executive authority get fused, as occurred during the French Revolution under the Jacobins (141–144). In stark contrast to the dictatorial practices of revolutionary France, the state of siege is depicted as a basically conservative constitutional device whereby the executive is temporarily permitted to engage even in otherwise illegal acts for the sake of preserving the status quo. Under the auspices of the state of siege, administrative power is concentrated in the hands of military commanders so that they can tackle concrete threats to public order. Even if doing so entails granting them substantial decision-making power, their decisions still lack a strictly legislative status. Military authorities issue temporary decrees appropriate to the specific necessities at hand. In contrast to standing general laws, however, their decrees lose any validity as soon as the crisis subsides and the state of siege ends. Similarly, even if the state of siege permits the military government to abrogate basic rights, such rights remain on the books: when the threats at hand have been successfully warded off, basic rights will again be respected.

At first look, Schmitt again appears to outline a relatively legalistic model of emergency powers, where constitutionally circumscribed military discretion differs sharply from lawless dictatorship. Limited to undertaking specific discretionary measures, crisis measures are to be rigorously distinguished from normal constitutional and legal devices, and they are not supposed to alter the normal operations of the constitutional system.

However, "Dictatorship and State of Siege" immediately deconstructs the dichotomy between dictatorship and state of siege, characterizing it as little more than a troublesome leftover from the French Enlightenment, to which Schmitt traces it. As he acknowledges, during a state of siege the traditional distinction between temporary measures and general laws in fact tends to get blurred. Admitting that this trend raises various jurisprudential problems, Schmitt observes that the German courts have nonetheless condoned it (1917b, 153). Although he remains coy in his discussion of this trend's sources, one of them seems manifest enough: if military governors during a state of siege are allowed to do whatever is necessary to counteract the threat at hand, what is to keep them from potentially setting major and indeed transformative legal changes into motion? The seemingly neat dividing line between the conservative—or at least stabilizing—institutions of the state of siege and dictatorship becomes messy. Legal praxis contradicts legal doctrine.

Schmitt then proceeds to offer an explanation for this tension. The French Enlightenment was predicated on an insufficiently appreciative assessment of both the historical primordiality and institutional creativity of the executive and state administration: the rationalistic French mistakenly sought to reduce executive discretion to an absolute minimum. Despite the ways French revolutionary praxis in actuality undermined the separation of powers, Schmitt notes, the French stubbornly held onto a dogmatic view of it (1917b, 141). Obfuscating the crucial fact that administrative authority should be conceived along the lines of an originary condition (*Urzustand*) prior to the realm of abstract legal norms and by no means reducible to them, conventional ideas of the state of siege obscure its special traits. When properly conceived, the state of siege represents a return to the origins of modern statehood, when administrative creativity unhampered by the modern rule of law, separation of powers, and constitutional government possessed predominance. "Within the space [of positive law], a return to the originary condition takes place, so to speak, the military commander acts like the administering state prior to the separation of powers: he decides on concrete measures as means to a concrete goal, without being hindered by statutory limits."[8] Notwithstanding claims to the contrary, administrative activity can never be completely contained or limited by general norms or other legal means. During a state of siege, the discretionary core of the modern administrative apparatus again rears its head (156–160).

Although Schmitt's 1917 essay never sufficiently defends these controversial claims, their implications for the state of siege are clear enough: it represents an attempt to recapture that originary law-free space (*rechtsfreier Raum*) by modern legal means. Within it military commanders act in a manner akin to bureaucrats under the auspices of early modern European absolutism, who had yet to succumb to naïve modern Enlightenment ideals of legality and constitutionalism. In Schmitt's account, emergency actors need to be able to act in a potentially unlimited fashion if they are to do their job properly. Who is to say ahead of time what measures may be necessary to defeat the potentially existential peril at hand?

By belittling the endeavor to subject the executive to general laws, Schmitt effectively undercut the possibility of a clear analytic separation between the state of siege and dictatorship. And by celebrating the existence of an original discretionary power intrinsic to the executive and administrative apparatus, allegedly repressed by a misbegotten Enlightenment-inspired legalism, he simultaneously provided a justification for substantial and perhaps unharnessed executive emergency discretion. Not surprisingly perhaps, the essay offered no discussion of the continuing importance of judicial independence, even as modestly interpreted in its sister piece from the same period. Schmitt saw Germany as subject to the constitutional mechanisms of the state of siege. Yet he creatively envisioned those strictures as legitimizing a law-free space, whose underlying dynamics were described as necessarily undermining efforts to tame executive power and the state's administrative apparatus by the rule of law and other Enlightenment-inspired legal innovations. Initial appearances to the contrary, Schmitt's wartime essay proffered, as Peter Caldwell astutely comments, "a radical rejection of 'western' constitutionalism" (1997, 61).

Schmitt's Munich superiors had asked him to justify the extension of military rule beyond the conclusion of hostilities. Read superficially, the essays shy away from providing direct support for this agenda. However, by suggesting that emergency government represented an authentic attempt to recapture the authentic originary condition of modern statehood, while questioning the normative desirability as well as practical viability of restraining executive discretion by normal legal means, his argument provided clear theoretical tools for doing so. Condoning both the ongoing fusion of military measures with general legislation and the spread of emergency rule into new arenas (e.g., the economy), it served his military superiors quite well. Perhaps best of all, it did so while at least appearing to remain loyal to a relatively traditional conception of the separation of powers, despite the fact that Schmitt's own argument in reality made mincemeat of the state of siege's more legalistic features.

ARTICLE 48: BETWEEN COMMISSARIAL AND SOVEREIGN DICTATORSHIP, 1921–1926

Schmitt's most sympathetic readers typically make a great deal of a 1924 lecture he gave in Jena at the annual meeting of German jurists, where as a law professor (now based in Bonn) with a growing reputation he offered a creative reinterpretation of Article 48 of the Weimar Constitution, Germany's first attempt to guarantee that emergency powers mesh with liberal democratic constitutionalism (Schmitt 1928b).[9] The lecture, "The Dictatorship of the Reich President According to Article 48 of Weimar Constitution," was subsequently reprinted as an addendum to the second edition of perhaps his most impressive scholarly tract from the 1920s, *Die Diktatur* (1928a). In the Jena presentation, Schmitt countered jurists who interpreted Article 48 as permitting only specified abrogations of a narrow range of basic rights. Instead, Schmitt expounded a

> latitudinarian conception of the President's [emergency] dictatorial power, maintaining that the dictator [i.e., president] might temporarily suspend almost all the articles of the Constitution, if necessary to save it, and not just the seven mentioned in Article 48 itself. Even though the President could not permanently alter the Constitution, he could temporarily prevent the operation of a large part of it. Schmitt advanced the idea that the operation of Article 48 itself provided for "an untouchable minimum of organization"—that is, there were several governmental organs (President, Cabinet, *Reichstag*) constitutionally joined together in the execution of those functions foreseen by Article 48.... Any temporary abridgement of other articles was not a serious and unconstitutional matter. (Rossiter 2002, 69)

According to the conventional scholarly interpretation even though Schmitt advocated an indisputably broad interpretation of presidential emergency powers, he still criticized the possible employment of Article 48 as an instrument of fundamental constitutional change (Schwab 1989, 29–43; Kennedy 2004, 159–168; Kalyvas 2011; Kennedy 2011). On this reading, he saw Article 48 as providing for a wide-ranging constitutional dictatorship (i.e., a temporary limited emergency government aimed at protecting Weimar's underlying constitutional and institutional framework). However, he opposed interpreting it as a constitutional conduit to unharnessed emergency dictatorship for the sake of basic political transformation.

Despite some clear textual support for this interpretation (Schmitt 2011, 313–320), it risks overlooking a number of illuminating ambiguities in Schmitt's overall account. Here as well, Schmitt initially evinced apparent fidelity to relatively legalistic ideas about emergency government while simultaneously deconstructing their underlying conceptual foundations. We can only make sense of this intellectual strategy, however, if proper attention is paid to the ways Schmitt's reflections on Article 48 build directly on his earlier wartime writings.

As he notes in the 1924 Jena lecture, Schmitt's reading of Article 48 depends on the crucial distinction between commissarial and sovereign dictatorship, as it had been previously articulated in the main body of *Die Diktatur* (1928a), with the former referring to temporary dictatorial power exercised for the purpose of upholding the constitutional status quo and the latter to dictatorial power pursuant to the creation of a new order. Schmitt interprets Article 48 as representing a specifically modern and rule of law-oriented (*rechtsstaatlich*) version of commissarial dictatorship, aiming under ideal circumstances at the complete legal regulation of emergency government: both the conditions of its invocation and the precise ways emergency power is employed should be legally codified. In this spirit, Schmitt insists, Article 48 pointed to the possibility of fully codifying emergency rule. However, he quickly adds, Weimar's various governments never finished the job: though Article 48 expressly called on the *Reichstag* to pass legislation providing for further codification, it never did so. Consequently, Schmitt concludes, Article 48 remains legally incomplete and thus provisional. "Even though it is valid law, there has been no thorough, finalized determination of Article 48.... The constitution remains open on this point" (2011, 309).[10] As we will see, this was a significant amendment to his overall argument.

Die Diktatur had built immediately on the wartime conceptual juxtaposition of state of siege to dictatorship. Significantly, it also smuggled in some of Schmitt's earlier skepticism about the ultimate value of the distinction. Executive discretion is briefly described in *Die Diktatur* as fundamental to the modern state (1928a, 12–13). Commissarial dictatorship refers to executive-dominated emergency government, where the executive is obliged to temporarily suspend basic rights and pass far-reaching individual measures for the sake of preserving political order. The traditional institutions of the state of siege represent an important example of it. Crucially, commissarial dictatorship allows emergency authorities to do whatever they consider necessary to overcome concrete threats at hand. Yet their acts are not supposed to possess the character of ordinary law: individual emergency measures are strictly delimited from standing general laws. In contrast, sovereign dictatorship entails full-scale revolutionary dictatorship, along the lines of the Jacobins and more recent political conjunctures, including the 1918 German Revolution. Its legal acts are transformative and thus also effectively permanent. According to Schmitt, the Weimar Constitutional Assembly exercised the powers of sovereign dictatorship when it created Germany's first republican system. Acting in the name of the people as a whole, conceived of as a constitutionally unbound pouvoir constituant, postwar Germany's revolutionary dictatorship destroyed the preexisting political order to create a novel one. Whereas commissarial dictatorship ostensibly rests on the traditional separation of powers, sovereign dictatorship does away with it (1928a, 148–149), in part by undermining any attempt to limit its undertaking to temporary measures.

However, the actual implications vis-à-vis Article 48 for the two basic types of dictatorship soon become rather more ambiguous. The detailed historical exegesis provided in *Die Diktatur* mentions some cases—for example, 1848 France—where commissarial and sovereign dictatorship apparently fused together (1928a, 200). *Die Diktatur* suggests that Article 48 is a highly legalistic—and thus problematic—version of commissarial dictatorship, since it mistakenly aims to subject emergency authority to complete legal codification. For Schmitt, this is a tendentious legacy of the liberal-bourgeois *Rechtsstaat*: building on his wartime enmity to the French Enlightenment-inspired attempt to subject originary executive and administrative authority to legality, he seems skeptical about both the viability and desirability of such attempts.[11] The 1924 Jena lecture then proceeds to describe manifold ways real-life legal practice conflicts with Article 48 when interpreted as an instrument of limited emergency rule (2011, 299–302). As Schmitt was aware, Article 48 was already being extensively employed by German governments as a launching pad for far-reaching executive legislation over a vast range of policy arenas, including state regulation of the economy.[12] Just as wartime legal praxis blurred the division between the state of siege and dictatorship, so too does real-life Weimar political and legal experience impair the closely related separation of sovereign from commissarial dictatorship. As in Schmitt's previous wartime writings, the tension between legal doctrine and legal praxis ultimately serves as evidence for the flawed character of the former.

To be sure, Schmitt did not rush to celebrate the conflation of emergency decrees with general laws, though in some writings from the mid-1920s he was already eagerly identifying the potentially fruitful political and institutional possibilities such trends proffered those hoping to strengthen Weimar's executive (see, e.g., 1925, 1). Yet as with the earlier binary divide between state of siege and dictatorship, by the end of the day he had taken major steps toward belittling the real-life significance of the differences between commissarial and sovereign dictatorship.

In Schmitt's narrative, commissarial dictatorship presupposes a basically coherent political unity where potentially explosive political and social divides have been defused. Otherwise, a new state-based order may still need to be created—by sovereign dictatorship—in the first place. The reestablishment of law and order presupposes that it had previously existed. Yet as Schmitt notes, it remains unclear whether Weimar Germany has in fact ever achieved the indispensable minimum of law and order. Operating amid more-or-less permanent civil disorder, Article 48 therefore should not be interpreted as an exclusively commissarial emergency instrument (1928a, 203–204; 1928b, 258–259).[13] Moreover, Germany's special historical situation helps explain Article 48's so-called provisional character. Even if the sovereign dictatorial powers exercised by Weimar's constitutional framers were supposed to be jettisoned in favor of legalistic (*rechtsstaatlich*) commissarial dictatorship along the lines hinted at in Article 48, this never transpired because Weimar Germany's more-or-less permanent abnormal situation necessitated "securing additional room to play" (*einen weiteren Spielraum sichern*) for a more far-reaching emergency dictatorship (2011, 313; translation modified; see also 1928a, 203–204). Even if Weimar's constitutional founders originally intended to grant the president limited constitutional commissarial powers, the President—acting via Article 48—still simultaneously represents the "residue" (*Residuum*) of the National Assembly's sovereign dictatorship (2011, 313).

So Schmitt ultimately envisioned Article 48 as *fusing* elements of both commissarial and sovereign dictatorship: Article 48 should not be interpreted as representing a resolute choice for one over the other. This peculiar scenario directly reflected a host of contradictory political and legal dynamics, Schmitt believed, that had plagued the German Republic's eventful history (1928a, 203–204). Unlike his earlier wartime writings, neither *Die Diktatur* nor the 1924 Jena lecture succumbed to crude Enlightenment bashing or a heavy-handed critique of French rationalism with heavily nationalistic overtones. Yet the results were similar. At least as far as Article 48 was concerned, the separation between limited commissarial (or constitutional) and unlimited sovereign (or transformative) dictatorship gets blurred. John McCormick rightly observes that even in the early *Die Diktatur* Schmitt already hinted at his preference for a "counter-theory of sovereign dictatorship," a right-wing authoritarian response to modern left-wing revolutionary notions of sovereign dictatorship (1998, 228). Crucially, Schmitt expressly identified Article 48 as one of its possible constitutional bases, seeing in it a residue of sovereign dictatorship.

As noted, during the 1920s Schmitt offered a number of express denouements of attempts to read Article 48 as potentially justifying a revolutionary transformation of the Weimar system. Even on his own conceptual terms, however, such claims can plausibly be interpreted as contextually and historically contingent and thus as potentially subject to dramatic reconsideration. On one reading of Schmitt's position, Article 48's commissarial features deserved to be considered preeminent only when the Weimar system as a whole could be seen viewed as having achieved political unity and stability. In contrast, to the extent that Weimar lacked the requisite stability, Article 48 as a residue of sovereign dictatorship deserved to be taken seriously. To the degree that Article 48 highlighted the unfinished and provisional character of the existing constitutional system, it invited significant—and potentially far-reaching—legal and constitutional change.

Revealingly, even in 1928, when the German Republic at least momentarily appeared to have achieved a measure of stability, Schmitt still doubted that his country had achieved sufficient political unity. "In the case of the [Weimar] state today, we are dealing with a people pieced together heterogeneously" and thus still lacking a modicum of political unity. Weimar remained "divided in many ways—culturally, socially, by class, race, and religion" (Schmitt 2000, 299) and the inadequate degree of political integration hitherto achieved rested, he added, on nothing more than the necessity of paying war reparations to the victorious Allies. Soon Schmitt would radicalize this line of argumentation, by 1930 describing Weimar as a politically incoherent pluralist party state whose profound internal fractures conflicted directly with political stability's necessary prerequisites (2001; 1931a).

The relatively commonplace view that Schmitt supported a limited commissarial—and basically constitutional—dictatorship during the 1920s does not ultimately hold up to careful scrutiny. Schmitt's writings from this period in fact support the critical view that "the gap between sovereign (constituent) and commissarial dictatorship could not be maintained" (Kalyvas 2011, 268). In contrast to much of the recent scholarship, one of Schmitt's own historical contemporaries, the U.S. political scientist Clinton Rossiter, is on the mark when he observes that even the otherwise impressive *Die Diktatur* "failed in the end to draw a sufficiently precise distinction between constitutional dictatorship and opportunistic Caesarism" (2002, 14 n10).

CROWN JURIST FOR AUTHORITARIAN PRESIDENTIALISM, 1930–1933

During Weimar's final hours, and with special intensity commencing during summer 1932, Schmitt served as crown jurist for an increasingly authoritarian set of executive-dominated emergency regimes, for which not only did he provide concrete legal advice[14] but in defense of whose constitutionally suspect practices he also penned a pair of fascinating books, *Der Hüter der Verfassung* (*The Guardian of the Constitution*), published in 1931, and *Legalität und Legitmität* (*Legality and Legitimacy*), published in 1932. Schmitt recounted the decline of elected legislatures, seeing in the Weimar parliament's dramatic disintegration impeccable evidence of a world-historical trend while simultaneously embracing the executive's ever-widening recourse to a broad interpretation of Article 48. Although he described his reform efforts as consistent with core elements of the Weimar system, in actuality he advocated a fundamental institutional transformation in which the Reich president, characterized in 1932 as ideally possessing a "rare type of authority" based on "the impression of a great political success; perhaps from the authoritarian residue of predemocratic times; or from the admiration of a quasi-democratic elite," would exercise plebiscitary rule via questions posed to a passive people, which would "only respond yes or no. They cannot advise, deliberate, or discuss. They cannot govern or administer. They also cannot set norms, but can only sanction norms by consenting to a draft set of norms laid before them. Above all, they cannot pose a question, but can only answer with yes or no to a question placed before them" (2004, 89–90).

For my limited purposes here, I highlight the ways Schmitt's views from this period, which both justified and helped contribute to the demise of Weimar democracy, built directly on his previous ideas about emergency government. As in his earliest writings from World War I, Schmitt regularly polemicized against those who associated authoritarian political trends—and his forceful advocacy of them—with dictatorship,[15] when in reality his own theory's conceptual layout suggests unambiguously that they deserved to be described as such. Here again, a certain legalistic veneer masked a radically antilegal agenda.

As early as World War I, Schmitt had condoned the extent to which emergency authority covered a wide range of novel social and economic matters. In 1931, he forthrightly argued that the modern state's irrepressible dependence on extensive regulatory and interventionist measures meant that the executive could rightfully declare an economic-financial emergency to pass controversial measures otherwise unacceptable to Germany's bedraggled legislature. Article 48, in short, permitted the promulgation of extensive social and economic regulation. Denying the executive such authority, he now bluntly contended, meant undermining the modern state's capacity to tackle severe economic and financial crises, which in Schmitt's eyes were widely and quite legitimately seen as potentially life-threatening (1931a, 115–131; 1931b, 235–261).[16] He now also openly endorsed the fusion of individual emergency measures with general law, arguing that the former should be seen as having the force of law. Since the economic state of emergency depended on complex, situation-specific measures, this second claim coalesced with the acknowledgement of the centrality of economic emergency government. Otherwise reasonable legalistic reservations about the fusion of general law and executive decrees, along the lines Schmitt himself occasionally raised during the 1920s (1931a, 118–131; 2004, 67–83), were described as having been swept aside by conventional legal and judicial practice, which had long tolerated it. In short, Schmitt reverted to a familiar theoretical strategy: when political and legal praxis conflicts with legal doctrine, the latter trumps the former, with Schmitt once again according normative status to highly troublesome factual trends. In 1931, he also reiterated his earlier reading of Article 48 as possessing an unfinished provisional character (1931a, 118). De facto emergency economic regulation, in conjunction with an ever-more expansive interpretation of the president's authority to pursue emergency legislation without clear parliamentary support, he noted, had at least partially filled in Article 48's original legal holes. By further expanding the scope of presidential prerogative, Article 48 had been partially completed. This de facto codification, however, merely functioned to give the executive vast leeway to act beyond parliament.

For Schmitt, the conflation of individual measures with general laws necessarily entailed a major blow against traditional views of the separation of powers, according to which general parliamentary lawmaking differed from the situation-specific orientation of the executive and administrative apparatus (2004, 71). As we saw already, Schmitt during World War I had already vehemently criticized the separation of powers; the ascent of an emergency regime that openly discarded it must have seemed like an empirical vindication of his basic intuitions about its congenital flaws. With Germany after 1930 to an ever greater degree ruled by an executive-dominated regime forced to undertake specialized economic and social measures, many of which seemed practically indistinguishable from general law, the result was a predictable blurring of the divide between commissarial and sovereign dictatorship: by permitting the Weimar executive to pursue far-reaching emergency acts with the force of law, the door was opened wide to massive institutional changes. Revealingly, *Legalität und Legitimität* chronicled—and oftentimes seemed to endorse—key ways the Reich president had garnered superior de facto as well as de jure power advantages vis-à-vis Weimar's embattled parliament (59–83).

Arguing that Germany faced a full-scale existential crisis, directly threatening his country with the imminent loss of a bare modicum of political unity,[17] Schmitt relied on the residual attributes of sovereign dictatorship he had previously identified as inhering in Article 48. An authoritarian presidential regime, ruling on the basis of Article 48—here interpreted as constituting little more than an open-ended launching pad for potentially transformative executive action—should replace the Weimar status quo. In effect, the Weimar Constitution's complex emergency power clauses were reduced to little more than a fig leaf for executive-dominated discretionary rule. Revealingly, *Legalität und Legitimität* conceded that the trends Schmitt defended were "contrary to the wording of the Weimar Constitution" (2004, 67).

Not surprisingly, Schmitt located the emerging presidential system's institutional basis in the administrative state (i.e., civil service and military), whose special institutional capacity for situation-specific individual measures he described as especially valuable to the management of the complex economic and social tasks essential to tackling the economic-financial emergency. The executive-based administrative state's originary discretionary power, whose unfortunate subjection to Enlightenment legalism Schmitt had ruefully eulogized during World War I, was now apparently shedding the deleterious Enlightenment and liberal legalism that so often had stood in its way.

What about the possibility of subjecting emergency government to judicial review, as in fact has occurred in many liberal democracies? Although conceding that such a possibility might still be open to polities resting on a widely shared (and probably classical) liberal political economy, where state intervention was narrowly circumscribed and rested on a broad consensus, in Germany and elsewhere it would inevitably mean that the judiciary would take on deeply controversial and thus eminently political tasks for which it was poorly suited.[18] Courts would disingenuously mask their political undertakings in misleading legalistic language, obfuscating the political choices at hand. Just as troubling, they would muck things up, undertaking decision-making tasks best left to others (1931a, 12–70). If the separation of powers were destined to decay because of the necessities of modern state economic intervention, the resulting institutional changes should strengthen the hand of the executive—in Schmitt's view, that branch most attuned to the day-to-day needs of modern social and economic affairs.

Though not the right moment to revisit the complicated as well as controversial issue of Schmitt's relationship to National Socialism, it remains telling that during the mid-1930s he similarly justified his enthusiasm for Germany's new regime on the basis of views about emergency government he had formulated as early as 1917. Schmitt's embrace of Nazism in 1933 was hardly predetermined by those ideas. By the same token, they help explain how and why his disastrous decision to jump into bed with the Nazis in 1933 represents more than personal or professional opportunism.[19] It would be naïve and perhaps disingenuous to ignore some of the more obvious ways Schmitt's Nazi-era writings build on his earlier arguments about emergency government.

In an otherwise sober 1936 survey of attempts by France, Great Britain, and the United States to tackle the economic crisis via emergency legislation, Schmitt at first glance might be taken as suggesting to his Nazi overlords the necessity of constructively learning from those liberal democracies similarly struggling with the dual tasks of overseeing the crisis and providing a coherent legal framework for a modern regulated economy. By the essay's conclusion, however, it again becomes clear that his real aim is to discredit modern constitutionalism and the rule of law. Because the Western liberal democracies remain disastrously mired in the anachronistic quest to maintain the separation of powers between the executive and legislative branches, Schmitt asserts, they were proving inept at dealing effectively with the novel regulatory tasks at hand. Schmitt even criticizes the authoritarian presidentialist regime he had previously prescribed for Weimar: like interwar Germany, and even the presidential regime it became after 1930, the liberal democracies failed in undertaking the "decisive step" toward dismantling the separation of powers (1936, 227–229). Only the Nazis had done so, Schmitt claims. Allegedly, their system of decision-making is fundamentally better attuned to the imperatives of emergency economic government.

In a related 1935 piece, "Die Rechtswissenschaft im Führerstaat" ("Legal Science in the Leader-State"), Schmitt pointedly argues that liberalism's preference for fixed, codified general norms, along with the separation of powers, creates a problematic time lag in its decision-making apparatus. By trying to separate lawmaking from execution, liberalism relies on general statutes that mesh poorly with the contemporary need for government to steer complicated, ever-changing present—and future-oriented economic matters. The temporal gap between law creation and execution in liberalism inexorably leaves state officials poorly equipped to pursue effective economic intervention: they "always come too late" by basing their decisions of legal relics oftentimes unrelated to present and prospective social and economic conditions. Here as well, Schmitt praises the Nazis for alone having "crossed the Rubicon" and finally dismantled parliamentary general law and the separation of powers in order to handle the regulatory imperatives of the modern interventionist state (1935, 439).[20] National Socialism supersedes the problem of a time lag that plagues liberalism by simply getting rid of the obsolete divide between law-making and legal application: in National Socialism, Schmitt appreciatively comments, "law is no longer an abstract norm referring to a past act of volition, but instead the volition and plan of the Führer" (439). Revealingly, no empirical evidence is provided to document the tendentious assertion that Nazism was better suited to the exigencies of the modern regulatory state.

CARL SCHMITT POST-9/11

Interest in Schmitt's ideas about emergency power has undergone a stunning scholarly revival in the aftermath of the 9/11 attacks on the World Trade Center and Pentagon, related terrorist attacks in the United Kingdom and Spain, and the so-called Global War on Terror promulgated by the George W. Bush Administration (Horton 2005; Scheuerman 2006a). One reason that this revival continues unabated even today probably stems from the many surprising continuities between U.S. President Barack Obama's counterterrorism policies and those of his conservative predecessor (Goldsmith 2012).

No short discussion could possibly hope to do justice to the complexity and richness of the debate: a vast range of scholars from a variety of fields has turned to Schmitt to make sense of contemporary developments.[21] At the risk of oversimplification, let me briefly and schematically describe three general strategies employed by contemporary U.S.-based political and legal thinkers who have tried to constructively engage Schmitt's ideas on emergency rule to investigate recent legal and political trends. In my view, none of them succeeds, chiefly because each accepts too much of Schmitt's underlying logic. Recent reworkings of Schmitt's views generally demonstrate at best a limited sensitivity to the specific political and historical contexts in which they originally emerged. Not surprisingly perhaps, they have a harder time circumventing their normative and political blind spots than the authors in question apparently recognize.

The first strategy might be described as *sneaking Schmitt in via the back door*. In this vein, political theorist Bonnie Honig admonishes Schmitt for relying on an overstated conceptual binary opposition between law (or rule of law) and emergency (see also Sarat 2010, 3). In opposition to Schmitt's (allegedly) crude opposition of law to emergencies, we should interpret exceptional and emergency politics as necessarily interwoven into ordinary politics and the normal rule of law. The state of exception should be "seen as part (even if an extreme part) of the daily rule of law-generated struggle between judicial and administrative power" (Honig 2009, 85). On this reading, Schmitt apparently missed the ways the emergency, which he associated with the existence of a legal space unregulated by general rules, cannot be conceptualized as neatly distinguishable from normal political and legal experience. Key elements of the state of emergency (e.g., far-reaching legal discretion) turn out to be constitutive of everyday democratic politics.

One consequence of this binary divide within Schmitt's thinking, Honig suggests, is the tendency to overstate the distinction between rule of law and "rule of men" (2009, 84). Another is then to try to circumvent Schmittian decisionism by unduly favoring the conventional liberal strategy of checking emergency power by turning to familiar legal-institutional devices (e.g., civil liberties and judicial review). However, if we recognize that exceptionalism permeates everyday legal and political affairs, we can begin to appreciate untapped possibilities for "forms of popular political action that engage in agonistic struggle with legal structures and institutions" (66). In short, the potentially positive role of democratic politics (in Honig's terms, agonistic cosmopolitics), where the conventional divide between legal generality and discretion gets blurred, is pushed inopportunely to the wayside by Schmitt's rigid conceptual framework.

The obvious failing with this position is that it purports to be critical when in reality it mirrors Schmitt's own thinking. As David Dyzenhaus accurately notes, "It is precisely Schmitt's point that the exception is the norm because it is a feature of every legal decision" (2011, 73). One can sensibly read Schmitt's reflections on emergency power as an analogous attempt to undermine what he considered to be an overstated normativistic juxtaposition of exception or emergency to general law: exceptional or emergency situations turn out not only to be ubiquitous, but they also cannot be neatly separated from so-called legal normalcy. This, in part, is why he was skeptical that emergencies could be tamed or regulated by constitutional devices (e.g., Article 48) and also why he believed that an element of so-called originary discretionary power was indispensable to political and legal affairs, despite conventional legal and constitutional ideas to the contrary.

Not surprisingly, at least some of what Honig says ends up echoing Schmitt. Like Schmitt, she not only criticizes but probably also caricatures the traditional intuition that the rule of law can be meaningfully distinguished from personalistic rule or the "rule of men." The binary opposition between rule of "law" and "men" is easily deconstructed by Honig only because, like Schmitt, she tends to equate the former with a straw man legal hyper-formalism along the lines occasionally endorsed by early modern jurisprudence (e.g., Montesquieu, Beccaria) but not by most modern liberals or democrats (Honig 2009, 82–86).[22] And even if we accept this misleading view of the rule of law, its proper supersession probably does not entail jettisoning "the quest to bind ourselves everywhere by law" for a celebration of law's "promisingly undecidable dimension" (86). Although Honig's progressive political aims differ fundamentally from Schmitt's, her insufficiently developed ideas about agonistic cosmopolitics hardly offer much reassurance to those who might legitimately want to hold on to the traditional view that the rule of law, separation of powers, and civil liberties, offer indispensable—and sometimes decisive—restraints on political and legal arbitrariness.

A second and closely related trend might then be categorized as *Carl Schmitt meets Critical Legal Studies* (CLS). Although jurists sympathetic to CLS share some of Schmitt's hostile views of liberal law, their sharply varying political standpoint would inevitably seem to doom any attempt at synthesis.[23] In fact, the recent CLS turn to Schmitt clashes with the former's progressive politics.

Mark Tushnet, a prominent CLS jurist, relies especially on Schmitt's *Political Theology* (1985a) to outline a number of provocative claims about the nexus between law and emergency rule. Like Honig, Tushnet sees in Schmitt a useful ally in the battle against conventional liberal legal and constitutionalist attempts to check emergency government. He similarly considers the standard divide between emergency and ordinary law misleading: "emergencies merely surface the usually hidden role of politics in determining the content of law" (Tushnet 2006, 886). The interpretation of even a seemingly unambiguous emergency constitutional clause is always fundamentally a political but not legal matter (886). Schmitt was apparently right to observe that no constitutional lawmaker could realistically anticipate all conceivable emergencies. Attempts to codify emergency powers via constitutional means therefore fail "to address the situation facing policy makers"; consequently, "one cannot use law to determine when legality should be suspended" (Tushnet 2005, 47). Even if traditional proponents of law-based government naively hope otherwise, political reality demands of us that we admit that constitutional provisions merely "provide executive officials with a fig leaf of legal justification for the expansive use of sheer power. What appears to be emergency power limited by the rule of law is actually unlimited emergency power" (49). In part perhaps because Schmitt's legal skepticism overlaps with some of Tushnet's own strong views about legal indeterminacy, he interprets Schmitt as having presciently grasped that emergency power is necessarily unchecked by the law (48). Emergency power is inherently "extra-constitutional," congenitally flawed attempts to restrain it by legal and constitutional mechanisms notwithstanding (48).

So how then to minimize the dangers of unlimited emergency power? For Tushnet, a certain kind of popular politics, interpreted as basically distinct from conventional liberal legal institutions and practices, might counter the specter of legally unchecked "black holes" (2008, 155). Only "the vigilance of the public acting, as it was put in the era of the American Revolution, 'out of doors,'" can protect us from abusive forms of emergency rule (2005, 50). Reminiscent of Honig, Tushnet seems to envision mass-based democratic political action as the best antidote to irresponsible emergency rule.[24]

Even if Tushnet's appeal to vigilant democratic publics sets him apart from Schmitt, the dramatic conceptual juxtaposition of mass politics (i.e., the idea of a people acting "out of [legal] doors") to conventional liberal legal ideals still oddly echoes the latter's own controversial quest to draw a sharp line between democracy and liberalism (Schmitt 1985b; 1996). In fact, it potentially reproduces its widely noted weaknesses. Democracy without civil liberties, the rule of law, or constitutionalism, conceived as operating according to logics at least partly distinguishable from normal or ordinary politics, probably risks culminating in some variety of executive-dominated rule over an easily manipulated populace. In such settings, the citizenry simply lacks effective recourse to time-tested legal and constitutional checks over political elites. Tushnet, like Honig, dramatically juxtaposes law to politics ultimately to blur normatively and politically significant distinctions between them.

History provides cases galore of political elites relying on the specter of crises, real or otherwise, to generate mass support while undertaking dubious illegal and unconstitutional action. Authoritarian emergency government and popular mobilization are by no means necessarily opposed. Vigilant and self-directed democratic publics, in contradistinction to a manipulated populace, can thrive only where civil liberties, the rule of law, and some measure of judicial independence remain intact and possess at least some autonomy vis-à-vis normal or ordinary politics. Having endorsed key components of Schmitt's theory of emergency power, it remains unclear that Tushnet can completely escape its snares.

A third innovative strategy in the ongoing reception of Schmitt's theory of emergency powers is best described as *mainstreaming Carl Schmitt*. This approach has been taken by two prominent legal scholars, Eric Posner and Adrian Vermeule, whose provocative *The Executive Unbound: After the Madisonian Republic* (2010) represents the most important attempt thus far to integrate Schmitt's emergency theory openly into mainstream U.S. legal scholarship. Echoing Schmitt, they believe that the modern administrative and interventionist state, in conjunction with more-or-less constant crises covering a broad range of political and economic matters, has debilitated what they call liberal legalism. In the United States (on which they focus), the modern administrative state generates a highly politicized rule by exception and not the rule by law, and its dominant institutional player is the executive (i.e., president) who now takes the form of a mass-based plebiscitarian figure poorly checked by legal and constitutional devices. In their analysis, no legal or constitutional innovation has succeeded in countering the ascent of a more-or-less permanent emergency-centered system resting on far-reaching administrative discretion.

In effect, Schmitt's own vision for a presidential emergency regime has *already* materialized in the United States. Unbeknownst to most Americans, his theory of emergency government correspondingly offers a perceptive starting point for understanding contemporary politics. Posner and Vermeule also directly follow Schmitt in looking askance at the liberal (and specifically Madisonian) idea of a separation of powers, arguing not only that the administrative and interventionist state has effectively dismantled it but also that reform strategies hoping to refurbish it are destined to fail (see, e.g., Shane 2009).

Yet Posner and Vermeule also endeavor to distance themselves from Schmitt by insisting that presidential emergency government is not quite as bad as one might first think: it turns out to be congruent with core liberal political ideals. By no means should we associate it with *tyranny* or *dictatorship*, terms that too often get sloppily bandied about even by serious scholars (Posner and Vermeule 2010, 176–205). They implicitly reject Schmitt's view that liberalism should be seen as a metaphysical whole, with its legal and political-institutional elements inextricably interconnected (Schmitt 1985b). Even absent the institutional paraphernalia of legal liberalism, effective *political* checks can operate to restrain the executive and prevent an authoritarian state along the lines endorsed by Schmitt. Akin to Tushnet, they think that by identifying some expressly political mechanisms we can drink Schmitt's medicine without suffering its nasty side effects. In contrast both to Tushnet and Honig, however, their antidote to Schmitt has little in common with radical democracy, instead seeing Schmitt's potentially useful legacy as consistent with a "realistic" understanding of existing liberal democracy.

Posner and Vermeule's volume is then filled with interesting ideas about how specifically political mechanisms do the work which liberal jurists previously expected of the rule of law and separation of powers. On their view, the existing U.S. political system is generally doing well at advancing the preferences of the median voter. Even if the executive remains the dominant institutional player, he or she has to stand for election. Fortunately, presidents typically worry about their future reputations; this encourages them to pursue a sensible political course. Presidents can and often do successfully send signals to the public communicating that their intentions are well motivated and that in fact voters might perhaps make the same decisions if they were in possession of the right information. By communicating properly (e.g., by appointing members of the opposing party to their cabinet), presidents can gain credibility, and voters might come to acknowledge the soundness of what the executive is doing (2010, 137–150). In societies having the requisite levels of wealth and education, liberal democracy can flourish even absent liberal legalism: relatively alert and well-educated citizens with sufficient resources can make sure that their government will act in sensible ways. Because the United States falls in this category, we need not worry too much about it reproducing the tragic history of Schmitt's Germany.

However, Posner and Vermeule never really put legitimate worries to rest that presidential emergency government comes at too high a price. The underlying problem is that they have implicitly accepted too many Schmittian intuitions. They also follow Schmitt in depending on a dramatic conceptual juxtaposition of liberal legalism to politics to discount the rule of law and constitutionalism. Thus, after showing that liberal legalism cannot restrain the administrative state, they are left with the idiosyncratic task of trying to prove that politics (conceived as fundamentally distinct from liberal legalism) can do the job while overlooking the legal and constitutional underpinnings (e.g., Congress' constitutional powers) of the executive's dependence on public opinion. Even the relatively limited array of political mechanisms they highlight requires conventional liberal-legal devices: what separates U.S.-style elections from those found in authoritarian regimes, for example, is a rich body of constitutional jurisprudence requiring that certain basic rules should be upheld during elections. Although Posner and Vermeule are perhaps right to observe that many traditional liberal-legal mechanisms have experienced decay, their institutional replacements are by no means disconnected altogether from liberal legalism.

If we decline to endorse their overstated juxtaposition of legalism to politics, things may not look quite as bleak for the rule of law and separation of powers. When Congress, for example, refuses to go along with the president's call to increase the debt ceiling, not just politics but also liberal legalism are still at work. The president's plebiscitarian appeal to the general populace can be effectively countered by power blocs within the U.S. House of Representatives that know how to use familiar constitutional devices to check executive power. In the Senate, the filibuster rule—a problematic offshoot of liberal legalism, to be sure, but a component of it nonetheless—allows a minority of senators to do the same.

Whatever the faults of his original analysis, Schmitt was right to see legal and political liberalism as two sides of the same coin: if you abandon core elements of the rule of law, separation of powers, and robust legislatures, then independent public opinion based in civil society and meaningful elections are also threatened. A political system dominated by an executive unchecked by legal and constitutional means is unlikely to take a desirable form. Civil rights will be insecure; the executive will dominate decision-making, elections will be a sham, and the welfare and regulatory states will constitute little more than devices by means of which dominant elites secure political stability and the social status quo.

Conclusion

To their credit, Posner and Vermeule still leave us with an important lesson. Even if their Schmitt-inspired diagnosis remains overstated, they identify sufficient grounds why those of us less willing to embrace Schmitt's theory of emergency power should still worry. If in fact the rule of law and the separation of powers are undergoing disintegration, liberals, democrats and others will need to think hard about the prospect of far-reaching institutional reforms to ward off the specter of authoritarian emergency regime along the lines so disturbingly diagnosed and embraced by Schmitt. To be sure, there is no reason to assume that Weimar's fate has to be repeated elsewhere. By the same token, Schmitt's vivid theoretical defense of emergency government highlights at least some of the dangers potentially awaiting those who continue to ignore evidence of ongoing democratic decay. Present-day scholars interested in the myriad political and legal challenges posed by dire emergencies will undoubtedly continue to turn to Carl Schmitt.[25] Like no other political or legal thinker in the last century, he placed the problem of emergency government on the intellectual front burner, and he consistently did so to unsettle those of us committed to liberal and democratic legal ideals. At the very least, his defense of emergency government calls out for a sufficient response by those of us who hope to preserve the rule of law and democratic constitutionalism: this is only the most obvious reason why it remains well worth our time to pay close attention to Schmitt's reflections on emergency power.

ACKNOWLEDGMENTS

I would like to thank Ben Kleinerman and Clem Fatovic for inviting me to present an earlier version of the essay at a wonderful conference devoted to emergency powers at Michigan State University and also Jens Meierhenrich and Oliver Simons for critical comments on earlier drafts.

NOTES

1. Unless noted otherwise, all translations of source material by the author.
2. A tendency to emphasize apparent discontinuities in Schmitt's thinking on emergencies bedevils even the best English-language literature, e.g., John P. McCormick 1998 (217–251).
3. For the historical and legal details, see Hans Boldt 1967; Heinz Kreutzer 1965; Christian Schudnagies 1994.
4. Quoted in Reinhard Mehring 2009 (88). This extension of the wartime emergency in fact happened (114–115). I have relied heavily on Mehring's biographical account of Schmitt. For a powerful critical discussion of Mehring's book, however, see Benno Teschke 2011.
5. For one refreshing exception to the general tendency, see Caldwell 1997 (55–62).
6. Some of Schmitt's readers simply miss the radicalism of his early views (Bendersky 1983, 19–20; Schwab 1989, 14–15).
7. I am citing Caldwell's 1997 (56) reliable translation of Schmitt 1917b (156).
8. Schmitt 1917b (160) as translated by Caldwell 1997 (59).
9. Unfortunately, a recent English translation by Ellen Kennedy (Schmitt 2011) deletes an important (5 pages) concluding section of the text as it appeared as an addendum to the second edition of *Die Diktatur*. The literature on Article 48 is massive. But see Boldt 1971 (79–98); Grau 1932 (274–295); Rossiter 2002 (29–74); Schulz 1965 (39–71); Watkins 1939.
10. Because of what is missing from Kennedy's incomplete and thereby potentially misleading English translation, see also Schmitt 1928b (254–259).
11. On Article 48, as a "typical" rule of law device, see Schmitt 1928a (201); Schmitt 1928b (239, 255–257).
12. On Weimar as economic state of emergency, see Rossiter 2002 (41–50); Watkins 1939 (73–85).
13. On the immanent conceptual tendency for commissarial dictatorship to collapse into its sovereign cousin, see the classic study by Hofmann 1964 (69–71).

14. For the particulars, see Mehring 2009 (281–302); see also Blasius 2001 (15–118).
15. For example, see Schmitt 1931a (117); 2004 (83).
16. Schmitt 1931a (115–131); 1931b. On the general problem of economic emergency rule, see Scheuerman 2000, 1869–1894. The most illuminating discussion of Schmitt's theory as it relates to changing social and economic conditions remains Maus 1980; see also Cristi 1998.
17. Schmitt 1931a (71–95), where Schmitt describes Weimar as a (deeply divided) "pluralist party state."
18. Schmitt 1931a (13–14), where he describes the U.S. constitutional order—and its strong Supreme Court—as resting on such political and social homogeneity.
19. This was the position—in opposition to those who interpret Schmitt's theoretical program as providing a defense of Weimar against rightist threats, including Nazism—I defended in Scheuerman 1999.
20. Note also the criticism of Italian fascism here for not having gone as far as the Nazis in dismantling the separation of powers. In its provocative critique of the "motorized law-maker," Schmitt's 1950 postwar *Die Lage der europäischen Rechtswissenschaft* builds upon these Nazi-era writings.
21. For surveys, written from alternative perspectives, see Scheuerman 2006b; Odysseos and Petito 2007.
22. For a useful riposte to such caricatures see Tamanaha 2004.
23. On the occasional jurisprudential common ground between Schmitt's jurisprudential views and CLS, see Scheuerman 1999. For a more cautious attempt than that described here by a prominent progressive legal scholar to use Schmitt see Levinson 2006.
24. See, however, his more modest embrace of a "moralized politics" in Tushnet 2008 (151).
25. For a survey of the many issues at hand, see the imposing study by Oren Gross and Fionnuala ni Aolain 2006.

References

Bendersky, J. 1983. *Carl Schmitt: Theorist for the Reich*. Princeton: Princeton University Press.

Blasius, D. 2001. *Carl Schmitt: Preussischer Staatsrat in Hitlers Reich*. Göttingen: Vandenhoeck & Ruprecht.

Boldt, H. 1967. *Rechtsstaat und Ausnahmezustand: Eine Studie über den Belagerungszustand als Ausnahmezustand des bürgerlichen Rechtsstaates im 19. Jahrhundert*. Berlin: Duncker & Humblot.

Boldt, H. 1971. "Article 48 of the Weimar Constitution, Its Historical and Political Implications." In *German Democracy and the Triumph of Hitler*, ed. A. Nicholls and E. Matthias. New York: St. Martin's, 79–97.

Caldwell, P. C. 1997. *Popular Sovereignty and the Crisis of German Constitutional Law: The Theory and Practice of Weimar Constitutionalism*. Durham: Duke University Press.

Cristi, R. 1998. *Carl Schmitt and Authoritarian Liberalism*. Cardiff: University of Wales Press.

Dyzenhaus, D. 2011. "Emergency, Liberalism, and the State." *Perspectives* 9: 69–78.

Grau, R. 1932. "Die Diktaturgewalt des Reichspräsidenten." In *Handbuch des Deutschen Staatsrechts*, 2nd ed., ed. G. Anschütz and R. Thoma. Tübingen: Mohr, 274–295.

Goldsmith, J. 2012. *Power and Constraint: The Accountable Presidency after 9/11*. New York: Norton.

Gross, O., and F. Aolain. 2006. *Law in Times of Crisis: Emergency Powers in Theory and Practice.* Cambridge: Cambridge University Press.

Hofmann, H. 1964. *Legitimität gegen Legalität: Der Weg der politischen Philosophie Carl Schmitts.* Neuwied: Luchterhand.

Honig, B. 2009. *Emergency Politics: Paradox, Law, Democracy.* Princeton: Princeton University Press.

Horton, S. 2005. "The Return of Carl Schmitt." *Balkinization.* Available at: http://balkin. blogspot.com/2005/11/return-of-carl-schmitt.html. (Accessed November 27, 2013).

Kalyvas, A. 2011. "Editor's Note." *Constellations* 18: 268–270.

Kennedy, E. 2004. *Constitutional Failure: Carl Schmitt in Weimar.* Durham: Duke University Press.

Kennedy, E. 2011. "Emergency Government within the Bounds of the Constitution: An Introduction to Carl Schmitt, 'The Dictatorship of the Reich President According to Article 48 R.V.'" *Constellations* 18: 284–298.

Kreutzer, H. 1965. "Der Ausnahmezustand im deutschen Verfassungsrecht." In *Der Staatsnotstand,* ed. E. Fraenkel. Berlin: Colloquium Verlag, 9–38.

Levinson, S. 2006. "Constitutional Norms in a State of Permanent Emergency." *Georgia Law Review* 40: 701–750.

Maus, I. 1980. *Bürgerliche Rechtstheorie und Faschismus: Zur sozialen Funktion und aktuellen Wirkung der Theorie Carl Schmitts,* 2nd ed. Munich: Fink.

McCormick, J. P. 1998. "The Dilemmas of Dictatorship: Carl Schmitt and Constitutional Emergency Powers." In *Law as Politics: Carl Schmitt's Critique of Liberalism,* ed. D. Dyzenhaus. Durham: Duke University Press, 217–251.

Mehring, R. 2009. *Carl Schmitt: Aufstieg und Fall: Eine Biographie.* Munich: Beck.

Odysseos, L. and P. Petito. eds. 2007. *The International Political Thought of Carl Schmitt: Terror, Liberal War, and the Crisis of Global Order.* London: Routledge.

Posner, E. A., and A. Vermeule. 2010. *The Executive Unbound: After the Madisonian Republic.* New York: Oxford University Press.

Rossiter, C. 2002. *Constitutional Dictatorship: Crisis Government in the Modern Democracies.* New Brunswick: Transaction.

Sarat, A. 2010. "Introduction." In *Sovereignty, Emergency, Legality,* ed. A. Sarat. Cambridge: Cambridge University Press, 1–15.

Scheuerman, W. E. 1999. *Carl Schmitt: The End of Law.* Lanham: Rowman & Littlefield.

Scheuerman, W. E. 2000. "The Economic State of Emergency." *Cardozo Law Review* 21: 1869–1894.

Scheuerman, W. E. 2006a. "Carl Schmitt and the Road to Abu Ghraib." *Constellations* 13: 108–124.

Scheuerman, W. E. 2006b. "Survey Article: Emergency Powers and the Rule of Law after 9/11." *Journal of Political Philosophy* 14: 61–84.

Schmitt, C. 1917a. "Die Einwirkungen des Kriegszustandes auf das ordentliche strafprozessuale Verfahren." *Zeitschrift für die gesamte Strafrechtswissenschaft* 38: 783–797.

Schmitt, C. 1917b. "Diktatur und Belagerungszustand: Eine Staatsrechtliche Studie." *Zeitschrift für die gesamte Strafrechtswissenschaft* 38: 138–161.

Schmitt, C. 1925. "Reichspräsident und Weimarer Verfassung." *Kölnische Zeitung* (March 15): 1.

Schmitt, C. 1928a. *Die Diktatur.* Munich: Duncker & Humblot.

Schmitt, C. 1928b. "Die Diktaturgewalt des Reichspräsidenten nach Artikel 48 der Weimarer Verfassung." In Schmitt 1928a, 213–259.

Schmitt, C. 1931a. *Hüter der Verfassung.* Tübingen: Mohr.

Schmitt, C. 1931b. "Die staatsrechtliche Bedeutung der Notverordnung, insbesondere ihre Rechtsgültigkeit." In Schmitt 1958, 236–261.

Schmitt, C. 1935. "Die Rechtswissenschaft im Führerstaat." *Zeitschrift der Akademie für Deutsches Recht* 2: 435–440.

Schmitt, C. 1936. "Vergleichender Überblick über die neueste Entwicklung des Problems der gesetzgeberischen Ermächtigungen: 'Legislative Delegationen.'" In Schmitt 1940, 214–229.

Schmitt, C. 1940. *Positionen und Begriffe im Kampf mit Weimar—Genf—Versailles, 1923–1939.* Hamburg: Hanseatische Verlagsanstalt.

Schmitt, C. 1950. *Die Lage der europäischen Rechtswissenschaft.* Tübingen: Universitäts-Verlag.

Schmitt, C. 1954. "Die staatsrechtliche Bedeutung der Notverordnung, insbesondere ihre Rechtsgültigkeit." In Schmitt 1958, 236–261.

Schmitt, C. 1958. *Verfassungsrechtliche Aufsätze aus den Jahren 1924–1954* Berlin: Duncker & Humblot.

Schmitt, C. 1985a. *Political Theology: Four Chapters on the Concept of Sovereignty,* trans. G. Schwab. Cambridge: MIT Press.

Schmitt, C. 1985b. *The Crisis of Parliamentary Democracy,* trans. E. Kennedy. Cambridge: MIT Press.

Schmitt, C. 1996. *The Concept of the Political,* trans. George Schwab. New Brunswick: Rutgers University Press.

Schmitt, C. 2000. "Liberal Rule of Law." In *Weimar: A Jurisprudence of Crisis,* ed. A. Jacobson and B. Schlink. Berkeley: University of California Press, 294–300.

Schmitt, C. 2001. "State Ethics and the Pluralist State." In *Weimar: A Jurisprudence of Crisis,* ed. A. Jacobsen and B. Schlink. Berkeley: University of California Press, 300–312.

Schmitt, C. 2004. *Legality and Legitimacy,* trans. and ed. J. Seitzer. Durham: Duke University Press.

Schmitt, C. 2011. "The Dictatorship of the Reich President According to Art. 48 of the Reich Constitution," trans. E. Kennedy. *Constellations* 18: 299–323.

Schudnagies, C. 1994. *Der Kriegs- oder Belagerungszustand im Deutschen Reich während des Ersten Weltkrieges.* Frankfurt: Lang.

Schulz, G. 1965. "Artikel 48 in politisch-historischer Sicht." In *Der Staatsnotstand,* ed. E. Fraenkel. Berlin: Colloquium Verlag, 39–71.

Schwab, G. 1989. *The Challenge of the Exception: An Introduction to the Political Ideas of Carl Schmitt between 1921 and 1936,* 2nd ed. New York: Greenwood.

Shane, P. 2009. *Madison's Nightmare: How Executive Power Threatens American Democracy.* Chicago: University of Chicago Press.

Tamanaha, B. 2004. *On the Rule of Law: History, Politics, Theory.* Cambridge: Cambridge University Press.

Teschke, B. 2011. "Decisions and Indecisions: Political and Intellectual Receptions of Carl Schmitt." *New Left Review* 67: 61–96.

Tushnet, M. 2005. "Emergencies and the Idea of Constitutionalism." In *The Constitution in Wartime: Beyond Alarmism and Complacency,* ed. M. Tushnet. Durham: Duke University Press, 39–54.

Tushnet, M. 2006. Meditations on Carl Schmitt. *Georgia Law Review* 40: 877–88.

Tushnet, M. 2008. "The Political Constitution of Emergency Powers: Some Conceptual Issues." In *Emergencies and the Limits of Legality,* ed. V. V. Ramraj. Cambridge: Cambridge University Press, 145–55.

Watkins, F. 1939. *The Failure of Constitutional Emergency Powers under the German Republic.* Cambridge: Harvard University Press.

CHAPTER 21

POLITONOMY

MARTIN LOUGHLIN

INTRODUCTION

IN HIS paper "Nomos—Nahme—Name," appended as the second of three concluding corollaries to the English translation of *Der Nomos der Erde im Völkerrecht des Jus Publicum Europaeum (The "Nomos" of the Earth in the International Law of the "Jus Publicum Europaeum;" hereinafter The "Nomos" of the Earth)*, Carl Schmitt comments that it seemed peculiar that when a new scholarly discipline emerged at the end of the eighteenth century it came to be known as *national economy* or *political economy*. How strange, he suggests, that with the extension of the concept of *nomos* from the household to the polity the term retained its linguistic relation to the household. Rather than being called *polito-nomy*, it was labeled *eco-nomy* (2006a, 339). As Schmitt would have been aware, there were particular reasons for this nomenclature: this eighteenth-century extension was primarily a consequence of the process by which Cameralist methods of managing the prince's household resources were extended to the task of establishing and maintaining the well-ordered commonwealth (Raeff 1983; Bourdieu 2004; Tribe 2006; Loughlin 2010, ch. 14). Schmitt was nevertheless making an astute observation, and one that in the light of more recent studies has assumed a heightened significance.

Work by such scholars as Michel Foucault (1978; 2007), Michael Mann (1993), Philip Gorski (2003), and Giorgio Agamben (2011) has identified this extension as being of pivotal significance for understanding the character of modern government. The transition that took place in the eighteenth century, Foucault argues, was "from an art of government to a political science," otherwise understood as a change "from a regime dominated by structures of sovereignty to one ruled by techniques of government" (1978, 217–218). But he goes on to suggest that, far from it dissipating as a consequence of the emergence of political economy, the question of sovereignty is presented with an ever-greater force. That question involves "an attempt to see what juridical and institutional form, what foundation in the law, could be given to the sovereignty that characterizes a state" (218). This is the central question with which Schmitt was concerned. It is a specifically juristic question. It is also the central question of a more precisely specified exercise of politonomy.

Politonomy, it is suggested, should not be taken to refer merely to the techniques of governmental management of the state's resources. In this more precise formulation, it is a broader science, one that seeks to specify the law by which the political manifests itself as a domain of reality. Schmitt is best known today as the quintessential theorist of the autonomy of the political (Bolsinger 2001; Schmitt 2007). Yet he also maintained that his entire scholarly contribution remained that of a jurist concerned to examine the constitution of modern political authority. In this respect, Schmitt can be placed within a line of political jurists who conceived public law broadly, as "an assemblage of rules, principles, canons, maxims, customs, usages, and manners that condition and sustain the activity of governing" (Loughlin 2003, 30).[1] I have previously referred to these jurists—a lineage including Bodin, Althusius, Lipsius, Grotius, Hobbes, Spinoza, Locke, and Pufendorf in the sixteenth and seventeenth centuries and extending to Montesquieu, Rousseau, Kant, Fichte, Smith, and Hegel in the eighteenth and nineteenth centuries—as engaging in an elaboration of public law as political jurisprudence (Loughlin 2010, ch. 6). This body of work seeks to elaborate the constitution of political authority.

Schmitt firmly situates himself within this lineage; he even claims to be its "last conscious representative" and "its last teacher and researcher in an existential sense" (1950, 75). This is significant, not least because at the core of these inquiries is the attempt to specify the law of the political. In this sense, these jurists can be understood to be engaged in politonomy. Schmitt recognizes that a "word bound to *nomos* is measured by *nomos* and subject to it," as is illustrated by the words *astronomy* and *gastronomy* (2006a, 338). Following this logic, it seems evident that his various studies—which extend from an explanation of the autonomy of the political (2007) through to an analysis of the foundational concepts of sovereignty (2005), legality (2004a), and constitutional order (2008a) and to his account of the order of ordering (2006b)—constitute a major contribution to the discipline of politonomy.

The objective of this chapter is to examine and evaluate Schmitt's scholarship as a contribution to politonomy. I begin by situating Schmitt as a jurist and especially as a *Staatsrechtler*, that is, as one who occupied a position within the distinctively German juristic tradition of state theory. Having situated him within that tradition, I consider whether Schmitt acknowledged a basic law of the political. I conclude that his position on this issue is ambivalent and that this ambivalence flows from his distrust of the scientific significance of general concepts. To the extent that he acknowledged any such law, I suggest that it is to be found implicitly within his embrace of institutionalism in the 1930s and later in his account of *nomos* as the basic law of appropriation, division, and production. Having focused on his jurisprudential arguments, I seek finally to situate Schmitt's work within the modern practice of political jurisprudence and to assess his general contribution to politonomy.

SCHMITT THE JURIST

On several occasions Schmitt comments that everything he published had been written as a scholarly contribution to jurisprudence and in particular as contributions to two fields of legal scholarship: constitutional law and international law. These disciplines, he explains, were the fields that were most directly exposed to "danger from 'the political'" (1950, 55). He goes on to argue that although no jurist working in these disciplines can escape this danger, the dominant legal philosophies of positivism and normativism that had emerged in the late nineteenth century seemed to have been devised as attempts to avoid this problem. Positivist public lawyers sought to exclude politics by the simple trick of presupposing the authority of the constitution as the fundamental law of the subject. And as its name suggests, normativism stands for the belief that law can be grasped as an autonomous discipline constructed according to, and bounded by, its own norms or laws.[2] Schmitt's essential point is that the prevailing tendency of lawyers to redefine the boundaries of their fields to exclude its political dimensions offered no scholarly solution. It could lead only to a skewed understanding of the nature of their discipline.

Rejecting the normativist claim about law's autonomous character, Schmitt contends that the modern concept of law is in fact derivative of the political. Positive law is, in other words, the product of political power. The modern jurist cannot avoid this fact; the most a jurist can do "is mitigate the danger [of exposure to the political] either by settling into remote neighboring areas, disguising himself as a historian or a philosopher, or by carrying to extreme perfection the art of caution and camouflage" (1950, 55). Schmitt refused to retreat, pouring scorn on jurists who deployed techniques of caution and camouflage. His work sought directly to engage with the relationship between the legal and the political: it constituted an exploration of the nature of public law elaborated from a perspective that asserts the primacy of the political.

Schmitt is sometimes regarded as an occasional writer (Löwith 1995), seen at his most incisive and stimulating when adopting a polemical argument in essay form. When his work is assessed as a contribution to political jurisprudence, however, he is revealed to be a more systematic thinker. Possessing an extensive knowledge of the historical and comparative study of the discipline, Schmitt's writing addresses the foundational questions in public law in a rigorous manner, and it displays an acute appreciation of the discipline's main points of tension. Viewed in its entirety, Schmitt's writing seeks systematically to elaborate on the nature of the relationship between the legal and the political and on that basis to build a concept of public law.

If correct, this assessment explains some of the confusion and controversy surrounding his work. In later life Schmitt writes, "I have always spoken and written as a lawyer and, accordingly, only to lawyers and for lawyers." It was his particular misfortune, he contends, "that the lawyers of my time had become technical managers of positive law, profoundly uninformed and uneducated, at best Goetheans and neutralized humanitarians" (1991, 17).[3] Consequently, he elaborates, those political and social theorists who had followed the lead of the lawyers' criticisms "would stumble with every word and every formulation and tear me apart like a desert fox" (17). There is a considerable degree of self-serving pathos in those words. Yet his core point remains. Schmitt's work is in danger of being misunderstood if examined purely as a contribution to social or political theory. It should be understood as the work of a jurist seeking to grasp the nexus between the legal and the political for the purpose of specifying the nature of modern public law.

This point takes us only so far. If law is not to be treated as an autonomous discipline and if the legal is to be derived from the political, then the scientific inquiry is simply pushed back one stage further. The question becomes: how is the autonomy of the political to be explained? This is the deeper question that needs to be examined if Schmitt's contribution to politonomy is to be assessed. In what respect, it might be asked, does Schmitt offer an account of the law of the political?

STATE THEORY

Schmitt's scholarship must first be situated within the German tradition of *Staatslehre*. During the eighteenth and nineteenth centuries, this doctrine of the state presented itself as a single discipline that embraced political theory, sociology, and law and aimed to offer a scientific understanding of the modern institution of the state (Kersten 2000). Schmitt acknowledges the importance of this movement but maintains that ever since the establishment of the German Reich in the 1870s there had been a progressive "decline of consciousness in the field of state theory" (1930, 14). This he attributes to the growing influence of positivist ideas in public law. Under the influence of positivist public lawyers such as Carl Friedrich von Gerber and Paul Laband, a new conceptualization of the subject held sway, in which all questions of history and politics were expelled from juristic consideration. The state was refashioned as a purely legal institution equipped with a special type of corporate personality; it was thus deemed to be an institution created by, and regulated in accordance with, the operations of positive public law (Gerber 1865; Laband 1876–1882; Stolleis 2001, ch. 8). Schmitt argues that, under the pervasive influence of these ideas, by 1914 the great tradition of state theory that had been developed over the previous two or three hundred years had been lost (1930, 16). No longer could any systematic and scientific account of public law be offered if it started by postulating the authority of (the positivist conception of) the state.

For Schmitt, the state is a modern institution that came into existence through intense political struggle. "The state that came into being in the seventeenth century and prevailed on the continent of Europe," he explains, "differs from all earlier kinds of political units" (2007, 34; see also 1941). Understood as an "organized political entity, internally peaceful, territorially enclosed, and impenetrable to aliens," he recognizes that the creation of this institution amounts to a specific historic achievement (2007, 47). Conceived as the outcome of struggle, its authority could not be taken for granted. Consequently, in the specific context of a crisis such as existed in the Weimar Republic, in which conditions of internal peace had not been established, the account of that regime's system of public law could not commence by assuming the authority of the state. A scientific account of public law had to be constructed from more basic elements of political understanding.

It is for this reason that Schmitt famously proclaims that the "concept of the state pre-supposes the concept of the political" (2007, 19). In the political circumstances prevailing in the Weimar Republic during the 1920s, it was evident that the logic of friend/enemy—Schmitt's criterion of the political—not only manifested itself externally, that is, with respect to interstate conflicts, but also emerged as a feature of the internal dynamics of the political unit. In such circumstances, Schmitt argues, a scientific account of public law could not be constructed on a foundation that assumed the authority of either the constitution or the state. A foundational account must first offer an explanation of the relationship between the legal and the political.

The account Schmitt presents is arguably as systematic and as radical as that of Thomas Hobbes, who had given us an image of life in the state of nature—which he characterized as that of a "war of all against all"—as the platform on which he might devise a rational solution to the problem of order. Conscious of the conditions of life in a state of nature, where insecurity reigns and force and fraud are the cardinal virtues, we are impelled to see the necessity, as a matter of self-preservation, of giving up our natural liberties and trading them for the protections offered by an absolute sovereign (Hobbes 1996, ch. 13). For Hobbes, the bargain to be struck is that between living free in a world of interminable conflict and living in peaceful conditions under the protection of a sov-ereign authority. In Hobbes's estimation, this bargain constitutes the fundamental law of the political.

From Schmitt's perspective, however, the stark contrast Hobbes had drawn between life in a state of nature and life under civil order reveals his account to be a formal legal exercise. If the concept of the political is derived from the existence of a distinc-tion between friend and enemy, then the transition Hobbes envisages from the state of nature, in which everyone is a potential enemy, to the civil state, in which all are bound to the sovereign's rule, is a transition that negates—or at least entirely externalizes—politics. Hobbes would appear to have given us a purely juristic concept of the state, in which the sovereign–subject relationship is conceived in entirely formal terms. Since all honor and all power are vested in the office of the sovereign, Hobbes evidently had no place for political struggle within the state. His theory is a juridical account that is anti-political in character (Strauss 1932, 108 n2).

For Schmitt, the contrast Hobbes drew between war (in a state of nature) and peace (in the state) is formal, abstract, and general. If political jurists are to acquire scientific knowledge of the institution of the state, they are obliged to have regard to the exis-tential conditions under which the authority of the state is established and maintained. He asserts that in reality the state is able to assure "total peace within…its territory" and to establish itself as "the decisive political entity" only through a historic struggle involving violence and domination (Schmitt 2007, 46). Only through such a process, argues Schmitt, could a "normal situation," which is "the pre-requisite for legal norms to be valid" (46), be established. Since tensions and conflicts continue to exist even in a well-ordered state, he recognizes that "this requirement for internal peace compels it [the state] in critical situations to decide also upon the domestic enemy" (46). He gives this as the reason that the sovereign power of decision must be retained to ensure the preservation of a constitutional state (47). Sovereign, Schmitt declares, is "he who decides on the exception" (2005, 5).

These political necessities are assumed to be of profound juristic significance. Any attempt to hide them behind abstract concepts or formal techniques leads only to a distortion of the nature of public law. Schmitt of course recognizes that within any well-ordered state law has "its own relatively independent domain" (2007, 66). The critical point is that although positive law might indeed occupy a relatively independent domain, it loses that autonomy the closer it intrudes on political matters. This is because political conflicts "can neither be decided by a previously determined general norm nor by the judgment of a disinterested and therefore neutral third party" (27; see also 1931). Only the politically engaged parties can settle an extreme case of conflict. If there is a threat to political existence then, even in a constitutional state "the battle must then be waged outside the constitution and the law" (2007, 47). This is because "unity and order lies in the political existence of the state, not in statutes, rules, and just any instrument containing norms" (65). For Schmitt, the most fundamental concept that grounds the modern understanding of law is neither the constitution nor the state: it is the concept of the political.

THE LAW OF THE POLITICAL

In *Political Theology*, Schmitt observes that "all law is situational law" (2005, 13). Given that he also proposes that the concept of the political grounds the meaning of the modern concept of law, it is evident that whatever meaning might be ascribed to the law of the political it is not a reference to positive law. This notion can be addressed only in the context of the broader tradition of public law as political jurisprudence.

From this perspective, the concept of the law of the political must refer to the laws, rules, and conditions that express and sustain the autonomy of the political. As has been indicated, public law in its broader conception is concerned with the rules, principles, canons, and maxims that condition and sustain the activity of governing. These various rules might now be divided into two main parts: constitutive rules and regulative rules. The former are those that establish a conceptual understanding of the political as a distinctive way of gaining knowledge of the world, whereas the latter are those by which the power of this way of acting in the world is sustained. For Bodin, who Schmitt acknowledges as having given us "the first depiction of modern public law" (Schmitt 2008a, 101), the constitutive rules are those that elaborate his concept of sovereignty, whereas the regulative rules are those that elaborate the principle that restraints on power generate power (Bodin 1962; Loughlin 2010, 62–70). The question is: does Schmitt acknowledge the existence of any such basic rules that constitute the political?

To address this question, Schmitt's understanding of the concept of the political must first be unpacked. Schmitt argues that the political acquires its specificity in contrast to other "relatively independent endeavors of human thought and action, particularly the moral, aesthetic and economic" (2007, 25–26). The essential criterion of the political is found in a binary distinction that is not reducible to other contrasts. This is the friend/enemy distinction. Two aspects of this criterion might be emphasized. The first is that the friend/enemy distinction should not be understood metaphorically: it has an existential meaning. Second, the political does not have a substance. That is, the political is not located in some discrete sector of social life called the political sphere; it is capable of manifesting itself in any aspect of group existence. The autonomous character of the political is thus founded on two basic conditions: first, the fact that existential conflicts emerge and divide humans according to the criterion of friend/enemy; and, second, that this criterion is formed as a consequence of there existing a particular "intensity of an association or dissociation of human beings" (38).

The conjunction of an existential meaning given to the concept of the political when combined with the lack of any constituted sphere of this autonomous practice would appear to suggest that there is not much on which any basic law of the political might found itself. In Schmitt's analysis, conflicts can arise in any social situation: they arise for a variety of unpredictable reasons, and they draw on a wide range of sources—theological, economic, ethnic, or cultural. It is difficult to see how any form of predictability, let alone normative rationality, can apply to this dimension of human experience.

This would suggest that Schmitt treats friend/enemy conflicts simply as an existential condition on which no further intellectual energy need be expended. Before yielding to this position, it should be noted that Schmitt believes that the friend/enemy criterion has a distinctive meaning. It is, he states, an entirely collective matter and also a public matter. That is, the criterion should not be understood "in a private-individualistic sense as a psychological expression of private emotions and tendencies" (2007, 28). The enemy "is solely the public enemy.... The enemy is *hostis*, not *inimicus*" (28). The enemy is not merely a competitor, nor is it a private adversary: "the enemy is solely the public enemy, because everything that has a relationship to such a collectivity of men, particularly to a whole nation, becomes public by virtue of such a relationship" (28). Elaborating, he explains that "an organized political entity"—that is, a state—must "decide for itself the friend–enemy distinction" (29–30).

Schmitt's account might be ambiguous, but it does indicate two things. It suggests, first, that the political is a bounded concept: it is bounded in that it is a distinction pertaining to a *group* and that this group has a *public* identity. The concept of the political must therefore, in some sense, be constituted by the criteria that enable us to identify a group as a group, as an organized political entity. It is also constituted by factors that enable us to distinguish between public and private concerns. These features suggest the formation of an institution (Searle 2005). If the constituent nature of this institution could be specified, then Schmitt's law of the political would be revealed. This, however, is not straightforward. This is so mainly because Schmitt doubts the capacity of general concepts to govern conduct, and he also doubts the value of undertaking general methodological inquiries (see Müller 1999, 63). Nonetheless, it should be emphasized that Schmitt treats the friend/enemy distinction as the essential criterion of the *concept of the political.*

Schmitt's political realism leads him to claim that political and legal concepts acquire meaning only when situated in a specific historical context. Concept formation is regarded as an immanent process that arises from an actual political situation. "All political concepts, images and terms," he suggests, "have a polemical meaning" (2007, 30). By this he means primarily that they "are focused on a specific conflict and are bound to a concrete situation whose ultimate consequence (which manifests itself in war or revolution) is a friend–enemy grouping" (30). As he explains in *The Concept of the Political*: "words such as state, republic, society, class, as well as sovereignty, constitutional state, absolutism, dictatorship, economic planning, neutral or total state, and so on, are incomprehensible if one does not know exactly who is to be affected, combated, refuted, or negated by such a term" (30–31). His general point is that, devoid of reference to such antagonisms, concepts become meaningless abstractions. "The critical moment in the history of a concept," Schmitt suggests, "is the moment in which its adversary is forgotten" (1930, 17; see also 1931, 128; 1933, 191). Unless noted otherwise, all translations of source material by the author.

Schmitt therefore maintains that both the nature and content of a concept are determined by the existence of a concrete antithesis. Generalizations are deceptive since abstract concepts do not carry an independent authority. For Schmitt, it would appear, concepts are either somehow found in a concrete reality or are tools to be used as weapons in the struggle for power. In most cases, as Jan-Werner Müller explains, "the exigencies of ideological combat and a strategic politics of concepts [*Begriffspolitik*] tended to override Schmitt's *Wissenschaftlichkeit*" (1999, 62). Schmitt's method must of necessity extend to the concept of the political itself. Consequently, if there is a law of the political, it cannot be founded on the appeal of some concept, whether of sovereignty, universal right, or the elaboration of the general will. This line of analysis might suggest that Schmitt held to the crude realist notion that might makes right and that that is all there is to say about the law of the political.

That is a conclusion that should be resisted, however, on the ground that in other writings Schmitt adopted a more nuanced position. In these contributions, he rejects the claim that concepts are merely the products of an extant political reality. In various essays, he recognizes that political struggles are invariably fought out through concepts and that these conceptual struggles are not entirely derivative. That is, they "are not merely 'ideological' delusions serving only propaganda purposes" (1932, 163). Rather, they are "only a case in point of the simple truth that all human activity bears a certain intellectual [*geistigen*] character" (163). Even in the context of political struggle, he acknowledges that there "has never in human history been an absence of such justifications and principles of legitimation" (163). Concepts, he seems to be saying, are drawn into conflictual struggle and used as weapons in those struggles, but they are not purely the product of these struggles. Rather, these power conflicts need to be legitimated through concepts at the level of political and constitutional theory (Bolsinger 2001, 37–40).

Schmitt thus seems not to be entirely consistent in his analysis of the significance of concepts and this makes it difficult to assess his stance on politonomy. He says both that "the content of world history... has always been a struggle for words and concepts"

(1933, 191) and that the "struggle over concepts is not a dispute about empty words but a war of enormous reality and presence" (198). But he also claims that the key point is "who interprets, defines and applies them" (1932, 179). Contrary to many political jurists, he asserts that in fact "*Caesar dominus et supra grammaticam*. The emperor is also ruler over grammar" (179; cf. Kant 1991, 58; see also Loughlin 2010, 178–180). If grammar is taken to be a metaphorical expression of the law of the political, then Schmitt appears to be saying that the sovereign determines not just the exception but also the political itself.

Our grasp of Schmitt's position with respect to the significance of concepts in understanding the phenomenon of the political might be advanced once his argument is situated within that of the German school of *Begriffsgeschichte*. This body of work, exemplified in the writings of Reinhart Koselleck, follows in the tradition of Schmitt. Their argument on the nature of concepts is insightful. Koselleck maintains that, whatever else it might be, a concept "bundles up the variety of historical experience together with a collection of theoretical and practical references into a relation that is given and can be experienced *only* through the concept" (2004, 85; emphasis added). Koselleck acknowledges that social and political concepts do not simply "define given states of affairs"; they aim in themselves to shape a state of affairs and thus to "reach into the future" (80). In this respect, he states, "a concept must remain ambiguous in order to be a concept," because a political concept is of necessity "the concentrate of several substantial meanings" (85). The claim that political concepts remain intrinsically contestable but have become the medium through which political struggles are fought out fits one strand of Schmitt's analysis. It also suggests that there is a conceptual frame through which the political is engaged.[4]

The ambiguous nature of Schmitt's position on the conceptual frame of the political casts a shadow over his work as an exercise of politonomy. Some believe this is an ambiguity he was content not only to maintain but also to exploit (see Müller 1999). From the juristic perspective, it might be said that this ambiguity flows from his reticence on whether there are in fact two different concepts of power at play in the domain of the political. In this domain, power not only signifies supremacy over the material means of rule (*potentia*) but also refers to the capacity to build unity through the establishment of authority (*potestas*) (Loughlin 2010, 164–177). Schmitt speaks mainly of the former aspect of power, on which he maintains a realist position. But occasionally, as in an early work in which he suggests that "to the political belongs the idea, because there is no politics without authority and no authority without an ethos of belief" (Schmitt 1996, 17), he is alluding to the idea of power as *potestas*. And when he invokes the idea of power as *potestas*, it might be emphasized that Schmitt is obliged to acknowledge the power-shaping capacity of concepts.

INSTITUTIONALISM

To take forward this analysis, it is necessary to shift register and directly address Schmitt's concept of law. As we have seen, he regarded all concepts of law as being historically situated. During the 1920s, Schmitt's primary task was to carry through a critique of the ahistorical abstractions of legal normativism. His basic thesis is that, by severing the norms of legal ordering from the facts of political existence, normativist jurists distort understanding of the true nature of law (see, e.g., 2005, ch. 2). In its place, Schmitt promotes a type of legal decisionism. Law, he argues, is essentially the product of will. In particular, the existence of a sovereign act of will can never be eliminated from the sphere of legal thought. In support of this argument, Schmitt seeks to show how normativist jurists, being interested only in the normal situation, are unable to account for exceptional circumstances. The norm may be destroyed in such exceptional circumstances, he explains, but the exception remains of juristic significance: "both elements, the norm as well as the decision, remain within the framework of the juristic" (2005, 12–13).

In his preface to the second edition of *Political Theology* in 1933, Schmitt begins to modify this claim. He writes, "I now distinguish not two but *three* types of legal thinking; in addition to the normativist and the decisionist types there is the institutional one" (2005, 2). "Whereas the pure normativist thinks in terms of impersonal rules, and the decisionist implements the good law of the correctly recognized political situation by means of a personal decision," Schmitt explains that "institutional legal thinking unfolds in institutions and organizations that transcend the personal sphere" (3). It is evident that Schmitt's advocacy of institutionalism is designed to grasp "the stable content inherent in every great political movement" (3). If, as he is now claiming, there is an inherent element that provides stability to political unity, what might this be? And, most importantly, does this element provide the key to Schmitt's politonomy?

Schmitt's institutional argument is most clearly presented in his 1934 book *On the Three Types of Juristic Thought* (2004b). In this work, Schmitt explains that all legal theories comprise three basic elements: norm; decision; and concrete-order formation. Legal theories are thus to be categorized according to the emphasis they place on each of these elements. Further, the type of political regime envisaged in this theory is invariably linked to the predominance given to one or other of these elements. "Every form of political life," he maintains, "stands in direct, mutual relationship with the specific mode of thought and argumentation of legal life" (45). In this work, Schmitt again criticizes normativism, but he also argues against the decisionism he seemed to be advocating in *Political Theology*. He argues instead in favor of a type of institutionalism that he calls concrete-order thinking.[5]

Normativists promote a purely conceptualistic understanding of law, law as a set of rules. The arguments of decisionists, by contrast, are reduced ultimately to factual analysis. Institutionalism, or concrete-order thinking, is Schmitt's attempt to finesse the distinction between normativity and facticity (2004b, 53). Rules and decisions are integral parts of legal order, but they carry meaning only as formulations of concrete order. Law as norm does not yield sound jurisprudence because a norm "cannot apply, administer, or enforce itself" (51), and decisionism is not sustainable because a legal decision does not spring from a normative vacuum (2005, 62). Legal order is maintained as an expression of the underlying concrete order. Rules and decisions achieve regularity by reliance on "concepts of what, in itself, is normal, the normal type and the normal situation" (54). Schmitt is therefore arguing that political unity is maintained only if there is a stable institutional structure in place, that is, that there is a concrete order that determines the meaning of legal norms and guides the exercise of legal decision-making. The question is: How is a stable institutional structure established and maintained?

With this question in mind, we turn to chapter 13 of Schmitt's *Constitutional Theory*, on the *Rechtsstaat* (2008a). His analysis of the nature of the *Rechtsstaat* follows what by now will be a familiar trajectory. He maintains that to invoke the idea of "the rule of law" is "an empty manner of speaking if it does not receive its actual sense through a certain opposition" (181). For Schmitt, the *Rechtsstaat* is a legislative state, that is, a state in which the authoritative expression of will takes the form of legislation and the legislature is itself bound by this law. This makes sense, he explains, only when a statute is expressed in the form of a general norm. The idea of the rule of law thus gestures toward the notion that law is not to be understood as *voluntas* (i.e., will or decision) but as *ratio* (i.e., norms or rules). Schmitt contends that the problem with this claim is that within any actually existing constitutional order the *Rechtsstaat* concept of law must be situated alongside an alternative concept of law, what he calls a political concept of law. This political concept remains a juristic concept: both form essential elements in modern constitutional thought.

By a political concept of law, Schmitt means a concept of law that "results from the political form of existence of the state" and arises "out of the concrete manner of the formation of the organization of rule" (2008a, 187). In the *Rechtsstaat* concept, law is essentially a norm—a rule of a general character. In the political concept, law is the expression of a concrete will; it takes the form of a command and is conceived as an act of sovereignty. The *Rechtsstaat*, he argues, seeks to suppress this political concept and establish a sovereignty of law, but this is a vain hope: without this political expression of law as will the *Rechtsstaat* formulation cannot exist.

Schmitt's analysis in *Constitutional Theory* emphasizes the dependence of norm on will. But in the light of his later argument about concrete-order thinking, it can be said that law as norm and law as will both rest on institutional ordering. He alludes to this point in chapter 13 of *Constitutional Theory* when he states that those who promote the concept of law as norm find themselves in a contradictory and confused position because "that which is directly lacking is the nomos" (184). Only in 1950, when he published *The "Nomos" of the Earth*, does he offer a systematic account of this crucial concept (2006b).

Nomos

Schmitt's objective in *The "Nomos" of the Earth* is to specify the original legal-constitutional meaning of *nomos* "in its energy and majesty" (2006b, 67) to demonstrate how jurists who translate *nomos* simply as law or, if they try to differentiate it from written law by defining it as custom, do not get to the root of the matter. In this sense, he seeks to elaborate on the meaning of *nomos* for the purpose of exposing a concept of law founded in concrete-order thinking.

The Greek noun *nomos*, Schmitt explains, derives from the Greek verb *nemein*, and, in common acceptance, *nemein* has three main meanings (in German): *nehmen* (to appropriate), *teilen* (to divide) and *weiden* (to pasture). In its first meaning it signifies a taking, especially a land appropriation. This forms the basis of the history of every settled people and "not only logically, but also historically, land-appropriation precedes the order that follows from it" (2006b, 48). *Nomos* thus signifies the constitution of "the original spatial order, the source of all further concrete order and all further law" (48) The constitutive process of a land-acquisition "is found at the beginning of the history of every settled people, every commonwealth, every empire" (48). Schmitt contends that "all subsequent law and everything promulgated and enacted thereafter as decrees and commands are *nourished* ... by this source" (48).

Nomos is an *ordo ordinans*, an order of ordering, that performs the constitutive act of establishing a spatially determined regime of rule. In the beginning, order was not established on the basis of consent or on some universal principle, or a basic norm. In the beginning, there was a land-grab, and only after the violence of that initial appropriation and division had been completed could "some degree of calculability and security" be achieved and *nomos* emerge as the expression of order (2006b, 341). This order evolves; it is not fully formed at the foundation, though it remains nourished by this source. *Nomos*, it would appear, holds the key to politonomy: it is an expression of the basic law of the political.

For Schmitt, the law of the political is revealed through the way the processes of appropriation, division, and production give rise to a substantive order of a political unity. Once this is grasped, the relation between *nomos*, state, and constitution becomes clear. For Schmitt, the state is "the concrete, collective condition of political unity" (2008a, 60). In modernity, it becomes the "master ordering concept" of this political unity (1941, 375).[6] It is similarly clear that Schmitt's concept of constitution (in its absolute sense) differs from the notion of constitutional law as that enacted in modern documentary form. Since the order that emerges within the state arises from "a pre-established, unified will" (2008a, 65), Schmitt argues that the state "does not *have* a constitution"; rather, "the state *is* constitution" (60). In this sense, the state/constitution is "an actually present condition, a *status* of unity and order" (60). The basic law of the state finds its authoritative expression not in enacted legal norms but in "the political existence of the state" (65). Once brought into alignment it is evident that state (the political unity), constitution (the status of unity and order), and *nomos* (the order of a concrete spatial unity) are, for all intents and purposes, synonyms.

Schmitt recognizes that, like *nomos*, state and constitution continue to evolve: the state expresses "the principle of the *dynamic emergence* of political unity, of the process of constantly renewed *formation* and *emergence* of this *unity* from a fundamental or ultimately effective *power* and *energy*" (2008a, 61). And he accepts that the "continuity of a constitution is manifest as long as the regress to this primary appropriation is recognizable and recognized" (2006b, 326 n6). If state highlights unity and constitution the form of that unity, then *nomos* accentuates the motive forces that shape the form of that unity: it is "the full immediacy of a legal power not mediated by laws; it is a constitutive historical event—an act of *legitimacy*, whereby the legality of a mere law first is made meaningful" (73). It is the law of the political.

Schmitt's institutionalism brings his legal thought much closer to Hegel's legal and political philosophy, in which "the state is a 'form (*Gestalt*), which is the complete realization of the spirit in being (*Dasein*)'; an 'individual totality', a *Reich* of objective reason and morality" (2004b, 78). This type of state, he emphasizes, is not an "order of a calculable and enforceable legal functionalism" (i.e., the product of decisionism), nor is it a "norm of norms" (normativism); instead, it "is the concrete order of orders, the institution of institutions" (78–79). But it should be emphasized that this is not Hegel's state in which the universal is willed; it more closely approximates his concept of *Notstaat*, the state based on necessity, an expression of the form within civil society "wherein the livelihood, happiness, and legal status of one man is interwoven with the livelihood, happiness, and rights of all" (Hegel 1952, §183).

For Schmitt, then, it seems evident that politonomy is founded on the concept of *nomos*. In *The "Nomos" of the Earth* he shows the distinctive contribution that *nomos* makes to the establishment of political order. The most basic claim is that law is tied to space, that is, to a defined and bounded territory that distinguishes inside and outside. Without this boundary, there can be no domain of the political. In this respect, it might be said that *nomos* is constitutive of the political. This space—this territory—is not merely a geographical notion. It is also a legal and political concept that concerns "the space between individuals in a group whose members are bound to, and at the same time separated and protected from, each other by all kinds of relationships, based on a common language, religion, a common history, customs and laws" (Arendt 1965, 262). The establishment of these relationships creates the space of political freedom. This freedom is always spatially limited, always an achievement, and always ordered. *Nomos* gives expression to that concrete order: an order initiated by a taking (involving force) and subsequently harnessed through institutionalization.

SCHMITT'S CONTRIBUTION TO POLITONOMY

Schmitt's contribution to politonomy can now be specified. As already noted, he is to be situated within a tradition of understanding public law as political jurisprudence. This body of thought recognizes the necessity of addressing the relationship between the legal within the political for the purpose of explaining the constitution of modern political authority. Rather than postulating the autonomy of law, thereby cutting off inquiry into the nature of the relationship between law and politics, political jurisprudence insists on the necessity of undertaking an inquiry into the character of the fundamental laws of the political. In this sense, political jurisprudence is an alternative formulation of the discipline of politonomy.

The status of this discipline within Western political thought might now be briefly explained. This tradition of Western political thought has evolved because, in the face of the common historical experience of living in regimes built on conflict, domination, and the threat of disorder, scholars have felt the lingering power of an image of human community as an ordered and peaceable existence. One highly influential strand of political thought has devoted itself to the task of overcoming that gulf. Starting with the Stoics, embraced by medieval Christian scholars and eventually secularized in Enlightenment thought, this line of thought claims that the laws of reason and the laws of nature can be revealed to operate in harmony. Reconciliation is achieved through the realization of a type of human association made accessible to us through the power of reason. Initially expressing an overarching, divinely sanctioned unity of the world, in its post-theological phase it presents itself as a set of principles of association that humans are impelled rationally to adopt and which they must strive to realize.

Politonomy, by contrast, is founded in opposition to this powerful strand of political thought. Expressing skepticism about the possibility of achieving reconciliation through transcendence, politonomy is born of a recognition of the essentially unbridgeable nature of this gulf (Hunter 2001). The power of "abstract universals" is to be acknowledged, but the "necessary conditions" cannot be ignored (Hegel 1952, §§29–33; see also Honneth 2010, 15). Politonomy appeals to reason but does not seek an escape from history. It often presents itself as a practical discourse that, although orientated to norms, always has regard to consequences. Rather than advocating reconciliation through the promotion of some overarching moral sensibility, politonomy seeks through phenomenological investigation to explain the immanent logic of political reason that sustains this distinctive way of ordering the world.

The first systematic exponent of this discipline was Jean Bodin. He laid its foundations through explication of the concept of sovereignty. This affirmed the absolute authority of the system of political rule and thereby asserted the autonomy of the political domain. But he proceeded to build on this foundation by carrying out an extensive comparative and historical inquiry into the governing practices of European states to elaborate a set of rules to be followed if the prince was to maintain his state. By bringing the concept of sovereignty establishing the *right* to rule into alignment with rules of civil prudence that maintained the *capacity* of rule, Bodin provided the basic template of the discipline of public law as political jurisprudence. Bodin's was a major contribution to politonomy.

In Bodin's framework, the concept of sovereignty outlined in book I and underpinned by the claim that the prince possesses "the most high, absolute, and perpetual power over the citizens and subjects in a commonwealth" specified the essential constitutive rule of the political domain (1962, 84). It is sometimes contended that Bodin's account of sovereignty is incoherent, since he claims that the sovereign's authority is absolute but also subject to certain limitations. That view misconstrues his overall objective. Bodin recognizes two main types of apparent limitation: those that concern the fundamental laws establishing and maintaining the office of the sovereign; and natural laws, which condition the sovereign's treatment of his subjects. These, however, are not, strictly speaking, limitations: they are illustrative of the conditions that define the nature of the office. Bodin sees that the autonomy of the political domain is established as a consequence of a distinction being drawn between public and private.

It should also be noted that book I forms only one aspect of Bodin's overall objective. While it seeks to establish the essential constitutive rules of the practice, the remaining five books outline the regulative rules. These are the rules that the prince must have regard if he is to maintain his state. Drawing on historical illustrations, Bodin sketches the political laws of governmental development. These include many regulative laws and practices that have become widely acknowledged: that the separation of the legislative and the executive power promotes liberty (1962, 277); that relative equality in wealth distribution promotes the stability of the state (569); that wars sustain democracies (422); that most self-styled democracies are disguised aristocracies (705); and that "the less the power of the sovereignty is (the true marks of majesty thereunto still reserved), the more it is assured" (517). The claim of formal absolute authority (*potestas*) thus merely laid the foundation for the emergence of a new field of knowledge, the political knowledge that is needed to establish, maintain, and extend the powers of civil government (*potentia*).

From our examination of Schmitt's work, it is evident that within the discipline of politonomy he maintained a realist position. It is for that reason that, although recognizing that Bodin "stands at the beginning of the modern theory of the state" (Schmitt 2005, 8) and acknowledging that "Bodin's work had a greater and more immediate impact than had any other book by a jurist in the history of law" (2006b, 127), he claims that Bodin's real achievement had been overlooked. Bodin's innovation, he argues, rests not so much in his definition of sovereignty as "the absolute and perpetual power of a republic" as on his recognition that the sovereign's defining characteristic is the ability, in an emergency, to rule contrary to the established laws. "When the time, place and individual circumstances demand it," Schmitt notes, Bodin accepted that "the sovereign can change and violate statutes" (2008a, 101). Rather than acknowledging the world-building character of the conjunction of Bodin's constitutive and regulative rules of politonomy, Schmitt emphasizes the decisionist quality of the sovereign's power to determine an issue that "cannot be settled normatively"—"that which advances the public good" (101).

Schmitt's reading of Bodin also signals his ambivalent relationship to Hobbes. Although praising Hobbes as "a great and truly systematic political thinker" (2007, 64), Schmitt was obliged also to acknowledge that Hobbes was "a spiritual forefather of the bourgeois law-and-constitutional state that materialized in the nineteenth century" (2008b, 67). And it is for this reason that, in contrast to the liberal leanings of such jurists as Bodin and Hobbes, Schmitt (2005, ch. 4) sought to resurrect the importance within politonomy of the work of Joseph de Maistre and Juan Donoso Cortés. He thus explains how "with an energy that rose to an extreme between the two revolutions of 1789 and 1848," Maistre and Donoso Cortés, "thrust the notion of the decision to the center of their thinking" (53). Schmitt's decisionism once again reveals his essentially realist stance.

While it is not possible within the bounds of this chapter comprehensively to situate Schmitt's oeuvre within this discipline of politonomy, his general orientation might be thrown into relief by contrasting his thought with that of another great public lawyer— Montesquieu. Like Schmitt, Montesquieu believed that the law of the political is not discovered through normative inquiry: it could be exposed only through empirical study of the history of government. Only by immersion in the various particulars of government, Montesquieu (1989, xliii) notes, can "the principles on which they are founded" be revealed. This was the ambition of his most important work on *The Spirit of the Laws*. The aim of his study was not to classify the laws enacted in particular regimes; those— the positive laws—are merely the products of a regime. Rather, it was to discern the laws that have determined the formation of those regimes. Montesquieu sought to identify "the law of the political." This—"the work of twenty years" (xliii)—was an exercise in politonomy.

Montesquieu therefore examines the historical development of governmental institutions for the purpose of identifying their spirit. His great breakthrough was achieved by virtue of developing an entirely modern concept of law (Althusser 1972, ch. 2). Before the modern era, law was conceived as command. This expressed a belief that the universe was the product of a divine creator, and it was by virtue of his will that order was established. In defining law purely as the command of the sovereign—the "mortal God" (Hobbes 1996, 9)—Hobbes broke the medieval chain of being. Nonetheless, his concept of law was otherwise entirely orthodox. Montesquieu, by contrast, argues that law is not command: it is the expression "of the necessary relations deriving from the nature of things" (1989, 3).

This modern conception of law as a relation applied to everything that exists, from God to the most basic units of physical existence (3). The laws of the physical world, Montesquieu explains, are rules that express a fixed and invariable relation and although accepting that "the intelligent world is far from being so well governed as the physical world," he contended that the concept of law as relation was similarly applicable to human interaction (4).

Through his meticulous investigations into the history of government, Montesquieu distinguishes between the objects of his studies—the laws and practices of regimes— and his findings: the laws that determine their form. He distinguishes in effect between *political laws*, the positive laws enacted to regulate government in particular regimes, and politonomy, the law of the political. Of particular importance is his claim that politonomy is directed toward causes rather than motives, and the main determining causes he identifies are those of climate and geography, customs and commerce, population and religion. These, he argues, are factors of which individuals might not be entirely conscious, but they invariably determine the type of regime that is established. The critical point is to locate a consonance of nature and principle. Each type of government (democracy, aristocracy, monarchy, and despotism) has both its nature, "that which makes it what it is," and its driving principle, "that which makes it act" (1989, 21). The power of any regime, he concludes, is determined by the degree to which nature and principle—the constitutive and the regulative—are united.

Montesquieu orientates his studies in politonomy toward the attempt to specify the laws of political and governmental development. This is a line of inquiry that takes its cue from book's II–VI of Bodin's *Six Books* and establishes an approach in which others, such as Hintze and Weber followed.[7] Especially with respect to his institutionalist work and the scheme of development laid down in *The "Nomos" of the Earth*, this is also a trajectory in which Schmitt can be situated. On the other hand, certain scholars have contended that this exercise in historical sociology provides only a partial account of politonomy, and this empirical orientation has the profound limitation, at least from a juristic perspective, of reducing the study of the political to that of an observa datum and of reducing the concept of political power to that of *potentia*. This type of claim derives mainly from the work of Rousseau.

Rousseau (1997) evidently grasps the difficulty of addressing the issue of political power in normative terms: in the *Discourse on Inequality*, for example, he recognizes that if we think of government as originating in a foundation, then the pact that might have been struck in the remote past was a deceptive and fraudulent device, drafted by the wealthy for the purpose of exploiting the poor. But he also claims that Montesquieu had created a great and useless science. The problem, he explains, was that Montesquieu did not really bury down to examine "the principles of political right." This type of exercise required a consideration of agency as well as structure. Montesquieu had remained "content to discuss the positive right of established governments," and this, Rousseau contends, is a rather different matter to that of revealing the principles of political right (Rousseau 1979, 458).

It is not my task here to determine the correct orientation of politonomy. My point is that it has evolved as a conjunction of constitutive and regulative laws and that it involves the dialectical interaction between power as *potestas* and power conceived as *potentia*. Schmitt's original contribution is to have staked his position within politonomy by promoting an understanding of the political in existential rather than conceptual terms—that is, in accordance with the criterion of friend/enemy rather than sovereignty as a representation of an autonomous conceptual world—and in conceiving power essentially as a capacity to decide (*potentia*) rather than as a quality generated through institutional forms of representation (*potestas*). He evidently is able to do so only by suppressing aspects of the conceptual and the rightful, and in that respect doubts will persist about the cogency of his theory. But by virtue of the rigor, insight, and brilliant style of delivery of his argument, Schmitt stakes his claim to recognition as one of the leading modern scholars of political jurisprudence.

This is a double-edged compliment. The fact that the most powerful twentieth-century exponent of political jurisprudence made such a disastrous exercise of political judgment has been used by some scholars to reject—or at very least to marginalize—the significance of an entire tradition of thought. Normativism appears once again to be the dominant influence in legal thought, and legal scholars commonly ignore the insights of political jurisprudence. By raising Schmitt's status to that of the exemplary figure of political jurisprudence, normativists seek to ensure that his own vain boast of being the last representative of the tradition will in fact come to pass.

CONCLUSION

Carl Schmitt's primary scholarly contribution was that of a jurist. To understand the significance of that contribution, his writing should be situated within the lineage of political jurisprudence. Political jurisprudence is a modern movement driven by the objective of establishing a rigorous and compelling account of the constitution of political authority in circumstances in which a hierarchically organized, religiously constituted universe has been supplanted by a world differentiated into various domains of thought and action. Only in modernity do we see the emergence of discrete spheres of human activity operating according to their own criteria and necessities: these include the scientific, the technical, the aesthetic, the legal, and the political. The founding assumption of the political jurists is that the modern form of law (i.e., positive law) is essentially the product of political power. Their overriding objective has been to offer an account of the way the domain of the political is constituted to render that modern form of positive law authoritative. This, we might say, is an exercise in politonomy.

The political jurists have constructed their various accounts on certain foundational concepts, most commonly those of the state and sovereignty. Schmitt's particular contribution is to have deployed a realist method in analyzing the nature and significance of these foundational elements. This is exhibited mainly in his work on the concept of the political, the character of sovereign authority, the nature of institutional ordering, and the uses made of the concept of legality. Although Schmitt's writing was— and remains—highly controversial, it continues to offer great insight into the nature of the relationship between law and politics. Whether we are trying to make sense of the recent extension in the constitutional jurisdiction of courts, figuring out how the conflicting claims of duties and rights might be balanced with respect to the values of security and liberty, or determining the status of the sovereign nation-state in a globalizing world, having a clear grasp of the relationship between the legal and the political remains the critical factor. Today, that relationship is often expressed polemically, whether as a complaint about the legalization of the political or of the politicization of the legal. This in itself is symptomatic of its deep-seated and enduring character. Schmitt's work may not hold answers to all these questions. But compelling answers are unlikely to be found without having taken seriously his distinctive contribution to the subject.

ACKNOWLEDGMENTS

An earlier version of this chapter was presented at the Swedish-Finnish Workshop titled "Friend or Foe? The Contemporary Relevance of Carl Schmitt," held at the University of Helsinki in June 2013. I record my thanks to participants in the workshop for their comments and especially to Panu Minkkinen.

NOTES

1. Operating under the influence of legal positivism, jurists today commonly define public law as a subset of positive law, treating public law as the law regulating relations between the institutions of government or between government and its subjects, in contrast to private law, which regulates relations between subjects. In this broader conception, public law includes a study of the juristic construction of public authority: it is concerned with the manner in which government is equipped with a rightful power (*potestas*) to rule through the instrumentality of positive law.

2. See, e.g., Kelsen 1992 (1): legal science must be "purified of all political ideology" and of "every element of the natural sciences."

3. Some sense of what Schmitt means by the term *Goetheans* is grasped from his comment in *"Nomos" of the Earth*: "The German language today is largely one of theologians—the language of Luther's bible translation—as well as a language of craftsmen and technicians (as Leibniz observed). In contrast to French, it is not a language of jurists or of moralists. German gives a heightened, even sublime significance to the word *Gesetz*. Poets and philosophers love the word, which acquired a sacred tone and a numinous power through Luther's bible translation. Even Goethe's *Urworte orphisch* is nourished by this source: *Nach dem Gesetz, nach dem du angetreten* [according to the law by which you began]" (2006, 70 n10). On the humanitarians, see Schmitt 1929.

4. This view of the nature and role of political concepts is now more widely accepted. Quentin Skinner acknowledges that in believing that concepts "not only alter over time, but are incapable of providing us with anything other than a series of changing perspectives on the world in which we live and have our being" (2002, 176), we are following in a tradition that stems from Nietzsche and Weber (and in whose company Schmitt would have felt at home). He joins with Koselleck (2004, 80) in maintaining that "we need to treat our normative concepts less as statements about the world than as tools and weapons of ideological debate" (Skinner, 2002, 176). In pursuing this line of argument about concepts, Skinner even prays in aid Foucault's (1980, 114) Nietzschean position that "the history which bears and determines us has the form of a war" (Skinner 2002, 177).

5. In the preface to *Political Theology*, Schmitt 2005 (2–3) admits that he had arrived at institutionalism as a result of his studies of "the profound and meaningful theory of institutions formulated by [the French public lawyer] Maurice Hauriou." But in *On the Three Types of Juristic Thought* he seems to have recognized that, with the establishment of the Nazi regime, it would be politic to call this *concrete-order thought* to avoid any association with neo-Thomism exhibited in Hauriou's work. See Bendersky's note in Schmitt 2004 (112 n59). On Hauriou, see Gray 2010.

6. Cf. the claims of Geertz 1980; Skinner 1989. Geertz: "That master noun of modern political discourse, *state*" (121). Skinner: "The state is ... the master noun of political argument" (123).

7. See Hintze 1970; 1975; Weber 1978; 1994. This line of inquiry has inspired a wide range of contemporary works including Ertman 1997; Mann 1986; 1993; 2012.

REFERENCES

Agamben, G. 2011. *The Kingdom and the Glory: For a Theological Genealogy of Economy and Government*, trans. L. Chiesa. Stanford: Stanford University Press.

Althusser, L. 1972. *Politics and History: Montesquieu, Rousseau, Marx*, trans. B. Brewster. London: Verso.

Arendt, H. 1965. *Eichmann in Jerusalem: A Report on the Banality of Evil*, rev. ed. New York: Penguin.

Bodin, J. 1962. *The Six Bookes of a Commonweale*, trans. R. Knolles, ed. K. D. McRae. Cambridge: Harvard University Press.

Bolsinger, E. 2001. *The Autonomy of the Political: Carl Schmitt's and Lenin's Political Realism*. Westport: Greenwood Press.

Bourdieu, P. 2004. "From the King's House to the Reason of State: A Model of the Genesis of the Bureaucratic Field." *Constellations* 11: 16–36.

Ertman, T. 1997. *Birth of the Leviathan: Building States and Regimes in Medieval and Early Modern Europe*. Cambridge: Cambridge University Press.

Foucault, M. 1978. "Governmentality." In *Essential Works of Foucault 1954–1984*, vol. 3: *Power*. London: Penguin, 201–222.

Foucault, M. 1980. *Power/Knowledge*. Brighton: Harvester.

Foucault, M. 2007. *Security, Territory, Population: Lectures at the Collège de France, 1977–78*, trans. G. Burchell. London: Palgrave.

Geertz, C. 1980. *Negara: The Theatre State in Nineteenth-Century Bali*. Princeton: Princeton University Press.

Gerber, C. F. von. 1865. *Grundzüge eines Systems des deutschen Staatsrechts*. Leipzig: Tauchnitz.

Gorski, P. S. 2003. *The Disciplinary Revolution: Calvinism and the Rise of the State in Early Modern Europe*. Chicago: University of Chicago Press.

Gray, C. B. 2010. *The Methodology of Maurice Hauriou*. Amsterdam: Rodopi.

Hegel, G. W. F. 1952. *Philosophy of Right*, trans. T. M. Knox. Oxford: Oxford University Press.

Hintze, O. 1970. *Staat und Verfassung: Gesammelte Abhandlungen zur Allgemeinen Verfassungsgeschichte*, 3rd ed., ed. G. Oestreich. Göttingen: Vandenhoeck & Ruprecht.

Hintze, O. 1975. *The Historical Essays of Otto Hintze*, ed. F. Gilbert. New York: Oxford University Press.

Hobbes, T. 1996. *Leviathan*, ed. R. Tuck. Cambridge: Cambridge University Press.

Honneth, A. 2010. *The Pathologies of Individual Freedom: Hegel's Social Theory*. Princeton: Princeton University Press.

Hunter, I. 2001. *Rival Enlightenments: Civil and Metaphysical Philosophy in Early Modern Germany*. Cambridge: Cambridge University Press.

Kant, I. 1991. "An Answer to the Question: 'What Is Enlightenment?'" In *Political Writings*, 2nd ed., ed. H. Reiss, trans. H. B. Nisbet. Cambridge: Cambridge University Press, 54–60.

Kelsen, H. 1992. *Introduction to the Problems of Legal Theory*, trans. B. L. Paulson and S. L. Paulson. Oxford: Clarendon Press.

Kersten, J. 2000. *Georg Jellinek und die klassische Staatslehre*. Tübingen: Mohr.

Koselleck, R. 2004. "Begriffsgeschichte and Social History." In *Futures Past: On the Semantics of Historical Time*, trans. K. Tribe. New York: Columbia University Press, 75–92.

Laband, P. 1876–1882. *Das Staatsrecht des deutschen Reiches*, 4 vols. Tübingen: Laupp.

Loughlin, M. 2003. *The Idea of Public Law*. Oxford: Oxford University Press.

Loughlin, M. 2010. *Foundations of Public Law*. Oxford: Oxford University Press.

Löwith, K. 1995. "The Occasional Decisionism of Carl Schmitt." In *Martin Heidegger and European Nihilism*, ed. R. Wolin. New York: Columbia University Press, 137–159.

Mann, M. 1986. *The Sources of Social Power*, vol. 1: *A History from the Beginning to 1760 AD*. Cambridge: Cambridge University Press.

Mann, M. 1993. *The Sources of Social Power*, vol. 2: *The Rise of Classes and Nation-States.* Cambridge: Cambridge University Press.

Mann, M. 2012. *The Sources of Social Power*, vol. 3: *Global Empire and Revolution.* Cambridge: Cambridge University Press.

Montesquieu, C. L. 1989. *The Spirit of the Laws*, trans. and ed. A. Cohler, B. Miller, and H. Stone. Cambridge: Cambridge University Press.

Müller, J.-W. 1999. "Carl Schmitt's Method: Between Ideology, Demonology and Myth." *Journal of Political Ideologies* 4: 61–85.

Raeff, M. 1983. *The Well-Ordered Police State: Social and Institutional Change through Law in the Germanies and Russia, 1600–1800.* New Haven: Yale University Press.

Rousseau, J.-J. 1979. *Emile, or On Education*, trans. A. Bloom. New York: Basic Books.

Rousseau, J.-J. 1997. "Discourse on the Origin and Foundations of Inequality among Men." In *The Discourses and Other Early Political Writing*, ed. V. Gourevitch. Cambridge: Cambridge University Press, 111–222.

Schmitt, C. 1929. "The Age of Neutralizations and Depoliticizations." In Schmitt 2007, 80–96.

Schmitt, C. 1930. *Hugo Preuss: Sein Staatsbegriff und seine Stellung in der deutschen Staatslehre.* Tübingen: Mohr.

Schmitt, C. 1931. *Der Hüter der Verfassung.* Tübingen: Mohr.

Schmitt, C. 1932. "Völkerrechtliche Formen des modernen Imperialismus." In Schmitt 1988, 162–180.

Schmitt, C. 1933. "Reich—Staat—Bund." In Schmitt 1988, 190–198.

Schmitt, C. 1941. "Staat als ein konkreter, an eine geschichtliche Epoche gebundener Begriff." In Schmitt 1958, 375–385.

Schmitt, C. 1950. *Ex Captivitate Salus: Erfahrungen der Zeit 1945–1947.* Cologne: Greven.

Schmitt, C. 1958. *Verfassungsrechtliche Aufsätze aus den Jahren 1924–1954: Materialien zu einer Verfassungslehre.* Berlin: Duncker & Humblot.

Schmitt, C. 1988. *Positionen und Begriffe im Kampf mit Weimar—Genf—Versailles, 1923–1939*, 2nd ed. Berlin: Ducker & Humblot.

Schmitt, C. 1991. *Glossarium: Aufzeichnungen der Jahre 1947–1951.* Berlin: Duncker & Humblot.

Schmitt, C. 1996. *Roman Catholicism and Political Form*, trans. G. L. Ulmen. Westport: Greenwood.

Schmitt, C. 2005. *Political Theology: Four Chapters on the Concept of Sovereignty*, trans. G. Schwab. Chicago: University of Chicago Press.

Schmitt, C. 2004a. *Legality and Legitimacy*, trans. and ed. J. Seitzer. Durham: Duke University Press.

Schmitt, C. 2004b. *On the Three Types of Juristic Thought*, trans. J. W. Bendersky. Westport: Praeger.

Schmitt, C. 2006a. "Nomos—Nahme—Name." In Schmitt 2006b, 336–350.

Schmitt, C. 2006b. *The "Nomos" of the Earth in the International Law of the "Jus Publicum Europaeum*," trans. G. L. Ulmen. New York: Telos Press.

Schmitt, C. 2007. *The Concept of the Political*, trans. G. Schwab. Chicago: University of Chicago Press.

Schmitt, C. 2008a. *Constitutional Theory*, trans. and ed. J. Seitzer. Durham: Duke University Press.

Schmitt, C. 2008b. *The Leviathan in the State Theory of Thomas Hobbes: Meaning and Failure of a Political Symbol*, trans. G. Schwab. Chicago: University of Chicago Press.

Searle, J. R. 2005. "What Is an Institution?" *Journal of Institutional Economics* 1: 1–22.

Skinner, Q. 1989. "The State." In *Political Innovation and Conceptual Change*, ed. T. Ball, J. Farr, and R. L. Hanson. Cambridge: Cambridge University Press, 90–131.

Skinner, Q. 2002. "Retrospect: Studying Rhetoric and Conceptual Change." In *Visions of Politics*, vol. 1: *Regarding Method*. Cambridge: Cambridge University Press, 175–187.

Stolleis, M. 2001. *Public Law in Germany, 1800–1914*. New York: Berghahn.

Strauss, L. 1932. "Notes on The Concept of the Political." In Schmitt 2007, 97–122.

Tribe, K. 2006. "Cameralism and the Sciences of the State." In *The Cambridge History of Eighteenth-Century Political Thought*, ed. M. Goldie and R. Wokler. Cambridge: Cambridge University Press, 525–546.

Weber, M. 1978. *Economy and Society*, ed. G. Roth and C. Wittich. Berkeley: University of California Press.

Weber, M. 1994. *Political Writings*, ed. P. Lassman and R. Spiers. Cambridge: Cambridge University Press.

CHAPTER 22

CARL SCHMITT AND INTERNATIONAL LAW

MARTTI KOSKENNIEMI

INTRODUCTION

IN THE course of World War II, Carl Schmitt began to emphasize that he was above all a jurist and not at all a political theorist or a philosopher. As war fortunes began to turn against Germany, he wrote on historical jurisprudence as the last carrier of the European Geist and an intellectual bulwark against the universalization of Anglo-American commercial and technologically oriented empire (Schmitt 1943). In a pluralistic world, only jurisprudence was left, representing "the unity of the legal will as opposed to the multiplicity of egoistic parties and factions" (1990, 49). There is no need to regard this as eccentric obfuscation. To have internalized the powerful German tradition of a historically based public law was already to occupy a polemical position against the neutralizations and depoliticizations of the liberal powers. It was to have learned the profoundly *political* tradition of European statehood and, with it, the idea of a shared European public law—*jus publicum Europaeum*—that transcended the spirit of single European nations and had for centuries enabled relative peace among Christians by pushing their friend/enemy confrontations into the spiritual darkness of the colonial world.

When Schmitt emphasized his own training as a jurist he did not have in mind a technical expert in this or that law. He abhorred the reduction of the legal profession to one dabbling with merely formal laws (*Gesetze*), products of the operation of the mechanized legislator. Against formal legality he put a substantive legitimacy in which the superlegality of law as *Recht* stood for the elements of the concrete political order (see Schmitt 1932). It was the latter that was represented by the European juridical tradition with which he wanted to associate himself. For Schmitt, the interwar international order—Versailles to Geneva—had been constituted by the allied powers' effort to legalize their territorial gains in Europe and to establish a permanent system of global control of which the League of Nations would be one aspect. To carry the European juridical tradition was to understand the superficial nature of the latter and the illegitimacy of the former. The traditional international law under which European States had confronted each other in peace and war as sovereign equals had, however, collapsed by World War II. As he had written already in 1939, the only means to prevent its replacement by a universal Anglo-American empire was to reconceive the territorial order of the world in terms of relations between hegemonic large spaces (*Grossräume*), one of which rightfully fell to be led by Germany (Schmitt 1939).

The booming Schmitt commentary of the past two decades has not spread into international law as much as one might have expected. Even as his international law texts have been reflected on by political theorists and international relations experts; international lawyers have not immersed themselves in Schmitt exegesis. This may result from their instinctive avoidance of conflictual items, inextricable from their self-image as representatives of a cosmopolitan peace project and their activist role in precisely the international institutions that Schmitt would have indicted as parts of Anglo-American global hegemony. In part, no doubt, this may also be explained by the predominantly technical and positivist orientation of the field. International lawyers do not see themselves as representatives of an intellectual discipline. Their humanitarian sensibilities are not based on any well-articulated theory but have been imbibed practically unconsciously with the profession's technical routines.

This is not to say that Schmitt would have no influence at all or that there would have been no overt discussion about him among international lawyers. The most widely used textbook on the history of international law, Wilhelm Grewe's *The Epochs of International Law*, is a Schmittian book. Grewe wrote most of this work in Berlin during the end phase of World War II as the Russians were approaching—in an atmosphere quite similar to that in which Schmitt himself composed his most important international law work. The book was published in Germany only in 1984, but as soon as the English translation came out in 2000 it ascended to the status of leading general treatment of its topic. The work depicts international law in a thoroughly realist way as a reflection of state power, its history portrayed as the succession of great imperial epochs following each other—a Spanish, French, and a British epoch followed by the twentieth-century Anglo-American condominium. The book's Schmittian politics are also visible in the way it laments the turn to a discriminatory concept of war under the League of Nations and wholly overlooks the crimes of the Nazi regime during World War II (Grewe 2000, 619–624; see also Fassbender 2002, 479–512).

In recent years, if international lawyers have dealt with Schmitt, this has been usually to restate the principles of the universalist humanitarianism that were the targets of his critique. Substantive engagement has been rare. Since the attacks on the World Trade Center in 2001, however, especially left-leaning lawyers began to suggest that Schmitt's analyses might provide a platform on which to discuss and challenge the prevailing system of global hegemony. After all, the unilaterally declared U.S. War on Terror in the aftermath of the 9/11 attacks seems to fit well Schmitt's description of the unlimited nature of the morally inspired discriminatory concept of war waged by liberal powers against those they regard as lawbreakers and enemies of humankind (see, e.g., Odysseos and Petito 2006, 1–7). The rhetoric of war has opened precisely the kind of semantic battlefield in which antagonisms may be intensified to justify dramatic extensions of social control at home and abroad (Mégret 2002, 361–399). The present international situation has also been analyzed as a normless normality in a Schmittian way (Gross 1999–2000). The use of the Camp Delta at Guantánamo for the indefinite detention of terrorist suspects brought in from across the world has symbolized this new global order of permanent exception. More perceptively, however, others have argued that Guantánamo and the related measures in Afghanistan and elsewhere should not at all be analyzed as an exception but rather as part of the normalcy of the Western-led international legal order (Johns 2005). To attack Guantánamo as a legal vacuum, after all, emanates from a legalism for which law is an intrinsically beneficial form of governance—instead of an instrument that can be used for the production of good as well as bad consequences. From a Schmittian perspective it is far from sufficient to point to something as an exception and as condemnable for *that* reason.

Schmittian themes sometimes emerge in historical studies of international law. In the 1980s Jörg Fisch challenged the claim that Europe had bought peace within the continent by externalizing warfare into the colonies. On the validity and historical significance of the principle of "no peace beyond the line," arguments still go both ways.[1] The same concerns the correctness of Schmitt's view of Europe's overseas empire as foundational for international law, especially to the extent that this resulted in a spatial order—a *nomos*—that consolidated Europe's global overlordship. The thesis has been accepted in most postcolonial international law literature; its opponents argue that international law rather mitigated the harshness of colonial rule. The opposing views are best visible in contrasting readings of the famous lectio on the Indians by Francisco de Vitoria in Salamanca in 1539.[2] In the German-speaking realm, Matthias Schmoeckel produced a thorough review of the content and uses of Schmitt's notion of large spaces (*Grossräume*), also with the view of its later applications (1994). Recently Schmitt may have ascended to official recognition in the field by the inclusion of a short biographical essay on him in the recent *Oxford Handbook of the History of International Law* (Fassbender 2012).

To understand why Schmitt's turn to international law was not (as it is sometimes suggested) only a strategic maneuver to avoid the attention of the SS with which (and with whose *völkisch* theory of law) he had come in conflict in the late 1930s but a logical extension of positions taken already in the 1920s, it is useful to put those writings, particularly his main international law work, *Der Nomos der Erde im Völkerrecht des Jus Publicum Europaeum* (1950), in the context of his legal theory and his view of the nature of the universal legal-political order (*nomos*). This is the intention of this chapter. I will begin with a brief overview of Schmitt's legal theory, as developed from the decisionism of his doctoral dissertation to the stress on the polemical nature of legal-constitutional concepts in his later work. I then situate the principal themes in Schmitt's interwar international law writings in the context of Weimar jurisprudence. The chapter then provides directions on how to read his main international law work *Nomos der Erde,* after which I turn to his postwar writings on the Cold War legal order and the vocabularies of world unity accompanying them. I conclude with reflections about the significance of Schmitt's writings for the theory and practice of international law today.

SCHMITT'S THEORY OF LAW

In his doctoral thesis *Gesetz und Urteil* of 1912 Schmitt took up a classical problem of legal hermeneutics: What guarantees the legal correctness of a judgment by a judge (*Richtigkeit der richterlichen Entscheidung*; 1969a, 1–20)? The title of the work—*Statute and Judgment*—lay out the perspective in a typically epigrammatic form. What is the relationship of the legal decision to the law that stood behind it? It had been a key pre-supposition of nineteenth-century German liberal jurisprudence that this relation could be described in terms of deduction and subsumption. A legitimate decision was arrived at by subsuming the individual case under the general formulation of the rule. It was unlikely that many actually believed judges to be decision automatons in this way. Liberal jurisprudence did highlight the difficulties in deduction–subsumption but assumed that the canons of interpretation would clarify the situation sufficiently so that the all-important values of legal certainty and predictability could be safeguarded. To accept that judges actually made choices or allowed their bias to intervene would have undermined the legitimacy of the legal system. Formal law (*Gesetz*) represented the will of the legislator, and in a democratic society the activity of judging was legitimate only if it came about as an application of the legislator's will to the single case or, if that will was unclear or absent, by the judge imagining itself as a legislator.[3]

Schmitt was neither the only nor the first jurist to have ridiculed the view of judges as decision-automatons. In Germany, the "jurisprudence of interests" as well as the "free law school" had already advocated a more complex hermeneutic that would anchor judging to the interests and policies of the community or the "moral values and cultural norms" underlying positive legislation (1969a, 38). They shared the liberal view of courts as part of the liberal society's self-government, however, and merely put forward her-meneutically more fine-tuned views of what legal correctness might mean. Schmitt felt no need to participate in the search of the legitimacy of the institutions of liberal law in this way. For him, the bases of the judicial decision remained ultimately mysterious and could not be constrained within interpretative techniques. There was as unbridgeable a gap between legal theory and practice, between doctrine and the activity of the judge as there was between the legislator's intent and the act of judgment. The positivist ideal of legitimacy constructed by the way legal decisions corresponding to a hypothesized leg-islative intent or a social consensus was mere ideological obfuscation. No rule or law, no interest or policy, no value or consensus validates legal practice. Instead, legal practice validates itself. Legal decisions are correct (*richtig*) to the extent they are actually taken as such in legal practice; legal certainty was thus upheld by the juristic class, the legal elite: its decision-making was a self-validating activity, based on nothing outside the mere fact of the practice of judging itself (1969a, 68–115; see further Rasch 2004, 93–103).

The decisionism that is commonly attached to Schmitt's name (but to which he himself came to be increasingly critical; see Schmitt 1993) emerged thus fully formed already in his first major work, intended as a contribution to the jurisprudence of modern industrial society.[4] Another key aspect of Schmitt's political jurisprudence that arose from the same context was his polemical theory of the meaning of such political and constitutional concepts as "state, republic, society, class, as well as sovereignty, constitutional state, absolutism, dictatorship, economic planning, neutral or total state and so on" (1969b, 30–31). In liberal theory, the meaning of such concepts appeared as a stable entity lying somewhere behind their linguistic form and was accessible by the interpretative techniques offered by legal training and practice. For Schmitt, the matter may appear so during periods of social consensus. That a stable jurisprudence emerges and judges appear to make predictable judgments is not a result of the stability of meanings, however, but of social cohesion and trust in the legislative mechanism (especially among the jurists). These are moments of normality when the power sustaining that cohesion, including the activity of courts and legislative bodies, appears obvious or unproblematic. The fragile surface of social life appears to sustain itself by very the force of its normality. However, as Schmitt argues with great force in the 1920s, this was a deceptive appearance. Every social normality relied on the exception, that is, on the power of the sovereign as the guarantor of the constitutional substance to send in the police. Every consensus was fragile and the meaning projected on the key legal concepts irreducibly dependent on what one wanted to do with them (see especially the analysis of sovereignty in *Political Theology*, 1985).

For Schmitt, the inherently polemical nature of the most important legal and political concepts meant that their meaning was constructed in confrontations that Schmitt analyzed through the friend/enemy distinction. They act as instruments to attack the enemy and to solidify the front against him (1969b, 25–37). Even legal-conceptual distinctions became meaningful only in the political confrontations to which they gave force and expression. They mean what they should mean to keep the defined adversary at bay, to attack, or to protect oneself against him. Ownership is always a tool in the struggle of social groups, while what constitutional concepts mean depends on how they should be used to protect the constitutional order against its enemies. Sometimes the distinctions were solidly entrenched so that their enforcement appears as merely the neutral application of the law. At revolutionary moments, however, the veil over law falls, and its operation appears in its nakedness as the repression of one group (a class, a race, a people) by another. Even consensus merely overshadows a victory won by somebody in the past and harbors the resentment of the vanquished that will use the resources of the legal system (including its semantic resources) to revenge as soon as it feels strong enough.

Schmitt's (qualified) decisionism and his polemical notion of legal and political concepts are quite crucial for his analysis of international law during the interwar period and after. Schmitt attacked above all the language of universal humanitarianism in Europe and the United States. He saw this language as an instrument with which the victorious powers sought to perpetuate German subordination and their own commercial-technological domination over the world. The dominant power, he wrote, is that "who can, with a concrete decision, determine what peace, or disarmament or intervention,

or public order or security means" (1988b, 179). In the interwar order, this interpretative power lay with the allied nations as they were implementing the Versailles restrictions over German sovereignty. After World War II, Schmitt applied this analysis to the
legal world revolution that had lifted the socialists and the Third World into a position
as challengers to the Western-liberal consensus. This demonstrated that the fluidity of
legal meanings could be captured by hegemonic or counterhegemonic parties alike as
part of their polemical strategies (see Schmitt 1987).

Schmitt's legal theory was based on a wholesale rejection of the terms of liberal jurisprudence in its positivist and natural law variants. Those two had been the predominant
theoretical avenues by which standard jurisprudence, as faithful servant of formal legality, had sought to protect the liberal (legislative) state. It had tried to link its legitimacy
either to the will of the legislator or to some underlying consensus of values. Schmitt saw
none of this as more than liberal polemic; it was both theoretically misguided and politically prone to failure. With Schmitt, law stepped out of its role as a lame instrument for
upholding the liberal consensus, turning instead into an expression of its underlying conflicts and struggles. Instead of positivism or natural law, Schmitt espoused a kind of *legal
expressionism* that highlighted the need of the jurist to know where the lines of social
struggle were drawn and what kind of decision, what kind of meaning, would be needed
to solidify the base of the legal order. The distinction between legality and legitimacy had
been well-known since Max Weber, one of Schmitt's spiritual fathers. Schmitt used it not
to highlight values or procedures, however, but to point to the elusive notion of substantive (concrete) order—*nomos*—on which everything about legal normality was based. In
the world of interwar international law and legality, he turned his concrete-order thinking against Versailles and Geneva, the legal system of the League of Nations and the associated neutralizations and depolitizations of Western legal humanism.

SCHMITT'S THEORY OF INTERNATIONAL LAW

Schmitt developed his jurisprudential and international law views in the context of
Weimar jurisprudence, the inheritor of the most impressive tradition of public and constitutional law in Europe.[5] This did not mean that he would have been oblivious of legal
developments elsewhere. He defined his own positions frequently against non-German
adversaries such as the French socialist Georges Scelle or the Polish-British liberal
Hersch Lauterpacht (see Schmitt 1988e). But most of his engagements took place the
Weimar context, often as polemical confrontations with colleagues and in terms that
looked back to the rich tradition of German public law.

From the 1860s German public law had been programmatically oriented to solidify-
ing the constitutional basis of the German Reich. It may be said that when unification
finally took place in 1871 it had already been in virtual existence through the writings
of the German public law experts for half a century, if not from Samuel Pufendorf's
famous analysis of the sui generis nature of the Roman-German empire from 1667 (see

Pufendorf 2007). At least in part, this is what Schmitt meant when, during World War II, he pointed to the role of jurisprudence as the sole inheritor of the European spirit. By the end of the nineteenth century, there existed a powerful tradition of legal argumentation on the nature of the German state and its place in the international world. The debates on the latter issue had been polarized between a state-centric view that saw international law as predominantly a part of the public law of the state—*äußeres Staatsrecht*, or external state law—and a weaker approach that conceptualized international law as an independent (cosmopolitan) legal order outside (and above) the state. The former, state-centric view had been by far more important in Germany than the latter. As the Hegelian jurist Adolf Lasson wrote in 1870, international law was weak, without a spiritual reference point or a teleology of its own. It could therefore exist only as an instrument for the coordination of state pursuits (*Koordinationsrecht*; see Lasson 1871). This view was substantially shared by the most important system-builder of fin-de-siècle public law of the Reich, Paul Laband, who took account of international law only in the form of treaties the Reich had concluded in accordance with its constitution (1909, 158, 161–165). In the influential articulation of the relations between national and international law of 1899 by Heinrich Triepel, international law did have existence as an independent legal order, but it was binding on the state only to the extent that the state itself had chosen to be bound by it through the treaties it had ratified (see Triepel 1899). This dualism (the separate existence of the two legal orders) was the most commonly accepted view of the matter and widely shared also outside Germany.

Throughout the nineteenth century, a dwindling cosmopolitan current, too, saw Germany bound by a tradition of European public law, based on the customs of European nations, general principles of law, and the work of incipient international institutions. After the terms of the Versailles Peace Treaty had been stated to Germany, however, that tradition had lost its legitimacy under German eyes. After 1918, German international lawyers, almost to a man and often contrary to their earlier positions, rejected the legal order that had been presented to them as *Diktatfrieden*. The few liberal-minded Germans who had worked for the advancement of international law and organization before and during the war such as Theodor Niemeyer or Walther Schücking lost much of their influence and were after 1933 removed from their positions—though it is ironic but significant that the commentary on the League of Nations' Covenant by the pacifist Schücking, written in collaboration with the Swiss Hans Wehberg, remained the most widely used work of its type through the interwar period.[6]

It was against this background that Schmitt developed his analysis of the interwar international legal system as a new kind of imperial universalism. Persistent themes in his analysis included the critique of the Versailles Peace Treaty as an index of a new liberal-imperial world order and analysis of the League of Nations as a perpetuation of allied control of Germany. He viewed the moral condemnation of Germany by the allies—visible above all in the war guilt clauses of the Versailles treaty—as part of a wider turn to a discriminating concept of war that constituted an application of the friend/enemy distinction as a constitutive aspect of the worldwide Anglo-American empire. In public speeches and writings in the 1920s, Schmitt focused on the allied occupation and neutralization of the Rhineland as one striking illustration of the new world order. In the previous periods, he writes, imperialism had operated predominantly through formal annexation of territories. The new imperialism, however, chose to use general and ambiguous formulae such as *occupation, control, sanctions,* and *right of investigation* to exercise potentially unlimited control over the subordinated people. Such expressions— spread all over the four peace treaties—allowed the allied states to determine when and how to intervene in the life of the German nation while at the same time refraining from turning the population of the territories into citizens of the victorious states. The aim was, in other words, to follow the old imperial strategy of reaping the benefits without taking on the burdens of expansion (see Schmitt 1988b; 1988c; 1988d; 1988e, 97–108).

The power of this new imperialism, Schmitt wrote, was strikingly demonstrated by the provisions that prohibited Germany from taking any action on its territory that could be understood as preparation for mobilization. Any road works, any construction of railways, or indeed any organization of public traffic might provide reason for intervention. In this way, the political and economic life of Germany had become dependent on what the Western allies would think necessary from the perspective of *their* peace and *their* security. Words such as *freedom, independence,* or *sovereignty* that remained part of interwar law, including the peace treaties, had become subservient to how their limits would be conceived by the victor states while much of the political conflict had come to be waged on the meaning of the status quo. For Britain and France, this referred to the stabilization of a situation that was inherently unstable. For Germany it pushed toward reforms—particularly under the controversial Article 19 of the Covenant of the League of Nations—to reestablish the normality of which the present situation appeared as a chronologically and territorially unlimited exception (1988e, 40–42, 43–44).

As Germany finally entered the League of Nations in 1926 Schmitt was still unable to see in the organization as a serious representative of European juridical traditions and even less an institution of a united humanity. It was striking, he wrote, how the United States was both absent from the League (the United States had not joined the organization despite President Woodrow Wilson's leading role in the drafting of the covenant and his pleas to Congress) and still profoundly implicated in everything that took place within it (see, e.g., 1988e, 90–93). The acceptance of the Monroe Doctrine in Article 21 of the covenant guaranteed that the league would never be able to intervene in the Western hemisphere while the United States was constantly present in the league through unofficial means and by proxy through its eighteen Latin American intermediaries. The league was neither universal nor really European. The fact that the covenant was part of the peace treaties constituted a striking manifestation of the fact that the league remained an instrument of the security needs of the Western allies.

Schmitt understood many new theories of international law as likewise aspects of this new, universal imperial order. The doctrine of monism, for example, according to which international treaties would be superior to national laws and the validity of the latter would derive from the international legal order, emerged as a key part of the ubiquitous critiques of sovereignty at the time. Its most brilliant German-language exponent was Hans Kelsen, joined also by the Viennese natural lawyer Alfred Verdross. Both also wrote on the existence of a universal international legal community of which particular states and legal systems would be members (see Kelsen 1928; Verdross 1923). Schmitt rejected all of this as an effort to introduce obscure legal notions that would override the national legal system and to allow constant meddling in domestic affairs. Internationalization—something that had been debated in the context of the Rhineland question—was simply the rule of those powers that were able to decide where it would apply and what it would mean. Everybody of course wants peace. But with the signature of the Kellogg-Briand pact on the "outlawry of war as an instrument of national diplomacy" in 1928, it had become plainly evident that the real question was not whether some were peaceful while others were not but "who decides what peace is, who on what are order and security, who on what is a passing and what a permanent situation" (Schmitt 1988b, 177). The critiques of sovereignty so popular in the West allowed the victorious states to address themselves as representatives of an international community and to intervene according to their interests. "Universal, worldwide general concepts in international law are typical weapons of interventionism" (1939, 41).

Another similar vehicle was the discriminating concept of war that had emerged in the war guilt clauses in the peace treaties and was then enshrined in the league covenant and the Kellogg-Briand pact. In the eighteenth and early nineteenth centuries, during the time of what Schmitt labeled the reign of the *jus publicum Europeaeum,* the right to go to war had been understood as part of a nation's sovereignty and of the arrangement under which Europeans had limited ideologically motivated (religious) warfare among themselves. War had been turned into a matter of state policy; as belligerents, all states would be equal. This had also been a crucial vehicle for limiting the means and the intensity of warfare. With the advent of the Anglo-American commercial empire at the end of the nineteenth century, however, and especially with the moralistic allied propaganda during the war of 1914–1918, war had once again been vested with a universal ideology. The belligerents would no longer be equal; one would be a fighter for peace, struggling on behalf of humanity, its adversary a morally and legally condemned lawbreaker. From the conceptual paradigm of interstate war, the discriminating concept of warfare moved into the conceptual world of criminal law: the adversary would not be a "just enemy" (*justus hostis*) but a *criminal* and an enemy of humanity against which no measure could be excessive. The limits of warfare would be lifted, and total war against whole populations would become a reality, manifested in Schmitt's imagination by the allied maritime blockade of German coasts.[7]

Throughout the interwar era Schmitt was very concerned and almost obsessed with the Monroe Doctrine under which, since 1823, the United States had purported to reject external intervention in the Western hemisphere, claiming its own superiority in the region. Was it a legal or a political principle? What did it actually entail in terms of obligations on third states? It was clearly in conflict with traditional international law under which nobody was entitled to claim an extensive hegemony. How could the world possibly have accepted the extraordinary powers arrogated by the United States? In the end, Schmitt held the Monroe Doctrine as a legal–political principle that was typical of an imperialist order: it had been declared unilaterally, and its meaning was completely dependent on how the United States chose to view it. From its originally noninterventionist motivation, it had come to underwrite constant American intervention in the Western Hemisphere, legally through the medium of the intervention treaties it had concluded with most Latin American states as well as its policies of recognition of the governments of the territory (1988e, 162–180; 1939, 21–39).

The new morally and economically driven empire had, among other things, replaced the classical international law distinction between civilized and uncivilized nations by the opposition between creditor and debtor countries. It had also inaugurated a humanitarian vocabulary of *peace, order*, and *security*, under which the United States and its British ally arrogated to themselves the right to determine what such words should mean, whose policy they would support, and whose policy they would condemn. As a kind of summary of these arguments, Schmitt concluded in 1932, "A people is only then conquered when it subordinates itself under a foreign vocabulary, a foreign understanding what the law, especially international law, is" (1988b, 179). Schmitt saw the only way to oppose the universal empire by taking his cue from the Monroe Doctrine itself and by suggesting the division of the world into large spaces (*Grossräume*). These would consist of (imperial) constellations of several states, united by their being within the radius of a leading state (Reich). In legal terms, this would mean the emergence of two different types of legal relationship: relations between states within each *Grossraum* and relations across the boundaries of two or more *Grossräume*. The former would be marked by the recognition of the leading position of the (imperial) center analogously to the Monroe Doctrine. By contrast, relations between states across the boundaries of such spaces would be based on formal equality, and any intervention would be prohibited. The concrete order formed of such large spaces (empires) would form an alternative to the single, universalistic empire of the Western powers (1939, 57, 69–88).[8]

THINKING THE *NOMOS*

During the war, Schmitt kept writing on international legal matters, the spatial revolution that he saw under way since late nineteenth century, revising the *Grossräume* idea and finally turning it to the theory of *nomos* as the basis for a postwar settlement (see further Mehring 2009, 424–433). He also began sketching the historical process of the emergence of two types of states: those based on land; and those finding their identity as maritime empires. There was even a dramatic, mythological contrast between the people of the land and people of the sea, behemoth and leviathan, he claimed. Schmitt's wartime musings on the concrete legal orders (*nomoi*) of world history highlight the way most European states had emerged through the occupation of land (*Landnahme*) and setting up a legal and political order over it. By contrast, ever since England first became a leading maritime power under Elizabeth I (1582–1603), it had come to think of itself as a political order of the seas—and thus a potentially global power (see Schmitt 1995; 395–398; 1981). Between the sixteenth and nineteenth centuries, England had carried out a spatial revolution (*Raumrevolution*) that came to oppose the powers of land to those of the sea, the one essentially limited, the other unlimited, including in its means of indiscriminate warfare that would strike at belligerents and neutrals, military as well as civilian targets (1981, 87–89). This also gave political direction for Schmitt's antisemitism: the dangerous search for an unlimited global legal order by a people that is not of the land thus brought together two of Schmitt's great enemies, both of which stood in the way of Germany's grasp for a large space in Central and Eastern Europe.[9]

The principal work that collects together Schmitt's wartime texts in a discussion of the decline of European international is *Nomos der Erde im Jus Publicum Europaeum*, first published in 1950. At the heart of this work stood a historical thesis about the three stages of international law. The medieval Respublica Christiana, a religiously based, homogenous order (for which the globe was not yet a geographical fact but a myth) was replaced in the sixteenth and seventeenth centuries by the territorial state that coexisted within a novel global consciousness. This thesis offered Schmitt the occasion to produce an influential view about the significance of the Spanish colonization of the Indies for international law. Focusing on the theological justifications provided by the Dominican cleric Francisco de Vitoria Schmitt was able to read his natural law as above all an instrument for conversion and colonization, stressing its theological (i.e., non-juridical) nature. It was true, Schmitt wrote, that Vitoria showed astonishing objectivity and neutrality in the conflict between the Spaniards and the Indians; to this extent he foreshadowed the global international law that was to come. On the other hand, he never depicted Indians at the same level as the Spaniards. There was and could be no symmetry between the Christian and the pagans. This made Vitoria a transitional figure against whose essentially theological perspective modern international law was born. From now on theologians should remain silent in matters that do not concern them (*silete theologi in munere alieno*): Schmitt repeated the famous slogan of the Protestant jurist Alberico Gentili as a kind of watershed between the old and the new (1950, 91–92). Vitoria had been critical of the jurists and argued that the matter of the conquest was to be dealt with by reference to passages in the Bible. By contrast, the new principle of delimitating European space brought in by Gentili and other Protestant jurists imported a sharp distinction between secular and ecclesiastic jurisdiction.[10]

The *jus publicum Europaeum* that came to regulate the relationship between European states in early modernity was consolidated through the great discoveries that opened up non-European territory as a field of unlimited land-taking. The great merit, for Schmitt, of this system lay in the manner it was able to limit inter-European warfare by conceiving it as a public law status between formally equal sovereigns, that is, by replacing the medieval notion of the *justa causa belli* by the formal concept of the *justus hostis*. This enabled treating enemies on an equal basis, through formal rules and without existential enmity (1950, 112–119). War became a duel, a *Kabinettkrieg*, a regulated procedure for resolving inter-European rivalries. But the political point of the book that Schmitt took over from his interwar writings was that this classical legal order was now being overcome by the universal extension of the Anglo-American commercial empire. The latter was accompanied by a humanitarian morality that was responsible for the "discriminating concept of war" and the consequent criminalization of the enemy (1950, 93–96, 232–255).

Nomos der Erde looked back with nostalgia toward the period between the sixteenth and late nineteenth centuries when the European order had been based on sovereign equality and limited warfare between European powers. In this history three Schmittian concepts play a central role: the concrete order; occupation of land; and statehood. His legal realism, we have seen, was based on the view of law as not merely *Gesetz* or *loi* but as concrete order. As *nomos* it expressed the unity of the human community, based on its fundamental political decision about who belongs to it. The relationship between order in the community and the land it inhabited was fundamental (*Ordnung/Ortung*). If land-taking (*Landnahme*) was the primal act of community, then the method of effective land distribution in a period provided its concrete order (1950, 13–20). Since the Great Discoveries, the *nomos* of the earth had consisted of the division of the globe into European and non-European territories. Order and limited warfare between sovereigns in the former had been made possible by channeling all further land-taking into the latter. At the end of the seventeenth century, this system had been supplemented by an aspect of the sea, dominated by the people of the sea—the English—with whom, however, a reasonable equilibrium had been attained by the Peace of Utrecht (1713). Central to this was the accepted safety valve of the unlimited opportunity for occupation of lands outside Europe (1950, 153).

This state-centric system of European public law, Schmitt wrote, had possessed the extraordinary merit of limiting inter-European warfare by channeling war to the colonies—"beyond the line" (1950, 112, 115–117, 123–140). This was an effect of the agnosticism of that law about matters of religion: *silete Theologi in munere alieno*! However, that system began to dismantle in the nineteenth century in connection with the spread of the universalist ideologies represented by the great maritime powers Britain and the United States. The Scramble for Africa and in particular the Berlin Conference (1884–1885) had been the last great act of European *Landnahme*. But even there signs of decay had been visible to the extent that claims had been made there to areas left unoccupied, perhaps not even been visited. The laws of colonial appropriation written into the Berlin Act thus remained a mere abstraction, no longer representing any concrete spatial order (1950, 188–200).

The civilizing ideas that the Anglo-American powers had flagged in the course of the nineteenth century, including at Berlin, had been essentially universalistic and without a basis in any firm system of land distribution. In the period between 1890 and World War I the United States itself had oscillated between isolationism and adherence to a universalistic-humanitarian principle of intervention, choosing the latter finally at Versailles in 1919 (Schmitt 1950, 200–201). The completion of the interwar system achieved a true spatial revolution; the demise of European public law had become a reality. From now on, there would be no specifically *European* but a *global* international law. This would be an unpolitical and technologically oriented law that would embrace equally all the populations of the world. In this law, the use of sea and air power and new worldwide technologies of mass destruction would turn every local conflict into a world war (290–298). Under it, the economically and technologically more advanced powers enjoyed an unlimited right of intervention, even through "police bombing" (299).

This narrative was dubious in regard to the nature of the land-taking that it postulated, its categorical view of the principle of no peace beyond the line, and its view of the benign and limited character of European warfare between the seventeenth and twentieth centuries. Moreover, Schmitt was in danger of characterizing *Le droit public de l'Europe* precisely in the formal and abstract terms that he ridiculed in attempts to defend the Weimar Constitution. The specificity of European public law, as understood by its predominant representatives such as Georg Friedrich von Martens or Johann Ludwig Klüber, lay precisely in its rigorous formalism, its absolute distance from the social lives of European nations. That Schmitt could possibly identify this superficial network of treaties and diplomatic protocols as the *nomos* of the world and still believe that what he was describing was neither a naturalist abstraction nor an empty *Vertragspositivismus* was possible only by recourse to a background assumption about the intrinsic worth of European statehood conceived in the prerevolutionary manner as absolutist statehood. Analogously to the Catholic Church he saw it as a political form that reduced the *complexio oppositorum* in Europe into a manageable set of territorial delimitations controlled by the balance of power between authoritarian units each of which was able to maintain internal order and direct expansive energies to an unlimited rivalry outside Europe.

Like many of Schmitt's works, *Nomos der Erde* was powerful but awkward and incoherent, full of brilliant insights and dubious generalizations. It was underlain by the circumstances of the war during which it was written but also by a political theology that refused to interpret international events by a secular philosophy of history but instead chose a sacred history where the endemic conflicts in the world would manifest theological struggle between the secular restrainer (*katekhon*) and the Antichrist.[11] Schmitt avoided foregrounding his political theology but provided references to it in the five corollaries that open the work and in several talks and papers he gave on world unity after the war. Schmitt was no nihilist, advocate of a bottomless, power-enchanted relativism, as he is sometimes portrayed. He did not attack the liberal powers because of their universalism but because of their *false* and *nihilistic* universalism. From his own perspective, the worldwide conflict between the leaders of the West and others was merely one aspect of the struggle between Christ and Antichrist in a world whose historical horizon was constituted not by progress but by salvation.[12] Unity under the Western powers would be Babylonian unity.

THEORIZING THE PARTISAN

In 1963 Schmitt published a small volume on the *Theory of the Partisan,* based on lectures given in the previous year in Pamplona (1992, 201–320).[13] Once again, his gaze was on the erosion of the formal distinctions of classical war: war and peace; combatant and noncombatant; enemy and the common criminal. Much of the work was written as a history of partisan warfare from the popular uprising against Napoleon's occupation forces in Spain in 1808–1813 to the teachings on guerrilla war by Mao Tse-tung, Ho-Chi Minh, and Che Guevara. Schmitt also discussed the actions of the French general Raoul Salan, leader of the OAS terrorist network (*"Organisation de l'armée secret"*) during the Algerian war of independence who, from having used partisan methods against the FNL (*"force nationale de libération"*) turned those methods against the French government itself (268–274).

But the weight of the book is in putting forward the structural and theoretical implications of partisan warfare—the way such war takes place outside the conventional international law distinctions and even *against* those distinctions as parts of the enemy order. The partisan, Schmitt suggests, not only operates within the logic of friend/enemy but also intensifies that contrast so that his actions are always political, unlike those of the pirate. The partisan will always be treated as an outlaw by his adversary, the regular occupying troops that are his immediate target. Although their actions are closely tied to the occupied land, partisans' ideological message is not territorially limited. To articulate the political nature of the struggle, the partisan often uses a third party, a state, as its friend that takes its case onto the international level as a global adversity—as the Soviet Union and China did with the liberation movements of the 1960s.

It is true, Schmitt writes, that the four Geneva Conventions of 1949 on the protection of victims of warfare, and especially their rules on occupation, aim at a compromise between the interests of the occupying power and the population. They also try to take account of irregular warfare by treating as combatants resistance fighters who are organized in a military fashion, bear arms openly and carry combatant insignia. But in fact, Schmitt claims, partisan warfare undermines any such regulations and remains disrespectful of the fragile equilibriums of classical law (1992, 225–238). Nevertheless, although partisan warfare is characterized by rule-breaking intensity, not all of it is alike. Schmitt made a distinction between the real enemy and the absolute enemy. The partisans fighting against Napoleonic occupation, for example, faced their adversaries as real enemies, defending a soil to which they were attached so that the recapture of the soil constituted the objective and limit of the enmity. By contrast, with Lenin and the requirement of absolute loyalty to the Party, the enemy, too, becomes absolute. The weight of the operations moves from the tactics of the battlefield to an overall political antagonism that has no territorial limit (299–305). No doubt, it is possible to see this contrast today in, for example, the actions of the opponent's of Israel's occupation of Palestine and the larger conflict between Islamic activists and parts of the secular West.

Until recently, Carl Schmitt's name appeared very rarely in postwar international law texts in Germany or elsewhere. This does not mean that his influence would have been negligible. Schmittian themes have been quite important in the development of the international relations especially in the United States.[14] As pointed out above, Schmitt's legacy in international law has been clearest in the widely read realist histories by Wilhelm Grewe and Karl-Heinz Ziegler that narrate the development of international law by reference to the succession of imperial epochs in which a hegemonic center (Rome,

Madrid, Paris, London, Washington) has radiated its political and cultural influence over the world.[15] More recently, and especially from the political Left, Schmittian perspectives have been used to analyze the effects on international law of the recourse to universalist moral vocabularies by the United States and its allies in their global War on Terror after 2001.

The points made already in *Nomos* regarding the breakdown of the formal distinctions of the classical laws of war have been found applicable to the new wars that are simultaneously international and national and where separating clearly between combatants and noncombatants has become virtually impossible. Against formal legality, the terrorist—like the partisan—relies on a deeper legitimacy from the perspective of which the law (North Atlantic Treaty Organization, United Nations, the coalition) is the crime and legality itself the enemy (Schmitt 1992, 289–294). With the end of the ("illegal") Iraq War (2003–2006) and the departure of the George W. Bush regime, the intensity of the conflict between the Islamic world and the West has not diminished. The effort to infuse the laws of war with a universal moral content continues at global institutions with the introduction of the notion of "responsibility to protect" as a wide authorization to engage in asymmetric war against enemies understood as criminals or outlaws.[16] The same implications are likewise entailed in the international community's actions against Somali pirates. In fact, as Schmitt pointed out in 1937, the (then) ongoing efforts to deal with piracy engaged the same conceptual logic as asymmetrical wars: "[they] relate to the impulse to replace war with collective arrangements of various types (international police, criminal punishment, proscriptions and sanctions), and to create some power capable of acting 'in the name of humanity'" (2011, 29). To respond to the demands of globalization, international law has increasingly turned from rigid formal rules to broad, often morally infused standards that vest their appliers with a wide degree of discretion (see Koskenniemi 2007, 9–15). Such deformalization has affected legal vocabularies as varied as those of *development, security, free trade*, and *human rights*. When giving concrete content to those notions, international institutions have tended to operate and be seen as representatives of an international community. This is part of what Schmitt used to treat in his postwar texts under the theme of world unity, aimed at by the economic and technical processes of world industries on one hand and by (Western) hegemonic humanitarianism on the other. In his last international law text, "The Legal World Revolution" (1978), Schmitt argues that a superlegality of progress was being used to construct an economic and technological world order beyond the territorial state (1987, 76–81). This could be prevented only by the emergence of a new *nomos*, controlled by the leading economic *Grossräume*, United States, China, the rest of Asia, Latin America, perhaps Europe. World unity was impossible for it would require the emergence of something like a patriotism of the species. But humanity could never become a political subject as there was nothing outside it against which it would exist. As long as that was the case, the vocabulary of humanity was therefore better understood as a political instrument, a tool for labeling one's adversary as "inhuman," as someone who was "worthless and must be destroyed" (1987, 88).

Conclusion

Carl Schmitt has been a problem for international lawyers. His critique of Anglo-American liberal universalism, initially put forward in writings against the League of Nations—a center, he assumed, for the enforcement of the preferences of the Anglo-American condominium—remain relevant for today's international legal theory and practice as well. The discriminatory concept of war, the demonization of the political adversary as an enemy of humankind and the instrumentalization of the law for the expansion of an economic-technical worldview are all familiar aspects of today's global world. Moreover, a turn to ethics has taken place in the field that is clearly vulnerable to some of Schmitt's more acerbic critiques. The expansion of human rights vocabularies and the rise of international criminal law illustrate efforts to enlist international for what seems self-evidently good and against what appears altogether evil. Schmitt would not have been surprised of the way every interest aims to parade in the garb of the right of the interest-holder. He would have expected nothing less from the "tyranny of values" of a faithless world (Schmitt 2011). Nor would he have found anything exceptional in the fact that when Western powers succeed in the setting up of an International Criminal Court, all of the accused will be from Africa. A concrete order reveals itself, he would have said.

International lawyers have had great difficulty integrating these facts into their conceptual world. Why? A realism that views law as a concrete order is not really novel or automatically against constructive work in international institutions. To the contrary: for most of the twentieth century, legal realism has been a minor but important part of the jurisprudential curriculum, providing a critical perspective on the operation of legal institutions. It is rather the case that work in international law has involved such strong *moral* commitment to the field's inherited rules, principles, and institutions that casting a cold and analytical eye on it has become very difficult. The problem is exacerbated by the weakness of the field and the manipulability of its central precepts. Attention to the way its rules or institutions may operate as part of some hegemonic project may appear as altogether disloyal and destructive in a legal system situated in a particularly complex and divisive context. Machiavelli, Montaigne, Hobbes, Hegel, and innumerable other thinkers have been making points not unlike those made by Schmitt; with each, jurists have felt themselves uncomfortable, often reacting by invoking precisely the humanitarian sentiments that have been the object of their dissections. Surely this is insufficient. International law is an important instrument for the realization of valuable purposes and its formality offers a useful platform to channel disagreement. It is hard to see how it could be able to serve those objectives if the field remains in denial about its inflated expectations and occasional hypocrisy and if no light is allowed on the way it inevitably prefers some interests and players over others. It is no coincidence that Schmittian themes are most in evidence among postcolonial lawyers, yet a robust defense of the field can begin only once jurists become more alert to the actual consequences the rules and institutions of international law in the worlds of power and politics.

No doubt, international law is a liberal project with a universalist ethos and vulnerable to many of Schmitt's critiques. In particular, its universality often appears as false universality, thinly hiding from sight the preferences of those who have succeeded in attaining a hegemonic position in its (universal) institutions. But it also operates as a polemical vocabulary that allows the indictment of those in power; without its idealism we could not even begin to distinguish between false and genuine universality. International law is not destroyed by Schmittian analyses. What they may do, instead, is disenchant ourselves from the assumption that every rule that presents itself as international law, and every institution that comes to us bearing the label of international community is for that very reason beyond criticism.

Notes

1. For a criticism of Schmitt and others advocating "no peace beyond the line," see Fisch 1984.
2. For the postcolonial reading, see, for example, Barreto 2013 (144–145, 150). For the opposing view, see Cavallar 2008 (181–209).
3. Schmitt rejected the view whereby in gap situations the judge ought to imagine himself of herself as a legislator. For, as he argued, the act of legislating general provisions and deciding in a single case were fundamentally different types of operation (1969, 65–66, 96–98).
4. Schmitt was critical of the type of decisionism he associated with Hobbes and that reduced all law to a voluntary decision by the sovereign. For him, that was simply the conceptual counterpart to normativism, the reduction of the law to positive laws (*Gesetze*). See, e.g., Schmitt 1932 (22–23). Especially in his later period of concrete-order thinking he characterized the decadent of nineteenth-century liberal jurisprudence in terms of an unstable oscillation between the two. Against both, he asserted the founding of the law on a prior substantive act or order (*nomos*). See especially Schmitt 1993.
5. See Michael Stolleis 1999. For the international law debates in Germany at that time, see Koskenniemi 2001 (179–265).
6. See Schücking and Wehberg 1921. On Schücking's context and activities, see Koskenniemi 2001 (213–222).
7. See Schmitt 1988a. Schmitt's attention to Allied means of warfare—maritime blockade and aerial war above all—was accompanied by his total nonchalance about the German unlimited submarine warfare or its violation of Belgium's neutrality. Among the Germans, however, these were not extreme positions. Most German international lawyers kept loyal silence about German violations while expressing moral outrage about consequences of the blockade to German civilians. See, e.g., Koskenniemi 2001 (234–235) and notes therein.
8. As an example of these, Schmitt listed alongside the system of the Monroe Doctrine also the British system of the "security of traffic lanes" and of the "freedom of seas," which in the nineteenth century extended British boundaries across world oceans (1939, 43–54).
9. Schmitt's *Grossraum* is not identical with Hitler's search for *Lebensraum*, but it cannot be denied that the timing of its emergence and much of its formulation was indistinguishable from the latter.

10. Schmitt saw the articulation of this new *nomos* first carried out by Spanish Dominican theologians, above all Francisco de Vitoria (1483–1546) whose writings on the American Indians did conceive a proper war with "just enemies" on both sides. In other respects, however, Vitoria's religious frame did not allow full equality between Christians and heathens. For this reason, he could credit the beginning of "modern international law" only in the Italian Protestant Alberico Gentili's exclamation, in 1588, that theologians ought to be silent about matters (such as just war) that do not concern them (Schmitt 1950, 71–85, 96).
11. The best theological interpretation of Schmitt's work is Meier 1998.
12. I have made this interpretation in much more detail in Koskenniemi 2004 (especially 500–502).
13. I have used the French text as in Schmitt 1992.
14. Especially through the work of Hans J. Morgenthau and other fathers of political realism. See, e.g., Brown 2007; Scheuerman 2007 (42–92).
15. Grewe 2000; Ziegler 1994. I critiqued Grewe's book in book reviews in Koskenniemi 2002 (496–501).
16. See now especially Orford 2011 (22–34) and for the parallel to Schmitt 2011 (125–138).

REFERENCES

Barreto, J. 2013. "Imperialism and Decolonization as Scenarios of Third World History." In *Human Rights from a Third World Perspective. Critique, History and International Law*, ed. J. Barreto. Cambridge: Cambridge Scholars.

Brown, C. 2007. "'The Twilight of International Morality'? Hans J. Morgenthau and Carl Schmitt on the end of *Jus Publicum Europaeum*." In *Realism Reconsidered: The Legacy of Hans J. Morgenthau*, ed. M. C. Williams. Oxford: Oxford University Press, 42–61.

Cavallar, G. 2008. "Vitoria, Grotius, Pufendorf, Wolff and Vattel: Accomplices of European Colonial Exploitation or True Cosmopolitans." *Journal of the History of International Law* 10: 181–209.

Fassbender, B. 2002. "Stories of War and Peace: On Writing the History of International Law in the 'Third Reich' and After." *European Journal of International Law* 13: 479–512.

Fassbender, B. 2012. "Carl Schmitt (1888–1985)." In *Oxford Handbook of the History of International Law*, ed. B. Fassbender and A. Peters Oxford: Oxford University Press, 1173–1178.

Fisch, J. 1984. *Die europäische Expansion und das Völkerrecht*. Stuttgart: Steiner.

Grewe, W. 2000. *The Epochs of International Law*, trans. M. Byers. Berlin: De Gruyter.

Gross, O. 1999–2000. "The Normless and Exceptionless Exception: Carl Schmitt's Theory of Emergency Powers and the Norm-Exception Dichotomy." *Cardozo Law Review* 21: 1825–1868.

Kelsen, H. 1928. *Der Begriff der Souveränität und die Theorie des Völkerrechts*, 2nd ed. Tübingen: Mohr.

Koskenniemi, M. 2001. *The Gentle Civilizer of Nations: The Rise and Fall of International Law 1870–1960*. Cambridge: Cambridge University Press.

Koskenniemi, M. 2002. "W. Grewe, *The Epochs of International Law*" [book review]. *International and Comparative Law Quarterly* 51.3: 746–751.

Koskenniemi, M. 2004. "International Law as Political Theology: How to Read *Nomos der Erde*?" *Constellations* 11.4: 492–511.

Koskenniemi, M. 2007. "The Fate of International Law: Between Technique and Politics." *Modern Law Review* 70: 1–31.

Laband, P. 1909. *Deutsches Reichsstaatsrecht*, 5th ed. Tübingen: Mohr.

Lasson, A. 1871. *Prinzip und Zukunft des Völkerrechts*. Berlin: Herz.

Mehring, R. 2009. *Carl Schmitt: Aufstieg und Fall. Eine Biografie*. Munich: Beck.

Mégret, F. 2002. "'War'? Legal Semantics and the Move to Violence." *European Journal of International Law* 13: 361–399.

Meier, H. 1998. *The Lesson of Carl Schmitt: Four Chapters on the Distinction between Political Theology and Political Philosophy*, trans. M. Brainard. Chicago: University of Chicago Press.

Odysseos, L, and Petito F. 2006. "Introducing the International Theory of Carl Schmitt: International Law, International Relations, and the Present Predicament(s)." *Leiden Journal of International Law* 19: 1–7.

Orford, A. 2011. *International Authority and the Responsibility to Protect*. Cambridge: Cambridge University Press.

Pufendorf, S. 2007. *The Present State of Germany*, ed. and with an introduction M. J. Seidler. Indianapolis: Liberty Fund.

Rasch, W. 2004. "Judgment: The Emergence of Legal Norms." *Cultural Critique* 57: 93–103.

Scheuerman, W. E. 2007. "Carl Schmitt and Hans Morgenthau: Realism and Beyond." In *Realism Reconsidered: The Legacy of Hans J. Morgenthau*, ed. M. C. Williams. Oxford: Oxford University Press, 62–91.

Schmitt, C. 1932. *Legalität und Legitimität*. Berlin: Duncker & Humblot.

Schmitt, C. 1939. *Die Völkerrechtliche Grossraumordnung: Mit Interventionsverbot für raum-fremde Mächte*. Berlin: Deutscher Rechtsverlag.

Schmitt, C. 1943. *Die Lage der europäischen Rechtswissenschaft*, trans. G. L. Ulmen as Schmitt, C. 1990. "The Plight of European Jurisprudence" *Telos* 83: 35–70.

Schmitt, C. 1950. *Der Nomos der Erde im Jus Publicum Europaeum*. Berlin: Duncker & Humblot.

Schmitt, C. 1969a. *Gesetz und Urteil: Eine Untersuchung zum Problem der Rechtspraxis*, 2nd ed. Munich: Beck.

Schmitt, C. 1969b. *The Concept of the Political*, trans. with an introduction by G. Schwab. Chicago: University of Chicago Press.

Schmitt, C. 1981. *Land und Meer: Eine weltgeschichtliche Betrachtung*. Stuttgart: Klett-Cotta.

Schmitt, C. 1985. *Political Theology: Four Chapters on the Concept of Sovereignty*, trans. G. Schwab. Cambridge: MIT Press.

Schmitt, C. 1987. "The Legal World Revolution." *Telos* 72: 73–98.

Schmitt, C. 1988a. *Positionen und Begriffe im Kampf mit Weimar—Genf—Versailles 1923–1939*. Berlin: Duncker & Humblot.

Schmitt, C. 1988b. "Die Rheinland als Objekt internationaler Politik." In Schmitt 1988a, 26–33.

Schmitt, C. 1988c. "Der Status quo und der Friede." In Schmitt 1988a, 33–42.

Schmitt, C. 1988d. "Völkerrechtliche Formen des modernen Imperialismus." In Schmitt 1988a, 162–180.

Schmitt, C. 1988e. *Die Wendung zum diskrimierenden Rechtsbegriff*. Berlin: Duncker & Humblot.

Schmitt, C. 1990. "The Plight of European Jurisprudence." *Telos* 83: 35–70.

Schmitt, C. 1992. "Théorie du partisan." In *La notion de politique/Théorie du partisan*, trans. M.-L. Steinhauser, preface by J. Freund. Paris: Flammarion, 205–305.

Schmitt, C. 1993. *Über die drei Arten der rechtwissenschaftlichen Denkens*, 3rd ed. Berlin: Duncker & Humblot.

Schmitt, C. 1995. "Das Meer gegen das Land (1941)." In *Staat, Grossraum, Nomos: Arbeiten aus den Jahren 1916–1969*. Berlin: Duncker & Humblot, 395–423.

Schmitt, C. 2011. "The Concept of Piracy (1937)." *Humanity* 2: 27–29.

Schmoeckel, M. 1994. *Die Grossraumtheorie: Ein Beitrag zur Geschichte der Völkerrechtswissenschaft im Dritten Reich, insbesondere der Kriegzeit*. Berlin: Duncker & Humblot.

Schücking, W., and H. Wehberg. 1921. *Die Satzung des Völkerbundes*. Berlin: Vahlen.

Stolleis, M. 1999. *Geschichte des öffentlichen Rechts in Deutschland*, vol. 3: 1914–1945. Munich: Beck.

Triepel, H. 1899. *Völkerrecht und Landesrecht*. Leipzig: Hirschfeld.

Verdross, A. 1923. *Die Einheit des rechtlichen Weltbildes auf Grundlage der Völkerrechtsverfassung*. Tübingen: Mohr.

Ziegler, K.-H. 1994. *Völkerrechtsgeschichte*. Munich: Beck.

CHAPTER 23

....

DEMYSTIFYING SCHMITT

....

ERIC A. POSNER AND ADRIAN VERMEULE

INTRODUCTION

....

CARL SCHMITT is too important to be left to the Schmitt specialists. To their credit, they were the first to recognize this. In recent years many of Schmitt's most important works have been given authoritative new translations (2008a; 2008b), while intellectual historians and political theorists have labored to set Schmitt's work in intellectual and historical context, explaining its content and significance for academics in other disciplines (e.g., Kennedy 2004; McCormick 1997; Scheuerman 1999, 2004).

The goal of open access to Schmitt's thinking, however, requires more than translation and historical context. Even when those indispensable first steps have been accomplished, there remains a barrier to entry for those who would draw on Schmitt's work to illuminate subjects such as the design and operation of constitutions, emergency powers, and the administrative state. The barrier is that Schmitt's work grows out of and exemplifies a continental tradition of legal and political theory that is heavily conceptual and laden with jurisprudential jargon. Especially for American lawyers whose interdisciplinary toolkit is drawn from the social sciences that flowered after World War II, Schmitt's thought seems relentlessly abstract and mystifying.

This chapter attempts to demystify some of Schmitt's core insights by interpreting them in light of simple causal intuitions and models drawn from the social sciences, including economics, law and economics, and political science. The aim is not exegetical or historical; of course we do not suggest that Schmitt thought in such terms or that the social-scientific interpretations we offer are the best contextual understanding of Schmitt's ideas from the internal point of view. Rather, the aim is deliberately acontextual and utilitarian. It is to make some of Schmitt's ideas usable for research in other disciplines and to illustrate a general approach to Schmitt that can be applied to all of his writings.

The first section focuses on Schmitt's distinction between legality and legitimacy and the associated idea that legitimacy often amounts to a strictly negative power on the part of mass publics to resist elite proposals, either through negative votes in referenda or through extralegal resistance. Although liberal theorists worried by the specter of a plebiscitary executive have cast these ideas in ominous terms, as a form of proto-fascist democracy by acclamation or "soccer-stadium democracy" (Holmes 1993, 49) we interpret the ideas in terms of recent work on the political foundations of constitutionalism. Schmitt's distinction between legality and legitimacy, we suggest, rests on the unimpeachable insight that constitutional rules amount to nothing more than parchment barriers unless supported by the equilibrium political strategies of officials, citizens, political parties, and other actors. In this setting, Schmitt's emphasis on the latent threat of mass violence amounts to nothing more than an attempt to dig down to the ultimate micro-foundations of constitutionalism.

The second section centers on Schmitt's distinction between the norm and the exception. This distinction is related to legality and legitimacy, because Schmitt claimed that legality and legitimacy are convergent in normal times and divergent in exceptional situations. Yet the distinction between norm and exception raises separate issues as well, because Schmitt famously claimed that the exception necessarily has the potential to intrude upon the "closed system" (2008a, 4) of constitutional legality in liberal regimes. We interpret this point in terms of the economic distinction between rules and standards and in terms of the lawyerly idea of purposive interpretation. Schmitt's idea of commissarial dictatorship as a form of dictatorship that may violate certain constitutional rules to protect and conserve the overall structure of the constitutional order is a form of standard-based purposivism writ large.

Interpreting Schmitt in our terms might just amount to a different form of translation, not from German to English but from jurisprudential to social-scientific terms. Yet we think there is more to it than that. Translating Schmitt's insights into the more concrete and pragmatic terms of the social sciences might make it possible also to cast at least some of them in the form of testable hypotheses, letting the fresh air of fact into the occasionally feverish world of Schmitt scholarship. The ultimate aim would be to test whether and to what extent Schmitt's work generalizes beyond Weimar, to other times and constitutional or political systems. This is an aim that will to some degree decontextualize his work, yet it is the logical conclusion of the Schmitt specialists' efforts to broaden access to his ideas.

LEGALITY AND LEGITIMACY

Schmitt's last major work before the collapse of Weimar was *Legality and Legitimacy*, published in 1932. The work is in some respects inevitably bound to time and place; in part, Schmitt was participating in the politically fraught legal polemics of the day, particularly involving President Paul von Hindenburg's use of the emergency powers granted by Article 48 of the Weimar Constitution. In this sense, *Legality and Legitimacy* is the hardest possible test case for our aim of interpreting Schmitt in generalizable social-scientific terms. Perhaps the work is so pervasively a creature of its background circumstances that it is hopeless to try to salvage any of its ideas from the wreck of Weimar, in many respects an outlier case for constitutional democracies. Yet we think that *Legality and Legitimacy* pioneers several major insights that political scientists and lawyers interested in constitutionalism have recently begun to appreciate and explore, in most cases seemingly without any awareness of Schmitt. Although the richness of *Legality and Legitimacy* means that one is somewhat spoiled for choice, this chapter examines the connections among legality, legitimacy, and the issue of the political foundations of constitutionalism.

Schmitt begins *Legality and Legitimacy* with a new typology of regimes, intended to supersede Aristotle's threefold classification of monarchy, aristocracy, and democracy (each of which has both healthy and degenerate forms—the degenerate forms being, respectively, tyranny, oligarchy, and mob rule). In Schmitt's taxonomy, there are legislative states in which the central locus of lawmaking is a representative parliament, jurisdiction states in which the courts develop freestanding legal norms, and governmental-administrative states in which the executive or the bureaucracy issues situation-specific decrees. One of the book's main theses is that the legislative state equates legitimacy with legality, which Schmitt argues is an impoverished account of legitimacy.

The problems with this equation are twofold. First, the general norms or rules of law enacted by representative legislatures through statutes typically assume a normal, stable state of affairs in which it is possible to imagine a "closed system of legality" (Schmitt 2008a, 4) covering the whole space of possible policies. In such an environment, legality and legitimacy are largely congruent. Where the political and economic environment changes rapidly, however, exceptions to general statutes become necessary and legality and legitimacy may diverge. This is the problem of the exception, which we take up in the next section.

A related but distinct problem, however, is logically antecedent to the distinction between the norm and the exception. In the legislative or parliamentary state, there is no role for direct political action by the masses, as opposed to the peaceful procedures of representative democracy; as Schmitt puts it, "a closed system of legality grounds the claim to obedience and justifies the suspension of every right of resistance" (2008a, 4). But it is unclear, Schmitt points out, how legality by itself could causally *motivate* compliance with law, whether or not as a normative matter it *justifies* compliance with law. The legislative state "assumes away the issue of 'obedience.' . . . Schmitt avers that contemporary legality does not account for *why* authority is obeyed" (McCormick 2008, xxi).

Schmitt here is offering a critique, quite explicitly, of Max Weber's famous classification of the grounds of legitimacy. Weber distinguished three sources of legitimacy: traditional; charismatic; and rational-legal. Schmitt in effect argues that the third cannot be sufficient by itself to support the legislative state and that in fact "legality is in direct opposition to legitimacy" (Schmitt 2008a, 9). More precisely, legality is neither necessary nor sufficient for legitimacy. As Schmitt put it: "Linguistic usage today has already proceeded so far that it perceives the legal as something 'merely formal' and in opposition to the legitimate. Without a sense of contradiction, for example, one can today consider a dissolution of the *Reichstag* 'strictly legal,' even though it is, in fact, a coup d'état, and, vice versa, a parliamentary dissolution might substantively conform to the spirit of the constitution, and yet not be legal" (9–10).

Schmitt's examples here are provocative, perhaps deliberately so, and instill in liberal legalists a sense of foreboding; they tend to read Schmitt as implicitly referring to the street violence of the early 1930s and perhaps even foreshadowing the events of 1933. There is a less lurid interpretation, however, in which Schmitt is pointing to the problem of parchment barriers. As James Madison notes, in the face of widespread public sentiment, legal rules in written or convention-based constitutions may be swept away.[1] Constitutions face a pervasive commitment problem: for self-sufficient national states, there is no enforcer external to society who can police attempts to deviate from the constitutional rules (Elster 2000, 58, 94–95; Acemoglu 2003, 622–623, 638). Rational, self-interested citizens and political agents have no clear incentive to obey and enforce the law, especially when the costs of doing so are concentrated while the benefits are diffused across society. The closed system of legality in the legislative state cannot, by itself, secure the political conditions for its own enforcement; obedience to or compliance with the law needs micro-foundations in the incentives and beliefs of political actors, including voters, officials, political parties, interest groups, and social movements. In the terms of legal theory, Schmitt anticipates the point that compliance with the capital-C Constitution is shaped and constrained by lower case-c constitutionalism.

A literature in political science addresses the political foundations of constitutionalism and attempts to identify conditions under which constitutions generally, or particular constitutional structures such as elections, can become incentive-compatible or self-enforcing for rational, self-interested agents (Weingast 1997, 245–263; 2007; Fearon 2006; Przeworski 1985, 35–38; for legal applications, see Levinson 2011). In one pioneering model, an incumbent government faces two or more political actors—perhaps classes, ethnic groups, or political parties. If either cooperates with the incumbent, then those two may join forces to prey upon the other political actor. The actors must then coordinate to block predation by the incumbent, which if it occurs would benefit the incumbent but reduce overall welfare. If the two actors have Assurance Game preferences, such that cooperation is the first choice for both, then the two may resist the incumbent so long as there is a focal point that allows them to coordinate their resistance. Even if the two actors have Prisoners' Dilemma preferences, such that defection (i.e., cooperation with the incumbent) would be the dominant strategy for each in a single-shot game, cooperation to resist the incumbent is an equilibrium[2] so long as the long-run benefits of doing so are sufficiently high, neither actor discounts the future too heavily, and what counts as a cooperative move is sufficiently clear. The last proviso means that focal points have a role even in the indefinitely repeated Prisoners' Dilemma game, insofar as the would-be cooperators need to possess common knowledge about what cooperation entails.

This model focuses on agency problems; the actors' problem is to prevent welfare-reducing exploitation by the incumbent. A different but compatible class of models puts micro-foundations under constitutionalism by attempting to specify conditions under which parties, classes, or other groups will or will not have incentives to rebel against the constitutional order or instead play within the rules of the political game. These models particularly resonate with the concerns that animated legal and political theorists situated within Weimar, whose constitution teetered precariously above a whirlpool of competing political movements, some of which aimed to subvert the constitution altogether.

The basic idea of these models is to endogenize elections rather than take them for granted. In one model, elections grant the winning party control of the state, which is assumed to be an indivisible good (see Przeworski 1991, ch. 1; 2005, 253–273). The losing factions then face the choice whether to fight or to wait for the next election cycle and take the chance of winning power for themselves. If the long-run net benefit of participating in the electoral system is greater than the net expected benefit of fighting now, rather than waiting for a turn in office, then each party will have self-interested incentives to play within the rules. In this account, elections are essentially a randomizing device that gives each party an equal (or at least sufficient) expectation of taking power in the future. Just as one might divide a toy between two children through taking turns, to prevent them from fighting over it, so too the indivisible good of state power is allocated intertemporally, in expectation, through elections.

A critique of this model is that elections are inefficiently expensive if they serve as little more than randomizing devices. An alternative model thus explains elections as focal points for coordinating resistance to leaders (Fearon 2006). Whether the leaders do or do not comply with the results of elections is an easily observable public signal that provides the crucial element of common knowledge; all concerned know that others know what has occurred, and so on. Leaders are disciplined by the "rebellion constraint" (Przeworski 2003, 135), and elections have no very elevated political function but do help to make democracy in a minimalist sense (Przeworski 1999) a political equilibrium.

Finally, the relationship between mass political action and democracy is explored from another angle in a model of the expansion of the franchise in democratic polities (see Acemoglu and Robinson 2006). In this model, the threat of mass rebellion induces wealthy elites to grant a broadly democratic franchise. Given reasonable assumptions about the distribution of wealth, a broad franchise ensures that the median voter will favor redistributive measures, so democratization in effect allows elites to commit to future redistribution. This model assumes that a commitment to an expanded franchise is credible, whereas a simple elite promise to enact redistributive policies would not be. However, this is hardly obvious; if mass rebellion is costly so that elites can simply renege on their promises to enact first-order redistributive measures, then perhaps elites can also renege on the grant of an expanded franchise (Fearon 2006). Yet violations of the franchise and of the results of elections may be more visible, and thus less costly for mass publics to monitor, than elite incumbents' undermining of redistributive policies. Here too, the relative clarity of electoral rules makes their violation a useful focal point for coordinating mass uprising against exploitative incumbents.

In Schmittian terms, models of the political foundations of constitutionalism both offer an account of legitimacy and connect legitimacy to constitutional legality. All the models interpret legitimacy as a game-theoretic equilibrium: a constitution is legitimate when it has micro-foundations in the preferences, beliefs, and choices of relevant actors, none of whom can do better by unilateral attempts to subvert the constitutional order. Legality by itself is insufficient to create legitimacy in this sense; writing a constitution on a piece of paper, by itself, does nothing to make the constitution incentive-compatible. Yet legality can play an indirect role in securing legitimacy as equilibrium: a written constitution or clearly defined constitutional conventions[3] may establish focal points that enable political actors to coordinate on action, including mass resistance or rebellion. In a sense, then, these models help to answer the question Schmitt posed to Weber, about what exactly legality has to do with legitimacy and what exactly grounds obedience to the legislative rule-of-law state.

Ironically, this answer may after all be compatible with Weber's views. Although Weber can be read to suggest that legality is itself a form of legitimacy, another reading is that, in Schmitt's paraphrase of Weber, "the most widely prominent form of legitimacy today is the *belief* in legality" (2008a, 9; emphasis added).[4] If the key point is public belief in legality, rather than legality as judged by the expert analyst, then we are not so far either from later sociological accounts of legitimacy in the jurisprudence of H. L. A. Hart (1961) or from the equilibrium accounts of the political foundations of constitutionalism that we have reviewed. In the latter accounts, public belief in legality is crucial; what matters is whether governmental violation of a clear constitutional rule, such as holding elections and respecting their results, becomes common knowledge among the public. In this sense, we may see *Legality and Legitimacy* as situated within a theoretical stream that runs from Weber all the way to the contemporary political science of constitutionalism. Within this stream, Schmitt has the honor of reviving Madison's critical question about parchment barriers—about why constitutional rules, written or indeed unwritten, have any causal efficacy in politics—and using the vivid context of Weimar, in which the political foundations of constitutionalism were patently problematic to put the question in its sharpest possible form.

Finally, the models of the political foundations of constitutionalism allow a demystifying and less ominous interpretation of Schmitt's insistence that the public's role under constitutionalism is in effect restricted to negative measures—either rejection of proposals in a referendum or, in extreme cases, resistance to the ruling power (Schmitt 2008a, 29–31, 87–90). In the models we have canvassed, political groups exert influence on incumbents and competitors for powers not through persuasion or democratic deliberation but through credible threats of resistance or armed conflict. In the lurid context of Weimar these ideas call up associations with torchlight rallies and thuggish street violence—soccer-stadium democracy—but this is to overlook that a credible threat of mass public resistance to exploitative action by incumbents can be necessary for the health of constitutionalism and democratic institutions. As Schmitt puts it, "the ancient problem of 'resistance against the tyrant' remains, that is, resistance against injustice and misuse of state power, and the functionalistic-formalistic hollowing out of the parliamentary legislative state is not able to resolve it" (29). Here, too, Schmitt's distinction between legality and legitimacy opens up a way of thinking about constitutionalism that proves more fruitful, because more politically realistic, than liberalism, which insists that legitimacy can straightforwardly be reduced to legality.

RULES, STANDARDS, AND EXECUTIVE PRIMACY

Schmitt famously declared that "sovereign is he who decides on the exception" (1985a, 5). This enigmatic statement, which underlies his critical view of parliamentary democracy, is related to two themes of American jurisprudence: the distinction between rules and standards; and the limits on executive power.

Let us begin with rules and standards. Schmitt did not use the modern law-and-economics argot, but his argument that legislatures cannot enact into law general rules that adequately guide and constrain executives during crises can be put into the modern idiom.[5] In law and economics, a rule is a norm that is specified in advance of the conduct that it regulates. A standard is a norm that is applied retroactively to conduct that has already occurred. For example, a simple traffic rule—speed limit of 60 miles per hour— is determined in advance and then is applied to drivers. The tort standard—drive with due care—does not specify in advance the speed or other attribute of driving behavior that will be sanctioned. A police officer or court will determine whether a driver has acted with due care on the spot or afterward. The legislature that enacts a standard puts off the determination of the norm by delegating that function to an enforcement agent or court.

To enact a sensible rule, the decision-maker must invest resources in predicting the future and evaluating future behavior. This investment is the cost of using rules. One does not incur this cost with standards because they are applied after the behavior has occurred. The benefit of using rules is that they render predictable the legal consequences of one's actions, enabling people to plan and deterring them from socially harmful behavior. By contrast, because standards are vague, decision-makers will have difficulties implementing them consistently and individuals will have a hard time predicting the legal consequences of their actions. Thus, it is better to use rules when the behavior in question recurs frequently and predictably—when the behavior is the norm (see Kaplow 1992, 557–629). The investment in determining the optimal rule is spread over a large set of actions. When a particular action does not recur frequently and predictably—when it is the exception—decision-making should be deferred until the action occurs, that is, a standard should be used.

It should be clear that law by standards is nearly the same as retroactive determination of law. The difference is that the standard is specified in advance, ruling out at least some behavior. The due care standard, for example, rules out a subsequent determination that driving at 150 miles per hour is lawful. Standards can be more or less specific; the more specific, the more they resemble a rule. Indeed, the choice between rules and standards is not binary; a perfectly specified rule and an extremely vague standard lie at the end of a spectrum, and all legal norms lie in between. Although we will continue to refer to rules and standards as ideal types, the continuous nature of this variable should be kept in mind.

The U.S. Congress enacts both rules (e.g., the Tax Code) and standards (e.g., antitrust law). Even highly complex rules, however, have pockets of vagueness—standards—that are left to courts to work out over time. And vague statutes gradually resolve themselves into sets of rules as judicial interpretations accumulate and form precedent. The same dynamic processes are familiar from the common law. In the bloodless language of law and economics, rules and standards reflect trade-offs, and it is not surprising, indeed it is predictable, that certain areas of the law are dominated by rules while other areas of the law are dominated by standards.

From this perspective, the subversive reputation of Schmitt's work on sovereignty might seem hard to understand. To understand why Schmitt's work is in fact radical, one should recall that lawyers who discuss rules and standards almost always do so in the context of the common law. When a legislature enacts a standard, it expects courts to interpret it in the course of resolving disputes between litigants. Judges are expected to be impartial, and various rules ensure that they usually are. Trial judges are monitored by appellate courts, and judicial decisions, while important for the litigants, do not have larger, systemic effects unless other judges in other courts find them persuasive. As judges decide cases, the vague standards gradually take on content and resolve into rules of varying specificity. Legislatures can intervene and overturn opinions that run counter to the original purposes of the statutes that are being interpreted. In interpreting statutes, and in other forms of common law development, judges in this way engage in retroactive lawmaking but of a type that is gradual and relatively predictable, that is subject to legislative veto, and hence that does not offend the rule of law.

Now consider the setting that interested Schmitt: the role of the executive. To understand Schmitt's argument, we need to introduce another concept from economics—agency costs. An agency relationship consists of two people: a principal and an agent (for a textbook treatment, see Laffont and Martimort 2001).[6] In the simplest models, the agent takes some action that benefits or harms the principal, and then the principal rewards or punishes the agent. For example, an employer (the principal) will reward a worker (the agent) with a high wage if the agent produces a high level of output and will sanction the worker with a low wage or some other penalty if the agent produces a low level of output.

In the standard agency model, the agent's level of effort stochastically determines the level of output. A high level of effort is more likely to produce a high level of output, but luck may intervene so that high effort leads to low output or low effort leads to high output. If the principal can observe the level of effort, the optimal contract simply rewards the agent who uses high effort and punishes the agent who uses low effort. But the model assumes that the principal cannot directly observe effort and can observe only output. Thus, a contract that rewards high output may inadvertently punish the high-effort worker who experiences bad luck. Nonetheless, the principal can spur a worker to high effort only by rewarding him for high output. If the worker is risk-averse, the principal may blunt the incentive somewhat, reducing the payoff slightly when output is high and increasing the payoff when output is low but maintaining a difference between them.

This model has been applied to political institutions (e.g., Besley 2007) and indeed is implicit in Madison's theory of separation of powers. Madison and the other founders feared an unconstrained government. Most of the direct power to do harm (as well as good) lay with the executive, who commands the troops. The executive is the agent; the people are the principal. The challenge was to design a constitution that gave the executive the power to govern while aligning his interests with those of the people.

Simplifying greatly, the original solution combined elections and separation of powers. The people elect (directly or indirectly) members of Congress who deliberate and determine policy, which is embodied in law. The president—also (indirectly) elected by the people—merely executes the law determined by Congress. The courts ensure that the president executes the law in good faith. The people reward the president who faithfully executes the law by reelecting him, and punishes the president who does not by ejecting him from office. The public also uses elections to select among candidates the one who seems most likely to take the rule of law seriously. Electoral mechanisms similarly discipline Congress. The overall picture is one where the people elect two agents—the president and Congress—and uses one of the agents (Congress) to help control the other (the president).

Madison's theory rested on a key assumption about legislative-executive relations that Schmitt clearly saw, in a different historical setting, but that has been mostly neglected by modern scholars. To control the president, Congress must enact law in the form of rules, not standards. Rules can constrain the president by making it clear in advance what he may do and not do; this makes it easy for Congress, the courts, and the people to determine later whether the president has complied with or broken the law. Standards cannot constrain the president, or at least not as well.

Consider a recent example. After 9/11, Congress enacted the Authorization for Use of Military Force (AUMF), which enabled the president to "use all necessary and appropriate force against those nations, organizations, or persons he determines planned, authorized, committed, or aided the terrorist attacks that occurred on September 11, 2001, or harbored such organizations or persons, in order to prevent any future acts of international terrorism against the United States by such nations, organizations or persons."[7] The president was also subject to a number of existing statutes, such as the Foreign Intelligence Surveillance Act (FISA) and federal statute prohibiting torture. The AUMF created a standard governing the deployment of forces against terrorist threats. Policy questions such as how much force to use, against whom, and where, were left to the president to answer. As a result, when the president expanded the "War on Terror" to Pakistan, no one could argue that the president had broken the law, whatever the merits of this decision as a matter of policy. By contrast, the wiretapping and interrogation

policies adopted by the George W. Bush Administration more clearly violated the relatively specific rules in FISA and the anti-torture statute.

Schmitt believed that constitution-writing assemblies and legislatures cannot enact
substantive laws that govern the executive during emergencies; the most the rule-maker
can specify in advance is who will exercise emergency powers (1985a, 7). The argument
falls out of the rules/standards analysis. Emergencies are, by their nature, unique and
costly or impossible to anticipate. Every threat to the nation is different. If emergencies
are unique, then their features cannot be predicted on the basis of the past, which means
that legislatures will not be able to use rules to govern the executive's behavior during
them. The cost of predicting the nature of the next security threat is too high, and given
their busy agendas, legislatures have little motivation to invest the resources in trying to
predict the future. Instead of enacting rules that govern the executive during emergencies, legislatures enact standards, in effect delegating to the executive the power to take
aggressive actions to defend the nation under ill-defined conditions and subject to ill-
defined constraints. In the United States, most emergency legislation takes the forms of
standards, and it exists alongside a constitutional understanding that the executive has
the primary responsibility for fending off foreign attacks and addressing other threats
and may draw on military and law enforcement resources to do so.

If Congress cannot regulate in advance of emergencies, might it not be able to regulate
once the emergency begins? The problem is that in the early stages of the emergency,
the legislature is hampered by its many-headed structure. Large bodies of people deliberate and act slowly (unless they act as mobs). The best that the legislature can do is
ratify the executive's actions by blessing it with a retroactive authorization or call a halt
to the executive's response by defunding it. As the emergency matures, the legislature
continues to be hampered. Crises unfold in an unpredictable fashion; secrecy will be at
a premium. Public deliberation compromises secrecy; the unpredictability of the threat
eliminates the value of lawmaking. The legislature's role in the emergency is marginal.
It can grant or withhold political support; and it can legislate along the margins. The
legislature may be able to undermine the executive response by defunding it, but it will
rarely do so because some response is always better than none. The problem for the legislature is that it cannot make policy in a fine-grained way; its choice—broad support
or none at all—is no choice at all. Anticipating a body of literature in positive political theory, Schmitt noted that "the extraordinary lawmaker [i.e., the President of the
Reich] can create accomplished facts in opposition to the ordinary legislature. Indeed,
especially consequential measures, for example, armed interventions and executions,
can, in fact, no longer be 'set aside' " (2008a, 69–70; internal quotation marks omitted).
The president's first-mover role—the "presidential power of unilateral action" (Moe and
Howell 1999, 132–179; see also Howell 2003, 24–55)—implies that he can create a new
status quo that constrains Congress' subsequent response, both in practical terms and
because the president can use his veto powers to block legislative attempts to restore the
status quo ante.

Courts face similar problems. Detailed statutes enacted before the emergency will
seem antiquated and inapt. Courts will feel pressure to interpret them loosely or use

procedural obstacles to avoid their application. For this reason, violations of FISA and the Anti-Torture Act never led to prosecutions. Vague statutes enacted before and after the emergency provide no rule of decision, and courts are reluctant to substitute their views about policy for those of the executive, which has far more expertise and resources. Commentators have urged courts to use constitutional norms or even international law to control the executive, but these norms also prove to be ambiguous standards rather than clear-cut rules. To apply such standards, courts would have to engage in judicial policymaking. But judges do not believe that they have the information or expertise to make policy during emergencies and so they have seldom taken this approach.

The upshot is that the Madisonian theory is a poor description of how modern democratic governments operate during emergencies and in anticipation of emergencies. Congress cannot realistically enact rules in advance, and cannot commit to enforce them if violated, so the policymaking authority during emergencies rests with the executive. Indeed, because the executive has responsibility for protecting the country during emergencies, only the executive has motivation to prepare for emergencies, which it does by putting into place institutions and agencies, and the legal authority on which they will rely. It is the executive that has constructed the national security state; Congress has mostly ratified the policies adopted by a series of presidents. Congress retains a very crude veto power; it can interfere with executive policymaking during emergencies only by withdrawing funds and, in effect, calling the emergency off. But Congress is highly constrained by the nature of the threat and can use this blunt instrument only in extreme circumstances. The current system, then, is better described as one of executive primacy than separation of powers. The president makes and executes policy subject to weak vetoes by Congress and the courts, which can be exercised only after the president has committed the country to a response to the perceived threat. Hence, the veto threats have little practical effect.

Although Schmitt saw clearly that the conditions of modern politics and the administrative state tended to generate a plebiscitary executive (2008a, 88–91), he went astray by arguing that such a system would eventually result in a Caesarist form of democracy by acclamation (1985b, 16–17). Electoral institutions remain an effective means to control the executive. Recall that the agency model requires that the principal must observe output (payoffs) and reward or punish the agent accordingly. In the United States, the public observes the output—security or no security—and holds the executive responsible. Democracy, albeit of a limited sort, continues to work. Schmitt believed that an executive with the power to declare emergencies and dictate policy during emergencies could use the same power to undermine electoral institutions, the press, and other checks. But that has not happened in the U.S. Abraham Lincoln, who enjoyed near-dictatorial powers, submitted to an election in 1864, as did Franklin Roosevelt in 1944. Perhaps it has not happened because of luck, but for the time being it does seem likely that the public would repudiate any president who used an emergency as an excuse for attacking democratic institutions. Indeed, it seems unlikely that his subordinates in the government would cooperate with him (see also Posner and Vermeule 2010).

Lincoln famously asked, "[a]re all the laws, *but one*, to go unexecuted, and the government itself go to pieces, lest that one be violated?" (1953, 430). Schmitt took a similar view, arguing that during an emergency a commissarial dictator must violate existing laws to save the state (see Schmitt 1921). This idea follows from the problem with rules: that they cannot provide adequate guidance for unique situations. If the legislature nonetheless enacts rules for emergencies, or general rules that lack exceptions for emergencies, the executive must be willing to violate them to save the nation. However alarming this proposition might seem, it follows from a standard notion in the law: the rule interpreter must enforce the purpose behind the rule when enforcement of the literal terms of the rule itself would have bad consequences. This notion is termed *purposivism* and, in the U.S., is associated with the *legal-process* approach to interpretation (see Hart and Sacks 2001). In this sense, Schmitt can be understood as a legal process or purposivist interpreter, writ very large. What is different in the emergency case is that the stakes are higher and that the executive rather than the courts takes primary responsibility for interpreting the rule. But there should be no great mystery about Schmitt's argument for executive primacy, which is perfectly straightforward—whether or not correct—when read in light of the modern distinction between rules and standards.

CONCLUSION

In a recent study of Tocqueville's thought, Jon Elster asks whether he has any "exportable" ideas of utility to the social sciences (2009, 9). Our question about Schmitt is similar. Intellectual historians and political theorists, whose disciplines weigh heavily any accusation that ideas have been ripped out of historical context, have done too little to mine from Schmitt's time- and place-bound writings a trove of ideas that may be useful in other times and places. We have attempted to indicate some of the directions in which profitable mining might occur and some of the areas of law and social science to which the resulting intellectual resources might be exported.

In short, Schmitt offers two major insights, which are in a certain sense the same insight. The first is a crucial distinction between legality and legitimacy and an analysis of the political conditions under which legality and legitimacy diverge. That analysis challenges simple versions of liberal legalism, challenges simple versions of the Weberian analysis of rational-legal authority, and connects constitutional theory with recent work in political economy and political science on the equilibrium foundations of constitutionalism.

The second insight is a crucial distinction between the norm and the exception, which underpins Schmitt's famous analysis of sovereignty. From our standpoint, however, many historians and theorists, fascinated by the conceptual foundations of Schmitt's analysis, have wasted their energies in sterile debates over sovereignty. They have failed to realize that in good pragmatic fashion Schmitt's insight is capable of standing on its own, even if its analytic foundations are obscure or infirm. The distinction between the norm and the exception was a pioneering claim about the role of rules and standards in constitutional emergencies and constitutionalism more generally. Emergencies just are situations in which constitutional governance by ex ante rules becomes increasingly costly, and in the extreme impossible. It is a liberal-legalist fantasy to think that constitutionalism can fully specify, ex ante, what should be done in emergencies or even who will decide what should be done in emergencies; the uniqueness of emergencies always threatens to render obsolete or irrelevant not only substantive policies but also even the procedural and institutional framework set up to regulate future policymaking.

From the lawyer's perspective, this generalizes to the macro-level of the constitutional regime as a whole a well-known insight within the legal system, about unanticipated cases and the inevitable limits of foresight on the part of lawmakers. Lawyers and judges engage in purposive, discretion-saturated interpretation of legal texts when unanticipated cases make the surface meaning of those texts inapposite, unworkable, or obsolete. Schmittian commissarial dictatorship is just the purposive approach to legal interpretation, writ very large and applied to the constitution as a whole.

These two main Schmittian insights, about legality and legitimacy on one hand and about constitutional rules and standards on the other, are really conjoined twins. In the ordinary case, the normal situation anticipated ex ante by the rules of a settled liberal constitutional and legal regime, legality and legitimacy are congruent. They diverge when exceptional circumstances—unique and unanticipated—overthrow normal routines and require new decisions that will inevitably have more or less of an ad hoc, all-things-considered character. Schmitt's insight—a great insight, fertile with collateral ideas and problems—was that liberal constitutionalism presupposes a certain type of stable political environment. The destabilization of Schmitt's own political environment laid the presupposition bare.

There is nothing mystical about that insight, however great it was. Schmitt's faintly ominous and deeply dramatized prose style, apparent even in translation; the continental conceptualisms that adorn his work; and the dark circumstances in which many of his most famous works were composed all conspire to throw an aura of mystery and profundity around what are ultimately straightforward, intelligible, and useful claims about the politics of liberal constitutionalism. A demystified version of Schmitt will extract the ore from his work, discard the tailings, and export what is useful to other sectors of the social sciences.

ACKNOWLEDGMENTS

We are grateful to Rachel Siegel for her research assistance.

Notes

1. Madison, J. (1961): "Will it be sufficient to mark, with precision, the boundaries of these departments, in the constitution of the government, and to trust to these parchment barriers against the encroaching spirit of power?... A mere demarcation on parchment of the constitutional limits of the several departments, is not a sufficient guard against those encroachments which lead to a tyrannical concentration of all the powers of government in the same hands." See also Madison, J. (1958): "[e]xperience proves the inefficacy of a bill of rights on those occasions when its controul is most needed. Repeated violations of these parchment barriers have been committed by overbearing majorities in every State. In Virginia I have seen the bill of rights violated in every instance where it has been opposed to a popular current."

2. By virtue of the folk theorem, noncooperation is also an equilibrium.

3. Conventions in the sense of norms, not assemblies.

4. Although the exact quote does not appear in Weber, the point is consistent with Weber's views. See the translator's note (126 n14).

5. Schmitt's views on the limits of parliamentary democracy can be found in Schmitt 1985b, among other places. This aspect of his thought, and its relationship to modern jurisprudential debates, is lucidly described in Scheuerman 2004 (124).

6. *Authorization for Use of Military Force Against Terrorists*, Pub.L. 107–40, 115 Stat. 224, §2(a).

7. We thank Fred Schauer for this point.

References

Acemoglu, D. 2003. "Why Not a Political Coase Theorem? Social Conflict, Commitment, and Politics." *Journal of Comparative Economics* 31: 620–652.

Acemoglu, D., and J. A. Robinson. 2006. *Economic Origins of Dictatorship and Democracy.* Cambridge: Cambridge University Press.

Besley, T. 2007. *Principled Agents? The Political Economy of Good Government.* Oxford: Oxford University Press.

Elster, J. 2000. *Ulysses Unbound: Studies in Rationality, Precommitment, and Constraints.* Cambridge: Cambridge University Press.

Elster, J. 2009. *Alexis de Tocqueville: The First Social Scientist.* Cambridge: Cambridge University Press.

Fearon, J. D. 2006. "Self-Enforcing Democracy." Paper presented at the 2006 Annual Meetings of the American Political Science Association, Philadelphia, PA, August 31–September 3.

Hart, H. L. A. 1961. *The Concept of Law.* Oxford: Clarendon Press.

Hart, H. L. A., and A. M. Sacks. 2001. *The Legal Process: Basic Problems in the Making and Application of Law*, ed. W. N. Eskridge Jr. and P. P. Frickey. New York: Foundation Press.

Holmes, S. 1993. *The Anatomy of Antiliberalism.* Cambridge: Harvard University Press.

Howell, H. G. 2003. *Power Without Persuasion: The Politics of Direct Presidential Action.* Princeton: Princeton University Press.

Kaplow, L. 1992. "Rules versus Standards: An Economic Analysis." *Duke Law Journal* 42: 557–629.

Kennedy, E. 2004. *Constitutional Failure: Carl Schmitt in Weimar.* Durham: Duke University Press.

Laffont, J.-J., and D. Martimort. 2001. *The Theory of Incentives: The Principal-Agent Model.* Princeton: Princeton University Press.

Levinson, D. 2011. "Parchment and Politics: The Positive Puzzle of Constitutional Commitment." *Harvard Law Review* 124: 657–746.

Lincoln, A. 1953. "Message to Congress in Special Session (July 4, 1861)." Reprinted in *Collected Works of Abraham Lincoln*, vol. 4, ed. R. P. Basler. New Brunswick: Rutgers University Press, 421–441.

Madison, J. 1961. "Federalist Papers Number 48: The Separation of Powers: II." Reprinted in *The Federalist by Alexander Hamilton, James Madison, and John Jay*, ed. B. F. Wright. Cambridge: Belknap Press of Harvard University Press, 343–347.

Madison, J. 1958. "Letter to Thomas Jefferson, October 17, 1788." Reprinted in *The Papers of Thomas Jefferson*, vol. 14, ed. J. P. Boyd. Princeton: Princeton University Press, 16–22.

McCormick, J. P. 1997. *Carl Schmitt's Critique of Liberalism: Against Politics as Technology.* Cambridge: Cambridge University Press.

McCormick, J. P. 2008. "Identifying or Exploiting the Paradoxes of Constitutional Democracy? An Introduction to Carl Schmitt's *Legality and Legitimacy*." In Schmitt 2008a, xiii–xliii.

Moe, T. M., and W. G. Howell. 1999. "The Presidential Power of Unilateral Action." *Journal of Law, Economics, and Organization* 15: 132–179.

Posner, E. A., and A. Vermeule. 2010. *The Executive Unbound: After the Madisonian Republic.* Oxford: Oxford University Press.

Przeworski, A. 1985. *Capitalism and Social Democracy.* Cambridge: Cambridge University Press.

Przeworski, A. 1991. *Democracy and the Market: Political and Economic Reforms in Eastern Europe and Latin America.* Cambridge: Cambridge University Press.

Przeworski, A. 1999. "Minimalist Conception of Democracy: A Defense." In *Democracy's Value*, ed. I. Shapiro and C. Hacker-Cordón. Cambridge: Cambridge University Press, 23–55.

Przeworski, A. 2003. "Why Do Political Parties Obey Results of Elections?" In *Democracy and the Rule of Law*, ed. A. Przeworski and J. M. Maravall. Cambridge: Cambridge University Press, 114–146.

Przeworski, A. 2005. "Democracy as an Equilibrium." *Public Choice* 123: 253–273.

Scheuerman, W. E. 1999. *Carl Schmitt: The End of Law.* Lanham: Rowman & Littlefield.

Scheuerman, W. E. 2004. *Liberal Democracy and the Social Acceleration of Time.* Baltimore: Johns Hopkins University Press.

Schmitt, C. 1921. *Die Diktatur.* Munich: Duncker & Humblot.

Schmitt, C. 1985a. *Political Theology*, trans. G. Schwab. Chicago: University of Chicago Press.

Schmitt, C. 1985b. *The Crisis of Parliamentary Democracy*, trans. E. Kennedy. Cambridge: MIT Press.

Schmitt, C. 2008a. *Legality and Legitimacy*, trans. and ed. J. Seitzer. Durham: Duke University Press.

Schmitt, C. 2008b. *Constitutional Theory*, trans. and ed. J. Seitzer. Durham: Duke University Press.

Weingast, B. R. 1997. "Political Foundations of Democracy and the Rule of Law." *American Political Science Review* 91: 245–263.

Weingast, B. R. 2007. "Self-Enforcing Constitutions: With an Application to Democratic Stability in America's First Century." Working Paper, Stanford: Hoover Institution, September.

PART V

THE CULTURAL
THOUGHT OF
CARL SCHMITT

CHAPTER 24

CARL SCHMITT AND MODERNITY

FRIEDRICH BALKE

INTRODUCTION

CARL SCHMITT's political and juridical thought is anchored in a specific diagnosis of modernity, which he describes at different points in his work. He develops the concept of the political to which his name is so famously connected because of how the location and address of the political become fundamentally questionable under modern conditions. The "modern" for Schmitt denotes that social and cultural situation in which the equation "state = politics" (Schmitt 2007a, 22) no longer holds. Modernity is characterized by the potential to politicize all social and cultural matters, so that the "total state" of the twentieth century proves to be the logical realization of the "identity of state and society" (22). The nineteenth-century liberal state knew "neutral" territories (religion, culture, education, economy), whereas in the era of the political, the state might seize any territory because it deems that "everything is at least potentially political." This is the reason that a reference to the state can no longer "assert for it a specifically political characteristic" (22). This fundamentally comprehensive jurisdiction of the "interventionist" state correlates with a characteristically modern critique of the former transcendence of the state. In contrast to Hegel's political philosophy, for Schmitt the state is no longer regarded as "qualitatively distinct from society and higher than it" (24).

In the 1920s Schmitt had found in Roman Catholicism an intellectual-historical alternative to the "methodology of the natural-technical sciences" (1996, 12). It was able to overrule a modernity no longer guided by last purposes and goals. The power of juridical rationalism lies in its ability to convert even the most ecstatic experiences, which are made possible by religion and were exploited by Romantic art, into an *institutional form*. Only shortly thereafter, Schmitt's *The Concept of the Political* dispenses with any anchoring of the political in an "idea" in favor of its definition as "the utmost degree of intensity of a union or separation" (2007a, 26). The political, understood as "the utmost degree of intensity," is no longer accessible to an institutional bracketing or juridical relativism, which is why the state forfeits the "monopoly on politics" (22).

The fact that the location and address of the political become suspect under the conditions of modernity reflects the famous formula of *Political Theology*, which insists on the necessity of a sovereign decision regarding the state of exception, although the precise subject of this decision and its institutional context are not specified. Despite its name, Schmitt's *Political Theology* does not take advantage of the abundance of ecclesiastical concepts to reassign them to the new territorial state and thereby increase its rank. This is the classic case of political theology investigated by Ernst Kantorowicz. For Schmitt, the political participates instead in a particular modern anomie, insofar as it develops under conditions that make *every* political form appear questionable. Schmitt understands modernity as an epoch in which all "classical distinctions" (12) made possible by the state as a "model of political unity" become obsolete (10). For this reason, Schmitt's diagnosis of the crisis of modernity is simply stated: "The epoch of statehood is now at an end. There is nothing more to say about that" (10). Because the institutional end to the epoch of statehood also calls into question state semantics, a teacher of constitutional law faces the problem of how to speak about politics at all after the end of the state, not to mention how to do this with juridical precision and authority. This paradox, characteristic of the jurist's discursive position, leads Schmitt to conclude that on the one hand, the end of the state brings "the whole superstructure of state-oriented concepts to an end" as well, but on the other hand, these concepts, which have lost their institutional foothold, are kept as "*classical* concepts," since a convincing alternative vocabulary is not available (10). The teacher of constitutional law must therefore use terms the classicism of which no longer guarantees their scientific validity. Schmitt expresses this teacher's difficult position in a way that marks the motivation behind his interest in Romanticism more generally and political romanticism in particular: "Of course today the word *classical* usually sounds equivocal and ambivalent, not to mention ironic" (10).

This knowledge of the untenability of classical concepts is what Schmitt derives from Romanticism. He understands Romanticism as the spearhead of a cultural movement that is not limited to the realms of literature and art. Irony is a central concept for early Romantic poetics, which accounts for the characteristic problem of modernity as a whole, namely how one should deal with a surviving set of concepts the validity of which has become suspect, but for which no fundamental alternative is available. It is therefore no coincidence that in the history of Schmitt's work, his early legal texts are flanked by literary and semiliterary works. Nor is it coincidental that his *Political Romanticism* identifies the rampant "general process of aestheticizing" (1986, 16) and privatization of Romanticism as the cardinal challenge for a concept of the political that is able to survive against the discursive and institutional amorphousness of modernity.

When Schmitt defines Romanticism as an "art without publicity and without representation" (1986, 15), he is at the same time naming publicity and representation as two central concepts for the establishment of *political* form, which likewise faced a crisis in the era of Romanticism. The idea that Romanticism produces deficient art, namely art "without works" (15), need not unsettle a jurist, except that he sees this widespread aestheticization of modern environments as an expression of resistance against "grand form" and "representation" more generally. This would fundamentally undermine the institution's claim to authoritatively shape human life (*vitam instituere*). In 1923 Schmitt could still write that "Catholicism is eminently political" and thereby confront it with every "economical thinking" (1996, 16) that he claimed was completely losing "a conviction about what is moral or lawful" (18). In *Roman Catholicism and Political Form*, Schmitt's second comprehensive diagnosis of modernity after *Political Romanticism*, he nostalgically refers to the medieval "ability to create representative figures—the pope, the emperor, the monk, the knight, the merchant." At the same time he inserts the Catholic Church as the "sole surviving contemporary example" into a series of institutions, namely the "House of Lords, the Prussian General Staff, the Académie Française, and the Vatican," that share a "superiority over an age of economic thinking" that lies in "the idea of representation" (19). Yet this is only a retrospective observation, from which Schmitt concludes that a *contemporary* concept of the political need not be dependent on representation any longer. *Political Romanticism* already contains his actual diagnosis of the crisis of modernity: "all ecclesiastical and state institutions and forms, all legal concepts and arguments, everything that is official, and even democracy itself since the time it assumed a constitutional form are perceived as empty and deceptive disguises, as a veil, a façade, a fake, or a decoration" (1986, 14). Romanticism disempowers the state, the government, and all political-public structures and processes, turning them into mere "scenery" or simulacrums that hide an actual or substantial reality. With this, it marks that critical moment of modernity at which the political withdraws from its "space of appearance" (Arendt 1998, 199–207). It instead becomes a space of action for indirect forces that operate in a realm cut off from the public sector and according to criteria that are guaranteed only by the adequacy or effectiveness of its own measures.

For this reason, the following considerations are not limited to a portrayal of this "Romantic-occasionalist" structure of the political around which Schmitt's thinking revolves. Instead, they start from the premise that what Schmitt called the "confused intermediate situation between form and formlessness" has left traces in various sociological, political, and cultural diagnoses of modernity, thereby raising questions that continue in the present day to "contain within themselves a real challenge" (Schmitt 1963, 12):

- With the theory of social systems developed by Niklas Luhmann, it becomes clear that the occasionalist structure of the Romantic denotes a basic requirement of modern communication standards. The communication that evades unilateral control prevents modern societies from finding their "own form," which also eliminates the possibility of their comprehensive and universally binding representation. Modern politics must operate under the condition of incomplete knowledge about its environment, which includes very different social spheres of activities, each with its own individual dynamics. It therefore no longer makes sense to recognize the state as "qualitatively distinct from" and "something higher" than society. The political can no longer align itself in polemical opposition to allegedly apolitical areas, because it must accept that essentially all problems that cannot be solved by other social systems will be transferred onto it. Systems theory thereby describes the aporias of that which Schmitt referred to in the 1920s as the "quantitative total state" (Schmitt 1958, 364), which cannot refuse to accept the increasing number of problems pushed toward it, but which at the same time must frustrate the expectation that it actually has the potential to effectively overcome these problems.[1]

- Modernity is not, however, only characterized by continually increasing expectations of the political system, which have led to the well-known symptoms of excessive demand on the welfare state. In various contexts, Michel Foucault, Giorgio Agamben, Judith Butler, and Zygmunt Bauman have pointed to the problem of the state of exception, which is characteristic of modernity on the whole, as a "paradigm of government" (Agamben 2005, 2). They have thus explicitly or implicitly followed Schmitt in revealing the continued efficacy of the mechanisms and effects of sovereign power under the conditions of post-totalitarian, constitutionally organized political systems. These authors are all the more indispensable for the determination of the relationship of Schmitt's political thought to modernity, insofar as they block the more comfortable path of engagement with Schmitt, which has been taken by large parts of the "exorcistic" Schmitt research. In this research, Schmitt is prematurely and far too exclusively defined by his role as an "awful jurist" who, as the gravedigger of the Weimar Constitution and crown jurist of the "Third Reich," is not of any immediate importance for our present constitutional age. The following considerations develop the central motif of the state of exception as a paradigm of government that has accompanied modern politics since the development of the state and throughout its changes in form in the twentieth century. Schmitt deserves our interest not only because of his important contribution to a still outstanding "theory of the state of exception in public law", but also because he described, as no other jurist has, the undercutting of the legislative and jurisdictional sphere through the expansion of executive power and the "indeterminate legal concepts" used for this purpose. This was doubtless done from a legitimizing perspective, yet one that need not be adopted by the reader interested in an analysis of the forms that lead a constitutional state to deem that a specific situation entitles it to make an exception in legal provisions.

- In the context of early modern government practices and theories of state, Walter Benjamin and Michel Foucault describe a no longer theologically oriented politics that operates immanently and self-referentially. For this politics, the task of the state consists exclusively in maintaining by means of extreme measures a particular political "status," which is threatened by turmoil and revolts. These are the circumstances that led Schmitt to coin the phrase "all law is 'situational law'" (2005, 13). Benjamin's studies of the concept of sovereignty in the baroque tragic drama and Foucault's analyses of modern reason of state are in accordance with one another on another point that is decisive for Schmitt's concept of the political—namely, that the modern state has not entirely left behind its origins in civil war, that is, in the most intense degree of separation between friend and foe. This is true even subsequent to its institutional formation, so that the state's relationship to the eventuality of a state of exception and to the necessity of sovereign "concrete actions" ("*Tathandlungen*") is indissoluble.

- Judith Butler, on the other hand, tries to determine the specific signature of a contemporary sovereignty by analyzing the mechanisms and functions of "governmental sovereignty." She does so in accordance with Schmitt's finding on the erosion of vertical topography, which assigned the sovereign state a preeminent position at the peak of the social order. This governmental sovereignty compensates for its loss of transcendence and visibility through its entrenchment in subaltern, bureaucratic decision-making bodies, which are explicitly removed from public surveillance and juridical review. Following Butler's considerations, one can see that the incorporation of an apocryphal sovereign authority into the order of the constitutional state should not be marginalized as a system error, but is rather already established in the founding documents of political liberalism. Correspondingly, it is no coincidence that following the events of September 11, 2001, the United States in particular resorted to John Locke's theory of executive prerogative to justify extralegal security forces.

- The degree to which Schmitt was preoccupied with modern bureaucratic administration as "domination through knowledge" (Weber 2013, 225), affected the exercise of political power is revealed using the example of his early "historico-philosophical essay." In this work, which appeared under the title "The Buribunks," Schmitt (1918) describes individuality as the mission and target of a new power economy. The decisive mutation in the field of power techniques that Foucault would later investigate under the term biopolitics was the object of Schmitt's satirical observation. In the "Buribunks," the enforcement of constant recording of life (of individuals and the population: *omnes et singulatim*) takes on the form of a dystopia. In this dystopia, authority refrains from all forms of theatrical self-display and assumes only a language of "observation and neutrality" in order to allow the "lower depths of social existence" that it had ignored for the longest time to appear (Foucault 1994, 172).

- With the increasing antisemitism of his newly domestically oriented distinction between friend and foe after 1933, Schmitt draws the most extreme conclusion possible from the situation of the discursive and institutional formlessness of modernity diagnosed in *Political Romanticism*. Bauman, in *Modernity and the Holocaust* (1989) and *Modernity and Ambivalence* (1991), describes a particular dialectic of order and definiteness that is characteristic for modernity as a whole and that leads to extensive political 'consolidation phantasms.' In these phantasms, Bauman discerns "the intense concerns of the modern era with boundary-drawing and boundary-maintenance" (1989, 40). The modern establishment of addresses, fixed places, and identities—both individual and collective—is paid for by the production of a shapeless, abject remnant, for which Bauman uses the term cultural "viscosity" (40). For Schmitt, Jewishness becomes a cipher for the impossibility of "looking behind the scenes" and establishing the political upon an "existential" distinction. Because Schmitt assumes an intrinsic mask-like character, latency, or indistinguishability of the ("inner") foe, his antisemitic writing is characterized by an inquisitorial furor that actually generates the foe as the product of a sovereign dissociation.

THE POLITICAL CHALLENGE
OF ROMANTIC OCCASIONALISM

Although Schmitt was by profession a jurist, or more accurately, a professor of constitutional law, interestingly enough his early publications include not only academic studies but also literary or semiliterary texts. In 1916 his literary critique of Theodor Däubler's monumental expressionist epic *Nordlicht* appeared, followed in 1919 by the expansive study *Political Romanticism*. On the one hand Schmitt is known as a political theologian; he renewed the classical relationship among sovereignty, decision, and the state of exception and ascribed a capacity for creating order to the political leader analogous to the same capacity in God the creator. On the other hand, Schmitt is a political theologian in a nondoctrinal sense, which was not recognized for a long time. The often cited formulation that "[a]ll significant concepts of the modern theory of the state are secularized theological concepts" (2005, 36) is a statement about the history of concepts that does not describe the horizon of Schmitt's political theory, unless one considers at the same time a sentence from his book *The Concept of the Political*: "The juridic formulas of the omnipotence of the state are, in fact, only superficial secularizations of theological formulas of the omnipotence of God" (2007a, 42). The trust in a theology that prescribes an eschatological horizon for politics is entirely foreign to Schmitt. Under the conditions of the twentieth century—after the end of philosophical and juridical rationalism, which thought it could ignore the state of exception—he sees the recurrence of the baroque constellation described by Walter Benjamin, in which church and secular actions are shaped by the "ideal of a complete stabilization" (Benjamin 1998, 65) of an order shattered by wars, revolts, and other catastrophes, "in a world which was denied direct access to a beyond" (79). As in baroque political thought, Schmitt "knows no eschatology,"[2] but instead dedicates himself to a policy in which government is indissoluble under the conditions of a state of exception. Even after its founding, the modern state remains oriented toward its site of emergence (*Entstehungsherd*)—civil war— which it simply tries to "suppress" with varying degrees of success.

Schmitt defines "the classical" in *The Concept of the Political* as the "possibility of unambiguous, clear distinctions" (1963, 11). From the perspective of a classical observer the present state of things must seem to be a "confused interim state between form and formlessness" (12). Before mentioning it in the later foreword to *The Concept of the Political*, Schmitt had already laid out a theory of modernity in his studies on "intellectual history." This theory reached far beyond the juridical sphere and was centered on a diagnosis that questioned any historical-philosophical or normative stylizing of this epoch. Instead, Schmitt deciphered the aesthetic radicalism of the period as the signature of that which is described by today's philosophy and sociology as the specifically modern relationships of communication. Modern society has no address at its disposal. It cannot be "reached" or targeted through any institution or system, not even a political one; it finds itself in a condition of "unresolvable indeterminacy" (Luhmann 1997, 866). Schmitt's *Political Romanticism*, which develops this theory against the backdrop of disintegrating metaphysical certainties and stabilities, describes how the classical, with its "obligation to achieve a grand and strict form or manifestation" (Schmitt 1986, 15), falls victim to the expansion of a neutralizing and functionalizing "discussion" culture for which ideas are now only points of contact, *occasiones*, for further ideas. In this situation, discourses as well as institutions become subject to a contingency pressure never known before, so that all establishments and concepts of a public nature, "all legal concepts and arguments, everything that is official, and even democracy itself since the time it assumed a constitutional form are perceived as empty and deceptive disguises, as a veil, a façade, a fake, or a decoration" (14). Instead of occupying a unique identity at their core, ideas are "no longer capable of representation" (15). They degenerate into communicative 'incitements,' insofar as they are now only judged on their surprise value—in other words, whether they succeed in building a bridge to something different and unexpected. They are incidents without substance that demand only brief attention and disintegrate in the very moment of their appearance.

The concept of the *occasio*, which Schmitt places at the center of his definition of the romantic ("subjectified occasionalism"), receives its real meaning through opposition: "It negates the concept of *causa*, in other words, the force of a calculable causality, and thus also every binding norm. It is a disintegrative concept. This is because everything that gives consistency and order to life and to what takes place...is incompatible with the idea of the merely occasional" (1986, 17). That cause and effect have lost their common measure, that there is no longer a "meaningful" proportionality or symmetry between them, that small causes can have large effects and large causes can have small effects, that there exists an "absolutely inadequate relationship" between them—above all Schmitt sees all of this as clearly exacerbating the problem of control, which is not least also a political problem, and more specifically, as aggravating the predictability of this "relation of the fanciful" (83). The specific modernity of Schmittean decisionism can be recognized in its own understanding of itself as a despairing answer to the challenge of the interminability and thematic "restlessness" of modern, mass-media-organized communication.

Schmitt's idea of occasionalism focuses on the same phenomenon that sociological systems theory treats under the keyword "meaning" ("*Sinn*"). For Luhmann, meaning "appears as a surplus of references to other possibilities of experience and action" (1995, 60). This referential surplus explains the emergence of the notion of an "infinite conversation" that is no longer restricted to the salon, but extends throughout all of society. As much as Schmitt's own formulation of political concepts—under the sign of political theology—is set in opposition to occasionalism, he was nevertheless deeply affected by it. Schmitt saw quite precisely how the "relation of the fanciful" had found its way into the political sphere and transformed its constitutive differentiations as well as all "substantive oppositions" into a play of differences that no longer represented a relation to things, to the "real" or "ontological" battles and conflicts. In Romanticism he sees the spearhead of a comprehensive process of political and societal de-realization. One of his chapter subheadings in *Political Romanticism* is symptomatic of this, understanding the movement of modern thought since the Cartesian division of being into two worlds (*res cogitans* and *res extensa*) as "La recherche de la Réalité" (Schmitt 1986, 51). This formulation at the same time names the compelling force behind his political thought. After all, although Schmitt already says openly in *Political Romanticism* that "all substantive oppositions and differences, good and evil, friend and enemy, Christ and Antichrist, can become aesthetic contrasts and means of intrigue in a novel" (16), just ten years later he suggests a concept of the political that perceives in its distinction between friend and enemy a guarantor for meaning that is non-functionalizing and non-fictionalizing, an original, ontological, and existential meaning. The state's "right to demand from its own members the readiness to die and unhesitatingly kill enemies" (2007a, 46) might still be a historical fact; few would deny this. But Schmitt knew that while this fact still guaranteed the intensity of political engagement in the age of mass media communication or of the "infinite conversation,"[3] it no longer guaranteed its truthfulness, authenticity, or "ontologicalness."

Undermining the Modern Rule of Law: Apocryphal Acts of Sovereignty

Schmitt's political theology, in which one seems to find the formula for his basic premodern position, is haunted by a modern uncertainty about the subject and the location of sovereignty, which have become problematic following the transfer of the highest authority to exert power from the ruler to the people in the course of democratic revolutions: "In the struggle of opposing interests and coalitions, absolute monarchy made the decision and thereby created the unity of the state. The unity that a people represents does not possess this decisionist character" (Schmitt 2005, 48–49). Schmitt thus throws decisionism into a fundamental crisis, insofar as it relies here on "the specific logic of the juristic thinking that culminates in a personal decision" (52). Schmitt's famous formula—"Sovereign is he who decides on the exception" (5)—is based on a situation in which it is no longer unquestionably clear *who* the sovereign *in concreto* is, and in which the state and its representatives can no longer readily lay claim to a monopoly on this ultimate discretionary competence. The sovereign himself is seized by the drift of occasionalism insofar as he is decreasingly able to presume the stability of a societal "situation" and can no longer muster the power for a "grand and strict form or manifestation"

(1986, 15). Under these conditions the following applies: "All law is 'situational law'" (2005, 13).

Schmitt's studies on constitutional theory show that modernity does not so much work toward a removal or constitutional taming of sovereignty as it promotes the development of a "system of apocryphal acts of sovereignty" (2008, 190). For this reason, his theory of sovereignty places the problem of arbitration at its center, the bearers of which, however, can no longer be conceived of according to the theological model of the immortal second body, which Ernst Kantorowicz (1957) develops in *Study in Medieval Political Theology* and its further historical transformations.[4] Schmitt's sovereign does not have a second body, which would guarantee the immortality of his dignity (*dignitas non moritur*). The "catalogue of representative predicates" with which the absolute monarchs "cloaked" their reign—Schmitt invokes, for example, "*majestas, splendor, excellentia, eminentia, honor* and *Gloria*" (1958, 268)—belongs irrevocably to the past. Schmitt reveals that he is rather a theorist of a *fluctuating empire* and of *delegated sovereignty*. His concept of sovereignty—far from being simply antiliberal or premodern—aligns itself in a systematic respect with John Locke's concept of the prerogative. Like Locke, Schmitt, too, is interested in the paradox of a temporal repeal or suspension of the law, which is implemented by juridical means.

The fact that Schmitt's famous opening sentence of *Political Theology* explicitly does not state the subject of this decision hints at the dynamics peculiar to sovereign power, which creates a "zone of anomie in which all legal determinations—and above all the very distinction between public and private—are deactivated" (Agamben 2005, 50). In other words, not only is it impossible to determine in advance the *extent* of power in the case of exception, but ambiguity also reigns over the *subject* of sovereignty, so that the state and its entities, which no longer function smoothly, rescind their power, allowing parastate groups or private citizens to seize control of the law on political actions.

THE LIBERAL CONSTRUCTION OF EXCEPTION: PREROGATIVE POWER

Judith Butler investigated the lawful suspension of constitutionally guaranteed legal protection using the example of the imprisonment of suspects whose right to a judicial verification of the rulings made against them was essentially denied. This was done in light of the security alert and national state of emergency following the events of September 11, 2001, in the United States. Although she only mentions Schmitt peripherally, she paints a forceful picture of something he described in his *Constitutional Theory* of 1928: "The ideal of the Rechtsstaat remains in place to thoroughly comprise all possibilities of state action in a system of norms and, through it, bind the state. In practical reality, however, a system of apocryphal acts of sovereignty forms." Schmitt continues, "If this practice is generally recognized today in all manifestations of the bourgeois

Rechtsstaat, that lies not in an intentional constitutional regime, but rather in the fact that a political concept of law proves itself stronger in opposition to the Rechtsstaat concept of law" (2008, 190). This sentence can be readily transferred from the historical context in which it originates to the present, "with every instance of conflict posing anew the problem of sovereignty" (187), but without this problem leading to the suspension of the state constitution or to the foundation of an "open dictatorship." As an example of the failure of the constitutional ideal of "the conformity of the entire state life to *general judicial forms*" (176), Schmitt invokes the

> [s]pecial treatment of *government acts* or specified *political acts* in the area of adjudication. In some countries, in particular France and the United States of America, where review of executive acts by an ordinary court with general jurisdiction or by an administrative court is permitted, the practice led to the exception of government acts or "political acts" from this court supervision, so that these acts escape any ordinary court or administrative court review. The demarcation of the political from other acts is certainly controversial. A definite, automatic distinguishing mark of the "government act" did not previously result in the aforementioned practice. (179–180)

Against this backdrop one can understand Butler's suggestion that on the one hand sovereignty is no longer embodied "as a unified locus for state power," but on the other this "does not foreclose the possibility that it might emerge as a reanimated anachronism within the political field unmoored from its traditional anchors" (Butler 2004, 53). Schmitt rejects the traditional "historical presentations that deal with the development of the concept of sovereignty," which he says are "like textbook compilations of abstract formulas from which definitions of sovereignty can be extracted" because they do not go beyond "the often-repeated but completely empty phraseology used to denote the highest power" (2005, 7–8). For jurists, the question of sovereignty is always directed "at the subject of sovereignty" (10), which is to be understood as an institutional position that can be occupied and organized in various ways and can be seized by various agencies of power so that they can speak and act "in the name of" a fictive reference (God, the people, the nation, security).

Without becoming involved in a detailed discussion of this difficulty in Schmitt, Butler nevertheless shows how the theory of sovereignty can be made fruitful as a placeholder for the analysis of political processes, particularly in liberal Western societies. Sovereignty once again enters the field of the arts of government, which originally developed—if one follows the history of governmentality as described by Foucault—in a polemical contrast with the exertion of ruling power in Europe (Foucault 2007). While the sovereign "exists in a relationship of singularity and externality, of transcendence, to his principality" (91), the arts of government are always manifold and conquer society and the state from within. It is inherent to the juridical construction of sovereign rule to "constantly try to make clear the discontinuity between the Prince's power and any other form of power" (94). Because our situation is characterized by governmentality, "and this implies, to a certain degree, a loss of sovereignty," there follows a compensation of this loss "through the resurgence of sovereignty within the field of governmentality. Petty sovereigns abound, reigning in the midst of bureaucratic army institutions mobilized by aims and tactics of power they do not inaugurate or fully control" (Butler 2004, 56). The petty sovereigns, who function separately from the public sphere and from representative acts, are "delegated with the power to render unilateral decisions, accountable to no law and without any legitimate authority" (56). Their power can therefore be called *prerogative*, and Butler, without specifically addressing this point, refers to a central argument of political liberalism, which John Locke propounds in chapter 14 of his *Second Treatise of Government*. This chapter is dedicated to the relationship between legislative power and executive power and thus leads to the central problem presented by Schmitt, who is very much aligned with Locke in his interest in the "many things…which the Law can by no means provide for, and those must necessarily be left to the discretion of him, that has the Executive Power in his hands" (Locke 1988, 374–375).

In this context, Locke defines the quasi-legal concept of the prerogative as the power "to act according to discretion, for the publick [sic] good, without the prescription of the Law, and sometimes even against it" (1988, 375). Locke constructs the prerogative as "the Peoples permitting their Rulers, to do several things of their own free choice, where the Law was silent, and sometimes too against the direct Letter of the Law" (377). Locke finds it decisive—in the same sense as Foucault when he describes the rise of modern *raison d'état*—to allow the ruler the prerogative, but at the same time to deny him any claim to godlike attributes or absolute reign. Schmitt's doctrine of public law addresses this very same discrepancy, insofar as it detaches the concept of sovereignty from its representative dimension and formulates it explicitly as a borderline concept. As such it is a concept "pertaining to the outermost sphere" (Schmitt 2005, 5), yet this sphere refers not to a point beyond human politics, but to the remote locations of bureaucratic decision making and enforcement, which one can designate as the realm of regulatory measures.

Sovereign Power as Speech Act

The political theology of Schmitt is based on a concept of delegated sovereignty, which allows the highest power of decision to be thought of together with the subalternity of those who receive this power. In this context, Foucault argued for the introduction of the "grotesque" or "Ubu-esque" as a category of sovereign exercise of power into the vocabulary of political theory. The grotesque "is not just a term of abuse or an insulting epithet," but must also be understood as a "precise category": "grotesque sovereignty" can be defined as "the maximization of effects of power on the basis of the disqualification of the one who produces them" (Foucault 2003, 11–12) and of the one who appears as a "nonentity" as measured by the political-theological perceptions of quasi-godlike transcendence and omnipotence of earthly rulers. According to Foucault, "[p]olitical power, at least in some societies, and anyway in our society, can give itself, and has usually given itself, the possibility of conveying its effects and, even more, of finding their source, in a place that is manifestly, explicitly, and readily discredited as odious, despicable, or ridiculous" (12). Schmitt's political theology is in this sense concerned with the "problem of the infamy of sovereignty, of the discredited sovereign" (13), so that it is not surprising when the literary "Satanism" of Baudelaire is not dismissed as an "incidental paradox," but is welcomed as "a powerful intellectual principle" (Schmitt 2005, 63) that demonstrates the inevitability of sovereignty precisely against its antithesis.

In the second chapter of *Political Theology*, which is seldom called upon with regard to Schmitt's concept of sovereignty, this concept is contingent on the "independent problem of the realization of law" (21): "Looked at normatively, the decision emanates from nothingness" (31–32). The detachment of the decision from the norm and from its own content is the core of that which Butler describes as the "unilateral judgment made by government officials" who, independently of the judicial evaluation of relevant facts, "simply deem that a given individual or, indeed, a group poses a danger to the state" (Butler 2004, 58–59). Schmitt identifies the problem of sovereignty as a problem in legal structure because his point of reference is not the bearer of sovereign power who stands at the center of public attention, but the specific structure of judicial or quasi-judicial rulings. Schmitt's sovereign is the *decider*, the one who judges and condemns[5] and whose sphere is bureaucracy. Schmitt explains that in certain cases the "legal force of a decision" separates itself from the "quality of content" of a decision (2005, 32). To Locke's statement, "The Law gives authority," Schmitt replies smugly, "But he did not recognize that the law does not designate to whom it gives authority" (32). According to Foucault, "[s]ince the nineteenth century, an essential feature of big Western bureaucracies has been that the administrative machine, with its unavoidable effects of power, works by using the mediocre, useless, imbecilic, superficial, ridiculous, worn-out, poor, and powerless functionary" (Foucault 2003, 12). The judgment's detachment from the law, while it is at the same time given the force of law, raises the "operation of 'deeming'" (Butler 2004, 76) to the status of a political, quasi-legislative decision, which need not rest upon a legal basis or be subject to judicial review in order to be valid and effective: "Outlawry can also be carried out in such a way that for members of certain religions or parties there is *suspicion* of a lack of peaceful or legal sentiments" (Schmitt 1963, 47).[6] In a state of exception the letter of the law is replaced by the political—that is, by the sovereign speech act of supposition or *opinion*:

> The act is warranted by the one who acts, and the "deeming" of someone as dangerous is sufficient to make that person dangerous and to justify his indefinite detention. The one who makes this decision assumes a lawless and yet fully effective form of power.... Those who decide on whether someone will be detained, and continue to be detailed, are government officials, not elected ones, and not members of the judiciary. They are, rather, part of the apparatus of governmentality; their decision, the power they wield to "deem" someone dangerous and constitute them effectively as such, is a sovereign power, a ghostly and forceful resurgence of sovereignty in the midst of governmentality. (Butler 2004, 59)

The temptation to neutralize the freedom-guaranteeing constitutionality in the name of security is ever present in decidedly liberal commonwealths, which on the one hand nominally hold to the constitutional ideal, according to which all pronouncements of the state authority must be strictly subjected to the rule of law, but on the other hand remain attached to the notion of an exception that cannot be subsumed under any norm and that is already inscribed in the founding acts of political liberalism.

"By All Means Necessary": The Origin of Schmitt's "Existential" Concept of Sovereignty

The fact that there exist "acts of state," or more precisely, speech acts that are institutionally allowed and sanctioned but have no legal foundation and are instead grounded "in another form of judgment" (Butler 2004, 67), hints at Schmitt's idea of a site of emergence (*Entstehungsherd*) in his concept of sovereignty. This site of emergence is not political theology, but *raison d'état*, which denotes the "transition from traditional sovereignty to modern politics."[7] The significance of the ruler's exercise of sovereignty over his subjects since the end of the sixteenth century "is not distinguished simply by his extension of a divine sovereignty over Earth" (Foucault 2007, 236). *Raison d'état* designates a kind of rationality "that will allow the maintenance and preservation of the state once it has been founded, in its daily functioning, in its everyday management" (238). This is also the systematic reason why Schmitt situates sovereignty within the conceptual opposition between state of exception and *normality*: "The norm requires a homogenous medium. This effective normal situation is not a mere 'superficial presupposition' that a jurist can ignore; that situation belongs precisely to its immanent validity.... All law is 'situational law'" (Schmitt 2005, 13). The necessity of maintaining a state in its "daily functioning, in its everyday management" demands the readiness of a sovereign to make an exception under certain conditions to the laws that he himself has put in place, according to his own determination. In the history of concepts, Schmitt's conception of the political draws conspicuously on the emergence of *politiques* (Foucault 2007, 245–246), which denotes a new group of statesmen who attempt to conceive of the rationality of government "existentially" and independently of normative and theological problems.

The question of raison d'état has inscribed itself onto Schmitt's concept of sovereignty, and it has *three characteristics* that have troubled the political sphere—as art of government—since this time. First is the renunciation of any reference to a natural or divine order: "Nothing of the cosmos, nature, or the divine is present in the definition of *raison d'État*" (257). Second, *raison d'état* is directed toward preserving a status quo, or in the case of a crisis, restoring it. Hence Schmitt's specific structural conservatism, which in essence has nothing to do with a particular political party or "ideological" preference. Ultimately, *raison d'état* does not have an "extraterrestrial" purpose; its goal is the state itself and its preservation at all costs: "There is no last day. There is no ultimate point" (258).[8] Alternatively, there is the "borderline case" of the state of exception, which has no eschatological potential, but instead marks the critical moment of political order in which the proper conditions must first be created, in order "[f]or a legal order to make sense" (Schmitt 2005, 13). With the state of exception Schmitt designates the inversion of the "outermost point," which no longer lies outside of or beyond the political order, but instead corresponds with the moment of its *immanent transgression*, or in other words, its breach, abrogation, or suspension: "In such a situation it is clear that the state remains, whereas law recedes" (12).

In the context of *raison d'état*, Schmitt negotiates his exception to the definition of sovereignty by referring to the government overthrow, or *coup d'état*. In the pertinent treatises, a *coup d'état* is in fact defined in relation to the *exception* made under certain conditions to the system of laws that "normal" government activity is subject to. A *coup d'état* does not simply entail the replacement of the current political order by another or a wholesale rejection of the legal order, but rather temporarily "retires" laws and legality. Under certain conditions the state acts directly upon itself, thus bypassing all rights, "swiftly, immediately, without rule, with urgency and necessity, and dramatically" (Foucault 2007, 262). Foucault cites Charron's formulation: "To retain justice in big things it is sometimes necessary to turn away from it in small things" (263). Foucault continues with a concrete example that plays a particular role in the texts of this raison d'état theorist and emerges by no means coincidentally from a context of disorder, revolt, and quasi-juridical discretion. In order to curb the revolts and atmosphere of turmoil, Charlemagne instituted courts that were peculiar in several ways. They remained "unknown to the public," judged "without knowledge of the facts, that is to say, without doing anything to establish the facts held against those they sentenced," and pronounced a judgment that "did not take the form of a trial, that is to say, there was no judicial ritual" (264). In the context of his theory on the state of siege, Schmitt made clear that his concept of sovereignty was derived from the tradition of *raison d'état*. Regarding the sovereign "concrete action" ("*Tathandlung*"), he says, "in its absolute factuality, in other words in its essence, it is not approachable through proper legal form" ("*Rechtsförmigkeit*"; Schmitt 2014, 151).

Calling on Schmitt's doctrine of sovereignty, Agamben was interested in "how certain subjects undergo a suspension of their ontological status as subjects when states of emergency are invoked" (Butler 2004, 67). When Schmitt calls the political that which creates an "internal enemy" who is set *hors la loi*, or declared an outlaw, and from whom the law has withdrawn itself (Schmitt 2007a, 46–48), so that the state becomes a party to civil war, he is describing a situation in which subjects lose their legal status entirely and enter a suspended zone in which only their bare or naked life remains dependent on the sovereign power. They are directly subject to this power, through which unilaterally wielded, undefined legal terms—for example, "in the name of national security" (Butler 2004, 85)—take the place of intersubjectively comprehensible and judicially verifiable grounds that could warrant the declaration that one lacks any rights.[9]

That which drove Schmitt into the arms of the Nazi regime after 1933 was not merely ideological motivation, as was typical for supporters of the conservative revolution. Schmitt was impressed with the readiness of this regime to erect its reign on the basis of an openly declared and perpetuated state of exception, which, without legal proceedings, transformed the practices of the declaration of a domestic enemy and preventative custody—in other words "indefinite detention"—into a means of *every-day* government practice. In doing so, the regime reconquered for everyday politics the very "tragedy of the coup d'état" that "can only appear, when necessary, in this theatrical and violent form" (Foucault 2007, 266). Speaking of Naudé's text on this topic, *Considérations politiques*, Foucault finds something "very Napoleonic in this text, something that quite remarkably makes one think of Hitlerian nights, of the night of the long knives" (266). To use a well-chosen phrase by Agamben, Schmitt revealed himself as the theorist and juridical apologist of the "floating *imperium*" (Agamben 2005, 51), of a sovereign power that is legally untamable and remains unanchored in any institutional body, and of a force of law that has been separated from the law itself. At the crucial moment, as Schmitt argued with regard to January 31, 1933, even legality may prove to be a medium of the suspension of the law, because the legal approach preserves the semblance of constitutional continuity and forges the important alliance between legal-minded bureaucracy and Nazi subversion (cf. Mommsen 1966).

An Early Analysis of Modern Biopolitics: "Die Buribunken"

Even before Schmitt finalized *Political Theology* (2005), which was centered on his "borderline concept" of sovereignty, he knew that the phase in which sovereignty was deemed sacrosanct was irrevocably past. The only remaining possibility was to reconstruct the regime of sovereign society on the terms of a very different power economy, whether in opposition to or paradoxically in alliance with it. Schmitt found no name for this power economy, even though he had tried to describe its mode of operation much earlier by literary means. Schmitt's "historical-philosophical experiment," "Die Buribunken" ("The Buribunks") published in *Summa*, the quarterly journal edited by Franz Blei (Schmitt 1918), is an early satire of the normalizing knowledge-power that had already been invented in the nineteenth century, of which Foucault would then write an analysis in the 1960s and 1970s. In the nineteenth century there was a systematic expansion of the ritual of confession, which initially belonged only to the religious and penal spheres but in the emerging study of human nature advanced to the most highly prized technique of truth production: "one goes about telling, with the greatest precision," according to Foucault, "whatever is most difficult to tell. One confesses in public and in private, to one's parents, one's educators, one's doctor, to those one loves; one admits to oneself, in pleasure and in pain, things it would be impossible to tell to anyone else, the things people write books about" (Foucault 1990, 59). In the act of confessing, one first brings forth only that which one claims to reveal; one produces the typically modern, no longer Christian "soul" that is "the element in which are articulated the effects of a certain type of power and the reference of a certain type of knowledge, the machinery by which the power relations give rise to a possible corpus of knowledge, and knowledge extends and reinforces the effects of this power" (Foucault 1979, 29).

In "The Buribunks," Schmitt describes a society that requires every member—and does everything possible to make an abiding preference out of this requirement—to keep a constant diary, with the encouragement to not only write about obscure stirrings of emotion, but also document the very rejection of this duty. Foucault highlighted the role of Christianity in creating a power in the Western world that seized "the ordinary preoccupations of life" and employed the ritual of confession for this purpose. Christians were obliged "to run the miniscule everyday world regularly through the mill of language, revealing the common faults, the imperceptible failings even, and down to the murky interplay of thoughts, intentions, and desires" (Foucault 1994, 166). Schmitt's satirical perspective on the secular ritual of confession must not obscure the fact that its origin points to a pastoral technique of power meant for the guidance of souls. Foucault refers to the "birth, consequently, of an immense possibility for discourse" (169) to sum up the effect of the incorporation of this originally religious technique of knowledge and power into modern political-administrative apparatuses. These use various methods of inquiry and analysis to transform everything that was previously only said to effect divine forgiveness into enduring textual traces such as "dossiers and archives" that "constitute, through time, a sort of constantly growing record of all the world's woes" (166).

If what Foucault calls "ordinary individuality" evaded detection and description for a long time, if it remained for centuries a privilege and ritual of the singular political power to view, observe, and recount it, and if "individualization is greatest where sovereignty is exercised and in the higher echelons of power" (1979, 192), then the new type of power detaches the procedures of individualization from the function of heroization—in other words, from the "pathos of *glorie* and *honneur*" (Schmitt 1958, 268)—and provides the business of inquiry with smaller and smaller differences between any two individuals. Individuality, the target of the new power economy, entirely gives up the "peculiarity of enhanced being that is capable of representation" (Schmitt 2008, 243), the presence of which Schmitt ties to the possibility of the political. The new variant of power, quite to the contrary, is more interested in the individual "case" the lower it is ranked, whether in regard to society (the worker), to medicine (the invalid), to pedagogy (the child), to psychology (the madman), or to justice (the criminal). Through the medium of literary discourse, Schmitt bears witness to the problem of the entry of "ordinary individuality" into the field of knowledge and to the origin of those "'ignoble' archives"—in "The Buribunks" it is a matter of an "obligatory collective diary" (Schmitt 1918, 101)—that are the result of an expansion of the political-"police" observation of "everything that happens," and in which the "birth of the sciences of man" (Foucault 1979, 191) has been accomplished: "Every Buribunk, male and female, is obligated to keep a diary for every second of his or her existence" (101).

The fact that the function of the obligatory collective diary—the details of which Schmitt enumerates extensively: daily inspection; local, regional, and central analysis; attachment of subject and personal indexes, which allow "the immediate identification of the respective circumstances of interest with regard to each individual" (1918, 101)—is to investigate and evaluate pathologies or deviations ("the smallest errors") is made clear by Schmitt's example of the utilization of the cataloged knowledge of confessions: "If, for example, a psychopathologist should be interested in the dreams that a certain class of Buribunks had during puberty, the pertinent material could be gathered immediately using the card catalogue" (101). Moreover, its self-referential function, which does not allow for outliers, is typical of modern power and its normalizing function: "The work of the psychopathologist, however, would likewise be subject to registration, so that a historian of psychopathology might be able to make a reliable determination in just a few hours as to the kind of psychopathological studies undertaken thus far, and at the same time—and this is the greatest advantage of double registration—to determine which psychopathological motives lie behind these psychopathological studies" (101). As one can see, the range of application of the pathological gaze also includes those who safeguard its effectiveness.

For the political theologian, the explosiveness of the power procedures of the "Buribunks" lies in the far-reaching epistemic analysis and social inclusion of "the other," which Schmitt would later call the enemy and whose exclusion he would make the epitome of the political. The power that is no longer dominantly repressive or "absorbing," but rather regulatory and normalizing, and that reorganizes the state on the basis of statistics, refuses to be given a limit, instead constantly assigning limits anew based on a flexible definition of "limiting values" and tolerance zones (cf. Link 1997), so that the "forbidden" never ceases to be controversial and constitutes a realm of intensely affective ambivalence. According to Schmitt's fictional reporter, it is important to consider "that there reigned in the realm of the Buribunks an unlimited, all-understanding, never indignant tolerance and the highest respect for personal freedom" (1918, 102)—as long as the claim to this freedom did not clash with the imperatives of "Buribunk" operations. In keeping the daily journal, not only the documentation of failures is expressly required, but also the very rejection of this institution, because "the absolute freedom of expression" is the "vital nerve" of Buribunk existence: "There is even a prestigious association that makes it its task to conceive of anti-Buribunk affairs in a Buribunkian manner, just as a special organization is set up to invoke impressive diary entries on the disgust and abhorrence of this very organization and on the protest against the duty of the diary" (102). The obligation to publish and utilize "experiences" encompasses its own negation—as far as this negation is published!

Against the backdrop of this analysis of "The Buribunks," one can recognize the degree to which Schmitt was aware of a fundamental shift in modern modalities of exercising power, a shift that changed every one of the classical terms available to describe the modern state. It seems that a power that itself encourages a "rebellious spirit"—as expressed with approval in "The Buribunks"—does not dismiss the differentiation between friend and enemy that Schmitt would later use to characterize the political, but it does assign a new role or function to this distinction. "The old power of death that symbolized sovereign power," writes Foucault, "was now carefully supplanted by the administration of bodies and the calculated management of life" (Foucault 1990, 139–140). The sovereign right over life and death is therefore not replaced by biopower, but put to its service, which is the reason the total wars of the twentieth century are "no longer waged in the name of a sovereign who must be defended; they are waged on behalf of the existence of everyone; entire populations are mobilized for the purpose of wholesale slaughter in the name of life necessity" (137). Schmitt likewise recognizes the "absolute limit" of "Buribunk" power in the fact that it only tolerates rebellion as long as it supplies society with productive energy. Biopower, with its interest in a total acquisition of life, or, in other words, its transformation into text, incorporates the sovereign right over life and death into one of its indispensable indexes: "Every entry on the refusal of keeping a diary must be justified and explained in detail. Anyone who actually refrains from keeping a diary, instead of writing that he refuses to do so, is abusing our common intellectual freedom and will be eliminated as a result of his antisocial disposition" (Schmitt 1918, 102).

The Declaration of Domestic Enemies as a Means of Self-Subversion of the State

One key aspect of the differentiation between friend and enemy with which Schmitt defines the political is that it does not function solely or even primarily with regard to "foreign affairs," as initially appears to be the case. In his programmatic text *The Concept of the Political*, Schmitt finds himself compelled to define the enemy more precisely as the foreigner with whom, in the most extreme case, existential conflicts are possible (2007a, 27). These conflicts are of an intensity that is not readily possible between institutionally and territorially definable political entities (states). The foreigner for Schmitt is therefore by no means the citizen of another political entity who comes from the outside and stays temporarily on one's "own" territory or seeks entry into the political community. The foreigner in the sense of *The Concept of the Political* can easily have access to all civil rights and still not belong to the political community. One sees in him a hidden or latent enmity, which is expressed through his own inherent challenge to the differentiation between friend and enemy (cf. Balke 1992). For Schmitt's purposes, the foreigner is the enemy who "assimilates" into a friend or claims for himself the position of the "neutral third party": "The foreigner, the one who is different, might pretend to be strictly 'critical,' 'objective,' 'neutral,' 'purely scientific,' and interject his foreign judgment using similar means of deception. His 'objectivity' is either only a political *disguise* or instead a complete, fundamentally deficient *disconnectedness*" (Schmitt 1933, 8).

The foreigner is thus he who remains "outside" even when he is actually—from a topographical or socializing perspective—"inside." " 'Being outside,' " writes Bauman, "casts the stranger in the position of *objectivity*: his is an outside, detached and autonomous vantage-point from which the insiders (complete with their world-view, including their map of friends and enemies) may be looked upon, scrutinized and censored. The very awareness of such an outside point of view (a point of view epitomized by the stranger's status) makes the natives feel uncomfortable, insecure in their home ways and truths" (Bauman 1991, 78). The natives might react to the supposed cognitive incongruity of the foreigner with exclusion measures of varying intensity. "A foreigner would be able to decide neither whether the 'exceptional case' is at hand, nor the further question as to which 'exceptional measures' will be vital in order to defend one's own existence and preserve one's own being—*in suo esse perseverare*" (Schmitt 1933, 8). With the formulation of "exceptional measures," found at the beginning of the third edition of the *Begriff des Politischen* in 1933, Schmitt makes the "regular" military emergency into an eliminatory state practice, explicitly identifying its object after 1933 as the Jewish citizens of the German state.

Schmitt's journalistic support, beginning after 1933 and reaching its preliminary high point in 1936, for the state-run measures of the Nazi regime against Jewish citizens makes the topos of the "fundamentally deficient disconnectedness" into the crux of his antisemitic polemic: "*The relationship of Jewish thought to the German spirit* is such: the Jew has a *parasitic, tactical* and *mongering* relationship to our intellectual work" (1936, 1197)—thus a relationship never concerned with its real "substance." The assimilation project that emerged together with the modern nation-state had made the affiliation to a homogenous "body public" dependent on an "essential change" of those who are to be assimilated. This was supposed to take place over the course of the acquisition of the majority culture (*Bildung*). To antisemitic essentialists it was clear that this project would fail and could only have one effect: the production of a specifically assimilatory subjectivity that had lost its original essence without ever having been able to reach a new essence. This subjectivity is attributed with speed, adaptability, and a "*mask-switching of demonic subtleness*" (1198). These features thus symbolically constitute that alterity that is the condition for the possibility of "existential" enmity. According to Schmitt, we have "no access to the inner being of the Jews," and we know "only their disparity to our kind" (1197), so that we can bear only a hostile relationship to them.

The "ultimate degree of intensity" of the friend/enemy distinction, which Schmitt makes a criterion of the political, refers to the diagnosis of a movement of subversion that takes place invisibly and in secret. When, in *Political Theology*, Schmitt sets liberalism, the essence of which is "negotiation," in opposition to the "decisive bloody battle," his work and his changing political and journalistic engagements can be read as a chain of attempts to identify subjects that attempt to withdraw from this kind of "definitive dispute" (2005, 63). After the war, in *Theory of the Partisan*, Schmitt would perceive the partisan as the epochal antagonist figure of the combatant in terms of international law. The danger he presents for the political order is that he "refuses to carry weapons openly" and "fights from ambush." The partisan is an irregular fighter who uses "the enemy's uniform, as well as true or false insignias and every type of civilian clothing as camouflage. Secrecy and darkness are his strongest weapons, which logically he cannot renounce without losing the space of irregularity, i.e., without ceasing to be a partisan" (2007b, 37). In retrospect, one can therefore say that Schmitt's antisemitism proves to be an effect of a construction of the Jew as an irregular fighter, a phantasm that became an underpinning of the state after 1933 and compelled the political regime, for its part, to follow the logic of the irregular "fight."

Bauman put forth the hypothesis "that the active or passive, direct or oblique involvement in the intense concerns of the modern era with boundary-drawing and boundary-maintenance was to remain the most distinctive and defining feature of the conceptual Jew." The conceptual Jew, according to Bauman, "has been historically construed as the universal 'viscosity' of the Western world." Furthermore, the conceptual Jew "has been located astride virtually every barricade erected by the successive conflicts that tore apart the Western society at its various stages and in various dimensions. The very fact that the conceptual Jew straddled so many different barricades, built on so many, ostensibly unrelated front lines, endowed his sliminess with the elsewhere unknown, exorbitant intensity" (Bauman 1989, 40). Schmitt's text, which has just been cited above and appeared in 1936 under the title "German Jurisprudence in Its Struggle against the Jewish Spirit," is obsessed with precisely this exorbitant "sliminess." Schmitt, too, sees the Jews—to use Bauman's wording—"astride the barricades," (41) so that following the logic of this image, the Jews do not feel as if they belong to any of the factions that are created by the respective barricades. "The Jews" embody the efficacy of those things that are strictly precluded by the binary logic of the political: the third party, ambiguity, permeability, the hybrid, and ambivalence, which according to Bauman is the decisive marker of modernity and simultaneously the reason for modernity's continual disconcertment about itself. The following formulation by Bauman applies to Schmitt: "The horror of mixing reflects the obsession with separating" (1991, 14). Because the Jews have no fixed identity, no "essence," or to use Nazi racial jargon, are not of a particular "kind," it is no wonder, according to Schmitt, that one sees them on so many different barricades. There exists "no deep problem in the fact that some Jews speak and write nationalistically, others internationalistically; that the theories they advocate are sometimes conservative, other times liberal, sometimes subjective, other times objective" (Schmitt 1936, 1197).

The Lower Levels of Extermination: Cleansing the Library

The fact that the Jews and their threatening "mask-like" nature embodied for Schmitt the ambiguity and contingency of modernity explains his vehement support of the state-operated measures of the Nazi regime to deprive a particular group of German citizens of rights and that he did not recoil at the *thought* of their physical extermination. In the context of an antisemitic comment in a letter to Ernst Jünger in 1935, Schmitt cited a sentence from Léon Bloy stating that war is senseless if it is not a war of obliteration.[10] If one returns to Schmitt's closing remarks on the occasion of the 1936 conference "Das Judentum in der Rechtswissenschaft" ("Judaism in Jurisprudence")[11] with the knowledge of the logic of the extermination process as it has been reconstructed by Raul Hilberg,[12] one can recognize in parts of the text that Schmitt commentators call especially "unintelligible" and "embarrassing"[13] the attempt to open up the specialized legal communication used for the lower levels of the extermination process. Schmitt is concerned with the transfer of measures initially aimed directly at people onto texts, and thus onto the field of the "intellect." Schmitt elaborates in detail the "tasks of the bibliography, of library technology and of citation," which can easily be mapped onto the levels distinguished by Hilberg of definition, expropriation, and concentration:

1. *Definition:* The task of a bibliography, as difficult as it might prove to be in practice, is indispensable, "because it is naturally essential to determine as precisely as possible who is a Jew, and who is not a Jew."

2. *Expropriation:* "Only when we have an exact catalogue can we continue to work with library technology towards the *cleansing of the libraries* in order to protect our students from confusion," which is caused by the impression, even in 1936, "as if the greater portion of legal scholarship had been produced by Jews."

3. *Concentration:* "As Reich Minister Dr. Frank [the later leader of the so-called General Government, on the territory of which the Nazi extermination camps would be built] has aptly noted, all legal texts by Jewish authors belong, according to library procedures, without differentiation in a special section, 'Judaica'" (Schmitt 1936, 1194–1195).

That the published texts by Jewish authors should be spatially separated, that is, "ghettoized," does not mean, however, a complete prohibition against contact with these texts and the thoughts expressed in them or that they should be physically destroyed. Only through the continued practice of separation from that which no longer seems "heterogeneous" to us can we continue the process of our own (interminable) homogenization, that is, purification, while halting our own *derealization.* The alarm caused by this text, which is perhaps Schmitt's most antisemitic, stems from the inquisitory[14] vigor and the quasi-epistemic pathos of precision with which he makes the case for turning toward the "practical questions" in the "treatment" of this "topic." Schmitt's concept of the political springs from the essential imperceptibility or latency of the enemy and makes the fight against this enemy dependent on bureaucratic practices that attempt to identify him, make him visible, and carry out his subsequent "dissociation." Jacques Derrida, whose reading of Schmitt's thought makes up the core of his essays *Politics of Friendship*, rightly suggested that for *the* political to exist for Schmitt, "one must know who everyone is, who is a friend and who is an enemy, and this knowing is not in the mode of theoretical knowledge but in one of a *practical identification*: knowing consists here in knowing how to identify the friend and the enemy" (Derrida 2005, 116). Nothing is as objectionable to Schmitt as modern power's abstractness, intangibility, and invisibility. In other words, he objects to the techniques of indirect rule and the façade-like quality of the official sphere of political representation. Schmitt's "struggle against the Jewish spirit" in this respect truly originates in a 'suffering' from the "structure of the romantic spirit" and its "rootlessness" (Schmitt 1986, 51). It is therefore performed as a "*recherche de la Réalité*," as the above-mentioned chapter of *Political Romanticism* is titled.

THE REALIZATION OF THE POLITICAL: THE DUAL STATE

Neither Schmitt's authoritarian nor his antisemitic dispositions are enough then, to explain his support for National Socialism. This support must instead be understood through his fundamental reassessment of the relationship between visibility and invisibility; that is, between the political space of appearance and the bureaucratic apparatus removed from the public sphere. Instead of portraying fascism and National Socialism as the rebirth of the strong state, which would once more equate the political with a "grand form" and powerful "representation," Schmitt takes a different approach. Beginning with his 1938 study on Hobbes's *Leviathan*, Schmitt conclusively moves the substance of the political "behind the scenes" and thereby confirms the Romantic understanding that everything essential is always hidden behind an empty and misleading disguise, to which he now adds the decoration of the leader cult. This is the lesson of Schmitt's 1930s reading of Hobbes: regardless of how authoritarian or absolute a state may be, it "can demand everything, but only ever superficially" (Schmitt 1982, 92). However, a power that "wants to become wholly public" and pushes "inner faith into the private sphere" must learn that the "soul of a people," as Schmitt formulates in deliberate allusion to Romantic topoi, proceeds "on the 'secret path' that leads inwards; then the counterforce of silence and stillness grows" (94). Once a political order has engaged with "the opposition between interior and exterior"—that is, once it has differentiated state and religion as distinct systems or social spheres of activity—then it has "already recognized the final dominance of the interior over the exterior, the invisible over the visible, stillness over noise, the hereafter over the mortal world" (95). In his cultural-historical treatise dedicated to Schmitt, *Critique and Crisis*, Reinhart Koselleck identifies the prerequisite to the subversion of the absolute state through the powers of a bourgeois cultural revolution in precisely this structural superiority of invisibility over visibility, private over public, silence over noise. Yet this was a hypocritical, self-delusional revolution that claimed to never contradict state order politically, but rather only morally and historico-philosophically (Koselleck 1973).

Under the conditions of the National Socialist state, Schmitt himself took the modern relegation of the political into the substate bureaucratic realm as an opportunity to reintroduce the differentiation between visibility and invisibility into the state itself. In this way he allowed for the resurrection of the state after its end (Balke 1996) in the form of the dual state (Fraenkel 1941; 2017). If the "real movement of reality" (Schmitt 1986, 14) is hidden behind the official state curtain, then sovereign power can only survive if it acts from the sidelines. This means that it has to maintain the façade of a normative state with proper jurisdiction, while *simultaneously* replacing it with a prerogative state. The legal basis for the prerogative state is the permanent state of exception, which relies on sovereign provisions for control. Ernst Fraenkel gets to the heart of this structure: "The political sphere is a vacuum as far as law is concerned. Of course it contains a certain element of factual order and predictability but only in so far as there is a certain regularity and predictability in the behavior of officials. There is, however, no legal regulation of the official bodies. The political sphere in the Third Reich . . . is regulated by arbitrary measures" (Fraenkel 1941, 3). For Schmitt, it is crucial not that the entire legal system is absorbed by the political, but that the political is granted the ability to suspend this order at any time according to sovereign opinion, or to individually disregard its own generally valid regulations. The political, as Schmitt had already determined in his 1928 *Constitutional Theory*, is not one power among many, but rather the *pouvoir constituant*, which is in permanent conflict with the constitutional principle of the measurability of all government actions. The political, as Fraenkel formulates following Schmitt, denotes an open-ended possibility, because "there is nothing which cannot be classified as 'political.' The possibility, however, of treating everything as if it were 'political' does not imply that this method is always resorted to" (57–58).

It is precisely this unpredictability of the political that Schmitt targets and that makes it possible to write in his *Political Romanticism* about a political occasionalism. This is because in every case it is the occasion (*occasio*) alone, as identified by a police-political decision maker, that determines what becomes political material; that is, material entrusted to a sovereign decision. Hannah Arendt, trained in the constitutional views of Schmitt, presented an analysis of the totalitarian state apparatus in which she revealed as a grandiose misunderstanding Schmitt's hope during the 1920s that the total regimes would restore the "great state" in "antique honesty." Schmitt himself dispensed of this "Roman" illusion no later than in the *Concept of the Political*, in which he revoked the politics' obligation to publicity or strict form. For Arendt, the totalitarian state apparatus in which politics—like Romanticism for Schmitt—was freed from all bondage and able to "expand immeasurably" (Schmitt 1986, 15) was characterized by "shapelessness" (Arendt 1979, 398), because its leadership "constantly shifts the actual center of power, often to other organizations, but without dissolving or even publicly exposing the groups that have thus been deprived of their power" (400). The notion that the political can no longer commit to a "great and rigorous form of visibility" is expressly confirmed in *The Origins of Totalitarianism*: "The only rule of which everybody in a totalitarian state may be sure is that the more visible government agencies are, the less power they carry" (403).

CONCLUSION

Starting from the discovery of a characteristically modern "intermediate situation between form and formlessness" (Schmitt 1963, 12), we can identify theories of modernity that take up the essence of Schmitt's diagnosis and question its sociological as well as cultural-historical conditions and consequences. It should be noted, however, that while these theories divide Schmitt's insights into modern paradoxes (Luhmann) and ambivalences (Bauman), they by no means espouse Schmitt's proposed solutions, which tie the political to the recovery of a great form and representation or to the development of an apocryphally or governmentally (Foucault, Butler) operating sovereign power. Various crisis diagnoses of modern politics, including Hannah Arendt's, find their basis in the hope that the "confused intermediate situation between form and formlessness" can be overcome through a new political visibility. Like Schmitt, whose work she knew intimately, Arendt derives the need to reclaim the political space of appearance from her description of a "consumers' society " (Arendt 1998, 126–135) that subjects all public affairs to the logic of the spectacle. Unlike the "Roman" Schmitt, however, she connects this space of appearance to the Greek polis democracy. For Arendt, this space of appearance "comes into being wherever men are together in the manner of speech and action, and therefore predates and precedes all formal constitution of the public realm and the various forms of government, that is, the various forms in which the public realm can be organized" (199). Schmitt, on the other hand, appreciates none other than Italian fascism for its state that wants "to be a state again with antique honesty, with visible bearers of power and representatives, but no façades and antechambers of invisible and irresponsible rulers and financiers" (Schmitt 1929, 114).

Because Schmitt cannot withhold his admiration for the classical image of the "great state" despite his insight into its political and sociological untenability, his political and journalistic involvement can be described as the continued search for substitutes for this erstwhile greatness. It is this search that ultimately leads to his role as a political supporter and constitutional apologist for the Nazi dictatorship. However, in the 1930s Schmitt is finally forced to recognize that the "great and rigorous form of visibility," which has become so problematic in the modern age, cannot be politically restored. The "romantic" destruction of the relation of expression between façade and subrepresentative powers is no longer reversible. A politics becomes totalitarian as soon as it accounts for the basic superiority of the secretly effective, subrepresentative powers, insofar as it consequently begins to operate from a covert standpoint itself. The sovereign dictatorship that established itself in Germany after 1933 therefore also included "secret orders and even secret laws" no longer guided by the "requirement of a public pronouncement of all legal norms" (1958, 434). In *hindsight*, Schmitt notes the fact that Hitler "deeply hated any stipulation based on forms or even institutions, and that a frown would have sufficed to eliminate" all attempts at formalization, and recognizes this as the "deliberate subjectivism and thereby fundamental abnormality of his regime" (434). Yet against the backdrop of 1947, Schmitt's explanation does not include the detail that this subjectivism and fundamental abnormality fit entirely within his own conception of the sovereign dictatorship.

Translated from the German by Jillian DeMair

NOTES

1. Unless noted otherwise, all translations of source material by the author or translator.
2. "The baroque knows no eschatology" (Benjamin 1998, 66).
3. Schmitt himself spoke of the victory of the "posterlike, insistent suggestion," or in other words, of the "symbol" (1985, 6).
4. It was only the French Revolution itself, according to Luhmann, that "would feel compelled after the murder of the king to *redefine* sovereignty through the organization of decisions"—and precisely not to simply abolish it or replace it through deliberation (2000, 341–342; emphasis added).
5. "The verdict is only a verdict if pronounced with almost unnatural assurance. There is no mercy in it and no caution and it accords best with its real nature when it is reached without reflection" (Canetti 1960, 345). The root of political judgment as a "disease" can be found, according to Canetti, in man's "profound need to arrange and rearrange in groups all the human beings he knows or can imagine; by dividing that loose amorphous mass into two opposing groups he gives it a kind of density. He draws up these groups as though in battle array; he makes them exclusive and fills them with enmity for each other" (346). With this observation, Canetti likewise casts light on the internal coherence between Schmitt's doctrine of sovereignty and his later *Concept of the Political*, in which he defines the distinction between friend and enemy as "the utmost degree of intensity of a union or separation, of an association or dissociation" (Schmitt 2007a, 26).
6. Emphasis added. Note omitted in Schwab's translation.
7. To use here the title of an essay by Luhmann (1993). This transition can be described in different terms as a transition from rivalry in stratified societies for opportunities for political power to sovereignty in functionally differentiated societies. Modern politics, as understood by systems theory, exists in the constitutional conditioning of sovereign exercise of power, although it is implied that this conditioning or limitation consistently more or less succeeds and can occasionally fail completely.
8. Benjamin formulates the same issue as follows: "Christendom or Europe is divided into a number of European Christian provinces whose historical actions no longer claim to be integrated in the process of redemption" (1998, 78).
9. Judith Butler quotes U.S. Department of Defense General Counsel Haynes, who replied to a reporter's question on the reasons for the indefinite imprisonment of "enemy combatants" as follows: "The people that we now hold at Guantanamo are held for a specific reason that is not tied specifically to any particular crime. They're not held—they're not being held on the basis that they are necessarily criminals" (2004, 74–75).
10. "*Eben lese ich bei Bloy* (le Vieux de la Montagne 1910) *den Satz: la guerre est dénuée de sens, quand elle n'est pas exterminatrice*" (Schmitt in Kiesel 1999, 49).
11. "Julius Streicher had done the inviting!" (Lauermann 1988, 51). Further "clues to Carl Schmitt's antisemitism" can also be found here.
12. This process extends over a series of stages: the definition of a population group; the exclusion of its members from public life, especially economically (dismissal, expropriation, deprivation of civil rights); their deportation and concentration; the exploitation of their labor to the point of starvation; and finally organized extermination, which occurs together with the confiscation of personal effects (cf. Hilberg 1985, 53–55, as well as Bauman 1989, 190).

13. For example, Helmuth Kiesel, in his afterword to the volume of Schmitt and Jünger correspondence, writes that Schmitt "contributed to the embarrassing tracing and marking of Jewish 'elements' in the German legal system" (Kiesel 1999, 862).

14. Raphael Gross emphasized the inquisitory signature of Carl Schmitt's *Political Theology*. Gross shows that Schmitt's state of exception refers to the situation in which the enemy does not openly reveal himself as such, so that his existence as a whole becomes problematic. The Spanish Inquisition was directed primarily against the *conversos*, who were accused of secretly continuing to hold to the Jewish faith and only using the appearance of Catholic orthodoxy in order to infiltrate the Christian state. Schmitt's conspicuous, obsessive hate for Spinoza can be explained precisely in light of this issue (cf. Gross 2000, 82–86). Schmitt is able to ascribe the "state-destroying" potency to the "*Blick des ersten liberalen Juden*" ("gaze of the first liberal Jew"), which Schmitt imagines in his *Leviathan* book, primarily because Spinoza descends from the Marranos, who eluded the grip of the inquisitor by escaping to Amsterdam (Schmitt 1982, 86).

References

Agamben, G. 2005. *State of Exception*, trans. K. Attell. Chicago: University of Chicago Press.

Arendt, H. 1979. *The Origins of Totalitarianism*, new ed. New York: Harvest.

Arendt, H.1998. *The Human Condition*, 2nd ed. Chicago: University of Chicago Press.

Balke, F. 1992. "Die Figur des Fremden bei Carl Schmitt und Georg Simmel." *Sociologia Internationalis* 30: 35–59.

Balke, F. 1996. *Der Staat nach seinem Ende: Die Versuchung Carl Schmitts*. Munich: Fink.

Bauman, Z. 1989. *Modernity and the Holocaust*. Ithaca: Cornell University Press.

Bauman, Z. 1991. *Modernity and Ambivalence*. Oxford: Polity.

Benjamin, W. 1998. *The Origin of German Tragic Drama*, trans. J. Osborne. London: Verso.

Butler, J. 2004. "Indefinite Detention." In *Precarious Life: The Powers of Mourning and Violence*. London: Verso, 50–100.

Canetti, E. 1960. "Judgement and Condemnation." In *Crowds and Power*, trans. C. Stewart. Harmondsworth: Penguin, 345–347.

Derrida, J. 2005. *The Politics of Friendship*, trans. G. Collins. London: Verso.

Foucault, M. 1979. *Discipline and Punish: The Birth of the Prison*, trans. A. Sheridan. New York: Vintage.

Foucault, M.1990. *The Will to Knowledge: The History of Sexuality*, vol. 1, trans. R. Hurley. London: Penguin.

Foucault, M. 1994. "Lives of Infamous Men." In *Power*, trans. R. Hurley, ed. J. D. Faubion. New York: New Press, 157–175.

Foucault, M. 2003. *Abnormal: Lectures at the Collège de France 1974–1975*, trans. G. Burchell. New York: Picador.

Foucault, M. 2007. *Security, Territory, Population: Lectures at the Collège de France 1977–78*, trans. G. Burchell. New York: Palgrave.

Fraenkel, E. 1941. *The Dual State: A Contribution to the Theory of Dictatorship*, trans. E. A. Shils. New York: Oxford University Press.

Fraenkel, E. 2017. *The Dual State: A Contribution to the Theory of Dictatorship*, expanded ed., trans. E. A. Shils, with an introduction by J. Meierhenrich. Oxford: Oxford University Press.

Gross, R. 2000. *Carl Schmitt and the Jews: The "Jewish Question," the Holocaust and German Legal Theory*, trans. J. Golb. Madison: University of Wisconsin Press.

Hilberg, R. 1985. *The Destruction of the European Jews*, vol. 1. New York: Holmes & Meier.

Kantorowicz, E. 1957. *The King's Two Bodies: A Study in Medieval Political Theology*. Princeton: Princeton University Press.

Kiesel, H. ed. 1999. *Ernst Jünger und Carl Schmitt: Briefwechsel 1930–1983*. Stuttgart: Klett-Cotta.

Koselleck, R. 1973. *Kritik und Krise: Eine Studie zur Pathogenese der bürgerlichen Welt*. Frankfurt: Suhrkamp.

Lauermann, M. 1988. "Versuch über Carl Schmitt im Nationalsozialismus." In *Carl Schmitt und die Liberalismuskritik*, ed. K. Hansen and H. Lietzmann. Opladen: Leske & Budrich, 37–51.

Link, J. 1997. *Versuch über den Normalismus: Wie Normalität produziert wird*. Opladen: Westdeutscher Verlag.

Locke, J. 1988. "The Second Treatise of Government." In *Two Treatises of Government*, ed. P. Laslett. Cambridge: Cambridge University Press, 265–428.

Luhmann, N. 1993. "Staat und Staatsräson im Übergang von traditionaler Herrschaft zu moderner Politik." In *Gesellschaftsstruktur und Semantik: Studien zur Wissenssoziologie der modernen Gesellschaft*, vol. 3. Frankfurt: Suhrkamp, 65–148.

Luhmann, N. 1995. *Social Systems*, trans. J. BednarzJr. Stanford: Stanford University Press.

Luhmann, N. 1997. *Gesellschaft der Gesellschaft*, vol. 2. Frankfurt: Suhrkamp.

Luhmann, N. 2000. *Die Politik der Gesellschaft*, ed. A. Kieserling. Frankfurt: Suhrkamp.

Mommsen, H. 1966. *Beamtentum im Dritten Reich: Mit ausgewählten Quellen zur nationalsozialistischen Beamtenpolitik*. Stuttgart: DVA.

Schmitt, C. 1918. "Die Buribunken: Ein geschichtsphilosophischer Versuch." *Summa* 4: 89–106.

Schmitt, C. 1929. "Wesen und Werden des faschistischen Staates." In Schmitt 1988, 124–130.

Schmitt, C. 1933. *Der Begriff des Politischen*, 3rd ed. Hamburg: Hanseatische Verlagsanstalt.

Schmitt, C. 1936. "Die deutsche Rechtswissenschaft im Kampf gegen den jüdischen Geist: Schlusswort auf der Tagung der Reichsgruppe Hochschullehrer des NSRB vom 3. und 4. Oktober 1936." *Deutsche Juristen-Zeitung* 41: 1193–1199.

Schmitt, C. 1958. *Verfassungsrechtliche Aufsätze aus den Jahren 1924–1954: Materialien zu einer Verfassungslehre*. Berlin: Duncker & Humblot.

Schmitt, C. 1963. *Der Begriff des Politischen: Text von 1932 mit einem Vorwort und drei Corollarien*. Berlin: Duncker & Humblot.

Schmitt, C. 1982. *Der Leviathan in der Staatslehre des Thomas Hobbes: Sinn und Fehlschlag eines politischen Symbols*. Cologne: Hohenheim.

Schmitt, C. 1985. *The Crisis of Parliamentary Democracy*, trans. E. Kennedy. Cambridge: MIT Press.

Schmitt, C. 1986. *Political Romanticism*, trans. G. Oaks. Cambridge: MIT Press.

Schmitt, C. 1988. *Positionen und Begriffe im Kampf mit Weimar—Genf—Versailles 1923–1939*, 2nd ed. Berlin: Duncker & Humblot.

Schmitt, C. 1996. *Roman Catholicism and Political Form*, trans. G. L. Ulmen. Westport: Greenwood Press.

Schmitt, C. 2005. *Political Theology: Four Chapters on the Concept of Sovereignty*, trans. G. Schwab. Chicago: University of Chicago Press.

Schmitt, C. 2007a. *The Concept of the Political*, trans. G. Schwab. Chicago: University of Chicago Press.

Schmitt, C. 2007b. *Theory of the Partisan: Intermediate Commentary on the Concept of the Political*, trans. G. L. Ulmen. New York: Telos Press.

Schmitt, C. 2008. *Constitutional Theory*, trans. and ed. J. Seitzer. Durham: Duke University Press.

Schmitt, C. 2014. *Dictatorship: From the Origin of the Modern Concept of Sovereignty to Proletarian Class Struggle*, trans. M. Hoelzl and G. Ward. Cambridge: Polity.

Weber, M. 2013. *Economy and Society: An Outline of Interpretative Sociology*, vol. 1, ed. G. Roth and C. Wittich. Berkeley: University of California Press.

CHAPTER 25

IS "THE POLITICAL" A ROMANTIC CONCEPT?

Novalis's Faith and Love or The King and Queen *with Reference to Carl Schmitt*

RÜDIGER CAMPE

INTRODUCTION

THIS CHAPTER suggests reading *Faith and Love or The King and Queen* by Novalis, the paradigmatic manifestation of political thought in Early German Romanticism, with an eye to Carl Schmitt's theory of the political as it developed in the 1920s and 1930s. The term Early Romanticism is used to identify a short period (1795–1805) in German literature and, even more so, literary and philosophical thought more than a hundred years before Schmitt. This group of young intellectuals was shaped politically by the experience of the French Revolution, the almost imminent breakdown of the Prussian state, and the dominance of Napoleon's new forms and techniques of government across the European continent. With regard to their position in philosophy, the brothers Friedrich and Wilhelm August Schlegel, Friedrich Schleiermacher, Friedrich Wilhelm Schelling, and Friedrich von Hardenberg (aka Novalis)—the "Friedrich"-pattern is no coincidence—were part of the unfolding of German Idealism, the further development and encyclopedic elaboration of the philosophical system Immanuel Kant had just formulated. Idealism sought to reflect on and reinterpret the very task of philosophy, which in these ambitious followers' view had come into the world with Kant. Whatever we may recognize as Kant's initial project today, for those who turned it into the starting point of the new, German, Idealism, it was the attempt to define philosophy in its entirety for the first time and comprehensively as a science (see Förster 2013; Behler 1987). Conceptualizing the turn of philosophy into science was what the Early Romantics pursued in their own writings as a continuation and further development of Kant's works, but also as that work's coming to terms with its own systemic nature. Transcending and completing Kant's project was, for the poets, philosophers, and scholars of Early Romanticism, one and the same. Theirs was an enormously hectic and yet concentrated, thematically far-reaching and yet deeply esoteric undertaking, with Johann Gottlieb Fichte's *Science of Knowledge* (1794) as its first moment of crystallization (see Frank 2004; Behler 1993).

The term and the distinction Schmitt introduced with the notion of "the political" can be seen as a characteristic product of Early Romanticism (see Vollrath 1987; Meier 2006; Bedorf and Röttgers 2010; Hebekus and Völker 2012). Distinguishing this or that political practice and this or that form of government from what renders all of these phenomena appearances of the political dimension of human life performs, we may argue, the very gesture of a transcendental critique (for a similar claim, see Marder 2009). "The political" emerges thus as the response to the question of what allows us to refer to procedures and events, constitutions and patterns of action as political in the first place. In his early publication *Gesetz und Urteil* (*Statute and Judgment*), Schmitt proposes a formula to define the "right decision of the judge" that evokes Kant's categorical imperative, transposed, as it were, into sociological and historical terms; a juridical decision, Schmitt explains in this early work, is the right decision only if we can convincingly assume that another judge makes the same judgment. "Another judge" refers in this phrasing to the type—the term taken in Max Weber's sense—of the modern, educated jurist (Schmitt 1912, 71).[1] Even if Schmitt does not use a formula such as "the juridical" in this context, it is easy to grasp how it echoes Kant's transcendental critique of morality on the one hand and prepares the way for Schmitt's own *Political Theology* as well *The Concept of the Political* on the other (2005; 1996).[2]

The formula is crafted in such a way as to maintain the full normative power of the judgment without binding it back to preexisting norms. Law, in this view, is not determined by values, norms, or principles that preexist outside the juridical sphere in a moral or social world. The defining case for the law is rather the morally and socially indifferent situation in which it is the function of the law to merely introduce a fixed mark and measure for distinguishing right from wrong. With each act of judgment, such original normativity of bringing distinction into the indifference of life is reinstated. What Schmitt later calls "political theology" and explicates in terms of "the political" are homologues to this early attempt in legal philosophy. Interestingly, what responds to the later dramatic state of exception and the existential situation of distinguishing friend from enemy is the colorless indifference of life with regard to the judgment-bound theory of civil law. We might even go so far as to say that each and every law presupposes the original act of introducing normativity, the model of "the political," in order to be law, and every essentially political act is directed toward the reconstitution of law.

The constellation proposed in this chapter, which invites a look at the Romantic poet Novalis from a Schmittian perspective, will lead us back to such a consideration of "the political" as a precondition for understanding the law, even if in more limited and, hopefully, precise terms (see the third section below). For the moment, however, an obvious objection must be answered: Even if we accept the claim that "the political" has a transcendental character, the question remains whether such an argument refers back specifically and necessarily to the Early Romantics. In support of this claim, I point to similar conceptual turns in the aesthetic and critical debates of the Schlegels, Schelling, and others. In their reinterpretation of traditional poetics and poetic criticism, they perform strikingly similar operations. The most famous example is the theory of "the tragic" as distinguished from what we know about tragedies, their history, their poetical rules, and the criticism of specific instances of the genre. "The tragic" in Schelling, Solger, and Hegel differs from poetics and the interpretation of tragedies in the same way as "the political," with Schmitt, is to be distinguished from constitutional forms and modes of government, the topics of political philosophy in the traditional sense (cf. Szondi 2002). More than that, the famous triad of literary genres—the epic, the dramatic, and the lyric—has come into discursive being with the Early Romantics in this same characteristic linguistic form of an adjective turned noun (see Staiger 1991). Such conceptualization in literary theory offers a remarkable prefiguration to Schmitt's construction of "the political."

And yet all of this is far from what Schmitt had to say about early and not so early Romantics. Despite the epistemic homology of "the political" and, consequently, of "political theology," with the Early Romantic notions of "the tragic" or "the epic, the dramatic and the lyric," Schmitt develops the construction of the political in exact opposition to what he sees as "political Romanticism." This point is discussed in more detail at the beginning of the first section below. It should, however, be noted here that in Schmitt's ideological evaluation, Romanticism signifies the ultimate destruction of original normativity. Political theology, as the sovereignty of decision in the state of exception, and the political, as separating friend from enemy, are for Schmitt both irreconcilably opposed to how the Romantics develop their notions and claims. The Romantic construction of ideas is, according to Schmitt, constitutively self-reflexive and aesthetic (Schmitt 1986; cf. Lima 1996, 107–136). Such ideas are therefore dependent on the subject, whose reflective possibilities generate them or whose aesthetic construction brings them into play. What Schmitt calls the "occasionalism" of Romantic theory (1986, 82–93) refers to the general structure of something "being dependent on" someone's beliefs, attitudes, or inclinations. The occasion of occasionalism is the coincidental circumstance under which a thought is shaped in the way it is shaped. Even if the "occasion" implies different connotations, the basic structure of "being dependent on" is equivalent to what we today call "contingency" (i.e., being contingent on something).[3] The suggestion of calling such a view on "political Romanticism" ideological is to underline the fact that with it, Schmitt observes and evaluates the procedures of reflection and aesthetic construction rather than giving an account of their function in the development of Kantianism and the unfolding of idealism. The question arises of why Schmitt is so focused on, and to what extent he has succeeded in, separating the systemic character of original normativity in judgment, decision, and distinction from the ideological picture of the Romantics' attitudes of reflection and aesthetic play, two sides that seem not necessarily opposed to each other in Early Romanticism.

Asking such a question does not entail catching Schmitt in an act of denial. It is not about demonstrating that the fiercest critic of political Romanticism has been, in the construction of the notion of the political, a Romantic himself. Neither is the goal to demonstrate that his ambivalence results from the problem of differentiation in the first place. This is not a critique of Schmitt or a deconstruction of his theory, although both tasks are important and justified. Rather, what is proposed with a closer look at Novalis's compilation of poems, fragments, and aphorisms under the title *Faith and Love or The King and Queen* is meant to trace Schmitt's striking ambivalence back to a primary and defining motif in Romanticism. What becomes Schmitt's ambivalence can thus be studied as if in the state of genesis and vital functioning in Novalis. In this sense, the following is a study in genealogy.

It is all the more so given the fact that *Faith and Love* forms a constitutive and early part of the history of "the political." In it we can identify a thinking of the political dimension of the law that helps clarify Schmitt's conceptual operations and his ambivalence toward Romanticism. Furthermore, through the particularities of its partial publication and nonpublication, its claim to hidden messages, and the obvious abuse in the hands of its addressees, the king and queen, *Faith and Love* offers itself to a genealogical study of "the political," even under the aspect of the material fabric and fate of its text (see the second section below; Novalis 1997, 85–100).[4]

The quality exhibited by these pieces of being a secret message is certainly motivated specifically by their political character, but it also is typical of the themes and character of this authorial personage in general. Novalis has always been a *poeta absconditus* of sorts, outside of German-speaking lands but also within them. Due to his early death, most of his works became accessible to a larger public only posthumously in a two-volume edition by Friedrich Schlegel and Ludwig Tieck (1802). While his fragmentary novel, *Henry of Ofterdingen*, and his cycle of poems, *Hymns to the Night*, have helped define Romantic prose and poetry in German literature, and his aphorisms, such as *Logological Fragments*, or essayistic writings, such as "Monologue," count among the most important Romantic writings on the conjunction of philosophy and poetry,[5] Novalis has always embodied the secret of Romantic thinking and writing like no other author. In addition, for the English reader it has long been difficult to access the important fragments and diaries that comprise his studies on philosophy, beginning with the *Fichte Studies* (2003b; cf. Molnár 1970), and his encyclopedic project, *Allgemeines Brouillon* (2007, translated as *Notes for a Romantic Encyclopedia*).

Together with his essay "Christendom or Europe" (1997, 137–152), the poems, fragments, and essayistic pieces collected under the name *Faith and Love or The King and Queen* form the densest and most coherent document of Novalis's political thinking. They exhibit the character of coded message in a programmatic way. *Faith and Love* is not only a tract on the political in poetic terms, it is also the performance of a political utterance in its own poetico-political tone. Addressing themselves to the Prussian king and queen, the poems and aphorisms are in need of poetic camouflage. The monarch, if he accepted the address, would turn into the centerpiece of a republic. In the politics of the address, a transformative function of the theory professed reveals itself; it defines the style of extreme intellectual political intervention, an intervention that hopes to side with the power by redefining the power's systemic conditions of being. As a political act, transcendental critique and transformative poetic invention go hand in hand. However, if one evaluates Schmitt's politics in the 1920s, or for that matter during the 1930s and 1940s—topics beyond the scope of this chapter—his interventions can well be seen as developing within the traces left by the Romantic poet when he sent his message to court.

The fate that *Faith and Love* experiences in the hands of king and queen (see second section below) links the type of discourse that is "the political" (discussed in the first section) with observations on this discourse's pragmatic conditions (analyzed in the third section). Concentrating on the Romantic *poeta absconditus* who prefigures Schmitt's political intervention means going back behind the legal theoretician's ambivalence in juxtaposing "the political" and "political Romanticism" in the days of the emerging "Third Reich."

The Nation-State and Its Visibility: Genealogy of a Discourse

> It is a great mistake of our states that one sees the state too little. The state should be visible everywhere, every person should be identified as a citizen. Could not badges and uniforms be generally introduced? Whoever regards such things as trivial is not familiar with an essential quality of our nature.
>
> Novalis 1997, "Faith and Love," fragment 19, 89[6]

This aphorism can be seen as the emblematic statement on the political in the group of texts that bear the title *Faith and Love or the King and Queen*. Novalis managed to publish parts of *Faith and Love* with Friedrich Schlegel's support under his nom de plume, "Novalis," in 1798 in the *Jahrbücher der Preussischen Monarchie unter der Regierung Friedrich Wilhelms III*, the Yearbooks of the Prussian monarchy under the reign of Frederick William III.[7] The new king had ascended the throne just the year before, and he was to oversee this most precarious phase of Prussian statehood, between the death of Frederick II ("Frederick the Great") in 1786 and the subsequent reign of Frederick William II in 1786–1797, with the French Revolution redefining European politics in 1789, on the one side, and on the other, Prussia's military defeat in the war with Napoleon in 1806 and the imposed ending of the Holy Roman Empire of the German Nation in the same year.

For a start, a brief commentary on the three sentences of aphorism 19 may provide an introduction to Novalis's political thinking. First comes the principle of visibility: "It is a great mistake of our states that one sees the state too little." The longing for and insistence upon the state's visibility is at the heart of modern political concerns. Characteristic of conservative thinking since the nineteenth century, it can also be found on the left side of the spectrum. The death of Louis XVI under the guillotine had left a void or rather yielded an opening in political imagination that cried out to be filled.[8] What we call "the political" since Schmitt and the early twentieth century was, beginning with the revolutionary regime in Paris, defined in no small part by a politics of visibility (e.g., the spectacles of the Revolution, staged, among others, by Jacques Louis David; see Ozouf 1988). Historian Christian Meier (1980) has argued that the origin of traditional political philosophy in ancient Greece is to be found in a reflexive gesture. According to Meier, political thinking emerges not so much as an act of constituting political order and organizing its institutional forms as by reflecting on existing political structures. Correspondingly, we may think of the modern theory of "the political" and its insistence on the visibility of the state as a reflection on the situation of European statehood after the French Revolution. The state's visibility as the essential concern of the political—the care of the political in the Heideggerian and Foucauldian sense of the term—is thus a matter of restaging the state's visibility in representation.

There is no reason to wonder why the state was not overly visible in Prussian lands as of 1798. When Frederick William III ascended the throne, Prussia had remained quiet in regard to the successful French Revolution during the preceding years, and the dissolution of the Holy Roman Empire lay no longer in the distant future. But Prussia's invisibility had other, and arguably even deeper, reasons than the French regicide and the imminence of the demise of the medieval empire a part of which it still was a part. There had never been much of a state to see in Berlin. Other than an old *Stadtpalais* from the seventeenth century, a wide avenue leading out of the city, *Unter den Linden*, and all sorts of military trappings, Berlin was still free from the heavy stamp of the national pomp that came later at the end of the nineteenth century. The *Forum Fridericianum*, however remarkably it was designed in the 1750s and 1760s with a royal opera house and library and various aristocratic palaces, never became a full reality (Engel 2001). Frederick II, who had planned the *Forum*, preferred to hide himself away in the invisibility of the park of Sanssouci, his *Ersatz* residence in Potsdam (designed and built 1745–1747 by von Knobelsdorff) from the late 1760s on. Those who wished to look at Berlin with faith and love, to refer to Novalis's Paulinian title,[9] had to content themselves with numbers and diagrammatic figures. Around the 1750s, Pastor Süssmilch, for one, brought his new scientific invention, population statistics, to bear in proving that, from the state's founding by the Great Elector in the seventeenth century onward, Berlin had grown more swiftly than either Paris or London, even if, as he reluctantly admitted, the older capitals still had the upper hand (Süssmilch 1752). We may in fact go so far as to claim that Prussia in 1798 still lacked a developed self-staging of the traditional, court-centered fabric. The country was a military and administrative machine, presenting itself in statistical tables and otherwise built within an old medieval empire, which for its part no longer had much more to offer than the tourist attraction of imperial coronations.[10]

Accordingly, the visibility that Novalis wishes to implement is not the visibility of bygone courtly representation. It is instead a secondary visibility, as though it were the visualization of Süssmilch's statistics through acts and events of actual life. "The state should be visible everywhere, every person should be identified as a citizen," Novalis continues in aphorism 19. "Could not badges and uniforms be generally introduced?" Citizens administered and counted in population figures are to be made visible as persons with badges and uniforms. In this continuation of his formula of visibility lies Novalis's conceptualization of what one might call Man's two bodies. Each and every citizen is here considered as a physical body that, at the same time, is part of the comprehensive representation of the body politic. Primary subjects of this representation are no longer princes and kings and the God-givenness of their dominion as with Ernst Kantorowicz's two bodies of the prince in Old Europe, but the bodies of governed subjects. Such bodies of biopolitics, as one might call them with Michel Foucault, are, it seems, in need of an additional representation as citizens of the administering state. Novalis actually suggests a broad spectrum of possibilities for such biopolitical, that is, secondary and reflexive, representation: medals for worthy housewives, the queen's performance as headmistress of the state in its welfare functions (upbringing, public health, public buildings), or depictions of king and queen in the interior of family homes instead of the official posts where they were traditionally presented to the public.

The venue for the publication of Novalis's essay, the *Jahrbücher*, since its inception in 1798 became an almost experimental forum for the visibility of the new Prussian state that was to come (Stamm-Kuhlmann 1992, 486–511).[11] A statistical publication in the traditional sense of the word, the *Jahrbücher* added documents of anecdotal evidence of the personal involvement of the prince and his family in the administration of the country; in its pages one may find poems of homage to the young royal couple, the king and queen, next to statistical treatises on Prussia's provinces. Data on the economy and military in Prussia are presented alongside—and surprisingly so—the cabinet orders issued by the king. The *Jahrbücher* bring together articles on political theory, descriptions of the royal couple's family life, reports from the capital's opera house, and news about the wars of the coalition against revolutionary France. The national architecture and iconography of Prussia developed by artists such as Johann Gottfried Schadow and Karl Friedrich Schinkel got their head start in its pages as well (see, among others, Bergdoll 1994; Mirsch 1998; Simon 1999). In his own contribution to the *Jahrbücher*, Novalis introduces a further meaning of the politics of visibility. In concluding aphorism 19 about how to fashion people and their biopolitical bodies as citizens, he remarks, "Whoever regards such things as trivial is not familiar with an essential quality of our nature." This final maxim seems in full harmony with the *Jahrbücher's* project to present the human, both bourgeois and corporeal, nature of king and queen to their people. But more precisely, it adds a hidden counter message: the people's many bodies should for their part become visible in the eyes of king and queen as both physical beings and members of the nation-state. The visibility of Man's two bodies, a human animal and a citizen, thus rephrases the formerly Christian grounding of political order with a fundamentally anthropological argument.

In what follows, the underlying claim is that such replacing of theology by anthropology is constitutively implied when we speak today of "political theology" and "the political" in the nineteenth or twentieth centuries. Visibility of the nation-state was in fact the central demand of those who coined the term "political theology" in the twentieth century. The relevant sources of this term are, first, Schmitt, and second the legal historian Ernst Kantorowicz.[12] For both, visibility means the embodiment of representation that occurs either in the persona of the legitimate ruler or in the act of usurping his power; in other words, in either Kantorowicz's figure of the prince or Schmitt's model situation of the dictator acting in the state of exception. Visibility, either of the king's body and princely insignia or in the dictator's decision, thus stands in for the *theologoumenon* of the unfounded foundation of a state's order. The demand for the state's visibility is the counterpart to a structural necessity implied in the concept of the political in political theology, the paradox of the unfounded foundation.

Both Kantorowicz and Schmitt work out the concept of political theology and the visibility of the political by reverting to theories and practices current before the Enlightenment and the modern age of mass societies and democracy. Kantorowicz for his part falls back on the medieval legal construction of the king as the *christomimetes*—the representative and actor of Christ—in order to let the ruler make his appearance as the incorporation of the state's visibility. In the case of Schmitt, it is the structural moment of decision in the state of exception that takes on theological momentum. The *creatio ex nihilo* of the God-creator is Schmitt's formula for the decision in the state of emergency, which he claims to find in Bodin's analysis of absolute sovereignty. For Kantorowicz and Schmitt, Enlightenment or modernity are complicit in forgetting what characterized political order and theory in Old Europe. According to them, the Enlightenment of the eighteenth century, along with the modern nation-states and mass societies of the following centuries, have forgotten and even erased the former theological concept of politics that either in the persona of the sovereign or in his sovereign act of decision used to supplement the state's foundation-without-a-foundation with irreducible, primordial visibility.

These brief remarks may suffice as a reminder of modern political theology's basic argumentative moves. The question to be raised in the present context is, however, this: Does modern political theology in fact hearken back to Kantorowicz's medieval theology or Schmitt's baroque origin of sovereignty? Or is their true point of departure rather the reflexive, anthropological, and biopolitical argument proffered by Novalis? Not that the gestures of looking back to the past were in themselves problematic in Kantorowicz and Schmitt as such. There is no doubt that Kantorowicz can find mouthpieces for his political theology of royal incorporation in the church fathers as well as in late medieval legal thought (Kantorowicz 1997, 42–86). Similarly, Bodin's search for the office of absolute power and Hobbes's discussion of sovereignty in *Leviathan* suggest themselves quite naturally as figures of appeal for Schmitt (Schmitt 2005, 7–10). A more detailed discussion would also have to stress the point that the two arguments fundamentally differ in how they conceive the historicity of political theology. For Kantorowicz, the history is one of documents and edicts, theological doctrines, and juridical statements. Schmitt's, by contrast, is a history of metaphysical worldviews.

According to his argument, Christianity opens and leaves room for the decision in the state of exception, which is a *creatio ex nihilo*, whereas it is the progression of modern enlightened and liberal thinking that tends to bar and increasingly "neutralize" the space for such sovereign action. But the phrase "one sees the state too little," the reflexive confirmation of the need of and desire for representation, is in fact different from both the doctrinal and the structural-metaphysical history of political theology. The insistence on visibility originates as such only with the situation of the state after the French Revolution, the defining context for Novalis and his contemporary Romantics. The demand for visibility, in any event, does not provide a ground for what exactly political theology falls back upon; it only motivates the gesture of reversion.

Keeping in mind this fundamental difference between Schmitt's and Kantorowicz's versions of political theology, Novalis may in fact be seen as anticipating both versions of historical argumentation in regard to their formal aspect. Novalis's slightly later essay "Christendom or Europe" (1997) is a starting point for every theory that places the legitimacy of state and moral order in the legendary Middle Ages, an "old time" before the Enlightenment. Even if this text does not argue explicitly in political terms, it still molds its thesis of the foundation of legitimate order upon Christian, theological, structures. "Christendom or Europe," one might argue, is a reference text for the discourse leading up to Kantorowicz' *King's Two Bodies* and the dogmatic history of political theology. *Faith and Love*, on the other hand, is an outspoken political text. As will be shown in greater detail, it is closely related to Schmitt's version, which sees the political in the unfounded foundation of a decision or a primary, irreducible distinction. One can therefore claim that the essential elements of political theology for both Kantorowicz and Schmitt—that is, the question of the unfounded foundation of the political, and hence the necessity of visibility for the state—find their formal templates in Novalis.

In speaking of political theology, I am thus not only addressing the prehistory of the undertaking that emerges under this name in the early twentieth century. Neither is the tradition of political theology meant as Kantorowicz and Schmitt themselves formulated it when they enlisted medieval Christology or the baroque sovereign respectively as models for their theories, however different their historical thinking was otherwise. What is at stake here is a tradition of posing the question of political theology, the question as to how the unfounded foundation of law is to be conceived. This tradition, such is the claim here, does go back before the twentieth century; but it does not begin as far back as the Middle Ages or the baroque period. Its moment comes in the closing years of the eighteenth century, during the late Enlightenment and early Romanticism— and perhaps even amid the Great Revolution itself. According to this assumption, the demand for the state's visibility and for reaching back toward a theological fundament of law begins in the same historical moment when forgetfulness of the visibility of the theological foundation of politics is starting to take hold. They are two sides of the same coin.

This is not only about correcting dates in intellectual history. What matters is rather the theoretical essence of political theology. It is no coincidence that Schmitt worked so emphatically to distinguish political theology, which he wished to refound, from what he termed "political Romanticism." His polemic against "political Romanticism" is aimed primarily at figures such as Friedrich Schlegel and Adam Müller, whereas Novalis appears less a target of attack. It is, however, a fragment by Novalis that is emblematic for what Schmitt eyes as "occasionalism," the "being-contingent-upon" subjective circumstances rather than original normativity. This is how Schmitt quotes the fragment in question and comments on it: "All the accidents of our lives are materials from which we can make what we want. Everything is the first element of an infinite series (up to this point, the sentence could still articulate a magical mysticism, but the conclusion is a manifestation of romanticism), the beginning of an endless novel."[13] The diatribe against "political Romanticism" opens up for Schmitt the demand for "political theology" and "the political."

The stark opposition between political Romanticism and political theology in Schmitt and its strategic sense can be clarified with a brief reference to *The Concept of the Political*. "The political," based as it is for Schmitt on distinguishing friend from enemy, is a differentiation that can only be actively drawn (1996, 25–45). In its political quality it can neither observe itself in its execution, nor be observed by others from the outside. Other registers of differentiation, such as that between beautiful and ugly in aesthetics, or between just and unjust in morality, are decisions that can and must be spoken about and reflected upon. Aesthetics and morality consist precisely in debate and reflection about those judgments. Differentiating between friend and enemy, however, is the absolute moment of drawing the distinction, a performance that cannot be mediated or objectified by any observation or reflection. The enemy is the Other per se, the political distinction being nothing less than the original form of differentiation in general. As soon as one tries to observe or discuss the distinction, the assumed purity of the performance, the purity of drawing the distinction is compromised (i.e., aestheticizied or moralized). Aestheticizing and moralizing the political distinction, then, are precisely key modes of what Schmitt calls "political Romanticism." For Schmitt it was the Romantics who—regardless of how far to the right or to the left they might have been engaged—always only *spoke about* political distinctions. "Political Romantics" missed "the political" because they destroyed its unobservable nature, the nature of pure emergence.

Seen against the foil of such a strict asymmetry between "political theology" and the forgetting of "the political" among "political Romantics," Novalis is here seen as the inventor of a *political theology* that is, however, essentially a *Romantic's* political theory. If this hypothesis is born out, then not only does the history of political theology demand a critical revision, but the theory itself undergoes a significant change. Viewed in this way, Novalis's theory of the political performs the political distinction and at the same time is its own self-observation. It articulates the absolute necessity of making the state visible and simultaneously shows the constructive means that are to be used to this end. Its figure is the catachresis—the metaphorical figure for which the proper word, the literal designation, is missing. This figure is a serious political argument in Novalis—but it is also and, despite Schmitt, a poetical play.

The Hermeneutic Chain of Command
at the Prussian Court: A Sovereign's
Problem of Reading

And what about the one who embodied this catachresis, the king? He was not amused. By the time the first two installments of *Faith and Love* appeared in the *Jahrbücher*, his displeasure had quickly made the rounds at the Berlin court, and any further publication was refused. How is the one who is declared to be a mere catachresis supposed to understand the text that generated him and made him into the visibility that is to complement the unfounded foundation?

As Novalis explains in aphorism 18 of *Faith and Love*, "The distinguishing character of the monarchy lies precisely in the fact of belief in a high-born person, of voluntary acceptance of an ideal person. I cannot choose a leader among my peers; I can entrust nothing to someone who is concerned as I am with the same question. The monarchy is a true system because it is bound to an absolute midpoint; to a being that belongs to humanity but not to the state. The king is a human being who has been called to a higher earthly destiny (*Fatum*). This poetic fiction (*Dichtung*) urges itself to Man with necessity" (Novalis 1997, fragment 18, 88; translation modified). Being a divine word and a fiction at the same time, the king incorporates the two contradictory strands of the modern, reflexive political theology. As a *Fatum*, the king in the vein of Kantorowicz's historical version of political theology refers to God's word, a word preceding himself and a word he can refer to. As a poetic fiction, he stands in for a systematic moment like Schmitt's decision in the state of emergency, the absolute beginning. Being *Fatum* and fiction at the same time, however, the king is a paradox. Only if God's word can also be understood as a fiction can the king *play* his role; only by assuming the fiction to recapitulate nothing other than God's word does he play his *role*. This is the paradox of the midpoint that makes the cosmological system a system (and, accordingly, the state a state):[14] without being itself of the same nature as the members of the "true system," the midpoint is the necessary requirement for the closure of system or state. But although the "absolute midpoint" does not share the mode of being of the physical parts of the system or state, this point can be spatially located and made visible in the middle of both, system and the state. The question then reads more precisely: Can a paradox understand what it means to be a paradox?

Friedrich Schlegel, the romantic intellectual par excellence and preferred object of Schmitt's scorn (1986, 37–39, 111–114, 132, 148), had conveyed Novalis's submission to the *Jahrbücher*. With great relish he reported that "the king is said to have been quite put off by some of the remarks in *Faith and Love*. He said, 'More is demanded of a king than he is capable of doing. It is repeatedly forgotten that he is only human.'"[15] Schlegel is even more tickled by the royal manifestation of what he later in a famous essay from the *Athenäum* will term incomprehensibility. "The king read *Faith and*

Love but didn't understand it. So he ordered the lieutenant colonel Köckeritz to read it. Since the lieutenant colonel in turn failed to understand it, he pulled the consistorial minister Niemeyer aside for advice. When the minister also didn't understand it, he was most taken aback and indignant, and declared that one of the two Schlegels must have written the piece."[16] The king reacts to his own failure to comprehend by activating a chain of command of understanding. But the military and the clergy, the two essential rungs in this hermeneutic order of service and rank, fail one after the other.

Two lines of comment suggest themselves here for us as the readers of this complex text—of Novalis's text in the first place but also of the king's hermeneutic chain of command, and finally, of Friedrich Schlegel's role as mediator of the text and narrator of the anecdote about the king's failure to understand it. The one comment would put the submission, the anecdote, and the political situation of 1789 in context with a series of similar occurrences, whose archetypical instance this one then would be. After Novalis and *Faith and Love*, we could think of Heinrich von Kleist again sending his dramatic pamphlet, the *Hermannsschlacht*, to the court in Berlin; in the twentieth century we might take Schmitt into consideration as he fabricates a legal opinion on the *Ermächtigungsgesetz* (see Breuer 2012; Blasius 2001) or Heidegger in the 1930s as he educates the youth of the *Bewegung* in the training camps of the Black Forest. It is a series of tragic comedies of political advising that seem to be characteristic of a certain type of illusionary claim of political intervention. Failures of understanding on the part of the advisees in all cases, they also are not entirely exempt from catastrophic success. This would be a genealogy of thinkers of the political in action. On the other hand, we might comment on Friedrich Schlegel, who is the emblematic figure of intrigue and political romanticism in Schmitt's sense of the word. For Schlegel, Novalis's assembled texts are obviously an aesthetic experiment in politics and nothing else, and the king's response a political anecdote that lends itself to satire and, as Schlegel would call it, transcendental buffoonery.

As important as both comments would be, they both fail to address, however, how *Fatum* and fiction relate and cooperate—in Novalis's texts, Schlegel's hermeneutic maneuvers and the king's stuttering response. In order to understand the simultaneity of *Fatum* and fiction, one could turn to aphorism 39, which occurs toward the end of the first—published—part of *Faith and Love*. In it, Novalis calls the king "the artist of artists" and the "poet, director and hero of the play" (the play, in other words, of the state as political system and theater piece; 1997, fragment 39, 95). Taken literally, this aphorism implies that the king plays the role ascribed to him by Novalis precisely by not understanding that he plays that role. Certainly the hero, who is director and poet at the same time, seems at first to know it all. But for the very same reason, he will miss the point that even "knowing it all" is a function of a play that he can write and direct only because he has a role in it. While playing his role, the king necessarily misses the right moment to come in or step out. In the play-act that makes him a king, regardless of how much power he has in that play, the king, in his role as poet-director-and-hero, does not have the capacity to understand that he wields power only by virtue of the play and within it.

True, the king is, as Novalis explains it, the only Man outside of the state; that is, outside of the system in which all men wear the uniforms of citizenry. But he does not stand in this position outside of the play or the system in such a way that he can freely view it from the outside. When Novalis characterizes the king as "poet, director and hero of the play," he seemingly sketches a portrait of the king of the *ancien régime*. He seems to make him an absolutist prince when he speaks of the king as the one who "holds all the threads of government in his hands" and from whose vantage point alone "all the machinery of state (can) be observed" (fragment 37, 94).

Novalis probably is first to take the baroque play and its practices strictly as meta-phor and model of political analysis, including the famous "place of the king." Reading Novalis's aphorism, one might think both of the baroque practice of the king acting in courtly performances and of the place of the king as a spectator in the theater where he occupies the ideal viewpoint vis-à-vis the perspectival construction of the stage. The theater play as Novalis describes it comes, however, without the baroque play's essential assumption: the assumption of God as the absolute outside for whom the stage can be the world and the world a stage. In Novalis's theater piece of people wearing the uni-forms of citizenship, by contrast, everyone is a player in a play that has no outside and therefore no onlookers or audience. The king alone, by virtue of his acting or viewing, or the acting of his viewing, seems to stand outside and inside the play at the same time. This has two consequences, which turn the king into the helpless idiot he is in Schlegel's anecdote. On the one hand, the place of the king is the trap of the epistemological sub-ject. The subject believes himself to be the origin of the world (of the system, of the play) that he views, while in fact he is only the fiction of such an origin. This king watches the play to the extent that he also simultaneously plays a role in it. On the other hand, the king is also the one whose real flesh and body is at stake in the play. In a theater play in which all members from the beginning have two bodies—the body of man and the uni-form of citizen—the king is the arbitrary but necessary fiction of man. His real, human body is his one and only uniform. As the epistemological subject and as mere flesh and body, this king stands outside of the play and at the same time is trapped in it. Novalis's king is *Fatum* and fiction, God-given and formal requirement, of system or statehood at the same time.

A last remark on Schlegel's anecdote may be in order, which appropriately concludes in making him (or his brother) the true author of *Faith and Love* in the king's view. Although the anecdote offers a perfect example of Schmitt's political Romanticism— that is, an ironic observation of a political event—it comprises deeper layers. When Schlegel refers to his report as a "most priceless anecdote," he obviously has in mind the hermeneutic chain of command put to work by the king. "Most priceless" is for him the fact that the king believes he can command anyone's (including his own) reading of a text. Precisely that had been the proper mark of Hobbes's sovereign. The sover-eign, according to Hobbes, was master of the interpretation of the relevant text, the law, whose author he was himself. Frederick William III is the perfect parody of this sover-eign in Schlegel's "priceless anecdote." In his essay "On Incomprehensibility," composed two years later, Schlegel appropriately analyzes incomprehensibility as the impossibility of understanding the self-conditioning of systems and states or the fiction of a foundation of worlds in general:

> But is incomprehensibility really something so unmitigatedly contemptible and bad? Methinks the salvation of families and nations rests upon it. If I am not wholly deceived, then states and systems, the most artificial productions of man, are often so artificial that one simply can't admire the wisdom of their creator enough. Only an incredibly minute quantity of it suffices: as long as its truth and purity remain inviolate and no blasphemous rationality dares approach its sacred confines. Yes, even man's most precious possession, his own inner happiness, depends in the last analysis, as anybody can easily verify, on some such point of strength that must be left in the dark, but that nonetheless shores up and supports the whole burden and would crumble the moment one subjected it to rational analysis. (Schlegel 1971, 268)

Does this mean an ironic, neutral play with words, or does it point the reader toward the most serious moment of a foundational politics of how to do things with words? Is incomprehensibility, according to this later essay by Schlegel, concerned with *Fatum* or fiction? It is as though "On Incomprehensibility" were a belated attempt by Schlegel to come to terms with "the priceless anecdote" of his friend's submission to the *Jahrbücher*.

Novalis on the Political Dimension of Law: For a Conceptual Genealogy of the Schmittian Political

How does the paradox of the king, his catachrestic nature, come about? And how does *Faith and Love* keep the paradox of *Fatum* and fiction in full vigor without destroying either the paradox or its own coherence? The final question, in other words, is whether Novalis can offer a tenable interpretation of the republican sovereign that neither ends in Schmittian "political Romanticism" (in merely ironic play, that is) nor calls for a pseudo-baroque sovereign who decides unswervingly in the state of exception (a sovereign parodied in Walter Benjamin's *The German Mourning Play*; 1998, 65).[17]

The first part of *Faith and Love*, which made its way into the *Jahrbücher* in two installments (first the poems, then the fragments specifically entitled *Faith and Love*), was dedicated to the theme of the state's visibility. Though it was a vain effort, Frederick William III ordered his men to understand the theory of visibility and his own existence as the paradoxical self-conditioning of system and state. Therefore, the next and last part of Novalis's submission, the *Political Aphorisms* (Novalis's original title), failed to reach the press. In the *Political Aphorisms* the king, lieutenant cornel Köckeritz, and minister Niemeyer all could have learned to understand that the question of the state's visibility is an eminent subject of political theory and indeed the decisive point for transforming traditional political philosophy into the theory of "the political." Only when referred to and distinguished from traditional political philosophy, the call for the state's visibility acquires its full meaning of what since the beginning of the twentieth century we call "the political." Whereas constitutions, forms of government, and theories of law have been the themes of political philosophy since Aristotle, "the political" is the answer to the post-Kantian question of what constitutes the political realm in the first place. Thus the transition from an *ancien régime* concept of sovereignty to the nation-state of the nineteenth and twentieth centuries occurs in Novalis together and in accordance with a shift in theory. The discussion shifts from political themes such as constitution and law to the understanding of what establishes the existence of the political dimension in human life in the first place.

A first hint at the transformation of traditional political philosophy into a theory of "the political" is, however, already to be found within the first two, published, install-ments. "One can only be interested in a constitution," Novalis writes there, "as one is in a letter [*Buchstaben*] for its own sake" (fragment 15, 87). When he recommends in this context the monarchy, the concern is not so much for a specific form of government as for the state having a form at all. The underlying assumption here is that the state's vis-ibility relates to its constitutional law as life does to the letter of the old law that "killeth" in St. Paul's theology. "Does not the mystical sovereign need a symbol, like every idea, and what symbol is more estimable and more appropriate than a gracious, excellent per-son?" (fragment 15, 87). A state's form—the visible form and the form of visibility—is monarchical for Novalis, even if, constitutionally, the state were a republic.

In what sense, however, can the king, the category of traditional constitutionalism, become a symbol in the sense of Kantian aesthetics? How, in other words, can politi-cal philosophy become a theory of "the political?" An ambiguous use of "expression" ("*Ausdruck*") intervenes here, making the transition from politics to the political pos-sible. Novalis introduces the notion in the context of law. "What is a law if it is not the expression of the will of a beloved person who is worthy of our respect?" (fragment 15, 87). The "expression of will" ("*Ausdruck des Willens*") has two meanings. "To give expression to a will" first can mean "to execute the speech act of making one's will known"; that is, "to decide." Thus, the—Hobbesian—monarch speaks through the law. On the other hand, however, expression can also be a visible manifestation, an aesthetic representation. The monarch presents a picture of himself in the law, a picture his sub-jects may then love and put their faith in. This second meaning is in accordance with the iconographic project of the *Jahrbücher*, which had been founded precisely to create a new imaginary of Prussia. "To give expression to one's will" is the very transition from legality to aesthetics and vice versa, because it designates both law *and* aesthetics, the *creatio ex nihilo* of decision *and* romantic irony. If we understand this ambivalence not only as a mere coincidence of meanings but also as the very statement of the ambiva-lence that is the essential structure in play, both meanings can be seen as *making* the transition to the other. The aesthetic representation is then not only a representation of something, but rather the act of producing a representation of something. The law, on the other hand, would mean not only the pure act of decision and announcement of a will, but also and already its being in appearance and showing itself.

The final, unpublished, part of *Faith and Love,* the *Political Aphorisms,* concentrates on the exposition of legal theory, which the published parts had only alluded to. Here Novalis traces the transformation of traditional political philosophy into the theory of "the political" in terms of the law. This is the topic of the remaining part of my commentary here.

In *Political Aphorisms,* Novalis first of all engages in the discussion of the traditional forms of government and their constitutions: democracy, oligarchy, and monarchy. This conventional way of treating the topics of political philosophy, however, captures only a superficial layer of the discussion. The thrust of the argument goes further than that. In every form of government, Novalis insists, the individual is exposed to the basic facticity of his or her being an integrated part of the state or system. The fact that the individual stands in relation to other individuals makes him and her subject to a heteronomous law or, more precisely, to the law as heteronomy in *any* state or system. The question as to whether this web of primary relations, the law of the state as a system, speaks in the name of all, many, or one singular person is of no immediate consequence in this basic respect. What the specific nature of the law is that socializes an individual is of secondary importance to the law's primary coming into being and its constitutive relation to the individual subject. "In all relative circumstances," Novalis writes, "the individual is once and for all exposed to caprice—and if I went into the wilderness—is not my essential interest [*Interesse*] still exposed there to the caprice of my individuality? The individuality, as such, is of his nature governed by *chance*" (fragment 63, 98).

The law, then, is essentially contingent, and its contingency is its essence. This argument affects the traditional distinction between the natural or essential and the positive or historically accidental law. "If Solon and Lycurgus gave true, general laws, laws for humanity, from what source did they take these? It is to be hoped that they took them from their humanity and their observation of it" (fragment 65, 98). Solon and Lycurgus, the heroes of the histories of positive law, thus appear as creators of "true, general laws"— that is, of natural laws. How can Novalis make such a paradoxical claim? The answer concerns a question of method. We can in fact take this view, if we inquire not after the structure of the law, but rather after its emergence. What we recognize in its completed form as a positive law used to be a natural law at the moment of its emergence. This is so because every law, in order to become law, must be the law of the one subjected to it. In law, the object or addressee always *becomes* the subject or agent. "Every true law is my law—let him pronounce and formulate it who will" (fragment 65, 98). In other words, every law to which the individual is subjected by chance rearticulates itself as the necessary law that the individual issues to himself or herself. Everyone subject to law becomes the subject of the law.

With this proposition—the proposition of the law as we may call it—Novalis arrives at the core of his politico-aesthetics. Both positive and natural law—the contingent, determined law and the normative idea of law—coincide when and if it is a matter of *my* law. It is contingently *and* necessarily law because it is the expression (in the double sense) of an "I." The mystical sovereign is the authoritative "I" that can and must both voice *and* represent the law. Novalis thus handily dispenses with the traditional discussions of constitution and law. The debate about the forms of government ends in the universal determination of the individual by the law, and this determination is located in the individual as having a necessary and contingent relation to the law at the same time. Every law is *necessarily coincidental* in respect to the individual. Even the most arbitrary law represents to the individual the necessity *that* a law presides over his relation to others and himself. But even a law that resembles the final redemption of the universal idea of justice is always a *determined and positive* one, if it is to order relations to oneself and others.

This paradoxical consequence, which the Romantic poet reaches in *Political Aphorisms*, seems as if to join immediately the sphere of legal and political theory Schmitt develops more than hundred years later. For Novalis, the essence of politics is similar to what the twentieth century jurist calls "the political," the condition of the possibility of politics. The necessarily contingent nature of law in *Political Aphorisms* describes the same structure as Schmitt's three main formulae of emerging normativity without preceding norms: the right judgment (in the sphere of civil law), the decision in the state of exception (with regard to constitutional law and sovereignty), and the distinction of friend and enemy (in the existential concept of the political). In Novalis, however, this structure does not emerge, as with Schmitt, through an investigation of the relation between the law and the judge or sovereign. This is Schmitt's exclusive point of view. For Schmitt, the law and its political moment is always and only a matter of the decider. Novalis, in contradistinction, approaches the normativity without norms from the point of view of the one who lives under the law. It is "my" relation to the law that is characterized by the fact that even outside of any state or society, "I" live always with others and, thus, under the law. And this fundamental—and fundamentally political— law is the law that, while being imposed upon me, is nevertheless "my own" law.

Two considerations may further illuminate this final point of solidarity and difference between Novalis and Schmitt. The first concerns the emergence of politics (or, in Schmittian diction, the political) within Novalis's philosophical, encyclopedic, project. What, we may ask, is the moment at which thinking becomes political; or what is the moment of politics in thinking for the poet and philosopher who participates in the unfolding of German idealism after Kant and Fichte? The other issue concerns the suggested distinction between Schmitt's decider and Novalis's individual under the law. Would not such a distinction, if it holds, contradict the first part of *Faith and Love*, the insistence on the visibility of the state and its politically theological nature? Would it not simply retract the emphasis on king and queen, which seems so central in the beginning, and undermine the comparison with Schmitt from the beginning? As for the first consideration, Novalis gives politics (or the political) its specific moment in thinking beginning with his *Fichte Studien*, his studies of Fichte (2003a). Morality, natural law, and politics, he notes in these studies with his usual attempt at schematizing things, are the three dimensions of practical philosophy (2003a, No. 51, 37). Politics is even of particular importance for the way in which, with Fichte and Novalis, practical philosophy comes as the middle phase in the process of Ego's turning from the immediately theoretical beginnings to the final theory that reflects on its practical nature, once again for theoretical purposes. Put differently, the freedom of Ego in practical philosophy, performed through the causality of reason, is in the final account revealed as the condition of understanding in the first place. "I should be free, says practical freedom. Theoretical freedom says I must be free. Politics is already grounded in the concept of the Ought for the practical I" (No. 96, 48). For the theoretical Ego, freedom has to be assumed so that the "I" can perform its own operations and, first and foremost, the operation of positing objects. That means, however, that the prerequisite of its own thinking is not accessible to the immediately theoretical Ego. Being the prerequisite for positing objects in theory, positing cannot be its own object. It becomes explicit only in the Ought of the practical Ego. This Ought in which the "I" relates to the "has-to-be" of theory is, for Novalis, the specific moment of politics, a specific moment within the sphere of the practical Ego and thereby in the development of Ego from immediate to reflected theory.

CONCLUSION

The political, in Novalis, emphasizes and isolates the function of the Ought as a decisive moment within the installation of the practical law in general. Each and every law includes the operation of Ought in its content as well as for its proclamation. In this double respect, the political Ought of the law (of practical philosophy) exposes what is presupposed in the "has-to-be" of the concepts and laws as forged and accepted by the theoretical Ego. The structural identity of this Ought with Schmitt's isolation of judgment, decision, and distinction is obvious. And yet Novalis demonstrates where, in thinking, it emerges as the political dimension of law rather than deducing it from the supposed nature of law or the existential quality of the political. This point leads to the other issue to be discussed here, the observation according to which, in *Political Aphorisms*, the necessity of the contingency of law is introduced from the point of view of the one who lives under the law rather than the one who gives the law. Expressed in this manner, the observation seems to contradict the earlier emphasis on king and queen in *Faith and Love*.

On closer inspection, however, any such juxtaposition of sovereign and subject of the law appears as exactly what Novalis rejects and transforms in his message to king and queen. The king enters and defines the sphere of the visibility of the state as a functional element. The fact that he plays the part of the sovereign precisely does *not* mean that he is both, physical body and body politic. Rather, the king is the one and only body in the comprehensive play of representation that is the "visibility of the state," including government, society, citizens, and institutions. It comes in full conformity with this picture of sovereign and state that in *Political Aphorisms*, the Ego recognizes itself in the end as the "I" that lives necessarily with others, or put differently, that accepts the law contingently imposed on it as "my" law and the necessity of law for the "I." The sovereign, as subject to the entirety of state and law, and the subject, as sovereign of the law imposed on her, are mirroring figures in Novalis's *Faith and Love*. The theory of politics that has emerged so far differs from Schmitt not because it excludes Schmitt's decider-concentrated theory but only, though importantly, because this Schmittian variant is only one possible realization of a broader range of possibilities opened up by Novalis.

With the phrase "Every true law is my law," Novalis, however, has not yet said it all. It is with an additional turn of thought that his address to king and queen in fact finally differs from Schmitt's theory of the political. If "Every true law is my law" were the final words, he would only have established that law, as "my" law, is present as if with one fell swoop. Novalis, however, claims that it is possible to *observe* and *describe* how law emerges *while* it emerges. The emergence of law is a matter of art. "Every true law is my law—let him pronounce and formulate it who will. But this pronouncement and formulation, or the observation of the original feeling and its representation, must not be so easy after all, otherwise would we have need of any special written laws? Must it not therefore be an art?" (1997, fragment 65, 98–100)

This is to say that *Faith and Love* is meant to develop the *romantic art of the political*. Only if understood in this comprehensive way—affirming as it were the Schmittian ambivalence as the vital function of politics—we see the theatrical playfulness and the serious biopolitical side of the state's high visibility at the same time. The uniforms that make men into citizens; the medals for housewives bestowed by the queen; the pictures of king and queen, faith and love, decorating private parlors, and especially those of women—all this can doubtless be taken seriously, and in these outward signs the quasi-familial organization of a population's "love of the institution" can be decoded. At the same time, all of that is obviously meant as an artful play. The point in re-reading Novalis's political statement today is not to be stuck with a Schmittian ambivalence between romantic play and the existential dimension of the political, but to recognize the productive genealogical intertwining of the two sides of the paradox. Even with such a qualification, thinking the political remains a burdened and precarious undertaking, but only if we allow for the mutual implication of the political and its aesthetic genealogy can it become productive to even embark on it.

Notes

1. The allusion to Kant's categorical imperative can be found in Schmitt 1969 (78). Unless noted otherwise, all translations of source material by the author.
2. Schematically, the decision in the state of exception may be called the legal a priori of "the political," while the friend/enemy distinction is the existential a priori.
3. In his comparative study on Carl Schmitt and Paul Valéry, Friedrich Balke 1996 (120–132) has convincingly argued that Schmitt's notion of occasionalism can be understood in terms of contingency as characteristic of the structure and function of modern societies (Niklas Luhmann, Anthony Giddens).
4. The translation leaves out a series of poems that form the introduction of Novalis's text (*Blumen; Flowers*); aphorisms 1–6 constitute a section of *Faith and Love* of their own under the subtitle *Vorrede* (*Preface*); aphorisms 44–68 stand under a title of their own, *Politische*

Aphorismen (*Political Aphorisms*). This section was separated from the body of the text of *Faith and Love* when the Prussian censor suppressed its further publication after the intervention of the king (cf. Novalis 1997, 176 n18; and 1999, vol. 2, 287–309; for commentary and notes, see 1999, vol. 3, 367–379).

5. The theme of secret language—"a language of tropes and riddles" (Novalis, "Faith and Love," fragment 1, 85)—is developed in the *Vorrede* (fragment 1–6), and it is carried out in the allegorical poems of *Blumen* (Novalis, "*Glaube und Liebe*," which, for example, allude to Goethe's *Fairy Tale* from *Conversations of German Refugees*, 288–290). The convergence proposed by Novalis between allegorical poetry and coded communication is central to the way political speech is seen as intrinsically poetical, and vice versa. A more detailed analysis would have to further determine the political as a specific mode of poetic speech in Novalis.

6. The German word "*Staat*" is usually rendered as nation-state, government, or society in English. While all these translations are occasionally used here, the solecism "state" is also employed as a reminder of the German term (cf. the standard translation of "Faith and Love") because of the implications that separate *Staat* from all three of its usual English translations.

7. Due to the critical reception at court, the text was not published as submitted by Novalis and Schlegel (cf. Novalis 1997, n12).

8. The notion of political imaginary is employed with an eye to Cornelius Castoriades (1987).

9. "And now abideth faith, hope, charity, these three; but the greatest of these is charity" (1 Cor. 13:13, King James Version). The Paulinian context has various ramifications in Novalis's *Faith and Love*: the Paulinian theology of the spirit and letter of the law is crucial throughout; the allegorical identification of Queen Louise (1776–1810) with Love ("the greatest of these") is an integral part of the nascent Louise cult and iconography in these years; one may speculate about the omission of Hope as silently pointing toward the royal children or the Prussian state's future; and finally, in Christian hagiography, fides, spes, and caritas are the three daughters of Sophia, who for Novalis was the theological center of the Sophia cult he developed after the death of his fiancée Sophie von Kühn (1782–1797).

10. Famously, Goethe records the coronation ceremonies for Emperor Joseph II in Frankfort in 1764 in his autobiography as the still impressive manifestations of an overage political institution, the Holy Roman Empire (Goethe 1987, 130–152).

11. As Stamm-Kuhlmann (1992) shows, the nineteenth-century Prussian iconography begins to unfold under, but not necessarily at the instigation of, Frederick William III. Only his son and successor, Frederick William IV (1795–1861), will be the "Romantic on the Prussian throne" also in this respect.

12. The reference here is to Kantorowicz 1997 and Schmitt 2005.

13. Schmitt continues: "This fragment... provides the real formula of the romantic" (1986, 83). He not only interrupts the quote by his own commentary but also slightly changes the wording. The actual fragment reads (*Pollen*, fragment 66): "All the chance events of our lives are materials from which we can make what we want. Whoever is rich in spirit, makes much out of his life. Every acquaintance, every incident would be for the thoroughly spiritual person the first element in an endless series, the beginning of an endless novel." Schmitt quotes from the version edited by Schlegel under the title *Pollen*, the translation rendered here follows, in slightly modified form, the translation of the original version in *Miscellaneous Fragments* (here fragment 65, 33).

14. As the context implies, Novalis uses the term "system" first of all in the sense of the cosmological system—the Newtonian constellation of sun and planets—as in Kant's *Universal*

Natural History and Theory of the Heavens (2012), and metaphorically for the nation-state or society.

15. These are in fact the words of the publisher Friedrich Unger, reported by Schlegel to Novalis. See Novalis 1999 (vol. 3, 376).

16. This is added by Schlegel to Unger's words as his own anecdote about the reception of the friend's submission at court (Novalis 1999, vol. 3, 376).

17. For the reference to Schmitt's formula of sovereignty as decision in the state of exception, which, however, makes it the sovereign's task to avoid such state of exception, see Benjamin 1998 (70–72), notably on the inability of the tyrant to decide.

References

Balke, F. 1996. *Der Staat nach seinem Ende: Die Versuchung Carl Schmitts*. Munich: Fink.

Bedorf, T., and K. Röttgers. eds. 2010. *Das Politische und die Politik*. Frankfurt: Suhrkamp.

Behler, E. 1993. *German Romantic Literary Theory*. New York: Cambridge University Press.

Behler, E. ed. 1987. *Philosophy of German Idealism*. New York: Continuum.

Benjamin, W. 1998. *The Origin of German Tragic Drama*, trans. J. Osborne. London, New York: Verso.

Bergdoll, B. 1994. *Karl Friedrich Schinkel: An Architecture for Prussia*. New York: Rizzoli.

Blasius, D. 2001. *Carl Schmitt: Preussischer Staatsrat in Hitlers Reich*. Göttingen: Vandenhoeck & Ruprecht.

Breuer, S. 2012. *Carl Schmitt im Kontext: Intellektuellenpolitik in der Weimarer Republik*. Berlin: Akademie Verlag.

Castoriades, C. 1987. *Imaginary Institution of Society*, trans. K. Blamey. Cambridge: Polity.

Engel, M. 2001. "Das Forum Fridericianum und die monumentalen Residenzplätze des 18. Jahrhunderts." Ph.D. diss., Free University Berlin.

Förster, E. 2013. *Twenty-Five Years of Philosophy: A Systematic Reconstruction*, trans. B. Bowman. Cambridge: Harvard University Press.

Frank, F. 2004. *Philosophical Foundations of Early German Romanticism*, trans. E. Millán-Zaibert. Albany: State University of New York Press.

Goethe, J. W. von. 1987. *From My Life: Poetry and Truth*. In *Collected Works*, vol. 4, ed. T. P. Saine and J. L. Sammons. Princeton: Princeton University Press.

Hebekus, U., and J. Völker. 2012. *Neue Philosophien des Politischen zur Einführung*. Hamburg: Junius.

The Holy Bible: King's James Version. 1978. Philadelphia: National.

Kant, I. 2012. "Universal Natural History and Theory of the Heavens." In *Kant: Natural Science*, trans. O. Reinhardt, ed. E. Watkins. New York: Cambridge University Press, 182–307.

Kantorowicz, E. 1997. *The King's Two Bodies: A Study in Medieval Political Theology*. Princeton: Princeton University Press.

Lima, L. C. 1996. *The Limits of Voice: Montaigne, Schlegel, Kafka*, trans. P. H. Britto. Stanford: Stanford University Press.

Marder, M. 2009. "From the Concept of the Political to the Event of Politics." *Telos* 147: 55–76.

Meier, C. 1980. *Entstehung des Politischen bei den Griechen*. Frankfurt: Suhrkamp.

Meier, H. 2006. *Carl Schmitt and Leo Strauss: The Hidden Dialogue*. Chicago: University of Chicago Press.

Mirsch, B. C. 1998. *Anmut und Schönheit: Schadows Prinzessinnengruppe und ihre Stellung in der Skulptur des Klassizismus*. Berlin: Deutscher Verlag für Kunstwissenschaft.

Molnár, G. von. 1970. *Novalis' "Fichte Studies": The Foundations of His Aesthetics*. The Hague: Mouton.

Novalis. 1997. *Philosophical Writings*, trans. and ed. M. M. Stoljar. Albany: State University of New York Press.

Novalis. 1999. *Werke, Tagebücher und Briefe Friedrich von Hardenbergs*, 3 vols, ed. H.-J. Mähl and R. Samuel. Darmstadt: Wissenschaftliche Buchgesellschaft.

Novalis. 2003a. *Fichte Studies*, trans. and ed. J. Kneller. New York: Cambridge University Press.

Novalis. 2003b. *Notes for a Romantic Encyclopedia: Das Allgemeine Brouillon*, trans. and ed. D. W. Wood. Albany: State University of New York Press.

Ozouf, M. 1988. *Festivals and the French Revolution*, trans. A. Sheridan. Cambridge: Harvard University Press.

Schlegel, F. 1971. "On Incomprehensibility." In *Friedrich Schlegel's Lucinde and the Fragments*, trans. P. Firchow. Minneapolis: University of Minnesota Press, 259–271.

Schmitt, C. 1969. *Gesetz und Urteil: Eine Untersuchung zum Problem der Rechtspraxis*, 2nd ed. Munich: Beck.

Schmitt, C. 1986. *Political Romanticism*, trans. G. Oakes. Cambridge: MIT Press.

Schmitt, C. 1996. *The Concept of the Political*, trans. G. Schwab. Chicago, London: University of Chicago Press.

Schmitt, C. 2005. *Political Theology: Four Chapters on the Concept of Sovereignty*, trans. G. Schwab. Chicago: University of Chicago Press.

Simon, H. 1999. "Die Bildpolitik des preussischen Königshauses im 19. Jahrhundert: Zur Ikonographie der preussischen Königin Luise (1776–1810)." *Wallraf-Richartz Jahrbuch* 60: 231–262.

Staiger, E. 1991. *Basic Concepts of Poetics*, trans. J. C. Hudson and L. T. Frank. University Park: Pennsylvania State University Press.

Stamm-Kuhlmann, T. 1992. *König in Preußens großer Zeit: Friedrich Wilhelm III., der Melancholiker auf dem Thron*. Berlin: Siedler.

Süssmilch, J. P. 1752. *Der königlichen Residentz Berlin schneller Wachsthum und Erbauung: In zweyen Abhandlungen erwiesen*. Berlin: Haude und Spener.

Szondi, P. 2002. *An Essay on the Tragic*, trans. P. Fleming. Stanford: Stanford University Press.

Vollrath, E. 1987. "Politisch, Das Politische." In *Historisches Wörterbuch der Philosophie*, vol. 7, ed. J. Ritter. Darmstadt: Wissenschaftliche Buchgesellschaft, 1071–1075.

CHAPTER 26

WALTER BENJAMIN'S ESTEEM FOR CARL SCHMITT

HORST BREDEKAMP

INTRODUCTION

WALTER BENJAMIN'S esteem for Carl Schmitt is one of the most perplexing cases in the intellectual history of the Weimar Republic. It arouses astonishment to this day, connecting as it does Benjamin, a victim of Nazism, to Schmitt, who, with his distinction between friend and fiend, developed a Manichean definition of the political and took a public stance in support of National Socialism soon after the *Machtergreifung* (Schmitt 1991; cf. Bendersky 1983; Koenen 1995; Mehring 2009, 304–436). The main document behind this sentiment is a letter Benjamin wrote to Schmitt in December 1930, announcing the shipment of his 1925 book on German tragic drama, the so-called *Trauerspiel* book:

> Esteemed Professor Schmitt,
>
> You will receive any day now from the publisher my book, *The Origin of the German Mourning Play*. With these lines I would like not merely to announce its arrival, but also to express my joy at being able to send it to you, at the suggestion of Mr. Albert Salomon. You will very quickly recognize how much my book is indebted to you for its presentation of the doctrine of sovereignty in the seventeenth century. Perhaps I may add that I have also derived from your later works, especially the "*Diktatur,*" a confirmation of my modes of research in the philosophy of art through yours in the philosophy of the state. If the reading of my book lets this feeling appear comprehensible, then the purpose of my sending it to you will be achieved.
>
> With my expression of special admiration,
>
> Yours very humbly
>
> Walter Benjamin[1]

The relationship expressed in this letter was repressed for decades as inconceivable or dismissed as a mere chance episode. Much to the contrary, however, it was no isolated incident, and it had complex and telling effects on Schmitt's reputation up to the present. Although he was forbidden to teach after 1945, Schmitt served as a kind of oracle for countless intellectuals and politicians in Germany and elsewhere in the decades before his death in 1985. It was even suggested that he "has more 'pupils' at universities in Germany and abroad than any other professor of his generation" (Meier 1998, 145; Laak 1993; Mehring 2009, 504–578). Finally, he continues to be the subject of increasing interest today, even and especially in the United States.[2]

What is particularly remarkable is the high regard Schmitt is held in by persons who at first seem foreign to him in their origin and thought. A key figure was Jacob Taubes, whose correspondence with Schmitt clearly shows his crucial role in the afterlife of the problem exposed (Kopp-Oberstebrink et al. 2012). His case is perhaps the most telling example of the extreme reluctance scholars in postwar Germany had even to touch on the matter. Therefore, it is of value to start with Taubes in tracing the steps and sidesteps of this complicated and thus all the more revealing story of the process through which the relationship between Benjamin and Schmitt became public.

Taubes was the son of a Viennese rabbi. After having held a position as professor of religion at Columbia University, he became professor of Judaic studies and hermeneutics at the Free University of Berlin in 1966. From then until his death in 1987, he played an essential and often controversial role in and around the philosophical faculty of the Free University, becoming a central figure of the student movement in the 1960s and even afterward remaining a restless source of intellectual shifts.

Jacob Taubes had been fascinated by the work of Schmitt since 1952, but after some professional contacts during the 1950s, there was complete silence from his side between 1960 and 1977, although Schmitt regularly sent him his publications. In the seething Berlin of 1967, Taubes invited Alexandre Kojève, the celebrated philosopher of "the end of history," to give a lecture at the Free University. For Taubes, the most startling event of Kojève's visit to Berlin was his sudden departure. Kojève announced that he was going to see Schmitt in Plettenberg, the only one "worth talking to" in Germany. Taubes was dismayed (1987, 24).

He was no less disturbed upon reading Benjamin's letter to Schmitt, which gradually became public between 1956 and 1974. Schmitt himself was the first to mention this letter, in a footnote in his book on Shakespeare in 1956 (1985, 64), as if putting a nugget of poison on a clean floor. However, the letter was not published in the first edition of Benjamin's correspondence in 1966. Later this became one of the flaws that provoked severe attacks on the editors.[3] At least by the beginning of 1968, the editors of Benjamin's collected works should have been alarmed, as Walter Boehlich, the chief lector of Suhrkamp publishing house, sent five letters to Schmitt in February and March 1968, asking for information about the circumstances in which Benjamin had sent his *Trauerspiel* book to Schmitt and about the intellectual impulses that Benjamin might have received from him. In his replies, Schmitt argued that he had never met Benjamin, but that they had been part of more or less the same circles and had shared the same friends, such as Albert Salomon, and that their ideas had converged; his book on Shakespeare should be seen as an intellectual dialogue with Benjamin from the first to the last page.[4]

Hans-Dietrich Sander, a critic of literature, who corresponded intensely with Schmitt after 1967, got hold of a copy of Benjamin's letter and thus became the first to publish most of it, in 1970 (Sander 1975, 173 n79). It was through this publication that it came to Taubes's attention. Taubes made the letter the core argument of a letter of his own, with which he intended to break his silence toward Schmitt in July 1970. However, Schmitt had suffered a heart attack, and the letter was never handed over to him (Kopp-Oberstebrink et al. 2012, 30).

Nevertheless, Taubes's undelivered letter to Schmitt remains a unique document, as it is the earliest known analytical reaction to Benjamin's esteem for Schmitt and vice versa (27–30). Taubes dealt exclusively with Schmitt's relationship to Benjamin, suggesting that both of them had tried to save metaphysics, from diametrically opposed poles— Benjamin by combining neo-Marxism and theology, Schmitt by mixing Catholicism and the forces of the counterrevolution: "If one accepts your own situational analysis of the era of world-civil-war, then you and Benjamin came down on the different sides of the barricades."[5] Even more telling is Taubes's insistence regarding the intellectual and political frame out of which Schmitt responded to Benjamin's admiration in his Hamlet book of 1956: "that is, one decade after the Nazi-diluvium. How was the constellation from your perspective in 1930? Could you still discover in Benjamin, who clearly preferred the most hackneyed communist platitudes to bourgeois depth, a spirit of your own spirit?"[6] Without question, Taubes was on Benjamin's side, but his harsh critique of Benjamin's externalized Marxism was a clear sign that he also tried to overcome the "abyss," as he called it, of what had separated Benjamin and Schmitt. Between the lines it becomes clear that this abyss was present in Taubes as well.[7]

Four years later, in 1974, the Benjamin letter was incorporated into the second edition of Benjamin's correspondences, and here it became public for the first time in its full length.[8] The "official" publication of the letter provoked public attempts to make sense of it (Rumpf 1976, 37–50). It may have given Taubes the last push to finally overcome his personal distance from Schmitt. A letter from Taubes to Gershom Scholem in March 1977 shows the deeply conflicting conclusions that Taubes drew from Benjamin's letter. Stating that Benjamin "adored" Schmitt without any hesitation, Taubes argues that Schmitt's devastating role in 1933 cannot be excused, but that he nevertheless remains "the most important thinker [Kopf] in Germany," and finally, that when Jürgen Habermas labels leaders of the 1968 movement "left fascists," he should better start with Benjamin, who, seen in this light, "presents not a small problem."[9] When Sander, the first editor of the Benjamin letter; Taubes; and others met two months later in May 1977, they conjointly sent a postcard to Schmitt, to which Taubes added one sentence: "The Benjamin-letter to you stands at the center of the discussion."[10]

In the same month, philosopher Hans Blumenberg, one of the most prominent intellectual figures in postwar Germany, wrote to Taubes that he should drop his tribunalistic attitude and get into personal contact with Schmitt. Blumenberg's letter is telling evidence of how the relationship with Schmitt was understood as a kind of litmus test determining to which degree acceptance or hypocrisy prevailed: "You praise yourself for keeping distance to a now almost ninety-year old because almost half a century ago he wrote truly abominable things? . . . [T]he intellectual posture of the judge . . . appalls me."[11]

Taubes abandoned his judgmental stance in response to Blumenberg's bitter reproach, telling himself: "You are not the judge" (Taubes in Kopp-Oberstebrink et al. 2012, 259). Assuming a rather Paulinian role, he became more interested in the views he had previously rejected so vehemently (Treml 2012, 283–286). In a letter from November 1977 that initiated the intense contact between Taubes and Schmitt during the following years, Taubes greeted Schmitt with "the hand reaching across an abyss."[12] By evoking the "abyss," Taubes repeated the same metaphor by which he had characterized the situation in his undelivered letter of July 1970. Schmitt's response, in which he referred to "Habakuk 2, 2ff. and 2 Thess. 2, 6ff. Abyssus vocat Abyssum,"[13] must have disarmed Taubes (Treml 2012, 295). In the years to come, Taubes visited Schmitt three times in Plettenberg, where he had "the most stormy conversations I have ever conducted in the German language."[14]

The intensity of the contact between Taubes and Schmitt became known, and Taubes, relentlessly engaging in conflicts of all kinds, was called to account for this relationship, as if in front of a "tribunal," at a panel discussion in the Maison Heinrich Heine in Berlin in 1986, a year after Schmitt's death. Taubes was taken to task for having visited Schmitt himself and of even, despite the gulf that had separated them, having respected his work. It seemed inconceivable that a scholar who characterized himself as an "arch-Jew" could have had anything to do with Schmitt.[15] Taubes defended himself with Schmitt's own dictum, which the latter had borrowed from his friend Theodor Däubler, a poet: "The enemy is the embodiment of your own question."[16] He then played his trump card: Benjamin's admiration for Schmitt. Taubes's main argument was Benjamin's letter to Schmitt of December 1930 (Taubes 1987, 26, 51).

An echo of this event could be heard months later (February 1987), when Taubes dedicated one of his four lectures in Heidelberg on Paulus's letter to the Romans to his relationship with Schmitt. Once again, the Benjamin letter played a key role. Taubes portrayed his relationship to Schmitt in the spirit of a testament, finishing his lecture with: "Dixi, and I did not save my soul, but I have reported to you how it came about."[17]

Two months later, Taubes died of cancer. In May of the same year, his book *Ad Carl Schmitt: Gegenstrebige Fügung* (1987) was published, documenting the exchanges between him and Schmitt. Translated into several languages, it became one of the most influential publications on Schmitt ever written. In it, Taubes called the Benjamin letter "a mine" that "disrupts our conception of the intellectual history of the Weimar period" (1987, 27). Without a doubt this dictum had an autobiographical undertone. Taubes took the Benjamin letter as a kind of talisman that guided him through his personal approach to Schmitt, a relationship that in his view became the most daring and most fruitful event in his whole intellectual life.[18]

REFLECTIONS ON THE STATUS
OF THE BENJAMIN LETTER

In the years that followed, new analyses dealt with the question of Schmitt's connection to the Frankfurt School,[19] and new approaches reflected the relationship between Schmitt and Benjamin (Güde 1985, 61–67; Turk 1986, 330–349). Susanne Heil's thorough revised dissertation (1996) provided a reliable basis for all further research and thus also for the first version of this chapter, published in 1999 (Bredekamp 1998; 1999). Giorgio Agamben dedicated a chapter of his book on the Schmittian *Ausnahmezustand* to the interrelationship between Benjamin and Schmitt (2004, 64–77; cf. Pan 2009). Furthermore, a number of new approaches have appeared, in part motivated by the new political frame of the "War on Terror" through which Benjamin's and Schmitt's concept of law gained renewed interest.[20]

Reinhard Mehring, in a countermove, argued against the "syncretistic amalgamation" of Benjamin and Schmitt, as performed by Taubes, Agamben, and others (Mehring 2010, 240). Taken aback by the in his view artificial excitement about the connection between Benjamin and Schmitt, he tried to demonstrate that Benjamin had had no deep-seated interest in Schmitt's publications, and that Schmitt had shown no interest in Benjamin before the mid-1950s, when he saw the chance of saving his own reputation by documenting Benjamin's admiration for him (Mehring 2010, 239–256).

There is no doubt that Benjamin's esteem for Schmitt was a most welcome tool for breaking out of his isolation in the late 1960s and 1970s. But it is equally true that his interest in Benjamin was far from being mere opportunism. Against Mehring's fundamental revocation, it was argued that by the time of Schmitt's reflections on Benjamin's *Trauerspiel* book, Benjamin had been more or less forgotten or was not yet known outside the circles of Adorno and Gershom Scholem (Adorno 1955, ix; cf. Tielke 2011, 270–272). As the (re)construction of Benjamin's fame did not happen before the first half of the 1960s, Schmitt's chapter on Benjamin in his Shakespeare book cannot be taken as jumping on the bandwagon (Bredekamp 1992, 120–122; Küpper and Skandris 2006, 17–56, esp. 22). Moreover, this is confirmed by a close reading of the marginal comments that Schmitt dedicated to the *Trauerspiel* book.[21]

All of these discussions and reflections confirm the paradigmatic character that the relationship between Schmitt and Benjamin had for postwar intellectual development in Germany and elsewhere. The greatest effect was the acknowledgment that a clear-cut distinction between good and bad, left and right was a product of a postwar construction of memory. Having overcome this product of good conscience, the essence of the relationship between Benjamin and Schmitt becomes even more telling.

ELEMENTS OF BENJAMIN'S
ESTEEM FOR SCHMITT

Gershom Scholem, who was closest to Benjamin, spoke of the "deep admiration" of his friend for Schmitt (Scholem 1982, 47; Schmidt 2000, 157 n2). This statement, which alone puts into perspective all attempts to relativize the relationship between Benjamin and Schmitt, was founded on a long-term perspective.

The connection between them did not come about by chance. Benjamin must have known that Schmitt had enjoyed considerable success as a literary critic and surrealistic writer,[22] as well as the high regard of poets such as Däubler and artists such as the Catholic-leaning Dadaist Hugo Ball (see Villinger 1995; Heil 1996, 10–47; Einem and Einem 1997, 59). It must have been in this ambience that Benjamin saw his own concept of art clarified in Schmitt's political theory.

The first source of Benjamin's interest in Schmitt can be found as early as 1923. In a letter to Gottfried Salomon in December of that year, Benjamin wrote that he had been reading texts on the doctrine of sovereignty in the baroque era while working on his Habilitation (Kambas 1982, 609). Without doubt he was referring to Schmitt's *Political Theology* (*Politische Theologie* 1996; 2004),which Benjamin cites as his political-theoretical basis in a central chapter of his Habilitation *The Origin of German Tragic Drama* (*Ursprung des deutschen Trauerspiels*), published two years later (Schmitt 1996; Benjamin 1974–1989, I.1, 203–430, esp. 246; 1985, 65).

In his short curriculum vitae of 1928, Benjamin confirms that his work on the *Trauerspiel* book was methodologically influenced by both the art historian Alois Riegl and the political thinker Schmitt: "This effort, undertaken on a larger scale in the above-mentioned *Ursprung des deutschen Trauerspiels*, embraces on the one hand the methodological ideas of Alois Riegl with his idea of the *Kunstwollen*, and on the other the contemporary essays of Schmitt, who in his analysis of political structure makes an analogous attempt to integrate phenomena that can only seemingly be isolated in different areas. Above all, however, it seems to me that such observation is the prerequisite for any penetrating physiognomic interpretation of works of art, to the extent that they are unique and inimitable."[23] The emphasis of this appraisal underlines that Benjamin's appreciation of Schmitt was by no means ephemeral.

His borrowings become obvious in his critique of parliamentary liberalism, which he says leads to compromises reflecting nothing of the violence that gave birth to parliament (Benjamin 1974, II.1, 190; cf. Rumpf 1976, 40), as well as in his longing for decision, as formulated in his piece on Goethe's *Elective Affinities* (*Wahlverwandtschaften*), written a year after he had read Schmitt's *Political Theology*,[24] and in his desire to argue from the *Grenzlinie* (borderline), as developed in the *Einbahnstraße* (*One-way Street*) (see Anglet 1995, 60).

It must be underlined that for Benjamin, Schmitt was a point of orientation not just in an affirmative way but as an impulse-giver who provoked radical conclusions that could also be controversial. This was the case with Benjamin's *Das Kunstwerk im Zeitalter seiner technischen Reproduzierbarkeit* (*The Work of Art in the Age of Mechanical Reproduction*; 2008). This book-length essay, which later became one of Benjamin's most famous writings, was inspired by Schmitt's *Politische Romantik* (*Political Romanticism*; 1919; 2011). In this fundamental critique of a modern liberalism lacking in seriousness, extremity, and depth, Schmitt had criticized the general trend of aestheticizing as a tool for privatizing intellectual life (1919, 21). Following this argument, Benjamin concluded that the aestheticizing of politics by fascism should be counteracted by the politicizing of the arts by communism (1974–1989, VII.1, 384; see Schöttker 2007, 155). Benjamin's essay, revealing the revolutionary potential of the reproduction of pictures, was encapsulated in this formula.

Schmitt's inspiring role for Benjamin's reproduction-thesis is confirmed even in 1940, the year of Benjamin's death. Benjamin had read Karl Löwith's article "Max Weber und seine Nachfolger" ("Max Weber and his Successors"), which had been published early that year (Löwith 1988, 166–176). However, Benjamin did not quote Löwith's essay as such, but instead Schmitt's lecture "Die europäische Kultur im Zwischenstadium der Neutralisierung" ("European Culture in the Intermediate Stage of Neutralization") of October 1929, which Löwith had cited at length.[25] In the quotation that Benjamin transcribed, Schmitt gave the example of the letterpress as a liberating, individualistic, and rebellious technical tool. As soon as mass media such as radio and film emerged, they would provoke monopolization and censorship, the two means of mass control. But this would not be a result of technology per se. According to Schmitt, letterpress and film show that technology as a neutral force could serve both "freedom and suppression, centralization and decentralization."[26]

Benjamin's answer to the question that Schmitt had brought forward in his lecture of 1929 was once again the politicization of the arts by means of unrolling the revolutionary potential of the categorically neutral technologies. Against the neutralizing forces of economy and technology, all areas of life should be politicized (Benjamin 1974–1989, VII.2, 673). It was the same response he had made in *The Work of Art in the Age of Mechanical Reproduction*. In 1940 Benjamin once more recognized the proximity of his and Schmitt's ideas, even in the frame of different conclusions.

BENJAMIN'S ULTIMATE RESPONSE TO SCHMITT

Also in 1940, during which Benjamin annotated his *The Work of Art in the Age of Mechanical Reproduction* with excerpts from one of Schmitt's articles, he wrote perhaps his most famous piece, "Über den Begriff der Geschichte" ("On the Concept of History"; Benjamin 2009). Benjamin's eighth thesis, followed by the famous picture of the *Angelus Novus* of destructive progress (see Werckmeister 1996, 239–267), again adopted Taubes's later theatrical description, "written eye to eye with the theses of Carl Schmitt."[27] Indeed,

Benjamin calls attention to the allusion by placing the words state of exception in quotation marks: "The tradition of the oppressed teaches us that the 'state of exception' in which we live is not the exception but the rule. We must attain to a conception of history that is in keeping with this insight. Then we shall clearly realize that it is our task to bring about a real state of exception, and this will improve our position in the struggle against Fascism."[28]

Benjamin here expands the thesis developed in his *Trauerspiel* book, that in the baroque the state of exception is impossible, not because it is superfluous, but because it exists permanently as a perpetual state of lawlessness, continuing to the present. What Schmitt views as the event of historical rupture, as the state of exception and a cessation, Benjamin sees as trapped in the permanence of a power that now, in the worst possible sense, truly is "barbarian." As in the *Trauerspiel* book, however, Benjamin once again concurs with Schmitt's demand for a true state of exception[29]—in order, now, to turn it against Schmitt's concept of history. Benjamin's conception of the shock-like liberation acquires the character of a last judgment of fascism.

As powerful as this image may seem, without knowledge of its real addressee it remains obscure.[30] It adopts Schmitt's state of exception in order to formulate a version of "political theology" that is immediately turned back against him. It is worth noting, moreover, that Benjamin, even while he seeks to attack Schmitt's *Politische Theologie* (*Political Theology*), remains caught in the framework of its conception. Theses 14–17, in which Benjamin seeks to "destroy" the idea of linear progress, likewise contain an echo of the time concept Schmitt attributed to the state of exception Schmitt's time-construct of the state of exception, inasmuch as they crystallize the idea of the "shock" in a "messianic cessation of activity."[31]

Benjamin's moving reflection on history uses Schmittian terms or at least parallel concepts in his critiques, shifting at will between political theory and the theory of art. As intriguing as the traces of Benjamin's reception of Schmitt's writings are: as such they cannot explain a closeness to the degree that even in 1940, the year of Benjamin's deadly flight from the Nazis, he could not resist quoting Schmitt. The explanation need be sought on a level that is located beyond the limits of historical circumstances.

Conceptions of Time in the Work of Schmitt

What Benjamin and Schmitt had in common were their attempts to define the character of time. Both were united in their opposition to the continuity of the lapsing time. This is the point at which the ideas of Benjamin and Schmitt converge. Schmitt's theoretical association of the political, art, and time appealed to Benjamin and finally ensnared him.

In a central passage of his *Trauerspiel* book, Benjamin addresses the significance of the "state of exception" (*Ausnahmezustand*) (Benjamin 1974–1989, I.1, 246; 1985, 65;

cf. Heil 1996, 128), a discussion that is based on Schmitt's dictum "sovereign is he who decides upon the state of exception" ("*Souverän ist, wer über den Ausnahmezustand entscheidet*"; Schmitt 1996, 13). In this idea, Schmitt saw the disparity between continuity and uniqueness expanded to include a concept of time that sought to distinguish between normality and exception. This idea is in fact the keystone of Schmitt's system of thought, at least during the years that were decisive for the relationship between Schmitt and Benjamin.[32]

The concept of the state of exception expresses Schmitt's conviction that democracy loses its foundation when different factions pursue their divergent interests to the point where a splintered political system is no longer able to guarantee the security of law. Under these circumstances, an extra-societal force, the sovereign, must suspend the laws in order to save them.

Up to this point, Schmitt's argument corresponds to the standard justification for dictatorial authority (Nippel 2011, 105–239). What lends it an art-theoretical twist, however, is his relentless politicization of the concept of time. According to Schmitt, it is logically impossible for the representatives of law and politics to create a limited sphere of time outside the framework of normality. Like the miracle for the theologian, the state of exception must come from the outside. Schmitt thus defines sovereignty as a "borderline concept" (*Grenzbegriff*), localized in the "outermost sphere" (1996, 13). It is founded in the intertwining of early modern state and art theory, as artists like Benvenuto Cellini and Leone Leoni, despite having been sentenced to death because of their crimes, were employed by sovereigns as subjects of activity, not by mercy, but by standing outside the frame of law (Bredekamp 2008). Through this they became symbols of the "outermost sphere." Because its place lies beyond the space of normality, sovereignty corresponds to an abnormal time. And since the framework of normality cannot be broken open from within, the state of exception must be declared by a person coming from the outside who interrupts the line of continuity. Political theory thus begins to approach political theology (Meier 1995, 7–19). It demands a court of appeal, the state of exception, located outside all frameworks, one that defines the character of time and even produces it. The state of exception in temporal terms may be described as the cessation of ordinary time.

The concept of a limited time beyond the continuity of the normal, in itself already an unusual idea, has the even stranger consequence of establishing itself as a "deadline" (*Frist*). The interpretation of the state of exception as a *Frist* is a function of Schmitt's arch-Catholic conception of the *katechon* or the "restrainer,"[33] a scheme in which history takes place in the space of time between the present and the coming of the Antichrist. It is the span of time in which the works of the Lawless One have not yet gained the upper hand, and the Antichrist has not yet appeared. The *katechon*, whatever form he may assume, produces history; without him, time itself would long ago have ended. He halts the flow of time leading toward the counter-era of the Antichrist, whether communism or the mechanization of the world: "[I]n the time of exception, the power of true life breaks through the crust of a mechanics caught in continuous repetition."[34] The reciprocal play of both together—the continuous time of normality as well as the shock of the state of exception—produces the history that is given to humanity as the *Frist*.

The construction of the *katechon* was used as an alternative to nihilism not only by the Catholic Schmitt but also by Protestants like Dietrich Bonhoeffer (cf. Schuller 1996, 402–405). Schmitt's ideas, moreover, have a diabolical, suggestive logic that has ensnared others besides Benjamin. Their marginal movement is exactly what it pretends to be; Schmitt's theory of time is a philosophical "borderline case" (*Grenzfall*), which posits a zone far beyond the known world. Accordingly, this theory seeks to nullify the rules of normal time and produce a moment of standstill and shock-like clarity.

This motif of the abrupt departure from the time of normality corresponds to the concepts of *shock*, the *now*, and *suddenness* from the canon of the avantgarde propagated by Ernst Jünger and Martin Heidegger as well as by André Breton and Louis Aragon (cf. Bohrer 1981, 52–54, 67, 73, 180, 183, 184, 211; Wolin 1992, 433). In his curriculum vitae, Benjamin emphasizes the proximity of his theory of art to Schmitt's dichotomy between continuity and uniqueness; in actuality, this dichotomy corresponds to the span between normality and the state of exception used by Schmitt in his concept of the *katechon*. And even the cinematic "shock effect" praised by Benjamin in *The Work of Art in the Age of Mechanical Reproduction*—an effect that, "like every shock, should be cushioned by intensified spiritual presence"—refers to the tension between normal time and uniqueness that Benjamin in his curriculum vitae had also found and praised in Schmitt's method (Benjamin 1974–1989, VII.1, 379 n16; Heil 1996, 91–98; Bredekamp 1992).

But the connection between Benjamin and Schmitt is more complex and contradictory than the mere adoption of Schmitt's concept of uniqueness would suggest. The link between the two thinkers can be established much more firmly via a relatively lengthy detour, one that leads to Thomas Hobbes's concept of political time and offers a key to both Benjamin and Schmitt.

HOBBES'S IMAGE OF THE LEVIATHAN AS THE CREATOR OF TIME

While Benjamin himself does not quote Hobbes, there can be no doubt that his fundamental theses are based on the latter's definition of the political. Thus it has been surmised that the image of the Leviathan should be viewed as a secret antithesis to the emptiness of the allegory. At the beginning of Benjamin's *Kritik der Gewalt* (*Critique of Violence*), where he deals with Spinoza, Hobbes is likewise present between the lines (Benjamin 1974–1989, II.1, 180; cf. Windisch 1997, 162).

Schmitt, on the other hand, who sought to reactivate the Hobbesian view of the state as rooted in elemental human fear, lays explicit claim to Hobbes as his intellectual "brother."[35] Of particular interest is the importance he attributes to the leviathan metaphor: "In the long history of political theories, richly laden with colorful images and symbols, icons and idols, paradigms and phantasms, emblems and allegories, this Leviathan is the most striking and powerful image. It transcends the framework of all intellectual theories or constructions."[36] Despite his criticism of the leviathan as an image inappropriate for the mechanistic Hobbesian state—a position he later repudiated (Holmes 1993, 50–53; Meier 1994, 160)—Schmitt attributes to this image the power to rupture the time of normality. The Old Testament metaphor of the leviathan is equivalent to the sovereign and thus possesses that time-producing quality that justifies sovereignty.

The same holds true for the anthropomorphic visualization of the leviathan. The frontispiece of Hobbes's book is the most authoritative answer imaginable to the experience of inescapable political chaos and years of civil war (see Figure 26.1).[37] Equipped with the bishop's crosier of spiritual power and the sword of secular authority, the giant bends men to his will. In the tradition of Arcimboldesque composite images, his body comprises more than three hundred people who, like a coat of mail, replace the skin and obviously extend into the body itself (see Figure 26.2). This double effect, whereby hundreds of people look toward a single head that itself returns our gaze, doubtless illustrates the decisive passage in chapter 17 of the *Leviathan* in which the birth of the state occurs through the transfer of the individual will to the sovereign: "This is more than Consent, or Concord; it is a reall Unitie of them all, in one and the same Person, made by Covenant of every man with every man.... This is the Generation of that great LEVIATHAN, or rather (to speak more reverently) of that Mortall God, to which we owe under the *Immortall* God, our peace and defence" (Hobbes 1991, 120).

"Generation" here means the creation not only of a body but also of time. The concept is related to the tradition of state effigies fashioned upon the death of a king in order to fill the period of the interregnum with a quasi-living representation of the state. Such effigies prepared the way for the process of visualization, without which the leviathan would scarcely have been conceivable.[38] The collection of royal effigies, dating back to the fourteenth century (Harvey and Mortimer 1994), demonstrated what was otherwise only visible to a supernatural eye, elevated above the flow of time: the chain of office holders, fragmented over time, but extending from the past into the future as a coherent composite figure. In *Leviathan*, Hobbes explores the question of the "Right of Succession" as if he were envisioning the royal effigies of Westminster Abbey:

> Of all these Formes of Government, the matter being mortall, so that not onely Monarchs, but also whole Assemblies dy, it is necessary for the conservation of the peace of men, that as there was order taken for an Artificiall Man, so there be order also taken, for an Artificiall Eternity of life; without which, men that are governed by an Assembly, should return into the condition of Warre in every age; and they that are governed by One man, as soon as their Governour dyeth. This Artificiall Eternity, is that which men call the Right of *Succession*. (Hobbes 1991, 135)[39]

In *Leviathan*, the artificial figure that represents the state claims this artificial eternity. The Leviathan is built to last.

FIGURE 26.1 Abraham Bosse, "Leviathan," etching, frontispiece to Thomas Hobbes, *Leviathan* (1651).

FIGURE 26.2 Body of Leviathan, detail of Figure 26.1.

THE STATE OF EXCEPTION:
HOBBES, SCHMITT, AND BENJAMIN

Common to both Hobbes and Schmitt is the preoccupation with a form of time posited beyond the continuum of normality. Like Hobbes's interregnum, Schmitt's state of exception constitutes the center around which all political considerations revolve. But while Hobbes theoretically extends the brief interregnum in order to transform the potentially endless time of anarchy into a period of authority and order through the permanence of the social contract and a living effigy—that is, the state—Schmitt is concerned with the duration of an unstable order, to which he opposes the moment of the "state of exception." Hobbes's objective is the permanence of the Leviathan, whereas

Schmitt emphasizes the exaltedness of the moment. Schmitt (1919), who attacked occasionalism as a delusion specific to German romanticism, is in fact its involuntary heir. Hobbes is political, Schmitt romantic.[40]

Benjamin occupies a middle ground between Hobbes and Schmitt. At first, his *Trauerspiel* book follows Schmitt's approach. Adopting the contrast between the serious case (*Ernstfall*), borderline concept (*Grenzbegriff*), and exception (*Ausnahme*), on the one hand, and the phenomenon of continuous normality on the other,[41] he emphasizes the significance of the "unique extreme." Moreover, the criteria by which Benjamin evaluates German tragic drama are taken from Schmitt: the sovereign, his relation to the state of exception, and his ability to make extreme decisions.[42] In his chapter on the theory of sovereignty, Benjamin makes reference to Schmitt's concept of sovereignty, which "emerges from a discussion of the state of exception."[43] Accordingly, one would expect Benjamin to follow Schmitt at this point, also, but such is not the case. Sovereignty, according to Benjamin, "makes it the most important function of the prince to avert this," that is, the state of exception. The shift of nuance is of utmost significance. For while Schmitt views the state of exception as the *conditio sine qua non* for the establishment of sovereignty, Benjamin sees sovereignty as existing in order to avoid the state of exception in the first place.

The following passage likewise underlines fundamental differences, despite the Schmittian influence: "The ruler is designated from the outset as the holder of dictatorial power if war, revolt, or other catastrophes should lead to a state of exception" (Benjamin 1974, I.1, 245). At first glance, the sentence reads like a summary of Schmitt's work on *Diktatur*. But while Schmitt views the sovereign, who establishes himself in the reciprocity of normal continuity and the state of exception, as both necessary and possible, Benjamin speaks of his absence.[44] His *Trauerspiel* shows rulers who are only seemingly able to govern the state of exception and, ideally, to exclude it. The symbol of the epoch is neither the clarity and permanence of the laws nor the moment of the sovereign's decision, but rather the "inability to decide" (*Entschlussunfähigkeit*) (cf. Turk 1986, 332) and the torsion of hesitation: "The prince, who is responsible for making the decision to proclaim the state of exception, reveals, at the first opportunity, that he is almost incapable of making a decision. Just as compositions with restful lighting are virtually unknown in mannerist painting, so it is that the theatrical figures of this epoch always appear in the harsh light of their changing resolve" (Benjamin 1974, I.1, 250; 1985, 71; translation modified).

Benjamin searches for traces of the true sovereign, but the rulers appear to him unable to find a way to the transcendence that would make possible an outer Archimedean point. The more the world moves aimlessly toward its end, the more history becomes bound to the world: "The religious man of the baroque era clings so tightly to the world because of the feeling that he is being driven along to a cataract with it. The baroque knows no eschatology; and for that very reason it possesses no mechanism by which all earthly things are gathered in together and exalted before being consigned to their end" (Benjamin 1974, I.1, 246; 1985, 66; see also Weber 1993, 153). The potentate is symbolized by the cold, unrestrained platter, whose actions fill up the permanent state of exception stochastically, without meaning or morality. His counterpart is the masquerade of the allegory, which transforms reality into changing masks of continual metamorphosis (see Weber 1992, 133; 1993, 154–159).

Benjamin criticizes authority as a masquerade of the chaotic state of nature, the endless repetition of change without substance, and the meaningless use of pliable allegories. He views history not as the pendulum swing of disintegrating order and its reestablishment in the state of exception, but as one-dimensional monotony—and thus to be lamented. Inasmuch as Benjamin views the absence of sovereignty as catastrophic, he remains, despite his "theological anarchism," within the Schmittian framework (Figal 1992, 253). He differs from Schmitt in his interpretation of history, but not with respect to the criteria for its evaluation.

Schmitt's Response to Benjamin

Schmitt did react to Benjamin's objections. In a series of letters in 1973, he mentions in passing that he had been occupied with Benjamin during the entire decade of the 1930s. First, he repeats the statement he had made to Walter Boehlich in 1968 by underlining that he was "in daily contact" with shared acquaintances like his colleague Karl Korsch, who was a leading member of intellectual left-wing circles of the Weimar Republic, which also included Berthold Brecht.[45] Then he deals with Benjamin's interpretation of the *Leviathan*. He suggests that his article of 1937 had implicitly criticized Benjamin's failure to deal with the symbolism of the Leviathan: "The important thing is the symbolism of the Leviathan, of which, strangely, W. Benjamin says nothing (as far as I can tell)."[46]

In the following remark, Schmitt explains that his influential book on Hobbes of 1938, which he himself characterized as his most significant, was intended as an answer to Benjamin's *Trauerspiel*: "Unfortunately, my attempt to respond to Benjamin by examining a great political symbol (the Leviathan in the political thought of Thomas Hobbes, 1938) went unnoticed" (Schmitt to Viesel, April 4, 1973, in Viesel 1988, 14).

At first glance, it may seem questionable whether Schmitt really had Benjamin in mind when he wrote his critique of Hobbes. It is possible that he, looking back in 1973, was seeking some share in Benjamin's fame. He may have viewed this as a welcome opportunity to disguise the book's open antisemitism by describing it as a veiled answer to a Jewish emigrant, in this way appearing to take him seriously and even honor him.[47] On the other hand, the question of the extent to which Schmitt sought to style himself in retrospect is of secondary significance. For regardless of whether it was consciously intended at the time or represented a later construction, Schmitt's preoccupation with the Leviathan brought him to a position that contradicted Benjamin's concept. His critical comments in the margins of the *Trauerspiel* book and the chapter on Benjamin in his book on Shakespeare (Mehring 2010, 241–254) correspond to the position he had developed in his *Leviathan* book of 1938.

Benjamin had written that in the age of the baroque, a state of exception was impossible because there was no authority that could instate or end it. The abrogation of law had become the condition of normality, approaching the Hobbesian state of nature and dissolving the dialectic between the status quo and the *Grenzbegriff*. Schmitt is concerned with the reconstruction of this reciprocal relationship. He attacks Benjamin's view of a persistent instability by critiquing its polar opposite, Hobbes's concept of the eternal, intact body politic. Hobbes's monster, according to Schmitt, cannot be as stable as it pretends to be. In the schemes of Jewish thinkers like Spinoza, "freedom of thought" works like a slow poison, undermining the foundations of the state, weakening its bones, and finally leading to its collapse (Schmitt 1982, 86). Schmitt sees this hollowing-out of the Leviathan as a process of decay, almost suggesting he had abandoned "exception" in favor of order. But there can be no question that he did not abandon the former, as the mere fact of his sympathy for pirates and interest in guerrillas proves (1942, 26; see 1995, 33 for the explanation of the concept of risk). In his criticism of those who undermine the Leviathan, moreover, there are undertones of cryptic satisfaction, for it is these situations that make possible a higher authority than the Leviathan itself: the sovereignty of the state of exception, which provokes the shock of uniqueness. Without the underminers, the reciprocity on which sovereignty exclusively depends would be impossible. Since the state of exception remains the core of his political thought, Schmitt's Leviathan book separates him from both Hobbes's concept of an earthly god of state and the perpetual absence of the Leviathan posited by Benjamin.

The explicit reference to Benjamin sixteen years later remains within the framework of this concept. In his book on Shakespeare, Schmitt confines his criticism to the two sentences in which Benjamin praises Shakespeare for having Christianized *Hamlet* (see Schmitt 1985, 63; see also Benjamin 1974, I.1, 335; 1985, 157–158). Schmitt maintained that since *Hamlet* is in no way a Christian play, Benjamin had trivialized it. In Schmitt's view, Shakespeare's England was "more barbaric" than Benjamin was ready to admit, "barbaric" in the sense that it was an antipode to the continental creation of the modern state, with its omnipresence of the political (1985, 65).

His use of the term *barbaric* is similar to Benjamin's confrontation of the "barbarians" Klee, Picasso, Brecht, Kraus, and others with the lifelessness of contemporary humanism.[48] According to Schmitt, Shakespeare's drama is interwoven with life beyond the stage and the elemental force of the exception. Schmitt defines Shakespeare's Hamlet as "play" (*Spiel*), but a play that reveals its opposite, the "crucial case" (*Ernstfall*). As play, the theater is the negation of the *Ernstfall*, yet without knowledge of the latter, it remains empty (42, 71 n15).

Schmitt's interpretation of *Hamlet* negates the autonomy of the work of art[49] in order to present it as the recipient of the "intrusion of time into the play": as an extreme form of the elemental, non-mechanical, and anomalous that demands the highest order, clarified and given form in sovereignty. In contrast to Benjamin's diagnosis that the state of exception is impossible because it already exists as a permanent state of lawlessness, here too Schmitt advocates the shock theory of the authoritarian avantgarde. Once again, political theory and the theory of art are intertwined.

CONCLUSION

In September 1980, in his penultimate letter to Michael Rumpf, who had been the first to analyze Benjamin's letter, Schmitt looked back on all of the quarrels. He came to the conclusion that the "decade-long quarrel around Walter Benjamin is a symptom of cryptical frontiers and fanatic hostilities.... The theme Benjamin contains many totally twisted signs."[50]

One wonders if Schmitt would have connected Jacques Derrida with this dictum. The "affinities" between Benjamin and Schmitt led Derrida to situate Benjamin's *Critique of Violence* (*Kritik der Gewalt*) on a level of divine violence in which even the Holocaust becomes thinkable.[51] Again and again, Derrida's comparison with texts by Schmitt is merely hinted at, causing his motive for the examination of Benjamin to remain vague. But in one passage, in which Derrida deals with the problem of time that arises in the moment of legislation, he does address the connection that was apparently constitutive of the "affinities" between Benjamin and Schmitt: "It is the moment when the justification of law hovers in the void or over the abyss, clinging to a purely performative act."[52] This moment may explain once again why Benjamin could orient himself so strongly to Schmitt. His esteem for Schmitt was based on art-theoretical considerations that, drawing from an iconology of time grounded in Hobbes, were able to sustain the longing for a time of exception.

Perhaps Benjamin saw Schmitt as the latter saw his enemy: "the embodiment of his own question." This "embodiment," however, was the aesthetically manifested state of exception, a trap from which Benjamin could not free himself even as he sought to turn it against itself. The aesthetic intersections were more powerful than the political fronts. To see this as a purely moral problem would be to ignore an elementary dilemma, one for which Schmitt and Benjamin each conceived his own solution: the filling of time with substance. One cannot confront it without first looking cold-bloodedly at the bottom of this Pandora's box.

Albert Salomon, Social Democrat and professor of political philosophy at the Deutsche Hochschule für Politik in Berlin—the one who had encouraged Benjamin to send his *Trauerspiel* book to Schmitt—organized a series of lectures called "Problems of Democracy" in the winter of 1929–1930. Schmitt was one of the participants. Shortly thereafter, Benjamin had a long discussion with Bertolt Brecht, which he summarized in four words. In their highly emotional nature, they embody Benjamin's paradoxical proximity to Schmitt in an almost hieroglyphic form: "Schmitt / Agreement Hate Suspicion."[53]

Translated from the German by Melissa Thorson Hause, Jackson Bond, and Katharina Lee Chichester

ACKNOWLEDGMENTS

I am grateful to Gerd Giesler, whose help was essential to giving this chapter its present shape. Many thanks also go to Helge Høibraaten (who provided the opportunity to discuss some of these problems at a symposium dedicated to Carl Schmitt at the University of Thondheim, Norway), Heinrich Meier, and Winfried Menninghaus for their comments and criticism, and to Joshua Gold for his research assistance. An earlier version of this chapter was dedicated to Stephen Holmes on his fiftieth birthday. I am delighted that eighteen years later, I can still count on his friendship unabatedly.

NOTES

1. "Sehr geehrter Herr Professor, / Sie erhalten dieser Tage vom Verlage mein Buch Ursprung des deutschen Trauerspiels. Mit diesen Zeilen möchte ich es Ihnen nicht nur ankündigen, sondern Ihnen auch meine Freude darüber aussprechen, daß ich es, auf Veranlassung von Herrn Albert Salomon, Ihnen zusenden darf. Sie werden sehr schnell bemerken, wieviel das Buch in seiner Lehre der Darstellung der Souveränität im 17. Jahrhundert Ihnen verdankt. Vielleicht darf ich Ihnen darüber hinausgehend sagen, daß ich auch Ihren späteren Werken, vor allem der Diktatur eine Bestätigung meiner kunstphilosophischen Forschungsweisen durch ihre staatsphilosophischen entnommen habe. Wenn Ihnen die Lektüre meines Buches dieses Gefühl verständlich erscheinen läßt, so ist die Absicht meiner Übersendung erfüllt. / Mit dem Ausdruck besonderer Hochschätzung / Ihr sehr ergebener / Walter Benjamin" (Benjamin to Schmitt, December 9, 1930, in Benjamin 1974–1989, 1.3: 887 and Benjamin 1997, 3: 558; Weber 1992a, 5). Unless noted otherwise, all translations of source material by the translators.
2. As early as 1987, Habermas expressed consternation regarding two translations of Schmitt into English (1987, 103–119). Mark Lilla's critical commentary on the latest Schmitt "boom" (1997, 38–40, 42–44) was met with sharp criticism by Ulmen 1996 (92–95) and Gottfried 1996 (95–97). Cf. also McCormick 1998 (830–854). A more recent example of the ever-growing importance of Schmitt's political theory is the dedication of an entire volume of *Constellations* 18.3 (2011) to him. See especially the article by Richard J. Bernstein 2011 (403–430).
3. Among others, Taubes spoke of censorship (quoted in Kopp-Oberstebrink et al. 2012, 34), but this obviously cannot be confirmed. On the other hand, it is a fact that all notes in the Trauerspiel-book that mentioned Schmitt's Diktatur were cut off from the reprint in the Gesammelte Schriften (Sander 1975, 173 n79; Treml 2012, 273–298).
4. Letters from Boehlich to Schmitt: February 22 and 29, March 6, 13, and 20, 1968 (Nachlass Carl Schmitt, Nordrhein-Westfälisches Hauptstaatsarchiv, Düsseldorf, RW 265, 1916–1920). Letters from Schmitt to Boehlich, March 4 and 11, 1968 (Burkhardt 2013, 188–190).
5. "Akzeptiert man Ihre eigene Situationsanalyse vom Zeitalter des Weltbürgerkriegs, so sind Sie und Benjamin auf den verschiedenen Seiten der Barrikaden gelandet" (Kopp-Oberstebrink et al. 2012, 28).
6. "Aber beim Hamlet schreiben wir schon 1956, also ein Jahrzehnt nach der Nazi-Sintflut. Wie sah die Konstellation von Ihrer Sicht aus? Konnten Sie in Benjamin, der eindeutig die abgegriffenste kommunistische Plattitüde dem bürgerlichen Tiefsinn vorzog, noch Geist von Ihrem Geist entdecken?" (Kopp-Oberstebrink et al. 2012, 29).

7. In 1973 Taubes offered a seminar on Benjamin and Schmitt in which problems that he had exposed in his letter were discussed (Kopp-Oberstebrink et al. 2012, 306; cf. Lehnert 2008, 267, 271).

8. See note 1.

9. "Carl Schmitt, den Benjamin, ohne Abstrich, bewunderte." "Ich (anerkenne) Schmitt auch heute noch als den bedeutendsten Kopf in Deutschland." "Wenn Habermas vom 'linken Faschismus' spricht, den er (zu Unrecht) bei Dutschke und Krahl vermutet, der aber bei Benjamin ein nicht kleines Problem darstellt" (March 16, 1977, quoted in Kopp-Oberstebrink and Treml 2013, 177).

10. "Der Benjamin Brief an Sie steht in der Mitte der Diskussion" (May 31, 1977, in Kopp-Oberstebrink et al. 2012, 32).

11. "Sie brüsten sich, den persönlichen Kontakt mit einem heute fast Neunzigjährigen zu meiden, weil er vor fast einem halben Jahrhundert wahrhaft abscheuliche Dinge geschrieben hat." "[D]as intellektuelle Schiedsgehabe…widert mich an" (Taubes to Schmitt, May 24, 1977, in Schmitz and Lepper 2007, 260; also in Kopp-Oberstebrink and Treml 2013, 174).

12. "Es grüßt Sie die Hand über einen Abgrund reichend" (Kopp-Oberstebrink et al. 2012, 35).

13. Schmitt to Taubes, November 29, 1977 (Kopp-Oberstebrink et al. 2012, 38).

14. "In Plettenberg hatt ich die stürmischsten Gespräche, die ich je in deutscher Sprache geführt habe" (Kopp-Oberstebrink et al. 2012, 251).

15. Taubes to Schmitt, September 18, 1978 (Kopp-Oberstebrink et al. 2012, 58). The letter was published under an incorrect date in Taubes 1987 (39; cf. also 46).

16. "Der Feind ist deine eigne Frage als Gestalt" (Däubler 1916, 58). This source was discovered by Meier 1998 (12, 35, 79, 91, 96); 1994 (76).

17. "Dixi, und ich habe meine Seele nicht gerettet, aber ich habe Ihnen erzählt, wie es gelaufen ist" (Kopp-Oberstebrink et al. 2012, 264).

18. The letter comes up continuously in Kopp-Oberstebrink et al. 2012 (27–33, 34, 37, 54, 154, 196, 252, 255).

19. On this complex of ideas, cf. Ellen Kennedy, who attributes antiliberal thought to the Frankfurt School as a whole (1986, 389; on Benjamin's letter, see 382 n5.) A series of critiques of Kennedy appeared in Telos 71: Jay 1987; Söllner 1987; Preuß 1987. See also Weber 1992 (123–137).

20. In this light, De Wilde has connected Benjamin's theory of law to that of Schmitt (2006, 188–200); cf. also De Wilde's thorough monograph (2008). Traverso 2007 (93–109) brings Taubes and Agamben into the picture in order to sharply distinguish political aims of Benjamin and Schmitt; and Lucca 2009 (87–111) follows this direction by hinting at 9/11.

21. They show an uncompromised approach that combines words of high appraisal with phrases of critique. More important, they reveal three different styles of comments, the first of which obviously stems from the first reading in 1930 (Thaler 2013, 246–251).

22. His surrealistic piece "Die Buribunken" ("The Buribunks") appeared in the magazine *Summa* (1918), in which authors such as Ernst Bloch, Hermann Broch, Max Scheler, and Robert Musil were also published.

23. "Dieser Versuch, den ich in größerem Maßstabe in dem erwähnten Ursprung des deutschen Trauerspiels unternahm, knüpft einerseits an die methodischen Ideen Alois Riegls in seiner Lehre vom Kunstwollen, andererseits an die zeitgenössischen Versuche

von Carl Schmitt an, der in seiner Analyse der politischen Gebilde einen analogen Versuch der Integration von Erscheinungen vornimmt, die nur scheinbar gebietsmäßig zu isolieren sind. Vor allem aber scheint mir eine derartige Betrachtung Bedingung jeder eindringlichen physiognomischen Erfassung der Kunstwerke in dem worin sie unvergleichlich und einmalig sind" (Benjamin 1974, 7.1, 219).

24. "Only the decision, not the choice, is recorded in the book of life. For choice is natural and may even suit the elements; the decision is transcendent" (*Nur die Entscheidung, nicht die Wahl ist im Buche des Lebens verzeichnet. Denn Wahl ist natürlich und mag sogar den Elementen eignen; die Entscheidung ist transzendent,* Benjamin 1974, I.1, 189; "Goethe's Elective Affinities," 1996a, 346, trans. S. Corngold; translation modified).

25. Schmitt had presented this paper in October 1929 in Barcelona. Published in the same year, it became part of the second edition of *The Concept of the Political* (*Der Begriff des Politischen*) (Schmitt 2007). It was published under the new title *Das Zeitalter der Neutralisierungen und Entpolitisierungen* (*The Age of Neutralizations and Depoliticizations*) (De Benoist 2003, 64, Br. B 65).

26. Schmitt 1963 (91); quoted by Löwith 1988 (173); quoted by Benjamin 1974 (7.2, 673).

27. "Dieser Text, eine Art Testament Walter Benjamins, steht Aug in Aug mit den Thesen Carl Schmitts" (Taubes 1987, 28; cf. Heil 1996, 158).

28. Benjamin, "Über den Begriff der Geschichte" (1974, I.2, 697; trans. Zohn 1969, 257, under the title "Theses on the Philosophy of History"; translation modified). Like Osborne, Zohn translates *Ausnahmezustand* as "state of emergency" (n39).

29. Michael Rumpf (1976, 46) emphasizes this point but does not discuss Benjamin's critical turn.

30. The image becomes no clearer if one takes into account Georges Sorel's gnoseological theory of the general strike, to which Benjamin referred in his "Kritik der Gewalt" (1974, II.1, 194), a theory that was also significant for Schmitt's conception of power; see Schmitt 1989 (147). Cf. Rumpf 1976 (41); Anglet 1995 (41, 49, 83, 101, esp. 102); Wolin 1992 (435).

31. Benjamin 1974 (I.2, 703); 1969 (263); translation modified. Cf. Poltermann and Sander 1981 (42).

32. On the legal aspect of the state of exception and its relation to the *Grenzsituation* ("borderline situation"), see Hofmann 1995 (65). Cf. also Weber 1992 (125). On the notion of the *Grenzsituation*, see Jaspers 1953 (20). Cf. generally Weber 1993 (148).

33. Schmitt refers to the second letter to the Thessalonians in the New Testament 2 Thess. 2:7. On Schmitt's frequent use of the term, see Meuter 1994 and Meier 1994 (46, 234–253) as well as Meier 1998 (56, 90).

34. "In der Ausnahme durchbricht die Kraft des wirklichen Lebens die Kruste einer in Wiederholung erstarrten Mechanik" (Schmitt 1996, 21; cf. Berthold 1993, 287, 294).

35. Schelsky even called Schmitt "a German Hobbes" (1981, 5). Schmitt published extensively on Hobbes (1936–1937, 622–632; 1982; 1965, 51–69). In his memoirs, written after 1945, Schmitt compares himself repeatedly to Hobbes (see 1950, 61, 63, 67, 68, 75, 78, 89; 1991, 81). On this subject, cf. Rumpf 1972 (57, 61–67) and the foundational discussion in Meier 1994 (157).

36. "In der langen, an bunten Bildern und Symbolen, an Ikonen und Idolen, an Paradigmen und Phantasmen, Emblemen und Allegorien überaus reichen Geschichte der politischen Theorien ist dieser Leviathan das stärkste und mächtigste Bild. Es sprengt den Rahmen jeder nur gedanklichen Theorie oder Konstruktion" (Schmitt 1982, 9).

37. The entire framework of this article was laid out in Bredekamp (2012). In an abbreviated form, the book was published as "Thomas Hobbes's Visual Strategies" (2007, 29–60).

38. The words "representation" and "image" were used synonymously for the first time on the occasion of the burial of Henry VII in 1509 (Hope 1907, 539, 555). Against this background, Hobbes's description of the Leviathan as a living machine is understandable. His introductory statement, "by Art is created that great LEVIATHAN called a COMMON-WEALTH, or STATE, (in latine CIVITAS) which is but an Artificiall Man," is clearly inspired by kings' effigies (Hobbes 1991, 9). Had he possessed knowledge of this tradition, Bates's (2012, 64–80) impressive attempt at reconstructing "The Robotic Soul" of the Leviathan could have gone deeper.

39. The resemblance of the Leviathan to the model of the effigies was noted already by Bourdieu 1991 (209), though only in passing, in a sentence explaining the principle of representation.

40. "The bucolic idyll has become—to exaggerate a little—a predatory idyll" (Kuhn 1933, 194; there Schmitt is also characterized as a "Romantic"; cf. Hofmann 1995, 162). In a contribution to a discussion published in *Recht und Institution*, Hermann Lübbe likewise calls Schmitt a "Romantic of the exceptional situation," driven by an "intellectual and aesthetic weakness for exceptional political positions" (1985, 99).

41. "The normal proves nothing, the exception proves everything" ("Das Normale beweist nichts, die Ausnahme beweist alles"; Schmitt 1996, 21).

42. "'The unique extreme.' The concept proceeds from the extreme" ("'Das Einmalig Extreme.' Vom Extremen geht der Begriff aus"; Benjamin 1974, I.1, 215; 1985, 35; translation modified; cf. Makropoulos 1989, 39–41 and Weber 1992, 124).

43. Benjamin 1974 (I.1, 245), referring to Schmitt 1989 (xiv, 16). Benjamin 1985 (65); translation modified. Osborne renders *Ausnahmezustand* as "state of emergency." Cf. the foundational essay by Weber 1992 (130) and the essay by Figal 1992 (262).

44. The German drama of the Counter-Reformation was formed "in an extremely violent effort, and this alone would mean that no sovereign genius gave the form its peculiar character" ("in einer höchst gewalttätigen Anstrengung und dies allein würde besagen, daß kein souveräner Genius dieser Form das Gepräge gegeben hat"; Benjamin 1974, I.1, 229; 1985, 49; translation modified).

45. Schmitt makes reference to a letter of July 7, 1932, in which Korsch urgently asks for a meeting to discuss the political development (Schmitt to Viesel, May 11, 1973, in Viesel 1988, 60; cf. Sander 1979, 135–154 and Lauermann 1999, 39–62, spec. 45). In addition, Schmitt played off this letter in his correspondence with Hans-Dietrich Sander, who was the first to publish Benjamin's letter to Schmitt (Lehnert 2008, 273, 303–305).

46. Viesel 1988 (16). The article mentioned is Schmitt, "Der Staat als Mechanismus bei Hobbes und Descartes."

47. As mentioned above, this opinion is fully developed by Mehring 2010 (245), who argues that Schmitt had not read Benjamin's *Trauerspiel*-book before he prepared his piece on Hamlet.

48. See Schmitt 1985 (64, 67); Benjamin, "Erfahrung und Armut" (1974, II.1, 215); and Heil 1996 (71).

49. "There is a powerful taboo of the autonomous work of art, isolated from its historical and sociological origin, a taboo of absolute form, the real taboo of an idealistic philosophy, a purity taboo, deeply rooted in the tradition of German learning. This taboo does not permit us to speak of the intrusion of time into the play" (Schmitt 1957, 7–9; reprint and annotated by Tommissen 1996, 13–19).

50. "Der jahrzehntelange Sreit um Walter Benjamin ist ein Symptom hintergründiger Fronten und fanatischer Feindschaften ... Das Thema Benjamin enthält viele total verdrehten [sic!] Wegweiser" (Rumpf 2014, 283).

51. Cf. Pan 2009 (48) and Honneth 2006 (193–210, esp. 209). Benjamin 1996a; 1996b (236–252).

52. Derrida 1994 (89) and 1996 (78); on the "affinities" between Schmitt and Benjamin, see 65, 67, 99, 110).

53. "Schmitt/Einverständnis Haß Verdächtigung" (diary entry, 21 April 21, 1930, Benjamin 1974, II.3, 1372). On the lectures, see Schmitt 1931; cf. Kambas 1982 (611).

REFERENCES

Adorno, T. W. 1955. "Einleitung." In *Walter Benjamin: Schriften*, ed. T. W. Adorno and G. Adorno, with collaboration of F. Podzus. Frankfurt: Suhrkamp, ix–xxvii.

Agamben, G. 2004. *Ausnahmezustand: Homo sacer II.1*. Frankfurt: Suhrkamp.

Anglet, K. 1995. *Messianität und Geschichte: Walter Benjamins Konstruktion der historischen Dialektik und deren Aufhebung ins Eschatologische durch Erik Peterson*. Berlin: Akademie Verlag.

Bates, D. 2012. *States of War: Enlightenment Origins of the Political*. New York: Columbia University Press.

Bendersky, J. W. 1983. *Carl Schmitt: Theorist for the Reich*. Princeton: Princeton University Press.

Benjamin, W. 1966. *Briefe*, 2 vols, ed. G. Sholem and T. W. Adorno. Frankfurt: Suhrkamp.

Benjamin, W. 1969. "Theses on the Philosophy of History," trans. H. Zohn. In *Illuminations: Essays and Reflections*. New York: Schocken, 253–264.

Benjamin, W. 1974–1989. *Gesammelte Schriften*, ed. R. Tiedemann and H. Schweppenhäuser. Frankfurt: Suhrkamp.

Benjamin, W. 1985. *The Origin of German Tragic Drama*, trans. J. Osborne. London, New York: Verso.

Benjamin, W. 1996. *Briefe*, 2 vols, ed. G. Scholem and T. W. Adorno. Frankfurt: Suhrkamp.

Benjamin, W. 1996a. "Goethe's Elective Affinities," trans. S. Corngold. In *Selected Writings, 1913–1926*, ed. M. Bullock and M. W. Jennings. Cambridge: Harvard University Press.

Benjamin, W. 1997. *Gesammelte Briefe*, 4 vols, ed. C. Gödde and H. Lonitz. Frankfurt: Suhrkamp.

Benjamin, W. 2008. *The Work of Art in the Age of Mechanical Reproduction*. London: Penguin.

Benjamin, W. 2009. *On the Concept of History*. New York: Classic Books America.

Bernstein, R. J. 2011. "The Aporias of Carl Schmitt." *Constellations* 18.3: 403–430.

Berthold, L. 1993. "Wer hält zur Zeit den Satan auf? Zur Selbstglossierung Carl Schmitts." *Leviathan* 21: 285–299.

Bohrer, K. H. 1981. *Plötzlichkeit: Zum Augenblick des ästhetischen Scheins*. Frankfurt: Suhrkamp.

Bourdieu, P. 1991. *Language and Symbolic Power*, trans. G. Raymond and M. Adamson, ed. J. B. Thompson. Cambridge: Harvard University Press.

Bredekamp, H. 1992. "Der simulierte Benjamin: Mittelalterliche Bemerkungen zu seiner Aktualität." In *Frankfurter Schule und Kunstgeschichte*, ed. A. Berndt et al. Berlin: Reimer, 117–140.

Bredekamp, H. 1998. "Von Walter Benjamin zu Carl Schmitt, via Thomas Hobbes." *Deutsche Zeitschrift für Philosophie* 46: 901–916.

Bredekamp, H. 1999. "From Walter Benjamin to Carl Schmitt, via Thomas Hobbes." *Critical Inquiry* 25: 247–266.

Bredekamp, H. 2007. "Thomas Hobbes's Visual Strategies." In *The Cambridge Companion to Hobbes' "Leviathan*," ed. P. Springborg. Cambridge, New York: Cambridge University Press, 29–60.

Bredekamp, H. 2008. *Der Künstler als Verbrecher: Ein Element der frühmodernen Rechts- und Staatstheorie.* Munich: Siemens Stiftung.

Bredekamp, H. 2012. *Thomas Hobbes: Der Leviathan. Das Urbild des modernen Staates und seine Gegenbilder 1651–2001.* Berlin: Akademie Verlag.

Burkhardt, K. ed. 2013. *Carl Schmitt und die Öffentlichkeit: Briefwechsel mit Journalisten, Publizisten und Verlegern aus den Jahren 1923 bis 1938.* Berlin: Duncker & Humblot.

Däubler, T. 1916. *Hymne an Italien.* Munich: Müller.

De Benoist, A. 2003. *Carl Schmitt: Bibliographie seiner Schriften und Korrespondenzen.* Berlin Akademie Verlag.

De Wilde, M. 2006. "Violence in the State of Exception: Reflections on Theologico-Political Motifs in Benjamin and Schmitt." In *Politica Theologies: Public Religions in a Post-secular World*, ed. H. de Vries and L. E. Sullivan. Fordham: Fordham University Press.

De Wilde, M. 2008. *Verwantschap in Extremen: Politieke Theologie bij Walter Benjamin en Carl Schmitt.* Amsterdam: Amsterdam University Press.

Derrida, J. 1994. *Force de loi: Le "Fondement mystique de l'autorité."* Paris: Galilée.

Derrida, J. 1996. *Gesetzeskraft: Der "mystische Grund der Autorität,"* trans. A. G. Düttmann. Frankfurt: Suhrkamp.

Einem, A., and C. Einem. 1997. "Carolus jocosus? Ein Blick in die Katakomben der Carl-Schmitt-Forschung." *Etappe* 13: 53–75.

Figal, G. 1992. "Vom Sinn der Geschichte: Zur Erörterung der politischen Theologie bei Carl Schmitt und Walter Benjamin." In *Dialektischer Negativismus: Michael Theunissen zum 60. Geburtstag*, ed. E. Angehrn et al. Frankfurt: Suhrkamp, 252–269.

Gottfried, P. 1996. "Letter to Robert B. Silvers, *The New York Review of Books*." *Telos* 109: 95–97.

Güde, F. 1985. "Der Schiffbrüchige und der Kapitän: Carl Schmitt und Walter Benjamin auf stürmischer See." *Kommune* 3: 61–67.

Habermas, J. 1987. "Die Schrecken der Autonomie: Carl Schmitt auf Englisch." In *Eine Art Schadensabwicklung: Kleine politische Schriften VI.* Frankfurt: Suhrkamp, 101–119.

Harvey, A., and R. Mortimer. 1994. *The Funeral Effigies of Westminster Abbey.* Woodbridge, Rochester: Boydell Press.

Heil, S. 1996. *Gefährliche Beziehungen: Walter Benjamin und Carl Schmitt.* Stuttgart: Metzler.

Hobbes, T. 1991. *Leviathan*, ed. R. Tuck. Cambridge: Cambridge University Press.

Hofmann, H. 1995. *Legitimität gegen Legalität: Der Weg der politischen Philosophie Carl Schmitts*, 3rd ed. Berlin: Duncker & Humblot.

Holmes, S. 1993. *The Anatomy of Antiliberalism.* Cambridge: Harvard University Press.

Honneth, A. 2006. "Zur Kritik der Gewalt." In *Benjamin-Handbuch: Leben—Werk—Wirkung*, ed. B. Lindner. Stuttgart: Metzler, 193–209.

Hope, W. H. St. J. 1907. "On the Funeral Effigies of the Kings and Queens of England, with Special Reference to Those in the Abbey of Westminster." *Archeologia: or Miscellaneous Tracts Relating to Antiquity* 60: 517–565.

Jaspers, K. 1953. *Einführung in die Philosophie.* Zurich: Artemis.

Jay, M. 1987. "Reconciling the Irreconcilable? Rejoinder to Kennedy." *Telos* 71: 76–80.

Kambas, C. 1982. "Walter Benjamin an Gottfried Salomon: Bericht über eine unveröffentlichte Korrespondenz." *Deutsche Vierteljahrsschrift für Literaturwissenschaft und Geistesgeschichte* 56: 601–621.

Kennedy, E. 1986. "Carl Schmitt und die 'Frankfurter Schule': Deutsche Liberalismuskritik im 20. Jahrhundert." *Geschichte und Gesellschaft* 12: 380–412.

Koenen, A. 1995. *Der Fall Carl Schmitt: Sein Aufstieg zum "Kronjuristen des Dritten Reiches."* Darmstadt: Wissenschaftliche Buchgesellschaft.

Kopp-Oberstebrink, et al. ed. 2012. *Jacob Taubes and Carl Schmitt: Briefwechsel mit Materialien.* Munich: Fink.

Kopp-Oberstebrink, H., and M. Treml. ed. 2013. *Hans Blumenberg und Jacob Taubes: Briefwechsel 1961–1981 und weitere Materialien.* Berlin: Suhrkamp.

Kuhn, H. 1933. Review of Carl Schmitt, *Der Begriff des Politischen. Kant-Studien* 38: 190–196.

Küpper, T., and T. Skandris. 2006. "Rezeptionsgeschichte." In *Benjamin-Handbuch: Leben—Werk—Wirkung*, ed. B. Lindner. Stuttgart: Metzler.

Laak D. van. 1993. *Gespräche in der Sicherheit des Schweigens: Carl Schmitt in der politischen Geistesgeschichte der frühen Bundesrepublik.* Berlin: Akademie Verlag.

Lauermann, M. 1999. "Politische Theologie des Klassenkampfs: Die Lektüre von Brechts *Die Massnahme durch* Carl Schmitt—ein soziologischer Versuch." In *Massnehmen: Bertold Brecht/ Hanns Eislers Lehrstück "Die Massnahme"*, ed. I. Gellert et al. Berlin: Theater der Zeit, 39–62.

Lehnert, E. and G. Maschke. ed. 2008. *Carl Schmitt und and Hans-Dietrich Sander: Werkstatt-Discorsi: Briefwechsel 1967–1981.* Schnellroda: Antaios.

Lilla, M. 1997. "The Enemy of Liberalism." *New York Review of Books*, May 15, 38–40, 42–44.

Löwith, K. 1988. "Max Weber und seine Nachfolger." *Maß und Wert* 3: 166–176. Reprinted in *Hegel und die Aufhebung der Philosophie im 19. Jahrhundert—Max Weber.* Stuttgart: Metzler, 408–418.

Lübbe, H. 1985. "Helmut Schelsky und die Institutionalisierung der Reflexion." In *Recht und Institution: Helmut Schelsky-Gedächtnissymposion Münster 1985*, ed. Rechtswissenschaftliche Fakultät der Universität Münster. Berlin: Duncker & Humblot, 59–70.

Lucca, J. 2009. "Walter Benjamin y Carl Schmitt: Palabras cruzadas de un diálogo mudo en un tiempo agitado." *Revista de Filosofía* 27: 87–111.

Makropoulos, M. 1989. *Modernität als ontologischer Ausnahmezustand? Walter Benjamins Theorie der Moderne.* Munich: Fink.

McCormick, J. P. 1998. "Political Theory and Political Theology: The Second Wave of Carl Schmitt in English." *Political Theory* 26: 830–854.

Mehring, R. 2009. *Carl Schmitt: Aufstieg und Fall.* Munich: Beck.

Mehring, R. 2010. "'Geist ist das Vermögen, Diktatur auszuüben': Carl Schmitts Marginalien zu Walter Benjamin." *Benjamin-Studien* 2: 239–256.

Meier, H. 1994. *Die Lehre Carl Schmitts: Vier Kapitel zur Unterscheidung politischer Theologie und politischer Philosophie.* Stuttgart: Metzler.

Meier, H. 1995. "Was ist Politische Theologie? Einführende Bemerkungen zu einem umstrittenen Begriff." In *Politische Theologie zwischen Ägypten und Israel*, 2nd ed., ed. J. Assmann. Munich: Siemens Stiftung, 7–19.

Meier, H. 1998. "Der Philosoph als Feind: Zu Carl Schmitts 'Glossarium.'" In *Carl Schmitt, Leo Strauss, und "Der Begriff des Politischen": Zu einem Dialog unter Abwesenden.* Stuttgart: Metzler, 141–152.

Meuter, G. 1994. *Der Katechon: Zu Carl Schmitts fundamentalistischer Kritik der Zeit.* Berlin: Duncker & Humblot.

Nippel, W. 2011. "Carl Schmitts 'kommissarische' und 'souveräne Diktatur': Französische Revolution und römische Vorbilder." In *Ideenpolitik: Geschichtliche Konstellation und gegenwärtige Konflikte*, ed. H. Bluhm et al. Berlin: Akademie Verlag, 105–140.

Pan, D. 2009. "Against Biopolitics: Walter Benjamin, Carl Schmitt, and Giorgio Agamben on Political Sovereignty and Symbolic Order." *German Quarterly* 82: 42–62.

Poltermann, A., and E. Sander. 1981. "Rede im Exil: Theologische Momente im Werk von Walter Benjamin." In *"Kritische Theorie" zwischen Theologie und Evolutionstheorie: Beiträge zu einer Auseinandersetzung mit der "Frankfurter Schule,"* ed. W. Kunstmann and E. Sander. Munich: Fink, 23–85.

Preuß, U. K. 1987. "The Critique of German Liberalism: Reply to Kennedy." *Telos* 71: 97–110.

Rumpf, H. 1972. *Carl Schmitt und Thomas Hobbes: Ideelle Beziehungen und aktuelle Bedeutung mit einer Abhandlung über die Frühschriften Carl Schmitts*. Berlin: Duncker & Humblot.

Rumpf, M. 1976. Radikale Theologie: Walter Benjamins Beziehung zu Carl Schmitt." In *Walter Benjamin: Zeitgenosse der Moderne*, ed. P. Gebhardt et al. Kronberg: Scriptor, 37–50.

Rumpf, M. ed. 2014. "Briefwechsel Michael Rumpf und Carl Schmitt." In *Schmittiana: Beiträge zu Leben und Werk Carl Schmitts* (Neue Folge), vol. 2, ed. Carl-Schmitt-Gesellschaft. Berlin: Duncker & Humblot, 275–285.

Sander, H.-D. 1975. *Marxistische Ideologie und allgemeine Kunsttheorie*. Tübingen: Mohr.

Sander, H.-D. 1979. "*Die Massnahme*, rechtsphilosophisch betrachtet: Carl Schmitt—Karl Korsch—Bertold Brecht." *Deutsche Studien* 17: 135–154.

Schelsky, H. 1981. *Thomas Hobbes: Eine politische Lehre*. Berlin: Duncker & Humblot.

Schmidt, C. 2000. *Der häretische Imperativ: Überlegungen zur theologischen Dialektik der Kulturwissenschaft in Deutschland*. Tübingen: Niemeyer.

Schmitt, C. 1918. "Die Buribunken: Ein geschichtsphilosophischer Versuch." *Summa* 4: 89–106.

Schmitt, C. 1919. *Politische Romantik*. Berlin: Duncker & Humblot.

Schmitt, C. 1931. *Probleme der Demokratie: Politische Wissenschaft*, 2nd ser. Berlin: Rothschild.

Schmitt, C. 1936–1937. "Der Staat als Mechanismus bei Hobbes und Descartes." *Archiv für Rechts- und Sozialphilosophie* 30: 622–632.

Schmitt, C. 1942. *Land und Meer: Eine weltgeschichtliche Betrachtung*. Leipzig: Reclam.

Schmitt, C. 1950. *Ex Captivitate Salus: Erfahrungen der Zeit 1945/47*. Cologne: Greven.

Schmitt, C. 1957. "Was habe ich getan?" *Dietsland-Europa* 2 [January]: 7–9. Reprinted and annotated by P. Tommissen, ed. 1996. *Schmittiana: Beiträge zu Leben und Werk Carl Schmitts*, vol. 5: 13–19.

Schmitt, C. 1963. *Begriff des Politischen*. Berlin: Duncker & Humblot.

Schmitt, C. 1965. "Die vollendete Reformation: Bemerkungen und Hinweise zu neuen *Leviathan*-Interpretationen." *Der Staat*, April 4, 51–69.

Schmitt, C. 1982. *Der Leviathan in der Staatslehre des Thomas Hobbes: Sinn und Fehlschlag eines politischen Symbols*, ed. G. Maschke. Cologne: Hohenheim.

Schmitt, C. 1985. *Hamlet oder Hekuba: Die Einbruch der Zeit in das Spiel*. Stuttgart: Klett-Cotta.

Schmitt, C. 1989. *Die Diktatur: Von den Anfängen des modernen Souveränitätsgedankens bis zum proletarischen Klassenkampf*, 5th ed. Berlin: Duncker & Humblot.

Schmitt, C. 1991. *Politische Romantik*, 5th ed. Berlin: Duncker & Humblot.

Schmitt, C. 1995. *Theorie des Partisanen: Zwischenbemerkungen zum Begriff des Politischen*, 4th ed. Berlin: Duncker & Humblot.

Schmitt, C. 1996. *Politische Theologie: Vier Kapitel zur Lehre von der Souveränität*, 7th ed. Berlin: Duncker & Humblot.

Schmitt, C. 2004. *Political Theology: Four Chapters on the Concept of Sovereignty*, trans. G. D. Schwab. Chicago: University of Chicago Press.

Schmitt, C. 2007. *The Concept of the Political*. Chicago: University of Chicago Press.

Schmitt, C. 2011. *Political Romanticism*. New Brunswick: Transaction.

Schmitz, A., and M. Lepper. ed. 2007. *Hans Blumenberg und Carl Schmitt: Briefwechsel 1971–1978 und weitere Materialien*. Frankfurt: Suhrkamp.

Scholem, G. 1982. *MiBerlin LiJerushalijim: Sichronot Ne'urim*. Tel Aviv: Am oved.

Schöttker, D. 2007. "Kommentar." In Walter Benjamin, *Das Kunstwerk im Zeitalter seiner technischen Reproduzierbarkeit und weitere Dokumente*, ed. Walter Benjamin. Frankfurt: Suhrkamp, 99–254.

Schuller, W. 1996. "Dennoch die Schwerter halten: Der Katechon Carl Schmitts." In *Geschichte—Tradition—Reflexion: Festschrift für Martin Hengel zum 70. Geburtstag*, 3 vols, ed. H. Cancik et al. Tübingen: Mohr, 389–408.

Söllner, A. 1987. "Beyond Carl Schmitt: Political Theory in the Frankfurt School." *Telos* 71: 81–96.

Taubes, J. 1987. *Ad Carl Schmitt: Gegenstrebige Fügung*. Berlin: Merve.

Thaler, J. 2013. "Genial." "Carl Schmitt liest Walter Benjamin." In *Lesespuren—Spurenlesen oder Wie kommt die Handschrift ins Buch? Von sprechenden und stummen Annotationen*, vols. 12/13, ed. M. Atze and V. Kaukoreit. Wien: Praesens, 246–251.

Tielke, M. 2011. "Die Bibliothek Carl Schmidts." In *Schmittiana: Beiträge zu Leben und Werk Carl Schmitts* (Neue Folge), vol. 1, ed. Carl-Schmitt-Gesellschaft. Berlin: Duncker & Humblot, 257–332.

Traverso, E. 2007. "'Relaciones peligrosas': Walter Benjamin y Carl Schmitt en el crepúsculo de Weimar." *Acta Poética* 28: 93–109.

Treml, M. 2012. "Paulinische Freundschaft: Korrespondenzen von Jacob Taubes und Carl Schmitt." In Kopp-Oberstebrink et al., 273–304.

Turk, H. 1986. "Politische Theologie? Zur Intention auf die Sprache bei Benjamin und Celan." In *Juden in der deutschen Literatur: Ein deutsch-israelisches Symposion*, ed. S. Moses and A. Schöne. Frankfurt: Suhrkamp, 330–349.

Ulmen, G. L. 1996. "Letter to the Editors, *New York Review of Books*." *Telos* 109: 92–95.

Viesel, H. 1988. *Jawohl, der Schmitt: Zehn Briefe aus Plettenberg*. Berlin: Support-Edition.

Villinger, I. 1995. *Carl Schmitts Kulturkritik der Moderne: Text, Kommentar; und Analyse der "Schattenrisse" des Johannes Negelinus*. Berlin: Akademie Verlag.

Weber, S. 1992. "Taking Exception to Decision: Theatrical-Theological Politics, Walter Benjamin and Carl Schmitt." In *Walter Benjamin, 1892-1940*, ed. U. Steiner. Frankfurt: Lang, 123–137.

Weber, S. 1992a. "Taking Exception to Decision: Walter Benjamin and Carl Schmitt." *Diacritics* 22: 5–18.

Weber, S. 1993. "Taking Exception to Decision." In *Enlightenments: Encounters between Critical Theory and Contemporary French Thought*, ed. H. Kunneman and H. de Vries. Kampen, Netherlands: Pharos, 141–161.

Werckmeister, K. 1996. "Walter Benjamin's 'Angel of History'; or the Transformation of the Revolutionary into the Historian." *Critical Inquiry* 22: 239–267.

Windisch, M. 1997. "'When There Is No Visible Power to Keep Them in Awe': Staatstheorie und Bildform bei Thomas Hobbes." *Zeitsprünge* 1: 117–165.

Wolin, R. 1992. "Carl Schmitt: The Conservative Revolutionary Habitus and the Aesthetics of Horror." *Political Theory* 20: 424–447.

CHAPTER 27

LEGITIMACY OF THE MODERN AGE?

Hans Blumenberg and Carl Schmitt

ALEXANDER SCHMITZ

INTRODUCTION

IN THIS chapter I consider Carl Schmitt as a thinker who continuously favored *relations* over positions, *forms of differentiation* over standpoints. The nature and limits of the concepts involved emerge situatively and by way of polemical reference to positions Schmitt marked as hostile.[1] Schmitt has often been read very differently. There are numerous interpretations seeing his ideas as adhering to a fixed idea, a center, an avowal of belief, and that use this as a basis for tying together the many strands of his thought (see Meier 2009; Groh 1998).[2] But already the most prominent concept used to pin down Schmitt's life and work, one repeatedly used by Schmitt himself to that end, poses difficulties. Namely, readers will search fruitlessly for a precise definition of what "political theology" is meant to be. Schmitt first used the term in 1922 in reference to a controversy between nineteenth-century Catholic counter-revolutionary publicists and their opponents, with the counter-revolutionaries arguing that all politics had a theological foundation. Already Bakunin, from whom Schmitt took the term, used it polemically. By fighting on the side of Bakunin's opponents, he entered that polemic context. In any event the concept's past emergence is not what mainly interested Schmitt. Rather, he saw "the present significance of those counter-revolutionary philosophers of state" as lying "in the determination with which they decide [*entscheiden*]. They intensify the moment of decision [*Dezision*] so greatly that in the end it annuls the thought of legitimacy from which it has emerged" (Schmitt 1934, 69; Hebekus 2009, 166–168).[3] Decision, then, creates its legitimacy from the intensity of a particular act of differentiation. And that decisions are made in the first place is more important than their content. These two dimensions of the decision accompany Schmitt's work while also indicating aspects of his modernity—and this whether or not we concur with his historical derivations.

In recent years the publication of Schmitt's diaries and correspondence has offered us a view of the intricate connections between his life and work. By contrast to the texts that he published in his lifetime, it becomes evident in these newly available materials that Schmitt's polemic not only is sparked by his opponents' positions but also in part appears astonishingly close to their positions. To describe this process, Schmitt borrowed an enigmatic formula from Theodor Däubler: "The enemy is our own question as figure" [Gestalt] (Schmitt 1950b, 90). The formula suggests that the vehemence with which Schmitt attacked certain positions may at times have been an expression of an affinity he had for them. If, for example, we apply the formula to Schmitt's *Political Romanticism* of 1919 and also consider the diaries written around that time, this early work appears to serve, among other things, as a rejection of a modern habitus that Carl Schmitt himself represents over a number of years, in an exemplary fashion. We can thus understand his critique of Romanticism as the exorcism of a specifically modern way of life pursued by Schmitt with his own person (Mehring 2009, 101–111). The intensity with which he struggles against Romanticism can thus be read as a sign of biographical closeness.

Some of Schmitt's interpreters, including Karl Löwith, noticed this pattern early on and criticized him on that basis. Löwith (1935) sees what he understands as Schmitt's opportunism vis-à-vis Nazism as stemming from his rejection of Romantic occasionalism. Precisely in respect to Schmitt's antisemitism, it is striking that the jurist was preoccupied with the line separating Judaism from Christianity over the course of his life, addressing it in various forms of correspondence with friends and opponents. Before 1933 the most impressive documentation of this is in the Schmitt-Ludwig Feuchtwanger correspondence; toward the end of his life Schmitt was still corresponding with Jacob Taubes, with whom he finally met (see Rieß 2007; Kopp-Oberstebrink, Palzhoff, and Treml 2012).

By examining the tense debate between Schmitt and Hans Blumenberg—the last such controversy to have an echo in Schmitt's published work—we can observe a line of continuation running through the jurist's life and writing. The debate's starting point was the first edition of Blumenberg's *Legitimität der Neuzeit* (*Legitimacy of the Modern Age*), appearing in 1966, which used succinct formulations to distance itself from Schmitt's *Political Theology*. Schmitt addressed and rebutted them in 1970, in the afterword to his *Political Theology II*. This was one basis for Blumenberg's decision to thoroughly revise *Legitimacy* (see Blumenberg 1974). It also led to a correspondence—involving only a few letters but nevertheless substantial—between the two authors in the 1970s; traces of this correspondence are evident in many of Blumenberg's works.

Continuity and identity in Schmitt's thought are not constituted by a specific position but by the will to decision and differentiation and an intensive search for an opponent from whom his own questions can be demarcated. As distinct as the positions of

Blumenberg and Schmitt may be, they share, alongside an interest in the threshold of the modern age, a certain view of the consequences of technological progress for the concept of human nature.

POLITICAL THEOLOGY II AS TESTAMENT

At the age of eighty-one, in 1969, Schmitt was working on his last full-length book, meant as his testament—as a text meant to fix a certain reading of his oeuvre for posterity. At this time, a copy of Blumenberg's first major book, *Legitimität der Neuzeit*, came into his possession. Blumenberg here models the transition between the medieval and modern periods in such a way that although the latter period indeed emerges from the former, it does not depend on it. In this framework he pays special attention to the concept of secularization, since it designates the developmental line upon which modernity, while dismissing its theological premises, at the same time refers to and depends on those premises. Blumenberg's anti-theological affect is catalyzed against this horizon of emancipation and simultaneous dependence. He positions himself against the voluntarism of the medieval concept of God, as it contradicts his picture of the person as a self-assertive being. For Blumenberg, the immanent constitution of modern rationality is legitimate because the idea of a despotic Christian God denies human beings the possibility of self-determination. Thus Blumenberg on the one hand understands the modern age as a response to the challenges of a theological absolutism, but on the other hand insists quite emphatically on the immanence of the development of scientific paradigms and modern rationality in general. This double logic of response and a new beginning without presuppositions served Schmitt as the starting point for a defense, against Blumenberg, of the identity and continuity of his conceptual work with political theology.

For Schmitt, Blumenberg's *Legitimität der Neuzeit* represented the final antithetical project in face of which he could demand satisfaction, and which he correspondingly countered in the closing pages of his last independently published work. At stake for both opponents were the foundation and justification of modern claims regarding the world and knowledge, together with modernity's picture of human beings. Blumenberg endowed questions of legitimacy with an anthropological dimension, in the process calling into doubt Schmitt's "avowal of faith" in *The Concept of the Political* (1963, 59–61). In doing so he was attacking Schmitt on just the field to which the latter had moved after his constitutional theory had, in Schmitt's self-assessment, reached its limits. Blumenberg's objections to the secularization thesis allowed Schmitt to once again place the object of his main argumentative and affective opposition on the table: the rule of economic-technical neutralizing regimes and the autism of a society seeking its salvation in social factors.

By the time of his confrontation with Blumenberg, Schmitt had officially been *persona non grata* in the German university system for a quarter of a century. Unofficially and semi-publicly, however, he was a presence; he was informed about the status of discussions that interested him (see van Laak 2002). The staging of spatial and temporal distance to those discussions was part of the self-stylization of the work of his old age. One thing becoming clear in this work is that after World War II Schmitt did not engage in any basic alteration of his earlier conceptual decisions. These were shaped in the 1920s and then adapted to suit altered problems and situations.

Testing the flexibility and applicability of his conceptual patterns to suit both new situations, positions, and ideas and the interpretation of his own case also characterized his confrontation with Blumenberg's *Legitimität der Neuzeit*. The text offered Schmitt a chance to remobilize many arguments at his disposal fifty years earlier. Already in his essay "The Buribunks" (1918) do we find a biting satire aimed at the "process-progress" ("*Prozess-Progreß*") of a life that completely circles within itself (Schmitt 2005, 453–471).[4] Schmitt adopts a similar approach in the afterword to *Political Theology II*. Already in "The Buribunks" we find an emphasis on modern self-assertion—here reduced to an act of permanent textualization. Put otherwise: the act of writing, through which the self merely asserts itself, has here become the only event worth narrating.

It is important to note that the legitimacy of the modern age, the basis for the controversy, was not only the focus of a specialized discussion about the concept of secularization. Rather, it directly concerned the historical present of the correspondents. With Hans Blumenberg and Carl Schmitt, a victim and someone who helped shape Nazi German policy stood face to face. Despite this fact, the confrontation was carried out in a tone stamped by astonishing courtesy—together with intractability in matters of substance and an exact awareness of the abysses present beneath the confrontation's stage. In one of the most noteworthy passages in his correspondence with Jacob Taubes, in a letter written in 1977, Blumenberg impressively articulates his lack of interest in a moral assessment of West German—and with it his own—history:

> [I have to] add one remark on how you have introduced the name Carl Schmitt and brought it into the right-left schema. I grant everyone the right to avoid personal contact with someone else and to bear him lifelong ill will, whatever he may have said or done. There is no remedy or law against that. But to bring this into a public or half-public self-representation or see it brought into one is as repugnant to me as are moral censors who hold heir judgment days in every nook and cranny, again post signs and distribute places on a scale between right and left, with it then being possible to decide who is carried along by the big turn and who not. Those who are properly placed receive all possible applause and argumentative help, all consideration and hermeneutic credit up to the edge of nonsense and beyond. They boast about avoiding contact with someone now nearly ninety because almost half a century ago he wrote truly revolting things whose genre has, however, not died out with other figures and approaches in the intellectual milieu, and in the urge for grandstanding and being cited that exists there. We undertake endless efforts to banish the spirit of moral judgment and revenge from our institutions, which to the contrary may be conceived and desired in our own cubbyholes. That is one of our

great accomplishments, in which the state even stands opposed to the majority will of our citizens. But anyone who has ever said the false thing from the false position is meant to remain the leper, and people adorn themselves with contempt for him. I say nothing against insurmountable personal resistance someone feels there and with which he has to come to terms; to the contrary, I also respect the inability to forget. But the affected intellectual judgments over "who still" and "who no longer" repel me. I have never had personal sympathy for Martin Heidegger, but I protest against his new censors. For this reason I would like to communicate the naked fact to you that in 1971 I sought out and found contact with Carl Schmitt. There will be more to say about this much later. (Blumenberg quoted in Kopp-Oberstebrink and Treml 2013, 173–174)[5]

To a large extent, Carl Schmitt's post-1945 writing was carried forward by the will to furnish posterity with reading instructions for his entire oeuvre. As a sequel to his half-century-old book on political theology (a book against which Erik Peterson had raised clear objections in 1935 in his *Monotheism as a Political Problem*), its second part, wrestling with the theological and scientific dismissal of just that theology, asserts the fundamental stability of what had been a lifelong theme.[6] For Schmitt, it may well have made sense to secure his position in view of the highly disparate discussions of the theme. But already contemporaries wondered about the reasons that the seemingly distant dispute with Peterson would here be taken up again; not only its context but also its significance had become opaque. Even confidants of Schmitt such as Ernst-Wolfgang Böckenförde and Reinhart Koselleck considered the debate with Blumenberg to carry more weight.

From Schmitt's perspective there were, however, good reasons for returning to the earlier controversy. In the first place, the basic question at issue was related to the situation that had emerged after the Second Vatican Council and the discussion of liberation theology. In this framework the origins and topicality of the catchphrase "political theology" were frequently no longer tied to Schmitt. "His" field was newly measured.[7] Of special significance for his recourse to the Peterson controversy was Schmitt's friendship with Hans Barion. Schmitt felt close to Barion particularly through their shared distaste for the Council, with both men interpreting its "pretensions" as "social revelation."[8] West Germany's self-conception was criticized in the same terms. But beyond such agreements and analogously to Peterson, the canonist Barion disagreed with Schmitt regarding a connection between theology and politics (Tommissen 2000, 569–571). He negatively answered the question of the Catholic Church's affinity with political form—of the possibility of a political theology in the sense of the Church as a "world-historical form of power." The last phrase, with a question mark at the end, was the title of a chapter Barion contributed to a 1968 *Festschrift* dedicated to Schmitt (Barion 1968, 54). Maintaining the connection between the political and the theological, that jurist's *Political Theology II* was a systematic rejoinder to Barion's position.

Where the theological dismissal of political theology proclaims a strict separation between *civitas dei* and *civitas terrena*, the scientific dismissal, for which Blumenberg

stands, does not even need this distinction. It confirms the self-sufficiency of immanence, as Schmitt observes in the afterword of *Political Theology II*:

> It is satisfied with a self-assertion, self confirmation, and self-authorization, one of
> the many composites with self, a so-called auto-composite allowing unpredictable
> new worlds to appear, which produce themselves and even the conditions of their
> own possibility, at least the laboratory conditions. That dismissal of every political
> theology with which we are concerned in our study wishes to have nothing to do
> with dismissals that are atheistic, anarchistic, or positivistic in nature. (1970, 12)

Nevertheless, as we will see the two "dismissals" end up depending on or emerging from
each other. For Schmitt, the process of neutralization of political-theological constellations has its conclusion in Blumenberg's *Legitimität der Neuzeit*, since the jurist believes
he can trace a line from Peterson to Löwith and onward to Blumenberg.

Blumenberg disputed the stability and continuity of Schmitt's political-theological theorization. In *Political Theology II* Schmitt offered what Blumenberg termed a
"most illuminating remark" on this theme "in a note": "Everything that I have expressed
about... political theology consists of statements of a jurist on the systematic structural
relationship between theological and legal concepts—a relationship that obtrudes in
the framework of both legal theory and legal practice" (Blumenberg in Schmitz and
Lepper 2007, 58). In response to the remark, in the revised edition of *Legitimacy* (entitled *Säkularisierung und Selbstbehauptung* and published in 1974), Blumenberg asked
whether in Schmitt's return to the theme the understanding of secularism had remained
the same, and thus whether it was actually at all justified to speak of a "political theology" at work in the realm of state-theory (58). Schmitt answered the question affirmatively twice in his correspondence with Blumenberg (104 and 109). He confirmed the
inherent stability of his political-theological theorization because it concerned such a
"highly polymorphous area" (Schmitt 1970, 41, 34).

Concerning this issue, Schmitt's writing reveals three distinct ancillary narratives
that, although genetically emerging from one another, are systematically intertwined
and are therefore condensed by him into a larger narrative. The first ancillary narrative
involves the "purely legal" state-theoretical dimension of the issue (Schmitt 1970, 26). It
tells of what Schmitt views as the heroic act with which the modern age begins, captured
in the call *Silete theologi in munere alieno*, "Let theologians keep silent about matters
outside their ken" (Schmitt 1950c, 131). Through this "redeployment" ("*Umbesetzung*"),
he argues, the rationality of the Roman Empire—a political formation that the Church,
in its capacity as a world-political power, no longer controlled—took effect in the framework of state theory.

Schmitt considers the transfer of theologically claimed authority to the account of
politics to be the decisive event allowing a nondiscriminatory concept of the enemy to
emerge within internal European affairs and pacifying conflict between states for a long
period—in part through a shift of more intensive conflict to the rest of the world (1950c,
112–114). In distinction to Blumenberg, for Schmitt what is decisive is not the redeployment, as such, with which the epochal threshold can be marked in analytic-historical

fashion. Rather, he understands the redeployment as making possible a realization of legal ideas, and hence of decisions. This dimension of the broader historical context involves a form of juridical political theology (Böckenförde 1983)[9] that Schmitt lays claim to for his argumentation—occasionally as a claim to sole representation, something largely deviating from the problem's core. This idea of secularization in no way approaches the act of redeployment as illegitimate, rather underscoring the nonsecular premises the secularized state cannot evade (Böckenförde 1967): something again important for the dispute with Blumenberg.

In Schmitt's eyes, the redeployment guarantees nothing less than the constantly threatened autonomy of modern law. In positioning himself after the war as the last "representative of European *jus publicum*" (1950a, 75), Schmitt is also positioning himself as the figure who intends to put a stop to law's total functionalization, its delivery to the powerful autonomous logic of economics, technology, and the natural sciences. The "tyranny of values" is Schmitt's late return to this problem. In this context, for the debate with Blumenberg he came up with an important formulation: jurists, he indicated, were in steady danger of being pulverized "between theology and technology" (see Schönberger 2011, 89–91).

The second subnarrative in *Political Theology* centers on the historical interpretive model that Blumenberg criticized and the suggestion of the illegitimacy of the modern situation connected to this. Here Schmitt describes the modernization process as one of decline. The metaphysical formulae through which society forms a picture of itself not only change but are simultaneously depoliticized and neutralized (1963, 79–95). This part of the narrative—especially if we keep in mind its beginning as an act of heroic realignment—has a melancholy character, confronting the plenitude of the beginning with a processual logic of depletion.[10] Almost inevitably, the present here receives a reckoning of its losses. One result of this logic of decline is the difference between legitimacy and legality; Schmitt describes its origin and development in several passages.[11] Even in the mode of decline, it here remains apparent that the long-term nature and stability of the structures renders their application to historically "unique" events possible and articulable.[12] Schmitt pleads for this continuity of political-theological structures vis-à-vis Blumenberg's intellectual justification of the modern age in terms of what renders it new.

The third subnarrative focuses on the "state after its end," for Schmitt the authentically modern situation marked by the triumph of economic-technical regimes of neutralization. At the beginning of the twentieth century, the jurist argues, *jus publicum Europaeum* foundered, since "as a central concept of international law, the traditional concept of the state no longer corresponds to truth and reality" (1939, 341–343). Historically and politically, Schmitt observes, this turning point was signified by the French Revolution, by Romanticism.[13] In this part of the narrative, the entire sense of direction of the relevant political-theological constellations changes—something that has been generally overlooked in the literature on Schmitt. These constellations, like all the others, are stamped by the rapid shift of significance that characterizes modernity in general.

This shift of perspective is perhaps most emphatically set out in the following passage: "Another example of these rapid developments is offered by the concept of political theology. This refers to transmittals of theological concepts and ideas to secular-political thinking, for instance the formula "'one God, one ruler of the world'" (Schmitt 1950a, 10). Both the structural analogy and a certain developmental line in conceptual history are addressed here: from the realm of theology to political-secular concepts, from transcendence to immanence, with the former legitimizing the latter. "I have now been instructed" (10), Schmitt continues in reference to Erik Peterson's above-mentioned thesis,

> that a political theology has become impossible as a result of the Christian dogma of the Trinity. I readily believe that. But from the beginning this question is concerned with something entirely different, namely the historical and sociological fact of a present reality that overwhelms us. Involved here is the mythization of the drives and ideal images of great masses steered by small groups. In its first stage, this mythization still worked with remainders of a secularized theology.... But the following stage has long since been beyond that and no longer needs any theological concepts. For the masses, pure immanence has become completely self-evident to a large degree. They have become... incapable of God. (10–11)

This approach to political theology was already at work in the text of 1922.[14]

In his take on modernity, Schmitt methodically addresses "myth," the general strike, and the proletarian revolution, political fictions and "irrational theories of the direct use of violence" (1926, 77–79). In this way he himself upends political-theological relations, considering metaphysical images as projections of political constellations (Assmann 1992, 36). The thesis of theology's dismissal that Schmitt confronts in *Political Theology II* concerns not only the "birth of politics from the spirit of theology," the first aspect of Schmitt's narrative, but also "an entire world of images and reflections, of vertical analogies (as long as they move from below to above)" (1970, 77). Political theology thus has a double directional sense in which, on the one hand, analogies move "from above to below" and, on the other hand, "from below to above." The theological objection wishes to keep the two sides apart; the scientific objection "trims" away the difference's ideal side, transforming it into autistic self-reference.

With these structural assumptions, Schmitt develops new fields of application extending into his late work. In the process, his theory of sovereignty is reformulated as a theory of history and contemplation. This permanent developmental work is manifest in the way almost every one of his important texts is treated as incomplete: it is being reshaped, modified, and supplemented with corollaries. Under changed political circumstances, Schmitt presents his *Concept of the Political* as an example of the application of political theology. One of the key statements in the afterword aimed at Blumenberg, the projection of his friend/enemy thesis onto political theology, is already foreshadowed in the preliminary remark to the second edition of *Political Theology*, where Schmitt registers the polemical position of both political and nonpolitical theology (1934, 7). He draws theology into the political division that he eschatologically deepens in opposition to Blumenberg as a gnostically divided Trinity in the afterword (Schmitt 1934, 41–43).[15]

Such transformations stand at least under the suspicion of opportunism because of their adaptability to various situations. In *Political Theology II* Schmitt cites Hans

Barion, alongside Hugo Ball, as that reader of his work capable of viewing his writings between 1919 and 1927 in their interconnection and correctly classifying them (Schmitt 1970, 28). For *Political Theology* this means especially the connection with the essay "Die Sichtbarkeit der Kirche" ("The Visibility of the Church"; 1917) and the monograph *Römischer Katholizismus und politische Form* (*Roman Catholicism and Political Form*; 1923). The latter publication, Schmitt explains in *Political Theology II*, does not propose "an affinity of the Church with certain forms of political unity (monarchy or democracy)." Rather, it

> defends the unique political form of the Roman Church as the world-historically visible representation of Christ become a man in historical reality, a representation manifesting its public presence in three forms: as aesthetic form in its great art, as a juridical form in the development of its canon law, and as a glorious and illustrious world-historical form of power. (1970, 23–24)

These paratexts of *Political Theology* of 1922 considerably broaden the field, moving—entirely in the sense of Blumenberg's remark—past a problem of state and legal theory in a narrower sense. It is significant that Schmitt only returned to this initial contextualization of his text in 1970. He had moved beyond it prior to the book's second edition, in November 1933. The preliminary comment in that edition contains, alongside the change of the meaning of political theology, the following remark:

> This second edition of *Political Theology* has remained unaltered. Today, after twelve years, it will be possible to judge the extent to which this small text, first published in March 1922, has stood firm. The debate with liberal normativism and its sort of "constitutional state" ["*Rechtsstaat*"] has remained word for word. Some abbreviations result merely from passages treating inessential things having been removed. (1934, 7)

In view of the changed political situation in the early 1930s, Schmitt considered the reference to the context in which the work was originally conceived, and which he had made explicit in the first edition, as inessential: "The four chapters of *Political Theology* were written in March 1922, at the same time as an essay on 'The Political Idea of Catholicism'" (1922, 2). In 1936/1937 he fell out of favor with Nazi officials because they did not want National Socialism to be portrayed as an instantiation of political theology.

From the Theological to the Scientific Dismissal of Political Theology: Peterson, Löwith, Blumenberg

These and additional "improvements" (Schmitt 1940, 314) were critically received by Schmitt's contemporaries. In particular, Karl Löwith, in 1935, not only underscored the extent to which Schmitt's decisionism operated occasionalistically and thus was to be seen as a form of the very Romanticism against which Schmitt so heatedly polemicized.[16] He also discussed Schmitt's "improvements" with reference to the modifications the jurist had made in the new printing of *The Concept of the Political*, which Löwith saw as an effort to make the text appealing to Nazi rulers. Schmitt responded in his *Positionen und Begriffe (Positions and Concepts)* with a reprinting of the eliminated passages and the following hate-laced note: "The present reprint was copied verbatim from the 1927 edition, which puts the reader in a better position to judge the efforts made by emigrant-run journals [*Emigranten-Zeitschriften*] to dismiss some of my later corrections as indecent changes of heart" (1940, 314).[17]

In any event, the critique of Löwith referred to in Schmitt's correspondence with Blumenberg was aimed in a more basic way at Erik Peterson, referred to by Schmitt as "Löwith's mystagogue" (Schmitz and Lepper 2007, 122). The line Schmitt traces from Peterson to Löwith and onward to Blumenberg can be reconstructed from the documents in the Schmitt archive and books he owned. In 1936 Peterson met Löwith in Rome. At this time Peterson, it appears, introduced Löwith to the rules of Christian historical interpretation (110–111), rules that in any case were decisively abbreviated and elided by Peterson when he formulated his dismissal thesis. Both this and the monotheism text in general are directed against "Reich theology,"[18] which laid claim to recognizing a realization of its eschatological visions in Nazism. There is little overlap with positions held by Schmitt.[19] Peterson's other explorations of the relationship between politics and theology are far more complicated than the dismissal thesis suggests. We may thus doubt that at this point Schmitt felt particularly stung by Peterson's work on monotheism. It is doubtful whether at a time that saw the publication of Schmitt works such as "Der Führer schützt das Recht" ("The Führer Protects the Law"), "Verfassung der Freiheit" ("The Constitution of Freedom"), and "Deutsche Rechtswissenschaft im Kampf gegen den jüdischen Geist" ("German Legal Studies in Its Struggle against the Jewish Spirit"), the jurist would have been interested in disputing a dismissal of political theology that had Eusebius of Caesarea as its main example. In any event, Schmitt and Peterson continued their correspondence beyond the monotheism book; a meeting took place in Italy in 1936 (Nichtweiß 1994, 727–730). Schmitt asked Peterson for bibliographical references for the *Leviathan* book; Peterson supplied them, and Schmitt then expressed his thanks in the published text (1938, 14).

Initially, then, Schmitt's texts only address Peterson's dismissal thesis indirectly and are concerned with problems that preoccupied both authors in the 1920s. One significant reference in this respect is found in Schmitt's "The State as a Mechanism in Hobbes and Descartes" (1936/1937). Discussing the question of which "philosophical systems make possible the concept of totality," Schmitt rejects the "view expressed by *E. Peterson* according to which 'total' concepts of the modern age are not meant as concepts but as myths, totalization thus meaning mythification" (1995, 146). Notably in "What Is Theology?" in 1925, Peterson had distinguished between theology and "myth." According to him, theology only existed between Christ's first and second coming, and, in this interim period mythical, totality-asserting depictions of reality deviating from dogma—mythic determinations affecting the political space at a remove from theology—were only possible within a pagan framework. In other words, from the perspective of dogma, totalizing concepts could only have mythical character (see Peterson 1994, 15–17). In Peterson's view, the self-assertions of modern rationality themselves constitute theological "fantasms" ("*Phantastereien*"; 32).

But legists are interested in other aspects of the modern age than are theologians. Schmitt justifies his interests with a reference to the redeployment within the modern conception of the state that took away theology's decisionary monopoly. At this point a sign emerges of what will later be at stake in the controversy over the Hobbes interpretation in *Leviathan*. In that context, Schmitt asserts the totality of the modern state in face of a putatively victorious "Jewish front" (1938, 108). This also means that against Peterson, he asserts the political-theological unity of the locus where the question *quis judicabit?* is answered. Schmitt adheres to the meaning of the mythical symbol of leviathan and the totalizing power of the "secular image of struggle" (10). In his answer of July 13, 1938, Peterson calls Schmitt's remarks "misguided" ("irrig") (as quoted in Nichtweiß 1994, 735). This marked an end to the correspondence between Peterson and Schmitt and of their exchange about the difference between theology and myth.

What Schmitt *did* return to was the question of the possibility of Christian historical interpretation. He believed that Peterson could only formulate the dismissal thesis because he had omitted a decisive historical-theological figure: the *katechon*. In lectures on the theory of meaning in the Christian Bible that Schmitt attended in 1924/1925, Peterson spoke about this figure in his explication of eschatological time and the relationship of Christ to the Antichrist:

> If the Lawless One is himself not yet with us, at least his spirit and powers already make their mark in the present… The reason that the Lawless One is presently not yet appearing is explained by Paul with a reference to the power that he once designates as τό Κατέχον and a second time as ό Κατέχων. It is the case that we cannot understand what is to be understood by this power. Everything presented on this in books and seminars is only speculation. (Peterson 2006, 445)[20]

Schmitt's most well-known comment on the *katechon*, his entry in the *Glossarium* of December 19, 1947, sounds like a late reply to the Peterson passage:

> I believe in the Katechon: for me it is the only possibility of understanding history as a Christian and finding it meaningful. The Katechon needs to be named for every epoch of the last 1,948 years. The place was never unoccupied; otherwise we would no longer be present… There are intermittent, temporary, fragmentarily scattered holders of this task. I am sure we can [sic] even agree on many concrete names extending to the present as soon as the concept is finally sufficiently clear. (1991, 63)

We may doubt that Schmitt ever achieved clarity concerning the concept.[21] What is certain is that it preoccupied him to a high degree and that he wanted to see others grapple with it. His notes in his personal copy of Peterson's monotheism book and other archival documents show that he saw the omission of the *katechon*—as an exemplary figure of the interconnection of spiritual and secular levels—as the basis for the possibility of the dismissal thesis.

Arguably, this omission and the connected work on "Practice in Christianity" that Peterson undertook but did not complete (Schmitz and Lepper 2007, 110) also led to the figure's absence in Löwith's writing and the restatement of the dismissal thesis in other terms. One of the formulations in *Meaning in History* that Schmitt found most provocative reads as follows:

> There is only one very particular history—that of the Jews—which as a political history can be interpreted strictly religiously. Within the biblical tradition, the Jewish prophets alone were radical philosophers of history because they had, instead of a philosophy, an unshakable faith in God's providential purpose for his chosen people, punishing and rewarding them for disobedience and obedience. (Löwith 1949, 194)

Löwith does not make clear the source of his observations. According to Schmitt, they were copied from Peterson. For Schmitt, they portray political theology as a Jewish phenomenon and deny Christians a sense of history ("a Christian history is nonsense"; Schmitt in Schmitz and Lepper 2007, 125; Löwith 1949, 195). In Schmitt's view, Löwith here offers a superficial dismissal of a genuinely Christian intertwining of "world history and salvation," which Schmitt wishes to preserve as "Force of History" ("*Geschichtskraft*"; Schmitz and Lepper 2007, 149).

This monomaniacal dispute with Peterson and Löwith also relates to Schmitt's confrontation with his own biography and the life decisions he made in 1933. For Schmitt, Blumenberg's position, i.e., the destruction of the cohesion between spiritual and secular levels, rests on a double exclusion. In order to formulate his dismissal thesis, Peterson leaves aside the figure of the *katechon*, within which *civitas terrena* and *civitas dei* intersect. In this only limitedly valid form, Schmitt argues, Peterson's reflection was adapted from Löwith. Blumenberg, in his critique of Löwith, can then undermine the spiritual-secular cohesion that has been distorted and weakened in a double sense, thus arriving at a radically immanent, purely scientific rebuttal of political theology: in short, a neutralization process.

CARL SCHMITT'S CONCEPT OF MIRACLES

In the course of celebrating the Eucharist, directly before Holy Communion, the congregation assembles in Christ's name and recites an act of unconditional faith: "Lord, I am not worthy that you should enter under my roof, but only say the word and my soul shall be healed." The background to this sentence in the Christian Bible is one of its miracle stories: In Carpernaum, Jesus encounters a centurion (Mt 8:5–13), who beseeches him to heal his gravely ill servant. Jesus assents, but the pious yet pagan centurion, being familiar with the laws of Israel, acknowledges them by declaring himself unworthy of having the Jew Jesus enter his house. Nevertheless the centurion repeats his request to Jesus: in the King James version, "Speak the word only." Jesus is astonished: "Verily I say unto you, I have not found so great faith, no, not in Israel." In the Vulgate version: *Non inveni tantam fidem in Israel*. In knowledge of the old law with simultaneous avowal of the new, the centurion emerges as the "first born of the Gentile church" (Luz 1990, 16) in that he transgresses the law of the Old Covenant. Although Jesus performs miracles in Israel, according to the Christian Bible, not Jews but Gentiles avow the new faith. It is they who will sit at the heavenly table together with Israel's patriarchs, while the Children of Israel will be thrown into darkness. Although, ever since the Second Vatican Council, the Catholic Church no longer prays for the "perfidious Jews," the asymmetry between Old and New Covenants remains a core element of the post-conciliar Eucharist.

Schmitt scribbled the formula *Tantam novitatem in Israel non inveni* ("I have not found such great novelty in Israel") to the left of the title page in his personal copy of Blumenberg's *Legitimität der Neuzeit*. Although Schmitt's antisemitism does not surface openly in his conflict with Blumenberg, the formula offers a compass for understanding his view of the book. In the formula, Schmitt blends the Christian Bible's miracle story with a passage from Augustine's *City of God*, suggesting, against Blumenberg, a model of emphatic temporality. Explaining this through a standard reference to the analogy proposed in *Political Theology* between sovereign decision and divine miracle is insufficient. For Schmitt here postponed a "detailed explanation of the significance the concept of the miracle has in this context" (1922, 37; 1934, 50) until a later date. This explanation finally arrived in 1938, with the publication of *The Leviathan in the State Theory of Thomas Hobbes* in 1938. After he had fallen into disfavor with the *Sicherheitsdienst* (SD) in Nazi Germany, Schmitt turned from the radically immanent movement-connected concepts that he had been propagating for several years to the field of political mythology. Indeed, one chapter in his Hobbes book is devoted to the question of belief in miracles (1938, 79–97).

Schmitt believes that as a result of its sovereign power, leviathan causes the "state's subjects," "*Staatsunterworfenen*," to believe in it "as in a miracle" (*als an ein Wunder, an ein Mirakel*; 1938, 80). Miraculous healing by laying on hands belonged to the royal office. Schmitt emphasizes the concrete and practical significance of belief in miracles for the kingdom, which had to defend its authority against the Roman pope.[22] Schmitt's comments on Hobbes's approach to belief in miracles offers another variant of political theology. On his argument, sovereign *auctoritas* reveals itself precisely through power not being dependent on truth. "But at this point," Schmitt comments, "at the apogee of a sovereign power effectuating a unity of religion and politics, the fracture in this otherwise so closed, irresistible unity becomes apparent" (1938, 84). Hobbes left this breach open by distinguishing between public and private creed. The "Jewish front" (108), he declares, has penetrated through this breach, hollowing out leviathan from within.

In *Political Theology II* Schmitt now suggests that a central difference between his position and Blumenberg's is manifest on historical-theoretical terrain. He cannot, he remarks,

> enter into what is in our context the central problem whose elucidation represents a special highpoint in Blumenberg's critique: the relationship of St. Augustine to Gnosis. I would need to comment on the interpretation of book 21, 1–8 of the *Civitas Dei* and also try to correctly interpret the difficult *tanta novitas* passage in book 12, ch. 21 of the *Civitas Dei*, with all its implications concerning eternal return and eternal bliss on the part of the human individual. (as quoted in Schmitz and Lepper 2007, 40–41)

At stake here are two sorts of historical interpretation, defined by Schmitt respectively as "Jewish" and "authentically Christian."

Once more Löwith's *Meaning in History* is behind Schmitt's reference to "the difficult *tanta novitas* passage." Contrary to Blumenberg, Löwith does not search for inconsistencies in Augustine's description but distinguishes between the theoretical and moral-theological sides of *The City of God*. In his view antique *theoria* is in no way theoretically refuted in Augustine's book, Christianity rather being described as moving past it through an absolute faith in the invisible and unprovable. "It is of secondary importance," Löwith contends, "that Augustine further argues that the newness of certain happenings is not extraneous to the 'order of nature'; for he conceives the latter not as physis but as a providential order provided for by god" (1949, 164). In Löwith's reading, in *The City of God* Augustine proposes, against the pagans, that the eternal return of the same is a belief grounded in evil and is hostile to true Christian bliss; Christian faith trusts in the incommensurably new entering world history with Christ. According to Schmitt, cyclical thinking, with its problematic atemporality, is superseded by a concrete event located within history—an event "of infinite singularity that can neither be possessed nor occupied" (in Schmitz and Lepper 2007, 149). But historicity cannot be based on this singular event. Schmitt thus combines it with the opposing model of repetition, his own historical schema in this way combining two incommensurable concepts. The guarantor of this procedure is Augustine, who argued that what in immortal nature happens in a singular moment has to be repeatable in mortal nature.

Schmitt acknowledges the validity of Löwith's observation that "[t]he problem of history cannot be solved within its own horizon" (1949, 191). Historical events in Löwith's view contain no sense as such; that is ascribed to each event in a social, cultural, or political framework. Schmitt's own conception of a political sphere that cannot be reduced to politics alone emerges from just that insight. The exception cannot be represented within either the historical or the political order. But the mere assumption of the exception's existence, the claim to transcendence, produces effects within immanence. Through an enigmatic reference to Kierkegaard (a thinker he does not mention in this work), Schmitt already applied this complicated conception of singularity and repetition, the momentous event and the cycle, to the sovereign's exception in *Political Theology* (1934, 22). The success of this interconnection within the sovereign's decision produces order. Analogously, Schmitt's no less significant reference in *Political Theology II* to the *tanta novitas* passage argues for the possibility that a singular event repeats itself. In the *katechon* Schmitt discovers a figure of history in which the infinite singularity of the historically real and the moment of repeatability can be projected upon each other. The Antichrist appears in ever-new incarnations; in ever-new incarnations the *katechon*, the one who withholds or restrains, steps forward against him. Schmitt forms the arc between parts 1 and 2 of *Political Theology* by moving his theoretical figure of sovereignty into history. From the sovereign's legal force, the *katechon*'s "force of history" (Schmitz and Lepper 2007, 149) emerges.

Schmitt defiantly adheres to this interconnection. It assures him that the past does not become permanently devalued, that the future does not emerge as a senseless form of "process-progress." The model of momentous event that Schmitt portrays as Christian is in his view not accessible to Judaism. He asserts that Blumenberg's philosophy of legitimacy refers constantly to the new, but cannot think the new. According to Schmitt, even after Blumenberg's exegesis, the synagogue remains blind to the breakthrough of eschatological time. Elements of the most traditional anti-Judaism are manifest in this conception of history; they are, however, shaped to address genuinely modern problems. When scrutinized carefully, Schmitt's position involves the steady construction of Jews (and Judaism) as the figure of the enemy, blamed for all of modernity's problems.[23] Within Schmitt's perspective, as an "obliterator of borders par excellence" (Weininger 1922, 413),[24] what he repetitively refers to as "*das Jüdische*," "the Jewish," is the figure that eludes all attempts at definition. Schmitt's constantly evoked stereotype defined the limits of his thinking, which he sought to defend against that of the "assimilated Jew" (Schmitt 1991, 18–19).[25]

DOES BLUMENBERG SUCCEED IN DISENCHANTING SCHMITT?

For Blumenberg, the spiritual/secular difference is not a starting point for considering history but the object of analysis—an object that the metaphorologist approaches in a historicizing (Schmitt would say corrosive) manner. By focusing on the origins of Christianity, as he does repeatedly in his writings, Blumenberg reveals the strategies and redeployments that furnish an event like the Christian revolution with its universalistic face—even through an elision of its own origin. Blumenberg's provocation is aimed at something essential since it does not concern displacements within a given system but its initial differentiations. In response to this challenge, Schmitt resorts to his political anthropology in *Political Theology II*. Eschatological images and constellations, the gnostic dualism of the creator-God and redeemer-God, here stand in the service of polemic intensification, although they are not its grounding.

In both the first edition of *Legitimität der Neuzeit* and the revised version, Blumenberg's critique of Schmitt centers on the abusive or at least abuse-enabling use of metaphors. For Blumenberg, political theology represents an active "taking at its word of secularized stylistic means" (in Schmitz and Lepper 2007, 31, 51). Political absolutism wrests theological absolutism's verbal means in order to shift them to consciousness "in the sphere of the familiar and sanctioned, that which is to be accepted as fatality" (31, 51). In the first edition of *Die Legitimität der Neuzeit*, the formulation is as follows: "The layer of secularized expression as a Trojan horse of ideas that would be considered unacceptable in naked directness—that, as well, needs to be considered when we methodologically distinguish the expressibility of theories from the responsiveness of human beings to them when it comes to the problem of secularized language" (31). Through cunning, the political sphere acquires an appearance of legitimacy. By alleging that its justification has been taken over from the field of theology, it renders the caprice of its actions invisible.

Blumenberg describes the foundations of such transmission in 1960, in his *Paradigmen zu einer Metaphorologie* (*Paradigms for a Metaphorology*; 1998), which involves a reinterpretation of the relationship between conceptual and metaphorical language. For a long time, philosophy considered metaphors preconceptual "remainders"—treated mainly in the course of transmission to the logicity of the conceptual sphere, with the transformation capable of being completed at any time. By contrast, Blumenberg describes metaphors as "basic elements of philosophical language" (1998, 10). Importantly, the study of "absolute metaphors," with which Blumenberg's metaphorology begins, concerns a preconceptual sphere that cannot be elevated into a sphere of concepts. It furnishes the grounding for conceptualization, offering "structure to a world" (25). "Absolute metaphors," which for Blumenberg offer the clearest view of the steady entwining of conceptual-historical and anthropological problems, "represent the never tangible, never assessable totality of reality" (25). In their pragmatic dimension, metaphors thus have an orientation function, with the metaphorologist seeking "to arrive at the substructure of thinking, the underground, the nutrient solution of systematic crystallization" (13). The metaphors that Blumenberg examines constitute the anteroom of thinking and pre-form "what can ever be apparent to us and what we can ascertain" (92).

Metaphorology is an analytical instrument allowing access to the threshold between a preconceptual and conceptual grasp of reality, particularly from a historicizing perspective. Its goal is not to produce orientation models for social integration; on the contrary, those "engaged in metaphorology" have already deprived themselves of the possibility "of finding answers in metaphors to those unanswerable questions" (1998, 24). Blumenberg does confirm the courage with which "spirit is ahead of itself in its images" (13). But in view of the possible results of such courage, it is incumbent on the metaphorologist to promptly contain such images. The prefigurations within which the spirit is ahead of itself could be mere feints and illusions. Hence already before his debate with Schmitt, in the context of metaphorological consideration of the "power of truth," Blumenberg encounters a central problem that—now again entirely a philosopher—he has rejected on ideological-critical grounds, with a reference to logical inconsistency and unclear relations between theory and practice.

What happens to metaphorology when it enters the realm of political mythologemes, when the relationship between power and truth is suddenly inverted? In the case of a "skeptic such as David Hume," Blumenberg sees the traditional form of that relation-ship "transformed, indeed perverted" (1998, 22). Where, he indicates, "the traditional conception of metaphor presents 'force' as a legitimate attribute of truth," "for Hume force has become the sole 'substance' of truth. 'Truth' is only the name for the fact that certain ideas prevail over other ideas in human consciousness through the quantum of energy adhering to them, thus constituting the status of belief.... Here truth no longer *has* power; rather, we theoretically legitimate what has power over us as that which is true" (22). It appears that although Blumenberg observes emotional grounds—grounds not ascribable to rational instances—for such power over individuals and society, and acknowledges its rationally impalpable status, he offers no space for further theoretical exploration of such irrationality. Schmitt's recourse to political metaphors and fictions, myth, and irrationalist theories of violence is theoretically and practically oriented pre-cisely toward that space, toward those moments in which power over human beings becomes its own legitimating authority and seals itself off from analysis.

Schmitt consistently underscored that political concepts are polemical concepts, which in the end means that his own conceptual models consistently seek to devise a concrete enemy. Here the positioning of the concepts does not depict but rather produce reality. In the revised edition of *Die Legitimität der Neuzeit*, Blumenberg comments as follows:

> "Political theology" is a metaphorical theology: the quasi-divine person of the sover-eign has legitimacy and must have it because legality does not yet exist or no longer exists for that person, for it is meant to initially or again constitute such legality. The enviable position in which "political theology" has placed itself through the instru-ment of asserted secularization consists in its discovery of the inventory of its figures, thus saving itself the cynicism of an open "theological politics." (Blumenberg, quoted in Schmitz and Lepper 2007, 67–69)

If we read secularization, with Hermann Lübbe, as "the metaphorically consistent [*kon-sequent*] insertion of non-religious contents into religiously pre-formed statements or systems of statements" (Lübbe 2003, 133; see Haverkamp 2003),[26] it would seem that Blumenberg's metaphorology thwarts the consequences of such insertions by revealing the invisibly underlaid schema of the self-founding of modern politics, and that Schmitt in this way is consigned to a masking of arbitrary assumptions that he suggests are a given presence when in fact he inserted them violently. From this perspective, his con-cepts of the political are simply atavistic remainders, a resentment-laden step back into a premodern world.

Schmitt's concepts of the political, which permanently circle around the problem of "visibility," do not render their own premises invisible. The radicalism and provo-cation of both *Political Theology* and *The Concept of the Political* must be seen in the revelation of the paradoxes of modern system-routines, hence the premise for the inser-tion. The polemic energy of these texts is directed against nothing more intensely than against intransitive laws of conservation and *procedural legitimation*. Schmitt counters the fact that the legal system has to dissemble the groundlessness of its application by constantly rendering that groundlessness visible. Hardly any other theory of the political has so aggressively displayed the violence of such acts of insertion, redeployment, and implementation.

As a "morphology of metaphorics," a political theology of modernism seeks "a first, phenomena-ordering cataloging within the many 'reflections and 'retro-reflections'" (Schmitt 1970, 33) where the "mythification of drives and ideals of large masses steered by small groups" (1950a, 11) is located. The theory of political fictions on which this assumption is based was already a part of Schmitt's early thinking, as set out in writings appearing before World War I as well as in various polemics in the 1920s. In these writings, Schmitt reflected on the indispensability of fictions for models of political order. In his view, such fictions had to be based not on criteria of truth but on the pure force of their execution.[27] In his words: "Fiction is a consciously arbitrary or false assumption" (1913, col. 805) whose "value and justification" lies in "inevitability" and "indispensability for the practice of thinking and acting" (1912, 240). No ignorance of their own situation is here imputed to those involved in the fictions; rather, their counterfactual status is clearly perceived and all the more effective. Suspicion of ideology and false consciousness here come to nothing. "Answers to unanswerable questions" (Blumenberg 1998, 24) are recognized to be necessary and vital in the orientation they offer—ethical questions remain intentionally elided.[28]

For Schmitt the locus of modern political activity is defined by what he considers a normatively completely empty will to decision and differentiation—and this beyond any historical derivation. In this sense the "metaphysical picture that a certain age makes of the world" (Schmitt 1934, 59) is no illusion needing to be destroyed but the indispensable metaphoric sphere in which a society secures its central distinctions. For Schmitt supra-personal "facilities and formations" in which "institutional legal thinking" unfolds (8) are grounded in genuinely aesthetic procedures. For this reason, the "political imaginary" of such institutions does not only correspond to what is readily manifest to society "as a form of its political organization" (59). Rather, the evidence is itself manufactured through, among other things, the polemical use of political-theological models. Schmitt's "radical conceptualization" works through the positions of his opponents until it reaches the realm of "the metaphysical and theological" (59).[29] He ascribes prognostic capacities to his procedure:

> I observed the events in Prague like a seismologist perceives an earthquake. Hence now Benesch takes on the role of an [Emil] Hacha and experiences how it feels. The whole thing unfolds in such a way that the model character of the German development from 1929 to 1933 becomes clear. My book *Legality and Legitimacy* is the only scientifically adequate account of this typical process. Many analogous casting-exchanges are still pending. What explains the fact that this model character was most realistically arrived at not in a sociological, mass-psychological, or economical study, but in one focused on legal theory and constitutional law such as this text on legality and legitimacy? What explains this is that a properly applied realism of concept (*"Begriffs-Realismus"*) of the sort belonging to the science of public law is superior to every other type of scientific contemplation. (Schmitt 1991, 107)

In his personal copy of Schmitt's *Glossarium*, Blumenberg noted that Schmitt claims conceptual realism—*Begriffsrealismus*—for the cases of "redeployment" described here. In working through the distinction between legitimacy and legality, the jurist had in fact revealed the aporias of the Weimar Constitution and shown how the constitution's enemy, having entered through "the door of legality," could close it "behind him and treat his political-party opponent, who then perhaps stepped against the closed door with his boots, as a common criminal" (Schmitz and Lepper 2007, 107).

What Blumenberg's Schmitt readings show are the consequences of the polemic position of this conceptual realism, in which analysis and decision can never be separated in a clear-cut manner. In the end it necessitates—this is Blumenberg's central argument—collaboration in designating "the nature of the human being" (34) and authorizes arbitrary characterizations of enemies. Blumenberg here takes the modernity of Schmittian conceptual structures seriously. The renunciation of differentiating the concept of decision that Blumenberg calls for hits home in a more significant way than would an uncovering of potential forms of substantialism—also a charge leveled against him and his "anthropological avowal of faith."[30] Blumenberg rejects Schmitt's implied "elevation of the *intensity of the decision*" (34) by pointing to the possibility of escaping from the "absolutisms of reality" (171). Rejection of such absolutistic demands is Blumenberg's life theme. He marks renunciation of decisions in certain situations as a specifically modern achievement of rationality.

While such abstinence does not preach the human being's disappearance, in Blumenberg's express view it is open to that very possibility. Where in Blumenberg's analysis technique was once conceived as an organ for gaining control of the world, the tables have meanwhile turned and rendered the human being into its prosthesis. Schmitt had diagnosed that "[t]he human being has abdicated before his self-perfecting tools" (Schmitz and Lepper 2007, 257 n8). Blumenberg speaks of an evaporation of the human character within a scientifically objectifying perspective: "The idea of science contains an actual vanishing from the theoretical scene of the human being as a person [*Gestalt*], an individual, a concrete figure" (Blumenberg 2006, 13). With his "morphology of political-theological metaphorics," Schmitt unceasingly warned of this vanishing of the human being that both he and Blumenberg diagnosed: "As long as the human being is an anthropomorphic, i.e. human-resembling being," Schmitt declared, "he will understand himself and his relationship to his counterparts through such 'images'" (1970, 33). The afterword aimed at Blumenberg presents the outline of a world trying to make do without such images. If we wish to argue for an intellectual achievement conveyed by Schmitt's arguments beyond their unsavory partisanship, then we can point to these concepts as marking the precarious situation that has emerged after the emptying out of the absolute. In the words of Reinhart Koselleck: "The human being [*Mensch*] from which the non-human being [*Unmensch*], the super-human and subhuman [*Übermensch/Untermensch*] are derived, only confirms a form of ideological arbitrariness that misses what follows from the concept of the human being: that he is an ambivalent being whose definition is a political risk" (2000, 103).

CONCLUSION

After World War II Carl Schmitt staged and stylized his persona and oeuvre in various role-templates. The figure of a Christian Epimetheus here has a sovereign, Promethean counterpart, just as the figure of the *katechon*, frequently used in the postwar period, can only unfold its delaying effects against the powers of acceleration. Through the situation of imprisoned Benito Cereno in Herman Melville's like-named story, Schmitt mirrors both the struggle over the "ship" of European history and his own role in National Socialism. Such stylizations have been properly criticized, because they demonstrate that Schmitt avoided any direct confrontation with that role. At the same time, they draw his readers into a labyrinth of images and challenge them to hold their ground there. One of Schmitt's assumptions is consistent throughout his work: that the form and limits of one's own identity can only be gained through such acts of identification and counter-identification.

As a self-proclaimed last representative of *jus publicum Europaeum*, Schmitt insists that the legitimacy of the modern age cannot be grasped from the perspective of immanent self-assertion. The liberal, secularized state subsists on preconditions that it itself cannot guarantee. The enduring task at the end of *Political Theology II* that Schmitt sets out for himself and his readers

> concerns the reality of an enemy whose real possibility I still recognize in a completely de-theologized counter-image. Observing its redeployment from the old political theology into what has the pretension of being a totally new, pure secularism and humane humanity ["*in eine der Prätention nach total neue, reine Weltlichkeit und humane Menschlichkeit*"] in actuality remains a lasting *officium* of every striving toward scientific knowledge. (Schmitz and Lepper 2007, 48)

Whether we wish to commit ourselves, in the way Schmitt suggests, to the "reality of the possibility" of an enemy is open to debate. With his advocacy of revelation against enlightenment, authority against anarchism, obedience to God against the self-empowerment of human beings, Schmitt tries to hold on to principles of decision and decisive battle beyond the dissolution of the sovereign state (Habermas 2012, 247–249).

At least two questions remain as far as Schmitt's confrontation with Blumenberg's *Die Legitimität der Neuzeit* is concerned. One involves the autonomy of law. Though perhaps not immediately threatened with pulverization between theology and technology, law has to assert itself in the face of the self-referentiality of many legal decisions as well as law's susceptibility to ideology. The second question requiring further reflection concerns the description of the human being. The technologization of the life-world that Schmitt severely criticized, yet melancholically observed, has led to a renunciation of meaning within it. But the economization of general circumstances has also led to technological progress being inscribed with a specific rationality (Müller 2008, 123–124). These facts present an ongoing challenge because the deliberate renunciation of meaning constitutes a loss. Neither Schmitt nor Blumenberg spelled out the pathologies of technologization as a deciding moment of modern rationality in this way. But we are in a position to illuminate this predicament on the basis of their intellectual exchange.

Translated from the German by Joel Golb

ACKNOWLEDGMENTS

The writing of this chapter was supported by funds from the Cultural Foundations of Social Integration Center of Excellence at the University of Konstanz, established under the framework of the *Exzellenzinitiative des Bundes und der Länder zur Förderung von Wissenschaft und Forschung an deutschen Hochschulen,* the German Federal and State Initiative for Academic Excellence. I am grateful to Joel Golb not only for providing the translation, but also for a productive discussion of difficult passages and various suggestions.

NOTES

1. For the correspondence between Blumenberg and Schmitt, the controversy as presented in the two authors' publications, and further documents and references, see Schmitz and Lepper 2007.
2. In the afterword of the third edition of *Die Lehre Carl Schmitts*, Meier (2009) discusses the correspondence with Blumenberg. Meier maintains that political theology constitutes the coherent center of Schmitt's thinking.
3. Unless noted otherwise, all translations of source material by the author or translator.
4. What I have said about the positions Schmitt criticizes applies to this satire. The positions are related to his own: Schmitt was a manic diary-writer who diligently recorded even the most negligible events of his life.
5. The letter prompted Taubes to seek contact with Schmitt. Taubes made his "summary" of Blumenberg's odd "letter of friendship and intensity" public (1987, 69–70). Blumenberg's letter in fact attests to growing intellectual and personal distance. He found it increasingly unacceptable that Taubes exhausted his intellectual energy confronting the life work of others without offering material of his own that could be subject to critique.
6. On the postwar literature, see the summary in van Laak 2002 (70–85). On *Political Theology II* as self-interpretation, see Mehring 2011 (105–108) and 2009 (549–554).
7. The course of these debates is summarized in Scholz 1978.
8. Carl Schmitt (as quoted in Tommissen 1994, 72) writes to Julien Freund thus: "[W]ith Hans Barion, the Bonn canonist who has just finished a furious demonstration, 'Das konziliare Utopia,' for the Mélanges d'Ebrach, a critique of the claims of *Vaticanum II* to offer us a *Sozialoffenbarung* (social revelation)." See also Barion (1967).
9. For relevant literature concerning the Schmitt-Blumenberg controversy, see Böckenförde 1983 (ch. 1).
10. Taubes describes the difference between Blumenberg and Schmitt on this point as follows: "Blumenberg discovers in the word secularization an illegitimate title; he rejects this concept, he says it doesn't hold up.... Blumenberg's idea is that the same substance gets passed on into other realms, it oozes, in the way that sludge oozes, from theology into

theory of law, from theory of law into literature. Blumenberg wants to cut this thread methodologically and says: The concept doesn't hold.... The upshot of this is: What Schmitt regards as realities, Blumenberg regards as metaphors. Blumenberg... is a metaphorologist. Schmitt asks: What is behind the metaphors? And he shows that there is an autism there, lurking behind the metaphors. An *autos*.... Anyway, that is the meaning of secularization: it's an illegitimate category. That something is secularized implies that it has been transferred from a legitimate place to an illegitimate one" (Taubes 2003, 68–69).

11. For Schmitt the "division of law into legality and legitimacy" is a late phenomenon characterizing the "position of European legal studies" since the nineteenth century. See Schmitt 1958 (422, 345–347); 1938 (102–104). The "development of a concept of legitimacy... from dynastic to democratic legitimacy" is already outlined in Schmitt 1923 (39) and 1934 (65). Blumenberg (in Schmitz and Lepper 2007, 61–62) seems to assume that for Schmitt the diachronic foundational context is central.
12. Reinhart Koselleck has examined the relationship between long-term structures and what is historically unique in many texts profiting from Carl Schmitt's terms of reference. Koselleck points Blumenberg to his essay "Zur historisch-politischen Semantik asymmetrischer Gegenbegriffe" (letter of December 16, 1975, German Literary Archive, Marbach) to bring differences in their positions to his attention. For examples of Koselleck's usage of this conceptual method, see also Koselleck 2000.
13. Schmitt perhaps here overlooks that what is at stake at this threshold is "no longer an exchange of metaphysical centers but the dissolution of the metaphysical schema in general" (Balke 1996, 114).
14. Instead of the "world ruler," the omnipotent legislator, the world architect and author are named here (see Schmitt 1922, 43). In reference to Rousseau's *législateur*, who can form both human individuality and collectivity because, according to the social contract, he is "*capable de changer la nature de l'homme*" (see 50). Schmitt notes that precisely this conception of a world architect has lost its plausibility with modernity's upheavals (43).
15. Cf. Groh 1998; 2004 (esp. 371–373); and Faber 2007.
16. See the text "Politischer Dezisionismus," published under the pseudonym Hugo Fiala (Fiala 1935).
17. On Schmitt's retouching, see Mehring 2009 (322–325, 335–339, 378–380).
18. See Erik Peterson's letter to Philipp Dessauer, presumably written in 1935/1936: "It was my book's intention to give a kick to 'Reich theology'" (Peterson 2004, 247).
19. However, see the work by Andreas Koenen 1995.
20. In *Political Theology II*, Schmitt 1970 (61 and 81) referred to those passages in Peterson's "Die Kirche" and "Die Kirche aus Juden und Heiden" in which the term *katechon* appeared.
21. For material relevant to the *katechon* in Schmitt's writing, see esp. Grossheutschi 1996 and Schuller 1996.
22. The historical source to which Schmitt 1938 (81) refers here is Marc Bloch's *Les rois thaumaturges* of 1924.
23. On the question of the extent to which Schmitt's concepts are also analytically discredited, see Gross 2007 and 2006 (44).
24. Ernst Hüsmert and Gerd Giesler 2005 (4–5) have pointed to affinities between Schmitt and Weininger.
25. This entry in Schmitt's *Glossarium* is without any doubt antisemitic. And yet its intended meaning is difficult to pin down conclusively, as Schmitt is here referencing a passage from

Peter F. Drucker's *The End of Economic Man* that points to the mutually dependent relationship that exists between the identification of the enemy and self-assertion: "'To the extent, that the problem of self-assertion and self-justification becomes more and more urgent, totalitarianism must invent new personifications of new demons. Compared to the Jews, even the communists are of doubtful value as demonic enemies.' For Jews always remain Jews, whereas the Communist can improve himself and change. This has nothing to do with a Nordic race etc. The assimilated Jew is the true enemy. It is pointless to demonstrate that the *Protocols of the Elders of Zion* are false." If we place the emphasis on "invent," then we have arrived at the modern, desubstantialized definition of the enemy that Blumenberg addresses.

26. According to Haverkamp 2013 (234–235), the correspondence shows "a parodistic intention" on the part of Blumenberg. One reason I cannot agree with this approach is that it does not do justice to the course of the Blumenberg-Schmitt controversy and reflects a highly particular interpretation of Blumenberg.

27. On the "effect-reality" of fictions, see Hebekus 2008 (45–75); 2009 (30–36).

28. Blumenberg extends his reflections on the rationality or irrationality of political mythologems most notably in the work leading up to his book *Arbeit am Mythos*. Though his explicit analysis of political mythology was not included in this text, it was published posthumously after the completion of my article. This publication casts a new light on the further development of Blumenberg's examination of Schmitt. Cf. Blumenberg 2014.

29. On Schmitt's conceptual politics, see Mehring 2006.

30. Schmitt's anthropology of the political turns vertical distinctions into horizontal ones. Defining political theology as the substantial core of his work possibly underestimates the modernity of this switch (see Balke 1990, 43).

References

Assmann, J. 1992. *Politische Theologie zwischen Ägypten und Israel*. Munich: Siemens Stiftung.

Balke, F. 1990. "Zur politischen Anthropologie Carl Schmitts." In *Die Autonomie des Politischen: Carl Schmitts Kampf um einen beschädigten Begriff*, ed. H.-G. Flickinger. Weinheim: Acta Humaniora, 37–65.

Balke, F. 1996. *Der Staat nach seinem Ende: Die Versuchung Carl Schmitts*. Munich: Fink.

Barion, H. 1967. "Das konziliare Utopia: Eine Studie zur Soziallehre des II. Vatikanischen Konzils." In *Säkularisation und Utopie: Ernst Forsthoff zum 65. Geburtstag*. Berlin: Kohlhammer, 187–233.

Barion, H. 1968. "'Weltgeschichtliche Machtform'? Eine Studie zur Politischen Theologie des II. Vatikanischen Konzils." In *Epirrhosis: Festgabe für Carl Schmitt zum 80. Geburtstag*, ed. H. Barion, et al. Berlin: Duncker & Humblot, 13–59.

Blumenberg, H. 1966. *Die Legitimität der Neuzeit*. Frankfurt: Suhrkamp.

Blumenberg, H. 1974. *Säkularisierung und Selbstbehauptung*. Frankfurt: Suhrkamp.

Blumenberg, H. 1998. *Paradigmen zu einer Metaphorologie*. Frankfurt: Suhrkamp.

Blumenberg, H. 2006. *Beschreibung des Menschen*, ed. M. Sommer. Frankfurt: Suhrkamp.

Blumenberg, H. 2014. *Präfiguration: Arbeit am politischen Mythos*, ed. A. Nicholls and F. Heidenreich. Berlin: Suhrkamp.

Böckenförde, E.-W. 1967. "Die Entstehung des Staates als Vorgang der Säkularisation." In *Säkularisation und Utopie: Ernst Forsthoff zum 65. Geburtstag*. Berlin: Kohlhammer, 75–94.

Böckenförde, E.-W. 1983. "Politische Theorie und politische Theologie." In *Der Fürst dieser Welt: Carl Schmitt und die Folgen*, ed. J. Taubes, Munich: Fink, 16–25.

Faber, R. 2007. "Politische Dämonologie: Über Carl Schmitts und anderer gegenrevolutionären Marcionismus." In *Politische Dämonologie: Über modernen Marcionismus*, ed. R. Faber. Würzburg: Königshausen & Neumann, 93–137.

Fiala, H. [K. Löwith]. 1935. "Politischer Dezisionismus." *Internationale Zeitschrift für Theorie des Rechts* 9: 101–123.

Groh, R. 1998. "Der Mythos vom entzweiten Gott: Carl Schmitt und Hans Blumenberg." In *Arbeit an der Heillosigkeit der Welt: Zur politisch-theologischen Mythologie und Anthropologie Carl Schmitts*, ed. R. Groh. Frankfurt: Suhrkamp, 156–184.

Gross, R. 2007. *Carl Schmitt and the Jews: The 'Jewish Question,' the Holocaust, and German Legal Theory*, trans. Joel Golb, introd. P. C. Caldwell, Madison: University of Wisconsin Press.

Gross, R. 2006. "Juden und das 'Jüdische' im Denken und Werk Carl Schmitts." In *Carl Schmitt in der Diskussion*, ed. I. Villinger. Plettenberg: Hagen, 35–44.

Grossheutschi, F. 1996. *Carl Schmitt und die Lehre vom Katechon*. Berlin: Duncker & Humblot.

Habermas, J. 2012. *Nachmetaphysisches Denken II: Aufsätze und Repliken*. Berlin: Suhrkamp.

Haverkamp, A. 2003. "La sécularisation comme métaphore: Hans Blumenberg interprète de la modernité." *Transversalités* 87: 15–28.

Haverkamp, A. 2013. "Prolegomena: Das Skandalon der Metaphorologie." In *Paradigmen zu einer Metaphorologie*, ed. H. Blumenberg. Berlin: Suhrkamp, 195–240.

Hebekus, U. 2008. "Der Wille zur Form: Politischer Ästhetizismus bei Georg Simmel, Ernst H. Kantorowicz und Alfred Rosenberg." In *Das Totalitäre der Klassischen Moderne*, ed. U. Hebekus and I. Stöckmann. Munich: Fink, 45–75.

Hebekus, U. 2009. *Ästhetische Ermächtigung: Zum politischen Ort der Literatur im Zeitraum der Klassischen Moderne*. Munich: Fink.

Koenen, A. 1995. *Der Fall Carl Schmitt: Sein Aufstieg zum "Kronjuristen des Dritten Reiches."* Darmstadt: Wissenschaftliche Buchgesellschaft.

Kopp-Oberstebrink, H., et al. eds. 2012. *Jacob Taubes and Carl Schmitt: Briefwechsel mit Materialien*. Munich: Fink.

Kopp-Oberstebrink, H., and M. Treml. eds. 2013. *Hans Blumenberg und Jacob Taubes: Briefwechsel 1961–1981 und weitere Materialien*. Berlin: Suhrkamp.

Koselleck, R. 2000. *Vergangene Zukunft: Zur Semantik geschichtlicher Zeiten*, 4th ed. Frankfurt: Suhrkamp.

Löwith, K. 1949. *Meaning in History: The Theological Implications of the Philosophy of History*. Chicago: University of Chicago Press.

Lübbe, H. 2003. *Säkularisierung: Geschichte eines ideenpolitischen Begriffs*. Freiburg: Alber.

Luz, U. 1990. *Das Evangelium nach Matthäus: Evangelisch-Katholischer Kommentar zum Neuen Testament*, vol. 1/2. Düsseldorf: Benziger.

Mehring, R. 1998. "Karl Löwith, Carl Schmitt, Jacob Taubes und das 'Ende der Geschichte.'" *Zeitschrift für Religions- und Geistesgeschichte* 48: 231–248.

Mehring, R. 2006. "Begriffssoziologie, Begriffsgeschichte, Begriffspolitik: Zur Form der Ideengeschichtsschreibung nach Carl Schmitt und Reinhart Koselleck." In *Politische Ideengeschichtsschreibung im 20. Jahrhundert: Konzepte und Kritik*, ed. H. Bluhm and J. Gebhardt. Baden-Baden: Nomos, 31–50.

Mehring, R. 2009. *Carl Schmitt: Aufstieg und Fall*. Munich: Beck.

Mehring, R. 2011. *Carl Schmitt zur Einführung*, 4th ed. Hamburg: Junius.

Meier, H. 2009. *Die Lehre Carl Schmitts: Vier Kapitel zur Unterscheidung Politischer Theologie und Politischer Philosophie*, 3rd ed. Stuttgart: Metzler.

Müller, O. 2008. "Natur und Technik als falsche Antithese: Die Technikphilosophie Hans Blumenbergs und die Struktur der Technisierung." *Philosophisches Jahrbuch* 115: 99–124.

Nichtweiß, B. 1994. *Erik Peterson: Neue Sicht auf Leben und Werk*, 2nd ed. Freiburg: Herder.

Peterson, E. 1935. *Der Monotheismus als politisches Problem*. Leipzig: Hegner.

Peterson, E. 1994. "Was ist Theologie?" In *Ausgewählte Schriften*, vol. 1: *Theologische Traktate*, ed. B. Nichtweiß. Würzburg: Echter, 9–43.

Peterson, E. 2004. "Translatio Imperii." In *Ausgewählte Schriften*, vol. 4: *Offenbarung des Johannes und politisch-theologische Texte*, ed. B. Nichtweiß and W. Löserhier. Würzburg: Echter, 247–248.

Peterson, E. 2006. "Satan und die Mächte der Finsternis." In *Ausgewählte Schriften*, vol. 7: *Der erste Brief an die Korinther und Paulus-Studien*, ed. H.-U. Weidemann. Würzburg: Echter, 441–450.

Rieß, R. ed. 2007. *Ludwig Feuchtwanger und Carl Schmitt: Briefwechsel 1918-1935*. Berlin: Duncker & Humblot.

Schmitt, C. 1912. "Richard Wagner und eine neue 'Lehre vom Wahn'." *Bayreuther Blätter* 35: 239–241.

Schmitt, C. 1913. "Juristische Fiktionen." *Deutsche Juristen-Zeitung* 18: 804–806.

Schmitt, C. 1917. "Die Sichtbarkeit der Kirche." *Summa* 2: 71–80.

Schmitt, C. 1918. "Die Buribunken: Ein geschichtsphilosophischer Versuch." *Summa* 4: 89–106.

Schmitt, C. 1922. *Politische Theologie: Vier Kapitel zur Lehre von der Souveränität*. Munich: Duncker & Humblot.

Schmitt, C. 1923. *Römischer Katholizismus und politische Form*, Hellerau: Hegner.

Schmitt, C. 1926. *Die geistesgeschichtliche Lage des heutigen Parlamentarismus*, 2nd ed. Munich: Duncker & Humblot.

Schmitt, C. 1934. *Politische Theologie: Vier Kapitel zur Lehre von der Souveränität*, 2nd ed. Munich: Duncker & Humblot.

Schmitt, C. 1936/1937. "Der Staat als Mechanismus bei Hobbes und Descartes." *Archiv für Rechts- und Sozialphilosophie* 30: 622–632.

Schmitt, C. 1938. *Der Leviathan in der Staatslehre des Thomas Hobbes: Sinn und Fehlschlag eines politischen Symbols*, Hamburg: Hanseatische Verlagsanstalt.

Schmitt, C. 1939. "Der Reichsbegriff im Völkerrecht." *Deutsches Recht* 9: 341–344.

Schmitt, C. 1940. *Positionen und Begriffe im Kampf mit Weimar—Genf—Versailles, 1923-1939*. Hamburg: Hanseatische Verlagsanstalt.

Schmitt, C. 1950a. *Donoso Cortés in gesamteuropäischer Interpretation*. Cologne: Greven.

Schmitt, C. 1950b. *Ex Captivitate Salus: Erfahrungen der Zeit 1945/47*. Cologne: Greven.

Schmitt, C. 1950c. *Der "Nomos" der Erde im Völkerrecht des "Jus Publicum Europaeum."* Cologne: Greven.

Schmitz, A., and Lepper, M. eds. 2007. *Hans Blumenberg und Carl Schmitt: Briefwechsel (1971-1978) und weitere Materialien*. Frankfurt: Suhrkamp.

Schmitt, C. 1958. *Verfassungsrechtliche Aufsätze aus den Jahren 1924 bis 1954: Materialien zu einer Verfassungslehre*. Berlin: Duncker & Humblot.

Schmitt, C. 1963. *Der Begriff des Politischen: Text von 1932 mit einem Vorwort und drei Corollarien*. Berlin: Duncker & Humblot.

Schmitt, C. 1970. *Politische Theologie II: Die Legende von der Erledigung jeder Politischen Theologie*. Berlin: Duncker & Humblot.

Schmitt, C. 1991. *Glossarium: Aufzeichnungen der Jahre 1947-1951*, ed. E. von Medem. Berlin: Duncker & Humblot.

Schmitt, C. 1995. *Staat, Großraum, Nomos: Arbeiten aus den Jahren 1916–1969*, ed. G. Maschke. Berlin: Duncker & Humblot.

Schmitt, C. 2005. *Die Militärzeit 1915 bis 1919: Tagebuch Februar bis Dezember 1915*, ed. E. Hüsmert and G. Giesler. Berlin: Akademie Verlag.

Schmitt, C. 2011. *Die Tyrannei der Werte*, 3rd ed. Berlin: Duncker & Humblot.

Schmitz, A. 2007. "Zur Geschichte einer Kontroverse, die nicht stattfand: Karl Löwith und Carl Schmitt (mit einem Dokument von Karl Löwith, 'Max Weber und Carl Schmitt' (FAZ vom 27. Juni 1964))." *Zeitschrift für Kulturphilosophie* 1: 365–383.

Schmitz, A., and Lepper, M. eds. 2007. *Hans Blumenberg und Carl Schmitt: Briefwechsel (1971–1978) und weitere Materialien*. Frankfurt: Suhrkamp.

Scholz, F. 1978. "Bemerkungen zur Funktion der Peterson-These in der neueren Diskussion um eine Politische Theologie." In *Monotheismus als politisches Problem? Erik Peterson und die Kritik der politischen Theologie*, ed. A. Schindler. Gütersloh: Mohn, 170–201.

Schönberger, C. 2011. "Werte als Gefahr für das Recht? Carl Schmitt und die Karlsruher Republik." In Schmitt 2011, 57–91.

Schuller, W. 1996. "Dennoch die Schwerter halten: Der Κατέχων Carl Schmitts." In *Festschrift für Martin Hengel*, vol. 2, ed. H. Cancik, et al. Tübingen: Mohr, 389–408.

Taubes, J. 1987. *Ad Carl Schmitt: Gegenstrebige Fügung*. Berlin: Merve.

Taubes, J. 2003. *The Political Theology of Paul*. Stanford: Stanford University Press.

Tommissen, P. ed. 1994. *Schmittiana: Beiträge zu Leben und Werk Carl Schmitts*, vol. 4. Berlin: Duncker & Humblot.

Tommissen, P. 2000. "Erster Einstieg in zwei Desiderate der Carl-Schmitt-Forschung." In *Staat—Souveränität—Verfassung: Festschrift für Helmut Quaritsch zum 70. Geburtstag*, ed. D. Murswiek. Berlin: Duncker & Humblot, 565–602.

van Laak, D. 2002. *Gespräche in der Sicherheit des Schweigens: Carl Schmitt in der politischen Geistesgeschichte der frühen Bundesrepublik*, 2nd ed. Berlin: Akademie Verlag.

Weininger, O. 1922. *Geschlecht und Charakter: Eine prinzipielle Untersuchung*, 23rd ed. Vienna: Braumüller.

CHAPTER 28

TRAGEDY AS EXCEPTION IN CARL SCHMITT'S *HAMLET OR HECUBA*

DAVID PAN

INTRODUCTION

CARL SCHMITT's 1956 *Hamlet or Hecuba: The Intrusion of the Time into the Play* seems at first glance to have only a peripheral significance for the main body of Schmitt's work. Presented originally as a lecture in Düsseldorf in 1955, this short book addresses a literary critical debate concerning Shakespeare's reasons for including key plot elements in *Hamlet*, most importantly the ambiguity of Hamlet's mother's guilt in the murder of Hamlet's father as well as Hamlet's indecision before carrying out his mission of revenge. Schmitt's main argument is that political events concerning James I's ascension to the throne were responsible for determining these crucial elements in the play and that these historical intrusions into the pure play are the basis for its enduring tragic quality. If these issues are in the first place of a purely literary critical nature, Schmitt's achievement is to demonstrate how such debates have far-reaching political and historical consequences. *Hamlet or Hecuba* is much more than just an occasional piece or an amateurish foray into a neighboring discipline; it makes an argument for both the political stakes of art and the mythic basis of politics.

Schmitt began work on these ideas as early as 1952, when he wrote the foreword to the German translation of Lilian Winstanley's *Hamlet and the Scottish Succession*, in which he first lays out the importance of historical events for the composition of Shakespeare's play, crediting Winstanley for demonstrating that "in Shakespeare's *Hamlet* there reappear, down to the finest detail, the concrete situations, events, and people of the historical moment contemporary with the life of James I and his mother Mary Stuart" (2010, 164–165). While this earlier essay already engages with the question of the mythic status of *Hamlet*, Schmitt's continuing investigation of this question over the next few years that culminated in *Hamlet or Hecuba* indicates that his interest is not just in literary critical issues but also in the reasons that literature is inseparable from politics and, conversely, that politics cannot be understood without an insight into issues of representation. *Hamlet or Hecuba* is perhaps Schmitt's most sustained attempt to address a pivotal question that underlies all of Schmitt's political theory—the importance of myth for political representation. His arguments concerning the relation between politics and metaphysics in *Political Theology* and the importance of representation for political power in *Roman Catholicism and Political Form* all presuppose a theory of representation and myth. If, as Schmitt argues in *Political Theology*, the exception precedes the norm, the basis of legal order lies in a political decision about ultimate values rather than a derivation of such values from absolute truths grounded in either religious revelation or the dictates of reason. In arguing that politics determines values, Schmitt is arguing not for the triumph of power over truth but for the relational quality of all values. Without a single incontrovertible source of values, they must derive from a mythic framework that grounds their legitimacy in a representational way, and Schmitt's political theory raises the question of an aesthetic theory of myth that he never adumbrates until *Hamlet or Hecuba*.

The key to this aesthetics of myth is contained in a section of the book titled "Source of the Tragic," in which he distinguishes the "reality" of tragedy from the mere play of the *Trauerspiel*, the German baroque tragic drama that grew out of the religious civil wars in Germany. Schmitt's argument here hinges on his distinguishing of historical reality from aesthetic play to identify true myth as the merging of the two. The inclusion of historical reality into the play constitutes the "surplus value" of genuine tragedy, which "lies in the objective reality of the tragic action itself, in the enigmatic concatenation and entanglement of indisputably real people in the unpredictable course of indisputably real events" and forms "the mute rock upon which the play founders, sending the foam of genuine tragedy rushing to the surface" (2009, 45).

In discussing Schmitt's theory of tragedy, both Carsten Strathausen and Eric Santner focus on this passage to develop their two interpretations of the opposition that Schmitt sets up between play and reality. Santner insists on the radical difference of an unalterable reality, comparing it to Franz Rosenzweig's notion of the "metaethical self" that arises in "a dimension of pure self-reference" (2010, 36). "It is this dimension that marks the self as constitutionally unfit for politics, that renders him un- or 'impolitical'" (36). In addition to his claim about the unpolitical nature of the metaethical self, Santner describes this dimension as the result of a conflict between two forms of life: a "part that remains excessive or *unheimlich* in relation to the whole—the political and economic home—to which it in some sense continues to belong" (37) and as a "tear in the fabric of a prior form of life" (46). This indication of a disjunction and resulting conflict between alternative forms of life reflects—in spite of Santner's attempt to imagine an impolitical self—on a political dynamic as the basis for the intrusion of reality into the play.

Schmitt's innovation is to describe this political dynamic simultaneously as an aesthetic one. Here Strathausen points out that Schmitt's mute rock of reality will eventually be eroded by the waves and that the seemingly unalterable reality is at its core simply another myth that eventually loses its authority and gives way to a new one. The opposition between art and reality dissolves into an opposition between competing myths that structure our understanding of reality. Consequently, for Strathausen, "conceptual knowledge is not opposed to myth but is itself mythical to the core." He affirms the "historical nature of conceptual knowledge" against Schmitt's "claim to be able to determine the 'real' core of historical reality" (2010, 11). In undermining the separation between play and reality that Schmitt tries to partially uphold, Strathausen indicates an alternative approach to the question of the relation of aesthetics and reality in Schmitt's text. Rather than the opposition between the two that Santner suggests, Strathausen imagines a continuum in which incontrovertible reality is simply a myth that has gained a metaphysical legitimacy in a particular society. The main opposition, then, would not be one between play and reality but between a socially accepted myth and a myth that does not (or does not yet, or no longer does) enjoy such acceptance. In this way, the question of myth also becomes immediately a political one in which competing myths must struggle for acceptance.

This conflictual nature of myth, combined with the insight into the dependence of conceptual knowledge on a foundational myth, indicates that there is in fact not an opposition between aesthetics, as a realm of artistic truths separate from everyday reality, and politics, as a sphere of power. Rather, Schmitt employs a kind of double vision, in which Drew Daniels, for example, demonstrates that King James's and Jean Bodin's discussions of sovereignty and demonology (i.e., their political and mythological concerns) cannot be separated into two different spheres but are rather two aspects of a single process (Schmitt 2010, 62–67). For the conflict between opposing mythic conceptions of the world is simultaneously a conflict between different ways of life, only one of which can establish the basic parameters that govern a single public sphere. As a consequence, the aesthetic struggle between opposing myths is simultaneously a political struggle between competing social orders.

This simultaneity stems from what Aryeh Botwinick describes as "the inescapability and insurmountability of playacting as the substance of human reality" (2010, 132). If we accept this view that there is no "hope or expectation of our return to an original scene of involvement from which our playacting might have taken off" (132), then there is no point in discussing an opposition between play and reality. Instead, we should focus our attention on different varieties of such role-playing. Here what we find in Schmitt's account is that his opposition between play and tragedy seems to recapitulate the primary opposition in politics that he identifies between the norm and the exception. Like the norm, the play functions as a self-enclosed game, with an internally coherent set of rules that allows for the uncomplicated functioning of its mechanisms. Just as the exception results from an external threat to a self-sufficient system of norms, the tragedy upsets the self-enclosed nature of the play through the intrusion of an external force. Moreover, both the exception and the tragedy are decision points, functioning to either confirm or to overturn the normal order of politics or of play by establishing a structuring myth that forms the metaphysical parameters for the game.

The relationship between these two oppositions—between norm and exception and play and tragedy—is not simply one of homology or analogy. Insofar as they both function according to mythic processes, they are both expressions of the same underlying aesthetic-political dynamic that founds the metaphysical parameters for a specific public sphere. In this conception, every political space is defined by a set of mythic conceptions that determine the legitimate speakers, the authoritative judges, the sacred texts, and the acceptable rhetorical rules. Schmitt's idea of politics is structured around his insight into the changing character of public spheres that shifts according to different representational schemas. As his treatment of *Hamlet* shows, the question of representation for Schmitt is simultaneously the question of political authority, and his approach to this question is fundamentally aesthetic to the extent that for him representation is not simply propaganda for a preexisting set of values but is itself constitutive for those values.

The next sections sketch out Schmitt's early theory of political representation of the Weimar era and its importance for his understanding of authority and the popular will as a whole. This analysis of the representational aspect of Schmitt's political theory provides the context for describing how *Hamlet or Hecuba* adumbrates the linked nature of aesthetic and political mechanisms implied by the political theory. The chapter then argues that the book contains a conflict between a *rhetorical* and *aesthetic* understanding of the mythic basis of political representation. While the first is based on direct political influences on the playwright and the contemporary audience that made certain topics taboo, the second depends on a more distanced understanding of the political conflicts that shape an epoch and its development. This second, aesthetic understanding of mythic representation is in fact similar to Walter Benjamin's approach to the problem in his book on the German tragic drama. Both Schmitt and Benjamin construct models of culture in which political and aesthetic issues are linked to such an extent that the two spheres in fact make up two views of the same unified phenomenon of political representation. I end with the idea that Schmitt rejects a modernization story in which myth gives way to reason. Instead, he affirms the way *Hamlet* does not overcome myth so much as inaugurate a new English mythic structure for the public sphere.

THE CENTRALITY OF REPRESENTATION

To understand the way aesthetics and politics function for Schmitt as two views on the same process, it is necessary to consider his theory of political representation. Discussions of Schmitt's ideas on this topic have often considered representation to be merely a way of providing propaganda for maintaining the power of a strong executive who establishes a more or less dictatorial rule.[1] From this perspective, the schema for understanding representation is to assume on the one hand that politics determine the structures of the state and on the other hand that representation provides the legitimation for these structures.[2] In his attempt to rehabilitate Schmitt for democratic theory,

Andreas Kalyvas (2008) argues that, contrary to this view, Schmitt's project, especially in his *Constitutional Theory*, is to develop his theory of representation as the prerequisite for a genuinely democratic politics. Though Schmitt argues that there is no higher law for the decision than the decision itself, the success of the decision is not at all a given but depends upon both the activity of the sovereign authority and the acclamation of the people. The role of representation in Schmitt's political theory is to establish the link between sovereignty and the popular will (146–162). To take seriously Schmitt's foray into literary criticism is part of an attempt to think through the legitimacy of a demo-cratic form of politics in which political structures and authority are established through the mediation of a popular will rather than simply through the ideas of an intellectual or political elite. Because Schmitt sees the idea of a rationally based order as part of a liberal attempt to pass off a particular order as a universal one, his alternative is to consider representation as the mechanism, and tradition as the space, where an order attains a concrete form. In his analysis, each separate legal and political order derives from a spe-cific cultural tradition, whose legitimacy lies in its ability to sum up and represent the popular will. His political theory is consequently incomplete without an explanation of the mythic, that is, metaphysical, basis of this legitimacy, and *Hamlet or Hecuba* presents a key text in this explanation.

On a social level, Schmitt's approach avoids managerial solutions that would install a bureaucratic elite as the determiner of ultimate values. His alternative is to imagine a democratic alternative in which a popular will establishes itself as the determiner of political structures. But the representation of the popular will is not simply a kind of referendum in which a simple majority establishes the rules. He recognizes in *Constitutional Theory* that a political unit must be founded on a set of basic principles that cannot be simply discarded through majority votes. Instead, such principles as are enshrined in a constitution must be established in a process that transcends the politi-cal opinions of the moment but at the same time represents a common political will (see Kalyvas 2008, 138–142; Kahn 2011). Though his turn to the sovereign decision has been criticized as an attempt to short-circuit democratic decision-making, his recognition of the fundamentally metaphysical and therefore rationally ungroundable quality of highest principles leads to an understanding of how the popular will underlies sovereign decisions.

Schmitt investigates different examples of how basic moral and metaphysical prin-ciples arise out of a common striving toward spiritual ideals. In describing the repre-sentational authority of the Catholic Church, he emphasizes in *Roman Catholicism and Political Form* that "all political forms and possibilities become nothing more than tools for the realization of an idea" (1996, 5). Because he contends that an idea lies at the foun-dation of every political order, Schmitt needs to explain how an idea establishes itself as the lived reality of a people. The issue of representation is consequently the issue of the *link* between politics and the idea. This linking role of representation is crucial for Schmitt because it differentiates for him a merely aesthetic process, which would be like the norm, from a representation in an emphatic sense, which would function like the exception. As Schmitt notes, "Representation is not a normative event, a process, and a procedure. It is, rather, something *existential*" (2008, 243). The existential character of the representation means for Schmitt that it is a final basis of existence, not just an aesthetic image or a form of entertainment. The representation exceeds a purely aesthetic play by having direct political consequences in a state of exception, and in this sense the representation coincides with the sovereign decision. By the same token, the decision does not establish itself through violence or pure power but through representation. The decision has a representational form, and representation has the significance of a decision.

Moreover, because the representation is not a normative event, like the decision it cannot be derived from the idea, neither as a corollary to an established principle nor as a kind of propagandistic legitimation of such a principle. The idea is not the source of the representation. Rather, if the decision and the representation converge within Schmitt's decisionism, the establishment of the representational link functions as the founding moment. This merging of the representation with the sovereign decision makes the decision into the moment in which the idea can manifest itself through the establishment of the link to the concrete situation. The forging of the link is the crucial activity, and this activity consists of grounding the seeming concreteness of the notion of the existential in something that is invisible: "To represent means to make an invisible being visible and present through a publicly present one. The dialectic of the concept is that the invisible is presupposed as absent and nevertheless is simultaneously made present" (243). Because the invisible is presupposed as absent and can be made present only in the representation, this representational process of making the invisible into something visible is for Schmitt the key action in establishing both a particular political form for a people and the presence of an idea. The aesthetic element here is not limited to the illusionary and playful but leads to an intensification beyond normal reality. "Something dead, something inferior or valueless, something lowly cannot be represented. It lacks the enhanced type of being that is capable of an *existence*, of rising into the public being" (243). In linking the political to the idea, the representation transforms reality into an aspect of an idea while at the same time establishing the presence of the idea. The heightened state of being that is enabled by the representation becomes the basis for political order. Yet the focus on existence differentiates the representation from an abstract idea that never gains political form. Ideas are not prior but come into public being only in an aesthetic process that links political existence to the idea through the mediation of the representation. Because the representation must therefore speak to the people and at the same time awaken its highest principles and most noble character, the theory of representation is Schmitt's method of linking popular will to metaphysical ideals and also an indication of the aesthetic element in the process of political will formation.

This idea of representation consequently provides the link between Schmitt's political and aesthetic theories. Just as the representation must merge idea with existence, thereby establishing both, the tragedy is distinctive for Schmitt because its way of linking aesthetic form to actual events contrasts with what he sees as the purely fictional character of the *Trauerspiel*, a German baroque genre of tragic dramas written in the same historical context of religious war as *Hamlet*. The state of exception, that is, a conflict between mythic orders, provides the background for both the decision and the tragedy. This conflict of metaphysical positions can be resolved only through the decision understood as representation. For it is only in this merging of idea and existence that a set of imagined structures are actualized in a political reality to become the basis for a normally functioning order.

THE AESTHETICS OF AUTHORITY

Because the representation is the source of political order for Schmitt, the key aspect of his notion of sovereignty is neither violence nor reason but authority. As opposed to Giorgio Agamben's approach, Schmitt tries to understand authority as part of a mechanism by which the political decision can gain credence within a reception sphere of reflective judgment. By understanding the decision as a judgment needing confirmation through the popular will, Schmitt is not limited, as Agamben is, to seeing authority as sovereign violence, the anomic opposite to the rule of law, and related immediately to bare life (Agamben 2005, 85–86).[3] Instead, Schmitt sees authority as containing its own form of legitimacy based in a public reception of the decision. Yet this public reception does not involve arguments and discourse either. While Kalyvas criticizes Schmitt for "excluding public deliberation and civic debate from the political expression of the constituent power" (Kalyvas 2008, 124), this objection ignores the circumstance that views about fundamental values that ground authority cannot be determined through rational debate. As value judgments, they cannot be referred to any logical arguments. Just as Hannah Arendt defines authority "in contradistinction to both coercion by force and persuasion through arguments" (1968, 93), Schmitt sees authority as an independent form of legitimation.

But as opposed to Arendt, Schmitt turns to aesthetic theory to understand authority, not as something bound up solely with a specific Greco-Roman or Christian tradition but as a phenomenon that can manifest itself in different times and places, depending on representational processes. Because Arendt, taking over an idea from republican Rome, argues that authority is derived from the ancestors leading back to the foundation of Rome and that the fall of Rome signaled the end of this type of traditional authority, the only modern form of political authority she recognizes derives from the foundation of states by means of popular revolutions. As a consequence, though she tries to avoid this result, her notion of authority must in the end affirm violence as the final ground of authority as well. She attempts to differentiate a nonviolent form of authority based on the ancient Roman use of a founding tradition from the past from a modern, Machiavellian invocation of political foundations as a violent action in the present (1968, 139). But in fact in both the Roman world and the modern one, the founding of the state must include the violence of an initial conquest in order to begin a tradition. The Roman avoidance of violence that she cites could occur only to the extent that their political order was already founded on a past violence and thus could dispense with a new violent foundation. Her pessimism regarding the ability of modern institutions to restore the lost efficacy of authority stems not from the passing of the Roman model but from her own conception that authority could only exist as a continuation of the Greco-Roman tradition. She is limited to this tradition, first, because it represents for her the only legitimate tradition that could ground authority nonviolently and, second, because she has not investigated the representational mechanisms of authority that would explain how it could function in a variety of different traditions.

Schmitt takes an alternative route by interpreting authority as an aesthetic phenomenon based on the merging of order and localization in the representation. Schmitt begins by affirming in 1922 the example of the Catholic Church, whose authority derives from the representational authority of Jesus Christ, and then of the Church, as the incarnation of a divine sovereignty. The institution of the Church represents to the people its sovereign authority as an incarnation of divine authority. By the time of his 1928 *Constitutional Theory*, though, Schmitt had developed his analysis of representation to take into account the authority of a general will of the people rather than of God. Instead of being based on arguments or on pure violence, the development of political authority adheres to structures familiar in the sphere of aesthetics, in which a particular producer creates an aesthetic experience that must be affirmed by recipients to have any value. The recipients of a work of art are not in a position to themselves produce the work of art, but they are the best judges of its validity. If, as Schmitt's arguments presume, a political judgment concerning values functions in the same way as Kantian reflective judgments on art (see Rasch 2004, 28), then the reception of the political judgment is also crucial to its validity. As with aesthetic judgments, political judgments would not be able to ground themselves on any objective principles but can only be affirmed by their link to the judgments of others. This intangible link between the sovereign and the popular will is the main issue in the question of political authority. As Samuel Weber points out, the key issue in Schmitt's conception of the political decision is not just the pronouncement of the judgment "but rather what agency or office is *actually capable of imposing* such a decision *effectively*" (2005, 35). This ability to impose a decision effectively depends on the response of an audience, and the question of sovereignty is linked to the issue of authority as the mechanism for grounding the idea in the popular will.

But though the people's existence is the primal basis of all political order, the people cannot form themselves into any kind of order until they recognize a common authority that would be the basis of their identity as a people. Even if the political will of a people is the source of the legitimation from which all political orders gain their power for Schmitt, and this will therefore retains an immediacy absent from laws and procedures, it cannot create a form and organization for itself. It is constantly in need of mediation by an organizing authority, and the resulting interaction between popular will and sovereign authority forms the representational mechanism for the functioning of every political order. But if a certain unity of the popular will is necessary for any political order, and Schmitt adheres to a single theory of representation as the mechanism for consolidating such a popular will, Schmitt also differentiates between a monarchy, in which the popular will recognizes the monarch as the embodiment of sovereignty, and a democracy, in which sovereignty is imagined as grounded in the general will of the people. "*Democratic legitimacy*, by contrast, rests on the idea that the state is the political unity of a *people*. The people are the subject of every definition of the state; the state is the political status of a people. The type and form of state existence is determined according to the principle of democratic legitimacy through the free will of the people" (Schmitt 2008, 138). Authority is an issue not just for monarchy or dictatorship but also for democracy, and Schmitt's identification of a democratic legitimacy that also has a claim to authority shows that he has a more general theory of authority that does not just apply to the Roman or the Catholic tradition but also seeks to explain the functioning of authority in any form of government.

While Stephanie Frank (2010, 89–93) argues persuasively that Schmitt shifts from God as the guarantor of sovereign authority in *Roman Catholicism and Political Form* to the people as the basis of sovereign authority in *Constitutional Theory*, it would be incorrect to conclude that Schmitt moves from one theory of representation in *Roman Catholicism and Political Form*, in which churchgoers are the audience of the Church as the divinely justified authority, to another theory in *Hamlet or Hecuba*, in which God becomes the audience for the play and the spectators. Rather, the shift is not in the mechanism of representation, but in the definition of the proper form of sovereign authority (the monarch, the Church, or the parliament) as well as the source of this authority (God or the people). In both cases, the ultimate source of authority is in fact a popular will that has coalesced in support of a particular representational form for this will. The difference between the Catholic Church and democracy lies in the way the former's authority is attributed to the idea of an institutional incarnation of God in a church hierarchy and the latter's authority derives from the idea of an institutional incarnation of the popular will in structures of government such as a parliament and a judicial system. In both cases, a specific institutional form of political authority must represent itself and its sovereignty to the people. While the Church's form of authority presumes a universally valid basis for sovereignty and the democratic form of authority only presumes a local unity of the people that make up the state, both forms of authority must speak to an audience of spectators because both depend on their representational ability to establish a unity of political will.

FROM *TRAUERSPIEL* TO TRAGEDY

Because Schmitt is so concerned with the link between politics and representation, he is at pains to purge representation of any hint of an illusionary aesthetic, that is, an aesthetic that is isolated and does not form the link that he is seeking. Schmitt's conception of the constitutive character of representation consequently depends on an opposition between two forms of art. Just as he foregrounds the exception over the norm in his political theory, he emphasizes the importance of mythic tragedy over the purely aesthetic play of the *Trauerspiel*. Just as the exception determines the norm, the tragedy sets the parameters for the play.

The primary difficulty with Schmitt's theory of political representation that divides *Hamlet or Hecuba* is that, in contrast to his understanding of the close ties between norm and exception, he is unable to articulate the complementary relationship between play and tragedy. His idea of representation is consequently based on rhetoric, whose authoritative power he poses against "a rapturously overpowering music" on one hand and "a mute practicality" on the other (1996, 23). As opposed to these two bad alternatives, Schmitt argues that rhetoric is able to establish a link between the idea and a political reality by creating a public sphere in which three specific parties are addressed and acquire "a special dignity" and "a noble value": "the representative," "the person represented," and "the third party whom they address" (20). In the case of the Catholic Church, the pope is the representative, Christ as God is what is represented, and the Catholic community is the addressee. Christ grounds the representation through a foundation in a concrete historical presence. The office of the pope extends this initial historical event into the future through a chain of representatives, whose authority ultimately derives from the political reality of Christ as the establisher of the Catholic community as a specific public sphere founded on Christian values.

Schmitt develops a notion of representation in which a particular figure derives authority, neither from a charismatic presence,[4] which would be an aesthetics detached from reality, nor from a material power, which would be a kind of violence, but from an office with a historical tradition that mediates between values and reality. Schmitt emphasizes that the pope is the only remaining representational figure in the modern age (19), primarily because his authority is "independent of charisma" and "the priest upholds a position that appears to be completely apart from his concrete personality" (14). At the same time, the pope's authority is also neither bureaucratic nor impersonal, "because his office is part of an unbroken chain linked with the personal mandate and concrete person of Christ" (14). The person of Christ grounds a historical tradition in which values and a "world-historical form of power" merge in the pope (20).

But if for Schmitt the "paradigm of representation is incarnation" (Kahn 2003, 73), there are two alternative ways of understanding this process. While the incarnation can describe the way in which the idea attains an historical embodiment in the moment of the decision, it can also describe the way in which the original historical presence of Christ grounds the entire rhetorical chain. Because the foundational moment of representation would in this latter case be a historical presence rather than itself a representation, the basis of representation seems to lie in a materiality that is devoid of values, a form of ultimate reality or naked power, thereby opening up Schmitt's theory to the criticism that his concept of rhetoric is indeed merely an alibi for violence rather than a genuine form of legitimation. Yet his insistence on the historical event, evident in *Roman Catholicism and Political Form*, contrasts with the idea of a representational dimension of the founding decision that he moves toward in *The Concept of the Political* and especially in *Constitutional Theory*. In terms of the example of the Catholic Church, what is missing in Schmitt's theory of representation is an account of the representational foundations of Christ's historical significance that goes beyond the fact of Christ's historical presence and explores the way in which this Christian story was able to gain its original truth.

In *Hamlet or Hecuba*, Schmitt makes an effort at such an explanation through his discussion of the way *Hamlet*, in transforming itself from *Trauerspiel* to tragedy, attains the status of myth. Though Schmitt puts together the building blocks of an essentially aesthetic theory of myth that would explain its functioning in both the ancient and the modern world, he continues to struggle with the ambiguity between a materialist explanation for the source of the tragic that would find its ultimate ground in an initial historical violence and an aesthetic explanation rooted in a representational process that determines ultimate values.

When Schmitt transfers his rhetorical schema from *Roman Catholicism and Political Form* over to *Hamlet*, the representative is the figure of Hamlet, the person represented is James I, and the third party whom they address is the Elizabethan audience. This particular audience is crucial for Schmitt, because he emphasizes that Shakespeare's drama is not based on the strict separation of art and reality on which German drama would be premised after the eighteenth century but rather exists within a public sphere that bridges between the two realms through the presence of the audience, which "establishes a public sphere [*Öffentlichkeit*] that encompasses the author, the director, the actors, and the audience itself and incorporates them all" (2009, 35). As a result, Shakespeare's theater "did not set up an opposition between the present of the play and the lived actuality of a contemporary present" (41). Schmitt argues here that, as opposed to the theater of "Corneille and Racine in the France of Louis XIV" (34) or of "Lessing, Goethe, Schiller, Grillparzer, and Hebbel" in Germany (41), Shakespearean theater was simply an extension of the representational forms that characterized political life outside of the theater, and Shakespeare's plays consequently did not function on a purely aesthetic level but on a political level as well.

The insistence on the link to the contemporary present is a call to recognize the political subtext of a literary stance. Rather than fleeing political questions by focusing on a purely aesthetic event, Schmitt argues for a political approach by interpreting Hamlet's reaction to the actor's play about Hecuba's weeping over the dead Priam as an example of a play that incites the audience to action. In this reading, the significance of the actor's play does not lie in its purely aesthetic effect but in its political function of linking the play to a particular "purpose or cause" (43). Schmitt rejects the aesthetic enjoyment of the play because it does not make sense for people to weep over something that has "no impact upon their actual existence and situation" (42–43). But the bad example of such an aesthetic reception ultimately creates the proper rhetorical effect of the play as a form of persuasion, that is, the example of the weeping actor moves Hamlet to action. For Schmitt this scene models for the audience the proper persuasive and rhetorical as opposed to the playful and aesthetic function of drama. In Schmitt's view, the legitimate role for Shakespeare's drama is not to create "aesthetic enjoyment" but rather a rhetorical effect in which the play's significance is not to be distinguished from the effect of political and religious forms of persuasion outside of the theater (43). Rather than creating disinterested enjoyment, the representation should be linked to a "purpose or cause" and has the function of moving people to action. A purely aesthetic approach would be an abdication of this political role.

Against the retreat into aesthetics, Schmitt argues that the play within the play in Act Three of *Hamlet* can avoid becoming untrue as play only because it includes "a realistic core of the most intense contemporary significance and timeliness" (43–44). The main significance of the play within the play lies in its ability to function rhetorically as part of the real historical conflicts that surrounded the original stagings of *Hamlet* in England. Specifically, Schmitt argues that, before James I's succession to the throne, the First Quarto version of the play of 1603 contained implicit support for James's bid, "a call to the irresolute James from the Essex-Southampton group before James's accession to the throne" (43 n31). The relevant line ("a crown bereft him") was removed in the later versions because James was already king. By functioning rhetorically to influence political events through persuasion, the drama turns the success of the play into an implicit form of acclamation for the crowning of James I. This rhetorical purpose maintains a grounding of the drama in reality that is ultimately the basis for its tragic effect.

But while Schmitt provides convincing examples for how *Hamlet* functioned rhetorically within the context of the English political situation of the time, these examples also demonstrate a slippage between rhetorical and aesthetic effects in Schmitt's analysis. This ambiguity results from the fact that, although Schmitt refers to the Elizabethan-era audience as the proper public sphere for the rhetorical effects that he cites, he also refers to the subsequent 350-year reception of Hamlet as the relevant audience for determining the status of the play as a mythic tragedy. The splitting of the addressee into both the Elizabethan audience and the critical Shakespeare reception leads to a conflict between the rhetorical effect on the former and what we can refer to as an aesthetic effect on the latter. So while Schmitt, relying on Lilian Winstanley (1921), provides a pertinent analysis of the rhetorical meaning of the play as it was performed in Shakespeare's time, his rhetorical analysis ultimately proves to be incomplete as an explanation for the play's subsequent mythic status and its tragic effect.

The conflict between rhetorical and aesthetic effects in his analysis becomes evident in Schmitt's examples of the intrusions of history into the play that ground its rhetorical function. He seeks to define how a historical circumstance comes to determine the structure of *Hamlet* by focusing on how Queen Gertrude's situation in the play mirrors that of Mary Stuart, who was suspected of having played a role in the death of her husband, Henry Lord Darnley, after she married his murderer, the Earl of Bothwell. Schmitt argues here that the refusal of the drama to make the queen clearly guilty or innocent of complicity with the elder Hamlet's murder was the result of a political situation in which Shakespeare could not make the queen guilty for fear of antagonizing Mary Stuart's son, James, but could not make the queen innocent out of consideration for a London audience that believed in Mary Stuart's guilt. In this historical intrusion into the structure of the play, Schmitt clearly identifies the political considerations that forced Shakespeare to create an ambiguity in the plot. As Johannes Türk (2008, 78) points out, the key to Schmitt's argument is that the political exigency forces the play to avoid the issue of the queen's guilt and thereby creates a lacuna in the structure of the play. The historical situation causes the otherwise pure play to become a serious tragedy to the extent that the play's structure must accommodate a piece of incontrovertible reality, not as a direct reference, but as an empty space. The structuring effect of an outside reality on an otherwise autonomous play transforms the play into tragedy by creating a link between the play and a political exigency that implies potential violence.

But the example of the taboo of the queen as the structural effect of the presence of Mary Stuart in the audience's consciousness remains inadequate as an explanation for the enduring significance of *Hamlet* to the extent that the audience for the mythic quality that Schmitt cites is not the same audience as the Elizabethan one that would have felt the need for the ambiguity concerning the queen's guilt. If the guarantors of *Hamlet*'s status as mythic tragedy consist of the critical commentary and artistic recreation within the long history of Shakespeare reception that Schmitt (2009, 7) cites at the beginning of his analysis, then the specific historical circumstances linking the taboo of the queen to the dispute over Mary Stuart would in fact be relatively insignificant for the tragic effect (cf. Strathausen 2010, 20–21). The eighteenth-, nineteenth-, and twentieth-century audiences no longer recall or feel concerned by the rhetorical context, and the mythic quality for subsequent generations that Schmitt wants to explain must in fact include some other mechanism. If Schmitt were to focus only on the issue of Mary Stuart's guilt as the source of the tragic effect, in spite of the lack of a meaningful rhetorical connection to non-Elizabethan audiences, he would have to fall back on the type of argumentation that he uses in *Roman Catholicism and Political Form*, namely, that the initial specific personage establishes the beginning of a chain of representative figures that leads into the present. But because the tragic effect is ultimately based on an initial rhetorical effect that has lost its direct significance, Schmitt would have to treat the tragic effect as one that is primarily based in the auratic status of *Hamlet* as a generally recognized myth and not in the particular aesthetic effect that the play would have on a later audience. In this way, Schmitt would emphasize a founding historical event for explaining the mythic quality, but only at the cost of depriving the work of art itself of an aesthetic basis for its own authority. This authority would have to be based ultimately in an institutional support that enshrines *Hamlet* as part of a literary canon. But such an emphasis on the institutionalization of a literary canon would feed into the same kind of separation of the aesthetic sphere from reality that Schmitt set out to dismantle. In fact, he seems to have recognized this problem with the Catholic Church after writing *Roman Catholicism and Political Form*, leading him to move away from it as a basis of political form in the course of the 1920s and toward his more nationalist stance of the Nazi era.

Schmitt does not confine himself then in *Hamlet or Hecuba* to the line of argument in *Roman Catholicism and Political Form*, and he outlines another mode of linking play to reality in his second example of how the historical intrusion transforms a play into a tragedy, not just for Elizabethan England but also for audiences that are centuries removed. This example explains the enduring significance by referring, not to a rhetorical effect that is based on the pure material facticity of an historical event but to an aesthetic one whose content includes a consciousness of a historical situation. Affirming that the transformation of the figure of the avenger into "a doubtful, problematic hero"

(2009, 21) is the key to the play's tragic quality, Schmitt argues that this transformation · of the typical revenge drama was determined by an intrusion into the play of the historical figure of King James. Schmitt argues not that the figure of Hamlet is supposed to directly refer to James but that this figure is determined by the indirect effect of the historical James, transforming the structure of the revenge drama so that the focus turns toward Hamlet's indecision: "The problematic of the figure of the avenger stems from the contemporary historical presence of Mary Stuart's son. The philosophizing and theologizing King James embodied namely the entire conflict of his age, a century of divided belief and religious civil war" (25). It is at this point that Schmitt's argument leads to a historical context that includes but also goes beyond the specific situation of James and Mary Stuart, indicating a broader historical reality of religious conflict. By incarnating the religious schism between Catholics and Protestants, James's situation created the impulse toward indecision in the avenger figure, and this indecision is thus the consequence for the play of a breakdown of a historical representational form. "In times of religious schisms the world and world history lose their secure forms, and a human problematic becomes visible out of which no purely aesthetic consideration could create the hero of a revenge drama. Historical reality is stronger than every aesthetic, stronger also than the most ingenious subject" (30). Schmitt sets up a stark contrast here between the reality of historical events and the relative of ephemerality of both aesthetic and subjective experience.

But even though Schmitt explicitly rejects an aesthetic explanation for the play's significance, his argument maps out a kind of rhetoric that is built around aesthetic insight to the extent that Hamlet's indecision in the play does not create a particular call to action but rather illuminates a human problematic. If the Reformation was a time in which Christianity as a political form was undergoing an extreme crisis of representation, the play integrates the effects of this historical transformation into its structure. However, if the play recapitulates in its structure a historical process, the effect is aesthetic to the extent that the recapitulation process does not encourage a specific action in the audience, but results in a new insight. Rather than promoting the play's direct participation in political representation for a particular cause or purpose, the play's link to history involves the ability of the play's inner development to create in the audience a disinterested awareness of the constraints built into a historical context. This historical consciousness might then have political consequences, in terms not of a specific cause or purpose but of a set-up of a representational foundation for a possible new structure of political identity.

As Strathausen (2010, 18–21) points out, the play's reference to this historical context is not in fact a case of an objective core of historical reality that breaks into the play, but, as a mythic construct, this objectivity of the historical is itself the result of an interpretive framework. If this dependence of reality on interpretation indicates a kind of "ontological relativism" in the sense that different cultural traditions will operate with their own distinctive metaphysical assumptions (24–26), the interpretive process is also constrained by the aesthetic structure of myths, which merge specific insights about a metaphysical situation with a set of interpretive decisions.

SCHMITT AND BENJAMIN

Such a sense of the structural effects of a work of art on an audience leads Schmitt's argument much closer to Walter Benjamin's approach to the play in *The Origin of German Tragic Drama*, and several sections of Schmitt's book include implicit and explicit responses to Benjamin's ideas on tragedy and *Trauerspiel*. When Schmitt writes that "tragedy originates only from a given circumstance that exists for all concerned—an incontrovertible reality for the author, the actors, and the audience" (2009, 45), he is insisting on the importance of historical context for determining the structure of a tragedy in the same way that Benjamin does in his own analysis of the spiritual effect that the Reformation had on both political life and dramatic form in the baroque period. Moreover, in his discussion of Hamlet's inaction, Schmitt accepts Benjamin's treatment of indecision as the primary characteristic of the baroque.[5]

Yet the two offer alternative interpretations for the nature of the historical context and the way this context determines the possibilities for drama. For Schmitt, the confessional struggles are the underlying historical reality that intrudes into the play in the person of James, who stood at the center of these conflicts. The source of the tragic is, however, still the concrete historical event that creates the "shadows" in the play that ground the tragic effect (44). While Schmitt draws attention to specific events such as the murder of James's father, Mary Stuart's guilt, and the fate of the Stuart house, all tied to the confessional struggles of the age, Benjamin focuses on how the religious struggles transformed the relationship between worldly event and spiritual meaning. The key for Benjamin is that in the baroque period "religious aspirations did not lose their importance: it was just that this century denied them a religious fulfillment, demanding of them, or imposing upon them, a secular solution instead" (1977, 79). The religious schisms were central for Benjamin, not directly because of the religious conflict but because these conflicts led to a hardening of positions in which the link between secular life and spiritual life was severed. Because religious structures had become stultified by the extreme polarizations, the universal validity of a Christian metaphysical context was undermined as well. The resulting confusion of metaphysical positions meant that spiritual concerns could no longer be fulfilled straightforwardly through action in the world, and such action began to have a futile character. As a consequence, "the German *Trauerspiel* is taken up entirely with the hopelessness of the earthly condition. Such redemption as it knows resides in the depths of this destiny itself rather than in the fulfillment of a divine plan of salvation" (81). The baroque drama remains imprisoned within worldly events and actions at the same time as it is suffused with a melancholy sense of their spiritual meaningless.

Based on this separation between action and meaning, Benjamin offers an alternative understanding of the lacunae that make up the tragedy in which the key is not the concrete historical event but the structure of those events that excludes certain outcomes. The tragedy reproduces this structure and its exclusions in such a way that they become clear to the audience. In the case of *Hamlet*, Benjamin emphasizes that its greatness as

a tragedy lies in the way that it was able to create a self-awareness of the spiritual emptiness of the world by reintegrating a spiritual perspective in a negative way, through
the reflection on melancholy that is created by Hamlet's indecision. As opposed to
the German *Trauerspiel*, which "was never able to awaken within itself the clear light
of self-awareness," Benjamin affirms that "it is only in [*Hamlet*] that melancholy self-
absorption attains Christianity" (158).

In his response to Benjamin, Schmitt (2009, 61–65) rejects the idea that *Hamlet* is
Christian in the medieval sense and insists that the play must be understood within
a historical development in England around 1600 from a medieval period, in which
religious issues were dominant, to a modern period characterized on one hand by
state-based institutions and on the other by the sea and the Industrial Revolution.
Yet when Benjamin writes that "only Shakespeare was capable of striking Christian
sparks from the baroque rigidity of the melancholic" (1977, 158), he is referring precisely to this situation of a transition away from a medieval situation in which worldly
events could be depicted as parts of a story of salvation. At the heart of the baroque
for Benjamin lies a spiritual emptiness in worldly actions that can be depicted only as
a lack. Shakespeare's achievement in *Hamlet* was to have allowed this situation to be
made palpable as a lack, which could be done only if Christianity could be invoked
as an absent desideratum. *Hamlet* is not Christian in the medieval sense but in the
baroque sense of a spiritual dimension that still maintains its authority in a private
sphere but has been cut off from a direct connection to worldly events (138). The
Christian aspect of *Hamlet* for Benjamin is not an explicit story of salvation but a spiritually grounded awareness of a melancholy imprisonment in a world of action that
has been decoupled from salvation.

If Schmitt overlooks this key aspect of Benjamin's argument, it is because he is overly
concerned with concrete historical events as the basis of tragedy and does not recognize Nietzsche's and Benjamin's focus on how the tragedy attains its effects through an
aesthetic reception of historical problems. In spite of Benjamin's (1977, 104) critique
of Nietzsche's aestheticism, he approvingly cites his explanation for how an aesthetic
structure can depict the lacunae of an age through the technique of musical dissonance (108–109). Translated into tragedy, this dissonance creates a situation in which
"the structure of the scenes and the visual images reveal a deeper wisdom than the
poet himself can put into words and concepts" (108; Nietzsche 1999, 105). The analogy between the events of the play and the spiritual situation of the spectators who
share a historical context creates the tragic effect through the structure of the drama's
development, which leaves gaps. The lacunae exist first in a historical reality as possibilities foreclosed by the structure of events, and the tragedy recreates those lacunae
in a way that makes visible what in reality is normally invisible because foreclosed as a
possibility. The gaps of tragedy are not the result of political considerations that can be
readily named but of a historical situation that forecloses certain events. The tragedy
makes the absent possibilities visible through the development of the inner dynamic
of the play.

CONCLUSION

Though Schmitt is reluctant to affirm the importance of aesthetic play, his contribution is to note that the aesthetic insights of an audience do not serve merely to establish a utopian element but also provide the basis for the development of a political will. While this means that political form cannot develop without an aesthetic truth, the other consequence is that every aesthetic truth has concrete political implications. In the case of *Hamlet*, the structure of the drama, while creating lacunae from the point of view of a Christian perspective, also establishes the representational foundations for a new political theology of the nation-state. Here, Schmitt's insistence on the mythic status of Shakespeare's *Hamlet* indicates that the age of myth is still with us and that the modern era is to be distinguished only by the specific selection of myths and not by its overcoming of myth itself.

Both Schmitt and Benjamin agree that the rise of *Hamlet* marks the beginning of the end of the confessional struggles. Schmitt argues that Hamlet's indecision reflected the undecidability of the religious civil wars, and Benjamin points out that these wars had disengaged spiritual questions from action in the world, thereby sundering the merging of real and ideal that Schmitt affirms to be essential to the legitimacy and stability of political representation and, with it, social order. But this does not mean that, as Carlo Galli argues, world and values must remain always separated in the modern world, nor does *Hamlet* reflect a "modern destruction of the traditional symbolic order" to become "one of the main myths of modernity as such" (2012, 71, 77). To simply note, as Franco Moretti does, "that the historical 'task' effectively accomplished by [tragic] form was precisely the destruction of the fundamental paradigm of the dominant culture" (1988, 42) would be to miss the structural role that tragedy played in the development of English culture in a direction that did not just delegitimize the absolute monarch but established the ground rules for a constitutional monarchy based on the identity of the English nation. The achievement of *Hamlet* lay not only in its lacunae but also in its adumbration of a mechanism for political representation that reestablishes the links between order and localization, merging aesthetics and politics in a way that cements the relationship between the political self-awareness of a people and sovereign authority.[6] If Hamlet's indecision indeed relates to the theological divisions of the age, the play does not end with an emptiness and a dearth of alternatives. Like the decision on the state of exception, it problematizes these divisions as a crisis of political representation in order to then sketch the outline of a new mode of representation that links popular will to sovereign authority.

Contrary to the idea that "with the modern tragedy, the principle of authority is dissolved" (Moretti 1988, 56), *Hamlet* establishes the outlines for a new concept of political authority that replaces a Christian framework with one that is based in the traditions of English language and history, including the history of its theaters, "for they are the abstract and brief chronicles of the time" (Shakespeare 1963, 2.2.494–495). Because Schmitt recognizes that "the people appear only in the public, and they first produce the public generally" (2008, 272), he can appreciate how the development of the English theater was coincident with that of the English nation, and he is therefore willing to speak the name of this new national order in a way that Benjamin was not, preferring instead to invoke a future age of freedom in an ultimate overcoming of myth itself. Schmitt seems to forget his own pronouncements about the primacy of the political, however, when he refers to the new order as the one of maritime existence and the Industrial Revolution rather than insisting more emphatically on the proper name of England, as if a merely technical innovation could be more significant than a political-theological one (2009, 67). But if Hamlet's attempt to link sovereign action with political representation founders in the play on the missing unity of the Danes, his tragedy marks out the path toward the development of a successful English national identity. Even if *Hamlet's* mythic significance is not based on the kind of intrusion of historical reality into the play that Schmitt describes in *Hamlet or Hecuba*, it does present the kind of merging of aesthetics and politics that Schmitt describes in his discussions of representation in *Roman Catholicism and Political Form* and *Constitutional Theory*. As in *Constitutional Theory*, the pendant to representation in *Hamlet* is identity, which means that the self-awareness of the audience is the foundation for the reality of the representation, whereby this audience is at once the theater audience and the developing English public sphere. In this sense, aesthetics and politics are not merely linked but become two aspects of a single process of representation.

Notes

1. See, e.g., Müller 2003; Scheuermann 1999; Cristi 1998; McCormick 1997; Holmes 1993; Kelly 2004 (113–134); Habermas 1992 (128–139); Wolin 1990 (389–416).
2. See, e.g., Victoria Kahn 2003 (74); Moretti 1988 (44–46).
3. Kahn's critique of Schmitt is also based on the idea that "for Schmitt, in contrast, sovereignty is not a category of legitimacy" (2003, 70).
4. On Schmitt's opposition to a charismatic mode of leadership elaborated by Max Weber, cf. Kalyvas 2008 (158–159); Schwab 1989 (71).
5. Samuel Weber's attempt to distinguish between Benjamin's focus on indecision and Schmitt's insistence on an "absolutely definitive and ultimate decision" fails to consider the arguments in *Hamlet or Hecuba* (1992, 18).
6. On the role of *Hamlet* in establishing a new national form of sovereignty, cf. Pan 2009 (111–118).

References

Agamben, G. 2005. *State of Exception*, trans. K. Attell. Chicago: University of Chicago Press.
Arendt, H. 1968. "What Is Authority?" In *Between Past and Future: Eight Exercises in Political Thought*. New York: Viking, 91–142.
Benjamin, W. 1977. *The Origin of German Tragic Drama*, trans. J. Osborne. London: Verso.

Botwinick, A. 2010. "Shakespeare in Advance of Hobbes: Pathways to the Modernization of the European Psyche as Charted in *The Merchant of Venice.*" *Telos* 153: 132–159.

Cristi, R. 1998. *Carl Schmitt and Authoritarian Liberalism.* Cardiff: University of Wales Press.

Daniels, D. 2010. "'Neither Simple Allusions Nor True Mirrorings': Seeing Double with Carl Schmitt." *Telos* 153: 62–67.

Frank, S. 2010. "Re-imagining the Public Sphere: Malebranche, Schmitt's Hamlet, and the Lost Theater of Sovereignty." *Telos* 153: 89–93.

Galli, C. 2012. "Hamlet: Representation and the Concrete." In *Political Theology and Early Modernity*, ed. G. L. Hammill et al. Chicago: University of Chicago Press, 60–83.

Habermas, J. 1992. "The Horrors of Autonomy: Carl Schmitt in English." In *The New Conservatism: Cultural Criticism and the Historians' Debate*, ed. S. Weber Nicholsen. Cambridge: MIT Press, 128–139.

Holmes, S. 1993. *The Anatomy of Anti-Liberalism.* Cambridge: Harvard University Press.

Kahn, P. 2011. *Political Theology: Four New Chapters on the Concept of Sovereignty.* New York: Columbia University Press.

Kahn, V. 2003. "Hamlet or Hecuba: Carl Schmitt's Decision." *Representations* 83: 67–96.

Kalyvas, A. 2008. *Democracy and the Politics of the Extraordinary: Max Weber, Carl Schmitt, and Hannah Arendt.* Cambridge: Cambridge University Press.

Kelly, D. 2004. "Carl Schmitt's Theory of Representation." *Journal of the History of Ideas* 65: 113–134.

McCormick, J. 1997. *Carl Schmitt's Critique of Liberalism: Against Politics as Technology.* Cambridge: Cambridge University Press.

Moretti, F. 1988. *Signs Taken for Wonders: Essays in the Sociology of Literary Forms*, trans. S. Fisher et al. London: Verso.

Müller, J.-W. 2003. *A Dangerous Mind: Carl Schmitt in Post-War European Thought.* New Haven: Yale University Press.

Nietzsche, F. 1999. *The Birth of Tragedy and Other Writings.* ed. R. Geuss and R. Speirs, trans. R. Speirs. Cambridge: Cambridge University Press.

Pan, D. 2009. "Afterword." In Schmitt 2009, 69–119.

Rasch, W. 2004. *Sovereignty and Its Discontents: On the Primacy of Conflict and the Structure of the Political.* London: Birkbeck Law Press.

Santner, E. L. 2010. "The Royal Remains: Carl Schmitt's *Hamlet or Hecuba.*" *Telos* 153: 30–50.

Scheuermann, W. 1999. *Carl Schmitt: The End of Law.* Lanham: Rowman & Littlefield.

Schmitt, C. 1996. *Roman Catholicism and Political Form*, trans. G. L. Ulmen. Westport: Greenwood Press.

Schmitt, C. 2008. *Constitutional Theory*, trans. and ed. J. Seitzer. Durham: Duke University Press.

Schmitt, C. 2009. *Hamlet or Hecuba: The Intrusion of the Time into the Play*, trans. D. Pan and J. R. Rust. New York: Telos Press.

Schmitt, C. 2010. "Foreword to the German Edition of Lilian Winstanley's *Hamlet and the Scottish Succession.*" *Telos* 153: 164–177.

Schwab, G. 1989. *The Challenge of the Exception: An Introduction to the Political Ideas of Carl Schmitt between 1921 and 1936.* New York: Greenwood Press.

Shakespeare, W. 1963. *Hamlet*, ed. C. Hoy. New York: Norton.

Strathausen, C. 2010. "Myth or Knowledge? Reading Carl Schmitt's *Hamlet or Hecuba.*" *Telos* 153: 7–29.

Türk, J. 2008. "The Intrusion: Carl Schmitt's Non-mimetic Logic of Art." *Telos* 142: 73–89.

Weber, S. 1992. "Taking Exception to Decision: Walter Benjamin and Carl Schmitt." *Diacritics* 22: 5–18.

Weber, S. 2005. *Targets of Opportunity: On the Militarization of Thinking*. New York: Fordham University Press.

Winstanley, L. 1921. *Hamlet and the Scottish Succession*. Cambridge: Cambridge University Press.

Wolin, R. 1990. "Carl Schmitt, Political Existentialism, and the Total State." *Theory & Society* 19: 389–416.

CHAPTER 29

·····

AT THE LIMITS
OF RHETORIC

*Authority, Commonplace, and the Role
of Literature in Carl Schmitt*

·····

JOHANNES TÜRK

Historical thinking is the thinking of singular situations and therefore of singular truths.

Schmitt 1955, 146[1]

On the contrary, the power of speech and discourse—rhetoric in its greatest sense—is a criterion [*ein Zeichen*] of human life.

Schmitt 1996b, 23

topos: *Definition* a traditional or conventional literary or rhetorical theme or topic; *Origin* Greek, short for *koinos topos*, literally, commonplace; *First Known Use*: 1936.

Merriam-Webster online, abbreviated

INTRODUCTION

·····

WHAT IS the relationship of Carl Schmitt's writing to rhetoric? While many of Schmitt's works betray his familiarity with rhetorical terms—from ethos and pathos to topos—their thematic occurrence is not easily translated into a systematic perspective. This chapter approaches the question of Schmitt's rhetoric by exploring a number of his political writings, such as *Römischer Katholizismus und politische Form* (*Roman Catholicism and Political Form*), *Der Begriff des Politischen* (*The Concept of the Political*), and *Die geistesgeschichtliche Lage des heutigen Parlamentarismus* (*The Crisis of Parliamentary Democracy*), which illustrate the significance of this dimension for central concerns of political theory. It then examines Schmitt's relationship to literature as *auctoritas* in readings of *Theodor Däublers "Nordlicht": Drei Studien über die Elemente, den Geist und die Aktualität des Werkes (Theodor Däubler's "The Northern Light": Three Studies about the Elements, the Spirit, and the Actuality of the Work)* and *Hamlet oder Hekuba (Hamlet or Hecuba)*.

A brief discussion will illustrate the stakes of this question. In his *"Völkerrechtliche Formen des modernen Imperialismus" ("Forms of Modern Imperialism in International Law")*, first published in 1933, Carl Schmitt investigates U.S. imperialism. In contrast to other forms of colonialism, American imperialism is, according to him, economic. The distinction between creditors and debtors has become the basis for an order of domination that politicizes the economic, considered to be a priori "peaceful" in the nineteenth century (Schmitt 2011, 30). More important, however, is the new legal form accompanying global power: the Monroe Doctrine and the Kellogg-Briand Pact of 1928 exemplify a scenario in which one country reserves for itself the right to "define, interpret, and apply" (44) legal terms. The Monroe Doctrine, at first a defensive declaration, thus becomes a justification for intervention in other parts of America. And the Kellogg Pact—apparently outlawing war while actually legitimizing it in the name of international principles—serves as the legal basis for American intervention in Cuba, Panama, and elsewhere.

The result of this process of "defining, interpreting, and applying" is, according to Schmitt, a profound confusion about the content of these concepts: military missions are not called war, peaceful occupations lead to casualties, and interventions are no longer acts of aggression but benevolent attempts to secure the integrity of a foreign country. Schmitt sees in the ability of the United States to operate with "elastic" and "open" concepts and to force other peoples to respect them as "a phenomenon of world-historical significance" (44). It is here that the legal scholar considers the relationship between power and language more explicitly than elsewhere:

> With those decisive political concepts the issue is who interprets, defines, and applies them; who says, by means of concrete decision, what is peace, what [is] disarmament, what intervention, what public order and security. It is one of the most important phenomena in the entire legal life of humanity that whoever has real power is also able to appropriate and determine concepts and words. *Caesar dominus et supra grammaticam*: the emperor is ruler over grammar as well. Imperialism forges for itself its own concepts, and false normativism and formalism only leads to a situation in which in the end nobody knows what is war and what is peace. I would like once again to caution against the misunderstanding according to which we are dealing with things here that [a people] can simply decide to do [*die man beliebig machen könnte*]. It is an expression of true political power if a great people [can] determine on its own the forms of speech and even the mode of thought of other peoples, the vocabulary, the terminology and the concepts. (44)

The confusion is not adequately explained from the perspective of a formal approach to law. Rather, the answer lies somewhere else; as this passage makes evident, for Schmitt the hermeneutic—interpreting, defining, and applying—is integral to rhetoric as a fundamental polemical dimension. Since antiquity, rhetoric has been understood as *ars persuadendi*, the knowledge about a communicative practice whose aim is to convince audiences, shape affairs, and influence decisions through narratives.

At its core, rhetoric conceives of language as the instrument of an *agon*, in which language is an instrument of power. Traditionally, the *ars rhetorica* crystallizes linguistic knowledge around the terms *orator* and *oratio*. Schmitt's essay draws on these two fundamental dimensions; the question of *who* determines the meaning of words is crucial. In Schmitt's view, they are defined through *concrete decisions*. The subjects of these decisions are "imperialism" and "a great people": a personification or *prosopopoeia*. And *what* is defined is a terminology that can be used to legitimize acts. Language is integral to a history of power: sovereignty ("Caesar") determines ("dominus") the universality of language ("grammaticam") while standing above it ("supra"). Thus rhetoric becomes visible as a central dimension of Schmitt's thought, located at the point where language and power meet in the context of a specific historical situation.

Grand Rhetoric

Schmitt's writing seeks to develop a voice that is engaged in the global metaphysical polemic that world history represents for him. The traditions of thought he mobilizes are all located along the fault lines of major ideological conflicts through which the modern age has emerged. Situated outside the traditional distinction between philosophy and rhetoric that has dominated the Western tradition since Plato's fundamental rejection of the sophists, his work claims validity on the basis of its relationship to serious concerns. In Schmitt's understanding, rhetoric lacks the ornamental character attributed to it since the eighteenth century. It rather grows out of a tradition in which the grammaticalization of the Latin language as a precondition of its universalization went hand in hand with global political aspirations. The Catholic Church inherited this Roman legacy, before the French in the seventeenth century began to question the unique status of Latin as a universal language.[2]

Schmitt's emphasis on the "grand rhetoric" (1996b, 22) of the Catholic Church in *Roman Catholicism and Political Form* is therefore of exemplary significance. As is well known, Schmitt defends the Catholic Church as an institution that is defined through a *complexio oppositorum*, capable of containing all forms of government (5–7). The book is less interested, as is sometimes suggested, in religious politics;[3] rather, it portrays the Catholic Church as an exemplary institution insofar as it is capable of absorbing contradictions based on a living form. It is characterized by the embodiment of representation capable of forming "representative figures" (19) such as the pope, the emperor, and the monk. And in this ability lies its superiority over the age of economic thinking, which only knows "exponents" and "private individuals" (2011, 20). Repeatedly, Schmitt insists that the forms of representation of the Catholic Church—from the ceremonial garments to the speech of its functionaries—are misunderstood if one thinks of them as ornamental. Rather, they are the result of a capability for form and imaging that stands in stark contrast to the "factory...lacking representation and imagery" (*Unbildlichkeit des modernen Betriebs*; 1996b, 22) characteristic of the contemporary world.

In this context, Schmitt develops a rudimentary theory of rhetoric. What Schmitt calls a "grand rhetoric" draws on the authority conveyed by this powerful institution to those representing it, and rhetoric becomes an expression of human dignity. In speech, the authority of representation manifests itself:

> But his discourse is only possible against the background of an imposing authority. It lapses neither into a discourse nor a dictate, nor a dialectic but moves in its architecture. Its grand diction is more than music; it is a form of human dignity which becomes visible in the rationality of forming speech. All this presupposes a hierarchy, because the spiritual resonance of grand rhetoric derives from the belief in the representation claimed by the orator. (1996b, 24; translation modified)

Only the authority of an institutional hierarchy can guarantee the belief that makes possible the resonance of grand rhetoric. It requires an "ethos of conviction" (17) that necessarily relates to an idea. And it requires a "pathos of moral or legal conviction" (18).

This rhetoric stands in the tradition of the *genus grande* defended by the church father Augustine in his *On Christian Doctrine*. Augustine adopts the legacy of rhetoric and ascribes it a pedagogical function. As Deborah Shuger has shown, serious thought has by no means been limited to the plain style or the *genus tenue*—a common, if historically false, association. Rather, the *genus grande* or *gravis oratio* was the style "engaged in a mortal struggle over the great, common, urgent issues of the commonwealth and, in a later era, of salvation" (Shuger 1984, 4). It is a style associated with dignity. Cicero describes it as "the greatest form of oratory, suited for the most important topics" (20), and its speaker is a *tragicus orator* (10–11). While Schmitt criticizes Romanticism as a movement that "employed historical events as the occasion for a distinctive literary productivity instead of apprehending them in a matter-of-fact way" (1986, 7), the rhetoric of the Catholic Church participates in the fundamental metaphysical struggles in the name of an idea. While Romanticism defines an occasion as what can give rise to the development of a potentiality, the Catholic Church encounters it with the ethos and pathos of a grand rhetoric shaping life. It is this seriousness or the serious case (*Ernstfall*) that endows the terms decision, emergency, and state of exception (*Ausnahmezustand*)—crucial for Schmitt's work—with their specific weight. Decisive questions are those that demand existential decisions. These terms express an intensity derived from the degree to which thought is implied in the questions that need to be solved.[4]

The most profound reason for Schmitt's alignment with the Catholic Church might not be biographical contingency, but rather its exemplary theory of rhetoric that authorizes the ethos and pathos to speak in the name of an idea.

Toward a Radical Topology: Polemical Displacements

For a worldview in which metaphysical assumptions have a structuring impact on world history, commonplaces are of central importance. They provide the matrix according to which the world is narrated and arguments are formed. It is therefore not surprising that the major domain in which Carl Schmitt's work unfolds its potential is topological. In his *Rhetoric*, Aristotle introduces the concept of "common place," or *topos coinos*, a term that will be translated into Latin as *locus communis* (2000, 31 I, 2, 1358a). According to him, commonplaces such as the more or less are general forms of intelligibility or ordering viewpoints that can be applied to any topic. Rather than being "clichés" or "stereotypical expressions" (Virno 2004), commonplaces are, according to him, forms that allow the organization of themes in language and places where one can find ways of structuring a narrative.

When the Roman rhetorician Quintilian in the first century AD revisits the knowledge of rhetorical places in his exhaustive account of how to find arguments, he already has to remind his reader what a commonplace is: "I do not call commonplaces those passages against luxury and adultery and the like, but the place where one can find latent arguments" ("locos appelo non, ut volgo nunc intelliguntur, in luxuriem et adulterium et simila, sed sedes argumentorum, in quibus latent"; Quintilianus 1997, V 10, 20). Commonplaces, therefore, are not a collection of quotes, but a system of places.

That commonplaces have a history is an observation whose implications for literature were unfolded by Robert Curtius, one of the major scholars of European literature in the first half of the twentieth century, who renewed interest in the study of topoi. Curtius defines commonplaces as a general matrix: "In the antique system of rhetoric topoi are the stockroom. There one found ideas of the most general sort—such as could be employed in every kind of oratory" (Curtius 1990, 79; translation modified). For him, commonplaces have a historical dimension. The emergence of new topoi, as well as their reception in later texts, points our attention to "genetics" and "formal elements" that define what he calls the *"genesis of new topoi"* (82; translation modified).

The central concern of Schmitt's work is to displace the topology in which the modern age understands itself. He expresses this more clearly than elsewhere in *The Concept of the Political*, in which the political is defined as its own sphere. The distinction defining the political in contrast to other spheres is, for Schmitt, the distinction between friend and enemy. The 1963 foreword, not included in the English translations, portrays his aim as "to bring order into a confused subject matter and to find a topological order for its concepts" (*"eine Topik der Begriffe"*; Schmitt 2002, 9). The political as it is generally perceived is not only the result of traditional assumptions and habitual arguments, but also of academic specialization: "The divisions based on the division of labor characteristic of our teaching and research in the humanities has confused the shared language" ("*Die arbeitsteilige Aufsplitterung unseres geisteswissenschaftlichen Lehr- und Forschungswesens hat die gemeinsame Sprache verwirrt*"; 15–16). While he draws on specific places and specialized knowledge, Schmitt aims at the reconstruction of a language that would no longer be confused. Here, as elsewhere, he suggests that a new set of distinctions is more appropriate to describe a current problem, that a different ensemble of assumptions is more fruitful to adequately capture the current situation, and that the question at hand is misrepresented by the metaphysical assumptions that have shaped the concept of the political. We consider here three more examples that illustrate Schmitt's search to displace architectures of commonplaces.

In *Legalität und Legitimität* (*Legality and Legitimacy*), Schmitt proposes that the modern world defines legitimacy as legality, whereas legality or the parliamentary state governed by lawgivers is only one form of legitimacy alongside states in which jurisdiction, institutions, or a monarch provide legitimacy. We have fallen prey to parliamentary democracy's polemical claim that its own assumption, the exclusive claim of norms to legitimacy, equals legitimacy as such. It is here that Schmitt contrasts "distinctions developed in previous situations" such as the antithesis of freedom and authority and the Aristotelian tripartite monarchy, aristocracy, and democracy, with the distinction between legality and legitimacy:

> It is not that the Aristotelian teaching is not modern and has been superseded. Today, however, the normative fiction of a closed system of legality emerges in a striking and undeniable opposition to the legitimacy of an instance of will that is actually present and in conformity with the law. This is currently the decisive contradiction, rather than that between the legitimacy of monarchy, aristocracy, oligarchy, or democracy, which mostly only obscures and confuses. (Schmitt 2004a, 6)

What is seemingly self-evident and cannot be refuted is the emergence of a legitimacy located outside our understanding of legitimacy, while key concepts of political thought, seemingly exhaustive, obscure the situation. New criteria need to be articulated to shed light on the evolving constellation whose reality endows the concepts with their relevance.

The essay "Nomos—Nahme—Name" lays the foundation for Schmitt's late work *Der Nomos der Erde im Völkerrecht des Jus Publicum Europaeum* (*The "Nomos" of the Earth in the International Law of the "Jus Publicum Europaeum;" The "Nomos" of the Earth*), which challenges our concept of law as such while sketching a new understanding of the development of Western law. Our understanding of the law forgets, the argument goes, its constitution, which becomes "semiconscious": "The *situation établie* rules all habits, including habits of thought and language. Normativism and positivism then become the most plausible and self-evident thing in the world, namely where there is no other horizon than the status quo" (1959, 97). The seeming plausibility and self-evidence is again the crucial point where our habits of thought and language join to obscure. Against the usurpation of the Greek *nomos* into the Roman law through its translation as *lex* by Cicero—a process through which it becomes equated with "norm" and eventually determines our seemingly self-evident understanding—Schmitt draws on a reading of Homer. Schmitt reinterprets the epic's use of *nomos* and demonstrates its etymological derivation from the verb *nemein*, which means to divide, to apportion, or to pasture, in order to establish an essential relationship between the law and the seizure of land (see 99–101). The topos that equals the law with a detached norm is replaced by a concept that is open to dimensions formerly perceived as external to legal history, particularly the seizure of land, its distribution, and the extension of the law into new elements.

Finally, *The Crisis of Parliamentary Democracy* argues against the current identification of parliamentarism with democracy, claiming that the ideas underlying them each belong to a distinct discursive tradition, but that those traditions have been historically conflated in the nineteenth-century state. This state has become a norm calibrating our thought and perception. In Schmitt's perspective, the twentieth century witnesses a decay of parliamentarism because its two defining features, discussion and publicity, are eroding. And this crisis makes evident that a thought informed by the current commonplaces cannot think to our age (see Schmitt 1985). The discovery of the heterogeneity of democracy and parliamentarism has consequences. For Schmitt, the tradition of democratic thinking is a tradition whose key term is, as Rousseau's *Social Contract* shows, identity, the identity of a general will, while parliamentarism is based on the assumption of representation (the difference between representation and identity is also crucial for Schmitt's *Verfassungslehre* (*Constitutional Theory*) (see Schmitt 2008, 239–240). Among the most radical consequences drawn from this observation is that democracy and totalitarianism are by no means in opposition; rather, because democracy implies the establishment of a shared will, it can be the latter's ally.

Schmitt relies on a counternarrative of legal history, on an etymological alternative, and on an unperceived conceptual disjunction in discursive history, to radically challenge and displace commonplaces that shape the perception of our time and to open horizons beyond the historical forces manifest in perceptual inabilities that become visible in an inadequacy to describe and understand the current political situation. For Schmitt, language is lagging behind the historical situation. This inherent belatedness is an anachronism that opens reality to the possibility of a polemical redefinition.

But he does not offer an outside perspective to contemporary debates; rather, all political concepts have for him "a polemical meaning" (Schmitt 1976, 30). He moves on the same plane of immanence as the positions he rejects. And he consequently not only refutes, but also relies on, knowledge sedimented in language as what one could call an architecture of commonplaces. Thus in *The Concept of the Political* he draws on the fact that all attempts to define "political" are inseparable from an inherent polemic meaning in order to establish plausibility for his claims: "But the fact that the substance of the political is contained in the context of a concrete antagonism is expressed in everyday language, even where the awareness of the extreme case [*Bewußtsein des Ernstfalles*] has been entirely lost" (30). Commonplaces as historically evolved linguistic patterns that define the contours of conceptual questions and the way in which concepts are located in relation to each other shape the intelligibility of the world and are therefore inherent in thought as well as in all knowledge.

THE LIMITS OF RHETORIC:
TOPOI COINOI AND *TOPOI IDIOI*

Schmitt's writing is located at the intersection of public interests and specific academic disciplines. While writing for a general audience on topics relevant beyond any particular professional environment, he engages with particular fields of expertise, from legal scholarship to political science. His texts are therefore inhabited by commonplaces as well as by special places. From the *topoi coinoi* Aristotle distinguishes the *topoi idioi* or special places, categories that derive their meaning from a particular ontological or epistemological area. They are specific to one domain of life and depend on the knowledge inherent in it. While the commonplaces are generic and, as Paulo Virno suggests, rudimentary elements of a "general intellect" (2004, 37), the special places belong to a "local" sphere of life and define the language appropriate to them.

In Aristotle's account, specific topics are inseparable from the particular kind of rhetoric they belong to: the deliberative, juridical, and epideictic genres are each defined through a kind of speaker, an addressee, as well as a topic. Deliberative rhetoric takes place in a political assembly whose members deliberate events to come, while juridical rhetoric addresses a judge who pronounces justice on events in the past. Each of these also inhabits a proximity to particular branches of knowledge: deliberative rhetoric lies near the knowledge of war, for example. In a significant passage, Aristotle defines the relationship between the two types of topoi:

> The first kind of topoi will not make a man practically wise about any particular class of things; because they do not deal with any particular subject matter; but as to the specific topics, the happier a man is in his choice of propositions, the more he will unconsciously produce a science quite different from Dialectic and Rhetoric. For if he once hits upon first principles, it will no longer be Dialectic or Rhetoric, but that science whose principles he has arrived at…the more they specialize in a subject, the more they transgress the limits of Rhetoric. (Aristotle 2000, 31 and 30; translation modified)

The *topos idios* describes the limit of rhetoric. Along its margin, knowledge permeates discourse and the discourse of rhetoric. By addressing a general audience while contributing to specific legal and political questions, Schmitt's writing inhabits this margin where the rhetorical is absorbed into specialized knowledge.

IN SHIFTING SAND: NORMAL TYPES,
APHORISM AND SYSTEM, CLASSICISM

Derived from a "normal situation" in which the current use becomes evident, topologies also fulfill a crucial function in Schmitt's writing: they occupy the place where the problem of reference would be located. The question of Schmitt's concept of language has received widely—and one is tempted to say wildly—differing interpretations. While some claim, based on early writings as well as on the persistence of the use of words like "essence," that Schmitt is an essentialist (see Meuter 1994, 62–64), for others he is a realist (Schmitt himself claims occasionally that every lawyer is naturally a conceptual realist) or a nominalist (see Groh 1998, 83–85, 255–257). A series of equations is necessary to arrive at any of these three popular answers. Schmitt himself seems, however, not particularly interested in developing a coherent theory of language, let alone of reference. Occasional remarks about the conceptual realism of all legal scholars do not contradict this. Rather, the question of how language relates to an existential situation receives a political answer that is more nuanced and at the same time remote from the contemporary linguistic concept of reference as well as from the tradition of conceptual realism and nominalism. There are two points at which Schmitt thinks of the relationship of language to the world as a question of topology.

First, if Schmitt speaks of the relation of language to an outside, he observes—as I have shown—how a topology relates to a situation it can fail to adequately capture, and he suggests how a different set of topoi could look that would allow a more accurate description. Here, historical commonplace can blind us to the real implications of a situation, as the example of parliamentarism and democracy shows. Schmitt's aim, therefore, is to deconstruct compounds and habitual connections in order to demonstrate their contingent affiliation and to replace them with a different conceptual architecture.

A crucial second point in which he outlines a complex relationship between meaning and existential reality becomes visible in his *Über die drei Arten des rechtswissenschaftlichen Denkens* (*On the Three Types of Juristic Thought*), first published in 1934. The book discovers a third type of juristic thought that complements normativism and decisionism, what Schmitt calls "concrete-order thinking" ("*konkretes Ordnungsdenken*"). Norms, decisions, and concrete order can each provide the basis from which all other legal ideas follow. From the perspective of "concrete-order thinking," norms or rules do not create order; they only have a regulating function within a preexisting order. Unlike the norm, which is an abstraction regulating many concrete cases (cf. Schmitt 2004b, 48–49), in this view the reality the law regulates is already ordered, is a "substantive institutional order" (55). It presupposes "typical figures" "growing out of the order of the concrete 'conditions,' for example, brave soldiers, duty-conscious bureaucrats, respectable comrades…the *bonus pater familias*" (55). Whereas the normative idea of law leads to a separation between norm and facticity, the perspective of concrete order grows out of commonplaces, types in which the factual is already normative: "We know that the norm presupposes a *normal* situation and *normal* types. Every order, including the 'legal order', is bound to concrete normal concepts, which are not derived from general norms, but rather such norms are generated by their specific order and for their specific order" (56). Norms are inherent in figurations produced by a social order. That Schmitt counts the "Führer of the movement" (56) among these figures is evidence of the fact that Nazi Germany seemed to speak to Schmitt's concern to find a correspondence of legal terms with a historical reality.

Schmitt sees his time as an interim phase in global history that is a history of meta-physical assumptions, a phase in which, as he writes, "the axis of concepts break." The conceptual order disintegrates; classical and revolutionary legal terms coexist and lead to confused notions of peace and partisan warfare (2002, 15). Although, for example, the concepts of the *jus publicum Europaeum*, the legal order established after the Thirty Years' War, persist, they have become incongruent with reality. In legal theory, this means that the time of systems has come to an end:

> The time of the systems is over. Three hundred years ago, when the epoch of European statehood was ascending, splendid systems of thought emerged. Today, one can no longer build that way. Today, only historic retrospection is possible.... The other, opposing possibility would be the leap into the aphorism. For me as a jurist it is impossible. In the dilemma between system and aphorism only one way out is left: to keep one's focus on the phenomena and to test the ever new questions of ever new tumultuous situations for their criteria. In this manner, one insight accrues to the other and a series of corollaries emerges.... Only a very specific category of such corollaries are relevant here, those that convey an overview of the relations in a conceptual field. They outline a conceptual field, in which concepts inform each other through the position in the conceptual field. (17)

What Schmitt's displacement of topoi therefore attempts is to build conceptual archi-tectures into shifting terrain. Although he seems at times to be faithful to classical legal thinking, his attempt to establish a systematic order is undermined by the provisional historical situation itself. If indeed, as he claims in *The Concept of the Political*, "the clas-sical is the possibility of unambivalent, clear distinctions" (11), then there can only be a certain degree of classicism, a continuously failing attempt to displace, replace, and anchor systematicity in a polemic in which not clarity, but the measure of possible clar-ity, is at stake. One can therefore describe many of Schmitt's texts with the rhetorical virtue of *claritas*, while simultaneously being aware of their esoteric nature.

In the Name of Literature: Criticism and Authority

In Schmitt's *Roman Catholicism and Political Form*, authority is, as mentioned above, established as the condition for speech. "But his discourse is only possible against the background of an imposing authority" (1996b, 24). Throughout his life, literature played a crucial role for him. Literature therefore becomes the place where Schmitt finds the authority in whose name he can speak, and on which he draws to legitimize the critique of his time and the values he suggests. It is a place of normative values and a voice of wis-dom he willingly serves. Although they formally belong to the genre of literary criticism, his essays on literature are also a school in which Schmitt develops his rhetoric. In more than one sense, literature therefore is exemplary. In Roman handbooks of rhetoric like Quintilian's *Institutionis Oratoriae*,[5] exemplum appears as a means used to prove a fact. A vital part of these examples is taken from poets. Literary and mythological as well as historical examples dispose the minds of listeners. Their persuasive influence emerges on the basis of their aesthetic qualities ("quabus delectantur"; V 11, 19). Quintilian mentions the story of the confrontation of the plebeians with patricians and the use of the story of the limbs that revolt against the stomach by Menenius Agrippa as a case in point. *Auctoritas*, the judgments of famous people as well as that of the general public, belong to the same category of external proofs (V 11, 36–38). But *exempla* are also paradigms that serve as models for the development of rhetorical style as well as for ethical attitudes.

This understanding of literary examples is a decisive dimension of Carl Schmitt's oeuvre. The literary appears as an exemplum. It appears as source, proof, and validation of critical and ethical positions rather than as a reference. It authorizes Schmitt's work and emerges in close proximity to cultural and literary developments of his time. Far from lacking an "aesthetic sensibility" (Kahn 2003), he appears as an "homme de lettre" (H. Muth)[6] engaging with artistic and cultural developments, who is close to key figures of the contemporary literary scene, from Hugo Ball to Ernst Jünger. Especially expressionist art influenced him in his early career, which has led critics to attempt to explain his thinking as "political expressionism" (cf. Kennedy 1988)—an equivalent to the radical opposition to the bourgeois conception of life in economic terms and social conformity in the early twentieth century. Kennedy sees in the tendency to the extreme and in the insistence on a moment of intensity of relations—both culminating in Schmitt's *The Concept of the Political* and *Politische Theologie* (*Political Theology*)—an equivalent to an expressionist aesthetic (cf. 250–251). In her view, Schmitt's understanding of political decision cannot be understood as a choice, but as the consequence of a metaphysical orientation (251). Schmitt's radical concepts are therefore inhabited by a moment that relates his work to an artistic context.

During the period when he was writing some of his most influential legal work, *Gesetz und Urteil* (*Statute and Judgment; 1912*), *Der Wert des Staates und die Bedeutung des Einzelnen* (*The Value of the State and the Significance of the Individual; 1917*), *Politische Romantik* (*Political Romanticism; 1923*), *Political Theology* (1922), and *Roman Catholicism and Political Form* (1923), he also published *Schattenrisse* (*Silhouettes; 1913*), *Theodor Däubler's "The Northern Light"* (1916), and "Die Buribunken" ("The Buribunks"; 1918), which are critical essays on cultural and literary topics. Although the legal philosopher focusing on questions of constitutional theory is his best known face, this is therefore at least partly the result of the light in which it has been cast.[7]

SCHATTENRISSE

The first of these writings, *Silhouettes*, was published under the pseudonym Johannes Negelinus.[8] It is a literary text Schmitt coauthored with his Jewish friend Fritz Eisler (cf. Mehring 2009, 2011). Whereas the authors of the letters used dog Latin to ridicule the scholarly world of Rome, Schmitt uses vulgar and hypertrophic language to caricature the culture of the early twentieth century (Villinger 1995, 131–132). This tone is already evident in the introduction, where the reader is addressed in what can only be read as exaggerated irony, interspersed with breaks in style: "The buckets of the present and the future are mounting and falling up and down (compare no. 7. In combination with no. 9), and the task is, to fill the soulless man of the mechanistic age with certainty, that the waves of culture are washing over us and that there is a time for everything" (Villinger 1995). He responds to the perceived nonsensical nature of contemporary politics, literature, and science with silhouettes whose black and white only reveals the sting of these portraits once the reader has deciphered a system of obscure references.

Preceding the introduction, for example, we find a systematic table, in which those portrayed are grouped as Suffering Germans, Loving Germans, Grinning Germans, Dead Germans, and Non-Germans. As Villinger shows in her commentary, the table references the eight-volume monograph *The Germans* by Moeller van den Bruck, a heavily judgmental series of portraits of representative figures of German history. Not only does Schmitt formulate a critique of some of the central figures—for example, the high value placed on the poet Richard Dehmel—he also criticizes the transfer of empirical psychological categories into historiography typical of the time (Villinger 1995, 149).

The work does not shy away from the German emperor himself; Wilhelm II is caricatured in the figure of Godfrey of Bouillon, a Frankish knight of the first crusade, whose presumed successes during the crusades had long been revealed as vastly exaggerated and who is used in contemporary satire to mock the colonial politics of Wilhelm II (Villinger 1995, 203–204): "The old warrior was sitting pensively in a lounge chair.... The old colonial fighter was miserable" (20). Seen by most interpreters as Schmitt's contribution to the "*Kulturkampf*," in which the Catholic legal scholar criticizes the culture of the empire and its literature, dominated by Prussian legal and scientific positivism, *Silhouettes* is recognized as an important step in the development of his writing and ideas.

Major traits of Schmitt's writing are emerging in this polemical and playful pamphlet: the strong contrasts turn the sketches into hyperbole, in which a system of values manifests itself. Through these portraits, the contours of the silhouettes are highlighted to the point where exemplarity and caricature become indistinguishable. Schmitt's critique draws on the reality it criticizes and establishes an intricate relationship to what it criticizes. The portraits are not arbitrary; rather, they create figurative types that can serve as a canvas for evaluative projections in an ongoing polemic.

DAS NORDLICHT

The most significant among these early writings is his study *Theodor Däubler's "The Northern Light*," published in 1916. If *Silhouettes* was a critique, *Theodor Däubler's "The Northern Light"* is a eulogy. It discusses Theodor Däubler's lyrical epic—an epic cycle consisting of rhymed poems in metric language—*Das Nordlicht (The Northern Light)*, whose three parts had first appeared in one volume in 1910 (see entry in *Kindler Neues Literatur Lexikon*, 1988–1991). The bilingual Däubler, born in 1876 in the Austro-Hungarian seaport Trieste to German parents, soon began an itinerant and productive life. The epic resulted from a period of several years spent roaming through Italy, and its publication brought Däubler considerable success in expressionist circles. In the 1920s his epics, poems, and literary criticism had established his moderate fame as a writer, manifest not only in literary prizes but also in the fact that he was president of the German PEN club. He died in 1934.

For Schmitt, Däubler represents a synthesis of European culture. Between the South and the North, the Latin and the German, Protestantism and Catholicism, his stature rises to historic proportions: "The entire beauty of the Mediterranean countries fills the soul of the man who is not only the epic poet of the European, but maybe also the first, in whom the longing for spiritual unity of the Occident has been fulfilled" (Schmitt 1916, 17). The largely forgotten oeuvre of the Italo-German writer had a considerable contemporary resonance, although he was never accepted as a major author of the period of literary modernism characterized by formal experimentation, from Dadaism and futurism to expressionism. It offers a mythical cosmogony that represents creation as a process reaching from the separation of sun and earth to their eventual reconciliation. The eponymous northern lights—according to "The Northern Light" the result of remnants of the sun in the form of lava in the depth of the earth—constitute the poem's central symbol. Through recurring images—the sun, the northern lights as final point of man's destiny, different cultural areas associated with specific stages of the sun's voyage, but also sounds that have a literal context from which they are dislocated—a symbolic dimension is established in which a spiritual significance emerges (entry in *Kindlers Neues Literatur Lexikon* 1988–1991).

The poem in three volumes represents the longing for a lost union that the end of the poem celebrates as an achievement of the spirit: "Tief überwunden sind des Zweifels Schemen: Die Welt versöhnt und übertönt der Geist" (Däubler 1910, 602). It has the formal structure of an astronomical figure, the ellipsis, and is held together through the experience of the persona of the poet, whose voice articulates the epic. It is he whom we follow in many different metamorphoses on his voyage through the Mediterranean in a first autobiographical part, as well as through the stages of human history in the second part of the poem, entitled "Sahara":

> I have now felt the world in me
> And slowly I consider what has happened;
> I could express myself to me
> As the creator to the creature, myself, in proximity
> *Ich habe jetzt die Welt in mir empfunden*
> *Und langsam überdenk ich, was geschah;*
> *Ich konnte mich, mir selber, klar bekunden,*
> *Ich war als Schöpfer mir Geschöpf ganz nah!*

(5)

As the third part, entitled "Pan-Orphic Intermezzo" (*Pan-Orphisches Intermezzo*), demonstrates, the poetic voice is identified with Orpheus and his search for Eurydice, a motif through which Däubler's epic becomes a quest for a poetic existence. The poem brings together ancient heritage and Christian modernity and culminates in the demand for a "new man." The superiority of the spirit manifests itself in the poet, who is conceived as a prophetic figure; he anticipates a possible reconciliation with the sun (Däubler 1910).[9]

As late as 1946, Schmitt claims Däubler had written "the epic of Europe" (*Ex Captivitate Salus*; Schmitt 2010, 46).[10] Looking back to 1910, he says that he "put himself into the service of Däubler's work" (51). Schmitt therefore establishes an authoritative figure as part of a counter-canon in which the seemingly untimely poet who is overshadowed by others emerges as the voice capturing his age. Literature is a place in which astute knowledge and a pertinent critique of the time is to be found. It is the unrecognized poet, as opposed to the mere writer, who reestablishes a spiritual authority.

The concrete influence of Däubler on Schmitt's work can be traced primarily in *The Value of the State and the Significance of the Individual* (1917), first published in 1914, a text that tries to argue for the irrelevance of the individual in relation to the state. It is important for the development of Schmitt's work, as it articulates the irreducible difference among power, state, and individual. Already the *exergon* "First is the command, the humans come later" ("*Zuerst ist das Gebot, die Menschen kommen später*"), a passage from *Das Nordlicht*, points to the importance of the poem. But its influence can also be traced throughout the study in crucial parts of the argument. One of the main theses of *The Value of the State and the Significance of the Individual* is that the law cannot be derived from any element outside itself, but rather emerges with the irreducible positioning of a norm. The central insight is presented as an intuition:

> "Eternity does not overtake itself on its ladder." (Däubler, *Das Nordlicht II*, S. 533.) Law cannot be deduced from the contemplation of nature, to which the living together of humans belongs, as far as it is merely a matter of the explanatory social sciences. Only the positing of a norm, and not nature, lays the foundation for the difference between law and unlawfulness. The sun is shining on the just as well as on the unjust. (Schmitt 1917, 31)

In the second passage, Däubler's portrait of the hasty, self-absorbed individual is quoted as the figure representing man before the foundational moment of the state:

> Because he who contemplates people—individually or on their mass—with a discerning gaze and sees how they only try to "hastily secure their individual happiness" (Däubler), will be moved that it was possible to bring an order into these wildly diverging interests. (84)

The third passage quotes the poem's derogatory designation of those incapable of transcending the world of duty by devoting themselves to a great cause—and therefore the lack of ethos—in order to criticize a view in which concrete institutions are confused with the state as a task:

> What is contemptible about the servile pettiness and pedantry of the "duty-gnomes" (Däubler), is the inability to devote themselves completely to a cause, the inability to abstraction and the confusion of what is here called a cause with the "office holding authority" and the concrete humans that are its organs. (92)

Here, as in *Theodor Däubler's "The Northern Light"*, Schmitt emphasizes the remarks on legal philosophy that ornament the "Iranian Rhapsody," a central part of the poem describing the foundation of the first state as the result of the realization of class distinctions by the farmers we see tilling the ground in the beginning of the part. When they encounter a foreign class of priests, the state results. It is here that Schmitt quotes the passage about the primacy of the command used in the *exergon* of *The Value of the State and the Significance of the Individual* as a "remarkable intuition":

> A surprising philosophic and historic intuition gives us the material for the colossal edifice. The deepest problem of legal and state philosophy is articulated clearly.... But the essential is, that an image is shown in response to the question about the state, the law, money...: the construction of the Persian castle in the "Iranian Rhepsody." The composition of this event gives a good example of this way of thinking and of seeing. (Schmitt 1916, 30)

The second sentence from the poem quoted here, which is the same he quoted in the *exergon* mentioned above—"An element, not a command produces legal moments" ("*Ein Element, nicht ein Gebot schafft Rechtsmomente*")—can be understood as an anticipation of Schmitt's attempt to understand the foundation of the law as related to the act of tilling and inhabiting a particular element, the land, in his late writings, especially in *Land und Meer* (*Land and Sea*), but also in *The "Nomos" of the Earth*.

Thus on the other hand we find in the poem a narration that embeds human history in a cosmogony and a mythopoetic quality that lays out parameters for an understanding of central trajectories of Schmitt's oeuvre. Much of his later work can be understood as an elaboration of aspects of Däubler's work and therefore as a part of the exemplary status of the poem and of literature as such. By articulating a symbolic dimension and elaborating into mythological narrative, the poem becomes an active force.

Beyond these thematic elements, the image is a central dimension. As we have seen, the "*Unbildlichkeit*" is a central feature of modernity for Schmitt. And alongside the institution of the Catholic Church, poetry is a source of imaging the world. Schmitt's characterization of Däubler dwells on the fact that not only is the poet an heir of hundreds of years of living Latin culture, but also his poetry is endowed with a "mythopoetic" force: "But the decisive fact is the power to the image" ("*Aber das Entscheidende ist die Kraft zum Bild*"; Schmitt 1916, 25). The force to create an image is the condition for the emergence of myth—an elaboration of a world of images that become symbols and carry a second meaning. The Ararat, for example, receives its value from its relation to the pyramid (29). The pyramid emerges as the symbol of the first period after the earth emerges from the floods and the sun reveals itself for the first time as the god of the sun, Ra. The mountain range of the Ararat, known in Indian and Iranian sources, is a counterweight to the dead grave of the pyramid. Humanity falls into it after the end of the period, but this grave entails the possibility of rebirth.

The force of the image shows not merely in the poem's narrative inventiveness; rather, it is a formal feature of the cycle of poems that Schmitt understands as a new development in the traditional framework of *ut pictura poiesis*. Based on a misinterpretation of Horace's equation of image and poetry, the phrase became a normative formula and emerged since late antiquity as a demand that literary representation should be pictorial, influencing both the concept of ekphrastic literature as well as allegorical and emblematic genres (see entry *ut pictura poiesis* in *Metzler Lexikon Literatur* 2007).

According to Schmitt, the thoughts in the poem have become images, whose relation has "the irrational rhythmicity of a painting or a symphony" rather than "following discursive-systematic rules." Schmitt continues:

> The path, on which the artistic transcendence of the enormous philosophic and cultural material is achieved appears to be the following: a process that has been experienced with acute intensity of vision is transformed at the moment of the experience into a painting and only then composed into poetry. In this way, an evolution of images emerges, a new, unparalleled pictura poiesis. (38)

This "artistic representation of second order" distinguishes itself from the understanding of the Horacian formula that Lessing develops in his commentary on Homer's description of Achilles's shield in his *Laocoon*:

> A lot remains incomprehensible if the tempo is not met.... In this way the misunderstanding is excluded, that the pictura poiesis discussed here has anything to do with the tiring enumeration of the details of an occurrence the way Lessing envisaged it. (Schmitt 1916, 42)

But what for Schmitt is truly exorbitant about Däubler's poems is their transformation of language. While Schmitt sees everyday language determined by a pragmatic purpose, and communication is used to create a utilitarian community, it is precisely this sociological dimension of language that disqualifies it as a medium for myth: "It is not possible to compose a myth in everyday language, not even a beautiful poem" (45).

As the use of the sound "Ra," also the name of an Egyptian god, exemplifies, Däubler's poem transcends for Schmitt the "naturalism" of everyday language: "Language entirely becomes an aesthetic medium without regard to the associations the same words carry with them in daily conversation" (45–46). The sound enters into manifold alliterations and assonances throughout the text that release the sign from the burden of instrumentality. Schmitt does not fail to see that Däubler does violence to language, and he also admits that the poetry inhabits a realm beyond a contemporary addressee with his standards of taste. But he insists that the language of these poems is not an ornament in the rhetorical sense, but rather "the essence of language" (50).

The proximity of these reflections on language to Walter Benjamin's philosophy has often been emphasized (see, e.g., Heil 1996, 164). In his "On Language as Such and the Language of Man" (1916), Benjamin claimed to unearth in language a metaphysical dimension expressing the essence of beings that has no relation to the spoken word (see, e.g., Menninghaus 1995). What Schmitt and Benjamin share is the sense that language does not exhaust itself in its instrumental function. While they are a part of the same discursive segment, the decisive contrast between them seems to be the role that imagination and the image plays in Schmitt. However, the status of the mediality in Schmitt is, as Heil points out, contradictory: on the one hand he claims "that here the word has become a medium of artistic vision" (Heil 1996, 49); on the other hand he claims the same language leaves mediality behind: "The depths of the world and of the soul reveal themselves in such words—in a language that has abandoned its medial character [*Mittelbarkeit*] in order to exclusively be the container [*Gefäß*] of wonderful images and thoughts" (55).

Schmitt is well aware of the fact that he is speaking about "contradictions" here. However, they are what characterizes faith. The artistic vision and its expression is, as he says, a gnosis related to the *visio dei* and does not belong to the same order. By the same token, he sees, in *Roman Catholicism and Political Form*, an institution that can assemble the contradictions of his time in Catholicism. In the above-mentioned passage, therefore, "container" is not of the same order as "medium." They are separated by the "leap into the metaphysical" ("*Sprung ins Metaphysische*"; 50): while the poet articulates his images in a language that serves him as a medium, the words are turned into a container for a symbolic meaning severed from communicative meaning. In the following passage, quoted by Schmitt, the relationship between language and processes of sound are indicated through the image of birds that are equated with rhythms. These rhythms are a part of a cosmogonic narrative in which they are a part of a spiritual journey:

> Suddenly infinite wings flap unbound
> The language of the Indians, full of glory, apart
> The feathers of the animal are rhythms, that sound
> *Da schlagen auf einmal unendliche Schwingen,*
> *Die Sprache der Inder, voll pracht auseinander:*
> *Die Federn des Tieres sind Rhythmen, die klingen*
>
> (Däubler 1910, II, 238)

In Schmitt's view, what gives Däubler's poetry its relevance and actuality is that it stands at a normative distance from the present moment, which Schmitt characterizes as a civilized yet empty bourgeois society, a society of circulation, technique, and organization, a "Betrieb" devoid of spirit in which means dominate ends (see 1916, 63–65). Däubler's poetry compensates its time: "It is as deep as the time is flat, as great as the time is small…the compensation of the age of spiritlessness; more than a timely book: the book of the aeon. It counterbalances the mechanistic age" (69). As such, it represents a "portendum"—a Ciceronian term that means "leading sign" or "miraculous sign": "the actuality is based on the relation to the innermost essence of time, whose grandiose negation this work represents" (70). *Portendum* also has the meaning of fantastic idea.

For Schmitt, Däubler's poem contrasts with the shallow contemporary literature he ironizes in his *Silhouettes*: rather than criticizing the contemporary world, it establishes a poem in which doubt is overcome and a mechanistic time finds its counterbalance as the source of authority and inspiration for the legal scholar and public intellectual. And it opens a trajectory on which Schmitt will continue his investigation of myth as a political force, from *The Crisis of Parliamentary Democracy* to *Der Leviathan in der Staatslehre des Thomas Hobbes* (*The Leviathan in the State Theory of Thomas Hobbes*). As the example of the leviathan will show, it is not a "visualization of a thought," but a "mythical symbol": "In the long history of political theories, a history exceedingly rich in colorful images and symbols, icons and idols, paradigms and phantasms, emblems and allegories, this leviathan is the strongest and most powerful image. It shatters the framework of every conceivable theory or construct" (Schmitt 1996a, 5). One can see in this early book of literary criticism the germ not only of Schmitt's legal philosophy of the same period, but beyond that, the central features and concerns of his entire oeuvre. Literature is attributed prophetic power, and the poet becomes a source not only of inspiration but also—and crucially—one of authority for the philosopher. And although Schmitt changes his view of the figures that accompany his intellectual biography, he remains faithful to them, as though he took on their mission. While much of the book—from the *ut pictura poiesis* debate to the discussion of Malfatti's Romantic use of the northern lights as a scientific and poetic fact—is written in the tone of a contribution to literary criticism, and therefore to an expert discussion, its existential tone, the persuasive power it attributes to values inherent in the poem, as well as its insistence on a different notion of literature and a counter-canon account for its role of exemplum.

SYNERGEIA VERSUS IDENTIFICATION: *HAMLET OR HECUBA*

Schmitt's second major contribution to literary criticism, *Hamlet or Hecuba*, published in 1956, is devoted to the question of how one of the three modern European myths, Hamlet, emerged. Alongside Don Quixote and Faust, Schmitt sees in the Shakespearean hero Hamlet a character in whose life the political destiny of modern Europe is expressed. But what is the lesson of *Hamlet*? Schmitt gives a surprising answer: literature can authorize action in the name of one's own destiny, for values that are not those offered in the immediate context, available for identification. In a reading that inscribes itself in a long textual tradition in which acting the role of Hecuba allows the reflection on identification and representation, Schmitt discovers in the play a reflection on the difference between acting in the name of one's duty and identifying with someone else's case.

Schmitt's reading of Shakespeare's drama *Hamlet* claims that the structure of the play that enables it to rise to the status of a myth is determined by its inability to mirror the political situation during which it was produced. Toward the end of her life, the pre-occupation with the childless Queen Elizabeth's succession gained particular urgency. It is during this time that Shakespeare was writing and performing *Hamlet*. He sup-ported the most apt successor, the Scottish king James I, whose great-grandmother was a daughter of Charles VII of England. But James's mother's lover, the Earl of Bothwell, had killed his father, Lord Darnley, and married his mother soon thereafter. Elizabeth in turn killed Mary Stuart.

It is the similarity to the taboo of the succession in the real political situation that, according to Schmitt, turns Hamlet into an inhibited and hesitant character. Schmitt describes this scenario as a "concrete situation" (2009, 18) or alternatively as the "real-istic core [*Wirklichkeitskern*] of most intense contemporary significance and timeli-ness" (43–44). The power that transforms *Hamlet* into a myth is, according to Schmitt, derived from the interaction between the play and this concrete, real situation that is present in the dramatic form, through what he calls "shadows" or "dark areas" (43–44). The irresolvable puzzles where the play leaves its meaning open—especially the guilt of the queen and the deformation of the figure of the avenger who becomes inhibited—are structurally open to the "intrusions" of the political reality into the sphere of the play (see also David Pan in this volume).

The scene preceding the mousetrap section in Shakespeare's play *Hamlet* (2000) is the crucial scene for Schmitt's interpretation. It is here that Hamlet realizes his situa-tion in an experience of difference to an actor. In the scene, Hamlet instructs the actors while they probe their art. Seeing the actor cry when he plays Hecuba, the Trojan king Priam's wife—she has seen her husband be dismembered and killed after the Achaians conquered Troy—Hamlet says:

> Tears in his eyes, distraction in his aspect,
> A broken voice, and his whole function suiting
> With forms to his conceit? And all for nothing!
> For Hecuba?
> What's Hecuba to him, or he to Hecuba,
> That he should weep for her? What would he do,
> Had he the motive and the cue for passion
> That I have?
>
> (Hamlet II.2)

In contrast to the assumption that the spectator is involved in the plot on stage that moves him to action, Schmitt reads in Hamlet's realization a disjunction between the literary experience of identification and a political decision: "Hamlet, however, does not weep for Hecuba. He is somewhat astonished to learn that there are people who, in the performance of their duties, weep over something that does not concern them in the least and has no impact on their actual existence and situation. Hamlet uses this knowledge to sternly reproach himself, to focus upon his own situation, and to compel himself to action and the fulfillment of his vow of vengeance" (Schmitt 2009, 45). In the above passage from act II, scene 2, it is clear what effect the play in the play has: Hamlet does not identify with the actor, nor does he identify with Hecuba. Instead, the crying of the actor motivates him to act in the name of his father's ghost and his own succession.[11]

The play restores the motivation to act, although it needs to respect the taboo of revenge and the guilt it cannot represent. The literary is therefore politically effective to the degree that it induces the ability to act through a difference with itself—or at least with literary reception understood as identification. Hamlet does not decide to do what virtue and reason ask him to do; instead, he realizes that what he is asked to do is different from what the scene on stage represents. Literature therefore provides a lesson on how to assume an ethos that is one's own. It authorizes and enables one to speak in the name of succession and a ghost, one's ideals, in a world in which "feeling with" threatens the ability to assume the burden of a political mission.

The scene in *Hamlet* inscribes itself in a tradition in which Hecuba stands for the impact of literature on the political. In Plato's early dialogue *Ion*, which questions the form and validity of the rhapsode's knowledge, the story of Hecuba and Priam is one of the exemplary constellations that present the rhapsode's work as a reenactment of literary scenes that invite the audience to share a certain form of madness:

> Soc. When you recite lines well and astonish the spectators, when you sing of Odysseus leaping onto the threshold and revealing himself to the suitors and pouring out the arrows at his feet, or of Achilles rushing at Hector, or something pitiful about Andromache or Hecuba and Priam—are you then in your right mind, or outside yourself? Does your soul, inspired, suppose you're in the midst the doings you describe in Ithaca or Troy, or wherever the lines have it?

> Ion. How clear to me is the proof you give, Socrates—for I'll tell you without concealment. When I say something pitiable, my eyes brim with tears, and when I say something fearful or terrible, my hair stands straight on end for fear and my heart pounds. (Plato 1998, 14–15)

Besides Andromache, who loses her husband, Hector, as well as her son, Astyanax—the first killed by Achilles, the second thrown off the wall in his mother's presence when Troy is conquered—Hecuba and her husband Priam are presented as the second theme that arouses pity and leads to the abandonment of one's identity in a collective mimetic process that endangers the polis.

However, the scene of the weeping actor also plays an important role in the tradition of juridical rhetoric. Here, it forms an integral part of the discussion of the tropes of visualization known as *evidentia* or *enargeia*. To represent something as if it was happening under one's eyes creates the impression that we are eyewitnesses to the scene and therefore to intense affective reactions. In order to achieve this effect on the audience, the legal representative is asked to take on the destiny of his client as if it were his own—a significant feature of rhetoric introduced into the tradition by Cicero, the major force behind the flourishing of Roman rhetoric as well as the Roman language in the first century BC.

In what constitutes the most prominent sum of rhetorical knowledge in antiquity, Marcus Fabius Quintilianus writes about this form of identification with explicit reference to Cicero:

> In this way we would say what we would say if the same had happened to us. I have frequently seen that actors and comedians, taking off their mask after a serious performance, were still crying when they stepped off the stage. But if, at the occasion of plays written by others, the representation through invented affects brings about such movement, what will we do, who have to contemplate how we can bring ourselves to be affected as if we were ourselves those threatened by the case. (Quintilianus 1997, VI.2, 35)

The *synergeia* or advocacy (see Campe 2008) that constitutes a central function of legal rhetoric and at the same time lies at the foundation of the profession of the rhetorician requires a technique of identification that exceeds the actor's achievement. The question "What will we do?" asks for the difference between professional advocacy in a juridical setting where something is at stake, on the one hand, and the identification with fictitious figures in a plot, on the other. And while emotions abound in the actor, the rhetorician requires a specific technique.

It is difficult not to read Shakespeare's mousetrap scene, and in this trajectory Schmitt's *Hamlet or Hecuba*, as an elaboration on this passage in Quintilian. Whereas the rhetorical tradition quotes the example of the actor in the context of the representation of a defendant, Schmitt's reading follows Shakespeare and turns the comparison into one between the actor assuming Hecuba's role and Hamlet, who on the level of the plot becomes aware of the difference between the affect of fiction and the implications action has in a real conflict.

If literary criticism—and Schmitt's book is a book of criticism in thematic as well as in formal respects—is for Schmitt a question of the exemplum and an exemplary function of literature, then what this exemplum teaches here is a lesson on the limits of rhetoric. It is a double lesson and a double limit: on the one hand, it teaches that the political dimension is located beyond identification and maybe even beyond the social as such. It is the "real case" that insists on tragic representation and myth but that cannot be arbitrarily reproduced and provoked. It is the measure compared to which everything else pales. And on the other hand, this limit or this lesson is only available in a reading "that transgresses the limits of Rhetoric," as Aristotle writes.

CONCLUSION

In more than one sense, Carl Schmitt's relationship to rhetoric is unique among his contemporaries. Due to his insistence on understanding history as a process in which a metaphysical dimension is at stake, his work is animated by an urgency that wants to transcend the narrow boundaries of academic discourse. His oeuvre is rhetorical to the degree that it defines itself as a voice in a polemic. It is out of this momentum that the Catholic Church and its grand rhetoric becomes a model that—although not emulated—allows Schmitt to rethink the relationship between institution and language.

The reflection on rhetorical knowledge invites an elucidation of a rhetorical dimension of Schmitt's texts. Topologies, that is, architectures of commonplaces, can be identified as a key concern of Schmitt's thought; his attempt to redefine the viewpoints that allow the construction of arguments in particular fields is evident in the case of *The Concept of the Political*, where the definition of a field is at stake, but it is also manifest in many if not all key texts. Topoi are also a fruitful way to configure the relation between the texts and the existential political situation at the heart of Schmitt's oeuvre. Which categories and types of arguments are adequate to think a new situation—and by definition historical situations are always new. In spite of his insistence on conceptual classicism or legal traditionalism, we have come to know Schmitt as an iconoclast who is willing to set aside traditional conceptual partitions such as monarchy, oligarchy, and democracy in the name of the present situation. These displacements of topologies are a core feature of his major work. And they are the point that guarantees its efficacy. Their nonarbitrary nature grounds his criticism of traditional conceptualization as well as his innovation in the service of a new existential conceptualization. That he believes he is able to anchor normativity in an existing topology shows how crucial the problem of rethinking reference and language in Schmitt is.

But what might constitute the most surprising viewpoint gained through a rhetorical perspective is the one on Schmitt's writings that are considered literary criticism. His book on Däubler's epic poem *The Northern Light* establishes the poet as an authoritative source; it draws on the poem to elaborate key insights of his legal work. Crucially, it is here that we find the first systematic reflection on symbol, image, and myth that will become key terms in his later thinking. And in *Hamlet or Hecuba*, Schmitt interprets Shakespeare's drama *Hamlet* as a reflection of the question Ciceronian rhetoric asks about identification and legal representation as an "acting in the name of." If the etymological origin of drama is the Greek word for "to act," *dramein*, then Schmitt's reading asks the question of action and of the difference between acting in one's own name and in one's own political reality versus acting in the name and reality of someone else. It is literature that provides Schmitt with an exemplary dimension in more than one sense; it is a proof as well as a paradigm for rhetorical style and a model for an ethos. As such, literature provides Schmitt with the necessary authority for his normative stances and his work. His critical writing can be seen as a series of studies in rhetoric, and a specific form of literature appears as the dimension from which his work emerges.

The Aristotelian distinction between *topoi coinoi* and *topoi idioi*, between common-places and special places, general assumptions and specific knowledge, constitutes a tension constitutive of Schmitt's oeuvre. In spite of their specialized nature as contributions to constitutional theory or literary criticism, his works are located at the limit of rhetoric. It is from this porous line that it still speaks to us.

NOTES

1. Unless noted otherwise, all translations of source material by the author.
2. I thank Hélène Merlin-Kajman for enriching my knowledge of this context.
3. Most famously by Hans Blumenberg 1988 (99–101).
4. The last decade has seen not only a renewed interest in Schmitt scholarship, but also the reemergence of Schmitt as a major interpreter of a contemporary reality. If his *Theory of the Partisan* is quoted in the context of reflections on terrorism, or if the return of the distinction between friend and enemy is diagnosed or lamented as it becomes visible in the erosion of international institutions, his conceptual suggestions return. And in spite of the fact that Schmitt is writing on historically specific topics such as the Weimar Constitution, the present recognizes that his scenarios are still relevant in spite of their emergence in the context of polemics, or rather, because of their emergence in a polemical context, Schmitt's conceptual suggestions delineate constellations we have not left behind. Friedrich Balke attributes to this relevance a symptomatic value (see Balke 1996, *Vorwort*).
5. Marcus Fabius Quintinlianus 1997.
6. See the excellent summary in Meuter 1994 (11–13), on which I draw here.
7. The relation between cultural criticism and legal scholarship through which Schmitt's work appears as an interdisciplinary endeavor par excellence has received different historical interpretations, from Heinrich Muth's understanding of the author as an "homme de lettre" to Ernst-Wolfgang Böckenförde's assumption that the Catholic position in the contemporary culture wars is a "key impetus" of his work (cf. Villinger 1995, 132–133). Such approaches, however, enclose Schmitt's work in the period of its origin—a task facilitated by the fact of his proximity to the Nazi regime that has earned him the title "crown jurist of the Third Reich." This shadow introduces an irrevocable historical and normative distance to a thinker whose main characteristic is an emphasis on actuality. If the status of Carl Schmitt's work as a classical text is still debated, it is largely due to this distance.
8. Magister Negelinus is the fictitious author of letter 18 in a series of letters entitled *Epistolae obscurorum*, written by Johannes Reuchlin and Ulrich von Hutten in 1515 to criticize contemporary scholasticism (Villinger 1995, introduction).
9. Däubler's poem thus is also an integral part of the contemporary debates around the figure of "*Der neue Mensch*" ("The New Man") manifesting itself as a major tendency, from Freundlich's 1912 sculpture *Großer Kopf* (Large Head) to Ernst Toller's Drama *Die Wandlung*, and the expressionist anthology of poems entitled *Menschheitsdämmerung*.
10. He now also reproaches himself for having misunderstood Däubler to be a Christian author, whereas his work really is the expression of a "poetic pantheism" (Schmitt 2010, 48). Another poet, Konrad Weiß, has become Schmitt's guide.

11. This is the argument of my reading of *Hamlet or Hecuba* in "The Intrusion: Carl Schmitt's Non-Mimetic Logic of Art" (Türk 2008).

References

Aristotle. 2000. *Art of Rhetoric*. Cambridge: Harvard University Press.

Balke, F. 1996. *Der Staat nach seinem Ende: Die Versuchung Carl Schmitts*. Munich: Fink.

Blumenberg, H. 1988. *Die Legitimität der Neuzeit*. Frankfurt: Suhrkamp.

Burdorf, D. and C. Fasbender. eds. 2007. *Metzler Lexikon Literatur: Begriffe und Definitionen*. Stuttgart: Metzler.

Campe, R. 2008. "An Outline for a Critical History of *Fürspache: Synegoria* and Advocacy." *Deutsche Vierteljahrsschrift für Literaturwissenschaft und Geistesgeschichte* 82: 355–381.

Curtius, E. R. 1990. *European Literature and Latin Middle Ages*. Princeton: Princeton University Press.

Däubler, T. 1910. *Das Nordlicht*. Leipzig: Müller.

Groh, R. 1998. *Arbeit an der Heillosigkeit der Welt. Zur politisch-theologischen Mythologie und Anthropologie Carl Schmitts*. Frankfurt: Suhrkamp.

Hammer, P. 2006. "Royal Marriage and the Royal Succession." In *A Concise Companion to English Renaissance Literature*, ed. D. B. Hamilton. Malden: Blackwell, 54–74.

Heil, S. 1996. *Gefährliche Beziehungen: Walter Benjamin und Carl Schmitt*. Stuttgart: Metzler.

Jens, W. ed. 1988–1991. *Kindlers Neues Literaturlexikon*. Munich: Kindler.

Kahn, V. 2003. "Hamlet or Hecuba: Carl Schmitt's Decision." *Representations* 83: 67–96.

Kennedy, E. 1988. "Carl Schmitt und Hugo Ball: Ein Beitrag zum Thema 'politischer Expressionismus.'" *Zeitschrift für Politik* 35: 143–162.

Mehring, R. 2009. *Die Hamburger Verlegerfamilie Eisler und Carl Schmitt*. Plettenberg: Carl-Schmitt-Gesellschaft.

Mehring, R. 2011. *Carl Schmitt zur Einführung*. Hamburg: Junius.

Menninghaus, W. 1995. *Walter Benjamins Theorie der Sprachmagie*. Frankfurt: Suhrkamp.

Meuter, G. 1994. *Der Katechon: Zu Carl Schmitts fundamentalistischer Kritik der Zeit*. Berlin: Duncker & Humblot.

Plato. 1998. *Ion*, trans. R. E. Allen. New Haven: Yale University Press.

Quintilianus, M. F. 1997. *Ausbildung des Redners*, trans. and ed. H. Rahn. Darmstadt: Wissenschaftliche Buchgesellschaft.

Rasch, W. 2004. "The Emergence of Legal Norms." *Cultural Critique* 57: 93–103.

Schmitt, C. 1917. *Der Wert des Staates und die Bedeutung des Einzelnen*. Hellerau: Hellerauer Verlag.

Schmitt, C. 1916. *Theodor Däublers "Nordlicht": Drei Studien über die Elemente, den Geist und die Aktualität des Werkes*. Munich: Müller.

Schmitt, C. 1918. "Die Buribunken: Ein geschichtsphilosophischer Versuch." *Summa* 4: 89–106.

Schmitt, C. 1955. "Die geschichtliche Struktur des heutigen Welt-Gegensatzes von Ost und West: Bemerkungen zu Ernst Jüngers Schrift 'Der gordische Knoten.'" In *Freundschaftliche Begegnungen: Festschrift für Ernst Jünger zum 60. Geburtstag*, ed. A. Mohler. Frankfurt: Klosterman, 93–107.

Schmitt, C. 1959. "Nomos—Nahme—Name." In *Der Beständige Aufbruch: Festschrift für Erich Przywara*, ed. S. Behn. Nuremberg: Gock und Lutz, 93–105.

Schmitt, C. 1976. *Concept of the Political*, trans. G. Schwab. New Brunswick: Rutgers University Press.

Schmitt, C. 1985. *The Crisis of Parliamentary Democracy*, trans. E. Kennedy. Cambridge: MIT Press.

Schmitt, C. 1986. *Political Romanticism*. Cambridge: MIT Press.

Schmitt, C. 1996a. *The Leviathan in the State Theory of Thomas Hobbes*, trans. G. Schwab. Westport: Greenwood Press.

Schmitt, C. 1996b. *Roman Catholicism and Political Form*, trans. G. L. Ulmen. Westport: Greenwood Press.

Schmitt, C. 2002. *Der Begriff des Politischen*. Berlin: Duncker & Humblot.

Schmitt, C. 2004a. *Legality and Legitimacy*, trans. J. Seitzer. Durham: Duke University Press.

Schmitt, C. 2004b. *On the Three Types of Juristic Thought*, trans. J. W. Bendersky. Westport: Praeger.

Schmitt, C. 2007. *Theory of the Partisan*, trans. G. L. Ulmen. New York: Telos Press.

Schmitt, C. 2008. *Constitutional Theory*. Durham: Duke University Press.

Schmitt, C. 2009. *Hamlet or Hecuba*, trans. D. Pan and J. Rust. New York: Telos Press.

Schmitt, C. 2010. *Ex Captivitate Salus*. Berlin: Duncker & Humblot.

Schmitt, C. 2011. "Forms of Modern Imperialism in International Law," trans. M. Hannah. In *Spatiality, Sovereignty and Carl Schmitt*, ed. S. Legg. London: Routledge, 29–45.

Shakespeare, W. 2000. *Hamlet*. The Arden Shakespeare. London: Thomson Learning.

Shuger, D. K. 1984. "The Grand Style and the 'Genera Dicendi' in Ancient Rhetoric." *Traditio* 40: 1–42.

Türk, J. 2008. "The Intrusion: Carl Schmitt's Non-Mimetic Logic of Art." *Telos* 142: 73–89.

Villinger, I. 1995. *Carl Schmitts Kulturkritik der Moderne: Text, Kommentar, und Analyse der Schattenrisse des Johannes Negelius*. Berlin: Akademie Verlag.

Virno, P. 2004. *A Grammar of the Multitude: For an Analysis of Contemporary Forms of Life*. Los Angeles: Semiotext(e).

....

CHAPTER 30

CARL SCHMITT'S
SPATIAL RHETORIC

....

OLIVER SIMONS

INTRODUCTION

BY THE end of the 1930s, space (*Raum*) had become a key term in the writings of Carl Schmitt. His essay "The Spatial Revolution: From Total War to Total Peace" appeared in the journal *Das Reich* in 1940 (1995f), "The *Großraum* Order of the International Law with a Ban on Intervention for Spatially Foreign Powers" (2011) followed in 1941. His article "Spatial Revolution: On the Spirit of the Western World" (1942) and *Land and Sea* (1997a; 2001) were published in 1942 and *The "Nomos" of the Earth in the International Law of the "Jus Publicum Europaeum"* (1997b; 2006a) in 1950, although Schmitt composed the majority of the latter text during the final year of the war. Space was not just one of the most popular terms of this period; it was also a multifaceted and incongruous concept. In the aforementioned titles alone, Schmitt associated space with war, international law, the history of ideas, and a narrative about the elements land and sea.

The appearance of space in such varying contexts is especially noteworthy since Schmitt repeatedly bemoaned the multitude of spatial concepts in circulation. Discussions about space were ubiquitous, Schmitt wrote, but determining what space actually *was* posed a serious conceptual challenge: "When asked, the scientists would reply that mathematical space is entirely different from the space of an electro-magnetic field and the latter in turn is completely different from the space as it is understood in psychology or in biology. That gives us half a dozen notions of space! There is no conceptual unity" (1997a, 28–29; 2001, 56). A bona fide science of space did not exist.[1]

How did Schmitt respond to this lack of conceptual unity? And what was the function of space in his writings toward the end of the 1930s? In this chapter I argue that space was not merely a subject matter or theme during this phase of his career; rather, I contend, it is linked to a rhetorical strategy and mode of argumentation that manifested itself most markedly in *Land and Sea* and *The "Nomos" of the Earth*. In each of these texts, Schmitt developed a distinctive spatial rhetoric and argumentation: *Land and Sea* belongs to a genre that Schmitt himself described as a "tale," a narrative, as it were, whereas *The "Nomos" of the Earth* is more concerned with conceptual definitions. The first two sections of this chapter discuss these two texts and their respective modes of argumentation in greater detail and show that Schmitt's selection of these genres was inextricably intertwined with his theory of space. In contrast to the recent spate of scholarship devoted to space and Schmitt (see, among others, Hooker 2009; Elden 2011; Minca and Rowan 2015a, 2015b), the focus of this chapter is the close relationship between Schmitt's spatial thought and the poetics of his writing. Both texts employ different, perhaps even incongruous genres. At the same time, grasping the logics of these modes of argumentation is crucial not only for understanding Schmitt's spatial theory but also for appreciating both texts' gestation. Because their modes of argumentation are so dissimilar, they can both be read as responses to a specific epistemological context. Juxtaposing *Land and Sea* to *The "Nomos" of the Earth* makes Schmitt's ambivalence toward the proliferation of spatial concepts comprehensible.

The final section of this chapter reconstructs this epistemic context. But instead of recapitulating the manifold influences on Schmitt or situating him among his contemporaries, that section views his spatial thought through the lens of more recent debates. The ongoing renaissance of Schmitt's writings can be most clearly observed in the appropriation of his spatial theory. But as we shall see, these appropriations are not always mindful of the historical difference between Schmitt's epistemological context and ours. Since the September 11, 2001, terrorist attacks, his theory of the state of exception has been frequently invoked. His concept of *nomos* also strikes some as an apt tool for comprehending the changing international system. Can we read *The "Nomos" of the Earth* as an introductory manual for a new world order?[2] How up to date is Schmitt's theory of space, and how salient has it been for contemporary discussions of space in the humanities? Was he a forerunner of the so-called *spatial turn*, as some have surmised (Mendieta 2011, 265)?

Giorgio Agamben's reflections on Schmitt's "topology" and the collaborative work *A Thousand Plateaus* by Gilles Deleuze and Felix Guattari serve as exemplary case studies in the final section. Both represent recent—and influential—reconfigurations of Schmitt's spatial thought. My analysis of their work demonstrates how and why they have appropriated Schmitt and points to major differences between Schmitt's theoretical perspective on space and Deleuze and Guattari's own spatial thought. The analytical distance between Schmitt and more recent theories is considerable. Schmitt's spatial theory, I contend, is deeply rooted in the epistemology of the early twentieth century, a peculiar intellectual soil from which it cannot be easily transplanted.

LAND AND SEA: SCHMITT AS NARRATOR

Some readers have referred to *Land and Sea: A World-Historical Reflection* as Schmitt's most poetic text (Köster 2002, 225; Mendieta 2011, 264), as one of his finest works (Quaritsch 1988, 113), or even, as Nikolaus Sombart wrote in his memoirs, as Schmitt's most beautiful and important book (Sombart 1984, 255). According to Sombart, *Land and Sea* is a "romantic fairy tale," and indeed, the genre of the text is surprising. As Schmitt observed in the dedication, he "told" (*"erzählt[e]"*) the short work to his daughter Anima, a point that he emphasized. In *Land and Sea* Schmitt combined his interest in symbols and images with a striking pleasure in his own imagination. Sombart interprets the dedication as a turning point in Schmitt's life, portraying him as having left solid ground to venture out on the open sea (1984, 255–257). But if the narrative constitutes a distinct change in Schmitt's mode of writing, perhaps even a "turn" (Quaritsch 1988, 113), how did this new genre inform his position as a thinker? Scholars seem to agree that Schmitt changed from a "combatant" into a "spectator" (113), that he substituted defensive interpretations for aggressive interventions (van Laak 2002, 28) and became eschatological during this period. Did this "esoteric move" merely obscure an "elemental determinism" (Hooker 2009, 70, 82)? And was this alternative form of exposition really less engaged than his political theory, possibly even devoid of ideology and politics (Kearns 2011, 80)?[3] In the next section I argue the contrary: Schmitt's spatial thought *is* part of his political theory, his spatial rhetoric nothing other than a political intervention.

Mythical Force: From *Leviathan* to *Land and Sea*

In spite of its brevity, *Land and Sea* contains many references to literary sources. Schmitt cited not only "myths and legends" of the earth that describe it as a "primal mother" (1997a, 1; 2001, 7), but also Goethe, Thales of Miletus, Heraclitus, Job, the Kabbalah, Heinrich Heine, and Herman Melville, among others. Schmitt drew from an entire archive of myths and literature, thus underlining the significance of his book for a cultural history of land and sea. And he also returned to some of his earlier works, his *Leviathan* in particular. This book from 1938 was a metareflection on symbols and metaphors in their relation to the political, a reflection that Schmitt appropriated and refined in *Land and Sea*.

The image of the leviathan, Schmitt wrote, is a "mythical symbol fraught with inscrutable meaning" and more than a mere visualization or illustration (2008a, 4; 2003, 9). He argued that the symbolic dimension of the leviathan is not subordinate to the political; the former is a condition of the latter, because a distinction between political and aesthetic discourses is ultimately impossible. This is precisely what Hobbes failed to recognize according to Schmitt, when he reduced the leviathan to a mere metaphor, a secondary representation arbitrarily related to its meaning.[4] Following the disappearance of the leviathan's biblical meaning as an adversary of the behemoth, the monster of the land, the political symbol also lost its unity. According to Schmitt, Hobbes's political theory was thus based on nothing more than an empty form. Instead of defining the state by its content, he conceived of it merely as a territory with arbitrary borders that imparted little to no shape or uniformity to the political entity. In the empty form of the state, the "soul of a people" (2008a, 61; 2003, 94) failed to find expression, and Hobbes did not realize "that in using this symbol he was conjuring up the invisible forces of an old, ambiguous myth. His work was overshadowed by the leviathan, and all his clear intellectual constructions and arguments were overcome in the vortex created by the symbol he conjured up. No clear chain of thought can stand up against the force of genuine, mythical images" (2008a, 81; 2003, 123).

The final sentence of this quote is particularly instructive in the context of this chapter. When Schmitt invoked the "force of genuine, mythical images," he did more than articulate his critique of a misunderstood myth; Schmitt's book on Hobbes was also a critique *through* myth, as if he were seeking to weaponize myth in order to mount a counterattack against Hobbes's reduction of the image. This mythical "force" is what motivated *Land and Sea* and defined the role of its narrative style. No other genre can more effectively conjure myth than narrative. I argue that this is exactly what *Land and Sea* tried to achieve. The step from Schmitt's *Leviathan* to *Land and Sea*, from the theory of a political symbol to a narrative, is therefore a consistent one. Whereas his *Leviathan* addressed myth thematically, *Land and Sea* is a narrative that approached myth from a formal perspective. Moreover, by narrating an elemental history of land and sea, Schmitt explored the preconditions of the leviathan and the behemoth and unveiled the history of the fundamental elements without which whales and land monsters could not even exist. *Land and Sea* radicalized Schmitt's earlier text on Hobbes and illustrated some of its fundamental principles. The narrative cannot be distinguished from his political writings; in fact, it must be understood as their founding discourse.

Contrary to conventional historical representations, "world-historical" events are not simply depicted chronologically in *Land and Sea*. The book presents elementary constellations whose orders obey a different logic than the traditional temporal continuum. The essence of world history is twofold, Schmitt argued: Each epoch is designated by a break with the previous era and is defined by a specific spatial order. Written against conventional histories and the linear flow of historical events, Schmitt's world history dealt with the discontinuities between epochs and their respective spatial logics. Removed from mere sequential history, Schmitt's world history replaced chronology with elementary constellations that, as preconditions of history, constitute spatial orders to which historical events are subordinated.

With that said, *Land and Sea* presented two narratives that must be distinguished from one another. The book reconstructed events that have occurred *within* a spatial order, and, more importantly, the narrative tackled the spatial orders themselves, whose constellations only become visible when they are taken in from an extra-historical standpoint. These spatial orders are discontinuous, marked by breaks and revolutions. As a consequence, *Land and Sea* was not a conventional history of

explorers and conquests but a metadiscourse on how such histories ought to be written. For this reason it was conceived as a narrative.

Schmitt argued, for example, that in the period from 500 to 1100, crusaders and merchants were driving forces of spatial expansion (Schmitt 1997a, 32; 2001, 62), but that a
revolution in spatial comprehension did not transpire during this phase. A fundamental break in the history of space was not possible until whale hunters and sea adven-
turers first discovered the globe and changed the world picture. As Jules Michelet and
as Melville's novel *Moby-Dick* demonstrate, the "global conscience of the Western and
Central Europeans, and ultimately, of the whole mankind was overhauled from top to
bottom" (1997a, 33; 2001, 64). The whale hunters of the sixteenth century were the first
"children of the sea" (1997a, 17; 2001, 35). Consequently, a new "world picture" (2001, 64)
developed. The "appearance of the cosmic dimension and of the concept of the infinite
void" (1997a, 34; 2001, 65) turned up in cosmology as well as in the foreshortened spatial depth of Renaissance painting: "People and objects were now sitting and moving in
space" (1997a, 36; 2001, 68). This new concept of space (1997a, 29; 2001, 57) also made
itself known in international law and political science. Empty space became a precursor
to national borders, which were henceforth understood as lines, most notably after the
1648 Peace of Westphalia established an entire system of sovereign states based on its
definition of territory.

Land and Sea dealt primarily with this first spatial revolution, but interestingly
enough, for Schmitt, the whale hunters were not the only discoverers of the sea. Schmitt
also wrote that the spatial revolution began in England. With the conquest of the world's
oceans, England established a new maritime presence and became an island capable of
terminating its connection to the continent. In Schmitt's eyes, it hoisted its anchor and
became a ship, or even a fish (1995b, 397). But he depicted England's maritime presence
as a potential threat; the leviathan England also represented the wave of liberalism that
threatened to flood the entire European continent. Schmitt juxtaposed two different versions of the same "world-historical" change, each written from a different perspective.
Whereas England's rise to global ascendancy imperiled the European order, Melville's
whaling tale allowed for a more positive version of this epoch-making upheaval; while
Schmitt perceived the threat from a terrestrial or continental point of view, his narrator
joined the whalers on their perilous adventures, following the lead of these masters of
the ocean. In *Land and Sea*, he did more than turn to a literary genre for his account of
the spatial revolution; by adopting the whalers' point of view, he also imitated the novel
in his own mode of writing. This strategy is crucial for our understanding of his choice
of genre: Schmitt's use of narrative lent meaning to spatial revolutions, first and foremost through its form, in which the new spatial consciousness manifested itself.

To illustrate this role of the narrative with a further example, when Schmitt observed
that the Dutch could sail across the ocean around 1600 without the aid of a rudder
thanks to the invention of new types of ships and sailing techniques, he associated
the spatial revolution with technological innovations. At the same time, however, he
wrote, technological progress was also responsible for man's loss of his original affinity with the sea: "The industrial revolution has transformed the children of the sea

into machine-builders and servants of machines" (1997a, 54; 2001, 98). Indeed, for Schmitt, the sea was "dangerous and fierce" (1991, 34). But while man's compulsion to use technology was needed to subdue this fear of the sea, this same technology developed a dynamic of its own (36). Man did not control his innovations as he would an instrument; on the contrary, he seemed to be driven by technology, particularly when it became "absolute." Yet this is precisely why a world-historical mediation of man's skills was needed. Although technology exposed mankind to new elements, the emergence of a new spatial consciousness was unthinkable without an interpretation of that technology. Melville's *Moby-Dick* did this successfully in its treatment of the sea and the activity of whaling; it is an indispensable exegesis of this elementary event. Not until the spatial revolution is depicted, its order symbolized, does it actually become a fundamental principle. Narrative lends meaning to the spatial revolution that a mere technological history cannot convey by allowing its readers to imitate and appropriate a new point of view. The spatial revolution is not fully realized until the creation of a narrative like *Moby-Dick* or Schmitt's *Land and Sea*.

Spatial Revolution, or How to Make an Epoch

Schmitt's decision to write *Land and Sea* in the form of a narrative can be understood only against this backdrop. As a narrator, he was able to determine his own position and point of view. More precisely, as a narrator he adopted different perspectives throughout the book, suggesting that each world-historical epoch corresponded with a unique way of perceiving the world.[5] In the opening, Schmitt described man as a "groundling": "He lives, moves, and walks on the firmly-grounded Earth. It is his standpoint and his base. He derives his points of view from it, which is also to say that his impressions are determined by it and his world outlook is conditioned by it" (1997a, 1; 2001, 7). But later his narrator takes a different stance, and the land perspective gives way to an ocean vantage point. When Schmitt wrote about the whaler, how he pursued his prey across the ocean armed with harpoons, he was also writing about the role and position of his own narrator: "Were it not for the whale, the fisherman would have never abandoned the shores. It was the whale that freed them from the coastline and lured them on to the high seas. In that way the maritime currents were discovered, as well as the northern passages. It was the whale that guided us" (1997a, 16; 2001, 34).

Melville's novel explored a space that had previously eluded description. His ocean is not only dangerous and evil; it also signified the inconceivable. Accordingly, Melville's novel attempted to draw on this space in the form of a narrative, as Schmitt himself did by devising a narrative meant to render the ocean comprehensible. After beginning with a land-based perspective, Schmitt's narrator later braved the sea, as if he had become a whaler. The whale, as both mammal and sea dweller, belonged to two distinct elements, and by following its tracks, both the whaler and the narrator hazarded a maritime existence. They were each thus brought into contact with a different element and were allowed to explore a new spatial order.

Finally, one should add that *Land and Sea* does more than deal with a bygone spatial revolution. At the end of the book the narrator marked a transition to a new era, a transition that manifests itself by means of another shift in perception. The concluding pages are not composed from a land- or sea-based perspective; instead, the text takes on a kind of bird's-eye view. In the narrative's final passages, a third mythical animal joins the leviathan and the behemoth, "quite likely in the figure of a big bird" (1997a, 58; 2001, 104–105). According to Schmitt, the new element signified by the mythical phoenix was fire, which is plausible when one recalls that the air raids of World War II were a very real threat at the time Schmitt was writing *Land and Sea*. In accordance with the general purpose of the book as a metahistorical reflection, however, Schmitt refused to register current historical events and instead focused on the more fundamental constellation of the elements; the history of land, sea, air, and fire; and a final turning point: the aerial perspective the narrator adopts at the end of the book. *Land and Sea* reflects a passage through the elements in a formal sense as well. Or, to put it differently, the spatial revolution was a distinct change in the narrative point of view. Thus, the spatial revolution cannot be separated from the act of narrating; the narrative itself has the force to overthrow a spatial order. This is how the narrative form changes spatial consciousness and how Schmitt's spatial rhetoric, as it appears in his earlier writings, is a form of political intervention and resistance.[6]

One should also add, however, that Schmitt described this new space only briefly. If every spatial revolution is a potential threat precisely because it changes the world order (like England's conquest of the sea) and because we need an additional, second narrative such as Melville's novel if we are to fully comprehend and realize this change, then the final passages on the new spatial order seem to lack such a turning point that might allow for the internalization of a new spatial consciousness. The ending of *Land and Sea* seems to be open and undecided because Schmitt's point of view does not provide him with a clear vision of the future. It is as if his narrative strategy came to an end when it approached his own time. Despite the new point of view, Schmitt did not rise to the challenge of this new world order. His narrative was retrospective and was not yet prepared to face the challenges of his present moment.

THE "NOMOS" OF THE EARTH, OR DEFINING CONCEPTS

The reader encounters the spatial revolution of the twentieth century only briefly at the end of *Land and Sea*. But in other texts that employ a different genre, Schmitt focused on the new spatial consciousness and new global order that became evident with the onset of World War II. Starting in the 1940s, Schmitt began to publish a series of works about the theories of *nomos* and *Großraum*, texts that sought to define space conceptually. His conceptual critique in these writings used a different approach from the narrative form discussed in the previous section and are directly related to the uncertainty of the new world order. Here Schmitt used definitions and demarcations, occupying himself with the science and theory of space instead of appropriating the point of view of whalers in a literary narrative. To be sure, here too one confronts the same fundamental assumption that underlies all of Schmitt's writings: space has lost significance, and since there are so many different conceptions of it, it is necessary to adopt a new, consistent understanding of space.

Although his conceptual writing seems to differ considerably from the tale of *Land and Sea*—according to Martti Koskenniemi, *The "Nomos" of the Earth* is yet another text that "is difficult to classify" (2004, 500)[7]—the methodological challenges of both projects are closely related: How does one write about space as a quasi-transcendental concept, as a condition of historical developments, and as a concept that is more coherent than the numerous different understandings of space in circulation? Not unlike *Land and Sea*, which sought to implement a new spatial consciousness in and through its own narrative, Schmitt's theory and definition of space in *The "Nomos" of the Earth* was concerned with the creation of a new spatial awareness. Schmitt's definitions were not merely descriptive or historical reflections on a given concept; they were claims and demands, postulations of a new understanding of space. Schmitt's *Nomos*, I contend, is as engaged as his political theory or *Land and Sea*, although he used a different strategy in it. This spatial theory was written from a terrestrial perspective; instead of following the whalers on their adventurous expeditions into the unknown, Schmitt retreated to an earthly position. He returned to an orderly conduct, and his writings on *nomos* were first and foremost attempts to bring order to space and its history. Schmitt sought security in the tried and tested. As the final section of this chapter shows, this conservative response was as significant for the challenges of his epistemological and historical context as the adventure tale of *Land and Sea*.

Naming Space

Schmitt's critique of the idea of concepts is well known from his earlier works. In *The Value of the State and the Significance of the Individual* from 1912, for example, he claimed that the consistency of political concepts had become endangered by a bewildering vortex of associations (2004, 46). In *Political Romanticism*, he wrote that not only was the idea of Romanticism afflicted by the term's own "dreadful confusion" (1986, 30; 1998, 35) but that the Romantics themselves suffered from a "lack of any relationship to a *causa*" (1986, 83; 1998, 91). Romantic ideas could no longer be clearly differentiated; they had become replaceable and lacked stable content. Everything "can become romantic. In such a world, all political or religious distinctions are dissolved into an interesting ambiguity" (1986, 158; 1998, 164). In his own response to the rootless and "nebulous" images of the Romantics (1986, 130; 1998, 132), Schmitt turned to the origin and etymology of "*Romantik*" (Romanticism), as if a better understanding of the word could eradicate the ambiguities of an entire era. The noun *Romantik* is derived from the word for novel,

Roman, and Schmitt's text is a treatment that attempted to do justice to the original meaning of the word (Schmitt 1986, 30; 1998, 35). "Germans," according to Schmitt, "lack the facility for making an easily managed, simple name out of a word, so that people can agree without a great deal of difficulty" (1986, 1; 1998, 5). As the following analysis of Schmitt's definitions of space shows, his conceptual demarcations of space were likewise quests for origins; his definitions always refer back to long-forgotten beginnings. In pursuit of his quest, however, his conceptual contributions became entangled in mythological speculations and fictions.

Among Schmitt's most peculiar etymological speculations is his text "Space and Rome" ("Raum und Rom"), an essay in which he endeavored to substantiate his understanding of meaningful space on the basis of phonetics, as if the essence of space could be divined from the word's phonetic features alone. German is a primal language, according to Schmitt, and *Raum*, or space, was a primal word of the German language (1995c, 491). According to Jacob and Wilhelm Grimm's *German Dictionary*, the German word *"Raum"* is related to both the Old Norse root *"rum"* and to the Latin *"e-ru-ere."* In contrast to *"rauh,"* or rough, *"rum"* refers to man's first cultivation of a wilderness. *Raum* and Rome, Schmitt concluded, must at one time have been the same word.

By way of this etymological speculation, Schmitt embarked on a search for truth, as if the ultimate concept signified by a word could be deduced from that word's supposed original meaning.[8] He thus posited an immediate correspondence between concept and thing. This is what the act of defining meant to him: identifying a direct and immediate correspondence between a concept and its referent. Schmitt was not seeking to make an etymological contribution; although he seemed to analyze the word *"Raum"* phonetically, his was not a historical analysis of a concept. Although he suggested in his speculations that he was locating original meanings, as if the content of a word were preserved in its language (see Meier 1988, 534), his finding was a founding act. Schmitt sought to affect the contemporary meaning of space, a strategy that is evident throughout his work on *nomos*.

When Schmitt wrote in the fourth "corollary" of *The "Nomos" of the Earth* that "the Greek word for the first measure of all subsequent measures, for the land-appropriation understood as the first partition and classification of space, for the primeval division and distribution, is *nomos*," the actual purpose of this alleged retrospection was his wish to "restore to the word *nomos* its energy and majesty" (2006a, 67; 1997b, 36). Because corollaries are theorems derived from preestablished principles, they presuppose a stringent, logical structure. But by "restoring" the word's power, Schmitt did more than merely trace its forgotten meaning; he also introduced a particular conception of legality. The act of returning power to the word is a kind of performative speech act, a proposition that enacts precisely what it portrays. Thus, Schmitt's text itself performed the very founding act *nomos* promotes.

Schmitt ostensibly strove for precision. But instead of presenting an unambiguous concept, his speculations led to ever more mythical images, even when the mode of representation would seem to curtail such a practice. At the very beginning of the text, for instance, Schmitt wrote: "In mythical language, the *earth* became known as the mother of law. This signifies a threefold root of law and justice" (2006a, 42; 1997b, 13). The imagery of this opening is consistent. The statement begins with "earth" as it is described in mythical texts and ends with "root"—concepts that belong to the same paradigm. Schmitt's language appears to mimetically correspond with the subject matter. Unlike *Land and Sea*, however, wherein the narrator embarked on an ocean voyage, the perspective adopted in *Nomos* consistently remains grounded and connected to the earth. Schmitt described the three roots as follows:

> First, the fertile earth contains within herself, within the womb of her fecundity, an inner measure, because human toil and trouble, human planting and cultivation of the fruitful earth is rewarded justly by her with growth and harvest. Every farmer knows the inner measure of his justice.

> Second, soil that is cleared and worked by human hands manifests firm lines, whereby definite divisions become apparent. Through the demarcation of fields, pastures, and forests, these lines are engraved and embedded. Through crop rotation and fallowing, they are even planted and nurtured. In these lines, the standards and rules of human cultivation of the earth become discernible. Third and last, the solid ground of the earth is delineated by fences, enclosures, boundaries, walls, houses, and other constructs. Then, the orders and orientations of human social life become apparent. (2006a, 42; 1997b, 13)

In keeping with this triad, earthbound law, which is related to *nomos*, also makes itself known in three ways: in the harvest, which compensates the farmer for his labor; in clearly delineated borders; and as the public mark of the order. For Schmitt, space was something that could be divided (Marzoa 2005, 307). The word "farmer" ("*Bauer*") derives from the words "building" ("*Bau*") and "site" ("*Stätte*"), according to Schmitt in "The *Großraum* Order of the International Law," and it is thereby associated with a form of space defined in terms of both space and content (2011, 123; 1995e, 319). Whereas the sea consists entirely of waves, which the law cannot hope to inscribe itself in, the space of law, as Schmitt explained it, should be understood in a wholly literal sense: as a system of law that, because of its attachment to the earth, creates a specific spatial form and can thus be most effectively represented in a text that textually reenacts the inaugural act of demarcation and ordering. The original act of the law is always the creation of earthbound locations. In the history of the law, this act consists of the appropriation of land and the founding of cities; in the poetics of legal history, this operation comes to the fore in Schmitt's own act of writing, which proceeds by way of definitions and restores to *nomos* its deep roots and meaning.

According to Schmitt's logic, *nomos* is a founding act of the law, and he conceived of his own work as a founding text of legal history. He described the appropriation of land as a founding act that establishes law, a primary demarcation and a "primary criterion embodying all subsequent criteria" (2006a, 45; 1997b, 16). But he also portrayed *nomos* as a concept capable of safeguarding the connection between order and location now that he had restored the concept's original meaning.

From a semiotic perspective, the history of law that Schmitt presented is an example of purely arbitrary concepts that had lost their original meaning. This history explained the gradual disorientation of legal concepts (2006a, 64; 1997b, 33). *Nomos* originally came from "*nemein*—a [Greek] word that means both 'to divide' and 'to pasture.' Thus, *nomos* is the immediate form in which the political and social order of a people becomes spatially visible—the initial measure and division of pastureland" (2006a, 70; 1997b, 39). Schmitt claimed that this origin was no longer visible for legal positivism, which inherently overlooked all origins and archetypes, and argued that positivism was only interested in the "law of appearance;" "home and origin are not core characteristics, which is why [the positivist] abolishes the link between order and orientation" (2006a, 72; 1997b, 41).

Writing *Nomos*: The History of Lines in International Law

The basic principle of *nomos*, its link between order (*Ordnung*) and location (*Ortung*), is its visibility, especially in its original denotation of "taking" and "dividing." Politically and cartographically, *nomos* manifests itself in the (literal) drawing of borders, the history of which Schmitt read as the development of international law. Instead of recapitulating the concepts of international law in legal terms, Schmitt wrote a history of the political line. "Global linear thinking has its own development and history. The most important examples of its numerous forms constitute a coherent progression from the discovery of America in 1492 to the American declarations of World War II" (2006a, 90; 1997b, 58). And instead of constituting an uninterrupted history, this "coherent progression" was marked by gaps because the intellectual structure of concepts about lines (boundaries) were shaped by the underlying spatial order. To recapitulate the structure of Schmitt's history of the line, the following pages briefly discuss three of his examples: the first global boundaries that divided Europe from the New World, the Monroe Doctrine, and the Congo Conference of 1884.

The new global lines by which the popes separated the Christian from the non-Christian world and by which Europe was distinguished from the New World were originally "conceived of only in terms of surface areas, i.e., superficially, with divisions drawn more or less geometrically: *more geometrico*" (2006a, 86; 1997b, 54). Nevertheless, these lines were constitutive of a new order. When Europe was differentiated from the New World, "the line set aside an area where force could be used freely and ruthlessly.... Everything that occurred 'beyond' the line remained outside the legal, moral, and political values recognized on this side of the line" (2006a, 94; 1997b, 62). For Schmitt, the space beyond this great divide was open to colonial powers and helped relieve the pressures that conflicts within Europe brought about. Colonialism was necessary if the nations of Europe were to peacefully coexist with their neighbors on the continent.

In the next period, the new line of the Western Hemisphere "upset the spatial order of the European world" (2006a, 100; 1997b, 69) and transformed space fundamentally. In 1832, with the Monroe Doctrine, the United States dissociated itself from Europe and demarcated a wide area in which European powers could not intervene. This area had a different structure than the European territorial state. Its outline signified a different mode of spatial thought because its boundaries constituted a line that could not be identified as a national border. Therefore, in Schmitt's understanding, the doctrine did more than factually divest European countries of permission to expand beyond European borders. For him, the Monroe Doctrine was a lynchpin event that was formative for the history of international law.

After the Congo Conference of 1884, this transformation of space became even more apparent. When the participating powers debated who would have jurisdiction over the last unoccupied space on the map of Africa, the Congo Basin, they decided to allocate the area to King Leopold of Belgium. At the same time, however, the Congo Basin was designated a free trade zone. This was decisive for Schmitt, as a structural transformation of space arose from the uncoupling of two different conceptions of space: the territorial definition, on the one hand, and the trade area, on the other. According to Schmitt, the establishment of the trade zone as neutral territory at the behest of the United States clearly demonstrated the imperial control of a superpower that was seeking to expand its influence over territories beyond its national borders. A further consequence of the Congo Conference was the collapse of the distinction between European and non-European territories in international law. From then on, the United States transferred its own conception of legality to the colonial territories and the colonies thereby lost their former status. The colonies no longer represented an exterior; they were no longer a separate space outside Europe but instead became part of an order that was becoming ever more diffuse: "Essentially, the whole enterprise already was a helpless confusion of lines dividing spheres of interest and influence, as well as of failed amity lines simultaneously overarched and undermined by a Eurocentrically conceived, free, global economy ignoring all territorial borders. In this confusion, the old *nomos* of the earth determined by Europe dissolved" (2006a, 226; 1997b, 200).

In its universal form, international law created a new space for a new world economy of free trade, but the freshly drawn lines lost their connection with territories (1995d, 245–250). Although they appeared to resemble the old lines of the *jus Europaeum*, they had become entirely arbitrary. For Schmitt, this development constituted a "headlong leap into the nothingness of a universality lacking any grounding in space or land" (2006a, 237; 1997b, 211). The original task of international law of containing combat and "prevent[ing] wars of annihilation" (2006a, 237; 1997b, 211) was abandoned. A spatial chaos, which showed itself in a political map of diffuse lines, was the consequence. The new lines no longer divided an inside from an outside and they were no longer a symbol of *nomos*. Space underwent fundamental changes because partition was no longer possible.

As becomes evident, the line served Schmitt as a type of narrative that led from mythical origins to a history of decay. When Schmitt wrote about the line ("*über die Linie*"), he did not wish to overstep boundaries; his object was to reflect on the form of the line itself (Odysseos 2007, 124). This reflection constituted a metadiscourse that, with the help of the simple yet fundamental form of the line, related a political history that led from the original significance of space—a fullness of meaning shaped by the line—to a purely geometrical "register's sheet" (Schmitt 2011, 120; 1995e, 316) that merely demarcated empty areas.

Schmitt's contributions to a theory of *nomos* have value that goes beyond diagnosis. His history of international law presents norms that he used to critically assess the development of legal concepts. The unity of order and location is fundamental to his definition of *nomos*, a type of precursor that history cannot change. In *Land and Sea: The World-Historical Reflection*, he distinguished between historical eras and their spatial preconditions: "Every basic order is a spatial order" (1997a, 37; 2001, 71). But in contrast to, for instance, Kant's transcendental philosophy, space is not a timeless structure in Schmitt's work. Although it is a precondition of historical periods, it is subject to revolutions. Schmitt's space is a transient historical order.

The Coming *Nomos*, or *Tatraum* Text

The final pages of this section on Schmitt's texts that define space return to the methodological challenge raised above: How can one describe the preconditions of one's own concepts? As the following deliberations show, this challenge presented problems for Schmitt. He was not always able to distinguish between his two levels of argumentation, the transcendental and factual preconditions. Historically specific terms sometimes slipped into descriptions of a transhistorical precondition. In this process, the polemical nature of his texts became more and more obvious, not least because of these slippages.

This lack of methodological rigor is particularly apparent in considerations of another of his key ideas, the concept of *Großraum*, which he discussed in several writings in the late 1930s (on the idea of *Großraum*, see Schmoeckel 1994; Voigt 2008). In his essay "Space and *Großraum*, in International Law" from 1940, Schmitt described *Großraum* as a "concrete, historical-political term of the present age" (1995d, 235). The term came from the word for the new continental economic zone (*Großraumwirtschaft*) and was supposedly based on the expansion of the energy industry as it delivered gas and electricity to more and more customers. For the first time, a new technical, industrial, and economic order arose that overcame the limitations and isolation of the small territories of earlier economies (236). In Schmitt's estimation, the new "large" geopolitical space (*Großraum*) was not the antithesis of a small geopolitical space (*Kleinraum*); it was the antithesis of universal claims to power (261). *Großraum* was Schmitt's answer to the empty space of universalism. "*Groß*," he wrote in "The *Großraum* Order of the International Law," "contains a meaning that is more than merely quantitative and mathematical-physical" (2011, 119; 1995d, 315). "*Groß*" impinged on territory itself.

Schmitt's lack of methodological rigor is very clear here. Since *nomos* is always concrete (Hooker 2009, 23), *Großraum* seems to take on an equally tangible meaning that must be differentiated from a concept of space as empty. Schmitt described *Großraum* as a space of action ("*Tatraum*") and as an achievement ("*Leistungsraum*"), a space filled by a people and its activities. However, the same term also has the function of a precondition that shapes the empirical world. Schmitt attempted to grasp the precondition of history—space as a priori—with the aid of a concept taken from his contemporary world. He thus granted transcendental status to his own contemporary history. Or to put it differently, he reconceptualized empirical space as a transhistorical phenomenon.

Does this mean that his spatial theory was not linked to its own historical moment? How can one not associate his *Großraum* with the foreign policy of the "Third Reich"? Although Schmitt insisted on a distinction between *Großraum* and empire (Reich), repeatedly asserting that the two were not the same thing (2011, 102; 1995d, 296), he reinforced his discourse on transhistorical space with references to the space of his own period. Since the links between concepts and their referents and between order (*Ordnung*) and geographical location (*Ortung*) form the foundation of his deliberations, is it not reasonable to transpose these two concepts and interpret the German Reich as the realization of the concept of *Großraum*? Schmitt's methodological lack of rigor was a direct consequence of his impulse to present his ideas in the most concrete way possible instead of attempting to explain them transcendentally and schematically.

For example, Schmitt's conception of land appropriation is coherent only if one assumes an empty territory in which the founding acts are still possible. In his passages on Great Britain's colonialism, on the "designation of a sphere outside the law and open to the use of force" (2006a, 98; 1997b, 66), he described a form of authority accorded to the British monarch that was held in check by Parliament. The colony is an exceptional space in which land acquisition is lawful. Since Schmitt saw this transoceanic space as something that stabilized Great Britain, passages such as these can be understood as a call to colonialism. After all, in the colonial discourse of his contemporaries, the German colonizer was usually presented as a diligent farmer who made fallow land productive, whereas the British colonizer merely sought financial gain and had no sense of the culture of the earth—culture in the sense of the Latin *colere*, to cultivate. The space described in *nomos* is at all times a motherly soil and a space of fertility (Aravamudan 2005, 228).

In Schmitt's 1939 lecture in Kiel, the concept of *Großraum* was a source of controversial interpretations. In this early introduction of the concept, delivered just two weeks after Hitler had invaded Czechoslovakia, Schmitt referred to the Monroe Doctrine of 1832. Shouldn't Germany, he asked, pursue its own *Großraum* as well (Kennedy 2004, 26; Kearns 2011, 80–81)? According to Schmitt's lecture, Hitler's invasion of Germany's neighbor was an entirely legitimate form of imperialism, if one defines the borders of the German *Großraum* accordingly. The concept of *Großraum* is still vague here (Bendersky 1983, 256), but his formulations suggested that one can always transform the abstract model of *Großraum* into an empirical phenomenon: "The new concept of the order of a new international law is our concept of Reich, which proceeds from a *völkisch Großraum* order upheld by a nation" (Schmitt 2011, 110–111; 1995d, 306). The distinction between *Großraum* and Reich is hazy, even when Schmitt indicated the difference between the two in the Kiel lecture. Admittedly, the temptation to position himself as a theorist of the new order brought him no support from the SS (Hell 2009, 297). On the contrary, after he seemed to be useful for a time (Müller 2003, 39), it was precisely this theoretical doctrine of spatial understanding that made him lose favor with the Nazis. A short while later, Hitler gave a speech at the *Reichstag* that referred to the Monroe Doctrine in response to Roosevelt's call to end aggression. Soon after this speech, Schmitt learned that Hitler believed that he himself had invented the idea of a German Monroe Doctrine. This was a further step in Schmitt's dissociation from National Socialism, but it also demonstrates the assimilability of Schmitt's terminology.

Schmitt's concept of *Großraum* corresponds to the German Reich in the same way that the philosophical concept of a lifeworld (*Lebenswelt*) corresponds to *Lebensraum* as it was propagated by the Nazi Party: *Lebenswelt* is an abstract concept, whereas *Lebensraum* draws on the empirical world. When Robert Kempner interrogated Schmitt after the war (Bendersky 1983, 270), the latter argued that his understanding of *Großraum* did not imply a space of expansion but rather an understanding of space that allowed him to abstractly delineate the new order. Nevertheless, Schmitt's spatial theory contains an insurmountable ambivalence. On the one hand, he treats these spatial ideas as theoretical concepts. On the other, he continually endows them with descriptions whose conceptualization cannot always be differentiated from Nazi ideology.[9] Does not the concept of *nomos* as taking, *Nahme*, therefore always imply bellicose and propagandistic overtones, particularly since free space had become increasingly scarce and no new and occupiable territories were found after 1884?

These ambiguities become even more apparent when one considers passages in which Schmitt attributed the emptying of space to Jewish thought. According to Schmitt, the degree to which Jewish authors had contributed to the development of an empty notion of space is striking. He names, among others, Georg Jellinek, Hans Kelsen and his students, and Georg Simmel. The Jewish people in general were "an important fermenting agent in the dissolution of concrete, spatially determined orders":

> The real misunderstanding of the Jewish people with respect to everything that concerns soil, land, and territory, is grounded in its style of political existence. The relation of a nation to a soil arranged through its own work of colonization and culture to the concrete forms of power that arise from this arrangement is incomprehensible to the spirit of the Jew. He does not, moreover, even wish to understand this, but rather only to conceptually seize these relations in order to set his own concepts in their place. (Schmitt 2011, 121–122; 1995d, 317–318)

In his responses to Kempner, Schmitt said that the concept of *Großraum* had "infiltrated" the German lexicon in 1923. It was therefore not his own etymological invention (1995a, 453). He also distanced himself from the Nazi doctrine, as his own theory was supposedly always based on rational concepts of space, not on biology (457). Indeed, it is true that a racial concept of space cannot be found in Schmitt's work, but what he meant by "rational concepts" remains unclear.[10] All of this is evidence of the fact that Schmitt did not always separate the various levels of his argumentation. His texts on *nomos* and *Großraum* are less a spatial theory than they are instances of spatial rhetoric deeply entangled in the discourses of his own time. The "space revolution," which Schmitt described in order to shed light on the restructuring of worldviews, is both an idea that had "infiltrated" the German-speaking world and a term that referred to concrete geopolitical developments. In a letter to Ernst Jünger in 1941, Schmitt, taking up a friend's recent postulation, dreamt up a spiral construction that represented a progressive development of spatial revolutions. This line began at the center of Germany and spiraled outward on the map of Europe, sequentially depicting the invasion of Czechoslovakia, the annexation of Austria, the Polish campaign, and ultimately the African offensive (Schmitt in Kiesel 1999, 125). Here, spatial revolution did not imply the intellectual transformation of a worldview; it referred to the military campaigns of the National Socialists.

Schmitt's methodological imprecision is one reason for the fundamental ambiguity of his writings. Another is the open-ended nature of his thoughts about a new world order. Multiple forms of a new *nomos* seemed possible, according to Schmitt. One superpower could triumph over another; new and independent *Großräume* could keep each other in check, thereby bringing about a pluralistic yet unified world order; or the return to an old *nomos* was also conceivable (Ulmen 1993, 49). While Schmitt failed to clearly formulate this new *nomos* (Legg 2011, 3), one can presume that it involved the unity of order (*Ordnung*) and location (*Ortung*). The correlation between the two is both the starting point and the conclusion of his book. Although the *jus Europaeum* could not be revived, it remained a criterion of his theory about space (see Scheuerman 2004).[11] While global politics had dissolved space and Europe was in a state of territorial chaos, it was impossible for Schmitt to disassociate his own theory from space; it was inconceivable for him that space might no longer serve as a suitable foundation for international law. And this shows all the more clearly the status of space in Schmitt's writing: he could not renounce his theory of (or rhetoric about) space because it defined the foundation and essence of international law and the strategy of his own writing.

What then is the *causa* of Schmitt's spatial theory? Do the unity of *Ordnung* and *Ortung* and the understanding of *nomos* as land appropriation constitute the *beginning* of the history that Schmitt reconstructed in an attempt to delineate space's loss of meaning? A different interpretation seems more plausible: Demanding a new spatial order and a new *nomos*, Schmitt delivered a lecture on the history of spatial forms that he intended, first and foremost, to *propagate* his model of space in the most effective way possible. In contrast to what he did in *Land and Sea*, Schmitt did not construct a narrative about *nomos*. He simply argued that *nomos* was a space of action (*Tatraum*) in which law could be actively implemented: *nomen actionis*. Schmitt's text imitated this procedure by positing and defining concepts or, to be more exact, by locating a myth from which it can derive itself and its laws.

Why are these two texts, written in such a short period of time, so incongruent? *Land and Sea* is a retrospective narrative that gives meaning to historical epochs and ends at its own world-historical point of origin. *The "Nomos" of the Earth* is a historical exercise of a different kind. Instead of exploring continental drifts and new spatial consciousness, it seems to be written from a terrestrial point of view, an earthly perspective that attempted to anchor the theory of space in a very concrete way. His orderly course of action was a different response to World War II. Schmitt's ambivalent writings about space, one could argue, manifest his uncertainty and ambivalence about the new world order and his clouded vision of the future. But this historical context does not explain the specific structural difference between his desire to transgress spatial orders in *Land and Sea* and his attempt to preserve and renew the origins of space in *The "Nomos" of the Earth*. The incongruence between these two modes of writing can be best understood if both texts are seen in their epistemological context, as two different responses to a new structure of thought about space. As the final section of this chapter shows, the nuances of this context become particularly evident when one takes more recent appropriations of Schmitt's theory into consideration. From that point of view it can be clearly seen why Schmitt is not contemporary and how deeply rooted he is in the epistemology of the early twentieth century.

Spatial Discourse after Schmitt

As I mentioned at the outset, Schmitt bemoaned the fact that there were "half a dozen notions of space" but no conceptual unity, let alone a proper science of space. Schmitt's theory of *nomos* was an attempt to lay the foundations for such a science. In addition to clarifying the meaning of *nomos*, he also engaged with contending ideas. He made explicit references to, for example, Max Planck; Friedrich Ratzel, the founder of political geography (Schmitt 1995d, 237); Karl Haushofer (Schmitt 1995e, 274), the editor of the *Zeitschrift für Geopolitik*; and Oswald Spengler. The list of authors who likely influenced Schmitt's theory of space could be expanded to include Martin Heidegger or Ernst Jünger, but it is doubtful whether an analysis of similarities and differences can shed further light on Schmitt's argumentative strategy. It seems more reasonable to place Schmitt's model of space in an epistemological context and in a structural relationship with his own era, not least because his oft-repeated thesis that empty, infinite space had come to an end was just as common in his day as talk of a spatial revolution or the establishment of a *Großraum*.

Around 1900, in the wake of the development of non-Euclidean geometries and the theory of relativity, space began to be no longer conceived as an empty enclosure or container in which phenomena could be displayed as if on a stage. Euclidean space became just one among many possible spaces, none of which is superior to any other. The rupture in spatial understanding Schmitt identified was a contemporary phenomenon and was by no means his own invention. The reactions to this break with empty, infinite space were anything but uniform. Whereas Heidegger and others attempted to comprehend space in a fundamentally different way and cross the barrier of three-dimensional space, other authors responded in the opposite manner, striving to stabilize the three-dimensional structure, as it were, in order to honor and conserve it. Schmitt can be associated with both reactions. To be sure, he registered the new spatial models of modern physics, citing Planck, for example, but at the same time, with his theory of *nomos*, he constructed a counter-concept based on visibility and the congruence of *Ordnung* and *Ortung*. Although Schmitt wrote that one must not depict space using past paradigms, that did not keep him from propagating a conception of *Ortung* that is inconsistent with the idea of a dynamic force field. This ambivalence demonstrates Schmitt's assimilation of the discourses of his contemporaries. However, his engagement with others who were thinking about space was not deep; his citations of their work are few and he disregarded the contexts of what they wrote. But precisely the inconsistencies in his considerations of space make it clear that his theory has its place in a specific historical context. Schmitt himself is a kind of transitional figure, since his spatial model is in fact interspersed with a variety of concepts. This is why his thought cannot be easily appropriated into current debates. In order to illustrate my claim, I examine two spatial theories that have revived some of his theoretical ideas about space.

Agamben's Topology

In the past few decades, Giorgio Agamben's contributions to a theory of the state of exception (*Ausnahmezustand*) have gone a long way toward popularizing Schmitt's oeuvre (Dean 2004, 12; see also Minca 2007; Aradau 2007; Butler 2006; Honig 2009; Rasch 2005). Agamben has taken Schmitt's definition of the state of exception almost verbatim from *Political Theology*, where Schmitt wrote the following about the sovereign who decrees the state of exception: "Although he stands outside the normally valid legal system, he nevertheless belongs to it, for it is he who must decide whether the constitution must be suspended in its entirety" (1988, 7; 2006a, 14). In *Homo Sacer*, Agamben described this curious position of the sovereign as a paradox: "The specification that the sovereign 'is at the same time outside and inside the juridical order' (emphasis added) is not insignificant: the sovereign, having the legal power to suspend the validity of the law, legally places himself outside the law. This means that the paradox can also be formulated this way: 'the law is outside itself', or: 'I, the sovereign, who am outside the law, declare that there is nothing outside the law'" (1998, 15). Agamben continues: "The topology implicit in the paradox is worth reflecting upon" (15). This afterthought is illuminating, for it illustrates that Agamben not only adopts Schmitt's definition of the sovereign but also reformulates it.

What exactly is the topology Agamben refers to? In mathematics, topology distinguishes itself from Euclidean geometry most notably in its refusal to insert its figures into a preexisting system of coordinates. Topology views spatial bodies solely from a relational point of view without reducing them to a given system of measurement. The advantage of topological delineation is its capacity to apprehend bodies that defy three-dimensional logic, such as a distorted Möbius strip or a Leyden jar, in which there is no distinction between inside and outside. Agamben seizes on these topological figures in outlining his version of the state of exception: "The state of nature and the state of exception are nothing but two sides of a single topological process in which what was presupposed as external (the state of nature) now reappears, as in a Möbius strip or a Leyden jar, in the inside (as a state of exception), and the sovereign power is this very impossibility of distinguishing between inside and outside, nature and law, *physis* and *nomos*" (1998, 37). In other words, the paradoxical point of departure is only paradoxical if observed from the familiar perspective of a three-dimensional schema. From a topological point of view, the thought of a body that is simultaneously inside and outside is not a contradiction at all. In his *State of Exception*, Agamben ranks Schmitt among the theorists who "complicate the topographical opposition into a more complex topological relation, in which the very limit of the juridical order is at issue" (2003, 23). Schmitt's work thereby obtains the status of a theory capable of grasping space in a new way. But are Schmitt's deliberations on space actually examples of topological thought?

If one proceeds from Schmitt's description of the Westphalian political order, this indeed appears to be the case. There Schmitt distinguished the regional planning of Europe, in which states are defined by borders and wars can be bounded, from an indeterminate outside, the New World, which belongs to a different logic, especially since its national borders have yet to be inscribed. This space not only represents an outside, it is also differently structured—though only, one must add, in order to be made available for land appropriations. The colony, according to Schmitt in "The *Großraum* Order of the International Law," "is the basic spatial fact of hitherto existing European international law" (2011, 114; 1995d, 310). On the one hand, Schmitt thereby appeared to put the colony into a topological relation with a Europe that is ascertained using geometry; on the other hand, the occupations of colonial territory are invariably conceived in accordance with the paradigm of land appropriation. Thus, such occupations can be understood both topologically and non-topologically.

As a consequence, Agamben's reading of Schmitt as a topological description of the state of exception appears to amend a precondition of Schmitt's thinking. Schmitt is mindful of borders and spatial appropriations, Agamben of relational concepts (see Coleman 2011, 131). By enlisting Schmitt's thought, Agamben goes beyond Schmitt, appropriating his theory for the purpose of revising one of its most vital foundations. The link between order and location, Agamben argues, has become so porous that the state of exception collapses along with the normal order (Agamben 1998, 38)—seeming to invert the hierarchy Schmitt sought to establish. A comparison of the two theorists therefore not only demonstrates an affinity between their theories; more important, it reveals a fundamental epistemological difference. The *purely* relational language of topology was not available to Schmitt. In this regard, one cannot overlook the extent to which Schmitt's own thought remained bound to his historical context. His insistence on location and visibility, on a space that provides orientation for its inhabitants, is possible only in relation to a system of measurement. One could argue that the coexistence of a relational space and a space of demarcations is indicative of Schmitt's relevance to contemporary issues. After all, the rise of non-Euclidean and topological spaces did not contradict the Euclidean model; it merely lost its status as an exclusively valid form of geometry. In other words, could Schmitt be seen as a forerunner of this diversification of spatial models? The analysis presented here suggests a different conclusion. As the previous sections have attempted to demonstrate, Schmitt wrote against a pluralistic understanding of space, and even if the European order is—topologically—related to an exterior, Schmitt had no doubt about the hierarchical order of these spaces. The exterior voids existed for the sole purpose of being conquered and occupied.

Deleuze and Guattari's *Nomos*

In their own way, Gilles Deleuze and Felix Guattari reveal the historical distance between Schmitt's work and their own. In recent years virtually no other theoretical discourse has been so closely connected to non-Euclidean spatial concepts as that of Deleuze. In their collaborative project *A Thousand Plateaus*, Deleuze and Guattari return not only to the work of Riemann but also, seemingly, to Schmitt's theory of land and sea (Werber 2007, 103–104). Their distinction between smooth and striated spaces at least appears to inherit Schmitt's differentiation between land and sea. Striated spaces are structured spaces defined by borders and fortifications; by contrast, smooth spaces, like the sea, lack contour—they are spaces of flowing transitions that cannot be ordered in a systematic fashion.

However, a more precise comparison of Schmitt and Deleuze reveals distinct discrepancies. As Friedrich Balke has shown, Schmitt overlooked an important detail in his text on *nomos*, namely nomadism, which is characterized by an entirely different relationship to property (1996, 317, 321; see also Werber 2007, 106). Nomadism presents a different form of spatial appropriation. Farmland and territorial enclosure are thus far from the only and most original roots of spatial understanding, though Schmitt suggested otherwise. Here, the suspicion is confirmed that Schmitt did not study the sources of his spatial theory with the faithful eye of a historian or a philologist; instead, he used them for a specific purpose.

The significance of *Verteilung* (distribution), which constitutes an aspect of *nomos*, is also less unambiguous than Schmitt suggested. As Balke demonstrates, the word has a twofold meaning; both Deleuze and Schmitt return to Emmanuel Laroche's *Histoire de la racine nem—en grec ancien* in their definitions of the concept. Deleuze cites that work as follows:

> Laroche shows that the idea of distribution in *nomos-nemo* does not stand in a simple relation to that of allocation.... The pastoral sense of *nemo* (to pasture) only

belatedly implied an allocation of land. Homeric society had neither enclosures nor property in pastures: it was not a question of distributing the land among the beasts but, on the contrary, of distributing the beasts themselves and dividing them up here and there across an unlimited space, but one without precise limits (for example, the expanse around a town)—whence, too, the theme of the "nomad." (1994, 309)

Deleuze describes *nomos* as an entirely different spatial condition than Schmitt did; whereas he employs the second meaning of distribution, Schmitt referred to the first meaning, *nomos* as allocation (Balke 1996, 320–321). According to Deleuze, *nomos* is

a completely other distribution which must be called nomadic, a nomadic *nomos*, without property, enclosure or measure. Here, there is no longer a division of that which is distributed but rather a division among those who distribute *themselves* in an open space—a space which is unlimited, or at least without precise limits. Nothing pertains or belongs to any person, but all persons are arrayed here and there in such a manner as to cover the largest possible space. (1994, 36)

It is precisely this "placelessness" that was associated with the Jews in Schmitt's work. Deleuze, however, argues that the nomad lives in a relational space, an outside of the state, a precondition of the measured space in which demarcations have yet to be drawn (Ojakangas 2004, 164). *Nomos* is not the order; it is an outside of order (166); the nomad fills the space instead of dividing and distributing it; smooth space is directional rather than dimensional. These distinctions are instructive, as they can be fleshed out with the spatial models of mathematics. In the work of Riemann, for instance, one must assume that space does not possess a homogenous metastructure but is instead capable of containing various and diverse subspaces. In this sense, smooth space is not simply the counterimage of striated space; it is a non-hierarchical open space of diversification and as such the precondition of any kind of ordering.

Multiple points of interest arise when comparing Schmitt's work with that of Deleuze and Guattari. First, it is once again made clear that the etymological roots Schmitt delineated are not beyond dispute. The quotations illustrate what I have herein described as Schmitt's process of positing: Schmitt called into existence a myth of origin and unity. Second, an epistemological difference comes to light in the comparison of the two theories. Schmitt depicted the sea as an entirely different space from the land and the new world of the colonies as a different order from Europe. He thereby presented a complex spatial model that contained diverse spatial types. The same holds true for Deleuze and Guattari. But while the French poststructuralists emphasize the interactions and transitions between these heterogeneous spaces (Deleuze and Guattari 2011, 524; Balke 1996, 337–339), in Schmitt's work, the significance of the free colonies was always the fact that they represent land that can be appropriated, thereby signifying a space to be occupied and striated. Whereas Schmitt primarily deployed his differential reasoning in order to lay down boundaries, Deleuze and

Guattari describe transitions; while Schmitt bemoaned the coexistence of multiple spatial concepts and wishes to unify them, Deleuze and Guattari are concerned with visualizing space as a framework of diverse constellations. For example, the Euclidean structure
is not simply annulled in their topology; it remains valid in a localized way. Deleuze and
Guattari's spatial model is characterized particularly by its ability to render this complexity conceivable. Their spatial model crosses the boundaries of the three-dimensional
schema, thereby transcending Schmitt's theory as well.

Conclusion

Schmitt's spatial reasoning belongs to his own time. Deeply intertwined with intellectual currents of the late nineteenth and early twentieth centuries, it is of limited
relevance for the comprehension of spatial developments in the twenty-first century.
Schmitt's theoretical language, not to mention his ideological standpoint, must be
understood in the context of the epistemological context from which it was derived.
While it is true that Schmitt perceptively identified a structural transformation of spatial understanding, so did many of his contemporaries. His attempts to craft a theoretical response to this intellectual development illustrate his status as a transitional
figure. Although he registered the spatial transformation, his response was ultimately
self-defeating: Because he responded to this specific historical situation by reasserting
a general hierarchy of spaces, he provided conceptual tools for retarding the progress
of the actually existing spatial revolution. Schmitt's position was ambivalent: on the
one hand, on the threshold of a new epoch, he saw the rise of a new order; on the other
hand, he attempted to safeguard a space that was about to vanish, seeing himself as a
katechon, as it were, a barrier capable of deferring the transition once more. His writings on space were directed toward preventing the dissolution of space. His was the
fight of a conservative against all forces that could, in his opinion, accelerate the disappearance of boundaries and demarcations: Jews, technology, or modernity in general. Here too it becomes evident that Schmitt's "spatial turn" was just as committed to
affecting practice as his political theory was.

   The spatial discourses of Agamben and Deleuze and Guattari invoke Schmitt's spatial rhetoric, but not without revising it. With the help of Deleuze and Guattari's terminology, I can, in closing, reiterate what I sought to achieve in this chapter. I have
argued that *Land and Sea* has an exceptional status because the narrative strove to
investigate different forms of space. *Land and Sea* was concerned with transitions; in it
Schmitt sympathized with and imitated whalers, as if daring to cross to the other side
of an epochal threshold. By contrast, Schmitt's conceptual definitions of *The "Nomos"
of the Earth*, although founded upon myths, performed a process of differentiation
and demarcation. It is almost as if Schmitt wrote *The "Nomos" of the Earth* against
Land and Sea, in an attempt to reinforce terrestrial boundaries against the open sea.

Notes

1. See also his essay "*Großraum* in International Law" ("Großraum im Völkerrecht"): "Es gibt mathematische, physikalische, geographische, biologische, psychologische, erkenntnistheoretische, metaphysische und noch manche andere Probleme des Raumbegriffs. Zerredungskünstler können sich hier entfalten; wer schikanieren oder ein Bein stellen will, hat es sehr leicht" (Schmitt 1995d, 234). Unless noted otherwise, all translations of source material by the author.

2. See Rasch 2005; Odysseos and Petito 2007; Odysseos 2007; Dean 2004; Elden 2011; Hooker 2009; Legg 2011. For example, Stephen Legg writes: "Although Schmitt refused to predict the coming *nomos*, his work provides endlessly provocative ways for considering the contemporary world." Other readers have noted the precariousness of his open-ended terminology in particular. Schmitt may indeed have raised questions that continue to be current, but according to Chantal Mouffe, who has objected to comparisons of Schmitt's and George W. Bush's conceptions of the political, the topicality of his questions does not necessarily ensure transmissable solutions (2005, 245; see also Legg 2011, 148). Stuart Elden notes in a similar vein, "It is precisely because he appears to be useful that he is so dangerous. The seductiveness is that he seems to transcend his circumstances and political view, when remaining deeply rooted in them. The anointing of Schmitt as a geopolitical theorist with contemporary relevance is thus a serious error, intellectually and politically" (2011, 102).

3. While scholars admittedly agree that Schmitt's style changed during this phase, the interpretations and justifications of this transformation could not conflict more. Kearns, for instance, reads these texts as direct consequences of Schmitt's nationalism, but others observe in *Land and Sea* a concealed resistance to National Socialism, especially since the Nazi Party had already long abandoned him by this point in his career (Mendieta 2011, 260).

4. In so doing, Hobbes supposedly contributed to a Jewish history of interpretation (Schmitt 2008a, 8; 2003, 16; see also Dean 2004, 13). Schmitt did not go into the details of this tradition—"Here we need not be detained by the details of the numerous depictions and combinations" (2008a, 9; 2003, 18)—but the fundamentally antisemitic tendency of his reading is very distinct. Schmitt held the Jews primarily responsible for the collapse of the state's mythical foundation (see Mehring 2008, 388).

5. According to Schmitt, existence was conditioned by space, but he also always had the potential to choose the elements he employed. "Man can choose, and at certain moments in his history, he may even go so far . . . as to change himself into a new form of his historical existence, by virtue of which he readjusts and reorganizes himself" (Schmitt 1997a, 5; 2001, 14). But man only possessed this power to choose when he fully recognized his own situation; then he could remove himself from history, even step outside of his own time period. The whaler, as depicted in Melville's *Moby-Dick*, provides a quintessential example of this decisiveness and vigor. In contrast to *Leviathan's* supposedly Jewish history of interpretation, which Schmitt described in his book on Hobbes, Melville's whaler leads a meaningful existence and has a relationship of immediacy with his element. Melville was a model for Schmitt's narrative and *Land and Sea* an answer to his own situation (Nowak 2008).

6. It is no coincidence that Schmitt at this time made frequent references to Benito Cereno, the captain from a novella by Melville. This novella portrays the story of a Spanish trading vessel drifting rudderless across the ocean. The ship's captain, Cereno, is powerless in the hands of mutinous black slaves, but he finally manages to save himself by leaping onto an

American ship. The mutineers are overpowered, and Cereno withdraws to a cloister. In *Ex Captivitate Salus* from 1950, Schmitt described this character as a symbol for intellectuals (Schmitt 2002, 21–22) and then characterized himself as the last representative of the *jus Europaeum* (75). As he noted to Ernst Jünger, Schmitt was particularly fascinated by Melville's ability to describe objective, elemental, and concrete situations (Schmitt in Kiesel 1999, 121). In Schmitt's understanding, narratives made situations tangible; instead of clearly portraying events historically, narratives provide more general interpretations that point beyond contemporary history. This is the position he adopted as the narrator of *Land and Sea*. By doing so, Schmitt removed himself from history. What's more, when Schmitt compared himself to Cereno, a fictional character from a different era whose destiny allegorically conveyed Schmitt's own situation, the inverse held as well: Schmitt's own life allegorically took on a more universal character.

7. "It is clearly not just a history of international law of a history of political thought or international relations. Schmitt's famous style, which prefers striking formulations and paradoxes—even his critics acknowledge their 'rare poetic quality'—over careful analysis, does nothing to make his narrative perspective any clearer. No conclusion emerges in *Nomos* to tie the critiques in a single thesis or position" (Koskenniemi 2004, 500). However, though the work's genre cannot be easily determined, Schmitt's approach is clear. The book is above all concerned with a conceptual definition of space.

8. Searching for etymological traces was quite conventional in the ancient world and during the Middle Ages, and modern linguistics continues to conduct etymological studies. However, whereas scholars in antiquity were still concerned with the affinity between concept and object, modern linguistics primarily analyzes phonetic shifts. Etymology can give an indication of the meanings that a concept might formerly have had, but research of this kind is deemed to be of purely historical interest.

9. In this way, the act of appropriation (*Nahme*), the original meaning of *nomos*, was for Schmitt ultimately a violent yet legitimate act: "Not every invasion or temporary occupation is a land-appropriation that founds an order. In world history, there have been many acts of force that have destroyed themselves quickly. Thus, every seizure of land is not a *nomos*, although, conversely, *nomos*, understood in our sense of the term, always includes a land-based order and orientation" (Schmitt 2006a, 80; 1997a, 48). If the *Nahme*, the taking, cannot be equated with an invasion, under what criteria can such an invasion be distinguished from the lawful *nomos*? (Balke 1996, 331).

10. As I have already shown, Schmitt derived his concept of space first and foremost from mythical origins. He did not write that empty space comes from Judaism, but this space was nevertheless "Jewish" in Schmitt's understanding of it, especially since he ascribed a completely different notion of space to Catholics, for instance: "Roman Catholic nations seem to love the soil, the maternal earth, very differently: all have their *terrisme*" (Schmitt 2008b, 18). In his *Leviathan*, Schmitt claimed that the Jewish-cabalist mode of interpretation was particularly responsible for the undermining of myth. He attributed the failure of the state to the Jews, and thus they were according to Schmitt, at least indirectly responsible for the emergence of the Reich (Gross 2007, 161–162; Kennedy 2004, 179–180; see also Balakrishan 2000, 205–207, 220). Schmitt always remains focused on space, never on race or "blood," which admittedly does not relativize his antisemitism. It was, in his estimation, above all the Jews who had detached themselves from space (Palaver 1996, 114–115).

11. As Koskenniemi writes, *"Nomos" of the Earth* is less "a history of international law than political manifesto against the moralization of warfare" (2004, 495).

References

Agamben, G. 1998. *Homo Sacer: Sovereign Power and Bare Life*, trans. D. Heller-Roazen. Stanford: Stanford University Press.

Agamben, G. 2003. *State of Exception*, trans. K. Attell. Chicago: University of Chicago Press.

Aradau, C. 2007. "Law Transformed: Guantánamo and the 'Other' Exception." *Third World Quarterly* 28: 489–501.

Aravamudan, S. 2005. "Carl Schmitt's The 'Nomos' of the Earth: Four Corollaries." *South Atlantic Quarterly* 104: 227–236.

Balakrishan, G. 2000. *The Enemy: An Intellectual Portrait of Carl Schmitt*. London: Verso.

Balke, F. 1996. *Der Staat nach seinem Ende: Die Versuchung Carl Schmitts*. Munich: Fink.

Bendersky, J. W. 1983. *Carl Schmitt: Theorist for the Reich*. Princeton: Princeton University Press.

Butler, J. 2006. *Precarious Life: The Powers of Mourning and Violence*. London: Verso.

Coleman, M. 2011. "Colonial War: Carl Schmitt's Deterritorializatin of Enmity." In Legg 2011, 127–142.

Dean, M. 2004. "A Political Mythology of World Order: Carl Schmitt's Nomos." *Theory, Culture & Society* 23: 1–22.

Deleuze, G. 1994. *Difference and Repetition*, trans. P. Patton. New York: Columbia University Press.

Deleuze, G., and F. Guattari. 2011. *A Thousand Plateaus: Capitalism and Schizophrenia*, trans. B. Massumi. Minneapolis: University of Minnesota Press.

Elden, S. 2011. "Reading Schmitt Geopolitically. Nomos, Territory and Großraum." In Legg 2011, 91–105.

Gross, R. 2007. *Carl Schmitt and the Jews: The "Jewish Question," the Holocaust, and German Legal Theory*. Madison: University of Wisconsin Press.

Hell, J. 2009. "*Katechon*: Carl Schmitt's Imperial Theology and the Ruins of the Future." *Germanic Review* 84: 283–326.

Honig, B. 2009. *Emergency Politics: Paradox, Law, Democracy*. Princeton: Princeton University Press.

Hooker, W. 2009. *Carl Schmitt's International Thought*. Cambridge: Cambridge University Press.

Kearns, G. 2011. "Echoes of Carl Schmitt among the Ideologists of the New American Empire." In Legg 2011, 74–90.

Kennedy, E. 2004. *Constitutional Failure: Carl Schmitt in Weimar*. Durham: Duke University Press.

Kiesel, H. ed. 1999. *Ernst Jünger und Carl Schmitt: Briefe 1930–1983*. Stuttgart: Klett-Cotta.

Koskenniemi, M. 2004. "International Law as Political Theology: How to Read *Nomos der Erde*?" *Constellations* 11: 492–511.

Köster, W. 2002. *Die Rede über den "Raum": Zur semantischen Karriere eines deutschen Konzepts*. Heidelberg: Synchron.

Legg, S. ed. 2011. *Spatiality, Sovereignty and Carl Schmitt: Geographies of the Nomos*. London: Routledge.

Marzoa, F. 2005. "Space and Nomos." *South Atlantic Quarterly* 104: 307–311.

Mehring, R. 2008. "'Raumrevolution' als Rechtsproblem: Zum politischen Kontext und Wandel von Carl Schmitts Großraumdenken." In Voigt 2008, 99–118.

Meier, C. 1988. "Zu Carl Schmitts Begriffsbildung: Das Politische und der Nomos." In Quaritsch 1988, 537–556.

Mendieta, E. 2011. "Land and Sea." In Legg 2011, 260–267.

Minca, C. 2007. "Agamben's Geographies of Modernity." *Political Geography* 26: 78–97.

Minca, C., and R. Rowan. 2015a. "The Question of Space in Carl Schmitt." *Progress in Human Geography* 39: 268–289.

Minca, C., and R. Rowan. 2015b. *On Schmitt and Space.* London: Routledge.

Mouffe, C. 2005. "Schmitt's Vision of a Multipolar World Order." *South Atlantic Quarterly* 104: 245–251.

Müller, J.-W. 2003. *A Dangerous Mind: Carl Schmitt in Post-War European Thought.* New Haven: Yale University Press.

Nowak, P. 2008. "Incarnations of Leviathan." In *Man and His Enemies,* ed. S. Minkow and P. Nowak. Bialystok: University of Bialystok Press, 285–300.

Odysseos, L. 2007. "Crossing the Line? Carl Schmitt on the 'Spaceless Universalism' of Cosmopolitanism and the War on Terror." In Odysseos and Petito 2007, 124–143.

Odysseos, L., and F. Petito. eds. 2007. *The International Political Thought of Carl Schmitt: Terror, Liberal War and the Crisis of Global Order.* London: Routledge.

Ojakangas, M. 2004. *A Philosophy of Concrete Life: Carl Schmitt and the Political Thought of Late Modernity.* Frankfurt: Lang.

Palaver, W. 1996. "Carl Schmitt on Nomos and Space." *Telos* 106: 105–127.

Quaritsch, H. ed. 1988. *Complexio Oppositorum über Carl Schmitt: Vorträge und Diskussionsbeiträge des 28. Sonderseminars 1986 der Hochschule für Verwaltungswissenschaften Speyer.* Berlin: Duncker & Humblot.

Rasch, W. 2005. "Introduction: Carl Schmitt and the New World Order." *South Atlantic Quarterly* 104: 177–183.

Scheuerman, W. 2004. "International Law as Historical Myth." *Constellations* 11: 537–550.

Schmitt, C. 1942. "Raumrevolution: Vom Geist des Abendlandes." *Deutsche Kolonialzeitung* 54: 219–221.

Schmitt, C. 1986. *Political Romanticism,* trans. G. Oakes. Cambridge: MIT Press.

Schmitt, C. 1988. *Political Theology: Four Chapters on the Concept of Sovereignty,* trans. G. Schwab. Cambridge: MIT Press.

Schmitt, C. 1991. "Die planetarische Spannung zwischen Ost und West und der Gegensatz von Land und Meer." In *Schmittiana: Beiträge zu Leben und Werk Carl Schmitts,* vol. 3, ed. P. Tommissen. Berlin: Duncker & Humblot, 19–44.

Schmitt, C. 1995a. "Antwort an Kempner." In Schmitt 1995g, 453–477.

Schmitt, C. 1995b. "Das Meer gegen das Land." In Schmitt 1995g, 395–400.

Schmitt, C. 1995c. "Raum und Rom—Zur Phonetik des Wortes Raum." In Schmitt 1995g, 491–495.

Schmitt, C. 1995d. "Raum und Großraum im Völkerrecht." In Schmitt 1995g, 234–268.

Schmitt, C. 1995e. "Völkerrechtliche Großraumordnung mit Interventionsverbot für raumfremde Mächte: Ein Beitrag zum Reichsbegriff im Völkerrecht." In Schmitt 1995g, 269–371.

Schmitt, C. 1995f. "Die Raumrevolution: Durch den totalen Krieg zum totalen Frieden." In Schmitt 1995g, 388–394.

Schmitt, C. 1995g. Staat, Großraum, Nomos: Arbeiten aus den Jahren 1916-1969, ed. G. Maschke. Berlin: Duncker & Humblot.

Schmitt, C. 1997a. *Land and Sea,* trans. S. Draghici. Washington: Plutarch Press.

Schmitt, C. 1997b. *Der Nomos der Erde im Völkerrecht des Jus Publicum Europaeum*, 4th ed. Berlin: Duncker & Humblot.

Schmitt, C. 1998. *Politische Romantik*, 6th ed. Berlin: Duncker & Humblot.

Schmitt, C. 2001. *Land und Meer: Eine weltgeschichtliche Betrachtung*, 4th ed. Stuttgart: Klett-Cotta.

Schmitt, C. 2002. *Ex Captivitate Salus: Erfahrungen der Zeit 1945/47*, 3rd ed. Berlin: Duncker & Humblot.

Schmitt, C. 2003. *Der Leviathan in der Staatslehre des Thomas Hobbes: Sinn und Fehlschlag eines politischen Symbols*, 3rd ed. Stuttgart: Klett-Cotta.

Schmitt, C. 2004. *Über den Wert des Staates und die Bedeutung des Einzelnen*, 2nd ed. Berlin: Duncker & Humblot.

Schmitt, C. 2006a. *The "Nomos" of the Earth in the International Law of the "Jus Publicum Europaeum,"* trans. G. L. Ulmen. New York: Telos Press.

Schmitt, C. 2006b. *Politische Theologie: Vier Kapitel zur Lehre von der Souveränität*, 9th ed. Berlin: Duncker & Humblot.

Schmitt, C. 2008a. *The Leviathan in the State Theory of Thomas Hobbes: Meaning and Failure of a Political Symbol*, trans. G. Schwab and E. Hilfstein. Chicago: University of Chicago Press.

Schmitt, C. 2008b. *Römischer Katholizismus und politische Form*, 5th ed. Stuttgart: Klett-Cotta.

Schmitt, C. 2011. "The *Großraum* Order of International Law with a Ban on Intervention for Spatially Foreign Powers: A Contribution to the Concept of *Reich* in International Law (1939–1941)." In *Writings on War*, trans. and ed. T. Nunan. Cambridge: Polity, 75–124.

Schmoeckel, M. 1994. *Die Großraumtheorie: Ein Beitrag zur Geschichte der Völkerrechtswissenschaft im Dritten Reich, insbesondere der Kriegszeit*. Berlin: Duncker & Humblot.

Simons, O. 2007. *Raumgeschichten: Topographien der Moderne in Philosophie, Wissenschaft und Literatur*. Munich: Fink.

Sombart, N. 1984. *Jugend in Berlin, 1933–1943: Ein Bericht*. Munich: Hanser.

Ulmen, G. 1993. "The Concept of Nomos: Introduction to Schmitt's 'Appropriation/Distribution/Production'." *Telos* 95: 39–51.

Van Laak, D. 2002. *Gespräche in der Sicherheit des Schweigens: Carl Schmitt in der politischen Geistesgeschichte der frühen Bundesrepublik*. Berlin: Akademie Verlag.

Voigt, R. ed. 2008. *Großraum-Denken: Carl Schmitts Kategorie der Grossraumordnung*. Stuttgart: Steiner.

Werber, N. 2007. *Die Geopolitik der Literatur: Eine Vermessung der medialen Weltraumordnung*. Munich: Hanser.

Index

CPSIA information can be obtained
at www.ICGtesting.com
Printed in the USA
BVHW050904160521
607210BV00001B/3